Human Values and Beliefs

Human Values and Beliefs:
A Cross-Cultural Sourcebook

*Political, Religious, Sexual, and Economic
Norms in 43 Societies: Findings from the
1990–1993 World Values Survey*

RONALD INGLEHART,
MIGUEL BASAÑEZ,
and
ALEJANDRO MORENO

Ann Arbor
THE UNIVERSITY OF MICHIGAN PRESS

2001 2000 1999 1998   4 3 2 1

A CIP catalog record for this book is available from the British Library.

Library of Congress Cataloging-in-Publication Data

Inglehart, Ronald.
    Human values and beliefs : a cross-cultural sourcebook :
political, religious, sexual, and economic norms in 43 societies : /
Ronald Inglehart, Miguel Basañez, and Alejandro Moreno.
      p.   cm.
    Includes index.
    ISBN 0-472-10833-6 (hardcover)
    1. Social values—Cross-cultural studies. I. Basañez, Miguel.
II. Menéndez Moreno, Alejandro. III. Title.
HM73.I544 1998
303.3'72—dc20   97-20731
                                            CIP

Contents

LIST OF TABLES BY TOPIC

ECOLOGY

V12 Protect environment: Give part of income
V13 Protect environment: Higher taxes
V14 Protect environment: Government
V15 Protect environment: Makes people too anxious
V16 Protect environment: Unemployment
V17 Protect environment: Not urgent
V26 Belongs to: Environmental organization
V44 Voluntary work in: Environmental organization
V32 Belongs to: Animal rights organization
V50 Voluntary work in: Animal rights organization
V290 Support for ecology movement
V291 Anti-nuclear energy movement

ECONOMY

V19 Belongs to: Social welfare
V25 Belongs to: Third World development organization
V37 Voluntary work in: Social welfare
V43 Voluntary work in: Third World development org.
V126 Management of business: Owners
V126 Management of business: Employee participation
V132 Financial satisfaction
V250 Income equality vs. individual incentives
V251 Ownership of business and industry
V252 Individual vs. state responsibility
V253 Unemployment
V254 Competition
V256 Accumulation of wealth
V264 Less emphasis on money
V266 Technological development
V281 Confidence in: Major companies
V283 Confidence in: TV/European Community
V335 Economy needs changes
V337 Individual freedom

EDUCATION

V21 Belongs to: Education/cultural organization
V39 Voluntary work in: Education/cultural organization
V271 Scientific advances
V274 Confidence in: Education system

EMOTIONS

V18 Happiness
V61 Reasons for voluntary work: Personal satisfaction
V56 Reasons for voluntary work: Compassion
V57 Reasons for voluntary work: Opportunity to give
V59 Reasons for voluntary work: Identify suffering
V63 Reasons for voluntary work: Give hope and dignity
V75 Reject neighbors: emotionally unstable
V84 Feeling excited
V85 Feeling restless
V86 Feeling proud
V87 Feeling lonely
V88 Feeling pleased
V89 Feeling bored
V90 Feeling "top of the world"
V91 Feeling depressed
V92 Feeling "going your way"
V93 Feeling upset

FAMILY

V5 Importance of family
V74 Reject neighbors: Large family
V180 Home satisfaction
V181 Marital status
V182 Married before
V183 Share with partner: Attitudes towards religion
V184 Share with partner: Moral attitudes
V185 Share with partner: Social attitudes

V241 Political interest
V242 Political action: Sign petition
V243 Political action: Join boycott
V244 Political action: Lawful demonstration
V245 Political action: Unofficial strikes
V246 Political action: Occupy buildings
V247 Freedom and equality
V248 Left-Right self-placement (% Left)
V248 Left-Right self-placement (% Center)
V248 Left-Right self-placement (% Right)
V249 Societal change (% Radical change)
V249 Societal change (% Gradual reform)
V249 Societal change (% Defend society)
V257 Country's goals: Economic growth
V257 Country's goals: Giving people more say in their jobs
V259 Country's goals: Maintain order
V259 Country's goals: Giving people more say in government decisions
V261 Country's goals: Stable economy
V261 Country's goals: Humane society
V268 Respect authority
V273 Confidence in: Armed forces
V275 Confidence in: Legal system
V276 Confidence in: Press
V277 Confidence in: Unions
V278 Confidence in: Police
V279 Confidence in: Parliament
V280 Confidence in: Civil service
V284 Confidence in: NATO
V285 Confidence in: Political system
V288 Country run by few big interests
V289 Trust in government
V292 Disarmament movement
V293 Human rights movement
V311 Fighting police
V315 Threaten strikers
V317 Assassinations
V336 Government should be made more open
V338 Helpless: Unjust law
V339 Political reform too rapid
V405 Materialist/Postmaterialist values (% Materialist)
V405 Materialist/Postmaterialist values (% Postmaterialist)

HEALTH

V33 Belongs to: Health voluntary organization
V51 Voluntary work in: Health voluntary organization
V83 State of health

INDIVIDUAL

V95 Free choice and control over own life
V96 Life satisfaction
V267 Individual development
V270 More natural lifestyle
V323 Boldness vs. caution
V324 New ideas vs. old ones
V325 Adapting to change
V326 Count on success
V327 Convince others
V328 Serve as model
V329 Get what I want
V330 Possessions
V331 Like responsibility
V332 Rarely unsure of self
V333 Give advice often

LEISURE AND FRIENDS

V6 Importance of friends
V7 Importance of leisure
V29 Belongs to: Sports/recreation organizations
V47 Voluntary work in: Sports/recreation organizations

MORALITY

V237 Abortion: Mother's health in risk
V238 Abortion: Handicapped child
V239 Abortion: Mother unmarried
V240 Abortion: Married couple do not want child
V296 Claim government benefits when not entitled
V297 Avoid transport fare
V298 Cheat on taxes
V299 Buy stolen goods
V300 Joyriding
V301 Marijuana/Hashish
V302 Keep money found
V303 Lying in your own interest

V306 Accept bribe
V309 Prostitution
V310 Divorce
V312 Euthanasia
V313 Suicide
V314 Hit car- No report
V318 Throw litter
V319 Drink and drive

RELIGION

V9 Importance of religion
V20 Belongs to: Religious organization
V38 Voluntary work in: Religious organization
V62 Reasons for voluntary work: Religious beliefs
V133 Think about the meaning of life
V134 Think of death
V135 Meaning of life: God exists
V136 Meaning of life: Get the best
V137 Meaning of life: Death inevitable
V138 Meaning of life: Belief in God
V139 Meaning of life: Death is a resting point
V140 Meaning of life: Sorrow
V141 Meaning of life: Life has no meaning
V142 Good and evil
V143 Belongs to religious denomination
V144 Which religion
V146 Raised religious
V147 Church attendance
V148 Religious services for: Birth
V149 Religious services for: Marriage
V150 Religious services for: Death
V151 Is Respondent religious?
V152 Church answers to: Moral problems
V153 Church answers to: Family life
V154 Church answers to: Spiritual needs
V155 Church answers to: Social problems
V156 Proper for churches to speak out on: Disarmament
V157 Proper for churches to speak out on: Abortion
V158 Proper for churches to speak out on: Third World problems
V159 Proper for churches to speak out on: Extramarital affairs

V160 Proper for churches to speak out on: Unemployment
V161 Proper for churches to speak out on: Racial discrimination
V162 Proper for churches to speak out on: Euthanasia
V163 Proper for churches to speak out on: Homosexuality
V164 Proper for churches to speak out on: Ecology
V165 Proper for churches to speak out on: Government policy
V166 Belief in God
V167 Belief in life after death
V168 Belief in soul
V169 Belief in devil
V170 Belief in hell
V171 Belief in heaven
V172 Belief in sin
V173 Belief in resurrection
V174 Belief in re-incarnation
V175 What is God?
V176 Importance of God
V177 Comfort in religion
V178 Prayer/Meditation
V179 How often pray
V272 Confidence in: Church

SOCIETY AND NATION

V28 Belongs to: Youth work organizations
V46 Voluntary work in: Youth work organizations
V55 Reasons for voluntary work: Solidarity
V64 Reasons for voluntary work: Community contribution
V66 Reasons for voluntary work: Social reasons
V69 Reject neighbors: Criminals
V70 Reject neighbors: Other race
V72 Reject neighbors: Drinkers
V76 Reject neighbors: Muslims
V77 Reject neighbors: Foreigners
V79 Reject neighbors: Drug addicts
V81 Reject neighbors: Jews
V82 Reject neighbors: Hindus
V94 Trust in people
V97 Reasons why people live in need: injustice
V97 Reasons why people live in need: laziness

V130 When jobs are scarce: Give priority to own nationality
V263 Willing to fight in war for own country
V282 Confidence in: Social security
V286 What makes people proud of their country
V295 Anti-apartheid movement
V320 Geographical groups: Town
V320 Geographical groups: Country
V320 Geographical groups: Cosmopolitan
V322 National pride
V341 Trust: Own nationality
V342 Trust: First domestic ethnic group
V343 Trust: Second domestic ethnic group
V344 Trust: First neighbor nationality
V345 Trust: Second neighbor nationality
V346 Trust: First superpower
V347 Trust: Second superpower

WORK

V4 Importance of work
V22 Belongs to: Trade unions
V40 Voluntary work in: Trade unions
V24 Belongs to: Community action organization
V42 Voluntary work in: Community action organization
V27 Belongs to: Professional associations
V45 Voluntary work in: Professional associations
V58 Reasons for voluntary work: Sense of duty
V60 Reasons for voluntary work: Worthwhile to do
V67 Reasons for voluntary work: Useful experience
V68 Reasons for voluntary work: Couldn't refuse
V99 Important aspects in a job: Good pay
V100 Important aspects in a job: Pleasant people

V101 Important aspects in a job: No pressure
V102 Important aspects in a job: Job security
V103 Important aspects in a job: Promotions
V104 Important aspects in a job: Respect
V105 Important aspects in a job: Good hours
V106 Important aspects in a job: Use initiative
V107 Important aspects in a job: Useful to society
V108 Important aspects in a job: Generous holidays
V109 Important aspects in a job: Meet people
V110 Important aspects in a job: Achieve something
V111 Important aspects in a job: Responsibility
V112 Important aspects in a job: Interesting
V113 Important aspects in a job: Meets abilities
V115 Pride in work
V116 Job satisfaction
V117 Decision-making freedom
V118 Why work: Get paid
V119 Why work: Do best
V120 Why work: Necessity
V121 Why work: Enjoyment
V122 Why work: Most important thing
V123 Why work: Never worked
V125 Efficient secretary gets paid more
V127 Following instructions at work: Always
V127 Following instructions at work: Must be convinced first
V128 When jobs are scarce: Men have more right to it
V129 When jobs are scarce: Force to retire early
V131 When jobs are scarce: Unfair to give jobs to the handicapped
V255 Hard work

LIST OF FIGURES AND TABLES BY NUMBER

FIGURES

xv

TABLES

FOREWORD

by Robert M. Worcester

One of the most difficult tasks in social science is that of gathering and interpreting cross-national survey data. The task is complicated by differences in culture, language, social context, education levels, political acceptability, and survey instrumentation. Researchers have their own experiences, feelings, and knowledge about how surveys should be conducted in their own country, and what is common practice in some is anathema in others. Cross-national survey research is difficult; to carry out comparable studies over time is a truly monumental undertaking. Yet all of these problems have been faced and surmounted in the World Values Surveys, coordinated by Ronald Inglehart.

This volume is a model of what a sourcebook should be, and will be extremely useful to anyone involved in the analysis of public opinion data. It contains the precise wording of the questions used in the survey, in their original sequence; details of sample sizes, fieldwork dates, and universe covered; it presents the overall responses for each question, in more than 40 countries, together with analyses by gender, age, income, political stance, and postmaterialist values; plus a clear and concise introductory summary; and finally, references and bibliography. This is a gold mine of fascinating findings that whet one's appetite for further exploration: I only wish that this sourcebook were accompanied by a CD-ROM disk containing the complete data! Fortunately, the original data are available from the ICPSR survey data archive at the University of Michigan.

Survey research is being undertaken in a growing number of countries, so that today it is possible to survey a majority of the world's population. This sourcebook will be useful not only to inform researchers about findings from the 1990–1993 World Values Survey, but also as a source of questionnaire wording, so that comparable survey results may be obtained to measure changes over time in order to provide an up-to-date picture of Human Values and Beliefs in global perspective.

Robert M. Worcester is president of Market Opinion Research International (MORI), past president of the World Association of Public Opinion Research and an adjunct professor at London School of Economics.

Introduction

This book enables the reader to examine the basic values and attitudes of the peoples of more than 40 societies around the world. Based on the 1990–93 World Values Survey, it provides standardized cross-cultural measures of people's values and goals concerning politics, economics, religion, sexual behavior, gender roles, family values, and ecological concerns.

These surveys cover a broader range of variation than has ever before been available for analyzing the belief systems of mass publics. They provide data from representative national samples of the publics of more than 40 societies representing 70 percent of the world's population and covering the full range of variation, from societies with per capita incomes as low as $300 per year, to societies with per capita incomes of more than $30,000 per year; from long-established democracies to authoritarian states; and from societies with market economies to societies that still had state-run economies at the time of the survey; and from societies that were historically shaped by a wide variety of religious and cultural traditions, from Christian to Islamic to Confucian. The 1990 World Values survey was carried out in Argentina, Austria, Belarus, Belgium, Brazil, Bulgaria, Canada, Chile, China, Czechoslovakia, Denmark, Estonia, Finland, France, Germany (with separate samples in the East and West regions), Great Britain, Hungary, Iceland, India, Ireland, Northern Ireland, Italy, Japan, South Korea, Latvia, Lithuania, Mexico, greater Moscow, the Netherlands, Nigeria, Norway, Poland, Portugal, Russia, Romania, Slovenia, South Africa, Spain, Sweden, Switzerland, Turkey, and the United States.[1]

This sourcebook enables the reader to compare the responses to almost 350 questions across societies covering the full spectrum of economic, political, and cultural variation. It also enables the reader to examine the differences between the responses of men and women in each society; and to examine generational differences; and differences linked with education; and whether the respondent identifies with the Left, Center, or

---

[1] In addition to a representative national sample from Russia, the 1990–1993 World Values Survey obtained a supplementary sample from greater Moscow. Though Moscow has a higher economic and educational level than the rest of Russia, the results from the two samples generally differ only marginally. Since survey research was still relatively new in the countries of the former USSR when these surveys were carried out, it is reassuring that the two samples (carried out independently by two different survey research organizations) provide generally similar findings. *Within* Russia, greater Moscow is a very distinctive region. But in global perspective we would expect to find that the results from Moscow would be in the same ballpark as those from Russia—and we do.

V4 WORK IMPORTANT

Please say, for each of the following, how important it is in your life: Work. (% "very important")

	Total	Gender Male	Gender Female	Age 16-29	Age 30-49	Age 50+	Education Lower	Education Medium	Education Upper	Income Lower	Income Middle	Income Upper	Political Affinity Left	Political Affinity Center	Political Affinity Right	Values Mat	Values Mixed	Values Postmat
India	86	89	84	94	86	86	85	87	87	89	86	86	90	84	85	88	86	83
Nigeria	94	94	95	94	94	95	96	95	92	94	93	96	97	91	96	95	94	88
China	64	66	60	58	66	67	63	65	67	65	64	63	na	na	na	64	65	52
Romania	69	71	67	53	68	79	76	63	67	72	67	67	65	69	68	73	66	59
Turkey	59	64	54	53	63	61	59	55	69	58	55	64	63	60	57	61	58	60
Poland	70	69	71	58	69	76	71	71	62	69	71	68	71	68	76	71	70	66
Bulgaria	57	59	54	39	57	67	66	54	53	56	57	58	58	58	58	60	56	46
Chile	75	76	74	69	77	80	76	76	73	79	76	70	73	75	80	82	74	70
Czechoslovakia	56	59	54	41	57	65	59	52	64	53	56	58	62	54	56	57	56	56
South Africa	79	83	75	81	80	72	83	80	57	85	83	59	80	74	75	76	80	81
Lithuania	42	41	42	23	41	59	54	36	49	48	35	40	na	na	na	47	42	34
Hungary	59	57	61	55	62	58	60	58	60	59	57	61	64	60	52	62	57	55
Argentina	76	76	76	67	75	84	82	76	65	79	78	66	70	74	73	82	74	72
Brazil	82	83	81	81	84	82	82	83	80	81	85	82	80	81	86	83	82	81
Mexico	67	71	63	65	71	66	68	71	63	66	67	70	70	66	69	67	67	67
Belarus	55	58	52	37	58	66	67	53	53	54	53	57	55	55	58	58	54	52
Russia	46	51	42	34	47	52	50	44	46	46	45	49	46	45	49	49	44	41
Moscow	47	49	44	35	44	59	60	44	46	46	45	51	43	52	56	50	46	44
Latvia	33	35	32	23	32	48	33	33	35	32	33	34	na	na	na	38	33	40
Estonia	32	34	31	17	35	43	34	29	37	30	34	34	na	na	na	33	31	36
Portugal	35	34	36	33	34	38	35	41	31	37	30	38	32	35	38	34	37	29
South Korea	69	70	69	62	71	78	75	70	66	66	73	70	69	67	72	74	66	65
Ireland	65	72	59	61	67	66	67	65	56	65	67	64	59	66	66	66	66	61
North Ireland	57	69	48	59	53	60	59	56	45	62	61	49	50	59	55	59	54	69
Slovenia	73	73	74	62	76	78	72	72	79	73	75	72	67	75	72	81	71	64
Spain	66	67	65	62	68	66	65	72	63	64	67	63	67	66	63	70	67	64
East Germany	61	64	58	55	63	62	62	56	58	54	63	65	63	59	62	50	65	55
Britain	51	61	41	63	53	40	49	48	52	40	54	61	48	51	58	51	52	47
Italy	62	65	60	60	57	68	62	63	59	65	60	59	59	64	69	66	62	59
Netherlands	49	58	45	44	40	66	56	48	41	44	49	45	41	45	58	52	53	42
Belgium	58	61	54	55	58	59	58	60	52	59	60	56	54	59	59	62	58	52
Austria	62	63	61	53	65	62	64	60	60	59	63	56	60	60	63	63	65	54
France	61	62	60	60	60	63	65	62	48	61	65	54	53	62	65	72	61	52
Canada	59	63	55	62	59	56	62	61	54	59	60	58	54	60	56	63	61	56
United States	62	65	59	69	61	61	61	66	59	66	61	61	57	63	63	60	64	59
Iceland	56	66	46	45	59	65	60	53	57	na	na	na	52	59	59	58	56	54
West Germany	35	40	30	27	37	38	36	31	38	33	32	39	30	38	37	31	39	30
Denmark	51	57	44	49	48	55	51	48	52	55	47	51	43	51	57	54	52	46
Finland	54	56	52	31	57	69	55	54	54	53	55	55	61	50	56	65	56	48
Norway	73	78	68	71	70	78	78	76	69	74	72	74	73	72	75	72	76	68
Sweden	67	70	63	57	66	75	77	62	57	62	70	68	64	67	69	67	69	62
Japan	41	51	31	26	43	46	44	41	36	48	38	39	42	40	47	42	41	38
Switzerland	52	56	48	48	53	53	54	50	51	51	53	51	42	51	58	54	52	48
Total	60	63	57	53	60	64	63	59	57	60	60	59	60	61	63	62	60	56

Ranking:

Nigeria	94
India	86
Brazil	82
South Africa	79
Argentina	76
Chile	75
Slovenia	73
Norway	73
Poland	70
Romania	69
South Korea	69
Mexico	67
Sweden	67
Spain	66
Ireland	65
China	64
Italy	62
Austria	62
United States	62
East Germany	61
France	61
Turkey	59
Hungary	59
Canada	59
Belgium	58
Bulgaria	57
North Ireland	57
Czechoslovakia	56
Iceland	56
Belarus	55
Finland	54
Switzerland	52
Britain	51
Denmark	51
Netherlands	49
Moscow	47
Russia	46
Lithuania	42
Japan	41
Portugal	35
West Germany	35
Latvia	33
Estonia	32

Note: Countries in the left column are ranked according to GNP per capita. / The percentages in the bottom row give each country an equal weight. / na=not ascertained.

Right in his or her society's political system; and according to whether the respondent has "Materialist," "Mixed," or "Postmaterialist" values (a distinction that is explained below). Finally, we show how each of the 43 societies ranked in response to the given question.

In order to present this material concisely, the responses to each question are dichotomized, with only the percentage ranking "high" being shown. For example, the first table presented in our data section shows the responses to the question, "How important is work in your life?" This table (V4) is reproduced here for illustrative purposes.[2] As the reader will note, only the percentage saying that work is "very important" is shown here. Reading down the first column, one finds that in India, 86 percent of the public rated work as "very important": the remaining 14 percent rated it as either "fairly important," "not very important," or "not at all important." The table doesn't show the breakdown among the other three categories.[3] This sacrifice of detail brings a huge gain in conciseness: if we were to report each response category for each variable, it would be necessary to expand the nearly 400 pages of tables and figures presented here into several thousand pages (this book presents the results of more than 100,000 cross-tabulations).

This mode of presentation facilitates cross-cultural comparisons. One can simply scan down the columns in each table in order to compare the proportions in each country that rated work as "very important." The countries are ranked according to their Gross National Product per capita, from the poorest to the richest country. This is done because many of the values and beliefs examined here are systematically related to a society's level of economic development, with the publics of richer countries consistently showing different outlooks from those of the publics of poorer societies. Table 1 shows the relative economic levels of these societies as indicated by their per capita GNP.

Ordering the countries according to economic level makes it easy to determine whether a given attitude or value is linked with development: as one scans down the first column, one can quickly note any systematic difference in outlook between rich and poor countries. It is also easy to identify which societies are deviant cases, falling higher or lower than their economic level would predict: one simply compares the order of the countries in the left-hand column (where they are ranked by GNP per capita) with their rankings in the right-hand column (where they are ranked by their level on the given variable).

---

[2] The tables are numbered according to their variable numbers in the ICPSR dataset. This question is variable 4; since the first three variables are the survey number, country code and interview number, respectively, they are not analyzed separately (the country is the row variable in all of these tables). The bottom row in these tables is based on the mean of all 43 societies in the column above it. This procedure gives equal weight to each country. Obviously, this does not reflect differences in population: if we weighted the sample according to population, China and India would outweigh the 41 other societies. Our reasoning is that, for most analytic purposes, Sweden is as interesting a case as China, though her substantive importance is far smaller. In these tables, "n.a." (or "not ascertained") indicates that the question was not asked in the given country. Although considerable care has gone into the preparation of this sourcebook, it is based on an immense body of data gathered from a wide range of cultures by a diverse group of investigators; some errors or inconsistencies may still be present. The authors will be grateful if any apparent errors are called to their attention by FAX (1-734-764-3341) or by E-mail (RFI@umich.edu).

[3] For those who are interested, this breakdown *does* appear in the frequencies for all 43 societies combined.

Table 1
GROSS NATIONAL PRODUCT PER CAPITA (1990)
AND ESTIMATED PURCHASING POWER COMPARISONS
FOR NATIONS IN THE 1990 WORLD VALUES SURVEY

	GNP/ capita	PPC estimate
India	$330	1,150
Nigeria	340	1,360
China	340	1,680
Romania	1,390	6,900
Turkey	1,780	4,840
Poland	1,790	4,500
Bulgaria	1,840	4,980
Chile	2,160	7,060
Czechoslovakia	2,470	6,280
South Africa	2,560	(N.A.)
Lithuania	2,710	5,410
Hungary	2,720	6,080
Argentina	2,790	5,120
Brazil	2,940	5,240
Mexico	3,030	7,170
Belarus	3,110	6,850
Russia	3,220	6,930
Moscow	(N.A.)	(N.A.)
Latvia	3,410	7,540
Estonia	3,830	8,090
Portugal	5,930	9,450
South Korea	6,330	8,320
Ireland	11,120	11,430
Northern Ireland	12,400	(N.A.)
Slovenia	12,450	(N.A.)
Spain	12,450	12,670
East Germany	14,220	(N.A.)
Britain	16,550	16,340
Italy	18,520	17,040
Netherlands	18,780	16,820
Belgium	18,950	17,510
Austria	20,140	17,690
France	20,380	18,430
Canada	20,440	19,320
United States	22,240	22,130
Iceland	23,170	(N.A.)
West Germany	23,650	19,770
Denmark	23,700	17,880
Finland	23,980	16,130
Norway	24,220	17,170
Sweden	25,110	17,490
Japan	26,930	19,390
Switzerland	33,610	21,780

Source: World Bank, *World Development Report, 1993*: pp. 238-239, 296-297 and 304.
Figures for Northern Ireland, Slovenia, and East Germany were extrapolated by the authors.

Though we very often find statistically significant relations between levels of economic development and beliefs and values, these relationships are virtually never monotonic: we almost always find deviant cases, sometimes dramatic ones. This reflects the fact that, although economic factors often seem to play an important role in shaping cross-cultural differences, it seems clear that they are not the *only* factors involved: these cultural differences seem to reflect the entire historical experience of given peoples, including political, social, technological, geographic, and other factors as well as economic influences.

In our first table of findings, for example, the publics of the poorest societies tend to place the greatest emphasis on work: having work may decide whether or not they survive. Accordingly, India and Nigeria rank at the very top. But we also find a tendency for the peoples of the Soviet successor states to place relatively *little* emphasis on work: five of the eight lowest-ranking societies formerly belonged to the Soviet Union. This is an interesting finding. Did the Soviet system lead to a diminishing emphasis on work? "They pretend to pay us and we pretend to work," was an outlook that many people expressed during the Soviet era. If the Soviet system did tend to erode emphasis on work, however, it probably did so gradually: orientations toward work are among the most central and enduring elements of a peoples' worldview. Thus, if there *was* a gradual erosion of emphasis on work during the Soviet era, one would expect to find it reflected in intergenerational differences, with the oldest generation still emphasizing work most and the youngest generation emphasizing it least of all. We can test this hypothesis by examining the age-group breakdowns on this same page. Table 2 moves to a second-order comparison, showing the size of the *difference* between the outlook of the youngest and oldest groups in each society, based on the data in Table V4.

The results tend to confirm our hypothesis. All six of the samples from the former Soviet Union show large differences between the outlook of the older and younger groups (ranging from 24 to 36 percentage points); and in every case the differences are in the predicted direction: the young place *less* emphasis on work than do the old. But it is also clear that younger people do not *necessarily* place less emphasis on work than older people—for in the United States, Canada, Great Britain, and South Africa, the young emphasize work *more* heavily than the old; and in many other societies (including both India and Nigeria) there is no significant difference between the views of young and old. However we *do* find a clear tendency for the young to place less emphasis on work in almost all of the former communist societies, and not just in the ex-Soviet Union. This is only moderately true of Hungary, East Germany, and China, which show intergenerational differences of only 3 to 9 points. But in the eleven other ex-communist societies, the young place much less emphasis on work than do the old, with the differences ranging from 18 to 36 percentage points. Indications of an intergenerational decline in emphasis on work are by no means limited to the ex-socialist societies. Most of the 43 societies examined here show some tendency in this direction—but it is most pronounced among the ex-communist societies, where we find eight of the nine largest intergenerational shifts away from emphasis on work.

We will not pursue our interpretation of Table V4 any farther. This discussion is simply intended to illustrate some of the many possible types of cross-cultural comparisons that this sourcebook facilitates. The reader will find a good deal of fascinating material in the more than 300 tables presented in the data section.

Table 2. Intergenerational Decline of
Emphasis on Work in Socialist Societies
(difference between oldest and youngest age groups
in percentage saying work is "very important" in their lives)

Great Britain	+23
South Africa	+ 9
U.S.	+ 8
Canada	+ 6
India	0
Nigeria	-1
N. Ireland	-1
Brazil	-1
Mexico	-1
France	-3
Hungary	**-3**
Spain	-3
Belgium	-4
Portugal	-5
Ireland	-5
Switzerland	-5
Denmark	-6
Norway	-7
E. Germany	**-7**
Italy	-8
Turkey	-8
Austria	-9
China	**-9**
W. Germany	-11
Chile	-11
S. Korea	-16
Argentina	-17
Sweden	-18
Poland	**-18**
Slovenia	**-18**
Russia	**-18**
Japan	-20
Iceland	-20
Netherlands	-22
Moscow	**-24**
Czechoslovakia	**-24**
Latvia	**-25**
Romania	**-26**
Estonia	**-26**
Bulgaria	**-28**
Belarus	**-29**
Lithuania	**-36**
Finland	-38

Source: 1990-93 World Values Survey, Table V4. In each country, the "oldest
group" consists of those 50 years and older; the "youngest group" consists of
those under 30 years of age. Ex-socialist societies are in **bold** type.

Most of the findings will seem intuitively plausible to the reader. For example, the tables show that religious beliefs tend to be much stronger among the publics of pre-industrial societies than among economically highly developed societies. These findings support the secularization thesis—and though the secularization thesis has been hotly debated, it is widely known, so the finding may not seem surprising to the reader. Nevertheless, there are some striking deviant cases, with the peoples of both the United States and Ireland showing a much more religious outlook than their economic levels would predict.

Some of the other findings will probably strike the reader as counterintuitive, however. For example (again, taking one of the first tables in the book), as Table V6 demonstrates, the Scandinavian peoples attach even greater importance to friends than do the peoples of Southern Europe: among the four Scandinavian countries, 60 percent rate friends as "very important" in their lives; while among the four Latin European publics, a mean of 36 percent give this response. This seems to contradict the stereotype of Latins as being relatively outgoing people who spend a great deal of time socializing—while Scandinavians are thought to be relatively stiff and introverted. One possibility is that the stereotypes are simply wrong, and always have been. But it is also possible that, because they have become some of the world's most affluent and secure societies within the last several decades, the peoples of Norway, Sweden, and Denmark have shifted their priorities, and now place greater emphasis on fulfilling their needs for belonging and social intercourse than on other needs (such as economic achievement) which formerly ranked higher. And it is even possible that, precisely because they *do* spend a relatively large amount of time socializing, the Latins have a great many friends, and can take them for granted; while the Scandinavians are in the opposite situation, and attach great importance to the few friends they possess. We will not attempt to decide which is the correct explanation here. Let us simply note that the finding itself is clear: Scandinavians attach considerably more importance to friends than Southern Europeans do. This is one of a great many interesting, and not always intuitively obvious findings, that emerge in the tables below.

In addition to presenting the overall responses for each society, these tables enable the reader to compare the responses of young and old, of men and women, and of the more educated and less educated within each society; and to compare the responses of those who identify with the Left, Center, and Right; or those who have Materialist, Mixed, or Postmaterialist values. The reader may wonder why we have chosen to provide these particular breakdowns from among the many that might have been given. They were chosen because they capture some of the most important and most theoretically interesting bases of variation. Let us briefly discuss them.

First of all, the following tables show how value systems vary between poor and rich societies; and between the more educated and less educated strata *within* each society. Both of these breakdowns reflect the concerns of modernization theory, a body of social thought that has been influential and controversial throughout the twentieth century.

The Implications of Modernization Theory

Economic, cultural, and political change go together in coherent patterns, with industrial societies showing fundamentally different characteristics from those of preindustrial societies: this is the central claim of modernization theory, and its two most influential proponents, Karl Marx and Max Weber, agreed on this point. They disagreed profoundly on *why* economic, cultural, and political changes go together. For Marx and his disciples, they are linked because economic and technological change determines political and cultural changes. For Weber and his disciples, they are linked because culture helps shape economic and political life.

Modernization theory gave rise to heated debate that stimulated influential subsequent work by Deutsch, Lerner, Inkeles and Smith, Bell, Toffler and many others. Still more recent work, analyzing evidence from the World Values surveys, suggests that the central claim of modernization theory is largely correct: economic change, cultural change, and political change are closely linked (Inglehart, 1997, forthcoming, and Inglehart, Nevitte and Basáñez 1996). Though we cannot predict exactly what will happen in a given society at a given time, some major trends are predictable in broad outline. When given processes of change are set in motion, certain characteristics are likely to emerge in the long run.

While conceding an important role to cultural factors, modernization theorists such as Bell (1973) viewed changes in the structure of the work force as the leading cause of cultural change. For Bell, the crucial milestone in the coming of "Postindustrial society" is reached when a majority of the work force is employed in the tertiary sector of the economy, producing neither raw materials, nor manufactured goods, but services. This leads to a massive expansion of formal education, driven by the need for an increasingly skilled and specialized work force. Other writers such as Lerner (1958) and Inkeles and Smith (1974) emphasized the importance of mass comunications and formal education as key factors shaping a "modern" worldview. Inglehart (1971, 1977, 1990) emphasizes the role of economic security in leading to gradual cultural changes.

The 1990 World Values survey investigated the hypothesis that economic development, cultural change and political change go together in coherent and even, to some extent, predictable patterns. This is a controversial claim. It implies that some trajectories of socioeconomic change are more likely than others—and consequently, that certain changes are foreseeable. Once a society has embarked on industrialization, for example, a whole syndrome of related changes, from mass mobilization to diminishing differences in gender roles, are likely to occur.

Though any simplistic linear version of modernization theory has long since been exploded, we *do* find strong empirical evidence that some scenarios of social change are far more probable than others. As Inglehart (1997) and Inglehart, Nevitte, and Basáñez (1996) demonstrate, the World Values surveys show coherent and far-reaching cultural patterns that are closely linked with economic development. In the long term, across many societies, once given processes are set in motion, certain important changes seem likely to happen. Industrialization, for example, tends to bring increasing urbanization, growing occupational specialization and higher levels of formal education in any society that undertakes it (Lerner, 1958; Deutsch, 1964). These are core elements of a trajectory that is generally called "Modernization."

This trajectory also tends to bring less obvious but equally important long term consequences, such as a shift from traditional religious values toward rational-bureaucratic norms; an increasing emphasis on economic achievement; rising levels of mass political participation and major changes in the types of issues that are most salient in the politics of the respective types of societies.

The modernization trajectory is linked with many other cultural changes. As this sourcebook shows, a wide range of cultural values are closely linked with a given society's level of economic development. For example, the sharply contrasting gender roles that characterize all preindustrial societies, tend to give way to increasingly similar gender roles in advanced industrial societies.

The Postmodern Shift

Economic development is linked with social change—but the process is not linear. Though a specific modernization syndrome becomes increasingly probable when societies move from an agrarian mode to an industrial mode, no trend goes on in the same direction forever. It eventually reaches a point of diminishing returns. Modernization is no exception. In the past few decades, advanced industrial societies have reached an inflection point and begun moving on a new trajectory that Inglehart (forthcoming) describes as "Postmodernization."

With Postmodernization, a new worldview is gradually replacing the outlook that has dominated industrializing societies since the Industrial Revolution. It reflects a shift in what people want out of life. It is transforming basic norms governing politics, work, religion, family, and sexual behavior. Thus, the process of economic development leads to two successive trajectories, Modernization and Postmodernization. Both of them are strongly linked with economic development but Postmodernization represents a later stage of development that is linked with very different beliefs from those that characterize Modernization. These belief systems are not mere consequences of economic or social changes, but shape socioeconomic conditions as well as being shaped by them, in reciprocal fashion.

Why Is the Postmodern Shift Occurring?

The shift toward Postmodern values is not the first time that a major cultural shift has occurred. The transition from agrarian society to industrial society was facilitated by a Modernization shift, from a worldview shaped by a steady-state economy, which discouraged social mobility and emphasized tradition, inherited status, and communal obligations, backed up by absolute religious norms; to a worldview that encouraged economic achievement, individualism and innovation, accompanied by increasingly secular and flexible social norms. Today, some of these trends linked with the transition from "Traditional" to "Modern" society have reached their limits in advanced industrial society, where change is taking a new direction.

This change of direction reflects the principle of diminishing marginal utility. Industrialization and modernization required breaking certain cultural constraints on accumulation that are found in any steady-state economy. In West European history, this was achieved by what Weber described as the rise of the Protestant Ethic, which was like a random mutation from a functional perspective. If it had occurred two centuries earlier it might have died out. In the environment of its time, it found a niche: technological developments were making rapid economic growth possible and the Calvinist worldview complemented these developments beautifully, forming a cultural-economic syndrome that led to the rise of capitalism and eventually, to the industrial revolution. Once this had occurred, economic accumulation (for individuals) and economic growth (for societies) became top priorities for an increasing part of the world's population, and are still the central goals for much of humanity. But eventually, diminishing returns from economic growth lead to a Postmodern shift.

Advanced industrial societies are now changing their basic value systems in a number of related ways. Increasing emphasis on individual economic achievement was one of the crucial changes that made modernization possible. This shift toward materialistic priorities entailed a deemphasis on communal obligations and an acceptance of social mobility: increasingly, social status became something that an individual could achieve, rather than something into which one was born. Economic growth came to be equated with progress and was seen as the hallmark of a successful society.

In postmodern society, this emphasis on economic achievement as the top priority is now giving way to an increasing emphasis on the quality of life. In a major part of the world, the disciplined, self-denying and achievement-oriented norms of industrial society are yielding to an increasingly broad latitude for individual choice of life styles and individual self-expression. The shift from "Materialist" values, emphasizing economic and physical security, to "Postmaterialist" values, emphasizing individual self-expression and quality life concerns, is the most amply documented aspect of this change; but it is only one component of a much broader syndrome of cultural change.

The theory of an intergenerational shift from Materialist to Postmaterialist value priorities is based on two key hypotheses (Inglehart, 1977):

1. *A Scarcity Hypothesis.* An individual's priorities reflect the socioeconomic environment: one places the greatest subjective value on those things that are in relatively short supply.
2. *A Socialization Hypothesis.* The relationship between socioeconomic environment and value priorities is not one of immediate adjustment: a substantial time lag is involved because, to a large extent, one's basic values reflect the conditions that prevailed during one's preadult years.

The recent economic history of advanced industrial societies has significant implications in the light of the scarcity hypothesis. For these societies are a striking exception to the prevailing historical pattern: they still contain poor people, but most of their population does *not* live under conditions of hunger and economic insecurity. This has led to a gradual shift in which needs for belonging, esteem, and intellectual and esthetic satisfaction became more prominent. Other things being equal, we would expect prolonged periods of high prosperity to encourage the spread of Postmaterialist values; economic decline would have the opposite effect.

The socialization hypothesis implies that neither an individual's values nor those of a society as a whole will change overnight. For the most part, fundamental value change takes place as younger birth cohorts replace older ones in the adult population of a society. Consequently, after a long period of rising economic and physical security, one should find substantial differences between the value priorities of older and younger groups: they have been shaped by different experiences in their formative years.

Materialist/Postmaterialist values have been measured by variable 257 through variable 262 in the questionnaire. Materialist priorities are tapped by emphasis on such goals as economic growth, fighting rising prices, maintaining order and fighting crime; while Postmaterialist values are reflected when top priority is given to such goals as giving people more say on the job or in government decisions, or protecting freedom of speech or moving toward a less impersonal, more humane society. Analyses by Abramson and Inglehart (1995) indicate that these items tap a meaningful and comparable dimension across virtually all of these societies.

The shift toward Postmaterialist values is only one aspect of a much broader Postmodern shift that involves changing political, religious, sexual, and other norms. The rise of Postmodern values manifests itself in a gradual intergenerational shift, as younger, more Postmaterialist birth cohorts replace older, more Materialist ones in the adult population. The orientations that are linked with this Postmodern shift are characterized by their age-related differences and their linkages with Materialist/Postmaterialist values, both of which are shown in the following tables.

Changing Religious Orientations, Gender Roles, And Sexual Norms

Postmaterialist values developed in the environment of the historically unprecedented economic growth and the welfare states that emerged after World War II. And they are part of a Postmodern shift that is reshaping the political outlook, religious orientations, gender roles, and sexual norms of advanced industrial society. Two factors contribute to the decline of traditional political, religious, social, and sexual norms in advanced industrial societies.

The first is that an increasing sense of security brings a diminishing need for absolute rules. Individuals under high stress have a need for rigid, predictable rules. They need to be sure of what is going to happen because they are in danger—their margin for error is slender and they need maximum predictability. Postmaterialists embody the opposite outlook: raised under conditions of relative security, they can tolerate more ambiguity; they are less likely to need the security of absolute rigid rules that religious sanctions provide. The psychological costs of deviating from whatever norms one grew up with are harder to bear if a person is under stress than if a person feels secure. Taking one's world apart and putting it together again is extremely stressful. But Post-materialists—people with relatively high levels of security—can more readily accept deviation from familiar patterns than people who feel anxiety concerning their basic existential needs. Consequently, Postmaterialists accept cultural change more readily than others.

The second reason is that societal and religious norms usually have a function. Such basic norms as "Thou shalt not kill" (the Judaeo-Christian version of a virtually universal social norm) obviously serve a societal function. Restricting violence to narrow, predictable channels is crucial to a society's viability. Without such norms, a society would tear itself apart.

Many religious norms such as "Thou shalt not commit adultery" or "Honor thy father and mother" are linked with maintaining the family unit. Various versions of these norms are also found in virtually every society because they serve crucial functions. But in advanced industrial society, some of these functions have dwindled.

The role of the family has become less crucial than it once was. Although the family was once the key economic unit, in advanced industrial society one's working life overwhelmingly takes place outside the home. Similarly, education now takes place mainly outside the family. Furthermore, the welfare state has taken over responsibility for survival. Formerly, whether children lived or died depended on whether their parents provided for them; and children cared for their parents when they reached old age.

Though the role of the family is still important, it is no longer a life or death relationship; to a large extent, its role has been taken over by the rise of the welfare state. Today, the new generation can survive if the family breaks up—or even if neither parent is around. One-parent families and childless old people have far better chances for survival under contemporary conditions than ever before.

Norms supporting the two-parent heterosexual family have been weakening for a variety of reasons, ranging from the rise of the welfare state to the drastic decline of infant mortality rates, which means that a couple no longer needs to produce four or five children in order for the population to reproduce itself. Experimentation and testing of the old rules takes place; gradually, new forms of behavior emerge that deviate from traditional norms, and the groups most likely to accept these new forms of behavior are the young more than the old; and the relatively secure, more than the insecure.

The Postmodern shift involves an intergenerational change in a wide variety of basic social norms, from cultural norms linked with ensuring survival of the species, to norms linked with the pursuit of individual well being. For example, Postmaterialists and the young are markedly more tolerant of homosexuality than are Materialists and the old. This is part of a pervasive pattern. Postmaterialists have been shaped by security during their formative years, and are far more permissive than Materialists in their attitudes toward abortion, divorce, extramarital affairs, prostitution, and euthanasia. Materialists, conversely, are likely to adhere to the traditional societal norms that favored child-bearing, but only within the traditional two-parent family—and that heavily stigmatized sexual activity outside that setting.

Traditional gender role norms from East Asia to the Islamic world to Western society discouraged women from taking jobs outside the home. Virtually all preindustrial societies emphasized child-bearing and child-rearing as the central goal of any woman, her most important function in life, and her greatest source of satisfaction. In recent years, this perspective has been increasingly called into question, as growing numbers of women postpone having children or forego them completely in order to devote themselves to careers outside the home. The sharply differentiated gender roles that characterize virtually all preindustrial societies, give way to increasingly similar gender roles in advanced industrial society.

As Table V128 in the data section demonstrates, we find large cross-national differences in attitudes toward equal employment opportunity for women. Outside of advanced industrial societies, much of the world still takes it for granted that practically everyone lives in a traditional family, with a male as their principal provider. People who see the world from this perspective are willing to accord men preferential employment opportunities.

Thus in Africa, South Asia, East Asia, and Eastern Europe, pluralities of the public feel that men have more right to a job than women (about half agree with this position, 5 to 10 percent are undecided, and less than half disagree). In Catholic Europe and Latin America, by contrast, solid pluralities of the public feel that men do *not* have more right to a job than women; in the U.S. and Canada, the public favors gender equality by an almost 3:1 margin (only 23 percent feel that men have more right to a job than women, while 72 percent disagree). And in Northern Europe, support for gender equality is overwhelming: only 17 percent agree that men have more right to a job than women, while 77 percent disagree.

The differences linked with Materialist/Postmaterialist values are also strong: 43 percent of the Materialists feel that men have more right to a job than women; 34 percent of the Mixed types and only 24 percent of the Postmaterialists take this position. The sizeable differences linked with Materialist/Postmaterialist values suggests that an inter-generational shift may be taking place—and this suggestion is supported by the fact that we also find sizeable differences between the attitudes of older and younger respondents: among those 50 and older, 44 percent feel that men have more right to a job; among those under 30 years of age, only 30 percent take this position, as Table V128 demonstrates.

Not surprisingly, women are more likely to favor equal employment opportunity than are men—the only surprising finding is the fact that the overall gender gap amounts to only 5 percentage points. Across these 43 societies, 38 percent of the men feel that their sex has more right to a job, while only 33 percent of the women agree. But we find relatively large gender differences in the less developed societies: in the ten lowest-income societies, fully 52 percent of the men agree that men have more right to a job than women; only 41 percent of the women agree, producing a gender gap of 11 points. In the ten richest societies, on the other hand, only 21 percent of the men say that man have more right to a job than women—and only 19 percent of the women take this view. In advanced industrial societies, there is a broad consensus favoring equal rights, and a gender gap of only two points.

Changing Values and Changing Political Cleavages

The pervasive cultural changes linked with Postmodernization have brought about a gradual shift in the issues underlying political cleavages in advanced industrial society.

The shift toward Postmodern values has brought a shift in the political agenda throughout advanced industrial society, moving it away from an emphasis on economic growth at any price, toward increasing concern for its environmental costs. It has also brought a shift from political cleavages based on social class conflict toward cleavages based on cultural issues and quality of life concerns. Economic conflicts are likely to remain important. But, while in the past they dominated the scene to such a degree that many influential thinkers accepted the Marxist view that economics was virtually the whole story, this now seems much less plausible. Today, economic conflicts are increasingly sharing the stage with new issues that were almost invisible a generation ago: in advanced industrial societies, environmental protection, abortion, ethnic conflicts, women's issues, and gay and lesbian emancipation are heated issues today—while the classic Marxist prescription, nationalization of industry, is virtually a forgotten cause.

As a result, a new dimension of political conflict has become increasingly salient. It reflects a polarization between modern and postmodern issue preferences. This new dimension is distinct from the traditional Left-Right conflict over ownership of the means of production and distribution of income. Its growing salience is transforming the meaning of Left and Right, and changing the social bases of Left and Right. Historically, the Left was based on the working class and the Right on the middle and upper classes. Today increasingly, support for the Left comes from middle class Postmaterialists, while a new Right draws support from less secure segments of the working class. A new Postmodern political cleavage pits culturally conservative, often xenophobic parties, disproportionately supported by Materialists; against change-oriented parties, often emphasizing environmental protection, and disproportionately supported by Postmaterialists.

Throughout most of the twentieth century, it was generally agreed that support for more state intervention in the economy was the crucial distinction between Left and Right. From a Marxist perspective, private ownership was the root problem, and nationalization of industry and state control of the economy constituted the core solution to all social problems. Abolishing private ownership of the means of production, it was thought, would eradicate exploitation, oppression, alienation, crime, and war.

The American Left also tended to view more state regulation and control of the economy as inherently good: liberals were those who supported a growing role for the state; conservatives were those who opposed it. Throughout most of the twentieth century, Western political elites continued to define the meanings of "Left" and "Right" in terms of state intervention in the economy and society.

This consensus has dissolved. It no longer seems self-evident that more state authority constitutes progress, even to those on the Left. One of the key developments of the past two decades has been a growing skepticism about the desirability and effectiveness of state planning and control, a growing concern for individual autonomy, and a growing respect for market forces. In recent years this outlook has been endorsed not only by conservatives but also by growing segments of the Left. As early as the 1960s, New Left groups emerged in the West that were highly critical of big government, viewed bureaucracy as dehumanizing, and called for devolution of decision-making power to local communities and to those directly affected by the decisions. Increasingly, those who support the Left are motivated by concerns for environmental protection, gender equality, the emancipation of sexual minorities and ethnic minorities. The following tables enable one to examine the degree to which given values and attitudes are linked with one's sense of affiliation with the Left or the Right in given societies.

A Cultural Map of the World

Figure 1 shows where each of the the 43 societies examined here falls on the two main dimensions of cross-cultural variation that we have just discussed, which are linked with the processes of "Modernization" and "Postmodernization" respectively (for a detailed discussion of the content of these dimensions and how they were derived, see Inglehart, forthcoming).

These two broad dimensions reflect most of the key values examined in the 1990 World Values survey. Since hundreds of questions were asked in these surveys, it would not be feasible to compare the values of all 43 publics on each topic separately. Figure 1 compares the orientations of these publics on two important dimensions that sum up the cross-national variation on scores of narrower values. These two dimensions tap:

1. **Traditional authority vs. Secular-Rational authority**. This dimension is based on a large number of items that reflect emphasis on obedience to traditional authority (usually religious authority), and adherence to family and communal obligations, and norms of sharing; or, on the other hand, a secular worldview in which authority is legitimated by rational-legal norms, linked with an emphasis on economic accumulation and individual achievement.

2. **Survival values vs. Well-being values**. This reflects the fact that in post-industrial society, historically unprecedented levels of wealth and the emergence of the welfare states have given rise to a shift from scarcity norms, emphasizing hard

work and self-denial, to postmodern values emphasizing the quality of life, emancipation of women and sexual minorities and related Postmaterialist priorities such as emphasis on self-expression.

Figure 1 sums up an immense amount of information. It is based on the responses to scores of questions, given by more than 60,000 respondents in 43 societies. There is a great deal of constraint among cultural systems. The first two dimensions that emerge from the principal components factor analysis depicted in Figure 1 account for fully 51% of the cross-national variation among 43 variables! Additional dimensions explain relatively small amounts of variance. And these dimensions are robust, showing little change if we drop some of the items, even high-loading ones.

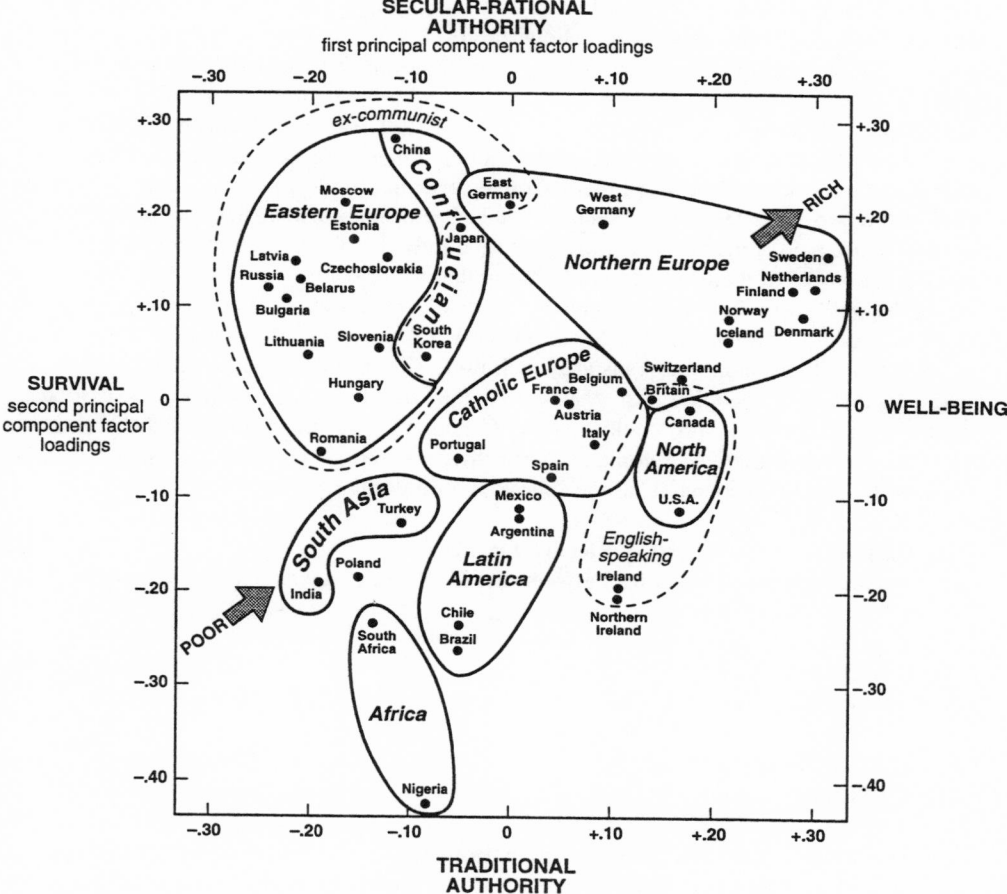

Figure 1. Where given societies fall on two key cultural dimensions.

Source: Ronald Inglehart, *Modernization and Postmodernization: Cultural, Economic and Political Change in 43 Societies* (Princeton: Princeton University Press, 1997).

Figure 1 shows the location of each society on these two dimensions. To make this possible, dummy variables were created for each of our 43 societies; they were mapped onto the two dimensions shaped by the worldviews of the respective publics. Societies that are close to each other on this figure, show relatively similar responses to most of the questions that were asked in the World Values Survey. For example, though the peoples of the United States and Canada differ in many ways, they have rather similar basic values in comparison with most other societies: accordingly, they are located close to each other on Figure 1.

Just how close are they? In order to provide a yardstick for cross-national comparisons, let us examine responses to the first six questions that were asked in the survey. The publics of each society were asked "Please say, for each of the following, how important it is in your life." They then rated the relative importance of "Work," "Family," "Friends," "Leisure," "Politics" and "Religion." This list covers a wide range of human concerns, and the various publics differed a great deal in how much importance they attached to the respective domains. The responses are shown in Tables V4 to V9; the right-hand column ranks each society from highest to lowest level of importance accorded to the given aspect of life.

Since 43 societies are ranked here, the greatest possible distance between two societies would occur if one were ranked 1st and the other were ranked 43rd: all 41 of the other societies would fall between them. Conversely, the smallest possible distance would occur if the two societies had consecutive ranks, with none of the other societies falling between them. And if the two societies were randomly distributed, about half of the other societies (about 21 of them) would fall between them.

The publics of the United States and Canada make rather similar ratings of these six aspects of life: on the average, there are only 3.3 other societies between them. The values of Canadians and Americans are much more similar to each other than they are to those of most other peoples. For example, the British are also relatively close to the Americans, but by no means as close as the Canadians. And the publics of the U.S. and China tend to give these six domains quite different ratings: on the average, they are separated by nearly 24 societies, as the following ratings show:

CULTURAL DISTANCE FROM THE U.S.
(mean number of societies between the U.S. and given society)

U.S.-Canada	3.3
U.S.-Britain	9.0
U.S.-France	16.7
U.S.-Japan	21.8
U.S.-Russia	22.2
U.S.-China	23.8

The foregoing comparison is written from a U.S. perspective, but the principle applies generally. One finds a similar pattern if one views the world from a Swedish perspective, for example. Sweden, Norway, and Denmark are located relatively near to each other on Figure 1; and accordingly, they tend to make rather similar ratings of the six aspects of life, as is demonstrated by their locations in the cross-national rankings in Tables V4–V9. On the average, only 3.8 societies fall between Sweden and Norway in these rankings; and only 5.8 societies fall between Sweden and Denmark. On the other hand, Sweden and China are separated by an average of more than 19 societies in these tables—as their relatively distant locations on Figure 1 suggest.

CULTURAL DISTANCE FROM SWEDEN
(mean number of societies between Sweden and given society)

Sweden-Norway	3.8
Sweden-Denmark	5.8
Sweden-France	13.6
Sweden-Russia	17.8
Sweden-Japan	18.2
Sweden-China	19.1

Given groups of nations take coherent positions on the two dimensions. For example, Norway, Iceland, Denmark, Finland, and Sweden—the five Nordic countries—form a compact cluster located in the upper right hand quadrant of figure 1: all five have similar cultures, ranking moderately high on the cultural outlook associated with secular-rational authority, and ranking very high on Postmodern values. But the fact that they are prosperous and traditionally Protestant welfare states seems more important than their geographic proximity. Thus The Netherlands, which is not a Nordic country but was historically Protestant and is today a prosperous welfare state, falls squarely into the middle of the Nordic group. Though geographically located next door to Belgium and sharing a common language with half of Belgium, The Netherlands is culturally much closer to the Nordic countries than to Belgium. Historically, The Netherlands has been shaped by Protestantism; even the Dutch Catholics today are remarkably Calvinist. And although the churches themselves are now a fading influence in West European society, religious traditions helped shape enduring *national* cultures that persist today. Thus, culturally, The Netherlands is located somewhere between Norway and Sweden. Finally, Switzerland—historically shaped by Calvinism and highly prosperous like the Nordic countries—falls at the edge of this cluster.

Belgium, France, Italy, Spain, Portugal, and Austria constitute another cluster in the cultural space of Figure 1. Though church attendance has declined drastically, all of these countries were historically Roman Catholic. Furthermore, this cluster is adjacent to a Latin American (and overwhelmingly Catholic) cluster containing Mexico, Argentina, Chile, and Brazil. These predominantly Catholic countries form a fairly coherent group. One could even expand it to include four other historically Roman Catholic countries, Poland, Hungary, Slovenia, and Lithuania. The latter countries are outliers, no doubt because of their divergent histories since 1945: the rising prosperity experienced by West European Catholic countries in recent decades has had less impact on them, and they are more permeated by Survival values than the rest of the Catholic group. On the modernization dimension, however, their values are almost as traditional as those of other Catholic countries (and they have more traditional values than the other ex-socialist countries). As Basáñez (1993) demonstrates, the Protestant-Catholic differences do not simply reflect the fact that the historically Protestant countries tend to be richer than the Catholic ones: controlling for GNP/capita, the value differences between them remain significant at the .001 level.

Nevertheless, there is no question that traditional orientations *are* closely related to a society's level of economic development. Almost all of the economically less-developed countries fall into the lower left-hand quadrant of Figure 1, with cultures that emphasize (1) traditional authority and (2) survival values. But interestingly enough, all five of the English-speaking societies (Britain, Canada, the U.S., Ireland, and Northern Ireland) fall into a cluster located in the lower right-hand quadrant: these societies place relatively strong emphasis on well-being values, but have much more traditional-religious values than most other countries at their economic level.

The former West German and East German regions of Germany were still independent states when these surveys were carried out, and were sampled separately. Though West Germany falls into the upper right-hand quadrant with the other West European societies, and East Germany into the upper left-hand quadrant containing most of the East European societies, the two societies are relatively close to each other on the two main cultural dimensions. This is significant. From 1945 to 1990, the communist regime made a massive effort to reshape East German culture to support a Marxist and atheistic authoritarian regime; while the Western powers launched a massive campaign, continued by the West German authorities, to remake political culture to support a market-oriented Western liberal democracy. The evidence indicates that 45 years under radically different regimes had an impact: by 1990, the two societies were some distance apart, especially along the Postmodernization dimension. But even more impressive is the fact that, in global perspective, the basic cultural values of the two societies were still relatively similar. This natural experiment indicates that, even when it makes a conscious and concerted effort to do so, the ability of a regime to reshape its underlying culture is limited. After 45 years under diametrically opposed political and economic institutions, East Germany and West Germany remained as similar to each other as are the United States and Canada.

Almost all of the socialist or ex-socialist societies fall into the upper left-hand quadrant: these societies are characterized by (1) survival values, and (2) a strong emphasis on state authority, rather than traditional authority. Poland is a striking exception, distinguished from the other socialist societies by her strong traditional-religious values. China is an outlier in the opposite direction—the least religious and most state-oriented society for which we have data. These societies' positions reflect their distinctive historical heritages. On one hand, adherence to the Catholic church has been a mainstay of the Polish struggle for independence from Russia since 1792. The church continued to play a vital role in this struggle throughout the 1980s, revitalizing the role of religion in the national culture.

China, on the other hand, has had a predominantly secular cultural system for two thousand years; and bureaucratic authority developed within the Confucian system long before it reached the West. Thus China and the Confucian-influenced societies of East Asia have had one major component of modern culture for a very long time. Until recently, they lacked the emphasis on science and technology, and the esteem for economic achievement that are its other main components; but their secular, bureaucratic heritage may have facilitated rapid economic development once these were attained. China's traditional low emphasis on religion and high emphasis on the state was almost certainly accentuated by four decades of socialism. Japan, another Confucian-influenced society, and both East and West Germany are also characterized by relatively strong emphasis on secular-rational authority.

Most of the socialist and ex-socialist societies are oriented toward secular-rational, rather than traditional-religious authority. This is certainly not surprising. Their people have lived for decades under socialist regimes in which religion was systematically repressed and in which it was natural to consider the state important because it dominated economic life, cultural life, and even one's chances of survival. The socialist states were probably the most heavily bureaucratized, centralized, and secularized societies in history, and they held science and technology in such esteem that their elites legitimated their power by the claim that they ruled, not through the unscientific and fallible process of majority rule, but according to the principles of scientific socialism. By these standards, the socialist states represented the culmination of modernization—and the fact that, on Figure 1, they are located near the Modernization pole of the Traditional Authority/ Secular-rational Authority dimension seems appropriate.

Institutional Determinism?

As we have seen, the historically Protestant countries of both Northern Europe and North America tend to cluster together to form one large group; similarly, the historically Roman Catholic countries of Western Europe, Latin America, and Eastern Europe tend to cluster together, forming another broad but reasonably cohesive cluster. Despite the enormous recent changes linked with economic and social modernization, and despite the tremendous sociopolitical changes brought by communist domination of five of these societies throughout the Cold War, the historically Catholic societies still manifest cultural values that are relatively similar to each other in global perspective—as do the historically Protestant societies.

When we view Poland as a Roman Catholic society, rather than as an East European society, she no longer constitutes an outlier but forms part of a large but relatively cohesive Catholic cluster embracing societies in Eastern Europe, Western Europe, and Latin America. From this perspective, it is Czechoslovakia rather than Poland that is the outlier: Czechoslovakia is the only traditionally Catholic society that has been sufficiently secularized that she falls into the reduced East European cluster, rather than the enlarged Catholic cluster that contains 15 of the 16 traditionally Catholic societies.

Similarly, we find a large but relatively coherent cluster of historically Protestant societies, embracing countries in both Europe and North America. The two types of societies do not overlap. As Figure 2 shows, Catholic societies form a group characterized by (1) more traditional, less secular-rational values, and (2) by greater emphasis on survival values, than is true of most Protestant societies. At first glance, this might seem to constitute strong evidence for an institutional determinist interpretation: one might conclude that the religious institutions of these societies led them to develop different cultures.

If institutional determinism is taken to mean simply that a society's institutions are among the factors that help shape its culture, the claim is undoubtedly correct. But institutional determinism is often pushed to a much more extreme claim than this: it is taken to mean that institutions alone determine a society's cultural values, so one needn't really take cultural factors into account: if one changes the institutions, the culture automatically changes accordingly. If one examines the evidence more closely, it is clear that this position is untenable.

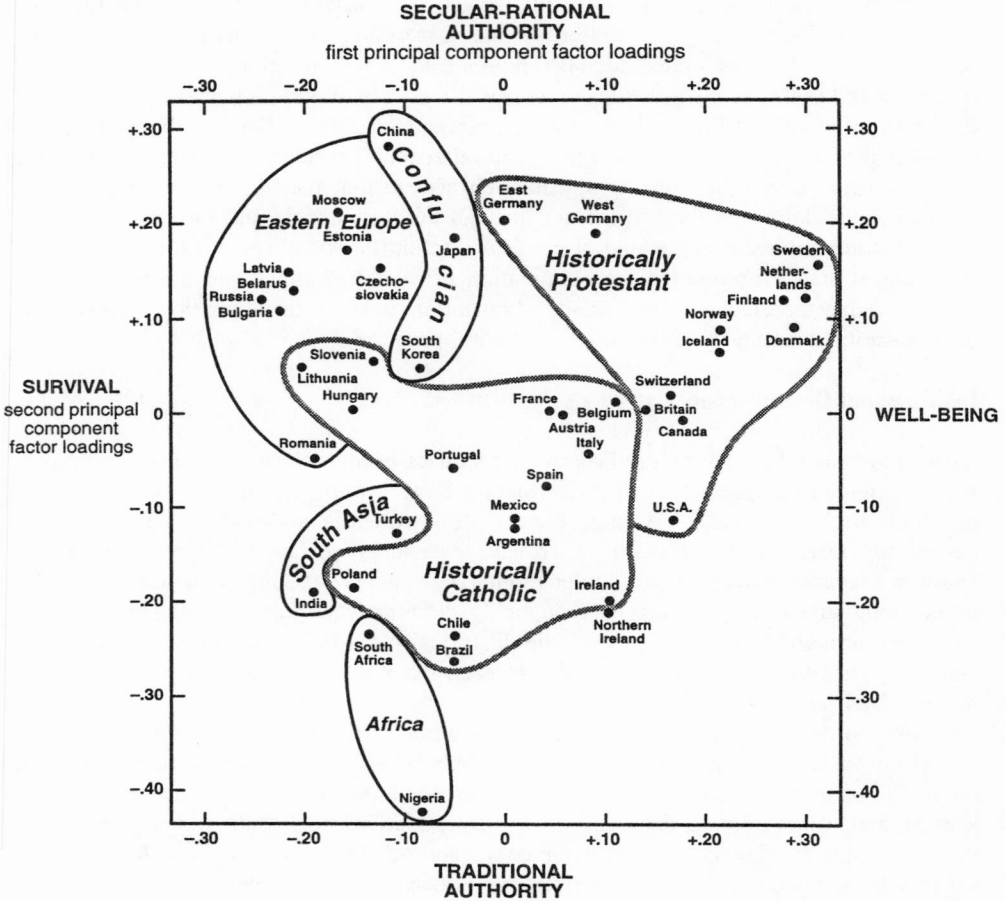

Figure 2. Where given societies fall on two key cultural dimensions.

Source: Ronald Inglehart, *Modernization and Postmodernization: Cultural, Economic and Political Change in 43 Societie*s (Princeton: Princeton University Press, 1997).

There are tremendous cultural differences between Protestant and Catholic societies, but for the most part they do not reflect the direct influence of the Catholic and Protestant churches *today*. For the direct influence of the church today is very slight in many of these countries. Though church attendance remains relatively high in Poland and Ireland (and the United States, to a lesser degree), it has fallen drastically in most of the historically Catholic countries of both Western and Eastern Europe; and it has fallen even more drastically in most of the historically Protestant societies—to the point where many observers now speak of the Nordic countries as post-Christian societies. Traditionally Catholic and Protestant societies still show very distinct values—even among segments of the population who have no contact whatever with the church. But these values persist as part of the cultural heritage of the given nations, and not through the direct influence of the religious institutions. This cultural heritage has been shaped not only by the religious institutions, but also by the economic, political, and social experience of the given people. An important aspect of this experience is the fact that the Protestant societies industrialized earlier than most of the Catholic societies (which may, in turn, be related to religious orientations as Weber argued—but is certainly not a case of direct institutional determinism).

These cultural differences reflect the entire historical experience of given societies, and not the influence of the respective churches today. This point becomes vividly evident when we examine the value systems of such societies as The Netherlands and Germany—both of which were historically predominantly Protestant societies, but (through the effects of different birth rates and different rates of religious erosion) now have about as many practicing Catholics as Protestants. Despite these changes in their religious makeup today, both The Netherlands and Germany show typically Protestant value systems. Furthermore, the Catholics and Protestants *within* these societies do not have markedly different value systems: the Dutch Catholics are more Dutch than Catholic in most of their social norms, and have very distinctive values from those of Catholics in traditionally Catholic societies.

As the reader examines the following tables, he or she will find that again and again, across scores of variables, the societies that are located near each other on Figure 1 show relatively similar values and beliefs; while those that are far apart on this figure show dissimilar values and beliefs.

There is a remarkable degree of coherence. Forty of the 43 societies fall into compact and historically meaningful clusters, such as Latin America or Eastern Europe or East Asia. There are only three relative outliers: Poland plus Ireland and Northern Ireland (with the latter two being closely linked). Both Poland and Ireland might be described as hyper-Catholic societies: historically Roman Catholic societies that for centuries were occupied and dominated by more powerful neighbors, and that responded to pressures toward cultural assimilation by an intense re-emphasis of their Roman Catholic heritage, as a means of preserving their national autonomy in the face of political domination. Ironically, this has led to a similar reaction on the part of the Irish Protestants, who constitute a small minority within Ireland as a whole. As a consequence, both Poland and Ireland societies manifest relatively traditional cultural values across a wide range of areas. Not only in religion, but also in politics, gender roles, sexual norms, and family values, their values are far more traditional than those generally found in industrial societies.

In their responses to these questions, the Japanese public shows a tendency to avoid extreme responses: they are less likely than most peoples to agree strongly or disagree strongly with given propositions, and less likely to describe themselves as "very satisfied" or "very dissatisfied" with aspects of their lives. This tendency has been noted by other analysts and seems to constitute an enduring cultural trait of the Japanese, who consider it immodest to stand out from the modal response. The Nigerian public seems to fall at the opposite pole: they are more likely to take extreme positions than most publics, being relatively apt to agree (or disagree) very strongly with given statements, or to describe themselves as "very satisfied" and "very dissatisfied" with aspects of life. To some extent, one can control for such cultural biases in cross-national comparisons by creating multi-item indices based on the difference between the proportion strongly endorsing one type of proposition, and the proportion strongly endorsing another type of proposition. Thus, in constructing an Achievement Motivation index, Granato, Inglehart, and Leblang (1996) subtract the proportion emphasizing one type of goal from the proportion emphasizing another (negatively correlated) type of goal.

The foregoing provides only a brief overview of the complex but coherent pattern of cross-national differences revealed in the World Values surveys. The tables in the data section enable one to delve into the rich body of evidence provided by these surveys in much greater detail, and to explore the implications of cross-cultural variations and their linkages with economic development and education; one can also explore the inter-generational differences that tend to be linked with Materialist/Postmaterialist values; the extent to which cultural values are linked with whether people identify with the Left or the Right; and the extent to which men and women have different beliefs and values.

The English-language version of the questionnaire used in the 1990 World Values surveys appears in the following section, providing the exact text of the questions asked in the respective countries. It also serves as a table of contents for the data tables, which appear in the same order as these questions. The next section is the heart of this book: it presents nearly 350 data tables, interspersed with graphs that place these detailed tables in their broader context. The data tables are followed by a section that provides information about the dates of fieldwork, sample sizes, and the people who conducted the surveys in the respective countries.

These surveys were carried out by a worldwide network of social scientists who cooperated in formulating the questionnaire and (in most cases) raised funding locally. Thus, this sourcebook was coauthored by the 80 following individuals: Rasa Alishauskiene, Vladimir Andreyenkov, Soo Young Auh, David Barker, Elena Bashkirova, Marek Boguszak, Pi-chao Chen, Marita Carballo de Cilley, Eric da Costa, Juan Diez Nicolas, Karel Dobbelaere, Mattei Dogan, Javier Elzo, Ustun Erguder, Yilmaz Esmer, Blanka Filipcova, Michael Fogarty, Luis de Franca, Christian Friesl, Yuji Fukuda, Ivan Gabal, Alec Gallup, George Gallup, Renzo Gubert, Peter Gundelach, Loek Halman, Elemer Hankiss, Stephen Harding, Gordon Heald, Felix Heunks, Carlos Huneeus, Kenji Iijima, J.C. Jesumo, Fridrik Jonsson, Ersin Kalaycioglu, Jan Kerkhofs, Hans-Dieter Klingemann, Renate Koecher, Marta Lagos, Max Larsen, Ola Listhaug, Jin-yun Liu, Nicolae Lotreanu, Leila Lotti, V.P. Madhok, Robert Manchin, Carlos Eduardo Meirelles Matheus, Anna Melich, Ruud de Moor, Neil Nevitte, Elisabeth Noelle-Neumann, Stefan Olafsson, Francisco Andres Orizo, R. C. Pandit, Juhani Pehkonen, Thorleif Petterson, Jacques-Rene Rabier, Andrei Raichev, Vladimir Rak, Helene Riffault, Ole Riis, Andrus Saar, Renata Siemienska, Kancho Stoichev, Kareem Tejumola, Noel Timms, Mikk Titma, Niko Tos, Jorge Vala, Andrei Vardomatski, Christine Woessner, Jiang Xingrong, Vladimir Yadov, Seiko Yamazaki, Catalin Zamfir, Brigita Zepa, Xiang Zongde, and Paul Zulehner. This joint undertaking has given rise to scores of publications, many (but by no means all) of which are listed in the final section of this book.

One of the most comprehensive overviews of findings (presenting contributions by authors from more than 30 societies) is a book edited by Juan Diez Nicolas and Ronald Inglehart, Tendencies mundiales de Cambio en los Valores sociales y politicos (Madrid: Libros de Fundesco, 1994). These contributions were first presented at a conference in El

Escorial Spain, held in honor of the 700th anniversary of the founding of Complutense University. An initial release of the 1990–1991 World Values Survey data, for the use of the investigators in this project, was prepared by Juan Diez Nicolas. We are grateful to Diez for organizing the 1993 conference and distributing the data; in doing so, he greatly facilitated collaboration within the World Values Survey network.

The authors are indebted to the National Science Foundation for a grant to Inglehart (SES 91-22433) that made possible the processing and documentation of the survey; to the U.S. Fulbright Commission which enabled Basáñez to spend the academic year 1995–1996 in Ann Arbor as a visiting Fulbright scholar; and to Salomon Brothers, who provided support for preparation of this sourcebook. Thanks are due to Julio Borquez, Georgia Aktan, and Bettina Schroeder for skillful and effective research assistance and to Juan Balderas, Arijit Banerjee, Pilgrim Spikes, Alejandro Basáñez, Ekaterina Beltran, and Chantal Beltran for excellent computer and administrative assistance.

Human beliefs and values are not just an epiphenomenon that is shaped by a society's economic infrastructure. The fact that the World Values surveys cover 43 societies, makes it possible to carry out statistically significant cross-level analyses, examining the impact of individual-level values and beliefs on societal-level phenomena such as fertility rates or political institutions. The results indicate that cultural factors play a major role in shaping the economic growth rates of given societies (Granato, Inglehart, and Lebland, 1996a and Granato, Inglehart, and Leblang, 1996b; Inglehart, 1997).

Moreover, an analysis of the empirical linkages between culture and democracy demonstrates that democracies have strikingly different political cultures from authoritarian societies. Almost without exception, stable democracies rank high on subjective well being and interpersonal trust, and authoritarian societies rank low on them. These linkages persist when we control for economic level and social structure: a prodemocratic political culture seems to play an important role in sustaining democratic institutions over the long term (Inglehart, 1990; Inglehart, Ellis, Granato, and Leblang, 1995; Inglehart, 1997).

The evidence suggests that the remarkably strong linkage found between political culture and democracy is more a matter of culture contributing to democracy, than of democracy determining culture. With economic development, cultural patterns tend to emerge that are increasingly supportive of democracy.

The authors hope that this sourcebook will be a useful tool to anyone concerned with the role of human values and beliefs in contemporary society. Those who wish to carry out more detailed analyses can obtain the original data from the ICPSR survey data archive at the University of Michigan, and other major data archives.

REFERENCES

Abramson, Paul R., and Ronald Inglehart. 1995. *Value Change in Global Perspective.* Ann Arbor: University of Michigan Press.

Basáñez, Miguel. 1993. "Protestant and Catholic Ethics: An Empirical Comparison." Paper presented at conference on *Changing Social and Political Values: A Global Perspective*, Complutense University, Madrid, September 27–October 1.

Basáñez, Miguel. 1993. "Is Mexico Headed Toward its Fifth Crisis?" In Riordan Roett (ed.) *Political and Economic Liberalization in Mexico.* Boulder: Lynne Rienner.

Bell, Daniel. 1973. *The Coming of Postindustrial Society.* New York: Basic Books.

Deutsch, Karl W. 1964. "Social Mobilization and Political Development." *American Political Science Review* 55:493–514.

Granato, Jim, Ronald Inglehart, and David Leblang. 1996a. "The Effect of Culture on Economic Development: Theory, Hypotheses and Some Empirical Tests." *American Journal of Political Science* (August).

Granato, Jim, Ronald Inglehart, and David Leblang. 1996b. "Cultural Values, Stable Democracy and Economic Development: A Reply." *American Journal of Political Science* (August).

Huber, John, and Ronald Inglehart. 1995. "Expert Interpretations of Party Space and Party Locations in 42 Societies," *Party Politics* 1, no. 1: 73–112.

Inglehart, Ronald. 1977. *The Silent Revolution: Changing Values and Political Styles.* Princeton: Princeton University Press.

Inglehart, Ronald. 1990. *Culture Shift in Advanced Industrial Society.* Princeton: Princeton University Press.

Inglehart, Ronald. 1997. *Modernization and Postmodernization: Cultural, Economic and Political Change in 43 Societies.* Princeton: Princeton University Press.

Inglehart, Ronald, Susan Ellis, Jim Granato, and David Leblang. 1996. "Economic Development, Political Culture and Democracy: Bringing the People Back In." Paper presented at the 1996 annual meeting of the Midwest Political Science Association, Chicago.

Inglehart, Ronald, Neil Nevitte, and Miguel Basáñez. 1996. *The North American Trajectory: Social Institutions and Social Change.* Hawthorne, NY: Aldine de Gruyter.

Inkeles, Alex and David Smith. 1974. *Becoming Modern: Individual Change in Six Developing Countries.* Cambridge, MA: Harvard University Press.

Lerner, Daniel. 1958. *The Passing of Traditional Society: Modernizing the Middle East.* New York: The Free Press.

World values survey 1990–1993 Weighted marginals

All these marginals are weighted (see technical note for details), except for 'V2 Country' which is shown both unweighted and weighted, to show the actual number of respondents in each country. For total percentages see * at the end of this section.

V2 Country (UNWEIGHTED)

Value label	Frequency	%
India	2,500	4.2
Nigeria	1,001	1.7
China	1,000	1.7
Romania	1,103	1.9
Turkey	1,030	1.7
Poland	938	1.6
Bulgaria	1,034	1.7
Chile	1,500	2.5
Czechoslovakia	1,396	2.4
South Africa	2,736	4.6
Lithuania	1,000	1.7
Hungary	999	1.7
Argentina	1,002	1.7
Brazil	1,782	3.0
Mexico	1,531	2.6
Belarus	1,015	1.7
Russia	1,961	3.3
Moscow	1,012	1.7
Latvia	903	1.5
Estonia	1,008	1.7
Portugal	1,185	2.0
South Korea	1,251	2.1
Ireland	1,000	1.7
North Ireland	304	.5
Slovenia	1,035	1.7
Spain	4,147	7.0
East Germany	1,336	2.3
Britain	1,484	2.5
Italy	2,018	3.4

Netherlands	1,017	1.7
Belgium	2,792	4.7
Austria	1,460	2.5
France	1,002	1.7
Canada	1,730	2.9
United States	1,839	3.1
Iceland	702	1.2
West Germany	2,101	3.6
Denmark	1,030	1.7
Finland	588	1.0
Norway	1,239	2.1
Sweden	1,047	1.8
Japan	1,011	1.7
Switzerland	1,400	2.4
Total	59,169	100
Valid cases	59,169	
Missing cases	0	

V2 Country (WEIGHTED)

Value label	Frequency	%
France	1,002	2.3
Britain	999	2.3
West Germany	1,002	2.3
Italy	1,002	2.3
Netherlands	996	2.3
Denmark	1,000	2.3
Belgium	1,000	2.3
Spain	1,013	2.4
Ireland	1,000	2.3
North Ireland	996	2.3
United States	1,000	2.3
Canada	1,000	2.3
Japan	1,000	2.3
Mexico	1,000	2.3
South Africa	1,000	2.3
Hungary	1,000	2.3
Norway	1,000	2.3
Sweden	1,000	2.3
Iceland	1,000	2.3
Argentina	1,000	2.3
Finland	1,000	2.3
South Korea	1,000	2.3
Poland	1,000	2.3
Switzerland	1,000	2.3
Brazil	1,000	2.3
Nigeria	1,000	2.3
Chile	1,000	2.3
Belarus	1,000	2.3
India	1,000	2.3
Czechoslovakia	1,000	2.3

East Germany	1,000	2.3
Slovenia	1,000	2.3
Bulgaria	1,000	2.3
Romania	1,000	2.3
China	1,000	2.3
Portugal	998	2.3
Austria	1,000	2.3
Turkey	1,000	2.3
Moscow	1,000	2.3
Lithuania	1,000	2.3
Latvia	1,000	2.3
Estonia	1,000	2.3
Russia	1,000	2.3
Total	43,012	100
Valid cases	43,012	

V4 Work important

Value label	Frequency	%
Very	25,308	60
Quite	13,422	32
Not very	2,665	6
Not at all	1,002	2
Total	43,012	100
Valid cases	42,397	
Missing cases	615	

V5 Family important

Value label	Frequency	%
Very	35,615	83
Quite	6,026	14
Not very	789	2
Not at all	251	1
Total	43,012	100
Valid cases	42,681	
Missing cases	331	

V6 Friends important

Value label	Frequency	%
Very	17,024	40
Quite	18,936	44
Not very	6,088	14
Not at all	585	1
Total	43,012	100
Valid cases	42,633	
Missing cases	379	

V7 Leisure important

Value label	Frequency	%
Very	14,685	35
Quite	18,712	44

Not very	7,629	18
Not at all	1,266	3
Total	43,012	100
Valid cases	42,293	
Missing cases	719	

V8 Politics important

Value label	Frequency	%
Very	4,947	12
Quite	11,595	28
Not very	15,860	38
Not at all	9,639	23
Total	43,012	100
Valid cases	42,041	
Missing cases	971	

V9 Religion important

Value label	Frequency	%
Very	11,145	27
Quite	10,571	25
Not very	11,287	27
Not at all	8,563	21
Total	43,012	100
Valid cases	41,566	
Missing cases	1,446	

V10 Discuss politics

Value label	Frequency	%
Often	9,198	22
At times	22,728	53
Never	10,722	25
Total	43,012	100
Valid cases	42,648	
Missing cases	364	

V11 Persuade friends

Value label	Frequency	%
Often	7,196	18
At times	15,998	41
Rarely	10,030	26
Never	6,088	16
Total	43,012	100
Valid cases	39,312	
Missing cases	3,700	

V12 Environment: income

Value label	Frequency	%
Agree+	9,568	26
Agree	18,214	49
Disagree	6,807	18

Disagree+	2,634	7
Total	43,012	100
Valid cases	37,224	
Missing cases	5,789	

V13 Environment: taxes

Value label	Frequency	%
Agree+	6,790	18
Agree	16,760	45
Disagree	9,850	26
Disagree+	3,874	10
Total	43,012	100
Valid cases	37,273	
Missing cases	5,739	

V14 Environment: no cost

Value label	Frequency	%
Agree+	9,514	26
Agree	11,887	32
Disagree	12,900	35
Disagree+	2,908	8
Total	43,012	100
Valid cases	37,209	
Missing cases	5,804	

V15 Environment: too anxious

Value label	Frequency	%
Agree+	5,853	16
Agree	13,357	37
Disagree	12,427	34
Disagree+	4,955	14
Total	43,012	100
Valid cases	36,592	
Missing cases	6,421	

V16 Environment: unemployment

Value label	Frequency	%
Agree+	3,012	9
Agree	9,167	26
Disagree	15,110	43
Disagree+	7,748	22
Total	43,012	100
Valid cases	35,038	
Missing cases	7,975	

V17 Environment: not urgent

Value label	Frequency	%
Agree+	2,360	6
Agree	5,943	15
Disagree	16,674	43
Disagree+	13,670	35

Total	43,012	100
Valid cases	38,648	
Missing cases	4,365	

V18 Happiness

Value label	Frequency	%
Very	9,653	23
Quite	22,552	54
Not very	8,215	20
Not at all	1,264	3
Total	43,012	100
Valid cases	41,684	
Missing cases	1,328	

V19   Social welfare

Value label	Frequency	%
Belongs	2,163	6
No	32,850	94
Total	43,012	100
Valid cases	35,013	
Missing cases	8,000	

V20 Religious organization

Value label	Frequency	%
Belongs	5,010	14
No	30,003	86
Total	43,012	100
Valid cases	35,013	
Missing cases	8,000	

V21 Education/cultural

Value label	Frequency	%
Belongs	3,545	10
No	31,467	90
Total	43,012	100
Valid cases	35,013	
Missing cases	8,000	

V22 Trade unions

Value label	Frequency	%
Belongs	7,881	23
No	27,131	78
Total	43,012	100
Valid cases	35,013	
Missing cases	8,000	

V23 Political parties

Value label	Frequency	%
Belongs	2,825	8

No	32,188	92
Total	43,012	100
Valid cases	35,013	
Missing cases	8,000	

V24 Community action

Value label	Frequency	%
Belongs	1,176	3
No	33,837	97
Total	43,012	100
Valid cases	35,013	
Missing cases	8,000	

V25 Third World development

Value label	Frequency	%
Belongs	820	2
No	34,193	98
Total	43,012	100
Valid cases	35,013	
Missing cases	8,000	

V26 Environment

Value label	Frequency	%
Belongs	1,555	4
No	33,458	96
Total	43,012	100
Valid cases	35,013	
Missing cases	8,000	

V27 Professional associations

Value label	Frequency	%
Belongs	2,809	8
No	32,203	92
Total	43,012	100
Valid cases	35,013	
Missing cases	8,000	

V28 Youth work

Value label	Frequency	%
Belongs	1,676	5
No	33,336	95
Total	43,012	100
Valid cases	35,013	
Missing cases	8,000	

V29 Sports/recreation

Value label	Frequency	%
Belongs	5,512	16
No	28,500	84

Total	43,012	100
Valid cases	34,012	
Missing cases	9,000	

V30 Women's groups

Value label	Frequency	%
Belongs	1,117	3
No	32,895	97
Total	43,012	100
Valid cases	34,012	
Missing cases	9,000	

V31 Peace movement

Value label	Frequency	%
Belongs	424	1
No	33,589	99
Total	43,012	100
Valid cases	34,012	
Missing cases	9,000	

V32 Animal rights

Value label	Frequency	%
Belongs	809	2
No	33,204	98
Total	43,012	100
Valid cases	34,012	
Missing cases	9,000	

V33 Health-voluntary

Value label	Frequency	%
Belongs	1,443	4
No	32,570	96
Total	43,012	100
Valid cases	34,012	
Missing cases	9,000	

V34 Other groups

Value label	Frequency	%
Belongs	2,028	6
No	31,984	94
Total	43,012	100
Valid cases	34,012	
Missing cases	9,000	

V35 None

Value label	Frequency	%
Mentioned	13,615	40
No	20,397	60
Total	43,012	100
Valid cases	34,012	

Missing cases   9,000

V36 Don't know

Value label	Frequency	%
Mentioned	5	1
No	33,551	99
Total	43,012	100
Valid cases	34,012	
Missing cases	9,000	

V37 Social welfare

Value label	Frequency	%
Works	1,453	4
No	32,560	96
Total	43,012	100
Valid cases	34,012	
Missing cases	9,000	

V38 Religious organization

Value label	Frequency	%
Works	2,139	6
No	31,874	94
Total	43,012	100
Valid cases	34,012	
Missing cases	9,000	

V39 Education/cultural

Value label	Frequency	%
Works	1,593	5
No	32,419	95
Total	43,012	100
Valid cases	34,012	
Missing cases	9,000	

V40 Trade unions

Value label	Frequency	%
Works	1,336	4
No	32,676	96
Total	43,012	100
Valid cases	34,012	
Missing cases	9,000	

V41 Political parties

Value label	Frequency	%
Works	1,243	4
No	32,770	96
Total	43,012	100
Valid cases	34,012	
Missing cases	9,000	

V42 Community action

Value label	Frequency	%
Works	773	2
No	33,239	98
Total	43,012	100
Valid cases	34,012	
Missing cases	9,000	

V43 Third World development

Value label	Frequency	%
Works	380	1
No	33,633	99
Total	43,012	100
Valid cases	34,012	
Missing cases	9,000	

V44 Environment

Value label	Frequency	%
Works	608	2
No	33,405	98
Total	43,012	100
Valid cases	34,012	
Missing cases	9,000	

V45 Professional associations

Value label	Frequency	%
Works	888	3
No	33,124	97
Total	43,012	100
Valid cases	34,012	
Missing cases	9,000	

V46 Youth work

Value label	Frequency	%
Works	1,204	4
No	32,809	97
Total	43,012	100
Valid cases	34,012	
Missing cases	9,000	

V47 Sports/recreation

Value label	Frequency	%
Works	2,334	7
Total	43,012	100
Valid cases	34,014	
Missing cases	8,998	

V48   Women's groups

Value label	Frequency	%

Works	571	2
No	33,443	98
Total	43,012	100
Valid cases	34,014	
Missing cases	8,998	

V49 Peace movement

Value label	Frequency	%
Works	222	1
No	33,792	99
Total	43,012	100
Valid cases	34,014	
Missing cases	8,998	

V50 Animal rights

Value label	Frequency	%
Works	285	1
No	33,729	99
Total	43,012	100
Valid cases	34,014	
Missing cases	8,998	

V51 Health-voluntary

Value label	Frequency	%
Works	678	2
No	33,336	98
Total	43,012	100
Valid cases	34,014	
Missing cases	8,998	

V52 Other groups

Value label	Frequency	%
Works	1,040	3
No	32,974	97
Total	43,012	100
Valid cases	34,014	
Missing cases	8,998	

V53 None

Value label	Frequency	%
Mentioned	16,996	50
No	17,017	50
Total	43,012	100
Valid cases	34,014	
Missing cases	8,998	

V54 Don't know

Value label	Frequency	%
Mentioned	1,311	4
No	32,686	96
Total	43,012	100
Valid cases	34,014	
Missing cases	8,998	

V55 Solidarity

Value label	Frequency	%
1 Import-	1,665	16
2	1,821	17
3	2,035	19
4	1,989	19
5 Import+	3,111	29
Total	43,012	100
Valid cases	10,622	
Missing cases	32,391	

V56 Compassion

Value label	Frequency	%
1 Import-	1,393	13
2	1,684	16
3	1,614	15
4	2,282	22
5 Import+	3,500	33
Total	43,012	100
Valid cases	10,471	
Missing cases	32,541	

V57 Opportunity to give

Value label	Frequency	%
1 Import-	2,243	22
2	1,902	18
3	1,793	17
4	1,944	19
5 Import+	2,429	24
Total	43,012	100
Valid cases	10,312	
Missing cases	32,701	

V58 Sense of duty

Value label	Frequency	%
1 Import-	1,097	10
2	1,736	16
3	1,631	15
4	2,531	24
5 Import+	3,616	34
Total	43,012	100
Valid cases	10,611	
Missing cases	32,401	

V59 Identify suffering

Value label	Frequency	%

1 Import-	1,589	15
2	1,860	18
3	1,673	16
4	2,195	21
5 Import+	3,051	29
Total	43,012	100
Valid cases	10,368	
Missing cases	32,645	

V60 Worthwhile to do

Value label	Frequency	%
1 Import-	1,847	18
2	1,957	19
3	1,805	17
4	2,243	21
5 Import+	2,656	25
Total	43,012	100
Valid cases	10,507	
Missing cases	32,505	

V61 Personal satisfaction

Value label	Frequency	%
1 Import-	2,478	24
2	2,274	22
3	1,947	19
4	1,744	17
5 Import+	2,099	20
Total	43,012	100
Valid cases	10,542	
Missing cases	32,470	

V62 Religious beliefs

Value label	Frequency	%
1 Import-	4,328	42
2	1,900	18
3	992	10
4	944	9
5 Import+	2,219	21
Total	43,012	100
Valid cases	10,383	
Missing cases	32,629	

V63 Give hope/dignity

Value label	Frequency	%
1 Import-	1,523	15
2	1,801	17
3	1,748	17
4	2,263	22
5 Import+	2,989	29
Total	43,012	100

Valid cases	10,324	
Missing cases	32,688	

V64 Community contribute

Value label	Frequency	%
1 Import-	1,299	12
2	1,861	18
3	1,798	17
4	2,438	23
5 Import+	3,126	30
Total	43,012	100
Valid cases	10,522	
Missing cases	32,490	

V65 Social/political change

Value label	Frequency	%
1 Import-	2,739	27
2	2,279	22
3	1,764	17
4	1,666	16
5 Import+	1,899	18
Total	43,012	100
Valid cases	10,347	
Missing cases	32,666	

V66 Social reasons

Value label	Frequency	%
1 Import-	1,633	15
2	2,029	19
3	1,885	18
4	2,376	22
5 Import+	2,737	26
Total	43,012	100
Valid cases	10,660	
Missing cases	32,353	

V67 Useful experience

Value label	Frequency	%
1 Import-	1,307	12
2	1,836	17
3	1,628	15
4	2,540	24
5 Import+	3,271	31
Total	43,012	100
Valid cases	10,583	
Missing cases	32,430	

V68 Couldn't refuse

Value label	Frequency	%

1 Import-	5,008	49
2	2,145	21
3	1,543	15
4	761	8
5 Import+	716	7
Total	43,012	100
Valid cases	10,173	
Missing cases	32,840	

V69 Neighbors: criminals

Value label	Frequency	%
Mention	20,030	49
No	20,983	51
Total	43,012	100
Valid cases	41,013	
Missing		2,000

V70 Neighbors: other race

Value label	Frequency	%
Mention	6,646	16
No	34,366	84
Total	43,012	100
Valid cases	41,013	
Missing cases	2,000	

V71 Neighbors: left wing

Value label	Frequency	%
Mention	15,308	37
No	25,705	63
Total	43,012	100
Valid cases	41,013	
Missing cases	2,000	

V72 Neighbors: drinkers

Value label	Frequency	%
Mention	24,258	59
No	16,755	41
Total	43,012	100
Valid cases	41,013	
Missing cases	2,000	

V73 Neighbors: right wing

Value label	Frequency	%
Mention	13,662	33
No	27,350	67
Total	43,012	100
Valid cases	41,013	
Missing cases	2,000	

V74 Neighbors: large family

Value label	Frequency	%

Mention	5,853	14
No	35,160	86
Total	43,012	100
Valid cases	41,013	
Missing cases	2,000	

V75 Neighbors: unstable

Value label	Frequency	%
Mention	14,351	35
No	26,662	65
Total	43,012	100
Valid cases	41,013	
Missing cases	2,000	

V76 Neighbors: muslims

Value label	Frequency	%
Mention	8,210	20
No	32,803	80
Total	43,012	100
Valid cases	41,013	
Missing cases	2,000	

V77 Neighbors: foreigners

Value label	Frequency	%
Mention	6,945	17
No	34,067	83
Total	43,012	100
Valid cases	41,013	
Missing cases	2,000	

V78 Neighbors: AIDS

Value label	Frequency	%
Mention	17,542	43
No	23,470	57
Total	43,012	100
Valid cases	41,013	
Missing cases	2,000	

V79 Neighbors: drug addicts

Value label	Frequency	%
Mention	27,312	67
No	13,701	33
Total	43,012	100
Valid cases	41,013	
Missing cases	2,000	

V80 Neighbors: homosex

Value label	Frequency	%
Mention	19,380	48

No	20,633	52
Total	43,012	100
Valid cases	40,012	
Missing cases	3,000	

V81 Neighbors: jews

Value label	Frequency	%
Mention	5,816	15
No	32,197	85
Total	43,012	100
Valid cases	38,012	
Missing cases	5,000	

V82 Neighbors: hindus

Value label	Frequency	%
Mention	4,981	13
No	33,031	87
Total	43,012	100
Valid cases	38,012	
Missing cases	5,000	

V83 State of health

Value label	Frequency	%
Good+	9,226	22
Good	15,296	37
Fair	13,408	32
Poor	3,032	7
Poor+	718	2
Total	43,012	100
Valid cases	41,680	
Missing cases	1,332	

V84 Feel excited

Value label	Frequency	%
Yes	23,138	55
No	18,660	45
Total	43,012	100
Valid cases	41,798	
Missing cases	1,214	

V85 Feel restless

Value label	Frequency	%
Yes	13,227	32
No	27,552	68
Total	43,012	100
Valid cases	40,779	
Missing cases	2,233	

V86 Feel proud

Value label	Frequency	%

Yes	16,916	41
No	24,786	59
Total	43,012	100
Valid cases	41,702	
Missing cases	1,311	

V87 Feel lonely

Value label	Frequency	%
Yes	7,989	19
No	33,755	81
Total	43,012	100
Valid cases	41,744	
Missing cases	1,268	

V88 Feel pleased

Value label	Frequency	%
Yes	29,382	70
No	12,346	30
Total	43,012	100
Valid cases	41,727	
Missing cases	1,285	

V89 Feel bored

Value label	Frequency	%
Yes	11,311	27
No	30,449	73
Total	43,012	100
Valid cases	41,760	
Missing cases	1,252	

V90 Feel 'top of the world'

Value label	Frequency	%
Yes	14,370	35
No	27,186	65
Total	43,012	100
Valid cases	41,556	
Missing cases	1,456	

V91 Feel depressed

Value label	Frequency	%
Yes	9,429	23
No	32,259	77
Total	43,012	100
Valid cases	41,729	
Missing cases	1,284	

V92 Feel 'going your way'

Value label	Frequency	%
Yes	20,037	49
No	20,519	51

Total	43,012	100
Valid cases	40,616	
Missing cases	2,396	

V93 Feel upset

Value label	Frequency	%
Yes	7,749	19
No	32,991	81
Total	43,012	100
Valid cases	40,740	
Missing cases	2,272	

V94 People trusted

Value label	Frequency	%
Trusted	14,240	35
Careful	26,347	65
Total	43,012	100
Valid cases	40,586	
Missing cases	2,426	

V95 Free choice/control

Value label	Frequency	%
1 None	1,689	4
2	805	2
3	1,760	4
4	2,242	5
5	6,708	16
6	4,915	12
7	6,423	15
8	7,840	19
9	3,770	9
0 A lot	5,736	14
Total	43,012	100
Valid cases	41,889	
Missing cases	1,123	

V96 Life satisfaction

Value label	Frequency	%
1 Satisfy-	1,429	3
2	750	2
3	1,825	4
4	2,098	5
5	5,374	13
6	4,552	11
7	6,236	15
8	9,051	21
9	5,157	12
0 Satisfy+	6,130	14
Total	43,012	100
Valid cases	42,601	

Missing cases	411

V97 Live in need: 1st reason

Value label	Frequency	%
Unlucky	5,056	13
Laziness	10,948	27
Injustice	16,319	40
Progress	6,428	16
None	1,715	4
Total	43,012	100
Valid cases	40,467	
Missing cases	2,545	

V98 Live in need: 2nd reason

Value label	Frequency	%
Unlucky	7,146	20
Laziness	8,853	24
Injustice	9,723	27
Progress	8,659	24
None	2,252	6
Total	43,012	100
Valid cases	36,633	
Missing cases	6,380	

V99 Good pay

Value label	Frequency	%
Mention	31,226	74
No	10,786	26
Total	43,012	100
Valid cases	42,012	
Missing cases	1,001	

V100 Pleasant people

Value label	Frequency	%
Mention	28,225	67
No	13,787	33
Total	43,012	100
Valid cases	42,012	
Missing cases	1,000	

V101 No pressure

Value label	Frequency	%
Mention	14,362	34
No	27,651	66
Total	43,012	100
Valid cases	42,012	
Missing cases	1,000	

V102 Job security

Value label	Frequency	%

Mention	23,836	57
No	18,176	43
Total	43,012	100
Valid cases	42,012	
Missing cases	1,000	

V103 Promotions

Value label	Frequency	%
Mention	14,909	36
No	27,103	65
Total	43,012	100
Valid cases	42,012	
Missing cases	1,000	

V104 Job respected

Value label	Frequency	%
Mention	16,606	40
No	25,406	61
Total	43,012	100
Valid cases	42,012	
Missing cases	1,000	

V105 Good hours

Value label	Frequency	%
Mention	19,141	46
No	22,871	54
Total	43,012	100
Valid cases	42,012	
Missing cases	1,000	

V106 Use initiative

Value label	Frequency	%
Mention	19,255	46
No	22,757	54
Total	43,012	100
Valid cases	42,012	
Missing cases	1,000	

V107 Useful to society

Value label	Frequency	%
Mention	18,664	44
No	23,348	56
Total	43,012	100
Valid cases	42,012	
Missing cases	1,000	

V108 Generous holidays

Value label	Frequency	%
Mention	12,164	29
No	29,849	71

Total	43,012	100
Valid cases	42,012	
Missing cases	1,000	

V109 Meet people

Value label	Frequency	%
Mention	18,025	43
No	23,988	57
Total	43,012	100
Valid cases	42,012	
Missing cases	1,000	

V110 Achieve something

Value label	Frequency	%
Mention	22,225	53
No	19,787	47
Total	43,012	100
Valid cases	42,012	
Missing cases	1,000	

V111 Responsible job

Value label	Frequency	%
Mention	17,554	42
No	24,458	58
Total	43,012	100
Valid cases	42,012	
Missing cases	1,000	

V112 Job interesting

Value label	Frequency	%
Mention	23,845	57
No	18,167	43
Total	43,012	100
Valid cases	42,012	
Missing cases	1,000	

V113 Meets abilities

Value label	Frequency	%
Mention	23,436	56
No	18,576	44
Total	43,012	100
Valid cases	42,012	
Missing cases	1,000	

V114 Important in job: none

Value label	Frequency	%
Mention	667	2
No	41,345	98
Total	43,012	100

Valid cases   42,012
Missing cases   1,000

V115 Pride in work

Value label	Frequency	%
A lot	11,302	43
Some	9,704	37
Little	3,472	13
None	1,814	7
Total	43,012	100
Valid cases	26,291	
Missing cases	16,721	

V116 Job satisfaction

Value label	Frequency	%
1 Satisfy-	742	3
2	433	2
3	1,068	4
4	1,232	4
5	3,031	11
6	2,732	10
7	3,866	14
8	5,710	20
9	3,844	14
10 Satisfy+	5,546	20
Total	43,012	100
Valid cases	28,205	
Missing cases	14,808	

V117 Decision-making freedom

Value label	Frequency	%
1 None	1,836	7
2	1,064	4
3	1,778	6
4	1,610	6
5	3,045	11
6	2,456	9
7	3,289	12
8	4,505	16
9	3,332	12
10 A lot	5,141	18
Total	43,012	100
Valid cases	28,055	
Missing cases	14,957	

V118 Why work: get paid

Value label	Frequency	%
Mention	5,669	13
No	37,343	87
Total	43,012	100

Valid cases   43,012
Missing cases   0

V119 Why work: do best

Value label	Frequency	%
Mention	14,614	34
No	28,399	66
Total	43,012	100
Valid cases	43,012	
Missing cases	0	

V120 Why work: necessity

Value label	Frequency	%
Mention	7,488	17
No	35,524	83
Total	43,012	100
Valid cases	43,012	
Missing cases	0	

V121 Why work: enjoyment

Value label	Frequency	%
Mention	12,107	28
No	30,906	72
Total	43,012	100
Valid cases	43,012	
Missing cases	0	

V122 Why work: most important

Value label	Frequency	%
Mention	5,184	12
No	37,828	88
Total	43,012	100
Valid cases	43,012	
Missing cases	0	

V123 Why work: never worked

Value label	Frequency	%
Mention	1,738	4
No	41,275	96
Total	43,012	100
Valid cases	43,012	
Missing cases	0	

V124 Why work:don't know

Value label	Frequency	%
Mention	1,019	2
No	41,950	98
Total	43,012	100
Valid cases	43,012	
Missing cases	0	

V125 Efficient paid more

Value label	Frequency	%
Fair	30,948	79
Unfair	8,016	21
Total	43,012	100
Valid cases	38,964	
Missing cases	4,048	

V126 Business managed

Value label	Frequency	%
Own run	14,192	36
Particip	16,449	42
State	1,897	5
Emp own	7,053	18
Total	43,012	100
Valid cases	39,590	
Missing cases	3,422	

V127 Following instructions

Value label	Frequency	%
Follow	12,419	32
Depends	8,870	23
Convince	17,649	45
Total	43,012	100
Valid cases	38,938	
Missing cases	4,074	

V128 Men more right to a job

Value label	Frequency	%
Agree	14,366	35
Neither	5,000	12
Disagree	21,442	53
Total	43,012	100
Valid cases	40,807	
Missing cases	2,205	

V129 Forced retirement

Value label	Frequency	%
Agree	17,936	45
Neither	4,855	12
Disagree	17,157	43
Total	43,012	100
Valid cases	39,947	
Missing cases	3,065	

V130 Jobs to own nationals

Value label	Frequency	%
Agree	28,331	70
Neither	2,967	7
Disagree	9,197	23
Total	43,012	100
Valid cases	40,496	
Missing cases	2,516	

V131 Handicappd work unfair

Value label	Frequency	%
Agree	8,507	22
Neither	5,735	15
Disagree	25,338	64
Total	43,012	100
Valid cases	39,580	
Missing cases	3,433	

V132 Financial satisfaction

Value label	Frequency	%
1 Satisfy-	3,249	8
2	1,683	4
3	3,056	7
4	3,148	8
5	6,495	16
6	4,922	12
7	5,469	13
8	6,213	15
9	3,105	8
10 Satisfy+	4,167	10
Total	43,012	100
Valid cases	41,508	
Missing cases	1,505	

V133 Think meaning of life

Value label	Frequency	%
Often	16,303	38
At times	17,096	40
Rarely	6,655	16
Never	2,511	6
Total	43,012	100
Valid cases	42,565	
Missing cases	447	

V134 Think of death

Value label	Frequency	%
Often	6,983	19
At times	14,472	38
Rarely	9,916	26
Never	6,314	17
Total	43,012	100
Valid cases	37,685	
Missing cases	5,328	

V135 Life: God exists

Value label	Frequency	%
Agree	13,315	39
Neither	5,255	15
Disagree	15,790	46
Total	43,012	100
Valid cases	34,360	
Missing cases	8,653	

V136 Life: get the best

Value label	Frequency	%
Agree	27,438	77
Neither	2,799	8
Disagree	5,318	15
Total	43,012	100
Valid cases	35,555	
Missing cases	7,458	

V137 Life: death inevitable

Value label	Frequency	%
Agree	27,667	77
Neither	2,532	7
Disagree	5,552	16
Total	43,012	100
Valid cases	35,750	
Missing cases	7,262	

V138 Life: belief in God

Value label	Frequency	%
Agree	11,675	36
Neither	4,128	13
Disagree	17,028	52
Total	43,012	100
Valid cases	32,831	
Missing cases	10,182	

V139 Life: death a rest

Value label	Frequency	%
Agree	29,351	85
Neither	1,952	6
Disagree	3,416	10
Total	43,012	100
Valid cases	34,719	
Missing cases	8,293	

V140 life: sorrow

Value label	Frequency	%
Agree	9,749	30
Neither	4,233	13
Disagree	18,824	57
Total	43,012	100

Valid cases	32,805	
Missing cases	10,207	

V141 Life: no meaning

Value label	Frequency	%
Agree	2,008	6
Neither	3,731	11
Disagree	29,819	84
Total	43,012	100
Valid cases	35,558	
Missing cases	7,455	

V142 Good & evil

Value label	Frequency	%
Guideline	12,413	31
Neither	4,061	10
Circumstance	23,318	59
Total	43,012	100
Valid cases	39,792	
Missing cases	3,221	

V143 Religious denominat

Value label	Frequency	%
Yes	27,852	70
No	11,889	30
Total	43,012	100
Valid cases	39,741	
Missing cases	3,272	

V144 Which religion

Value label	Frequency	%
Catholic	14,818	50
Protestant	7,939	27
Non-conf	1,308	4
Jew	94	0
Muslim	1,424	5
Hindu	1,185	4
Buddhist	348	1
Other	2,604	9
Total	43,012	100
Valid cases	29,720	
Missing cases	13,292	

V145 Ever member

Value label	Frequency	%
Catholic	3,038	50
Protestant	2,127	35
Non-conf	197	3
Jew	19	0
Muslim	70	1
Hindu	27	0

Buddhist	42	1
Other	586	10
Total	43,012	100
Valid cases	6,105	
Missing cases	36,907	

V146 Raised religious

Value label	Frequency	%
Yes	26,560	64
No	15,084	36
Total	43,012	100
Valid cases	41,644	
Missing cases	1,368	

V147 Attend services

Value label	Frequency	%
Once+/wk	2,952	8
Once/wk	6,383	17
Once/mo	4,370	11
Xmas/eas	3,460	9
Holidays	2,603	7
Once/yr	3,393	9
Less	4,590	12
Never	10,750	28
Total	43,012	100
Valid cases	38,500	
Missing cases	4,513	

V148 Services: birth

Value label	Frequency	%
Yes	27,108	70
No	11,484	30
Total	43,012	100
Valid cases	38,592	
Missing cases	4,421	

V149 Services: marriage

Value label	Frequency	%
Yes	28,454	74
No	10,120	26
Total	43,012	100
Valid cases	38,573	
Missing cases	4,439	

V150 Services: death

Value label	Frequency	%
Yes	31,010	80
No	7,827	20
Total	43,012	100
Valid cases	38,837	

Missing cases	4,175	

V151 Is respondent religious

Value label	Frequency	%
Yes	24,502	63
No	12,160	31
Atheist	2,113	6
Total	43,012	100
Valid cases	38,775	
Missing cases	4,238	

V152 Answers: moral problems

Value label	Frequency	%
Yes	14,344	52
No	13,342	48
Total	43,012	100
Valid cases	27,686	
Missing cases	15,326	

V153 Answers: family life

Value label	Frequency	%
Yes	13,301	48
No	14,652	52
Total	43,012	100
Valid cases	27,953	
Missing cases	15,060	

V154 Answers: spiritual needs

Value label	Frequency	%
Yes	18,951	68
No	9,066	32
Total	43,012	100
Valid cases	28,017	
Missing cases	14,996	

V155 Answers: social problems

Value label	Frequency	%
Yes	11,027	40
No	16,368	60
Total	43,012	100
Valid cases	27,395	
Missing cases	15,617	

V156 Speak out: disarmament

Value label	Frequency	%
Yes	18,932	61
No	11,880	39
Total	43,012	100
Valid cases	30,812	
Missing cases	12,201	

V157 Speak out: abortion

Value label	Frequency	%
Yes	17,311	56
No	13,794	44
Total	43,012	100
Valid cases	31,105	
Missing cases	11,908	

V158 Speak out: Third World

Value label	Frequency	%
Yes	21,304	70
No	8,963	30
Total	43,012	100
Valid cases	30,267	
Missing cases	12,745	

V159 Speak out: affairs

Value label	Frequency	%
Yes	16,022	52
No	14,858	48
Total	43,012	100
Valid cases	30,879	
Missing cases	12,133	

V160 Speak out: unemployment

Value label	Frequency	%
Yes	16,269	53
No	14,662	47
Total	43,012	100
Valid cases	30,931	
Missing cases	12,081	

V161 Speak out: racial discrimination

Value label	Frequency	%
Yes	21,459	69
No	9,573	31
Total	43,012	100
Valid cases	31,032	
Missing cases	11,981	

V162 Speak out: euthanasia

Value label	Frequency	%
Yes	17,607	61
No	11,171	39
Total	43,012	100
Valid cases	28,778	
Missing cases	14,234	

V163 Speak out: homosexuality

Value label	Frequency	%
Yes	13,979	46
No	16,272	54
Total	43,012	100
Valid cases	30,251	
Missing cases	12,761	

V164 Speak out: ecology

Value label	Frequency	%
Yes	19,150	64
No	10,853	36
Total	43,012	100
Valid cases	30,003	
Missing cases	13,010	

V165 Speak out: government

Value label	Frequency	%
Yes	9,783	33
No	20,089	67
Total	43,012	100
Valid cases	29,872	
Missing cases	13,141	

V166 Belief in God

Value label	Frequency	%
Yes	24,910	77
No	7,368	23
Total	43,012	100
Valid cases	32,278	
Missing cases	10,735	

V167 Life after death

Value label	Frequency	%
Yes	17,057	54
No	14,741	46
Total	43,012	100
Valid cases	31,797	
Missing cases	11,215	

V168 Belief in soul

Value label	Frequency	%
Yes	23,267	70
No	9,965	30
Total	43,012	100
Valid cases	33,232	
Missing cases	9,780	

V169 Belief in devil

Value label	Frequency	%
Yes	10,870	32

No	22,776	68
Total	43,012	100
Valid cases	33,646	
Missing cases	9,367	

V170 Belief in hell

Value label	Frequency	%
Yes	10,499	32
No	22,825	69
Total	43,012	100
Valid cases	33,324	
Missing cases	9,688	

V171 Belief in heaven

Value label	Frequency	%
Yes	17,467	53
No	15,706	47
Total	43,012	100
Valid cases	33,172	
Missing cases	9,840	

V172 Belief in sin

Value label	Frequency	%
Yes	21,031	62
No	12,869	38
Total	43,012	100
Valid cases	33,901	
Missing cases	9,112	

V173 Resurrection

Value label	Frequency	%
Yes	14,212	44
No	18,005	56
Total	43,012	100
Valid cases	32,217	
Missing cases	10,796	

V174 Re-incarnation

Value label	Frequency	%
Yes	9,952	32
No	21,004	68
Total	43,012	100
Valid cases	30,957	
Missing cases	12,056	

V175 What is God

Value label	Frequency	%
Personal	12,262	34
Spirit	13,200	37
Confused	5,958	17

No God	4,521	13
Total	43,012	100
Valid cases	35,941	
Missing cases	7,072	

V176 Importance of God

Value label	Frequency	%
1 Not at all	6,331	17
2	2,166	6
3	2,211	6
4	1,631	4
5	3,715	10
6	2,595	7
7	2,565	7
8	3,188	9
9	2,413	6
10 Very	10,753	29
Total	43,012	100
Valid cases	37,568	
Missing cases	5,444	

V177 Comfort in religion

Value label	Frequency	%
Yes	19,516	58
No	13,976	42
Total	43,012	100
Valid cases	33,492	
Missing cases	9,520	

V178 Prayer/meditation

Value label	Frequency	%
Yes	22,879	63
No	13,213	37
Total	43,012	100
Valid cases	36,092	
Missing cases	6,921	

V179 How often pray

Value label	Frequency	%
Often	9,228	27
At times	7,575	22
Rarely	3,351	10
Crisis	3,584	11
Never	10,047	30
Total	43,012	100
Valid cases	33,786	
Missing cases	9,226	

V180 Home satisfaction

Value label	Frequency	%

1 Satisfy-	1,188	3
2	554	1
3	1,140	3
4	1,412	3
5	3,769	9
6	3,226	8
7	5,145	12
8	8,875	21
9	6,724	16
10 Satisfy+	10,401	25
Total	43,012	100
Valid cases	42,434	
Missing cases	579	

V181 Marital status

Value label	Frequency	%
Married	26,707	62
Living	2,093	5
Divorced	1,571	4
Separate	650	2
Widow	2,788	7
Single	9,152	21
Total	43,012	100
Valid cases	42,961	
Missing cases	51	

V182 Married before

Value label	Frequency	%
Yes-more	2,453	8
Yes-once	15,020	47
No	14,374	45
Total	43,012	100
Valid cases	31,947	
Missing cases	11,065	

V183 Partner: religion

Value label	Frequency	%
Mention	19,431	50
No	19,581	50
Total	43,012	100
Valid cases	39,013	
Missing cases	4,000	

V184 Partner: moral

Value label	Frequency	%
Mention	23,760	61
No	15,252	39
Total	43,012	100
Valid cases	39,013	
Missing cases	4,000	

V185 Partner: social

Value label	Frequency	%
Mention	22,017	56
No	16,996	44
Total	43,012	100
Valid cases	39,013	
Missing cases	4,000	

V186 Partner: politics

Value label	Frequency	%
Mention	15,411	40
No	23,602	61
Total	43,012	100
Valid cases	39,013	
Missing cases	4,000	

V187 Partner: sex

Value label	Frequency	%
Mention	20,965	54
No	18,048	46
Total	43,012	100
Valid cases	39,013	
Missing cases	4,000	

V188 Partner: none

Value label	Frequency	%
Mention	1,357	4
No	37,656	97
Total	43,012	100
Valid cases	39,013	
Missing cases	4,000	

V189 Partner: don't know

Value label	Frequency	%
Mention	1,731	4
No	37,282	96
Total	43,012	100
Valid cases	39,013	
Missing cases	4,000	

V190 Parents: religion

Value label	Frequency	%
Mention	23,400	60
No	15,613	40
Total	43,012	100
Valid cases	39,013	
Missing cases	4,000	

V191 Parents: moral

Value label	Frequency	%
Mention	26,689	68
No	12,323	32
Total	43,012	100
Valid cases	39,013	
Missing cases	4,000	

V192 Parents: social

Value label	Frequency	%
Mention	23,940	61
No	15,073	39
Total	43,012	100
Valid cases	39,013	
Missing cases	4,000	

V193 Parents: politics

Value label	Frequency	%
Mention	15,138	39
No	23,875	61
Total	43,012	100
Valid cases	39,013	
Missing cases	4,000	

V194 Parents: sex

Value label	Frequency	%
Mention	9,342	24
No	29,671	76
Total	43,012	100
Valid cases	39,013	
Missing cases	4,000	

V195 Parents: none

Value label	Frequency	%
Mention	3,338	8
No	39,674	92
Total	43,012	100
Valid cases	43,012	
Missing cases	0	

V196 Parents: don't know

Value label	Frequency	%
Mention	2,915	8
No	36,097	93
Total	43,012	100
Valid cases	39,013	
Missing cases	4,000	

V197 Sexual freedom

Value label	Frequency	%
Agree	9,914	25
Depends	8,176	21
Disagree	21,379	54
Total	43,012	100
Valid cases	39,469	
Missing cases	3,543	

V198 Faithfulness

Value label	Frequency	%
Very	32,830	82
Rather	6,123	15
Not very	883	2
Total	43,012	100
Valid cases	39,836	
Missing cases	3,176	

V199 Adequate income

Value label	Frequency	%
Very	16,595	42
Rather	18,513	47
Not very	4,508	11
Total	43,012	100
Valid cases	39,616	
Missing cases	3,396	

V200 Same background

Value label	Frequency	%
Very	8,156	21
Rather	13,989	35
Not very	17,408	44
Total	43,012	100
Valid cases	39,552	
Missing cases	3,460	

V201 Mutual respect

Value label	Frequency	%
Very	33,113	84
Rather	5,940	15
Not very	537	1
Total	43,012	100
Valid cases	39,590	
Missing cases	3,422	

V202 Shared religion

Value label	Frequency	%
Very	10,251	26
Rather	11,322	29
Not very	17,881	45
Total	43,012	100
Valid cases	39,455	
Missing cases	3,558	

V203 Good housing

Value label	Frequency	%
Very	15,757	40
Rather	19,172	48
Not very	4,775	12
Total	43,012	100
Valid cases	39,705	
Missing cases	3,308	

V204 Politics

Value label	Frequency	%
Very	4,243	11
Rather	10,383	26
Not very	24,774	63
Total	43,012	100
Valid cases	39,399	
Missing cases	3,613	

V205 Understanding

Value label	Frequency	%
Very	30,514	77
Rather	8,385	21
Not very	826	2
Total	43,012	100
Valid cases	39,725	
Missing cases	3,288	

V206 Away from in-laws

Value label	Frequency	%
Very	16,736	42
Rather	11,885	30
Not very	10,825	27
Total	43,012	100
Valid cases	39,447	
Missing cases	3,566	

V207 Happy sexual life

Value label	Frequency	%
Very	24,288	63
Rather	12,319	32
Not very	1,869	5
Total	43,012	100
Valid cases	38,476	
Missing cases	4,536	

V208 Share household chores

Value label	Frequency	%
Very	14,838	38

Rather	16,398	42
Not very	7,417	19
Total	43,012	100
Valid cases	38,653	
Missing cases	4,360	

V209 Children

Value label	Frequency	%
Very	26,121	68
Rather	9,466	25
Not very	3,061	8
Total	43,012	100
Valid cases	38,649	
Missing cases	4,364	

V210 Common interests

Value label	Frequency	%
Very	16,269	41
Rather	18,175	46
Not very	5,131	13
Total	43,012	100
Valid cases	39,576	
Missing cases	3,437	

V211 How many children

Value label	Frequency	%
1 child	7,357	25
2 child	12,047	40
3 child	5,663	19
4 child	2,458	8
5 child	1,129	4
6+ child	1,296	4
Total	43,012	100
Valid cases	29,951	
Missing cases	13,062	

V212 How many at home

Value label	Frequency	%
1 child	8,571	40
2 child	8,283	39
3 child	2,866	14
4 child	906	4
5 child	360	2
6+ child	270	1
Total	43,012	100
Valid cases	21,256	
Missing cases	21,756	

V213 Ideal number of children

Value label	Frequency	%

None	534	1
1child	1,767	4
2child	20,484	50
3child	11,932	29
4child	4,216	10
5child	863	2
6child	400	1
7child	88	0
8child	70	0
9child	336	1
10+child	211	1
Total	43,012	100
Valid cases	40,901	
Missing cases	2,112	

V214 Child needs parents

Value label	Frequency	%
Agree	35,469	91
Disagree	3,632	9
Total	43,012	100
Valid cases	39,101	
Missing cases	3,911	

V215 Woman needs child

Value label	Frequency	%
Needs	24,144	61
No need	15,529	39
Total	43,012	100
Valid cases	39,672	
Missing cases	3,340	

V216 Marriage outdated

Value label	Frequency	%
Yes	5,366	14
No	33,834	86
Total	43,012	100
Valid cases	39,200	
Missing cases	3,812	

V217 Woman single parent

Value label	Frequency	%
Approve	15,021	37
Depends	9,329	23
No	16,349	40
Total	43,012	100
Valid cases	40,699	
Missing cases	2,313	

V218 Working mother

Value label	Frequency	%
Agree+	12,122	31
Agree	14,222	37
Disagree	10,018	26
Disagree+	2,560	7
Total	43,012	100
Valid cases	38,923	
Missing cases	4,090	

V219 Child will suffer

Value label	Frequency	%
Agree+	9,959	26
Agree	16,610	43
Disagree	9,902	26
Disagree+	2,016	5
Total	43,012	100
Valid cases	38,487	
Missing cases	4,525	

V220 Women want home and child

Value label	Frequency	%
Agree+	9,785	27
Agree	15,354	42
Disagree	9,101	25
Disagree+	2,146	6
Total	43,012	100
Valid cases	36,386	
Missing cases	6,627	

V221 Housewife fulfilled

Value label	Frequency	%
Agree+	8,818	24
Agree	15,203	41
Disagree	10,078	27
Disagree+	2,759	8
Total	43,012	100
Valid cases	36,857	
Missing cases	6,155	

V222 Way to independence

Value label	Frequency	%
Agree+	8,419	23
Agree	15,653	42
Disagree	10,658	29
Disagree+	2,502	7
Total	43,012	100
Valid cases	37,232	
Missing cases	5,780	

V223 Both contribute

Value label	Frequency	%
Agree+	13,056	34
Agree	16,609	44
Disagree	7,205	19
Disagree+	1,165	3
Total	43,012	100
Valid cases	38,035	
Missing cases	4,978	

V224 Respect parents

Value label	Frequency	%
Always	30,083	74
Earn it	10,441	26
Total	43,012	100
Valid cases	40,534	
Missing cases	2,478	

V225 Parent's duty

Value label	Frequency	%
Sacrifice	27,228	65
Neither	5,569	13
Own life	8,949	21
Total	43,012	100
Valid cases	41,747	
Missing cases	1,266	

V226 Good manners

Value label	Frequency	%
Mention	32,124	75
No	10,888	25
Total	43,012	100
Valid cases	43,012	
Missing cases	0	

V227 Independence

Value label	Frequency	%
Mention	19,613	46
No	23,399	54
Total	43,012	100
Valid cases	43,012	
Missing cases	0	

V228 Hard work

Value label	Frequency	%
Mention	20,153	47
No	22,860	53
Total	43,012	100
Valid cases	43,012	
Missing cases	0	

V229 Responsibility

Value label	Frequency	%
Mention	31,005	72
No	12,008	28
Total	43,012	100
Valid cases	43,012	

V230 Imagination

Value label	Frequency	%
Mention	8,930	21
No	34,083	79
Total	43,012	100
Valid cases	43,012	
Missing cases	0	

V231 Tolerance/respect

Value label	Frequency	%
Mention	30,082	70
No	12,930	30
Total	43,012	100
Valid cases	43,012	
Missing cases	0	

V232 Thrift

Value label	Frequency	%
Mention	15,491	36
No	27,521	64
Total	43,012	100
Valid cases	43,012	
Missing cases	0	

V233 Determination

Value label	Frequency	%
Mention	14,630	34
No	28,382	66
Total	43,012	100
Valid cases	43,012	
Missing cases	0	

V234 Religious faith

Value label	Frequency	%
Mention	10,905	25
No	32,108	75
Total	43,012	100
Valid cases	43,012	
Missing cases	0	

V235 Unselfishness

Value label	Frequency	%
Mention	11,841	28

No	31,171	73
Total	43,012	100
Valid cases	43,012	
Missing cases	0	

V236 Obedience

Value label	Frequency	%
Mention	13,940	32
No	29,072	68
Total	43,012	100
Valid cases	43,012	
Missing cases	0	

V237 Abortion: mother's health

Value label	Frequency	%
Approve	34,635	88
Disapprove	4,697	12
Total	43,012	100
Valid cases	39,331	
Missing cases	3,681	

V238 Abortion: handicapped

Value label	Frequency	%
Approve	29,554	75
Disapprove	9,873	25
Total	43,012	100
Valid cases	39,427	
Missing cases	3,585	

V239 Abortion: mother not married

Value label	Frequency	%
Approve	13,837	35
Disapprove	25,223	65
Total	43,012	100
Valid cases	39,061	
Missing cases	3,952	

V240 Abortion: not want child

Value label	Frequency	%
Approve	17,076	43
Disapprove	22,255	57
Total	43,012	100
Valid cases	39,331	
Missing cases	3,682	

V241 Interested in politics

Value label	Frequency	%
Very	6,362	15
Some	15,561	37
Not very	11,464	28
Not at all	8,189	20

Total	43,012	100
Valid cases	41,575	
Missing cases	1,437	

V242 Sign petition

Value label	Frequency	%
Havedone	16,289	43
Mightdo	12,566	34
Never	8,651	23
Total	43,012	100
Valid cases	37,528	
Missing cases	5,485	

V243 Join boycott

Value label	Frequency	%
Havedone	3,328	9
Mightdo	13,140	37
Never	18,921	54
Total	43,012	100
Valid cases	35,389	
Missing cases	7,623	

V244 Lawful demonstration

Value label	Frequency	%
Havedone	8,092	21
Mightdo	15,402	40
Never	14,858	39
Total	43,012	100
Valid cases	38,352	
Missing cases	4,660	

V245 Unofficial strikes

Value label	Frequency	%
Havedone	2,062	6
Mightdo	8,261	23
Never	25,272	71
Total	43,012	100
Valid cases	35,595	
Missing cases	7,417	

V246 Occupy building

Value label	Frequency	%
Havedone	803	2
Mightdo	5,080	14
Never	29,687	84
Total	43,012	100
Valid cases	35,569	
Missing cases	7,443	

V247 Freedom & equality

Value label	Frequency	%
Freedom	21,755	54
Neither	2,582	6
Equality	15,918	40
Total	43,012	100
Valid cases	40,254	
Missing cases	2,758	

V248 Left-Right self placement

Value label	Frequency	%
1 Left	1,522	5
2	1,139	4
3	2,893	9
4	3,076	10
5	9,721	30
6	4,781	15
7	3,194	10
8	2,860	9
9	1,078	3
10 Right	1,701	5
Total	43,012	100
Valid cases	31,964	
Missing cases	11,049	

V249 Societal change

Value label	Frequency	%
Radical	4,442	12
Reform	26,274	71
Defend	6,418	17
Total	43,012	100
Valid cases	37,134	
Missing cases	5,878	

V250 Income equality

Value label	Frequency	%
1 Equality	4,131	10
2	1,693	4
3	2,520	6
4	2,205	5
5	4,428	11
6	2,992	7
7	4,603	11
8	7,049	17
9	3,681	9
10 Individual	7,305	18
Total	43,012	100
Valid cases	40,605	
Missing cases	2,407	

V251 Ownership of business

Value label	Frequency	%
1 Private	6,871	18
2	3,721	10
3	5,240	14
4	3,928	10
5	7,356	19
6	2,968	8
7	2,135	6
8	2,420	6
9	1,342	3
10 Government	2,940	8
Total	43,012	100
Valid cases	38,922	
Missing cases	4,091	

V252 Responsibility

Value label	Frequency	%
1 Individual	6,272	15
2	3,575	9
3	4,538	11
4	3,590	9
5	6,168	15
6	3,068	8
7	2,903	7
8	3,582	9
9	2,112	5
10 State	4,846	12
Total	43,012	100
Valid cases	40,652	
Missing cases	2,360	

V253 Unemployed

Value label	Frequency	%
1 Take any job	7,730	20
2	3,293	9
3	3,954	10
4	3,355	9
5	5,117	13
6	2,801	7
7	2,905	8
8	3,514	9
9	1,851	5
10 Refuse	4,129	11
Total	43,012	100
Valid cases	38,649	
Missing cases	4,364	

V254 Competition

Value label	Frequency	%
1 Good	12,053	30

2	5,591	14
3	6,292	16
4	4,478	11
5	5,309	13
6	1,692	4
7	1,270	3
8	1,291	3
9	681	2
10 Harmful	1,410	4
Total	43,012	100
Valid cases	40,067	
Missing cases	2,946	

V255 Hard work

Value label	Frequency	%
1 Good	8,572	21
2	4,313	11
3	4,917	12
4	3,974	10
5	5,683	14
6	2,543	6
7	2,670	7
8	3,063	8
9	1,749	4
10 No luck	3,109	8
Total	43,012	100
Valid cases	40,593	
Missing cases	2,420	

V256 Wealth accumulation

Value label	Frequency	%
1 Greed	2,495	6
2	1,423	4
3	2,104	5
4	2,271	6
5	5,864	15
6	3,794	10
7	4,468	12
8	6,135	16
9	3,449	9
10 Others	6,957	18
Total	43,012	100
Valid cases	38,961	
Missing cases	4,051	

V257 Country's goals(1)-#1

Value label	Frequency	%
Economy	23,358	58
Defense	2,610	7
More say	10,740	27

Beauty	3,510	9
Total	43,012	100
Valid cases	40,218	
Missing cases	2,794	

V258 Country's goals(1)-#2

Value label	Frequency	%
Economy	7,957	21
Defense	5,696	15
More say	14,682	38
Beauty	10,432	27
Total	43,012	100
Valid cases	38,767	
Missing cases	4,245	

V259 Country's goals(2)-#1

Value label	Frequency	%
Order	15,853	38
More say	10,821	26
Prices	9,366	22
Speech	5,804	14
Total	43,012	100
Valid cases	41,844	
Missing cases	1,168	

V260 Country's goals(2)-#2

Value label	Frequency	%
Order	8,809	22
More say	9,728	24
Prices	12,127	30
Speech	10,058	25
Total	43,012	100
Valid cases	40,723	
Missing cases	2,290	

V261 Country's goals(3)-#1

Value label	Frequency	%
Economy	22,287	53
Humane	8,848	21
Ideas	3,592	9
Crime	7,267	17
Total	43,012	100
Valid cases	41,994	
Missing cases	1,018	

V262 Country's goals(3)-#2

Value label	Frequency	%
Economy	7,910	19
Humane	10,417	26
Ideas	7,555	19

Crime	15,018	37
Total	43,012	100
Valid cases	40,900	
Missing cases	2,113	

V263 Willing to fight for country

Value label	Frequency	%
Yes	27,481	75
No	8,953	25
Total	43,012	100
Valid cases	36,573	
Missing cases	6,440	

V264 Less emphasis on money

Value label	Frequency	%
Good	23,810	60
Neither	6,929	18
Bad	8,683	22
Total	43,012	100
Valid cases	39,421	
Missing cases	3,591	

V265 Decrease work importance

Value label	Frequency	%
Good	9,633	25
Neither	4,625	12
Bad	25,074	64
Total	43,012	100
Valid cases	39,332	
Missing cases	3,681	

V266 Technological development

Value label	Frequency	%
Good	29,781	73
Neither	6,567	16
Bad	4,756	12
Total	43,012	100
Valid cases	41,105	
Missing cases	1,907	

V267 Individual development

Value label	Frequency	%
Good	35,499	86
Neither	4,060	10
Bad	1,814	4
Total	43,012	100
Valid cases	41,374	
Missing cases	1,639	

V268 Respect authority

Value label	Frequency	%
Good	22,718	58
Neither	8,488	22
Bad	8,072	21
Total	43,012	100
Valid cases	39,278	
Missing cases	3,734	

V269 Emphasis family life

Value label	Frequency	%
Good	37,719	91
Neither	2,947	7
Bad	930	2
Total	43,012	100
Valid cases	41,596	
Missing cases	1,417	

V270 Natural lifestyle

Value label	Frequency	%
Good	34,489	83
Neither	4,793	12
Bad	2,149	5
Total	43,012	100
Valid cases	41,430	
Missing cases	1,582	

V271 Scientific advances

Value label	Frequency	%
Help	18,367	48
Both	14,568	38
Harm	5,326	14
Total	43,012	100
Valid cases	38,261	
Missing cases	4,752	

V272 Confidence: church

Value label	Frequency	%
A lot	10,480	25
Quite	12,661	31
Not very	12,237	30
Not at all	6,118	15
Total	43,012	100
Valid cases	41,496	
Missing cases	1,516	

V273 Confidence: armed forces

Value label	Frequency	%
A lot	7,271	18
Quite	14,228	34

Not very	13,625	33
Not at all	6,319	15
Total	43,012	100
Valid cases	41,443	
Missing cases	1,570	

V274 Confidence: education system

Value label	Frequency	%
A lot	8,332	20
Quite	18,012	43
Not very	12,703	31
Not at all	2,471	6
Total	43,012	100
Valid cases	41,518	
Missing cases	1,495	

V275 Confidence: legal syst

Value label	Frequency	%
A lot	5,669	14
Quite	15,854	38
Not very	15,178	37
Not at all	4,688	11
Total	43,012	100
Valid cases	41,388	
Missing cases	1,624	

V276 Confidence: press

Value label	Frequency	%
A lot	3,276	8
Quite	14,039	34
Not very	18,547	45
Not at all	5,460	13
Total	43,012	100
Valid cases	41,321	
Missing cases	1,691	

V277 Confidence: unions

Value label	Frequency	%
A lot	3,094	8
Quite	11,837	29
Not very	17,802	44
Not at all	7,803	19
Total	43,012	100
Valid cases	40,537	
Missing cases	2,476	

V278 Confidence: police

Value label	Frequency	%
A lot	5,669	14
Quite	16,540	41

Not very	13,085	32
Not at all	5,382	13
Total	43,012	100
Valid cases	40,675	
Missing cases	2,337	

V279 Confidence: parliament

Value label	Frequency	%
A lot	4,570	11
Quite	14,356	35
Not very	15,880	39
Not at all	6,287	15
Total	43,012	100
Valid cases	41,093	
Missing cases	1,919	

V280 Confidence: civil serv

Value label	Frequency	%
A lot	3,494	9
Quite	14,302	35
Not very	17,442	43
Not at all	5,686	14
Total	43,012	100
Valid cases	40,924	
Missing cases	2,088	

V281 Confidence: companies

Value label	Frequency	%
A lot	3,742	9
Quite	13,925	34
Not very	16,964	42
Not at all	5,938	15
Total	43,012	100
Valid cases	40,569	
Missing cases	2,444	

V282 Confidence: social security

Value label	Frequency	%
A lot	5,780	14
Quite	16,046	39
Not very	14,113	35
Not at all	4,966	12
Total	43,012	100
Valid cases	40,905	
Missing cases	2,107	

V283 Confidence: T.V. / European Community

Value label	Frequency	%
A lot	3,329	11

Quite	11,274	38
Not very	10,516	36
Not at all	4,505	15
Total	43,012	100
Valid cases	29,624	
Missing cases	13,388	

V284 Confidence: NATO

Value label	Frequency	%
A lot	2,598	9
Quite	9,504	33
Not very	10,727	37
Not at all	6,278	22
Total	43,012	100
Valid cases	29,107	
Missing cases	13,905	

V285 Confidence: political system

Value label	Frequency	%
A lot	1,879	10
Quite	4,685	26
Not very	6,487	36
Not at all	4,957	28
Total	43,012	100
Valid cases	18,007	
Missing cases	25,005	

V286 Proud of: first mention

Value label	Frequency	%
Science	2,617	24
Politics	778	7
Sports	1,438	13
Culture	2,716	25
Economy	681	6
Health	974	9
None	1,578	14
Total	43,012	100
Valid cases	10,980	
Missing cases	32,032	

V287 Proud of: second ment

Value label	Frequency	%
Science	1,367	15
Politics	778	9
Sports	1,364	15
Culture	1,932	22
Economy	990	11
Health	954	11
None	1,246	14
Total	43,012	100

Valid cases	8,889	
Missing cases	34,123	

V288 Country run by

Value label	Frequency	%
Intersts	6,303	56
Everyone	5,033	44
Total	43,012	100
Valid cases	11,336	
Missing cases	31,676	

V289 Trust government

Value label	Frequency	%
Always	1,273	11
Most	3,491	31
Some	4,933	43
Never	1,765	15
Total	43,012	100
Valid cases	11,461	
Missing cases	31,551	

V290 Ecology movement

Value label	Frequency	%
Approve+	24,466	59
Approve	14,795	36
Disapprove	1,418	3
Disapprove+	496	1
Total	43,012	100
Valid cases	41,175	
Missing cases	1,838	

V291 Anti-nuclear energy

Value label	Frequency	%
Approve+	16,088	40
Approve	14,268	36
Disapprove	6,470	16
Disapprove+	3,024	8
Total	43,012	100
Valid cases	39,850	
Missing cases	3,162	

V292 Disarmament

Value label	Frequency	%
Approve+	18,774	47
Approve	12,849	32
Disapprove	4,685	12
Disapprove+	3,945	10
Total	43,012	100
Valid cases	40,252	

Missing cases   2,761

V293 Human rights

Value label	Frequency	%
Approve+	25,232	63
Approve	12,889	32
Disapprove	1,559	4
Disapprove+	691	2
Total	43,012	100
Valid cases	40,372	
Missing cases	2,641	

V294 Women's movement

Value label	Frequency	%
Approve+	12,629	32
Approve	17,770	45
Disapprove	6,120	16
Disapprove+	2,619	7
Total	43,012	100
Valid cases	39,138	
Missing cases	3,875	

V295 Anti-apartheid

Value label	Frequency	%
Approve+	18,779	51
Approve	12,557	34
Disapprove	3,519	10
Disapprove+	2,327	6
Total	43,012	100
Valid cases	37,182	
Missing cases	5,831	

V296   Claim benefits

Value label	Frequency	%
1 Never	26,350	63
2	3,887	9
3	2,899	7
4	1,574	4
5	2,200	5
6	1,346	3
7	798	2
8	735	2
9	451	1
10 Always	1,670	4
Total	43,012	100
Valid cases	41,911	
Missing cases	1,101	

V297 Avoid transport fare

Value label	Frequency	%

1 Never	24,406	62
2	3,846	10
3	3,028	8
4	1,696	4
5	2,300	6
6	1,394	4
7	755	2
8	650	2
9	382	1
10 Always	1,091	3
Total	43,012	100
Valid cases	39,548	
Missing cases	3,465	

V298 Cheat on tax

Value label	Frequency	%
1 Never	24,465	59
2	3,968	10
3	3,280	8
4	1,883	5
5	2,574	6
6	1,300	3
7	938	2
8	836	2
9	497	1
10 Always	1,449	4
Total	43,012	100
Valid cases	41,192	
Missing cases	1,821	

V299 Buy stolen goods

Value label	Frequency	%
1 Never	31,990	77
2	3,143	8
3	1,980	5
4	1,050	3
5	1,259	3
6	643	2
7	371	1
8	332	1
9	210	1
10 Always	569	1
Total	43,012	100
Valid cases	41,548	
Missing cases	1,464	

V300 Joyriding

Value label	Frequency	%
1 Never	33,706	85
2	2,267	6

3	1,124	3
4	602	2
5	616	2
6	411	1
7	162	0
8	167	0
9	106	0
10 Always	439	1
Total	43,012	100
Valid cases	39,600	
Missing cases	3,412	

V301 Marijuana/hashish

Value label	Frequency	%
1 Never	35,661	84
2	1,972	5
3	1,247	3
4	736	2
5	973	2
6	546	1
7	264	1
8	274	1
9	151	0
10 Always	701	2
Total	43,012	100
Valid cases	42,524	
Missing cases	488	

V302 Keep money found

Value label	Frequency	%
1 Never	18,603	49
2	3,474	9
3	3,092	8
4	1,915	5
5	3,718	10
6	2,061	5
7	1,221	3
8	1,211	3
9	746	2
10 Always	2,332	6
Total	43,012	100
Valid cases	38,373	
Missing cases	4,640	

V303 Lying own interest

Value label	Frequency	%
1 Never	20,485	48
2	4,887	12
3	4,578	11
4	2,499	6

5	3,871	9
6	2,241	5
7	1,226	3
8	1,037	2
9	460	1
10 Always	1,049	3
Total	43,012	100
Valid cases	42,332	
Missing cases	681	

V304 Married have affair

Value label	Frequency	%
1 Never	23,477	56
2	3,638	9
3	3,059	7
4	2,039	5
5	3,901	9
6	2,167	5
7	975	2
8	944	2
9	496	1
10 Always	1,277	3
Total	43,012	100
Valid cases	41,972	
Missing cases	1,040	

V305 Sex under age

Value label	Frequency	%
1 Never	25,139	65
2	2,499	6
3	2,065	5
4	1,393	4
5	2,625	7
6	1,496	4
7	908	2
8	921	2
9	557	1
10 Always	1,401	4
Total	43,012	100
Valid cases	39,003	
Missing cases	4,009	

V306 Accept bribe

Value label	Frequency	%
1 Never	31,968	76
2	3,635	9
3	2,329	6
4	1,048	3
5	1,293	3
6	698	2

7	382	1
8	293	1
9	196	1
10 Always	518	1
Total	43,012	100
Valid cases	42,359	
Missing cases	654	

V307 Homosexuality

Value label	Frequency	%
1 Never	24,474	59
2	1,858	5
3	1,746	4
4	1,320	3
5	3,857	9
6	1,742	4
7	961	2
8	1,268	3
9	865	2
10 Always	3,122	8
Total	43,012	100
Valid cases	41,211	
Missing cases	1,802	

V308 Prostitution

Value label	Frequency	%
1 Never	25,380	61
2	2,731	7
3	2,598	6
4	1,704	4
5	3,631	9
6	1,844	4
7	1,007	2
8	1,036	3
9	496	1
10 Always	1,498	4
Total	43,012	100
Valid cases	41,924	
Missing cases	1,088	

V309 Abortion

Value label	Frequency	%
1 Never	11,940	29
2	2,589	6
3	3,322	8
4	2,491	6
5	7,426	18
6	4,330	11

7	1,975	5
8	2,412	6
9	1,389	3
10 Always	3,109	8
Total	43,012	100
Valid cases	40,982	
Missing cases	2,030	

V310 Divorce

Value label	Frequency	%
1 Never	8,628	21
2	1,717	4
3	2,784	7
4	2,506	6
5	8,865	21
6	5,092	12
7	2,600	6
8	3,135	8
9	1,723	4
10 Always	4,856	12
Total	43,012	100
Valid cases	41,905	
Missing cases	1,107	

V311 Fighting the police

Value label	Frequency	%
1 Never	21,068	50
2	4,251	10
3	3,699	9
4	2,141	5
5	4,338	10
6	2,803	7
7	1,048	3
8	923	2
9	453	1
10 Always	1,170	3
Total	43,012	100
Valid cases	41,893	
Missing cases	1,119	

V312 Euthanasia

Value label	Frequency	%
1 Never	14,593	38
2	2,605	7
3	2,538	7
4	1,759	5
5	4,668	12
6	2,461	6
7	2,004	5
8	2,595	7

9	1,468	4
10 Always	4,010	10
Total	43,012	100
Valid cases	38,702	
Missing cases	4,310	

V313 Suicide

Value label	Frequency	%
1 Never	24,152	60
2	3,090	8
3	2,419	6
4	1,547	4
5	3,662	9
6	1,879	5
7	873	2
8	891	2
9	433	1
10 Always	1,317	3
Total	43,012	100
Valid cases	40,265	
Missing cases	2,747	

V314 Hit car-no report

Value label	Frequency	%
1 Never	25,040	64
2	4,079	10
3	2,868	7
4	1,534	4
5	2,197	6
6	1,160	3
7	553	1
8	515	1
9	253	1
10 Always	862	2
Total	43,012	100
Valid cases	39,061	
Missing cases	3,951	

V315 Threaten strikers

Value label	Frequency	%
1 Never	29,474	73
2	3,440	9
3	2,190	5
4	1,125	3
5	1,689	4
6	816	2
7	402	1
8	387	1
9	242	1
10 Always	812	2

Total	43,012	100
Valid cases	40,576	
Missing cases	2,437	

V316 Kill in self-defense

Value label	Frequency	%
1 Never	8,988	22
2	1,925	5
3	2,359	6
4	1,946	5
5	5,180	13
6	3,306	8
7	2,448	6
8	3,630	9
9	2,561	6
10 Always	7,926	20
Total	43,012	100
Valid cases	40,269	
Missing cases	2,743	

V317 Assassinations

Value label	Frequency	%
1 Never	29,604	77
2	2,513	7
3	1,491	4
4	888	2
5	1,543	4
6	948	3
7	347	1
8	334	1
9	188	1
10 Always	695	2
Total	43,012	100
Valid cases	38,550	
Missing cases	4,462	

V318 Throw litter

Value label	Frequency	%
1 Never	27,484	71
2	3,752	10
3	2,774	7
4	1,377	4
5	1,483	4
6	654	2
7	295	1
8	236	1
9	142	0
10 Always	425	1
Total	43,012	100
Valid cases	38,623	

Missing cases   4,390

V319 Drink & drive

Value label	Frequency	%
1 Never	33,143	80
2	3,241	8
3	1,814	4
4	917	2
5	974	2
6	531	1
7	211	1
8	160	0
9	111	0
10 Always	479	1
Total	43,012	100
Valid cases	41,582	
Missing cases	1,431	

V320 Geographical group-#1

Value label	Frequency	%	
Town	16,920	40	
Region	8,053	19	
Country	12,401	29	
Continent	1,390	3	
World	2,910	7	534
	1		
Total	43,012	100	
Valid cases	42,208		
Missing cases	804		

V321 Geographical group-#2

Value label	Frequency	%	
Town	8,942	23	
Region	11,204	29	
Country	11,470	29	
Continent	3,633	9	
World	3,202	8	508
	1		
Total	43,012	100	
Valid cases	38,960		
Missing cases	4,053		

V322 Proud of nationality

Value label	Frequency	%
Very	19,352	47
Quite	15,766	38
Not very	4,749	12
Not at all	1,485	4
Total	43,012	100
Valid cases	41,352	

Missing cases   1,661

V323 Boldness vs. caution

Value label	Frequency	%
1 Cautious	5,655	14
2	2,374	6
3	3,553	9
4	3,133	8
5	6,504	16
6	3,581	9
7	4,033	10
8	5,163	13
9	2,431	6
10 Bold	4,455	11
Total	43,012	100
Valid cases	40,882	
Missing cases	2,130	

V324 New ideas vs. old ones

Value label	Frequency	%
1 Old best	5,230	13
2	2,601	6
3	3,635	9
4	3,427	9
5	9,038	22
6	4,641	12
7	3,584	9
8	3,498	9
9	1,578	4
10 New best	3,110	8
Total	43,012	100
Valid cases	40,342	
Missing cases	2,671	

V325 Adapting to change

Value label	Frequency	%
1 Worry	3,219	8
2	1,803	5
3	2,858	7
4	2,821	7
5	6,632	17
6	4,099	11
7	4,467	12
8	5,367	14
9	2,676	7
10 Welcome	4,691	12
Total	43,012	100
Valid cases	38,633	
Missing cases	4,380	

V326 Count on success

Value label	Frequency	%
Mention	18,767	44
No	24,245	56
Total	43,012	100
Valid cases	43,012	
Missing cases	0	

V327 Convince others

Value label	Frequency	%
Mention	11,418	27
No	31,594	74
Total	43,012	100
Valid cases	43,012	
Missing cases	0	

V328 Serve as model

Value label	Frequency	%
Mention	6,905	16
No	36,107	84
Total	43,012	100
Valid cases	43,012	
Missing cases	0	

V329 Get what I want

Value label	Frequency	%
Mention	13,996	33
No	29,017	68
Total	43,012	100
Valid cases	43,012	
Missing cases	0	

V330 Possessions

Value label	Frequency	%
Mention	5,755	13
No	37,257	87
Total	43,012	100
Valid cases	43,012	
Missing cases	0	

V331 Like responsibility

Value label	Frequency	%
Mention	19,701	46
No	23,311	54
Total	43,012	100
Valid cases	43,012	

V332 Rarely unsure of self

Value label	Frequency	%
Mention	14,582	34

No	28,430	66
Total	43,012	100
Valid cases	43,012	
Missing cases	0	

V333 Give advice often

Value label	Frequency	%
Mention	16,478	38
No	26,535	62
Total	43,012	100
Valid cases	43,012	
Missing cases	0	

V334 Characteristic-none

Value label	Frequency	%
Mention	4,416	10
No	38,596	90
Total	43,012	100
Valid cases	43,012	
Missing cases	0	

V335 Economy needs changes

Value label	Frequency	%
Agree+	18,565	48
Agree	12,781	33
Neither	4,055	11
Disagree	2,474	6
Disagree+	760	2
Total	43,012	100
Valid cases	38,634	
Missing cases	4,379	

V336 Government more open

Value label	Frequency	%
Agree+	18,888	48
Agree	15,028	38
Neither	3,388	9
Disagree	1,464	4
Disagree+	516	1
Total	43,012	100
Valid cases	39,285	
Missing cases	3,728	

V337 Individual freedom

Value label	Frequency	%
Agree+	7,882	22
Agree	11,239	31
Neither	7,318	20
Disagree	6,837	19
Disagree+	2,713	8

Total	43,012	100
Valid cases	35,989	
Missing cases	7,024	

V338 Helpless: unjust law

Value label	Frequency	%
Agree+	11,782	31
Agree	9,693	25
Neither	4,389	12
Disagree	7,855	21
Disagree+	4,536	12
Total	43,012	100
Valid cases	38,256	
Missing cases	4,757	

V339 Political reform rapid

Value label	Frequency	%
Agree+	5,608	15
Agree	7,869	21
Neither	7,788	21
Disagree	9,792	27
Disagree+	5,909	16
Total	43,012	100
Valid cases	36,966	
Missing cases	6,046	

V340 Trust: family

Value label	Frequency	%
Trust+	33,717	81
Trust	5,639	14
Neither	1,117	3
Not much	523	1
Not at all	547	1
Total	43,012	100
Valid cases	41,544	
Missing cases	1,469	

V341 Trust: own countrymen

Value label	Frequency	%
Trust+	8,212	20
Trust	18,468	45
Neither	9,063	22
Not much	3,875	10
Not at all	1,206	3
Total	43,012	100
Valid cases	40,824	
Missing cases	2,188	

V342 Trust: first domestic ethnic group

Value label	Frequency	%
Trust+	2,494	14
Trust	4,984	28
Neither	5,116	28
Not much	2,661	15
Not at all	2,851	16
Total	43,012	100
Valid cases	18,106	
Missing cases	24,907	

V343 Trust: second domestic ethnic group

Value label	Frequency	%
Trust+	2,069	12
Trust	4,807	27
Neither	5,108	28
Not much	2,631	15
Not at all	3,431	19
Total	43,012	100
Valid cases	18,045	
Missing cases	24,967	

V344 Trust: first neighbor nationality

Value label	Frequency	%
Trust+	1,430	8
Trust	4,078	24
Neither	5,680	33
Not much	2,974	17
Not at all	2,934	17
Total	43,012	100
Valid cases	17,096	
Missing cases	25,916	

V345 Trust: second neighbor nationality

Value label	Frequency	%
Trust+	953	6
Trust	3,479	20
Neither	5,535	32
Not much	3,545	20
Not at all	3,924	23
Total	43,012	100
Valid cases	17,435	
Missing cases	25,577	

V346 Trust: 1st superpower

Value label	Frequency	%
Trust+	1,169	6
Trust	3,992	22
Neither	5,902	32
Not much	3,471	19
Not at all	3,689	20

Total	43,012	100
Valid cases	18,225	
Missing cases	24,788	

V347 Trust: 2nd superpower

Value label	Frequency	%
Trust+	858	6
Trust	3,062	20
Neither	5,175	34
Not much	2,989	20
Not at all	3,241	21
Total	43,012	100
Valid cases	15,325	
Missing cases	27,687	

V348 Born in this country

Value label	Frequency	%
Yes	14,856	93
Lat Amer	559	4
Usa	239	2
Asia	79	1
Europe	118	1
Africa	9	0
Other	54	0
Total	43,012	100
Valid cases	15,915	
Missing cases	27,098	

V450 Values: Materialist /Postmaterialist

Value label	Frequency	%
Materialist	11,011	27
Mixed	24,017	58
Postmaterialist	6,326	15
Total	43,012	100
Valid cases	41,355	
Missing cases	1,658	

* Please note that SPSS shows the total of marginals as 100 percent with all variables. However, in some cases the sum may come to 1 point above or below (99 or 101%), due to rounding. This also explains one percent differences between some graphs and tables.

TABLES AND FIGURES

TABLE OF FREQUENCIES

Each cell shows the actual number of respondents ("n") in a given country (row) by each breakdown (column).
In some cases the number of respondents is small. When analyzing those cases, the specific "n" must be taken into account.

	Total	Gender		Age			Education			Income			Political Affinity			Values		
		Male	Female	16-29	30-49	50+	Lower	Medium	Upper	Lower	Middle	Upper	Left	Center	Right	Mat	Mixed	Postmat
India	2500	1337	1163	946	1124	430	473	1119	908	742	845	842	587	806	568	931	1230	141
Nigeria	1001	598	403	538	394	57	169	430	402	313	359	217	173	348	271	351	559	73
China	1000	599	399	303	443	254	241	421	240	383	297	301	na	na	na	497	434	54
Romania	1103	545	558	275	399	429	382	436	285	285	441	374	168	480	262	480	542	81
Turkey	1030	512	518	371	420	233	637	258	135	338	364	305	222	454	222	259	563	208
Poland	938	454	482	187	381	365	368	464	106	361	289	283	130	328	196	284	539	89
Bulgaria	1034	485	544	223	440	368	248	475	273	383	282	295	229	351	164	281	622	92
Chile	1500	714	786	539	586	374	511	579	403	501	547	422	393	671	240	359	806	270
Czechoslovakia	1396	671	724	329	588	475	444	728	224	438	548	406	296	663	404	366	879	146
South Africa	2736	1258	1478	971	1149	615	635	1639	442	599	738	1119	669	665	607	1050	1492	194
Lithuania	1000	464	536	300	348	352	230	652	118	457	333	203	na	na	na	254	558	117
Hungary	999	478	521	170	398	431	472	430	84	428	422	132	126	458	124	449	503	40
Argentina	1002	474	528	270	379	353	404	268	241	228	327	200	115	403	140	253	555	194
Brazil	1782	892	890	691	690	401	528	1000	252	636	452	591	466	576	457	720	934	128
Mexico	1531	836	695	678	596	257	979	230	322	673	479	299	253	582	386	336	841	156
Belarus	1015	466	549	255	507	253	155	437	423	323	385	298	577	285	96	328	571	64
Russia	1961	837	1124	453	817	691	459	754	748	614	592	487	392	673	133	762	1083	116
Moscow	1012	443	555	224	487	300	110	341	546	384	393	218	579	245	77	257	575	125
Latvia	903	364	539	255	432	216	84	543	276	238	258	393	na	na	na	217	506	75
Estonia	1008	454	554	298	428	281	222	580	206	456	257	293	na	na	na	297	573	59
Portugal	1185	565	620	371	379	435	890	145	150	566	309	249	249	470	357	414	562	118
South Korea	1251	586	665	405	609	236	229	550	472	467	454	274	163	440	608	564	530	139
Ireland	1000	480	520	247	372	381	530	380	90	270	289	334	111	491	296	232	565	191
North Ireland	304	128	176	76	118	110	195	80	29	70	79	81	28	158	93	65	186	45
Slovenia	1035	487	548	245	415	375	430	382	223	419	408	195	150	408	90	289	678	68
Spain	4147	1929	2218	1253	1486	1408	2698	688	761	603	1152	1676	1410	1009	558	916	2062	781
East Germany	1336	613	723	316	504	516	909	200	227	444	396	490	436	562	224	158	840	301
Britain	1484	691	793	337	508	639	1064	260	160	489	312	300	336	675	333	286	878	268
Italy	2018	965	1053	635	739	644	1739	227	52	761	532	131	623	628	263	467	1008	470
Netherlands	1017	441	576	251	433	333	382	327	308	291	250	249	294	340	296	105	545	337
Belgium	2792	1363	1429	718	990	1084	1150	1091	551	518	453	572	471	848	661	559	1376	611
Austria	1460	568	892	280	541	639	597	718	121	414	584	416	146	612	530	199	899	362
France	1002	473	529	279	360	363	485	334	183	331	258	236	331	301	160	200	522	241
Canada	1730	861	869	403	772	545	423	752	555	394	588	479	236	839	376	193	1031	424
United States	1839	900	899	330	728	749	439	783	617	530	630	536	253	858	476	299	1069	405
Iceland	702	355	347	218	307	177	219	190	287	na	na	na	192	223	233	178	450	74
West Germany	2101	1002	1099	520	715	866	1310	556	235	649	602	681	539	880	427	288	1142	580
Denmark	1030	516	514	269	404	357	255	308	447	359	299	239	225	382	327	157	666	152
Finland	588	304	284	115	342	131	108	262	218	171	230	185	108	188	222	34	384	170
Norway	1239	635	604	283	515	441	254	491	494	310	421	306	312	440	389	347	737	116
Sweden	1047	539	490	252	407	327	351	455	222	224	293	404	258	347	330	143	639	229
Japan	1011	483	528	214	472	317	231	557	223	255	348	293	99	334	190	225	480	79
Switzerland	1400	641	759	255	576	568	586	664	150	453	474	175	256	508	326	190	886	324
Total	59169	28406	30681	16548	23698	18776	23225	22184	13409	17768	17969	16179	12601	19929	12112	15239	32500	8907

Note: Countries in the left column are ranked according to GNP per capita. / na=not ascertained.

V4-V9. How important are the following in your life?

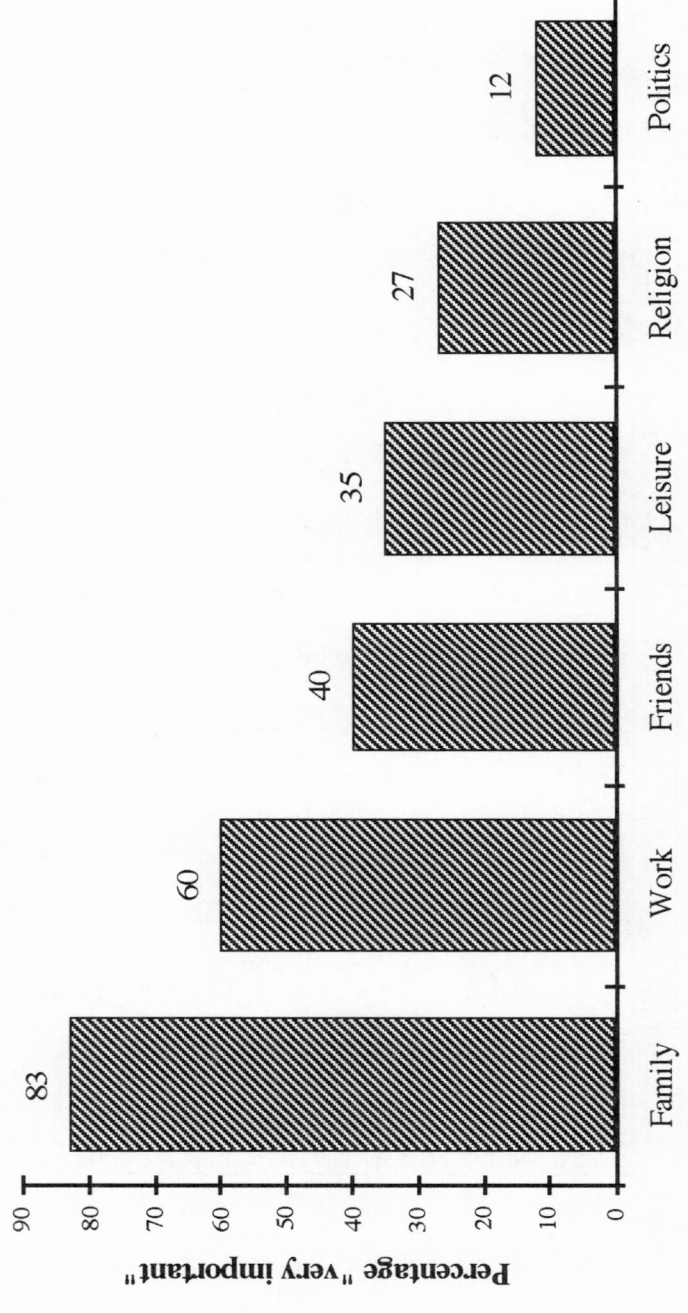

V4 WORK IMPORTANT

Please say, for each of the following, how important it is in your life: Work. (% "very important")

	Total	Gender		Age			Education			Income			Political Affinity			Values		
		Male	Female	16-29	30-49	50+	Lower	Medium	Upper	Lower	Middle	Upper	Left	Center	Right	Mat	Mixed	Postmat
India	86	89	84	86	87	86	85	87	87	89	86	86	90	84	85	88	86	83
Nigeria	94	94	95	94	94	95	86	95	92	94	93	96	97	91	96	95	94	88
China	64	66	60	58	66	67	63	65	67	65	64	63	na	na	na	64	65	52
Romania	69	71	67	53	68	79	76	63	67	72	67	67	65	69	68	73	66	59
Turkey	59	64	54	53	63	61	59	55	69	58	55	64	63	60	57	61	58	60
Poland	70	69	71	58	69	76	71	71	62	69	71	68	71	68	76	71	70	66
Bulgaria	57	59	54	39	57	67	66	54	53	56	57	58	58	58	58	60	56	46
Chile	75	76	74	69	77	80	76	76	73	79	76	70	73	75	80	82	74	70
Czechoslovakia	56	59	54	41	57	65	59	52	64	53	56	58	62	54	56	57	56	56
South Africa	79	83	75	81	80	72	83	80	57	85	83	59	80	74	75	76	80	81
Lithuania	42	41	42	23	41	59	54	36	49	48	35	40	na	na	na	47	42	34
Hungary	59	57	61	55	62	58	60	58	60	59	57	61	64	60	52	62	57	55
Argentina	76	76	76	67	75	84	82	76	65	79	78	66	70	74	73	82	74	72
Brazil	82	83	81	81	84	82	82	83	80	81	85	82	80	81	86	83	82	81
Mexico	67	71	63	65	71	66	68	71	63	66	67	70	70	66	69	67	67	67
Belarus	55	58	52	37	58	66	67	53	53	54	53	57	55	55	58	58	54	52
Russia	46	51	42	34	47	52	50	44	46	46	45	49	46	45	49	49	44	41
Moscow	47	49	44	35	44	59	60	44	46	46	45	51	43	52	56	50	46	44
Latvia	33	35	32	23	32	48	33	33	35	32	33	34	na	na	na	38	33	40
Estonia	32	34	31	17	35	43	34	29	37	30	34	34	na	na	na	33	31	36
Portugal	35	34	36	33	34	38	35	41	31	37	30	38	32	35	38	34	37	29
South Korea	69	70	69	62	71	78	75	70	66	66	73	70	69	67	72	74	66	65
Ireland	65	72	59	61	67	66	67	65	56	65	67	64	59	66	66	66	66	61
North Ireland	57	69	48	59	53	60	59	56	45	62	61	49	50	59	55	59	54	69
Slovenia	73	73	74	62	76	78	72	72	79	73	75	72	67	75	72	81	71	64
Spain	66	67	65	62	68	66	65	72	63	64	67	63	67	66	63	70	67	64
East Germany	61	64	58	55	63	62	62	56	58	54	63	65	63	59	62	50	65	55
Britain	51	61	41	63	53	40	49	56	53	40	54	61	48	51	58	51	52	47
Italy	62	65	60	60	57	68	62	63	59	65	60	59	59	64	69	66	62	59
Netherlands	49	58	45	44	40	68	56	48	41	44	49	45	41	45	58	52	53	42
Belgium	58	61	54	55	58	62	58	60	52	59	60	56	54	59	59	62	58	52
Austria	62	63	61	53	65	62	64	60	60	59	63	62	60	60	63	63	65	54
France	61	62	60	60	60	63	65	62	48	61	65	54	53	62	65	72	61	52
Canada	59	63	55	62	59	56	62	61	54	59	60	58	54	60	56	63	61	56
United States	62	65	59	69	61	66	61	66	59	66	61	61	57	63	63	60	64	59
Iceland	56	66	46	45	59	65	60	53	57	na	na	na	52	59	59	58	56	54
West Germany	35	40	30	27	37	38	36	31	38	33	32	39	30	38	37	31	39	30
Denmark	51	57	44	49	48	55	51	48	52	55	47	51	43	51	57	54	52	46
Finland	54	56	52	31	57	69	55	54	54	53	55	55	61	50	56	65	61	48
Norway	73	78	68	71	70	78	78	76	69	74	72	74	73	72	75	72	76	68
Sweden	67	70	63	57	66	75	77	62	63	62	70	68	64	67	69	67	69	62
Japan	41	51	31	26	43	46	44	41	36	48	38	39	42	40	47	42	41	38
Switzerland	52	56	48	48	53	53	54	50	51	51	53	51	42	51	58	54	52	48
Total	60	63	57	53	60	64	63	59	57	60	60	59	60	61	63	62	60	56

Ranking:

Nigeria	94
India	86
Brazil	82
South Africa	79
Argentina	76
Chile	75
Slovenia	73
Norway	73
Poland	70
Romania	69
South Korea	69
Mexico	67
Sweden	67
Spain	66
Ireland	65
China	64
Italy	62
Austria	62
United States	62
East Germany	61
France	61
Turkey	59
Hungary	59
Canada	59
Belgium	58
Bulgaria	57
North Ireland	57
Czechoslovakia	56
Iceland	56
Belarus	55
Finland	54
Switzerland	52
Britain	51
Denmark	51
Netherlands	49
Moscow	47
Russia	46
Lithuania	42
Japan	41
Portugal	35
West Germany	35
Latvia	33
Estonia	32

Note: Countries in the left column are ranked according to GNP per capita. / The percentages in the bottom row give each country an equal weight. / na=not ascertained.

V5 FAMILY IMPORTANT

Please say, for each of the following, how important it is in your life: Family. (% "very important")

	Total	Gender		Age			Education			Income			Political Affinity			Values		
		Male	Female	16-29	30-49	50+	Lower	Medium	Upper	Lower	Middle	Upper	Left	Center	Right	Mat	Mixed	Postmat
India	77	73	81	73	80	77	81	78	74	76	76	78	70	74	79	80	75	67
Nigeria	94	93	96	94	94	97	96	94	93	92	93	98	95	94	94	95	94	93
China	62	60	66	56	64	66	69	59	56	61	65	62	na	na	na	64	59	61
Romania	83	82	84	75	88	85	86	82	82	80	85	83	81	86	76	87	82	72
Turkey	87	85	89	85	90	86	89	88	78	85	88	88	87	88	85	88	88	83
Poland	91	87	94	84	93	92	91	90	95	92	90	90	94	89	94	80	92	90
Bulgaria	76	72	79	64	78	82	82	76	71	78	76	73	76	77	77	80	75	64
Chile	86	84	86	81	89	86	84	85	88	83	87	88	84	86	86	86	85	88
Czechoslovakia	86	82	90	79	89	88	84	85	93	81	91	86	88	87	86	86	87	86
South Africa	90	88	92	88	92	91	88	92	90	88	90	92	91	91	86	91	90	89
Lithuania	65	57	72	56	73	66	61	65	75	66	68	61	na	na	na	68	65	60
Hungary	89	86	91	92	90	86	86	91	87	84	93	90	92	90	86	90	88	90
Argentina	91	89	94	86	93	93	91	90	93	89	94	92	90	92	92	91	91	92
Brazil	91	89	92	90	91	92	89	91	93	87	92	94	88	92	85	88	91	85
Mexico	85	84	86	83	88	84	86	83	86	82	88	87	81	88	85	76	85	82
Belarus	77	76	77	73	79	77	83	76	75	81	80	68	78	76	68	81	79	69
Russia	79	73	83	73	83	78	78	79	80	81	79	76	76	77	81	80	79	68
Moscow	78	71	83	73	80	76	85	78	75	78	78	72	79	76	75	78	77	80
Latvia	73	65	78	69	75	73	65	73	75	75	71	72	na	na	na	71	72	72
Estonia	69	58	77	64	72	69	63	69	73	73	70	60	na	na	na	62	68	59
Portugal	65	61	68	61	65	68	65	73	56	64	67	62	56	68	66	66	66	62
South Korea	93	94	92	89	95	95	93	93	93	90	95	95	88	92	95	90	93	89
Ireland	91	88	95	92	93	90	90	93	91	88	92	93	90	92	91	97	94	93
North Ireland	94	91	97	91	97	95	93	98	91	90	97	94	89	95	95	97	94	75
Slovenia	81	75	86	73	84	83	79	81	83	80	81	79	75	82	79	85	80	80
Spain	82	79	85	76	86	83	82	82	81	78	83	83	81	86	83	83	87	80
East Germany	85	82	87	76	88	87	85	82	87	80	87	88	84	87	91	85	90	87
Britain	89	87	90	87	88	86	88	92	88	87	89	92	89	91	85	93	88	84
Italy	88	86	91	83	93	90	89	84	73	87	90	86	86	91	na	93	89	73
Netherlands	82	80	83	74	86	86	85	89	71	73	85	88	71	88	87	83	89	73
Belgium	84	80	87	74	88	87	83	85	82	82	86	88	78	85	85	84	86	78
Austria	86	83	88	81	88	87	88	85	84	83	89	85	88	86	83	87	88	83
France	82	77	86	77	83	85	79	87	81	76	88	86	78	85	92	81	81	82
Canada	92	87	96	89	92	94	92	93	89	89	92	91	89	93	91	93	91	92
United States	92	91	94	92	93	92	91	94	92	91	93	93	88	91	93	90	93	91
Iceland	91	88	94	85	95	91	92	92	90	na	na	na	90	91	76	90	92	92
West Germany	71	68	74	54	76	77	75	64	67	68	72	75	63	75	85	73	74	65
Denmark	88	84	92	81	91	90	89	88	88	84	90	93	89	90	84	88	89	86
Finland	84	79	90	81	89	82	85	85	80	76	86	88	91	82	84	89	84	83
Norway	88	84	92	82	91	88	87	86	90	81	89	89	86	90	89	89	87	85
Sweden	87	83	91	85	89	86	87	84	91	90	77	92	84	88	81	89	87	84
Japan	78	77	79	68	85	75	76	79	79	78	79	80	76	77	88	84	79	77
Switzerland	88	84	91	81	89	89	88	89	81	83	89	89	84	88	89	92	88	83
Total	83	80	86	78	86	84	83	84	82	81	85	84	83	86	85	85	84	80

Ranking:

Nigeria	94
North Ireland	94
South Korea	93
Canada	92
United States	92
Poland	91
Argentina	91
Brazil	91
Ireland	91
Iceland	91
South Africa	90
Hungary	89
Britain	89
Italy	88
Denmark	88
Norway	88
Switzerland	88
Turkey	87
Sweden	87
Chile	86
Czechoslovakia	86
Austria	86
Mexico	85
East Germany	85
Belgium	84
Finland	84
Romania	83
Spain	82
Netherlands	82
France	82
Slovenia	81
Russia	79
Moscow	78
Japan	78
India	77
Belarus	77
Bulgaria	76
Latvia	73
West Germany	71
Estonia	69
Lithuania	65
Portugal	65
China	62

Note: Countries in the left column are ranked according to GNP per capita. / The percentages in the bottom row give each country an equal weight. / na=not ascertained.

V6 FRIENDS IMPORTANT

Please say, for each of the following, how important it is in your life: Friends and acquaintances. (% "very important")

	Total	Gender		Age			Education			Income			Political Affinity			Values			Ranking:
		Male	Female	16-29	30-49	50+	Lower	Medium	Upper	Lower	Middle	Upper	Left	Center	Right	Mat	Mixed	Postmat	
India	30	30	30	32	29	27	28	30	31	30	29	30	29	26	32	35	27	28	Sweden 69
Nigeria	53	52	53	55	49	64	66	53	48	47	52	59	50	51	60	56	52	47	Norway 68
China	22	23	20	30	19	16	23	22	20	22	19	22	na	na	na	21	22	19	Netherlands 63
Romania	25	31	19	35	22	20	21	28	24	25	22	27	27	23	26	18	29	36	Brazil 57
Turkey	55	54	57	55	55	56	56	53	56	57	52	55	59	53	58	55	57	51	Turkey 55
Poland	23	23	22	23	20	26	24	22	21	25	25	22	21	20	30	19	25	21	Ireland 55
Bulgaria	38	42	35	47	38	34	31	40	40	35	41	42	35	40	41	36	37	52	United States 54
Chile	19	17	22	18	17	25	20	18	21	18	17	22	19	19	22	18	19	22	Nigeria 53
Czechoslovakia	27	29	26	38	22	26	27	27	23	32	24	25	22	29	28	25	27	31	North Ireland 53
South Africa	23	23	24	29	19	22	21	25	22	21	23	23	29	21	19	23	23	28	Denmark 53
Lithuania	19	20	19	30	16	13	15	21	15	17	19	23	na	na	na	13	20	24	South Korea 52
Hungary	28	28	27	40	27	23	23	32	29	25	30	28	23	30	28	28	27	35	Switzerland 52
Argentina	51	49	53	51	48	55	48	53	54	49	47	50	47	50	51	47	49	63	Argentina 51
Brazil	57	56	59	49	60	67	63	55	55	59	55	59	53	56	61	58	57	59	Canada 51
Mexico	25	25	25	22	28	26	26	27	20	26	22	29	27	21	27	24	25	25	Iceland 49
Belarus	37	34	39	42	36	32	42	37	34	36	35	39	37	37	33	30	41	32	Britain 48
Russia	29	32	27	37	25	29	27	29	31	26	29	31	29	29	32	24	33	30	Belgium 46
Moscow	40	36	44	43	37	44	40	40	39	37	41	43	41	39	40	43	38	42	Spain 45
Latvia	16	15	18	24	13	14	17	18	13	17	15	16	na	na	na	15	19	10	Finland 43
Estonia	23	23	23	37	18	15	23	26	16	22	27	19	na	na	na	20	23	27	France 41
Portugal	20	20	21	22	15	23	19	21	27	20	20	20	22	18	23	17	21	28	Moscow 40
South Korea	52	47	56	67	45	43	40	53	56	57	45	50	55	52	51	49	52	60	Bulgaria 38
Ireland	55	49	59	63	50	54	54	54	58	54	53	57	59	51	61	50	56	55	Slovenia 38
North Ireland	53	46	58	50	43	66	54	43	72	63	42	52	46	50	57	57	51	51	Italy 38
Slovenia	38	41	35	40	32	42	43	35	33	40	36	37	32	38	40	40	37	32	Belarus 37
Spain	45	45	45	53	44	40	43	46	53	41	46	45	48	42	51	43	47	49	West Germany 37
East Germany	34	30	37	43	28	33	33	36	34	40	31	31	34	34	33	33	31	41	Austria 35
Britain	48	43	52	53	41	51	45	54	58	49	44	52	50	47	50	48	49	45	East Germany 34
Italy	38	40	36	51	33	33	37	41	46	35	36	40	42	37	33	36	35	46	Japan 34
Netherlands	63	57	65	72	57	62	62	63	64	66	59	57	65	64	61	63	62	64	India 30
Belgium	46	46	46	56	43	42	42	46	53	43	52	47	51	43	48	41	44	55	Russia 29
Austria	35	30	38	46	31	33	36	33	36	36	32	37	39	33	33	33	35	36	Hungary 28
France	41	44	38	48	37	39	40	40	44	39	39	44	43	42	39	31	40	51	Czechoslovakia 27
Canada	51	47	55	54	45	52	48	54	50	57	50	47	46	53	51	47	52	50	Romania 25
United States	54	51	58	48	47	63	67	50	51	65	52	52	57	52	53	52	51	60	Mexico 25
Iceland	49	46	52	55	41	56	49	47	50	na	na	na	50	48	50	52	48	50	Poland 23
West Germany	37	35	38	51	32	32	34	40	42	33	32	38	38	36	34	31	35	40	South Africa 23
Denmark	53	48	57	61	47	52	48	54	54	57	46	48	55	52	49	47	51	63	Estonia 23
Finland	43	42	43	54	38	46	49	44	50	54	39	36	42	44	38	53	45	36	China 22
Norway	68	62	74	80	65	64	67	69	67	65	66	67	67	71	64	69	69	61	Portugal 20
Sweden	69	63	76	77	65	68	68	71	69	67	72	66	66	69	70	63	71	68	Chile 19
Japan	34	35	34	53	31	26	28	36	35	35	32	31	35	31	37	33	33	41	Lithuania 19
Switzerland	52	47	56	66	46	51	51	51	55	55	48	47	59	50	46	52	52	52	Latvia 16
Total	40	39	41	46	36	40	40	40	41	40	38	40	42	41	43	38	40	42	

Note: Countries in the left column are ranked according to GNP per capita. / The percentages in the bottom row give each country an equal weight. / na=not ascertained.

V7 LEISURE IMPORTANT

Please say, for each of the following, how important it is in your life: Leisure time. (% "very important")

	Total	Gender Male	Gender Female	Age 16-29	Age 30-49	Age 50+	Education Lower	Education Medium	Education Upper	Income Lower	Income Middle	Income Upper	Political Affinity Left	Political Affinity Center	Political Affinity Right	Values Mat	Values Mixed	Values Postmat
India	17	17	16	18	16	16	15	15	20	15	15	19	18	14	19	17	17	17
Nigeria	68	68	68	70	67	65	74	68	65	67	64	69	69	67	70	69	67	69
China	14	14	14	18	12	13	13	13	15	13	16	13	na	na	na	14	14	21
Romania	25	28	23	31	28	20	20	28	29	22	27	26	24	25	30	20	28	39
Turkey	24	23	26	27	24	20	24	22	32	24	24	25	24	23	25	25	24	24
Poland	35	33	36	35	39	30	30	37	37	32	35	37	32	36	36	26	37	41
Bulgaria	36	35	37	47	37	29	26	39	41	37	35	36	30	42	35	31	36	50
Chile	33	30	36	28	33	39	37	29	33	34	32	33	35	31	32	37	31	31
Czechoslovakia	30	34	26	37	29	25	29	32	25	27	30	30	26	30	29	26	31	33
South Africa	29	31	27	36	26	20	22	33	27	26	31	30	35	27	29	26	29	37
Lithuania	17	18	15	22	18	11	12	18	18	17	14	20	na	na	na	17	17	16
Hungary	32	35	30	38	33	29	29	36	36	29	33	39	36	34	29	32	31	48
Argentina	40	40	40	40	43	38	37	46	39	35	42	39	44	40	39	35	38	53
Brazil	52	51	52	48	54	54	51	53	49	52	52	54	54	45	57	49	53	56
Mexico	28	28	29	28	30	25	29	27	27	30	24	32	38	29	25	25	29	31
Belarus	37	37	37	37	36	39	36	37	37	36	37	36	40	31	36	35	38	37
Russia	29	29	29	34	30	24	24	30	31	28	28	28	28	27	35	26	29	43
Moscow	33	31	35	33	33	34	37	32	33	35	31	36	34	33	32	34	33	36
Latvia	21	20	22	23	20	22	24	22	18	23	18	22	na	na	na	22	22	20
Estonia	25	28	23	31	25	18	26	27	19	24	28	24	na	na	na	27	25	20
Portugal	16	18	15	20	15	14	14	26	16	15	14	18	18	16	15	12	18	19
South Korea	25	24	26	35	22	16	16	27	28	29	21	27	29	31	20	21	26	36
Ireland	32	30	33	35	37	25	29	36	30	27	29	37	38	29	37	28	32	37
North Ireland	31	40	25	25	36	30	31	33	31	23	27	41	50	30	30	22	31	44
Slovenia	28	29	26	31	26	28	29	26	28	28	28	26	24	27	30	27	28	28
Spain	38	41	35	45	42	28	35	43	47	31	38	42	46	32	34	34	38	49
East Germany	36	36	34	47	32	34	36	41	34	35	37	37	36	39	33	22	36	45
Britain	45	51	39	44	44	46	45	39	55	43	41	53	50	43	48	38	46	49
Italy	33	38	28	45	33	25	32	35	41	26	39	34	36	31	35	29	32	41
Netherlands	51	49	51	57	49	46	47	53	52	49	52	51	56	49	48	43	50	54
Belgium	41	42	39	49	43	32	40	41	42	38	47	40	45	39	36	40	40	43
Austria	37	36	37	48	37	31	35	37	42	31	37	40	44	38	32	32	35	43
France	31	34	29	40	34	22	30	31	37	28	33	35	37	26	26	25	28	43
Canada	42	42	41	40	42	43	43	43	39	42	42	38	37	42	45	36	43	42
United States	43	45	41	40	43	44	45	44	41	41	42	44	43	43	39	41	43	43
Iceland	36	36	36	37	32	41	38	37	33	na	na	na	37	37	34	36	35	41
West Germany	40	43	37	55	42	29	36	47	40	34	42	43	44	41	30	28	40	44
Denmark	48	48	48	58	51	38	34	55	51	44	49	55	52	48	46	43	48	50
Finland	47	51	42	54	51	29	44	48	46	44	49	46	48	46	44	35	48	46
Norway	42	41	44	49	46	34	34	46	43	37	48	45	46	42	40	43	43	40
Sweden	55	54	56	62	56	49	56	60	44	57	54	54	58	55	51	51	57	54
Japan	24	25	24	43	23	14	15	24	34	24	19	30	33	23	25	22	25	33
Switzerland	47	47	47	56	47	44	49	48	38	50	46	41	51	46	42	55	46	48
Total	**35**	**36**	**34**	**39**	**35**	**31**	**33**	**36**	**35**	**33**	**35**	**36**	**39**	**36**	**35**	**32**	**35**	**39**

Ranking:

Nigeria	68
Sweden	55
Brazil	52
Netherlands	51
Denmark	48
Finland	47
Switzerland	47
Britain	45
United States	43
Canada	42
Norway	42
Belgium	41
Argentina	40
West Germany	40
Spain	38
Belarus	37
Austria	37
Bulgaria	36
East Germany	36
Iceland	36
Poland	35
Chile	33
Moscow	33
Italy	33
Hungary	32
Ireland	32
North Ireland	31
France	31
Czechoslovakia	30
South Africa	29
Russia	29
Mexico	28
Slovenia	28
Romania	25
Estonia	25
South Korea	25
Turkey	24
Japan	24
Latvia	21
India	17
Lithuania	17
Portugal	16
China	14

Note: Countries in the left column are ranked according to GNP per capita. / The percentages in the bottom row give each country an equal weight. / na=not ascertained.

V8 POLITICS IMPORTANT

Please say, for each of the following, how important it is in your life: Politics. (% "very important" or "quite important")

	Total	Gender		Age			Education			Income			Political Affinity			Values		
		Male	Female	16-29	30-49	50+	Lower	Medium	Upper	Lower	Middle	Upper	Left	Center	Right	Mat	Mixed	Postmat
India	40	46	32	44	38	36	30	42	42	41	40	39	48	38	45	39	43	48
Nigeria	39	42	35	40	37	51	48	35	40	37	43	35	32	40	55	40	39	38
China	59	60	58	48	61	68	52	63	63	63	57	56	na	na	na	58	62	49
Romania	21	27	15	16	25	20	15	22	29	19	22	22	17	19	31	15	23	46
Turkey	28	34	21	26	29	28	24	26	48	24	23	38	45	23	28	18	26	42
Poland	42	44	41	36	44	44	38	42	58	43	39	45	45	42	55	42	41	47
Bulgaria	46	50	43	51	46	43	36	49	52	41	46	52	52	48	58	37	49	59
Chile	31	35	27	34	29	29	25	31	39	26	30	39	52	25	31	20	30	49
Czechoslovakia	36	38	34	33	37	36	27	36	52	35	35	37	44	27	46	29	37	43
South Africa	59	64	53	66	55	49	48	64	62	57	61	58	77	56	68	49	62	69
Lithuania	51	56	47	41	52	59	47	50	66	50	54	48	na	na	na	52	51	58
Hungary	26	30	22	27	27	25	17	32	43	18	28	45	38	29	32	24	28	30
Argentina	31	32	30	25	32	35	25	32	38	27	31	35	51	32	39	22	31	44
Brazil	42	43	41	42	42	43	35	40	65	37	37	51	43	47	47	36	44	60
Mexico	41	46	35	40	42	43	40	40	46	37	43	47	61	38	45	40	39	59
Belarus	37	44	31	25	39	47	40	28	46	32	41	38	38	35	44	34	38	40
Russia	37	43	33	27	38	44	29	33	47	32	40	45	51	38	48	34	39	49
Moscow	41	45	36	26	39	55	34	32	48	39	39	46	46	35	38	40	41	50
Latvia	44	48	41	35	44	54	44	40	51	38	49	44	na	na	na	42	46	57
Estonia	42	46	38	30	47	47	34	40	55	37	45	45	na	na	na	35	46	53
Portugal	22	24	20	20	17	28	18	26	34	19	20	27	32	21	20	19	22	33
South Korea	71	72	71	73	69	73	71	72	70	70	73	70	79	71	69	67	74	78
Ireland	28	30	26	22	31	30	28	26	45	27	26	31	38	25	37	24	28	34
North Ireland	28	25	31	26	26	32	24	33	40	34	28	29	36	24	39	23	27	42
Slovenia	25	30	21	23	26	26	20	25	34	24	24	29	36	32	34	24	26	23
Spain	22	26	19	21	28	18	19	27	33	17	21	29	36	20	23	16	23	35
East Germany	57	61	54	58	61	53	51	62	76	53	49	67	70	54	53	32	58	66
Britain	43	46	41	39	46	43	37	55	58	37	48	53	51	37	56	40	41	54
Italy	31	39	23	35	32	27	29	47	48	29	35	50	44	31	34	21	29	47
Netherlands	53	59	50	45	56	56	46	51	61	50	58	60	62	46	62	42	52	58
Belgium	26	29	23	28	26	24	16	29	40	20	28	34	34	27	32	16	24	41
Austria	35	43	30	29	39	36	33	37	39	29	37	40	47	36	37	26	34	43
France	33	37	29	30	31	36	28	32	47	26	32	46	46	30	35	20	32	47
Canada	48	47	49	39	45	59	42	46	55	43	50	52	55	47	57	44	46	57
United States	52	53	50	48	49	56	49	50	57	49	52	56	56	53	59	45	50	62
Iceland	26	28	24	24	27	27	21	24	31	na	na	na	30	23	29	17	28	39
West Germany	42	51	35	38	43	44	36	47	65	37	41	48	53	38	53	28	42	52
Denmark	43	46	41	41	44	45	29	39	55	43	41	50	59	40	43	25	44	63
Finland	26	33	18	26	25	29	32	24	25	30	26	23	32	24	29	27	24	30
Norway	50	51	50	49	50	52	51	42	59	45	51	55	60	46	54	41	54	62
Sweden	45	44	46	41	44	52	40	43	59	44	44	48	53	38	52	40	43	56
Japan	54	58	50	38	54	65	59	51	57	55	50	61	61	58	70	53	54	71
Switzerland	41	46	37	45	39	42	36	43	54	40	42	43	61	41	46	32	38	56
Total	**39**	**43**	**36**	**36**	**40**	**42**	**35**	**40**	**50**	**37**	**40**	**44**	**48**	**37**	**44**	**33**	**40**	**50**

Ranking:

South Korea	71
China	59
South Africa	59
East Germany	57
Japan	54
Netherlands	53
United States	52
Lithuania	51
Norway	50
Canada	48
Bulgaria	46
Sweden	45
Latvia	44
Britain	43
Denmark	43
Poland	42
Brazil	42
Estonia	42
West Germany	42
Mexico	41
Moscow	41
Switzerland	41
India	40
Nigeria	39
Belarus	37
Russia	37
Czechoslovakia	36
Austria	35
France	33
Chile	31
Argentina	31
Italy	31
Turkey	28
Ireland	28
North Ireland	28
Hungary	26
Belgium	26
Iceland	26
Finland	26
Slovenia	25
Portugal	22
Spain	22
Romania	21

Note: Countries in the left column are ranked according to GNP per capita. / The percentages in the bottom row give each country an equal weight. na=not ascertained.
Unlike the series V4-V9, this table includes the percentage "very important" or "quite important."

V9 RELIGION IMPORTANT

Please say, for each of the following, how important it is in your life: Religion. (% "very important")

	Total	Gender		Age			Education			Income			Political Affinity			Values			Ranking:	
		Male	Female	16-29	30-49	50+	Lower	Medium	Upper	Lower	Middle	Upper	Left	Center	Right	Mat	Mixed	Postmat		
India	49	47	51	44	49	61	58	54	40	57	48	42	48	46	48	55	44	41	Nigeria	85
Nigeria	85	81	92	83	88	93	94	87	80	87	83	89	85	82	89	91	83	76	South Africa	66
China	01	02	01	01	01	03	03	01	00	01	01	02	na	na	na	02	01	04	Turkey	61
Romania	42	35	48	29	35	57	59	32	34	45	43	37	41	37	43	48	38	33	Brazil	57
Turkey	61	58	64	53	61	74	75	46	25	70	64	48	39	63	75	69	63	47	Poland	53
Poland	53	49	56	46	44	63	68	46	27	53	53	51	49	46	52	56	51	46	United States	53
Bulgaria	12	09	14	13	09	14	17	11	06	11	12	10	07	08	17	12	10	15	Chile	51
Chile	51	44	59	42	53	64	62	47	45	59	51	42	44	52	52	58	49	48	India	49
Czechoslovakia	11	09	13	03	09	20	22	06	08	15	09	11	05	11	16	13	11	08	Ireland	48
South Africa	66	58	74	63	66	73	68	67	54	67	70	58	63	63	67	67	67	61	Romania	42
Lithuania	16	10	21	06	08	31	34	10	12	23	11	07	na	na	na	19	14	15	Argentina	40
Hungary	23	16	30	13	13	36	32	15	16	31	19	09	10	22	27	25	21	15	Mexico	34
Argentina	40	32	47	27	39	51	48	35	33	48	40	35	23	37	50	45	41	30	North Ireland	34
Brazil	57	50	64	48	58	71	66	56	41	65	52	52	49	51	65	64	54	43	Italy	34
Mexico	34	29	40	28	35	49	35	40	27	38	31	32	22	33	39	35	33	30	Canada	31
Belarus	12	09	15	06	10	23	28	10	09	15	12	10	13	09	18	16	10	14	South Korea	26
Russia	12	07	16	07	07	21	21	10	08	14	11	07	07	09	15	15	10	12	Austria	25
Moscow	11	07	15	10	10	14	18	12	10	13	11	10	11	11	11	12	10	18	Iceland	24
Latvia	07	05	08	09	04	11	18	07	03	06	07	07	na	na	na	07	07	07	Switzerland	24
Estonia	05	04	05	03	04	07	07	04	03	06	03	04	na	na	na	05	04	05	Hungary	23
Portugal	17	09	24	06	12	32	23	06	04	29	09	05	10	13	23	21	14	03	Spain	21
South Korea	26	31	21	22	26	32	36	24	23	29	22	27	23	28	25	27	24	28	Netherlands	19
Ireland	48	41	54	22	42	71	58	40	25	68	46	36	25	45	57	57	47	39	Portugal	17
North Ireland	34	27	40	28	31	43	37	31	24	37	29	23	21	34	36	32	33	33	Slovenia	17
Slovenia	17	12	22	13	11	27	29	11	06	26	13	09	14	14	20	18	18	12	Lithuania	16
Spain	21	13	27	09	16	34	23	17	12	28	18	15	11	20	32	28	19	13	East Germany	16
East Germany	16	12	19	08	14	21	16	18	11	19	16	12	06	18	23	17	15	16	Britain	16
Britain	16	11	21	06	11	27	17	14	17	21	11	11	13	15	18	20	15	14	Belgium	15
Italy	34	27	42	25	25	49	35	28	40	41	31	20	19	44	38	41	34	28	Finland	15
Netherlands	19	23	17	09	15	35	25	15	16	20	19	16	08	18	32	22	22	12	Norway	15
Belgium	15	11	19	06	13	24	16	17	12	18	14	14	06	14	23	16	15	11	France	14
Austria	25	17	30	13	20	35	33	20	14	38	22	18	28	20	29	38	27	13	West Germany	13
France	14	12	16	08	10	23	15	12	15	11	15	16	08	13	27	19	12	14	Bulgaria	12
Canada	31	25	36	21	23	47	45	28	23	38	33	19	20	32	33	41	29	28	Belarus	12
United States	53	50	56	46	47	61	59	55	46	61	51	45	33	53	62	55	55	47	Russia	12
Iceland	24	20	28	13	23	39	36	23	16	na	na	na	17	26	27	29	22	20	Czechoslovakia	11
West Germany	13	09	16	05	07	23	15	10	11	20	10	09	07	13	20	23	13	07	Moscow	11
Denmark	09	05	12	03	07	15	12	05	09	13	06	04	05	09	10	08	09	06	Sweden	10
Finland	15	13	16	11	11	26	22	13	12	21	11	13	10	16	14	28	13	14	Denmark	09
Norway	15	12	19	09	10	25	25	11	14	23	10	13	10	17	17	16	15	10	Latvia	07
Sweden	10	07	14	08	09	14	08	09	15	09	11	09	06	08	13	07	11	08	Japan	06
Japan	06	04	07	08	05	08	10	05	03	10	05	04	06	05	06	05	06	03	Estonia	05
Switzerland	24	17	30	16	18	33	23	24	26	32	20	12	18	20	29	31	25	16	China	01
Total	27	23	31	20	23	37	34	24	20	32	25	22	22	28	33	31	26	22		

Note: Countries in the left column are ranked according to GNP per capita. / The percentages in the bottom row give each country an equal weight. / na=not ascertained.

V10. When you get together with your friends, would you say you discuss political matters...

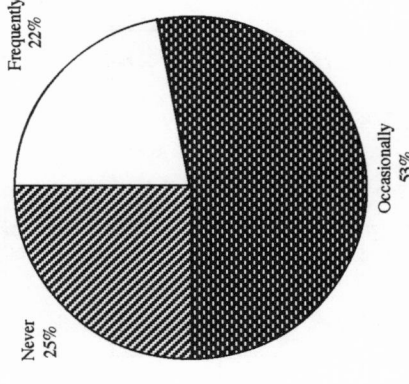

Frequently
22%

Never
25%

Occasionally
53%

V11. When you yourself hold a strong opinion do you ever find yourself persuading your friends, relatives or fellow workers to share your views?

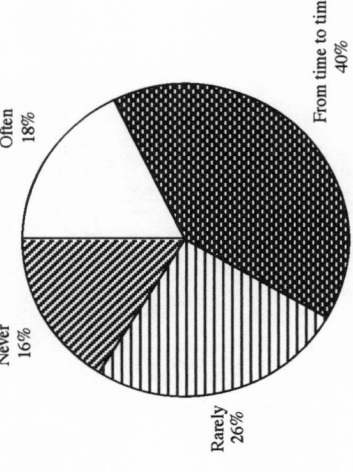

Often
18%

Never
16%

Rarely
26%

From time to time
40%

V10 DISCUSS POLITICS

When you get together with your friends, would you say you discuss political matters frequently, occasionally or never?
(% "frequently" or "occasionally")

	Total	Gender		Age			Education			Income			Political Affinity			Values			Ranking:	
		Male	Female	16-29	30-49	50+	Lower	Medium	Upper	Lower	Middle	Upper	Left	Center	Right	Mat	Mixed	Postmat		
India	73	83	62	79	72	62	46	75	85	66	75	79	84	78	74	74	78	86	Latvia	96
Nigeria	63	69	54	66	60	57	63	56	71	58	69	63	52	68	78	58	66	65	Estonia	95
China	89	92	84	89	91	85	81	94	98	88	90	88	na	na	na	85	93	100	Lithuania	94
Romania	66	76	56	68	72	59	49	69	84	60	65	72	59	67	77	57	72	82	East Germany	94
Turkey	56	67	46	57	59	49	46	67	82	46	55	70	75	54	58	47	54	74	Moscow	92
Poland	83	89	77	82	88	77	70	89	98	83	81	85	89	87	87	80	83	89	Belarus	91
Bulgaria	88	91	86	94	93	79	69	94	98	86	91	89	91	93	95	83	90	98	Czechoslovakia	90
Chile	60	67	53	67	60	50	40	66	75	43	63	76	75	58	64	43	63	76	China	89
Czechoslovakia	90	93	88	87	94	88	83	93	96	88	92	91	92	89	93	85	92	96	Norway	89
South Africa	70	76	65	73	73	59	51	77	96	58	69	90	86	77	88	65	72	79	Bulgaria	88
Lithuania	94	96	93	93	98	92	87	96	98	92	97	96	na	na	na	91	97	94	South Korea	88
Hungary	76	80	72	81	83	67	65	85	92	65	84	90	87	79	83	73	77	90	Switzerland	86
Argentina	67	73	61	64	71	65	52	74	82	58	63	81	84	74	75	53	70	75	West Germany	84
Brazil	55	63	48	56	60	47	39	57	84	42	56	68	62	61	56	48	58	78	Poland	83
Mexico	74	80	67	74	76	67	70	72	87	68	78	82	90	73	77	71	76	80	Russia	83
Belarus	91	93	88	89	94	86	79	90	95	87	92	94	94	89	85	88	91	94	Slovenia	82
Russia	83	88	80	84	90	74	69	84	91	78	86	86	91	87	85	77	87	92	Finland	82
Moscow	92	97	89	92	95	88	74	93	96	91	93	95	96	92	86	91	93	96	Denmark	79
Latvia	96	96	97	95	98	94	88	97	98	96	98	96	na	na	na	95	98	99	Sweden	79
Estonia	95	95	94	92	98	93	87	96	99	94	95	95	na	na	na	95	96	93	Iceland	78
Portugal	53	63	45	59	53	48	44	65	81	39	55	72	64	52	57	42	59	73	Hungary	76
South Korea	88	82	94	88	90	86	73	89	95	82	92	94	91	89	87	85	90	98	Canada	75
Ireland	58	68	50	48	64	59	51	62	83	44	58	71	64	56	70	56	58	63	Mexico	74
North Ireland	56	63	51	59	53	57	49	63	83	49	47	78	61	51	71	60	52	67	Netherlands	74
Slovenia	82	85	79	83	87	76	72	88	92	74	87	88	89	92	90	82	81	91	India	73
Spain	50	61	41	57	59	37	44	61	72	38	51	66	69	53	53	43	53	69	United States	72
East Germany	94	96	92	95	98	89	92	96	99	91	95	96	98	93	92	88	94	96	South Africa	70
Britain	66	71	62	62	72	63	60	79	82	57	79	75	66	65	78	60	65	77	Austria	69
Italy	58	71	46	66	78	52	55	76	88	54	68	83	68	58	63	46	57	75	Argentina	67
Netherlands	74	79	72	67	81	72	66	74	84	74	76	87	80	77	78	61	73	82	Romania	66
Belgium	53	56	50	51	56	51	39	55	76	43	53	66	58	56	64	36	52	71	Britain	66
Austria	69	76	64	67	72	67	64	70	83	58	70	79	72	71	74	54	67	81	Japan	66
France	65	73	59	61	68	66	56	69	83	57	67	80	78	66	76	50	65	80	France	65
Canada	75	77	73	66	78	79	64	73	86	67	76	85	83	75	87	67	75	81	Nigeria	63
United States	72	76	68	65	73	75	65	69	82	64	73	82	78	74	74	70	71	77	Chile	60
Iceland	78	81	75	75	85	68	70	77	85	na	na	na	80	78	83	68	80	89	Ireland	58
West Germany	84	92	77	82	89	81	80	88	97	80	86	89	91	83	88	71	84	91	Italy	58
Denmark	79	85	73	80	82	73	61	79	88	74	82	87	87	75	85	62	81	89	Turkey	56
Finland	82	85	78	78	82	83	79	81	84	83	77	86	88	81	85	74	78	91	North Ireland	56
Norway	89	91	86	87	92	85	81	85	96	87	93	92	93	88	93	83	90	97	Brazil	55
Sweden	79	82	76	76	81	80	72	80	89	75	78	83	83	77	86	73	79	85	Portugal	53
Japan	66	76	58	53	67	74	69	64	70	63	67	71	81	73	77	65	69	81	Belgium	53
Switzerland	86	92	82	86	88	85	82	87	99	81	90	90	96	90	92	74	85	96	Spain	50
Total	75	80	70	74	78	71	65	78	88	69	76	83	80	74	79	68	76	85		

Note: Countries in the left column are ranked according to GNP per capita. / The percentages in the bottom row give each country an equal weight. / na=not ascertained.

V11 PERSUADE FRIENDS

When you yourself hold a strong opinion do you ever find yourself persuading your friends, relatives, or fellow workers to share your views?
IF SO, does it happen often, from time to time, or rarely? (% "often")

	Total	Gender		Age			Education			Income			Political Affinity			Values		
		Male	Female	16-29	30-49	50+	Lower	Medium	Upper	Lower	Middle	Upper	Left	Center	Right	Mat	Mixed	Postmat
India	14	18	10	14	14	12	07	13	18	13	11	18	18	14	13	13	16	13
Nigeria	29	35	20	29	31	19	25	27	34	29	30	27	31	29	36	23	32	37
China	16	17	16	17	18	12	17	18	14	19	16	14	na	na	na	16	16	28
Romania	32	34	29	30	32	33	27	31	39	32	29	33	35	30	41	27	33	48
Turkey	19	21	17	17	20	19	17	19	28	16	18	24	18	17	23	16	19	22
Poland	11	13	09	08	11	13	08	11	22	11	08	15	16	11	12	09	12	14
Bulgaria	27	28	26	31	30	20	16	27	37	20	26	38	31	27	32	27	25	36
Chile	24	26	21	23	23	25	23	22	26	23	23	26	27	23	24	19	23	33
Czechoslovakia	na	na	na	na	na	na	na	na	na	na	na	na	na	na	na	na	na	na
South Africa	19	23	15	22	18	16	13	22	22	15	20	22	22	21	25	16	21	19
Lithuania	33	39	27	33	34	31	28	32	43	28	37	35	na	na	na	31	33	41
Hungary	30	34	27	43	34	22	22	39	33	22	35	42	36	31	38	28	32	30
Argentina	24	26	23	33	24	18	19	31	27	20	22	33	26	23	37	19	25	30
Brazil	20	19	21	17	21	24	22	20	19	20	22	19	21	19	21	19	21	22
Mexico	16	17	16	16	14	21	16	18	17	15	16	19	21	13	19	13	18	14
Belarus	28	33	23	26	28	28	16	23	36	24	26	34	29	27	28	27	28	30
Russia	22	25	20	20	24	22	15	19	30	22	22	25	34	21	26	19	24	33
Moscow	35	37	34	30	34	40	24	35	37	31	37	40	37	32	36	33	35	38
Latvia	19	19	19	18	20	20	22	18	21	17	15	22	na	na	na	15	21	24
Estonia	23	27	20	19	29	18	16	21	38	20	18	33	na	na	na	23	24	34
Portugal	13	14	11	17	12	09	09	22	18	10	09	21	14	12	14	11	13	20
South Korea	na	na	na	na	na	na	na	na	na	na	na	na	na	na	na	na	na	na
Ireland	10	11	10	15	10	07	08	12	18	08	07	14	13	09	12	07	11	13
North Ireland	05	08	03	03	07	06	04	09	03	03	07	07	07	04	07	05	05	09
Slovenia	10	13	08	09	12	09	08	10	14	08	09	15	17	10	10	06	12	12
Spain	14	17	12	20	15	10	12	21	20	10	12	21	17	13	22	11	15	22
East Germany	19	22	17	15	22	19	18	16	25	18	20	20	20	18	23	14	19	21
Britain	10	10	09	12	08	10	09	09	14	08	10	09	12	09	10	08	10	13
Italy	20	22	17	21	25	15	19	26	29	18	19	28	21	17	25	16	20	24
Netherlands	19	25	16	20	17	19	16	16	24	21	16	24	22	19	18	23	24	34
Belgium	13	14	11	18	13	10	09	13	19	11	12	14	13	14	16	10	12	16
Austria	11	12	10	07	15	09	11	10	13	09	09	15	15	12	11	05	10	15
France	10	10	09	10	09	10	09	11	21	08	10	13	12	07	16	05	09	14
Canada	15	16	15	18	15	14	11	15	18	16	15	18	21	14	12	05	16	19
United States	16	19	14	23	18	13	12	16	21	18	14	19	21	14	19	16	17	16
Iceland	16	20	12	22	15	10	11	16	19	na	11	15	16	12	21	12	16	23
West Germany	12	15	10	12	13	12	11	11	19	11	11	15	15	10	16	07	10	15
Denmark	34	37	32	42	34	29	23	38	38	35	31	39	46	29	34	24	34	47
Finland	07	09	04	11	05	06	09	07	06	08	06	07	06	05	09	09	07	06
Norway	14	17	11	18	16	10	10	12	19	12	14	20	16	11	19	08	16	21
Sweden	15	16	15	17	17	11	10	17	19	15	10	19	15	11	18	11	14	19
Japan	07	10	04	05	07	09	09	06	07	07	06	08	18	07	05	05	08	08
Switzerland	na	na	na	na	na	na	na	na	na	na	na	na	na	na	na	na	na	na
Total	18	21	16	20	19	17	15	19	23	17	17	22	21	17	21	15	19	23

Ranking:

Moscow	35
Denmark	34
Lithuania	33
Romania	32
Hungary	30
Nigeria	29
Belarus	28
Bulgaria	27
Chile	24
Argentina	24
Estonia	23
Russia	22
Brazil	20
Italy	20
Turkey	19
South Africa	19
Latvia	19
East Germany	19
Netherlands	19
China	16
Mexico	16
United States	16
Iceland	16
Canada	15
Sweden	15
India	14
Spain	14
Norway	14
Portugal	13
Belgium	13
West Germany	12
Poland	11
Austria	11
Ireland	10
Slovenia	10
Britain	10
France	10
Finland	07
Japan	07
North Ireland	05

Note: Countries in the left column are ranked according to G.N.P. per capita. / The percentages in the bottom row give each country an equal weight. / na=not ascertained.

V12-V17. Statements about the environment

Percentage "strongly agree" or "agree"

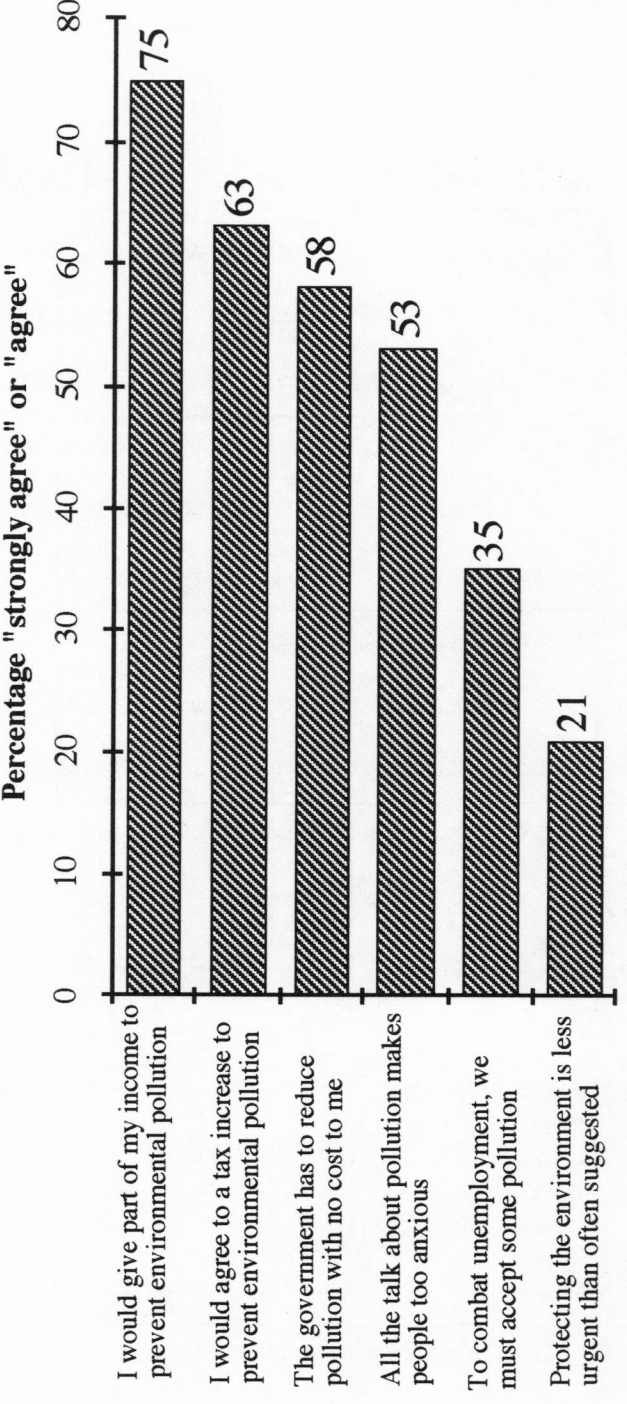

I would give part of my income to prevent environmental pollution — 75

I would agree to a tax increase to prevent environmental pollution — 63

The government has to reduce pollution with no cost to me — 58

All the talk about pollution makes people too anxious — 53

To combat unemployment, we must accept some pollution — 35

Protecting the environment is less urgent than often suggested — 21

V12 ENVIRONMENT: INCOME

I would give part of my income if I were certain that the money would be used to prevent environmental pollution.
(% "strongly agree" or "agree")

	Total	Gender		Age			Education			Income			Political Affinity			Values			Ranking:	
		Male	Female	16-29	30-49	50+	Lower	Medium	Upper	Lower	Middle	Upper	Left	Center	Right	Mat	Mixed	Postmat		
India	81	83	78	85	79	76	66	81	87	80	80	82	86	85	76	77	85	89	Slovenia	89
Nigeria	78	79	76	77	80	74	78	77	79	74	81	78	73	82	81	78	78	76	Turkey	87
China	78	77	80	80	78	76	74	78	84	80	81	71	na	na	na	75	82	79	Chile	84
Romania	na	na	na	na	na	na	na	na	na	na	na	na	na	na	na	na	na	na	Moscow	84
Turkey	87	86	88	89	86	86	86	89	90	82	89	91	88	89	85	84	87	91	Portugal	84
Poland	na	na	na	na	na	na	na	na	na	na	na	na	na	na	na	na	na	na	South Korea	84
Bulgaria	83	82	84	85	86	78	73	85	88	77	85	86	89	84	84	81	83	83	Denmark	84
Chile	84	83	85	88	84	79	79	88	85	79	86	87	81	86	87	83	84	89	Bulgaria	83
Czechoslovakia	79	79	79	81	82	75	73	81	81	74	82	81	78	79	83	70	82	88	Netherlands	83
South Africa	na	na	na	na	na	na	na	na	na	na	na	na	na	na	na	na	na	na	Sweden	82
Lithuania	75	77	72	77	75	73	77	73	78	73	75	77	na	na	na	70	75	83	India	81
Hungary	60	62	59	78	63	51	51	68	72	48	67	76	64	64	70	59	62	63	Mexico	81
Argentina	62	62	62	65	62	60	54	66	71	50	65	69	72	72	68	50	64	73	Belarus	80
Brazil	72	68	76	75	69	72	73	74	65	75	70	71	71	72	74	76	69	70	Norway	80
Mexico	81	79	84	83	80	77	78	82	89	79	84	82	77	82	85	82	81	85	Czechoslovakia	79
Belarus	80	79	81	76	81	81	78	80	80	78	84	77	81	81	77	76	82	89	Nigeria	78
Russia	78	76	79	79	77	78	76	79	77	77	79	78	77	81	77	80	76	81	China	78
Moscow	84	85	83	82	85	83	81	85	84	81	86	86	86	82	83	83	84	85	Russia	78
Latvia	78	76	79	83	74	77	77	79	75	82	74	77	78	na	na	67	81	81	Latvia	78
Estonia	77	73	81	77	78	76	70	79	80	76	74	82	na	na	na	70	79	91	Iceland	78
Portugal	84	82	87	88	85	80	82	89	89	77	88	90	83	87	85	85	85	82	Estonia	77
South Korea	84	84	85	89	83	80	72	85	90	80	84	89	85	84	85	82	85	89	Lithuania	75
Ireland	69	69	70	68	72	68	64	74	83	65	65	77	74	74	63	67	67	80	North Ireland	75
North Ireland	75	74	76	72	77	75	73	80	76	72	74	81	93	74	74	66	77	78	Canada	74
Slovenia	89	89	89	93	90	84	84	92	92	84	91	95	91	94	93	85	89	95	United States	74
Spain	72	73	72	78	75	65	70	78	77	60	78	77	78	73	70	62	78	81	Brazil	72
East Germany	63	65	61	61	66	61	61	62	71	56	67	66	65	65	59	49	63	69	Spain	72
Britain	68	67	68	73	69	63	62	76	85	60	73	76	63	72	71	56	67	82	Ireland	69
Italy	68	66	69	73	66	65	66	79	86	65	70	86	73	70	66	63	65	79	Britain	68
Netherlands	83	83	83	84	85	79	76	82	93	80	85	91	87	84	85	72	82	91	Italy	68
Belgium	56	55	58	62	58	52	47	59	69	55	57	64	59	61	59	45	55	71	Japan	68
Austria	60	61	59	64	67	52	54	62	74	46	62	70	60	62	63	40	60	70	Finland	67
France	61	57	65	67	60	59	59	60	69	55	64	68	63	63	51	50	63	68	East Germany	63
Canada	74	74	73	76	73	72	65	75	83	69	75	81	83	71	78	59	74	82	Argentina	62
United States	74	76	73	78	73	74	68	73	80	68	73	83	83	75	76	70	74	81	France	61
Iceland	78	77	79	76	77	83	79	73	81	na	na	na	80	85	70	76	77	88	Hungary	60
West Germany	52	51	54	55	54	49	47	57	72	45	51	61	58	52	48	38	50	65	Austria	60
Denmark	84	82	87	86	87	80	74	89	88	80	87	91	88	85	84	74	86	91	Belgium	56
Finland	67	63	71	71	68	61	59	63	74	66	64	71	71	68	63	48	64	75	West Germany	52
Norway	80	78	83	83	82	76	73	80	83	66	82	83	80	84	79	76	74	88		
Sweden	82	81	82	81	84	78	79	81	86	82	76	84	87	77	82	74	81	87		
Japan	68	71	65	69	64	75	62	66	78	60	70	75	63	74	76	72	69	75		
Switzerland	na	na	na	na	na	na	na	na	na	na	na	na	na	na	na	na	na	na		
Total	75	74	75	77	75	72	70	76	81	70	76	79	77	76	75	68	75	81		

Note: Countries in the left column are ranked according to GNP per capita. na=not ascertained. The percentages in the bottom row give each country an equal weight.

V13 ENVIRONMENT: TAXES

I would agree to an increase in taxes if the extra money is used to prevent environmental pollution. (% "strongly agree" or "agree")

	Total	Gender Male	Gender Female	Age 16-29	Age 30-49	Age 50+	Education Lower	Education Medium	Education Upper	Income Lower	Income Middle	Income Upper	Political Affinity Left	Political Affinity Center	Political Affinity Right	Values Mat	Values Mixed	Values Postmat
India	66	69	62	71	65	58	53	65	72	63	65	68	73	67	65	61	71	72
Nigeria	59	59	59	60	59	46	57	59	59	53	62	60	61	58	63	60	58	56
China	82	82	83	79	83	86	82	81	87	82	85	81	na	na	na	80	85	81
Romania	na	na	na	na	na	na	na	na	na	na	na	na	na	na	na	na	na	na
Turkey	72	71	73	76	72	68	71	74	76	66	75	76	74	72	72	68	73	77
Poland	na	na	na	na	na	na	na	na	na	na	na	na	na	na	na	na	na	na
Bulgaria	70	72	69	76	72	66	60	72	77	66	70	76	73	70	74	68	71	74
Chile	76	77	75	79	76	72	75	76	78	71	79	78	78	78	75	75	75	84
Czechoslovakia	67	67	68	64	68	69	66	66	73	61	69	72	66	64	75	57	70	78
South Africa	na	na	na	na	na	na	na	na	na	na	na	na	na	na	na	na	na	na
Lithuania	66	68	63	68	69	60	59	66	75	63	66	70	na	na	70	61	66	75
Hungary	35	34	35	47	34	30	28	38	48	27	39	44	40	37	40	36	34	35
Argentina	50	52	49	54	50	48	45	53	56	44	49	55	56	57	55	44	51	56
Brazil	71	70	71	73	70	68	71	72	61	70	73	69	69	73	73	71	71	67
Mexico	67	66	68	69	66	65	66	70	70	66	66	71	63	69	70	71	66	65
Belarus	67	64	71	67	68	67	66	68	67	65	72	64	67	69	66	69	68	66
Russia	66	64	68	67	66	67	62	67	68	65	65	71	73	68	62	65	67	71
Moscow	69	69	70	68	68	72	73	70	68	68	71	70	69	71	76	70	70	66
Latvia	64	63	64	66	62	65	67	63	64	62	64	65	na	na	na	56	65	80
Estonia	59	57	61	56	61	58	52	59	65	56	61	60	na	na	na	47	63	77
Portugal	65	64	67	69	64	63	65	68	65	62	69	65	69	67	64	64	67	67
South Korea	76	72	79	73	78	77	65	77	80	70	77	84	64	76	79	79	73	73
Ireland	51	53	48	50	48	53	47	53	62	50	49	54	53	53	49	45	50	59
North Ireland	65	68	63	69	62	66	61	74	69	62	70	72	74	64	65	62	63	80
Slovenia	69	71	68	73	70	67	62	70	81	62	69	84	74	76	71	67	70	78
Spain	60	60	59	65	63	52	58	64	66	49	66	63	65	62	54	51	67	66
East Germany	65	65	64	69	67	59	62	71	71	60	68	67	66	67	62	47	66	71
Britain	70	73	67	73	71	67	67	72	83	62	77	80	70	70	74	59	71	79
Italy	54	55	53	55	52	55	52	68	60	51	59	70	56	58	55	54	52	59
Netherlands	69	68	70	69	72	66	65	69	74	66	74	76	74	67	70	57	67	77
Belgium	41	42	39	43	41	39	33	42	52	41	40	50	42	48	46	29	41	51
Austria	52	51	53	59	56	46	49	54	57	41	53	62	54	57	53	39	51	62
France	54	54	55	60	51	54	50	59	58	50	56	60	60	58	47	46	53	67
Canada	64	63	65	66	62	65	59	64	67	61	65	71	74	63	64	57	62	74
United States	64	66	62	66	64	63	53	65	71	57	63	74	74	65	65	57	64	71
Iceland	60	60	60	55	61	65	58	56	66	na	na	na	78	59	52	55	60	72
West Germany	49	47	51	48	51	49	44	53	69	43	46	57	53	49	49	36	48	59
Denmark	70	64	75	67	74	66	63	66	77	64	76	70	80	70	64	61	71	77
Finland	56	54	58	58	55	58	55	50	65	53	54	61	58	54	57	45	54	63
Norway	73	69	78	77	76	67	63	73	78	75	76	72	78	76	67	69	74	86
Sweden	77	75	80	74	79	75	77	75	79	74	73	80	84	75	73	69	77	81
Japan	51	56	45	44	51	55	45	48	65	43	51	61	58	56	60	55	52	62
Switzerland	na	na	na	na	na	na	na	na	na	na	na	na	na	na	na	na	na	na
Total	**63**	**63**	**63**	**65**	**64**	**61**	**59**	**64**	**69**	**59**	**65**	**68**	**66**	**64**	**63**	**58**	**64**	**70**

Ranking:

China	82
Sweden	77
Chile	76
South Korea	76
Norway	73
Turkey	72
Brazil	71
Bulgaria	70
Britain	70
Denmark	70
Moscow	69
Slovenia	69
Netherlands	69
Czechoslovakia	67
Mexico	67
Belarus	67
India	66
Lithuania	66
Russia	66
Portugal	65
North Ireland	65
East Germany	65
Latvia	64
Canada	64
United States	64
Spain	60
Iceland	60
Nigeria	59
Estonia	59
Finland	56
Italy	54
France	54
Austria	52
Ireland	51
Japan	51
Argentina	50
West Germany	49
Belgium	41
Hungary	35

Note: Countries in the left column are ranked according to GNP per capita. / The percentages in the bottom row give each country an equal weight. / na=not ascertained.

V14 ENVIRONMENT: NO COST

The Government has to reduce environmental pollution but it should not cost me any money. (% "strongly agree" or "agree")

	Total	Gender		Age			Education			Income			Political Affinity			Values			Ranking:	
		Male	Female	16-29	30-49	50+	Lower	Medium	Upper	Lower	Middle	Upper	Left	Center	Right	Mat	Mixed	Postmat		
India	52	50	55	49	54	58	66	55	43	58	51	48	54	52	48	57	49	46	Portugal	92
Nigeria	61	59	64	62	60	57	67	61	59	65	57	65	69	57	60	70	58	44	Italy	80
China	46	46	46	40	46	53	47	48	38	43	45	51	na	na	na	53	38	53	Spain	76
Romania	na	na	na	na	na	na	na	na	na	na	na	na	na	na	na	na	na	na	Hungary	75
Turkey	56	54	57	55	55	59	60	50	46	63	52	51	54	50	61	63	54	51	Bulgaria	74
Poland	na	na	na	na	na	na	na	na	na	na	na	na	na	na	na	na	na	na	France	74
Bulgaria	74	72	76	71	74	76	79	76	65	75	75	71	71	73	71	77	74	64	Argentina	72
Chile	58	59	57	52	58	67	71	55	47	68	60	42	55	58	54	71	56	44	Belarus	72
Czechoslovakia	46	45	47	43	45	50	56	43	38	52	45	41	51	48	37	60	43	34	Estonia	72
South Africa	na	na	na	na	na	na	na	na	na	na	na	na	na	na	na	na	na	na	Moscow	71
Lithuania	69	69	69	61	66	78	75	69	57	72	68	62	na	na	na	74	69	56	Latvia	71
Hungary	75	75	75	63	70	84	84	68	58	83	71	59	68	74	71	76	74	65	Lithuania	69
Argentina	72	70	74	64	73	76	81	70	56	82	73	60	70	69	61	82	70	64	Brazil	65
Brazil	65	65	66	60	67	72	80	62	48	74	65	57	62	62	67	72	62	52	North Ireland	63
Mexico	40	41	38	35	41	51	44	39	27	45	36	35	38	37	37	45	38	35	Belgium	62
Belarus	72	74	70	70	71	76	79	73	68	73	70	73	73	69	71	75	71	68	Nigeria	61
Russia	49	50	47	43	49	53	54	49	45	51	51	42	44	45	46	49	49	43	Austria	61
Moscow	71	66	74	71	69	73	85	73	66	76	68	68	73	67	70	77	69	69	Ireland	60
Latvia	71	71	71	63	72	78	76	73	67	72	71	70	na	na	na	79	69	67	Chile	58
Estonia	72	74	71	71	73	73	79	72	66	72	76	70	na	na	na	80	70	59	West Germany	57
Portugal	92	92	91	88	93	94	91	92	92	90	94	91	93	92	90	93	92	89	Turkey	56
South Korea	50	54	47	48	51	54	68	53	39	54	52	40	52	51	50	53	51	37	Slovenia	56
Ireland	60	57	62	53	63	60	70	53	31	66	66	50	56	57	60	66	61	50	Britain	56
North Ireland	63	67	60	58	61	69	72	48	41	80	59	51	80	62	61	69	64	51	Japan	56
Slovenia	56	54	57	45	54	65	69	54	37	67	53	40	46	51	53	65	55	26	United States	53
Spain	76	75	77	68	76	82	80	71	63	85	76	68	70	76	75	83	74	70	India	52
East Germany	48	46	49	33	41	63	53	36	38	60	44	40	44	46	51	72	46	36	Canada	52
Britain	56	53	59	56	50	62	64	42	29	68	47	39	61	58	46	62	57	45	Finland	51
Italy	80	78	81	76	80	82	83	61	61	84	75	63	80	77	78	84	81	73	South Korea	50
Netherlands	17	16	17	15	15	22	25	15	09	22	13	06	13	16	17	31	18	09	Russia	49
Belgium	62	61	64	55	62	68	73	62	44	66	63	49	61	58	56	75	65	45	East Germany	48
Austria	61	59	62	50	55	71	68	57	56	73	61	47	66	58	58	79	63	44	China	46
France	74	72	76	69	75	77	79	76	56	83	74	61	71	72	78	85	78	57	Czechoslovakia	46
Canada	52	51	53	53	52	53	63	54	42	61	52	40	43	54	48	63	56	38	Norway	44
United States	53	52	54	50	52	55	69	55	39	64	51	44	39	51	55	64	53	45	Mexico	40
Iceland	28	28	27	30	27	26	39	27	19	na	na	47	20	29	31	33	28	14	Sweden	36
West Germany	57	56	59	49	54	65	66	48	33	67	59	47	50	60	60	76	60	42	Denmark	29
Denmark	29	31	27	26	24	36	42	32	20	35	27	24	18	32	32	44	29	16	Iceland	28
Finland	51	52	50	45	49	63	59	59	39	61	52	42	47	55	52	79	54	40	Netherlands	17
Norway	44	44	44	38	41	52	58	47	34	64	51	40	41	45	41	51	44	22		
Sweden	36	36	36	33	31	43	45	33	26	38	39	32	27	36	40	50	37	24		
Japan	56	52	60	64	56	51	59	60	44	64	56	48	42	55	42	50	56	42		
Switzerland	na	na	na	na	na	na	na	na	na	na	na	na	na	na	na	na	na	na		
Total	58	57	58	53	57	63	66	56	45	65	57	51	54	56	55	66	57	47		

Note: Countries in the left column are ranked according to GNP per capita. / The percentages in the bottom row give each country an equal weight. / na=not ascertained.

V15 ENVIRONMENT: TOO ANXIOUS

All the talk about pollution makes people too anxious. (% "strongly agree" or "agree")

	Total	Gender		Age			Education			Income			Political Affinity			Values		
		Male	Female	16-29	30-49	50+	Lower	Medium	Upper	Lower	Middle	Upper	Left	Center	Right	Mat	Mixed	Postmat
India	66	65	68	70	64	60	61	70	63	67	66	65	66	71	62	68	65	67
Nigeria	70	73	65	70	70	69	72	69	70	68	69	74	65	69	76	72	68	70
China	33	35	31	33	32	37	41	34	24	35	31	33	na	na	na	38	29	32
Romania	na	na	na	na	na	na	na	na	na	na	na	na	na	na	na	na	na	na
Turkey	50	51	48	47	49	56	57	42	33	58	52	39	46	47	53	54	51	42
Poland	na	na	na	na	na	na	na	na	na	na	na	na	na	na	na	na	na	na
Bulgaria	68	67	69	67	68	70	78	72	56	65	73	66	63	69	57	76	68	46
Chile	71	72	71	72	69	73	77	72	63	75	72	65	67	72	72	78	71	65
Czechoslovakia	58	57	59	55	57	62	68	56	46	59	60	55	60	60	53	62	57	54
South Africa	na	na	na	na	na	na	na	na	na	na	na	na	na	na	na	na	na	na
Lithuania	31	30	32	25	30	38	39	30	20	35	32	21	na	na	na	37	31	19
Hungary	78	76	79	71	78	80	81	76	70	81	78	66	74	77	78	81	76	66
Argentina	53	52	54	47	50	61	62	51	41	62	52	43	36	55	53	63	51	45
Brazil	63	62	65	58	62	75	77	61	42	75	62	53	63	59	66	68	61	53
Mexico	62	63	60	59	63	66	65	59	54	63	61	57	52	61	63	70	61	52
Belarus	64	64	65	54	63	77	68	63	64	66	63	66	64	60	79	70	62	57
Russia	26	26	27	23	25	31	35	25	23	28	26	26	23	25	29	28	26	20
Moscow	52	51	54	40	49	67	79	54	46	58	51	43	48	54	65	60	51	44
Latvia	61	55	66	51	61	73	78	66	47	66	60	61	na	na	na	67	64	37
Estonia	49	45	53	44	44	63	57	52	34	47	55	48	na	na	na	56	48	33
Portugal	66	66	67	58	71	71	73	61	48	72	66	59	70	67	62	77	62	54
South Korea	49	55	43	48	47	56	61	57	34	51	55	34	44	49	50	54	45	42
Ireland	39	38	47	39	37	41	46	32	24	48	39	31	34	42	35	38	54	40
North Ireland	64	66	62	53	64	71	71	56	41	72	70	48	71	65	63	74	57	54
Slovenia	84	84	85	78	84	89	85	88	77	88	86	75	80	82	86	87	84	80
Spain	61	59	63	55	60	69	66	55	48	71	62	56	57	64	63	65	63	53
East Germany	43	38	47	33	35	57	48	39	28	54	41	35	34	47	47	58	46	30
Britain	54	53	54	50	49	60	57	51	36	62	44	43	47	56	53	67	54	38
Italy	53	53	54	44	52	61	55	41	33	58	48	39	51	57	54	65	62	43
Netherlands	31	38	29	28	26	43	40	38	14	33	29	22	18	34	36	59	31	21
Belgium	44	41	46	32	41	53	53	42	30	47	41	34	40	41	43	51	54	30
Austria	51	55	49	42	49	58	53	51	37	58	51	48	62	50	49	62	62	38
France	59	57	60	52	56	66	67	59	39	66	59	40	51	60	61	70	52	43
Canada	48	51	45	46	45	53	60	47	39	54	49	40	39	47	48	60	49	39
United States	46	47	46	40	43	51	53	50	37	51	45	34	26	48	49	51	48	39
Iceland	25	24	25	19	22	37	34	28	15	na	na	na	21	23	26	38	21	14
West Germany	34	34	34	28	29	42	40	26	18	38	36	28	22	37	42	49	38	19
Denmark	54	52	56	47	52	62	63	55	49	57	55	49	42	60	54	64	55	41
Finland	35	38	32	27	31	52	45	41	23	46	36	24	33	40	34	46	39	24
Norway	55	55	54	43	50	68	73	59	42	63	51	49	46	59	52	63	54	34
Sweden	53	53	54	52	50	58	66	53	33	63	61	46	49	58	50	59	60	33
Japan	50	50	50	52	44	58	65	54	30	56	52	44	36	43	53	55	46	38
Switzerland	na	na	na	na	na	na	na	na	na	na	na	na	na	na	na	na	na	na
Total	53	53	53	47	51	60	61	52	40	58	54	47	49	55	55	61	53	42

Ranking:

Slovenia 84	Latvia 61	Sweden 53	Ireland 39
Hungary 78	Spain 61	Moscow 52	Finland 35
Chile 71	France 59	Austria 51	West Germany 34
Nigeria 70	Czechoslovakia 58	Turkey 50	China 33
Bulgaria 68	Norway 55	Japan 50	Lithuania 31
India 66	Britain 54	Estonia 49	Netherlands 31
Portugal 66	Denmark 54	South Korea 49	Russia 26
Belarus 64	Argentina 53	Canada 48	Iceland 25
North Ireland 64	Italy 53	United States 46	
Brazil 63		Belgium 44	
Mexico 62		East Germany 43	

Note: Countries in the left column are ranked according to GNP per capita. / The percentages in the bottom row give each country an equal weight. / na=not ascertained.

V16 ENVIRONMENT: UNEMPLOYMENT

If we want to combat unemployment in this country, we shall just have to accept environmental problems. (% "strongly agree" or "agree")

	Total	Gender		Age			Education			Income			Political Affinity			Values		
		Male	Female	16-29	30-49	50+	Lower	Medium	Upper	Lower	Middle	Upper	Left	Center	Right	Mat	Mixed	Postmat
India	62	62	62	60	63	65	68	65	57	72	56	59	60	66	59	64	61	61
Nigeria	63	66	59	63	62	69	66	64	61	61	65	65	59	62	69	68	61	60
China	26	26	26	25	26	26	41	21	19	32	22	22	na	na	na	29	22	26
Romania	na	na	na	na	na	na	na	na	na	na	na	na	na	na	na	na	na	na
Turkey	44	44	44	39	46	48	50	36	31	52	41	39	37	47	43	42	48	35
Poland	na	na	na	na	na	na	na	na	na	na	na	na	na	na	na	na	na	na
Bulgaria	26	24	28	27	24	28	35	28	15	24	24	28	25	24	24	27	27	12
Chile	57	58	57	56	54	66	63	58	50	61	57	53	53	61	55	61	56	58
Czechoslovakia	44	45	44	39	42	50	50	42	39	45	45	41	45	44	41	49	43	38
South Africa	na	na	na	na	na	na	na	na	na	na	na	na	na	na	na	na	na	na
Lithuania	17	17	17	13	14	24	26	15	13	17	18	15	na	na	na	20	18	08
Hungary	59	55	63	50	59	62	64	55	44	64	57	44	59	61	56	57	59	66
Argentina	29	26	32	30	28	30	29	29	27	34	28	28	22	31	33	32	29	26
Brazil	47	44	51	46	44	55	62	46	21	59	45	36	41	43	53	52	47	21
Mexico	30	31	30	27	30	40	31	33	26	31	30	30	20	31	33	33	30	23
Belarus	22	22	22	14	23	27	27	23	19	21	23	21	20	24	24	26	21	10
Russia	14	12	15	14	12	16	20	14	10	16	11	13	11	13	16	16	12	14
Moscow	16	15	17	13	14	22	34	17	12	19	12	16	13	18	26	18	17	08
Latvia	11	13	09	08	08	19	20	10	10	08	09	13	13	18	na	15	17	10
Estonia	18	18	17	15	17	23	19	19	14	18	18	17	na	na	na	17	09	20
Portugal	53	51	55	46	53	62	63	36	33	62	55	39	51	57	46	66	50	31
South Korea	47	49	44	42	46	58	68	53	29	55	47	35	45	48	45	48	50	32
Ireland	36	37	35	31	36	40	43	30	20	45	40	26	25	38	35	36	48	31
North Ireland	44	39	48	34	44	51	52	32	26	48	41	31	25	38	42	51	38	26
Slovenia	62	65	58	53	62	67	66	60	59	64	63	56	60	63	67	60	45	66
Spain	42	42	42	32	43	50	47	36	28	48	44	33	37	43	43	52	62	31
East Germany	31	26	35	20	26	43	36	26	16	39	28	26	24	32	36	39	41	21
Britain	32	32	32	27	23	44	37	23	19	46	25	20	32	31	30	39	33	22
Italy	49	48	49	40	47	55	50	40	30	55	42	36	44	50	56	57	32	47
Netherlands	22	26	20	18	16	35	30	21	13	25	16	19	13	21	29	33	46	15
Belgium	37	37	38	28	33	48	44	36	28	40	40	32	32	39	36	42	25	33
Austria	33	34	31	27	32	36	34	33	27	35	37	28	42	31	38	39	38	25
France	38	35	41	32	34	46	46	34	25	47	37	23	35	34	27	48	35	28
Canada	30	30	30	31	25	35	43	30	20	40	27	23	23	30	38	39	39	26
United States	31	29	32	26	25	38	44	31	22	40	30	23	22	29	38	37	30	38
Iceland	28	29	27	25	23	42	41	30	18	39	30	23	22	27	31	38	31	31
West Germany	21	21	20	15	15	29	26	12	12	na	22	15	14	20	31	35	27	14
Denmark	33	27	40	29	28	44	25	12	28	25	35	23	20	36	33	43	22	12
Finland	22	23	20	13	18	40	37	35	11	37	21	14	20	25	24	52	35	17
Norway	33	37	29	25	27	46	44	36	25	32	28	33	24	33	35	38	24	12
Sweden	36	37	34	27	31	46	44	36	22	41	35	32	29	35	40	47	32	21
Japan	22	23	20	18	20	28	31	22	15	25	24	16	20	19	24	23	41	18
Switzerland	na	na	na	na	na	na	na	na	na	na	na	na	na	na	na	na	20	na
Total	35	35	35	30	33	42	43	33	25	40	34	30	33	37	39	41	35	27

Ranking:

Nigeria	63
India	62
Slovenia	62
Hungary	59
Chile	57
Portugal	53
Italy	49
Brazil	47
South Korea	47
Turkey	44
Czechoslovakia	44
North Ireland	44
Spain	42
France	38
Belgium	37
Ireland	36
Sweden	36
Austria	33
Denmark	33
Norway	33
Britain	32
East Germany	31
United States	31
Mexico	30
Canada	30
Argentina	29
Iceland	28
China	26
Bulgaria	26
Belarus	22
Netherlands	22
Finland	22
Japan	22
West Germany	21
Estonia	18
Lithuania	17
Moscow	16
Russia	14
Latvia	11

Note: Countries in the left column are ranked according to GNP per capita. / The percentages in the bottom row give each country an equal weight. / na=not ascertained.

V17 ENVIRONMENT: NOT URGENT

Protecting the environment and fighting pollution is less urgent than often suggested. (% "strongly agree" or "agree")

	Total	Gender		Age			Education			Income			Political Affinity			Values		
		Male	Female	16-29	30-49	50+	Lower	Medium	Upper	Lower	Middle	Upper	Left	Center	Right	Mat	Mixed	Postmat
India	37	35	41	36	38	38	49	39	31	43	38	33	42	36	35	38	37	34
Nigeria	66	66	67	67	66	59	74	68	62	61	68	72	63	68	68	71	64	55
China	32	33	32	30	33	34	38	31	26	32	33	32	na	na	na	35	30	30
Romania	na	na	na	na	na	na	na	na	na	na	na	na	na	na	na	na	na	na
Turkey	26	26	27	20	27	34	33	19	12	36	23	19	24	24	28	28	28	19
Poland	na	na	na	na	na	na	na	na	na	01	00	00	20	17	17	na	na	na
Bulgaria	19	18	19	14	17	23	30	17	10	15	19	19	20	17	17	22	18	08
Chile	40	40	40	37	40	44	47	39	32	48	40	30	36	38	46	47	40	32
Czechoslovakia	17	18	17	14	16	20	18	18	13	18	18	16	20	17	15	24	15	12
South Africa	09	08	09	08	09	08	14	07	01	12	12	01	10	07	06	07	09	12
Lithuania	13	13	13	09	13	18	20	12	10	19	09	09	na	na	na	15	13	09
Hungary	39	41	37	27	42	41	48	35	15	46	36	28	31	40	42	41	37	46
Argentina	29	31	28	35	28	26	32	28	25	37	31	24	25	33	28	32	29	25
Brazil	30	28	32	26	31	36	44	27	15	37	28	24	27	26	35	33	28	26
Mexico	30	31	29	29	28	36	33	31	20	34	28	26	23	29	32	32	29	22
Belarus	20	22	18	16	19	27	35	20	15	19	21	20	18	21	26	25	18	12
Russia	12	11	12	13	10	13	17	11	09	13	09	13	10	12	13	13	11	07
Moscow	12	11	13	11	09	16	27	14	07	15	10	09	10	09	25	15	11	08
Latvia	09	09	09	08	06	16	18	10	05	08	12	08	na	na	na	11	09	09
Estonia	09	09	09	07	07	15	16	09	03	08	10	10	na	na	na	13	08	02
Portugal	24	26	23	21	26	26	29	19	12	31	21	16	23	26	24	32	21	13
South Korea	22	23	21	15	23	32	40	24	10	23	25	16	20	22	22	24	22	14
Ireland	26	27	24	21	25	29	33	19	10	34	23	22	22	26	25	26	27	22
North Ireland	30	30	30	25	34	29	35	26	21	34	25	23	36	33	25	32	33	14
Slovenia	31	35	27	22	32	36	35	31	24	34	30	26	31	30	31	34	32	11
Spain	25	26	25	20	24	32	27	21	21	32	26	20	20	26	33	27	25	18
East Germany	11	10	12	08	09	15	13	09	05	14	10	10	08	13	12	19	11	09
Britain	22	21	23	18	18	29	25	18	12	30	19	12	17	22	22	24	23	16
Italy	18	20	17	18	18	22	19	19	07	20	14	13	19	17	22	22	19	13
Netherlands	17	24	14	12	13	27	23	17	09	18	11	14	07	18	24	28	19	09
Belgium	19	18	20	15	18	21	22	19	11	20	21	11	16	19	17	23	20	10
Austria	19	19	19	17	18	21	21	19	17	20	21	16	28	16	19	30	20	12
France	19	20	18	15	19	21	20	18	16	22	18	17	17	18	26	27	18	14
Canada	22	24	20	21	20	26	32	20	17	29	20	17	14	22	23	25	24	15
United States	29	28	28	25	22	36	37	27	24	35	26	22	19	27	35	31	29	25
Iceland	15	17	12	11	13	23	20	16	09	na	na	na	11	16	16	22	14	01
West Germany	12	14	10	07	10	17	15	07	06	15	13	09	08	12	17	24	13	04
Denmark	18	18	18	16	12	28	26	16	14	23	17	12	12	17	21	27	18	09
Finland	13	15	11	13	12	19	21	15	08	22	13	07	11	15	15	19	15	09
Norway	16	21	12	15	14	20	24	16	13	17	14	18	13	16	19	19	16	08
Sweden	16	19	13	14	15	19	23	13	12	17	19	14	12	14	19	19	18	12
Japan	12	15	09	07	08	22	21	11	07	17	12	07	09	10	17	11	10	15
Switzerland	na	na	na	na	na	na	na	na	na	na	na	na	na	na	na	na	na	na
Total	**22**	**23**	**21**	**19**	**21**	**26**	**29**	**21**	**15**	**25**	**21**	**18**	**20**	**23**	**25**	**26**	**22**	**16**

Ranking:

Nigeria	66	Belgium	19
Chile	40	Austria	19
Hungary	39	France	19
India	37	Italy	18
China	32	Denmark	18
Slovenia	31	Czechoslovakia	17
Brazil	30	Netherlands	17
Mexico	30	Norway	16
North Ireland	30	Sweden	16
Argentina	29	Iceland	15
United States	29	Lithuania	13
Turkey	26	Finland	13
Ireland	26	Russia	12
Spain	25	Moscow	12
Portugal	24	West Germany	12
South Korea	22	Japan	12
Britain	22	East Germany	11
Canada	22	South Africa	09
Belarus	20	Latvia	09
Bulgaria	19	Estonia	09

Note: Countries in the left column are ranked according to GNP per capita. / The percentages in the bottom row give each country an equal weight. / na=not ascertained.

V18. Taking all things together, would you say you are...

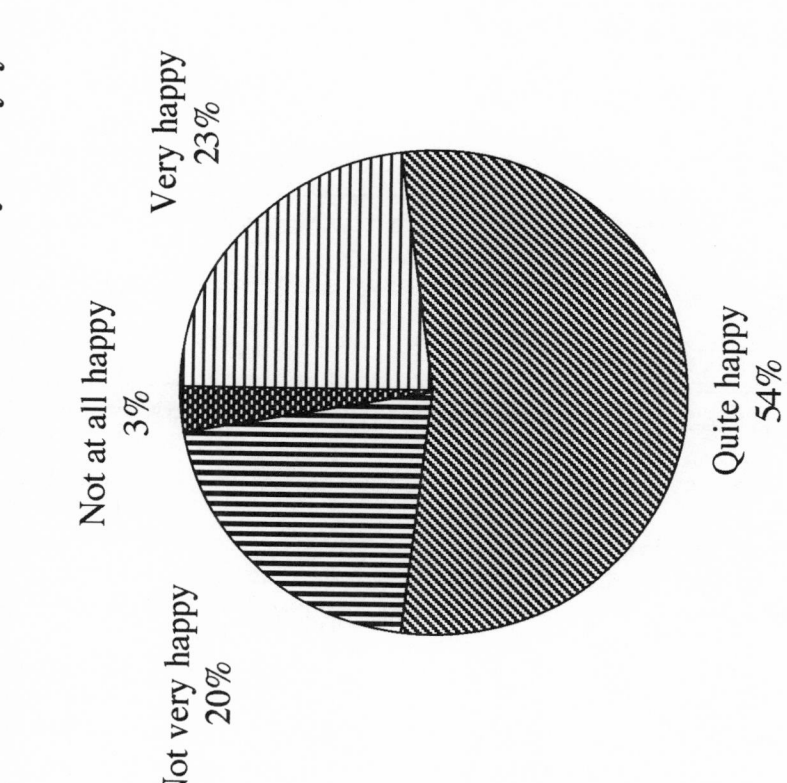

Very happy
23%

Not at all happy
3%

Quite happy
54%

Not very happy
20%

V18 HAPPINESS

Taking all things together, would you say you are very happy, quite happy, not very happy, or not at all happy. (% "very happy")

	Total	Gender		Age			Education			Income			Political Affinity			Values			Ranking:	
		Male	Female	16-29	30-49	50+	Lower	Medium	Upper	Lower	Middle	Upper	Left	Center	Right	Mat	Mixed	Postmat		
India	24	22	27	26	24	19	18	24	27	18	25	27	25	20	29	24	25	22	Netherlands	48
Nigeria	40	35	47	43	34	34	48	41	35	33	42	47	36	39	47	45	36	42	Ireland	44
China	28	29	28	26	33	24	22	32	28	33	29	21	na	na	na	27	29	26	Denmark	43
Romania	06	08	05	04	08	06	06	05	09	05	05	09	05	05	10	05	07	11	United States	41
Turkey	29	22	37	30	30	28	33	25	21	26	31	32	25	29	30	26	35	20	Iceland	41
Poland	10	10	09	09	10	10	10	10	09	08	10	12	10	09	12	10	10	09	Sweden	41
Bulgaria	07	05	08	10	05	07	07	08	04	03	07	12	07	07	05	08	07	04	Nigeria	40
Chile	33	32	35	34	35	31	35	35	30	29	34	38	30	35	34	30	35	34	Belgium	40
Czechoslovakia	05	06	04	07	03	07	05	05	05	05	05	06	04	05	07	04	06	06	Britain	38
South Africa	24	22	26	24	24	23	17	26	35	14	24	35	21	29	27	27	22	24	North Ireland	37
Lithuania	04	03	04	05	02	04	03	03	06	03	04	04	na	na	14	03	03	07	Switzerland	36
Hungary	11	09	13	14	11	10	09	12	12	09	12	13	10	11	14	11	11	10	Chile	33
Argentina	33	34	32	36	35	29	33	32	35	29	33	36	27	32	32	29	35	32	Argentina	33
Brazil	21	20	22	17	22	27	26	18	23	23	17	24	17	18	26	23	20	18	Austria	30
Mexico	26	24	30	28	27	22	25	29	28	22	27	30	22	25	31	26	26	30	Canada	30
Belarus	06	08	05	07	05	09	07	06	07	05	08	07	06	06	08	08	06	05	Turkey	29
Russia	06	06	06	09	06	06	07	06	07	07	05	06	05	07	11	07	06	04	Norway	29
Moscow	06	05	07	09	05	07	07	06	06	07	05	07	05	05	18	01	06	08	China	28
Latvia	02	02	02	04	01	01	00	02	06	01	03	01	na	na	na	02	02	00	Mexico	26
Estonia	03	04	03	05	03	02	01	05	02	03	03	04	na	na	na	03	04	04	France	25
Portugal	13	13	12	14	15	09	14	09	08	12	11	14	12	11	16	16	11	07	India	24
South Korea	10	08	12	11	10	10	11	09	13	09	10	13	08	40	11	10	11	11	South Africa	24
Ireland	44	37	50	49	42	42	41	46	49	39	46	48	39	40	51	42	47	38	Brazil	21
North Ireland	37	31	42	41	36	36	30	44	66	31	29	37	29	41	34	32	36	44	Spain	20
Slovenia	09	07	11	13	08	08	08	11	09	07	10	13	08	11	06	09	10	05	Finland	20
Spain	20	20	21	22	21	19	20	23	21	16	19	22	20	20	21	19	23	20	Japan	18
East Germany	14	14	14	14	14	13	14	12	12	13	13	15	13	13	17	09	14	17	Italy	16
Britain	38	37	39	36	35	42	37	40	40	33	43	41	35	35	47	41	39	34	West Germany	16
Italy	16	18	15	19	17	14	17	12	14	15	18	16	12	20	17	15	16	16	East Germany	14
Netherlands	48	43	50	51	49	43	49	50	45	42	53	52	40	49	59	46	56	38	Portugal	13
Belgium	40	39	41	45	41	36	39	41	40	37	45	44	35	43	44	37	41	42	Hungary	11
Austria	30	31	29	40	31	26	29	31	33	25	30	35	35	31	28	24	31	32	Poland	10
France	25	21	28	29	29	19	21	27	29	18	28	35	28	24	33	34	23	29	South Korea	10
Canada	30	28	32	28	31	29	28	31	29	24	30	35	19	31	28	19	30	28	Slovenia	09
United States	41	39	42	42	39	41	42	40	40	35	40	46	35	39	47	41	40	41	Bulgaria	07
Iceland	41	37	46	39	41	45	42	44	39	na	21	33	41	42	41	48	41	26	Romania	06
West Germany	16	16	17	18	16	16	18	18	12	11	16	21	14	17	20.	14	17	15	Belarus	06
Denmark	43	42	44	43	43	38	39	48	41	34	45	52	36	44	46	40	45	37	Russia	06
Finland	20	19	22	32	16	22	17	20	23	28	17	18	19	24	21	19	21	20	Moscow	06
Norway	29	28	31	35	28	29	30	31	28	28	33	33	24	32	32	31	30	24	Czechoslovakia	05
Sweden	41	35	47	47	39	39	38	43	37	45	31	47	37	40	42	49	40	38	Lithuania	04
Japan	18	15	21	21	18	16	17	21	13	16	17	20	16	16	17	19	16	18	Estonia	03
Switzerland	36	35	36	44	36	32	39	33	37	30	37	35	29	35	37	47	35	32	Latvia	02
Total	23	21	24	25	23	22	22	24	24	20	23	25	22	24	27	23	23	22		

Note: Countries in the left column are ranked according to GNP per capita. / The percentages in the bottom row give each country an equal weight. / na=not ascertained.

V19-V36. Membership in voluntary organizations

Percentage "belong to"

Organization	Percentage
None	40
Trade unions	23
Sports/recreation	16
Religious organization	14
Education/cultural	10
Political parties	8
Professional association	8
Social welfare services	6
Other groups	6
Youth work	5
Environment	4
Health-voluntary	4
Local community action	3
Women's groups	3
Human rights	2
Animal rights	2
Peace movement	1

V19 SOCIAL WELFARE

Please look carefully at the following list of voluntary organizations and activities and say which, if any, do you belong to?
Social welfare services for elderly, handicapped, or deprived people. (% "belong to")

	Total	Gender		Age			Education			Income			Political Affinity			Values		
		Male	Female	16-29	30-49	50+	Lower	Medium	Upper	Lower	Middle	Upper	Left	Center	Right	Mat	Mixed	Postmat
India	na	na	na	na	na	na	na	na	na	na	na	na	na	na	na	na	na	na
Nigeria	na	na	na	na	na	na	na	na	na	na	na	na	na	na	na	na	na	na
China	04	04	04	03	04	05	05	04	03	03	04	04	na	na	na	03	04	06
Romania	02	02	02	00	03	02	01	02	04	01	03	02	01	03	02	01	02	04
Turkey	na	na	na	na	na	na	na	na	na	na	na	na	na	na	na	na	na	na
Poland	na	na	na	na	na	na	na	na	na	na	na	na	na	na	na	na	na	na
Bulgaria	04	04	03	04	03	05	04	03	03	03	03	04	04	03	04	03	04	03
Chile	05	03	06	02	05	08	05	05	04	03	05	06	03	05	07	05	05	05
Czechoslovakia	na	na	na	na	na	na	na	na	na	na	na	na	na	na	na	na	na	na
South Africa	na	na	na	na	na	na	na	na	na	na	na	na	na	na	na	na	na	na
Lithuania	01	01	01	00	01	02	00	01	02	01	00	01	01	na	na	02	01	00
Hungary	02	02	03	01	02	03	02	02	04	03	01	03	01	02	02	01	03	03
Argentina	02	02	03	02	02	03	03	02	03	02	02	04	02	03	05	01	03	02
Brazil	10	09	11	06	12	14	09	09	15	09	08	13	10	11	09	10	10	13
Mexico	05	03	06	06	03	05	04	05	06	03	05	05	04	05	04	04	05	03
Belarus	na	na	na	na	na	na	na	na	na	na	na	na	na	na	na	na	na	na
Russia	02	02	02	01	02	04	02	03	02	02	02	03	03	02	02	02	02	01
Moscow	na	na	na	na	na	na	na	na	na	na	na	na	na	na	na	na	na	na
Latvia	02	02	02	01	01	03	05	02	01	01	01	02	02	03	05	01	01	00
Estonia	02	02	01	01	01	03	01	02	02	01	01	02	na	na	na	01	02	05
Portugal	05	03	06	02	04	08	06	05	02	07	04	03	04	05	06	04	05	06
South Korea	06	05	07	03	08	08	04	05	09	02	06	12	09	05	06	07	05	08
Ireland	07	05	09	05	05	11	07	07	12	05	08	08	07	08	06	06	07	12
North Ireland	09	03	13	08	07	11	09	09	17	09	09	14	na	11	09	06	10	07
Slovenia	01	01	02	00	01	02	01	01	03	01	03	01	02	02	03	02	01	03
Spain	03	03	03	01	02	05	03	03	02	04	02	03	03	04	05	03	03	03
East Germany	10	06	12	04	08	15	10	09	09	13	09	07	08	13	07	11	09	10
Britain	07	06	09	03	06	10	07	05	11	10	06	06	07	08	07	09	07	07
Italy	04	04	04	04	04	05	04	06	03	03	06	02	07	06	04	04	04	05
Netherlands	15	14	16	08	16	23	17	14	16	18	15	12	15	13	21	19	18	12
Belgium	12	11	13	09	10	15	10	13	13	12	12	13	12	10	14	11	11	15
Austria	06	05	06	07	07	05	05	06	10	04	07	07	08	07	05	03	05	09
France	07	07	06	03	04	12	06	07	09	05	06	11	08	08	10	05	07	08
Canada	08	06	10	06	08	11	08	07	11	09	09	08	09	09	10	09	07	11
United States	09	07	11	06	08	11	07	08	12	07	08	11	09	10	09	07	09	12
Iceland	16	15	16	06	10	20	15	19	14	na	na	na	12	15	21	17	15	16
West Germany	07	06	09	03	07	10	07	08	09	04	08	07	07	08	07	09	07	07
Denmark	06	03	08	03	07	06	06	04	07	06	05	07	08	05	05	02	05	08
Finland	11	08	13	03	11	18	10	08	14	13	07	12	14	09	10	27	10	09
Norway	11	10	12	05	10	16	17	08	11	12	11	11	10	11	12	14	10	10
Sweden	08	05	10	04	07	11	04	06	16	06	06	10	06	06	11	06	08	08
Japan	02	02	02	01	02	03	04	01	02	00	03	02	04	02	03	01	02	05
Switzerland	09	07	10	03	09	11	07	10	09	08	10	13	11	09	09	08	09	09
Total	**06**	**05**	**07**	**04**	**06**	**09**	**06**	**06**	**08**	**06**	**06**	**07**	**07**	**07**	**08**	**06**	**06**	**07**

Ranking:

Iceland	16
Netherlands	15
Belgium	12
Finland	11
Norway	11
Brazil	10
East Germany	10
North Ireland	09
United States	09
Switzerland	09
Canada	08
Sweden	08
Ireland	07
Britain	07
France	07
West Germany	07
South Korea	06
Austria	06
Denmark	06
Chile	05
Mexico	05
Portugal	05
China	04
Bulgaria	04
Italy	04
Spain	03
Romania	02
Hungary	02
Argentina	02
Russia	02
Latvia	02
Estonia	02
Japan	02
Lithuania	01
Slovenia	01

Note: Countries in the left column are ranked according to GNP per capita. / The percentages in the bottom row give each country an equal weight. / na=not ascertained.

V20 RELIGIOUS ORGANIZATION

Please look carefully at the following list of voluntary organizations and activities and say which, if any, do you belong to?
Religious or church organizations. (% "belong to")

	Total	Gender		Age			Education			Income			Political Affinity			Values		
		Male	Female	16-29	30-49	50+	Lower	Medium	Upper	Lower	Middle	Upper	Left	Center	Right	Mat	Mixed	Postmat
India	na	na	na	na	na	na	na	na	na	na	na	na	na	na	na	na	na	na
Nigeria	na	na	na	na	na	na	na	na	na	na	na	na	na	na	na	na	na	na
China	01	01	02	00	02	02	01	01	01	01	01	02	na	na	na	02	01	00
Romania	05	05	05	02	05	07	02	03	01	05	05	04	04	06	05	06	04	05
Turkey	na	na	na	na	na	na	na	na	na	na	na	na	na	na	na	na	na	na
Poland	na	na	na	na	na	na	na	na	na	na	na	na	na	na	na	na	na	na
Bulgaria	02	01	03	01	02	04	02	03	02	04	01	02	00	02	06	03	03	00
Chile	18	15	21	12	20	23	21	17	16	21	16	16	13	18	17	24	15	18
Czechoslovakia	na	na	na	na	na	na	na	na	na	na	na	na	na	na	na	na	na	na
South Africa	na	na	na	na	na	na	na	na	na	na	na	na	na	na	na	na	na	na
Lithuania	03	03	04	01	02	07	08	02	03	05	03	01	04	na	na	03	na	04
Hungary	11	09	13	05	09	16	14	07	12	10	10	01	04	11	23	13	10	05
Argentina	07	06	08	08	07	06	05	09	08	06	06	07	02	09	11	05	08	07
Brazil	22	19	25	18	21	30	25	20	23	24	20	22	18	23	26	23	21	24
Mexico	14	12	17	12	14	17	15	15	09	13	13	15	12	12	16	18	13	08
Belarus	na	na	na	na	na	na	na	na	na	na	na	na	na	na	na	na	na	na
Russia	01	01	01	00	01	02	02	01	01	02	01	01	01	01	01	01	01	00
Moscow	na	na	na	na	na	na	na	na	na	na	na	na	na	na	na	na	na	00
Latvia	03	03	04	03	02	05	11	01	01	03	02	03	na	na	na	01	04	na
Estonia	04	03	04	04	04	03	04	04	01	06	03	02	na	na	na	02	04	05
Portugal	11	08	13	10	06	14	13	03	08	12	09	10	08	10	13	11	10	08
South Korea	39	45	33	32	43	39	40	40	36	37	38	42	26	42	40	41	38	32
Ireland	14	12	16	12	12	17	12	15	21	09	15	16	11	15	16	10	14	17
North Ireland	25	16	32	16	25	31	20	35	31	23	22	34	18	24	33	32	25	16
Slovenia	03	03	03	05	02	02	03	02	04	03	03	03	02	03	08	03	03	03
Spain	04	03	05	03	04	05	04	04	06	05	04	05	03	05	10	05	04	04
East Germany	20	18	22	13	21	24	19	23	22	24	21	16	10	22	33	18	19	26
Britain	16	12	19	09	15	21	13	18	30	17	14	18	13	15	20	17	15	18
Italy	08	07	08	11	07	07	07	13	12	08	10	04	03	14	05	05	08	10
Netherlands	33	37	32	25	35	40	36	35	28	27	37	39	23	32	49	35	36	30
Belgium	12	11	13	06	11	16	09	12	16	13	13	14	06	12	18	08	12	14
Austria	16	16	16	16	18	13	14	17	17	14	16	18	11	17	18	10	15	19
France	06	06	07	03	04	11	05	07	07	05	08	06	05	05	14	07	06	06
Canada	25	20	30	14	22	34	26	24	25	25	27	24	15	25	28	27	25	24
United States	49	49	49	41	48	54	45	46	57	43	51	53	37	53	56	51	50	48
Iceland	50	50	49	45	50	56	47	55	49	43	51	na	53	47	49	47	51	51
West Germany	16	14	18	10	14	21	15	16	25	18	16	16	13	16	23	18	17	14
Denmark	07	06	07	04	09	06	05	06	08	06	06	08	05	05	07	03	08	05
Finland	18	17	18	14	15	28	21	15	19	24	13	18	15	25	19	35	16	17
Norway	11	09	13	10	11	13	13	09	13	14	10	11	06	13	12	11	11	12
Sweden	10	10	11	10	10	10	09	10	14	11	09	12	08	12	11	13	11	08
Japan	07	08	05	05	05	10	06	06	05	09	06	06	10	07	06	07	08	05
Switzerland	11	09	13	07	11	13	09	11	14	14	09	10	10	11	14	09	12	09
Total	14	13	15	11	14	17	15	14	16	14	13	14	12	16	20	15	14	14

Ranking:

Iceland	50
United States	49
South Korea	39
Netherlands	33
North Ireland	25
Canada	25
Brazil	22
East Germany	20
Chile	18
Finland	18
Britain	16
Austria	16
West Germany	16
Mexico	14
Ireland	14
Belgium	12
Hungary	11
Portugal	11
Norway	11
Switzerland	11
Sweden	10
Italy	08
Argentina	07
Denmark	07
Japan	07
France	06
Romania	05
Estonia	04
Spain	04
Lithuania	03
Latvia	03
Slovenia	03
Bulgaria	02
China	01
Russia	01

Note: Countries in the left column are ranked according to GNP per capita. / The percentages in the bottom row give each country an equal weight. / na=not ascertained.

V21 EDUCATION/CULTURAL

Please look carefully at the following list of voluntary organizations and activities and say which, if any, do you belong to? Education, art, music, or cultural activities. (% "belong to")

	Total	Gender Male	Gender Female	Age 16-29	Age 30-49	Age 50+	Education Lower	Education Medium	Education Upper	Income Lower	Income Middle	Income Upper	Political Affinity Left	Political Affinity Center	Political Affinity Right	Values Mat	Values Mixed	Values Postmat
India	na	na	na	na	na	na	na	na	na	na	na	na	na	na	na	na	na	na
Nigeria	na	na	na	na	na	na	na	na	na	na	na	na	na	na	na	na	na	na
China	07	08	06	09	05	09	04	08	13	05	08	10	na	na	na	06	09	13
Romania	02	02	01	02	02	01	01	01	04	02	02	01	03	03	01	01	02	05
Turkey	na	na	na	na	na	na	na	na	na	na	na	na	na	na	na	na	na	na
Poland	04	04	05	04	06	02	01	04	07	04	06	03	05	03	07	03	04	07
Bulgaria	04	04	05	04	06	02	01	04	07	05	09	05	10	09	12	05	08	17
Chile	09	10	09	11	10	07	04	10	16	05	09	16	na	na	na	04	05	08
Czechoslovakia	na	na	na	na	na	na	na	na	na	na	na	na	na	na	na	na	na	na
South Africa	na	na	na	na	na	na	na	na	na	na	na	na	na	na	na	na	na	na
Lithuania	07	08	07	09	08	05	05	06	20	07	06	10	02	04	02	05	07	12
Hungary	03	02	03	05	02	02	01	02	13	01	03	05	04	06	09	03	02	03
Argentina	06	06	06	09	06	03	02	07	12	03	07	10	11	06	na	03	07	08
Brazil	05	05	05	06	05	04	03	04	13	03	05	07	06	04	na	04	05	12
Mexico	12	11	12	14	10	09	10	12	16	11	12	12	18	10	11	12	12	12
Belarus	na	na	na	na	na	na	na	na	na	na	na	na	na	na	na	na	na	na
Russia	05	04	05	05	06	04	03	04	08	04	05	06	09	06	04	04	05	08
Moscow	na	na	na	na	na	na	na	na	na	na	na	na	na	na	na	na	na	na
Latvia	07	05	08	07	07	06	02	05	12	05	07	07	na	na	na	07	06	11
Estonia	11	11	12	09	14	09	06	10	20	10	10	14	18	10	11	08	13	22
Portugal	08	09	06	08	11	03	05	05	17	05	07	12	10	09	05	07	13	13
South Korea	11	11	11	14	11	07	05	09	16	10	10	15	14	10	11	10	11	16
Ireland	10	08	12	16	10	07	04	11	41	02	09	19	20	08	13	06	10	15
North Ireland	11	06	14	15	11	08	15	15	45	03	09	23	04	11	15	08	13	09
Slovenia	03	04	03	06	03	02	02	02	08	03	03	07	07	04	02	02	03	07
Spain	06	07	06	09	09	02	04	08	15	03	06	11	10	06	06	03	07	14
East Germany	09	09	08	10	09	07	06	10	17	07	07	11	13	06	07	06	07	13
Britain	10	08	12	09	10	11	05	13	35	08	10	16	10	11	13	09	09	16
Italy	04	05	04	06	05	03	05	14	12	06	06	07	06	05	02	02	04	07
Netherlands	36	36	36	39	39	27	22	36	52	36	32	45	43	32	36	22	32	45
Belgium	17	18	16	19	22	12	08	18	34	11	17	27	21	20	21	07	16	31
Austria	08	12	06	08	09	07	08	08	11	06	07	13	10	08	10	03	08	10
France	09	08	10	10	09	08	06	10	15	08	08	14	12	10	05	02	07	19
Canada	18	16	19	17	20	16	08	15	29	11	19	24	28	17	19	13	16	25
United States	20	16	23	19	26	15	10	14	35	11	18	31	29	20	19	15	18	29
Iceland	14	11	17	13	18	09	06	14	20	na	na	16	18	14	12	10	14	24
West Germany	12	13	11	10	13	12	09	14	23	10	10	16	13	12	13	07	12	15
Denmark	13	12	13	13	14	11	02	14	18	10	12	19	17	11	14	04	13	18
Finland	20	16	24	17	21	22	13	16	29	22	15	25	19	20	20	12	20	23
Norway	14	15	12	12	17	11	06	09	22	12	15	17	20	11	13	11	13	22
Sweden	13	10	16	10	16	13	07	13	21	12	13	14	12	13	14	10	13	15
Japan	06	04	08	07	07	05	03	07	07	06	06	09	08	06	07	06	06	08
Switzerland	07	07	07	05	09	06	05	08	11	05	08	11	13	08	05	03	06	12
Total	**10**	**10**	**11**	**11**	**11**	**08**	**06**	**10**	**20**	**08**	**10**	**14**	**14**	**10**	**11**	**07**	**10**	**15**

Ranking:

Netherlands	36
United States	20
Finland	20
Canada	18
Belgium	17
Iceland	14
Norway	14
Denmark	13
Sweden	13
Mexico	12
West Germany	12
Estonia	11
South Korea	11
North Ireland	11
Ireland	10
Britain	10
Chile	09
East Germany	09
France	09
Portugal	08
Austria	08
China	07
Lithuania	07
Latvia	07
Switzerland	07
Argentina	06
Spain	06
Japan	06
Brazil	05
Russia	05
Bulgaria	04
Italy	04
Hungary	03
Slovenia	03
Romania	02

Note: Countries in the left column are ranked according to GNP per capita. / The percentages in the bottom row give each country an equal weight. / na=not ascertained.

V22 TRADE UNIONS

Please look carefully at the following list of voluntary organizations and activities and say which, if any, do you belong to? Trade unions. (% "belong to")

	Total	Gender		Age			Education			Income			Political Affinity			Values		
		Male	Female	16-29	30-49	50+	Lower	Middle	Upper	Lower	Middle	Upper	Left	Center	Right	Mat	Mixed	Postmat
India	na	na	na	na	na	na	na	na	na	na	na	na	na	na	na	na	na	na
Nigeria	na	na	na	na	na	na	na	na	na	na	na	na	na	na	na	na	na	na
China	02	02	01	02	02	01	01	02	02	00	02	04	na	na	na	01	02	06
Romania	20	23	17	23	31	07	11	25	24	22	19	19	16	21	23	18	21	17
Turkey	na	na	na	na	na	na	na	na	na	na	na	na	na	na	na	na	na	na
Poland	na	na	na	na	na	na	na	na	na	na	na	na	na	na	na	na	na	na
Bulgaria	19	20	19	13	27	14	11	22	25	21	20	19	20	24	18	17	20	19
Chile	06	10	02	05	08	04	04	07	07	03	08	07	08	08	02	04	06	10
Czechoslovakia	na	na	na	na	na	na	na	na	na	na	na	na	na	na	na	na	na	na
South Africa	na	na	na	na	na	na	na	na	na	na	na	na	na	na	na	na	na	na
Lithuania	43	41	45	33	58	37	25	46	59	38	50	41	na	na	na	45	44	39
Hungary	32	29	34	25	38	29	24	39	38	25	36	44	49	34	26	36	28	33
Argentina	01	02	01	01	01	02	01	02	02	01	02	02	03	01	05	00	01	03
Brazil	06	10	03	05	01	06	05	06	12	05	02	09	09	07	05	04	07	11
Mexico	04	05	03	03	08	03	04	01	04	03	05	04	07	07	03	04	04	02
Belarus	na	na	na	na	na	na	na	na	na	na	na	na	na	na	na	na	na	na
Russia	62	65	59	63	76	44	48	64	68	56	65	68	68	68	48	57	64	74
Moscow	na	na	na	na	na	na	na	na	na	na	na	na	na	na	na	na	na	na
Latvia	52	52	52	42	60	47	49	51	55	51	51	53	na	na	na	57	52	56
Estonia	59	58	60	49	70	53	47	63	62	56	63	61	na	na	na	58	60	68
Portugal	05	07	03	03	07	04	05	05	04	05	05	04	08	03	04	07	04	05
South Korea	07	06	09	05	10	05	09	09	05	08	09	05	09	08	07	08	07	08
Ireland	09	13	05	09	13	05	06	11	14	03	03	14	15	11	06	06	09	14
North Ireland	12	20	06	12	17	06	10	14	17	03	11	26	11	11	15	02	14	20
Slovenia	19	21	18	21	29	07	11	23	28	17	20	22	23	21	17	19	19	25
Spain	04	07	01	02	08	02	03	05	07	02	03	08	09	03	02	01	05	08
East Germany	56	60	53	53	63	51	54	54	65	44	60	64	71	48	54	49	57	58
Britain	14	19	09	13	19	10	13	15	17	09	21	19	19	15	10	13	13	20
Italy	06	09	03	03	10	05	05	13	04	06	08	11	10	05	03	04	05	11
Netherlands	17	26	14	09	21	20	15	18	18	12	25	21	23	15	16	14	16	20
Belgium	16	19	12	15	20	12	12	17	21	13	26	20	21	14	17	10	15	25
Austria	19	29	13	15	23	18	19	21	16	13	23	21	25	24	15	13	19	24
France	05	08	03	03	06	07	04	05	09	04	04	10	10	04	04	02	06	08
Canada	12	16	07	08	18	08	06	14	13	03	14	17	16	12	11	08	11	15
United States	09	13	05	03	11	10	06	12	08	06	12	10	16	11	07	08	11	11
Iceland	60	61	58	65	65	45	55	58	63	na	na	na	66	61	54	58	58	74
West Germany	15	23	09	15	19	12	15	15	14	12	20	16	26	13	11	10	15	19
Denmark	49	52	46	51	62	33	35	55	54	34	70	59	65	50	40	49	48	61
Finland	36	37	35	28	44	21	21	38	41	28	38	41	49	28	36	27	35	39
Norway	42	45	38	32	49	39	37	40	46	31	52	52	53	44	33	37	42	54
Sweden	59	61	56	48	71	53	56	57	67	69	55	64	70	63	49	55	58	64
Japan	07	11	04	09	09	04	05	08	09	04	10	08	17	07	06	06	08	11
Switzerland	06	12	02	03	08	06	06	06	07	05	09	10	13	07	04	04	05	10
Total	23	25	20	20	28	18	18	24	26	18	24	25	26	21	18	20	23	27

Ranking:

Russia	62
Iceland	60
Estonia	59
Sweden	59
East Germany	56
Latvia	52
Denmark	49
Lithuania	43
Norway	42
Finland	36
Hungary	32
Romania	20
Bulgaria	19
Slovenia	19
Austria	19
Netherlands	17
Belgium	16
West Germany	15
Britain	14
North Ireland	12
Canada	12
Ireland	09
United States	09
South Korea	07
Japan	07
Chile	06
Brazil	06
Italy	06
Switzerland	06
Portugal	05
France	05
Mexico	04
Spain	04
China	02
Argentina	01

Note: Countries in the left column are ranked according to GNP per capita. / The percentages in the bottom row give each country an equal weight. / na=not ascertained.
The Chinese questionnaire translated "Trade Unions" (V22 and V40) as "Trading Associations," which was chosen by very few people. "Professional Associations" was translated as "occupational organizations," which evokes the (government-sponsored) labor unions; thus, for China, V27 is functionally equivalent to V22.

V23 POLITICAL PARTIES

Please look carefully at the following list of voluntary organizations and activities and say which, if any, do you belong to?
Political parties or groups. (% "belong to")

Country	Total	Gender		Age			Education			Income			Political Affinity			Values		
		Male	Female	16-29	30-49	50+	Lower	Medium	Upper	Lower	Middle	Upper	Left	Center	Right	Mat	Mixed	Postmat
India	na	na	na	na	na	na	na	na	na	na	na	na	na	na	na	na	na	na
Nigeria	na	na	na	na	na	na	na	na	na	na	na	na	na	na	na	na	na	na
China	35	38	31	22	41	39	23	38	52	29	41	39	na	na	na	31	40	06
Romania	03	04	01	01	03	04	01	02	05	02	03	02	04	02	05	02	02	05
Turkey	na	na	na	na	na	na	na	na	na	na	na	na	na	na	na	na	na	na
Poland	11	15	08	06	15	10	07	11	18	10	11	14	19	12	10	11	11	10
Bulgaria	05	07	03	05	05	05	03	06	06	03	05	06	12	03	03	00	05	13
Chile	05	07	03	na	na	na	na	na	na	na	na	na	na	na	na	na	na	na
Czechoslovakia	na	na	na	na	na	na	na	na	na	na	na	na	na	na	na	na	na	na
South Africa	na	na	na	na	na	na	na	na	na	na	na	na	na	na	na	na	na	na
Lithuania	07	11	05	04	09	09	03	08	13	07	07	08	na	na	na	04	09	08
Hungary	02	04	01	02	02	03	01	03	08	01	03	02	06	02	05	02	03	01
Argentina	02	03	01	02	02	02	01	01	05	01	03	02	04	02	03	03	05	12
Brazil	05	06	03	04	06	03	04	03	11	03	04	07	07	03	05	04	05	08
Mexico	05	08	03	06	06	04	06	03	04	06	06	04	12	04	06	04	05	08
Belarus	na	na	na	na	na	na	na	na	na	na	na	na	na	na	na	na	na	na
Russia	11	16	08	06	13	13	05	05	22	07	11	18	18	13	17	11	12	08
Moscow	na	na	na	na	na	na	na	na	na	15	21	19	na	na	na	12	20	33
Latvia	18	23	15	14	21	19	14	14	30	07	19	10	na	na	na	06	09	12
Estonia	08	10	07	04	10	09	04	07	17	07	07	08	na	na	na	03	05	14
Portugal	05	07	03	06	04	04	03	06	10	04	05	09	09	04	05	03	05	02
South Korea	05	03	06	02	06	06	07	04	04	02	04	05	04	04	04	03	03	06
Ireland	04	05	03	02	05	04	04	03	07	03	03	01	06	01	02	00	02	04
North Ireland	02	02	02	01	01	03	01	03	08	02	03	08	07	05	04	02	03	06
Slovenia	03	04	02	02	04	04	01	03	08	02	03	04	06	02	04	01	03	03
Spain	02	04	01	02	03	02	01	03	04	01	02	04	05	08	01	06	11	10
East Germany	11	15	08	08	13	10	12	12	15	11	12	10	14	08	09	06	11	09
Britain	06	06	06	03	05	07	04	10	07	05	06	12	07	04	04	01	05	11
Italy	05	08	03	06	06	04	08	12	08	08	09	11	07	07	12	08	08	09
Netherlands	08	13	07	03	06	16	08	08	10	08	09	11	09	07	12	08	08	08
Belgium	06	08	04	05	06	07	04	11	14	04	08	13	06	06	10	04	13	12
Austria	12	19	07	05	14	13	12	11	04	08	14	05	23	12	03	08	02	06
France	03	04	02	00	03	04	02	02	04	02	03	05	06	06	11	01	07	09
Canada	07	09	06	05	08	08	06	06	10	08	08	12	11	12	11	05	07	17
United States	14	16	12	09	15	16	12	10	23	14	12	20	20	11	19	09	16	22
Iceland	15	18	12	12	19	19	20	10	14	10	14	12	18	05	12	05	07	10
West Germany	07	11	04	05	09	10	05	10	14	06	06	09	11	05	10	07	07	09
Denmark	07	07	07	02	06	10	08	04	08	05	06	16	08	11	17	06	07	18
Finland	14	17	10	08	14	18	17	12	15	15	11	16	18	13	16	12	13	20
Norway	14	17	11	08	12	19	12	13	15	14	12	16	15	07	09	10	09	14
Sweden	10	12	08	04	10	15	12	08	13	12	12	13	19	07	09	10	09	05
Japan	02	03	01	01	02	03	04	01	01	02	02	03	07	02	07	05	02	11
Switzerland	09	14	05	03	09	11	06	11	14	06	11	18	13	07	15	05	09	11
Total	**08**	**10**	**06**	**05**	**09**	**09**	**06**	**08**	**12**	**06**	**08**	**10**	**11**	**06**	**09**	**06**	**08**	**11**

Ranking:

China	35
Latvia	18
Iceland	15
United States	14
Finland	14
Norway	14
Austria	12
Bulgaria	11
Russia	11
East Germany	11
Sweden	10
Switzerland	09
Estonia	08
Netherlands	08
Lithuania	07
Canada	07
West Germany	07
Denmark	07
Britain	06
Belgium	06
Chile	05
Brazil	05
Mexico	05
Portugal	05
South Korea	05
Italy	05
Ireland	04
Romania	03
Slovenia	03
France	03
Hungary	02
Argentina	02
North Ireland	02
Spain	02
Japan	02

Note: Countries in the left column are ranked according to GNP per capita. / The percentages in the bottom row give each country an equal weight. / na=not ascertained.

V24 COMMUNITY ACTION

Please look carefully at the following list of voluntary organizations and activities and say which, if any, do you belong to?
Local community action on issues like poverty, employment, housing, racial equality. (% "belong to")

Country	Total	Gender Male	Gender Female	Age 16-29	Age 30-49	Age 50+	Edu Lower	Edu Medium	Edu Upper	Inc Lower	Inc Middle	Inc Upper	Pol Left	Pol Center	Pol Right	Values Mat	Values Mixed	Values Postmat
India	na	na	na	na	na	na	na	na	na	na	na	na	na	na	na	na	na	na
Nigeria	na	na	na	na	na	na	na	na	na	na	na	na	na	na	na	na	na	na
China	01	01	00	01	01	01	01	00	01	01	01	00	na	na	na	01	01	00
Romania	01	02	01	00	01	01	01	01	03	01	01	02	02	02	00	01	02	01
Turkey	na	na	na	00	01	01	01	01	03	na	na	na	na	na	na	na	na	na
Poland	na	na	na	na	na	na	na	na	na	na	na	na	na	na	na	na	na	na
Bulgaria	02	02	02	01	01	02	00	03	02	02	02	02	02	03	02	02	02	02
Chile	04	04	05	03	05	05	04	04	04	03	05	04	06	03	05	04	04	07
Czechoslovakia	na	na	na	na	na	na	na	na	na	na	na	na	na	na	na	na	na	na
South Africa	na	na	na	na	na	na	na	na	na	na	na	na	na	na	na	na	na	na
Lithuania	02	02	02	01	03	02	02	02	04	02	02	03	na	na	na	02	02	01
Hungary	01	02	01	02	01	01	01	02	02	01	01	05	02	02	00	01	02	03
Argentina	01	02	01	02	02	01	01	01	02	02	02	01	01	02	01	01	01	02
Brazil	08	08	08	06	11	06	08	07	11	07	09	10	08	07	10	06	09	11
Mexico	04	04	05	04	05	03	04	04	04	03	05	06	06	04	04	03	05	02
Belarus	na	na	na	na	na	na	na	na	na	na	na	na	na	na	na	na	na	na
Russia	03	02	03	01	03	03	02	03	03	02	02	04	03	03	05	03	05	na
Moscow	na	na	na	na	na	na	na	na	na	na	na	na	na	na	na	na	02	01
Latvia	05	06	05	04	06	07	06	04	08	03	07	06	na	na	na	04	06	na
Estonia	05	06	05	00	07	05	02	04	09	03	06	06	06	03	01	03	06	08
Portugal	02	01	02	01	02	02	02	01	01	02	01	01	02	01	02	02	02	01
South Korea	13	08	16	06	17	14	13	12	13	10	14	17	09	12	14	14	12	08
Ireland	03	03	03	01	04	04	03	04	04	02	04	05	03	04	04	02	03	06
North Ireland	02	00	03	01	03	02	02	03	00	01	01	05	04	04	01	03	02	02
Slovenia	06	07	05	02	06	08	05	04	11	05	06	07	00	09	01	03	06	10
Spain	01	02	01	01	02	01	03	01	01	01	02	01	02	02	02	01	01	02
East Germany	03	03	03	03	03	04	02	02	03	02	02	03	02	03	05	01	01	02
Britain	04	03	04	02	04	04	03	05	04	04	03	04	05	03	04	03	02	05
Italy	02	02	01	02	02	02	02	02	01	02	03	04	05	03	04	03	03	07
Netherlands	05	05	05	03	06	06	05	05	05	04	04	06	07	04	01	01	05	03
Belgium	05	05	04	06	05	04	05	05	09	04	04	07	07	04	05	04	05	07
Austria	02	03	02	03	02	04	03	02	03	02	03	03	08	03	03	01	02	09
France	03	04	02	01	03	06	04	04	06	02	03	05	03	03	06	02	03	03
Canada	05	05	06	04	05	07	04	04	07	05	03	05	05	06	05	04	03	05
United States	05	06	05	04	06	06	03	03	08	04	06	06	06	05	06	05	04	08
Iceland	02	02	01	04	02	01	01	01	02	01	na	01	05	01	00	00	02	05
West Germany	02	02	02	01	03	05	02	05	06	02	06	01	01	07	02	01	05	07
Denmark	05	05	05	02	06	05	05	05	06	05	06	05	05	02	04	01	05	08
Finland	03	03	03	04	03	03	05	02	04	05	03	03	06	05	03	05	02	07
Norway	03	03	03	02	04	02	01	02	04	03	03	03	06	02	03	02	02	08
Sweden	02	02	02	02	03	02	02	03	05	04	04	05	05	03	01	02	02	09
Japan	00	00	00	01	00	00	00	00	00	00	00	02	01	00	01	02	03	04
Switzerland	03	04	03	01	03	05	00	04	02	02	04	05	05	03	05	02	03	05
Total	03	03	03	02	04	04	03	03	05	03	04	04	04	04	04	03	03	05

Ranking:

South Korea	13
Brazil	08
Slovenia	06
Latvia	05
Estonia	05
Netherlands	05
Belgium	05
Canada	05
United States	05
Denmark	05
Chile	04
Mexico	04
Britain	04
Russia	03
Ireland	03
East Germany	03
France	03
Finland	03
Norway	03
Switzerland	03
Bulgaria	02
Lithuania	02
Portugal	02
North Ireland	02
Italy	02
Austria	02
Iceland	02
West Germany	02
Sweden	02
China	01
Romania	01
Hungary	01
Argentina	01
Spain	01
Japan	00

Note: Countries in the left column are ranked according to GNP per capita. / The percentages in the bottom row give each country an equal weight. / na=not ascertained.

V25 THIRD WORLD DEVELOPMENT

Please look carefully at the following list of voluntary organizations and activities and say which, if any, do you belong to?
Third world development or human rights. (% "belong to")

	Total	Gender Male	Gender Female	Age 16-29	Age 30-49	Age 50+	Education Lower	Education Medium	Education Upper	Income Lower	Income Middle	Income Upper	Political Affinity Left	Political Affinity Center	Political Affinity Right	Values Mat	Values Mixed	Values Postmat
India	na	na	na	na	na	na	na	na	na	na	na	na	na	na	na	na	na	na
Nigeria	na	na	na	na	na	na	na	na	na	na	na	na	na	na	na	na	na	na
China	01	01	01	00	01	00	00	01	01	01	01	00	na	na	na	01	01	01
Romania	00	00	00	00	00	00	00	00	00	00	00	00	01	00	00	00	00	01
Turkey	na	na	na	na	na	na	na	na	na	na	na	na	na	na	na	na	na	na
Poland	02	na	na	na	na	na	na	na	na	na	na	na	na	na	na	na	na	na
Bulgaria	02	02	01	01	01	02	01	01	01	01	02	01	01	01	01	03	01	00
Chile	01	01	01	01	01	02	02	01	01	01	01	02	01	01	01	01	01	03
Czechoslovakia	na	na	na	na	na	na	na	na	na	na	na	na	na	na	na	na	na	na
South Africa	na	na	na	na	na	na	na	na	na	na	na	na	na	na	na	na	na	na
Lithuania	01	02	01	00	02	01	01	01	02	01	01	01	01	00	00	01	01	01
Hungary	00	00	00	01	00	01	00	00	00	00	00	01	00	00	01	00	00	01
Argentina	00	00	00	00	01	01	01	01	00	00	00	01	01	02	01	01	01	03
Brazil	01	01	01	01	02	01	01	01	03	01	01	02	01	02	02	01	01	02
Mexico	01	01	00	01	01	00	00	01	01	01	02	00	na	00	na	00	01	01
Belarus	na	na	na	na	na	na	na	na	na	na	na	na	na	na	na	na	na	na
Russia	00	00	00	00	01	00	00	00	00	00	00	01	01	00	00	00	01	00
Moscow	na	na	na	na	na	na	na	na	na	na	na	na	na	na	na	02	01	01
Latvia	01	01	02	01	01	02	01	01	02	00	00	03	na	na	na	00	01	01
Estonia	01	01	00	00	01	00	00	01	02	01	01	00	na	na	na	00	01	00
Portugal	01	01	01	01	00	00	00	02	03	00	03	01	00	01	01	01	01	02
South Korea	02	01	03	01	03	02	02	02	03	02	03	03	03	03	02	01	02	04
Ireland	02	01	02	02	02	01	02	01	02	03	01	01	00	02	01	00	03	04
North Ireland	03	04	02	01	05	00	01	04	10	03	01	04	00	04	05	00	00	08
Slovenia	00	00	00	00	00	00	00	00	00	00	00	01	00	00	01	00	00	00
Spain	01	01	01	01	01	01	01	00	03	01	01	01	01	01	01	01	01	02
East Germany	01	02	01	01	01	01	01	04	06	02	03	03	04	02	02	01	02	05
Britain	02	03	02	01	02	03	01	02	04	01	01	02	01	01	01	01	01	02
Italy	01	01	01	01	01	01	02	01	02	01	01	02	01	01	01	01	01	02
Netherlands	14	13	14	08	18	14	09	12	21	13	14	20	22	09	13	03	05	19
Belgium	07	07	06	06	08	05	04	07	10	05	09	08	12	06	06	03	05	14
Austria	02	00	03	01	03	01	02	02	04	02	01	06	03	02	03	00	01	03
France	03	03	03	01	03	03	03	04	04	03	02	06	04	03	04	01	03	06
Canada	05	05	04	03	04	06	04	06	07	06	05	05	08	04	05	03	03	08
United States	02	02	02	03	02	01	01	01	03	01	01	03	04	04	03	03	02	03
Iceland	03	02	05	02	05	03	04	03	06	02	03	03	04	01	03	03	03	07
West Germany	02	02	02	03	03	01	03	02	05	02	02	03	05	02	01	02	01	04
Denmark	03	02	04	02	03	04	02	04	05	05	05	07	04	03	03	03	05	08
Finland	06	05	07	03	06	08	04	05	08	07	05	06	09	04	05	03	05	15
Norway	05	05	05	04	06	04	02	04	10	06	05	09	09	04	04	02	03	08
Sweden	09	06	12	09	11	08	04	08	19	10	09	09	14	08	08	06	08	17
Japan	00	00	00	01	00	00	00	00	00	00	00	00	01	00	00	00	00	00
Switzerland	na	na	na	na	na	na	na	na	na	na	na	na	na	na	na	na	na	na
Total	**02**	**02**	**03**	**02**	**03**	**02**	**02**	**01**	**04**	**02**	**02**	**03**	**04**	**02**	**02**	**01**	**02**	**04**

Note: Countries in the left column are ranked according to GNP per capita. / The percentages in the bottom row give each country an equal weight. / na=not ascertained.

Ranking:

Netherlands	14
Sweden	09
Belgium	07
Finland	06
Canada	05
Norway	05
North Ireland	03
France	03
Iceland	03
Denmark	03
Bulgaria	02
South Korea	02
Ireland	02
Britain	02
Austria	02
United States	02
West Germany	02
China	01
Chile	01
Lithuania	01
Brazil	01
Mexico	01
Latvia	01
Estonia	01
Portugal	01
Spain	01
East Germany	01
Italy	01
Romania	00
Hungary	00
Argentina	00
Russia	00
Slovenia	00
Japan	00

V26 ENVIRONMENT

Please look carefully at the following list of voluntary organizations and activities and say which, if any, do you belong to? Conservation, the environment, ecology. (% "belong to")

	Total	Gender Male	Gender Female	Age 16-29	Age 30-49	Age 50+	Educ. Lower	Educ. Medium	Educ. Upper	Income Lower	Income Middle	Income Upper	Pol. Left	Pol. Center	Pol. Right	Values Mat	Values Mixed	Values Postmat
India	na	na	na	na	na	na	na	na	na	na	na	na	na	na	na	na	na	na
Nigeria	na	na	na	na	na	na	na	na	na	na	na	na	na	na	na	na	na	na
China	01	01	01	01	01	01	01	01	01	00	01	01	01	01	01	01	01	02
Romania	01	02	01	01	01	01	01	01	01	01	01	02	01	02	01	01	01	02
Turkey	na	na	na	na	na	na	00	01	02	01	na	01	01	02	01	01	01	04
Poland	na	na	na	na	na	na	na	na	na	na	na	na	na	na	na	na	na	na
Bulgaria	04	04	03	03	05	03	01	04	06	03	02	05	04	03	06	04	04	na
Chile	02	02	01	02	02	03	01	01	03	02	02	01	02	02	01	00	03	03
Czechoslovakia	na	na	na	na	na	na	na	na	na	na	na	na	na	na	na	na	na	na
South Africa	na	na	na	na	na	na	na	na	na	na	na	na	na	na	na	na	na	na
Lithuania	02	03	01	03	03	01	01	02	04	02	02	02	na	na	na	02	03	03
Hungary	01	02	00	01	01	02	00	02	06	00	01	05	01	02	03	01	02	03
Argentina	00	00	00	00	00	00	00	00	00	00	00	00	01	00	00	00	00	00
Brazil	03	03	03	03	04	00	03	03	04	02	03	04	04	02	04	00	03	06
Mexico	03	03	02	03	03	03	03	02	03	02	04	04	04	03	03	02	03	02
Belarus	na	na	na	na	na	na	na	na	na	na	na	na	na	na	na	na	na	na
Russia	02	02	01	01	03	01	01	02	02	01	01	03	03	02	01	01	02	03
Moscow	na	na	na	na	na	na	na	na	na	na	na	na	na	na	na	na	na	na
Latvia	04	04	04	06	na	05	06	04	05	04	06	04	na	na	na	06	03	08
Estonia	03	04	02	02	03	02	01	02	07	02	02	06	na	na	na	01	03	02
Portugal	01	02	01	03	01	01	01	01	04	01	00	04	02	01	01	00	01	07
South Korea	02	02	02	01	02	03	03	02	04	03	02	02	02	01	03	00	01	07
Ireland	02	02	03	02	02	03	01	03	07	01	02	05	02	01	03	01	02	02
North Ireland	02	02	03	04	02	02	01	04	10	01	02	06	06	01	03	01	01	03
Slovenia	02	02	01	02	01	03	01	03	05	00	00	03	00	03	02	00	03	02
Spain	01	02	01	02	02	01	01	01	03	01	02	03	04	01	01	02	01	04
East Germany	04	05	03	05	04	02	03	03	06	03	03	04	03	04	04	06	04	02
Britain	06	06	06	05	08	06	03	09	13	03	07	04	04	04	05	00	03	07
Italy	03	04	02	02	03	01	02	06	09	04	05	09	09	06	02	03	05	12
Netherlands	24	24	24	21	28	22	19	22	33	20	30	34	34	23	20	11	24	29
Belgium	08	09	07	07	10	06	06	08	12	06	07	13	12	09	07	03	07	15
Austria	03	04	03	04	03	03	03	03	04	01	03	05	04	03	03	01	02	05
France	02	04	01	01	02	02	02	03	03	02	03	02	03	03	02	01	01	05
Canada	08	09	06	07	09	06	02	07	12	04	07	11	15	06	09	07	06	11
United States	09	09	08	08	11	06	03	07	14	05	07	14	19	09	05	04	08	15
Iceland	05	05	05	05	06	03	02	03	08	na	na	na	10	02	04	06	04	15
West Germany	05	05	04	06	05	02	03	06	11	04	04	06	10	03	04	04	03	08
Denmark	13	13	12	09	15	12	04	12	18	09	12	19	19	13	11	00	10	10
Finland	05	06	05	03	06	08	05	04	07	05	07	05	09	13	05	03	13	21
Norway	04	05	03	04	06	03	01	03	07	05	05	07	07	05	02	06	05	07
Sweden	11	10	10	08	15	07	07	08	21	09	11	13	17	10	08	08	08	19
Japan	01	01	01	01	01	01	02	01	01	00	02	01	02	02	01	01	02	01
Switzerland	11	11	10	10	12	10	07	12	18	09	11	18	19	11	09	02	09	20
Total	05	05	04	04	05	04	03	04	08	03	05	07	08	05	04	02	04	07

Ranking:

Netherlands	24
Denmark	13
Sweden	11
Switzerland	11
United States	09
Belgium	08
Canada	08
Britain	06
Iceland	05
West Germany	05
Finland	05
Bulgaria	04
Latvia	04
East Germany	04
Norway	04
Brazil	03
Mexico	03
Estonia	03
Italy	03
Austria	03
Chile	02
Lithuania	02
Russia	02
South Korea	02
Ireland	02
North Ireland	02
Slovenia	02
France	02
China	01
Romania	01
Hungary	01
Portugal	01
Spain	01
Japan	01
Argentina	00

Note: Countries in the left column are ranked according to GNP per capita. / The percentages in the bottom row give each country an equal weight. / na=not ascertained.

V27 PROFESSIONAL ASSOCIATIONS

Please look carefully at the following list of voluntary organizations and activities and say which, if any, do you belong to? Professional associations. (% "belong to")

Country	Total	Gender Male	Gender Female	Age 16-29	Age 30-49	Age 50+	Education Lower	Education Medium	Education Upper	Income Lower	Income Middle	Income Upper	Political Left	Political Center	Political Right	Values Mat	Values Mixed	Values Postmat
India	na	na	na	na	na	na	na	na	na	na	na	na	na	na	na	na	na	na
Nigeria	26	26	25	15	33	26	25	23	35	22	31	26	na	na	na	na	na	na
China	02	02	02	01	02	02	00	01	06	02	02	02	01	03	03	02	02	07
Romania	02	02	02	01	02	02	00	01	06	02	02	02	na	na	na	02	02	07
Turkey	na	na	na	na	na	na	na	na	na	na	na	na	na	na	na	na	na	na
Poland	05	05	05	05	07	03	02	03	12	04	05	07	07	05	07	03	05	08
Bulgaria	03	05	03	05	07	03	02	02	08	01	03	07	05	03	02	01	03	06
Chile	03	04	03	01	05	04	01	02	08	00	01	08	06	03	04	01	03	06
Czechoslovakia	na	na	na	na	na	na	na	na	na	na	na	na	na	na	na	na	na	na
South Africa	na	na	na	na	na	na	01	02	13	02	03	05	na	na	na	04	02	04
Lithuania	03	03	04	01	03	03	01	06	18	03	07	12	10	06	04	04	06	13
Hungary	06	07	02	07	08	03	03	00	09	03	01	08	05	03	03	01	03	02
Argentina	03	04	02	00	05	02	01	00	16	00	04	08	06	03	04	02	05	15
Brazil	05	07	03	03	06	04	02	03	06	02	03	16	03	03	04	02	03	03
Mexico	03	03	03	02	04	02	02	01	06	01	03	05	03	03	04	01	03	03
Belarus	na	na	na	02	02	na	02	01	03	na	na	02	05	00	01	01	03	02
Russia	02	02	02	02	02	01	02	01	03	01	02	07	na	na	na	na	na	na
Moscow	na	na	na	na	na	na	na	na	na	05	06	07	na	na	na	06	06	12
Latvia	06	08	05	04	07	08	04	04	12	05	06	05	na	na	na	06	05	09
Estonia	04	05	03	02	06	04	03	03	11	03	03	09	07	04	04	05	04	05
Portugal	04	05	03	05	05	03	03	05	10	06	03	27	13	13	10	04	13	17
South Korea	13	08	17	12	13	14	03	07	24	00	11	11	08	05	13	11	13	09
Ireland	05	05	05	06	05	04	01	06	22	01	02	16	04	08	05	01	05	11
North Ireland	07	09	05	13	07	06	03	13	17	03	05	11	11	08	14	03	07	12
Slovenia	06	08	04	05	07	05	01	05	17	03	07	06	04	07	04	03	06	04
Spain	02	03	02	02	04	01	01	02	08	01	01	10	04	01	04	03	03	05
East Germany	06	10	04	05	08	05	04	07	31	05	05	25	09	08	04	04	07	14
Britain	11	14	08	07	15	10	06	17	31	05	10	14	12	11	15	04	10	16
Italy	04	06	02	03	06	02	02	14	12	02	05	24	05	03	04	04	11	06
Netherlands	12	17	10	11	11	12	07	08	21	07	12	24	10	14	14	05	11	13
Belgium	07	09	04	04	09	04	03	06	15	02	09	12	09	06	07	05	05	09
Austria	06	09	04	05	06	06	03	07	21	02	05	10	06	05	08	03	05	08
France	05	07	07	03	06	06	06	03	33	07	05	28	06	05	23	05	05	11
Canada	16	17	15	13	19	15	05	09	31	06	14	26	26	13	16	12	13	23
United States	15	17	13	10	19	14	08	10	28	11	08	14	21	12	14	10	13	38
Iceland	15	17	13	09	20	14	10	08	28	06	08	17	22	08	15	05	10	10
West Germany	09	15	04	06	12	09	07	08	21	07	09	14	12	11	16	07	13	16
Denmark	12	17	07	06	17	12	07	08	18	07	12	24	16	11	20	12	15	17
Finland	15	18	13	08	18	15	12	09	24	12	19	26	16	18	16	15	16	23
Norway	16	21	11	07	22	16	07	12	26	09	11	25	14	18	16	10	11	14
Sweden	12	14	09	06	13	16	04	10	28	04	04	06	14	08	16	10	11	05
Japan	04	08	01	02	05	05	04	03	07	04	04	25	03	06	08	04	04	20
Switzerland	14	20	08	11	17	11	10	15	21	07	17	25	14	16	17	08	12	12
Total	**08**	**10**	**06**	**06**	**10**	**08**	**04**	**07**	**17**	**04**	**08**	**14**	**10**	**08**	**09**	**06**	**08**	**12**

Ranking:

China	26
Canada	16
Norway	16
United States	15
Iceland	15
Finland	15
Switzerland	14
South Korea	13
Netherlands	12
Denmark	12
Sweden	12
Britain	11
West Germany	09
North Ireland	07
Belgium	07
Hungary	06
Latvia	06
Slovenia	06
East Germany	06
Austria	06
Bulgaria	05
Brazil	05
Ireland	05
France	05
Estonia	04
Portugal	04
Italy	04
Japan	04
Chile	03
Lithuania	03
Argentina	03
Mexico	03
Romania	02
Russia	02
Spain	02

Note: Countries in the left column are ranked according to GNP per capita. / The percentages in the bottom row give each country an equal weight. / na=not ascertained.
The Chinese questionnaire translated "Trade Unions" (V22 and V40) as "Trading Associations," which was chosen by very few people. "Professional Associations" was translated as "occupational organizations," which evokes the (government-sponsored) labor unions; thus, for China, V27 is functionally equivalent to V22.

V28 YOUTH WORK

Please look carefully at the following list of voluntary organizations and activities and say which, if any, do you belong to?

Youth work (e.g., scouts guides, youth clubs, etc.) (% "belong to")

	Total	Gender Male	Gender Female	Age 16-29	Age 30-49	Age 50+	Education Lower	Education Medium	Education Upper	Income Lower	Income Middle	Income Upper	Pol. Aff. Left	Pol. Aff. Center	Pol. Aff. Right	Values Mat	Values Mixed	Values Postmat
India	na	na	na	na	na	na	na	na	na	na	na	na	na	na	na	na	na	na
Nigeria	na	na	na	na	na	na	na	na	na	na	na	na	na	na	na	na	na	na
China	09	08	11	17	08	02	06	12	10	08	13	08	01	01	01	08	10	11
Romania	01	01	01	02	00	01	01	01	00	01	01	01	01	01	01	00	01	00
Turkey	na	na	na	na	na	na	na	na	na	na	na	na	na	na	na	na	na	na
Poland	02	02	02	03	02	01	00	02	03	01	02	02	02	03	02	01	02	na
Bulgaria	06	06	05	08	05	03	03	07	08	03	06	08	06	06	04	03	06	09
Chile	na	na	na	na	na	na	na	na	na	na	na	na	na	na	na	na	na	na
Czechoslovakia	na	na	na	na	na	na	na	na	na	na	na	na	na	na	na	na	na	na
South Africa	na	na	na	na	na	na	na	na	na	na	na	na	na	na	na	na	na	na
Lithuania	05	05	05	11	03	01	02	06	05	04	04	05	na	na	na	03	06	na
Hungary	02	02	02	03	02	01	00	03	06	01	02	05	02	02	02	02	02	03
Argentina	02	03	00	02	02	01	01	02	06	00	02	03	03	03	01	01	01	03
Brazil	04	05	03	06	02	01	02	04	06	03	04	04	04	04	na	02	05	06
Mexico	04	04	04	06	03	03	04	04	04	03	06	03	04	03	06	04	05	02
Belarus	na	na	na	na	na	na	na	na	na	na	na	na	na	na	na	na	na	na
Russia	03	03	03	04	04	01	00	03	05	03	02	04	05	03	05	na	na	na
Moscow	na	na	na	na	04	01	na	03	05	na	02	04	05	03	05	01	04	na
Latvia	02	02	02	04	na	02	04	02	01	02	01	02	na	na	na	01	na	01
Estonia	03	03	01	04	02	02	04	03	03	01	03	02	na	na	na	02	02	03
Portugal	03	03	03	06	02	00	06	05	07	02	04	05	02	04	01	01	03	11
South Korea	07	07	07	10	06	03	03	06	09	05	06	08	08	08	06	03	07	11
Ireland	06	07	05	13	07	02	04	08	11	01	09	08	06	07	06	07	07	10
North Ireland	11	09	12	21	12	03	05	20	28	00	08	22	04	13	09	03	11	13
Slovenia	02	03	01	03	02	01	05	01	05	02	02	05	07	02	00	09	01	07
Spain	02	02	02	03	02	01	02	02	03	01	02	03	03	02	03	01	02	07
East Germany	03	04	02	09	02	00	03	04	02	04	02	03	03	03	04	01	03	04
Britain	04	04	05	04	08	02	05	05	14	02	06	06	04	04	05	03	04	05
Italy	03	04	03	06	04	04	06	10	01	03	04	04	03	04	02	01	04	06
Netherlands	07	07	07	09	07	06	07	07	11	07	08	06	03	06	08	03	03	06
Belgium	08	09	07	16	07	05	04	10	13	08	06	11	10	07	10	05	09	06
Austria	03	03	02	06	02	01	02	03	05	01	03	03	06	03	02	05	02	04
France	03	03	03	05	03	04	03	04	03	02	06	05	05	04	05	01	03	06
Canada	10	09	10	10	12	07	04	10	12	06	05	05	07	10	10	03	09	11
United States	13	12	15	12	19	09	07	11	19	10	12	19	07	15	16	05	13	15
Iceland	08	10	06	13	08	03	05	10	12	na	06	na	06	09	10	05	07	na
West Germany	04	04	03	07	04	01	03	05	06	02	04	05	04	03	02	01	03	03
Denmark	05	05	04	05	05	03	04	07	05	03	06	06	05	05	05	03	05	07
Finland	05	07	04	05	06	04	07	04	06	04	05	07	05	06	05	03	05	07
Norway	06	07	05	11	06	03	02	07	07	05	07	07	06	06	06	03	04	09
Sweden	09	09	09	14	10	03	07	10	12	08	06	12	10	08	10	08	09	11
Japan	01	01	01	01	01	00	00	01	01	00	02	01	01	08	00	01	01	03
Switzerland	04	05	03	09	04	02	02	03	15	04	03	06	06	03	03	02	03	06
Total	**05**	**05**	**05**	**08**	**05**	**02**	**03**	**06**	**08**	**03**	**05**	**06**	**05**	**05**	**05**	**03**	**05**	**07**

Ranking:

United States	13
North Ireland	11
Canada	10
China	09
Sweden	09
Belgium	08
Iceland	08
South Korea	07
Netherlands	07
Chile	06
Ireland	06
Norway	06
Lithuania	05
Denmark	05
Finland	05
Brazil	04
Mexico	04
Britain	04
West Germany	04
Switzerland	04
Russia	03
Estonia	03
Portugal	03
East Germany	03
Italy	03
Austria	03
France	03
Bulgaria	02
Hungary	02
Argentina	02
Latvia	02
Slovenia	02
Spain	02
Romania	01
Japan	01

Note: Countries in the left column are ranked according to GNP per capita. / The percentages in the bottom row give each country an equal weight. / na=not ascertained

V29 SPORTS/RECREATION

Please look carefully at the following list of voluntary organizations and activities and say which, if any, do you belong to? Sports or recreation. (% "belong to")

	Total	Gender		Age			Education			Income			Political Affinity			Values			Ranking:
		Male	Female	16-29	30-49	50+	Lower	Medium	Upper	Lower	Middle	Upper	Left	Center	Right	Mat	Mixed	Postmat	
India	na	na	na	na	na	na	na	na	na	na	na	na	na	na	na	na	na	na	Netherlands 43
Nigeria	na	na	na	na	na	na	na	na	na	na	na	na	na	na	na	na	na	na	Denmark 34
China	04	05	04	07	03	03	05	05	05	03	06	04	04	04	02	03	05	11	Norway 33
Romania	03	05	01	06	02	02	01	05	05	02	04	04	04	04	02	02	04	05	West Germany 32
Turkey	na	na	na	na	na	na	na	na	na	na	na	na	na	na	na	na	na	na	Sweden 32
Poland	na	na	na	na	na	na	na	na	na	na	na	na	na	na	na	na	na	na	Iceland 30
Bulgaria	04	06	03	06	05	02	01	04	08	03	04	06	03	05	09	02	05	09	Ireland 24
Chile	12	21	04	15	13	07	08	15	14	09	14	15	15	12	12	08	13	15	Canada 23
Czechoslovakia	na	na	na	na	na	na	na	na	na	na	na	na	na	na	na	na	na	na	Finland 23
South Africa	na	na	na	na	na	na	na	na	na	na	na	na	na	na	na	na	na	na	East Germany 21
Lithuania	08	12	04	14	07	02	04	08	14	06	07	12	05	na	na	06	07	11	Belgium 20
Hungary	04	07	02	10	04	02	02	07	07	02	06	08	05	06	03	05	04	05	United States 20
Argentina	05	07	03	06	06	03	03	06	09	01	04	12	06	07	06	02	06	06	Britain 18
Brazil	08	13	04	10	09	03	04	09	14	05	11	10	10	09	08	07	09	10	South Korea 17
Mexico	08	10	06	10	08	04	07	06	13	06	10	09	10	07	10	08	09	06	North Ireland 17
Belarus	na	na	na	na	na	na	na	na	na	na	na	na	na	na	na	na	na	na	Austria 17
Russia	05	08	04	09	06	02	02	05	08	04	04	08	09	05	09	04	06	09	France 16
Moscow	na	na	na	na	na	na	na	na	na	na	na	na	na	na	na	na	na	na	Estonia 14
Latvia	09	14	05	15	08	04	06	10	08	05	09	11	na	na	na	08	10	12	Portugal 14
Estonia	14	21	09	23	13	08	10	16	16	14	15	16	na	na	na	13	15	24	Chile 12
Portugal	14	21	07	18	14	09	11	19	20	09	14	20	20	14	12	14	15	14	Italy 10
South Korea	17	14	20	17	19	16	10	16	22	14	16	27	14	19	17	17	18	16	Latvia 09
Ireland	24	33	16	37	26	12	14	32	44	07	21	40	31	24	25	16	24	31	Japan 09
North Ireland	17	22	14	36	16	06	12	19	52	04	13	38	07	22	14	12	19	20	Lithuania 08
Slovenia	08	13	04	16	09	03	04	10	13	05	10	11	13	11	11	06	08	19	Brazil 08
Spain	06	10	03	10	07	02	04	10	10	04	05	09	09	07	05	03	06	13	Mexico 08
East Germany	21	29	15	34	23	12	19	24	29	13	24	27	26	22	17	11	23	24	Slovenia 08
Britain	18	24	12	23	22	11	13	27	35	12	22	33	18	19	20	12	19	22	Spain 06
Italy	10	15	06	19	12	03	06	16	23	06	15	20	14	10	10	04	10	17	Argentina 05
Netherlands	43	41	43	52	46	27	33	45	52	34	46	55	46	43	43	28	44	47	Russia 05
Belgium	20	26	14	28	20	14	13	21	31	15	21	26	20	20	27	14	19	27	China 04
Austria	17	25	12	24	22	10	12	20	21	10	20	21	16	19	17	13	16	24	Bulgaria 04
France	16	20	12	21	17	10	11	17	27	10	17	25	18	17	15	05	17	22	Hungary 04
Canada	23	29	17	29	26	15	16	24	27	13	25	31	25	24	26	23	22	25	Romania 03
United States	20	25	15	27	26	12	11	19	29	11	20	30	19	23	21	14	20	26	
Iceland	30	38	23	40	32	15	20	38	33	na	na	na	33	28	32	30	30	31	
West Germany	32	40	25	40	40	21	29	39	37	22	36	38	34	33	33	21	35	34	
Denmark	34	40	27	49	38	17	14	41	40	20	37	50	36	30	39	26	37	32	
Finland	23	29	16	28	26	11	23	24	22	21	23	25	26	23	21	24	22	24	
Norway	33	37	28	40	41	19	13	33	43	22	37	41	34	32	37	30	33	42	
Sweden	32	40	23	43	36	18	27	35	33	32	26	40	33	33	33	29	32	34	
Japan	09	10	07	09	11	05	05	08	13	04	11	11	15	08	10	08	09	10	
Switzerland	na	na	na	na	na	na	na	na	na	na	na	na	na	na	na	na	na	na	
Total	**16**	**21**	**12**	**23**	**18**	**09**	**11**	**19**	**23**	**11**	**17**	**22**	**19**	**18**	**18**	**13**	**17**	**20**	

Note: Countries in the left column are ranked according to GNP per capita. / The percentages in the bottom row give each country an equal weight. / na=not ascertained.

V30 WOMEN'S GROUPS

Please look carefully at the following list of voluntary organizations and activities and say which, if any, do you belong to? Women's groups. (% "belong to")

Country	Total	Gender Male	Gender Female	Age 16-29	Age 30-49	Age 50+	Education Lower	Education Medium	Education Upper	Income Lower	Income Middle	Income Upper	Political Affinity Left	Political Affinity Center	Political Affinity Right	Values Mat	Values Mixed	Values Postmat	Ranking
India	na	na	na	na	na	na	na	na	na	na	na	na	na	na	na	na	na	na	Belgium 09
Nigeria	na	na	na	na	na	na	na	na	na	na	na	na	na	na	na	na	na	na	Netherlands 08
China	03	00	08	02	04	na	02	04	04	02	04	04	na	na	na	03	03	na	United States 08
Romania	01	00	01	00	01	01	01	01	00	01	01	00	01	00	01	00	01	01	East Germany 07
Turkey	na	na	na	na	na	na	na	na	na	na	na	na	na	na	na	na	na	na	Canada 07
Poland	na	na	na	na	na	na	na	na	na	na	na	na	na	na	na	na	na	na	Iceland 07
Bulgaria	02	00	03	na	01	02	01	02	02	02	01	02	02	02	02	01	02	00	West Germany 06
Chile	03	01	04	03	02	03	02	03	02	01	04	03	02	03	03	02	02	05	Ireland 05
Czechoslovakia	na	na	na	na	na	na	na	na	na	na	na	na	na	na	na	na	na	na	North Ireland 05
South Africa	na	na	na	na	na	na	na	na	na	na	na	na	na	na	na	na	na	na	Britain 05
Lithuania	03	00	05	02	03	02	00	04	01	03	03	01	na	na	na	04	02	03	Austria 04
Hungary	01	00	02	01	00	02	01	01	01	01	01	02	00	01	02	02	00	00	China 03
Argentina	01	00	01	00	02	01	01	00	00	00	00	01	00	01	02	01	01	01	Chile 03
Brazil	02	01	02	01	02	02	03	01	02	02	02	01	02	01	02	01	02	03	Lithuania 03
Mexico	02	01	03	03	02	02	02	02	02	01	02	04	02	02	03	02	02	02	South Korea 03
Belarus	na	na	na	na	na	na	na	na	na	na	na	na	na	na	na	na	na	na	Finland 03
Russia	02	01	03	01	03	02	02	02	na	03	02	02	03	02	02	02	02	02	Norway 03
Moscow	na	na	na	na	na	na	na	na	na	na	na	na	na	na	na	01	na	02	Sweden 03
Latvia	01	00	01	01	01	01	02	01	01	01	00	01	00	na	na	01	na	00	Japan 03
Estonia	02	00	03	01	03	02	01	03	01	02	01	02	na	na	na	03	02	00	Bulgaria 02
Portugal	00	00	00	00	00	00	00	00	02	00	00	02	00	00	01	00	00	03	Brazil 02
South Korea	03	06	01	02	05	03	03	03	04	01	04	06	03	02	04	04	04	01	Mexico 02
Ireland	05	00	09	02	05	06	03	06	07	03	04	07	05	04	06	04	05	05	Russia 02
North Ireland	05	00	09	00	05	09	05	05	07	06	04	07	04	04	09	09	05	00	Estonia 02
Slovenia	00	00	00	00	00	00	00	01	00	00	01	01	00	01	00	00	00	02	Denmark 02
Spain	01	00	01	00	01	01	01	00	01	01	01	01	02	00	01	01	01	01	Romania 01
East Germany	07	00	12	03	07	09	07	07	04	08	07	05	07	06	07	11	06	07	Hungary 01
Britain	05	00	10	00	04	10	05	06	05	08	03	03	02	06	04	07	05	04	Argentina 01
Italy	00	00	01	01	00	00	00	01	00	00	00	04	00	00	00	00	00	01	Latvia 01
Netherlands	08	00	11	03	11	09	10	06	08	08	10	08	08	08	09	11	07	09	Spain 01
Belgium	09	02	16	03	11	12	08	11	07	06	12	11	03	09	14	07	11	07	France 01
Austria	04	01	06	03	06	03	03	04	06	05	04	05	02	03	06	02	04	06	Portugal 00
France	01	00	02	01	01	01	00	02	02	01	01	02	02	01	00	01	00	03	Slovenia 00
Canada	07	01	12	03	06	11	08	06	07	07	07	06	06	07	07	08	06	07	Italy 00
United States	08	01	16	05	08	10	06	08	12	07	07	08	12	10	06	06	08	11	
Iceland	07	00	13	01	11	11	09	05	06	na	12	11	09	05	06	08	11	10	
West Germany	06	00	11	02	05	09	07	05	05	08	05	05	04	07	06	09	06	07	
Denmark	02	00	03	01	02	02	02	01	02	02	02	03	02	01	01	01	01	05	
Finland	03	01	06	03	02	08	07	02	03	08	02	06	04	04	03	06	03	02	
Norway	03	00	06	03	02	04	03	03	03	04	03	02	04	04	03	04	03	04	
Sweden	03	00	06	01	03	05	02	03	05	04	03	03	03	02	04	04	02	04	
Japan	03	01	05	02	03	04	04	03	02	03	04	03	04	04	03	04	02	01	
Switzerland	na	na	na	na	na	na	na	na	na	na	na	na	na	na	na	na	na	na	
Total	03	01	06	02	04	04	03	03	03	03	03	04	03	03	04	04	03	03	

Note: Countries in the left column are ranked according to GNP per capita. / The percentages in the bottom row give each country an equal weight. / na=not ascertained.

V31 PEACE MOVEMENT

Please look carefully at the following list of voluntary organizations and activities and say which, if any, do you belong to?
Peace movement. (% "belong to")

	Total	Gender		Age			Education			Income			Political Affinity			Values		
		Male	Female	16-29	30-49	50+	Lower	Medium	Upper	Lower	Middle	Upper	Left	Center	Right	Mat	Mixed	Postmat
India	na	na	na	na	na	na	na	na	na	na	na	na	na	na	na	na	na	na
Nigeria	na	na	na	na	na	na	na	na	na	na	na	na	na	na	na	na	na	na
China	01	00	01	00	00	01	00	01	01	00	01	01	01	na	na	00	00	00
Romania	00	00	00	00	00	01	01	00	00	00	00	00	01	00	00	00	00	00
Turkey	na	na	na	na	na	na	na	na	na	na	na	na	na	na	na	na	na	na
Poland	01	na	01	na	na	na	na	01	02	01	01	01	na	na	na	00	02	na
Bulgaria	01	01	01	01	01	02	00	01	02	01	01	00	00	01	02	00	01	02
Chile	01	01	00	01	00	01	00	01	02	na	na	na	01	01	00	00	00	na
Czechoslovakia	na	na	na	na	na	na	na	na	na	na	na	na	na	na	na	na	na	na
South Africa	na	na	na	na	na	na	na	na	na	na	na	na	na	na	na	01	na	na
Lithuania	01	01	00	00	01	01	01	00	02	01	01	00	na	00	02	01	01	01
Hungary	01	01	00	00	01	01	00	01	01	00	00	02	00	00	02	00	00	01
Argentina	00	00	00	00	00	00	00	01	00	00	03	01	00	01	03	02	02	04
Brazil	02	02	02	02	03	02	03	02	03	03	02	01	03	02	01	02	02	01
Mexico	01	01	01	02	01	01	02	01	01	02	01	02	02	02	01	01	01	00
Belarus	01	na	01	na	00	02	na	01	02	na	01	02	02	01	00	01	01	00
Russia	01	01	01	na	01	01	01	01	00	01	01	02	na	na	na	01	01	00
Moscow	na	na	na	na	na	01	01	02	00	01	01	01	na	na	na	01	01	00
Latvia	01	01	02	na	na	01	01	02	00	01	01	02	na	na	na	01	02	00
Estonia	01	02	01	01	01	01	01	01	02	00	01	02	01	na	01	00	01	03
Portugal	01	01	00	01	00	00	00	01	02	00	03	03	01	02	03	00	03	01
South Korea	02	01	03	01	03	02	04	01	02	01	00	02	04	00	01	00	01	01
Ireland	01	00	01	01	01	00	00	01	02	00	01	01	02	01	00	00	01	01
North Ireland	01	00	01	00	01	00	01	00	03	00	02	04	04	01	00	00	01	02
Slovenia	00	00	00	00	00	00	00	00	00	00	00	00	00	00	00	01	00	00
Spain	01	01	01	01	01	01	01	02	02	03	00	01	02	02	01	02	01	02
East Germany	02	01	02	01	03	02	01	02	03	00	01	01	04	01	00	01	01	05
Britain	01	01	01	01	01	01	01	01	02	00	01	04	02	00	01	00	01	03
Italy	01	01	01	02	02	00	01	02	02	01	03	05	05	03	01	02	02	05
Netherlands	03	03	03	01	03	03	03	03	03	03	02	03	06	01	00	02	01	06
Belgium	02	03	02	02	03	02	01	01	05	01	01	03	06	01	00	01	01	01
Austria	01	01	00	01	01	01	01	02	07	00	01	03	01	01	00	00	00	01
France	01	01	01	01	01	00	01	02	02	06	01	02	06	02	02	01	01	05
Canada	02	01	03	02	02	03	01	01	03	03	03	02	08	02	00	00	02	05
United States	02	02	02	01	03	02	02	01	03	03	02	03	03	01	01	00	02	04
Iceland	01	01	01	01	02	01	01	02	02	00	00	03	05	01	01	00	01	05
West Germany	02	02	02	03	02	02	02	03	07	02	01	02	05	02	01	00	02	05
Denmark	02	02	03	03	03	01	03	01	02	03	02	02	06	01	00	00	02	02
Finland	02	02	02	00	02	04	01	02	02	02	01	02	03	01	02	00	02	05
Norway	02	01	01	02	02	01	04	01	02	01	01	04	05	02	02	01	03	05
Sweden	03	02	03	03	04	02	01	03	07	02	03	00	01	01	00	03	01	05
Japan	01	00	01	00	01	01	00	01	00	01	01	na	na	na	na	01	na	00
Switzerland	na	na	na	na	na	na	na	na	na	na	na	na	na	na	na	01	01	02
Total	**01**	**01**	**01**	**01**	**01**	**01**	**01**	**01**	**02**	**01**	**01**	**02**	**03**	**01**	**01**	**01**	**01**	**02**

Note: Countries in the left column are ranked according to GNP per capita. / The percentages in the bottom row give each country an equal weight. / na=not ascertained.

Ranking:

Netherlands	03
Sweden	03
Brazil	02
South Korea	02
East Germany	02
Belgium	02
Canada	02
United States	02
West Germany	02
Denmark	02
Finland	02
Norway	02
China	01
Bulgaria	01
Chile	01
Lithuania	01
Hungary	01
Mexico	01
Russia	01
Latvia	01
Estonia	01
Portugal	01
Ireland	01
North Ireland	01
Spain	01
Britain	01
Italy	01
Austria	01
France	01
Iceland	01
Japan	01
Romania	00
Argentina	00
Slovenia	00

V32 ANIMAL RIGHTS

Please look carefully at the following list of voluntary organizations and activities and say which, if any, do you belong to? Animal rights. (% "belong to")

	Total	Gender		Age			Education			Income			Political Affinity			Values			Ranking:	
		Male	Female	16-29	30-49	50+	Lower	Medium	Upper	Lower	Middle	Upper	Left	Center	Right	Mat	Mixed	Postmat		
India	na	na	na	na	na	na	na	na	na	na	na	na	na	na	na	na	na	na	Netherlands	13
Nigeria	00	na	na	na	na	na	na	na	na	na	01	01	na	na	na	na	na	na	Belgium	08
China	00	00	01	00	00	01	00	00	00	00	00	00	na	na	na	00	01	00	Sweden	07
Romania	00	00	00	00	00	00	00	01	00	01	00	00	01	00	00	00	00	00	United States	05
Turkey	na	na	na	na	na	na	na	na	na	na	na	na	na	na	na	na	na	na	West Germany	05
Poland	na	na	na	na	na	na	na	na	na	na	na	na	na	na	na	na	na	na	Austria	04
Bulgaria	02	03	02	02	02	02	01	02	03	02	02	03	02	02	02	01	02	03	Denmark	04
Chile	01	02	01	01	01	02	01	01	02	01	01	02	01	02	01	01	01	02	Canada	03
Czechoslovakia	na	na	na	na	na	na	na	na	na	na	na	na	na	na	na	na	na	na	Bulgaria	02
South Africa	na	na	na	na	na	na	na	na	na	na	na	na	na	na	na	na	na	na	Brazil	02
Lithuania	01	01	00	01	01	01	00	02	01	01	02	01	na	na	na	00	01	02	Latvia	02
Hungary	01	02	01	02	01	01	01	02	01	01	02	02	02	01	03	00	02	08	East Germany	02
Argentina	00	00	00	00	00	00	00	00	00	00	00	00	00	01	00	00	00	00	Britain	02
Brazil	02	02	01	02	02	01	01	02	01	01	02	02	02	01	02	02	02	05	France	02
Mexico	01	01	01	01	01	02	02	00	01	01	01	02	00	01	02	02	01	00	Iceland	02
Belarus	na	na	na	na	na	na	na	na	na	na	na	na	na	na	na	na	na	na	Finland	02
Russia	01	01	01	01	01	01	01	01	01	01	00	02	02	01	00	01	02	00	Norway	02
Moscow	na	na	na	na	na	na	na	na	na	na	na	na	na	na	na	na	na	na	Chile	01
Latvia	02	na	02	03	na	02	04	03	01	na	04	03	na	na	na	01	03	00	Lithuania	01
Estonia	01	01	00	01	01	00	01	01	03	01	01	00	na	na	na	00	01	00	Hungary	01
Portugal	01	02	00	01	01	01	01	01	01	02	00	02	00	02	01	01	01	02	Mexico	01
South Korea	01	01	01	01	01	01	00	00	00	01	01	01	00	01	00	01	01	01	Russia	01
Ireland	01	01	01	02	01	01	01	01	02	00	01	01	04	00	01	00	01	02	Estonia	01
North Ireland	01	01	02	00	03	00	01	01	05	03	01	03	00	03	00	00	01	04	Portugal	01
Slovenia	01	01	00	01	01	00	01	01	04	01	00	01	02	00	01	02	01	02	South Korea	01
Spain	01	01	01	00	01	01	01	01	02	01	01	02	02	01	02	00	01	01	Ireland	01
East Germany	02	02	01	02	01	02	02	01	05	02	02	01	04	02	01	03	02	01	North Ireland	01
Britain	02	02	03	04	02	01	02	03	04	01	03	05	03	02	02	02	01	06	Slovenia	01
Italy	01	02	01	02	02	01	02	03	03	01	02	04	03	01	02	00	01	04	Spain	01
Netherlands	13	11	13	09	14	15	11	14	14	12	14	17	17	14	10	07	13	15	Italy	01
Belgium	08	09	07	07	09	07	08	08	07	09	07	05	08	08	08	07	09	08	China	00
Austria	04	04	05	04	04	05	04	05	06	03	04	03	05	05	03	05	05	05	Romania	00
France	02	02	03	05	05	03	01	03	04	02	05	03	02	02	05	02	01	05	Argentina	00
Canada	03	03	03	02	03	03	02	03	03	02	02	02	02	02	04	02	02	04	Japan	00
United States	05	06	05	05	06	05	04	05	07	05	05	07	10	05	04	04	06	06		
Iceland	02	03	02	03	02	02	03	03	06	na	na	na	05	02	01	05	02	01		
West Germany	05	05	05	04	05	05	04	06	06	04	05	07	04	04	06	04	05	05		
Denmark	04	04	04	05	05	03	01	05	05	02	05	01	04	04	05	04	03	08		
Finland	02	02	01	01	02	02	02	02	01	02	02	02	02	01	01	03	02	01		
Norway	02	01	02	01	02	02	00	01	03	02	01	06	01	06	08	01	02	03		
Sweden	07	06	07	06	08	06	06	07	09	07	08	06	07	06	00	06	07	09		
Japan	00	00	00	00	00	01	00	00	00	00	00	00	00	00	00	00	00	00		
Switzerland	na	na	na	na	na	na	na	na	na	na	na	na	na	na	na	na	na	na		
Total	02	02	02	02	03	02	02	03	03	02	03	03	03	03	02	02	02	03		

Note: Countries in the left column are ranked according to GNP per capita. / The percentages in the bottom row give each country an equal weight. / na=not ascertained.

V33 HEALTH-VOLUNTARY

Please look carefully at the following list of voluntary organizations and activities and say which, if any, do you belong to?   (% "belong to")
Voluntary organizations concerned with health.

	Total	Gender Male	Gender Female	Age 16-29	Age 30-49	Age 50+	Education Lower	Education Medium	Education Upper	Income Lower	Income Middle	Income Upper	Political Affinity Left	Political Affinity Center	Political Affinity Right	Values Mat	Values Mixed	Values Postmat
India	na	na	na	na	na	na	na	na	na	na	na	na	na	na	na	na	na	na
Nigeria	na	na	na	na	na	na	na	na	na	na	na	na	na	na	na	na	na	na
China	02	02	01	02	01	01	00	02	03	01	03	01	01	00	na	01	03	00
Romania	01	01	00	01	01	00	00	00	01	00	00	01	01	00	00	00	01	03
Turkey	na	na	na	na	na	na	na	na	na	na	na	na	na	na	na	na	na	na
Poland	na	na	na	na	na	na	na	na	na	na	na	na	na	na	na	na	na	na
Bulgaria	02	03	02	01	02	03	02	03	02	02	03	02	02	02	04	01	02	03
Chile	03	03	02	02	03	04	02	03	03	01	03	04	02	03	03	02	02	04
Czechoslovakia	na	na	na	na	na	na	na	na	na	na	na	na	na	na	na	na	na	na
South Africa	na	na	na	na	na	na	na	na	na	na	na	na	na	na	na	na	na	na
Lithuania	01	02	01	02	01	02	01	02	02	01	01	01	na	na	na	02	02	01
Hungary	04	02	05	02	05	03	04	04	07	04	04	08	05	05	02	04	03	05
Argentina	02	02	02	01	02	03	02	02	03	01	01	02	na	03	02	02	01	03
Brazil	03	04	03	03	05	03	04	02	08	02	04	04	04	03	05	02	04	06
Mexico	02	02	02	01	02	04	02	02	02	01	02	03	04	02	01	02	01	03
Belarus	na	na	na	na	na	na	na	na	na	na	na	na	na	na	na	na	na	na
Russia	01	00	01	01	01	01	01	01	01	01	01	01	01	01	01	01	01	00
Moscow	na	na	na	na	na	na	na	na	na	na	na	na	na	na	na	na	na	na
Latvia	02	01	03	02	03	02	00	03	02	02	02	03	na	na	na	03	02	01
Estonia	02	02	02	00	02	01	01	01	01	02	02	01	na	na	na	01	02	00
Portugal	03	04	02	03	02	02	03	03	01	02	04	01	na	03	02	03	03	00
South Korea	15	13	16	11	17	16	17	13	16	12	15	21	17	13	16	16	13	17
Ireland	03	02	04	03	04	03	02	05	04	01	02	06	04	03	04	02	03	05
North Ireland	03	02	04	03	03	05	03	04	07	03	05	05	04	03	05	03	04	02
Slovenia	01	02	01	00	02	01	01	01	01	01	01	01	03	01	01	01	01	00
Spain	01	01	01	00	02	01	01	02	03	01	01	02	02	01	02	01	01	02
East Germany	05	03	07	06	05	05	05	06	04	04	06	05	05	05	07	03	05	06
Britain	04	04	04	03	05	05	03	03	10	05	04	03	04	04	04	02	04	04
Italy	03	02	03	02	03	02	02	03	09	03	03	04	03	03	04	01	03	04
Netherlands	20	18	20	11	23	25	19	18	22	14	24	22	19	20	23	20	22	17
Belgium	04	04	04	03	04	04	03	03	07	03	05	06	05	04	05	03	04	06
Austria	03	04	03	03	04	03	03	04	03	03	04	04	06	04	02	02	04	03
France	03	04	02	02	03	04	02	03	05	03	02	06	04	03	03	02	02	05
Canada	09	07	10	06	09	11	08	08	11	11	09	08	15	09	07	06	08	11
United States	08	06	09	06	07	09	07	06	10	05	08	10	07	09	07	06	08	08
Iceland	05	03	07	03	06	04	06	04	05	05	04	05	05	05	04	04	04	06
West Germany	04	05	04	04	04	05	04	05	07	05	04	05	06	04	06	05	04	03
Denmark	06	04	07	04	05	08	04	06	07	03	06	10	07	03	06	03	06	05
Finland	07	06	08	04	08	07	05	05	11	07	07	08	08	06	07	18	06	07
Norway	12	09	16	05	10	20	07	09	13	14	12	09	13	11	14	16	11	10
Sweden	02	03	02	02	02	03	01	02	04	02	02	03	02	02	03	02	02	02
Japan	01	01	01	01	01	01	01	01	01	00	02	01	02	02	01	00	01	03
Switzerland	na	na	na	na	na	na	na	na	na	na	na	na	na	na	na	na	na	na
Total	04	04	05	03	05	05	04	04	06	04	05	06	06	05	05	04	04	05

Ranking:

Netherlands	20
South Korea	15
Norway	12
Canada	09
United States	08
Finland	07
Denmark	06
East Germany	05
Iceland	05
Hungary	04
Britain	04
Belgium	04
West Germany	04
Chile	03
Brazil	03
Portugal	03
Ireland	03
North Ireland	03
Italy	03
Austria	03
France	03
China	02
Bulgaria	02
Argentina	02
Mexico	02
Latvia	02
Estonia	02
Sweden	02
Romania	01
Lithuania	01
Russia	01
Slovenia	01
Spain	01
Japan	01

Note: Countries in the left column are ranked according to GNP per capita. / The percentages in the bottom row give each country an equal weight. / na=not ascertained.

V34 OTHER GROUPS

Please look carefully at the following list of voluntary organizations and activities and say which, if any, do you belong to?
Other groups. (% "belong to")

	Total	Gender		Age			Education			Income			Political Affinity			Values		
		Male	Female	16-29	30-49	50+	Lower	Medium	Upper	Lower	Middle	Upper	Left	Center	Right	Mat	Mixed	Postmat
India	na	na	na	na	na	na	na	na	na	na	na	na	na	na	na	na	na	na
Nigeria	na	na	na	na	na	na	na	na	na	na	na	na	na	na	na	na	na	na
China	02	02	02	02	02	02	02	01	04	01	02	03	01	02	02	03	01	02
Romania	02	03	01	01	02	02	02	01	05	03	02	02	01	02	02	01	02	06
Turkey	na	na	na	na	na	na	na	na	na	na	na	na	na	na	na	na	na	na
Poland	na	na	na	na	na	na	na	na	na	na	na	na	na	na	na	na	na	na
Bulgaria	03	04	03	04	02	03	03	04	02	03	04	02	03	03	na	04	03	02
Chile	04	04	03	01	05	04	03	04	05	02	04	05	05	03	06	02	04	05
Czechoslovakia	na	na	na	na	na	na	na	na	na	na	na	na	na	na	na	na	na	na
South Africa	na	na	na	na	na	na	na	na	na	na	na	na	na	na	na	na	na	na
Lithuania	02	02	02	01	02	03	01	02	03	02	01	02	na	na	na	na	02	03
Hungary	02	02	02	01	02	02	02	02	01	02	01	04	05	01	04	02	02	00
Argentina	03	04	02	02	04	03	02	03	05	01	04	04	06	02	04	01	02	05
Brazil	00	00	00	00	00	01	00	08	00	00	00	00	00	00	01	01	00	01
Mexico	02	02	01	01	02	01	01	02	02	01	02	02	02	01	03	01	01	01
Belarus	na	na	na	01	na	na	01	na	na	01	na	na	02	na	na	02	01	na
Russia	02	02	02	01	02	03	02	02	03	na	02	03	03	03	01	02	02	03
Moscow	na	na	na	na	na	na	na	na	na	na	na	na	na	03	na	na	02	03
Latvia	04	05	04	06	04	03	04	na	03	04	04	05	na	na	na	02	05	05
Estonia	04	05	04	03	07	02	02	na	07	05	03	05	na	na	na	04	05	02
Portugal	03	04	na	03	03	02	02	03	04	02	na	na	na	na	na	04	na	03
South Korea	04	03	06	05	04	03	03	04	06	04	05	05	05	06	03	04	02	11
Ireland	02	03	01	01	03	02	02	02	01	04	02	02	05	06	04	04	03	03
North Ireland	07	07	06	05	11	02	03	02	01	11	08	12	08	07	10	01	03	13
Slovenia	05	08	02	05	04	14	06	04	17	07	06	07	07	08	04	03	07	13
Spain	04	04	05	02	07	04	04	04	06	04	04	05	06	04	04	05	04	10
East Germany	08	10	07	06	09	08	07	12	11	06	10	08	06	06	09	04	05	07
Britain	08	08	08	05	10	08	07	11	10	05	09	12	10	07	10	05	09	08
Italy	02	02	02	01	02	03	02	04	10	02	02	04	08	03	04	08	08	02
Netherlands	09	14	08	07	10	14	07	04	13	07	02	12	03	02	11	01	03	11
Belgium	05	06	04	05	05	06	04	06	06	08	06	08	05	06	07	10	09	08
Austria	06	09	03	05	05	07	05	07	03	04	05	06	06	06	06	05	04	05
France	05	06	05	04	05	07	04	05	09	04	05	06	06	03	08	04	06	06
Canada	13	14	12	15	15	13	11	13	09	11	14	14	08	13	16	10	13	14
United States	10	13	08	10	10	12	08	13	13	18	10	13	21	11	12	06	11	12
Iceland	10	11	09	07	11	11	07	12	11	na	na	na	11	09	10	06	12	12
West Germany	09	11	07	10	08	09	09	09	08	10	08	10	10	09	10	07	09	05
Denmark	11	12	10	05	11	09	12	09	08	13	08	12	09	10	14	12	10	06
Finland	09	10	09	08	08	15	09	12	09	12	07	09	10	11	09	21	10	12
Norway	19	23	16	18	21	17	17	18	22	18	14	13	08	19	20	21	07	na
Sweden	19	18	19	07	20	24	17	15	29	20	14	22	22	16	20	16	19	31
Japan	05	07	03	02	07	04	02	06	06	02	06	06	08	06	05	18	18	21
Switzerland	na	na	na	na	na	na	na	na	na	na	na	na	na	na	na	na	na	na
Total	06	07	05	04	07	07	05	06	08	05	06	07	08	06	07	06	06	08

Ranking:

Norway	19
Sweden	19
Canada	13
Denmark	11
United States	10
Iceland	10
Netherlands	09
West Germany	09
Finland	09
East Germany	08
Britain	08
North Ireland	07
Austria	06
Slovenia	05
Belgium	05
France	05
Japan	05
Chile	04
Latvia	04
Estonia	04
South Korea	04
Spain	04
Bulgaria	03
Argentina	03
Portugal	03
China	02
Romania	02
Lithuania	02
Hungary	02
Mexico	02
Russia	02
Ireland	02
Italy	02
Brazil	00

Note: Countries in the left column are ranked according to GNP per capita. / The percentages in the bottom row give each country an equal weight. / na=not ascertained.

V37-V54. Unpaid voluntary work in voluntary organizations

Percentage "do unpaid work for"

Category	Percentage
None	50
Sports/recreation	7
Religious organization	6
Education/cultural	5
Social welfare	4
Trade unions	4
Political parties	4
Youth work	4
Professional association	3
Other groups	3
Local community action	2
Environment	2
Women's groups	2
Health-voluntary	2
Human rights	1
Peace movement	1
Animal rights	1

V37 SOCIAL WELFARE

Please look at the following list of voluntary organizations and activities and say which, if any, are you currently doing unpaid voluntary work for? Social welfare services for elderly, handicapped, or deprived people. (% "do unpaid voluntary work")

	Total	Gender		Age			Education			Income			Political Affinity			Values		
		Male	Female	16-29	30-49	50+	Lower	Medium	Upper	Lower	Middle	Upper	Left	Center	Right	Mat	Mixed	Postmat
India	na	na	na	na	na	na	na	na	na	na	na	na	na	na	na	na	na	na
Nigeria	na	na	na	na	na	na	na	na	na	na	na	na	na	na	na	na	na	na
China	16	18	13	13	16	19	13	19	15	12	22	15	na	na	na	14	18	17
Romania	02	02	02	00	02	02	01	02	04	01	03	01	01	03	02	01	02	04
Turkey	na	na	na	na	na	na	na	na	na	na	na	na	na	na	na	na	na	na
Poland	na	na	na	na	na	na	na	na	na	na	na	na	na	na	na	na	na	na
Bulgaria	02	03	01	03	na	na	na	02	02	01	02	02	02	02	01	01	02	08
Chile	04	03	04	02	02	01	04	04	03	02	04	05	02	04	05	03	03	07
Czechoslovakia	na	na	na	na	na	na	na	na	na	na	na	na	na	na	na	na	na	na
South Africa	na	na	na	na	na	na	na	na	na	na	na	na	na	na	na	na	na	na
Lithuania	01	01	01	00	01	01	00	01	02	02	00	na	na	na	na	01	01	01
Hungary	02	02	02	02	01	02	01	02	02	02	01	03	01	02	02	02	02	03
Argentina	02	01	03	02	02	02	02	02	02	00	02	03	01	02	04	02	02	01
Brazil	06	06	07	04	08	09	06	05	12	06	05	08	06	07	06	06	07	05
Mexico	03	02	04	04	02	04	02	03	04	02	02	04	02	03	03	02	03	03
Belarus	na	na	na	na	na	na	na	na	na	na	na	na	na	na	na	na	na	na
Russia	01	01	02	00	01	02	01	01	02	01	01	02	02	01	02	01	01	01
Moscow	na	na	na	na	na	na	na	na	na	na	na	na	na	na	na	na	na	na
Latvia	04	03	05	03	04	07	04	na	04	03	06	03	na	na	na	03	05	01
Estonia	01	01	01	01	01	02	01	01	02	01	00	02	na	na	na	00	02	04
Portugal	03	02	03	02	02	03	03	03	02	02	03	02	02	na	03	03	03	02
South Korea	07	07	08	05	09	09	08	06	09	06	08	09	02	08	03	03	03	01
Ireland	07	05	08	04	06	10	06	07	12	04	07	08	09	08	07	08	07	07
North Ireland	05	02	07	05	03	06	04	06	07	04	04	08	08	06	05	06	06	10
Slovenia	01	01	01	01	02	na	01	01	03	01	02	02	00	06	05	03	06	02
Spain	04	02	04	02	04	04	02	04	05	04	02	04	02	02	04	02	01	04
East Germany	04	03	06	01	04	07	04	04	05	07	03	03	04	05	04	04	02	04
Britain	05	05	05	02	04	07	04	03	08	07	04	05	03	06	04	06	05	07
Italy	06	04	08	04	06	07	05	05	08	07	04	05	03	05	05	03	02	04
Netherlands	09	06	10	03	09	08	08	10	08	02	05	02	02	03	03	03	02	04
Belgium	06	06	07	05	06	07	05	07	11	06	07	07	08	06	08	11	10	07
Austria	03	02	03	02	03	03	01	03	04	01	03	04	05	06	08	04	06	08
France	05	05	06	02	04	10	04	05	08	04	05	09	05	06	09	03	03	04
Canada	06	04	08	03	06	08	07	05	08	07	07	05	06	06	07	05	05	07
United States	06	05	08	04	04	08	05	04	09	05	05	06	03	03	07	06	05	08
Iceland	10	11	11	05	12	12	07	11	11	05	na	na	08	na	na	11	10	07
West Germany	03	02	04	01	02	05	03	03	03	03	04	03	09	12	12	04	06	03
Denmark	02	01	03	02	03	03	03	03	03	02	05	02	04	02	02	01	03	03
Finland	08	05	10	00	06	16	03	01	09	10	07	08	01	02	08	05	02	03
Norway	04	04	05	02	04	07	03	07	06	10	05	05	12	04	06	24	07	05
Sweden	03	02	03	01	04	05	03	02	07	03	04	03	02	05	06	06	04	03
Japan	02	02	05	01	02	02	01	01	02	01	02	03	02	03	03	03	02	02
Switzerland	na	na	na	na	na	na	na	na	na	na	na	na	na	na	na	na	na	na
Total	04	04	05	03	04	06	04	04	06	04	04	05	04	04	05	05	04	05

Ranking:

China	16
Iceland	10
Netherlands	09
Finland	08
South Korea	07
Ireland	07
Brazil	06
Belgium	06
Canada	06
United States	06
North Ireland	05
Britain	05
France	05
Chile	04
Latvia	04
East Germany	04
Norway	04
Spain	04
Mexico	03
Portugal	03
Italy	03
Austria	03
West Germany	03
Sweden	03
Romania	02
Bulgaria	02
Hungary	02
Argentina	02
Denmark	02
Japan	02
Lithuania	01
Russia	01
Estonia	01
Slovenia	01

Note: Countries in the left column are ranked according to GNP per capita. / The percentages in the bottom row give each country an equal weight. / na=not ascertained.

V38 RELIGIOUS ORGANIZATION

Please look at the following list of voluntary organizations and activities and say which, if any, are you currently doing unpaid voluntary work for? Religious or church organizations. (% "do unpaid voluntary work")

	Total	Gender Male	Gender Female	Age 16-29	Age 30-49	Age 50+	Education Lower	Education Medium	Education Upper	Income Lower	Income Middle	Income Upper	Political Affinity Left	Political Affinity Center	Political Affinity Right	Values Mat	Values Mixed	Values Postmat
India	na	na	na	na	na	na	na	na	na	na	na	na	na	na	na	na	na	na
Nigeria	na	na	na	na	na	na	na	na	na	na	na	na	na	na	na	na	na	na
China	02	02	02	01	02	03	03	01	01	02	02	02	na	na	na	03	01	04
Romania	04	04	04	02	05	06	06	03	05	05	05	04	04	05	05	05	04	05
Turkey	na	na	na	na	na	na	na	na	na	na	na	na	na	na	na	na	na	na
Poland	na	na	na	na	na	na	na	na	na	na	na	na	na	na	na	na	na	na
Bulgaria	02	02	03	03	03	02	01	03	03	04	01	02	01	02	06	01	03	00
Chile	12	10	13	09	12	17	13	11	12	14	11	11	09	13	13	12	11	15
Czechoslovakia	na	na	na	na	na	na	na	na	na	na	na	na	na	na	na	na	na	na
South Africa	na	na	na	na	na	na	na	na	na	na	na	na	na	na	na	na	na	na
Lithuania	03	03	03	01	01	06	06	02	03	04	03	01	na	na	na	02	03	05
Hungary	03	03	02	00	02	04	03	02	02	04	02	01	03	02	02	04	02	03
Argentina	05	04	05	06	05	05	04	06	05	04	04	05	01	06	07	03	06	05
Brazil	13	10	15	11	12	17	13	11	16	13	09	14	09	14	13	13	12	12
Mexico	10	08	12	09	09	12	10	10	07	09	09	11	09	09	10	10	10	06
Belarus	01	na	01	na	na	01	na	na	01	01	01	00	01	01	02	na	01	na
Russia	01	01	01	01	01	01	01	01	01	01	01	00	01	01	02	01	01	00
Moscow	na	na	na	na	na	na	na	na	na	na	03	na	na	na	na	na	na	na
Latvia	03	03	03	04	03	03	01	04	02	03	03	03	na	na	na	03	03	03
Estonia	01	01	01	00	01	01	01	01	01	02	00	01	na	na	na	01	01	02
Portugal	06	05	07	07	05	07	07	02	06	06	05	06	04	07	07	07	05	07
South Korea	07	08	07	06	08	09	06	07	08	07	07	09	08	08	07	07	08	09
Ireland	07	05	09	06	07	07	06	08	07	02	08	08	05	07	08	05	07	09
North Ireland	10	07	13	08	13	09	14	15	21	04	06	16	04	10	15	12	10	07
Slovenia	02	02	02	04	01	01	01	01	03	01	03	03	02	03	06	02	02	02
Spain	07	05	07	04	07	07	05	07	07	04	05	07	04	09	09	07	07	05
East Germany	09	09	08	04	12	08	09	08	08	08	10	08	04	09	14	06	08	13
Britain	06	04	08	02	06	08	04	11	12	06	05	08	05	06	07	05	05	09
Italy	06	06	07	05	05	06	09	11	09	08	06	05	03	11	05	04	06	09
Netherlands	10	10	09	05	11	13	09	08	11	07	10	12	05	10	15	05	11	09
Belgium	07	07	07	04	07	08	05	07	10	08	08	09	03	06	13	04	07	10
Austria	06	05	06	03	07	06	05	06	08	08	05	05	06	04	09	05	06	06
France	05	04	06	02	04	08	03	07	06	04	05	05	03	03	12	05	06	04
Canada	16	11	20	11	13	22	16	15	16	16	19	13	13	16	19	19	15	13
United States	29	28	30	21	30	31	25	28	32	20	32	32	16	31	35	31	28	29
Iceland	04	02	05	03	04	03	03	04	04	na	na	na	02	03	06	03	04	04
West Germany	07	06	08	05	06	09	07	06	12	07	07	07	04	07	11	08	07	07
Denmark	02	02	03	02	04	02	03	03	02	02	02	03	04	02	03	00	01	01
Finland	07	07	06	05	05	11	07	06	07	07	04	09	02	05	09	15	05	08
Norway	06	05	07	04	05	08	07	05	05	07	06	05	02	07	07	07	05	06
Sweden	03	03	02	02	03	04	02	02	05	05	03	03	02	04	02	06	03	01
Japan	03	03	02	01	02	04	05	02	01	04	01	03	04	03	02	03	03	03
Switzerland	na	na	na	na	na	na	na	na	na	na	na	na	na	na	na	na	na	na
Total	**07**	**06**	**07**	**05**	**07**	**08**	**06**	**07**	**08**	**06**	**06**	**07**	**05**	**07**	**09**	**07**	**06**	**07**

Ranking:

United States	29
Canada	16
Brazil	13
Chile	12
Mexico	10
North Ireland	10
Netherlands	10
East Germany	09
South Korea	07
Ireland	07
Belgium	07
West Germany	07
Finland	07
Spain	07
Portugal	06
Britain	06
Italy	06
Austria	06
Norway	05
Argentina	05
France	05
Romania	04
Iceland	04
Lithuania	03
Hungary	03
Latvia	03
Sweden	03
Japan	03
China	02
Bulgaria	02
Slovenia	02
Denmark	02
Russia	01
Estonia	01

Note: Countries in the left column are ranked according to GNP per capita. / The percentages in the bottom row give each country an equal weight. / na=not ascertained.

V39 EDUCATION/CULTURAL

Please look at the following list of voluntary organizations and activities and say which, if any, are you currently doing unpaid voluntary work for? Education, art, music, or cultural activities. (% "do unpaid voluntary work")

	Total	Gender		Age			Education			Income			Political Affinity			Values		
		Male	Female	16-29	30-49	50+	Lower	Medium	Upper	Lower	Middle	Upper	Left	Center	Right	Mat	Mixed	Postmat
India	na	na	na	na	na	na	na	na	na	na	na	na	na	na	na	na	na	na
Nigeria	na	na	na	na	na	na	na	na	na	na	na	na	na	na	na	na	na	na
China	08	09	08	10	07	09	07	09	12	07	10	09	01	na	01	06	09	19
Romania	02	02	01	02	07	01	00	01	04	02	02	01	01	03	01	01	01	05
Turkey	na	na	na	na	na	na	na	na	na	na	na	na	na	na	na	na	na	na
Poland	na	na	na	na	na	na	na	na	na	na	na	na	na	na	na	na	na	na
Bulgaria	03	03	02	04	03	01	00	02	06	02	02	03	02	03	02	02	02	08
Chile	06	07	06	07	06	05	02	07	11	03	07	09	07	07	06	03	06	11
Czechoslovakia	na	na	na	na	na	na	na	na	na	na	na	na	na	na	na	na	na	na
South Africa	na	na	na	na	na	na	na	na	na	na	na	na	na	na	na	na	na	na
Lithuania	06	06	05	07	06	04	04	04	16	06	04	08	na	na	na	04	05	06
Hungary	02	02	02	04	02	01	00	02	10	01	03	04	02	03	01	02	02	03
Argentina	04	04	04	04	05	03	02	05	06	02	06	05	08	03	05	02	04	05
Brazil	03	04	02	03	02	03	02	03	07	01	03	04	03	02	04	02	03	06
Mexico	05	05	06	08	03	05	05	05	07	04	05	08	11	04	05	04	06	07
Belarus	na	na	na	na	na	na	na	na	na	na	na	na	na	na	na	na	na	na
Russia	03	02	03	01	04	02	01	01	05	02	03	03	05	03	05	03	02	05
Moscow	na	na	na	na	na	na	na	na	na	na	na	na	na	na	na	na	na	na
Latvia	05	04	05	04	04	na	01	na	na	01	06	06	na	na	na	na	05	04
Estonia	07	08	07	05	09	07	03	06	15	06	06	11	11	04	05	04	08	17
Portugal	04	06	03	06	05	02	03	03	10	02	03	08	05	05	02	04	03	10
South Korea	03	02	04	03	03	03	01	03	04	04	04	04	04	02	04	02	04	04
Ireland	04	04	04	05	05	03	02	05	14	01	04	07	06	04	05	02	03	08
North Ireland	03	02	04	04	11	02	02	04	10	00	04	06	00	03	04	03	03	02
Slovenia	03	04	03	05	04	01	01	04	08	02	03	06	07	04	03	02	03	09
Spain	04	05	04	05	07	01	01	05	11	00	04	05	05	04	04	04	04	09
East Germany	04	04	03	04	04	03	03	03	08	02	04	04	06	03	03	03	03	06
Britain	03	03	04	02	03	04	01	04	10	03	03	04	03	03	04	03	02	06
Italy	03	03	02	04	03	02	02	07	02	02	04	05	03	03	01	02	02	04
Netherlands	11	08	11	07	15	08	06	14	13	08	12	13	11	10	12	08	11	11
Belgium	07	09	06	07	10	06	03	08	14	04	09	12	09	08	09	03	06	13
Austria	04	07	03	04	05	04	05	04	04	03	04	07	06	04	05	03	04	05
France	05	05	05	04	05	05	03	04	10	03	06	07	07	06	03	01	04	10
Canada	09	08	10	09	11	08	04	08	15	06	09	13	13	09	11	06	09	11
United States	10	08	12	07	15	07	06	06	17	05	10	14	15	10	09	06	09	14
Iceland	05	05	06	06	06	02	02	06	07	na	na	na	07	07	03	02	06	07
West Germany	04	05	03	04	05	04	03	05	09	03	05	05	05	04	05	03	04	04
Denmark	05	06	03	05	05	05	00	06	06	04	05	07	08	03	04	01	04	07
Finland	09	09	08	08	08	11	08	05	13	11	06	10	07	06	12	06	08	09
Norway	05	07	04	05	06	05	02	04	08	04	06	06	08	05	04	05	05	10
Sweden	03	03	03	03	04	03	01	03	07	05	02	04	04	04	03	02	03	05
Japan	03	02	04	02	04	02	01	03	04	02	03	05	02	04	05	04	03	05
Switzerland	na	na	na	na	na	na	na	na	na	na	na	na	na	na	na	na	na	na
Total	05	05	05	05	06	04	03	05	09	03	05	07	06	05	05	03	05	08

Ranking:

Netherlands	11
United States	10
Canada	09
Finland	09
China	08
Estonia	07
Belgium	07
Chile	06
Lithuania	06
Mexico	05
Latvia	05
France	05
Iceland	05
Denmark	05
Norway	05
Argentina	04
Portugal	04
Ireland	04
East Germany	04
Austria	04
West Germany	04
Spain	04
Bulgaria	03
Brazil	03
Russia	03
South Korea	03
North Ireland	03
Slovenia	03
Britain	03
Italy	03
Sweden	03
Japan	03
Romania	02
Hungary	02

Note: Countries in the left column are ranked according to GNP per capita. / The percentages in the bottom row give each country an equal weight. / na=not ascertained.

V40 TRADE UNIONS

Please look at the following list of voluntary organizations and activities and say which, if any, are you currently doing unpaid voluntary work for? Trade unions. (% "do unpaid voluntary work")

	Total	Gender Male	Gender Female	Age 16-29	Age 30-49	Age 50+	Educ. Lower	Educ. Medium	Educ. Upper	Income Lower	Income Middle	Income Upper	Pol. Left	Pol. Center	Pol. Right	Values Mat	Values Mixed	Values Postmat
India	na	na	na	na	na	na	na	na	na	na	na	na	na	na	na	na	na	na
Nigeria	na	na	na	na	na	na	na	na	na	na	na	na	na	na	na	na	na	na
China	01	01	01	01	01	01	00	01	01	na	02	01	na	na	na	01	01	02
Romania	14	16	12	18	22	05	07	19	17	17	13	14	11	15	17	14	15	11
Turkey	na	na	na	na	na	na	na	na	na	na	na	na	na	na	na	na	na	na
Poland	na	na	na	na	na	na	na	na	na	na	na	na	na	na	na	na	na	na
Bulgaria	05	05	05	04	06	03	02	05	07	05	04	05	04	07	02	03	05	07
Chile	02	04	01	01	03	01	01	02	03	01	03	03	03	03	01	01	01	06
Czechoslovakia	na	na	na	na	na	na	na	na	na	na	na	na	na	na	na	na	na	na
South Africa	na	na	na	na	na	na	na	na	na	na	na	na	na	na	na	na	na	na
Lithuania	09	08	11	08	13	07	04	10	15	10	09	09	07	na	na	09	10	11
Hungary	05	04	05	02	07	04	06	06	12	03	05	10	07	06	01	05	05	03
Argentina	01	01	00	00	01	01	01	00	00	01	00	01	02	00	01	00	00	02
Brazil	02	02	01	01	02	02	02	01	05	02	02	02	02	02	01	01	02	03
Mexico	02	03	01	01	03	02	02	00	02	02	02	03	04	02	01	02	02	01
Belarus	na	na	na	na	na	na	na	na	na	na	na	na	na	na	na	na	na	na
Russia	09	07	10	08	11	07	04	06	14	05	09	13	13	10	07	06	11	10
Moscow	na	na	na	na	na	na	na	na	na	na	na	na	na	na	na	na	na	na
Latvia	09	08	10	08	10	na	07	10	08	11	08	09	na	na	na	12	09	09
Estonia	11	09	13	05	15	11	07	12	14	09	13	12	na	na	na	10	12	14
Portugal	01	02	01	01	01	02	02	01	02	02	01	00	02	02	00	02	01	01
South Korea	01	01	02	02	02	02	01	01	02	01	01	02	02	01	02	01	02	01
Ireland	01	02	01	00	02	01	00	02	03	00	02	03	02	01	02	00	01	02
North Ireland	02	05	00	00	03	03	01	03	00	01	03	03	04	01	04	00	02	04
Slovenia	02	03	01	00	04	01	03	02	03	02	02	03	02	02	03	02	02	03
Spain	01	04	00	01	04	00	01	01	04	00	01	01	05	00	00	00	01	04
East Germany	10	12	09	09	14	08	09	13	12	05	12	14	17	07	09	05	10	12
Britain	01	02	01	01	01	01	01	01	03	01	03	00	02	03	01	02	01	02
Italy	03	04	01	01	04	02	03	05	03	03	04	02	05	01	03	02	02	05
Netherlands	01	01	01	01	01	02	01	03	02	03	01	03	01	01	02	00	01	01
Belgium	02	03	01	02	03	02	03	03	02	03	03	02	03	02	02	01	02	04
Austria	02	05	01	00	04	02	03	03	02	03	03	03	06	03	01	01	01	04
France	02	04	01	01	03	03	02	05	04	02	03	05	05	01	03	03	03	06
Canada	04	05	02	03	05	03	05	07	05	07	10	02	06	05	05	09	08	08
United States	02	03	01	03	03	02	03	07	08	02	07	10	07	06	05	05	06	12
Iceland	03	02	04	01	05	02	03	03	04	na	03	03	06	01	03	02	03	05
West Germany	02	05	01	01	04	02	02	03	02	01	03	07	03	03	01	01	01	03
Denmark	03	04	02	01	04	02	03	03	05	02	03	11	08	03	02	03	03	06
Finland	08	09	07	06	09	08	07	07	10	07	07	11	17	06	06	09	08	08
Norway	06	07	06	03	10	04	02	07	08	02	07	10	07	06	05	05	06	12
Sweden	06	08	05	04	09	05	06	06	08	08	06	07	08	06	05	08	05	10
Japan	01	03	00	01	02	02	01	01	01	01	02	02	08	00	01	02	01	03
Switzerland	na	na	na	na	na	na	na	na	na	na	na	na	na	na	na	na	na	na
Total	**04**	**05**	**03**	**03**	**06**	**03**	**03**	**04**	**05**	**03**	**04**	**05**	**06**	**03**	**03**	**03**	**04**	**05**

Ranking:

Romania	14
Estonia	11
East Germany	10
Lithuania	09
Russia	09
Latvia	09
Finland	08
Norway	06
Sweden	06
Bulgaria	05
Hungary	05
Canada	04
Italy	03
Iceland	03
Denmark	03
Chile	02
Brazil	02
Mexico	02
North Ireland	02
Slovenia	02
Belgium	02
Austria	02
France	02
United States	02
West Germany	02
China	01
Argentina	01
Portugal	01
South Korea	01
Ireland	01
Britain	01
Netherlands	01
Spain	01
Japan	01

Note: Countries in the left column are ranked according to GNP per capita. / The percentages in the bottom row give each country an equal weight. / na=not ascertained
The Chinese questionnaire translated "Trade Unions" (V22 and V40) as "Trading Associations," which was chosen by very few people. "Professional Associations" was translated as "occupational organizations," which evokes the (government-sponsored) labor unions; thus, for China. V27 is functionally equivalent to V22.

V41 POLITICAL PARTIES

Please look at the following list of voluntary organizations and activities and say which, if any, are you currently doing unpaid voluntary work for? Political parties or groups. (% "do unpaid voluntary work")

	Total	Gender Male	Gender Female	Age 16-29	Age 30-49	Age 50+	Education Lower	Education Medium	Education Upper	Income Lower	Income Middle	Income Upper	Political Affinity Left	Political Affinity Center	Political Affinity Right	Values Mat	Values Mixed	Values Postmat
India	na	na	na	na	na	na	na	na	na	na	na	na	na	na	na	na	na	na
Nigeria	na	na	na	na	na	na	na	na	na	na	na	na	na	na	na	na	na	na
China	26	29	21	14	32	30	14	29	38	19	30	31	na	na	na	22	31	28
Romania	02	03	01	01	02	03	01	02	05	02	03	02	03	01	05	02	02	06
Turkey	na	na	na	na	na	na	na	na	na	na	na	na	na	na	na	na	na	na
Poland	05	07	03	03	06	04	02	03	10	04	04	05	07	06	02	05	04	05
Bulgaria	02	03	01	02	02	02	02	03	02	02	03	03	06	01	02	00	02	06
Chile	na	03	01	02	06	04	02	03	02	02	03	03	06	06	02	05	04	na
Czechoslovakia	na	na	na	na	na	na	na	na	na	na	na	na	na	na	na	na	na	na
South Africa	na	na	na	na	na	na	na	na	na	na	na	na	na	na	na	na	na	na
Lithuania	04	06	02	02	06	03	01	03	11	03	05	05	na	na	na	01	06	03
Hungary	01	03	00	00	02	01	00	01	06	01	01	02	02	01	03	01	01	08
Argentina	01	01	01	01	01	01	01	01	02	00	01	01	02	01	01	00	01	01
Brazil	02	04	01	01	01	02	01	01	05	01	01	03	02	02	03	01	01	01
Mexico	03	04	02	02	03	03	03	01	03	04	03	03	04	02	03	02	03	06
Belarus	na	na	na	na	na	na	na	na	na	na	na	na	na	na	na	na	na	na
Russia	05	06	04	02	05	05	02	02	09	03	04	08	09	05	07	03	06	07
Moscow	na	na	na	na	na	na	na	na	na	na	na	na	na	na	na	na	na	na
Latvia	06	07	05	06	06	07	04	05	09	04	07	07	na	na	na	07	na	na
Estonia	04	06	03	01	07	04	01	04	10	04	03	07	na	na	na	06	06	08
Portugal	03	04	02	04	03	03	02	04	07	02	02	06	06	02	03	03	05	07
South Korea	02	02	03	01	03	01	03	02	02	02	03	03	03	02	03	03	03	00
Ireland	02	03	02	02	03	01	02	02	02	00	03	03	05	01	03	01	02	04
North Ireland	01	01	01	00	01	01	01	01	00	01	03	03	05	01	03	01	02	04
Slovenia	01	03	00	03	01	01	00	01	00	01	01	00	04	00	01	01	01	02
Spain	01	01	01	01	04	00	00	01	04	00	01	01	06	00	03	01	01	00
East Germany	06	08	04	05	08	04	05	04	12	05	07	06	08	04	07	02	01	04
Britain	02	02	02	01	02	02	01	04	04	02	01	03	03	01	03	03	06	07
Italy	04	05	02	05	05	02	03	04	12	03	04	07	05	05	02	03	01	04
Netherlands	02	04	02	05	02	02	03	08	02	02	03	02	03	05	02	03	03	08
Belgium	02	02	02	02	02	01	02	03	03	03	02	03	02	02	03	03	02	02
Austria	03	06	02	01	04	01	04	03	03	01	02	05	08	04	03	01	04	03
France	02	02	01	01	04	03	01	02	03	04	04	05	04	00	01	01	01	04
Canada	04	05	03	04	04	03	03	03	05	02	04	04	05	03	06	03	04	03
United States	05	05	05	04	05	05	03	03	08	02	05	07	07	04	06	03	04	02
Iceland	04	05	04	03	05	05	04	05	04	04	05	04	05	03	06	02	06	04
West Germany	03	04	02	02	04	03	02	05	06	02	03	04	05	02	04	02	02	05
Denmark	02	02	02	01	03	02	03	01	02	01	03	03	04	02	04	02	02	03
Finland	07	10	03	01	07	10	10	07	06	05	05	09	08	05	02	02	06	08
Norway	04	05	03	01	04	04	07	03	05	07	03	06	04	05	04	09	06	07
Sweden	04	05	03	02	04	06	03	04	06	02	04	04	08	04	02	04	03	05
Japan	01	03	00	01	02	02	01	01	01	01	02	02	08	00	02	04	04	03
Switzerland	na	na	na	na	na	na	na	na	na	na	na	na	na	na	na	na	na	na
Total	04	05	03	02	05	04	03	04	06	03	04	05	05	02	03	03	04	06

Ranking:

China	26
Finland	07
Latvia	06
East Germany	06
Bulgaria	05
Russia	05
United States	05
Lithuania	04
Estonia	04
Italy	04
Canada	04
Iceland	04
Norway	04
Sweden	04
Mexico	03
Portugal	03
Austria	03
West Germany	03
Romania	02
Chile	02
Brazil	02
South Korea	02
Ireland	02
Britain	02
Netherlands	02
Belgium	02
France	02
Denmark	02
Hungary	01
Argentina	01
North Ireland	01
Slovenia	01
Spain	01
Japan	01

Note: Countries in the left column are ranked according to GNP per capita. / The percentages in the bottom row give each country an equal weight. / na=not ascertained.

V42 COMMUNITY ACTION

Please look at the following list of voluntary organizations and activities and say which, if any, are you currently doing unpaid voluntary work for? Local community action on issues like poverty, employment, housing, racial equality. (% "do unpaid voluntary work")

Country	Total	Gender Male	Gender Female	Age 16-29	Age 30-49	Age 50+	Educ Lower	Educ Medium	Educ Upper	Income Lower	Income Middle	Income Upper	Pol Left	Pol Center	Pol Right	Values Mat	Values Mixed	Values Postmat
India	na	na	na	na	na	na	na	na	na	na	na	na	na	na	na	na	na	na
Nigeria	na	na	na	na	na	na	na	na	na	na	na	na	na	na	na	na	na	na
China	05	05	04	04	05	05	05	03	07	04	05	05	na	na	na	05	04	00
Romania	01	01	01	00	01	01	00	01	01	00	01	01	01	01	00	01	01	00
Turkey	na	na	na	na	na	na	na	na	na	na	na	na	na	na	na	na	na	na
Poland	na	na	na	na	na	na	na	na	na	na	na	na	na	na	na	na	na	na
Bulgaria	02	02	02	01	02	01	00	02	02	02	02	02	02	02	01	01	02	00
Chile	03	03	03	02	04	04	03	04	03	02	04	04	05	03	04	03	03	04
Czechoslovakia	na	na	na	na	na	na	na	na	na	na	na	na	na	na	na	na	na	na
South Africa	na	na	na	na	na	na	na	na	na	na	na	na	na	na	na	na	na	na
Lithuania	02	02	01	01	03	01	02	02	03	02	01	02	na	na	na	02	01	02
Hungary	02	02	01	02	02	01	01	02	02	01	02	03	na	02	00	01	02	03
Argentina	01	01	01	02	01	01	01	01	02	00	01	01	02	01	01	01	01	02
Brazil	04	04	05	04	06	03	03	04	08	03	05	07	03	04	06	03	05	07
Mexico	03	02	04	03	03	02	02	03	04	02	02	05	04	03	03	01	04	02
Belarus	na	na	na	na	na	na	na	na	na	na	na	na	na	na	na	na	na	na
Russia	02	02	02	00	02	03	02	02	02	02	02	02	01	02	04	03	02	01
Moscow	na	10	08	na	10	14	na	05	10	08	09	08	na	na	na	09	09	11
Latvia	08	08	08	02	05	05	05	08	10	08	09	10	09	09	na	09	09	05
Estonia	04	06	02	01	05	05	04	04	07	03	05	05	04	03	03	02	05	02
Portugal	01	01	01	01	01	01	00	01	01	00	01	02	01	01	01	01	01	01
South Korea	03	02	05	02	04	03	04	03	04	03	05	03	05	04	03	03	04	04
Ireland	03	03	03	01	04	03	03	03	03	01	04	03	03	03	03	02	03	04
North Ireland	02	02	02	01	03	01	02	02	00	03	03	04	04	03	00	02	03	07
Slovenia	03	04	02	02	04	01	01	02	07	03	03	05	04	03	03	02	03	07
Spain	01	01	01	01	01	00	01	01	01	01	01	01	01	01	01	00	01	04
East Germany	01	02	01	00	01	03	02	01	01	01	01	02	01	01	02	01	01	02
Britain	01	01	01	01	01	01	01	02	01	02	01	00	02	01	02	01	01	03
Italy	01	02	01	01	01	01	01	01	03	02	01	02	02	00	02	01	01	02
Netherlands	03	02	03	01	03	03	04	02	05	04	03	02	04	02	01	00	02	04
Belgium	03	04	02	04	03	02	03	03	05	03	03	04	06	02	03	02	02	06
Austria	01	02	01	01	02	01	03	03	03	01	02	02	01	03	02	01	01	02
France	03	04	04	04	04	05	04	03	04	03	04	04	04	05	04	03	03	04
Canada	04	04	04	04	04	05	06	03	06	03	05	04	04	03	04	03	04	06
United States	03	03	03	01	03	05	02	02	05	03	04	05	04	03	04	03	03	04
Iceland	01	00	01	01	00	01	01	01	00	na	01	01	00	02	00	00	01	00
West Germany	01	01	01	00	01	02	02	01	03	01	02	03	00	03	01	01	01	01
Denmark	02	02	02	00	04	01	03	03	03	03	03	03	05	03	02	01	02	03
Finland	03	03	03	04	03	03	04	03	03	04	03	05	02	03	02	03	02	05
Norway	01	01	01	01	02	01	00	02	02	01	01	02	02	01	01	03	01	03
Sweden	01	01	01	01	01	01	00	00	03	01	01	01	02	01	01	01	00	03
Japan	01	01	00	00	01	01	01	01	00	00	01	01	01	01	01	00	00	01
Switzerland	na	na	na	na	na	na	na	na	na	na	na	na	na	na	na	na	na	na
Total	02	03	02	02	03	03	02	02	03	02	03	03	03	02	02	02	02	03

Ranking:

Latvia	08
China	05
Brazil	04
Estonia	04
Canada	04
Chile	03
Mexico	03
South Korea	03
Ireland	03
Slovenia	03
Netherlands	03
Belgium	03
France	03
United States	03
Finland	03
Bulgaria	02
Lithuania	02
Hungary	02
Russia	02
North Ireland	02
Denmark	02
Romania	01
Argentina	01
Portugal	01
East Germany	01
Britain	01
Italy	01
Austria	01
Iceland	01
West Germany	01
Norway	01
Sweden	01
Spain	01
Japan	01

Note: Countries in the left column are ranked according to GNP per capita. / The percentages in the bottom row give each country an equal weight. / na=not ascertained.

V43 THIRD WORLD DEVELOPMENT

Please look at the following list of voluntary organizations and activities and say which, if any, are you currently doing unpaid voluntary work for? Third world development or human rights. (% "do unpaid voluntary work")

	Total	Gender Male	Gender Female	Age 16-29	Age 30-49	Age 50+	Education Lower	Education Medium	Education Upper	Income Lower	Income Middle	Income Upper	Political Affinity Left	Political Affinity Center	Political Affinity Right	Values Mat	Values Mixed	Values Postmat
India	na	na	na	na	na	na	na	na	na	na	na	na	na	na	na	na	na	na
Nigeria	na	na	na	na	na	na	na	na	na	na	na	na	na	na	na	na	na	na
China	00	00	00	00	00	00	00	00	01	00	01	00	00	00	00	00	00	00
Romania	00	00	00	00	01	00	00	00	01	00	00	00	00	00	00	00	00	01
Turkey	na	na	na	na	na	na	na	na	na	na	na	na	na	na	na	na	na	na
Poland	na	na	na	na	na	na	na	na	na	na	na	na	na	na	na	na	na	na
Bulgaria	01	03	00	02	01	01	00	02	02	01	01	02	01	01	01	01	01	00
Chile	01	01	01	01	01	01	00	02	01	01	01	01	02	01	00	01	01	02
Czechoslovakia	na	na	na	na	na	na	na	na	na	na	na	na	na	na	na	na	na	na
South Africa	na	na	na	na	na	na	na	na	na	na	na	na	na	na	na	na	na	na
Lithuania	01	01	01	00	01	01	00	01	01	01	02	00	na	na	na	01	01	01
Hungary	00	01	00	00	00	01	00	00	01	00	00	02	01	00	00	00	00	03
Argentina	00	00	00	00	01	00	00	00	00	00	00	01	01	00	01	00	00	01
Brazil	01	01	01	00	01	01	01	02	02	01	00	01	00	01	01	01	01	02
Mexico	01	01	01	00	01	01	00	00	01	01	01	01	00	01	01	00	01	02
Belarus	na	na	na	na	na	na	na	na	na	na	na	na	na	na	na	na	na	na
Russia	00	01	00	01	00	00	00	00	01	00	00	01	01	00	01	00	01	00
Moscow	na	01	00	01	00	00	00	00	01	00	00	01	01	00	01	00	01	00
Latvia	04	06	03	04	04	05	na	04	04	03	03	05	na	na	na	04	04	05
Estonia	01	01	01	01	01	01	01	01	02	01	00	02	na	na	na	01	01	00
Portugal	01	01	01	01	00	00	00	03	00	00	01	01	00	01	01	00	01	02
South Korea	02	01	02	00	03	02	01	02	03	01	02	03	01	01	03	02	02	01
Ireland	01	01	02	02	01	01	01	02	04	00	01	02	02	01	01	00	01	03
North Ireland	00	01	00	00	01	01	00	00	00	00	00	01	02	01	00	00	01	00
Slovenia	01	01	00	00	01	01	01	01	01	01	00	02	01	00	02	01	00	00
Spain	01	01	01	01	00	01	00	04	01	00	01	01	01	00	00	00	01	01
East Germany	00	00	00	00	00	00	00	01	00	02	00	00	00	00	00	00	00	01
Britain	00	00	02	00	01	00	00	01	03	02	00	00	01	00	01	01	01	03
Italy	01	01	01	01	01	01	01	02	04	01	01	02	01	01	01	01	00	03
Netherlands	03	02	03	01	04	04	02	03	04	05	02	03	05	02	03	01	03	04
Belgium	03	05	02	03	05	03	03	03	07	03	04	05	06	03	03	02	02	08
Austria	01	00	01	01	01	00	01	01	03	01	01	01	02	01	01	00	01	01
France	01	02	01	01	01	02	01	01	04	02	02	02	02	01	01	01	01	03
Canada	03	03	02	02	01	04	02	02	04	02	03	03	04	02	03	02	02	05
United States	01	01	01	00	01	01	01	01	01	00	01	01	02	00	00	01	00	01
Iceland	00	00	01	01	00	01	00	01	01	00	na	01	00	00	00	02	00	01
West Germany	01	01	01	01	01	00	01	01	03	00	01	01	02	01	00	01	01	01
Denmark	01	00	01	01	01	00	00	01	01	00	00	00	02	01	00	00	01	03
Finland	02	02	03	02	01	05	04	02	02	04	01	02	03	02	02	03	02	03
Norway	01	01	01	00	02	01	00	02	01	01	01	01	03	01	01	00	01	03
Sweden	03	02	05	04	03	02	03	03	08	02	04	03	04	03	04	01	03	06
Japan	00	00	00	00	00	00	00	00	00	00	00	00	00	00	01	00	00	00
Switzerland	na	na	na	na	na	na	na	na	na	na	na	na	na	na	na	na	na	na
Total	**01**	**01**	**01**	**01**	**01**	**01**	**01**	**01**	**02**	**01**	**01**	**02**	**02**	**01**	**01**	**01**	**01**	**02**

Ranking:

Latvia	04
Netherlands	03
Belgium	03
Canada	03
Sweden	03
South Korea	02
Finland	02
Bulgaria	01
Chile	01
Lithuania	01
Brazil	01
Mexico	01
Estonia	01
Portugal	01
Ireland	01
Slovenia	01
Britain	01
Italy	01
Austria	01
France	01
United States	01
West Germany	01
Denmark	01
Norway	01
Spain	01
China	00
Romania	00
Hungary	00
Argentina	00
Russia	00
North Ireland	00
East Germany	00
Iceland	00
Japan	00

Note: Countries in the left column are ranked according to GNP per capita. / The percentages in the bottom row give each country an equal weight. / na=not ascertained.

V44 ENVIRONMENT

Please look at the following list of voluntary organizations and activities and say which, if any, are you currently doing unpaid voluntary work for? Conservation, the environment, ecology. (% "do unpaid voluntary work")

	Total	Gender		Age			Education			Income			Political Affinity			Values			Ranking:	
		Male	Female	16-29	30-49	50+	Lower	Medium	Upper	Lower	Middle	Upper	Left	Center	Right	Mat	Mixed	Postmat		
India	na	na	na	na	na	na	na	na	na	na	na	na	na	na	na	na	na	na	Latvia	05
Nigeria	na	na	na	na	na	na	na	na	na	na	na	na	na	na	na	na	na	na	Canada	04
China	02	03	01	02	02	02	00	01	03	01	04	01	01	02	01	02	02	04	United States	04
Romania	01	01	01	01	01	01	00	01	02	01	01	01	01	02	01	01	01	03	Bulgaria	03
Turkey	na	na	na	na	na	na	na	na	na	na	na	na	na	na	na	na	na	na	Netherlands	03
Poland	na	na	na	na	na	na	na	na	na	na	na	na	na	na	na	na	na	na	Belgium	03
Bulgaria	03	05	02	03	05	01	02	04	04	02	05	04	04	04	02	03	04	03	Finland	03
Chile	01	01	00	01	01	01	00	01	01	01	01	01	02	00	00	01	01	02	Sweden	03
Czechoslovakia	na	na	na	na	na	na	na	na	na	na	na	na	na	na	na	na	na	na	China	02
South Africa	na	na	na	na	na	na	na	na	na	na	na	na	na	na	na	na	na	na	Lithuania	02
Lithuania	02	03	01	02	02	01	03	02	03	02	01	02	na	na	na	01	02	06	Mexico	02
Hungary	01	02	01	01	01	02	02	02	04	00	01	05	02	02	02	01	01	00	Estonia	02
Argentina	00	00	00	00	00	00	00	00	00	00	00	00	01	00	00	00	00	00	South Korea	02
Brazil	01	02	00	02	02	00	02	01	03	01	01	02	02	01	02	01	01	03	East Germany	02
Mexico	02	02	02	02	02	03	02	03	02	02	03	03	03	02	03	01	03	01	Britain	02
Belarus	na	na	na	na	na	na	na	na	na	na	na	na	na	na	na	na	na	na	France	02
Russia	01	01	02	01	02	01	00	01	03	01	01	02	03	02	00	01	02	04	Iceland	02
Moscow	na	na	na	na	na	na	na	na	na	na	na	na	na	na	na	na	na	na	Romania	01
Latvia	05	06	05	06	03	07	05	05	05	03	05	07	na	na	na	04	05	07	Chile	01
Estonia	02	03	01	02	02	01	02	03	04	01	02	04	02	01	03	01	03	00	Hungary	01
Portugal	01	01	00	02	01	00	00	01	02	01	00	02	03	00	01	00	01	04	Brazil	01
South Korea	02	02	03	01	03	03	01	03	02	02	03	03	03	02	03	02	03	00	Russia	01
Ireland	01	00	01	01	01	00	00	01	02	00	00	01	03	00	01	00	01	02	Portugal	01
North Ireland	01	00	02	01	00	02	01	00	03	00	00	03	00	01	01	00	02	00	Ireland	01
Slovenia	01	02	01	02	02	02	01	02	04	02	01	04	03	02	01	01	01	04	North Ireland	01
Spain	01	01	00	04	01	00	01	01	01	00	01	01	02	04	00	00	01	09	Slovenia	01
East Germany	02	03	01	04	03	01	01	03	02	02	01	03	04	02	03	00	02	04	Spain	01
Britain	02	02	02	00	03	02	01	03	03	01	02	03	04	01	01	01	02	04	Italy	01
Italy	01	02	01	03	01	00	01	02	04	02	02	04	04	00	01	01	02	03	Austria	01
Netherlands	03	03	02	01	03	04	03	02	02	02	02	04	04	02	02	00	02	04	West Germany	01
Belgium	03	04	01	02	04	04	02	03	04	02	02	04	04	03	01	01	02	06	Denmark	01
Austria	01	02	01	02	02	01	01	02	01	00	01	02	03	02	01	01	02	02	Norway	01
France	02	02	01	01	02	02	01	02	02	01	01	02	01	02	02	01	02	03	Japan	01
Canada	04	03	04	04	03	04	02	03	06	04	03	04	04	04	05	04	03	05	Argentina	00
United States	04	03	04	02	05	03	02	04	05	03	03	05	07	04	04	02	03	06		
Iceland	02	02	02	01	02	02	01	02	04	na	01	na	04	01	01	02	02	03		
West Germany	01	02	01	03	02	01	02	02	03	02	01	02	04	02	01	00	01	02		
Denmark	01	01	01	01	01	01	01	00	01	01	01	01	02	01	01	01	01	01		
Finland	03	05	01	02	03	05	05	00	04	02	02	03	06	03	02	03	02	05		
Norway	01	01	01	00	01	03	00	00	02	00	01	02	07	04	02	01	01	03		
Sweden	03	03	02	03	02	02	01	02	03	02	03	03	04	02	01	01	02	06		
Japan	01	01	02	00	02	02	02	01	01	00	02	02	01	02	01	01	02	03		
Switzerland	na	na	na	na	na	na	na	na	na	na	na	na	na	na	na	na	na	na		
Total	02	02	02	02	02	02	01	02	03	01	02	03	03	02	01	01	02	03		

Note: Countries in the left column are ranked according to GNP per capita. / The percentages in the bottom row give each country an equal weight. / na=not ascertained.

V45 PROFESSIONAL ASSOCIATIONS

Please look at the following list of voluntary organizations and activities and say which, if any, are you currently doing unpaid voluntary work for? Professional associations. (% "do unpaid voluntary work")

	Total	Gender		Age			Education			Income			Political Affinity			Values		
		Male	Female	16-29	30-49	50+	Lower	Medium	Upper	Lower	Middle	Upper	Left	Center	Right	Mat	Mixed	Postmat
India	na	na	na	na	na	na	na	na	na	na	na	na	na	na	na	na	na	na
Nigeria	na	na	na	na	na	na	na	na	na	na	na	na	na	na	na	na	na	na
China	17	18	16	11	23	14	16	15	23	17	21	14	00	02	02	16	18	20
Romania	02	02	01	01	02	02	00	01	04	02	01	02	00	02	02	02	01	05
Turkey	na	na	na	na	na	na	na	na	na	na	na	na	na	na	na	na	na	na
Poland	na	na	na	na	na	na	na	na	na	na	na	na	na	na	na	na	na	na
Bulgaria	02	03	02	02	03	02	00	02	06	02	02	04	03	03	03	01	03	03
Chile	01	02	01	01	02	02	00	01	03	00	02	02	03	01	03	01	01	03
Czechoslovakia	na	na	na	na	na	na	na	na	na	na	na	na	na	na	na	na	na	na
South Africa	na	na	na	na	na	na	na	na	na	na	na	na	na	na	na	na	na	na
Lithuania	01	02	01	00	02	02	01	01	08	01	01	03	na	na	na	02	01	02
Hungary	02	02	01	02	02	01	01	01	08	01	02	05	04	01	01	01	02	03
Argentina	01	01	00	00	01	01	00	00	02	00	01	01	00	01	01	01	00	01
Brazil	02	03	01	02	02	01	01	01	09	01	01	05	02	03	02	01	02	05
Mexico	01	01	01	02	02	02	01	01	03	02	01	03	02	01	02	01	02	01
Belarus	na	na	na	na	na	na	na	na	na	na	na	na	na	na	na	na	na	na
Russia	01	01	01	00	02	00	00	00	02	01	01	01	03	01	00	00	01	02
Moscow	na	na	na	na	na	na	na	na	na	na	na	na	na	na	na	na	na	na
Latvia	03	05	02	04	03	03	01	02	02	03	04	03	na	na	na	02	04	04
Estonia	02	03	02	01	03	03	01	01	06	02	02	04	na	na	na	02	02	05
Portugal	01	01	na	01	01	00	00	02	05	00	01	01	02	01	00	01	01	01
South Korea	02	02	03	02	03	02	02	03	02	01	03	03	02	01	04	02	01	04
Ireland	01	02	01	00	02	01	00	01	07	00	01	02	05	01	01	01	01	02
North Ireland	01	02	01	01	03	00	03	03	08	01	01	03	00	02	02	01	02	02
Slovenia	02	04	01	02	02	03	01	01	06	00	01	05	05	03	01	00	02	06
Spain	01	01	01	01	04	01	00	01	05	00	00	01	04	01	01	01	02	01
East Germany	03	04	01	01	04	02	01	03	07	01	03	04	03	03	02	01	03	03
Britain	02	02	02	01	04	01	01	02	06	01	03	03	02	02	02	01	02	03
Italy	01	02	01	01	03	01	02	03	06	01	04	05	03	02	01	01	02	03
Netherlands	02	02	01	01	02	03	01	03	03	01	01	04	02	02	02	00	02	05
Belgium	02	03	01	02	03	01	02	02	05	00	01	04	01	01	00	01	01	01
Austria	01	01	00	01	02	01	02	02	02	01	03	03	01	03	02	01	01	06
France	03	04	01	02	03	02	03	03	09	03	01	06	03	01	02	01	01	02
Canada	05	06	05	04	06	04	04	03	10	03	03	06	03	04	06	02	04	07
United States	05	07	04	03	07	06	03	03	10	03	05	09	07	05	06	03	05	07
Iceland	03	03	03	02	03	03	01	02	05	na	01	na	03	02	02	04	03	06
West Germany	02	03	01	02	02	01	01	02	05	01	01	03	01	01	02	01	02	04
Denmark	03	04	01	02	04	02	02	03	04	02	02	05	04	02	02	02	02	03
Finland	07	09	06	04	09	06	05	04	12	05	05	12	10	06	07	09	06	09
Norway	03	04	02	01	05	03	03	03	04	01	03	06	04	03	03	03	03	07
Sweden	03	04	02	02	03	02	03	03	05	03	03	04	05	03	03	01	03	04
Japan	01	03	00	01	02	02	01	02	03	01	02	01	01	02	03	01	01	03
Switzerland	na	na	na	na	na	na	na	na	na	na	na	na	na	na	na	na	na	na
Total	03	04	02	02	04	02	02	02	06	02	03	04	03	02	03	02	03	04

Ranking:

China	17
Finland	07
Canada	05
United States	05
Latvia	03
East Germany	03
France	03
Iceland	03
Denmark	03
Norway	03
Sweden	03
Romania	02
Bulgaria	02
Hungary	02
Brazil	02
Estonia	02
South Korea	02
Slovenia	02
Britain	02
Netherlands	02
Belgium	02
West Germany	02
Chile	01
Lithuania	01
Argentina	01
Mexico	01
Russia	01
Portugal	01
Ireland	01
North Ireland	01
Italy	01
Austria	01
Spain	01
Japan	01

Note: Countries in the left column are ranked according to GNP per capita. / The percentages in the bottom row give each country an equal weight. / na=not ascertained.

The Chinese questionnaire translated "Trade Unions" (V22 and V40) as "Trading Associations," which was chosen by very few people. "Professional Associations" was translated as "occupational organizations," which evokes the (government-sponsored) labor unions; thus, for China, V27 is functionally equivalent to V22.

V46 YOUTH WORK

Please look at the following list of voluntary organizations and activities and say which, if any, are you currently doing unpaid voluntary work for? Youth work (e.g., scouts guides, youth clubs, etc.) (% "do unpaid voluntary work")

	Total	Gender		Age			Education			Income			Political Affinity			Values		
		Male	Female	16-29	30-49	50+	Lower	Medium	Upper	Lower	Middle	Upper	Left	Center	Right	Mat	Mixed	Postmat
India	na	na	na	na	na	na	na	na	na	na	na	na	na	na	na	na	na	na
Nigeria	na	na	na	na	na	na	na	na	na	na	na	na	na	na	na	na	na	na
China	10	10	11	17	na	04	09	12	11	08	14	10	na	na	na	09	11	13
Romania	01	01	01	02	08	00	00	01	00	01	01	01	01	01	01	00	01	00
Turkey	na	na	na	na	na	na	na	na	na	na	na	na	na	na	na	na	na	na
Poland	na	na	na	na	na	na	na	na	na	na	na	na	na	na	na	na	na	na
Bulgaria	01	01	01	03	01	00	00	01	02	01	01	01	01	01	01	00	01	04
Chile	04	05	03	05	03	02	02	04	07	02	04	05	04	04	03	02	04	06
Czechoslovakia	na	na	na	na	na	na	na	na	na	na	na	na	na	na	na	na	na	na
South Africa	na	na	na	na	na	na	na	na	na	na	na	na	na	na	na	na	na	na
Lithuania	04	04	04	08	03	00	02	04	04	04	03	05	02	na	na	03	04	04
Hungary	01	01	02	02	02	01	00	02	04	01	01	02	02	01	02	01	02	00
Argentina	02	03	01	02	02	01	01	02	03	00	02	03	01	03	01	01	01	04
Brazil	02	03	01	03	01	02	01	02	04	02	01	03	02	02	02	01	02	05
Mexico	02	03	02	03	02	02	02	02	03	02	03	03	02	01	04	02	02	02
Belarus	na	na	na	na	na	na	na	na	na	na	na	na	na	na	na	na	na	na
Russia	03	02	03	02	03	02	00	02	05	02	03	03	05	02	03	na	03	03
Moscow	na	na	na	na	na	na	na	na	na	na	na	na	na	na	na	na	na	na
Latvia	03	04	03	06	03	01	04	03	04	02	06	02	na	na	na	03	04	03
Estonia	02	02	02	03	02	01	01	02	02	02	01	02	02	01	04	02	02	00
Portugal	02	02	02	05	02	00	01	05	06	01	03	04	03	03	01	01	02	09
South Korea	03	03	03	03	03	03	01	03	04	02	03	04	04	02	04	02	04	04
Ireland	05	06	04	09	06	01	03	06	08	01	06	06	04	06	04	02	06	06
North Ireland	08	06	09	13	09	03	03	15	24	08	08	15	04	09	08	06	09	02
Slovenia	01	02	01	02	02	01	01	01	04	01	01	03	05	01	02	02	01	01
Spain	01	01	01	05	01	00	00	01	07	00	02	04	01	01	04	01	01	04
East Germany	02	03	01	05	02	00	02	03	01	02	01	02	03	02	02	01	02	03
Britain	03	02	04	01	06	03	01	06	08	02	04	05	03	04	04	03	03	05
Italy	03	03	02	05	03	01	03	05	01	04	04	02	02	04	01	03	02	05
Netherlands	07	05	06	08	04	05	03	05	09	06	07	04	05	05	07	04	06	06
Belgium	05	07	04	11	03	04	03	07	08	03	03	08	08	04	06	03	05	09
Austria	02	02	01	04	02	01	01	01	05	01	02	02	05	02	03	01	01	03
France	03	03	03	05	02	03	01	04	03	01	03	03	03	04	03	01	03	05
Canada	07	06	08	07	09	05	05	08	08	06	07	08	07	08	07	04	07	09
United States	10	09	12	07	14	07	06	09	14	08	10	13	05	11	11	09	10	10
Iceland	05	07	03	07	05	03	03	05	07	03	na	na	02	06	06	04	06	03
West Germany	02	03	02	05	03	01	02	04	03	01	04	03	04	02	03	01	02	04
Denmark	03	02	03	04	04	01	02	05	02	03	03	03	03	02	02	02	03	05
Finland	05	07	03	05	06	02	06	03	06	05	05	06	04	05	05	03	04	07
Norway	04	04	03	06	04	02	02	04	05	02	05	04	04	04	04	04	03	05
Sweden	07	06	08	09	08	02	05	08	10	05	05	09	08	07	07	06	07	08
Japan	01	01	01	01	02	00	01	01	00	00	02	01	02	01	00	01	01	01
Switzerland	na	na	na	na	na	na	na	na	na	na	na	na	na	na	na	na	na	na
Total	04	04	03	05	04	02	02	04	06	02	04	05	04	04	04	03	04	05

Ranking:

China	10
United States	10
North Ireland	08
Canada	07
Sweden	07
Ireland	05
Netherlands	05
Belgium	05
Iceland	05
Finland	05
Chile	04
Lithuania	04
Norway	04
Russia	03
Latvia	03
South Korea	03
Britain	03
Italy	03
France	03
Denmark	03
Argentina	02
Brazil	02
Mexico	02
Estonia	02
Portugal	02
East Germany	02
Austria	02
West Germany	02
Romania	01
Bulgaria	01
Hungary	01
Slovenia	01
Spain	01
Japan	01

Note: Countries in the left column are ranked according to GNP per capita. / The percentages in the bottom row give each country an equal weight. / na=not ascertained.

V47 SPORTS/RECREATION

Please look at the following list of voluntary organizations and activities and say which, if any, are you currently doing unpaid voluntary work for? Sports or recreation. (% "do unpaid voluntary work")

	Total	Gender		Age			Education			Income			Political Affinity			Values		
		Male	Female	16-29	30-49	50+	Lower	Medium	Upper	Lower	Middle	Upper	Left	Center	Right	Mat	Mixed	Postmat
India	na	na	na	na	na	na	na	na	na	na	na	na	na	na	na	na	na	na
Nigeria	na	06	na	na	na	na	na	na	na	na	na	na	na	na	na	na	na	na
China	06	05	01	09	05	04	04	06	09	05	07	06	04	04	02	04	07	13
Romania	03	05	01	06	02	01	01	05	03	02	04	02	04	04	02	02	04	05
Turkey	na	na	na	na	na	na	na	na	na	na	na	na	na	na	na	na	na	na
Poland	na	na	na	na	na	na	na	na	na	na	na	na	na	na	na	na	na	na
Bulgaria	04	05	02	06	04	02	01	05	05	03	04	05	01	06	04	01	04	09
Chile	07	11	03	07	07	04	04	08	07	05	09	06	06	06	06	05	07	09
Czechoslovakia	na	na	na	na	na	na	na	na	na	na	na	na	na	na	na	na	na	na
South Africa	na	na	na	na	na	na	na	na	na	na	na	na	na	na	na	na	na	na
Lithuania	07	11	03	14	05	02	05	07	09	na	na	na	na	na	na	na	na	na
Hungary	02	03	01	03	02	01	01	03	02	06	05	10	03	02	01	05	06	11
Argentina	02	03	01	03	02	01	01	03	07	01	02	03	01	03	01	02	02	00
Brazil	04	06	02	04	04	02	02	04	07	00	02	04	03	04	01	02	02	02
Mexico	05	06	03	06	04	02	04	02	08	03	04	05	05	04	05	03	04	04
Belarus	na	na	na	na	na	na	na	na	na	na	na	na	na	na	na	na	na	na
Russia	03	05	02	05	04	01	01	03	04	02	03	05	04	03	04	03	05	05
Moscow	na	na	na	na	na	na	na	na	na	na	na	na	na	na	na	na	na	na
Latvia	09	11	08	09	10	07	04	09	11	07	12	08	na	na	na	03	03	04
Estonia	08	13	05	13	08	05	05	09	10	07	10	10	07	na	na	07	10	09
Portugal	06	11	02	10	06	03	05	10	10	04	06	11	08	na	na	08	08	12
South Korea	03	02	04	02	04	03	02	03	03	02	04	04	07	06	07	07	06	10
Ireland	07	12	03	09	10	03	06	08	11	03	09	09	03	03	03	02	04	01
North Ireland	06	09	03	08	06	04	05	06	07	01	08	11	07	07	08	05	08	06
Slovenia	03	05	01	04	04	01	01	04	05	02	03	05	07	06	04	00	07	09
Spain	04	07	01	05	05	01	04	04	07	01	04	05	05	05	03	03	03	07
East Germany	11	17	06	16	12	07	04	13	17	04	15	14	05	04	01	01	04	11
Britain	na	na	na	na	na	na	na	na	na	04	15	na	12	12	13	04	12	14
Italy	06	10	03	12	07	02	05	05	08	na	na	na	12	07	07	03	05	11
Netherlands	08	11	07	08	10	07	06	05	18	04	09	16	08	07	07	08	09	08
Belgium	06	08	04	07	07	05	04	07	09	08	08	13	09	10	08	04	06	10
Austria	07	12	04	10	09	05	06	08	07	04	06	na	07	06	08	08	07	09
France	06	08	04	05	07	06	04	08	09	04	10	07	07	08	08	08	07	09
Canada	12	15	09	14	15	08	08	15	12	04	05	13	07	07	08	02	08	07
United States	08	10	07	07	13	04	03	09	11	08	13	15	11	14	15	15	12	11
Iceland	14	19	09	17	16	08	na	18	15	04	08	13	06	10	09	06	09	09
West Germany	11	16	06	13	14	06	09	12	15	06	14	12	13	14	14	16	13	15
Denmark	11	16	07	17	13	05	04	17	13	08	11	16	11	11	13	07	11	11
Finland	16	22	10	18	19	07	14	19	17	16	16	16	12	09	15	12	12	11
Norway	14	18	10	14	19	08	06	14	17	16	18	18	20	15	14	21	16	16
Sweden	17	22	11	24	20	07	15	19	15	19	13	21	13	18	17	15	18	17
Japan	03	05	01	02	03	03	02	02	05	01	05	03	17	18	17	03	04	03
Switzerland	na	na	na	na	na	na	na	na	na	00	00	00	04	05	03	na	na	na
Total	07	10	05	09	08	04	05	08	09	05	08	09	08	08	08	06	08	09

Ranking:

Sweden	17
Finland	16
Iceland	14
Norway	14
Canada	12
East Germany	11
West Germany	11
Denmark	11
Latvia	09
Estonia	08
Netherlands	08
United States	08
Chile	07
Lithuania	07
Ireland	07
Austria	07
China	06
Portugal	06
North Ireland	06
Italy	06
Belgium	06
France	06
Mexico	05
Bulgaria	04
Brazil	04
Spain	04
Romania	03
Russia	03
South Korea	03
Slovenia	03
Japan	03
Hungary	02
Argentina	02

Note: Countries in the left column are ranked according to GNP per capita. / The percentages in the bottom row give each country an equal weight. / na=not ascertained.

V48 WOMEN'S GROUPS

Please look at the following list of voluntary organizations and activities and say which, if any, are you currently doing unpaid voluntary work for? Women's groups. (% "do unpaid voluntary work")

| | | Gender | | Age | | | Education | | | Income | | | Political Affinity | | | Values | | | Ranking: |
	Total	Male	Female	16-29	30-49	50+	Lower	Medium	Upper	Lower	Middle	Upper	Left	Center	Right	Mat	Mixed	Postmat	
India	na	na	na	na	na	na	na	na	na	na	na	na	na	na	na	na	na	na	Canada 05
Nigeria	na	na	na	na	na	na	na	na	na	na	na	na	na	na	na	na	na	na	United States 05
China	03	01	07	01	04	03	02	03	04	02	04	04	00	00	01	03	03	04	China 03
Romania	00	00	01	00	01	00	00	01	00	00	01	00	00	00	01	00	00	01	East Germany 03
Turkey	na	na	na	na	na	na	na	na	na	na	na	na	na	na	na	na	na	na	Netherlands 03
Poland	na	na	na	na	na	na	na	na	na	na	na	na	na	na	na	na	na	na	Belgium 03
Bulgaria	01	01	02	02	01	01	00	02	02	01	01	01	00	02	01	01	01	00	Iceland 03
Chile	02	01	02	02	01	02	02	02	01	01	02	02	01	02	02	01	01	03	West Germany 03
Czechoslovakia	na	na	na	na	na	na	na	na	na	na	na	na	na	na	na	na	na	na	Finland 03
South Africa	na	na	na	na	na	na	na	na	na	na	na	na	na	na	na	na	na	na	Chile 02
Lithuania	02	00	04	01	02	02	03	03	01	02	03	01	na	na	na	03	01	03	Lithuania 02
Hungary	01	00	01	01	00	01	01	01	00	01	01	00	01	00	01	00	01	00	Latvia 02
Argentina	00	00	01	00	00	01	00	00	00	00	00	00	00	00	02	01	00	01	Estonia 02
Brazil	01	01	01	01	02	01	01	02	01	02	01	01	02	01	01	01	01	01	South Korea 02
Mexico	01	00	02	01	01	02	02	00	01	01	00	03	02	01	01	01	00	02	Ireland 02
Belarus	na	na	na	na	na	na	na	na	na	na	na	na	na	na	na	na	na	na	North Ireland 02
Russia	01	01	01	00	02	01	00	02	00	01	01	00	03	01	00	01	01	00	Austria 02
Moscow	na	na	na	na	na	na	na	na	na	na	na	na	na	na	na	na	na	na	Sweden 02
Latvia	02	01	02	01	02	02	02	02	02	01	02	02	na	01	na	04	01	00	Japan 02
Estonia	02	00	03	01	01	01	02	00	00	02	00	00	02	01	00	03	01	02	Bulgaria 01
Portugal	00	00	00	00	00	00	00	00	00	00	00	00	00	00	00	00	00	00	Hungary 01
South Korea	02	03	02	01	03	03	02	02	03	01	02	03	02	02	03	03	01	03	Brazil 01
Ireland	02	00	04	00	02	01	03	02	03	04	03	03	00	02	03	03	03	00	Mexico 01
North Ireland	02	01	03	00	02	05	03	00	03	04	03	03	00	03	01	03	00	08	Russia 01
Slovenia	00	00	00	00	01	00	00	00	00	00	00	00	00	00	00	00	00	00	France 01
Spain	00	00	00	01	00	04	01	02	02	03	03	03	03	03	01	03	02	03	Denmark 01
East Germany	03	00	05	01	03	04	02	02	02	03	03	03	03	03	01	02	01	03	Norway 01
Britain	na	na	02	00	00	00	na	na	na	na	na	na	na	na	na	na	na	na	Romania 00
Italy	00	00	00	00	00	00	00	00	00	00	00	01	00	00	00	00	00	03	Argentina 00
Netherlands	03	03	03	01	02	04	02	02	04	04	03	04	04	02	03	03	02	02	Portugal 00
Belgium	03	01	05	01	01	04	02	02	04	03	02	04	02	01	03	02	03	04	Slovenia 00
Austria	02	00	04	01	03	04	02	02	02	02	03	02	02	02	03	02	01	01	Spain 00
France	01	00	02	00	01	01	02	01	01	01	01	01	01	01	02	01	04	04	Italy 00
Canada	05	01	08	02	04	07	00	07	05	06	04	05	05	05	03	08	04	04	
United States	05	01	09	00	05	06	04	04	06	03	03	06	04	06	03	05	04	05	
Iceland	03	00	06	01	04	05	05	03	03	05	03	na	04	02	03	05	02	03	
West Germany	03	00	05	01	03	04	03	02	03	03	01	03	03	01	02	03	01	01	
Denmark	01	01	01	00	01	01	00	00	01	00	00	01	03	01	01	06	03	04	
Finland	03	01	06	03	02	08	05	03	03	07	01	01	08	05	03	02	01	03	
Norway	01	00	02	01	01	00	01	00	01	01	01	02	01	01	01	04	02	01	
Sweden	02	00	04	01	01	03	02	02	03	02	02	03	04	01	03	03	01	00	
Japan	02	00	03	01	01	03	02	02	02	02	02	03	04	00	03	03	01	na	
Switzerland	na	na	na	na	na	na	na	na	na	na	na	na	na	na	na	na	na	na	
Total	02	00	03	01	02	02	02	02	02	02	02	02	02	02	02	02	01	02	

Note: Countries in the left column are ranked according to GNP per capita. / The percentages in the bottom row give each country an equal weight. / na=not ascertained.

V49 PEACE MOVEMENT

Please look at the following list of voluntary organizations and activities and say which, if any, are you currently doing unpaid voluntary work for? Peace movement. (% "do unpaid voluntary work")

	Total	Gender		Age			Education			Income			Political Affinity			Values		
		Male	Female	16-29	30-49	50+	Lower	Medium	Upper	Lower	Middle	Upper	Left	Center	Right	Mat	Mixed	Postmat
India	na	na	na	na	na	na	na	na	na	na	na	na	na	na	na	na	na	na
Nigeria	na	na	na	na	na	na	na	na	na	na	na	na	na	na	na	na	na	na
China	00	00	01	01	00	00	00	00	00	00	00	00	00	00	00	00	01	00
Romania	00	00	00	00	00	00	00	00	00	00	00	00	00	00	00	00	00	00
Turkey	na	na	na	na	na	na	na	na	na	na	na	na	na	na	na	na	na	na
Poland	na	na	na	na	na	na	na	na	na	na	na	na	na	na	na	na	na	na
Bulgaria	01	01	01	02	01	01	00	01	02	01	01	01	00	01	01	01	01	01
Chile	01	01	00	01	00	01	00	01	01	01	01	01	01	00	00	00	01	01
Czechoslovakia	na	na	na	na	na	na	na	na	na	na	na	na	na	na	na	na	na	na
South Africa	na	na	na	na	na	na	na	na	na	na	na	na	na	na	na	na	na	na
Lithuania	01	01	00	01	01	01	01	01	02	01	01	01	na	na	na	01	na	03
Hungary	00	00	00	00	00	00	00	00	02	00	01	00	01	00	01	01	00	00
Argentina	00	00	00	00	00	00	00	00	00	00	00	00	00	00	01	00	00	01
Brazil	01	02	00	01	01	01	02	01	02	02	00	01	01	00	01	01	01	04
Mexico	01	01	01	00	01	02	01	01	00	01	02	01	01	02	01	00	01	01
Belarus	na	na	na	na	na	na	na	na	na	na	na	na	na	na	na	na	na	na
Russia	01	01	01	00	02	01	01	00	02	01	01	02	03	01	00	01	01	00
Moscow	na	na	na	na	na	na	na	na	na	na	na	na	na	na	na	na	na	na
Latvia	01	na	01	01	na	na	02	01	na	02	01	01	na	na	na	01	01	na
Estonia	01	01	01	02	01	01	01	01	02	01	01	01	na	na	na	01	01	03
Portugal	00	01	00	01	00	00	00	01	01	00	00	01	na	na	na	01	01	00
South Korea	02	02	02	01	03	03	02	02	03	02	02	04	01	00	00	02	00	01
Ireland	00	00	00	01	00	03	02	03	00	02	02	00	02	01	04	01	02	01
North Ireland	00	00	00	00	01	00	00	00	00	00	00	00	01	00	00	na	na	na
Slovenia	00	00	00	00	01	00	00	00	01	00	00	01	01	01	00	00	01	00
Spain	01	01	01	01	00	00	01	01	01	00	02	01	01	01	00	01	00	04
East Germany	01	02	00	01	03	00	02	02	01	02	02	00	02	01	04	01	00	01
Britain	00	00	01	00	00	00	00	00	00	01	00	00	01	01	00	00	00	01
Italy	01	01	01	01	01	00	01	00	01	01	01	04	01	00	na	na	na	02
Netherlands	01	01	01	01	01	00	01	01	01	01	00	02	01	01	00	00	01	01
Belgium	01	02	01	01	01	01	01	02	02	01	02	01	02	01	01	01	00	00
Austria	00	00	00	00	01	00	00	01	01	00	00	00	01	01	00	00	01	01
France	01	01	01	01	01	01	01	00	01	01	01	01	01	01	00	00	01	00
Canada	02	01	02	02	01	01	02	01	02	02	02	01	03	01	00	01	01	03
United States	01	01	01	00	01	01	01	01	01	01	01	01	04	01	02	01	01	01
Iceland	01	01	00	01	01	01	01	01	00	01	00	00	01	01	00	01	00	00
West Germany	00	01	01	01	01	00	00	00	01	00	00	00	02	00	00	00	00	00
Denmark	00	00	00	00	01	00	00	00	00	00	01	00	01	00	00	00	00	02
Finland	01	02	01	00	01	01	01	00	01	01	01	01	04	01	00	00	00	01
Norway	00	01	00	00	00	02	03	01	00	00	01	00	00	00	00	01	01	01
Sweden	02	02	02	02	02	01	01	02	03	01	02	02	02	01	01	01	01	04
Japan	01	01	00	01	01	01	01	01	00	01	01	02	03	01	02	01	01	00
Switzerland	na	na	na	na	na	na	na	na	na	na	na	na	na	na	na	na	na	na
Total	01	01	01	01	01	01	01	01	01	01	01	01	01	01	00	00	01	01

Ranking:

South Korea	02
Canada	02
Sweden	02
Bulgaria	01
Chile	01
Lithuania	01
Brazil	01
Mexico	01
Russia	01
Latvia	01
Estonia	01
Spain	01
East Germany	01
Italy	01
Netherlands	01
Belgium	01
France	01
United States	01
West Germany	01
Finland	01
Japan	01
China	00
Romania	00
Hungary	00
Argentina	00
Portugal	00
Ireland	00
North Ireland	00
Slovenia	00
Austria	00
Iceland	00
Denmark	00
Norway	00

Note: Countries in the left column are ranked according to GNP per capita. / The percentages in the bottom row give each country an equal weight. / na=not ascertained.

V50 ANIMAL RIGHTS

Please look at the following list of voluntary organizations and activities and say which, if any, are you currently doing unpaid voluntary work for? Animal rights. (% "do unpaid voluntary work")

	Total	Gender Male	Gender Female	Age 16-29	Age 30-49	Age 50+	Education Lower	Education Medium	Education Upper	Income Lower	Income Middle	Income Upper	Political Affinity Left	Political Affinity Center	Political Affinity Right	Values Mat	Values Mixed	Values Postmat
India	na	na	na	na	na	na	na	na	na	na	na	na	na	na	na	na	na	na
Nigeria	na	na	na	na	na	na	na	na	na	na	na	na	na	na	na	na	na	na
China	00	00	00	00	00	00	00	00	01	00	00	01	na	na	na	00	00	00
Romania	00	00	00	00	00	00	00	01	00	01	00	00	na	na	na	00	00	00
Turkey	na	na	na	na	na	na	na	na	na	na	na	na	na	na	na	na	na	na
Poland	01	na	na	na	na	na	na	na	na	na	na	na	na	na	na	na	na	na
Bulgaria	01	02	01	02	01	01	00	02	02	01	02	01	00	01	01	01	01	02
Chile	01	01	00	01	00	01	00	01	00	01	01	01	01	01	00	01	00	01
Czechoslovakia	na	na	na	na	na	na	na	na	na	na	na	na	na	na	na	na	na	na
South Africa	na	na	na	na	na	na	na	na	na	na	na	na	na	na	na	na	na	na
Lithuania	01	02	00	02	01	01	01	01	01	01	01	01	na	na	na	00	01	03
Hungary	01	01	00	02	01	00	00	01	01	00	01	01	02	01	01	00	01	03
Argentina	00	00	00	00	00	00	00	00	00	00	00	00	00	00	00	00	00	00
Brazil	01	01	01	01	01	00	01	00	01	01	00	01	01	00	01	01	01	03
Mexico	00	01	00	00	00	01	00	00	00	00	00	02	00	00	01	00	01	00
Belarus	na	na	na	na	na	na	na	na	na	na	na	na	na	na	na	na	na	na
Russia	01	01	01	02	01	00	00	01	01	01	00	na	01	01	00	01	01	01
Moscow	na	na	na	na	na	na	na	na	na	na	na	na	na	na	na	na	na	na
Latvia	02	03	02	02	02	02	02	03	01	02	03	02	na	na	na	02	02	04
Estonia	00	01	00	01	00	01	00	00	01	00	00	00	na	na	01	00	01	00
Portugal	01	01	00	01	01	01	01	01	01	01	00	02	00	02	00	00	00	02
South Korea	02	02	02	01	03	02	04	02	01	02	03	02	04	01	03	02	02	01
Ireland	00	01	00	00	01	00	00	00	00	00	01	01	00	01	00	00	00	04
North Ireland	01	00	01	00	02	00	01	00	00	00	00	01	00	01	00	00	00	04
Slovenia	01	01	01	01	01	00	01	01	01	01	00	02	01	01	01	00	01	02
Spain	01	01	01	01	00	01	00	01	01	01	01	01	01	01	01	01	01	01
East Germany	01	01	01	01	01	00	01	01	01	01	01	00	01	01	00	01	01	01
Britain	na	na	na	na	na	na	na	na	na	na	na	na	na	na	na	na	na	na
Italy	01	01	01	01	01	01	01	01	00	01	01	04	01	00	02	01	00	02
Netherlands	01	02	01	00	02	02	02	01	01	02	01	01	02	01	01	00	02	01
Belgium	02	02	02	02	02	02	02	02	02	03	02	02	03	01	01	02	02	02
Austria	01	01	01	01	01	01	01	01	03	00	01	03	04	01	01	01	01	01
France	01	01	01	02	01	01	01	01	01	02	02	00	01	02	00	02	01	01
Canada	01	01	01	02	02	01	01	02	01	02	02	00	01	02	02	01	01	02
United States	02	02	03	01	03	02	02	01	02	02	03	01	02	02	01	00	02	01
Iceland	00	00	00	01	00	01	00	01	01	01	na	01	01	00	00	01	00	00
West Germany	02	02	01	02	03	02	02	02	02	02	02	03	01	02	02	02	02	00
Denmark	00	00	00	00	00	00	00	00	00	00	00	00	00	00	00	01	00	01
Finland	01	01	01	02	01	01	02	01	01	01	01	01	02	01	01	03	01	02
Norway	00	00	00	01	01	01	01	00	00	00	00	00	02	00	00	00	00	01
Sweden	01	02	01	01	02	01	01	02	01	01	00	02	02	01	01	02	01	04
Japan	00	00	00	01	00	01	00	00	00	00	00	01	01	00	00	01	00	00
Switzerland	na	na	na	na	na	na	na	na	na	na	na	na	na	na	na	na	na	na
Total	01	01	01	01	01	01	01	01	01	01	01	01	01	01	01	01	01	02

Ranking:

Latvia	02
South Korea	02
Belgium	02
United States	02
West Germany	02
Bulgaria	01
Chile	01
Lithuania	01
Hungary	01
Brazil	01
Russia	01
Portugal	01
North Ireland	01
Slovenia	01
Spain	01
East Germany	01
Italy	01
Netherlands	01
Austria	01
France	01
Canada	01
Finland	01
Sweden	01
China	00
Romania	00
Argentina	00
Mexico	00
Estonia	00
Ireland	00
Iceland	00
Denmark	00
Norway	00
Japan	00

Note: Countries in the left column are ranked according to GNP per capita. / The percentages in the bottom row give each country an equal weight. / na=not ascertained.

V51 HEALTH-VOLUNTARY

Please look at the following list of voluntary organizations and activities and say which, if any, are you currently doing unpaid voluntary work for? Voluntary organizations concerned with health. (% "do unpaid voluntary work")

	Total	Gender		Age			Education			Income			Political Affinity			Values		
		Male	Female	16-29	30-49	50+	Lower	Medium	Upper	Lower	Middle	Upper	Left	Center	Right	Mat	Mixed	Postmat
India	na	na	na	na	na	na	na	na	na	na	na	na	na	na	na	na	na	na
Nigeria	na	na	na	na	na	na	na	na	na	na	na	na	na	na	na	na	na	na
China	00	02	01	01	02	01	00	02	03	01	02	02	na	na	na	01	03	00
Romania	00	00	00	01	01	00	00	00	01	00	00	01	01	00	00	00	00	03
Turkey	na	na	na	na	na	na	na	na	na	na	na	na	na	na	na	na	na	na
Poland	na	na	na	na	na	na	na	na	na	na	na	na	na	na	na	na	na	na
Bulgaria	02	03	02	03	02	02	00	02	05	02	03	02	01	03	04	01	02	05
Chile	02	02	02	02	02	03	02	02	02	01	02	04	02	02	03	02	02	03
Czechoslovakia	na	na	na	na	na	na	na	na	na	na	na	na	na	na	na	na	na	na
South Africa	na	na	na	na	na	na	na	na	na	na	na	na	na	na	na	na	na	na
Lithuania	01	01	01	01	01	01	00	01	01	00	01	01	na	na	na	01	01	01
Hungary	02	02	03	01	03	02	01	02	05	02	03	04	na	na	na	01	02	00
Argentina	02	02	02	00	02	03	02	02	03	01	01	02	03	03	02	02	01	03
Brazil	02	02	02	00	02	03	01	01	06	01	01	03	02	03	02	02	01	04
Mexico	01	01	01	01	01	02	01	01	01	02	02	02	02	02	01	01	01	02
Belarus	na	na	na	na	na	na	na	na	na	na	na	na	na	na	na	na	na	na
Russia	01	00	01	01	01	01	00	00	02	01	01	01	01	01	01	01	01	na
Moscow	na	na	na	na	na	na	na	na	na	na	na	na	na	na	na	na	na	na
Latvia	02	02	02	02	02	02	02	02	na	02	02	02	na	na	na	na	na	na
Estonia	01	01	01	01	01	01	00	01	01	00	01	02	na	na	na	03	02	00
Portugal	02	03	01	03	01	02	02	00	01	02	01	00	02	02	na	00	01	00
South Korea	03	02	04	02	04	03	03	03	03	03	04	05	03	02	04	03	02	00
Ireland	02	02	03	01	02	03	01	02	03	02	01	03	04	03	02	03	03	04
North Ireland	02	01	03	03	02	03	03	01	02	01	01	04	02	02	02	01	03	03
Slovenia	01	01	00	00	01	00	00	01	01	01	01	02	na	na	na	02	03	02
Spain	01	01	01	01	01	00	00	00	04	00	01	01	01	01	na	01	01	01
East Germany	02	02	03	03	02	02	02	04	02	01	03	03	02	01	04	01	02	03
Britain	na	na	na	na	na	na	na	na	na	na	na	na	na	na	na	na	na	na
Italy	02	02	02	na	02	02	na	na	08	02	na	04	02	na	03	na	02	na
Netherlands	03	01	04	02	05	03	03	05	03	03	05	03	03	02	07	01	02	03
Belgium	02	03	02	02	03	02	02	02	05	01	03	03	03	02	02	01	02	04
Austria	02	03	02	01	01	02	01	02	03	01	02	03	03	03	02	02	02	02
France	02	02	02	02	02	02	01	01	03	01	01	04	04	02	03	01	03	03
Canada	07	06	08	04	07	09	07	06	08	09	06	06	10	07	06	04	07	08
United States	05	04	07	03	05	06	04	04	08	04	04	08	04	06	04	04	05	05
Iceland	04	03	05	04	04	03	05	02	04	04	02	na	04	05	03	03	03	08
West Germany	01	01	01	02	01	01	01	02	01	01	01	02	01	01	02	01	01	02
Denmark	01	00	01	00	01	01	00	01	02	01	01	01	01	01	01	01	01	01
Finland	04	03	06	03	05	05	02	03	08	04	04	06	06	02	05	02	04	05
Norway	03	02	04	03	03	04	02	01	05	03	03	03	02	03	04	12	02	04
Sweden	01	02	01	01	01	00	01	01	02	01	01	01	00	01	01	01	01	01
Japan	01	01	01	01	01	01	01	00	00	01	01	00	00	00	00	00	01	na
Switzerland	na	na	na	na	na	na	na	na	na	na	na	na	na	na	na	na	na	na
Total	02	02	02	02	02	02	02	02	03	02	02	03	03	02	02	02	02	03

Ranking:

Canada	07
United States	05
Iceland	04
Finland	04
South Korea	03
Netherlands	03
Norway	03
China	02
Bulgaria	02
Chile	02
Hungary	02
Argentina	02
Brazil	02
Latvia	02
Portugal	02
Ireland	02
North Ireland	02
East Germany	02
Italy	02
Belgium	02
Austria	02
France	02
Lithuania	01
Mexico	01
Russia	01
Estonia	01
Slovenia	01
Spain	01
West Germany	01
Denmark	01
Sweden	01
Japan	01
Romania	00

Note: Countries in the left column are ranked according to GNP per capita. / The percentages in the bottom row give each country an equal weight. / na=not ascertained.

V52 OTHER GROUPS

Please look at the following list of voluntary organizations and activities and say which, if any, are you currently doing unpaid voluntary work for? Other groups. (% "do unpaid voluntary work")

	Total	Gender Male	Female	Age 16-29	30-49	50+	Education Lower	Medium	Upper	Income Lower	Middle	Upper	Political Affinity Left	Center	Right	Values Mat	Mixed	Postmat
India	na	na	na	na	na	na	na	na	na	na	na	na	na	na	na	na	na	na
Nigeria	na	na	na	na	na	na	na	na	na	na	na	na	na	na	na	na	na	na
China	02	01	02	02	02	01	03	01	03	01	02	02	00	02	02	02	01	02
Romania	02	02	01	01	02	02	01	01	04	02	02	02	00	02	02	01	02	06
Turkey	na	na	na	na	na	na	na	na	na	na	na	na	na	na	na	na	na	na
Poland	na	na	na	na	na	na	na	na	na	na	na	na	na	na	na	na	na	na
Bulgaria	02	02	02	01	02	03	03	02	02	03	03	01	02	03	02	02	01	03
Chile	03	03	03	01	04	03	02	03	03	02	04	03	03	03	05	02	03	04
Czechoslovakia	na	na	na	na	na	na	na	na	na	na	na	na	na	na	na	na	na	na
South Africa	na	na	na	na	na	na	na	na	na	na	na	na	na	na	na	na	na	na
Lithuania	02	02	02	01	01	03	01	01	03	02	01	01	01	01	01	01	01	03
Hungary	01	01	01	01	01	01	01	01	00	00	01	01	01	01	02	01	01	00
Argentina	02	03	01	02	03	02	01	03	03	00	03	03	04	03	01	01	02	04
Brazil	00	00	00	00	00	00	00	00	00	00	00	00	00	00	00	00	00	01
Mexico	01	01	01	01	01	01	01	01	01	01	02	01	02	01	02	00	01	02
Belarus	na	na	na	na	na	na	na	na	na	na	na	na	na	na	na	na	na	na
Russia	02	02	02	02	03	02	02	02	04	03	02	03	02	03	02	02	02	04
Moscow	na	na	na	na	na	na	na	na	na	na	na	na	na	na	na	na	na	na
Latvia	02	03	01	02	02	01	01	02	03	01	01	02	03	02	00	01	02	04
Estonia	02	03	02	02	04	01	00	02	05	03	01	03	03	02	03	02	02	02
Portugal	02	02	01	01	02	01	01	03	01	01	01	02	00	01	02	02	02	01
South Korea	03	02	04	01	04	03	02	04	03	02	04	05	04	02	04	02	04	02
Ireland	02	02	01	01	03	01	01	02	01	01	02	02	01	01	02	01	01	03
North Ireland	02	02	02	01	03	02	01	02	02	03	00	04	07	03	00	00	02	04
Slovenia	03	05	01	02	03	03	02	03	03	03	03	03	03	03	03	03	03	03
Spain	01	01	01	04	01	01	01	01	01	00	01	02	01	04	04	01	04	01
East Germany	04	05	03	02	04	04	03	07	05	03	04	05	04	04	04	04	04	03
Britain	na	na	na	na	na	na	na	na	na	na	na	na	na	na	na	na	na	na
Italy	02	02	01	01	02	02	02	03	02	02	02	02	03	01	03	01	02	02
Netherlands	05	05	05	03	05	06	03	04	07	04	05	05	05	03	06	05	05	05
Belgium	03	03	02	03	03	02	02	03	04	04	02	03	03	03	03	02	03	04
Austria	03	06	02	02	04	03	02	05	02	02	04	04	05	03	05	04	03	03
France	04	04	04	03	04	05	05	09	09	08	04	07	07	09	10	02	05	04
Canada	09	08	09	08	09	09	08	09	10	08	10	09	08	09	09	09	09	08
United States	06	07	05	04	07	07	06	06	07	05	07	06	05	07	07	05	06	07
Iceland	04	05	04	04	04	06	03	07	04	na	04	na	06	03	04	03	05	00
West Germany	04	05	03	06	04	03	04	04	04	04	04	04	05	03	06	03	04	04
Denmark	04	05	02	03	05	02	01	04	04	03	04	06	03	03	06	03	04	03
Finland	07	08	06	03	05	14	03	05	11	08	04	09	05	06	09	21	05	08
Norway	07	08	05	06	07	06	05	06	09	05	07	08	06	06	09	05	06	07
Sweden	09	10	09	04	09	11	07	08	16	10	08	10	12	08	08	09	09	10
Japan	04	05	03	01	06	03	02	04	05	05	05	05	03	05	06	05	04	05
Switzerland	na	na	na	na	na	na	na	na	na	na	na	na	na	na	na	na	na	na
Total	**03**	**04**	**03**	**02**	**04**	**03**	**03**	**03**	**04**	**03**	**03**	**04**	**04**	**03**	**04**	**03**	**03**	**04**

Ranking:

Canada	09
Sweden	09
Finland	07
Norway	07
United States	06
Netherlands	05
East Germany	04
France	04
Iceland	04
West Germany	04
Denmark	04
Japan	04
Chile	03
South Korea	03
Slovenia	03
Belgium	03
Austria	03
China	02
Romania	02
Bulgaria	02
Lithuania	02
Argentina	02
Russia	02
Latvia	02
Estonia	02
Portugal	02
Ireland	02
North Ireland	02
Italy	02
Hungary	01
Mexico	01
Spain	01
Brazil	00

Note: Countries in the left column are ranked according to GNP per capita. / The percentages in the bottom row give each country an equal weight. / na=not ascertained.

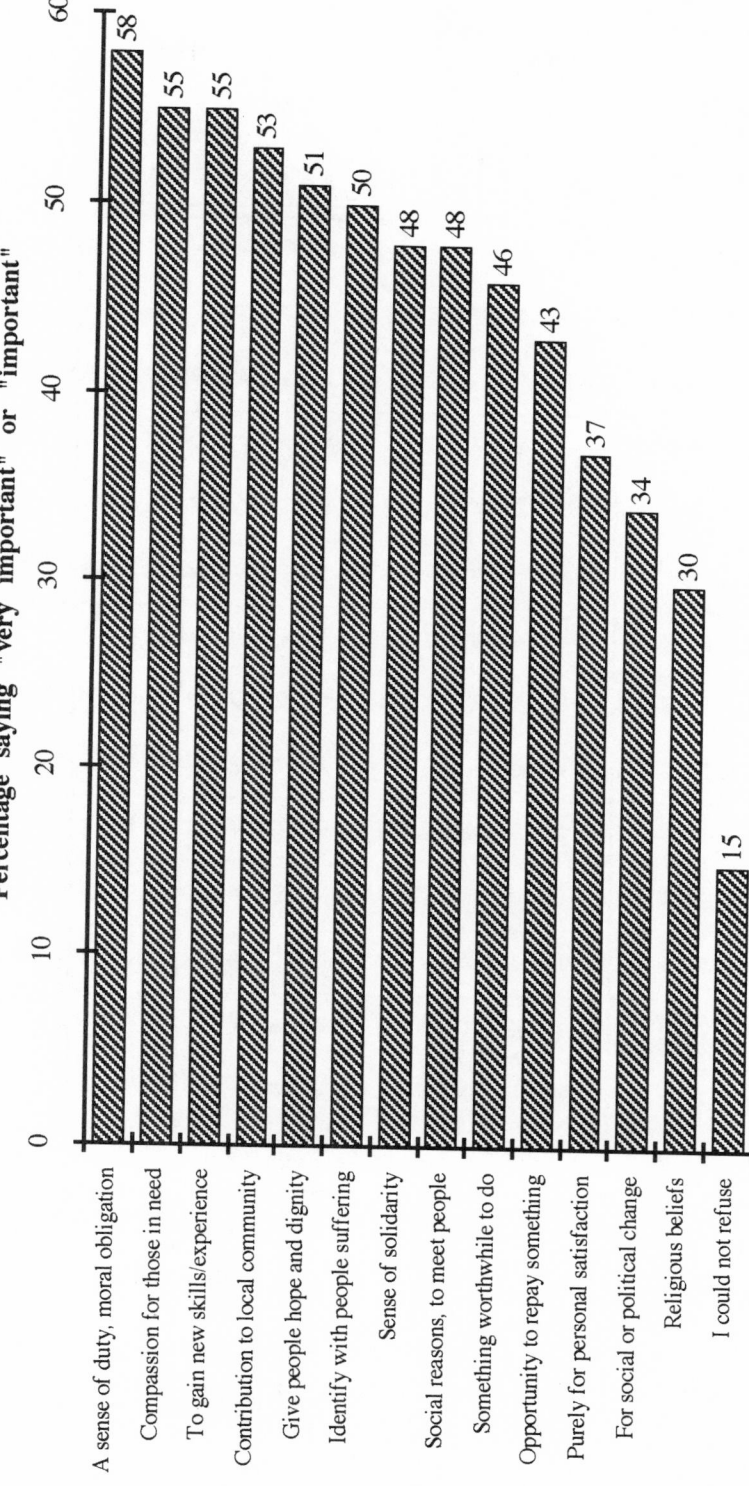

V55-V68. Reasons for doing voluntary work

Percentage saying "very important" or "important"

Reason	Percentage
A sense of duty, moral obligation	58
Compassion for those in need	55
To gain new skills/experience	55
Contribution to local community	53
Give people hope and dignity	51
Identify with people suffering	50
Sense of solidarity	48
Social reasons, to meet people	48
Something worthwhile to do	46
Opportunity to repay something	43
Purely for personal satisfaction	37
For social or political change	34
Religious beliefs	30
I could not refuse	15

V55 SOLIDARITY

Thinking about your reasons for doing voluntary work, how important has been the following reason in your own case?

"A sense of solidarity with the poor and disadvantaged." (% "very important"—codes 4 or 5)

	Total	Gender		Age			Education			Income			Political Affinity			Values		
		Male	Female	16-29	30-49	50+	Lower	Medium	Upper	Lower	Middle	Upper	Left	Center	Right	Mat	Mixed	Postmat
India	na	na	na	na	na	na	na	na	na	89	78	87	na	na	na	na	na	na
Nigeria	84	86	79	82	87	76	85	83	84	62	61	54	81	86	82	83	86	74
China	59	60	59	46	61	69	56	61	58	61	46	36	45	44	38	60	59	58
Romania	41	41	41	25	42	54	44	33	50	46	46	36	na	na	na	42	40	40
Turkey	na	na	na	na	na	na	na	na	na	na	na	na	na	na	na	na	na	na
Poland	na	na	na	na	na	na	na	na	na	na	na	na	na	na	na	na	na	na
Bulgaria	55	48	64	62	52	55	64	56	53	59	39	62	56	51	50	84	79	74
Chile	79	77	81	74	80	84	85	79	73	87	80	70	76	81	76	79	na	na
Czechoslovakia	na	na	na	na	na	na	na	na	na	na	na	na	na	na	na	na	na	na
South Africa	na	na	na	na	na	na	na	na	na	na	na	na	na	na	na	na	na	na
Lithuania	47	42	51	39	43	63	50	46	46	48	43	46	41	49	47	52	45	51
Hungary	47	39	56	44	50	45	48	57	50	53	67	56	53	68	74	46	48	50
Argentina	65	58	72	59	61	76	79	79	61	76	81	74	74	75	79	79	67	76
Brazil	78	71	85	76	78	79	80	71	69	80	81	74	60	73	66	82	76	68
Mexico	68	65	70	67	70	65	66	71	69	68	72	61	na	na	na	65	68	71
Belarus	na	na	na	na	na	na	na	na	na	na	na	na	41	46	54	na	na	na
Russia	47	44	50	40	47	54	50	49	46	49	49	44	na	na	na	49	45	58
Moscow	na	na	na	na	na	na	na	na	na	55	41	44	na	na	na	45	50	21
Latvia	45	37	50	40	48	43	42	47	40	55	41	44	na	na	na	32	24	17
Estonia	27	23	31	30	21	36	37	28	21	27	23	30	na	na	na	60	66	48
Portugal	62	59	65	48	60	84	72	63	35	68	68	52	66	66	57	60	66	48
South Korea	na	na	na	na	na	na	na	na	na	na	na	na	50	39	49	52	41	48
Ireland	45	42	47	36	40	59	45	44	47	45	40	47	33	49	35	50	43	42
North Ireland	43	39	46	38	36	59	61	21	50	70	45	28	52	47	00	62	41	44
Slovenia	46	52	36	35	46	56	46	47	46	62	44	36	54	65	56	64	58	60
Spain	59	55	64	56	58	64	62	60	61	na	67	63	62	61	59	64	63	62
East Germany	63	57	69	52	61	71	65	55	53	59	65	26	47	43	31	64	44	37
Britain	41	34	48	30	36	49	45	38	31	55	42	32	43	55	49	35	49	44
Italy	50	41	62	40	47	64	51	48	34	60	45	30	40	34	37	46	35	36
Netherlands	36	36	36	23	38	45	36	39	53	39	31	36	56	55	61	46	61	54
Belgium	55	53	61	48	51	71	62	53	53	69	59	50	60	55	54	53	55	56
Austria	55	50	60	42	54	63	59	53	53	62	54	52	54	56	56	53	53	62
France	57	57	57	58	50	62	65	55	50	58	63	39	46	48	50	68	45	50
Canada	48	48	48	43	46	55	58	47	37	57	49	43	42	45	43	64	45	42
United States	45	43	47	45	42	50	55	50	49	60	43	37	51	52	45	50	46	56
Iceland	47	40	54	38	47	57	47	44	49	na	48	43	64	46	19	42	49	28
West Germany	51	43	59	52	46	54	49	50	56	51	48	38	35	27	46	39	26	59
Denmark	26	19	38	18	26	38	49	18	26	29	25	41	62	48	31	29	49	26
Finland	53	45	63	27	50	71	70	50	49	58	50	38	40	37	39	53	38	46
Norway	36	32	42	24	31	53	52	29	37	45	31	38	47	41	17	34	43	43
Sweden	43	33	53	40	41	46	41	38	51	43	42	38	53	31	48	43	34	49
Japan	33	33	33	44	22	49	48	25	36	33	26	41	na	na	na	29	34	43
Switzerland	na	na	na	na	na	na	na	na	na	na	na	na	na	na	na	na	na	na
Total	51	47	55	45	49	59	57	49	49	57	50	47	53	52	48	54	51	49

Ranking:

	Ranking
Nigeria	84
Chile	79
Brazil	78
Mexico	68
Argentina	65
East Germany	63
Portugal	62
China	59
Spain	59
Belgium	57
France	57
Bulgaria	55
Austria	55
Finland	53
West Germany	51
Italy	50
Canada	48
Lithuania	47
Hungary	47
Russia	47
Iceland	47
Slovenia	46
Latvia	45
Ireland	45
United States	45
North Ireland	43
Sweden	43
Romania	41
Britain	41
Netherlands	36
Norway	36
Japan	33
Estonia	27
Denmark	26

Note: Countries in the left column are ranked according to GNP per capita. / The percentages in the bottom row give each country an equal weight. / na=not ascertained.

V56 COMPASSION

Thinking about your reasons for doing voluntary work, how important has been the following reason in your own case? "Compassion for those in need." (% "very important"—codes 4 or 5)

Country	Total	Gender Male	Gender Female	Age 16-29	Age 30-49	Age 50+	Education Lower	Education Medium	Education Upper	Income Lower	Income Middle	Income Upper	Political Affinity Left	Political Affinity Center	Political Affinity Right	Values Mat	Values Mixed	Values Postmat
India	na	na	na	na	na	na	na	na	na	na	na	na	na	na	na	na	na	na
Nigeria	92	92	91	91	91	94	94	91	91	88	91	95	90	92	93	93	92	87
China	63	62	65	52	66	70	61	66	60	68	62	59	na	na	na	66	61	65
Romania	39	34	47	26	40	49	45	31	46	37	46	33	45	42	33	40	40	29
Turkey	na	na	na	na	na	na	na	na	na	na	na	na	na	na	na	na	na	na
Poland	na	na	na	na	na	na	na	na	na	na	na	na	na	na	na	na	na	na
Bulgaria	69	59	80	69	69	67	57	72	65	70	67	69	67	60	86	67	71	61
Chile	69	68	70	65	65	80	79	69	60	84	67	57	63	71	62	74	69	65
Czechoslovakia	na	na	na	na	na	na	na	na	na	na	na	na	na	na	na	na	na	na
South Africa	na	na	na	na	na	na	na	na	na	na	na	na	na	na	na	na	na	na
Lithuania	70	65	73	62	68	83	74	68	71	73	69	61	na	na	na	78	70	61
Hungary	49	46	53	55	50	45	56	51	43	47	60	25	61	49	40	53	47	40
Argentina	51	47	55	55	46	55	71	39	46	62	54	37	39	47	57	61	52	42
Brazil	79	78	79	79	79	78	81	81	69	81	80	77	80	77	76	82	79	66
Mexico	na	na	na	na	na	na	na	na	na	na	na	na	na	na	na	na	na	na
Belarus	na	na	na	na	na	na	na	na	na	na	na	na	na	na	na	na	na	na
Russia	58	54	61	51	56	67	63	59	57	61	61	56	56	60	56	64	54	68
Moscow	na	na	na	na	na	na	na	na	na	na	na	na	na	na	na	na	na	na
Latvia	68	64	70	59	68	77	75	70	62	68	66	70	na	na	na	na	na	na
Estonia	53	47	60	58	51	54	63	56	45	55	51	53	na	na	na	72	71	50
Portugal	48	43	53	35	50	65	61	36	20	60	53	35	38	50	51	59	49	48
South Korea	na	na	na	na	na	na	na	na	na	na	na	na	na	na	na	60	44	17
Ireland	54	45	63	44	44	76	57	51	53	59	46	54	na	na	na	na	na	na
North Ireland	65	52	73	43	70	78	77	53	58	70	75	56	54	50	61	52	52	60
Slovenia	59	61	55	50	60	63	80	61	60	81	75	38	67	68	63	67	65	58
Spain	52	47	58	52	49	73	52	52	37	62	64	38	53	58	31	72	55	50
East Germany	73	70	77	61	72	83	76	69	68	00	67	76	36	58	58	70	54	36
Britain	70	65	75	65	71	71	78	65	54	68	73	64	66	77	71	74	73	75
Italy	37	32	44	21	35	59	40	28	10	45	37	06	71	73	66	68	70	73
Netherlands	33	30	34	14	37	42	47	35	21	27	35	30	29	46	41	53	39	29
Belgium	47	43	52	41	41	58	64	49	29	61	49	35	16	40	39	56	35	24
Austria	68	64	72	63	67	72	69	68	66	70	67	67	38	47	47	54	53	40
France	50	47	53	45	42	59	57	50	42	59	52	46	64	70	68	69	70	63
Canada	71	66	75	65	71	74	77	71	67	74	73	64	38	57	58	63	50	46
United States	76	72	80	73	75	78	80	77	72	79	73	64	74	71	75	69	70	74
Iceland	58	54	62	52	61	58	61	55	58	61	53	57	60	56	61	59	57	na
West Germany	56	51	63	55	61	58	51	51	62	55	53	57	54	57	56	60	57	52
Denmark	24	22	28	20	20	39	35	22	23	27	23	25	21	25	24	21	25	27
Finland	59	55	65	44	58	70	78	64	49	66	62	52	25	48	57	77	57	57
Norway	48	41	58	37	44	62	68	46	44	57	45	50	68	48	49	50	50	29
Sweden	51	43	58	46	51	54	53	48	51	54	51	46	57	50	42	49	53	46
Japan	16	13	21	18	12	22	24	19	07	25	09	14	19	08	24	14	21	00
Switzerland	na	na	na	na	na	na	na	na	na	na	na	na	na	na	na	na	na	na
Total	57	52	61	50	56	65	63	55	50	60	58	51	53	56	56	62	57	51

Ranking:

Nigeria	92
Brazil	79
United States	76
East Germany	73
Canada	71
Lithuania	70
Britain	70
Bulgaria	69
Chile	69
Latvia	68
Austria	68
North Ireland	65
China	63
Slovenia	59
Finland	59
Russia	58
Iceland	58
West Germany	56
Ireland	54
Estonia	53
Spain	52
Argentina	51
Sweden	51
France	50
Hungary	49
Portugal	48
Norway	48
Belgium	47
Romania	39
Italy	37
Netherlands	33
Denmark	24
Japan	16

Note: Countries in the left column are ranked according to GNP per capita. / The percentages in the bottom row give each country an equal weight. / na=not ascertained.

V57 OPPORTUNITY TO GIVE

Thinking about your reasons for doing voluntary work, how important has been the following reason in your own case? "An opportunity to repay something, give something back." (% "very important"—codes 4 or 5)

	Total	Gender		Age			Education			Income			Political Affinity			Values		
		Male	Female	16-29	30-49	50+	Lower	Medium	Upper	Lower	Middle	Upper	Left	Center	Right	Mat	Mixed	Postmat
India	na	na	na	na	na	na	na	na	na	na	na	na	na	na	na	na	na	na
Nigeria	54	55	51	55	54	39	53	57	51	65	46	52	54	52	59	51	54	63
China	16	17	16	22	13	17	17	14	16	20	16	13	28	22	24	14	18	19
Romania	23	22	24	24	21	25	19	20	28	19	24	25	28	22	24	21	23	29
Turkey	na	na	na	na	na	na	na	na	na	na	na	na	na	na	na	na	na	na
Poland	na	na	na	na	na	na	na	na	na	na	na	na	na	na	na	48	56	50
Bulgaria	54	58	50	66	57	40	50	61	48	49	51	61	50	55	52	72	62	68
Chile	66	66	66	62	69	68	68	61	71	64	71	62	67	65	73	72	62	68
Czechoslovakia	na	na	na	na	na	na	na	na	na	na	na	na	na	na	na	na	na	na
South Africa	na	na	na	na	na	na	na	na	na	na	na	na	na	na	na	na	na	na
Lithuania	46	42	49	31	44	68	49	42	56	52	44	36	61	33	21	52	44	51
Hungary	37	36	38	42	38	32	36	43	23	38	45	14	21	25	50	40	36	00
Argentina	32	38	25	19	29	44	40	19	34	38	30	29	21	25	50	21	35	32
Brazil	75	70	81	74	79	70	75	76	72	74	77	76	73	74	75	72	77	76
Mexico	na	na	na	na	na	na	na	na	na	na	na	na	na	na	na	na	na	na
Belarus	na	na	na	na	na	na	na	na	na	na	na	na	na	na	na	na	na	na
Russia	51	52	51	47	50	56	62	55	46	57	49	47	37	56	59	53	50	47
Moscow	na	na	na	na	na	na	na	na	na	na	na	na	na	na	na	na	na	na
Latvia	46	43	48	30	49	57	36	52	38	39	42	53	na	na	na	55	46	50
Estonia	57	50	65	60	52	66	73	60	45	57	51	63	na	na	na	66	52	57
Portugal	44	42	45	42	35	55	44	46	42	49	39	38	43	49	41	45	42	44
South Korea	na	na	na	na	na	na	na	na	na	na	na	na	na	na	na	na	na	na
Ireland	63	55	71	56	56	79	62	68	53	81	59	62	58	63	69	57	67	63
North Ireland	66	62	68	65	64	70	62	77	50	91	65	56	17	70	71	75	69	42
Slovenia	50	45	60	63	50	41	50	54	48	54	56	41	33	53	54	54	52	38
Spain	30	33	27	25	28	39	38	28	20	na	33	30	21	28	35	41	29	29
East Germany	49	46	53	46	49	53	52	49	43	44	51	51	46	48	46	56	52	42
Britain	65	65	65	64	68	63	68	60	63	67	65	63	64	68	59	40	71	65
Italy	15	12	19	11	13	23	15	21	00	17	12	16	12	17	19	27	15	08
Netherlands	42	38	43	36	45	42	40	49	36	43	41	41	32	46	43	45	47	33
Belgium	45	40	51	47	39	52	55	41	42	58	51	38	38	42	50	59	46	41
Austria	47	42	52	46	49	45	53	43	41	47	50	41	48	49	44	49	50	41
France	22	25	19	26	25	17	30	14	23	31	18	18	16	29	21	32	20	24
Canada	70	69	71	61	74	72	73	69	69	71	71	69	69	70	70	71	70	71
United States	71	68	74	61	74	71	76	71	69	72	71	71	68	73	71	65	70	78
Iceland	38	44	32	45	36	35	37	33	42	37	35	40	37	35	40	46	39	22
West Germany	42	42	42	41	41	44	42	42	44	45	42	39	39	42	42	49	40	42
Denmark	22	21	22	25	21	20	26	27	17	31	16	21	11	24	26	21	21	23
Finland	48	52	43	33	50	52	67	50	41	54	55	37	49	43	49	59	52	38
Norway	22	20	26	17	19	30	32	20	21	32	21	20	19	22	24	27	22	13
Sweden	42	46	37	51	38	40	43	45	35	46	44	39	44	44	41	50	45	36
Japan	38	36	42	00	47	36	39	40	36	17	32	56	41	53	35	21	44	43
Switzerland	na	na	na	na	na	na	na	na	na	na	na	na	na	na	na	na	na	na
Total	45	44	46	42	45	47	48	46	41	49	45	43	41	47	47	47	46	42

Ranking:

Brazil	75
United States	71
Canada	70
Chile	66
North Ireland	66
Britain	65
Ireland	63
Estonia	57
Nigeria	54
Bulgaria	54
Russia	51
Slovenia	50
East Germany	49
Finland	48
Austria	47
Lithuania	46
Latvia	45
Belgium	45
Portugal	44
Netherlands	42
West Germany	42
Sweden	42
Iceland	38
Japan	38
Hungary	37
Argentina	32
Spain	30
Romania	23
France	22
Denmark	22
Norway	22
China	16
Italy	15

Note: Countries in the left column are ranked according to GNP per capita. / The percentages in the bottom row give each country an equal weight. / na=not ascertained.

V58 SENSE OF DUTY

Thinking about your reasons for doing voluntary work, how important has been the following reason in your own case? "A sense of duty, moral obligation." (% "very important"—codes 4 or 5)

	Total	Gender		Age			Education			Income			Political Affinity			Values		
		Male	Female	16-29	30-49	50+	Lower	Medium	Upper	Lower	Middle	Upper	Left	Center	Right	Mat	Mixed	Postmat
India	na	na	na	na	na	na	na	na	na	na	na	na	na	na	na	na	na	na
Nigeria	89	90	87	88	89	91	88	89	89	87	88	93	88	88	91	87	91	79
China	74	75	73	73	75	74	71	72	81	72	88	74	na	88	na	75	73	81
Romania	53	53	53	50	50	60	55	50	56	36	60	58	47	53	53	53	53	56
Turkey	na	na	na	na	na	na	na	na	na	na	na	na	na	na	na	na	na	na
Poland	na	na	na	na	na	na	na	na	na	na	na	na	na	na	na	na	na	na
Bulgaria	79	75	84	74	86	71	62	86	75	78	76	80	76	76	87	80	78	87
Chile	77	77	76	75	78	78	78	77	75	75	76	79	79	75	78	81	77	71
Czechoslovakia	na	na	na	na	na	na	na	na	na	na	na	na	na	na	na	na	na	na
South Africa	na	na	na	na	na	na	na	na	na	na	na	na	na	na	na	na	na	na
Lithuania	80	74	84	73	78	91	76	81	80	79	85	72	na	na	na	80	81	85
Hungary	73	69	77	80	69	74	68	73	75	74	72	71	67	76	67	67	77	80
Argentina	70	76	63	61	71	75	88	60	65	76	69	64	63	69	64	72	70	67
Brazil	73	69	78	68	74	80	77	74	68	76	73	71	67	74	73	74	73	69
Mexico	na	na	na	na	na	na	na	na	na	na	na	na	na	na	na	na	na	na
Belarus	na	na	na	na	na	na	na	na	na	na	na	na	na	na	na	na	na	na
Russia	73	75	72	64	74	78	72	71	75	71	70	76	77	75	78	75	72	73
Moscow	na	na	na	na	na	na	na	na	na	na	na	na	na	na	na	na	na	na
Latvia	78	76	79	66	81	83	64	76	82	73	79	80	na	na	na	na	na	na
Estonia	77	74	80	73	77	81	71	79	76	72	79	81	na	na	na	80	79	71
Portugal	43	41	45	26	46	64	55	21	25	61	37	31	38	44	44	84	73	89
South Korea	na	na	na	na	na	na	na	na	na	na	na	na	38	44	44	58	35	25
Ireland	55	52	57	50	55	59	65	47	47	58	54	55	50	57	57	na	na	na
North Ireland	55	52	57	57	53	57	53	57	58	64	55	50	17	55	63	55	60	44
Slovenia	61	63	57	59	59	67	60	66	58	61	67	54	55	66	33	75	52	54
Spain	66	70	62	55	70	73	73	73	51	00	67	52	64	66	72	72	61	41
East Germany	74	72	76	62	75	81	72	72	82	68	77	75	78	73	68	79	64	61
Britain	62	62	63	62	62	63	66	59	56	67	60	60	49	66	67	79	74	73
Italy	53	49	58	44	51	60	52	60	59	58	60	32	50	58	62	70	65	53
Netherlands	45	51	43	32	45	57	48	45	44	42	41	50	50	43	54	63	50	55
Belgium	49	46	53	43	46	57	55	49	44	53	47	52	45	45	54	49	49	39
Austria	70	70	70	59	72	75	72	69	69	65	74	68	66	71	70	52	53	47
France	56	54	58	49	55	60	64	54	49	57	53	53	50	52	70	67	73	65
Canada	67	66	67	64	67	68	71	68	62	67	68	64	65	66	70	69	54	54
United States	68	71	65	65	66	70	76	68	64	72	65	69	61	68	74	68	67	69
Iceland	45	46	43	35	45	58	43	41	48	na	na	na	46	40	52	55	40	52
West Germany	56	58	53	49	53	63	57	54	55	60	53	55	48	56	65	64	59	49
Denmark	44	43	44	35	46	48	61	41	41	42	46	46	39	48	44	43	42	49
Finland	59	62	55	52	56	70	74	56	57	57	58	62	60	50	63	77	57	58
Norway	40	42	37	28	39	50	55	35	40	48	39	41	50	38	40	42	39	43
Sweden	44	48	38	39	44	48	49	40	42	46	48	43	43	42	49	56	45	36
Japan	43	44	41	09	42	57	57	42	34	35	35	47	47	39	46	26	59	20
Switzerland	na	na	na	na	na	na	na	na	na	na	na	na	na	na	na	na	na	na
Total	62	62	62	55	62	68	65	61	60	61	63	61	56	60	62	67	62	60

Ranking:

Nigeria	89
Lithuania	80
Bulgaria	79
Latvia	78
Chile	77
Estonia	77
China	74
East Germany	74
Hungary	73
Brazil	73
Russia	73
Argentina	70
Austria	70
United States	68
Canada	67
Spain	66
Britain	62
Slovenia	61
Finland	59
France	56
West Germany	56
Ireland	55
North Ireland	55
Romania	53
Italy	53
Belgium	49
Netherlands	45
Iceland	45
Denmark	44
Sweden	44
Portugal	43
Japan	43
Norway	40

Note: Countries in the left column are ranked according to GNP per capita. / The percentages in the bottom row give each country an equal weight. / na=not ascertained.

V59 IDENTIFY SUFFERING

Thinking about your reasons for doing voluntary work, how important has been the following reason in your own case? "Identifying with people who were suffering." (% "very important"—codes 4 or 5)

	Total	Gender		Age			Education			Income			Political Affinity			Values		
		Male	Female	16-29	30-49	50+	Lower	Medium	Upper	Lower	Middle	Upper	Left	Center	Right	Mat	Mixed	Postmat
India	na	na	na	na	na	na	na	na	na	na	na	na	na	na	na	na	na	na
Nigeria	88	89	87	87	90	89	94	89	86	92	85	88	87	87	89	87	90	83
China	63	64	61	59	61	71	70	62	56	66	63	59	na	na	na	65	62	58
Romania	33	29	39	28	28	47	43	25	37	28	34	37	37	39	22	33	34	28
Turkey	na	na	na	na	na	na	na	na	na	na	na	na	na	na	na	na	na	na
Poland	na	na	na	na	na	na	na	na	na	na	na	na	na	na	na	na	na	na
Bulgaria	72	64	80	74	71	71	67	77	67	71	62	79	54	73	81	70	72	68
Chile	70	69	70	64	74	71	78	69	62	75	75	60	74	67	65	69	68	72
Czechoslovakia	na	na	na	na	na	na	na	na	na	na	na	na	na	na	na	na	na	na
South Africa	na	na	na	na	na	na	na	na	na	na	na	na	na	na	na	na	na	na
Lithuania	69	77	63	64	72	71	55	70	79	66	75	68	na	na	na	67	70	76
Hungary	44	39	49	40	43	48	52	48	32	56	46	22	56	41	60	44	45	25
Argentina	49	47	50	38	42	66	56	47	45	57	51	46	53	45	55	57	42	57
Brazil	77	72	83	73	77	84	83	81	60	84	79	71	73	74	83	80	77	67
Mexico	na	na	na	na	na	na	na	na	na	na	na	na	na	na	na	na	na	na
Belarus	na	na	na	na	na	na	na	na	na	na	na	na	na	na	na	na	na	na
Russia	46	39	51	32	46	55	52	46	44	52	41	47	46	49	38	47	44	57
Moscow	na	na	na	na	na	na	na	na	na	na	na	na	na	na	na	na	na	na
Latvia	77	72	82	71	79	80	79	75	81	77	76	80	na	na	na	83	75	86
Estonia	64	67	61	50	71	62	56	65	65	64	64	64	na	na	na	66	61	81
Portugal	35	36	34	28	41	41	43	29	18	47	39	21	23	42	27	47	32	13
South Korea	na	na	na	na	na	na	na	na	na	na	na	na	na	na	na	na	na	na
Ireland	42	36	48	36	33	62	40	44	47	50	42	40	44	40	45	44	41	43
North Ireland	55	36	67	52	52	64	60	48	58	54	55	55	67	61	44	40	62	46
Slovenia	27	29	24	17	30	29	23	38	21	38	33	14	17	25	33	41	24	19
Spain	53	52	53	39	49	71	63	54	35	00	67	na	40	56	64	61	50	53
East Germany	78	72	84	64	77	86	80	79	69	80	77	76	72	79	78	88	77	77
Britain	55	52	57	46	51	61	60	57	35	62	47	51	52	56	55	61	55	54
Italy	38	30	49	30	35	49	39	30	39	42	39	15	28	47	35	53	38	30
Netherlands	45	41	47	24	53	49	47	46	43	42	48	49	42	42	51	57	47	41
Belgium	56	52	61	43	50	72	62	59	46	63	51	53	40	54	66	60	62	48
Austria	72	65	78	61	72	78	77	69	73	76	73	67	71	72	73	78	74	65
France	41	40	42	38	32	50	48	39	35	52	33	36	39	38	42	46	40	41
Canada	57	50	63	55	53	64	66	57	53	52	61	44	48	57	63	58	58	56
United States	58	57	58	58	52	64	67	61	50	72	51	54	45	62	51	64	56	57
Iceland	39	36	41	35	34	54	43	31	41	43	34	na	40	38	40	43	36	45
West Germany	60	54	66	51	60	65	59	60	62	61	58	59	53	63	62	58	60	59
Denmark	21	17	25	13	20	30	30	20	19	26	21	22	15	22	22	25	20	20
Finland	34	29	41	16	27	57	60	33	26	53	24	25	31	30	33	65	32	28
Norway	26	21	33	11	24	39	46	24	22	34	23	24	22	27	25	31	26	10
Sweden	33	26	41	23	31	45	38	27	35	33	38	29	34	33	30	40	35	25
Japan	44	44	43	50	39	52	67	37	38	58	26	52	50	40	36	46	47	54
Switzerland	na	na	na	na	na	na	na	na	na	na	na	na	na	na	na	na	na	na
Total	52	49	55	45	51	61	58	51	48	56	52	49	47	50	51	57	52	50

Ranking:

Nigeria	88
East Germany	78
Brazil	77
Latvia	77
Bulgaria	72
Austria	72
Chile	70
Lithuania	69
Estonia	64
China	63
West Germany	60
United States	58
Canada	57
Belgium	56
North Ireland	55
Britain	55
Spain	53
Argentina	49
Russia	46
Netherlands	45
Hungary	44
Japan	44
Ireland	42
France	41
Iceland	39
Italy	38
Portugal	35
Finland	34
Romania	33
Sweden	33
Slovenia	27
Norway	26
Denmark	21

Note: Countries in the left column are ranked according to GNP per capita. / The percentages in the bottom row give each country an equal weight. / na=not ascertained.

V60 WORTHWHILE TO DO

Thinking about your reasons for doing voluntary work, how important has been the following reason in your own case? "Time on my hands, wanted something worthwhile to do." (% "very important"—codes 4 or 5)

	Total	Gender		Age			Education			Income			Political Affinity			Values		
		Male	Female	16-29	30-49	50+	Lower	Medium	Upper	Lower	Middle	Upper	Left	Center	Right	Mat	Mixed	Postmat
India	na	na	na	na	na	na	na	na	na	na	na	na	na	na	na	na	na	na
Nigeria	62	66	55	65	59	52	62	65	60	71	54	62	60	57	74	54	na	na
China	72	72	71	73	71	72	66	73	73	71	71	72	na	na	na	72	68	56
Romania	31	35	25	39	26	31	28	28	36	25	35	32	40	31	29	30	30	42
Turkey	na	na	na	na	na	na	na	na	na	na	na	na	na	na	na	na	na	na
Poland	51	na	na	na	na	na	na	na	na	na	na	na	na	na	na	45	53	55
Bulgaria	65	48	54	58	51	45	64	47	54	50	48	54	46	49	56	73	65	59
Chile	na	65	65	69	59	70	71	66	58	71	69	53	61	66	67	na	na	na
Czechoslovakia	na	na	na	na	na	na	na	na	na	na	na	na	na	na	na	na	na	na
South Africa	na	na	na	na	na	na	na	na	na	na	na	na	na	na	na	na	na	na
Lithuania	66	62	70	70	61	69	71	65	68	68	70	57	na	na	na	65	69	70
Hungary	48	49	46	55	39	56	62	48	32	53	52	30	47	47	53	51	42	80
Argentina	49	47	51	60	38	57	50	49	51	50	52	53	39	44	63	53	46	51
Brazil	79	75	82	80	77	79	81	81	69	79	82	76	76	79	81	78	80	74
Mexico	na	na	na	na	na	na	na	na	na	na	na	na	na	na	na	na	na	na
Belarus	na	na	na	na	na	na	na	na	na	na	na	na	na	na	na	52	51	57
Russia	52	49	54	57	46	57	63	55	47	54	52	51	55	48	55	na	na	na
Moscow	na	na	na	na	na	na	na	na	na	na	na	na	na	na	na	na	na	na
Latvia	39	32	45	38	36	48	56	43	31	43	32	41	na	na	na	44	41	28
Estonia	30	27	33	47	20	33	43	32	22	27	29	36	na	na	na	36	26	33
Portugal	52	52	52	55	52	46	55	54	44	53	44	60	na	na	na	52	56	46
South Korea	na	52	57	54	52	na	58	54	45	57	51	50	49	46	60	58	52	na
Ireland	29	26	32	29	29	30	53	51	51	41	33	25	17	34	28	66	51	49
North Ireland	33	24	38	40	24	39	39	21	15	63	23	47	33	32	32	38	26	25
Slovenia	51	50	52	66	44	62	65	53	25	57	62	48	45	40	50	71	62	56
Spain	53	50	59	59	49	58	65	52	53	64	58	49	43	50	63	58	55	56
East Germany	52	55	57	59	52	54	59	54	53	61	58	47	56	52	41	52	52	49
Britain	31	28	34	23	22	41	39	51	51	45	43	45	26	31	32	66	52	29
Italy	62	60	64	66	52	69	65	21	18	40	36	31	58	63	68	38	29	51
Netherlands	55	50	56	50	52	62	65	53	57	na	30	26	58	63	68	71	62	56
Belgium	56	54	59	59	46	66	65	52	47	68	58	49	54	56	52	75	56	49
Austria	56	55	57	50	52	63	59	54	45	64	58	47	52	59	53	64	56	55
France	50	48	51	41	45	59	55	42	28	61	43	45	43	48	64	62	55	52
Canada	37	33	40	39	35	39	68	36	24	45	36	31	29	36	43	37	56	51
United States	31	34	28	34	25	36	40	36	24	40	30	26	29	31	33	43	55	36
Iceland	43	40	47	46	38	51	49	42	41	na	na	na	45	44	41	37	55	33
West Germany	50	50	50	38	48	52	51	49	49	54	49	47	51	50	49	50	42	41
Denmark	52	49	56	48	48	56	64	55	48	52	51	51	42	54	62	58	48	52
Finland	64	62	65	58	58	73	68	65	62	61	61	62	61	53	68	67	53	40
Norway	47	41	55	40	40	57	61	52	36	61	48	39	47	65	44	50	62	71
Sweden	65	61	70	66	63	67	66	68	57	70	69	58	67	65	63	67	45	37
Japan	36	32	41	50	32	37	35	29	46	53	33	26	33	33	28	31	43	69
Switzerland	na	na	na	na	na	na	na	na	na	na	na	na	na	na	na	31	43	27
Total	50	48	52	53	45	54	56	49	45	55	51	45	47	49	52	54	50	49

Ranking:

Brazil	79
China	72
Lithuania	66
Chile	65
Sweden	65
Finland	64
Nigeria	62
Italy	62
Belgium	56
Austria	56
Netherlands	55
Spain	53
Russia	52
Portugal	52
East Germany	52
Denmark	52
Bulgaria	51
Slovenia	51
France	50
West Germany	50
Argentina	49
Hungary	48
Norway	47
Iceland	43
Latvia	39
Canada	37
Japan	36
North Ireland	33
Romania	31
Britain	31
United States	31
Estonia	30
Ireland	29

Note: Countries in the left column are ranked according to GNP per capita. / The percentages in the bottom row give each country an equal weight. / na=not ascertained.

V61 PERSONAL SATISFACTION

Thinking about your reasons for doing voluntary work, how important has been the following reason in your own case? "Purely for personal satisfaction." (% "very important"—codes 4 or 5)

	Total	Gender Male	Gender Female	Age 16-29	Age 30-49	Age 50+	Education Lower	Education Medium	Education Upper	Income Lower	Income Middle	Income Upper	Political Affinity Left	Political Affinity Center	Political Affinity Right	Values Mat	Values Mixed	Values Postmat
India	na	na	na	na	na	na	na	na	na	na	na	na	na	na	na	na	na	na
Nigeria	63	60	70	66	60	59	69	64	61	56	66	68	69	65	63	70	61	55
China	21	21	23	25	18	23	26	18	21	22	20	21	na	na	na	20	21	22
Romania	41	46	33	38	32	57	51	34	43	43	48	30	43	42	39	39	41	46
Turkey	na	na	na	na	na	na	na	na	na	na	na	na	na	na	na	na	na	na
Poland	na	na	na	na	na	na	na	na	na	na	na	na	na	na	na	na	na	na
Bulgaria	53	52	54	65	53	44	40	58	51	47	50	63	36	59	65	41	56	61
Chile	44	46	42	47	36	52	58	40	35	53	43	36	36	45	47	58	42	35
Czechoslovakia	na	na	na	na	na	na	na	na	na	na	na	na	na	na	na	na	na	na
South Africa	na	na	na	na	na	na	na	na	na	na	na	na	na	na	na	na	na	na
Lithuania	66	63	68	69	60	68	75	62	69	66	66	65	na	na	na	67	69	54
Hungary	24	28	19	20	20	31	42	20	14	24	26	18	22	21	40	24	22	50
Argentina	54	54	54	72	47	52	55	59	57	38	54	67	74	57	46	64	50	56
Brazil	69	67	73	70	70	66	72	69	67	68	73	69	69	66	71	71	70	64
Mexico	na	na	na	na	na	na	na	na	na	na	na	na	na	na	na	na	na	na
Belarus	na	na	na	na	na	na	na	na	na	na	na	na	na	na	na	na	na	na
Russia	27	27	28	39	24	25	27	28	27	26	30	25	22	29	29	32	23	41
Moscow	na	na	na	na	na	na	na	na	na	na	na	na	na	na	na	na	na	na
Latvia	58	60	57	65	52	62	30	63	52	49	49	66	17	57	38	60	58	47
Estonia	36	37	35	49	33	29	45	37	30	37	45	28	36	24	43	37	37	27
Portugal	47	47	46	45	43	52	52	33	40	49	45	45	38	42	57	58	38	43
South Korea	48	na	na	na	na	na	na	na	na	na	na	na	na	na	na	na	na	na
Ireland	38	42	36	43	39	29	49	44	36	55	47	43	31	38	42	46	36	37
North Ireland	35	45	29	30	35	39	33	17	11	28	50	19	17	37	38	50	33	31
Slovenia	34	33	36	45	30	31	64	19	33	31	36	34	36	24	43	44	36	06
Spain	54	55	54	52	62	46	58	54	48	58	33	64	59	49	52	56	54	56
East Germany	48	48	47	43	46	53	49	20	36	63	47	43	46	50	39	69	47	43
Britain	34	35	32	43	28	34	44	38	35	38	31	31	37	35	27	46	36	37
Italy	30	29	31	31	29	29	33	47	37	29	30	15	30	26	38	50	33	31
Netherlands	20	28	17	19	18	24	18	21	20	20	20	22	21	18	18	44	36	06
Belgium	28	28	28	26	27	30	36	24	25	28	24	31	30	26	23	34	29	20
Austria	53	47	58	54	49	53	56	50	56	63	53	45	57	55	49	54	54	49
France	39	36	42	39	41	37	25	25	21	26	31	33	54	35	53	44	42	34
Canada	45	43	46	46	45	44	48	47	37	45	48	39	26	25	20	58	44	39
United States	43	45	40	47	40	44	43	47	40	48	41	41	44	40	46	40	44	44
Iceland	32	32	32	34	28	38	36	38	26	53	51	46	21	32	37	35	34	15
West Germany	50	50	50	39	55	52	52	47	49	26	51	46	54	45	53	54	49	49
Denmark	23	23	22	23	24	18	25	25	21	26	21	24	26	21	20	17	31	20
Finland	43	41	45	50	36	52	62	38	41	48	48	35	49	48	56	60	45	34
Norway	11	11	10	11	09	14	18	10	09	13	11	11	11	12	10	14	10	06
Sweden	19	18	20	18	17	24	26	20	12	25	15	18	15	23	16	20	19	18
Japan	28	17	43	54	28	18	24	28	31	33	22	24	22	23	39	25	29	20
Switzerland	na	na	na	na	na	na	na	na	na	na	na	na	na	na	na	na	na	na
Total	**40**	**40**	**40**	**43**	**37**	**40**	**44**	**38**	**36**	**40**	**40**	**38**	**38**	**38**	**41**	**44**	**40**	**36**

Ranking:
Brazil 69 · Lithuania 66 · Nigeria 63 · Latvia 58 · Argentina 54 · Spain 54 · Bulgaria 53 · Austria 53 · West Germany 50 · East Germany 48 · Portugal 47 · Canada 45 · Chile 44 · United States 43 · Finland 43 · Romania 41 · France 39 · Ireland 38 · Estonia 36 · North Ireland 35 · Slovenia 34 · Britain 34 · Iceland 32 · Italy 30 · Belgium 28 · Japan 28 · Russia 27 · Hungary 24 · Denmark 23 · China 21 · Netherlands 20 · Sweden 19 · Norway 11

Note: Countries in the left column are ranked according to GNP per capita. / The percentages in the bottom row give each country an equal weight. / na=not ascertained.

V62 RELIGIOUS BELIEFS

Thinking about your reasons for doing voluntary work, how important has been the following reason in your own case? "Religious beliefs." (% "very important"—codes 4 or 5)

	Total	Gender		Age			Education			Income			Political Affinity			Values			Ranking	
		Male	Female	16-29	30-49	50+	Lower	Medium	Upper	Lower	Middle	Upper	Left	Center	Right	Mat	Mixed	Postmat		
India	na	na	na	na	na	na	na	na	na	na	na	na	na	na	na	na	na	na	Nigeria	84
Nigeria	84	80	92	84	83	91	86	89	79	86	80	90	90	80	89	89	83	74	Chile	64
China	07	06	09	08	06	08	08	07	04	09	05	07	na	na	na	10	03	14	Brazil	62
Romania	24	18	32	14	20	42	51	14	22	23	27	21	29	24	21	32	20	13	United States	60
Turkey	na	na	na	na	na	na	na	na	na	na	na	na	na	na	na	na	na	na	Spain	46
Poland	na	na	na	na	na	na	na	na	na	na	na	na	na	na	na	na	na	na	Argentina	45
Bulgaria	18	14	24	10	18	26	18	22	13	30	07	14	06	11	42	17	22	10	Canada	44
Chile	64	58	70	55	63	77	80	54	60	74	59	58	55	65	61	70	66	54	Italy	41
Czechoslovakia	na	na	na	na	na	na	na	na	na	na	na	na	na	na	na	na	na	na	North Ireland	40
South Africa	na	na	na	na	na	na	na	na	na	na	na	na	na	na	na	na	na	na	Portugal	36
Lithuania	32	27	36	19	25	58	49	30	23	39	33	11	17	28	43	41	30	29	Ireland	34
Hungary	28	30	27	15	22	44	54	22	21	36	24	29	17	49	55	35	23	20	Lithuania	32
Argentina	45	36	53	42	46	46	44	48	41	57	37	47	52	63	65	56	47	32	Britain	32
Brazil	62	54	71	53	63	74	74	63	43	76	61	51	na	na	na	69	58	54	Austria	29
Mexico	na	na	na	na	na	na	na	na	na	na	na	na	na	na	na	na	na	na	Hungary	28
Belarus	na	na	na	na	na	na	na	na	na	na	na	na	na	na	na	na	na	na	East Germany	28
Russia	13	08	17	15	10	17	25	14	10	15	14	09	08	14	17	13	13	17	Belgium	28
Moscow	na	na	na	na	na	na	na	na	na	na	na	na	na	na	na	na	na	na	West Germany	28
Latvia	24	15	32	17	30	23	10	24	26	31	26	19	na	na	na	18	27	15	Netherlands	25
Estonia	11	06	16	09	10	16	14	10	11	12	12	09	na	na	na	04	11	17	Romania	24
Portugal	36	24	53	24	32	60	46	31	15	55	29	22	26	39	38	42	31	25	Latvia	24
South Korea	na	na	na	na	na	na	na	na	na	na	na	na	na	na	na	na	na	na	France	24
Ireland	28	29	38	16	29	55	40	29	26	35	27	24	14	32	42	37	33	34	Norway	20
North Ireland	34	21	51	25	33	50	35	40	50	36	23	24	00	35	58	75	32	31	Japan	20
Slovenia	12	13	12	21	09	13	21	10	11	15	15	09	07	12	18	14	13	06	Bulgaria	18
Spain	46	41	51	28	38	73	56	45	29	00	33	29	21	47	73	62	51	26	Finland	17
East Germany	28	22	34	13	28	37	28	32	23	35	27	24	12	31	37	34	27	27	Iceland	16
Britain	32	21	42	12	27	42	31	37	27	36	23	24	20	30	38	34	31	27	Sweden	15
Italy	41	34	53	38	33	56	41	48	30	55	34	20	24	52	41	49	41	37	Russia	13
Netherlands	25	30	24	18	22	37	31	22	24	25	24	29	09	27	38	27	31	38	Slovenia	12
Belgium	28	24	34	15	24	43	36	29	21	34	25	23	10	25	42	29	33	23	Estonia	11
Austria	29	23	34	21	24	37	31	27	30	36	27	25	22	25	35	37	29	25	Denmark	10
France	24	18	30	18	14	35	33	19	20	26	33	12	11	26	48	33	24	17	China	07
Canada	44	39	48	35	34	61	65	43	33	52	48	29	28	45	46	56	43	36		
United States	60	59	61	53	55	69	68	64	53	63	63	53	43	64	66	65	60	58		
Iceland	16	14	18	14	13	28	22	10	17	22	23	26	11	19	18	18	16	13		
West Germany	28	22	36	18	24	39	34	19	27	37	23	09	17	29	35	47	28	22		
Denmark	10	08	14	07	10	15	17	10	09	17	06	17	05	14	09	03	13	06		
Finland	17	15	19	07	14	29	39	16	11	26	14	12	13	15	16	33	14	18		
Norway	20	14	27	18	14	30	33	14	19	29	17	17	11	20	24	23	18	17		
Sweden	15	12	18	15	13	19	13	15	17	17	12	15	09	19	13	15	19	06		
Japan	20	19	22	18	14	32	37	18	13	44	09	13	20	24	13	17	23	07		
Switzerland	na	na	na	na	na	na	na	na	na	na	na	na	na	na	na	na	na	na		
Total	31	26	36	23	28	42	38	30	26	36	29	26	21	33	39	36	31	25		

Note: Countries in the left column are ranked according to GNP per capita. / The percentages in the bottom row give each country an equal weight. / na=not ascertained.

V63 GIVE HOPE/DIGNITY

Thinking about your reasons for doing voluntary work, how important has been the following reason in your own case? "To help give disadvantaged people hope and dignity." (% "very important"—codes 4 or 5)

	Total	Gender Male	Gender Female	Age 16-29	Age 30-49	Age 50+	Educ Lower	Educ Medium	Educ Upper	Income Lower	Income Middle	Income Upper	Pol Left	Pol Center	Pol Right	Values Mat	Values Mixed	Values Postmat
India	na	na	na	na	na	na	na	na	na	na	na	na	na	na	na	na	na	na
Nigeria	86	86	86	86	na	na	84	88	85	90	82	85	81	85	87	82	89	83
China	56	57	55	46	57	67	55	59	52	57	56	55	55	45	na	56	57	56
Romania	44	47	38	36	42	54	40	37	54	40	45	45	55	45	39	40	45	52
Turkey	na	na	na	na	na	na	na	na	na	na	na	na	na	na	na	na	na	na
Poland	na	na	na	na	na	na	na	na	na	na	na	na	na	na	na	na	na	na
Bulgaria	60	52	69	62	56	64	42	66	56	71	44	58	54	52	77	75	55	62
Chile	78	74	81	71	80	82	84	76	73	82	77	72	75	76	80	80	77	76
Czechoslovakia	na	na	na	na	na	na	na	na	na	na	na	na	na	na	na	na	na	na
South Africa	na	na	na	na	na	na	na	na	na	na	na	na	na	na	na	na	na	na
Lithuania	69	63	74	62	68	79	70	71	62	73	67	63	na	na	na	66	75	61
Hungary	52	48	57	53	57	45	48	53	54	53	59	39	50	53	53	49	55	50
Argentina	63	59	67	63	59	70	65	63	62	62	64	55	67	64	68	71	61	62
Brazil	83	79	87	82	84	82	85	84	76	85	82	82	83	83	82	81	84	82
Mexico	na	na	na	na	na	na	na	na	na	na	na	na	na	na	na	na	na	na
Belarus	na	na	na	na	na	na	na	na	na	na	na	na	na	na	na	na	na	na
Russia	42	38	44	36	41	47	50	41	40	47	35	42	35	48	39	42	41	46
Moscow	na	na	na	na	na	na	na	na	na	na	na	na	na	na	na	na	na	na
Latvia	51	42	57	43	52	57	27	52	51	55	51	49	na	na	na	48	55	43
Estonia	36	31	40	41	33	37	35	45	19	31	41	38	na	na	na	41	32	42
Portugal	52	47	60	41	51	72	65	45	25	70	52	36	46	56	48	60	48	37
South Korea	64	54	65	48	56	73	68	62	60	65	67	60	62	63	61	70	62	51
Ireland	52	48	56	40	47	67	65	51	46	45	51	49	51	60	49	48	58	53
North Ireland	61	48	68	44	55	71	62	58	48	70	60	53	65	55	56	52	49	42
Slovenia	37	36	38	18	36	41	36	34	26	42	38	33	39	34	31	46	34	29
Spain	59	54	65	48	56	73	55	47	44	100	67	41	41	62	72	70	62	51
East Germany	64	54	74	57	64	67	65	62	60	65	67	60	62	63	61	63	58	67
Britain	56	52	60	50	52	63	62	51	53	63	54	49	51	56	49	48	49	56
Italy	51	44	57	44	51	60	51	58	26	56	51	30	44	55	35	66	55	47
Netherlands	32	24	35	18	40	29	36	34	26	29	32	30	31	23	41	59	31	28
Belgium	48	43	54	37	41	65	55	47	44	48	57	41	47	46	51	57	47	46
Austria	57	50	62	52	55	60	58	57	53	58	70	49	58	56	58	56	58	55
France	59	56	64	50	52	70	66	62	48	65	64	50	51	62	65	82	55	61
Canada	63	56	68	63	56	71	74	63	56	75	64	50	58	62	65	65	61	67
United States	65	65	66	66	63	67	76	64	62	68	64	64	62	66	64	56	63	71
Iceland	53	47	59	45	56	53	53	48	57	50	45	47	51	56	54	54	53	44
West Germany	48	42	55	44	43	55	49	48	22	50	45	29	48	50	47	07	46	33
Denmark	24	19	32	16	26	31	38	22	23	24	29	24	29	23	22	24	26	33
Finland	47	43	52	23	47	59	75	42	41	53	52	35	47	48	38	53	49	42
Norway	44	37	52	39	41	49	58	37	45	51	29	39	44	43	44	43	46	33
Sweden	44	35	54	42	41	49	36	44	49	43	59	33	49	40	43	41	44	44
Japan	32	32	31	13	25	48	38	29	31	31	29	39	47	33	23	35	30	na
Switzerland	na	na	na	na	na	na	na	na	na	na	na	na	na	na	na	na	na	na
Total	**54**	**49**	**58**	**47**	**52**	**60**	**57**	**53**	**49**	**58**	**54**	**49**	**53**	**54**	**54**	**56**	**54**	**52**

Ranking:

Nigeria	86
Brazil	83
Chile	78
Lithuania	69
United States	65
East Germany	64
Argentina	63
Canada	63
North Ireland	61
Bulgaria	60
Spain	59
France	59
Austria	57
China	56
Britain	56
Iceland	53
Hungary	52
Portugal	52
Ireland	52
Latvia	51
Italy	51
Belgium	48
West Germany	48
Finland	47
Romania	44
Norway	44
Sweden	44
Russia	42
Slovenia	37
Estonia	36
Netherlands	32
Japan	32
Denmark	24

Note: Countries in the left column are ranked according to GNP per capita. / The percentages in the bottom row give each country an equal weight. / na=not ascertained.

V64 COMMUNITY CONTRIBUTION

Thinking about your reasons for doing voluntary work, how important has been the following reason in your own case? "To make a contribution to my local community." (% "very important"—codes 4 or 5)

	Total	Gender		Age			Education			Income			Political Affinity			Values		
		Male	Female	16-29	30-49	50+	Lower	Medium	Upper	Lower	Middle	Upper	Left	Center	Right	Mat	Mixed	Postmat
India	na	na	na	na	na	na	na	na	na	na	na	na	na	na	na	na	na	na
Nigeria	87	88	86	87	88	83	91	87	86	89	82	93	92	84	89	86	89	78
China	59	60	56	51	60	63	59	61	56	61	59	55	40	39	31	56	62	57
Romania	36	39	32	24	35	49	35	35	38	23	44	37	40	39	31	39	37	20
Turkey	na	na	na	na	na	na	na	na	na	na	na	na	na	na	na	na	na	na
Poland	na	na	na	na	na	na	na	na	na	na	na	na	na	na	na	na	na	na
Bulgaria	70	74	64	58	73	72	53	73	69	62	66	79	72	71	58	78	68	57
Chile	68	66	69	61	69	73	73	69	61	75	70	56	72	63	67	72	67	65
Czechoslovakia	na	na	na	na	na	na	na	na	na	na	na	na	na	na	na	na	na	na
South Africa	na	na	na	na	na	na	na	na	na	na	na	na	na	na	na	na	na	na
Lithuania	36	39	34	31	35	46	28	39	33	35	36	40	na	na	na	36	40	31
Hungary	66	63	68	60	63	73	60	77	44	65	64	70	67	66	67	69	65	40
Argentina	69	69	69	67	66	74	67	67	70	68	73	56	71	68	64	66	71	67
Brazil	67	63	73	65	70	67	68	69	65	68	69	67	63	66	68	68	67	67
Mexico	na	na	na	na	na	na	na	na	na	na	na	na	na	na	na	na	na	na
Belarus	na	na	na	na	na	na	na	na	na	na	na	na	na	na	na	na	na	na
Russia	61	60	62	54	63	65	58	61	63	68	56	61	65	70	49	62	60	70
Moscow	na	na	na	na	na	na	na	na	na	na	na	na	na	na	na	na	na	na
Latvia	54	54	54	46	54	61	36	56	51	55	60	49	na	na	na	56	53	58
Estonia	44	48	40	36	45	49	37	44	46	43	46	43	na	na	na	45	44	42
Portugal	60	59	61	54	56	72	69	66	32	65	61	52	59	57	62	74	53	51
South Korea	na	na	na	na	na	na	na	na	na	na	na	na	na	na	na	na	na	na
Ireland	75	70	79	69	78	74	80	74	59	74	75	71	56	80	76	75	78	67
North Ireland	68	66	69	75	62	70	67	73	75	54	70	72	17	76	71	75	71	46
Slovenia	59	64	49	48	64	58	60	65	53	74	57	49	59	51	69	72	56	47
Spain	50	50	50	41	52	56	51	51	46	na	50	50	47	45	67	43	51	56
East Germany	45	45	45	44	42	49	46	45	40	42	48	43	34	52	44	40	45	48
Britain	66	59	73	73	60	70	66	66	70	77	63	59	75	65	62	86	59	73
Italy	59	58	60	55	55	67	59	58	61	65	55	45	51	63	58	64	59	56
Netherlands	48	52	46	36	49	56	50	50	45	35	60	45	33	48	56	65	45	48
Belgium	45	49	42	35	42	59	52	38	49	48	50	44	40	45	52	39	50	43
Austria	39	44	34	31	35	48	42	37	42	43	37	38	34	40	41	38	43	31
France	56	59	53	36	57	64	63	58	44	69	62	46	62	52	48	46	61	54
Canada	67	67	67	56	70	71	72	64	67	67	70	64	62	66	67	63	66	71
United States	69	67	70	69	71	66	68	68	70	68	66	72	66	69	70	65	69	70
Iceland	64	67	62	63	63	70	73	59	63	66	71	75	63	76	59	65	69	44
West Germany	38	36	39	36	26	47	43	31	32	47	33	33	32	34	49	45	40	31
Denmark	50	46	55	51	54	39	63	47	49	47	47	55	52	38	60	50	49	52
Finland	50	50	50	56	46	56	65	54	41	58	49	43	54	44	50	50	53	43
Norway	69	68	70	60	72	70	70	69	68	66	71	75	63	72	70	75	65	73
Sweden	47	49	46	46	54	36	59	44	41	60	46	44	49	48	45	53	48	46
Japan	44	43	46	33	57	28	33	47	48	40	46	41	63	51	31	35	46	60
Switzerland	na	na	na	na	na	na	na	na	na	na	na	na	na	na	na	na	na	na
Total	57	57	57	51	57	61	58	58	54	58	58	55	56	59	59	59	58	53

Ranking:

Country	Ranking
Nigeria	87
Ireland	75
Bulgaria	70
Argentina	69
United States	69
Norway	69
Chile	68
North Ireland	68
Brazil	67
Canada	67
Hungary	66
Britain	66
Iceland	64
Russia	61
Portugal	60
China	59
Slovenia	59
Italy	59
France	56
Latvia	54
Spain	50
Denmark	50
Finland	50
Netherlands	48
Sweden	47
East Germany	45
Belgium	45
Estonia	44
Japan	44
Austria	39
West Germany	38
Romania	36
Lithuania	36

Note: Countries in the left column are ranked according to GNP per capita. / The percentages in the bottom row give each country an equal weight. / na=not ascertained.

V65 SOCIAL/POLITICAL CHANGE

Thinking about your reasons for doing voluntary work, how important has been the following reason in your own case?
"To bring about social or political change." (% "very important"—codes 4 or 5)

	Total	Gender		Age			Education			Income			Political Affinity			Values		
		Male	Female	16-29	30-49	50+	Lower	Medium	Upper	Lower	Middle	Upper	Left	Center	Right	Mat	Mixed	Postmat
India	na	na	na	na	na	na	na	na	na	na	na	na	na	na	na	na	na	na
Nigeria	61	63	56	60	62	55	64	59	65	60	60	58	55	60	73	55	67	43
China	32	34	28	29	34	32	28	30	43	39	39	29	30	26	40	28	35	47
Romania	29	37	17	28	28	29	25	30	35	25	26	34	na	na	na	24	27	54
Turkey	na	na	na	na	na	na	na	na	na	na	na	na	na	na	na	na	na	na
Poland	na	na	na	na	na	na	na	na	na	na	na	na	na	na	na	na	na	na
Bulgaria	64	66	61	64	68	54	54	59	76	54	57	75	68	68	52	65	61	67
Chile	44	50	38	44	45	42	42	44	47	41	41	51	64	39	40	42	61	44
Czechoslovakia	na	na	na	na	na	na	na	na	na	na	na	na	na	na	na	na	na	na
South Africa	na	na	na	na	na	na	na	na	na	na	na	na	na	na	na	na	na	na
Lithuania	41	54	31	25	51	51	35	42	43	47	47	48	na	na	na	33	44	50
Hungary	31	34	29	25	36	28	26	39	29	36	36	29	22	31	50	20	41	40
Argentina	33	36	29	22	30	44	29	28	38	32	32	41	44	27	43	21	30	47
Brazil	50	53	45	52	51	43	39	51	62	39	52	57	60	45	49	38	53	72
Mexico	na	na	na	na	na	na	na	na	na	na	na	na	na	na	na	na	na	na
Belarus	na	na	na	na	na	na	na	na	na	na	na	na	na	na	na	na	na	na
Russia	63	64	62	55	66	63	62	63	64	62	63	65	71	65	61	63	61	74
Moscow	na	na	na	na	na	na	na	na	na	na	na	na	na	na	na	na	na	na
Latvia	60	62	58	48	65	64	50	60	62	60	61	59	na	na	na	58	59	75
Estonia	33	40	27	23	41	27	15	34	39	27	29	44	na	na	na	38	33	40
Portugal	32	35	27	29	41	27	26	35	41	26	28	39	44	31	26	25	33	53
South Korea	na	na	na	na	na	na	na	na	na	na	na	na	na	na	na	na	na	na
Ireland	25	30	22	26	27	22	13	27	35	13	28	25	33	23	28	26	22	31
North Ireland	21	17	23	19	21	22	27	21	25	10	10	22	50	22	17	18	21	23
Slovenia	30	33	25	17	34	31	21	28	36	35	35	29	34	28	08	28	31	28
Spain	32	37	26	26	39	28	30	30	36	30	33	36	44	25	35	17	27	51
East Germany	54	61	47	60	56	47	52	51	63	56	56	61	62	53	49	30	54	60
Britain	25	24	27	16	22	31	36	24	24	23	23	22	37	23	21	16	31	27
Italy	35	38	32	29	42	35	38	49	49	36	36	35	41	36	28	32	35	40
Netherlands	21	20	22	19	23	21	21	20	28	15	15	28	35	15	18	09	18	30
Belgium	27	30	24	26	25	30	28	28	37	26	27	25	38	27	25	30	20	33
Austria	31	33	30	25	35	31	23	32	32	31	31	36	39	31	30	16	31	38
France	33	32	33	34	35	30	40	30	34	35	35	28	46	29	19	12	30	46
Canada	40	39	41	39	42	38	38	36	44	43	43	39	52	38	44	32	38	50
United States	42	42	42	41	45	41	46	38	44	40	40	40	60	40	39	31	40	53
Iceland	30	29	32	24	35	27	33	24	32	na	na	na	36	26	33	22	28	55
West Germany	35	38	31	39	39	29	29	37	49	29	32	42	50	25	35	27	32	45
Denmark	30	31	30	24	33	32	27	20	35	27	29	38	38	32	26	14	30	41
Finland	36	41	28	27	37	39	23	29	38	38	38	44	49	32	34	20	33	45
Norway	29	27	31	25	32	26	34	28	31	23	23	37	39	29	23	26	27	46
Sweden	31	27	37	34	34	27	32	25	44	32	40	26	45	24	28	16	29	46
Japan	26	21	32	09	29	26	24	21	29	17	17	34	35	30	16	17	28	40
Switzerland	na	na	na	na	na	na	na	na	na	na	na	na	na	na	na	na	na	na
Total	37	39	34	32	39	36	31	35	42	34	36	40	46	34	34	29	36	46

Note: Countries in the left column are ranked according to GNP per capita. / The percentages in the bottom row give each country an equal weight. / na=not ascertained.

Ranking:

Bulgaria	64
Russia	63
Nigeria	61
Latvia	60
East Germany	54
Brazil	50
Chile	44
United States	42
Lithuania	41
Canada	40
Finland	36
Italy	35
West Germany	35
Argentina	33
Estonia	33
France	33
China	32
Portugal	32
Spain	32
Hungary	31
Austria	31
Sweden	31
Slovenia	30
Iceland	30
Denmark	30
Romania	29
Norway	29
Belgium	27
Japan	26
Ireland	25
Britain	25
North Ireland	21
Netherlands	21

V66 SOCIAL REASONS

Thinking about your reasons for doing voluntary work, how important has been the following reason in your own case? "For social reasons, to meet people." (% "very important"—codes 4 or 5)

	Total	Gender Male	Gender Female	Age 16-29	Age 30-49	Age 50+	Education Lower	Education Medium	Education Upper	Income Lower	Income Middle	Income Upper	Political Affinity Left	Political Affinity Center	Political Affinity Right	Values Mat	Values Mixed	Values Postmat
India	na	na	na	na	na	na	na	na	na	na	na	na	na	na	na	na	na	na
Nigeria	70	74	63	70	69	64	74	70	68	73	62	76	71	69	74	67	73	59
China	37	40	32	50	33	32	40	36	37	36	38	38	30	37	32	31	40	57
Romania	34	36	31	39	26	40	28	31	40	27	38	34	30	37	32	32	32	50
Turkey	na	na	na	na	na	na	na	na	na	na	na	na	na	na	na	na	na	na
Poland	na	na	na	na	na	na	na	na	na	na	na	na	na	na	na	na	na	na
Bulgaria	62	69	55	66	65	55	43	69	61	57	56	72	68	67	52	69	58	70
Chile	41	44	38	44	39	42	48	42	34	48	45	29	42	41	42	48	44	32
Czechoslovakia	na	na	na	na	na	na	na	na	na	na	na	na	na	na	na	na	na	na
South Africa	na	na	na	na	na	na	na	na	na	na	na	na	na	na	na	na	na	na
Lithuania	84	79	88	82	85	85	90	84	79	84	88	77	78	na	73	81	87	88
Hungary	61	65	57	85	52	62	52	66	61	60	63	58	78	56	73	59	61	80
Argentina	24	31	17	25	24	23	23	30	19	15	31	27	29	23	23	25	21	29
Brazil	65	64	66	72	61	60	63	68	58	66	70	61	61	62	71	62	66	68
Mexico	na	na	na	na	na	na	na	na	na	na	na	na	na	na	na	na	na	na
Belarus	na	na	na	na	na	na	na	na	na	na	na	na	na	na	na	na	na	na
Russia	67	63	71	64	67	70	65	68	67	67	71	64	71	70	72	65	68	71
Moscow	na	na	na	na	na	na	na	na	na	na	na	na	na	na	na	na	na	na
Latvia	68	65	71	71	69	64	36	73	64	67	65	72	na	na	na	69	71	59
Estonia	68	65	70	83	65	60	70	72	59	68	79	58	na	na	na	70	65	77
Portugal	32	34	30	32	30	36	37	26	24	35	29	35	22	30	40	38	28	35
South Korea	55	53	57	na	50	56	56	56	51	58	59	48	55	56	47	55	53	61
Ireland	37	35	38	43	33	26	39	31	26	42	29	34	29	33	36	38	36	25
North Ireland	46	35	39	43	38	30	36	43	25	46	50	47	17	41	38	58	37	23
Slovenia	47	49	43	58	45	42	64	44	43	43	49	39	39	45	62	52	50	28
Spain	37	40	34	44	35	34	40	42	29	na	33	40	34	39	43	21	40	48
East Germany	55	53	57	na	50	56	56	56	51	58	59	48	55	56	47	55	53	61
Britain	37	35	38	40	30	42	45	18	35	46	29	35	43	31	36	55	53	61
Italy	46	48	43	51	45	41	47	47	24	43	52	47	46	44	45	40	41	50
Netherlands	58	64	56	52	56	67	67	51	59	50	71	59	53	61	56	57	65	52
Belgium	55	55	54	56	55	53	62	50	54	62	57	53	55	55	50	62	53	55
Austria	57	56	59	69	52	56	57	58	48	61	68	52	60	56	56	69	56	54
France	59	56	61	50	72	51	58	64	53	39	38	29	66	60	50	33	64	64
Canada	35	34	36	42	32	34	42	38	28	30	24	34	31	36	35	48	36	31
United States	26	27	26	30	23	29	32	29	21	30	24	23	12	26	34	26	27	25
Iceland	49	50	48	64	44	39	55	44	48	na	na	na	42	55	51	60	49	27
West Germany	58	60	56	67	58	53	59	60	52	59	65	52	57	61	57	54	57	61
Denmark	56	55	57	66	55	46	68	55	54	63	50	56	53	54	62	55	58	54
Finland	73	74	73	87	71	72	89	70	72	85	73	64	64	75	76	88	71	74
Norway	53	53	53	63	52	47	55	60	46	62	51	47	47	54	53	54	53	46
Sweden	66	63	68	79	62	61	67	68	58	68	67	61	64	69	63	66	67	64
Japan	65	63	68	79	66	58	62	65	68	74	65	53	60	64	58	60	69	67
Switzerland	na	na	na	na	na	na	na	na	na	na	na	na	na	na	na	na	na	na
Total	52	53	51	58	50	49	54	52	47	55	54	49	48	51	51	54	53	52

Ranking:	
Lithuania	84
Finland	73
Nigeria	70
Latvia	68
Estonia	68
Russia	67
Sweden	66
Brazil	65
Japan	65
Bulgaria	62
Hungary	61
France	59
Netherlands	58
West Germany	58
Austria	57
Denmark	56
East Germany	55
Belgium	55
Norway	53
Iceland	49
Slovenia	47
Italy	46
Chile	41
China	37
North Ireland	37
Spain	37
Britain	37
Canada	35
Romania	34
Ireland	34
Portugal	32
United States	26
Argentina	24

Note: Countries in the left column are ranked according to GNP per capita. / The percentages in the bottom row give each country an equal weight. / na=not ascertained.

V67 USEFUL EXPERIENCE

Thinking about your reasons for doing voluntary work, how important has been the following reason in your own case?
"To gain new skills and useful experience." (% "very important"—codes 4 or 5)

		Gender		Age			Education			Income			Political Affinity			Values		
	Total	Male	Female	16-29	30-49	50+	Lower	Medium	Upper	Lower	Middle	Upper	Left	Center	Right	Mat	Mixed	Postmat
India	na	na	na	na	na	na	na	na	na	na	na	na	na	na	na	na	na	na
Nigeria	80	82	76	84	75	73	76	84	77	80	75	84	82	78	81	76	82	85
China	64	68	57	72	66	52	55	66	73	62	62	69	37	40	34	57	69	81
Romania	37	39	34	49	32	34	34	37	38	32	42	35	37	40	34	36	38	38
Turkey	na	na	na	na	na	na	na	na	na	na	na	na	na	na	na	na	na	na
Poland	na	na	na	na	na	na	na	na	na	na	na	na	na	na	na	na	na	na
Bulgaria	53	55	51	73	55	34	25	66	48	53	50	56	50	65	36	55	48	68
Chile	69	69	68	73	68	63	72	68	66	76	66	65	68	71	66	67	68	71
Czechoslovakia	na	na	na	na	na	na	na	na	na	na	na	na	na	na	na	na	na	na
South Africa	na	na	na	na	na	na	na	na	na	na	na	na	na	na	na	na	na	na
Lithuania	83	84	81	88	84	74	61	87	89	82	82	86	na	na	na	74	86	89
Hungary	67	71	64	85	65	62	52	77	61	65	67	71	72	66	80	62	69	100
Argentina	41	46	35	55	42	29	32	44	48	19	52	41	33	44	52	43	35	51
Brazil	81	78	84	87	81	72	77	85	75	79	86	81	81	80	82	81	81	85
Mexico	na	na	na	na	na	na	na	na	na	na	na	na	na	na	na	na	na	na
Belarus	na	na	na	na	na	na	na	na	na	na	na	na	na	na	na	na	na	na
Russia	63	62	65	70	69	48	54	62	67	59	69	63	69	67	58	59	65	73
Moscow	na	na	na	na	na	na	na	na	na	na	na	na	na	na	na	na	na	na
Latvia	62	62	63	64	65	55	43	69	55	61	65	61	na	na	na	61	64	59
Estonia	71	70	72	81	70	62	72	75	63	72	75	64	na	na	na	69	68	88
Portugal	62	64	59	74	51	51	60	55	68	54	54	75	62	61	61	65	62	66
South Korea	na	na	na	na	na	na	na	na	na	na	na	na	na	na	na	na	na	na
Ireland	27	26	27	30	30	19	26	29	24	30	27	24	17	28	29	24	26	28
North Ireland	46	45	46	52	52	30	46	53	25	30	45	44	33	51	33	50	50	25
Slovenia	53	52	56	71	55	35	64	51	51	53	60	43	44	49	62	59	56	33
Spain	46	49	42	57	44	39	50	43	42	50	33	50	44	51	40	32	49	52
East Germany	66	71	61	70	67	61	65	65	68	61	71	64	70	64	61	63	66	67
Britain	37	36	38	55	42	26	43	23	35	40	42	29	40	42	26	31	40	34
Italy	55	55	55	63	51	51	55	54	57	53	57	50	58	53	50	61	53	55
Netherlands	59	53	62	63	63	51	53	56	67	61	67	50	70	51	53	54	58	63
Belgium	47	46	48	54	49	38	50	43	48	39	50	47	52	49	39	45	44	53
Austria	66	66	65	79	67	57	58	71	62	58	69	67	65	70	63	66	65	68
France	45	53	36	64	51	30	41	48	44	44	53	40	41	57	42	18	50	49
Canada	54	56	53	68	53	45	55	58	50	55	59	47	54	52	56	60	53	56
United States	43	42	43	57	42	40	41	53	35	48	43	40	38	47	42	45	43	42
Iceland	61	58	64	69	60	53	62	67	57	na	50	63	51	65	66	67	60	58
West Germany	60	60	61	74	64	49	55	67	66	56	61	63	62	63	56	45	61	66
Denmark	65	61	71	71	71	45	64	66	66	68	63	64	72	61	63	69	64	69
Finland	76	76	77	87	80	60	62	79	78	73	76	78	63	75	84	67	77	77
Norway	59	54	65	70	59	51	45	62	60	68	55	57	54	57	63	60	58	57
Sweden	70	65	77	85	68	61	66	75	68	69	75	67	74	71	68	70	70	73
Japan	39	36	42	54	46	19	33	43	36	44	36	39	35	40	42	33	44	33
Switzerland	na	na	na	na	na	na	na	na	na	na	na	na	na	na	na	na	na	na
Total	58	58	58	68	59	48	53	60	57	56	59	57	55	58	55	55	58	61

Ranking:

Lithuania	83
Brazil	81
Nigeria	80
Finland	76
Estonia	71
Sweden	70
Chile	69
Hungary	67
East Germany	66
Austria	66
Denmark	65
China	64
Russia	63
Latvia	62
Portugal	62
Iceland	61
West Germany	60
Netherlands	59
Norway	59
Italy	55
Canada	54
Bulgaria	53
Slovenia	53
Belgium	47
North Ireland	46
Spain	46
France	45
United States	43
Argentina	41
Japan	39
Romania	37
Britain	37
Ireland	27

Note: Countries in the left column are ranked according to GNP per capita. / The percentages in the bottom row give each country an equal weight. / na=not ascertained.

V68 COULDN'T REFUSE

Thinking about your reasons for doing voluntary work, how important has been the following reason in your own case?
"I did not want to, but could not refuse." (% "very important"—codes 4 or 5)

	Total	Gender		Age			Education			Income			Political Affinity			Values		
		Male	Female	16-29	30-49	50+	Lower	Medium	Upper	Lower	Middle	Upper	Left	Center	Right	Mat	Mixed	Postmat
India	na	na	na	na	na	na	na	na	na	na	na	na	na	na	na	na	na	na
Nigeria	31	32	28	30	32	24	37	32	27	36	24	34	32	25	39	34	28	na
China	13	15	10	15	14	09	21	09	11	15	12	13	na	na	na	13	12	18
Romania	27	23	32	30	26	25	26	28	27	23	34	22	29	27	25	34	23	17
Turkey	na	na	na	na	na	na	na	na	na	na	na	na	na	na	na	na	na	na
Poland	na	na	na	na	na	na	na	na	na	na	na	na	na	na	na	na	na	na
Bulgaria	13	13	13	03	14	18	09	18	09	16	23	04	13	14	12	19	16	00
Chile	20	23	17	17	20	25	33	17	11	26	21	14	22	21	18	28	22	10
Czechoslovakia	na	na	na	na	na	na	na	na	na	na	na	na	na	na	na	na	na	na
South Africa	na	na	na	na	na	na	na	na	na	na	na	na	na	na	na	na	na	na
Lithuania	26	23	29	26	27	23	21	30	16	28	27	19	na	na	na	na	na	na
Hungary	18	19	18	25	22	10	04	26	11	17	20	17	00	22	29	23	29	22
Argentina	07	08	06	09	08	02	05	05	05	05	04	13	00	06	14	22	17	00
Brazil	36	34	38	35	35	37	46	35	26	46	39	29	34	33	40	11	05	06
Mexico	na	na	na	na	na	na	na	na	na	na	na	na	na	na	na	42	34	20
Belarus	na	na	na	na	na	na	na	na	na	na	na	na	na	na	na	na	na	na
Russia	23	20	25	26	21	23	28	24	21	22	30	19	22	24	19	na	na	na
Moscow	na	na	na	na	na	na	na	na	na	na	na	na	na	na	na	24	21	31
Latvia	28	25	31	25	29	31	31	28	28	36	35	19	na	na	na	na	na	na
Estonia	18	15	21	25	14	18	17	21	12	20	13	21	na	na	na	21	32	14
Portugal	15	11	20	14	22	08	15	22	19	16	19	07	26	na	15	16	19	18
South Korea	na	na	na	na	na	na	08	04	00	16	19	07	na	na	na	19	15	03
Ireland	05	05	05	01	na	05	08	04	00	07	04	07	06	02	09	23	na	04
North Ireland	16	17	15	05	08	14	20	17	05	09	15	12	17	24	04	11	06	04
Slovenia	08	11	03	05	11	06	05	06	12	08	09	09	07	10	00	36	14	08
Spain	08	08	07	03	05	16	13	10	02	00	00	10	08	09	11	14	06	06
East Germany	14	14	13	07	16	14	15	10	13	13	18	11	11	18	10	11	08	07
Britain	10	07	12	02	12	10	15	12	01	14	13	01	02	11	12	10	16	08
Italy	06	05	08	02	05	09	06	05	00	05	06	05	05	07	05	12	11	05
Netherlands	07	06	07	07	06	08	07	07	00	05	10	06	04	10	07	09	07	02
Belgium	11	08	14	06	08	18	16	11	07	18	09	09	07	13	08	17	06	06
Austria	18	15	22	17	20	17	18	19	20	19	19	17	16	12	19	21	12	03
France	10	12	09	12	07	12	12	08	11	17	05	04	08	12	09	23	20	14
Canada	12	12	12	09	11	16	15	08	08	12	12	10	13	13	12	11	12	07
United States	14	13	13	13	10	19	18	16	09	18	14	08	08	13	18	08	13	10
Iceland	05	07	03	06	03	08	07	04	05	07	04	05	08	03	05	21	12	14
West Germany	13	17	10	09	15	15	17	10	08	14	15	13	11	11	22	08	05	03
Denmark	08	09	08	05	10	09	15	09	06	01	13	11	07	06	12	11	17	10
Finland	23	25	19	13	19	35	39	17	22	22	23	22	18	25	26	14	08	08
Norway	13	13	13	06	14	16	17	17	08	39	10	11	06	15	14	33	18	27
Sweden	10	09	11	08	07	17	12	10	09	11	09	09	10	09	12	12	13	15
Japan	10	12	07	13	09	10	05	11	12	11	14	09	06	15	08	04	17	09
Switzerland	na	na	na	na	na	na	na	na	na	na	na	na	na	na	na	na	na	na
Total	15	15	15	13	15	16	18	15	12	17	16	13	12	15	15	18	15	11

Ranking:

Brazil	36
Nigeria	31
Latvia	28
Romania	27
Lithuania	26
Russia	23
Finland	23
Chile	20
Hungary	18
Estonia	18
Austria	18
North Ireland	16
Portugal	15
East Germany	14
United States	14
China	13
Bulgaria	13
West Germany	13
Norway	13
Canada	12
Belgium	11
Britain	10
France	10
Sweden	10
Japan	10
Slovenia	08
Spain	08
Denmark	08
Argentina	08
Netherlands	07
Italy	07
Ireland	06
Iceland	05

Note: Countries in the left column are ranked according to GNP per capita. / The percentages in the bottom row give each country an equal weight. / na=not ascertained.

V69-V82. On this list are various groups of people. Could you please sort out any that you would not like to have as neighbors?

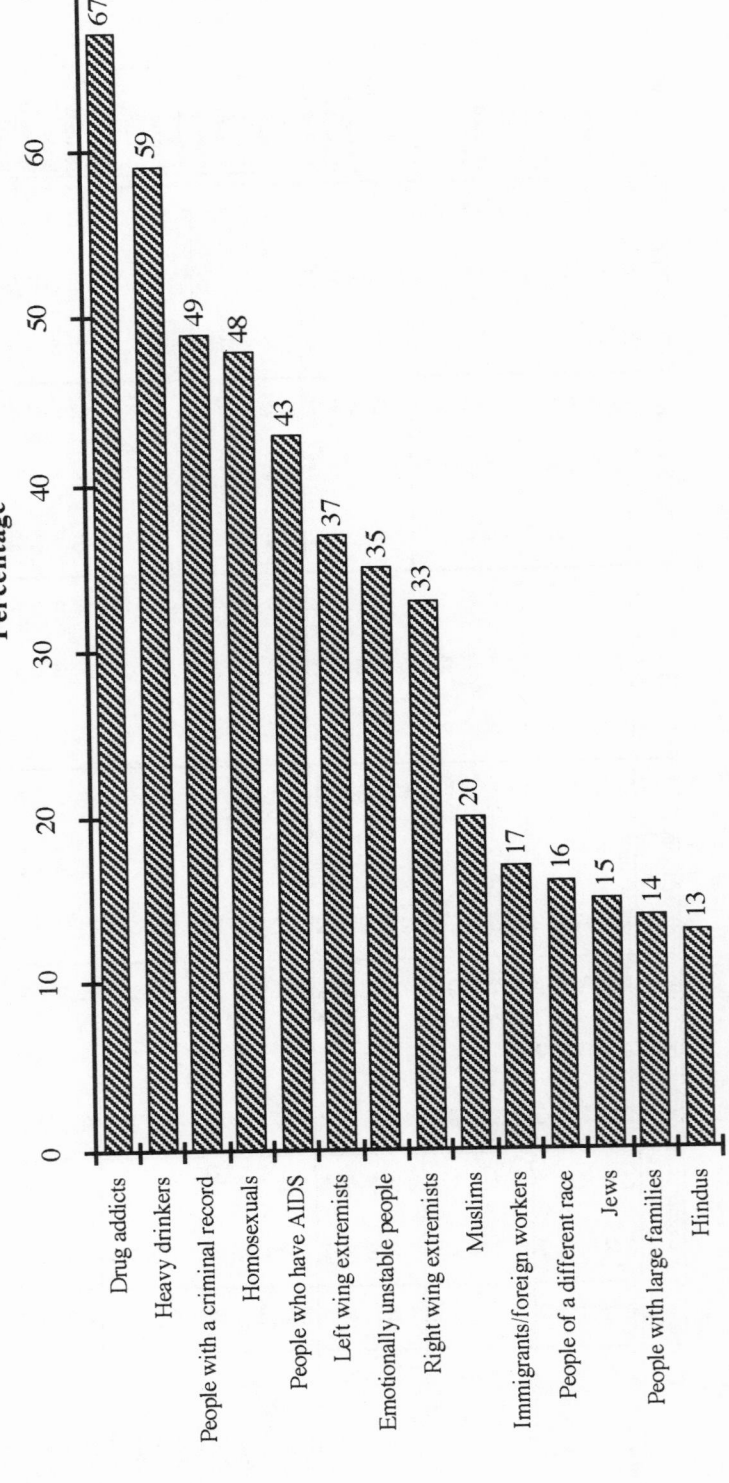

V69 NEIGHBORS: CRIMINALS

On this list are various groups of people. Could you please sort out any that you would not like to have as neighbors?
People with a criminal record (% "mentioned")

	Total	Gender		Age			Education			Income			Political Affinity			Values		
		Male	Female	16-29	30-49	50+	Lower	Medium	Upper	Lower	Middle	Upper	Left	Center	Right	Mat	Mixed	Postmat
India	93	93	93	93	92	93	94	93	92	93	94	91	92	92	93	94	93	90
Nigeria	80	81	80	81	79	77	79	79	82	73	88	80	81	85	78	83	79	78
China	41	40	44	35	44	45	42	43	37	44	43	35	70	na	na	41	43	32
Romania	67	62	71	64	63	72	70	70	58	68	68	64	70	67	63	70	66	52
Turkey	81	79	82	80	79	85	86	74	68	81	84	76	69	83	85	86	82	72
Poland	na	na	na	na	na	na	na	na	na	na	na	na	na	na	na	na	na	na
Bulgaria	70	69	71	66	68	74	74	68	69	71	72	69	71	71	62	78	69	54
Chile	46	46	46	46	42	52	49	46	42	52	43	42	43	43	54	55	46	36
Czechoslovakia	72	67	76	64	70	79	76	69	71	74	74	67	76	71	69	81	69	63
South Africa	na	na	na	na	na	na	na	na	na	na	na	na	na	na	na	na	na	na
Lithuania	69	62	74	65	70	71	72	66	77	71	65	68	75	79	na	72	68	64
Hungary	77	73	81	74	72	84	79	77	75	80	77	68	75	79	69	80	76	65
Argentina	41	41	42	34	40	48	43	41	39	42	41	43	31	43	46	49	41	33
Brazil	52	52	51	49	51	57	58	49	47	55	49	49	48	48	58	55	51	36
Mexico	69	64	74	66	69	74	69	70	67	72	67	66	65	68	73	74	69	62
Belarus	72	69	75	68	72	76	70	71	74	68	74	72	71	77	70	74	72	64
Russia	63	56	68	55	61	70	64	62	64	58	66	64	63	63	65	68	60	57
Moscow	60	51	67	50	61	64	59	57	61	58	63	56	58	62	61	68	58	56
Latvia	63	59	65	60	65	62	58	61	69	61	65	63	na	na	na	68	62	60
Estonia	63	62	65	57	62	72	63	62	68	59	68	66	na	na	na	66	61	73
Portugal	59	59	59	50	57	70	62	43	60	61	59	57	55	62	59	68	57	50
South Korea	31	28	34	35	30	25	32	29	32	35	30	27	39	31	29	26	36	37
Ireland	52	50	53	41	48	63	56	48	39	57	50	49	35	55	54	54	53	45
North Ireland	46	45	47	32	42	59	50	38	41	47	49	43	43	44	52	62	45	29
Slovenia	37	37	38	41	37	35	37	39	36	37	36	40	35	40	34	36	37	47
Spain	36	36	37	27	33	46	39	33	25	41	39	30	30	40	44	43	36	26
East Germany	35	32	37	32	31	41	38	27	27	39	35	31	27	39	34	52	36	25
Britain	41	40	42	32	34	53	42	39	41	44	34	37	35	39	50	50	42	30
Italy	48	46	50	41	46	54	49	38	39	49	46	49	44	47	47	55	49	37
Netherlands	28	28	28	31	22	35	31	28	26	32	23	26	20	29	35	40	30	22
Belgium	28	27	30	23	26	34	32	28	23	30	26	28	23	28	30	33	30	21
Austria	32	32	32	23	28	40	35	32	24	36	31	28	32	27	39	39	35	22
France	20	19	20	16	15	26	27	12	14	23	16	16	13	22	33	33	19	10
Canada	42	40	44	36	41	50	46	44	37	41	40	43	33	44	44	50	44	34
United States	50	46	53	55	45	51	54	50	46	51	49	51	45	48	54	56	50	42
Iceland	24	26	22	27	20	28	28	23	21	na	na	na	20	22	27	28	24	12
West Germany	28	25	30	17	23	37	31	23	19	31	29	23	19	27	37	45	30	13
Denmark	28	28	27	32	24	29	25	33	27	30	25	30	20	28	34	34	30	16
Finland	34	32	35	35	33	34	32	33	35	27	34	39	22	34	42	38	34	32
Norway	37	35	38	30	32	47	45	37	32	41	33	36	32	36	41	43	36	21
Sweden	35	34	36	36	29	41	36	34	37	36	34	33	28	33	41	44	35	28
Japan	50	49	50	46	48	55	51	49	51	49	51	50	56	47	50	59	48	38
Switzerland	07	05	08	07	04	08	08	05	07	07	05	07	05	05	11	11	06	05
Total	49	47	51	45	47	54	51	47	46	51	49	48	44	48	50	55	49	41

Ranking:

India	93
Turkey	81
Nigeria	80
Hungary	77
Czechoslovakia	72
Belarus	72
Bulgaria	70
Lithuania	69
Mexico	69
Romania	67
Russia	63
Latvia	63
Estonia	63
Moscow	60
Portugal	59
Brazil	52
Ireland	52
United States	50
Japan	50
Italy	48
Chile	46
North Ireland	46
Canada	42
China	41
Argentina	41
Britain	41
Slovenia	37
Norway	37
Spain	36
East Germany	35
Sweden	35
Finland	34
Austria	32
South Korea	31
Netherlands	28
Belgium	28
West Germany	28
Denmark	28
Iceland	24
France	20
Switzerland	07

Note: Countries in the left column are ranked according to GNP per capita. / The percentages in the bottom row give each country an equal weight. / na=not ascertained.

V70 NEIGHBORS: OTHER RACE

On this list are various groups of people. Could you please sort out any that you would not like to have as neighbors? People of a different race (% "mentioned")

	Total	Gender		Age			Education			Income			Political Affinity			Values			Ranking:	
		Male	Female	16-29	30-49	50+	Lower	Medium	Upper	Lower	Middle	Upper	Left	Center	Right	Mat	Mixed	Postmat		
India	35	32	38	33	36	37	46	36	28	42	36	25	31	30	34	35	33	28	South Korea	58
Nigeria	31	31	31	34	28	33	34	34	27	32	30	30	31	26	37	26	35	25	Slovenia	40
China	12	10	14	10	12	15	12	12	08	09	13	14	na	na	na	14	09	07	Bulgaria	39
Romania	28	28	28	21	29	31	33	27	23	26	29	27	30	28	26	32	26	14	India	35
Turkey	34	31	37	30	33	42	48	14	07	45	34	20	23	32	43	39	37	20	Turkey	34
Poland	na	na	na	na	na	na	na	na	na	na	na	na	na	na	na	na	na	na	Nigeria	31
Bulgaria	39	38	40	34	37	44	50	39	29	37	38	42	38	39	35	47	38	26	Czechoslovakia	31
Chile	11	11	10	10	08	16	16	08	08	12	11	08	09	11	13	13	11	09	Romania	28
Czechoslovakia	31	30	33	29	28	38	35	31	25	35	31	28	31	32	30	36	32	19	Finland	25
South Africa	na	na	na	na	na	na	na	na	na	na	na	na	na	na	na	na	na	na	Hungary	23
Lithuania	20	19	21	19	17	24	21	19	25	21	17	23	na	na	na	22	18	21	Lithuania	20
Hungary	23	23	23	11	21	30	24	22	17	26	21	17	19	21	22	22	23	28	Estonia	19
Argentina	03	03	03	01	03	04	02	04	01	03	03	04	01	03	05	02	03	04	Mexico	17
Brazil	05	05	05	04	04	07	09	03	01	08	04	02	04	03	07	05	05	00	Belarus	17
Mexico	17	16	17	17	16	17	17	18	15	15	15	22	09	18	16	18	17	11	Belgium	17
Belarus	17	17	17	15	17	17	23	17	15	18	17	16	15	16	23	18	15	19	Portugal	16
Russia	11	10	11	10	09	13	14	10	10	12	08	09	08	11	11	12	10	08	Latvia	13
Moscow	11	12	11	09	10	15	19	11	10	11	09	15	10	11	20	12	11	14	Italy	13
Latvia	13	15	12	13	13	13	13	12	14	13	14	13	na	na	na	13	13	11	China	12
Estonia	19	20	18	17	18	22	24	18	18	19	18	20	09	na	na	20	19	22	Spain	12
Portugal	16	17	14	10	17	19	19	06	12	18	14	12	16	13	19	22	13	10	East Germany	12
South Korea	58	58	58	70	55	43	41	62	62	58	57	58	63	57	57	53	63	63	Norway	12
Ireland	06	07	05	04	05	08	09	03	00	09	08	03	06	04	07	07	06	04	Chile	11
North Ireland	07	09	05	03	02	16	04	04	03	09	06	04	04	06	10	15	05	00	Russia	11
Slovenia	40	40	39	41	41	37	39	40	39	38	40	39	41	40	36	37	41	41	Moscow	11
Spain	12	11	12	06	09	18	13	09	06	17	11	07	09	13	16	13	10	10	Japan	11
East Germany	12	13	11	10	08	17	14	10	06	16	10	09	07	12	17	22	11	08	West Germany	10
Britain	09	09	09	04	09	12	10	07	06	12	05	09	08	08	10	10	09	06	Britain	09
Italy	13	14	13	10	10	20	15	05	05	16	06	00	09	11	14	18	15	04	France	09
Netherlands	06	08	05	02	03	13	08	04	04	06	07	06	02	06	10	15	05	03	United States	09
Belgium	17	17	18	10	15	24	23	16	10	17	17	15	08	17	21	23	18	10	Austria	08
Austria	08	08	08	04	05	12	12	06	04	12	07	06	10	07	10	12	08	06	Iceland	08
France	09	11	08	06	08	13	13	05	08	12	07	09	09	08	19	13	10	06	North Ireland	07
Canada	05	05	05	04	06	05	06	05	04	06	05	05	03	04	06	07	04	06	Denmark	07
United States	09	09	08	11	05	10	14	08	06	10	07	09	05	09	09	15	05	03	Sweden	07
Iceland	08	10	05	04	06	15	11	08	05	na	na	na	05	06	12	11	07	03	Ireland	06
West Germany	10	08	11	07	06	15	13	07	03	12	10	07	07	08	16	21	10	03	Netherlands	06
Denmark	07	08	05	06	05	10	09	04	04	11	06	05	04	07	10	10	07	04	Brazil	05
Finland	25	30	20	26	23	30	23	25	26	24	23	28	11	27	33	29	26	22	Canada	05
Norway	12	16	09	08	08	20	22	12	08	16	12	07	11	10	13	18	11	05	Argentina	03
Sweden	07	08	05	08	05	08	09	07	02	09	05	05	03	08	06	08	07	03	Switzerland	02
Japan	11	10	12	07	07	18	17	09	07	11	12	06	12	07	14	11	09	06		
Switzerland	02	03	02	07	01	04	03	02	01	03	02	01	01	02	04	05	02	01		
Total	16	17	16	14	15	20	19	15	12	18	16	15	14	15	19	19	16	13		

Note: Countries in the left column are ranked according to GNP per capita. / The percentages in the bottom row give each country an equal weight. / na=not ascertained.

V71 NEIGHBORS: LEFT WING

On this list are various groups of people. Could you please sort out any that you would not like to have as neighbors?
Left wing extremists (% "mentioned")

	Total	Gender		Age			Education			Income			Political Affinity			Values		
		Male	Female	16-29	30-49	50+	Lower	Medium	Upper	Lower	Middle	Upper	Left	Center	Right	Mat	Mixed	Postmat
India	74	75	74	76	74	73	73	77	72	72	77	72	77	73	74	74	75	79
Nigeria	48	51	45	47	48	61	49	49	48	42	55	41	36	51	53	43	52	48
China	na	na	na	na	na	na	na	na	na	na	na	na	na	na	na	na	na	na
Romania	45	47	43	40	47	47	41	45	51	49	44	44	44	46	52	43	45	na
Turkey	70	68	73	66	69	78	79	61	45	73	73	64	46	77	78	81	72	51
Poland	na	na	na	na	na	na	na	na	na	na	na	na	na	na	na	na	na	na
Bulgaria	69	70	67	70	65	72	70	68	70	71	72	67	70	70	66	75	67	65
Chile	47	46	47	43	44	56	50	44	45	49	43	46	35	48	58	54	47	35
Czechoslovakia	38	39	36	31	37	43	38	35	46	40	37	35	31	37	45	34	40	35
South Africa	na	na	na	na	na	na	na	na	na	na	na	na	na	na	na	na	na	na
Lithuania	65	65	65	58	67	69	64	65	69	65	63	67	na	na	na	65	67	61
Hungary	21	26	17	15	22	22	18	23	27	20	22	23	18	23	25	21	21	20
Argentina	49	52	46	38	47	59	50	43	49	53	47	48	35	52	54	55	49	40
Brazil	12	14	11	08	12	19	18	09	11	15	12	10	08	12	18	13	12	09
Mexico	26	27	25	25	25	30	25	28	27	22	25	34	12	31	31	30	26	21
Belarus	40	43	38	33	40	47	38	38	44	40	39	43	37	44	46	44	39	39
Russia	41	42	40	38	42	42	38	41	43	37	45	38	44	44	43	43	40	37
Moscow	23	27	20	21	23	26	18	24	23	23	24	23	21	27	26	25	23	22
Latvia	69	69	69	64	69	73	63	69	70	65	68	72	na	na	na	76	69	53
Estonia	66	71	61	61	67	70	67	66	65	63	71	66	na	na	na	69	66	66
Portugal	33	32	33	29	29	40	31	32	41	33	25	41	23	33	42	37	31	34
South Korea	18	20	17	29	14	08	11	17	23	20	17	15	40	20	12	11	21	40
Ireland	29	32	26	21	29	34	31	26	31	31	28	30	23	32	27	27	30	29
North Ireland	35	35	34	21	27	52	34	43	14	42	38	34	23	34	43	27	34	29
Slovenia	31	32	30	34	33	28	29	33	32	28	34	32	14	35	29	48	34	18
Spain	25	26	24	17	23	33	26	26	22	29	25	25	21	26	30	26	23	37
East Germany	58	63	54	51	62	59	56	59	64	55	56	62	48	60	70	56	58	60
Britain	34	41	28	21	34	42	32	41	37	34	29	38	16	32	57	39	36	22
Italy	30	33	28	22	30	36	31	26	26	30	30	32	20	34	38	33	32	24
Netherlands	42	55	38	31	42	56	41	42	45	38	43	52	35	40	58	44	45	39
Belgium	34	36	32	28	33	39	34	33	37	27	33	37	26	36	43	30	35	36
Austria	43	48	40	34	45	46	46	42	43	40	44	44	42	44	48	37	45	43
France	24	28	19	20	20	29	22	22	30	24	19	28	19	26	38	23	25	23
Canada	27	31	23	19	29	31	27	27	28	27	27	29	22	28	32	25	28	26
United States	31	35	27	23	29	37	28	32	32	31	30	33	22	35	34	30	31	30
Iceland	30	35	25	25	24	47	40	30	22	40	na	na	19	30	40	36	30	14
West Germany	51	52	50	42	49	57	54	45	48	50	52	54	37	53	66	57	54	44
Denmark	06	07	05	04	05	09	06	08	05	08	05	04	04	05	10	05	07	01
Finland	12	16	07	19	09	13	13	10	14	13	11	14	02	10	20	15	12	12
Norway	19	25	12	14	15	26	30	16	15	20	18	19	14	17	24	23	18	15
Sweden	24	27	21	21	18	34	27	24	20	27	23	23	14	21	36	27	26	19
Japan	77	78	77	77	78	77	75	78	79	74	81	77	75	75	87	80	80	72
Switzerland	15	19	12	10	14	19	15	16	13	13	18	19	16	23	23	15	18	09
Total	38	41	36	34	37	43	38	38	38	38	39	39	29	37	43	40	39	35

Ranking:

Japan	77
India	74
Turkey	70
Bulgaria	69
Latvia	69
Estonia	66
Lithuania	65
East Germany	58
West Germany	51
Argentina	49
Nigeria	48
Chile	47
Romania	45
Austria	43
Netherlands	42
Russia	41
Belarus	40
Czechoslovakia	38
North Ireland	35
Britain	34
Belgium	34
Portugal	33
Slovenia	31
United States	31
Italy	30
Iceland	30
Ireland	29
Canada	27
Mexico	26
Spain	25
France	24
Sweden	24
Moscow	23
Hungary	21
Norway	19
South Korea	18
Switzerland	15
Brazil	12
Finland	12
Denmark	06

Note: Countries in the left column are ranked according to GNP per capita. / The percentages in the bottom row give each country an equal weight. / na=not ascertained.
The surveys in the Baltic countries asked about "extremists" (not "Left-wing extremists") in V71, and about "people of other nationalities" in V73.

V72 NEIGHBORS: DRINKERS

On this list are various groups of people. Could you please sort out any that you would not like to have as neighbors? Heavy drinkers (% "mentioned")

	Total	Gender		Age			Education			Income			Political Affinity			Values		
		Male	Female	16-29	30-49	50+	Lower	Medium	Upper	Lower	Middle	Upper	Left	Center	Right	Mat	Mixed	Postmat
India	91	90	91	90	91	91	90	92	89	90	92	90	91	89	92	93	90	92
Nigeria	72	71	75	74	69	70	68	73	73	67	78	71	72	75	70	75	71	70
China	58	54	63	56	58	58	56	55	60	56	60	57	na	na	na	59	56	56
Romania	79	74	84	76	76	84	81	81	75	80	81	76	84	83	75	81	78	77
Turkey	87	85	89	88	86	87	90	82	82	88	88	85	81	87	89	89	88	81
Poland	na	na	na	na	na	na	na	na	na	na	na	na	na	na	na	na	na	na
Bulgaria	73	69	76	74	72	73	75	72	74	71	76	74	76	72	66	80	72	62
Chile	52	47	56	50	52	54	53	51	52	53	51	50	47	53	54	56	51	50
Czechoslovakia	74	67	80	69	69	82	78	70	75	76	75	70	76	73	74	74	74	73
South Africa	na	na	na	na	na	na	na	na	na	na	na	na	na	na	na	na	na	na
Lithuania	92	88	95	90	92	93	87	92	96	92	92	91	na	na	na	91	93	92
Hungary	82	78	85	79	78	86	79	84	85	82	79	88	85	83	81	82	82	73
Argentina	45	41	49	35	43	56	51	41	40	47	46	43	42	44	51	50	47	35
Brazil	41	39	44	39	36	55	54	36	37	48	38	35	36	41	46	43	42	28
Mexico	56	52	60	54	57	58	55	53	61	54	56	59	55	58	57	55	59	52
Belarus	82	78	85	83	81	81	74	83	83	77	84	83	86	78	76	80	84	81
Russia	82	74	87	82	80	84	78	82	84	81	85	79	83	83	80	83	81	82
Moscow	82	73	90	80	81	85	76	80	85	81	82	84	83	79	78	83	82	86
Latvia	85	83	86	86	85	82	76	86	86	81	83	88	na	na	na	88	84	83
Estonia	90	87	92	89	91	89	87	89	94	90	89	90	na	na	na	88	91	90
Portugal	51	48	55	44	47	62	53	48	49	54	46	56	43	54	52	59	48	44
South Korea	17	14	19	21	16	12	12	16	19	16	15	22	22	16	16	14	19	19
Ireland	34	30	38	31	30	41	39	31	22	44	32	29	32	33	35	35	35	30
North Ireland	43	39	46	33	36	57	41	48	41	50	35	40	36	44	45	49	45	27
Slovenia	45	42	47	49	42	44	43	45	47	45	40	53	47	45	41	42	45	47
Spain	40	38	42	33	36	49	41	40	36	44	41	37	36	41	49	44	39	36
East Germany	72	65	77	65	70	78	71	71	74	74	70	72	73	72	67	79	72	68
Britain	48	43	53	38	40	61	47	51	51	52	47	42	43	49	51	58	47	41
Italy	51	47	56	42	51	58	52	48	36	52	46	55	51	53	48	58	51	45
Netherlands	60	57	62	56	60	65	63	59	58	57	63	63	59	61	61	74	60	57
Belgium	50	47	53	48	47	54	51	50	49	46	48	53	48	50	54	50	52	45
Austria	60	54	63	55	57	64	65	56	56	65	56	61	56	62	61	56	61	58
France	50	44	55	46	45	57	51	48	49	54	48	48	44	52	59	54	51	46
Canada	55	50	59	48	55	60	54	55	55	52	57	53	55	54	59	53	55	54
United States	60	57	62	60	59	60	62	57	63	62	61	57	54	59	66	63	59	59
Iceland	61	59	63	63	58	64	62	62	60	na	na	na	61	65	58	66	61	49
West Germany	64	56	72	52	63	72	66	61	62	69	61	63	57	67	66	75	66	57
Denmark	34	34	34	42	28	35	30	39	33	36	34	33	27	33	39	47	33	24
Finland	54	53	56	58	53	53	55	51	58	47	58	55	48	53	65	59	54	55
Norway	32	34	31	31	26	40	44	27	31	34	28	31	28	32	34	39	31	22
Sweden	45	46	43	50	37	49	47	43	44	47	43	42	38	44	48	58	43	44
Japan	58	51	65	53	57	65	59	58	58	61	61	52	63	55	63	61	58	53
Switzerland	23	20	25	20	19	28	24	22	22	25	24	24	22	24	24	29	23	18
Total	59	56	63	57	57	63	59	58	59	60	59	59	55	57	58	63	59	55

Ranking:

Lithuania	92
India	91
Estonia	90
Turkey	87
Latvia	85
Hungary	82
Belarus	82
Russia	82
Moscow	82
Romania	79
Czechoslovakia	74
Bulgaria	73
Nigeria	72
East Germany	72
West Germany	64
Iceland	61
Netherlands	60
Austria	60
United States	60
China	58
Japan	58
Mexico	56
Canada	55
Finland	54
Chile	52
Portugal	51
Italy	51
Belgium	50
France	50
Britain	48
Argentina	45
Slovenia	45
Sweden	45
North Ireland	43
Brazil	41
Spain	40
Ireland	34
Denmark	34
Norway	32
Switzerland	23
South Korea	17

Note: Countries in the left column are ranked according to GNP per capita. / The percentages in the bottom row give each country an equal weight. / na=not ascertained.

V73 NEIGHBORS: RIGHT WING

On this list are various groups of people. Could you please sort out any that you would not like to have as neighbors?
Right wing extremists (% "mentioned")

	Total	Gender		Age			Education			Income			Political Affinity			Values		
		Male	Female	16-29	30-49	50+	Lower	Medium	Upper	Lower	Middle	Upper	Left	Center	Right	Mat	Mixed	Postmat
India	65	64	66	64	65	66	66	65	64	64	66	63	71	69	51	63	67	73
Nigeria	36	38	33	36	37	33	27	36	39	38	38	29	35	37	35	31	37	47
China	na	na	na	na	na	na	na	na	na	na	na	na	na	na	na	na	na	na
Romania	42	45	40	36	42	46	40	41	47	46	42	40	47	44	38	42	41	52
Turkey	71	73	70	72	70	72	74	64	68	74	70	69	70	76	61	76	71	66
Poland	na	na	na	na	na	na	na	na	na	na	na	na	na	na	na	na	na	na
Bulgaria	65	69	62	65	63	69	67	64	69	68	68	64	66	70	59	71	65	61
Chile	46	49	43	43	46	50	47	43	49	46	44	48	48	44	49	48	46	45
Czechoslovakia	36	38	35	30	34	43	34	35	45	39	36	34	40	37	35	37	37	29
South Africa	na	na	na	na	na	na	na	na	na	na	na	na	na	na	na	na	na	na
Lithuania	10	11	10	12	08	11	10	10	12	09	10	12	na	na	11	09	10	11
Hungary	20	25	16	14	20	23	17	21	32	19	20	24	25	23	14	21	19	30
Argentina	46	48	44	36	44	56	46	41	47	50	45	47	50	47	42	52	45	43
Brazil	08	11	06	06	10	10	10	06	13	07	07	10	10	09	06	07	09	14
Mexico	27	27	27	27	28	27	27	26	30	23	28	37	30	30	27	26	29	25
Belarus	42	47	37	35	42	47	43	40	43	42	43	39	42	44	42	42	42	44
Russia	41	43	38	38	42	41	36	40	44	35	44	38	47	43	39	40	41	40
Moscow	26	27	25	21	27	30	26	22	30	26	26	28	27	27	26	26	25	38
Latvia	05	05	06	06	05	06	06	06	04	05	07	05	na	na	na	05	06	03
Estonia	09	09	09	11	08	09	14	09	05	09	09	10	na	na	na	10	09	05
Portugal	30	31	28	25	28	36	27	29	39	30	24	36	36	30	26	30	30	33
South Korea	27	29	26	29	25	29	33	26	26	31	26	23	26	25	30	27	28	26
Ireland	21	24	19	17	21	25	30	21	23	22	23	22	26	25	15	18	21	28
North Ireland	29	33	26	18	27	37	34	31	27	31	30	32	25	27	33	40	25	28
Slovenia	33	33	33	34	34	31	29	36	36	30	35	34	33	36	33	30	34	16
Spain	29	32	27	23	29	33	28	30	34	33	29	30	32	28	28	30	34	38
East Germany	70	75	66	69	76	64	66	72	84	65	69	76	81	68	60	65	70	34
Britain	28	34	34	18	28	33	24	35	38	26	27	30	24	26	37	34	25	28
Italy	34	38	30	25	34	39	34	31	27	34	34	36	34	38	25	32	35	25
Netherlands	48	58	45	41	49	56	42	47	57	46	49	62	56	47	47	41	46	55
Belgium	38	42	34	36	36	41	36	42	47	34	34	43	45	39	38	31	38	46
Austria	42	47	39	33	45	44	43	42	41	40	42	44	47	45	43	33	42	48
France	33	36	30	32	34	33	30	31	44	31	29	42	44	31	28	21	31	48
Canada	25	29	20	17	28	27	22	24	27	25	24	30	36	25	22	21	24	28
United States	31	35	26	21	30	36	28	29	35	30	30	35	37	33	29	29	30	33
Iceland	29	34	24	22	24	46	37	27	23	na	na	na	24	28	34	30	29	23
West Germany	62	62	62	60	63	62	58	65	74	61	63	65	73	59	58	54	60	73
Denmark	07	09	05	07	07	06	04	08	07	08	06	07	14	06	05	03	07	08
Finland	07	09	05	09	07	05	06	08	09	07	09	05	08	07	07	09	07	07
Norway	22	29	15	19	20	27	29	20	21	21	09	24	27	21	22	22	22	30
Sweden	29	33	24	26	27	35	31	27	32	31	27	28	31	29	29	25	29	32
Japan	79	80	79	79	80	78	77	79	82	76	82	78	80	79	83	82	80	81
Switzerland	18	22	14	21	17	18	18	16	28	19	20	22	36	18	12	12	16	29
Total	**34**	**37**	**32**	**31**	**34**	**37**	**34**	**34**	**37**	**34**	**34**	**36**	**40**	**37**	**34**	**33**	**34**	**37**

Ranking:

Japan	79
Turkey	71
East Germany	70
India	65
Bulgaria	65
West Germany	62
Netherlands	48
Chile	46
Argentina	46
Romania	42
Belarus	42
Austria	42
Russia	41
Belgium	38
Nigeria	36
Czechoslovakia	36
Italy	34
Slovenia	33
France	33
United States	31
Portugal	30
North Ireland	29
Spain	29
Iceland	29
Sweden	29
Britain	28
Mexico	27
South Korea	27
Moscow	26
Canada	25
Norway	22
Ireland	21
Hungary	20
Switzerland	18
Lithuania	10
Estonia	09
Brazil	08
Denmark	07
Finland	07
Latvia	05

Note: Countries in the left column are ranked according to GNP per capita. / The percentages in the bottom row give each country an equal weight. / na=not ascertained.
The surveys in the Baltic countries asked about "extremists" (not "Right-wing extremists") in V73, and about "people of other nationalities" in V73.

V74 NEIGHBORS: LARGE FAMILY

On this list are various groups of people. Could you please sort out any that you would not like to have as neighbors?
People with large families (% "mentioned")

	Total	Gender Male	Gender Female	Age 16-29	Age 30-49	Age 50+	Education Lower	Education Medium	Education Upper	Income Lower	Income Middle	Income Upper	Pol. Affinity Left	Pol. Affinity Center	Pol. Affinity Right	Values Mat	Values Mixed	Values Postmat
India	35	38	32	37	35	33	27	35	40	34	37	35	40	36	35	34	38	40
Nigeria	33	36	30	33	34	30	28	33	36	33	33	36	30	30	38	31	35	38
China	19	18	20	16	19	21	20	16	19	19	18	19	na	na	na	19	19	15
Romania	22	22	22	23	22	20	15	23	29	21	22	22	25	22	25	19	24	24
Turkey	41	41	40	43	38	41	39	42	46	38	42	41	38	43	41	43	41	39
Poland	na	na	na	na	na	na	na	na	na	na	na	na	na	na	na	na	na	na
Bulgaria	24	25	24	24	25	24	23	27	21	23	18	27	21	23	26	21	26	22
Chile	14	14	13	13	12	16	17	14	10	17	14	10	12	15	12	15	14	12
Czechoslovakia	15	16	14	13	15	17	14	14	17	15	15	14	14	14	16	14	16	09
South Africa	na	na	na	na	na	na	na	na	na	na	na	na	na	na	na	na	na	na
Lithuania	17	19	16	17	16	19	14	17	25	16	19	17	na	na	na	19	16	19
Hungary	07	08	07	04	06	10	09	06	05	08	07	06	06	08	07	08	07	08
Argentina	05	05	04	03	03	08	05	05	03	04	04	04	00	05	06	05	05	05
Brazil	06	08	05	05	07	08	10	04	03	09	05	03	06	03	09	06	07	02
Mexico	23	22	24	23	23	20	22	25	25	21	25	23	15	26	23	20	24	25
Belarus	16	15	17	14	17	15	19	16	14	17	12	17	15	14	21	17	14	22
Russia	12	12	12	14	10	14	12	13	11	10	11	13	11	13	12	14	12	07
Moscow	11	11	12	09	12	13	16	11	11	12	09	13	10	11	14	11	11	12
Latvia	12	15	10	14	10	12	10	13	10	09	11	14	na	na	na	13	12	13
Estonia	11	12	11	13	08	14	13	12	09	08	13	15	na	na	na	13	11	07
Portugal	15	19	12	11	16	19	16	13	15	18	11	15	19	15	14	22	13	13
South Korea	79	82	77	79	80	80	78	78	81	79	77	85	80	78	80	81	78	78
Ireland	03	03	03	02	03	02	03	01	03	03	02	02	05	03	01	03	03	01
North Ireland	09	09	09	07	06	13	09	09	07	12	09	09	04	06	16	06	11	02
Slovenia	40	41	39	40	42	37	40	39	41	39	40	38	45	41	40	37	40	47
Spain	10	10	11	08	07	14	11	07	09	15	10	08	08	11	14	09	10	09
East Germany	07	07	07	05	04	11	09	02	05	10	06	05	06	09	08	15	06	05
Britain	11	11	10	05	10	15	11	11	12	12	10	12	12	09	14	15	10	07
Italy	12	15	10	12	11	14	13	10	14	11	10	09	09	14	11	13	13	09
Netherlands	06	10	05	04	06	10	07	05	07	09	05	07	06	06	09	12	07	04
Belgium	08	09	08	08	08	10	10	06	07	07	09	06	06	08	09	11	08	07
Austria	05	06	05	06	04	06	06	05	04	06	05	04	07	04	06	03	06	04
France	08	08	07	08	07	08	07	08	09	10	06	07	09	08	11	08	08	08
Canada	06	06	06	05	06	08	08	06	06	08	06	07	04	05	09	08	06	06
United States	08	08	08	08	07	09	10	06	09	12	07	07	07	08	09	07	08	08
Iceland	02	03	02	02	01	05	04	03	00	na	na	na	02	02	03	03	02	01
West Germany	08	07	09	06	05	12	09	07	06	11	07	07	07	08	10	16	08	05
Denmark	03	03	03	03	01	05	04	03	03	05	02	03	03	03	04	03	03	02
Finland	04	04	04	04	03	05	07	02	03	02	04	02	02	05	03	09	03	04
Norway	06	08	05	05	05	09	12	05	05	09	05	04	07	05	05	08	06	04
Sweden	05	06	05	05	03	09	07	05	02	08	08	05	04	06	06	06	06	01
Japan	06	06	06	02	05	09	10	05	04	08	05	05	06	05	07	07	04	04
Switzerland	01	01	01	02	00	01	01	00	00	01	01	01	04	01	01	06	04	01
Total	**14**	**15**	**14**	**14**	**13**	**16**	**15**	**14**	**14**	**15**	**14**	**14**	**14**	**14**	**16**	**15**	**14**	**13**

Ranking:

South Korea	79
Turkey	41
Slovenia	40
India	35
Nigeria	33
Bulgaria	24
Mexico	23
Romania	22
China	19
Lithuania	17
Belarus	16
Czechoslovakia	15
Portugal	15
Chile	14
Russia	12
Latvia	12
Italy	12
Moscow	11
Estonia	11
Britain	11
Spain	10
North Ireland	09
Belgium	08
France	08
United States	08
West Germany	08
Hungary	07
East Germany	07
Brazil	06
Netherlands	06
Canada	06
Norway	06
Japan	06
Argentina	05
Austria	05
Sweden	05
Finland	04
Ireland	03
Denmark	03
Iceland	02
Switzerland	01

Note: Countries in the left column are ranked according to GNP per capita. / The percentages in the bottom row give each country an equal weight. / na=not ascertained.

V75 NEIGHBORS: UNSTABLE

On this list are various groups of people. Could you please sort out any that you would not like to have as neighbors?
Emotionally unstable people (% "mentioned")

	Total	Gender		Age			Education			Income			Political Affinity			Values		
		Male	Female	16-29	30-49	50+	Lower	Medium	Upper	Lower	Middle	Upper	Left	Center	Right	Mat	Mixed	Postmat
India	69	69	70	69	71	67	65	71	69	68	70	70	72	66	70	74	66	73
Nigeria	57	58	57	59	55	63	52	60	57	52	64	56	56	60	55	58	58	58
China	46	43	50	41	47	49	43	46	47	45	46	46	na	na	na	47	45	41
Romania	64	63	66	64	63	65	63	67	61	65	64	63	71	66	61	65	64	57
Turkey	72	70	73	77	69	67	73	71	68	74	71	70	70	73	69	70	73	70
Poland	na	na	na	na	na	na	na	na	na	na	na	na	na	na	na	na	na	na
Bulgaria	53	55	52	56	52	54	53	55	51	50	55	59	52	56	47	61	53	37
Chile	28	30	27	26	27	33	31	28	26	30	28	26	25	29	32	28	29	28
Czechoslovakia	33	32	34	26	32	38	36	33	29	36	35	28	34	32	34	31	35	26
South Africa	na	na	na	na	na	na	na	na	na	na	na	na	na	na	na	na	na	na
Lithuania	48	47	49	40	46	57	54	47	47	52	47	44	na	na	na	49	49	43
Hungary	23	24	23	17	20	30	24	22	23	26	24	15	27	24	21	25	22	20
Argentina	22	25	19	18	19	27	22	20	21	23	23	20	19	24	24	21	22	20
Brazil	16	19	14	14	14	24	22	13	17	16	16	16	16	13	20	15	18	13
Mexico	38	39	36	38	40	33	37	38	40	34	40	44	37	40	38	40	40	37
Belarus	63	61	64	65	62	61	61	64	62	59	66	62	64	62	59	61	66	61
Russia	51	49	53	56	50	50	45	55	52	47	54	49	52	48	52	51	52	49
Moscow	50	50	50	47	53	49	49	48	52	48	50	54	52	50	39	53	49	54
Latvia	54	51	55	53	53	55	54	54	56	54	50	57	na	na	na	57	52	55
Estonia	37	38	37	37	35	41	38	39	31	38	34	39	na	na	na	35	38	42
Portugal	47	43	50	38	47	56	46	49	50	46	41	55	47	44	53	53	44	48
South Korea	17	17	17	21	17	12	12	18	19	19	16	18	18	17	18	15	19	20
Ireland	30	29	31	32	31	28	30	30	29	32	31	30	27	30	34	29	30	32
North Ireland	23	29	19	24	20	27	25	26	17	29	16	25	07	24	30	29	25	09
Slovenia	36	34	39	37	35	37	36	35	40	34	38	37	35	37	31	31	38	43
Spain	25	26	24	22	24	27	26	22	24	25	25	25	24	25	28	25	24	26
East Germany	20	22	19	21	20	20	22	16	15	20	20	20	17	20	26	26	21	14
Britain	28	29	28	25	25	34	27	28	36	27	27	31	26	27	35	34	28	23
Italy	34	33	35	30	36	35	35	28	33	35	33	27	28	36	30	36	35	30
Netherlands	15	17	12	12	12	24	17	12	17	19	11	16	10	15	21	25	15	13
Belgium	21	22	19	21	21	21	22	19	22	15	20	24	15	19	21	20	22	17
Austria	20	18	21	27	15	21	23	19	13	21	18	23	19	20	26	21	21	18
France	17	15	19	16	17	18	17	16	19	18	17	20	13	19	22	20	16	15
Canada	30	30	30	30	32	27	25	32	31	28	27	24	23	29	36	24	31	27
United States	43	44	41	44	45	39	41	41	46	43	42	45	35	44	47	40	45	40
Iceland	33	39	26	42	27	31	32	35	31	na	na	na	26	31	38	33	34	24
West Germany	31	33	29	33	30	30	34	26	21	32	31	30	25	31	33	42	32	22
Denmark	11	12	10	16	10	09	06	13	13	12	12	11	12	09	14	13	12	08
Finland	24	26	22	16	20	30	13	21	28	23	26	24	21	23	31	09	25	25
Norway	22	24	20	21	19	26	27	20	22	22	25	18	21	22	31	27	25	25
Sweden	17	19	15	18	16	16	17	19	14	18	17	16	12	19	18	23	21	14
Japan	62	65	59	61	63	61	64	62	59	62	62	62	59	61	70	64	64	53
Switzerland	04	04	05	02	04	06	04	04	03	05	05	03	03	04	06	04	05	04
Total	35	36	35	35	34	37	35	35	34	35	35	35	32	34	36	36	35	32

Ranking:

Turkey	72
India	69
Romania	64
Belarus	63
Japan	62
Nigeria	57
Latvia	54
Bulgaria	53
Russia	51
Moscow	50
Lithuania	48
Portugal	47
China	46
United States	43
Mexico	38
Estonia	37
Slovenia	36
Italy	34
Czechoslovakia	33
Iceland	33
West Germany	31
Ireland	30
Canada	30
Chile	28
Britain	28
Spain	25
Finland	24
Hungary	23
North Ireland	23
Argentina	22
Norway	22
Belgium	21
East Germany	20
Austria	20
South Korea	17
France	17
Sweden	17
Brazil	16
Netherlands	15
Denmark	11
Switzerland	04

Note: Countries in the left column are ranked according to GNP per capita. / The percentages in the bottom row give each country an equal weight. / na=not ascertained.

V76 NEIGHBORS: MUSLIMS

On this list are various groups of people. Could you please sort out any that you would not like to have as neighbors?
Muslims (% "mentioned")

	Total	Gender		Age			Education			Income			Political Affinity			Values		
		Male	Female	16-29	30-49	50+	Lower	Medium	Upper	Lower	Middle	Upper	Left	Center	Right	Mat	Mixed	Postmat
India	29	28	30	30	27	29	31	30	25	33	30	22	29	27	26	31	26	23
Nigeria	24	24	25	25	23	25	20	27	23	33	18	23	25	18	30	19	30	16
China	12	11	14	09	13	14	16	09	13	11	15	09	na	na	na	12	12	07
Romania	35	35	34	30	34	38	36	38	26	34	35	33	46	34	31	38	33	25
Turkey	55	51	58	53	54	57	69	38	19	66	59	36	35	54	67	60	60	34
Poland	na	na	na	na	na	na	na	na	na	na	na	na	na	na	na	na	na	na
Bulgaria	41	40	42	36	38	47	50	42	30	38	43	41	39	40	40	47	41	29
Chile	12	13	11	11	08	18	17	10	07	14	12	09	10	14	09	14	11	09
Czechoslovakia	49	46	51	45	46	54	55	47	42	53	48	45	44	50	49	53	49	40
South Africa	na	na	na	na	na	na	na	na	na	na	na	na	na	na	na	36	35	29
Lithuania	34	33	35	35	33	35	33	34	39	34	32	37	18	18	20	19	19	10
Hungary	18	17	19	15	16	22	20	18	08	20	18	11	00	07	07	06	06	05
Argentina	06	07	05	05	06	07	05	07	04	06	06	05	00	na	na	na	na	na
Brazil	na	na	na	na	na	na	na	na	18	16	18	24	11	21	21	18	20	13
Mexico	19	17	21	20	18	17	18	25	22	15	23	25	22	24	25	25	23	20
Belarus	24	22	26	26	25	16	18	16	13	15	15	13	15	15	17	16	15	12
Russia	16	14	16	17	14	19	23	15	13	16	13	17	13	14	25	18	14	13
Moscow	15	19	12	13	13	22	29	27	22	27	28	25	07	15	19	25	26	25
Latvia	26	23	28	33	24	21	25	21	14	22	20	20	na	na	na	21	21	17
Estonia	21	23	19	25	18	21	21	10	15	19	15	18	14	15	26	25	16	11
Portugal	18	19	17	17	17	16	16	19	26	17	25	21	26	22	19	18	23	11
South Korea	21	22	20	24	21	17	18	10	10	21	14	09	11	13	16	11	15	27
Ireland	13	15	12	08	13	16	15	07	10	16	11	10	07	15	19	25	14	13
North Ireland	15	19	12	07	11	17	15	10	11	17	14	10	10	14	20	16	15	13
Slovenia	38	38	37	39	40	34	37	37	39	36	39	37	41	38	41	36	38	11
Spain	14	13	14	09	11	25	24	16	12	24	17	20	15	21	27	26	22	11
East Germany	20	21	20	15	19	23	18	16	12	20	14	17	15	14	22	19	18	13
Britain	17	18	16	09	15	19	16	07	11	16	11	05	12	14	15	21	15	10
Italy	15	16	15	12	12	19	15	11	10	11	10	12	07	11	19	22	14	07
Netherlands	12	15	10	09	09	30	29	26	20	25	23	28	20	24	34	30	15	06
Belgium	26	29	24	25	11	30	19	11	08	18	15	10	19	11	18	20	21	19
Austria	14	15	14	11	11	18	23	14	09	20	16	16	12	17	38	21	11	10
France	18	19	16	13	11	23	12	10	09	13	10	10	07	10	14	12	15	09
Canada	10	11	10	08	10	14	18	13	11	18	10	11	05	14	19	14	15	08
United States	14	15	12	11	09	19	15	11	09	na	na	na	08	09	17	14	28	08
Iceland	12	14	09	10	09	24	24	14	13	22	19	17	14	19	27	31	21	11
West Germany	20	20	20	15	18	24	17	21	11	20	15	12	10	14	21	19	21	13
Denmark	15	20	11	16	12	30	12	09	10	09	08	13	05	11	12	12	16	09
Finland	10	14	06	14	08	11	33	23	13	24	21	15	18	21	23	27	10	09
Norway	21	26	17	16	12	19	23	16	08	21	19	13	08	20	19	22	18	13
Sweden	17	20	14	18	12	24	36	29	21	30	30	22	25	22	32	30	26	17
Japan	29	28	29	33	23	34	na	na	na	na	na	na	na	na	na	na	26	17
Switzerland	na	na	na	na	na	na	na	na	na	na	na	na	na	na	na	na	na	na
Total	**21**	**22**	**21**	**20**	**19**	**24**	**24**	**20**	**16**	**23**	**20**	**18**	**18**	**20**	**25**	**24**	**22**	**15**

Ranking:

Turkey	55
Czechoslovakia	49
Bulgaria	41
Slovenia	38
Romania	35
Lithuania	34
India	29
Japan	29
Latvia	26
Belgium	26
Nigeria	24
Belarus	24
Estonia	21
South Korea	21
Norway	21
East Germany	20
West Germany	19
Mexico	19
Hungary	18
Portugal	18
France	18
Britain	17
Sweden	17
Russia	16
Moscow	15
North Ireland	15
Italy	15
Denmark	15
Spain	14
Austria	14
United States	14
Ireland	13
China	12
Chile	12
Netherlands	12
Iceland	12
Canada	10
Finland	10
Argentina	06

Note: Countries in the left column are ranked according to GNP per capita. / The percentages in the bottom row give each country an equal weight. / na=not ascertained.

V77 NEIGHBORS: FOREIGNERS

On this list are various groups of people. Could you please sort out any that you would not like to have as neighbors?
Immigrants/foreign workers (% "mentioned")

	Total	Gender		Age			Education			Income			Political Affinity			Values		
		Male	Female	16-29	30-49	50+	Lower	Medium	Upper	Lower	Middle	Upper	Left	Center	Right	Mat	Mixed	Postmat
India	37	35	39	32	40	38	49	37	29	45	39	26	37	32	33	37	34	36
Nigeria	26	26	27	28	25	23	29	26	26	28	24	26	31	22	27	25	28	23
China	13	11	16	10	14	13	12	11	15	11	17	10	na	na	na	14	11	15
Romania	30	30	31	28	29	33	30	32	28	28	32	29	42	32	27	33	29	21
Turkey	28	28	28	26	28	31	37	18	07	38	28	16	22	27	33	30	31	19
Poland	na	na	na	na	na	na	na	na	na	na	na	na	na	na	na	na	na	na
Bulgaria	34	33	36	26	34	40	40	36	26	32	36	36	32	33	37	38	34	27
Chile	12	13	11	12	10	15	16	11	09	14	13	08	13	12	10	15	12	09
Czechoslovakia	34	32	36	31	33	37	38	34	26	40	32	31	35	36	30	38	34	22
South Africa	na	na	na	na	na	na	na	na	na	na	na	na	na	na	na	na	na	na
Lithuania	15	16	14	15	13	17	12	15	18	16	12	16	na	na	na	16	14	15
Hungary	22	21	23	14	20	27	25	21	12	25	21	17	19	23	19	24	21	18
Argentina	02	02	03	01	03	02	02	03	00	03	03	01	01	02	01	02	02	03
Brazil	04	04	04	03	04	05	08	03	00	06	05	01	02	03	06	03	05	01
Mexico	18	17	19	18	15	21	16	22	19	17	17	20	12	19	19	18	18	14
Belarus	17	16	18	15	18	18	22	17	15	20	16	15	15	17	22	19	15	17
Russia	12	11	13	10	12	13	15	12	10	13	10	11	10	11	22	13	11	10
Moscow	13	14	12	05	14	18	25	10	13	12	12	17	12	14	18	16	12	14
Latvia	31	31	31	31	30	32	42	30	30	39	32	25	na	na	na	32	30	32
Estonia	17	18	16	20	16	16	22	16	16	17	19	16	na	na	na	18	18	14
Portugal	10	10	09	08	08	12	11	03	08	11	08	07	09	09	10	15	07	06
South Korea	53	51	55	62	51	43	37	55	60	52	53	56	57	54	53	49	57	60
Ireland	05	06	05	02	04	04	08	02	00	09	05	04	05	06	05	04	06	05
North Ireland	07	13	03	04	03	15	08	06	00	07	07	04	00	07	11	12	09	05
Slovenia	40	38	41	42	41	37	43	39	34	40	40	38	43	39	40	36	41	43
Spain	11	10	11	06	08	16	12	08	07	15	11	06	09	12	15	12	11	09
East Germany	19	20	17	17	16	22	22	17	08	22	18	16	13	19	26	29	11	15
Britain	12	13	11	06	10	17	13	10	09	15	07	11	11	10	14	16	18	08
Italy	15	15	14	10	11	20	16	10	09	15	11	05	09	15	15	18	11	07
Netherlands	07	09	06	03	04	16	10	06	04	09	05	04	03	06	12	19	16	07
Belgium	21	21	20	16	18	26	26	19	13	19	19	18	11	19	26	25	23	12
Austria	20	21	20	17	18	24	26	18	08	26	19	15	21	18	24	33	20	14
France	13	13	12	08	11	18	18	10	06	16	10	11	09	11	29	15	16	07
Canada	06	06	05	04	07	06	06	06	04	07	05	05	04	06	05	08	16	05
United States	10	10	09	07	08	12	07	09	07	12	07	10	05	10	11	09	20	12
Iceland	08	09	07	06	05	16	11	07	05	na	14	na	03	06	13	09	11	07
West Germany	16	17	16	14	14	20	20	12	08	19	14	14	10	15	25	34	08	03
Denmark	12	14	10	12	08	15	14	13	09	17	09	08	08	13	12	18	16	07
Finland	05	06	03	05	07	07	09	05	02	09	08	03	01	06	05	03	11	07
Norway	16	20	12	11	12	23	27	17	09	12	03	11	13	14	18	26	04	06
Sweden	09	10	07	12	06	10	13	09	04	12	15	06	03	11	18	11	13	06
Japan	17	15	18	18	13	22	21	17	12	17	17	12	16	13	10	17	11	11
Switzerland	02	02	01	02	01	02	03	01	00	02	02	02	01	02	03	04	02	01
Total	**17**	**17**	**17**	**15**	**16**	**20**	**20**	**16**	**13**	**19**	**17**	**15**	**15**	**16**	**19**	**20**	**17**	**14**

Ranking:

South Korea	53
Slovenia	40
India	37
Bulgaria	34
Czechoslovakia	34
Latvia	31
Romania	30
Turkey	28
Nigeria	26
Hungary	22
Belgium	21
Austria	20
East Germany	19
Mexico	18
Belarus	17
Estonia	17
Japan	17
West Germany	16
Norway	16
Lithuania	15
Italy	15
China	13
Moscow	13
France	13
Chile	12
Russia	12
Britain	12
Denmark	12
Spain	11
Portugal	10
United States	10
Sweden	09
Iceland	08
North Ireland	07
Netherlands	07
Canada	06
Ireland	05
Finland	05
Brazil	04
Argentina	02
Switzerland	02

Note: Countries in the left column are ranked according to GNP per capita. / The percentages in the bottom row give each country an equal weight. / na=not ascertained.

V78 NEIGHBORS: AIDS

On this list are various groups of people. Could you please sort out any that you would not like to have as neighbors?
People who have AIDS (% "mentioned")

	Total	Gender Male	Gender Female	Age 16-29	Age 30-49	Age 50+	Education Lower	Education Medium	Education Upper	Income Lower	Income Middle	Income Upper	Political Affinity Left	Political Affinity Center	Political Affinity Right	Values Mat	Values Mixed	Values Postmat
India	93	93	92	91	94	91	93	93	92	91	94	92	91	92	95	94	92	93
Nigeria	79	78	81	81	76	77	79	79	79	73	87	76	80	81	76	83	78	70
China	76	75	77	80	76	72	77	80	74	80	77	70	74	na	na	76	77	82
Romania	66	63	69	55	66	73	77	64	54	70	70	58	66	66	58	71	65	41
Turkey	89	89	89	86	91	88	92	88	76	88	91	86	85	89	89	88	91	83
Poland	na	na	na	na	na	na	na	na	na	na	na	na	na	na	na	na	na	na
Bulgaria	63	62	63	61	59	68	70	64	54	63	64	61	60	62	56	69	62	51
Chile	41	41	40	39	37	50	48	39	34	46	40	35	43	39	40	50	39	32
Czechoslovakia	64	58	70	59	61	72	75	60	57	67	65	61	67	63	62	72	63	53
South Africa	na	na	na	na	na	na	na	na	na	na	na	na	na	na	na	na	na	na
Lithuania	78	75	80	67	81	84	82	77	75	82	78	68	na	na	na	79	79	72
Hungary	66	63	69	59	67	68	66	68	56	66	68	61	67	68	62	66	66	60
Argentina	32	34	29	23	27	43	36	28	27	36	33	29	18	35	27	44	31	19
Brazil	24	24	23	19	21	36	41	18	07	36	21	13	16	19	31	30	21	10
Mexico	57	54	61	53	58	67	59	59	50	60	56	55	46	59	58	66	58	41
Belarus	73	73	73	68	72	78	76	72	72	67	75	76	73	73	73	77	72	66
Russia	68	63	72	59	66	76	72	71	63	69	69	64	62	66	66	75	65	47
Moscow	58	55	61	45	62	62	72	57	55	59	58	57	56	58	69	66	59	44
Latvia	65	63	66	58	67	68	68	67	60	66	63	65	na	na	na	72	64	57
Estonia	63	60	65	60	58	72	72	62	54	62	62	65	na	na	na	64	62	56
Portugal	44	46	42	35	47	51	50	28	36	48	44	39	43	43	48	54	43	29
South Korea	04	04	04	04	05	02	05	04	04	05	05	03	03	05	04	03	04	08
Ireland	35	37	33	27	31	43	41	30	19	45	35	28	32	35	35	38	35	31
North Ireland	28	20	34	12	28	38	32	23	07	34	33	12	14	29	32	43	26	11
Slovenia	41	41	41	41	41	40	42	40	39	40	42	39	37	43	40	41	40	44
Spain	33	33	34	22	30	45	37	29	21	44	33	26	26	31	42	40	32	25
East Germany	20	19	20	14	16	27	22	14	15	23	19	17	14	20	26	32	20	10
Britain	23	24	23	13	19	32	24	22	17	26	18	23	20	20	29	29	24	13
Italy	44	43	44	31	40	54	46	30	20	48	38	27	37	44	45	55	46	26
Netherlands	13	16	12	10	07	24	18	11	09	13	10	10	08	13	16	26	13	07
Belgium	24	24	24	16	22	31	30	22	15	24	24	18	14	23	29	30	25	15
Austria	32	34	32	24	28	40	37	31	17	35	31	30	38	29	38	39	35	22
France	15	14	15	10	12	22	19	11	10	18	11	12	09	15	22	22	15	08
Canada	21	24	17	16	18	27	22	22	15	25	21	16	18	19	22	30	21	15
United States	28	31	24	27	21	34	36	27	24	31	30	23	16	27	36	33	30	19
Iceland	18	21	15	10	15	32	26	16	13	na	na	na	15	14	25	23	17	11
West Germany	29	27	30	18	25	37	34	20	17	31	30	24	21	28	36	49	29	16
Denmark	09	11	07	07	06	14	13	10	06	13	08	06	06	09	13	13	10	03
Finland	24	26	23	22	22	33	29	28	18	28	24	22	22	25	29	38	23	24
Norway	25	29	21	19	20	36	42	27	16	31	23	21	22	21	30	35	22	11
Sweden	18	20	15	17	13	25	22	17	12	24	16	15	12	18	21	24	19	11
Japan	77	79	75	78	73	82	78	78	71	78	78	75	74	72	81	79	78	63
Switzerland	na	na	na	na	na	na	na	na	na	na	na	na	na	na	na	na	na	na
Total	**44**	**44**	**44**	**38**	**42**	**50**	**49**	**42**	**37**	**47**	**45**	**40**	**37**	**40**	**43**	**50**	**44**	**35**

Ranking:

India	93
Turkey	89
Nigeria	79
Lithuania	78
Japan	77
China	76
Belarus	73
Russia	68
Romania	66
Hungary	66
Latvia	65
Czechoslovakia	64
Bulgaria	63
Estonia	63
Moscow	58
Mexico	57
Portugal	44
Italy	44
Chile	41
Slovenia	41
Ireland	35
Spain	33
Argentina	32
Austria	32
West Germany	29
North Ireland	28
United States	28
Norway	25
Brazil	24
Belgium	24
Finland	24
Britain	23
Canada	21
East Germany	20
Iceland	18
Sweden	18
France	15
Netherlands	13
Denmark	09
South Korea	04

Note: Countries in the left column are ranked according to GNP per capita. / The percentages in the bottom row give each country an equal weight. / na=not ascertained.

V79 NEIGHBORS: DRUG ADDICTS

On this list are various groups of people. Could you please sort out any that you would not like to have as neighbors?
Drug addicts (% "mentioned")

	Total	Gender		Age			Education			Income			Political Affinity			Values		
		Male	Female	16-29	30-49	50+	Lower	Medium	Upper	Lower	Middle	Upper	Left	Center	Right	Mat	Mixed	Postmat
India	93	93	93	93	93	92	93	95	90	93	92	92	94	91	92	96	91	91
Nigeria	77	75	78	77	76	74	75	76	78	72	83	74	78	81	72	80	74	75
China	76	75	78	77	77	73	75	78	76	78	77	71	na	na	na	77	75	83
Romania	76	74	78	68	75	82	80	75	73	80	77	72	79	79	66	80	74	64
Turkey	92	92	92	90	93	93	94	92	85	91	94	91	88	92	94	94	93	87
Poland	na	na	na	na	na	na	na	na	na	na	na	na	na	na	na	na	na	na
Bulgaria	69	67	71	67	71	68	70	72	66	68	72	72	66	74	64	75	69	58
Chile	55	52	58	50	54	64	58	54	52	59	53	52	49	55	58	61	55	46
Czechoslovakia	81	77	84	78	80	83	83	78	83	81	82	78	82	80	80	82	80	77
South Africa	na	na	na	na	na	na	na	na	na	na	na	na	na	na	na	na	na	na
Lithuania	89	89	89	82	91	94	94	87	90	91	88	85	na	na	na	93	89	82
Hungary	84	80	87	79	85	84	83	87	76	84	83	84	79	88	79	85	83	78
Argentina	50	50	50	34	50	63	57	46	42	52	51	48	33	50	58	62	50	36
Brazil	58	60	57	54	57	69	68	56	47	66	54	53	51	54	67	65	57	34
Mexico	69	67	72	65	70	79	69	70	68	72	68	66	63	71	72	74	70	63
Belarus	82	79	85	80	83	82	76	83	84	79	85	82	83	85	78	85	83	67
Russia	86	84	88	82	87	88	88	85	86	86	87	84	86	86	83	89	85	83
Moscow	82	79	84	77	83	83	84	80	82	84	80	81	80	85	79	85	83	74
Latvia	89	88	89	85	92	87	88	90	88	84	91	89	na	na	na	90	88	89
Estonia	87	87	87	82	89	88	87	86	88	87	85	87	na	na	na	93	85	81
Portugal	61	61	60	50	62	69	64	51	53	63	61	59	52	61	66	71	58	50
South Korea	04	05	04	05	04	02	04	05	04	04	05	03	04	05	04	03	05	07
Ireland	64	65	64	54	68	68	70	61	47	74	64	59	58	64	69	71	64	60
North Ireland	59	60	58	51	48	76	61	63	38	66	58	47	43	56	69	74	60	38
Slovenia	47	46	47	47	47	46	44	50	47	46	46	51	44	48	49	48	46	54
Spain	54	55	53	42	52	65	57	45	48	62	54	48	48	55	60	61	52	44
East Germany	59	62	59	56	56	65	64	58	51	59	61	58	56	59	61	72	61	45
Britain	62	64	61	61	40	51	60	63	55	57	42	59	60	61	70	71	62	52
Italy	60	61	61	49	60	66	62	47	41	63	56	57	55	62	61	69	62	47
Netherlands	73	73	73	71	70	79	78	74	65	65	74	78	65	77	75	82	74	69
Belgium	53	53	52	45	53	56	56	51	49	53	53	51	50	50	56	60	54	42
Austria	60	62	59	55	56	65	64	58	51	59	61	60	55	60	63	65	63	50
France	44	43	45	39	40	66	51	39	36	47	42	38	34	48	59	55	49	29
Canada	63	63	63	57	65	66	60	65	62	60	66	61	63	62	68	69	64	58
United States	79	78	80	77	81	77	77	79	80	77	80	81	73	81	81	84	78	58
Iceland	74	76	72	71	74	77	70	76	75	na	na	na	75	74	75	78	74	61
West Germany	60	59	61	48	58	68	65	54	46	62	60	58	48	62	67	77	64	45
Denmark	54	60	47	63	50	51	51	58	53	54	54	54	49	52	58	62	55	43
Finland	68	67	69	74	67	63	69	66	68	59	72	70	60	71	74	65	68	67
Norway	55	58	53	56	51	60	62	55	51	55	54	58	50	53	62	63	54	67
Sweden	65	68	63	69	61	65	64	65	66	64	62	66	58	62	71	77	65	42
Japan	91	92	90	95	91	88	84	93	93	89	93	91	86	93	94	91	93	59
Switzerland	32	32	31	23	29	38	36	29	27	34	31	34	22	36	38	41	34	21
Total	67	67	67	63	66	70	68	66	63	67	67	65	60	65	67	73	67	59

Ranking:

India	93
Turkey	92
Japan	91
Lithuania	89
Latvia	89
Estonia	87
Russia	86
Hungary	84
Belarus	82
Moscow	82
Czechoslovakia	81
United States	79
Nigeria	77
China	76
Romania	76
Iceland	74
Netherlands	73
Bulgaria	69
Mexico	69
Finland	68
Sweden	65
Ireland	64
Canada	63
Britain	62
Portugal	61
Italy	60
Austria	60
West Germany	60
North Ireland	59
East Germany	59
Brazil	58
Chile	55
Norway	55
Spain	54
Denmark	54
Belgium	53
Argentina	50
Slovenia	47
France	44
Switzerland	32
South Korea	04

Note: Countries in the left column are ranked according to GNP per capita. / The percentages in the bottom row give each country an equal weight. / na=not ascertained.

V80   NEIGHBORS: HOMOSEXUALS

On this list are various groups of people. Could you please sort out any that you would not like to have as neighbors? Homosexuals (% "mentioned")

	Total	Gender		Age			Education			Income			Political Affinity			Values		
		Male	Female	16-29	30-49	50+	Lower	Medium	Upper	Lower	Middle	Upper	Left	Center	Right	Mat	Mixed	Postmat
India	91	92	91	91	91	92	91	91	92	92	91	75	92	90	92	94	91	90
Nigeria	76	76	76	77	76	70	75	74	79	69	84	75	78	80	72	82	73	71
China	72	71	73	74	73	69	70	77	70	73	75	67	na	na	na	71	74	72
Romania	75	73	77	67	75	82	81	75	68	76	78	71	79	78	67	82	72	61
Turkey	92	93	90	90	94	91	93	94	80	92	94	89	87	92	94	93	93	86
Poland	na	na	na	na	na	na	na	na	na	na	na	na	na	na	na	na	na	na
Bulgaria	68	67	68	66	70	65	67	70	65	66	72	69	62	72	63	73	68	55
Chile	58	57	58	56	56	63	60	56	58	60	57	55	56	55	61	63	57	50
Czechoslovakia	59	59	58	57	53	66	69	55	50	62	59	55	62	58	55	66	57	50
South Africa	na	na	na	na	na	na	na	na	na	na	na	na	na	na	na	na	na	na
Lithuania	87	88	87	82	90	90	88	88	86	88	89	84	na	na	na	89	88	80
Hungary	75	77	74	71	79	74	75	77	69	75	78	70	75	78	73	76	75	75
Argentina	39	44	34	28	37	50	46	34	32	42	41	36	18	43	42	53	37	26
Brazil	30	35	25	27	27	42	42	27	21	35	28	25	25	26	40	35	29	18
Mexico	60	60	60	54	63	70	62	60	54	64	57	59	47	61	67	66	60	49
Belarus	79	78	80	80	79	79	76	81	79	76	83	78	79	83	73	81	80	67
Russia	81	79	81	80	82	79	79	82	80	77	83	79	80	81	75	82	81	70
Moscow	71	68	72	68	74	67	59	75	70	74	68	68	69	74	77	77	71	58
Latvia	78	79	78	75	80	80	81	81	73	80	79	78	na	na	na	84	77	76
Estonia	73	74	72	68	73	79	78	73	68	72	74	74	na	na	na	81	71	51
Portugal	50	57	43	41	49	58	55	40	36	54	48	46	47	48	55	61	48	33
South Korea	04	06	03	05	04	02	05	05	03	04	04	04	06	04	04	03	06	04
Ireland	33	35	31	25	30	42	40	27	18	42	36	21	21	34	37	38	33	29
North Ireland	48	51	46	34	42	65	50	50	28	57	48	41	18	45	62	55	51	24
Slovenia	43	42	43	44	43	41	43	44	40	42	43	42	39	45	46	42	42	54
Spain	27	28	26	15	23	40	29	25	18	36	27	22	20	26	41	35	25	20
East Germany	34	39	30	26	28	45	39	29	22	37	37	29	25	36	44	46	36	25
Britain	31	36	26	21	25	43	35	25	19	37	25	24	27	30	35	39	32	19
Italy	39	41	38	27	34	52	42	23	12	45	31	23	29	44	37	53	40	24
Netherlands	09	15	06	07	04	16	12	08	06	09	06	04	03	07	15	22	09	02
Belgium	24	27	20	18	19	32	30	23	13	26	22	17	19	21	27	32	24	14
Austria	43	49	40	36	39	50	49	41	30	50	44	35	49	42	47	52	47	29
France	24	26	23	15	22	34	31	19	16	32	18	21	14	28	37	33	28	12
Canada	30	37	23	26	26	33	36	31	23	34	28	25	23	30	31	36	30	24
United States	39	45	32	40	33	43	44	40	33	44	40	32	20	30	48	44	40	30
Iceland	20	28	12	13	19	31	27	18	16	na	na	na	15	19	26	28	19	10
West Germany	34	38	31	23	27	45	40	24	23	38	34	29	23	33	46	57	37	17
Denmark	12	15	09	09	08	18	18	11	09	16	10	07	07	11	16	19	12	03
Finland	25	34	16	25	22	34	31	29	18	25	27	24	18	27	32	32	23	28
Norway	20	26	13	17	13	29	35	20	11	27	18	11	17	18	21	26	18	10
Sweden	18	22	12	18	12	23	25	16	09	24	19	11	14	17	20	25	19	10
Japan	69	75	62	68	66	73	69	70	64	65	73	71	63	68	76	71	70	56
Switzerland	na	na	na	na	na	na	na	na	na	na	na	na	na	na	na	na	na	na
Total	**49**	**51**	**46**	**44**	**47**	**54**	**52**	**47**	**42**	**52**	**49**	**45**	**40**	**46**	**49**	**55**	**49**	**40**

Ranking:

Turkey	92	Slovenia	43
India	91	Austria	43
Lithuania	87	Argentina	39
Russia	81	Italy	39
Belarus	79	United States	39
Latvia	78	East Germany	34
Nigeria	76	West Germany	33
Romania	75	Ireland	31
Hungary	75	Britain	31
Estonia	73	Brazil	30
China	72	Canada	30
Moscow	71	Spain	27
Japan	69	Finland	25
Bulgaria	68	Belgium	24
Mexico	60	France	24
Czechoslovakia	59	Iceland	20
Chile	58	Norway	20
Portugal	50	Sweden	18
North Ireland	48	Denmark	12
		Netherlands	09
		South Korea	04

Note: Countries in the left column are ranked according to GNP per capita. / The percentages in the bottom row give each country an equal weight. / na=not ascertained.

V81 NEIGHBORS: JEWS

On this list are various groups of people. Could you please sort out any any that you would not like to have as neighbors? Jews (% "mentioned")

	Total	Gender Male	Gender Female	Age 16-29	Age 30-49	Age 50+	Education Lower	Education Medium	Education Upper	Income Lower	Income Middle	Income Upper	Pol. Aff. Left	Pol. Aff. Center	Pol. Aff. Right	Values Mat	Values Mixed	Values Postmat	Ranking	
India	53	49	57	47	52	65	93	46	39	62	56	39	50	49	45	55	47	48	Turkey	59
Nigeria	35	35	36	37	33	37	39	36	33	34	35	35	39	31	36	31	38	33	India	53
China	na	na	na	na	na	na	na	na	na	na	na	na	na	na	na	na	na	na	Slovenia	37
Romania	28	28	29	23	29	30	34	28	21	31	28	26	35	29	26	34	26	10	Nigeria	35
Turkey	59	58	61	60	58	61	72	44	29	71	62	42	40	59	74	64	64	42	Bulgaria	30
Poland	na	na	na	na	na	na	na	na	na	na	na	na	na	na	na	na	na	na	Romania	28
Bulgaria	30	30	30	29	27	35	39	32	19	28	31	28	25	27	34	34	31	na	Japan	28
Chile	16	16	15	15	13	21	22	13	11	20	15	11	16	16	14	20	16	19	Czechoslovakia	23
Czechoslovakia	23	22	24	26	20	24	27	23	15	25	22	23	25	24	17	29	22	09	Belarus	21
South Africa	na	na	na	na	na	na	na	na	na	na	na	na	na	na	na	na	na	14	Mexico	19
Lithuania	18	16	19	16	17	20	19	18	15	21	14	17	na	na	na	19	18	15	Portugal	19
Hungary	10	10	11	07	10	12	13	07	05	12	10	05	06	09	11	10	11	10	Lithuania	18
Argentina	06	07	04	05	05	07	06	06	03	07	05	06	02	05	09	05	06	06	Chile	16
Brazil	na	na	na	na	na	na	na	na	na	na	na	na	na	na	na	na	na	06	Russia	13
Mexico	19	17	20	18	18	22	19	20	17	17	21	20	na	na	21	23	18	14	Estonia	13
Belarus	21	23	20	24	19	23	24	23	19	23	21	21	11	19	21	25	19	19	Italy	13
Russia	13	15	11	14	11	13	15	15	09	12	12	09	13	11	20	13	13	10	Belgium	13
Moscow	12	12	11	11	12	12	17	12	10	14	10	10	10	10	21	16	10	10	Moscow	12
Latvia	09	08	09	11	08	07	18	09	05	10	08	08	na	na	na	11	09	03	Spain	12
Estonia	13	15	11	17	10	13	20	12	08	12	13	14	na	na	na	13	13	07	Austria	11
Portugal	19	19	20	18	20	20	24	07	12	25	16	15	15	17	25	30	15	08	Hungary	10
South Korea	na	na	na	na	na	na	na	na	na	na	na	na	na	na	na	na	na	na	Latvia	09
Ireland	06	06	07	04	07	08	10	03	00	10	06	04	09	06	05	08	06	05	Norway	09
North Ireland	06	06	07	03	03	12	08	04	00	09	01	03	00	07	07	08	08	00	East Germany	08
Slovenia	37	38	36	42	39	33	35	39	40	33	41	37	37	39	38	33	39	38	Britain	07
Spain	12	12	12	07	10	18	14	07	07	16	13	09	10	13	19	15	11	10	France	07
East Germany	08	09	07	05	06	11	10	06	03	11	07	06	04	08	14	11	08	06	Iceland	07
Britain	07	07	07	03	06	11	08	05	05	10	03	06	08	06	06	10	07	03	West Germany	07
Italy	13	13	13	08	12	17	14	06	08	14	06	05	08	13	13	10	14	07	Argentina	06
Netherlands	03	03	03	02	02	06	04	03	01	03	01	01	02	02	04	07	03	01	Ireland	06
Belgium	13	13	13	10	13	15	16	12	09	14	13	11	07	11	19	19	13	08	North Ireland	06
Austria	11	12	11	08	09	15	15	10	03	18	10	07	14	08	15	18	12	07	Canada	06
France	07	09	05	03	06	10	10	03	04	09	05	07	06	07	11	10	08	03	Sweden	06
Canada	06	05	06	04	06	06	05	06	05	06	06	05	01	05	05	10	05	05	United States	05
United States	05	05	05	05	04	06	07	05	03	08	03	04	05	06	04	08	06	03	Finland	05
Iceland	07	10	05	04	05	16	11	07	04	16	13	09	10	06	10	04	06	03	Netherlands	03
West Germany	07	07	07	05	06	10	09	06	03	08	07	06	04	06	09	11	06	05	Denmark	03
Denmark	03	04	03	03	01	05	06	03	02	06	02	01	05	06	03	12	08	02		
Finland	05	07	02	05	03	10	04	04	04	07	03	05	01	04	05	05	03	01		
Norway	09	12	06	06	08	12	15	10	05	11	09	05	02	06	08	12	04	05		
Sweden	06	06	06	06	02	08	10	05	01	08	07	03	09	08	08	14	07	03		
Japan	28	29	28	34	21	34	35	29	18	32	30	19	27	22	32	30	26	17		
Switzerland	na	na	na	na	na	na	na	na	na	na	na	na	na	na	na	na	na	na		
Total	**16**	**16**	**16**	**15**	**14**	**18**	**20**	**14**	**11**	**18**	**15**	**13**	**14**	**15**	**18**	**19**	**16**	**11**		

Note: Countries in the left column are ranked according to GNP per capita. / The percentages in the bottom row give each country an equal weight. / na=not ascertained.

V82 NEIGHBORS: HINDUS

On this list are various groups of people. Could you please sort out any that you would not like to have as neighbors? Hindus (% "mentioned")

	Total	Gender Male	Gender Female	Age 16-29	Age 30-49	Age 50+	Education Lower	Education Medium	Education Upper	Income Lower	Income Middle	Income Upper	Political Affinity Left	Political Affinity Center	Political Affinity Right	Values Mat	Values Mixed	Values Postmat
India	02	02	na	02	02	04	02	na	03	03	02	02	02	01	02	02	02	02
Nigeria	22	22	24	23	21	28	27	25	18	27	15	26	23	18	24	18	25	22
China	na	na	na	na	na	na	na	na	na	na	na	na	na	na	na	na	na	na
Romania	na	na	na	na	na	na	na	na	na	na	na	na	na	na	na	na	na	na
Turkey	51	47	55	53	49	52	64	35	22	63	52	34	39	47	62	55	55	36
Poland	na	na	na	na	na	na	na	na	na	na	na	na	na	na	na	na	na	na
Bulgaria	22	22	21	19	21	23	24	24	15	20	19	21	23	21	22	20	23	16
Chile	13	13	13	12	11	17	17	12	08	17	12	08	10	15	11	18	13	07
Czechoslovakia	76	74	78	77	74	77	77	77	71	75	78	75	76	76	77	81	75	69
South Africa	na	na	na	na	na	na	na	na	na	na	na	na	na	na	na	na	na	na
Lithuania	na	na	na	na	na	na	na	na	na	na	na	na	na	na	na	na	na	na
Hungary	14	12	15	09	13	16	17	11	05	16	13	07	09	13	13	14	14	13
Argentina	03	03	03	03	03	04	04	04	01	04	03	03	00	02	06	04	03	02
Brazil	na	na	na	na	na	na	na	na	na	na	na	na	na	na	na	na	na	na
Mexico	14	12	16	15	13	14	14	14	13	12	16	16	06	15	16	14	14	09
Belarus	na	na	na	na	na	na	na	na	na	07	05	04	05	05	13	06	06	08
Russia	06	07	05	06	06	06	07	08	04	06	05	07	04	06	14	09	05	04
Moscow	06	07	06	04	05	10	13	06	05	06	05	07	04	06	14	09	05	04
Latvia	na	na	na	na	na	na	na	na	na	na	na	na	na	na	na	na	na	na
Estonia	na	na	na	na	na	na	na	na	na	na	na	na	na	na	na	na	na	na
Portugal	17	17	16	17	16	18	19	06	16	19	15	15	13	15	22	25	13	12
South Korea	na	11	09	06	09	15	na	na	05	15	11	05	09	09	11	na	10	08
Ireland	10	11	09	06	09	12	14	05	01	15	11	05	00	10	12	17	09	00
North Ireland	09	09	09	04	06	16	10	10	03	10	09	04	00	10	14	38	43	47
Slovenia	42	41	43	42	42	42	44	41	40	40	41	47	39	42	52	14	11	09
Spain	11	11	11	06	09	17	13	08	07	15	13	08	09	11	17	22	15	10
East Germany	15	15	15	10	13	19	18	11	05	18	14	13	09	16	20	15	12	07
Britain	12	12	12	07	09	18	13	11	08	14	08	12	10	10	15	18	14	05
Italy	13	12	14	08	11	18	14	05	08	15	07	04	03	05	09	16	05	04
Netherlands	05	06	05	05	04	09	07	06	04	05	04	05	10	14	21	23	16	11
Belgium	16	16	11	13	15	20	19	17	04	19	17	13	15	09	14	17	12	06
Austria	11	11	11	08	09	15	15	09	05	17	09	08	06	08	14	11	09	05
France	08	09	07	06	08	09	11	06	03	12	06	07	08	11	10	14	10	08
Canada	10	11	10	09	10	12	11	11	04	12	10	09	04	07	09	07	08	03
United States	07	08	07	07	05	08	11	07	04	10	05	06	05	07	11	11	08	03
Iceland	08	09	07	06	04	18	13	08	04	na	na	na	09	13	15	25	13	07
West Germany	13	13	14	09	13	16	17	07	05	16	12	10	06	06	06	08	06	03
Denmark	06	07	04	07	04	08	07	07	05	09	05	03	07	07	08	12	06	04
Finland	06	07	04	07	04	09	09	05	07	09	03	06	01	13	15	21	13	05
Norway	14	17	11	10	12	18	22	17	07	14	15	08	12	12	08	12	10	04
Sweden	09	09	08	08	05	14	15	08	02	12	12	04	03	12	08	12	10	04
Japan	28	28	27	33	21	34	35	29	17	31	30	19	26	21	32	29	25	17
Switzerland	na	na	na	na	na	na	na	na	na	na	na	na	na	na	na	na	na	na
Total	16	16	16	14	14	19	19	14	10	18	15	13	13	15	19	19	16	11

Ranking:

Czechoslovakia	76
Turkey	51
Slovenia	42
Japan	28
Nigeria	22
Bulgaria	22
Portugal	17
Belgium	16
East Germany	15
Hungary	14
Mexico	14
Norway	14
Chile	13
Italy	13
West Germany	13
Britain	12
Spain	11
Austria	11
Ireland	10
Canada	10
North Ireland	09
Sweden	09
France	08
Iceland	08
United States	07
Russia	06
Moscow	06
Denmark	06
Finland	06
Netherlands	05
Argentina	03
India	02

Note: Countries in the left column are ranked according to GNP per capita. / The percentages in the bottom row give each country an equal weight. / na=not ascertained.
The Slovenian survey and the Lithuanian, Latvian, and Estonian surveys asked about "Gypsies," rather than "Hindus," in V82.

V83. All in all, how would you describe your state of health these days?

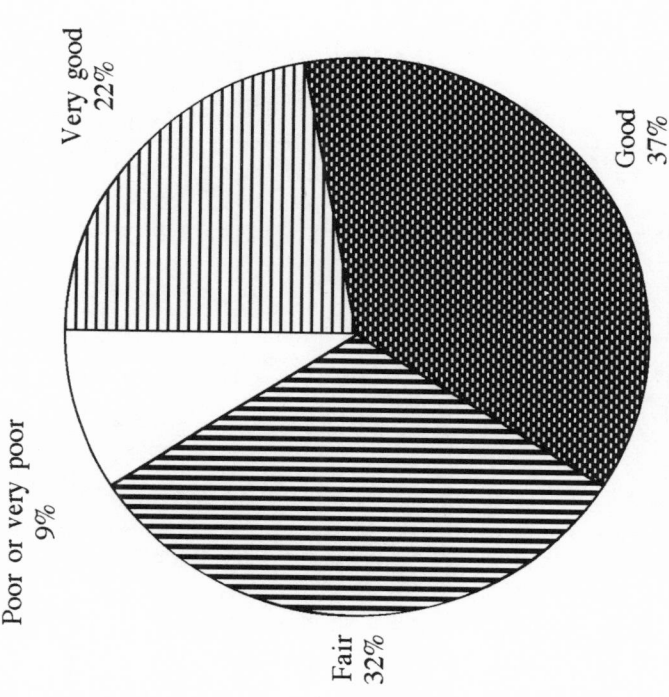

V83 STATE OF HEALTH

All in all, how would you describe your state of health these days? Would you say it is very good, good, fair, poor, or very poor?
(% "very good" or "good")

	Total	Gender		Age			Education			Income			Political Affinity			Values		
		Male	Female	16-29	30-49	50+	Lower	Medium	Upper	Lower	Middle	Upper	Left	Center	Right	Mat	Mixed	Postmat
India	63	66	60	71	62	47	47	64	70	55	65	68	58	65	72	64	66	65
Nigeria	78	77	81	79	77	76	84	75	79	71	82	84	83	77	78	81	76	86
China	56	61	48	61	57	49	52	62	52	54	57	58	na	49	na	53	61	41
Romania	47	55	40	58	52	36	39	53	50	36	47	56	46	49	51	43	51	48
Turkey	60	64	57	67	62	47	57	63	68	54	64	64	64	57	64	53	61	68
Poland	38	45	32	68	42	19	24	47	46	29	39	48	41	41	38	37	38	39
Bulgaria	51	58	45	71	58	32	34	53	66	43	53	65	53	52	57	46	53	57
Chile	54	61	49	63	55	41	40	60	66	38	56	71	56	58	58	48	56	62
Czechoslovakia	44	49	39	68	44	27	32	49	51	35	45	52	42	46	42	35	46	53
South Africa	68	69	66	77	68	48	51	74	85	55	68	83	67	71	72	69	67	68
Lithuania	43	52	36	67	44	23	28	50	41	37	48	51	na	na	na	36	43	53
Hungary	31	36	27	62	38	13	17	44	49	22	38	43	42	34	32	27	35	38
Argentina	60	64	56	65	62	54	52	62	71	45	62	71	50	65	66	59	59	65
Brazil	69	76	63	82	68	49	53	75	81	60	71	79	72	72	68	64	72	80
Mexico	69	68	69	75	68	52	63	79	77	64	67	81	73	66	74	62	70	78
Belarus	27	35	21	37	31	10	20	30	27	23	29	31	27	32	22	28	29	19
Russia	26	35	20	47	26	13	18	30	28	23	23	31	33	27	31	21	29	33
Moscow	29	39	20	42	31	15	23	31	29	30	29	29	30	28	26	27	28	33
Latvia	32	35	30	53	25	21	18	34	32	29	31	35	na	na	na	26	33	34
Estonia	36	43	30	61	33	14	29	38	37	32	38	39	na	na	na	29	38	55
Portugal	44	55	35	61	47	26	37	64	56	33	51	53	43	46	44	40	46	53
South Korea	na	na	na	na	na	na	na	na	na	na	na	na	na	na	na	na	na	na
Ireland	82	83	81	94	89	66	72	92	91	65	86	91	87	81	83	77	82	86
North Ireland	77	84	73	88	84	63	71	86	93	66	82	90	61	81	76	75	75	87
Slovenia	43	49	37	62	47	26	34	50	48	32	45	61	49	47	42	39	44	50
Spain	57	60	55	69	66	41	54	68	64	43	61	66	62	57	57	53	61	62
East Germany	55	63	49	76	66	32	51	66	61	40	58	67	62	53	56	32	56	65
Britain	75	79	71	86	84	60	70	89	82	63	86	83	72	76	77	74	74	79
Italy	55	60	50	73	61	39	54	65	70	48	65	71	58	53	63	50	54	63
Netherlands	74	73	75	84	77	60	65	80	80	64	77	83	71	78	77	66	79	72
Belgium	72	75	70	85	78	58	62	76	84	65	73	82	73	74	76	66	73	79
Austria	62	64	61	84	73	43	51	70	69	45	66	73	60	65	60	45	61	73
France	66	65	67	82	73	48	59	72	75	56	73	72	70	67	61	61	66	74
United States	79	81	79	89	87	66	64	85	86	68	84	88	83	80	79	76	81	81
Iceland	74	78	70	80	81	55	62	79	80	64	83	91	76	74	76	73	79	83
West Germany	56	62	51	82	69	31	50	68	65	na	59	71	61	58	53	38	56	65
Denmark	78	82	74	90	86	59	68	84	86	62	88	90	84	74	82	67	80	85
Finland	76	78	74	87	82	50	72	86	86	63	78	86	66	76	81	70	75	79
Norway	75	76	73	88	79	61	51	75	86	61	80	86	74	76	77	69	77	78
Sweden	80	83	77	90	88	69	74	84	82	75	71	89	80	79	84	82	79	84
Japan	44	48	41	51	48	34	37	44	53	43	44	47	44	46	47	44	43	55
Switzerland	81	83	79	88	88	69	79	81	87	71	86	89	84	83	80	78	79	86
Total	59	63	55	73	63	43	49	64	66	49	61	68	62	62	62	54	60	64

Ranking:

Ireland	82
Switzerland	81
Canada	80
Sweden	80
United States	79
Nigeria	78
Denmark	78
North Ireland	77
Finland	76
Britain	75
Norway	75
Netherlands	74
Iceland	74
Belgium	72
Brazil	69
Mexico	69
South Africa	68
France	66
India	63
Austria	62
Turkey	60
Argentina	60
Spain	57
China	56
West Germany	56
East Germany	55
Italy	55
Chile	54
Bulgaria	51
Romania	47
Czechoslovakia	44
Portugal	44
Japan	44
Lithuania	43
Slovenia	43
Poland	38
Estonia	36
Latvia	32
Hungary	31
Moscow	29
Belarus	27
Russia	26

Note: Countries in the left column are ranked according to GNP per capita. / The percentages in the bottom row give each country an equal weight. / na=not ascertained.

V84-V93. We are interested in the way people are feeling these days. During the past few weeks, did you ever feel...

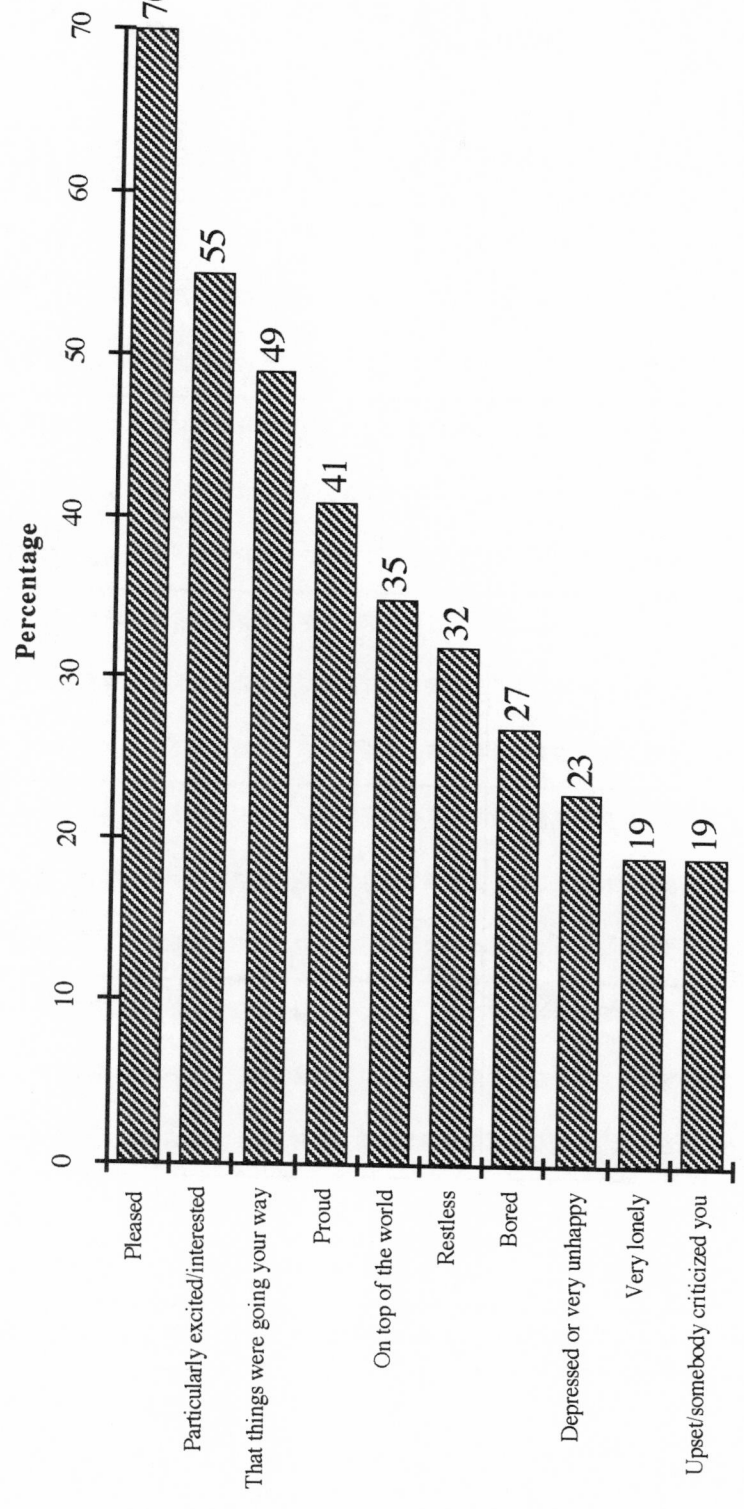

V84 FEEL EXCITED

We are interested in the way people are feeling these days. During the past few weeks, did you ever feel...
Particularly excited or interested in something (% "yes")

	Total	Gender		Age			Education			Income			Political Affinity			Values		
		Male	Female	16-29	30-49	50+	Lower	Medium	Upper	Lower	Middle	Upper	Left	Center	Right	Mat	Mixed	Postmat
India	53	57	48	60	51	42	37	54	60	49	52	58	57	53	56	54	55	63
Nigeria	71	71	70	73	69	65	72	70	71	63	72	73	72	68	75	68	72	70
China	43	47	36	51	39	38	43	43	44	46	44	37	na	na	na	40	44	57
Romania	38	39	38	49	41	28	31	42	41	34	38	42	34	38	43	32	43	47
Turkey	40	42	39	45	38	38	34	47	56	32	40	50	50	42	35	36	39	50
Poland	79	78	79	67	81	83	77	77	93	82	74	80	83	78	85	80	78	75
Bulgaria	57	52	61	65	58	51	39	61	66	53	62	58	54	64	63	54	58	56
Chile	68	68	68	71	69	63	60	70	77	62	69	75	71	68	69	58	70	77
Czechoslovakia	61	61	60	55	65	60	55	61	70	58	62	62	64	59	63	56	63	62
South Africa	64	65	63	69	65	50	43	72	87	47	66	85	73	69	75	59	65	71
Lithuania	54	51	55	47	54	59	57	53	48	56	54	49	na	na	na	57	53	51
Hungary	70	72	68	73	73	66	66	75	68	68	69	76	79	72	72	72	68	73
Argentina	62	62	61	67	64	55	53	67	70	54	62	66	83	66	67	52	63	69
Brazil	65	66	63	69	66	55	61	65	72	62	64	67	68	67	63	62	65	75
Mexico	70	70	71	76	69	56	65	75	83	65	72	80	77	69	73	70	70	75
Belarus	53	59	49	59	55	45	41	51	61	51	57	51	58	50	41	50	56	55
Russia	39	42	37	50	39	33	29	38	47	36	39	44	43	42	45	35	42	43
Moscow	58	65	53	64	60	52	39	55	64	54	59	65	64	54	55	51	60	70
Latvia	51	53	49	55	51	45	41	51	52	51	52	49	na	na	na	45	53	52
Estonia	53	54	52	57	56	45	45	53	62	49	54	59	na	na	na	48	56	70
Portugal	44	43	46	54	41	37	42	47	50	46	43	45	48	43	47	49	43	47
South Korea	na	na	na	na	na	na	na	na	76	48	58	72	66	56	66	51	60	70
Ireland	59	60	59	72	63	47	50	68	76	48	53	67	75	46	55	51	51	51
North Ireland	51	58	47	67	50	42	42	65	76	34	53	54	75	36	44	52	49	50
Slovenia	50	58	43	49	50	50	42	50	65	48	50	54	55	57	62	56	70	72
Spain	33	35	32	45	34	25	29	38	48	27	33	61	38	35	35	28	35	44
East Germany	71	77	65	72	75	65	69	74	72	65	73	74	70	71	78	51	71	80
Britain	55	57	53	62	64	42	48	66	78	40	61	71	54	56	57	48	55	62
Italy	40	41	40	53	39	33	39	48	47	38	43	44	45	36	44	34	39	50
Netherlands	69	72	68	73	68	65	57	71	80	64	72	79	76	65	72	56	70	72
Belgium	54	57	51	68	57	42	46	58	62	50	51	61	53	56	62	46	52	66
Austria	49	53	47	60	53	41	44	50	63	41	50	55	50	53	49	37	50	54
France	47	50	44	55	53	34	42	49	54	41	48	56	50	48	43	34	46	62
Canada	72	72	73	78	76	63	60	71	83	62	75	81	82	71	76	73	71	76
United States	67	66	69	76	73	59	56	65	79	58	69	75	75	68	68	64	65	76
Iceland	62	61	63	71	65	45	54	62	69	na	na	74	64	60	63	55	62	76
West Germany	63	68	59	75	71	51	56	75	78	54	62	74	72	61	62	49	63	71
Denmark	52	52	53	62	57	40	34	56	61	46	54	60	59	48	53	45	52	63
Finland	49	53	45	62	48	41	51	46	52	45	50	52	44	46	53	29	49	53
Norway	62	65	59	68	67	51	42	60	74	57	64	70	62	62	66	51	65	74
Sweden	67	69	63	69	69	60	51	71	82	65	61	72	67	64	70	56	64	82
Japan	28	30	27	36	31	20	20	30	31	27	29	30	38	32	24	26	30	39
Switzerland	36	41	32	38	37	34	32	36	54	33	42	36	43	38	37	34	35	39
Total	**55**	**57**	**54**	**62**	**57**	**48**	**47**	**58**	**65**	**50**	**56**	**61**	**61**	**56**	**58**	**50**	**56**	**63**

Ranking:

Poland	79
Canada	72
Nigeria	71
East Germany	71
Hungary	70
Mexico	70
Netherlands	69
Chile	68
United States	67
Sweden	67
Brazil	65
South Africa	64
West Germany	63
Argentina	62
Iceland	62
Norway	62
Czechoslovakia	61
Ireland	59
Moscow	58
Bulgaria	57
Britain	55
Lithuania	54
Belgium	54
India	53
Belarus	53
Estonia	53
Denmark	52
Latvia	51
North Ireland	51
Slovenia	50
Austria	49
Finland	49
France	47
Portugal	44
China	43
Turkey	40
Italy	40
Russia	39
Romania	38
Switzerland	36
Spain	33
Japan	28

Note: Countries in the left column are ranked according to GNP per capita. / The percentages in the bottom row give each country an equal weight. / na=not ascertained.

V85 FEEL RESTLESS

We are interested in the way people are feeling these days. During the past few weeks, did you ever feel...
So restless you couldn't sit long in a chair (% "yes")

	Total	Gender		Age			Education			Income			Political Affinity			Values			Ranking:	
		Male	Female	16-29	30-49	50+	Lower	Medium	Upper	Lower	Middle	Upper	Left	Center	Right	Mat	Mixed	Postmat		
India	27	30	23	29	26	26	23	28	28	28	27	27	30	26	31	28	27	26	East Germany	55
Nigeria	27	28	25	31	21	25	24	28	27	26	26	27	28	25	29	19	32	22	Turkey	48
China	28	29	27	32	27	26	30	27	28	32	29	22	na	na	na	25	29	46	Chile	48
Romania	45	39	51	51	45	41	42	49	43	47	46	42	45	45	50	41	47	53	West Germany	48
Turkey	48	44	52	56	46	38	45	52	52	44	46	53	54	48	44	42	50	51	Romania	45
Poland	37	30	42	23	36	44	43	33	31	44	32	31	34	31	43	39	34	35	Moscow	45
Bulgaria	43	39	47	34	47	44	43	43	43	47	43	38	45	42	43	39	46	36	Hungary	44
Chile	48	47	49	48	49	47	52	46	45	55	48	39	45	47	52	45	50	47	Bulgaria	43
Czechoslovakia	27	24	31	25	29	27	28	27	28	27	28	27	32	24	28	27	28	27	Netherlands	43
South Africa	32	29	35	31	32	36	34	31	37	30	34	32	37	31	32	34	31	31	Brazil	40
Lithuania	30	27	32	30	31	29	32	29	30	30	28	31	na	na	na	29	30	29	Britain	39
Hungary	44	47	42	49	43	44	48	43	38	49	43	33	54	41	48	45	45	43	Poland	37
Argentina	28	27	30	30	26	30	32	28	23	33	32	26	22	32	27	34	27	25	Belarus	37
Brazil	40	36	43	39	42	36	44	39	34	42	43	35	39	38	44	41	40	30	North Ireland	35
Mexico	32	32	31	36	30	27	31	34	34	32	31	32	24	34	40	33	33	25	Austria	35
Belarus	37	33	41	44	37	32	30	40	37	39	37	35	39	32	41	36	39	44	Canada	34
Russia	32	29	34	34	32	31	27	34	33	37	31	31	31	30	40	32	32	30	United States	34
Moscow	45	43	46	44	46	42	46	48	42	48	45	38	46	46	46	41	47	40	South Africa	32
Latvia	26	24	28	37	26	16	18	29	24	24	28	27	na	na	na	22	28	28	Mexico	32
Estonia	32	31	33	40	33	21	28	32	35	32	32	31	na	na	na	30	33	42	Russia	32
Portugal	21	16	25	18	25	19	24	20	08	25	20	17	19	21	22	23	21	14	Estonia	32
South Korea	na	na	na	na	na	na	na	na	na	na	na	na	na	na	na	na	na	na	Lithuania	30
Ireland	26	24	28	32	30	18	25	26	28	23	28	28	na	na	na	33	na	43	China	28
North Ireland	35	30	39	46	36	27	33	38	45	30	35	40	34	26	22	23	25	33	Argentina	28
Slovenia	26	26	26	30	21	28	27	38	45	30	35	40	36	35	33	29	35	49	Belgium	28
Spain	26	24	28	31	26	23	26	26	29	26	25	26	26	27	27	28	26	24	India	27
East Germany	55	53	57	63	56	49	53	61	58	51	58	58	59	55	51	48	54	62	Nigeria	27
Britain	39	38	39	39	45	33	40	35	38	36	39	40	36	43	35	37	40	39	Czechoslovakia	27
Italy	19	16	21	23	18	16	19	18	13	19	17	16	20	18	18	18	19	18	Denmark	27
Netherlands	43	37	45	47	42	39	44	43	41	44	41	37	47	38	42	52	45	37	Latvia	26
Belgium	28	28	29	38	29	21	24	31	32	28	24	30	32	29	29	23	28	34	Ireland	26
Austria	35	30	38	44	34	31	32	34	52	34	34	38	45	35	33	33	34	38	Slovenia	26
France	22	21	23	31	24	14	25	21	16	24	23	22	24	20	22	24	21	23	Spain	26
Canada	34	35	33	44	35	24	32	34	36	38	21	28	36	33	33	29	35	35	Iceland	25
United States	34	34	34	40	37	29	34	33	35	39	34	33	32	36	31	29	35	35	Norway	25
Iceland	25	28	22	33	25	14	23	28	25	na	na	na	25	26	26	25	25	26	France	22
West Germany	48	42	53	54	52	41	46	50	54	49	48	47	54	48	52	48	45	54	Sweden	22
Denmark	27	29	24	30	17	33	19	28	31	30	23	29	38	25	22	22	26	34	Portugal	21
Finland	18	21	16	29	19	08	20	16	20	17	20	17	19	18	17	09	19	18	Italy	19
Norway	25	28	22	39	24	19	20	31	22	29	21	26	28	24	25	24	27	17	Finland	18
Sweden	22	21	24	38	19	14	17	29	18	23	25	17	26	23	19	20	21	27	Japan	16
Japan	16	18	15	16	19	13	15	15	20	16	13	17	21	15	16	17	18	18		
Switzerland	na	na	na	na	na	na	na	na	na	na	na	na	na	na	na	na	na	na		
Total	32	31	34	37	33	28	32	33	33	34	32	31	35	32	33	31	33	33		

Note: Countries in the left column are ranked according to GNP per capita. / The percentages in the bottom row give each country an equal weight. / na=not ascertained.

V86 FEEL PROUD

We are interested in the way people are feeling these days. During the past few weeks, did you ever feel...
Proud because someone had complimented you on something you had done (% "yes")

	Total	Gender		Age			Education			Income			Political Affinity			Values		
		Male	Female	16-29	30-49	50+	Lower	Medium	Upper	Lower	Middle	Upper	Left	Center	Right	Mat	Mixed	Postmat
India	36	37	34	42	33	29	25	36	42	34	35	38	42	38	38	35	38	47
Nigeria	50	49	51	51	49	46	52	51	48	45	50	59	47	53	56	48	53	44
China	27	27	27	27	28	24	28	26	26	28	29	23	na	40	na	25	29	25
Romania	37	39	36	36	37	39	44	34	33	36	39	38	36	40	34	38	38	31
Turkey	47	44	50	51	47	42	46	47	50	46	48	47	47	49	42	44	48	48
Poland	30	28	33	35	27	31	37	27	24	30	27	34	29	26	40	32	29	35
Bulgaria	33	28	38	37	34	30	34	37	27	30	39	34	29	39	34	33	34	25
Chile	44	45	44	46	44	43	41	48	43	43	43	47	43	44	51	44	44	47
Czechoslovakia	12	12	13	13	13	11	15	11	11	12	13	12	07	13	16	13	11	18
South Africa	55	53	56	56	57	49	36	61	81	39	57	77	61	64	67	53	54	69
Lithuania	16	17	16	13	16	20	21	15	15	18	16	13	na	na	na	21	15	13
Hungary	23	25	21	26	25	20	18	26	30	19	24	31	27	22	32	21	24	25
Argentina	39	39	39	40	42	35	39	38	39	36	36	46	34	43	46	38	39	41
Brazil	47	45	49	51	46	41	42	48	52	45	50	46	50	48	46	46	47	52
Mexico	50	50	51	54	48	46	48	50	58	46	50	61	51	50	52	51	51	52
Belarus	28	26	29	30	25	32	28	32	24	28	27	29	28	27	35	30	27	28
Russia	21	18	22	26	19	19	19	19	24	19	23	21	21	21	24	21	20	23
Moscow	33	33	33	39	32	32	41	36	30	33	34	21	34	30	44	35	34	31
Latvia	31	31	31	40	26	29	25	32	30	29	29	32	na	na	na	29	31	35
Estonia	29	28	30	37	28	22	26	30	31	29	27	31	na	na	na	28	28	51
Portugal	24	25	24	25	26	22	25	16	28	25	22	25	22	24	30	29	25	15
South Korea	na	na	na	na	na	na	na	na	na	na	na	na	na	na	na	na	na	na
Ireland	50	47	54	62	52	42	44	57	61	42	48	60	53	52	50	46	49	61
North Ireland	43	45	43	53	42	38	40	53	45	36	42	52	57	40	48	43	46	38
Slovenia	40	41	38	39	39	41	43	40	34	42	40	34	40	40	51	44	39	31
Spain	21	22	21	27	22	17	20	25	23	17	22	25	23	22	25	24	22	21
East Germany	65	61	69	67	67	63	63	70	70	64	64	67	68	66	62	51	67	67
Britain	55	49	60	60	57	51	51	65	63	51	56	57	53	58	51	54	57	51
Italy	39	39	38	44	39	35	39	40	36	40	36	39	42	35	45	36	37	46
Netherlands	58	51	61	64	59	49	53	58	64	61	56	56	63	56	59	49	61	56
Belgium	46	45	47	55	47	40	44	46	52	44	46	50	47	47	47	42	48	47
Austria	70	64	74	79	78	60	63	73	87	61	70	79	69	74	68	61	67	83
France	35	33	36	41	38	26	33	33	42	31	39	37	39	27	40	35	32	40
Canada	64	60	68	70	66	58	61	61	70	64	66	67	72	62	63	67	63	66
United States	68	65	72	79	72	61	64	67	74	63	68	73	68	69	69	68	67	73
Iceland	43	42	45	51	49	25	35	43	51	na	na	na	42	44	47	42	44	47
West Germany	74	72	76	82	77	67	70	80	84	70	74	79	76	76	74	64	73	83
Denmark	45	43	46	55	46	36	36	49	48	43	40	49	52	40	46	44	44	50
Finland	37	38	36	48	36	29	40	33	40	36	39	36	34	34	38	35	36	40
Norway	46	42	51	56	49	38	36	46	52	45	45	52	45	46	48	46	47	49
Sweden	55	49	61	62	57	46	48	56	63	51	55	57	57	50	59	48	54	62
Japan	20	21	19	30	18	17	17	21	21	21	16	24	24	22	23	21	22	17
Switzerland	15	17	14	16	15	16	16	16	08	16	16	19	17	15	16	17	17	11
Total	41	39	42	46	41	36	38	42	44	38	40	44	43	42	45	39	41	43

Ranking:

West Germany	74
Austria	70
United States	68
East Germany	65
Canada	64
Netherlands	58
South Africa	55
Britain	55
Sweden	55
Nigeria	50
Mexico	50
Ireland	50
Turkey	47
Brazil	47
Belgium	46
Norway	46
Denmark	45
Chile	44
North Ireland	43
Iceland	43
Slovenia	40
Argentina	39
Italy	39
Romania	37
Finland	37
India	36
France	35
Bulgaria	33
Moscow	33
Latvia	31
Poland	30
Estonia	29
Belarus	28
China	27
Portugal	24
Hungary	23
Russia	21
Spain	21
Japan	20
Lithuania	16
Switzerland	15
Czechoslovakia	12

Note: Countries in the left column are ranked according to GNP per capita. / The percentages in the bottom row give each country an equal weight. / na=not ascertained.

V87 FEEL LONELY

We are interested in the way people are feeling these days. During the past few weeks, did you ever feel...

Very lonely or remote from other people (% "yes")

	Total	Gender		Age			Education			Income			Political Affinity			Values		
		Male	Female	16-29	30-49	50+	Lower	Medium	Upper	Lower	Middle	Upper	Left	Center	Right	Mat	Mixed	Postmat
India	21	22	20	25	19	20	17	23	22	22	19	24	27	23	17	23	21	21
Nigeria	22	22	23	25	20	14	18	23	23	21	21	23	23	22	20	20	23	23
China	10	09	12	16	08	08	11	11	06	11	11	07	na	na	na	09	11	15
Romania	24	18	30	28	21	25	26	25	21	34	22	20	26	23	na	25	23	26
Turkey	34	31	38	38	32	34	35	33	33	39	35	27	36	35	31	33	35	35
Poland	16	12	20	13	13	21	20	14	13	22	13	13	15	14	18	18	15	17
Bulgaria	19	16	21	20	15	22	23	16	17	24	17	11	18	16	23	24	17	13
Chile	37	33	41	38	36	37	41	35	35	45	36	29	36	37	37	41	36	35
Czechoslovakia	18	13	23	16	19	19	24	16	14	27	14	15	18	19	18	18	19	15
South Africa	28	26	29	29	26	28	35	24	21	35	27	19	32	24	26	27	28	28
Lithuania	14	11	17	15	11	18	21	12	11	19	10	11	na	na	na	18	13	12
Hungary	18	15	21	11	15	24	24	13	10	25	15	09	18	16	22	18	13	20
Argentina	24	22	26	23	22	28	28	23	21	32	22	21	26	23	23	23	18	20
Brazil	32	26	37	34	31	30	37	31	21	37	35	24	34	28	34	32	25	23
Mexico	26	26	27	27	23	30	27	27	25	28	28	22	25	26	27	28	33	26
Belarus	19	13	24	24	17	18	22	20	17	21	19	17	20	15	23	16	28	22
Russia	24	18	28	25	21	26	25	23	23	27	19	20	20	15	23	16	20	30
Moscow	20	16	23	28	17	19	27	21	18	25	21	14	24	24	26	25	23	24
Latvia	16	12	18	21	15	11	26	15	15	21	18	13	18	24	16	19	19	22
Estonia	18	11	23	21	15	18	23	17	15	21	14	14	na	na	na	10	16	16
Portugal	14	13	16	15	18	11	16	10	13	17	15	13	na	na	na	15	18	19
South Korea	na	na	na	na	na	na	na	na	na	na	14	13	14	13	15	15	15	13
Ireland	15	12	17	13	11	19	17	11	11	23	na	na	na	na	na	na	na	na
North Ireland	14	10	17	15	13	16	16	11	07	23	12	12	13	16	22	18	13	15
Slovenia	11	08	13	10	08	14	14	10	06	17	10	11	13	12	15	11	16	26
Spain	17	14	19	17	13	19	17	15	17	23	06	06	13	08	07	09	11	11
East Germany	35	28	41	35	30	41	37	38	25	48	15	12	15	16	15	19	12	09
Britain	19	17	21	19	19	41	21	14	14	27	33	25	31	37	32	45	34	33
Italy	12	09	16	08	19	20	12	09	14	15	14	13	23	19	16	21	20	16
Netherlands	15	13	15	15	13	17	16	15	14	20	10	05	14	10	14	14	13	16
Belgium	16	13	18	14	15	18	18	14	14	19	10	11	19	09	11	14	12	09
Austria	24	19	28	23	22	27	26	23	26	33	16	10	15	18	13	21	15	12
France	18	15	22	23	18	16	22	16	19	25	21	21	31	26	23	28	24	24
Canada	17	16	19	19	17	16	22	14	13	21	19	13	19	18	19	18	19	19
United States	19	17	20	20	18	19	22	16	19	22	16	16	21	17	16	18	17	18
Iceland	11	10	12	13	09	12	16	09	08	na	20	13	25	17	14	16	20	17
West Germany	36	28	43	34	31	41	37	34	35	46	06	na	11	14	08	11	10	11
Denmark	13	10	16	13	13	13	14	11	14	20	35	30	40	34	31	44	32	39
Finland	21	22	19	22	21	19	31	15	22	25	09	08	16	14	08	14	12	18
Norway	13	11	14	12	11	15	21	11	10	17	16	23	22	22	20	21	21	19
Sweden	07	07	08	10	08	05	05	09	08	07	09	09	16	11	09	13	13	17
Japan	13	12	14	19	12	10	12	13	13	13	10	05	10	07	06	04	08	07
Switzerland	05	05	05	05	04	07	05	05	06	08	11	12	12	13	11	10	15	06
Total	19	16	22	20	17	20	22	18	17	25	04	02	06	05	04	05	06	03

Ranking:

Chile	37
West Germany	36
East Germany	35
Turkey	34
Brazil	32
South Africa	28
Mexico	26
Romania	24
Argentina	24
Russia	24
Austria	24
Nigeria	22
India	21
Finland	21
Moscow	20
Bulgaria	19
Belarus	19
Britain	19
United States	19
Czechoslovakia	18
Hungary	18
Estonia	18
France	18
Spain	17
Canada	17
Poland	16
Latvia	16
Belgium	16
Ireland	15
Netherlands	15
Lithuania	14
Portugal	14
North Ireland	14
Denmark	13
Norway	13
Japan	13
Italy	12
Slovenia	11
Iceland	11
China	10
Sweden	07
Switzerland	05

Note: Countries in the left column are ranked according to GNP per capita. / The percentages in the bottom row give each country an equal weight. / na=not ascertained.

V88 FEEL PLEASED

We are interested in the way people are feeling these days. During the past few weeks, did you ever feel...
Pleased about having accomplished something (% "yes")

	Total	Gender Male	Gender Female	Age 16-29	Age 30-49	Age 50+	Education Lower	Education Medium	Education Upper	Income Lower	Income Middle	Income Upper	Pol. Aff. Left	Pol. Aff. Center	Pol. Aff. Right	Values Mat	Values Mixed	Values Postmat
India	45	48	41	51	43	38	28	45	53	37	43	52	56	43	47	47	46	53
Nigeria	72	72	73	73	73	65	63	72	77	66	75	78	67	74	75	72	72	82
China	67	68	65	66	69	63	65	72	60	66	69	66	na	na	na	65	69	54
Romania	78	77	79	69	79	82	80	77	77	70	81	81	76	80	78	79	78	68
Turkey	77	78	75	80	78	70	74	80	82	69	84	77	77	79	73	70	77	85
Poland	73	75	72	81	70	73	72	74	75	71	72	76	73	74	75	69	74	80
Bulgaria	65	65	65	65	71	59	56	68	70	63	68	68	61	67	69	64	65	63
Chile	76	76	75	73	78	75	75	77	75	74	77	76	69	77	81	74	76	75
Czechoslovakia	65	67	63	64	61	70	65	64	67	67	64	64	65	62	71	63	67	60
South Africa	61	62	61	59	66	57	43	68	89	41	63	88	67	69	74	63	60	67
Lithuania	65	70	61	60	63	72	68	64	67	66	63	67	na	na	na	61	68	67
Hungary	55	56	55	49	55	59	55	55	62	53	56	62	58	59	55	58	54	48
Argentina	69	68	70	68	75	64	69	65	76	62	73	73	69	72	80	79	69	74
Brazil	78	77	79	75	79	82	80	76	82	78	79	80	77	79	80	66	67	76
Mexico	67	67	67	71	69	56	65	66	76	61	69	77	73	67	69	66	64	76
Belarus	63	70	58	60	66	61	60	63	65	60	67	62	65	61	68	65	64	64
Russia	51	54	50	53	55	47	45	52	55	51	52	54	57	50	54	48	53	57
Moscow	61	66	57	62	60	61	60	61	61	58	63	63	63	58	61	62	61	60
Latvia	68	68	67	68	68	66	70	67	68	70	68	66	na	na	na	78	64	68
Estonia	66	67	65	69	68	61	58	69	69	64	69	68	na	na	na	66	68	68
Portugal	65	69	62	69	67	60	64	65	68	63	62	72	64	67	66	67	66	63
South Korea	na	na	na	na	na	na	na	na	na	na	na	na	na	na	na	na	na	na
Ireland	69	70	68	75	69	66	63	75	80	60	68	78	70	70	71	67	68	77
North Ireland	67	71	65	71	70	63	62	75	86	59	67	79	75	68	69	66	69	67
Slovenia	76	79	73	72	76	78	72	78	78	74	80	72	80	74	79	78	75	78
Spain	45	47	43	56	47	35	42	54	49	34	47	49	48	46	46	44	46	50
East Germany	93	93	93	92	94	93	92	95	95	92	92	95	94	92	93	88	94	94
Britain	73	74	72	72	79	69	69	79	87	65	77	82	69	76	74	70	74	71
Italy	66	70	62	63	68	65	65	70	56	64	69	72	67	64	70	64	64	82
Netherlands	80	83	79	86	79	75	73	79	90	79	78	86	85	80	78	76	80	77
Belgium	71	72	71	77	74	65	66	73	78	68	73	89	72	74	85	66	72	90
Austria	86	88	85	85	90	83	83	88	89	83	87	89	80	89	69	84	85	75
France	68	69	66	70	69	64	64	69	74	63	70	72	89	85	85	63	67	86
Canada	85	83	86	84	87	84	83	84	87	83	88	88	87	85	85	86	86	89
United States	84	84	84	85	86	82	80	83	89	82	82	88	87	85	85	82	84	74
Iceland	79	77	81	80	82	72	75	80	81	na	na	na	73	78	85	82	79	90
West Germany	89	91	88	92	91	86	87	90	95	85	89	93	89	90	89	81	91	90
Denmark	86	84	88	91	87	81	81	88	87	82	88	92	89	82	89	88	85	89
Finland	88	89	88	92	87	87	86	90	87	88	90	88	87	89	88	94	87	92
Norway	88	88	88	88	88	88	85	86	92	88	87	90	87	89	88	89	87	90
Sweden	91	91	91	93	89	94	93	91	90	91	91	93	91	90	93	91	92	90
Japan	37	43	33	35	40	35	29	39	42	36	36	43	39	42	44	42	39	44
Switzerland	48	53	45	44	48	50	51	47	43	46	51	53	45	51	50	54	48	47
Total	70	72	69	71	72	68	67	72	75	67	71	74	72	72	73	70	71	72

Ranking:

East Germany	93
Sweden	91
West Germany	89
Finland	88
Norway	88
Austria	86
Denmark	86
Canada	85
United States	84
Netherlands	80
Iceland	79
Romania	78
Brazil	78
Turkey	77
Chile	76
Slovenia	76
Poland	73
Britain	73
Nigeria	72
Belgium	71
Argentina	69
Ireland	69
Latvia	68
France	68
China	67
Mexico	67
North Ireland	67
Estonia	66
Italy	66
Bulgaria	65
Czechoslovakia	65
Lithuania	65
Portugal	65
Belarus	63
South Africa	61
Moscow	61
Hungary	55
Russia	51
Switzerland	48
India	45
Spain	45
Japan	37

Note: Countries in the left column are ranked according to GNP per capita. / The percentages in the bottom row give each country an equal weight. / na=not ascertained.

V89 FEEL BORED

We are interested in the way people are feeling these days. During the past few weeks, did you ever feel... Bored (% "yes")

	Total	Gender		Age			Education			Income			Political Affinity			Values		
		Male	Female	16-29	30-49	50+	Lower	Medium	Upper	Lower	Middle	Upper	Left	Center	Right	Mat	Mixed	Postmat
India	28	28	28	31	26	27	24	30	27	28	30	27	36	na	23	26	28	36
Nigeria	32	33	31	36	28	21	25	35	32	35	32	27	28	33	31	29	35	26
China	31	29	35	37	28	22	34	32	29	34	27	32	na	na	na	26	35	54
Romania	39	33	44	55	33	31	37	44	33	44	39	35	39	38	40	37	39	44
Turkey	66	64	69	71	64	64	66	67	67	70	67	61	73	65	63	61	68	69
Poland	25	22	27	28	22	27	31	22	18	29	23	22	21	29	23	26	24	24
Bulgaria	24	21	26	21	28	21	20	25	26	27	23	20	22	22	32	24	21	38
Chile	35	31	39	42	33	21	38	36	30	40	36	27	36	34	36	38	35	33
Czechoslovakia	17	18	16	23	16	15	19	18	11	18	15	20	16	18	17	21	16	11
South Africa	33	33	34	37	30	30	40	31	21	43	32	21	35	30	28	31	34	32
Lithuania	37	32	41	44	39	29	40	37	31	40	36	29	na	na	na	40	36	37
Hungary	10	11	09	12	08	11	13	08	06	13	10	01	12	07	11	09	10	10
Argentina	24	20	28	29	21	24	26	28	15	33	22	16	26	26	23	25	25	21
Brazil	42	38	46	41	43	41	43	43	37	43	44	38	47	41	40	43	42	39
Mexico	30	29	31	31	26	36	31	30	27	33	28	29	28	27	35	29	31	28
Belarus	40	36	44	53	37	34	31	43	41	41	38	42	43	34	43	36	42	47
Russia	35	30	38	40	31	35	33	40	31	37	32	33	32	34	35	37	33	36
Moscow	35	35	36	47	32	31	39	37	34	35	34	37	35	38	34	36	35	34
Latvia	29	25	31	38	27	21	29	30	25	30	23	31	na	na	na	25	29	28
Estonia	45	41	48	48	49	35	45	46	44	45	43	47	na	na	na	43	45	48
Portugal	30	25	36	25	28	37	33	23	26	39	27	21	32	28	32	34	28	27
South Korea	na	na	na	na	na	na	na	na	na	na	na	na	na	na	na	na	na	na
Ireland	23	22	23	31	21	19	25	18	28	23	22	22	29	23	18	23	23	26
North Ireland	29	28	30	36	36	16	32	24	24	30	35	21	50	27	25	28	29	29
Slovenia	13	12	14	16	11	14	18	11	06	16	11	09	15	14	13	13	13	13
Spain	22	20	24	26	17	24	22	18	24	27	21	18	22	21	22	23	21	19
East Germany	21	22	20	32	17	19	22	25	14	24	20	20	21	21	20	20	21	26
Britain	33	32	34	45	34	25	35	31	25	33	30	31	40	35	23	31	35	32
Italy	23	20	26	26	21	23	23	22	14	24	20	21	25	21	27	23	24	22
Netherlands	17	17	17	26	14	12	16	17	19	18	17	14	25	12	16	17	15	21
Belgium	17	16	18	21	17	15	20	15	16	22	13	15	20	20	12	18	16	17
Austria	09	08	10	14	06	10	09	09	08	11	08	09	11	07	11	13	08	09
France	23	21	25	32	20	20	28	19	19	28	21	18	23	22	21	27	23	21
Canada	29	30	28	42	28	19	29	30	28	35	27	25	33	28	25	27	29	28
United States	32	32	32	55	29	25	32	31	33	35	35	26	40	30	29	31	31	35
Iceland	22	21	22	25	25	11	23	17	23	na	na	na	na	na	na	31	31	35
West Germany	27	25	29	37	24	23	27	28	21	34	26	21	29	23	20	34	21	24
Denmark	14	16	12	20	13	10	13	14	14	16	12	13	21	13	08	13	24	28
Finland	29	30	28	37	32	15	33	25	32	25	29	33	28	26	26	27	12	20
Norway	28	28	27	47	23	20	23	31	26	31	24	29	28	26	26	27	29	29
Sweden	19	18	20	32	18	10	16	23	17	18	18	18	22	17	18	11	20	32
Japan	17	20	15	28	12	19	21	17	15	21	15	15	11	19	14	16	18	24
Switzerland	05	06	04	10	03	05	05	05	07	07	03	06	07	04	03	02	05	17
Total	**27**	**26**	**28**	**34**	**26**	**23**	**28**	**27**	**24**	**30**	**26**	**24**	**28**	**25**	**25**	**27**	**27**	**29**

Ranking:

Turkey	66
Estonia	45
Brazil	42
Belarus	40
Romania	39
Lithuania	37
Chile	35
Russia	35
Moscow	35
South Africa	33
Britain	33
Nigeria	32
United States	32
China	31
Mexico	30
Portugal	30
Latvia	29
North Ireland	29
Canada	29
Finland	29
India	28
Norway	28
West Germany	27
Poland	25
Bulgaria	24
Argentina	24
Ireland	23
Italy	23
France	23
Spain	22
Iceland	22
East Germany	21
Sweden	19
Czechoslovakia	17
Netherlands	17
Belgium	17
Japan	17
Denmark	14
Slovenia	13
Hungary	10
Austria	09
Switzerland	05

Note: Countries in the left column are ranked according to GNP per capita. / The percentages in the bottom row give each country an equal weight. / na=not ascertained

V90 FEEL 'TOP OF THE WORLD'[1]

We are interested in the way people are feeling these days. During the past few weeks, did you ever feel...
On top of the world/feeling that life is wonderful (% "yes")

	Total	Gender		Age			Education			Income			Political Affinity			Values		
		Male	Female	16-29	30-49	50+	Lower	Medium	Upper	Lower	Middle	Upper	Left	Center	Right	Mat	Mixed	Postmat
India	25	28	22	28	24	23	15	23	33	19	26	31	29	26	30	22	28	35
Nigeria	49	50	47	49	49	40	54	49	45	44	48	52	54	45	52	46	49	59
China	55	54	58	50	57	60	58	56	48	55	60	51	na	na	na	58	53	47
Romania	20	21	19	23	21	16	19	19	23	18	19	22	20	21	22	13	24	27
Turkey	73	74	73	76	76	65	71	79	75	67	77	75	70	74	74	66	75	77
Poland	36	37	35	37	30	42	41	34	24	33	36	40	35	34	43	36	36	36
Bulgaria	08	07	08	12	07	06	07	09	05	05	09	10	04	10	08	07	09	01
Chile	37	34	39	28	39	46	47	33	29	44	34	31	33	36	40	43	37	27
Czechoslovakia	25	28	24	34	20	26	26	26	22	27	25	31	22	24	29	21	26	31
South Africa	41	40	42	41	43	34	24	47	64	20	46	64	45	48	51	41	40	44
Lithuania	16	16	16	21	12	16	19	15	14	17	17	12	na	na	na	13	17	19
Hungary	13	12	15	14	11	15	14	11	19	12	13	18	17	13	19	13	15	05
Argentina	35	38	32	36	34	34	38	34	32	40	31	32	34	31	36	34	34	35
Brazil	38	37	40	35	42	39	43	38	30	40	40	36	39	36	43	40	39	29
Mexico	32	32	32	33	31	32	31	37	31	28	34	36	29	31	36	38	29	35
Belarus	19	18	21	25	19	15	22	20	17	17	20	20	20	17	22	21	19	20
Russia	14	13	15	20	13	12	13	16	13	15	13	15	12	14	15	14	15	10
Moscow	19	18	19	28	15	17	26	20	16	21	17	20	18	16	31	18	18	22
Latvia	25	23	26	33	20	23	31	25	22	26	23	24	na	na	na	21	25	28
Estonia	11	10	12	19	08	06	11	11	10	11	11	11	na	na	na	09	12	10
Portugal	29	35	25	34	28	27	30	30	27	27	32	28	24	32	29	33	30	25
South Korea	na	na	na	na	na	na	na	na	na	na	na	na	na	na	na	na	na	na
Ireland	42	39	45	48	44	37	39	46	55	37	43	48	36	40	48	40	43	42
North Ireland	42	45	40	45	41	42	40	43	30	43	35	42	39	41	48	45	42	42
Slovenia	15	15	15	19	12	15	19	13	10	16	14	13	13	13	17	13	16	10
Spain	13	13	13	14	12	13	12	14	15	13	12	15	15	14	17	15	12	12
East Germany	40	42	39	51	42	31	39	39	43	32	41	46	38	40	46	23	39	50
Britain	45	46	44	49	43	44	44	49	47	41	45	51	39	47	46	41	45	46
Italy	20	20	21	29	17	18	21	16	14	21	20	14	18	22	22	17	21	22
Netherlands	52	46	55	60	55	41	48	52	57	47	56	57	52	50	57	41	57	50
Belgium	37	39	36	46	37	32	34	40	38	34	36	41	35	42	40	32	39	38
Austria	31	30	33	47	34	22	28	32	41	24	33	38	29	36	29	16	31	40
France	33	32	35	43	34	24	33	32	36	30	35	36	34	32	30	33	33	37
Canada	56	53	58	56	54	58	54	56	57	57	52	59	49	58	58	55	57	56
United States	56	57	56	60	55	56	57	59	53	52	57	59	55	56	61	52	57	58
Iceland	63	61	65	66	65	55	65	63	61	na	na	na	60	61	67	69	62	49
West Germany	44	43	45	60	51	30	38	55	51	37	45	52	48	44	41	33	42	54
Denmark	64	63	66	72	66	57	53	73	65	59	67	73	64	62	70	58	66	66
Finland	20	18	23	33	19	14	22	17	24	23	20	18	18	20	19	12	19	24
Norway	59	58	60	62	53	64	64	61	55	58	60	59	56	61	59	62	59	54
Sweden	77	75	80	80	77	77	80	76	74	81	69	81	75	78	78	78	79	73
Japan	12	11	13	19	10	09	10	12	12	11	11	14	12	13	12	09	14	17
Switzerland	11	09	14	17	11	09	13	11	07	12	09	11	11	09	13	09	12	11
Total	**35**	**34**	**35**	**39**	**34**	**32**	**35**	**36**	**35**	**32**	**34**	**36**	**34**	**35**	**38**	**32**	**35**	**35**

Ranking:

Sweden	77
Turkey	73
Denmark	64
Iceland	63
Norway	59
Canada	56
United States	56
China	55
Netherlands	52
Nigeria	49
Britain	45
West Germany	44
Ireland	42
North Ireland	42
South Africa	41
East Germany	40
Brazil	38
Chile	37
Belgium	37
Poland	36
Argentina	35
France	33
Mexico	32
Austria	31
Portugal	29
India	25
Czechoslovakia	25
Latvia	25
Romania	20
Italy	20
Finland	20
Belarus	19
Moscow	19
Lithuania	16
Slovenia	15
Russia	14
Hungary	13
Spain	13
Japan	12
Estonia	11
Switzerland	11
Bulgaria	08

Note: Countries in the left column are ranked according to GNP per capita. / [1] The percentages in the bottom row give each country an equal weight. / na=not ascertained.

V91 FEEL DEPRESSED

We are interested in the way people are feeling these days. During the past few weeks, did you ever feel...
Depressed or very unhappy (% "yes")

	Total	Gender		Age			Education			Income			Political Affinity			Values			Ranking:	
		Male	Female	16-29	30-49	50+	Lower	Medium	Upper	Lower	Middle	Upper	Left	Center	Right	Mat	Mixed	Postmat		
India	25	26	24	27	24	23	28	26	23	26	27	23	30	24	20	23	25	28	Turkey	56
Nigeria	37	39	34	41	32	30	34	40	34	41	33	34	35	39	33	35	39	26	East Germany	47
China	17	17	17	21	18	12	17	18	17	18	19	14	na	na	na	15	19	32	West Germany	45
Romania	32	25	40	34	32	32	37	32	26	47	31	24	37	32	31	35	30	35	Nigeria	37
Turkey	56	51	61	57	55	57	58	50	57	61	53	52	58	57	47	53	56	61	South Africa	34
Poland	28	21	35	17	27	35	37	22	26	36	22	25	25	26	32	35	25	23	Romania	32
Bulgaria	20	15	35	16	20	21	22	20	15	22	17	18	18	17	24	23	18	14	Austria	30
Chile	29	25	34	28	31	29	35	25	28	37	29	21	29	28	31	33	29	24	Chile	29
Czechoslovakia	21	15	26	16	22	23	25	19	21	26	19	19	24	19	31	24	20	18	Lithuania	29
South Africa	34	32	36	35	32	36	43	31	20	45	33	20	36	28	29	36	33	34	Poland	28
Lithuania	29	22	36	26	28	34	39	27	25	33	29	22	na	na	na	34	28	25	Brazil	28
Hungary	22	20	23	13	16	30	29	15	10	30	16	15	21	19	24	34	22	18	Russia	27
Argentina	23	18	26	18	22	27	27	25	17	29	21	19	24	21	20	21	24	16	India	25
Brazil	28	22	33	24	31	27	34	26	19	33	28	20	29	24	29	25	24	16	Moscow	24
Mexico	23	23	22	24	20	26	23	24	20	24	22	24	19	22	26	29	26	27	Argentina	23
Belarus	21	13	27	22	20	21	19	22	20	25	19	18	22	20	16	25	22	19	Mexico	23
Russia	27	21	31	22	27	29	31	26	25	31	25	18	22	28	16	20	21	23	Hungary	22
Moscow	24	17	29	27	22	25	27	23	23	24	24	23	24	26	18	31	24	29	Netherlands	22
Latvia	15	10	18	18	13	16	20	16	12	16	10	18	24	na	na	21	25	21	Finland	22
Estonia	18	12	23	17	19	17	19	17	11	18	16	20	na	na	na	14	15	12	Czechoslovakia	21
Portugal	15	13	16	10	15	19	17	11	09	20	10	11	na	12	16	17	18	14	Belarus	21
South Korea	na	na	na	na	na	na	na	na	na	na	na	na	15	na	na	15	15	10	Britain	21
Ireland	16	12	19	11	12	22	20	12	08	21	15	12	na	na	24	15	na	na	Bulgaria	20
North Ireland	14	09	18	13	12	17	16	10	14	20	15	07	15	16	15	19	15	15	Denmark	20
Slovenia	13	09	17	10	11	17	18	10	08	18	10	08	21	13	16	20	11	18	United States	19
Spain	18	13	23	15	16	22	20	15	14	25	18	13	17	17	09	15	12	13	Japan	19
East Germany	47	39	54	44	43	52	47	49	43	54	47	41	48	47	41	52	48	42	Estonia	18
Britain	21	18	23	18	21	21	21	17	21	26	18	16	22	22	17	19	22	18	Spain	18
Italy	16	10	21	14	15	19	16	13	11	19	15	12	15	15	15	17	16	17	China	17
Netherlands	22	16	24	20	24	22	24	23	19	25	18	21	26	15	21	23	21	24	Canada	17
Belgium	14	12	16	15	13	14	17	12	13	14	15	12	17	12	14	16	13	12	Norway	17
Austria	30	22	35	24	27	34	35	26	29	37	27	27	31	28	32	37	30	26	Ireland	16
France	15	11	19	17	16	13	19	12	11	21	13	11	15	15	18	18	16	12	Italy	16
Canada	17	16	19	25	16	15	22	15	17	23	16	14	17	18	15	18	17	17	Latvia	15
United States	19	17	22	19	20	18	25	19	16	23	20	15	25	16	14	19	19	21	Portugal	15
Iceland	07	07	07	07	07	07	07	04	07	na	12	07	08	06	08	06	07	05	France	15
West Germany	45	37	51	46	42	46	45	43	47	52	44	38	51	41	37	53	42	45	North Ireland	14
Denmark	20	14	26	19	20	19	19	19	19	24	18	15	26	19	14	18	19	22	Belgium	14
Finland	22	21	24	25	25	13	26	18	25	23	21	23	22	21	19	09	22	24	Slovenia	13
Norway	17	14	20	17	16	18	19	18	15	20	14	16	20	16	14	17	16	16	Sweden	10
Sweden	10	08	12	12	09	08	07	11	12	09	12	07	11	08	10	04	10	11	Iceland	07
Japan	19	18	20	22	19	17	18	19	19	20	17	20	24	18	16	18	20	19	Switzerland	07
Switzerland	07	05	09	07	06	09	08	07	08	11	06	04	07	09	05	07	08	06		
Total	**23**	**19**	**26**	**22**	**22**	**24**	**26**	**21**	**20**	**27**	**21**	**19**	**24**	**22**	**21**	**24**	**22**	**22**		

Note: Countries in the left column are ranked according to GNP per capita. / The percentages in the bottom row give each country an equal weight. / na=not ascertained.

V92 FEEL 'GOING YOUR WAY'

We are interested in the way people are feeling these days. During the past few weeks, did you ever feel...
That things were going your way (% "yes")

	Total	Gender Male	Female	Age 16-29	30-49	50+	Education Lower	Medium	Upper	Income Lower	Middle	Upper	Political Affinity Left	Center	Right	Values Mat	Mixed	Postmat
India	35	36	33	37	34	31	27	31	43	29	34	42	39	37	31	34	39	30
Nigeria	58	57	60	58	59	51	56	58	58	49	62	65	57	55	61	58	58	60
China	52	51	52	46	56	51	45	56	50	54	52	49	na	na	na	51	53	42
Romania	61	63	60	57	60	64	63	59	62	44	61	74	58	61	66	63	61	51
Turkey	76	75	77	73	79	75	76	74	80	69	80	79	74	76	77	74	76	78
Poland	59	63	55	59	59	60	56	62	54	51	61	67	55	58	66	54	61	67
Bulgaria	36	36	37	44	39	29	32	36	41	26	39	49	33	36	41	34	37	46
Chile	54	53	54	52	54	55	52	56	52	53	53	55	47	55	61	55	52	53
Czechoslovakia	21	22	21	26	15	25	24	21	14	21	18	25	15	18	31	19	21	25
South Africa	49	48	49	49	50	44	33	55	69	31	54	64	50	57	58	51	46	56
Lithuania	35	38	32	43	35	28	31	36	36	29	41	38	na	na	na	29	36	42
Hungary	36	33	39	44	39	30	31	41	37	30	41	41	36	39	45	35	39	28
Argentina	41	41	41	51	41	34	38	41	44	35	43	45	35	46	44	38	42	44
Brazil	58	59	57	61	55	58	59	57	59	56	58	62	57	57	64	60	56	57
Mexico	48	49	47	47	51	46	46	52	53	43	51	58	46	51	53	45	51	47
Belarus	48	53	44	48	50	45	54	45	50	42	52	50	48	51	49	51	48	41
Russia	51	52	50	58	49	48	45	51	53	50	52	52	49	57	49	52	50	45
Moscow	46	51	41	48	47	42	44	51	43	45	46	46	45	43	57	48	44	48
Latvia	27	29	25	32	24	26	25	27	26	19	28	31	na	na	na	26	26	33
Estonia	45	53	39	54	45	37	38	48	47	43	45	51	na	na	na	40	48	59
Portugal	65	70	60	72	68	55	63	72	67	58	66	74	65	66	66	65	67	71
South Korea	na	na	na	na	na	na	na	na	na	na	na	na	na	na	na	na	na	na
Ireland	68	69	68	77	71	59	60	75	86	57	69	77	na	71	71	66	69	70
North Ireland	68	67	68	75	68	63	64	71	83	64	67	75	61	70	69	66	69	69
Slovenia	53	54	52	64	57	42	48	59	54	47	56	62	49	56	57	53	53	53
Spain	40	42	39	46	42	35	37	48	47	30	42	51	43	43	43	36	42	49
East Germany	37	40	35	42	38	35	39	39	31	34	36	41	32	38	47	29	36	45
Britain	63	64	62	69	66	57	61	68	72	57	67	77	59	67	63	59	64	66
Italy	41	44	38	45	43	37	42	35	37	38	42	46	40	40	52	41	41	42
Netherlands	35	33	35	38	37	27	32	37	35	28	37	38	32	35	38	20	40	32
Belgium	38	38	37	41	38	35	36	39	37	37	34	42	41	38	38	40	38	36
Austria	56	58	55	62	59	51	55	58	54	50	60	59	55	56	57	49	57	59
France	53	51	54	61	54	45	44	59	65	43	54	65	53	52	54	54	51	57
Canada	70	70	70	72	71	68	64	69	76	59	74	78	72	71	74	66	69	76
United States	72	72	72	74	75	68	68	72	75	64	74	78	72	73	74	64	72	77
Iceland	84	84	85	84	87	80	85	82	85	na	na	na	81	82	88	89	83	82
West Germany	53	56	51	60	55	48	51	56	60	47	54	60	53	56	55	49	54	54
Denmark	38	38	37	37	37	39	34	42	37	34	35	44	28	39	44	40	38	31
Finland	40	42	37	40	35	52	41	39	40	46	36	39	42	42	40	47	39	40
Norway	na	na	na	na	na	na	na	na	na	na	na	na	na	na	na	na	na	na
Sweden	73	75	71	75	72	75	75	72	73	75	64	79	74	73	73	74	73	76
Japan	15	18	12	21	17	09	10	15	20	14	15	16	20	16	18	16	17	14
Switzerland	28	29	26	29	28	27	28	27	29	27	30	29	35	26	31	23	28	29
Total	49	51	48	53	50	46	47	51	52	43	50	54	49	52	54	48	50	51

Ranking:

Iceland	84
Turkey	76
Sweden	73
United States	72
Canada	70
Ireland	68
North Ireland	68
Portugal	65
Britain	63
Romania	61
Poland	59
Nigeria	58
Brazil	58
Austria	56
Chile	54
Slovenia	53
France	53
West Germany	53
China	52
Russia	51
South Africa	49
Mexico	48
Belarus	48
Moscow	46
Estonia	45
Argentina	41
Italy	41
Spain	40
Finland	40
Belgium	38
Denmark	38
East Germany	37
Bulgaria	36
Hungary	36
India	35
Lithuania	35
Netherlands	35
Switzerland	28
Latvia	27
Czechoslovakia	21
Japan	15

Note: Countries in the left column are ranked according to GNP per capita. / The percentages in the bottom row give each country an equal weight. / na=not ascertained.

V93 FEEL UPSET

We are interested in the way people are feeling these days. During the past few weeks, did you ever feel...
Upset because somebody criticized you (% "yes")

	Total	Gender Male	Gender Female	Age 16-29	Age 30-49	Age 50+	Education Lower	Education Medium	Education Upper	Income Lower	Income Middle	Income Upper	Political Affinity Left	Political Affinity Center	Political Affinity Right	Values Mat	Values Mixed	Values Postmat	Ranking
India	20	20	20	22	20	16	16	22	20	19	20	21	30	19	16	17	21	34	Turkey 48
Nigeria	24	25	24	26	23	16	22	27	23	23	22	29	21	22	27	22	25	27	Brazil 27
China	08	08	10	12	07	06	09	09	05	10	08	07	na	na	na	08	08	13	Chile 26
Romania	23	22	24	25	23	21	27	22	20	24	26	19	26	20	26	21	25	19	Russia 26
Turkey	48	44	53	52	47	45	53	42	39	52	52	40	44	50	49	45	50	47	Finland 26
Poland	25	23	28	26	25	26	32	20	26	30	22	24	21	25	25	25	25	25	Poland 25
Bulgaria	na	na	na	na	na	na	na	na	na	na	na	na	na	na	na	na	na	na	Czechoslovakia 25
Chile	26	25	28	27	29	22	29	25	25	30	26	23	27	25	28	29	26	24	Nigeria 24
Czechoslovakia	25	24	25	27	25	23	27	25	18	23	26	25	27	24	23	29	24	19	West Germany 24
South Africa	22	22	21	24	21	17	19	22	30	19	22	26	25	19	31	23	21	23	Romania 23
Lithuania	16	15	16	13	16	18	18	16	10	18	14	13	na	na	na	18	15	14	Latvia 23
Hungary	18	18	17	19	18	16	20	18	06	22	13	16	21	16	18	17	19	10	South Africa 22
Argentina	20	17	22	28	18	15	17	22	20	23	18	18	24	19	24	20	20	19	Moscow 22
Brazil	27	23	31	26	28	27	31	27	18	32	28	20	27	24	30	30	25	27	East Germany 22
Mexico	19	19	19	20	17	20	19	19	18	18	20	19	17	19	18	22	19	16	France 22
Belarus	17	17	18	17	18	16	14	18	18	18	17	15	16	16	27	19	17	17	India 20
Russia	26	22	28	27	27	23	25	25	28	27	27	23	26	24	24	26	26	23	Argentina 20
Moscow	22	21	23	30	22	17	19	26	20	24	22	17	24	18	26	20	22	27	Netherlands 20
Latvia	23	19	25	28	23	17	24	24	16	26	23	21	na	na	na	22	24	15	Mexico 19
Estonia	16	14	18	18	16	13	17	16	16	16	15	17	na	na	na	16	17	10	Denmark 19
Portugal	15	12	17	18	12	14	15	15	15	14	15	16	13	15	17	17	14	16	Hungary 18
South Korea	na	na	na	na	na	na	na	na	na	na	na	na	na	na	na	na	na	na	Slovenia 18
Ireland	12	11	13	16	11	11	11	13	13	10	10	14	14	11	13	11	12	14	Belgium 18
North Ireland	11	07	14	13	14	18	10	15	06	12	10	10	14	10	12	11	10	16	Canada 18
Slovenia	18	16	20	14	20	20	21	18	14	23	18	10	17	16	18	19	17	24	Belarus 17
Spain	10	10	09	13	10	07	09	07	16	10	10	11	10	09	10	08	10	13	Italy 17
East Germany	22	21	24	28	22	19	23	21	20	21	23	23	19	25	20	14	21	25	Austria 17
Britain	15	14	16	17	18	11	14	16	18	12	14	19	15	15	16	23	17	16	United States 17
Italy	17	17	17	16	17	18	18	15	06	19	17	21	20	16	17	16	17	18	Lithuania 16
Netherlands	20	12	23	22	21	15	20	23	17	20	21	20	24	20	16	25	17	23	Estonia 16
Belgium	18	15	20	22	18	15	18	19	17	19	17	17	18	19	18	16	19	15	Portugal 15
Austria	17	14	18	18	18	15	18	16	18	14	19	19	19	17	18	14	17	17	Britain 15
France	22	22	23	23	25	19	24	21	22	26	22	27	21	24	22	22	21	27	Iceland 15
Canada	18	18	18	21	20	13	16	17	21	17	19	18	26	18	16	20	17	19	Sweden 14
United States	17	16	17	19	19	13	15	17	18	13	18	18	19	16	17	16	16	20	Norway 13
Iceland	15	14	16	20	14	10	15	13	16	16	13	11	17	14	16	15	15	12	Ireland 12
West Germany	24	21	26	27	27	19	23	24	26	25	23	25	27	22	23	23	22	28	North Ireland 11
Denmark	19	19	20	24	22	13	19	20	20	17	18	27	23	19	18	16	19	25	Spain 10
Finland	26	26	27	27	30	16	26	21	33	21	24	33	30	20	30	29	26	27	China 08
Norway	13	14	12	15	13	11	12	12	14	15	10	14	14	13	12	12	14	13	Japan 07
Sweden	14	12	17	19	14	13	11	16	18	16	13	11	16	14	16	15	13	17	Switzerland 07
Japan	07	08	07	06	09	06	07	07	09	08	06	08	08	08	09	07	09	05	
Switzerland	07	06	08	07	08	06	06	07	09	06	08	07	10	08	04	05	07	08	
Total	19	18	20	21	20	16	19	19	18	20	19	19	21	19	20	19	19	20	

Note: Countries in the left column are ranked according to GNP per capita. / The percentages in the bottom row give each country an equal weight. / na=not ascertained.

V94. Generally speaking, would you say that most people can be trusted or that you can't be too careful in dealing with people?

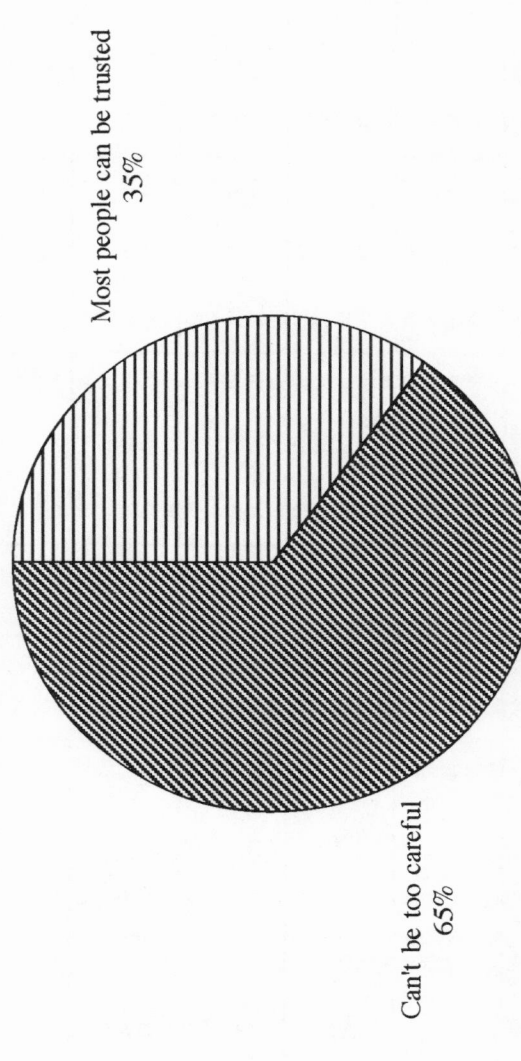

Most people can be trusted
35%

Can't be too careful
65%

V94 PEOPLE TRUSTED

Generally speaking, would you say that most people can be trusted or that you can't be too careful in dealing with people?
(% "most people can be trusted")

	Total	Gender		Age			Education			Income			Political Affinity			Values		
		Male	Female	16-29	30-49	50+	Lower	Medium	Upper	Lower	Middle	Upper	Left	Center	Right	Mat	Mixed	Postmat
India	35	37	34	34	36	36	34	33	39	36	33	38	33	34	41	34	35	39
Nigeria	23	24	22	23	24	19	21	25	23	27	22	23	22	23	29	19	25	25
China	60	61	60	58	58	67	54	60	68	59	61	61	na	na	na	61	61	60
Romania	16	17	15	13	16	18	16	16	17	15	16	16	18	17	17	12	18	26
Turkey	10	10	10	09	11	10	08	09	20	11	06	13	17	09	07	07	09	17
Poland	35	35	34	32	34	36	30	37	40	33	30	41	33	33	39	35	33	40
Bulgaria	30	32	29	32	34	26	22	28	43	31	29	30	36	35	24	28	31	35
Chile	23	23	22	25	22	21	20	20	29	20	22	27	28	22	22	19	23	28
Czechoslovakia	28	29	26	23	27	21	25	28	33	26	27	31	30	27	28	23	30	27
South Africa	28	27	30	27	28	32	30	26	38	30	27	30	32	29	33	30	26	36
Lithuania	31	33	29	33	34	26	21	33	38	23	38	37	na	na	na	23	31	48
Hungary	25	26	23	29	26	22	17	31	36	17	27	41	36	26	28	24	25	30
Argentina	23	26	21	24	26	20	19	25	30	19	24	33	44	22	29	19	20	38
Brazil	07	07	07	05	07	08	07	06	10	06	07	08	06	07	10	06	07	09
Mexico	34	35	31	34	33	34	34	33	33	34	30	36	34	34	33	35	35	25
Belarus	26	25	26	27	26	23	19	25	29	22	27	28	20	22	22	24	26	28
Russia	38	38	37	35	35	42	40	36	38	39	37	39	35	35	34	40	36	38
Moscow	34	34	33	36	33	34	28	29	38	32	34	39	36	31	32	23	36	47
Latvia	19	20	18	11	17	34	21	16	25	19	20	19	na	na	na	17	36	23
Estonia	28	31	25	23	29	30	28	25	35	27	28	29	na	na	na	26	21	23
Portugal	21	21	22	24	22	18	19	21	31	19	27	19	20	22	22	26	27	41
South Korea	34	34	37	34	36	32	26	32	41	31	37	36	35	35	34	17	23	22
Ireland	47	47	48	44	46	51	44	49	63	37	50	56	50	44	57	32	35	40
North Ireland	44	49	40	35	38	31	33	44	47	34	51	58	54	41	47	47	48	48
Slovenia	17	22	13	16	18	18	10	17	32	12	19	27	27	19	22	43	43	49
Spain	32	34	30	30	36	29	29	34	46	25	33	41	36	33	28	15	16	40
East Germany	26	29	23	25	31	21	22	31	36	22	27	28	29	22	29	28	33	38
Britain	44	46	41	20	28	47	39	49	63	43	42	53	41	43	51	18	25	30
Italy	34	36	33	45	45	31	33	44	47	31	39	51	40	35	33	42	43	49
Netherlands	56	52	57	62	58	45	44	59	66	49	55	68	63	55	51	28	43	50
Belgium	33	33	33	36	35	30	25	36	45	30	37	41	36	33	39	30	56	62
Austria	32	36	29	35	33	30	27	34	42	27	30	39	30	34	34	23	32	45
France	23	24	22	20	28	20	15	29	33	16	20	36	32	19	18	27	30	40
Canada	52	52	53	45	56	55	39	51	65	45	51	62	57	54	55	10	22	35
United States	52	48	55	42	52	56	41	49	63	47	50	59	62	52	48	38	50	63
Iceland	44	39	49	35	50	42	34	43	52	na	na	na	55	41	38	30	46	62
West Germany	38	38	38	40	40	35	33	45	50	33	36	45	42	40	36	27	38	46
Denmark	58	57	58	63	62	49	45	55	68	51	58	69	70	54	56	40	58	75
Finland	63	62	63	66	60	67	51	55	75	61	61	67	63	61	66	50	61	70
Norway	65	66	64	67	71	57	57	63	77	54	72	74	68	65	68	56	66	87
Sweden	66	68	63	62	73	61	57	65	83	67	55	75	73	61	70	56	64	78
Japan	42	39	45	45	44	37	27	43	55	32	41	52	42	49	40	43	44	49
Switzerland	43	46	41	46	48	38	37	43	70	39	51	46	61	43	43	33	40	59
Total	35	36	35	34	37	34	30	36	45	32	35	41	40	35	36	30	35	43

Ranking:

Sweden	66
Norway	65
Finland	63
China	60
Denmark	58
Netherlands	56
Canada	52
United States	52
Ireland	47
North Ireland	44
Britain	44
Iceland	44
Switzerland	43
Japan	42
Russia	38
West Germany	38
India	35
Poland	35
Mexico	34
Moscow	34
South Korea	34
Italy	34
Belgium	33
Spain	32
Austria	32
Lithuania	31
Bulgaria	30
Czechoslovakia	28
South Africa	28
Estonia	28
Belarus	26
East Germany	26
Hungary	25
Nigeria	23
Chile	23
Argentina	23
France	23
Portugal	21
Latvia	19
Slovenia	17
Romania	16
Turkey	10
Brazil	07

Note: Countries in the left column are ranked according to GNP per capita. / The percentages in the bottom row give each country an equal weight. / na=not ascertained.

V95 FREE CHOICE/CONTROL

Some people feel they have completely free choice and control over their lives, and other people feel that what they do has no real effect on what happens to them. Please use the ten-point scale (1=none at all and 10=a great deal) to indicate how much freedom of choice and control you feel you have over the way your life turns out. (% "a great deal"—codes 7 to 10)

	Total	Gender		Age			Education			Income			Political Affinity			Values			Ranking:	
		Male	Female	16-29	30-49	50+	Lower	Medium	Upper	Lower	Middle	Upper	Left	Center	Right	Mat	Mixed	Postmat		
India	50	54	46	49	51	50	40	49	56	44	49	56	52	48	56	48	54	61	Finland	79
Nigeria	57	56	58	56	56	68	56	56	59	47	58	67	62	51	62	54	59	57	Canada	77
China	63	66	59	54	67	69	61	67	60	61	64	66	na	na	na	64	65	43	United States	77
Romania	49	57	42	52	53	44	44	47	59	38	46	62	47	52	54	46	50	67	North Ireland	75
Turkey	31	33	29	34	32	23	26	34	47	31	26	38	46	27	24	24	30	43	Sweden	74
Poland	52	53	51	57	56	46	50	53	55	45	51	62	51	52	54	51	52	60	South Korea	73
Bulgaria	28	31	26	33	29	24	22	30	30	23	27	37	25	29	39	24	31	24	Mexico	70
Chile	61	67	56	58	62	66	56	59	69	54	60	72	64	60	61	56	62	65	Iceland	70
Czechoslovakia	42	48	37	54	38	38	33	46	47	43	43	43	41	37	52	32	45	51	Argentina	68
South Africa	57	56	57	52	59	60	50	57	77	45	55	78	57	66	60	59	55	57	Norway	67
Lithuania	55	57	52	64	55	46	51	56	56	52	52	64	na	na	na	44	56	63	Switzerland	66
Hungary	50	49	50	54	47	50	52	47	50	51	48	52	48	48	55	48	51	50	Ireland	65
Argentina	68	68	67	73	67	64	67	69	66	64	70	70	63	67	75	70	67	67	Britain	65
Brazil	63	67	58	62	62	64	60	64	62	62	61	65	61	59	68	62	62	66	Denmark	64
Mexico	70	69	70	71	71	66	67	69	79	66	71	76	74	69	74	68	71	77	China	63
Belarus	40	42	38	39	43	35	36	36	46	39	41	38	42	36	38	38	41	41	Brazil	63
Russia	47	52	43	53	47	42	42	45	51	43	45	53	51	45	56	44	47	55	West Germany	63
Moscow	44	50	39	46	48	37	39	43	46	40	45	52	46	40	51	39	46	46	Chile	61
Latvia	48	49	47	56	45	45	46	49	46	42	48	51	na	na	na	44	49	49	Nigeria	57
Estonia	50	56	45	55	51	44	46	50	54	46	50	56	52	47	na	46	52	66	South Africa	57
Portugal	52	54	49	56	54	45	48	63	56	47	54	56	47	50	57	50	51	59	Belgium	57
South Korea	73	70	75	81	70	65	58	72	80	70	71	78	71	70	76	71	72	80	Austria	57
Ireland	65	66	64	72	68	58	60	69	78	55	65	71	60	63	72	60	66	68	Spain	56
North Ireland	75	77	73	82	73	73	72	75	100	71	76	82	67	74	77	66	75	89	Lithuania	55
Slovenia	44	49	40	53	44	38	39	43	56	35	49	55	52	47	53	38	45	63	East Germany	53
Spain	56	58	55	56	56	57	48	57	57	54	54	56	55	56	68	50	61	56	Poland	52
East Germany	53	54	51	54	52	52	55	46	50	56	51	51	50	52	59	50	51	57	Portugal	52
Britain	65	67	62	67	67	61	62	69	72	59	69	74	57	62	75	69	64	63	Italy	52
Italy	52	57	47	55	55	40	50	68	65	45	58	66	53	51	56	43	52	61	Netherlands	52
Netherlands	52	56	51	64	51	40	40	53	65	54	48	60	53	55	50	38	52	56	India	50
Belgium	57	60	53	60	60	52	51	59	61	51	56	61	55	56	65	53	55	62	Hungary	50
Austria	57	58	57	66	62	49	56	56	69	50	58	63	56	56	61	55	55	65	Estonia	50
France	45	45	45	47	48	40	42	44	55	40	48	50	44	43	49	43	46	45	Romania	49
Canada	77	76	78	81	77	72	70	76	82	69	80	81	79	74	83	79	75	79	Latvia	48
United States	77	77	78	80	78	76	76	75	81	69	79	83	76	77	81	75	77	79	Russia	47
Iceland	70	72	68	80	74	52	56	71	80	na	na	na	69	65	78	62	72	82	France	45
West Germany	63	65	62	69	61	62	60	68	67	60	60	67	62	63	66	55	63	68	Moscow	44
Denmark	64	71	58	76	70	49	45	66	75	54	64	77	69	59	71	58	67	66	Slovenia	44
Finland	79	79	79	83	83	65	72	79	82	76	81	79	80	71	84	79	78	80	Czechoslovakia	42
Norway	67	65	69	81	73	51	40	70	78	57	72	77	81	67	72	63	69	71	Belarus	40
Sweden	74	70	77	81	76	65	64	77	81	73	66	79	71	73	77	76	70	79	Turkey	31
Japan	29	30	27	43	30	17	14	28	43	19	27	37	45	29	29	27	30	45	Japan	29
Switzerland	66	67	65	70	64	66	64	67	68	64	65	71	64	62	70	75	63	68	Bulgaria	28
Total	57	59	55	61	58	52	51	58	63	51	56	63	57	55	62	53	57	62		

Note: Countries in the left column are ranked according to GNP per capita. / The percentages in the bottom row give each country an equal weight. / na=not ascertained.

V96 LIFE SATISFACTION

All things considered, how satisfied are you with your life as a whole these days? Please use this card to help with your answer.
(Ten-point scale: 1=Dissatisfied and 10=Satisfied); (% "satisfied"—codes 7 to 10)

	Total	Gender Male	Gender Female	Age 16-29	Age 30-49	Age 50+	Education Lower	Education Medium	Education Upper	Income Lower	Income Middle	Income Upper	Political Affinity Left	Political Affinity Center	Political Affinity Right	Values Mat	Values Mixed	Values Postmat
India	53	52	54	54	53	52	41	54	59	40	41	56	48	50	66	54	56	60
Nigeria	54	49	62	57	50	49	60	55	52	41	58	65	53	50	59	59	52	51
China	68	68	67	57	71	74	70	68	61	65	72	68	na	na	na	70	68	44
Romania	44	47	42	41	45	46	42	41	53	26	41	62	48	42	49	43	46	37
Turkey	48	44	51	51	48	42	49	44	53	41	47	57	48	45	52	46	49	48
Poland	57	57	57	64	57	55	56	58	58	48	58	69	48	55	66	57	57	61
Bulgaria	25	27	24	32	23	24	23	26	26	16	26	37	24	26	32	20	28	20
Chile	70	73	67	64	72	74	72	69	68	67	68	74	67	68	75	67	70	70
Czechoslovakia	50	53	47	55	46	51	44	50	68	47	51	51	49	44	60	44	51	55
South Africa	51	52	50	49	53	53	38	55	81	32	52	78	47	60	64	55	49	52
Lithuania	44	46	42	45	45	42	44	42	52	40	47	45	na	na	na	43	43	43
Hungary	44	44	44	52	43	41	38	49	49	35	49	55	48	46	46	42	45	45
Argentina	69	67	71	69	69	68	67	70	74	59	69	74	65	69	73	67	70	69
Brazil	68	71	65	67	66	73	69	66	72	66	69	70	78	68	73	67	69	64
Mexico	72	70	75	74	72	68	69	77	81	68	73	79	75	72	78	73	72	77
Belarus	33	33	34	31	37	28	33	30	36	29	36	34	32	31	42	38	31	33
Russia	32	32	31	31	30	34	32	31	32	29	32	34	32	29	46	32	32	27
Moscow	35	34	35	35	35	35	33	32	37	32	37	38	36	28	45	35	36	33
Latvia	40	40	39	44	34	46	42	39	42	34	40	43	na	na	na	35	39	49
Estonia	45	48	42	55	42	39	43	44	48	41	49	47	na	na	na	43	47	44
Portugal	63	68	59	67	66	58	63	62	67	57	68	68	59	62	66	63	63	61
South Korea	61	62	61	62	63	55	45	59	72	50	63	74	59	59	66	61	61	59
Ireland	80	79	81	80	80	80	78	81	88	73	80	87	78	79	84	79	81	78
North Ireland	83	82	84	75	86	86	83	80	93	79	84	89	79	83	88	79	86	80
Slovenia	47	51	43	57	45	41	40	48	56	34	52	63	45	51	54	46	46	55
Spain	66	69	64	68	69	62	66	69	67	55	68	71	64	68	74	64	69	66
East Germany	59	61	58	63	63	54	59	63	58	52	60	66	60	56	69	51	59	65
Britain	74	76	73	76	74	74	73	78	79	70	76	82	66	73	83	78	74	72
Italy	71	73	70	73	74	67	71	74	65	68	74	74	69	73	68	72	71	69
Netherlands	85	87	84	87	85	83	81	85	90	77	88	94	84	88	86	77	88	84
Belgium	79	79	78	82	79	75	75	81	81	74	80	85	77	80	83	76	79	83
Austria	64	65	63	66	69	58	64	62	74	58	65	68	61	65	66	55	61	74
France	59	58	59	55	61	60	55	62	65	48	63	69	60	58	58	56	59	60
Canada	84	84	84	84	84	85	77	85	86	74	85	91	82	83	87	87	83	85
United States	81	80	80	79	80	81	80	79	83	70	82	90	75	80	88	79	80	84
Iceland	85	84	86	87	85	82	86	83	85	na	na	na	83	85	87	84	86	82
West Germany	71	72	71	76	74	67	69	75	78	64	71	79	69	75	74	59	74	74
Denmark	86	89	83	91	88	79	78	90	87	78	90	94	86	85	89	82	87	85
Finland	79	77	81	79	81	75	79	79	81	76	82	78	81	75	82	76	78	82
Norway	78	75	80	80	81	72	69	77	83	72	80	84	74	79	79	75	78	75
Sweden	84	84	84	83	85	75	81	85	86	83	77	90	83	83	87	87	80	75
Japan	53	51	55	52	56	48	56	56	55	43	52	64	52	51	64	56	50	59
Switzerland	86	86	86	83	88	85	87	85	82	84	86	89	81	84	92	89	86	84
Total	**62**	**63**	**62**	**63**	**63**	**61**	**60**	**63**	**66**	**55**	**63**	**69**	**62**	**63**	**69**	**61**	**63**	**62**

Ranking:

Denmark	86
Switzerland	86
Netherlands	85
Iceland	85
Canada	84
Sweden	84
North Ireland	83
United States	81
Ireland	80
Belgium	79
Finland	79
Norway	78
Britain	74
Mexico	72
Italy	71
West Germany	71
Chile	70
Argentina	69
China	68
Brazil	68
Spain	66
Austria	64
Portugal	63
South Korea	61
East Germany	59
France	59
Poland	57
Nigeria	54
India	53
Japan	53
South Africa	51
Czechoslovakia	50
Turkey	48
Slovenia	47
Estonia	45
Romania	44
Lithuania	44
Hungary	44
Latvia	40
Moscow	35
Belarus	33
Russia	32
Bulgaria	25

Note: Countries in the left column are ranked according to GNP per capita. / The percentages in the bottom row give each country an equal weight. / na=not ascertained.

V97. Why are there people in this country who live in need? Here are four possible reasons. Which one reason do you consider to be most important?

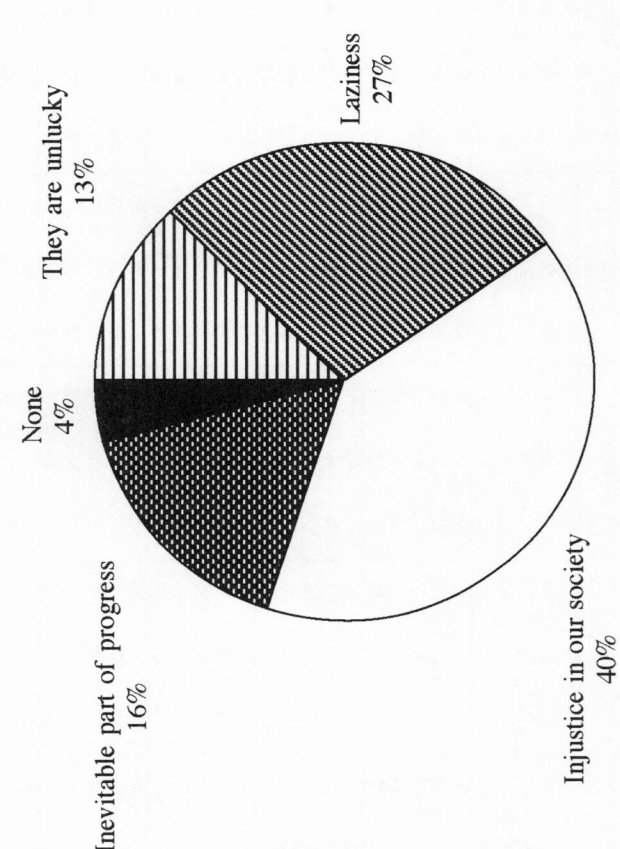

Inevitable part of progress
16%

None
4%

They are unlucky
13%

Laziness
27%

Injustice in our society
40%

V97 LIVE IN NEED: INJUSTICE

Why are there people in this country who live in need? Here are four possible reasons. Which one reason do you consider to be most important? (% "Because there is injustice in our society")

	Total	Gender Male	Gender Female	Age 16-29	Age 30-49	Age 50+	Education Lower	Education Medium	Education Upper	Income Lower	Income Middle	Income Upper	Political Affinity Left	Political Affinity Center	Political Affinity Right	Values Mat	Values Mixed	Values Postmat
India	33	33	33	34	33	32	33	34	32	33	34	32	37	34	27	30	36	31
Nigeria	48	49	46	45	52	46	48	45	50	46	49	50	51	50	43	47	47	49
China	36	37	35	35	38	36	36	35	43	33	39	38	na	na	na	35	36	55
Romania	36	32	39	34	41	32	34	39	33	44	40	25	36	35	40	38	34	34
Turkey	37	43	31	40	40	28	31	44	55	36	35	41	57	34	33	26	37	51
Poland	59	61	58	59	61	58	58	62	53	64	56	57	52	61	61	53	62	59
Bulgaria	52	53	51	55	58	41	36	55	63	55	54	48	50	54	68	44	51	70
Chile	41	45	37	43	44	33	33	43	48	36	42	45	60	38	30	32	40	57
Czechoslovakia	27	25	28	28	29	23	25	27	28	26	28	25	28	26	27	27	27	27
South Africa	58	61	55	63	58	48	56	61	48	60	63	46	70	52	45	42	64	76
Lithuania	51	50	52	52	58	43	40	52	65	48	55	51	na	na	na	44	52	63
Hungary	39	41	37	40	41	37	39	39	44	41	39	35	41	38	46	39	38	54
Argentina	49	51	48	47	49	51	50	48	50	50	55	43	70	48	41	49	44	64
Brazil	40	43	37	46	41	30	27	45	50	37	41	45	48	42	33	36	42	49
Mexico	32	31	33	33	32	30	30	32	37	34	34	25	48	31	24	27	33	41
Belarus	60	61	59	64	61	54	39	67	61	62	59	60	65	59	41	50	64	78
Russia	50	51	50	54	56	41	44	49	55	48	52	50	57	51	42	43	54	68
Moscow	55	54	56	56	55	53	43	53	58	54	53	59	58	50	49	48	56	64
Latvia	65	69	62	61	68	64	56	63	71	67	67	62	na	na	na	63	66	69
Estonia	57	57	57	56	61	52	48	58	63	58	57	54	na	na	na	59	58	58
Portugal	39	41	38	40	45	34	36	46	49	37	44	38	54	37	33	32	44	52
South Korea	35	32	37	41	34	27	32	33	39	35	36	32	50	36	31	27	38	56
Ireland	36	34	38	39	38	31	41	39	57	42	34	40	46	37	30	27	35	49
North Ireland	25	23	26	41	27	11	24	20	41	24	27	20	50	27	13	13	26	39
Slovenia	44	42	45	40	45	44	41	48	42	48	44	36	44	43	36	45	43	47
Spain	44	44	44	53	47	34	39	51	58	35	45	51	55	44	36	33	44	63
East Germany	47	47	46	47	47	46	47	49	43	44	48	47	46	45	53	41	44	56
Britain	34	34	35	39	37	30	33	34	43	32	36	35	51	36	17	24	34	48
Italy	43	45	41	42	46	41	42	47	49	45	43	35	57	37	34	36	42	54
Netherlands	39	29	43	44	40	32	37	36	46	46	37	29	55	35	28	34	34	47
Belgium	33	33	33	43	36	24	29	34	39	34	34	33	47	32	23	26	31	45
Austria	25	22	27	36	25	21	22	26	30	23	26	27	32	26	25	18	22	36
France	42	38	45	40	48	38	41	43	43	42	47	39	49	41	29	38	41	49
Canada	32	30	33	29	35	31	33	30	35	35	31	31	52	30	28	25	30	39
United States	33	31	34	29	36	30	29	30	40	30	30	40	49	30	28	21	31	46
Iceland	27	27	26	34	31	12	21	25	33	na	na	na	43	24	17	23	25	46
West Germany	31	31	31	38	32	27	29	32	41	33	32	27	47	27	22	21	27	45
Denmark	29	26	32	32	32	24	27	32	29	30	33	26	51	29	18	20	27	48
Finland	20	18	21	15	22	18	28	18	18	21	17	21	36	20	11	19	18	23
Norway	49	45	53	56	48	46	47	53	45	52	49	38	61	48	37	49	48	53
Sweden	35	31	40	42	34	30	38	36	29	35	37	31	45	35	26	31	33	45
Japan	29	23	35	42	27	22	26	29	30	38	29	21	35	30	15	25	30	38
Switzerland	na	na	na	na	na	na	na	na	na	na	na	na	na	na	na	na	na	na
Total	**40**	**40**	**41**	**43**	**43**	**35**	**37**	**41**	**45**	**41**	**42**	**39**	**50**	**38**	**33**	**35**	**40**	**51**

Ranking:

Latvia	65
Belarus	60
Poland	59
South Africa	58
Estonia	57
Moscow	55
Bulgaria	52
Lithuania	51
Russia	50
Argentina	49
Norway	49
Nigeria	48
East Germany	47
Slovenia	44
Spain	44
Italy	43
France	42
Chile	41
Switzerland	na
Brazil	40
Hungary	39
Portugal	39
Netherlands	39
Turkey	37
China	36
Romania	36
Ireland	36
South Korea	35
Sweden	35
Britain	34
India	33
Belgium	33
United States	33
Mexico	32
Canada	32
West Germany	31
Denmark	29
Japan	29
Czechoslovakia	27
Iceland	27
North Ireland	25
Austria	25
Finland	20

Note: Countries in the left column are ranked according to GNP per capita. / The percentages in the bottom row give each country an equal weight. / na=not ascertained.

V97 LIVE IN NEED: LAZINESS

Why are there people in this country who live in need? Here are four possible reasons. Which one reason do you consider to be most important? (% "Because of laziness and lack of will power")

	Total	Gender		Age			Education			Income			Political Affinity			Values			Ranking:	
		Male	Female	16-29	30-49	50+	Lower	Medium	Upper	Lower	Middle	Upper	Left	Center	Right	Mat	Mixed	Postmat		
India	40	42	38	43	39	38	28	41	45	36	38	46	42	39	44	44	38	44	Czechoslovakia	43
Nigeria	24	22	26	24	23	32	25	26	20	23	23	26	24	24	27	25	24	13	India	40
China	12	13	12	11	13	14	13	13	09	13	11	13	na	na	na	12	12	13	United States	40
Romania	34	36	32	29	27	43	39	27	37	28	34	37	34	38	29	37	31	35	Turkey	39
Turkey	39	34	44	33	39	49	46	33	20	42	41	35	26	42	44	47	40	27	Mexico	39
Poland	20	18	21	15	19	24	26	15	20	19	22	19	22	15	20	27	17	15	Austria	37
Bulgaria	27	29	24	19	17	42	45	22	17	26	27	29	28	28	17	34	26	12	South Korea	36
Chile	35	34	35	31	32	44	40	33	30	38	36	30	19	37	44	43	34	25	Chile	35
Czechoslovakia	43	43	43	36	40	52	48	41	40	45	43	41	40	43	46	44	44	37	Romania	34
South Africa	22	21	22	18	22	28	19	22	30	15	19	34	18	24	34	29	19	13	Hungary	34
Lithuania	25	26	24	18	18	37	42	21	15	30	20	21	na	na	na	32	24	13	Argentina	34
Hungary	34	32	36	24	31	41	38	31	28	36	31	34	29	32	38	35	34	11	Russia	34
Argentina	34	31	37	36	37	29	33	37	33	30	29	42	18	34	43	32	38	24	Japan	33
Brazil	27	24	30	22	28	35	38	25	14	31	25	25	21	22	35	34	23	21	North Ireland	32
Mexico	39	39	39	38	39	42	39	41	36	40	36	39	27	38	50	42	39	31	Canada	32
Belarus	27	26	27	20	26	35	48	21	25	25	27	28	23	30	41	36	24	10	Italy	30
Russia	34	32	35	28	30	44	38	34	32	36	33	35	28	32	44	40	31	23	East Germany	29
Moscow	27	28	27	22	26	34	39	29	24	26	31	24	25	29	33	36	25	20	Bulgaria	27
Latvia	17	14	19	19	15	19	23	19	11	16	16	19	na	na	na	20	17	12	Brazil	27
Estonia	24	23	25	21	22	29	27	24	21	21	27	26	08	na	na	23	24	19	Belarus	27
Portugal	24	24	25	18	27	28	27	17	20	24	23	26	16	26	28	29	22	24	Moscow	27
South Korea	36	32	39	24	37	53	40	37	32	33	36	41	23	35	40	43	33	17	Britain	27
Ireland	21	22	21	15	18	29	25	19	08	21	23	19	17	23	22	25	21	18	Finland	26
North Ireland	32	30	33	16	28	46	40	22	07	41	35	20	25	34	31	41	31	18	Lithuania	25
Slovenia	24	26	21	21	19	31	30	19	20	26	21	25	20	23	28	25	23	25	Nigeria	24
Spain	24	24	23	20	23	28	26	25	15	25	24	23	18	29	31	31	24	15	Estonia	24
East Germany	29	31	28	29	27	32	31	28	25	32	30	27	28	30	29	35	31	23	Portugal	24
Britain	27	28	26	20	23	34	29	26	15	31	25	24	20	26	36	33	26	21	Slovenia	24
Italy	30	30	30	27	28	33	31	24	14	27	31	28	18	36	35	34	33	18	Spain	24
Netherlands	14	18	12	13	12	17	17	15	09	10	17	13	08	12	23	24	16	08	Iceland	23
Belgium	22	23	22	17	19	28	26	21	17	22	20	22	13	21	30	29	21	16	West Germany	23
Austria	37	43	32	24	37	42	40	35	31	41	37	31	34	35	37	44	40	25	South Africa	22
France	15	16	15	15	13	19	18	14	13	18	15	10	11	16	19	21	16	09	Belgium	22
Canada	32	35	29	35	29	33	33	34	28	36	31	30	22	33	33	38	34	25	Ireland	21
United States	40	40	40	39	36	45	44	45	30	49	40	32	28	42	44	46	43	28	Poland	20
Iceland	23	27	20	27	22	28	25	23	22	na	na	na	17	18	31	24	25	11	Latvia	17
West Germany	23	25	21	25	20	27	25	21	15	23	22	23	16	24	29	32	25	12	Sweden	16
Denmark	14	18	11	18	10	16	17	15	12	15	13	11	04	13	20	23	15	04	France	15
Finland	26	29	22	29	22	32	26	26	25	26	27	26	14	24	36	31	27	22	Netherlands	14
Norway	11	15	07	09	10	14	16	09	10	11	10	14	07	11	15	13	12	05	Denmark	14
Sweden	16	20	13	18	10	22	20	15	13	17	21	13	12	15	20	23	18	09	China	12
Japan	33	38	29	22	37	36	35	34	31	27	35	40	30	33	50	31	36	32	Norway	11
Switzerland	na	na	na	na	na	na	na	na	na	na	na	na	na	na	na	na	na	na		
Total	27	28	27	23	25	33	31	26	22	28	27	27	22	28	33	32	27	19		

Note: Countries in the left column are ranked according to GNP per capita. / The percentages in the bottom row give each country an equal weight. / na=not ascertained.

V99-V114. Here are some aspects of a job that people say are important. Which ones do you personally think are important in a job?

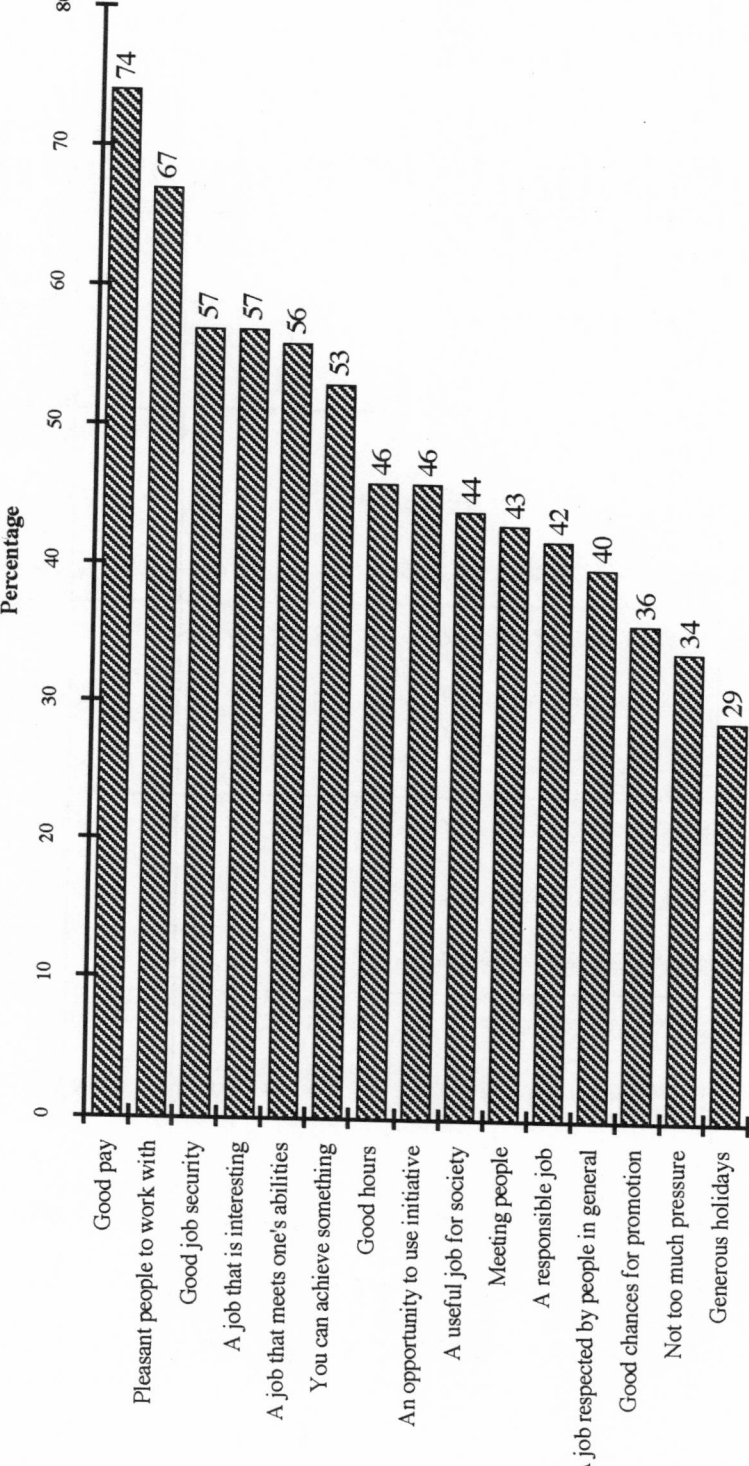

V99 GOOD PAY

Here are some aspects of a job that people say are important. Please look at them and tell me which ones you personally think are important in a job? "Good pay" (% "mentioned")

	Total	Gender Male	Gender Female	Age 16-29	Age 30-49	Age 50+	Education Lower	Education Medium	Education Upper	Income Lower	Income Middle	Income Upper	Political Affinity Left	Political Affinity Center	Political Affinity Right	Values Mat	Values Mixed	Values Postmat	Ranking country	Ranking
India	87	86	88	88	87	85	89	88	84	88	89	91	82	89	93	88	87	84	Nigeria	93
Nigeria	93	94	91	93	92	98	95	93	91	93	93	91	91	92	93	92	93	95	Turkey	90
China	68	66	70	67	72	63	74	63	68	67	67	70	na	na	na	69	67	59	Bulgaria	90
Romania	76	77	74	79	76	73	81	77	66	76	77	75	76	75	77	77	75	73	India	87
Turkey	90	90	89	91	90	88	91	86	87	88	90	89	87	91	90	92	91	84	Belarus	87
Poland	na	na	na	na	na	na	na	na	na	na	na	na	na	na	na	na	na	na	Estonia	86
Bulgaria	90	91	90	92	91	89	91	91	88	91	93	88	88	90	91	89	90	90	United States	86
Chile	77	79	76	78	78	75	77	77	78	77	76	79	77	77	79	78	80	72	Iceland	86
Czechoslovakia	83	85	81	88	86	76	85	84	75	82	82	85	83	84	81	86	82	80	Hungary	85
South Africa	84	85	82	86	85	78	89	82	75	87	85	77	82	84	83	85	84	79	South Africa	84
Lithuania	79	81	77	76	82	79	80	80	71	78	84	75	na	na	na	82	80	70	Argentina	84
Hungary	85	88	83	91	86	82	85	86	86	84	86	84	86	85	85	88	83	80	Czechoslovakia	83
Argentina	84	84	84	85	82	85	82	86	86	89	81	83	80	87	83	86	83	83	Russia	83
Brazil	82	83	80	82	81	81	83	81	81	83	81	79	81	79	83	83	81	75	Brazil	82
Mexico	79	79	78	77	81	78	80	74	79	77	82	77	78	78	78	78	81	71	Slovenia	82
Belarus	87	86	87	89	88	82	85	90	85	87	88	86	87	86	93	91	86	88	Moscow	80
Russia	83	86	81	86	86	76	82	85	81	83	82	83	84	83	80	83	82	82	Lithuania	79
Moscow	80	84	77	88	81	73	81	83	78	79	80	82	81	83	73	81	80	80	Mexico	79
Latvia	69	75	64	72	73	57	69	69	68	65	69	71	na	na	na	71	69	68	Portugal	79
Estonia	86	90	83	88	89	79	83	87	85	86	85	87	na	86	na	88	86	86	Japan	78
Portugal	79	79	79	81	75	81	78	78	81	78	78	82	76	80	80	83	77	74	Chile	77
South Korea	18	21	16	21	17	17	25	15	19	18	17	21	17	22	16	20	18	13	Romania	76
Ireland	73	77	69	79	72	70	70	75	81	70	74	75	75	72	77	71	75	70	Canada	76
North Ireland	74	80	69	84	76	64	72	78	76	73	72	83	71	77	69	66	77	73	Spain	75
Slovenia	82	85	79	86	81	80	85	83	76	86	82	77	76	82	84	83	81	87	North Ireland	74
Spain	75	75	74	70	75	78	74	74	73	76	75	76	76	75	72	80	76	66	Ireland	73
East Germany	71	77	66	79	72	66	72	70	68	68	72	74	73	72	71	72	72	69	West Germany	73
Britain	69	75	63	79	73	58	70	63	66	64	73	73	70	70	65	72	69	67	Sweden	73
Italy	72	74	69	72	73	71	73	66	56	71	68	79	72	69	68	77	72	66	Italy	72
Netherlands	69	73	67	74	68	65	69	73	64	66	66	72	63	69	69	81	74	59	East Germany	71
Belgium	71	75	66	72	70	71	74	69	67	68	70	72	71	69	74	73	72	65	Belgium	71
Austria	60	67	55	64	60	58	59	61	55	61	59	59	62	64	54	67	59	57	Latvia	69
France	54	56	52	55	55	47	54	55	51	54	52	57	52	50	61	55	55	51	Britain	69
Canada	76	78	74	81	77	69	75	75	77	72	76	76	74	78	71	80	77	71	Netherlands	69
United States	86	88	83	91	88	82	86	86	86	83	88	87	83	86	87	88	86	85	China	68
Iceland	86	89	83	90	87	79	80	88	88	na	na	na	82	87	88	91	83	89	Finland	66
West Germany	73	77	70	79	76	68	74	73	70	71	77	74	75	73	73	75	74	72	Austria	60
Denmark	55	66	44	71	61	36	43	63	55	47	62	61	55	56	55	55	55	56	Norway	60
Finland	66	68	63	76	68	50	65	63	68	59	65	71	66	65	65	71	66	64	Denmark	55
Norway	60	66	54	68	62	52	51	63	61	54	61	63	58	55	64	60	60	58	France	54
Sweden	73	79	67	80	72	70	76	73	68	76	70	74	73	75	69	76	72	74	South Korea	18
Japan	78	79	78	85	85	65	64	80	88	73	81	83	79	80	74	81	81	77		
Switzerland	na	na	na	na	na	na	na	na	na	na	na	na	na	na	na	na	na	na		
Total	75	78	73	79	76	71	75	75	73	74	75	76	74	75	75	77	75	72		

Note: Countries in the left column are ranked according to GNP per capita. / The percentages in the bottom row give each country an equal weight. / na=not ascertained.

V100 PLEASANT PEOPLE

Here are some aspects of a job that people say are important. Please look at them and tell me which ones you personally think are important in a job? "Pleasant people to work with" (% "mentioned")

	Total	Gender		Age			Education			Income			Political Affinity			Values		
		Male	Female	16-29	30-49	50+	Lower	Medium	Upper	Lower	Middle	Upper	Left	Center	Right	Mat	Mixed	Postmat
India	69	71	67	74	70	56	54	73	72	65	71	69	74	69	66	74	71	67
Nigeria	85	85	84	85	84	91	87	85	83	81	86	83	84	84	85	81	86	96
China	55	55	56	55	56	54	49	55	63	52	59	56	na	na	na	52	58	65
Romania	56	54	58	63	59	50	44	63	62	50	58	59	57	58	61	54	58	58
Turkey	86	89	83	89	86	81	85	89	87	86	85	88	85	88	88	79	89	87
Poland	na	na	na	na	na	na	na	na	na	na	na	na	na	na	na	na	na	na
Bulgaria	63	62	64	70	63	59	57	66	65	61	67	65	60	65	65	66	62	67
Chile	57	57	56	59	54	57	59	54	57	56	59	53	56	57	58	56	58	50
Czechoslovakia	83	79	86	84	83	82	84	82	82	83	81	85	82	84	82	81	83	86
South Africa	40	36	45	41	39	41	39	41	42	39	41	46	36	41	37	40	41	39
Lithuania	73	70	76	77	74	69	73	74	72	73	76	70	na	na	na	69	74	74
Hungary	65	62	68	68	66	63	62	66	71	64	65	64	64	69	63	68	63	65
Argentina	61	62	60	63	57	64	61	60	63	60	63	61	61	61	57	63	60	61
Brazil	58	56	60	60	56	60	62	57	57	61	60	54	59	58	58	60	58	55
Mexico	69	68	70	71	68	66	68	70	70	67	69	71	62	71	72	68	70	62
Belarus	82	79	84	83	83	80	82	82	82	80	83	82	83	84	83	84	82	80
Russia	71	73	70	75	72	68	70	73	71	69	72	72	69	73	68	71	73	61
Moscow	72	71	73	77	72	67	72	76	70	71	73	73	75	72	60	75	72	71
Latvia	55	52	58	60	57	46	49	55	58	58	53	55	62	49	52	54	57	48
Estonia	77	71	81	77	78	75	73	78	76	80	75	71	na	na	na	74	80	85
Portugal	80	79	80	84	79	77	75	79	89	73	80	87	78	81	85	82	81	85
South Korea	14	13	14	19	11	11	17	15	11	20	11	07	10	17	13	13	14	13
Ireland	64	60	67	74	59	61	59	68	72	65	64	62	60	59	71	62	64	66
North Ireland	68	66	69	79	65	64	67	69	72	67	67	74	68	66	73	68	68	71
Slovenia	82	82	82	89	82	77	78	87	80	82	82	80	85	83	88	82	81	87
Spain	62	64	60	67	62	58	60	66	64	57	66	68	67	66	56	57	64	68
East Germany	65	59	76	75	69	71	72	76	66	73	74	68	72	72	68	75	71	71
Britain	65	59	71	75	66	60	64	69	70	64	65	70	62	68	63	67	66	63
Italy	50	51	50	59	49	46	50	51	41	49	52	53	49	49	52	45	51	55
Netherlands	93	93	93	96	92	92	91	94	96	92	91	96	93	94	94	92	94	93
Belgium	68	69	66	77	69	60	63	68	60	62	70	72	73	69	64	64	66	77
Austria	62	63	62	74	59	60	62	63	60	66	63	59	69	63	60	61	61	67
France	53	52	54	66	51	46	49	59	56	51	53	58	54	52	54	50	54	59
Canada	73	72	75	79	76	65	65	75	77	72	71	76	74	74	71	61	74	76
United States	74	72	77	73	77	73	69	74	78	73	72	78	74	74	74	66	75	79
Iceland	89	87	92	93	88	86	88	91	89	76	na	na	89	91	88	92	88	88
West Germany	76	73	79	82	78	72	76	79	74	76	81	77	77	77	73	77	76	79
Denmark	77	72	82	87	78	68	69	83	77	73	82	76	80	78	73	75	77	82
Finland	64	62	66	77	59	65	60	60	65	60	65	65	61	61	66	65	64	63
Norway	80	76	84	88	79	76	79	83	89	79	82	75	78	83	78	83	80	82
Sweden	91	90	91	96	89	89	91	92	87	93	90	90	88	93	89	92	90	91
Japan	78	80	77	90	82	65	67	81	84	75	79	84	82	79	78	81	90	80
Switzerland	na	na	na	na	na	na	na	na	na	na	na	na	na	na	na	na	na	na
Total	69	67	70	74	68	65	66	71	70	67	69	69	69	70	68	68	69	70

Ranking:

Netherlands	93
Sweden	91
Iceland	89
Turkey	86
Nigeria	85
Czechoslovakia	83
Belarus	82
Slovenia	82
Portugal	80
Norway	80
Japan	78
Estonia	77
Denmark	77
West Germany	76
United States	74
Lithuania	73
Canada	73
Moscow	72
East Germany	72
Russia	71
India	69
Mexico	69
North Ireland	68
Belgium	68
Hungary	65
Britain	65
Ireland	64
Finland	64
Bulgaria	63
Spain	62
Austria	62
Argentina	61
Brazil	58
Chile	57
Romania	56
China	55
Latvia	55
France	53
Italy	50
South Africa	40
South Korea	14

Note: Countries in the left column are ranked according to GNP per capita. / The percentages in the bottom row give each country an equal weight. / na=not ascertained.

V101 NO PRESSURE

Here are some aspects of a job that people say are important. Please look at them and tell me which ones you personally think are important in a job? "Not too much pressure" (% "mentioned")

Country	Total	Gender		Age			Education			Income			Political Affinity			Values		
		Male	Female	16-29	30-49	50+	Lower	Medium	Upper	Lower	Middle	Upper	Left	Center	Right	Mat	Mixed	Postmat
India	48	49	48	51	49	41	42	52	47	49	51	45	48	49	45	49	51	47
Nigeria	64	64	65	66	64	54	70	67	60	60	70	61	60	63	64	68	63	59
China	30	27	34	26	32	31	33	30	26	27	33	31	na	na	na	31	29	26
Romania	37	39	34	38	36	37	38	37	34	32	38	39	39	38	34	41	33	37
Turkey	78	80	75	81	77	74	75	80	85	74	78	81	78	81	77	77	76	84
Poland	na	na	na	na	na	na	na	na	na	na	na	na	na	na	na	na	na	na
Bulgaria	35	31	38	35	34	34	38	38	29	32	40	33	35	37	37	39	32	34
Chile	46	44	47	45	45	48	50	47	40	46	49	41	44	45	48	44	47	44
Czechoslovakia	58	56	60	50	55	66	69	54	47	63	58	52	53	61	56	65	57	47
South Africa	29	28	31	32	29	25	37	28	09	38	32	10	30	24	19	27	30	33
Lithuania	40	32	47	35	43	42	45	40	34	41	46	37	na	na	na	41	41	35
Hungary	46	45	47	43	46	37	47	44	45	47	46	38	38	47	43	50	42	45
Argentina	41	42	40	43	43	37	37	47	38	38	37	41	43	41	34	42	39	45
Brazil	40	41	39	41	40	38	41	40	35	40	41	38	44	37	38	41	38	42
Mexico	47	49	44	47	46	48	49	48	38	46	50	42	40	48	47	45	47	40
Belarus	60	62	58	63	58	62	52	62	61	55	63	61	61	62	59	60	60	56
Russia	19	18	20	23	21	15	19	22	17	20	17	18	16	19	24	21	18	16
Moscow	49	54	46	50	49	50	48	43	54	48	46	60	54	48	46	48	48	58
Latvia	19	19	18	22	17	18	25	20	14	18	20	18	19	18	na	18	18	19
Estonia	32	30	33	33	32	31	34	34	25	30	34	33	na	na	na	37	30	24
Portugal	41	41	41	42	37	43	42	43	38	42	40	38	46	43	40	44	41	40
South Korea	08	08	08	08	08	08	09	09	07	08	09	06	10	06	09	08	07	10
Ireland	26	25	28	26	25	29	29	25	21	30	30	20	31	25	29	25	28	24
North Ireland	20	20	21	17	20	23	25	11	17	27	11	19	18	22	31	22	20	20
Slovenia	48	46	50	51	52	43	46	53	45	51	50	41	41	45	56	51	48	37
Spain	38	41	36	44	40	33	36	45	44	33	41	42	44	40	34	35	39	45
East Germany	19	19	19	19	16	22	22	20	08	20	25	14	14	20	24	27	18	16
Britain	19	18	21	21	21	17	20	15	21	19	21	17	23	19	14	17	19	22
Italy	31	33	30	35	32	29	32	27	29	30	29	25	33	28	31	30	31	36
Netherlands	44	38	46	49	43	39	45	48	38	47	50	31	43	40	47	55	44	39
Belgium	26	25	26	23	27	26	25	27	24	25	31	26	23	24	29	25	26	25
Austria	17	16	17	21	17	14	16	18	13	17	17	16	19	17	14	18	16	17
France	08	08	07	09	09	06	08	06	10	06	10	06	10	06	05	07	08	08
Canada	28	27	30	26	28	30	33	28	25	34	27	21	27	30	24	25	29	26
United States	33	32	33	32	31	34	38	32	29	35	33	27	32	31	30	35	32	31
Iceland	35	38	33	41	27	44	38	37	32	na	33	24	37	35	33	43	33	32
West Germany	28	29	27	34	29	24	30	27	18	28	33	24	29	27	25	32	28	27
Denmark	16	15	17	20	14	14	16	16	15	18	17	10	19	15	13	15	15	19
Finland	20	21	19	25	20	18	20	17	24	16	22	22	19	23	19	27	20	20
Norway	23	23	24	22	21	27	28	24	21	17	24	22	26	23	22	25	22	26
Sweden	48	47	51	53	40	53	56	49	35	48	50	42	41	56	42	43	52	39
Japan	42	37	47	50	45	34	36	43	47	40	40	46	40	45	38	48	43	44
Switzerland	na	na	na	na	na	na	na	na	na	na	na	na	na	na	na	na	na	na
Total	35	35	35	36	35	34	37	35	32	35	36	32	35	36	34	37	35	34

Ranking:

Turkey	78
Nigeria	64
Belarus	60
Czechoslovakia	58
Moscow	49
India	48
Slovenia	48
Sweden	48
Mexico	47
Chile	46
Hungary	46
Netherlands	44
Japan	42
Argentina	41
Portugal	41
Lithuania	40
Brazil	40
Spain	38
Romania	37
Bulgaria	35
Iceland	35
United States	33
Estonia	32
Italy	31
China	30
South Africa	29
Canada	28
West Germany	28
Ireland	26
Belgium	26
Norway	23
North Ireland	20
Finland	20
Russia	19
Latvia	19
East Germany	19
Britain	19
Austria	17
Denmark	16
South Korea	08
France	08

Note: Countries in the left column are ranked according to GNP per capita. / The percentages in the bottom row give each country an equal weight. / na=not ascertained.

V102 JOB SECURITY

Here are some aspects of a job that people say are important. Please look at them and tell me which ones you personally think are important in a job? "Good job security" (% "mentioned")

	Total	Gender		Age			Education			Income			Political Affinity			Values		
		Male	Female	16-29	30-49	50+	Lower	Medium	Upper	Lower	Middle	Upper	Left	Center	Right	Mat	Mixed	Postmat
India	74	77	71	78	73	70	62	78	76	69	76	76	78	74	75	78	77	74
Nigeria	88	88	89	86	90	93	85	88	89	90	88	84	86	87	89	88	88	97
China	44	41	48	36	47	48	48	43	32	45	46	40	na	na	na	45	42	37
Romania	43	43	44	48	46	38	48	47	32	45	45	40	51	45	37	48	42	26
Turkey	83	84	82	80	84	85	85	81	75	86	82	79	86	83	81	83	83	83
Poland	na	na	na	na	na	na	na	na	na	na	na	na	na	na	na	na	na	na
Bulgaria	57	55	58	58	60	52	47	64	55	55	61	59	57	62	56	62	56	53
Chile	69	72	66	70	68	67	66	68	73	67	70	70	69	69	67	64	71	71
Czechoslovakia	71	69	73	67	72	73	75	71	65	72	74	70	78	73	64	78	70	71
South Africa	68	70	66	67	68	68	69	68	58	67	70	67	61	71	68	72	66	64
Lithuania	38	38	37	32	34	46	53	34	26	39	38	34	na	na	na	37	38	34
Hungary	72	72	71	75	73	69	71	74	67	71	73	67	75	72	66	76	69	68
Argentina	63	65	62	63	62	65	64	68	57	69	61	62	60	65	54	68	63	59
Brazil	71	70	71	69	71	73	70	72	67	70	76	67	69	72	70	70	72	71
Mexico	63	65	61	64	64	62	65	64	59	63	63	63	64	62	64	62	65	55
Belarus	37	41	33	35	34	44	43	38	32	37	36	38	37	34	45	38	36	33
Russia	38	36	40	37	41	36	40	41	34	38	40	40	32	37	46	43	36	27
Moscow	25	31	21	25	25	25	42	27	20	26	22	31	25	25	29	28	24	22
Latvia	22	23	21	25	22	19	31	24	14	23	23	20	na	na	na	19	24	15
Estonia	40	41	39	39	39	42	47	40	32	41	38	41	na	na	na	41	41	42
Portugal	73	74	73	73	72	75	76	69	67	74	71	75	73	75	76	79	73	63
South Korea	35	34	36	28	37	42	40	32	36	34	39	36	31	33	38	38	34	28
Ireland	61	63	59	58	58	67	62	62	52	62	64	58	51	60	69	65	62	56
North Ireland	62	70	56	57	69	57	61	66	52	63	63	64	50	62	66	62	61	67
Slovenia	73	73	73	73	77	68	72	76	70	75	73	70	70	71	79	77	72	69
Spain	67	69	65	66	67	68	67	70	63	70	71	66	69	67	72	70	68	63
East Germany	72	75	70	77	73	68	73	73	68	66	78	73	74	72	72	67	74	70
Britain	57	63	51	62	56	55	57	57	56	59	55	56	56	58	58	62	57	53
Italy	61	57	64	49	58	70	63	47	35	67	57	37	60	60	55	73	61	50
Netherlands	40	44	38	43	35	44	41	44	35	41	43	31	40	36	47	58	42	32
Belgium	39	40	37	37	36	43	45	38	27	43	34	33	36	37	34	44	41	31
Austria	65	69	62	61	61	70	70	64	50	73	65	57	62	65	65	80	66	54
France	35	33	37	32	35	38	37	38	25	42	36	26	30	37	37	44	37	27
Canada	67	68	66	66	67	68	71	70	60	68	67	63	61	69	66	68	69	62
United States	72	72	70	71	72	71	72	72	71	70	74	71	68	75	71	74	73	68
Iceland	57	56	57	61	51	62	58	58	54	na	na	na	68	75	56	63	56	47
West Germany	73	72	73	69	73	75	77	67	62	74	78	67	60	54	56	85	75	65
Denmark	52	54	49	55	56	46	54	57	49	49	53	54	50	54	50	52	53	51
Finland	53	53	53	49	55	55	57	54	49	50	53	54	48	52	56	52	52	51
Norway	78	74	82	72	78	81	85	82	70	80	79	71	78	78	75	86	75	72
Sweden	65	63	68	65	61	71	72	65	55	71	68	62	67	68	61	66	69	56
Japan	58	59	57	63	61	54	58	57	60	60	58	56	54	57	59	64	59	49
Switzerland	na	na	na	na	na	na	na	na	na	na	na	na	na	na	na	na	na	na
Total	58	59	57	57	58	59	60	59	52	59	59	55	59	61	61	62	58	53

Ranking:

Nigeria	88
Turkey	83
Norway	78
India	74
Portugal	73
Slovenia	73
West Germany	73
Hungary	72
East Germany	72
United States	72
Czechoslovakia	72
Brazil	71
Chile	69
South Africa	68
Spain	67
Canada	67
Austria	65
Sweden	65
Argentina	63
Mexico	63
North Ireland	62
Ireland	61
Italy	61
Japan	58
Bulgaria	57
Britain	57
Iceland	57
Finland	53
Denmark	52
China	44
Romania	43
Estonia	40
Netherlands	40
Belgium	39
Lithuania	38
Russia	38
Belarus	37
South Korea	35
France	35
Moscow	25
Latvia	22

Note: Countries in the left column are ranked according to GNP per capita. / The percentages in the bottom row give each country an equal weight. / na=not ascertained.

V103 PROMOTIONS

Here are some aspects of a job that people say are important. Please look at them and tell me which ones you personally think are important in a job? "Good chances for promotion" (% "mentioned")

	Total	Gender		Age			Education			Income			Political Affinity			Values		
		Male	Female	16-29	30-49	50+	Lower	Medium	Upper	Lower	Middle	Upper	Left	Center	Right	Mat	Mixed	Postmat
India	72	74	70	75	73	64	57	76	75	66	73	76	75	72	75	76	73	72
Nigeria	89	89	88	88	89	93	89	87	90	88	89	89	87	88	89	89	89	89
China	27	26	29	29	30	21	25	23	41	24	30	28	na	na	na	25	29	30
Romania	30	31	28	38	28	25	22	34	33	28	27	33	33	30	34	26	31	40
Turkey	61	60	62	63	59	61	62	60	56	64	63	55	51	67	61	54	65	59
Poland	na	na	na	na	na	na	na	na	na	na	na	na	36	41	36	37	35	na
Bulgaria	36	38	34	44	33	35	32	38	37	34	38	41	51	47	49	46	50	46
Chile	49	53	45	51	45	50	46	50	51	46	49	50	35	28	30	29	31	45
Czechoslovakia	30	30	30	30	31	29	28	31	31	32	30	28	36	41	40	37	38	27
South Africa	38	40	36	37	39	37	34	40	36	35	37	41	na	na	na	13	17	39
Lithuania	16	16	15	19	13	16	23	14	11	17	14	16	39	46	36	44	43	15
Hungary	42	41	44	41	44	42	41	43	42	43	42	40	40	49	47	47	44	25
Argentina	45	47	43	44	43	47	42	52	41	48	40	47	40	53	53	55	52	45
Brazil	53	54	52	52	52	56	55	53	51	54	54	52	53	53	53	60	62	53
Mexico	61	61	62	62	60	60	61	57	66	57	62	64	57	62	64	22	20	60
Belarus	22	21	23	26	20	23	16	22	24	17	21	29	22	20	32	17	18	31
Russia	17	19	16	20	16	17	13	18	19	15	17	22	21	18	23	17	18	15
Moscow	19	21	17	24	19	15	13	17	21	17	18	23	19	18	20	06	09	22
Latvia	09	10	08	13	08	04	06	08	10	06	09	09	na	na	na	13	12	08
Estonia	12	14	11	15	12	10	14	12	16	12	11	14	na	na	na	58	58	17
Portugal	57	57	56	63	53	55	53	62	67	56	54	60	56	56	63	02	02	57
South Korea	02	01	03	02	03	01	04	02	02	02	03	01	02	03	02	32	39	03
Ireland	38	37	38	45	33	37	32	43	44	32	38	40	35	33	48	46	42	41
North Ireland	41	46	38	41	39	45	38	49	45	50	34	43	29	47	40	60	62	36
Slovenia	62	68	58	73	64	54	63	64	60	60	63	67	63	65	76	31	35	74
Spain	33	37	31	38	31	33	32	39	36	30	35	40	34	34	35	24	29	36
East Germany	28	31	25	36	26	25	28	26	30	25	28	31	29	27	28	41	33	28
Britain	35	38	32	46	34	31	31	43	47	30	39	43	30	36	40	30	29	37
Italy	28	29	27	31	25	28	28	27	29	27	26	26	26	26	31	39	37	25
Netherlands	35	40	30	38	26	42	33	34	38	35	34	35	29	36	40	32	34	31
Belgium	31	34	27	46	31	31	31	30	32	26	31	27	27	31	32	29	27	29
Austria	33	41	29	29	24	29	30	36	37	28	34	37	34	35	32	23	34	33
France	25	30	20	29	24	22	22	26	26	22	26	26	25	26	26	43	52	23
Canada	49	50	49	56	49	44	41	51	52	49	49	50	51	48	49	58	57	45
United States	58	62	54	67	58	52	54	58	60	56	60	58	61	56	62	42	33	60
Iceland	37	42	31	49	28	35	37	37	35	na	na	na	32	31	44	39	47	45
West Germany	43	46	40	50	44	38	41	48	43	37	46	46	34	46	46	10	18	39
Denmark	16	20	11	31	13	08	06	17	20	14	14	20	10	15	21	35	28	15
Finland	30	32	28	51	23	28	32	28	30	32	28	30	19	30	37	17	19	32
Norway	19	21	17	26	17	16	16	18	22	19	18	19	16	16	26	34	42	22
Sweden	41	44	37	57	30	41	33	46	43	39	39	39	28	38	51	23	27	40
Japan	23	28	19	32	23	18	12	24	32	17	22	32	23	23	29	na	na	24
Switzerland	na	na	na	na	na	na	na	na	na	na	na	na	na	na	na	na	na	na
Total	36	39	34	42	34	35	34	38	38	35	36	38	36	39	42	36	37	37

Note: Countries in the left column are ranked according to GNP per capita. / The percentages in the bottom row give each country an equal weight. / na=not ascertained.

Ranking:

Nigeria	89
India	72
Slovenia	62
Turkey	61
Mexico	61
United States	58
Portugal	57
Brazil	53
Chile	49
Canada	49
Argentina	45
West Germany	43
Hungary	42
North Ireland	41
Sweden	41
South Africa	38
Ireland	38
Iceland	37
Bulgaria	36
Britain	35
Netherlands	35
Spain	33
Austria	33
Belgium	31
Romania	30
Czechoslovakia	30
Finland	30
East Germany	28
Italy	28
China	27
France	25
Japan	23
Belarus	22
Moscow	19
Norway	19
Russia	17
Lithuania	16
Denmark	16
Estonia	12
Latvia	09
South Korea	02

Here are some aspects of a job that people say are important. Please look at them and tell me which ones you personally think are important in a job? "A job respected by people in general" (% "mentioned")

	Total	Gender		Age			Education			Income			Political Affinity			Values		
		Male	Female	16-29	30-49	50+	Lower	Medium	Upper	Lower	Middle	Upper	Left	Center	Right	Mat	Mixed	Postmat
India	59	60	57	62	59	52	44	61	64	54	57	63	61	62	62	61	62	69
Nigeria	74	73	57	74	74	74	79	75	70	69	72	74	75	70	78	74	74	71
China	47	45	50	46	49	44	44	45	56	42	50	48	na	na	na	41	52	54
Romania	55	52	58	44	53	64	62	52	50	53	56	56	57	58	48	58	54	44
Turkey	87	87	87	88	87	84	86	89	88	84	88	89	84	89	87	83	89	88
Poland	na	na	na	na	na	na	na	na	na	na	na	na	na	na	na	na	na	na
Bulgaria	58	55	60	56	58	59	57	61	55	55	63	60	56	62	60	63	57	58
Chile	60	58	60	56	58	66	67	57	54	63	60	56	57	61	58	60	59	59
Czechoslovakia	33	34	33	27	34	36	38	31	34	35	33	32	38	33	32	35	33	30
South Africa	22	21	23	22	21	24	25	21	20	23	23	17	20	16	25	22	22	23
Lithuania	28	28	27	18	28	35	35	24	31	31	26	23	na	na	na	28	26	27
Hungary	16	19	14	14	16	17	13	17	25	15	14	24	16	17	13	17	15	13
Argentina	43	42	43	39	45	44	42	43	42	44	40	41	39	43	41	44	44	39
Brazil	58	55	62	56	58	62	64	57	51	58	57	57	55	57	64	62	55	59
Mexico	54	54	54	51	54	61	55	55	51	54	55	51	46	54	57	59	53	49
Belarus	42	41	43	36	44	45	39	39	46	41	42	44	40	47	45	49	39	41
Russia	40	40	40	33	39	46	43	41	37	40	41	40	34	42	43	45	38	28
Moscow	30	29	32	28	28	35	32	30	30	30	31	32	31	29	31	33	30	30
Latvia	31	35	29	26	34	33	35	30	30	33	32	30	na	na	na	32	32	28
Estonia	38	41	35	32	40	42	38	37	41	38	35	40	na	na	na	36	41	46
Portugal	59	58	61	54	57	67	62	55	51	64	53	58	59	59	66	66	57	59
South Korea	07	08	07	06	07	10	09	07	07	07	06	10	09	06	08	08	07	05
Ireland	29	27	31	29	27	32	26	33	34	30	29	26	24	26	38	28	31	27
North Ireland	20	20	21	24	15	24	17	29	17	22	15	23	18	13	32	28	31	22
Slovenia	59	59	59	57	57	63	63	60	51	60	61	54	57	56	67	63	58	57
Spain	37	40	35	34	38	40	38	33	38	36	40	41	38	37	39	38	40	36
East Germany	51	50	51	42	49	58	51	53	46	50	51	51	48	52	53	55	52	45
Britain	27	29	25	22	28	30	24	31	39	27	26	34	23	25	33	29	26	28
Italy	40	41	40	37	40	43	41	37	29	43	35	38	38	38	39	44	41	36
Netherlands	55	55	54	50	57	56	51	56	57	53	54	53	56	53	58	55	53	57
Belgium	40	40	40	38	39	42	39	38	44	36	35	42	37	39	44	37	41	41
Austria	35	35	34	33	32	38	36	33	37	34	35	35	37	32	36	38	37	27
France	17	19	15	14	15	22	20	16	12	18	16	17	19	14	16	22	17	14
Canada	36	36	36	34	38	35	33	36	38	39	34	37	40	35	39	28	37	36
United States	44	44	43	41	42	46	45	37	52	39	41	50	46	42	47	44	43	46
Iceland	45	45	46	48	49	49	49	40	46	na	na	na	42	43	51	52	43	46
West Germany	42	42	42	38	37	48	44	37	42	42	40	44	27	45	50	47	45	34
Denmark	13	17	09	20	09	12	06	14	17	12	11	16	08	13	18	14	14	10
Finland	24	29	19	30	21	28	32	18	28	20	23	30	21	22	29	35	22	28
Norway	30	27	33	25	26	39	20	29	29	32	31	27	30	30	30	33	30	28
Sweden	43	42	45	37	41	50	49	37	45	46	45	39	39	44	44	42	46	35
Japan	26	28	24	25	26	27	21	24	35	23	22	35	23	24	36	30	26	27
Switzerland	na	na	na	na	na	na	na	na	na	na	na	na	na	na	na	na	na	na
Total	40	40	40	38	40	43	41	39	41	40	39	41	39	40	44	42	41	39

Ranking:

Turkey	87
Nigeria	74
Chile	60
India	59
Portugal	59
Slovenia	59
Bulgaria	58
Brazil	58
Romania	55
Netherlands	55
Mexico	54
East Germany	51
China	47
Iceland	45
United States	44
Argentina	43
Sweden	43
Belarus	42
West Germany	42
Russia	40
Italy	40
Belgium	40
Estonia	38
Spain	37
Canada	36
Austria	35
Czechoslovakia	33
Latvia	31
Moscow	30
Norway	30
Ireland	29
Lithuania	28
Britain	27
Japan	26
Finland	24
South Africa	22
North Ireland	20
France	17
Hungary	16
Denmark	13
South Korea	07

Note: Countries in the left column are ranked according to GNP per capita. / The percentages in the bottom row give each country an equal weight. / na=not ascertained.

V105 GOOD HOURS

Here are some aspects of a job that people say are important. Please look at them and tell me which ones you personally think are important in a job? "Good hours" (% "mentioned")

	Total	Gender Male	Gender Female	Age 16-29	Age 30-49	Age 50+	Education Lower	Education Medium	Education Upper	Income Lower	Income Middle	Income Upper	Political Affinity Left	Political Affinity Center	Political Affinity Right	Values Mat	Values Mixed	Values Postmat
India	55	55	55	59	55	47	42	60	56	52	57	55	57	57	55	57	58	51
Nigeria	80	80	81	82	79	91	85	82	76	82	80	75	78	76	81	77	82	84
China	37	35	43	37	39	34	39	37	33	36	38	37	na	na	na	36	38	35
Romania	36	35	36	41	35	33	33	41	31	33	38	35	38	37	36	36	36	32
Turkey	88	88	88	91	88	84	87	88	89	87	87	90	86	92	84	84	89	90
Poland	na	na	na	na	na	na	na	na	na	na	na	na	na	na	na	na	na	na
Bulgaria	55	47	62	60	57	49	49	60	51	52	61	54	51	61	56	59	52	65
Chile	48	46	49	48	44	52	54	48	40	54	46	42	47	47	45	52	48	43
Czechoslovakia	59	54	63	61	58	58	65	58	48	62	59	55	59	60	56	64	58	49
South Africa	na	na	na	na	na	na	na	na	na	na	na	na	na	na	na	na	na	na
Lithuania	54	51	58	55	55	53	56	55	48	56	59	44	na	61	na	53	55	52
Hungary	60	56	62	63	60	57	57	62	60	60	60	52	57	61	57	64	57	43
Argentina	44	42	45	46	42	44	43	48	38	40	44	39	43	45	45	47	43	42
Brazil	46	44	48	45	45	49	56	45	31	51	48	38	47	41	47	51	43	40
Mexico	56	56	57	55	57	56	58	54	51	55	57	55	57	57	54	58	57	48
Belarus	59	53	63	57	60	57	56	60	58	60	58	57	60	58	62	61	58	48
Russia	46	38	52	49	51	39	44	50	44	52	46	42	44	43	55	49	45	44
Moscow	55	49	60	60	58	46	55	60	52	58	55	53	57	56	42	60	52	59
Latvia	34	32	35	32	38	29	36	37	27	36	30	35	na	na	na	36	34	24
Estonia	58	52	63	61	59	55	58	61	52	62	60	51	na	na	na	60	59	59
Portugal	62	58	65	62	57	66	63	53	63	66	61	54	63	61	64	68	59	55
South Korea	11	13	10	12	12	09	14	13	08	13	13	06	08	12	12	13	11	05
Ireland	46	43	49	51	43	46	48	44	39	50	50	39	50	44	47	50	46	42
North Ireland	42	42	42	42	42	42	46	43	14	50	34	38	36	42	41	46	41	38
Slovenia	39	40	39	29	39	46	45	38	31	47	38	27	33	38	47	44	38	27
Spain	43	47	40	43	44	43	43	46	43	48	45	44	47	38	40	44	43	44
East Germany	40	37	43	48	38	39	41	45	34	40	44	37	40	39	43	49	38	40
Britain	37	34	39	36	40	30	27	29	38	28	38	31	43	37	26	31	36	35
Italy	39	40	39	42	40	37	36	35	31	32	38	37	40	39	36	44	41	38
Netherlands	47	44	48	53	47	41	50	51	40	54	45	38	46	46	45	49	47	46
Belgium	40	36	43	41	41	38	41	41	36	38	40	39	44	37	38	38	42	37
Austria	35	31	37	41	39	28	32	37	34	35	36	34	34	36	32	39	33	36
France	26	24	28	29	30	19	24	28	28	26	28	26	28	24	27	26	29	21
Canada	52	49	54	51	54	49	53	55	47	53	52	47	53	54	43	52	53	47
United States	55	53	57	58	54	55	58	55	54	56	54	53	58	54	52	59	55	53
Iceland	64	60	69	68	62	64	69	64	61	na	na	na	63	66	62	71	63	58
West Germany	48	45	50	57	52	39	48	48	44	47	54	45	52	46	42	45	47	52
Denmark	32	29	34	36	34	26	27	37	30	28	38	29	36	32	29	31	31	37
Finland	37	34	40	48	35	32	36	36	39	32	37	41	36	40	36	44	36	38
Norway	32	30	34	31	31	34	37	32	29	36	33	27	33	33	29	36	30	31
Sweden	64	61	68	68	64	59	68	64	58	72	63	57	66	68	56	67	63	63
Japan	55	50	61	70	58	42	43	59	58	50	58	55	57	55	49	59	57	57
Switzerland	na	na	na	na	na	na	na	na	na	na	na	na	na	na	na	na	na	na
Total	48	45	50	51	48	45	48	49	44	49	48	44	49	48	46	50	48	45

Note: Countries in the left column are ranked according to GNP per capita. / The percentages in the bottom row give each country an equal weight. / na=not ascertained.

Ranking:

Turkey	88
Nigeria	80
Iceland	64
Sweden	64
Portugal	62
Hungary	60
Czechoslovakia	59
Belarus	59
Estonia	58
Mexico	56
India	55
Bulgaria	55
Moscow	55
United States	55
Japan	55
Lithuania	54
Canada	52
Chile	48
West Germany	48
Netherlands	47
Brazil	46
Russia	46
Ireland	46
Argentina	44
Spain	43
North Ireland	42
East Germany	40
Belgium	40
Slovenia	39
Italy	39
China	37
Britain	37
Finland	37
Romania	36
Austria	35
Latvia	34
Denmark	32
Norway	32
France	26
South Korea	11

V106 USE INITIATIVE

Here are some aspects of a job that people say are important. Please look at them and tell me which ones you personally think are important in a job? "An opportunity to use initiative" (% "mentioned")

		Gender		Age			Education			Income			Political Affinity			Values		
	Total	Male	Female	16-29	30-49	50+	Lower	Medium	Upper	Lower	Middle	Upper	Left	Center	Right	Mat	Mixed	Postmat
India	54	56	51	56	54	47	35	56	60	48	50	61	60	60	51	57	56	60
Nigeria	82	83	81	81	85	86	83	81	83	84	83	79	81	84	82	80	84	92
China	52	56	45	54	54	46	41	54	68	46	57	55	na	na	na	44	60	69
Romania	38	41	35	45	40	32	24	40	52	36	35	44	35	40	45	31	40	65
Turkey	81	86	76	84	81	75	76	89	90	78	78	87	86	82	81	70	82	90
Poland	na	na	na	na	na	na	na	na	na	na	na	na	na	na	na	na	na	na
Bulgaria	47	50	44	54	50	39	30	46	65	42	50	53	50	49	56	43	47	64
Chile	55	61	51	55	53	58	51	56	60	48	57	61	52	57	58	48	56	64
Czechoslovakia	55	60	51	54	58	53	48	56	67	56	55	55	61	53	58	45	58	62
South Africa	28	32	24	25	29	31	14	32	55	18	23	51	36	34	33	27	28	29
Lithuania	29	35	24	27	30	30	30	27	39	28	26	37	na	na	na	23	29	40
Hungary	37	39	34	34	40	34	28	41	56	32	35	52	44	39	39	36	36	48
Argentina	55	60	50	53	60	50	43	63	66	42	51	65	63	60	57	47	54	68
Brazil	51	52	50	50	52	51	48	49	64	48	52	55	51	53	52	47	51	70
Mexico	60	62	58	60	61	56	58	57	68	53	61	69	61	59	67	56	60	69
Belarus	40	43	37	40	40	40	29	36	48	35	38	47	41	37	48	33	42	61
Russia	29	34	25	29	30	27	21	27	35	26	30	33	36	31	31	25	30	37
Moscow	40	48	34	43	41	37	27	34	46	37	41	46	45	39	34	31	42	50
Latvia	17	26	12	17	18	17	10	16	24	13	15	21	na	na	na	14	18	28
Estonia	30	37	24	30	35	23	17	30	44	28	28	35	na	na	na	25	31	56
Portugal	55	61	49	62	50	52	48	69	70	51	50	64	58	55	59	54	31	71
South Korea	15	09	19	19	13	11	07	12	22	12	14	19	22	14	13	10	54	26
Ireland	50	52	49	61	51	43	39	61	74	37	50	62	53	48	58	42	17	61
North Ireland	38	40	36	45	33	37	30	45	66	26	42	49	39	37	39	29	50	58
Slovenia	55	63	49	61	58	48	48	58	66	50	57	64	65	59	67	29	39	47
Spain	37	41	33	47	37	29	31	45	55	28	39	45	43	36	36	54	56	74
East Germany	58	64	53	66	66	46	50	66	82	48	57	68	69	56	52	27	41	48
Britain	46	50	43	52	50	40	38	63	72	36	48	63	39	47	54	32	60	67
Italy	45	53	39	54	51	36	30	41	64	40	53	59	50	43	47	46	44	52
Netherlands	64	69	62	73	61	58	43	60	64	61	60	78	69	66	64	33	45	59
Belgium	41	44	38	50	41	35	50	65	79	30	39	53	44	41	46	49	64	70
Austria	42	46	40	50	46	34	31	42	59	29	42	54	47	44	44	26	40	56
France	38	42	34	42	37	35	36	43	64	29	38	52	41	39	45	23	40	57
Canada	54	54	54	54	57	50	30	41	54	48	55	62	57	54	58	25	54	52
United States	52	52	52	47	55	51	42	56	61	41	52	63	56	52	57	50	50	60
Iceland	55	59	50	62	57	42	45	46	65	na	na	na	56	50	61	44	55	60
West Germany	59	64	54	66	67	48	51	52	67	46	61	70	63	60	60	33	60	77
Denmark	44	46	42	57	51	32	46	66	84	41	45	54	51	41	46	35	43	72
Finland	45	49	42	50	44	43	23	46	54	40	43	54	33	46	52	56	47	59
Norway	45	48	42	57	45	38	41	40	55	39	48	54	44	42	54	40	43	48
Sweden	71	71	70	73	73	66	65	71	78	74	65	73	67	70	75	60	72	74
Japan	34	40	30	37	37	29	22	34	47	27	34	43	41	37	41	32	39	44
Switzerland	na	na	na	na	na	na	na	na	na	na	na	na	na	na	na	na	na	na
Total	47	51	44	51	49	42	38	49	61	41	46	55	52	49	52	39	48	59

Ranking:

Nigeria	82
Turkey	81
Sweden	71
Netherlands	64
Mexico	60
West Germany	59
East Germany	58
Chile	55
Czechoslovakia	55
Argentina	55
Portugal	55
Slovenia	55
Iceland	55
India	54
Canada	54
China	52
United States	52
Brazil	51
Ireland	50
Bulgaria	47
Britain	46
Italy	45
Finland	45
Norway	45
Denmark	44
Austria	42
Belgium	41
Belarus	40
Moscow	40
Romania	38
North Ireland	38
France	38
Hungary	37
Spain	37
Japan	34
Estonia	30
Lithuania	29
Russia	29
South Africa	28
Latvia	17
South Korea	15

Note: Countries in the left column are ranked according to GNP per capita. / The percentages in the bottom row give each country an equal weight. / na=not ascertained.

V107 USEFUL TO SOCIETY

Here are some aspects of a job that people say are important. Please look at them and tell me which ones you personally think are important in a job? "A useful job for society" (% "mentioned")

	Total	Gender Male	Gender Female	Age 16-29	Age 30-49	Age 50+	Education Lower	Education Medium	Education Upper	Income Lower	Income Middle	Income Upper	Political Affinity Left	Political Affinity Center	Political Affinity Right	Values Mat	Values Mixed	Values Postmat	Ranking:	
India	60	61	59	63	60	52	45	62	64	58	56	63	67	63	59	62	62	62	Turkey	91
Nigeria	83	83	82	83	82	84	79	84	83	83	82	81	78	81	86	81	83	92	Nigeria	83
China	55	56	55	50	57	60	49	58	61	54	57	56	na	na	na	51	60	59	Czechoslovakia	64
Romania	48	46	50	40	48	52	46	48	50	47	49	47	44	50	45	49	47	46	Slovenia	63
Turkey	91	94	89	91	92	90	90	94	94	90	91	93	90	93	92	90	91	94	India	60
Poland	na	na	na	na	na	na	na	na	na	na	na	na	na	na	na	na	na	na	Portugal	60
Bulgaria	53	53	53	53	54	51	47	55	58	46	60	59	48	57	58	56	53	57	Belarus	57
Chile	55	56	55	55	53	59	55	54	58	52	57	55	55	57	55	55	53	59	Argentina	56
Czechoslovakia	64	62	65	58	62	69	68	60	67	67	62	62	70	61	65	62	65	64	Mexico	56
South Africa	23	22	24	25	21	23	23	23	20	23	26	18	27	22	22	20	25	26	China	55
Lithuania	47	50	44	38	43	57	54	42	55	49	45	44	na	na	na	44	46	51	Chile	55
Hungary	49	46	51	39	48	53	46	51	52	47	51	47	52	50	52	51	47	43	Brazil	55
Argentina	56	56	56	56	55	58	52	57	64	53	58	56	60	59	54	53	57	59	Iceland	54
Brazil	55	52	57	51	56	59	55	53	58	56	53	56	57	52	57	55	53	59	Bulgaria	53
Mexico	56	58	55	56	56	57	57	52	58	53	57	59	56	54	62	57	56	60	Moscow	51
Belarus	57	55	59	55	56	60	50	52	64	47	61	58	58	56	55	55	59	55	Hungary	49
Russia	48	48	48	42	49	52	42	48	52	47	50	50	49	50	47	48	49	41	Romania	48
Moscow	51	50	52	51	48	57	44	46	56	52	51	53	54	54	51	48	52	59	Russia	48
Latvia	32	36	30	27	32	39	36	32	33	30	36	31	na	na	na	29	35	35	East Germany	48
Estonia	36	40	33	36	36	36	36	32	36	36	37	36	na	na	na	37	37	48	Netherlands	48
Portugal	60	59	61	59	57	65	59	65	61	61	61	58	66	59	67	63	60	65	Lithuania	47
South Korea	28	21	33	21	32	27	22	23	36	26	27	36	23	26	30	27	28	28	Italy	47
Ireland	30	28	31	28	24	37	27	29	48	28	29	31	32	30	33	27	30	34	United States	42
North Ireland	22	23	22	21	19	27	20	25	31	22	19	25	14	23	23	22	23	22	Sweden	42
Slovenia	63	63	63	58	62	66	61	65	63	64	64	61	66	61	68	66	62	59	Japan	42
Spain	40	43	38	41	40	40	37	47	49	36	42	49	44	41	41	34	43	49	Canada	41
East Germany	48	48	48	43	48	50	45	54	53	50	47	46	51	46	45	51	45	52	Spain	40
Britain	30	30	29	27	29	32	25	34	49	31	28	36	36	29	26	27	27	28	Estonia	36
Italy	47	47	46	46	47	47	46	55	51	48	47	46	46	50	43	46	45	40	Norway	36
Netherlands	48	53	47	42	47	56	47	43	55	49	49	45	51	46	51	49	47	48	West Germany	35
Belgium	32	32	32	30	30	34	31	30	37	32	31	29	32	31	33	27	32	35	Latvia	32
Austria	32	29	34	34	29	33	33	30	33	32	32	33	36	30	32	31	32	33	Belgium	32
France	32	32	25	27	26	20	27	27	33	25	30	20	27	29	26	21	30	34	Austria	32
Canada	41	41	40	42	39	41	36	38	48	44	39	41	53	41	43	30	40	45	Ireland	30
United States	42	42	41	43	44	40	40	36	52	37	42	46	55	40	41	35	41	49	Britain	30
Iceland	54	56	52	43	56	66	56	52	54	na	na	na	54	57	52	55	53	62	South Korea	28
West Germany	35	32	37	32	32	38	33	32	49	35	34	36	36	33	37	32	35	38	France	28
Denmark	21	20	22	23	21	20	16	19	25	22	21	20	27	19	21	20	19	32	South Africa	23
Finland	20	21	19	20	18	25	23	15	25	18	19	23	22	21	19	32	16	28	North Ireland	22
Norway	36	34	39	31	37	38	39	34	37	40	39	30	40	38	30	36	36	46	Denmark	21
Sweden	42	39	45	42	38	44	47	39	40	45	43	38	44	43	36	39	43	37	Finland	20
Japan	42	45	39	36	43	44	35	39	56	39	39	51	44	45	46	43	45	51		
Switzerland	na	na	na	na	na	na	na	na	na	na	na	na	na	na	na	na	na	na		
Total	**45**	**45**	**45**	**43**	**45**	**48**	**43**	**45**	**50**	**44**	**46**	**46**	**48**	**46**	**46**	**44**	**45**	**49**		

Note: Countries in the left column are ranked according to GNP per capita. / The percentages in the bottom row give each country an equal weight. / na=not ascertained.

V108 GENEROUS HOLIDAYS

Here are some aspects of a job that people say are important. Please look at them and tell me which ones you personally think are important in a job? (% "mentioned") "Generous holidays"

Country	Total	Gender Male	Gender Female	Age 16-29	Age 30-49	Age 50+	Education Lower	Education Medium	Education Upper	Income Lower	Income Middle	Income Upper	Political Affinity Left	Political Affinity Center	Political Affinity Right	Values Mat	Values Mixed	Values Postmat
India	28	27	29	28	28	27	26	30	26	28	27	26	22	28	30	29	29	19
Nigeria	51	50	53	52	52	47	55	54	46	50	50	52	55	43	57	54	50	49
China	15	12	19	18	15	12	16	13	19	11	18	18	na	na	na	14	16	22
Romania	35	34	35	42	36	29	35	40	25	31	38	33	36	35	37	34	36	27
Turkey	44	42	46	49	40	44	48	37	39	48	42	42	40	44	47	44	48	35
Poland	na	na	na	na	na	na	na	na	na	na	na	na	na	na	na	na	na	na
Bulgaria	33	27	38	41	33	27	32	35	28	31	38	30	28	36	32	40	30	29
Chile	23	24	22	17	24	28	27	22	19	25	23	18	21	23	23	22	22	23
Czechoslovakia	38	38	38	42	41	32	41	37	34	38	38	38	33	40	38	41	37	36
South Africa	08	08	08	09	09	04	10	07	06	12	07	04	10	06	09	08	08	10
Lithuania	40	36	44	43	41	38	43	39	40	39	44	36	na	na	na	44	39	41
Hungary	37	37	37	39	38	36	37	37	38	36	38	34	36	38	35	39	36	33
Argentina	30	34	27	29	31	30	30	33	27	28	27	30	27	31	31	32	29	31
Brazil	18	17	18	18	16	20	27	15	10	24	17	13	16	14	23	19	18	12
Mexico	33	34	31	32	32	34	36	32	23	35	31	27	29	30	35	36	31	26
Belarus	53	49	57	55	53	53	54	57	49	52	52	56	54	51	63	56	52	48
Russia	43	40	45	47	46	37	45	45	39	46	44	39	37	44	51	47	41	34
Moscow	46	40	51	46	50	40	50	48	44	47	45	46	46	46	38	48	44	53
Latvia	31	31	31	30	34	26	30	31	30	29	35	29	na	na	na	34	30	21
Estonia	32	32	32	40	32	23	33	34	24	30	36	31	na	na	na	35	30	31
Portugal	47	47	48	45	40	57	51	43	36	55	45	37	49	47	51	52	47	38
South Korea	08	09	07	08	09	05	11	09	06	09	10	03	10	08	07	08	08	08
Ireland	29	28	29	32	26	29	30	27	31	30	33	25	40	26	30	32	29	24
North Ireland	27	33	23	20	23	17	30	24	17	31	24	30	29	25	28	32	26	33
Slovenia	29	29	29	29	29	21	30	31	23	31	28	26	29	28	29	30	28	29
Spain	32	34	29	33	29	32	31	33	34	32	33	33	35	26	33	31	32	33
East Germany	29	32	26	34	28	26	30	30	24	27	33	27	26	29	33	39	27	28
Britain	25	28	23	25	26	25	25	20	32	25	25	25	29	26	19	21	26	25
Italy	19	24	15	14	15	25	23	23	16	20	18	16	22	18	18	17	22	19
Netherlands	35	37	35	37	33	36	37	37	33	39	33	35	22	32	33	47	34	33
Belgium	30	30	30	31	31	28	29	32	27	28	34	31	32	27	28	31	30	28
Austria	16	17	15	19	16	15	15	16	15	15	16	16	17	17	16	18	16	15
France	15	15	14	19	16	14	16	12	16	14	18	14	16	13	11	16	15	14
Canada	26	28	23	24	27	26	29	26	24	27	27	21	29	26	24	19	27	22
United States	31	30	30	29	33	29	35	31	27	29	31	35	34	28	33	35	30	29
Iceland	17	20	13	17	17	17	18	15	16	na	na	na	16	17	17	19	15	16
West Germany	34	36	32	44	38	25	32	38	32	29	39	36	37	33	28	28	33	39
Denmark	17	19	14	25	19	13	13	19	18	16	18	18	20	19	13	16	21	17
Finland	20	22	18	15	19	15	22	18	23	13	23	23	20	17	22	21	16	18
Norway	09	09	08	09	09	09	09	08	10	07	09	11	09	10	07	10	08	13
Sweden	35	34	37	37	33	35	39	33	32	42	31	31	34	36	33	30	38	31
Japan	52	51	53	69	56	34	39	54	60	47	54	53	50	51	50	55	56	52
Switzerland	na	na	na	na	na	na	na	na	na	na	na	na	na	na	na	na	na	na
Total	**30**	**30**	**30**	**32**	**30**	**27**	**31**	**30**	**27**	**30**	**31**	**29**	**30**	**29**	**30**	**31**	**30**	**28**

Ranking:

Belarus	53
Japan	52
Nigeria	51
Portugal	47
Moscow	46
Turkey	44
Russia	43
Lithuania	40
Czechoslovakia	38
Hungary	37
Romania	35
Netherlands	35
Sweden	35
West Germany	34
Bulgaria	33
Mexico	33
Estonia	32
Spain	32
Latvia	31
United States	31
Argentina	30
Belgium	30
Ireland	29
Slovenia	29
East Germany	29
India	28
North Ireland	27
Canada	26
Britain	25
Chile	23
Finland	20
Italy	19
Brazil	18
Iceland	17
Denmark	17
Austria	16
China	15
France	15
Norway	09
South Africa	08
South Korea	08

Note: Countries in the left column are ranked according to GNP per capita. / The percentages in the bottom row give each country an equal weight. / na=not ascertained.

V109 MEET PEOPLE

Here are some aspects of a job that people say are important. Please look at them and tell me which ones you personally think are important in a job? "Meeting people" (% "mentioned")

	Total	Gender		Age			Education			Income			Political Affinity			Values		
		Male	Female	16-29	30-49	50+	Lower	Medium	Upper	Lower	Middle	Upper	Left	Center	Right	Mat	Mixed	Postmat
India	45	48	42	48	45	38	32	49	48	43	42	49	51	47	45	48	47	49
Nigeria	68	71	64	67	69	65	68	67	69	65	68	68	69	63	71	66	69	75
China	26	27	23	28	28	19	25	28	22	26	29	23	na	na	na	21	30	32
Romania	27	24	29	33	25	24	24	29	27	25	25	30	28	30	26	24	28	36
Turkey	68	75	62	72	69	61	65	72	78	65	66	75	70	71	66	56	71	76
Poland	na	na	na	na	na	na	na	na	na	na	na	na	na	na	na	na	na	na
Bulgaria	44	43	45	49	45	39	32	51	44	38	49	50	44	47	48	44	44	54
Chile	39	39	39	40	36	42	44	39	34	40	41	33	36	39	39	39	39	38
Czechoslovakia	54	50	58	59	53	54	58	54	47	55	54	54	56	54	55	52	55	57
South Africa	na	na	na	na	na	na	na	na	na	na	na	na	na	na	na	na	na	na
Lithuania	59	52	65	57	58	61	60	58	59	59	61	54	na	na	na	53	61	59
Hungary	40	36	44	39	37	43	40	38	48	40	39	39	41	40	45	43	37	48
Argentina	50	50	49	47	49	52	49	51	49	49	48	48	47	49	50	51	49	51
Brazil	42	40	43	41	39	47	49	40	35	49	45	37	40	39	44	42	40	48
Mexico	47	46	48	47	44	51	48	47	41	45	45	48	40	51	46	49	46	42
Belarus	53	49	57	53	51	58	49	52	56	49	55	55	53	54	55	55	52	58
Russia	27	26	28	28	27	26	24	27	29	23	27	29	22	28	27	26	27	25
Moscow	48	44	52	51	46	49	46	53	46	49	49	45	52	46	40	48	48	53
Latvia	39	31	43	39	38	38	38	40	36	40	35	41	46	42	na	38	43	25
Estonia	57	46	66	58	57	56	53	61	52	58	58	55	na	na	na	55	58	64
Portugal	53	52	55	57	52	51	52	58	56	51	54	56	52	56	57	55	53	58
South Korea	24	24	24	24	26	17	20	32	17	25	24	24	18	27	23	24	25	21
Ireland	35	31	39	41	30	36	34	36	37	25	37	31	35	29	48	38	35	31
North Ireland	16	16	17	12	18	18	15	21	10	22	20	10	11	17	19	22	16	09
Slovenia	56	57	56	67	56	50	54	60	53	57	56	54	51	60	64	58	55	60
Spain	35	38	33	40	35	33	35	35	38	31	39	40	38	35	37	32	36	44
East Germany	50	41	58	51	49	51	51	49	48	51	52	49	52	49	45	51	49	52
Britain	43	39	48	51	44	39	42	46	47	42	43	48	42	44	40	45	43	46
Italy	43	43	44	52	46	36	42	51	57	42	44	49	46	42	45	35	45	51
Netherlands	71	67	73	75	72	68	62	76	78	69	73	78	77	71	72	61	69	80
Belgium	45	43	48	54	46	39	42	43	54	40	40	51	47	46	46	37	46	52
Austria	39	37	41	45	41	35	38	39	50	35	41	43	47	37	40	38	38	43
France	39	33	45	48	41	30	34	46	41	36	47	40	41	41	39	36	40	44
Canada	42	41	44	45	41	41	42	43	42	48	40	41	47	44	37	28	45	39
United States	38	33	43	38	35	40	41	36	38	41	34	39	43	37	36	33	38	41
Iceland	59	52	66	67	54	58	59	59	59	50	53	na	59	58	61	67	56	58
West Germany	55	50	59	58	56	51	53	55	64	50	53	62	53	55	53	44	55	60
Denmark	43	41	45	51	45	36	34	47	45	43	43	42	44	42	43	40	43	52
Finland	30	30	30	44	24	34	28	28	33	28	34	28	25	22	37	24	29	33
Norway	41	37	46	41	40	43	44	42	38	42	42	34	41	42	39	38	43	41
Sweden	64	61	67	71	61	62	63	66	60	66	59	63	61	67	63	62	65	63
Japan	48	45	50	55	47	43	36	49	56	41	46	57	47	46	51	48	48	56
Switzerland	na	na	na	na	na	na	na	na	na	na	na	na	na	na	na	na	na	na
Total	45	43	47	49	44	43	43	47	46	44	45	45	45	45	46	43	45	48

Ranking:

Netherlands	71
Nigeria	68
Turkey	68
Sweden	64
Lithuania	59
Iceland	59
Estonia	57
Slovenia	56
West Germany	55
Czechoslovakia	54
Belarus	53
Portugal	53
Argentina	50
East Germany	50
Moscow	48
Japan	48
Mexico	47
India	45
Belgium	45
Bulgaria	44
Britain	43
Italy	43
Denmark	43
Brazil	42
Canada	42
Norway	41
Hungary	40
Chile	39
Latvia	39
Austria	39
France	39
United States	38
Ireland	35
Spain	35
Finland	30
Romania	27
Russia	27
China	26
South Korea	24
North Ireland	16

Note: Countries in the left column are ranked according to GNP per capita. / The percentages in the bottom row give each country an equal weight. / na=not ascertained.

V110 ACHIEVE SOMETHING

Here are some aspects of a job that people say are important. Please look at them and tell me which ones you personally think are important in a job? "A job in which you feel you can achieve something" (% "mentioned")

	Total	Gender		Age			Education			Income			Political Affinity			Values		
		Male	Female	16-29	30-49	50+	Lower	Medium	Upper	Lower	Middle	Upper	Left	Center	Right	Mat	Mixed	Postmat
India	61	63	59	65	60	53	44	63	67	54	57	69	63	na	64	63	64	69
Nigeria	91	92	91	93	91	90	92	91	92	90	91	94	95	90	93	90	93	95
China	38	40	34	43	37	33	27	38	53	36	39	39	60	na	na	29	45	65
Romania	63	63	63	66	64	60	56	64	70	57	64	65	na	65	65	62	62	78
Turkey	86	89	84	88	88	79	83	90	95	84	86	89	88	89	85	80	87	91
Poland	na	na	na	na	na	na	na	na	na	na	na	na	na	na	na	na	na	na
Bulgaria	42	45	39	50	45	34	28	46	50	39	44	47	45	45	48	41	41	64
Chile	58	59	58	62	56	57	58	60	58	56	60	59	59	57	60	56	59	61
Czechoslovakia	48	51	45	51	49	44	43	51	50	45	50	49	50	45	53	40	50	57
South Africa	na	na	na	na	na	na	na	na	na	na	na	na	na	na	na	na	na	na
Lithuania	44	47	42	44	43	47	50	42	48	43	42	50	na	na	na	38	47	47
Hungary	58	58	58	64	60	54	48	67	69	52	59	69	65	60	61	61	55	70
Argentina	50	54	47	52	50	49	46	51	57	51	44	57	51	54	54	51	48	57
Brazil	53	51	54	49	54	56	54	50	58	51	54	53	50	55	53	54	50	60
Mexico	66	67	65	66	66	65	66	64	69	64	64	74	65	69	67	64	67	68
Belarus	42	43	42	48	40	40	36	40	47	35	42	50	41	43	50	41	43	41
Russia	28	32	24	34	28	23	19	27	33	23	27	33	34	28	32	23	31	30
Moscow	41	44	38	46	42	36	31	34	47	39	43	42	46	38	31	37	41	53
Latvia	27	34	22	34	24	23	26	23	33	22	27	28	na	na	na	20	28	31
Estonia	43	46	39	45	45	37	34	40	57	44	40	43	65	na	na	38	45	56
Portugal	68	68	67	75	65	63	63	77	78	63	66	76	65	69	73	64	71	77
South Korea	24	18	29	30	23	16	10	18	38	18	24	34	29	24	24	18	26	40
Ireland	60	60	60	63	59	59	53	66	79	52	60	66	60	59	66	57	59	67
North Ireland	74	73	66	71	66	51	55	71	83	54	66	69	61	65	59	54	64	71
Slovenia	71	74	68	75	74	65	65	76	80	69	69	77	70	73	77	69	71	77
Spain	39	44	35	45	40	34	36	46	49	34	42	44	43	39	40	33	42	47
East Germany	68	69	67	69	74	62	65	68	80	59	70	74	71	66	65	63	68	71
Britain	66	64	68	69	68	63	60	77	85	59	69	78	65	64	75	65	66	70
Italy	51	53	50	61	54	43	50	60	65	47	52	70	54	48	54	41	51	62
Netherlands	45	50	43	54	39	37	38	44	53	45	44	47	42	49	45	43	47	43
Belgium	40	39	39	45	38	39	38	41	43	36	34	47	38	41	44	32	42	43
Austria	49	52	47	59	49	44	47	49	57	43	49	55	53	48	50	39	49	54
France	42	41	43	42	44	40	39	45	43	38	43	47	46	43	43	42	41	47
Canada	74	73	74	74	76	71	65	75	79	70	75	77	77	73	75	58	75	77
United States	71	73	69	71	71	72	66	68	80	68	71	77	73	71	77	65	71	77
Iceland	83	83	82	83	86	77	79	82	86	85	84	85	84	83	82	82	83	85
West Germany	62	65	59	65	63	59	60	64	72	55	62	68	59	64	65	55	62	67
Denmark	55	55	56	61	57	49	47	59	58	52	56	58	59	52	60	53	55	61
Finland	54	57	52	61	52	56	51	50	61	49	56	58	52	55	56	50	52	61
Norway	69	66	73	75	71	64	56	67	79	64	71	70	71	67	72	64	71	77
Sweden	85	80	89	80	88	84	84	83	88	85	84	85	82	84	88	81	86	85
Japan	48	50	45	57	51	36	31	49	62	39	50	58	55	51	49	49	51	58
Switzerland	na	na	na	na	na	na	na	na	na	na	na	na	na	na	na	na	na	na
Total	**56**	**57**	**55**	**60**	**56**	**52**	**50**	**57**	**64**	**51**	**55**	**60**	**59**	**58**	**60**	**52**	**56**	**63**

Ranking:

Country	%	Country	%
Nigeria	91	Brazil	53
Turkey	86	Italy	51
Sweden	85	Argentina	50
Iceland	83	Austria	49
Canada	74	Czechoslovakia	48
Slovenia	71	Japan	48
United States	71	Netherlands	45
Norway	69	Lithuania	44
Portugal	68	Estonia	43
East Germany	68	Bulgaria	42
Mexico	66	Belarus	42
Britain	66	France	42
Romania	63	Moscow	41
North Ireland	62	Belgium	40
West Germany	62	Spain	39
India	61	China	38
Ireland	60	Russia	28
Chile	58	Latvia	27
Hungary	58	South Korea	24
Denmark	55		
Finland	54		

Note: Countries in the left column are ranked according to GNP per capita. / The percentages in the bottom row give each country an equal weight. / na=not ascertained.

V111 RESPONSIBLE JOB

Here are some aspects of a job that people say are important. Please look at them and tell me which ones you personally think are important in a job? "A responsible job" (% "mentioned")

		Gender		Age			Education			Income			Political Affinity			Values		
	Total	Male	Female	16-29	30-49	50+	Lower	Medium	Upper	Lower	Middle	Upper	Left	Center	Right	Mat	Mixed	Postmat
India	65	68	60	68	65	57	49	66	70	60	64	68	70	66	64	69	67	65
Nigeria	84	84	83	86	81	93	83	85	83	83	83	81	79	81	88	80	86	88
China	22	25	18	21	24	21	23	22	23	23	26	19	na	na	na	19	25	30
Romania	28	30	26	30	30	25	21	29	35	23	28	32	26	29	32	24	30	40
Turkey	78	83	74	77	82	72	73	84	90	74	78	84	79	82	75	71	79	86
Poland	na	na	na	na	na	na	na	na	na	na	na	na	na	na	na	na	na	na
Bulgaria	28	33	24	27	28	27	19	30	34	22	31	34	30	31	32	29	28	28
Chile	52	57	48	52	50	57	53	50	54	50	55	50	53	53	50	52	51	57
Czechoslovakia	48	51	45	38	48	55	48	46	53	48	49	47	53	45	48	42	51	43
South Africa	25	28	22	24	26	25	26	25	26	24	25	26	26	22	27	25	25	28
Lithuania	24	25	22	15	21	33	34	21	18	25	22	23	na	na	na	21	24	22
Hungary	51	51	51	41	53	53	46	54	60	48	52	52	53	55	55	53	49	50
Argentina	58	62	55	55	59	60	55	60	59	60	57	57	56	62	54	62	56	59
Brazil	59	61	57	58	58	65	60	59	59	58	61	60	57	61	61	60	58	62
Mexico	57	57	57	56	56	63	58	55	55	55	58	59	51	60	60	59	56	56
Belarus	27	31	24	23	27	32	35	23	28	23	27	32	26	27	32	30	26	23
Russia	21	22	20	15	22	23	17	21	22	19	21	23	20	18	23	21	21	10
Moscow	22	25	19	16	22	25	26	21	21	23	21	21	21	21	27	22	22	19
Latvia	12	13	12	13	13	10	13	13	11	14	10	12	na	na	na	10	14	12
Estonia	17	19	15	15	18	17	16	16	20	16	15	19	na	na	na	16	17	25
Portugal	54	56	52	56	56	50	53	55	57	52	58	52	51	55	59	56	55	53
South Korea	23	21	24	20	25	21	19	28	18	23	24	23	21	23	22	23	22	17
Ireland	41	40	41	47	35	42	36	44	53	36	37	46	46	37	47	40	40	43
North Ireland	35	41	30	38	30	37	30	44	41	34	25	44	29	32	42	43	34	31
Slovenia	53	58	48	52	52	54	51	53	55	53	50	60	55	51	63	54	50	68
Spain	32	36	29	29	34	33	31	36	35	30	35	36	33	36	37	31	35	32
East Germany	49	52	46	47	51	48	45	52	61	45	43	57	54	50	42	44	49	52
Britain	42	45	39	39	45	40	37	50	59	36	43	53	37	41	48	49	38	47
Italy	32	39	26	35	33	30	32	36	31	32	32	38	31	32	34	30	34	31
Netherlands	43	59	37	45	38	47	33	43	54	41	43	51	40	45	47	32	44	43
Belgium	38	42	34	43	38	35	33	39	46	35	38	42	35	41	43	34	39	40
Austria	45	52	41	47	46	43	45	45	47	41	45	48	45	46	45	42	45	48
France	53	56	51	56	51	54	48	57	61	47	52	64	49	58	61	47	54	59
Canada	56	58	55	58	57	54	52	57	58	58	53	60	58	56	55	54	57	55
United States	56	56	56	54	57	56	54	53	62	50	58	62	58	57	58	56	55	60
Iceland	36	40	32	41	34	34	33	36	37	na	54	63	33	32	41	36	35	45
West Germany	54	61	47	52	56	52	50	56	68	45	54	63	51	55	59	45	55	58
Denmark	42	46	39	52	43	32	29	46	47	36	49	46	43	38	49	36	44	47
Finland	30	33	26	38	27	29	35	23	35	32	26	32	25	25	36	38	27	34
Norway	43	44	43	48	41	42	40	43	45	41	46	46	41	40	49	44	43	47
Sweden	72	71	72	73	69	73	71	71	73	75	69	72	64	72	77	67	72	72
Japan	48	52	45	42	52	46	39	48	58	42	49	58	52	46	58	51	53	56
Switzerland	na	na	na	na	na	na	na	na	na	na	na	na	na	na	na	na	na	na
Total	43	46	40	43	43	43	40	44	47	41	43	46	45	45	49	42	43	45

Ranking:

Country	%
Nigeria	84
Turkey	78
Sweden	72
India	65
Brazil	59
Argentina	58
Mexico	57
Canada	56
United States	56
Portugal	54
West Germany	54
Slovenia	53
France	53
Chile	52
Hungary	51
East Germany	49
Czechoslovakia	48
Japan	48
Austria	45
Netherlands	43
Norway	43
Britain	42
Denmark	42
Ireland	41
Belgium	38
Iceland	36
North Ireland	35
Spain	32
Italy	32
Finland	30
Romania	28
Bulgaria	28
Belarus	27
South Africa	25
Lithuania	24
South Korea	23
China	22
Moscow	22
Russia	21
Estonia	17
Latvia	12

Note: Countries in the left column are ranked according to GNP per capita. / The percentages in the bottom row give each country an equal weight. / na=not ascertained.

V112   JOB INTERESTING

Here are some aspects of a job that people say are important. Please look at them and tell me which ones you personally think are important in a job? "A job that is interesting" (% "mentioned")

	Total	Gender		Age			Education			Income			Political Affinity			Values		
		Male	Female	16-29	30-49	50+	Lower	Medium	Upper	Lower	Middle	Upper	Left	Center	Right	Mat	Mixed	Postmat
India	64	65	64	70	63	54	50	67	68	62	65	66	64	66	65	68	66	63
Nigeria	83	82	84	85	82	77	82	85	81	82	65	83	79	81	87	82	84	86
China	34	34	34	41	32	28	32	33	42	33	36	33	na	na	na	27	40	48
Romania	43	44	42	51	43	38	36	46	49	36	46	45	39	44	52	41	43	58
Turkey	49	49	48	52	47	47	50	44	54	44	48	53	44	54	48	44	52	45
Poland	na	na	na	na	na	na	na	na	na	na	na	na	na	na	na	na	na	na
Bulgaria	51	51	52	61	56	40	32	56	65	45	57	58	52	53	58	48	52	67
Chile	50	54	47	51	48	53	49	49	54	48	50	52	49	49	55	46	51	52
Czechoslovakia	69	68	70	71	70	66	65	70	75	68	69	70	68	69	71	68	68	73
South Africa	na	na	na	na	na	na	na	na	na	na	na	na	na	na	na	na	na	na
Lithuania	64	68	60	73	61	59	61	64	66	62	63	70	na	na	na	59	65	71
Hungary	51	52	51	60	54	45	38	61	76	42	56	64	59	53	53	52	50	63
Argentina	51	52	50	51	51	50	45	55	53	50	45	52	57	53	45	53	48	56
Brazil	46	44	48	48	42	48	51	44	42	48	48	42	45	45	46	49	44	44
Mexico	60	59	61	61	59	59	59	57	64	55	61	66	56	61	62	58	61	61
Belarus	73	72	73	79	71	68	62	73	76	67	75	75	74	72	78	72	73	78
Russia	67	67	67	75	68	61	54	69	72	64	66	72	73	69	69	62	70	73
Moscow	69	71	67	77	71	60	64	68	71	71	68	69	71	73	64	65	71	77
Latvia	60	64	57	66	61	49	46	59	65	54	61	62	na	na	na	55	60	68
Estonia	68	68	69	71	71	61	60	69	74	70	68	66	na	na	na	62	71	86
Portugal	53	51	55	58	51	50	50	60	57	52	50	56	53	55	55	56	52	57
South Korea	07	07	07	10	07	03	04	07	09	10	05	07	07	08	06	05	09	09
Ireland	70	68	72	79	65	68	64	76	79	64	72	73	74	70	72	68	70	73
North Ireland	69	70	68	74	66	68	61	79	93	60	68	79	54	70	74	69	69	69
Slovenia	76	76	76	87	77	68	71	80	80	73	77	80	76	79	79	74	76	85
Spain	47	50	43	55	46	41	42	54	62	41	46	56	54	45	50	42	48	56
East Germany	65	66	63	73	64	60	62	66	74	61	62	70	72	62	60	55	65	69
Britain	72	71	74	78	75	67	68	82	83	63	77	82	68	74	75	77	69	78
Italy	56	56	57	61	59	51	56	64	58	53	60	67	58	58	55	51	57	63
Netherlands	60	71	57	69	56	57	41	68	75	53	62	72	70	58	59	43	61	66
Belgium	47	48	46	54	47	42	41	47	58	45	48	49	53	47	48	42	47	50
Austria	56	60	53	68	58	48	52	56	73	50	55	62	53	57	57	51	53	66
France	59	57	61	67	61	50	52	64	67	52	57	70	65	59	62	45	62	66
Canada	72	72	73	75	73	69	62	73	80	71	74	75	78	73	73	66	73	74
United States	69	69	70	74	71	66	61	67	78	65	67	75	77	70	65	66	67	79
Iceland	76	76	77	84	76	68	76	81	76	81	na	na	77	71	80	73	77	80
West Germany	71	73	69	79	77	62	68	75	81	66	72	76	74	73	69	60	81	81
Denmark	63	67	59	78	67	47	39	67	74	53	68	72	67	61	65	54	65	70
Finland	65	64	66	80	63	57	68	58	73	66	64	65	67	60	69	59	63	71
Norway	64	65	63	77	63	57	52	64	70	63	66	67	60	62	70	61	64	71
Sweden	80	80	79	84	80	77	72	83	85	81	77	81	77	79	83	73	80	84
Japan	36	41	33	58	35	24	20	37	51	30	36	42	34	38	37	36	40	44
Switzerland	na	na	na	na	na	na	na	na	na	na	na	na	na	na	na	na	na	na
Total	60	61	59	67	60	54	53	62	67	56	60	63	61	60	62	56	60	66

Ranking:

Nigeria	83
Sweden	80
Slovenia	76
Iceland	76
Belarus	73
Britain	72
Canada	72
West Germany	71
Ireland	70
Czechoslovakia	69
Moscow	69
North Ireland	69
United States	69
Estonia	68
Russia	67
East Germany	65
Finland	65
India	64
Lithuania	64
Norway	64
Denmark	63
Mexico	60
Latvia	60
Netherlands	60
France	59
Italy	56
Austria	56
Portugal	53
Bulgaria	51
Hungary	51
Argentina	51
Chile	50
Turkey	49
Spain	47
Belgium	47
Brazil	46
Romania	43
Japan	36
China	34
South Korea	07

Note: Countries in the left column are ranked according to GNP per capita. / The percentages in the bottom row give each country an equal weight. / na=not ascertained.

V113 MEETS ABILITIES

Here are some aspects of a job that people say are important. Please look at them and tell me which ones you personally think are important in a job? "A job that meets one's abilities" (% "mentioned")

	Total	Gender Male	Gender Female	Age 16-29	Age 30-49	Age 50+	Education Lower	Education Medium	Education Upper	Income Lower	Income Middle	Income Upper	Political Affinity Left	Political Affinity Center	Political Affinity Right	Values Mat	Values Mixed	Values Postmat	Ranking:	
India	67	69	65	70	67	61	52	70	71	62	67	71	72	65	65	74	67	67	Turkey	90
Nigeria	86	87	86	88	84	86	88	87	85	88	86	86	84	87	89	85	87	92	Nigeria	86
China	66	65	66	66	66	64	57	68	75	65	66	67	na	na	na	63	69	69	Czechoslovakia	81
Romania	52	53	51	59	56	44	37	57	65	46	52	58	42	54	61	45	55	73	Netherlands	74
Turkey	90	92	88	92	91	85	87	93	98	85	91	93	91	91	91	87	89	96	Iceland	72
Poland	na	na	na	na	na	na	na	na	na	na	na	na	na	na	na	na	na	na	Japan	71
Bulgaria	52	52	51	52	49	54	59	52	45	51	54	52	47	53	53	57	51	50	West Germany	70
Chile	59	59	59	57	57	64	61	59	55	58	61	56	57	59	57	61	58	57	India	67
Czechoslovakia	81	81	81	76	82	83	78	81	85	82	82	79	83	79	82	80	81	83	China	66
South Africa	32	28	34	32	30	34	28	32	42	28	29	40	34	35	33	32	31	34	Hungary	66
Lithuania	56	60	52	51	57	58	57	55	56	53	59	55	na	na	na	49	57	62	Brazil	66
Hungary	66	64	67	55	70	65	58	72	74	61	66	77	70	71	67	69	63	65	Mexico	65
Argentina	59	62	55	56	59	60	56	62	61	58	57	58	52	65	61	57	60	57	East Germany	65
Brazil	66	65	66	66	68	61	60	68	69	62	67	70	65	67	68	64	67	64	Slovenia	61
Mexico	65	64	65	67	64	60	64	61	68	60	68	68	65	66	66	63	65	72	Chile	59
Belarus	50	48	51	51	51	44	37	47	57	43	50	55	50	48	52	47	50	56	Argentina	59
Russia	54	53	56	56	57	50	43	57	59	51	55	58	57	53	47	53	55	63	Austria	58
Moscow	38	40	38	41	40	33	20	34	45	35	40	41	41	40	29	39	37	46	Portugal	57
Latvia	44	44	45	42	45	46	48	43	46	42	45	46	na	na	na	41	47	47	United States	57
Estonia	55	56	53	50	57	55	55	55	54	57	51	54	65	62	72	50	58	71	Lithuania	56
Portugal	57	60	55	61	56	55	54	63	65	53	59	61	63	57	60	56	59	68	Canada	56
South Korea	31	28	33	21	34	37	36	32	26	29	34	31	31	28	31	32	32	19	Denmark	56
Ireland	50	50	50	52	49	50	44	55	66	42	53	54	51	47	59	44	49	61	Estonia	55
North Ireland	41	41	40	37	39	46	35	54	61	37	37	52	32	41	43	43	44	33	Russia	54
Slovenia	61	62	60	62	65	55	51	68	68	57	62	69	63	62	72	61	60	74	Italy	54
Spain	46	48	45	48	45	45	45	46	52	42	46	55	47	45	49	45	48	50	Sweden	53
East Germany	65	67	64	68	67	62	54	75	76	58	67	69	72	63	60	54	67	66	Romania	52
Britain	42	44	40	41	45	40	38	46	60	37	42	49	39	42	46	39	42	44	Bulgaria	52
Italy	54	58	51	53	53	56	54	55	61	56	53	63	55	55	53	49	57	57	Belarus	50
Netherlands	74	78	72	79	71	72	63	72	88	72	77	82	79	75	74	61	73	81	Ireland	50
Belgium	49	53	46	57	49	45	43	47	66	43	45	58	50	51	53	35	50	62	Belgium	49
Austria	58	60	57	65	56	56	54	60	63	54	57	63	62	63	59	52	57	63	Spain	46
France	43	45	41	45	42	42	38	48	46	39	43	49	44	45	45	36	42	54	Finland	45
Canada	56	55	58	55	57	57	54	55	61	58	57	56	59	57	57	44	58	59	Latvia	44
United States	57	57	57	56	54	59	55	52	64	55	55	60	65	57	55	54	57	58	France	43
Iceland	72	72	71	77	69	70	63	74	76	na	na	na	70	74	72	71	70	80	Norway	43
West Germany	70	74	68	75	71	67	68	70	83	66	73	73	73	71	67	62	71	76	Britain	42
Denmark	56	57	55	61	59	50	49	60	57	54	58	59	59	52	58	53	57	59	North Ireland	41
Finland	45	44	45	57	40	47	47	37	53	41	46	47	38	44	49	53	43	48	Moscow	38
Norway	43	40	45	47	37	46	43	39	46	46	44	38	40	44	45	42	43	48	South Africa	32
Sweden	53	51	56	53	50	57	52	54	57	55	54	53	45	55	57	41	55	53	South Korea	31
Japan	71	70	72	77	70	68	63	73	74	66	70	76	75	70	73	72	73	68		
Switzerland	na	na	na	na	na	na	na	na	na	na	na	na	na	na	na	na	na	na		
Total	57	57	56	58	57	56	53	58	63	54	57	60	57	57	58	54	57	61		

Note: Countries in the left column are ranked according to GNP per capita. / The percentages in the bottom row give each country an equal weight. / na=not ascertained.

V115. How much pride, if any, do you take in the work that you do?

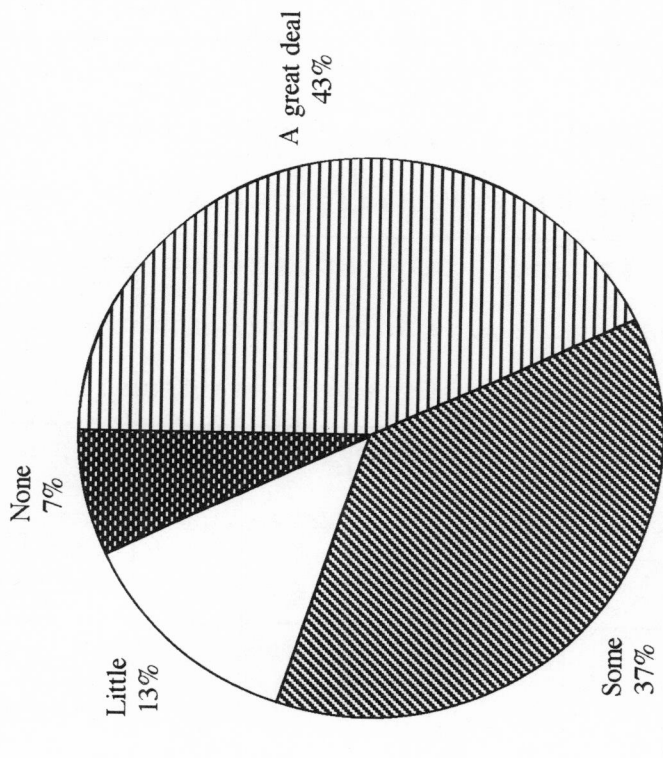

A great deal
43%

Some
37%

Little
13%

None
7%

V115 PRIDE IN WORK

How much pride, if any, do you take in the work that you do? A great deal, some, little, none. (% "a great deal")

	Total	Gender		Age			Education			Income			Political Affinity			Values		
		Male	Female	16-29	30-49	50+	Lower	Medium	Upper	Lower	Middle	Upper	Left	Center	Right	Mat	Mixed	Postmat
India	51	51	50	46	53	49	34	47	59	38	48	63	50	52	57	52	52	52
Nigeria	65	63	70	60	69	69	57	59	74	54	68	78	64	61	66	68	63	66
China	23	26	17	21	21	27	18	25	22	22	25	20	na	na	na	23	23	13
Romania	19	24	14	13	20	30	32	11	24	20	16	23	20	21	16	17	22	12
Turkey	39	37	43	34	40	45	36	32	56	28	37	47	43	33	36	30	38	47
Poland	36	40	32	24	35	49	44	32	41	31	35	43	38	33	40	40	35	36
Bulgaria	19	21	17	17	17	26	20	17	23	13	19	26	16	23	26	18	20	23
Chile	65	67	62	65	65	67	66	62	68	58	64	73	59	65	75	64	64	70
Czechoslovakia	14	14	14	13	11	20	15	14	12	15	14	12	14	14	14	13	14	12
South Africa	68	65	72	60	70	70	51	69	90	40	63	88	68	77	73	73	64	65
Lithuania	19	20	18	13	16	29	26	15	30	21	17	20	na	na	na	23	17	21
Hungary	28	29	28	26	28	32	24	32	30	27	29	31	28	28	34	30	27	26
Argentina	66	63	70	52	69	75	71	61	66	59	68	65	53	67	66	69	68	59
Brazil	49	48	51	39	53	64	56	48	43	51	50	47	40	46	58	52	47	44
Mexico	49	49	50	43	54	49	46	48	60	39	52	64	46	55	55	45	51	56
Belarus	20	20	21	11	20	34	22	19	22	18	18	26	21	19	24	23	19	22
Russia	19	21	17	14	17	28	21	16	20	17	19	23	17	17	28	21	17	20
Moscow	28	30	27	20	25	41	44	28	26	30	28	27	25	28	45	40	25	29
Latvia	08	12	05	09	06	13	10	08	08	09	08	08	na	na	na	08	07	08
Estonia	13	13	13	11	13	15	09	12	18	11	10	18	11	na	12	13	14	12
Portugal	72	72	72	60	77	83	71	74	74	68	73	76	68	71	76	71	72	68
South Korea	24	20	27	25	23	27	19	20	32	18	25	33	21	21	27	20	27	28
Ireland	78	79	77	68	82	85	79	76	84	81	74	82	72	77	87	81	78	75
North Ireland	81	81	82	69	84	91	83	80	73	87	85	75	64	82	88	80	80	89
Slovenia	29	31	26	25	31	27	37	28	22	30	30	24	27	28	25	33	29	13
Spain	45	47	41	44	42	53	43	50	48	40	40	51	40	51	58	45	46	44
East Germany	33	31	36	32	34	34	35	31	37	31	34	34	44	34	30	28	35	32
Britain	84	83	85	76	87	89	83	85	88	82	84	87	80	84	87	90	83	82
Italy	31	32	29	29	30	35	32	27	21	26	33	24	25	32	41	41	30	26
Netherlands	29	36	26	24	31	38	34	26	28	33	30	20	29	28	27	34	32	26
Belgium	35	33	38	35	34	37	33	38	32	28	39	36	29	35	45	34	35	35
Austria	33	31	36	32	34	34	35	31	37	31	34	34	44	34	30	28	35	32
France	16	19	12	14	14	21	19	14	13	17	18	13	12	18	18	16	16	16
Canada	74	74	75	72	74	80	74	74	74	64	71	80	75	71	82	65	77	70
United States	88	88	88	80	89	93	87	86	91	86	87	90	91	89	88	83	88	91
Iceland	76	75	79	67	80	84	80	73	77	na	na	na	76	71	85	80	74	80
West Germany	18	19	17	15	19	21	19	15	23	10	14	23	14	19	26	17	21	14
Denmark	78	79	76	73	78	84	70	80	78	73	77	81	73	79	82	75	77	80
Finland	59	58	61	51	63	50	53	57	64	57	52	69	47	59	65	50	60	59
Norway	63	65	60	50	70	63	59	60	67	48	65	75	65	58	71	55	66	69
Sweden	72	71	73	57	75	80	69	69	81	72	69	75	73	67	78	72	73	68
Japan	36	40	29	27	37	41	37	33	41	36	35	40	37	34	48	40	35	34
Switzerland	na	na	na	na	na	na	na	na	na	na	na	na	na	na	na	na	na	na
Total	44	44	43	38	45	49	44	42	47	39	43	47	44	47	52	44	44	43

Ranking:

United States	88
Britain	84
North Ireland	81
Ireland	78
Denmark	78
Iceland	76
Canada	74
Portugal	72
Sweden	72
South Africa	68
Argentina	66
Nigeria	65
Chile	65
Norway	63
Finland	59
India	51
Brazil	49
Mexico	49
Spain	45
Turkey	39
Poland	36
Japan	36
Belgium	35
Austria	33
Italy	31
Slovenia	29
Netherlands	29
Hungary	28
Moscow	28
South Korea	24
China	23
East Germany	22
Belarus	20
Romania	19
Bulgaria	19
Lithuania	19
Russia	19
West Germany	18
France	16
Czechoslovakia	14
Estonia	13
Latvia	08

Note: Countries in the left column are ranked according to GNP per capita. / The percentages in the bottom row give each country an equal weight. / na=not ascertained.

V116 JOB SATISFACTION

Overall, how satisfied or dissatisfied are you with your job?

(% "satisfied"—codes 7 to 10 from a ten-point scale where 1=Dissatisfied and 10=Satisfied)

	Total	Gender		Age			Education			Income			Political Affinity			Values			Ranking:	
		Male	Female	16-29	30-49	50+	Lower	Medium	Upper	Lower	Middle	Upper	Left	Center	Right	Mat	Mixed	Postmat		
India	58	58	59	56	60	57	39	58	66	41	63	70	54	56	70	59	61	62	Denmark	88
Nigeria	68	63	78	67	69	71	64	64	73	57	68	87	68	64	66	71	66	70	Switzerland	88
China	63	65	60	50	66	72	62	64	62	62	65	64	na	na	na	67	64	26	Sweden	85
Romania	56	63	49	48	58	66	50	50	70	46	48	72	65	55	55	61	53	59	Canada	82
Turkey	36	35	40	30	42	32	31	33	56	25	30	49	41	34	31	28	38	40	Iceland	82
Poland	78	75	81	80	69	87	84	73	78	75	80	80	79	75	81	82	76	78	United States	81
Bulgaria	47	52	43	42	48	50	47	45	52	33	47	62	43	47	51	50	46	49	Norway	81
Chile	70	72	66	64	72	77	68	70	72	61	69	80	65	72	75	68	69	76	Netherlands	80
Czechoslovakia	58	58	58	51	57	68	58	58	60	55	59	60	62	55	61	62	57	54	Belgium	80
South Africa	64	62	66	58	65	69	46	67	82	33	64	83	63	68	76	66	61	67	Poland	78
Lithuania	61	61	61	54	59	70	70	60	59	58	62	66	na	na	na	67	57	68	Mexico	78
Hungary	66	66	67	60	67	70	62	69	66	62	69	69	69	67	62	67	66	63	Ireland	78
Argentina	72	71	74	66	70	82	76	71	69	66	75	66	63	70	74	74	72	71	North Ireland	78
Brazil	70	71	70	65	73	79	75	70	67	68	75	72	65	67	78	73	68	72	Finland	77
Mexico	78	78	77	76	80	76	74	81	87	71	82	86	77	81	85	74	79	83	Argentina	72
Belarus	44	44	44	32	47	51	48	43	44	41	42	51	45	42	49	49	42	43	West Germany	72
Russia	49	50	48	44	48	55	58	45	49	48	48	54	49	47	60	49	49	45	Britain	71
Moscow	48	51	45	40	47	54	52	46	48	46	46	54	45	47	65	51	49	38	Chile	70
Latvia	52	51	54	54	49	58	53	53	51	51	50	55	na	na	na	52	54	54	Brazil	70
Estonia	58	59	56	53	58	63	53	58	62	56	61	58	na	na	na	58	60	56	Italy	70
Portugal	66	66	65	57	68	79	69	57	65	67	59	71	60	66	75	73	63	59	Nigeria	68
South Korea	57	56	57	60	56	54	54	54	69	44	60	74	52	52	62	55	58	61	Slovenia	68
Ireland	78	81	74	71	79	87	79	78	80	76	81	80	69	78	85	82	77	78	Japan	68
North Ireland	78	77	78	64	82	85	83	67	73	65	78	79	71	83	72	74	78	77	Hungary	66
Slovenia	68	70	64	65	68	70	62	68	71	59	66	85	72	70	65	73	66	67	Portugal	66
Spain	62	65	56	59	63	62	60	65	63	45	57	69	57	60	75	59	64	61	Austria	66
East Germany	62	65	60	57	62	70	66	59	55	61	61	64	59	64	68	68	63	60	South Africa	64
Britain	71	72	70	67	71	77	73	69	66	73	72	69	62	73	75	74	71	67	China	63
Italy	70	72	65	66	69	75	70	73	52	64	72	78	65	70	74	70	71	65	Spain	62
Netherlands	80	84	78	75	81	85	82	76	82	66	71	92	74	82	85	89	84	75	East Germany	62
Belgium	80	79	81	77	80	84	80	81	77	71	80	83	79	79	82	82	81	78	Lithuania	61
Austria	66	71	61	65	68	59	63	66	71	58	66	68	64	67	69	63	64	70	France	59
France	59	57	60	54	60	61	52	58	70	48	59	68	60	55	64	56	60	57	India	58
Canada	82	82	83	79	82	88	78	83	82	71	81	87	79	82	88	90	82	81	Czechoslovakia	58
United States	81	81	81	72	81	88	84	80	81	78	79	84	82	81	84	82	82	79	Estonia	58
Iceland	82	80	83	75	86	83	76	82	85	na	na	na	80	75	88	82	81	83	South Korea	57
West Germany	72	73	71	70	74	73	70	71	84	66	68	79	68	75	79	73	74	71	Romania	56
Denmark	88	91	85	85	89	90	86	90	88	88	88	89	87	90	88	84	89	91	Latvia	52
Finland	77	78	76	67	80	78	79	76	78	76	75	79	83	71	82	71	77	77	Russia	49
Norway	81	82	80	74	83	85	81	81	82	75	81	87	79	81	84	80	82	81	Moscow	48
Sweden	85	86	86	81	83	92	85	84	89	86	82	89	82	84	90	88	86	82	Bulgaria	47
Japan	68	62	73	59	64	78	74	64	70	69	61	74	62	64	72	70	65	69	Belarus	44
Switzerland	88	88	87	76	89	94	87	88	89	84	89	90	81	88	94	95	87	86	Turkey	36
Total	67	68	67	62	68	72	66	66	70	61	66	73	66	68	73	69	67	66		

Note: Countries in the left column are ranked according to GNP per capita. / The percentages in the bottom row give each country an equal weight. / na=not ascertained.

V117 DECISION-MAKING FREEDOM

How free are you to make decisions in your job? Please use this card (1=none at all and 10=a great deal) to indicate how much decision-making freedom you feel you have. (% "a great deal"—codes 7 to 10)

Country	Total	Gender Male	Gender Female	Age 16-29	Age 30-49	Age 50+	Education Lower	Education Medium	Education Upper	Income Lower	Income Middle	Income Upper	Political Affinity Left	Political Affinity Center	Political Affinity Right	Values Mat	Values Mixed	Values Postmat
India	52	53	50	48	54	56	47	50	56	43	51	62	49	47	59	55	51	54
Nigeria	64	59	73	59	65	80	74	63	60	54	67	70	60	61	67	65	63	61
China	44	47	40	33	46	53	41	49	41	44	42	47	na	51	na	46	44	30
Romania	48	53	43	39	51	56	40	43	62	47	41	57	42	51	54	38	53	58
Turkey	58	58	56	55	55	76	60	53	63	54	52	67	63	55	57	58	57	59
Poland	71	67	75	73	59	84	78	65	73	68	68	79	78	67	69	73	71	73
Bulgaria	37	46	28	28	42	34	21	36	49	26	41	46	38	41	42	37	39	41
Chile	61	64	55	53	63	71	66	56	63	62	55	68	59	61	67	59	61	66
Czechoslovakia	45	46	44	37	47	48	40	43	60	43	46	45	50	42	48	45	46	39
South Africa	54	52	56	44	55	62	35	56	75	26	48	73	53	60	67	58	51	54
Lithuania	52	60	46	51	53	53	50	49	69	48	49	66	na	na	na	52	50	64
Hungary	52	51	53	41	51	61	46	55	57	46	54	59	54	53	49	50	52	59
Argentina	70	72	69	62	72	77	72	71	69	56	69	69	68	70	67	72	70	70
Brazil	66	66	66	58	71	71	67	64	69	62	60	73	62	66	69	66	65	68
Mexico	62	64	59	59	64	68	60	61	69	51	67	76	64	64	69	59	62	74
Belarus	32	33	30	22	34	36	21	29	38	28	29	38	32	30	32	30	33	35
Russia	40	42	39	35	42	41	36	34	49	37	40	45	44	39	52	38	41	47
Moscow	42	45	39	37	41	47	32	38	46	37	41	51	45	34	53	41	40	51
Latvia	50	52	48	46	48	58	31	48	56	46	47	53	na	na	na	54	46	54
Estonia	52	56	49	44	55	56	46	49	66	47	52	60	na	na	na	48	54	58
Portugal	59	55	64	52	60	68	56	60	67	60	52	65	56	61	59	61	55	73
South Korea	63	61	65	55	65	68	55	60	71	50	63	85	59	57	68	65	63	54
Ireland	63	68	54	53	63	75	65	56	80	61	60	66	51	64	69	70	61	59
North Ireland	64	69	57	64	60	71	61	67	67	59	59	69	57	71	54	77	65	42
Slovenia	48	56	39	37	48	63	26	49	65	34	48	68	52	50	55	52	46	54
Spain	53	53	54	45	57	56	50	54	65	41	45	62	43	53	67	54	53	52
East Germany	47	51	42	35	50	54	45	43	55	40	43	52	43	50	47	42	47	48
Britain	66	76	52	59	64	78	64	68	74	57	65	75	58	66	73	58	69	65
Italy	59	61	57	55	65	64	51	57	62	53	60	73	59	59	61	58	58	60
Netherlands	70	81	66	63	72	83	73	66	83	63	67	83	72	66	71	60	72	69
Belgium	65	66	63	57	67	71	61	62	74	53	60	74	59	64	76	60	61	73
Austria	62	65	58	59	64	59	65	58	69	54	60	67	66	63	61	57	60	66
France	56	56	52	47	56	70	51	57	78	51	57	57	52	54	74	61	55	55
Canada	68	69	66	66	71	78	64	66	72	58	71	73	69	66	77	68	68	70
United States	72	75	67	63	74	80	73	71	73	63	68	80	73	73	74	71	72	72
Iceland	63	66	56	51	72	64	45	63	74	na	na	na	61	58	71	56	64	74
West Germany	51	53	49	41	56	54	47	51	69	38	43	63	48	50	59	45	52	53
Denmark	74	79	68	66	76	79	58	77	78	63	71	84	70	68	83	69	75	75
Finland	69	74	64	61	71	70	58	66	74	68	65	75	67	62	79	62	75	69
Norway	64	71	55	50	68	68	65	61	66	57	64	72	60	63	70	62	64	68
Sweden	79	80	78	67	78	89	79	75	86	80	73	82	79	77	81	76	79	80
Japan	66	64	69	59	62	78	74	61	73	70	61	69	61	65	71	69	65	63
Switzerland	73	74	73	62	76	78	73	72	82	65	75	79	66	76	77	72	73	75
Total	58	61	56	51	60	65	54	57	66	51	56	66	58	58	64	57	58	60

Ranking:

Sweden	79
Denmark	74
Switzerland	73
United States	72
Poland	71
Argentina	70
Netherlands	70
Finland	69
Canada	68
Brazil	66
Britain	66
Japan	66
Belgium	65
Nigeria	64
North Ireland	64
Norway	64
South Korea	63
Ireland	63
Iceland	63
Mexico	62
Austria	62
Chile	61
Portugal	59
Italy	59
Turkey	58
France	56
South Africa	54
Spain	53
India	52
Lithuania	52
Hungary	52
Estonia	52
West Germany	51
Latvia	50
Romania	48
Slovenia	48
East Germany	47
Czechoslovakia	45
China	44
Moscow	42
Russia	40
Bulgaria	37
Belarus	32

Note: Countries in the left column are ranked according to GNP per capita. / The percentages in the bottom row give each country an equal weight. / na=not ascertained.

V118-V123. Why people work. Irrespective of whether you have a job, or not, which statement comes closest to what you think?

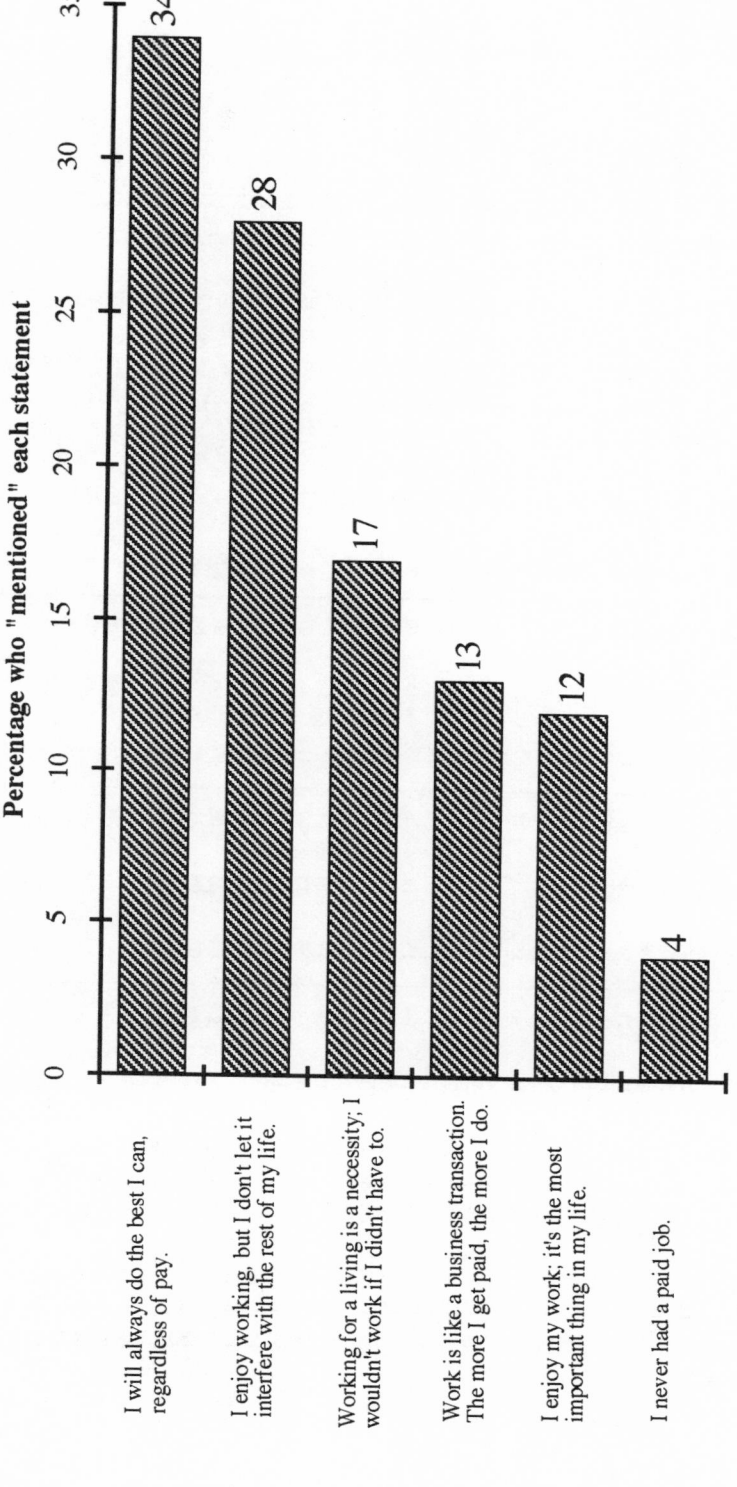

Percentage who "mentioned" each statement

I will always do the best I can, regardless of pay. — 34

I enjoy working, but I don't let it interfere with the rest of my life. — 28

Working for a living is a necessity; I wouldn't work if I didn't have to. — 17

Work is like a business transaction. The more I get paid, the more I do. — 13

I enjoy my work; it's the most important thing in my life. — 12

I never had a paid job. — 4

V118 WHY WORK: GET PAID

Here are some statements about why people work. Irrespective of whether you have a job, or not, which of them comes closest to what you think? "Work is like a business transaction. The more I get paid, the more I do; the less I get paid, the less I do" (% "mentioned")

	Total	Gender		Age			Education			Income			Political Affinity			Values		
		Male	Female	16-29	30-49	50+	Lower	Medium	Upper	Lower	Middle	Upper	Left	Center	Right	Mat	Mixed	Postmat
India	21	21	20	22	20	18	26	22	16	27	20	16	20	22	19	16	24	21
Nigeria	27	27	26	28	27	09	30	26	18	25	26	31	27	24	33	25	28	26
China	19	19	18	21	19	14	30	16	11	20	16	19	19	na	na	20	17	15
Romania	20	24	17	26	19	17	20	20	20	21	22	19	17	19	22	16	23	25
Turkey	15	17	13	12	16	20	17	14	07	16	16	14	16	14	18	21	14	11
Poland	17	24	10	16	24	10	13	20	18	15	19	18	17	19	17	15	18	15
Bulgaria	24	32	18	28	29	17	21	26	25	26	23	24	21	26	25	21	25	30
Chile	14	15	13	15	14	14	19	13	09	19	13	10	14	14	10	15	15	09
Czechoslovakia	17	24	10	23	18	11	18	18	09	14	16	20	12	18	17	16	17	16
South Africa	09	12	06	07	12	06	10	09	08	07	09	10	08	11	09	09	09	08
Lithuania	22	29	16	28	22	16	21	23	17	19	24	27	20	22	na	19	22	26
Hungary	24	31	17	29	27	18	22	26	18	23	25	21	20	26	25	19	27	28
Argentina	08	11	05	13	08	03	10	08	05	06	10	06	11	07	09	08	08	08
Brazil	13	17	09	12	16	10	15	13	08	14	14	12	13	13	11	14	13	09
Mexico	na	na	na	na	na	na	na	na	na	na	na	na	na	na	na	na	na	na
Belarus	25	32	19	29	22	25	25	28	21	27	25	22	26	23	23	24	24	22
Russia	23	35	14	32	25	16	23	26	21	21	26	23	25	24	26	20	25	29
Moscow	19	27	13	25	20	13	17	26	16	18	20	21	20	19	25	20	20	18
Latvia	16	26	10	24	16	08	18	16	16	18	15	16	na	na	na	14	17	15
Estonia	23	34	14	31	25	13	22	26	16	20	22	28	na	na	na	26	23	22
Portugal	09	10	08	09	08	10	10	04	10	11	09	07	12	07	08	10	10	05
South Korea	na	na	na	na	na	na	na	na	na	na	13	09	18	12	07	na	12	na
Ireland	11	15	07	16	11	08	12	10	07	na	13	09	na	12	07	09	12	09
North Ireland	09	13	07	18	07	06	08	13	07	12	06	07	11	11	02	03	11	07
Slovenia	12	15	10	17	11	10	15	11	09	13	12	11	16	13	11	13	12	10
Spain	07	08	06	06	07	07	07	04	06	09	06	06	07	06	06	10	06	05
East Germany	12	18	06	17	11	10	14	08	07	11	12	12	09	12	18	10	13	09
Britain	07	10	04	11	06	05	08	05	03	10	06	04	07	06	06	10	06	09
Italy	08	11	05	10	07	08	08	05	11	10	07	07	06	08	11	08	07	09
Netherlands	02	04	01	02	02	02	03	02	01	02	01	02	02	02	02	05	02	01
Belgium	10	12	08	09	12	08	11	09	08	09	10	08	10	11	09	12	10	07
Austria	09	11	08	11	08	09	09	09	09	09	11	07	12	08	12	13	09	07
France	09	11	07	10	09	08	09	10	09	09	08	08	08	06	10	08	09	11
Canada	09	11	07	11	08	08	10	08	09	11	09	07	09	08	10	07	08	10
United States	12	16	08	14	13	11	13	13	11	12	14	10	14	12	11	14	13	11
Iceland	07	10	03	09	08	03	06	10	05	na	na	na	04	07	09	08	07	04
West Germany	09	11	07	11	10	07	10	09	04	08	11	08	11	11	10	10	10	07
Denmark	11	14	07	15	10	08	10	12	10	08	12	11	13	11	10	10	12	09
Finland	18	24	11	24	18	12	15	22	14	17	17	19	19	20	14	15	20	14
Norway	09	13	05	13	07	09	09	10	08	12	08	09	07	08	12	10	09	09
Sweden	08	10	05	08	09	06	08	09	05	10	07	08	09	09	07	09	08	08
Japan	14	17	11	21	14	10	14	13	17	15	13	14	09	14	18	14	15	18
Switzerland	na	na	na	na	na	na	na	na	na	na	na	na	na	na	na	na	na	na
Total	**14**	**18**	**10**	**17**	**14**	**11**	**15**	**14**	**11**	**14**	**14**	**13**	**13**	**13**	**14**	**14**	**14**	**13**

Ranking:

Nigeria	27
Belarus	25
Bulgaria	24
Hungary	24
Russia	23
Estonia	23
Lithuania	22
India	21
Romania	20
China	19
Moscow	19
Finland	18
Poland	17
Czechoslovakia	17
Latvia	16
Turkey	15
Chile	14
Japan	14
Brazil	13
Slovenia	12
East Germany	12
United States	12
Ireland	11
Denmark	11
Belgium	10
South Africa	09
Portugal	09
North Ireland	09
Austria	09
France	09
Canada	09
West Germany	09
Norway	09
Argentina	08
Italy	08
Sweden	08
Spain	07
Britain	07
Iceland	07
Netherlands	02

Note: Countries in the left column are ranked according to GNP per capita. / The percentages in the bottom row give each country an equal weight. / na=not ascertained.

V119 WHY WORK: DO BEST

Here are some statements about why people work. Irrespective of whether you have a job, or not, which of them comes closest to what you think? "I will always do the best I can, regardless of pay" (% "mentioned")

	Total	Gender		Age			Education			Income			Political Affinity			Values			Ranking:	
		Male	Female	16-29	30-49	50+	Lower	Medium	Upper	Lower	Middle	Upper	Left	Center	Right	Mat	Mixed	Postmat		
India	52	56	48	54	51	50	34	52	62	46	50	60	61	52	49	58	51	52	Finland	58
Nigeria	02	02	03	02	03	00	02	02	03	03	02	03	01	02	04	02	02	04	Norway	54
China	38	38	38	27	40	46	34	38	40	38	39	34	na	na	na	40	35	43	Ireland	53
Romania	19	17	21	12	18	24	21	17	18	16	20	21	15	18	20	20	18	21	India	52
Turkey	39	43	36	38	42	37	34	47	52	34	41	43	40	45	34	38	37	48	Netherlands	46
Poland	19	18	20	13	24	17	17	19	27	19	18	21	19	21	18	18	21	15	Iceland	45
Bulgaria	16	15	18	12	17	18	15	16	17	13	18	20	20	17	18	20	16	05	Belgium	44
Chile	40	42	39	40	39	43	34	42	45	34	40	48	38	41	45	35	41	47	Czechoslovakia	41
Czechoslovakia	41	36	46	34	40	47	38	39	55	42	41	41	45	40	40	38	43	38	Chile	40
South Africa	20	23	17	13	27	20	11	21	49	09	17	42	23	24	31	22	19	18	Britain	40
Lithuania	29	25	32	16	27	42	34	26	37	34	23	28	na	na	na	27	31	23	Italy	40
Hungary	36	35	36	32	34	39	34	35	45	32	37	47	39	37	33	38	34	30	Turkey	39
Argentina	39	38	39	35	38	42	31	41	51	31	41	46	38	42	36	32	41	42	Argentina	39
Brazil	16	15	17	17	15	14	12	15	24	13	14	19	18	19	12	15	15	26	China	38
Mexico	na	na	na	na	na	na	na	na	na	na	na	na	na	na	na	na	na	na	France	38
Belarus	22	17	26	13	22	30	22	19	24	23	21	22	19	30	16	20	23	20	North Ireland	37
Russia	36	31	40	19	35	49	39	30	41	37	39	37	33	39	33	41	34	32	Spain	37
Moscow	22	18	24	11	19	35	25	16	25	23	21	21	20	25	30	22	23	14	Austria	37
Latvia	19	17	21	12	18	31	18	18	24	17	21	20	na	na	na	19	20	20	Canada	37
Estonia	21	16	25	09	22	32	20	19	30	22	20	21	na	na	na	22	21	19	Denmark	37
Portugal	33	34	33	31	34	35	30	41	39	27	37	38	31	37	33	29	35	46	Hungary	36
South Korea	na	na	na	na	na	na	na	na	na	na	na	na	na	na	na	29	na	na	Russia	36
Ireland	53	51	55	45	49	62	54	49	61	52	53	55	42	53	60	38	53	48	United States	34
North Ireland	37	37	38	34	31	46	35	41	38	40	29	33	25	34	47	58	38	20	Portugal	33
Slovenia	29	29	29	29	29	29	23	33	34	23	31	38	39	30	31	45	29	35	Lithuania	29
Spain	37	40	34	35	37	37	37	34	37	37	35	39	37	30	37	27	37	40	Slovenia	29
East Germany	27	21	32	17	26	34	27	23	32	33	25	23	25	28	37	37	25	28	East Germany	27
Britain	40	39	41	39	37	43	39	42	42	39	39	37	38	41	42	38	42	35	West Germany	24
Italy	40	43	38	36	44	43	40	44	43	39	42	35	40	43	36	37	41	41	Belarus	22
Netherlands	46	43	46	42	49	44	43	46	47	37	50	50	45	45	49	40	47	48	Moscow	22
Belgium	44	43	45	41	41	50	43	47	43	45	42	48	46	45	47	38	46	47	Estonia	21
Austria	37	36	37	32	38	38	35	37	41	37	36	38	45	33	40	42	39	46	South Africa	20
France	38	37	39	34	34	46	38	39	38	38	40	37	33	43	43	35	40	33	Romania	19
Canada	37	39	35	42	36	32	37	36	36	33	36	38	43	35	34	38	35	37	Poland	19
United States	34	36	32	45	31	32	37	35	31	34	35	31	32	34	31	36	34	33	Latvia	19
Iceland	45	44	45	39	47	48	43	44	47	na	na	na	39	50	45	33	45	50	Bulgaria	16
West Germany	24	21	26	19	22	28	24	20	30	25	20	25	18	26	27	42	24	21	Brazil	16
Denmark	37	32	42	31	32	47	42	38	34	43	34	32	31	36	41	26	39	29	Nigeria	02
Finland	58	52	64	55	57	64	57	55	62	56	64	54	57	57	62	56	58	59		
Norway	54	49	59	47	52	59	58	54	51	56	55	47	47	58	54	58	54	41		
Sweden	na	na	na	na	na	na	na	na	na	na	na	na	na	na	na	na	na	na		
Japan	na	na	na	na	na	na	na	na	na	na	na	na	na	na	na	na	na	na		
Switzerland	na	na	na	na	na	na	na	na	na	na	na	na	na	na	na	na	na	na		
Total	34	32	35	29	33	38	32	33	38	32	33	35	34	36	35	34	34	33		

Note: Countries in the left column are ranked according to GNP per capita. / The percentages in the bottom row give each country an equal weight. / na=not ascertained.

V120 WHY WORK: NECESSITY

Here are some statements about why people work. Irrespective of whether you have a job, or not, which of them comes closest to what you think? "Working for a living is a necessity; I wouldn't work if I didn't have to" (% "mentioned")

Column groups: Gender (Male, Female); Age (16-29, 30-49, 50+); Education (Lower, Medium, Upper); Income (Lower, Middle, Upper); Political Affinity (Left, Center, Right); Values (Mat, Mixed, Postmat).

Country	Total	Male	Female	16-29	30-49	50+	Edu Lower	Edu Medium	Edu Upper	Inc Lower	Inc Middle	Inc Upper	Pol Left	Pol Center	Pol Right	Mat	Mixed	Postmat	Ranking
India	19	20	18	20	18	19	18	19	20	17	22	18	19	23	18	16	23	16	United States 34
Nigeria	02	01	02	01	03	00	01	01	02	02	01	02	01	01	03	01	02	04	Russia 29
China	23	22	23	23	22	24	25	23	15	27	18	23	na	na	na	25	21	26	Bulgaria 28
Romania	21	21	21	23	24	17	18	24	20	24	21	19	23	22	21	22	21	15	Spain 28
Turkey	16	13	19	19	13	16	18	13	13	21	12	15	19	14	16	17	18	09	Hungary 27
Poland	05	05	06	05	08	02	04	07	05	07	04	05	06	04	06	07	04	10	Belarus 27
Bulgaria	28	23	32	28	27	29	35	30	17	32	26	25	28	26	27	27	28	25	Canada 27
Chile	23	19	27	22	23	25	32	21	15	30	22	16	21	23	21	28	23	15	Estonia 26
Czechoslovakia	12	09	14	16	11	10	16	12	05	13	12	11	11	13	11	18	10	10	Moscow 25
South Africa	06	08	05	04	08	07	07	06	05	06	06	05	09	06	04	06	06	11	Denmark 25
Lithuania	21	18	24	20	21	23	24	22	14	24	25	10	24	27	na	27	21	13	Latvia 24
Hungary	27	25	29	27	26	28	31	25	14	33	24	13	24	27	27	27	28	18	China 23
Argentina	16	16	15	15	15	17	20	13	10	20	17	13	16	18	11	19	15	14	Chile 23
Brazil	20	20	20	22	17	20	23	19	14	21	24	15	22	16	25	21	19	18	Portugal 23
Mexico	na	na	na	na	na	na	na	na	na	na	na	na	na	na	na	na	na	na	Ireland 22
Belarus	27	23	30	29	26	27	28	28	24	25	27	28	27	26	26	27	26	28	North Ireland 22
Russia	29	23	34	34	32	23	25	32	29	29	27	29	29	27	27	28	31	25	France 22
Moscow	25	19	30	25	25	25	30	24	24	25	25	27	24	24	27	30	23	22	Romania 21
Latvia	24	15	30	24	25	20	32	26	16	31	24	19	na	na	na	25	24	16	Lithuania 21
Estonia	26	21	31	26	25	28	34	25	22	31	26	20	24	22	23	30	25	22	Britain 21
Portugal	23	22	24	24	23	22	26	20	12	26	25	15	24	22	12	29	22	12	Belgium 21
South Korea	na	na	na	na	na	na	na	na	na	na	na	na	na	na	na	na	na	na	Brazil 20
Ireland	22	21	23	20	26	20	25	20	14	24	24	20	25	21	21	na	na	24	India 19
North Ireland	22	16	27	24	30	13	26	14	21	22	32	17	21	23	12	23	23	20	Italy 19
Slovenia	17	15	18	19	16	16	18	16	14	23	15	08	11	15	12	18	17	10	Finland 18
Spain	28	30	26	27	29	27	29	27	22	27	30	27	29	28	22	26	29	27	Slovenia 17
East Germany	11	06	14	10	11	11	11	13	07	11	12	10	09	11	12	18	09	11	Turkey 16
Britain	21	19	23	20	22	22	25	15	13	23	18	20	24	22	18	23	21	22	Argentina 16
Italy	19	18	20	21	22	17	20	13	08	19	17	18	19	17	17	20	21	15	West Germany 15
Netherlands	07	07	07	08	07	05	07	08	06	11	03	06	08	06	06	06	08	05	Sweden 15
Belgium	21	20	21	21	22	19	22	22	15	20	21	17	21	21	18	22	21	18	Iceland 13
Austria	22	19	24	23	25	09	10	10	04	12	10	06	18	09	08	15	09	09	Czechoslovakia 12
France	22	19	24	09	10	09	10	22	19	12	10	26	18	09	20	15	09	09	East Germany 11
Canada	27	28	26	32	27	23	28	28	26	28	30	22	31	27	22	29	29	24	Norway 11
United States	34	37	31	40	35	31	29	38	32	41	33	30	29	35	36	38	32	36	Austria 10
Iceland	13	12	15	18	10	13	16	13	11	na	na	na	17	12	10	14	13	15	Netherlands 07
West Germany	15	17	14	21	15	12	16	16	09	18	17	12	20	14	11	16	15	16	South Africa 06
Denmark	25	25	25	23	30	22	32	28	18	30	28	17	24	27	22	27	27	17	Poland 05
Finland	18	22	14	14	19	21	20	21	15	19	18	17	26	21	13	41	17	18	Nigeria 02
Norway	11	10	12	10	12	09	11	10	11	09	09	13	10	11	10	12	10	08	
Sweden	15	15	15	18	14	14	19	16	10	15	20	11	17	14	11	16	15	16	
Japan	na	na	na	na	na	na	na	na	na	na	na	na	na	na	na	na	na	na	
Switzerland	na	na	na	na	na	na	na	na	na	na	na	na	na	na	na	na	na	na	
Total	**19**	**18**	**20**	**20**	**20**	**18**	**21**	**19**	**15**	**22**	**20**	**16**	**20**	**18**	**17**	**22**	**19**	**17**	

Note: Countries in the left column are ranked according to GNP per capita. / The percentages in the bottom row give each country an equal weight. / na=not ascertained.

V121 WHY WORK: ENJOYMENT

Here are some statements about why people work. Irrespective of whether you have a job, or not, which of them comes closest to what you think? "I enjoy working but I don't let it interfere with the rest of my life" (% "mentioned")

	Total	Gender		Age			Education			Income			Political Affinity			Values		
		Male	Female	16-29	30-49	50+	Lower	Medium	Upper	Lower	Middle	Upper	Left	Center	Right	Mat	Mixed	Postmat
India	44	46	42	48	44	38	29	44	54	39	45	49	50	51	39	44	49	53
Nigeria	01	01	02	01	02	00	01	01	02	02	01	02	01	01	02	01	01	03
China	26	23	30	33	28	13	25	26	31	25	28	24	na	na	na	21	30	35
Romania	23	23	23	30	26	16	15	28	27	21	22	26	23	25	26	21	26	22
Turkey	12	13	11	15	13	06	09	17	19	08	11	18	14	12	14	08	11	19
Poland	21	23	18	19	30	12	10	27	32	18	21	25	21	22	24	17	22	24
Bulgaria	18	14	21	21	19	14	11	18	24	17	18	17	15	19	18	15	18	23
Chile	25	26	23	30	22	20	21	26	27	22	25	27	24	26	25	17	26	28
Czechoslovakia	20	20	20	22	24	12	14	23	19	16	21	21	20	19	21	15	20	29
South Africa	13	15	11	09	17	11	10	13	22	08	13	18	13	13	12	13	13	10
Lithuania	28	28	28	33	30	22	17	30	37	25	26	37	na	na	na	24	29	38
Hungary	27	26	27	31	30	22	18	34	41	20	31	33	28	33	23	25	27	33
Argentina	20	19	20	24	23	12	17	21	22	16	19	22	23	21	21	20	18	23
Brazil	27	25	28	31	28	19	15	32	32	20	27	34	27	32	24	25	29	24
Mexico	na	na	na	na	na	na	na	na	na	na	na	na	na	na	na	na	na	na
Belarus	26	26	26	28	29	19	16	26	30	23	26	29	28	22	27	24	26	36
Russia	22	20	24	31	25	14	15	26	23	20	21	26	25	25	23	18	24	31
Moscow	28	27	29	32	30	22	21	28	30	28	30	25	32	23	21	25	28	34
Latvia	29	28	30	29	33	23	17	29	33	24	29	34	na	na	na	28	29	31
Estonia	24	23	25	27	25	19	14	26	36	20	29	25	25	30	24	23	25	27
Portugal	26	27	25	35	30	15	21	38	36	18	27	39	na	na	na	23	28	37
South Korea	na	na	na	na	na	na	na	na	na	na	na	na	na	na	na	na	na	na
Ireland	41	42	41	54	45	30	33	51	50	32	38	49	na	na	na	34	41	na
North Ireland	44	46	42	43	51	36	40	53	48	33	52	53	52	47	39	37	na	53
Slovenia	15	16	14	21	16	09	12	14	23	13	15	19	46	42	41	11	15	27
Spain	16	16	15	22	17	10	12	26	23	10	17	21	13	17	17	12	16	23
East Germany	38	38	37	47	42	28	34	49	42	29	42	41	17	19	18	25	27	40
Britain	35	34	36	39	40	28	32	41	44	28	41	39	42	36	34	38	39	38
Italy	29	31	28	36	32	22	29	33	37	23	37	39	31	37	34	22	34	41
Netherlands	33	35	33	38	34	28	31	33	36	32	36	35	35	28	30	27	28	38
Belgium	37	38	36	44	40	31	31	39	44	30	39	45	34	36	32	31	31	41
Austria	47	46	48	55	53	39	41	52	55	38	48	54	42	39	38	39	38	41
France	21	22	20	25	26	14	16	21	33	16	20	31	36	51	46	13	45	58
Canada	48	49	48	48	50	47	47	50	46	46	50	50	25	22	18	48	22	25
United States	42	40	45	37	45	41	37	42	45	44	37	46	51	50	47	36	48	49
Iceland	27	24	30	28	28	24	24	24	31	36	na	na	47	42	41	27	42	47
West Germany	42	42	42	47	46	37	39	49	48	36	44	48	31	26	25	33	41	51
Denmark	67	65	69	68	70	63	59	72	69	61	74	73	45	44	40	64	68	72
Finland	47	46	47	43	49	44	34	45	55	41	47	52	74	67	66	38	47	48
Norway	65	62	67	72	66	59	51	67	69	59	70	67	41	45	53	62	66	72
Sweden	58	56	61	60	61	55	54	59	60	58	55	63	65	59	56	52	59	59
Japan	na	na	na	na	na	na	na	na	na	na	na	na	na	na	na	na	na	na
Switzerland	na	na	na	na	na	na	na	na	na	na	na	na	na	na	na	na	na	na
Total	31	31	31	35	34	25	25	34	37	27	32	36	33	33	31	27	32	37

Ranking:

Denmark	67
Norway	65
Sweden	58
Canada	48
Austria	47
Finland	47
India	44
North Ireland	44
United States	42
West Germany	42
Ireland	41
East Germany	38
Belgium	37
Britain	35
Netherlands	33
Latvia	29
Italy	29
Lithuania	28
Moscow	28
Hungary	27
Brazil	27
Iceland	27
China	26
Belarus	26
Portugal	26
Chile	25
Estonia	24
Romania	23
Russia	22
Poland	21
France	21
Czechoslovakia	20
Argentina	20
Bulgaria	18
Spain	16
Slovenia	15
South Africa	13
Turkey	12
Nigeria	01

Note: Countries in the left column are ranked according to GNP per capita. / The percentages in the bottom row give each country an equal weight. / na=not ascertained.

V122 WHY WORK: MOST IMPORTANT THING

Here are some statements about why people work. Irrespective of whether you have a job, or not, which of them comes closest to what you think? "I enjoy my work; it's the most important thing in my life" (% "mentioned")

	Total	Gender		Age			Education			Income			Political Affinity			Values			Ranking:	
		Male	Female	16-29	30-49	50+	Lower	Medium	Upper	Lower	Middle	Upper	Left	Center	Right	Mat	Mixed	Postmat		
India	65	71	58	67	66	59	49		68	64	66	65	70	67	67	69	65	75	India	65
Nigeria	01	01	01	01	01	00	01	01	01	01	01	01	01	01	02	01	01	03	China	40
China	40	42	37	30	43	47	41	41	36	45	36	38	na	na	na	40	42	35	Slovenia	22
Romania	16	17	16	07	16	23	22	12	15	18	17	14	17	17	13	18	15	15	Brazil	20
Turkey	09	11	08	09	10	09	11	06	07	10	11	06	08	09	10	07	09	12	Norway	20
Poland	na	na	na	na	na	na	na	na	na	na	na	na	na	na	na	na	na	na	Chile	19
Bulgaria	11	14	09	05	07	20	15	07	14	10	10	14	14	10	09	12	11	12	Austria	18
Chile	19	22	16	13	21	25	25	16	17	24	19	13	16	19	21	21	18	16	East Germany	17
Czechoslovakia	10	10	09	05	06	18	14	07	11	14	09	06	11	09	09	12	09	06	Denmark	17
South Africa	na	na	na	na	na	na	na	na	na	na	na	na	na	na	na	na	na	na	Romania	16
Lithuania	12	12	13	07	10	19	21	10	11	16	09	10	na	na	17	14	12	11	Canada	16
Hungary	14	13	16	07	10	22	17	12	05	16	13	14	15	17	16	17	10	15	United States	16
Argentina	10	11	09	07	08	14	14	09	10	15	09	10	07	07	24	13	10	06	Hungary	14
Brazil	20	21	20	14	21	30	29	17	15	27	18	15	17	16	na	23	19	14	Belarus	14
Mexico	na	na	na	na	na	na	na	na	na	na	na	na	na	na	na	na	na	na	Russia	14
Belarus	14	15	13	08	14	20	18	13	14	13	15	13	14	11	24	18	12	09	Lithuania	12
Russia	14	15	13	06	11	23	17	11	15	15	14	16	16	13	15	16	13	13	Ireland	12
Moscow	09	10	09	07	07	15	18	07	09	10	08	11	08	11	13	09	10	08	North Ireland	12
Latvia	10	12	09	07	07	21	16	09	10	09	10	11	na	na	na	11	10	11	Finland	12
Estonia	05	07	04	02	06	06	04	05	07	04	06	06	na	na	na	05	05	05	Bulgaria	11
Portugal	10	11	10	06	10	15	12	05	08	13	09	08	13	09	10	12	10	07	Sweden	11
South Korea	17	na	na	na	na	na	na	na	na	na	na	na	na	na	na	14	13	na	Czechoslovakia	10
Ireland	12	16	08	07	11	17	16	08	10	16	14	08	04	16	17	14	13	09	Argentina	10
North Ireland	12	20	06	08	07	20	14	11	00	14	14	12	07	09	08	09	13	13	Latvia	10
Slovenia	22	22	22	10	23	29	24	22	19	22	23	21	17	22	26	27	21	13	Portugal	10
Spain	05	07	04	04	04	07	06	04	05	07	05	06	04	07	08	06	06	04	Turkey	09
East Germany	17	18	16	09	14	24	19	08	14	21	13	16	18	16	16	17	18	15	Moscow	09
Britain	08	11	05	05	07	10	08	06	11	11	07	09	05	08	11	09	07	09	Italy	09
Italy	09	10	08	04	07	14	09	07	06	11	08	05	11	10	08	11	09	07	Belgium	09
Netherlands	07	10	06	05	05	14	08	07	05	09	07	04	08	07	08	12	09	04	Britain	08
Belgium	09	10	07	06	09	10	10	08	07	11	07	07	08	09	10	10	09	06	West Germany	08
Austria	18	18	18	09	18	22	22	15	17	22	17	16	18	15	22	23	20	11	Netherlands	07
France	04	06	02	02	02	07	06	03	01	06	03	01	04	04	05	07	04	02	Iceland	06
Canada	16	17	14	13	12	21	18	15	14	19	16	13	13	14	19	15	16	15	Estonia	05
United States	16	19	13	12	11	22	20	14	15	20	15	12	17	17	16	16	17	15	Spain	05
Iceland	06	08	04	03	06	08	08	06	04	09	na	na	06	05	06	07	05	04	France	04
West Germany	08	08	07	03	05	12	09	06	07	09	07	07	05	08	10	11	08	05	Nigeria	01
Denmark	17	19	15	11	16	24	20	13	19	19	17	13	10	19	21	22	17	16		
Finland	12	14	10	03	08	31	25	11	06	20	10	07	14	10	12	29	12	09		
Norway	20	25	14	10	16	30	36	17	15	22	19	17	17	22	19	26	18	16		
Sweden	11	13	09	06	11	16	16	09	10	14	12	09	10	11	12	13	11	10		
Japan	na	na	na	na	na	na	na	na	na	na	na	na	na	na	na	na	na	na		
Switzerland	na	na	na	na	na	na	na	na	na	na	na	na	na	na	na	na	na	na		
Total	14	16	12	09	13	20	17	12	12	17	14	13	13	13	16	16	14	12		

Note: Countries in the left column are ranked according to GNP per capita. / The percentages in the bottom row give each country an equal weight. / na=not ascertained.

V123 WHY WORK: NEVER WORKED

Here are some statements about why people work. Irrespective of whether you have a job, or not, which of them comes closest to what you think? "I never had a paid job" (% "mentioned")

	Total	Gender Male	Gender Female	Age 16-29	Age 30-49	Age 50+	Education Lower	Education Medium	Education Upper	Income Lower	Income Middle	Income Upper	Political Affinity Left	Political Affinity Center	Political Affinity Right	Values Mat	Values Mixed	Values Postmat	Ranking	Ranking
India	00	00	00	00	00	00	00	00	00	00	00	00	00	00	00	00	00	00	South Africa	52
Nigeria	00	00	00	00	00	00	00	00	00	00	00	00	00	00	00	00	00	00	Poland	37
China	03	03	04	08	01	01	01	05	03	03	04	02	04	na	na	02	04	06	Spain	09
Romania	04	02	06	03	03	04	07	02	02	05	02	04	04	03	03	05	03	03	Chile	08
Turkey	05	00	09	04	04	07	07	02	00	07	05	02	04	03	05	05	05	01	Italy	08
Poland	37	29	45	46	12	59	56	27	18	42	38	31	35	33	35	42	34	37	Belgium	06
Bulgaria	02	02	03	05	01	02	02	02	03	01	03	02	02	02	01	03	02	02	Turkey	05
Chile	08	04	11	08	07	08	09	06	07	10	07	05	10	06	09	09	08	06	Portugal	05
Czechoslovakia	00	00	01	00	00	01	01	00	00	01	00	00	00	01	01	01	01	00	Romania	04
South Africa	52	42	61	67	35	56	62	51	15	71	54	24	47	45	43	51	52	53	Argentina	04
Lithuania	01	01	01	02	00	00	01	01	00	00	01	03	na	na	na	00	01	02	China	03
Hungary	03	01	05	01	02	05	02	02	02	04	03	01	02	03	01	03	04	03	Hungary	03
Argentina	04	01	07	03	03	06	05	05	02	08	02	01	03	03	03	06	03	04	Netherlands	03
Brazil	02	01	03	02	01	04	04	02	02	02	02	03	02	02	02	02	03	04	Austria	03
Mexico	na	na	na	na	na	na	na	na	na	na	na	na	na	na	na	na	na	na	France	03
Belarus	01	00	01	00	00	02	01	00	00	00	01	01	01	00	01	01	01	00	Bulgaria	02
Russia	00	00	00	01	00	00	00	00	00	00	01	01	00	00	00	01	01	00	Brazil	02
Moscow	01	00	01	01	01	00	01	01	01	01	01	01	01	01	00	01	01	02	Ireland	02
Latvia	00	01	00	02	00	00	01	01	00	01	00	00	na	na	na	01	00	00	North Ireland	02
Estonia	01	01	01	03	00	01	02	01	00	01	03	00	na	na	na	01	01	00	Canada	02
Portugal	05	01	08	02	02	09	06	02	02	06	03	03	03	01	09	05	03	03	United States	02
South Korea	na	na	na	na	na	na	na	na	na	na	na	na	na	na	na	na	na	na	Lithuania	01
Ireland	02	01	04	02	01	04	03	01	03	04	01	02	02	02	01	03	02	03	Belarus	01
North Ireland	02	00	03	04	00	02	01	03	03	01	03	01	00	01	02	05	00	04	Moscow	01
Slovenia	01	00	02	00	01	03	03	01	00	03	01	00	na	na	01	02	02	01	Estonia	01
Spain	09	03	15	09	07	11	09	06	11	13	08	06	06	10	14	10	10	05	Slovenia	01
East Germany	00	00	00	01	00	00	00	00	01	00	00	00	00	00	00	00	00	00	Britain	01
Britain	01	00	00	00	01	01	01	01	00	01	01	00	01	01	01	01	00	01	West Germany	01
Italy	08	02	13	08	03	11	08	06	05	08	05	00	05	09	10	10	07	04	Norway	01
Netherlands	03	01	03	04	01	03	03	02	03	06	01	00	03	01	03	05	01	00	Sweden	01
Belgium	06	03	09	11	04	06	09	04	05	06	07	04	07	05	06	07	07	05	India	00
Austria	03	01	04	01	01	05	05	01	01	05	02	01	03	02	02	04	03	01	Nigeria	00
France	03	01	05	06	01	03	05	02	03	03	03	02	02	03	03	07	03	02	Czechoslovakia	00
Canada	02	00	03	01	00	04	04	01	03	04	03	00	02	02	01	02	02	01	Russia	00
United States	02	01	04	03	01	03	05	02	01	02	02	02	02	01	02	04	02	01	Latvia	00
Iceland	00	00	00	00	00	00	00	00	00	na	01	00	00	01	00	00	00	00	East Germany	00
West Germany	01	01	02	02	00	02	02	02	01	02	01	00	01	01	02	01	01	01	Iceland	00
Denmark	00	00	01	00	00	01	00	01	00	00	00	00	00	00	01	01	00	00	Denmark	00
Finland	00	00	00	00	00	01	01	00	00	00	01	00	00	00	00	00	00	00	Finland	00
Norway	01	00	02	00	00	02	03	00	00	02	00	00	00	01	02	02	01	00		
Sweden	01	01	01	01	00	01	01	00	00	00	00	01	01	00	00	02	00	01		
Japan	na	na	na	na	na	na	na	na	na	na	na	na	na	na	na	na	04	na		
Switzerland	na	na	na	na	na	na	na	na	na	na	na	na	na	na	na	na	04	na		
Total	04	03	06	05	02	06	06	04	02	06	04	03	04	04	05	05	04	04		

Note: Countries in the left column are ranked according to GNP per capita. / The percentages in the bottom row give each country an equal weight. / na=not ascertained.

V125 EFFICIENT PAID MORE

Imagine two secretaries, of the same age, doing practically the same job. One finds out that the other earns $50 a week more than she does. The better paid secretary, however, is quicker, more efficient, and more reliable at her job. In your opinion, is it fair or not fair that one secretary is paid more than the other? (% "fair")

	Total	Gender		Age			Education			Income			Political Affinity			Values		
		Male	Female	16-29	30-49	50+	Lower	Medium	Upper	Lower	Middle	Upper	Left	Center	Right	Mat	Mixed	Postmat
India	78	77	na	79	na	79	77	77	82	77	78	78	na	na	na	85	77	76
Nigeria	80	82	76	80	79	82	80	77	100	75	87	78	85	82	69	85	77	73
China	97	98	95	97	97	95	94	98	94	97	97	96	na	na	na	97	97	98
Romania	88	90	85	88	90	86	80	90	94	85	89	89	84	87	92	86	89	93
Turkey	72	75	69	70	72	74	71	73	72	69	72	76	70	73	72	69	71	78
Poland	na	na	na	na	na	na	na	na	na	na	na	na	na	na	na	na	na	na
Bulgaria	86	88	84	90	84	86	78	87	92	88	87	88	88	88	90	83	87	92
Chile	62	61	63	59	64	65	56	62	70	56	61	71	60	61	69	60	61	71
Czechoslovakia	44	51	38	47	43	43	36	47	49	44	41	49	35	40	55	43	44	45
South Africa	na	na	na	na	na	na	na	na	na	na	na	na	na	na	na	na	na	na
Lithuania	94	95	92	94	94	92	89	95	94	92	95	96	na	na	na	94	93	97
Hungary	90	90	90	92	92	88	85	95	100	85	94	96	91	92	94	90	91	83
Argentina	83	84	82	78	86	84	82	83	84	75	81	90	81	85	84	83	83	84
Brazil	78	80	76	75	78	82	73	78	88	74	78	80	74	85	76	77	78	82
Mexico	85	86	84	85	85	88	84	86	87	84	87	86	84	86	84	85	86	83
Belarus	93	92	93	92	94	91	91	92	94	93	91	94	94	89	95	90	94	95
Russia	94	94	94	96	94	92	88	95	97	92	95	96	97	94	95	93	94	96
Moscow	94	94	94	95	95	91	93	94	96	94	94	94	95	94	90	93	94	96
Latvia	95	97	93	94	95	94	94	93	96	94	95	95	na	na	na	94	95	94
Estonia	95	95	95	95	97	92	92	95	98	96	94	94	na	na	na	92	96	93
Portugal	74	74	73	72	77	73	71	77	80	67	81	78	66	74	80	69	75	85
South Korea	73	70	76	76	71	76	65	72	80	68	72	83	71	70	76	72	74	75
Ireland	73	71	74	67	76	73	67	78	80	67	71	78	63	73	79	73	72	75
North Ireland	71	72	70	64	70	78	68	79	69	70	67	80	50	75	72	69	72	67
Slovenia	91	92	90	92	91	91	88	91	97	90	91	94	89	93	93	94	94	96
Spain	75	75	75	72	74	78	74	77	77	72	72	78	72	80	79	77	75	72
East Germany	96	97	96	97	97	95	95	97	99	96	97	96	98	96	96	95	97	96
Britain	79	81	77	76	80	80	76	83	88	75	80	87	70	79	88	82	77	79
Italy	79	83	75	80	80	77	77	91	77	74	84	93	77	81	84	79	76	83
Netherlands	68	78	65	62	68	76	69	67	69	62	66	80	57	72	78	72	72	62
Belgium	72	75	70	73	70	74	67	74	79	73	66	75	68	76	76	72	72	75
Austria	90	92	89	87	91	90	89	91	84	90	90	89	86	91	90	87	91	89
France	79	78	79	76	79	79	74	82	85	71	79	88	75	81	86	70	79	88
Canada	82	84	81	80	83	83	75	84	87	79	85	87	85	82	86	75	83	84
United States	86	86	85	82	88	86	81	84	92	78	89	90	87	86	86	84	85	89
Iceland	75	76	75	72	78	76	70	79	77	70	na	na	68	79	82	72	79	67
West Germany	85	87	83	80	85	87	86	82	84	80	85	88	81	87	87	89	84	84
Denmark	76	80	72	74	78	77	67	78	81	72	75	85	67	76	87	70	79	72
Finland	74	77	70	72	77	68	66	72	80	72	72	79	66	75	76	47	74	79
Norway	54	60	48	51	55	55	45	50	63	49	52	66	42	51	70	53	55	49
Sweden	62	69	55	59	64	64	55	62	75	62	54	69	50	62	74	60	62	63
Japan	59	58	60	53	60	61	57	57	65	59	63	58	55	61	67	58	61	59
Switzerland	69	73	66	62	71	70	63	73	73	63	71	77	56	74	76	65	69	70
Total	79	81	78	78	80	80	75	80	83	76	79	84	73	79	81	77	79	80

Ranking:

China	97
East Germany	96
Latvia	95
Estonia	95
Lithuania	94
Russia	94
Moscow	94
Belarus	93
Slovenia	91
Hungary	90
Austria	90
Romania	88
Bulgaria	86
United States	86
Mexico	85
West Germany	85
Argentina	83
Canada	82
Nigeria	80
Britain	79
Italy	79
France	79
India	78
Brazil	78
Denmark	76
Spain	75
Iceland	75
Portugal	74
Finland	74
South Korea	73
Ireland	73
Turkey	72
Belgium	72
North Ireland	71
Switzerland	69
Netherlands	68
Chile	62
Sweden	62
Japan	59
Norway	54
Czechoslovakia	44

Note: Countries in the left column are ranked according to GNP per capita. / The percentages in the bottom row give each country an equal weight. / na=not ascertained.

V126. There is a lot of discussion about how business and industry should be managed. Which of these four statements comes closest to your opinion?

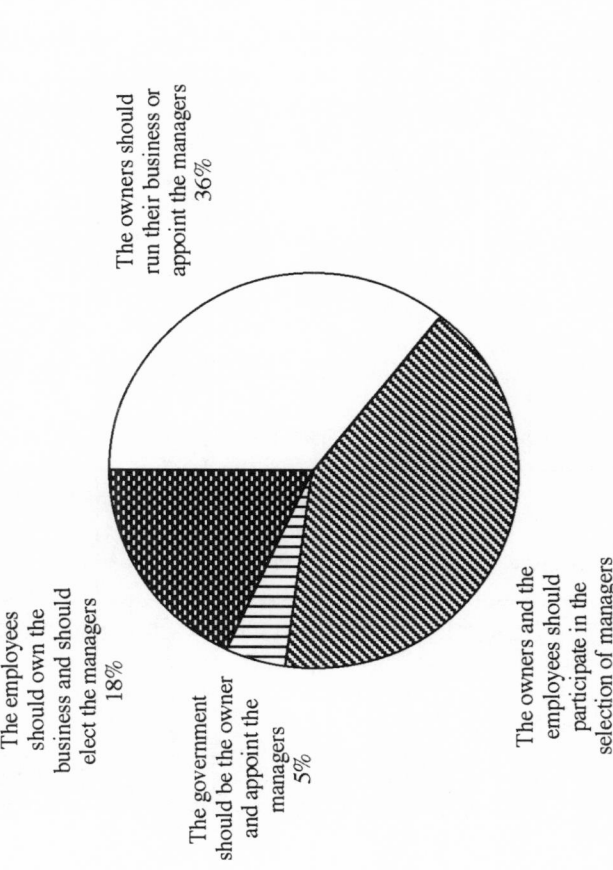

The employees
should own the
business and should
elect the managers
18%

The government
should be the owner
and appoint the
managers
5%

The owners and the
employees should
participate in the
selection of managers
41%

The owners should
run their business or
appoint the managers
36%

V127. Following instructions at work

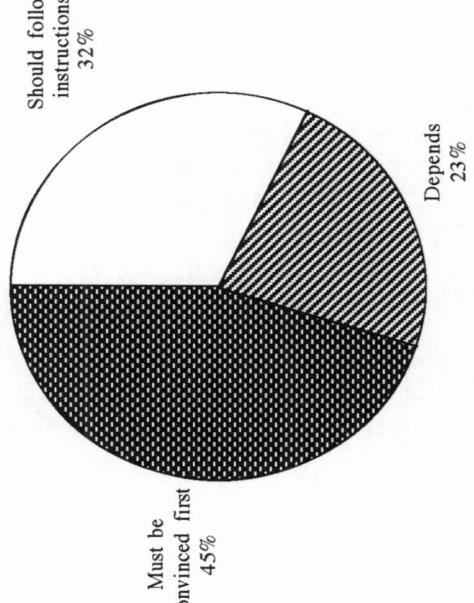

Should follow
instructions
32%

Depends
23%

Must be
convinced first
45%

V126 OWNERS SHOULD RUN BUSINESSES

There is a lot of discussion about how business and industry should be managed. Which of these four statements comes closest to your opinion? (% "The owners should run their business or appoint the managers")

	Total	Gender		Age			Education			Income			Political Affinity			Values			Ranking:	
		Male	Female	16-29	30-49	50+	Lower	Medium	Upper	Lower	Middle	Upper	Left	Center	Right	Mat	Mixed	Postmat		
India	22	23	21	22	20	28	26	24	18	23	21	22	17	21	24	23	21	20	United States	57
Nigeria	53	49	58	51	54	58	61	50	52	50	52	55	56	51	51	59	48	53	North Ireland	55
China	22	22	23	24	22	21	22	22	26	17	23	28	na	na	na	23	22	22	Nigeria	53
Romania	35	35	35	44	35	30	25	33	43	32	31	43	25	36	45	23	42	58	Canada	53
Turkey	27	25	28	26	26	31	27	27	24	25	28	28	20	30	29	33	28	16	Switzerland	51
Poland	15	17	13	15	15	16	13	14	24	11	16	19	11	15	20	14	16	14	Austria	50
Bulgaria	38	40	36	47	42	26	25	37	49	39	31	42	37	40	44	30	38	56	Portugal	48
Chile	24	22	25	20	24	29	26	22	23	23	22	28	16	24	30	31	23	17	Iceland	48
Czechoslovakia	34	40	29	38	35	30	25	38	40	32	32	39	24	31	47	30	35	39	West Germany	48
South Africa	40	40	40	34	43	48	40	39	47	38	34	53	28	42	51	50	36	26	Mexico	47
Lithuania	38	41	36	47	39	30	31	40	45	33	40	48	na	na	na	31	38	46	Denmark	47
Hungary	24	26	23	19	27	24	22	23	40	20	24	39	23	21	31	27	22	25	Belgium	46
Argentina	31	35	28	23	34	36	33	33	29	30	28	37	23	32	39	37	31	26	Britain	44
Brazil	32	35	29	26	33	39	35	30	35	31	29	35	26	33	35	37	30	21	Japan	44
Mexico	47	46	47	43	46	57	46	47	49	40	46	59	32	46	54	49	47	46	Ireland	43
Belarus	09	11	08	11	09	08	09	06	12	08	09	11	09	09	08	07	09	16	Italy	43
Russia	11	14	09	16	12	08	08	11	14	10	12	14	16	12	10	07	13	24	Estonia	42
Moscow	14	15	12	19	15	08	04	11	17	10	15	15	17	09	na	11	12	22	Finland	42
Latvia	31	35	29	35	30	31	25	30	37	30	32	33	na	na	na	25	33	39	South Africa	40
Estonia	42	46	38	43	42	41	43	38	49	37	41	49	32	46	54	36	43	51	Bulgaria	38
Portugal	48	49	46	46	47	50	47	46	51	45	41	56	09	09	08	55	48	32	Lithuania	38
South Korea	23	23	22	12	25	34	29	22	20	18	24	30	16	21	25	29	20	07	Romania	35
Ireland	43	46	41	40	42	47	43	46	33	40	42	48	25	41	52	56	42	32	Czechoslovakia	34
North Ireland	55	49	60	51	45	70	55	55	59	49	51	54	48	56	55	70	56	34	Netherlands	33
Slovenia	26	30	21	29	26	22	21	24	34	20	25	36	27	29	36	25	26	28	Brazil	32
Spain	31	32	31	22	31	42	33	33	23	41	27	30	21	33	45	45	30	14	East Germany	32
East Germany	32	33	31	29	27	38	34	27	29	35	33	27	20	33	51	35	33	25	Norway	32
Britain	44	45	43	42	44	47	44	47	44	39	42	50	30	40	62	50	46	31	Argentina	31
Italy	43	43	43	40	45	43	42	50	47	40	48	60	33	46	56	53	43	33	Latvia	31
Netherlands	33	37	32	30	33	36	34	32	32	27	31	42	18	34	46	42	35	27	Spain	31
Belgium	46	46	46	40	44	52	48	45	44	42	42	50	31	44	58	53	46	39	Sweden	30
Austria	50	53	48	37	48	58	56	46	45	54	49	47	45	48	53	57	53	39	Turkey	27
France	24	23	24	20	19	32	25	20	28	19	23	28	12	26	45	31	25	15	Slovenia	26
Canada	53	55	52	50	51	59	60	55	46	53	53	52	36	55	56	65	54	43	Chile	24
United States	57	56	57	52	51	65	62	56	54	55	57	58	38	58	62	66	58	47	Hungary	24
Iceland	48	56	40	48	50	45	46	52	47	na	na	na	30	45	65	49	50	37	France	24
West Germany	48	51	44	39	45	55	50	44	40	45	46	50	32	51	60	58	51	36	South Korea	23
Denmark	47	52	42	46	44	52	47	50	46	44	45	53	26	46	65	51	51	26	India	22
Finland	42	48	36	39	44	42	40	47	38	38	42	47	19	41	57	46	44	38	China	22
Norway	32	37	27	28	32	35	33	35	29	26	33	36	15	32	46	40	30	21	Poland	15
Sweden	30	34	26	27	33	45	29	31	29	33	23	26	37	18	29	42	39	31	Moscow	14
Japan	44	45	42	36	46	44	44	44	44	48	36	50	27	46	52	49	44	28	Russia	11
Switzerland	51	51	51	43	49	55	49	54	45	44	48	57	23	51	66	59	55	34	Belarus	09
Total	36	37	34	34	35	38	35	36	37	33	34	40	26	36	45	40	36	31		

Note: Countries in the left column are ranked according to GNP per capita. / The percentages in the bottom row give each country an equal weight. / na=not ascertained.

V126 EMPLOYEE PARTICIPATION IN MANAGEMENT

There is a lot of discussion about how business and industry should be managed. Which of these four statements comes closest to your opinion? (% "The owners and the employees should participate in the selection of managers")

	Total	Gender		Age			Education			Income			Political Affinity			Values			Ranking:	
		Male	Female	16-29	30-49	50+	Lower	Medium	Upper	Lower	Middle	Upper	Left	Center	Right	Mat	Mixed	Postmat		
India	48	49	46	50	47	44	39	47	51	46	46	51	48	51	52	49	48	41	South Korea	68
Nigeria	31	35	26	30	33	33	28	32	32	34	34	25	23	35	35	29	32	35	Sweden	65
China	40	40	41	37	42	41	35	38	49	40	44	37	na	na	na	35	45	41	Norway	62
Romania	33	34	32	37	34	30	31	36	31	32	35	32	31	34	27	35	32	30	France	61
Turkey	38	40	37	38	39	36	35	46	36	31	42	42	37	39	37	34	38	44	Netherlands	57
Poland	42	38	45	51	40	39	37	48	29	43	41	40	39	46	43	40	41	46	Spain	53
Bulgaria	23	25	23	24	25	22	19	22	29	23	25	26	24	27	21	20	25	24	Finland	51
Chile	47	48	46	50	46	42	38	49	54	40	48	52	54	46	44	39	47	53	India	48
Czechoslovakia	43	38	48	43	46	40	44	43	41	46	46	42	43	47	38	40	43	48	Chile	47
South Africa	45	45	45	48	44	41	43	46	46	43	50	40	51	42	38	40	49	51	Hungary	47
Lithuania	19	18	20	21	18	19	16	19	26	17	20	22	na	na	na	19	20	21	Argentina	47
Hungary	47	44	50	62	47	42	43	54	42	47	48	44	45	47	50	42	51	53	Japan	47
Argentina	47	42	52	48	49	45	43	46	52	43	47	47	40	49	45	44	48	48	East Germany	46
Brazil	43	42	45	47	44	37	34	46	52	38	47	46	48	47	36	36	48	51	Italy	46
Mexico	42	41	43	45	43	30	40	44	44	47	41	34	48	44	38	38	43	40	Denmark	46
Belarus	23	21	24	24	23	19	20	26	20	19	24	23	23	22	23	23	23	25	South Africa	45
Russia	18	18	19	22	17	17	19	19	17	19	16	17	21	18	15	18	18	21	Britain	44
Moscow	23	22	23	24	23	22	14	22	25	24	23	21	22	25	23	20	26	14	Belgium	44
Latvia	31	30	32	34	31	29	32	29	35	32	32	30	na	na	na	35	30	37	Czechoslovakia	43
Estonia	26	23	30	24	28	26	22	28	26	28	25	24	na	na	na	27	25	26	Brazil	43
Portugal	36	34	39	35	37	37	36	37	36	37	40	34	43	37	30	30	37	49	West Germany	43
South Korea	68	68	68	76	67	57	56	70	72	69	68	64	64	69	68	64	69	80	Switzerland	43
Ireland	42	40	44	46	44	38	39	44	57	38	43	41	53	44	36	37	42	50	Poland	42
North Ireland	36	40	33	42	45	22	32	45	38	40	42	42	38	38	37	37	36	52	Mexico	42
Slovenia	37	34	41	44	38	30	34	40	37	32	41	40	42	38	26	24	36	49	Ireland	42
Spain	53	53	54	60	56	44	52	54	58	44	56	53	58	54	49	31	38	49	Austria	42
East Germany	46	47	45	50	52	37	43	55	47	41	46	50	51	48	37	44	56	61	China	40
Britain	44	43	45	46	45	42	42	47	50	43	46	45	48	50	31	35	46	53	Turkey	38
Italy	46	45	46	48	45	45	46	44	44	47	45	32	52	47	38	38	43	53	Slovenia	37
Netherlands	57	54	59	57	59	55	55	56	62	61	60	54	69	56	48	37	47	54	Canada	37
Belgium	44	44	43	48	45	38	38	45	49	42	47	43	53	46	35	42	56	64	Iceland	37
Austria	42	40	43	50	44	36	37	44	47	38	42	46	45	46	39	35	44	51	Portugal	36
France	61	61	62	63	66	55	57	66	63	62	63	61	69	60	49	34	39	51	North Ireland	36
Canada	37	36	38	41	40	30	29	36	44	34	37	40	47	38	33	53	60	70	United States	35
United States	35	36	35	36	40	29	28	35	41	34	35	36	50	35	29	26	36	46	Romania	33
Iceland	37	30	45	43	36	32	40	35	37	na	na	na	46	43	26	28	33	45	Nigeria	31
West Germany	43	41	45	51	44	37	41	47	46	45	43	43	53	42	35	37	36	43	Latvia	31
Denmark	46	43	50	43	49	42	45	46	48	48	49	41	61	49	31	32	40	53	Estonia	26
Finland	51	46	57	57	49	51	52	46	57	53	51	49	65	55	39	39	45	61	Bulgaria	23
Norway	62	57	68	63	63	59	61	59	66	64	63	60	75	65	50	43	49	57	Belarus	23
Sweden	65	61	69	63	64	69	64	65	64	71	69	60	76	66	55	56	65	66	Moscow	23
Japan	47	46	48	50	44	49	48	46	47	46	54	40	60	45	40	58	63	71	Lithuania	19
Switzerland	43	41	44	45	44	40	45	40	44	50	46	35	58	45	32	35	47	55	Russia	18
Total	42	40	43	45	43	38	38	43	44	41	43	41	48	44	37	36	42	47		

Note: Countries in the left column are ranked according to GNP per capita. / The percentages in the bottom row give each country an equal weight. / na=not ascertained.

V127 FOLLOWING INSTRUCTIONS: ALWAYS

People have different ideas about following instructions at work. Some say that one should follow instructions of one's superiors even when one does not fully agree with them. Others say that one should follow one's superior's instructions only when one is convinced that they are right. With which of these two opinions do you agree? (% "Should follow instructions")

	Total	Gender Male	Gender Female	Age 16-29	Age 30-49	Age 50+	Education Lower	Education Medium	Education Upper	Income Lower	Income Middle	Income Upper	Political Affinity Left	Political Affinity Center	Political Affinity Right	Values Mat	Values Mixed	Values Postmat
India	25	26	25	23	25	33	36	26	20	30	25	22	18	28	29	26	24	25
Nigeria	38	38	38	37	39	32	45	40	33	39	36	40	37	33	39	38	37	47
China	21	22	20	16	19	32	18	21	20	21	22	21	na	na	na	26	18	11
Romania	25	24	25	19	22	31	32	19	24	29	26	20	31	23	19	28	24	14
Turkey	27	26	28	24	27	30	30	23	19	32	25	24	19	27	33	32	29	15
Poland	na	na	na	na	na	na	na	na	na	na	na	na	na	na	na	na	na	na
Bulgaria	18	19	17	14	13	25	29	16	11	20	13	18	24	16	10	23	17	07
Chile	41	43	39	37	40	49	47	38	38	46	42	35	37	42	41	43	43	32
Czechoslovakia	17	17	17	13	13	24	23	14	16	19	15	18	19	16	16	25	14	12
South Africa	na	na	na	na	na	na	na	na	na	na	na	na	na	na	na	na	na	na
Lithuania	08	09	07	03	06	14	15	06	07	09	06	07	na	na	na	11	07	03
Hungary	28	27	30	21	28	32	35	23	18	33	25	26	22	26	28	30	27	23
Argentina	35	41	30	33	35	38	41	35	28	38	34	36	15	36	42	42	36	25
Brazil	19	20	17	15	19	25	33	15	03	26	18	12	15	17	22	19	18	16
Mexico	39	39	39	35	39	50	41	39	32	42	34	39	22	40	44	48	37	23
Belarus	19	21	16	10	19	28	24	16	20	18	17	21	17	16	33	23	16	14
Russia	19	18	19	13	15	27	25	18	16	22	18	18	16	18	24	25	16	15
Moscow	18	23	15	12	16	26	21	19	18	15	20	23	14	22	30	13	17	09
Latvia	13	16	10	09	14	14	13	12	14	07	12	16	na	na	na	21	14	10
Estonia	13	14	12	08	09	23	19	11	11	15	11	10	na	na	na	21	09	05
Portugal	45	44	46	39	42	54	50	39	34	48	44	41	34	46	52	50	45	27
South Korea	09	09	09	05	09	14	20	07	06	10	08	09	06	08	10	12	08	01
Ireland	47	49	45	44	41	55	51	42	48	50	47	47	30	48	50	52	49	35
North Ireland	55	55	56	58	48	62	55	54	66	60	48	58	54	58	52	60	54	60
Slovenia	20	20	19	16	17	25	24	18	15	26	16	15	15	19	16	20	20	18
Spain	31	31	32	23	29	41	35	29	16	42	26	27	26	32	37	45	28	17
East Germany	45	49	42	40	45	48	47	40	41	45	46	44	40	48	49	54	46	38
Britain	44	45	43	44	41	46	44	45	39	45	46	45	36	44	51	50	46	31
Italy	30	32	29	25	28	36	31	23	19	32	26	35	25	31	37	40	30	20
Netherlands	37	40	36	33	35	45	43	38	30	38	38	35	28	37	46	42	40	31
Belgium	33	34	32	24	30	41	36	34	23	38	36	27	30	32	36	43	33	22
Austria	40	40	39	31	35	47	41	39	27	45	40	34	36	38	41	48	42	31
France	36	35	37	32	33	42	38	37	27	36	33	35	31	37	43	46	38	24
Canada	52	52	53	47	50	59	57	55	45	55	51	51	42	52	56	54	56	46
United States	62	64	60	59	58	68	59	66	60	64	63	61	54	63	66	67	63	58
Iceland	38	42	34	34	40	39	48	35	31	na	na	na	27	45	42	48	36	27
West Germany	41	41	41	30	40	48	45	34	32	44	36	42	33	40	53	58	43	29
Denmark	35	36	34	36	31	41	39	38	32	36	40	30	26	36	40	46	36	21
Finland	15	17	12	12	13	22	25	14	10	18	14	13	08	13	18	21	16	10
Norway	62	64	59	66	63	58	53	60	68	56	63	66	54	59	71	61	63	58
Sweden	44	45	43	38	43	51	49	39	46	41	43	48	37	45	53	49	47	36
Japan	33	39	27	22	33	40	38	30	34	36	35	31	33	35	42	48	29	22
Switzerland	na	na	na	na	na	na	na	na	na	na	na	na	na	na	na	na	na	na
Total	32	33	31	28	30	38	36	30	28	34	31	31	28	34	38	38	32	24

Ranking:

United States	62
Norway	62
North Ireland	55
Canada	52
Ireland	47
Portugal	45
East Germany	45
Britain	44
Sweden	44
Chile	41
West Germany	41
Austria	40
Mexico	39
Nigeria	38
Iceland	38
Netherlands	37
France	36
Argentina	35
Denmark	35
Belgium	33
Japan	33
Spain	31
Italy	30
Hungary	28
Turkey	27
India	25
Romania	25
China	21
Slovenia	20
Brazil	19
Belarus	19
Russia	19
Bulgaria	18
Moscow	18
Czechoslovakia	17
Finland	15
Latvia	13
Estonia	13
South Korea	09
Lithuania	08

Note: Countries in the left column are ranked according to GNP per capita. / The percentages in the bottom row give each country an equal weight. / na=not ascertained.

V127 FOLLOWING INSTRUCTIONS: MUST BE CONVINCED

People have different ideas about following instructions at work. Some say that one should follow instructions of one's superiors even when one does not fully agree with them. Others say that one should follow one's superior's instructions only when one is convinced that they are right. With which of these two opinions do you agree? (% "Must be convinced first")

	Total	Gender		Age			Education			Income			Political Affinity			Values			Ranking:	
		Male	Female	16-29	30-49	50+	Lower	Medium	Upper	Lower	Middle	Upper	Left	Center	Right	Mat	Mixed	Postmat		
India	55	55	55	56	55	52	46	54	54	52	58	59	61	55	47	57	54	53	Brazil	78
Nigeria	49	47	50	49	47	53	43	49	50	50	46	50	48	52	49	50	50	36	Romania	75
China	34	34	35	31	36	34	36	37	31	35	30	32	na	na	na	34	35	32	Bulgaria	65
Romania	75	76	75	81	78	69	68	81	76	73	78	72	69	77	81	73	76	86	Hungary	59
Turkey	54	54	54	54	55	53	53	56	57	52	59	42	66	53	47	48	52	66	Slovenia	58
Poland	na	na	na	na	na	na	na	na	na	na	na	na	na	na	na	na	na	na	Russia	56
Bulgaria	65	64	67	67	70	59	51	70	71	61	69	71	60	70	71	63	66	68	India	55
Chile	49	48	50	51	51	43	44	51	51	48	47	53	52	48	50	49	47	57	Belarus	55
Czechoslovakia	51	51	51	47	53	52	48	52	56	52	52	47	54	51	52	40	56	51	Turkey	54
South Africa	na	na	na	na	na	na	na	na	na	na	na	na	na	na	na	na	na	na	Moscow	54
Lithuania	33	35	31	42	37	21	22	36	35	22	34	33	na	na	na	27	34	34	Denmark	54
Hungary	59	60	59	67	60	56	55	65	55	56	62	58	64	64	57	58	60	73	Spain	52
Argentina	50	47	54	53	51	48	47	51	55	51	51	43	63	50	47	41	51	60	Czechoslovakia	51
Brazil	78	77	80	82	79	72	65	82	92	77	88	79	82	81	77	77	79	83	Argentina	50
Mexico	38	39	36	41	37	31	37	39	38	38	39	33	47	37	38	33	38	50	Nigeria	49
Belarus	55	51	58	55	55	54	46	57	56	56	53	68	57	52	47	53	55	63	Chile	49
Russia	56	53	59	58	57	54	55	55	58	58	57	53	58	56	54	55	57	59	South Korea	48
Moscow	54	51	56	55	52	55	58	54	52	57	51	55	57	52	46	48	57	52	Netherlands	48
Latvia	45	47	44	58	43	34	39	46	45	47	40	31	na	na	na	43	45	49	France	48
Estonia	44	44	43	49	44	37	42	45	41	44	43	27	na	na	na	39	45	38	Italy	46
Portugal	39	40	38	43	40	34	35	50	44	37	40	45	51	37	34	33	41	54	Latvia	45
South Korea	48	43	52	43	47	58	52	48	45	50	43	39	50	47	49	46	49	52	Finland	45
Ireland	41	38	44	45	47	35	39	46	37	39	42	42	56	43	35	41	39	50	Estonia	44
North Ireland	38	36	39	38	43	31	40	38	35	36	46	35	43	35	42	35	40	33	Britain	43
Slovenia	58	59	57	57	58	58	56	57	64	56	62	49	59	62	60	59	58	49	Belgium	43
Spain	52	51	53	57	54	46	51	49	49	53	52	58	55	50	48	45	55	59	Ireland	41
East Germany	36	33	38	28	33	37	36	39	30	37	36	33	37	34	34	32	35	40	Sweden	41
Britain	43	43	44	45	46	40	45	39	39	43	44	42	48	45	36	42	41	52	Portugal	39
Italy	46	46	46	44	47	47	46	45	39	49	49	17	52	48	44	38	47	58	Mexico	38
Netherlands	48	46	48	53	47	43	56	50	57	50	49	45	54	52	39	44	47	51	North Ireland	38
Belgium	43	43	43	49	44	36	41	42	49	41	50	47	46	44	42	36	42	53	Austria	38
Austria	38	36	39	45	44	29	35	39	42	32	41	44	47	39	36	30	37	44	East Germany	36
France	48	49	46	49	53	41	45	46	56	50	54	47	56	45	43	38	48	57	China	34
Canada	29	30	27	29	30	27	25	26	35	27	32	30	39	29	30	23	27	35	Norway	34
United States	23	21	24	25	23	21	22	23	22	24	21	26	28	21	22	15	22	28	Lithuania	33
Iceland	33	28	38	28	35	36	31	34	35	na	24	23	39	28	32	26	35	37	Iceland	33
West Germany	24	23	24	29	22	22	20	29	29	25	24	23	30	22	21	15	23	30	Canada	29
Denmark	54	51	57	53	58	49	54	54	53	54	50	55	62	51	50	47	52	66	West Germany	24
Finland	45	42	49	41	45	50	47	45	46	44	48	45	49	51	42	42	44	49	United States	23
Norway	34	32	37	31	33	37	42	35	29	42	31	30	41	37	26	34	33	40	Japan	11
Sweden	41	42	41	45	42	38	39	44	39	44	43	38	48	43	34	35	41	48		
Japan	11	13	09	15	10	10	12	11	09	13	09	11	18	10	09	10	12	13		
Switzerland	na	na	na	na	na	na	na	na	na	na	na	na	na	na	na	na	na	na		
Total	**45**	**45**	**46**	**47**	**47**	**43**	**43**	**47**	**47**	**46**	**47**	**44**	**51**	**46**	**44**	**41**	**46**	**50**		

Note: Countries in the left column are ranked according to GNP per capita. / The percentages in the bottom row give each country an equal weight. / na=not ascertained.

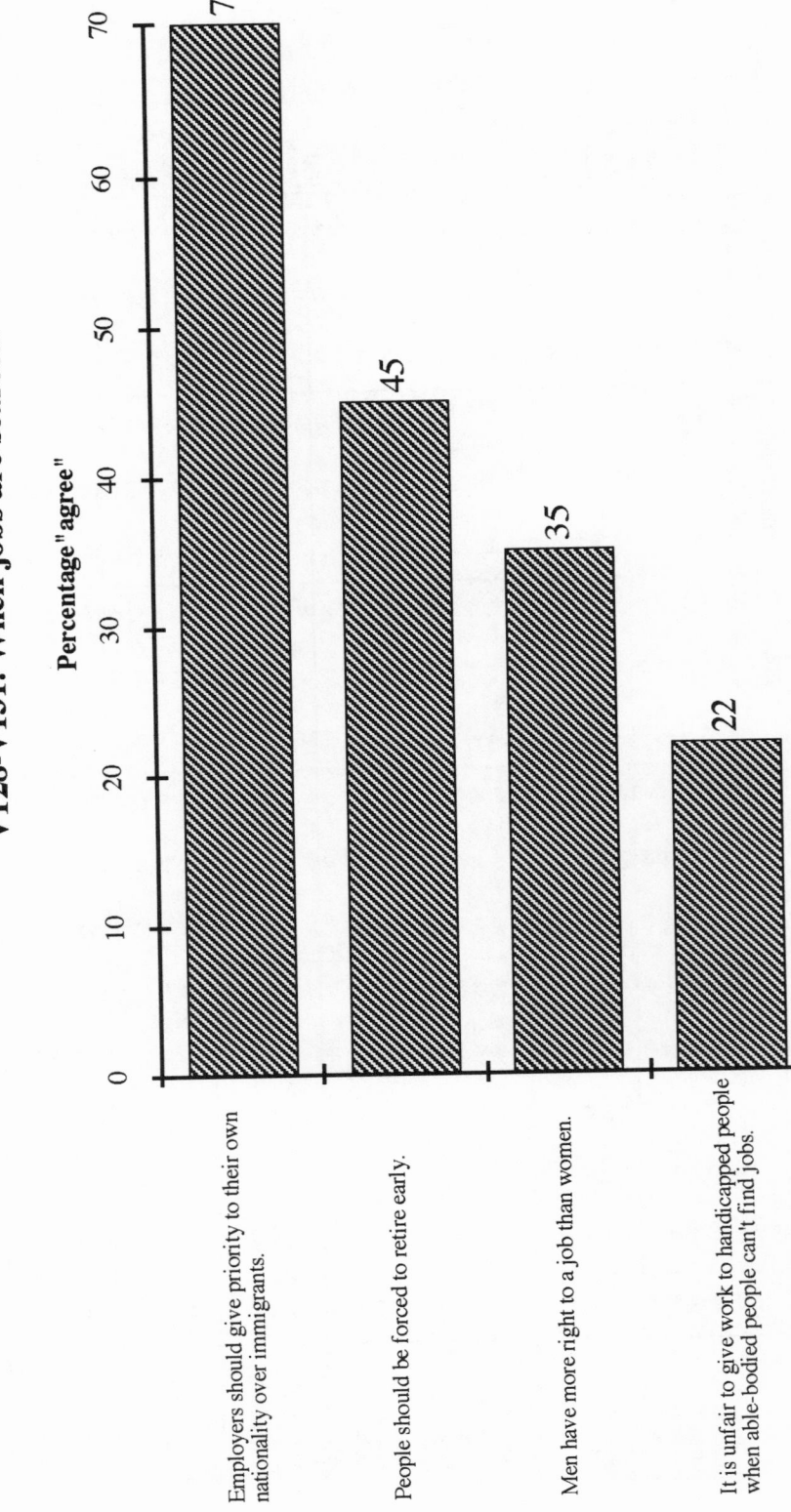

V128-V131. When jobs are scarce...

Percentage "agree"

70

45

35

22

Employers should give priority to their own nationality over immigrants.

People should be forced to retire early.

Men have more right to a job than women.

It is unfair to give work to handicapped people when able-bodied people can't find jobs.

V128 MEN MORE RIGHT TO A JOB

Do you agree or disagree with the following statement?

"When jobs are scarce, men have more right to a job than women." (% "agree")

	Total	Gender		Age			Education			Income			Political Affinity			Values		
		Male	Female	16-29	30-49	50+	Lower	Medium	Upper	Lower	Middle	Upper	Left	Center	Right	Mat	Mixed	Postmat
India	49	56	41	49	49	55	55	51	43	58	45	46	54	51	43	53	46	42
Nigeria	48	51	44	49	47	52	55	47	48	46	52	46	52	48	51	48	48	48
China	41	50	29	35	45	43	48	42	32	40	39	46	na	na	na	41	39	57
Romania	42	46	38	31	42	49	55	38	31	38	44	42	46	41	43	45	42	27
Turkey	51	57	44	42	51	63	61	42	21	59	53	38	36	48	71	58	53	36
Poland	55	58	52	39	50	67	63	52	40	58	56	50	53	48	62	59	53	54
Bulgaria	46	57	36	39	42	53	54	44	39	51	44	42	46	46	45	48	44	52
Chile	37	38	37	32	34	50	48	35	26	44	39	27	34	37	38	46	37	26
Czechoslovakia	55	57	52	45	52	64	62	54	42	59	52	55	53	55	55	59	55	43
South Africa	45	53	38	42	45	50	57	42	23	53	47	30	37	45	52	48	43	45
Lithuania	66	71	63	61	66	71	73	65	59	65	68	68	na	na	na	70	65	63
Hungary	42	41	44	26	38	54	54	34	21	52	39	25	34	42	48	46	40	40
Argentina	24	27	22	19	22	30	31	19	18	30	27	21	20	23	28	30	24	17
Brazil	38	40	36	36	35	48	50	35	27	47	34	32	32	36	43	43	35	32
Mexico	23	28	16	19	22	34	26	22	14	28	20	17	14	23	23	31	19	16
Belarus	38	46	31	36	36	42	36	34	42	43	38	38	39	36	32	42	35	40
Russia	40	46	36	41	38	42	41	39	41	42	43	38	41	39	44	39	41	40
Moscow	42	44	39	33	44	45	49	39	42	41	39	46	40	46	40	48	41	34
Latvia	34	38	32	34	31	41	49	33	10	38	35	32	na	na	na	38	35	26
Estonia	45	46	43	44	41	51	51	44	41	44	39	49	na	na	na	42	35	38
Portugal	34	35	32	22	27	51	41	20	16	43	30	22	na	na	na	37	27	19
South Korea	42	38	32	25	48	56	56	39	39	38	43	50	32	28	41	42	28	20
Ireland	36	36	35	12	33	53	47	25	17	48	37	26	40	36	47	47	41	28
North Ireland	34	37	32	12	34	49	40	28	12	40	33	25	29	36	37	42	34	30
Slovenia	29	34	25	18	26	40	39	23	22	35	29	17	18	31	43	33	36	20
Spain	31	30	31	16	29	44	37	17	16	48	28	22	20	28	27	45	28	19
East Germany	31	35	31	20	28	41	35	25	20	36	30	29	25	26	34	46	31	14
Britain	34	31	36	14	27	51	39	21	22	43	26	29	21	35	41	41	35	25
Italy	43	45	41	24	37	61	46	26	08	54	31	21	30	33	37	62	42	20
Netherlands	22	26	21	12	21	37	36	19	11	24	21	25	36	46	45	46	23	24
Belgium	38	38	38	23	33	52	50	35	20	43	38	16	12	18	35	52	39	15
Austria	50	54	48	29	46	64	60	45	37	60	50	29	31	36	37	72	52	21
France	33	35	31	23	32	42	41	30	17	43	29	25	44	48	54	52	33	34
Canada	19	18	20	15	15	27	31	20	09	23	22	10	27	33	41	30	20	17
United States	24	26	23	20	16	35	32	26	16	28	26	19	11	20	19	32	25	12
Iceland	06	06	06	06	05	07	08	07	03	na	na	na	17	25	28	07	06	04
West Germany	31	37	27	17	25	45	39	21	15	39	30	25	03	05	08	56	34	14
Denmark	11	07	14	05	05	21	22	08	06	16	07	05	22	29	46	19	09	05
Finland	15	16	15	11	14	22	22	13	14	21	12	14	04	14	10	21	17	11
Norway	16	17	15	05	10	31	39	12	08	25	12	10	14	13	16	23	14	15
Sweden	08	07	09	04	05	14	14	05	03	08	08	06	14	15	16	18	07	06
Japan	34	38	30	24	30	47	50	31	24	38	35	32	04	11	07	37	34	18
Switzerland	na	na	na	na	na	na	na	na	na	na	na	na	na	na	na	na	na	na
Total	**35**	**38**	**33**	**26**	**33**	**45**	**44**	**31**	**25**	**41**	**35**	**31**	**29**	**33**	**38**	**43**	**35**	**27**

Ranking:

Lithuania	66
Poland	55
Czechoslovakia	55
Turkey	51
Austria	50
India	49
Nigeria	48
Bulgaria	46
South Africa	45
Estonia	45
Italy	43
Romania	42
Hungary	42
Moscow	42
South Korea	42
China	41
Russia	40
Brazil	38
Belarus	38
Belgium	38
Chile	37
Ireland	36
Latvia	34
Portugal	34
North Ireland	34
Britain	34
Japan	34
France	33
Spain	31
East Germany	31
West Germany	31
Slovenia	29
Argentina	24
United States	24
Mexico	23
Netherlands	22
Canada	19
Norway	16
Finland	15
Denmark	11
Sweden	08
Iceland	06

Note: Countries in the left column are ranked according to GNP per capita. / The percentages in the bottom row give each country an equal weight. / na=not ascertained.

V129 FORCED RETIREMENT

Do you agree or disagree with the following statement?
"When jobs are scarce, people should be forced to retire early." (% "agree")

Country	Total	Gender Male	Gender Female	Age 16-29	Age 30-49	Age 50+	Educ. Lower	Educ. Medium	Educ. Upper	Income Lower	Income Middle	Income Upper	Pol. Left	Pol. Center	Pol. Right	Values Mat	Values Mixed	Values Postmat
India	36	40	31	33	38	38	41	35	35	44	33	33	36	34	35	37	35	25
Nigeria	48	46	51	49	48	37	53	48	46	39	52	54	61	45	47	49	47	47
China	39	38	41	37	45	31	41	37	40	37	41	40	na	na	na	39	36	57
Romania	65	61	68	58	70	64	75	65	51	64	65	65	68	66	62	71	63	43
Turkey	56	59	53	56	58	54	62	50	44	61	59	48	51	56	61	59	60	45
Poland	57	54	60	37	59	64	61	58	38	60	52	58	52	55	61	58	57	58
Bulgaria	74	69	78	78	76	69	73	77	68	73	73	73	74	75	72	73	74	77
Chile	37	34	40	32	38	45	49	32	29	49	38	22	32	37	35	49	35	26
Czechoslovakia	68	66	71	62	70	71	72	67	64	68	69	68	69	68	67	68	68	71
South Africa	20	21	19	20	20	20	21	19	18	16	22	21	19	19	24	24	17	20
Lithuania	64	63	65	60	62	69	71	63	58	68	61	62	na	na	na	67	65	55
Hungary	41	42	40	26	42	46	50	35	24	42	40	36	36	42	43	43	40	35
Argentina	25	25	24	32	22	22	28	27	19	28	21	24	24	22	30	31	23	20
Brazil	34	32	36	31	32	41	50	30	12	48	30	21	31	26	37	38	32	25
Mexico	23	24	21	21	32	30	26	21	14	25	21	21	15	22	25	26	23	13
Belarus	60	60	61	58	64	55	64	59	61	61	60	60	63	58	53	61	60	64
Russia	64	61	67	63	69	59	63	66	63	68	66	64	68	64	60	64	66	64
Moscow	60	56	62	57	61	60	57	60	60	58	61	61	60	60	55	64	59	58
Latvia	48	46	49	44	49	50	42	48	49	44	54	47	na	na	na	51	47	52
Estonia	57	55	59	54	58	57	56	57	59	58	53	59	na	na	na	59	57	52
Portugal	60	56	63	48	61	70	64	54	47	68	60	45	64	55	59	69	57	46
South Korea	29	28	29	19	30	41	45	36	22	32	27	29	27	29	28	30	29	19
Ireland	47	47	47	34	48	54	57	36	30	60	49	36	40	50	43	53	47	39
North Ireland	43	41	45	27	50	46	49	35	24	45	46	27	43	43	43	41	47	27
Slovenia	60	58	62	57	61	61	67	64	43	68	58	49	50	57	60	67	60	41
Spain	62	63	61	56	64	64	66	60	45	71	61	56	64	67	69	68	59	56
East Germany	64	69	60	61	70	61	64	63	65	59	66	67	59	67	69	63	64	64
Britain	43	44	42	37	40	50	48	35	31	50	48	34	48	40	45	45	45	37
Italy	54	52	57	51	51	59	55	52	47	62	48	41	52	55	55	62	53	48
Netherlands	42	42	42	46	36	46	51	37	36	41	44	37	30	46	47	53	45	34
Belgium	49	48	50	48	49	50	55	48	41	56	52	48	44	50	40	59	48	44
Austria	44	44	44	40	45	45	44	45	45	44	45	43	51	45	40	49	46	37
France	49	48	50	45	49	52	54	50	34	54	49	40	46	48	53	54	51	41
Canada	31	33	29	27	29	36	44	30	23	41	30	24	27	31	31	46	30	26
United States	16	17	14	15	12	19	20	17	11	20	16	11	11	14	33	21	15	12
Iceland	37	37	36	31	36	46	38	35	36	na	na	na	39	41	33	41	36	32
West Germany	50	51	49	55	50	47	53	48	40	51	52	48	53	48	25	53	53	43
Denmark	24	27	22	23	24	26	28	26	21	25	24	25	24	25	25	31	25	15
Finland	59	59	60	49	62	61	53	64	57	57	58	64	67	59	60	63	60	57
Norway	30	30	31	24	26	38	41	31	24	35	27	27	29	30	30	33	32	10
Sweden	09	10	08	10	06	11	10	10	05	09	09	08	08	09	13	17	08	07
Japan	10	10	09	08	07	14	13	08	10	12	08	10	08	10	13	09	11	10
Switzerland	na	na	na	na	na	na	na	na	na	na	na	na	na	na	na	na	na	na
Total	45	44	45	41	45	47	49	44	38	48	45	42	43	44	44	49	45	39

Ranking:

Bulgaria	74
Czechoslovakia	68
Romania	65
Lithuania	64
Russia	64
East Germany	64
Spain	62
Belarus	60
Moscow	60
Portugal	60
Slovenia	60
Finland	59
Poland	57
Estonia	57
Turkey	56
Italy	54
West Germany	50
Belgium	49
France	49
Nigeria	48
Latvia	48
Ireland	47
Austria	44
North Ireland	43
Britain	43
Netherlands	42
Hungary	41
China	39
Chile	37
Iceland	37
India	36
Brazil	34
Canada	31
Norway	30
South Korea	29
Argentina	25
Denmark	24
Mexico	23
South Africa	20
United States	16
Japan	10
Sweden	09

Note: Countries in the left column are ranked according to GNP per capita. / The percentages in the bottom row give each country an equal weight. / na=not ascertained.

V130 JOBS PREFERENCE TO OWN NATIONALITY

Do you agree or disagree with the following statement?
"When jobs are scarce, employers should give priority to own nationality over immigrants." (% "agree")

	Total	Gender		Age			Education			Income			Political Affinity			Values		
		Male	Female	16-29	30-49	50+	Lower	Medium	Upper	Lower	Middle	Upper	Left	Center	Right	Mat	Mixed	Postmat
India	84	82	86	85	85	81	85	86	82	87	82	82	83	81	84	86	82	84
Nigeria	80	79	81	80	80	76	84	79	79	79	78	82	89	83	73	82	78	78
China	65	63	67	58	66	71	67	65	60	66	64	64	na	na	na	70	62	45
Romania	75	72	78	69	75	79	82	74	67	76	76	73	80	75	72	81	73	55
Turkey	75	77	72	72	74	80	77	75	64	77	78	68	70	74	77	81	74	68
Poland	67	68	67	49	66	78	74	65	59	70	66	65	69	64	71	75	64	63
Bulgaria	87	85	88	84	87	88	86	88	86	85	89	87	90	89	80	92	86	81
Chile	83	82	83	81	82	88	86	82	80	86	84	79	82	84	83	84	83	82
Czechoslovakia	88	87	89	87	87	90	91	88	82	91	89	84	86	89	89	92	87	82
South Africa	74	73	74	74	76	69	73	75	67	73	77	70	74	72	69	75	74	69
Lithuania	92	90	94	95	89	93	92	93	87	93	93	89	na	na	na	92	92	95
Hungary	87	85	88	88	85	89	89	87	74	90	86	78	82	89	84	89	86	74
Argentina	60	59	61	61	63	57	61	60	60	63	62	58	49	63	71	63	61	55
Brazil	82	82	81	81	83	81	85	80	79	84	81	79	84	77	84	82	81	80
Mexico	83	83	82	82	83	85	82	81	84	85	82	80	85	82	78	86	82	81
Belarus	56	56	56	54	54	63	69	57	51	59	55	54	57	53	56	60	54	48
Russia	63	60	65	64	58	67	71	64	56	64	65	56	54	61	70	66	62	48
Moscow	69	64	72	64	66	75	77	70	65	68	68	70	68	65	76	73	70	53
Latvia	80	73	84	82	79	80	86	82	73	84	80	78	na	na	na	85	79	81
Estonia	82	79	84	83	81	82	79	84	73	83	76	84	na	na	na	83	83	81
Portugal	88	89	86	86	88	89	87	89	87	87	88	88	92	86	87	86	88	91
South Korea	72	72	73	67	73	80	78	72	70	73	72	75	67	70	75	77	71	61
Ireland	69	67	70	64	67	74	76	63	52	74	71	66	60	73	67	73	70	61
North Ireland	62	59	65	46	61	76	68	55	46	71	60	52	48	62	66	69	63	46
Slovenia	79	78	80	83	77	79	80	82	72	84	79	72	68	79	82	84	79	59
Spain	75	74	75	71	70	81	77	74	64	84	72	70	71	71	79	81	74	62
East Germany	69	70	69	67	65	74	75	61	53	70	70	67	57	72	78	81	73	53
Britain	51	46	55	43	46	60	56	43	33	58	45	43	47	51	54	59	53	36
Italy	74	73	74	64	71	81	76	59	44	75	69	64	65	75	81	86	75	58
Netherlands	30	37	28	25	23	46	37	30	22	32	24	27	15	30	45	55	34	17
Belgium	66	65	66	58	62	74	71	67	53	69	59	62	49	68	70	77	69	48
Austria	77	81	75	74	73	83	81	76	68	78	77	76	74	76	78	83	80	69
France	63	64	62	49	62	75	72	60	47	72	57	56	46	68	84	78	68	41
Canada	53	53	52	53	52	53	62	54	43	59	54	44	42	56	49	61	54	44
United States	51	52	51	45	44	62	58	52	46	58	51	45	40	54	52	57	52	45
Iceland	87	86	88	85	84	94	92	91	80	na	na	na	81	87	90	91	87	73
West Germany	62	63	61	50	59	70	71	48	40	65	64	57	46	64	72	83	66	42
Denmark	53	52	54	50	45	64	69	57	41	59	55	39	36	57	57	77	52	27
Finland	71	75	66	65	68	84	71	78	62	75	73	64	66	72	75	82	70	69
Norway	59	57	60	51	48	76	76	66	43	66	51	51	44	59	65	73	57	27
Sweden	35	33	37	36	29	41	47	36	12	38	37	29	25	40	34	53	36	21
Japan	65	65	64	64	65	65	64	65	65	59	67	68	55	62	72	69	67	54
Switzerland	na	na	na	na	na	na	na	na	na	na	na	na	na	na	na	na	na	na
Total	70	69	71	66	68	75	75	69	61	72	69	66	63	69	72	77	70	60

Note: Countries in the left column are ranked according to GNP per capita. / The percentages in the bottom row give each country an equal weight. / na=not ascertained.

Ranking:

Lithuania	92
Czechoslovakia	88
Portugal	88
Bulgaria	87
Hungary	87
Iceland	87
India	84
Chile	83
Mexico	83
Brazil	82
Estonia	82
Nigeria	80
Latvia	80
Slovenia	79
Austria	77
Romania	75
Turkey	75
Spain	75
South Africa	74
Italy	74
South Korea	72
Finland	71
Moscow	69
Ireland	69
East Germany	69
Poland	67
Belgium	66
China	65
Japan	65
Russia	63
France	63
North Ireland	62
West Germany	62
Argentina	60
Norway	59
Belarus	56
Canada	53
Denmark	53
Britain	51
United States	51
Sweden	35
Netherlands	30

V131 HANDICAPPED WORK UNFAIR

Do you agree or disagree with the following statement?

"It is unfair to give work to handicapped people when able-bodied people can't find jobs." (% "agree")

	Total	Gender		Age			Education			Income			Political Affinity			Values		
		Male	Female	16-29	30-49	50+	Lower	Medium	Upper	Lower	Middle	Upper	Left	Center	Right	Mat	Mixed	Postmat
India	22	23	21	23	21	24	24	23	20	27	22	19	26	22	17	22	21	25
Nigeria	36	37	35	38	33	29	44	36	33	35	37	36	39	38	38	37	37	28
China	35	37	33	33	38	33	39	37	29	37	35	33	41	36	40	36	34	42
Romania	39	37	40	37	37	41	48	38	28	39	43	34	21	25	32	44	35	31
Turkey	26	26	26	27	24	27	31	21	13	29	26	22	21	25	na	25	29	18
Poland	42	44	41	38	37	50	47	42	24	42	43	44	37	39	47	47	45	35
Bulgaria	46	49	43	50	43	46	56	48	32	45	47	47	41	48	43	44	45	44
Chile	21	23	20	18	19	29	29	19	14	30	22	11	20	21	21	27	20	15
Czechoslovakia	31	32	30	31	29	32	36	29	24	34	30	28	32	29	31	32	31	24
South Africa	23	26	20	24	23	21	30	22	07	31	23	10	23	17	24	23	23	23
Lithuania	56	54	57	49	56	61	58	55	55	56	58	51	21	23	na	62	54	50
Hungary	25	27	22	21	24	27	32	18	12	31	21	19	21	23	25	25	26	10
Argentina	11	13	08	11	09	12	15	10	05	16	08	09	06	09	12	14	11	05
Brazil	19	21	17	18	17	24	30	17	03	27	17	12	17	17	24	21	18	11
Mexico	24	26	22	24	22	31	28	24	15	27	25	18	19	25	24	33	22	15
Belarus	39	42	37	44	35	44	39	42	37	43	38	38	39	39	38	44	38	27
Russia	42	42	43	39	39	49	49	42	39	45	46	37	36	44	48	44	43	29
Moscow	31	32	30	31	27	36	47	39	22	30	32	28	27	32	48	40	31	17
Latvia	34	38	31	35	32	36	54	36	25	28	37	36	na	na	na	34	36	32
Estonia	30	31	29	33	27	31	31	32	32	28	29	33	25	21	24	35	28	27
Portugal	23	23	24	17	24	29	30	15	07	31	22	15	21	13	16	30	20	12
South Korea	14	12	16	07	14	28	24	14	10	17	11	16	07	10	05	16	14	10
Ireland	09	11	07	04	08	12	12	05	05	16	07	05	07	06	05	06	09	08
North Ireland	06	07	06	05	02	12	08	05	00	09	06	01	07	06	05	06	08	00
Slovenia	39	44	34	34	34	46	50	37	21	49	36	24	29	34	45	47	36	23
Spain	23	23	23	18	20	30	27	12	13	38	20	14	20	22	22	29	19	17
East Germany	16	18	14	18	14	18	18	15	10	18	13	17	12	18	16	19	17	13
Britain	07	08	07	05	05	11	09	04	04	10	03	05	06	07	08	11	08	03
Italy	18	19	17	13	14	25	19	17	17	22	11	17	14	18	20	26	18	09
Netherlands	10	12	08	08	07	17	11	13	06	12	10	07	06	10	13	18	12	06
Belgium	16	17	15	13	14	20	22	14	09	20	15	12	15	14	15	20	16	11
Austria	18	21	16	14	16	21	20	18	10	22	17	15	21	17	18	14	19	14
France	10	10	09	05	08	14	13	05	05	13	08	04	07	08	08	09	10	05
Canada	08	10	07	05	05	13	11	09	04	10	09	06	06	09	12	13	11	07
United States	10	11	08	08	07	13	14	10	07	11	11	07	05	10	07	05	06	06
Iceland	05	06	05	05	03	08	10	02	03	na	na	na	04	04	04	05	06	00
West Germany	16	18	14	12	14	16	19	12	06	20	16	12	11	15	23	23	19	14
Denmark	09	10	08	06	04	10	17	06	04	14	05	06	08	08	09	13	10	05
Finland	05	07	03	05	04	10	11	09	09	08	04	05	02	05	08	19	09	07
Norway	06	07	06	05	05	09	11	07	07	06	05	05	04	07	06	07	09	03
Sweden	05	05	06	03	05	11	08	04	08	07	08	03	08	04	12	09	06	07
Japan	07	08	06	05	05	na	07	07	07	07	07	07	08	04	na	na	na	na
Switzerland	na	na	na	na	na	na	na	na	na	na	na	na	na	na	na	na	na	na
Total	22	23	21	20	20	25	27	21	15	25	22	19	18	19	22	25	22	16

Ranking:

Lithuania	56
Bulgaria	46
Poland	42
Russia	42
Romania	39
Belarus	39
Slovenia	39
Nigeria	36
China	35
Latvia	34
Czechoslovakia	31
Moscow	31
Estonia	30
Turkey	26
Hungary	25
Mexico	24
South Africa	23
Portugal	23
Spain	23
India	22
Chile	21
Brazil	19
Italy	18
Austria	18
East Germany	16
Belgium	16
West Germany	14
South Korea	11
Argentina	11
Netherlands	10
France	10
United States	10
Ireland	09
Denmark	09
Canada	08
Britain	07
Japan	07
North Ireland	06
Norway	06
Iceland	05
Finland	05
Sweden	05

Note: Countries in the left column are ranked according to GNP per capita. / The percentages in the bottom row give each country an equal weight. / na=not ascertained.

V132 FINANCIAL SATISFACTION

How satisfied are you with the financial situation of your household?

(% "satisfied"—codes 7 to 10 from a ten-point scale where 1=Dissatisfied and 10=Satisfied)

	Total	Gender Male	Gender Female	Age 16-29	Age 30-49	Age 50+	Education Lower	Education Middle	Education Upper	Income Lower	Income Middle	Income Upper	Political Affinity Left	Political Affinity Center	Political Affinity Right	Values Mat	Values Mixed	Values Postmat	Ranking	
India	47	45	50	48	48	45	36	48	53	29	48	64	41	45	63	48	49	54	Switzerland	83
Nigeria	38	31	47	39	36	39	39	37	38	21	41	58	38	31	41	41	37	32	Netherlands	75
China	47	45	49	41	44	57	47	50	38	42	47	50	na	na	32	51	45	22	Belgium	70
Romania	29	33	26	28	30	30	27	29	33	09	23	53	31	29	32	28	31	27	Canada	68
Turkey	21	20	22	24	21	16	18	24	29	09	16	42	19	20	23	20	21	22	Italy	67
Poland	30	30	29	32	29	30	28	29	39	14	25	54	30	30	29	31	29	37	Denmark	66
Bulgaria	17	21	14	21	19	14	14	17	20	08	11	35	21	15	18	18	17	18	Sweden	63
Chile	41	43	40	47	37	40	35	46	43	24	40	62	41	42	46	35	44	44	United States	62
Czechoslovakia	30	31	28	27	24	38	32	28	31	25	29	36	30	26	36	28	30	29	Austria	61
South Africa	34	32	35	31	35	35	19	38	60	12	33	62	29	39	48	36	32	36	West Germany	60
Lithuania	na	na	na	na	na	na	na	na	na	na	na	na	na	na	na	na	na	na	Ireland	59
Hungary	30	30	30	31	30	29	27	29	41	22	33	46	25	32	37	29	30	33	Finland	59
Argentina	36	38	34	44	32	33	30	35	46	20	33	51	24	37	52	33	37	35	North Ireland	58
Brazil	37	38	36	37	33	44	40	35	39	32	35	43	32	38	41	39	36	38	Britain	56
Mexico	51	51	52	51	54	46	49	48	61	43	50	69	43	53	63	55	51	46	Norway	56
Belarus	27	31	24	22	29	31	35	25	27	18	29	35	26	26	41	33	24	28	Iceland	53
Russia	27	28	27	25	25	32	29	26	29	19	28	38	28	25	31	27	28	25	Mexico	51
Moscow	26	29	24	30	23	31	34	24	26	18	28	39	26	25	39	26	27	26	Spain	48
Latvia	21	21	21	22	17	29	19	20	23	13	19	27	na	na	na	21	21	20	India	47
Estonia	31	30	31	34	23	39	34	27	38	17	39	47	na	na	na	28	33	37	China	47
Portugal	43	46	40	44	46	39	39	49	54	33	37	63	40	40	51	46	42	42	Portugal	43
South Korea	40	40	40	40	40	38	28	34	52	29	37	63	35	33	46	41	38	41	East Germany	43
Ireland	59	58	60	57	52	66	54	63	69	50	52	70	46	55	72	61	59	54	France	42
North Ireland	58	58	57	59	52	63	56	58	69	40	57	72	54	57	62	55	60	53	Chile	41
Slovenia	23	27	19	33	19	21	19	24	27	08	22	56	22	27	27	21	23	28	Japan	41
Spain	48	51	45	52	49	31	45	54	55	34	47	62	46	46	55	46	49	52	South Korea	40
East Germany	43	44	43	38	46	43	43	41	46	33	45	50	44	44	44	37	44	44	Nigeria	38
Britain	56	60	54	56	55	58	53	64	65	40	60	74	44	55	70	58	56	58	Brazil	37
Italy	67	66	67	68	66	67	66	69	63	60	72	81	64	68	70	67	67	58	Argentina	36
Netherlands	75	81	73	72	76	79	72	75	81	55	87	94	70	76	84	67	79	65	South Africa	34
Belgium	70	72	69	70	71	70	65	73	76	57	73	82	63	73	80	59	79	77	Estonia	31
Austria	61	63	60	69	63	55	60	60	69	53	64	65	48	63	63	66	69	78	Poland	30
France	42	43	41	38	40	47	38	44	47	26	42	62	42	36	53	57	59	68	Czechoslovakia	30
Canada	68	69	68	62	67	76	67	69	69	53	69	82	42	36	74	38	42	44	Hungary	30
United States	62	66	58	48	58	71	63	59	65	44	62	77	63	68	71	72	68	69	Romania	29
Iceland	53	57	49	49	51	61	56	55	50	na	na	na	60	60	61	59	64	58	Belarus	27
West Germany	60	61	59	48	60	66	60	60	61	48	61	71	52	48	62	53	55	42	Russia	27
Denmark	66	68	65	65	61	73	68	68	64	55	61	74	52	62	69	55	63	58	Moscow	26
Finland	59	57	63	46	60	71	63	56	61	51	70	66	56	65	75	68	68	55	Slovenia	23
Norway	56	56	57	45	52	68	61	52	59	46	60	67	57	51	72	68	61	53	Turkey	21
Sweden	63	66	60	57	61	73	64	62	64	66	45	77	49	60	61	54	58	54	Latvia	21
Japan	41	40	42	47	37	44	38	40	46	27	39	56	46	39	50	62	65	60	Bulgaria	17
Switzerland	83	81	84	71	83	87	84	82	79	73	88	93	78	83	84	88	82	81		
Total	**46**	**45**	**45**	**44**	**44**	**49**	**44**	**46**	**50**	**34**	**45**	**60**	**43**	**46**	**54**	**45**	**46**	**45**		

Note: Countries in the left column are ranked according to GNP per capita. / The percentages in the bottom row give each country an equal weight. / na=not ascertained.

V133. How often, if at all, do you think about the meaning and purpose of life?

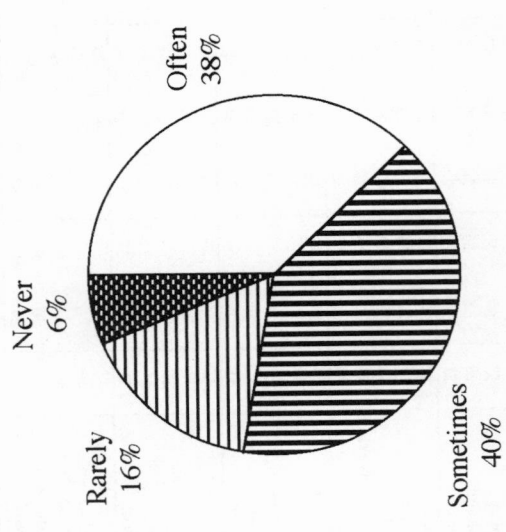

Often
38%

Never
6%

Rarely
16%

Sometimes
40%

V134. Do you ever think about death?

Often
19%

Sometimes
38%

Never
17%

Rarely
26%

V133 THINK MEANING OF LIFE

How often, if at all, do you think about the meaning and purpose of life? Often, sometimes, rarely, never. (% "often")

	Total	Gender Male	Gender Female	Age 16-29	Age 30-49	Age 50+	Education Lower	Education Medium	Education Upper	Income Lower	Income Middle	Income Upper	Political Affinity Left	Political Affinity Center	Political Affinity Right	Values Mat	Values Mixed	Values Postmat
India	34	35	32	34	33	35	27	32	39	31	29	40	43	30	34	35	32	45
Nigeria	59	61	55	57	61	60	63	55	61	55	63	60	64	61	61	63	58	49
China	32	34	28	39	31	24	31	34	31	36	28	30	na	na	na	30	31	57
Romania	45	39	51	44	49	41	36	47	53	50	43	44	46	43	51	43	44	59
Turkey	38	40	36	38	38	40	38	37	40	36	39	41	41	40	31	33	40	43
Poland	34	29	38	25	35	37	42	28	29	38	33	30	29	31	37	35	34	30
Bulgaria	44	38	50	46	43	45	47	43	44	41	43	48	40	45	48	42	45	42
Chile	53	50	56	55	55	50	52	53	56	50	53	59	54	53	52	50	53	61
Czechoslovakia	31	28	35	27	30	39	34	29	34	35	31	29	32	29	35	26	33	35
South Africa	57	57	57	52	60	59	56	56	66	54	56	61	60	56	60	56	58	53
Lithuania	41	38	44	40	38	45	47	39	44	47	38	34	na	na	na	43	41	51
Hungary	45	41	48	47	44	45	48	44	33	47	45	34	45	47	50	46	43	51
Argentina	57	53	61	55	61	55	54	58	62	54	57	60	64	57	59	49	57	67
Brazil	44	43	44	37	46	52	47	40	51	44	42	45	47	41	43	44	41	58
Mexico	40	38	42	41	41	36	37	41	47	35	41	47	44	40	42	35	39	50
Belarus	35	29	41	38	33	36	30	33	39	37	34	35	38	30	31	34	35	43
Russia	41	36	45	39	43	40	40	39	43	45	39	40	46	40	44	42	40	46
Moscow	38	32	43	39	39	36	31	37	40	40	37	35	38	38	40	34	38	43
Latvia	36	25	44	44	33	35	32	38	35	36	39	35	na	na	na	30	39	38
Estonia	35	28	42	33	36	36	33	35	38	37	32	36	na	na	na	36	39	32
Portugal	43	41	45	42	47	42	41	43	49	47	39	40	43	47	38	40	45	40
South Korea	39	42	37	51	35	31	28	37	47	40	34	43	45	36	40	33	40	63
Ireland	34	29	38	21	32	45	35	33	34	36	30	35	26	32	41	37	32	39
North Ireland	33	26	39	21	31	45	35	32	28	36	32	34	38	28	38	34	38	27
Slovenia	37	33	40	38	43	29	34	41	35	38	35	38	43	40	43	32	38	41
Spain	26	24	28	29	26	24	23	31	36	24	24	32	26	26	32	18	27	36
East Germany	40	34	45	30	39	47	39	44	39	42	38	39	39	39	46	34	42	38
Britain	36	33	40	25	38	41	35	39	38	38	38	37	37	35	38	37	36	37
Italy	47	42	52	47	46	48	46	55	56	52	44	50	47	52	47	42	49	49
Netherlands	30	29	31	23	34	33	28	25	39	40	22	36	33	25	36	28	30	31
Belgium	29	26	31	28	32	25	25	30	34	26	33	31	27	31	31	24	29	33
Austria	28	22	32	21	30	30	27	29	31	30	24	31	36	29	27	30	27	30
France	39	34	44	39	42	37	37	40	45	37	36	44	40	41	33	31	39	48
Canada	43	41	46	42	45	43	46	38	49	50	43	42	53	40	47	41	41	50
United States	48	48	50	41	46	53	50	47	50	51	49	43	45	46	53	46	48	51
Iceland	36	27	46	31	35	46	44	35	32	na	28	na	33	42	34	39	35	41
West Germany	30	26	34	25	28	35	29	30	37	28	25	27	32	29	30	31	29	33
Denmark	29	22	36	20	30	35	30	27	30	25	27	27	30	27	32	27	27	38
Finland	38	31	46	32	39	41	46	33	41	34	38	35	44	37	36	55	37	36
Norway	31	27	36	24	27	42	41	24	34	41	27	28	27	33	33	28	33	36
Sweden	24	20	29	22	23	28	22	23	30	22	32	21	26	22	25	22	25	23
Japan	21	22	21	23	21	20	16	20	29	22	18	25	38	24	24	17	25	26
Switzerland	44	41	47	46	46	41	41	44	57	47	48	42	58	43	43	35	42	54
Total	**38**	**35**	**42**	**36**	**39**	**40**	**38**	**38**	**42**	**40**	**37**	**39**	**41**	**38**	**40**	**36**	**38**	**43**

Note: Countries in the left column are ranked according to GNP per capita. / The percentages in the bottom row give each country an equal weight / na=not ascertained.

Ranking:

Nigeria	59
South Africa	57
Argentina	57
Chile	53
United States	48
Italy	47
Romania	45
Hungary	45
Bulgaria	44
Brazil	44
Switzerland	44
Portugal	43
Canada	43
Lithuania	41
Russia	41
Mexico	40
East Germany	40
South Korea	39
France	39
Turkey	38
Moscow	38
Finland	38
Slovenia	37
Latvia	36
Britain	36
Iceland	36
Belarus	35
Estonia	35
India	34
Poland	34
Ireland	34
North Ireland	33
China	32
Czechoslovakia	31
Norway	31
Netherlands	30
West Germany	30
Belgium	29
Denmark	29
Austria	28
Spain	26
Sweden	24
Japan	21

V134 THINK OF DEATH

Do you ever think about death? Would you say often, sometimes, rarely, never.
(% "often")

	Total	Gender		Age			Education			Income			Political Affinity			Values		
		Male	Female	16-29	30-49	50+	Lower	Medium	Upper	Lower	Middle	Upper	Left	Center	Right	Mat	Mixed	Postmat
India	12	11	12	08	12	19	15	10	10	11	10	13	13	11	na	11	12	11
Nigeria	44	44	43	41	46	48	56	42	40	39	49	41	49	48	42	49	42	36
China	02	02	02	02	02	03	02	01	03	02	02	02	na	na	na	02	01	09
Romania	20	15	24	13	15	28	27	14	17	30	17	15	na	na	na	21	17	26
Turkey	43	39	46	32	42	61	52	32	18	52	43	33	30	43	48	51	42	32
Poland	na	na	na	na	na	na	na	na	na	na	na	na	16	17	17	18	17	17
Bulgaria	18	11	23	13	14	24	24	16	14	20	16	13	27	32	29	18	17	29
Chile	31	26	36	26	29	42	37	27	30	34	30	29	na	na	na	30	32	na
Czechoslovakia	na	na	na	na	na	na	na	na	na	na	na	na	na	na	na	na	na	na
South Africa	na	na	na	na	na	na	na	na	na	na	na	na	na	na	na	25	19	16
Lithuania	20	11	29	14	14	32	35	16	16	27	19	10	10	14	20	23	16	18
Hungary	18	10	25	11	11	27	24	13	13	25	13	11	34	29	30	19	16	18
Argentina	29	24	34	26	30	31	27	32	32	31	28	28	23	18	24	24	19	28
Brazil	22	17	27	17	23	29	27	20	17	25	21	19	16	16	21	17	17	23
Mexico	18	18	19	15	18	25	19	19	15	19	19	17	10	08	13	22	09	11
Belarus	10	07	13	06	09	18	14	10	09	15	07	09	11	14	17	13	16	20
Russia	18	11	24	10	14	30	27	14	17	19	19	16	na	na	na	13	12	12
Moscow	13	10	15	11	11	16	14	11	13	14	12	12	na	14	na	09	14	07
Latvia	13	07	16	12	11	15	19	12	11	10	12	15	na	na	na	12	12	12
Estonia	13	08	16	08	12	18	15	12	12	14	08	13	20	17	24	22	20	15
Portugal	20	10	29	11	19	31	24	10	13	25	20	12	22	17	na	na	na	na
South Korea	na	na	na	na	na	na	na	na	na	na	na	na	na	na	na	25	18	19
Ireland	20	13	26	09	15	32	22	18	16	27	16	18	16	18	22	20	18	11
North Ireland	18	12	22	08	14	28	22	11	03	22	18	07	25	16	18	10	06	11
Slovenia	08	06	09	05	05	12	07	09	07	11	05	07	08	08	08	18	19	20
Spain	19	13	24	15	16	25	20	14	19	24	17	17	14	20	25	18	12	11
East Germany	13	10	16	08	09	21	14	13	09	22	10	08	08	15	14	20	19	19
Britain	19	14	23	13	17	25	20	19	14	22	17	15	19	19	19	20	19	19
Italy	32	25	38	22	28	41	31	35	46	36	29	28	30	33	37	35	31	29
Netherlands	14	12	15	09	15	19	16	09	17	17	13	14	18	10	17	15	16	17
Belgium	16	12	20	11	18	17	16	13	16	19	17	16	16	16	16	20	16	12
Austria	15	08	20	10	13	20	17	13	19	19	13	15	20	18	22	22	18	23
France	20	16	23	17	18	23	23	16	19	20	21	19	20	20	19	16	18	21
Canada	19	16	22	16	17	23	20	16	21	23	18	18	20	17	21	23	21	21
United States	21	19	24	16	18	27	27	22	16	30	15	18	20	17	19	16	20	12
Iceland	18	13	24	15	17	25	22	17	16	na	na	na	17	17	21	27	18	15
West Germany	18	12	24	09	13	28	19	16	18	13	13	17	20	22	15	15	18	26
Denmark	19	11	27	10	19	26	22	17	19	12	12	13	19	15	15	21	15	13
Finland	15	09	20	13	11	25	26	13	12	16	13	13	11	15	15	12	15	10
Norway	14	10	18	10	12	21	20	12	13	17	10	14	12	10	13	11	12	11
Sweden	12	08	16	10	12	13	09	12	17	11	11	08	13	12	12	10	13	17
Japan	12	10	13	09	11	15	11	12	13	na	na	14	na	na	na	na	na	na
Switzerland	na	na	na	na	na	na	na	na	na	na	na	na	na	na	na	na	na	na
Total	**19**	**14**	**23**	**13**	**17**	**25**	**22**	**16**	**17**	**22**	**17**	**16**	**19**	**19**	**20**	**20**	**18**	**18**

Note: Countries in the left column are ranked according to GNP per capita. / The percentages in the bottom row give each country an equal weight. / na=not ascertained.

Ranking:

Nigeria	44
Turkey	43
Italy	32
Chile	31
Argentina	29
Brazil	22
United States	21
Romania	20
Lithuania	20
Portugal	20
Ireland	20
France	20
Spain	19
Britain	19
Canada	19
Denmark	19
Bulgaria	18
Hungary	18
Mexico	18
Russia	18
North Ireland	18
Iceland	18
West Germany	18
Belgium	16
Austria	15
Finland	15
Netherlands	14
Norway	14
Moscow	13
Latvia	13
Estonia	13
East Germany	13
India	12
Sweden	12
Japan	12
Belarus	08
Slovenia	08
China	02

V135-V141. Statements about the meaning of life

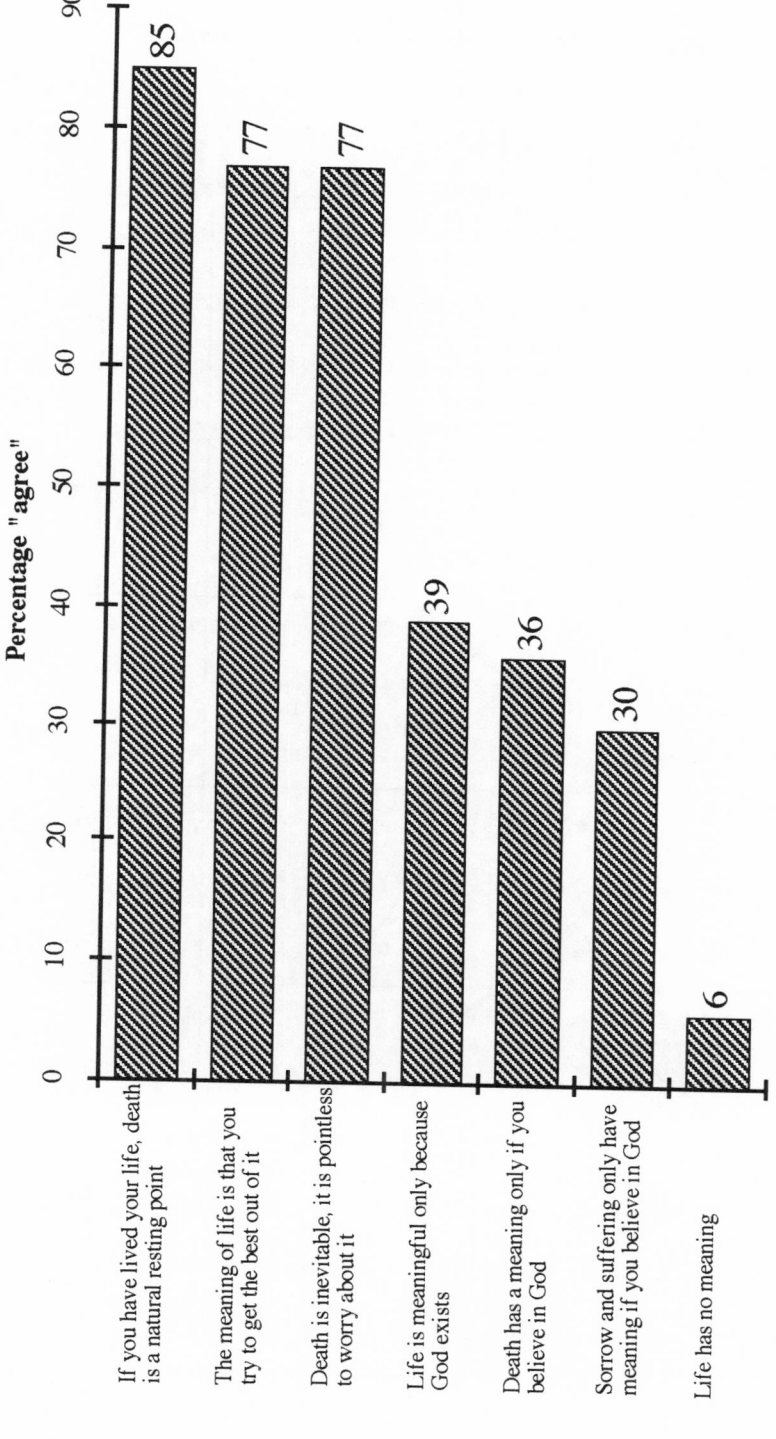

Percentage "agree"

V135 LIFE: GOD EXISTS

I am going to read out a list of statements about the meaning of life. Please indicate whether you agree or disagree with each of them.

"Life is meaningful only because God exists" (% "agree")

	Total	Gender		Age			Education			Income			Political Affinity			Values		
		Male	Female	16-29	30-49	50+	Lower	Medium	Upper	Lower	Middle	Upper	Left	Center	Right	Mat	Mixed	Postmat
India	61	57	65	55	62	70	76	62	52	67	62	54	60	58	55	62	58	58
Nigeria	92	91	93	91	92	93	98	92	89	93	91	93	93	90	93	96	90	90
China	83	84	80	76	83	89	78	85	81	85	80	82	na	na	na	83	83	74
Romania	55	49	61	45	47	69	73	47	43	61	58	48	61	52	50	63	50	44
Turkey	na	na	na	na	na	na	na	na	na	na	na	na	na	na	na	na	na	na
Poland	na	na	na	na	na	na	na	na	na	na	na	na	na	na	na	na	na	na
Bulgaria	16	12	20	13	13	22	29	13	09	17	16	11	08	12	21	17	15	18
Chile	62	55	68	51	61	77	76	55	52	74	62	46	52	62	62	73	61	46
Czechoslovakia	na	na	na	na	na	na	na	na	na	na	na	na	na	na	na	na	na	na
South Africa	na	na	na	na	na	na	na	na	na	na	na	na	na	na	na	na	na	na
Lithuania	28	23	32	12	18	52	59	19	15	38	22	17	15	27	40	34	26	27
Hungary	31	26	36	13	19	49	47	16	13	45	22	15	33	52	60	33	29	25
Argentina	51	50	52	43	46	63	61	44	43	62	54	37	50	71	77	61	52	38
Brazil	74	69	79	68	73	86	90	70	53	86	73	60	67	53	60	80	71	58
Mexico	52	49	56	47	50	70	56	52	41	57	47	48	31	53	60	66	47	42
Belarus	17	14	20	09	14	31	32	17	11	22	14	14	16	14	22	21	14	12
Russia	23	14	29	14	17	35	38	22	15	31	20	16	12	20	25	28	19	18
Moscow	18	13	22	17	14	26	34	20	14	18	19	17	16	18	na	21	16	17
Latvia	16	10	20	13	13	26	35	16	11	18	15	16	na	na	na	16	15	16
Estonia	11	09	14	08	11	16	19	11	06	15	10	08	40	40	54	12	11	08
Portugal	46	37	55	26	44	67	59	15	23	60	40	29	40	40	54	57	42	17
South Korea	na	na	na	na	na	na	na	na	na	na	na	na	na	na	na	na	na	na
Ireland	64	61	67	41	63	80	73	56	48	80	62	55	38	63	72	71	65	53
North Ireland	68	60	74	48	64	86	76	56	48	81	67	53	50	67	72	83	66	51
Slovenia	24	19	28	15	18	37	39	15	10	33	20	12	15	17	34	31	22	11
Spain	37	27	45	17	30	57	42	27	11	52	33	26	22	37	51	51	33	19
East Germany	22	17	25	11	19	31	22	25	16	31	21	14	09	23	35	29	20	22
Britain	36	28	44	16	28	55	39	30	26	47	30	23	23	35	39	46	35	31
Italy	41	33	48	30	32	55	41	35	29	49	32	23	35	50	44	49	39	34
Netherlands	23	26	21	12	20	39	29	18	21	23	23	21	25	18	40	36	25	14
Belgium	27	22	33	12	21	43	32	26	21	35	37	25	10	26	36	33	28	19
Austria	38	33	41	22	33	49	45	33	34	47	25	29	34	33	43	53	39	26
France	29	26	31	16	20	47	33	24	25	32	35	25	17	32	46	35	29	23
Canada	35	31	38	27	29	49	47	34	28	46	24	25	27	35	38	39	36	30
United States	61	59	63	54	57	69	64	65	55	69	61	53	39	60	71	66	65	48
Iceland	28	21	34	14	23	54	45	24	18	na	na	na	21	32	28	34	27	16
West Germany	30	22	38	13	20	48	35	23	23	39	27	23	16	20	44	46	31	19
Denmark	19	13	25	07	11	39	36	12	15	30	14	07	15	32	33	25	20	07
Finland	28	26	31	13	23	54	40	29	22	24	24	24	15	35	38	48	36	30
Norway	27	23	30	12	19	46	51	19	22	37	20	23	21	39	71	32	25	15
Sweden	14	13	16	10	10	25	18	12	14	15	17	12	09	17	18	20	17	06
Japan	18	17	20	09	14	31	31	16	12	23	19	14	08	15	24	22	16	12
Switzerland	na	na	na	na	na	na	na	na	na	na	na	na	na	na	na	na	na	na
Total	**38**	**33**	**42**	**27**	**33**	**52**	**49**	**33**	**29**	**46**	**36**	**31**	**28**	**38**	**44**	**45**	**37**	**29**

Ranking:

Nigeria	92
China	83
Brazil	74
North Ireland	68
Ireland	64
Chile	62
India	61
United States	61
Romania	55
Mexico	52
Argentina	51
Portugal	46
Italy	41
Austria	38
Spain	37
Britain	36
Canada	35
Hungary	31
West Germany	30
France	29
Lithuania	28
Iceland	28
Finland	28
Belgium	27
Norway	27
Slovenia	24
Russia	23
Netherlands	23
East Germany	22
Denmark	19
Moscow	18
Japan	18
Belarus	17
Bulgaria	16
Latvia	16
Sweden	14
Estonia	11

Note: Countries in the left column are ranked according to GNP per capita. / The percentages in the bottom row give each country an equal weight. / na=not ascertained.

V136 LIFE: GET THE BEST

I am going to read out a list of statements about the meaning of life. Please indicate whether you agree or disagree with each of them.
"The meaning of life is that you try to get the best out of it" (% "agree")

	Total	Gender		Age			Education			Income			Political Affinity			Values		
		Male	Female	16-29	30-49	50+	Lower	Medium	Upper	Lower	Middle	Upper	Left	Center	Right	Mat	Mixed	Postmat
India	86	87	85	87	87	82	83	87	86	87	82	88	89	84	82	92	82	83
Nigeria	77	79	73	77	75	82	82	78	73	76	77	79	79	76	81	77	76	78
China	60	59	61	64	62	52	68	60	56	58	62	62	na	na	na	61	60	61
Romania	77	76	78	77	76	78	79	78	73	75	75	81	78	78	75	80	76	71
Turkey	na	na	na	na	na	na	na	na	na	na	na	na	na	na	na	na	na	na
Poland	na	na	na	na	na	na	na	na	na	na	na	na	na	na	na	na	na	na
Bulgaria	79	76	81	81	76	80	85	80	71	81	77	77	79	75	76	81	81	65
Chile	88	89	88	87	89	89	90	87	87	89	88	87	88	88	90	89	90	83
Czechoslovakia	na	na	na	na	na	na	na	na	na	na	na	na	na	na	na	na	na	na
South Africa	na	na	na	na	na	na	na	na	na	na	na	na	na	na	na	na	na	na
Lithuania	59	62	57	62	56	61	64	59	52	62	60	54	na	na	na	61	61	53
Hungary	92	92	91	90	91	92	92	91	92	91	93	90	93	91	93	92	91	92
Argentina	89	89	89	89	88	89	95	83	85	91	89	87	85	86	92	92	89	85
Brazil	86	87	85	86	85	87	89	86	76	88	85	83	83	83	90	87	85	79
Mexico	85	84	86	85	85	85	84	89	85	83	86	86	85	83	85	88	86	80
Belarus	41	44	38	47	39	39	51	43	36	39	39	45	43	37	44	43	40	36
Russia	35	42	30	42	34	31	39	33	34	37	37	29	29	38	33	35	35	29
Moscow	33	37	29	42	32	26	43	41	25	33	34	30	31	35	33	39	31	27
Latvia	53	56	52	57	52	51	65	57	43	58	48	54	na	na	na	62	50	54
Estonia	59	63	56	64	56	57	62	59	57	56	59	64	na	na	na	62	57	62
Portugal	67	70	65	72	63	65	65	70	75	69	65	68	71	67	67	70	67	65
South Korea	na	na	na	na	na	na	na	na	na	na	na	na	na	na	na	na	na	na
Ireland	82	81	82	89	83	76	84	81	73	83	84	78	85	81	80	82	82	80
North Ireland	90	91	90	92	91	88	91	88	86	91	94	84	93	91	87	88	91	93
Slovenia	84	86	83	85	82	85	85	86	81	88	82	83	78	86	86	86	84	80
Spain	84	86	83	86	86	82	85	87	78	83	88	83	88	82	79	87	83	84
East Germany	83	83	83	87	80	84	85	79	77	84	83	83	85	85	81	85	85	79
Britain	92	93	91	96	90	90	93	88	86	91	92	93	88	94	91	93	93	87
Italy	66	65	68	63	65	70	69	49	57	70	65	48	67	64	63	70	68	61
Netherlands	94	91	95	93	95	94	96	96	89	93	95	91	91	94	96	98	95	91
Belgium	89	89	89	90	87	89	90	88	86	90	86	88	88	87	89	89	90	88
Austria	85	83	85	87	82	86	87	84	81	87	86	82	85	86	82	88	84	83
France	89	87	90	91	91	84	89	89	88	92	90	84	88	90	85	89	90	86
Canada	83	81	84	88	80	83	86	83	81	83	83	80	75	84	83	85	85	77
United States	84	82	85	80	82	86	87	84	80	89	80	82	80	87	86	85	84	83
Iceland	92	93	90	94	90	92	94	92	90	na	na	na	89	94	91	96	92	84
West Germany	80	80	79	84	79	78	82	77	72	81	81	77	78	81	78	83	80	78
Denmark	91	89	93	90	91	92	96	91	88	91	92	89	86	93	91	93	92	85
Finland	51	52	49	57	45	63	48	52	50	50	53	49	53	52	51	66	52	47
Norway	94	95	94	96	93	95	95	96	93	94	94	95	92	95	96	97	94	94
Sweden	83	83	83	90	83	77	84	84	79	81	84	83	80	83	85	80	84	81
Japan	84	86	83	79	88	83	82	85	85	83	86	85	88	84	85	90	84	82
Switzerland	na	na	na	na	na	na	na	na	na	na	na	na	na	na	na	na	na	na
Total	**77**	**78**	**76**	**79**	**76**	**76**	**80**	**77**	**73**	**77**	**77**	**75**	**78**	**79**	**79**	**79**	**77**	**74**

Ranking:

Netherlands	94
Norway	94
Hungary	92
Britain	92
Iceland	92
Denmark	91
North Ireland	90
Argentina	89
Belgium	89
France	89
Chile	88
India	86
Brazil	86
Mexico	85
Austria	85
Slovenia	84
Spain	84
United States	84
Japan	84
East Germany	83
Canada	83
Sweden	83
Ireland	82
West Germany	80
Bulgaria	79
Nigeria	77
Romania	77
Portugal	67
Italy	66
China	60
Lithuania	59
Estonia	59
Latvia	53
Finland	51
Belarus	41
Russia	35
Moscow	33

Note: Countries in the left column are ranked according to GNP per capita. / The percentages in the bottom row give each country an equal weight. / na=not ascertained.

V137 LIFE: DEATH INEVITABLE

I am going to read out a list of statements about the meaning of life. Please indicate whether you agree or disagree with each of them. "Death is inevitable, it is pointless to worry about it" (% "agree")

	Total	Gender		Age			Education			Income			Political Affinity			Values		
		Male	Female	16-29	30-49	50+	Lower	Medium	Upper	Lower	Middle	Upper	Left	Center	Right	Mat	Mixed	Postmat
India	79	80	78	79	79	79	74	80	81	80	74	83	83	79	76	86	75	76
Nigeria	82	82	82	80	84	88	84	80	83	84	82	82	80	81	83	81	82	86
China	96	96	95	93	98	96	95	96	95	96	94	97	84	89	83	88	87	84
Romania	87	87	87	85	87	88	85	88	87	85	88	na	na	na	na	na	na	na
Turkey	na	na	na	na	na	na	na	na	na	na	na	na	na	na	na	na	na	na
Poland	na	na	na	na	na	na	na	na	na	na	na	na	na	na	na	na	na	na
Bulgaria	89	90	88	89	89	88	89	90	86	90	90	88	86	91	91	85	92	84
Chile	68	70	67	67	70	69	72	67	67	70	71	65	69	69	68	70	70	63
Czechoslovakia	na	na	na	na	na	na	na	na	na	na	na	na	na	na	na	na	na	na
South Africa	na	na	na	na	na	na	na	na	na	na	na	na	na	na	na	na	na	na
Lithuania	36	36	36	22	35	48	48	34	24	42	33	25	na	na	na	39	36	25
Hungary	90	89	91	90	89	91	91	89	88	91	90	85	87	91	90	89	92	83
Argentina	81	83	79	77	82	82	84	78	76	84	82	77	70	81	80	82	81	78
Brazil	74	76	73	73	73	79	78	75	63	78	75	71	73	74	72	76	74	66
Mexico	75	74	77	75	76	74	77	70	74	75	78	74	75	77	72	74	76	76
Belarus	83	83	83	82	80	91	89	84	80	83	82	84	83	82	81	83	82	79
Russia	74	72	75	73	72	77	79	75	70	76	73	73	72	75	79	75	74	71
Moscow	81	82	80	77	81	83	87	82	78	80	82	81	82	79	83	79	81	81
Latvia	77	79	75	73	76	83	86	79	70	80	75	77	na	na	na	79	77	74
Estonia	86	85	86	83	85	91	90	85	84	87	85	84	na	na	na	87	87	82
Portugal	78	78	77	78	77	78	79	77	73	80	78	74	77	76	78	79	75	84
South Korea	na	na	na	na	na	na	na	na	na	na	na	na	na	na	na	na	na	na
Ireland	86	89	83	89	87	83	86	86	84	82	89	86	85	88	85	88	86	84
North Ireland	87	86	88	85	92	84	88	82	97	94	83	89	82	90	88	91	87	91
Slovenia	86	90	83	85	86	88	87	87	84	86	88	86	80	88	85	86	87	82
Spain	73	75	71	71	74	73	74	71	70	78	73	67	72	68	70	78	71	67
East Germany	63	63	62	62	60	65	65	55	58	63	64	60	64	62	62	63	65	55
Britain	90	92	89	89	90	92	92	88	84	92	88	90	90	91	91	93	90	89
Italy	70	71	69	68	68	74	71	63	57	71	70	70	71	70	73	74	69	68
Netherlands	71	76	69	68	69	75	76	70	66	71	71	72	68	77	66	69	72	70
Belgium	82	81	82	80	80	84	85	81	77	86	79	81	78	82	79	84	82	80
Austria	59	65	55	58	53	64	62	57	55	62	60	54	62	60	52	69	61	47
France	83	85	82	82	81	86	85	85	75	84	81	83	77	87	82	89	85	76
Canada	85	87	84	82	83	90	88	85	82	88	83	86	79	90	85	87	87	85
United States	81	79	83	72	80	85	82	83	77	86	80	77	78	82	81	81	81	82
Iceland	91	93	88	90	90	93	90	92	90	na	na	na	91	89	92	94	89	89
West Germany	52	57	48	50	51	54	58	45	35	55	52	48	49	53	52	56	55	43
Denmark	86	88	84	86	86	87	88	88	84	88	88	83	82	87	88	92	86	81
Finland	74	77	71	69	71	87	77	77	69	72	79	69	76	71	78	79	74	72
Norway	72	76	68	76	71	71	78	73	68	75	72	68	75	73	70	74	71	76
Sweden	82	86	79	82	82	83	85	84	74	79	82	85	80	82	84	86	83	79
Japan	47	51	43	39	45	56	52	47	43	45	50	48	41	47	51	51	47	45
Switzerland	na	na	na	na	na	na	na	na	na	na	na	na	na	na	na	na	na	na
Total	77	79	76	75	77	80	80	76	73	78	77	75	76	78	77	79	77	74

Ranking:

China	96
Iceland	91
Hungary	90
Britain	90
Bulgaria	89
Romania	87
North Ireland	87
Estonia	86
Ireland	86
Slovenia	86
Denmark	86
Canada	85
Belarus	83
France	83
Nigeria	82
Belgium	82
Sweden	82
Argentina	81
Moscow	81
United States	81
India	79
Portugal	78
Latvia	77
Mexico	75
Brazil	74
Russia	74
Finland	74
Spain	73
Norway	72
Netherlands	71
Italy	70
Chile	68
East Germany	63
Austria	59
West Germany	52
Japan	47
Lithuania	36

Note: Countries in the left column are ranked according to GNP per capita. / The percentages in the bottom row give each country an equal weight. / na=not ascertained.

V138 LIFE: BELIEF IN GOD

I am going to read out a list of statements about the meaning of life. Please indicate whether you agree or disagree with each of them. "Death has a meaning only if you believe in God" (% "agree")

	Total	Gender		Age			Education			Income			Political Affinity			Values		
		Male	Female	16-29	30-49	50+	Lower	Medium	Upper	Lower	Middle	Upper	Left	Center	Right	Mat	Mixed	Postmat
India	43	41	47	39	43	53	60	43	36	50	43	38	42	39	40	46	40	38
Nigeria	81	83	78	82	80	79	84	82	78	85	76	85	79	77	85	81	82	76
China	na	na	na	na	na	na	na	na	na	na	na	na	na	na	na	na	na	na
Romania	46	38	54	36	40	58	61	38	37	50	49	39	43	45	44	50	43	39
Turkey	na	na	na	na	na	na	na	na	na	na	na	na	na	na	na	na	na	na
Poland	na	na	na	na	na	na	na	na	na	na	na	na	na	na	na	na	na	na
Bulgaria	17	11	21	14	14	22	23	15	13	18	16	13	08	14	25	18	16	21
Chile	63	59	66	55	64	72	73	60	54	71	60	56	54	63	65	72	62	53
Czechoslovakia	na	na	na	na	na	na	na	na	na	na	na	na	na	na	na	na	na	na
South Africa	na	na	na	na	na	na	na	na	na	na	na	na	na	na	na	na	na	na
Lithuania	49	41	56	41	40	62	61	45	47	53	46	43	na	na	na	51	47	49
Hungary	33	28	37	18	20	51	48	18	25	44	26	17	20	28	40	34	32	29
Argentina	56	53	58	47	53	65	62	52	51	64	59	48	34	56	67	62	56	47
Brazil	67	63	71	59	69	79	84	62	51	81	65	55	59	64	70	74	63	56
Mexico	48	44	53	44	46	64	51	45	40	51	44	45	31	46	55	59	46	36
Belarus	17	14	20	14	16	21	23	17	14	20	14	17	17	13	24	19	15	24
Russia	22	17	25	20	17	29	31	21	17	28	17	19	20	21	21	21	22	29
Moscow	21	14	25	20	18	25	22	20	21	21	20	22	22	20	17	21	17	29
Latvia	20	17	22	18	19	23	25	20	17	21	23	17	na	na	na	18	20	18
Estonia	14	13	14	17	12	14	17	14	11	16	13	12	na	na	na	10	15	16
Portugal	39	29	49	21	38	58	49	17	20	51	36	24	30	32	52	51	34	19
South Korea	na	na	na	na	na	na	na	na	na	na	na	na	na	na	na	na	na	na
Ireland	63	58	68	47	60	76	72	54	52	75	63	53	37	61	75	71	64	51
North Ireland	58	51	64	49	54	69	61	58	41	70	54	51	54	57	58	60	59	52
Slovenia	21	16	25	13	17	30	32	16	10	29	17	14	14	16	28	22	21	16
Spain	40	30	48	26	32	57	44	31	26	55	36	31	25	40	60	51	36	24
East Germany	21	18	24	15	18	27	23	21	15	26	24	14	09	23	36	23	20	22
Britain	36	29	42	22	31	49	39	27	31	45	30	24	28	37	38	44	38	25
Italy	48	40	55	39	39	60	49	44	27	55	41	33	30	59	58	57	48	38
Netherlands	15	17	14	08	14	23	20	13	11	11	13	13	05	12	26	31	15	08
Belgium	27	24	30	13	22	42	31	26	23	35	23	26	13	28	38	32	28	22
Austria	38	34	40	32	33	44	45	33	28	44	36	34	47	32	41	54	39	26
France	28	23	32	19	21	42	31	24	27	30	24	31	18	31	41	36	28	20
Canada	35	31	39	23	29	42	31	24	27	26	15	09	08	21	22	23	28	20
United States	49	45	53	38	41	61	56	54	38	59	49	37	30	46	57	59	48	42
Iceland	29	24	35	23	24	52	40	32	19	39	23	27	22	32	32	39	27	22
West Germany	29	23	34	14	22	41	33	21	22	36	23	27	17	31	39	46	31	16
Denmark	18	12	24	07	08	33	31	16	13	27	15	09	08	21	22	23	19	10
Finland	15	14	16	11	08	35	22	17	08	26	12	08	14	18	12	23	14	11
Norway	23	21	25	13	19	35	42	18	20	33	18	20	22	24	23	27	22	13
Sweden	15	14	16	12	11	22	18	14	13	16	16	12	09	18	17	16	08	13
Japan	11	09	12	06	10	17	17	10	08	15	09	12	05	09	14	16	08	na
Switzerland	na	na	na	na	na	na	na	na	na	na	na	na	na	na	na	na	na	na
Total	**35**	**31**	**39**	**27**	**31**	**46**	**42**	**31**	**28**	**42**	**33**	**29**	**27**	**35**	**41**	**41**	**34**	**29**

Ranking:

Nigeria	81
Brazil	67
Chile	63
Ireland	63
North Ireland	58
Argentina	56
Lithuania	49
United States	49
Mexico	48
Italy	48
Romania	46
India	43
Spain	40
Portugal	39
Austria	38
Britain	36
Canada	35
Hungary	33
Iceland	29
West Germany	29
France	28
Belgium	27
Norway	23
Russia	22
Moscow	21
Slovenia	21
East Germany	21
Latvia	20
Denmark	18
Bulgaria	17
Belarus	17
Netherlands	15
Finland	15
Sweden	15
Estonia	14
Japan	11

Note: Countries in the left column are ranked according to GNP per capita. / The percentages in the bottom row give each country an equal weight. / na=not ascertained.

V139 LIFE: DEATH A REST

I am going to read out a list of statements about the meaning of life. Please indicate whether you agree or disagree with each of them.
"If you have lived your life, death is a natural resting point" (% "agree")

	Total	Gender		Age			Education			Income			Political Affinity			Values		
		Male	Female	16-29	30-49	50+	Lower	Medium	Upper	Lower	Middle	Upper	Left	Center	Right	Mat	Mixed	Postmat
India	77	76	78	77	76	77	77	77	77	77	71	82	79	76	76	82	72	81
Nigeria	89	88	90	89	88	93	90	88	89	92	85	88	90	87	91	88	91	86
China	93	92	94	90	92	97	93	92	93	95	90	93	na	na	na	93	92	93
Romania	84	84	84	75	85	89	86	82	84	85	85	83	82	83	84	87	82	81
Turkey	na	na	na	na	na	na	na	na	na	na	na	na	na	na	na	na	na	na
Poland	na	na	na	na	na	na	na	na	na	na	na	na	na	na	na	na	na	na
Bulgaria	63	58	68	62	64	63	67	64	60	68	64	57	60	67	67	69	62	57
Chile	83	82	83	78	83	88	87	80	81	86	81	81	81	82	83	81	84	80
Czechoslovakia	na	na	na	na	na	na	na	na	na	na	na	na	na	na	na	na	na	na
South Africa	na	na	na	na	na	na	na	na	na	na	na	na	na	na	na	na	na	na
Lithuania	89	87	90	87	86	93	91	88	88	89	88	88	na	na	na	86	90	92
Hungary	91	90	91	90	87	94	92	91	81	93	89	87	88	92	87	90	90	95
Argentina	85	81	88	74	86	92	92	85	73	90	86	77	77	86	82	87	86	80
Brazil	88	90	87	86	88	92	90	88	87	90	89	86	88	88	86	90	87	90
Mexico	82	80	84	81	82	84	82	82	82	82	83	78	81	81	80	82	81	83
Belarus	90	90	89	88	90	92	91	90	89	90	90	89	92	88	84	87	92	81
Russia	92	90	94	88	93	94	94	90	94	92	94	92	94	92	91	93	92	91
Moscow	92	93	92	87	92	96	96	91	92	91	93	92	92	92	89	92	93	90
Latvia	72	68	75	66	73	76	75	72	72	74	74	69	na	na	na	78	73	66
Estonia	83	82	85	79	83	88	91	81	83	81	87	83	na	na	na	84	83	91
Portugal	62	62	63	52	61	73	67	54	52	69	56	57	62	59	66	69	59	56
South Korea	na	na	na	na	na	na	na	na	na	na	na	na	na	na	na	na	na	na
Ireland	92	90	93	86	91	96	95	89	82	95	94	88	81	92	94	93	93	85
North Ireland	89	84	92	82	89	93	92	85	79	91	92	86	96	89	87	91	88	91
Slovenia	93	94	92	88	95	95	91	94	95	93	94	92	93	94	91	93	94	85
Spain	72	69	75	62	73	79	77	64	60	79	72	68	71	65	73	81	72	58
East Germany	87	85	89	85	85	90	89	83	83	85	89	87	88	87	83	90	88	84
Britain	88	86	90	85	86	91	90	83	82	92	88	82	88	89	87	88	89	85
Italy	78	79	78	76	75	83	79	73	80	79	81	78	79	80	79	83	77	77
Netherlands	78	78	79	78	78	80	83	79	73	75	85	79	76	80	76	87	78	76
Belgium	85	86	85	80	85	89	88	84	80	86	83	84	85	83	85	85	85	88
Austria	83	83	84	80	82	86	85	81	83	85	81	84	84	87	79	86	83	82
France	91	91	91	88	91	94	90	92	93	92	91	92	92	92	90	92	94	87
Canada	86	85	87	82	86	90	91	86	80	89	86	85	80	88	86	85	87	87
United States	83	79	87	77	81	87	86	82	80	88	82	78	76	82	84	84	85	76
Iceland	88	85	91	86	90	87	90	90	85	na	83	84	90	86	90	90	85	89
West Germany	85	83	86	79	83	89	87	80	84	87	83	82	86	85	87	89	85	81
Denmark	89	90	89	85	90	93	88	91	89	88	90	89	90	89	92	88	89	85
Finland	89	87	91	85	86	96	90	88	90	91	88	89	90	89	91	88	89	90
Norway	92	91	92	89	91	95	95	93	88	93	92	90	92	93	91	94	91	89
Sweden	90	89	91	86	92	91	93	89	89	93	91	90	93	90	90	93	91	86
Japan	64	63	65	50	62	75	65	64	62	65	64	68	71	66	67	67	65	62
Switzerland	na	na	na	na	na	na	na	na	na	na	na	na	na	na	na	na	na	na
Total	84	83	85	80	84	88	87	83	82	86	84	83	84	84	84	86	84	82

Ranking:

China	93	Canada	86
Slovenia	93	Argentina	85
Russia	92	Belgium	85
Moscow	92	West Germany	85
Ireland	92	Romania	84
Norway	92	Chile	83
Hungary	91	Estonia	83
France	91	Austria	83
Belarus	90	United States	83
Sweden	90	Mexico	82
Nigeria	89	Italy	78
Lithuania	89	Netherlands	78
North Ireland	89	India	77
Denmark	89	Latvia	72
Finland	89	Spain	72
Brazil	88	Japan	64
Britain	88	Bulgaria	63
Iceland	88	Portugal	62
East Germany	87		

V140 LIFE: SORROW

I am going to read out a list of statements about the meaning of life. Please indicate whether you agree or disagree with each of them.

"In my opinion, sorrow and suffering only have meaning if you believe in God" (% "agree")

	Total	Gender Male	Gender Female	Age 16-29	Age 30-49	Age 50+	Education Lower	Education Medium	Education Upper	Income Lower	Income Middle	Income Upper	Pol. Aff. Left	Pol. Aff. Center	Pol. Aff. Right	Values Mat	Values Mixed	Values Postmat
India	42	39	45	37	42	53	59	41	34	49	41	37	41	na	39	45	na	na
Nigeria	72	72	72	74	69	75	83	76	63	81	63	75	70	63	78	74	71	63
China	na	na	na	na	na	na	na	na	na	na	na	na	na	na	na	na	na	na
Romania	43	35	51	33	35	57	58	38	32	47	45	37	48	40	39	49	39	31
Turkey	na	na	na	na	na	na	na	na	na	na	na	na	na	na	na	na	na	na
Poland	na	na	na	na	na	na	na	na	na	na	na	na	na	na	na	na	na	na
Bulgaria	18	12	22	16	14	24	27	15	15	20	18	14	09	18	23	19	17	22
Chile	60	55	65	50	61	72	74	55	48	71	61	47	49	60	63	71	59	46
Czechoslovakia	na	na	na	na	na	na	na	na	na	na	na	na	na	na	na	na	na	na
South Africa	na	na	na	na	na	na	na	na	na	na	na	na	na	na	na	na	na	na
Lithuania	32	29	35	16	25	52	56	25	27	39	29	21	na	na	na	36	30	30
Hungary	36	31	40	18	25	53	53	22	13	49	28	19	23	34	37	38	34	32
Argentina	52	47	57	43	50	62	61	51	38	64	57	42	28	52	61	64	53	38
Brazil	58	54	62	50	58	72	78	52	40	74	56	43	51	52	63	67	53	45
Mexico	39	35	44	34	38	53	42	38	30	42	36	35	21	38	44	46	37	31
Belarus	14	10	17	10	12	21	27	13	10	17	12	13	13	12	21	18	12	15
Russia	17	13	21	12	13	26	28	17	12	23	15	12	13	17	17	19	17	14
Moscow	14	11	17	11	13	20	23	15	13	13	14	16	14	12	17	17	13	13
Latvia	21	15	25	19	20	25	31	23	14	27	21	18	na	na	na	22	21	16
Estonia	13	13	14	09	13	20	21	12	10	14	14	12	na	na	na	13	12	15
Portugal	35	28	41	19	31	53	46	12	12	48	33	16	31	27	44	47	29	17
South Korea	na	na	na	na	na	na	na	na	na	na	na	na	na	na	na	na	na	na
Ireland	44	41	48	28	39	60	55	32	38	57	45	34	24	44	50	48	46	35
North Ireland	39	34	42	25	35	52	44	35	15	51	37	32	36	40	36	37	40	28
Slovenia	22	19	25	17	17	31	34	15	13	30	16	17	18	15	31	23	22	21
Spain	32	23	39	17	26	48	36	23	19	48	28	24	18	33	50	42	29	15
East Germany	18	14	22	08	15	29	21	15	13	27	16	11	06	21	32	26	17	19
Britain	23	18	28	09	17	37	27	13	14	32	15	11	20	21	24	29	23	17
Italy	43	35	50	33	40	52	44	36	35	51	37	32	29	54	44	49	43	34
Netherlands	15	18	14	06	14	27	23	13	09	14	12	15	06	14	26	35	17	06
Belgium	22	18	26	08	17	37	26	21	20	30	29	24	10	22	34	28	22	18
Austria	32	26	36	22	27	33	39	28	25	42	29	19	35	28	34	46	33	23
France	21	16	26	11	18	33	25	18	18	23	20	11	14	20	36	30	21	15
Canada	33	29	36	22	29	46	46	31	25	44	31	25	28	34	31	49	31	28
United States	35	32	39	27	27	47	43	39	25	48	34	24	20	32	41	48	34	30
Iceland	18	12	25	07	16	36	32	18	09	33	22	21	13	16	23	24	17	10
West Germany	26	19	31	11	19	39	30	19	17	22	13	17	14	26	37	40	28	14
Denmark	15	11	19	06	11	26	26	12	11	13	05	08	07	15	20	22	15	05
Finland	09	09	08	03	05	23	17	09	03	18	11	04	04	12	08	28	09	05
Norway	16	14	18	07	11	28	34	11	12	27	11	11	12	18	17	19	14	10
Sweden	08	07	08	04	05	14	12	05	07	07	09	05	05	08	09	10	08	06
Japan	17	13	22	07	14	31	26	17	10	20	17	17	07	12	22	25	14	12
Switzerland	na	na	na	na	na	na	na	na	na	na	na	na	na	na	na	na	na	na
Total	**29**	**25**	**33**	**20**	**26**	**41**	**39**	**25**	**21**	**37**	**27**	**23**	**22**	**29**	**35**	**36**	**28**	**23**

Ranking:

Nigeria	72
Chile	60
Brazil	58
Argentina	52
Ireland	44
Romania	43
Italy	43
India	42
Mexico	39
North Ireland	39
Hungary	36
Portugal	35
United States	35
Canada	33
Lithuania	32
Spain	32
Austria	32
West Germany	26
Britain	23
Slovenia	22
Belgium	22
Latvia	21
France	21
Bulgaria	18
East Germany	18
Iceland	18
Russia	17
Japan	17
Norway	16
Netherlands	15
Denmark	15
Belarus	14
Moscow	14
Estonia	13
Finland	09
Sweden	08

Note: Countries in the left column are ranked according to GNP per capita. / The percentages in the bottom row give each country an equal weight. / na=not ascertained.

V141 LIFE: NO MEANING

I am going to read out a list of statements about the meaning of life. Please indicate whether you agree or disagree with each of them.
"Life has no meaning" (% "agree")

	Total	Gender		Age			Education			Income			Political Affinity			Values		
		Male	Female	16-29	30-49	50+	Lower	Medium	Upper	Lower	Middle	Upper	Left	Center	Right	Mat	Mixed	Postmat
India	07	06	08	07	na	06	09	07	20	10	07	07	08	07	16	07	08	06
Nigeria	19	16	23	18	18	23	23	16	04	21	17	19	17	22	16	18	18	26
China	05	05	05	06	04	05	08	04	04	06	04	04	na	na	na	06	04	06
Romania	06	05	07	05	07	06	07	06	02	08	05	06	04	05	07	07	05	08
Turkey	na	na	na	na	na	na	na	na	na	na	na	na	na	na	na	na	na	na
Poland	na	na	na	na	na	na	na	na	na	na	na	na	na	na	na	na	na	na
Bulgaria	08	07	09	07	06	10	12	08	03	09	07	05	05	06	08	11	07	06
Chile	10	11	08	08	10	12	15	08	06	13	08	07	11	08	08	09	10	07
Czechoslovakia	na	na	na	na	na	na	na	na	na	na	na	na	na	na	na	na	na	na
South Africa	na	na	na	na	na	na	na	na	na	na	na	na	na	na	na	na	na	na
Lithuania	05	04	05	02	03	08	12	03	00	07	03	03	na	na	na	03	05	04
Hungary	06	05	06	03	04	08	08	04	04	08	04	04	07	05	04	05	06	08
Argentina	03	03	02	04	03	02	03	03	02	03	03	02	06	03	02	04	02	03
Brazil	07	08	06	04	07	12	15	04	02	11	06	05	07	06	10	08	08	03
Mexico	11	13	08	09	11	15	13	09	06	13	09	09	09	13	08	11	10	11
Belarus	07	07	07	05	07	08	10	05	04	07	05	04	07	04	13	08	06	03
Russia	05	05	05	06	05	04	07	03	04	07	03	04	03	05	06	05	04	06
Moscow	05	04	06	03	03	08	11	05	04	06	04	04	04	04	10	05	05	03
Latvia	03	03	04	03	03	04	09	03	02	05	03	02	na	na	na	02	03	06
Estonia	04	04	04	04	03	06	05	03	04	04	04	03	na	na	na	04	04	05
Portugal	07	09	06	04	08	09	08	06	03	11	05	04	10	06	05	07	07	06
South Korea	na	na	na	na	na	na	na	na	na	na	na	na	na	na	na	na	na	na
Ireland	05	06	04	04	05	05	07	03	02	08	04	03	na	05	04	04	06	03
North Ireland	03	05	02	03	03	04	05	01	00	04	00	02	07	04	na	02	03	02
Slovenia	04	04	04	03	04	06	07	03	03	05	04	04	04	02	02	05	04	06
Spain	10	09	11	08	08	13	11	08	07	17	08	07	07	07	12	09	08	12
East Germany	03	02	03	02	03	03	03	02	01	03	02	02	07	03	04	05	02	02
Britain	05	07	04	05	05	06	05	03	08	06	05	03	08	04	06	06	05	05
Italy	04	04	05	02	03	07	04	06	00	07	07	03	03	03	05	05	05	05
Netherlands	02	03	02	02	02	03	07	03	02	03	01	02	01	02	02	02	03	01
Belgium	05	04	05	04	05	05	05	05	07	08	04	07	05	03	03	06	05	04
Austria	03	02	04	01	04	05	04	03	02	03	04	02	06	02	04	02	04	03
France	10	11	09	09	10	11	15	05	05	15	06	07	09	08	09	12	10	07
Canada	08	07	09	05	07	13	13	06	06	09	10	06	06	09	08	21	06	08
United States	04	05	03	03	03	06	09	03	02	05	04	03	03	04	04	04	04	03
Iceland	04	06	02	04	04	05	06	04	02	03	na	na	05	05	02	07	03	06
West Germany	02	02	02	01	03	03	04	03	03	03	02	02	03	02	03	04	02	03
Denmark	02	02	02	03	02	03	03	03	02	02	02	03	02	03	01	02	02	04
Finland	03	04	02	03	03	05	06	03	02	05	02	03	05	05	02	03	04	02
Norway	03	04	03	03	04	03	03	04	03	03	02	04	05	03	02	05	02	03
Sweden	08	08	07	06	06	11	10	07	07	06	11	07	07	08	07	03	08	09
Japan	04	05	03	01	03	08	09	03	03	03	06	04	06	01	05	03	04	04
Switzerland	na	na	na	na	na	na	na	na	na	na	na	na	na	na	na	na	na	na
Total	06	06	06	05	05	07	08	05	04	07	05	05	06	05	06	06	05	06

Ranking:

Nigeria	19
Mexico	11
Chile	10
Spain	10
France	10
Bulgaria	08
Canada	08
Sweden	08
India	07
Brazil	07
Belarus	07
Portugal	07
Romania	06
Hungary	06
China	05
Lithuania	05
Russia	05
Moscow	05
Ireland	05
Britain	05
Belgium	05
Estonia	04
Slovenia	04
Italy	04
United States	04
Iceland	04
Japan	04
Argentina	03
Latvia	03
North Ireland	03
East Germany	03
Austria	03
Finland	03
Norway	03
Netherlands	02
West Germany	02
Denmark	02

Note: Countries in the left column are ranked according to GNP per capita. / The percentages in the bottom row give each country an equal weight. / na=not ascertained.

V142. Good and evil

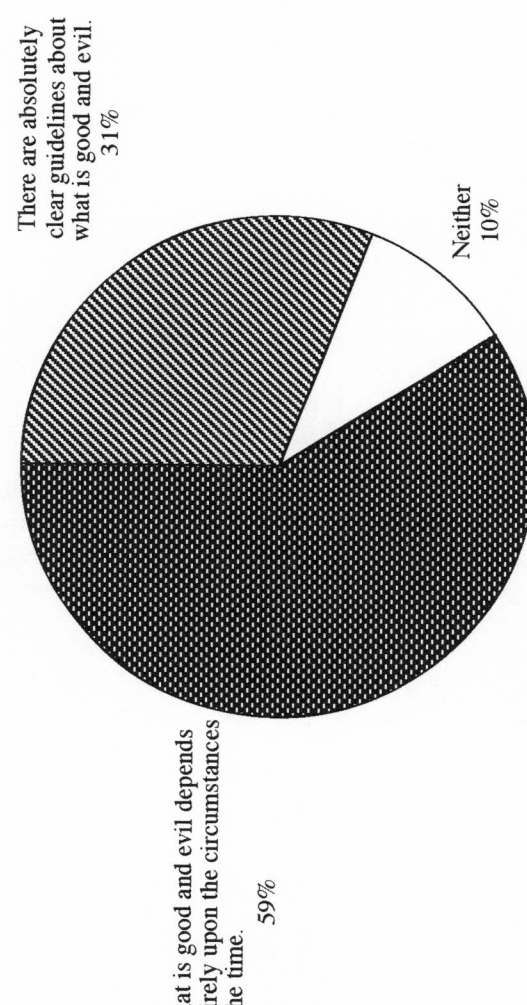

There are absolutely
clear guidelines about
what is good and evil.
31%

Neither
10%

What is good and evil depends
entirely upon the circumstances
at the time.
59%

V142 GOOD & EVIL

Here are two statements* which people sometimes make when discussing good and evil. Which one comes closest to your own point of view?
(% "There are absolutely clear guidelines about what is good and evil. These always apply to everyone, whatever the circumstances")

	Total	Gender		Age			Education			Income			Political Affinity			Values			Ranking:	
		Male	Female	16-29	30-49	50+	Lower	Medium	Upper	Lower	Middle	Upper	Left	Center	Right	Mat	Mixed	Postmat		
India	45	44	47	43	46	50	55	46	41	53	43	41	43	46	47	47	44	35	Nigeria	60
Nigeria	60	57	66	60	60	67	70	60	57	62	60	61	74	61	55	67	58	48	South Africa	52
China	35	35	34	21	37	48	34	17	34	35	38	33	na	na	na	40	31	20	North Ireland	51
Romania	23	23	23	13	24	29	34	20	20	22	25	22	25	22	24	25	23	15	United States	50
Turkey	34	34	34	28	34	45	38	29	25	38	35	27	27	33	41	44	32	28	Bulgaria	47
Poland	33	35	32	25	32	38	33	32	37	35	31	33	39	32	36	35	33	24	Brazil	46
Bulgaria	47	46	48	43	49	49	46	51	43	43	52	45	44	45	54	52	46	41	India	45
Chile	35	37	34	30	36	42	40	32	33	39	36	31	36	33	37	40	35	29	Italy	45
Czechoslovakia	na	na	na	na	na	na	na	na	na	na	na	na	na	na	na	na	na	na	Ireland	42
South Africa	52	49	53	48	51	60	53	51	49	52	50	54	47	53	52	58	48	50	Mexico	38
Lithuania	23	21	25	16	18	36	33	21	16	27	21	18	na	na	na	31	21	20	Britain	36
Hungary	17	15	19	14	14	21	22	12	14	19	16	13	11	17	18	19	14	18	China	35
Argentina	33	34	33	32	31	37	36	35	27	36	35	26	35	33	34	42	32	27	Chile	35
Brazil	46	47	45	42	47	51	49	45	43	49	43	46	40	44	50	49	44	42	Turkey	34
Mexico	38	37	40	34	38	50	41	34	32	40	35	39	30	36	43	44	36	29	Spain	34
Belarus	26	29	23	28	24	26	24	27	24	27	24	26	26	24	29	26	25	27	Poland	33
Russia	31	30	32	25	30	36	35	29	30	31	31	32	32	27	37	32	30	31	Argentina	33
Moscow	24	23	25	20	23	29	25	24	24	24	25	23	25	23	24	27	25	13	Belgium	33
Latvia	27	25	29	23	27	32	42	28	23	30	26	26	na	na	na	33	27	25	Norway	32
Estonia	23	23	23	19	23	27	26	24	18	22	25	22	na	na	na	27	20	17	Russia	31
Portugal	31	32	31	26	29	39	35	27	22	34	32	27	30	32	33	38	28	28	Portugal	31
South Korea	23	21	24	16	24	31	27	22	22	21	24	26	22	21	26	23	23	20	Canada	31
Ireland	42	43	40	24	38	57	47	36	29	52	43	33	24	43	44	52	40	34	Austria	28
North Ireland	51	40	59	29	50	67	54	49	35	66	49	37	36	52	51	63	50	38	Latvia	27
Slovenia	21	22	21	21	23	19	31	22	16	23	22	17	18	23	23	21	22	17	Belarus	26
Spain	34	32	35	22	32	45	38	27	22	48	33	24	27	33	41	46	31	18	West Germany	26
East Germany	23	22	23	15	21	29	25	20	18	28	20	24	20	23	26	32	23	18	Finland	26
Britain	36	35	37	20	32	50	40	29	28	42	35	30	31	34	43	42	36	30	Moscow	24
Italy	45	43	46	27	44	57	46	37	36	49	43	45	36	53	43	55	45	35	France	24
Netherlands	23	31	21	15	22	35	31	22	16	25	20	23	12	22	33	40	28	11	Romania	23
Belgium	33	33	33	19	31	45	38	34	24	40	36	31	27	34	37	38	36	24	Lithuania	23
Austria	28	28	28	15	24	37	31	25	24	31	28	24	22	24	36	37	29	20	Estonia	23
France	24	25	24	15	21	35	27	22	22	23	27	22	17	27	33	31	26	16	South Korea	23
Canada	31	32	29	24	30	38	38	32	22	30	33	26	23	32	32	35	31	25	East Germany	23
United States	50	47	52	43	47	55	55	54	40	53	50	44	35	49	58	57	53	37	Netherlands	23
Iceland	11	12	10	10	08	17	16	07	10	na	na	na	08	13	12	13	11	10	Switzerland	22
West Germany	26	25	26	14	21	36	29	21	19	28	26	24	18	26	33	40	27	15	Slovenia	21
Denmark	10	11	09	08	07	15	15	09	08	13	10	06	06	10	11	14	10	05	Sweden	19
Finland	26	28	23	17	23	40	27	27	23	30	24	23	23	23	31	38	26	22	Hungary	17
Norway	32	34	29	21	29	42	43	29	28	37	26	34	27	34	33	37	30	28	Japan	15
Sweden	19	20	18	10	17	30	23	17	16	24	19	17	16	19	20	23	19	17	Iceland	11
Japan	15	19	11	04	16	20	17	15	13	16	18	12	14	18	17	16	16	12	Denmark	10
Switzerland	22	24	21	15	20	28	23	23	15	24	21	16	13	23	24	29	25	12		
Total	31	31	31	24	30	39	35	29	26	35	31	29	27	32	35	37	31	25		

Note: Countries in the left column are ranked according to GNP per capita. / The percentages in the bottom row give each country an equal weight. / na=not ascertained.
*The other statement offered was: "There can never be absolutely clear guidelines about what is good and evil. What is good and evil depends entirely upon the circumstances at the time."

V143 RELIGIOUS DENOMINATION

Do you belong to a religious denomination? (% "yes")

	Total	Gender Male	Gender Female	Age 16-29	Age 30-49	Age 50+	Education Lower	Education Medium	Education Upper	Income Lower	Income Middle	Income Upper	Political Affinity Left	Political Affinity Center	Political Affinity Right	Values Mat	Values Mixed	Values Postmat	Ranking:	
India	99	99	99	99	99	98	100	99	98	99	99	99	98	99	99	99	99	99	India	99
Nigeria	95	93	99	94	na	na	95	96	93	95	96	95	97	96	94	97	93	95	Iceland	98
China	04	03	04	03	03	05	04	03	03	03	04	04	na	na	na	05	03	02	Turkey	97
Romania	94	92	96	90	92	99	97	93	93	93	95	94	94	95	91	98	92	91	Ireland	96
Turkey	97	97	98	96	98	98	98	97	93	97	98	96	92	99	99	100	98	94	Nigeria	95
Poland	na	na	na	na	na	na	na	na	na	na	na	na	na	na	na	na	na	na	Romania	94
Bulgaria	34	29	38	29	25	48	54	27	25	39	32	28	22	30	38	37	33	31	Denmark	92
Chile	82	76	87	77	82	89	86	80	80	85	81	80	73	84	88	88	81	75	Switzerland	92
Czechoslovakia	56	52	59	36	48	80	68	49	55	60	55	53	55	56	55	65	54	46	North Ireland	91
South Africa	na	na	na	na	na	na	na	na	na	na	na	na	na	na	na	na	na	na	Norway	90
Lithuania	63	54	71	52	56	80	83	59	50	71	60	50	na	na	65	72	63	55	West Germany	89
Hungary	58	54	62	38	49	75	71	48	41	67	54	43	34	58	65	59	58	45	Finland	89
Argentina	84	80	88	80	83	90	86	85	82	86	87	81	61	84	93	89	86	74	Brazil	88
Brazil	88	86	90	86	86	95	91	88	82	90	86	86	84	88	92	91	87	85	Austria	86
Mexico	85	82	88	82	85	92	86	86	81	85	86	83	72	86	89	91	84	79	Mexico	85
Belarus	30	24	35	25	28	40	44	31	24	36	31	24	28	27	48	34	29	22	Spain	85
Russia	37	28	44	34	30	48	50	35	32	42	36	32	29	35	40	40	35	41	Italy	85
Moscow	24	15	30	27	18	30	30	27	20	24	26	20	24	19	23	26	21	27	Argentina	84
Latvia	37	28	43	30	34	50	60	36	30	41	37	33	na	na	na	39	37	37	Chile	82
Estonia	13	09	16	10	11	19	18	13	07	16	11	10	na	na	na	14	11	14	Sweden	82
Portugal	72	63	81	63	74	80	79	59	57	79	67	65	61	70	81	79	69	58	United States	77
South Korea	72	75	69	59	77	81	74	72	71	69	71	77	64	70	74	74	73	57	Slovenia	74
Ireland	96	95	97	92	96	99	99	95	88	97	98	93	82	98	99	100	96	92	Canada	74
North Ireland	91	85	94	87	89	95	91	94	86	93	91	85	89	90	91	91	91	87	Portugal	72
Slovenia	74	70	77	66	71	82	84	72	57	84	72	56	53	71	77	83	72	54	South Korea	72
Spain	85	79	89	79	83	90	87	82	74	88	85	79	74	90	92	91	86	72	Belgium	68
East Germany	35	30	39	24	33	44	36	36	32	43	35	28	17	41	48	41	33	39	Lithuania	63
Britain	58	50	65	45	55	68	55	62	67	59	52	62	47	58	68	68	56	53	France	62
Italy	85	80	90	82	82	90	87	77	76	89	84	75	74	92	91	92	86	77	Hungary	58
Netherlands	51	49	52	43	52	59	55	54	43	44	50	53	29	54	71	64	53	44	Britain	58
Belgium	68	63	74	55	64	81	73	68	62	69	64	69	46	71	80	74	71	56	Czechoslovakia	56
Austria	86	84	87	89	82	87	86	86	84	85	85	87	68	85	90	90	87	80	Netherlands	51
France	62	61	62	47	56	78	62	60	62	60	60	65	48	70	79	68	63	53	Russia	37
Canada	74	70	78	67	71	84	78	75	70	74	74	74	63	75	80	85	75	69	Latvia	37
United States	77	75	80	71	74	83	77	77	77	73	78	79	60	80	83	81	78	70	East Germany	35
Iceland	98	96	99	97	98	99	99	98	97	na	na	na	97	98	97	98	na	93	Bulgaria	34
West Germany	89	87	92	87	86	93	91	89	81	89	91	88	82	91	94	94	91	84	Belarus	30
Denmark	92	90	93	90	90	95	94	93	89	94	92	90	83	94	95	94	94	80	Moscow	24
Finland	89	85	93	87	90	88	91	87	90	88	91	86	78	89	93	88	90	87	Estonia	13
Norway	90	89	92	89	87	94	95	92	86	91	89	87	83	95	91	95	91	72	China	04
Sweden	82	78	86	80	83	82	83	81	80	84	76	84	79	81	85	83	82	81		
Japan	na	na	na	na	na	na	na	na	na	na	na	na	na	na	na	na	na	na		
Switzerland	92	90	94	89	90	96	93	93	85	92	92	91	83	94	95	96	93	88		
Total	70	66	73	64	68	77	75	69	65	71	68	66	65	75	80	74	70	64		

Note: Countries in the left column are ranked according to GNP per capita. / The percentages in the bottom row give each country an equal weight. / na=not ascertained.

V144 WHICH RELIGION
(% Roman Catholic)

	Total	Gender		Age			Education			Income			Political Affinity			Values		
		Male	Female	16-29	30-49	50+	Lower	Medium	Upper	Lower	Middle	Upper	Left	Center	Right	Mat	Mixed	Postmat
India	02	02	01	01	02	02	00	02	02	02	01	02	01	02	03	02	02	01
Nigeria	23	23	23	26	22	09	16	23	26	25	24	21	22	23	25	20	25	28
China	na	na	na	na	na	na	na	na	na	na	na	na	na	na	na	na	na	na
Romania	02	02	03	02	02	03	na	02	03	na	03	03	02	02	03	02	02	07
Turkey	01	01	01	01	01	01	01	00	02	01	01	01	00	01	00	01	01	00
Poland	97	97	97	95	97	97	97	97	94	95	98	98	97	95	98	97	96	97
Bulgaria	00	00	01	02	00	00	00	01	00	00	01	00	00	00	00	00	01	00
Chile	83	85	81	84	84	81	77	87	85	78	82	91	84	84	87	79	84	87
Czechoslovakia	88	89	86	90	88	87	88	89	85	85	87	92	84	89	89	89	87	91
South Africa	12	11	12	13	10	13	11	13	11	10	13	10	14	12	10	11	12	11
Lithuania	92	93	91	93	88	93	97	90	84	92	94	85	na	na	na	91	92	94
Hungary	73	74	73	72	77	71	73	73	71	72	74	75	56	74	74	73	74	78
Argentina	90	88	92	89	90	91	89	90	93	89	90	92	83	92	92	94	89	88
Brazil	79	80	78	80	76	80	78	79	79	79	84	74	78	81	78	79	79	76
Mexico	93	93	93	91	95	95	93	93	95	94	95	93	91	94	95	95	93	93
Belarus	22	21	22	20	27	16	21	24	18	24	24	14	25	18	18	17	25	36
Russia	00	00	00	00	00	00	00	00	00	00	00	00	00	00	00	00	00	00
Moscow	02	04	02	00	01	05	00	00	05	00	02	08	03	02	00	02	03	03
Latvia	42	46	40	42	48	33	39	45	37	48	41	36	na	na	na	51	36	39
Estonia	03	00	05	07	04	00	00	04	07	01	07	03	na	na	na	00	05	13
Portugal	97	99	96	99	96	97	97	96	98	98	97	98	99	96	98	99	97	99
South Korea	23	26	20	28	25	13	21	23	24	25	22	20	26	27	19	22	24	29
Ireland	97	97	97	98	96	97	97	98	95	97	97	96	99	96	98	96	97	98
North Ireland	32	36	29	45	35	22	35	24	36	31	18	29	58	36	13	14	36	44
Slovenia	97	96	98	94	96	99	96	97	98	96	97	98	94	95	99	97	96	97
Spain	99	99	98	99	97	97	99	98	98	99	98	99	99	98	99	99	98	98
East Germany	49	52	47	47	50	41	44	63	56	38	57	57	48	45	56	37	50	53
Britain	15	17	13	29	13	11	16	17	08	15	16	17	20	15	12	09	15	25
Italy	98	98	99	99	98	99	98	98	100	98	98	100	95	100	100	100	98	97
Netherlands	59	57	60	63	60	55	61	61	54	55	58	56	43	69	55	60	61	58
Belgium	97	95	98	96	96	98	97	97	96	97	92	96	94	97	99	98	97	95
Austria	91	92	91	93	89	92	91	92	89	91	92	91	90	90	94	90	92	90
France	94	93	95	92	95	95	94	95	92	93	98	94	90	96	98	97	93	94
Canada	56	56	56	62	59	49	56	55	58	58	56	58	59	58	49	68	54	55
United States	36	38	34	36	37	35	38	38	32	35	36	38	26	40	32	34	38	32
Iceland	01	00	01	01	00	00	00	01	01	00	na	na	00	00	00	01	01	00
West Germany	50	50	51	49	50	51	53	47	44	51	53	48	45	51	56	52	51	47
Denmark	01	01	01	01	01	01	01	00	01	01	00	01	01	01	01	01	00	01
Finland	00	00	00	00	00	02	00	00	01	00	00	01	00	00	01	00	00	00
Norway	01	01	00	01	00	00	01	01	01	02	00	02	01	01	00	00	01	01
Sweden	01	01	01	02	00	00	00	00	01	02	00	00	00	00	00	00	00	02
Japan	00	00	00	00	00	01	00	00	00	00	01	00	00	00	01	01	00	00
Switzerland	51	52	50	59	50	48	50	53	43	54	49	50	44	45	58	60	51	45
Total	**46**	**47**	**46**	**48**	**47**	**45**	**46**	**47**	**46**	**47**	**48**	**47**	**45**	**47**	**46**	**46**	**47**	**48**

Ranking:

Spain	99
Italy	98
Poland	97
Portugal	97
Ireland	97
Slovenia	97
Belgium	97
France	94
Mexico	93
Lithuania	92
Austria	91
Argentina	90
Czechoslovakia	88
Chile	83
Brazil	79
Hungary	73
Netherlands	59
Canada	56
Switzerland	51
West Germany	50
East Germany	49
Latvia	42
United States	36
North Ireland	32
Nigeria	23
South Korea	23
Belarus	22
Britain	15
South Africa	12
Estonia	03
India	02
Romania	02
Moscow	02
Turkey	01
Iceland	01
Denmark	01
Norway	01
Sweden	01
Bulgaria	00
Russia	00
Finland	00
Japan	00

Note: Countries in the left column are ranked according to GNP per capita. / The percentages in the bottom row give each country an equal weight. / na=not ascertained.

V146 RAISED RELIGIOUS

Were you brought up religiously at home? (% "yes")

	Total	Gender		Age			Education			Income			Political Affinity			Values		
		Male	Female	16-29	30-49	50+	Lower	Medium	Upper	Lower	Middle	Upper	Left	Center	Right	Mat	Mixed	Postmat
India	94	93	95	93	95	94	96	95	91	95	93	88	91	94	95	94	93	94
Nigeria	94	91	98	93	94	93	94	93	94	93	94	95	97	95	93	95	93	92
China	07	08	06	04	08	08	06	06	06	07	08	04	na	na	na	08	06	06
Romania	77	73	81	61	73	91	91	73	65	78	77	73	78	74	74	83	74	59
Turkey	78	75	81	73	76	89	86	70	56	82	68	58	60	79	89	90	77	65
Poland	98	97	98	97	97	98	99	98	93	97	98	96	97	98	96	98	97	98
Bulgaria	38	37	39	30	29	53	56	33	28	44	34	22	30	35	40	42	36	36
Chile	78	74	82	76	78	82	76	81	77	77	79	81	78	77	80	78	78	76
Czechoslovakia	52	49	54	34	44	73	63	46	48	58	47	57	52	50	52	56	51	42
South Africa	88	87	90	90	88	86	85	90	88	87	92	81	86	88	90	87	90	83
Lithuania	66	64	68	50	60	85	84	63	51	79	66	57	na	na	na	74	65	62
Hungary	69	64	74	41	60	88	80	59	57	79	63	51	48	69	69	72	68	45
Argentina	80	76	84	74	81	84	81	81	78	83	76	83	70	80	83	86	81	71
Brazil	75	74	77	73	77	77	70	77	81	75	76	89	75	75	80	75	75	78
Mexico	85	83	87	84	85	88	84	90	84	85	85	83	86	81	87	88	83	87
Belarus	19	15	23	10	17	34	36	19	14	23	16	10	18	15	34	24	17	17
Russia	19	16	21	07	12	34	32	15	14	22	13	12	12	16	22	26	15	11
Moscow	14	11	16	12	11	19	29	15	10	16	14	02	12	16	13	17	13	06
Latvia	29	28	30	18	27	47	51	29	23	31	22	14	na	na	na	34	29	22
Estonia	15	12	18	06	11	32	25	13	10	17	12	00	na	na	na	18	14	15
Portugal	79	74	84	71	82	85	84	69	69	82	80	67	71	80	83	83	76	76
South Korea	na	na	na	na	na	na	na	na	na	na	na	na	na	na	na	na	na	na
Ireland	94	93	95	92	94	96	95	94	90	97	93	92	88	94	95	94	94	94
North Ireland	84	79	88	78	81	91	86	78	81	79	84	85	82	82	87	89	83	78
Slovenia	75	72	77	65	70	85	84	72	62	81	69	56	64	73	75	79	74	56
Spain	91	89	93	86	93	94	94	88	84	92	89	85	86	94	94	95	91	86
East Germany	48	43	53	28	42	67	51	44	43	56	39	40	29	55	62	67	45	47
Britain	59	52	66	34	56	77	60	55	64	73	54	54	54	57	67	62	60	56
Italy	94	93	95	91	94	97	95	91	90	95	91	100	88	82	97	97	94	90
Netherlands	71	70	72	62	74	78	76	71	67	65	74	70	58	76	81	75	72	67
Belgium	85	84	86	76	83	92	85	86	82	85	81	85	73	87	92	85	85	83
Austria	83	82	83	79	78	88	85	81	74	84	82	80	74	79	88	93	83	76
France	71	72	71	57	72	81	72	70	73	69	72	73	64	75	83	79	72	64
Canada	78	73	82	69	77	86	82	78	75	78	78	78	74	78	80	83	78	76
United States	81	79	82	70	78	87	80	81	81	80	81	86	69	82	84	81	81	79
Iceland	76	70	82	65	77	88	77	77	75	na	na	na	74	79	76	76	78	67
West Germany	63	57	68	48	59	74	66	56	64	63	65	60	56	64	72	71	64	56
Denmark	43	37	49	32	40	56	54	38	41	46	41	38	29	45	51	48	43	34
Finland	51	49	54	34	48	75	64	49	48	69	51	49	46	50	55	62	50	52
Norway	46	45	46	38	41	57	58	42	44	50	39	45	40	45	51	47	46	35
Sweden	31	30	32	19	29	43	32	26	40	31	36	30	29	30	35	30	31	32
Japan	22	22	23	11	21	31	25	22	21	22	23	23	34	20	35	24	24	20
Switzerland	78	76	80	67	75	86	80	78	72	79	75	74	68	78	81	89	79	69
Total	**64**	**61**	**66**	**55**	**62**	**73**	**69**	**62**	**60**	**66**	**62**	**59**	**62**	**67**	**72**	**68**	**63**	**59**

Ranking:

Poland	98
India	94
Nigeria	94
Ireland	94
Italy	94
Spain	91
South Africa	88
Mexico	85
Belgium	85
North Ireland	84
Austria	83
United States	81
Argentina	80
Portugal	79
Turkey	78
Chile	78
Canada	78
Switzerland	78
Romania	77
Iceland	76
Brazil	75
Slovenia	75
Netherlands	71
France	71
Hungary	69
Lithuania	66
West Germany	63
Britain	59
Czechoslovakia	52
Finland	51
East Germany	48
Norway	46
Denmark	43
Bulgaria	38
Sweden	31
Latvia	29
Japan	22
Belarus	19
Russia	19
Estonia	15
Moscow	14
China	07

Note: Countries in the left column are ranked according to GNP per capita. / The percentages in the bottom row give each country an equal weight. / na=not ascertained.

V147 ATTEND SERVICES

Apart from weddings, funerals, and christenings, about how often do you attend religious services these days?
(% "once a month" or more)

Country	Total	Gender Male	Gender Female	Age 16-29	Age 30-49	Age 50+	Education Lower	Education Medium	Education Upper	Income Lower	Income Middle	Income Upper	Pol. Aff. Left	Pol. Aff. Center	Pol. Aff. Right	Values Mat	Values Mixed	Values Postmat
India	71	66	76	66	74	73	77	72	65	71	72	69	69	72	74	72	70	65
Nigeria	88	87	91	87	90	91	87	87	90	88	88	92	93	87	89	89	88	88
China	01	01	01	00	01	02	01	01	00	01	00	01	na	na	na	01	00	00
Romania	31	24	38	18	21	47	48	21	23	33	32	27	30	26	33	38	25	22
Turkey	38	67	09	31	39	47	39	40	32	41	42	33	22	40	59	44	37	35
Poland	85	79	91	88	82	86	91	86	62	86	83	86	75	86	87	88	83	88
Bulgaria	09	06	12	08	06	14	14	07	09	12	10	05	03	09	13	10	09	13
Chile	47	39	53	36	49	58	52	44	42	46	49	44	37	49	47	54	45	40
Czechoslovakia	21	18	23	17	12	34	31	16	14	25	17	21	13	21	25	27	18	20
South Africa	na	na	na	na	na	na	na	na	na	na	na	na	na	na	na	na	na	na
Lithuania	na	na	na	na	na	na	na	na	na	na	na	na	na	na	na	na	na	na
Hungary	34	28	39	18	25	46	40	28	25	39	30	30	24	31	47	38	31	18
Argentina	55	48	61	49	58	56	56	56	53	56	53	53	43	56	62	62	51	61
Brazil	50	45	55	45	48	64	64	46	40	55	49	45	40	49	57	55	48	43
Mexico	63	57	70	60	62	73	63	73	56	63	62	63	48	63	68	71	61	53
Belarus	06	04	07	04	04	12	15	05	04	07	07	04	05	03	13	08	04	08
Russia	06	03	08	04	04	10	10	05	05	07	06	05	04	06	06	07	06	05
Moscow	09	05	11	07	08	11	07	07	10	06	11	08	09	07	12	09	08	11
Latvia	09	05	11	06	06	16	20	09	05	07	07	11	na	na	na	07	10	03
Estonia	na	na	na	na	na	na	na	na	na	na	na	na	na	na	na	na	na	na
Portugal	41	32	50	31	33	58	49	18	32	55	31	29	27	39	51	47	38	27
South Korea	64	68	61	53	67	76	71	66	59	61	65	67	51	66	66	67	63	58
Ireland	88	84	91	80	87	94	90	88	73	92	90	82	66	89	92	91	88	81
North Ireland	69	55	78	57	68	77	67	70	76	64	68	66	64	71	63	75	69	58
Slovenia	35	33	37	34	29	42	45	32	23	44	31	25	24	30	47	43	33	27
Spain	39	26	49	20	33	58	42	30	31	49	35	31	22	45	63	45	38	22
East Germany	20	16	23	12	20	25	21	24	15	26	19	16	08	22	32	26	18	22
Britain	24	17	30	13	21	32	20	29	35	28	17	22	18	24	27	27	21	26
Italy	53	43	63	44	48	65	54	53	49	57	54	42	33	69	62	61	53	47
Netherlands	30	31	29	20	29	42	35	28	26	26	31	29	15	30	47	34	32	25
Belgium	31	25	36	16	25	46	30	31	31	32	29	35	16	32	48	32	31	29
Austria	44	37	49	35	38	53	52	39	32	50	43	40	38	37	54	54	46	35
France	17	15	18	07	10	31	17	16	19	15	17	20	10	16	35	21	16	15
Canada	40	32	47	29	35	56	48	37	38	42	43	34	30	43	43	53	41	33
United States	58	56	60	48	57	63	60	53	62	54	59	58	37	59	69	65	60	47
Iceland	09	07	12	07	09	14	11	08	09	na	na	na	08	10	10	07	10	10
West Germany	34	25	42	17	25	51	38	28	25	39	30	31	18	37	46	50	36	22
Denmark	11	07	15	03	07	22	18	07	10	13	08	08	05	11	15	10	12	05
Finland	11	09	13	11	07	20	15	11	09	19	07	08	09	13	10	24	10	12
Norway	13	09	16	09	10	18	17	09	14	17	11	09	06	14	15	12	13	10
Sweden	10	09	12	09	09	14	09	08	16	09	10	12	09	11	12	11	11	09
Japan	14	12	16	07	10	26	20	14	10	18	13	15	14	12	22	17	14	15
Switzerland	43	36	48	28	38	53	40	45	43	51	40	30	33	39	55	51	43	35
Total	**36**	**32**	**39**	**28**	**33**	**44**	**40**	**34**	**32**	**39**	**35**	**33**	**28**	**37**	**44**	**40**	**35**	**31**

Ranking:

Country	Rank
Nigeria	88
Ireland	88
Poland	85
India	71
North Ireland	69
South Korea	64
Mexico	63
United States	58
Argentina	55
Italy	53
Brazil	50
Chile	47
Austria	44
Switzerland	43
Portugal	41
Canada	40
Spain	39
Turkey	38
Slovenia	35
Hungary	34
West Germany	34
Romania	31
Belgium	31
Netherlands	30
Britain	24
Czechoslovakia	21
East Germany	20
France	17
Japan	14
Norway	13
Denmark	11
Finland	11
Sweden	10
Bulgaria	09
Moscow	09
Latvia	09
Iceland	09
Belarus	06
Russia	06
China	01

Note: Countries in the left column are ranked according to GNP per capita. / The percentages in the bottom row give each country an equal weight. / na=not ascertained.

V148-V150. Do you personally think it is important to hold a religious service for any of the following events?

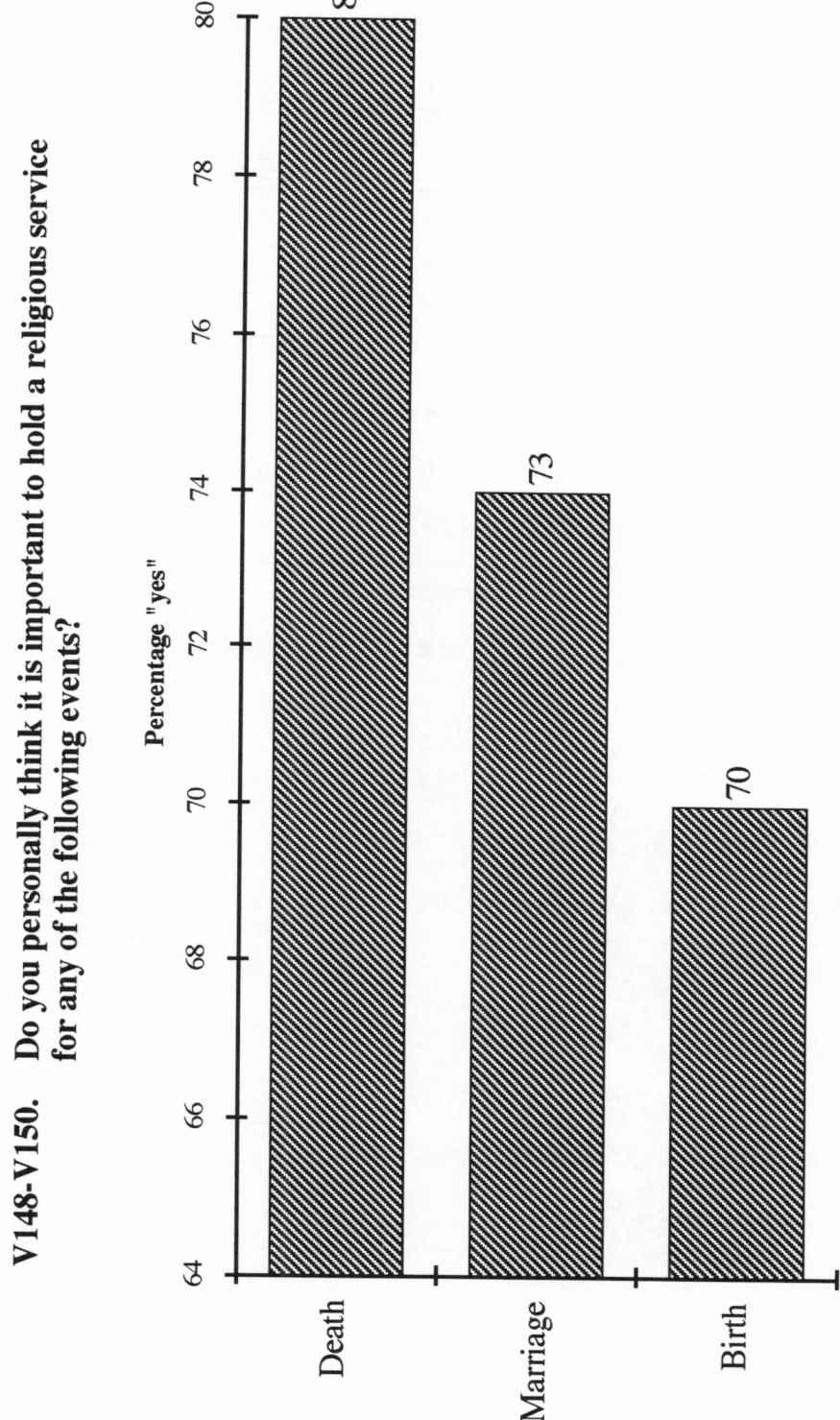

V148 SERVICES: BIRTH

Do you personally think it is important to hold a religious service for any of the following events? Birth (% "yes")

	Total	Gender		Age			Education			Income			Political Affinity			Values			Ranking:	
		Male	Female	16-29	30-49	50+	Lower	Medium	Upper	Lower	Middle	Upper	Left	Center	Right	Mat	Mixed	Postmat		
India	74	70	80	68	76	82	90	76	64	80	74	69	66	74	77	75	72	65	Poland	95
Nigeria	92	90	94	93	89	93	94	90	92	88	90	96	90	92	93	93	92	85	Ireland	94
China	04	03	05	06	03	04	04	03	05	03	05	06	na	na	na	04	04	08	Nigeria	92
Romania	86	83	89	82	86	89	91	84	83	87	89	82	81	85	84	87	86	81	Lithuania	87
Turkey	42	34	50	39	40	50	52	29	23	49	43	34	24	41	51	48	44	30	Austria	87
Poland	95	93	97	95	95	96	97	95	86	95	97	93	91	94	94	96	94	93	Romania	86
Bulgaria	78	76	80	75	78	80	82	77	77	81	80	71	70	78	85	78	77	82	Italy	86
Chile	77	73	80	77	76	76	78	77	76	80	75	75	71	78	84	78	78	71	Latvia	84
Czechoslovakia	52	49	54	46	46	62	62	48	43	54	50	52	38	53	56	58	50	45	Belarus	83
South Africa	78	77	78	79	75	78	80	77	73	81	77	71	78	77	76	76	79	73	North Ireland	83
Lithuania	87	82	91	85	86	89	93	85	82	90	86	80	na	na	na	91	87	82	Brazil	81
Hungary	79	76	81	69	71	89	85	73	72	88	73	66	61	79	83	79	80	55	Hungary	79
Argentina	67	59	74	66	65	71	71	68	60	72	66	61	43	65	71	75	70	50	Slovenia	79
Brazil	81	79	83	81	79	85	85	81	71	86	82	74	79	78	84	86	78	72	Bulgaria	78
Mexico	76	72	81	74	76	82	77	78	71	79	72	75	61	74	82	81	75	60	South Africa	78
Belarus	83	80	85	81	82	85	96	87	73	86	79	83	83	80	88	89	80	73	Russia	78
Russia	78	69	84	78	75	81	85	82	68	83	77	70	65	79	78	83	75	68	Chile	77
Moscow	76	71	80	74	76	78	86	78	72	79	75	72	76	74	74	79	75	70	Mexico	76
Latvia	84	79	87	84	83	85	92	85	77	86	85	82	na	na	na	86	83	76	Moscow	76
Estonia	66	59	72	64	63	71	74	64	62	65	67	66	na	na	na	72	63	53	Portugal	75
Portugal	75	71	78	68	73	84	81	63	63	85	66	67	64	74	84	85	71	60	India	74
South Korea	na	na	na	na	na	na	na	na	na	na	na	na	na	na	na	na	na	na	Spain	74
Ireland	94	91	96	92	92	96	96	93	85	94	95	92	81	95	95	95	94	92	Belgium	74
North Ireland	83	86	81	82	81	87	87	76	76	83	85	75	79	82	82	91	80	87	West Germany	72
Slovenia	79	77	82	78	77	83	87	80	62	88	80	61	56	79	82	88	78	61	Denmark	69
Spain	74	67	80	61	70	88	81	65	53	87	73	63	56	82	89	87	75	50	Canada	68
East Germany	39	35	41	23	35	51	41	38	30	49	35	32	19	44	55	49	37	39	Argentina	67
Britain	66	62	70	61	60	74	68	65	55	68	65	61	61	70	66	71	67	60	Iceland	67
Italy	86	80	91	81	83	91	87	77	75	90	84	75	71	93	92	94	87	75	Estonia	66
Netherlands	48	43	49	44	47	52	51	49	42	44	48	46	28	51	65	54	50	43	Britain	66
Belgium	74	69	78	64	69	85	79	74	63	76	70	72	55	84	82	83	76	59	Norway	66
Austria	87	84	90	84	86	90	89	87	83	90	87	86	78	84	92	94	89	79	France	65
France	65	63	67	58	58	78	72	62	54	69	62	58	47	72	79	79	69	47	Finland	58
Canada	68	66	70	69	63	74	76	68	61	72	67	65	56	71	70	82	70	59	United States	57
United States	57	54	60	57	52	61	62	57	52	54	55	58	50	57	60	64	57	52	Sweden	56
Iceland	67	64	71	67	64	73	73	74	59	75	72	na	60	67	72	72	69	42	Czechoslovakia	52
West Germany	72	67	76	57	65	85	78	64	55	75	72	68	55	75	85	87	77	55	Netherlands	48
Denmark	69	66	72	68	61	79	77	67	66	70	70	62	50	71	78	80	72	47	Turkey	42
Finland	58	54	63	50	54	75	63	57	58	64	52	61	37	60	66	71	58	57	East Germany	39
Norway	66	66	67	60	58	80	80	66	60	72	63	62	54	71	71	74	67	40	Japan	36
Sweden	56	52	60	56	48	64	57	56	53	54	51	58	45	56	64	60	59	45	China	04
Japan	36	35	37	26	35	44	45	36	28	35	40	35	33	35	37	42	34	28		
Switzerland	na	na	na	na	na	na	na	na	na	na	na	na	na	na	na	na	na	na		
Total	70	66	73	66	67	76	76	69	63	73	69	66	60	72	76	76	70	60		

Note: Countries in the left column are ranked according to GNP per capita. / The percentages in the bottom row give each country an equal weight. / na=not ascertained.

V149 SERVICES: MARRIAGE

Do you personally think it is important to hold a religious service for any of the following events? Marriage (% "yes")

	Total	Gender		Age			Education			Income			Political Affinity			Values		
		Male	Female	16-29	30-49	50+	Lower	Medium	Upper	Lower	Middle	Upper	Left	Center	Right	Mat	Mixed	Postmat
India	79	74	84	73	81	86	91	79	72	82	78	77	68	78	85	80	77	68
Nigeria	95	94	97	97	94	91	96	96	94	95	95	98	97	95	96	96	96	89
China	13	12	13	21	10	07	10	13	14	12	10	15	na	na	na	11	13	17
Romania	92	90	94	88	92	94	95	90	91	92	94	89	90	91	93	92	92	89
Turkey	76	75	78	71	77	85	87	66	47	83	79	66	54	79	88	82	80	61
Poland	97	96	98	98	96	97	98	97	88	97	98	94	95	96	97	96	97	94
Bulgaria	81	79	83	80	81	81	80	80	83	83	83	75	71	82	87	81	80	87
Chile	87	84	90	85	88	90	90	88	83	90	87	85	79	89	93	92	88	79
Czechoslovakia	50	48	52	44	45	59	60	46	42	53	49	47	36	51	55	54	49	43
South Africa	93	92	94	94	93	91	95	93	87	95	94	88	92	93	91	93	93	92
Lithuania	84	78	89	82	80	89	93	81	78	87	82	78	na	na	na	89	82	80
Hungary	76	74	78	69	67	87	82	70	70	84	71	63	60	74	83	77	77	53
Argentina	73	66	80	73	69	78	78	74	65	77	74	69	46	71	79	81	76	57
Brazil	82	82	82	80	80	78	89	81	67	88	83	73	79	78	87	88	79	69
Mexico	82	79	85	80	82	88	82	85	79	83	79	83	67	80	86	89	80	73
Belarus	62	63	61	53	60	75	84	63	53	63	61	61	60	62	64	70	56	66
Russia	62	56	67	59	58	69	73	64	54	65	61	58	53	59	56	65	61	59
Moscow	56	54	57	55	53	62	68	60	51	58	55	55	56	57	61	57	54	59
Latvia	79	73	83	75	79	83	88	79	75	81	78	79	na	na	na	79	80	70
Estonia	64	56	71	64	61	69	71	63	60	64	64	66	na	na	na	68	63	55
Portugal	79	73	84	72	76	88	86	58	69	88	71	71	64	79	88	87	76	58
South Korea	na	na	na	na	na	na	na	na	na	na	na	na	na	na	na	na	na	na
Ireland	94	92	96	92	93	97	96	94	85	96	96	92	83	95	96	94	95	92
North Ireland	93	91	96	93	89	98	94	93	93	94	96	89	89	91	97	95	93	93
Slovenia	76	74	78	77	72	79	87	75	57	85	75	61	52	75	80	85	75	52
Spain	74	67	80	59	69	89	81	63	53	87	72	62	56	79	91	86	74	50
East Germany	46	43	49	35	42	57	48	49	38	55	44	40	25	54	60	56	44	48
Britain	80	76	84	77	75	87	82	81	68	82	77	78	73	83	84	85	82	71
Italy	83	77	88	78	78	90	84	72	76	88	81	68	64	92	87	93	84	71
Netherlands	52	51	52	48	50	58	54	56	45	45	53	52	27	59	70	63	55	44
Belgium	76	73	79	67	70	87	80	76	67	76	72	76	57	80	83	84	77	64
Austria	85	81	87	82	83	88	87	84	82	87	84	83	76	81	89	93	88	74
France	68	65	70	63	59	80	75	65	54	71	64	62	49	77	83	82	71	49
Canada	64	57	71	67	54	73	70	60	62	64	66	54	46	65	74	82	84	71
United States	70	68	73	65	57	83	70	64	61	72	62	58	48	60	72	91	84	60
Iceland	66	59	73	67	59	75	85	71	62	77	66	64	58	75	74	89	87	46
West Germany	75	70	79	67	66	87	72	66	57	na	74	72	57	68	74	74	66	57
Denmark	68	65	70	64	54	80	81	65	57	77	66	54	46	79	86	91	79	74
Finland	64	57	71	67	57	73	71	60	60	64	62	58	48	65	74	72	68	42
Norway	70	68	73	65	61	83	70	64	61	72	62	64	58	60	72	72	65	60
Sweden	59	57	61	67	51	63	63	59	55	56	55	60	47	58	67	66	63	45
Japan	56	53	60	49	53	65	63	59	45	59	56	52	44	56	59	60	53	50
Switzerland	na	na	na	na	na	na	na	na	na	na	na	na	na	na	na	na	na	na
Total	73	70	77	71	70	80	79	72	66	76	73	69	62	76	81	79	74	64

Ranking:

Poland	97
Nigeria	95
Ireland	94
South Africa	93
North Ireland	93
Romania	92
Chile	87
United States	86
Austria	85
Lithuania	84
Italy	83
Brazil	82
Mexico	82
Canada	82
Bulgaria	81
Britain	80
India	79
Latvia	79
Portugal	79
Turkey	76
Hungary	76
Slovenia	76
Belgium	76
West Germany	75
Spain	74
Argentina	73
Norway	70
France	68
Iceland	66
Estonia	64
Denmark	64
Finland	64
Belarus	62
Russia	62
Sweden	59
Moscow	56
Japan	56
Netherlands	52
Czechoslovakia	50
East Germany	46
China	13

Note: Countries in the left column are ranked according to GNP per capita. / The percentages in the bottom row give each country an equal weight. / na=not ascertained.

V150 SERVICES: DEATH

Do you personally think it is important to hold a religious service for any of the following events? Death (% "yes")

	Total	Gender		Age			Education			Income			Political Affinity			Values			Ranking:	
		Male	Female	16-29	30-49	50+	Lower	Medium	Upper	Lower	Middle	Upper	Left	Center	Right	Mat	Mixed	Postmat		
India	75	71	79	68	89	84	89	75	68	77	75	91	63	75	80	76	72	68	Ireland	97
Nigeria	90	89	93	91	89	91	91	92	88	92	88	91	91	90	89	91	90	86	North Ireland	96
China	11	11	11	15	09	09	10	09	10	11	10	11	na	na	na	12	09	17	Turkey	95
Romania	89	88	90	80	88	95	95	84	88	88	92	86	84	89	88	91	87	86	Poland	95
Turkey	95	95	95	92	97	97	97	95	86	97	96	92	89	96	99	97	96	90	Iceland	93
Poland	95	94	97	97	96	95	96	96	93	95	98	94	94	95	95	96	95	94	Nigeria	90
Bulgaria	87	85	88	89	86	86	89	86	86	89	87	82	79	86	93	87	86	92	Romania	89
Chile	82	80	85	80	83	85	82	83	84	82	83	82	76	85	86	83	84	77	Lithuania	89
Czechoslovakia	62	62	61	62	56	68	71	59	51	64	58	64	53	62	66	64	61	57	Austria	88
South Africa	86	83	89	88	86	85	89	85	82	87	88	79	90	84	76	84	87	88	Bulgaria	87
Lithuania	89	85	92	86	87	92	94	88	80	91	88	85	na	na	na	93	89	83	Italy	87
Hungary	86	84	88	86	80	91	90	81	88	92	84	74	72	86	86	85	88	68	United States	87
Argentina	67	58	74	59	63	76	68	65	62	70	67	61	40	65	73	76	68	48	Japan	87
Brazil	76	75	78	74	74	85	79	76	71	78	78	73	72	76	79	79	75	68	South Africa	86
Mexico	81	76	86	81	79	85	81	85	77	82	79	80	67	80	85	87	80	68	Hungary	86
Belarus	76	73	79	74	78	74	89	78	70	79	74	76	75	76	80	80	74	68	Britain	86
Russia	74	66	80	76	71	76	80	77	68	80	74	70	67	74	68	75	74	70	Latvia	85
Moscow	76	70	81	80	75	74	84	80	71	84	75	79	76	73	72	77	73	82	Canada	84
Latvia	85	81	88	85	85	86	92	87	79	87	85	85	na	na	na	86	86	74	West Germany	83
Estonia	72	66	77	73	68	78	79	70	70	71	74	73	na	na	na	77	69	74	Finland	83
Portugal	79	75	82	73	77	86	84	64	69	89	68	72	65	78	87	85	76	62	Chile	82
South Korea	na	na	na	na	na	na	na	na	na	na	na	na	na	na	na	na	na	na	Mexico	81
Ireland	97	95	98	96	96	98	98	97	90	98	98	95	88	98	97	97	97	95	Slovenia	81
North Ireland	96	92	98	95	93	99	96	93	100	00	99	na	96	94	99	97	95	98	Norway	81
Slovenia	81	78	83	84	76	83	91	78	63	89	78	68	63	81	83	87	80	58	Denmark	80
Spain	75	68	81	61	69	90	82	64	54	82	72	64	57	81	91	87	74	52	Sweden	80
East Germany	61	58	63	55	56	69	63	62	50	69	58	56	36	69	77	74	58	62	Portugal	79
Britain	86	81	90	83	82	91	88	85	74	86	82	85	77	89	87	90	87	79	Belgium	79
Italy	87	81	93	83	85	91	88	79	79	90	87	75	73	94	92	93	88	79	Brazil	76
Netherlands	62	56	64	62	62	61	64	66	55	90	62	58	42	67	78	71	64	56	Belarus	76
Belgium	79	76	81	72	74	87	83	80	68	83	77	77	61	83	85	85	80	69	Moscow	76
Austria	88	84	90	86	86	90	88	87	87	88	86	87	77	86	92	94	90	79	India	75
France	73	70	75	71	65	82	79	70	62	73	72	67	56	79	87	86	76	58	Spain	75
Canada	84	80	87	85	78	88	89	85	77	86	84	79	69	85	85	93	85	74	Russia	74
United States	87	86	88	90	84	88	88	88	85	87	89	84	76	88	91	92	89	78	France	73
Iceland	93	89	97	93	92	94	95	95	90	95	na	na	87	96	94	97	94	77	Estonia	72
West Germany	83	79	86	74	79	91	88	77	71	88	84	79	68	87	92	94	87	69	Argentina	67
Denmark	80	74	85	81	74	85	88	80	76	81	81	74	64	84	85	86	82	63	Czechoslovakia	62
Finland	83	77	88	76	80	94	85	82	81	86	81	81	67	83	88	91	84	78	Netherlands	62
Norway	81	79	84	77	77	89	89	81	77	83	80	78	71	86	83	86	83	59	East Germany	61
Sweden	80	77	83	87	72	84	85	79	74	82	79	78	75	78	85	84	83	70	China	11
Japan	87	86	88	83	84	93	91	88	80	88	88	85	81	88	90	92	85	80		
Switzerland	na	na	na	na	na	na	na	na	na	na	na	na	na	na	na	na	na	na		
Total	80	76	83	78	77	84	84	79	74	79	79	76	71	83	85	84	80	72		

Note: Countries in the left column are ranked according to GNP per capita. / The percentages in the bottom row give each country an equal weight. / na=not ascertained.

V152-V155. Generally speaking, do you think that your church is giving, in your country, adequate answers to...

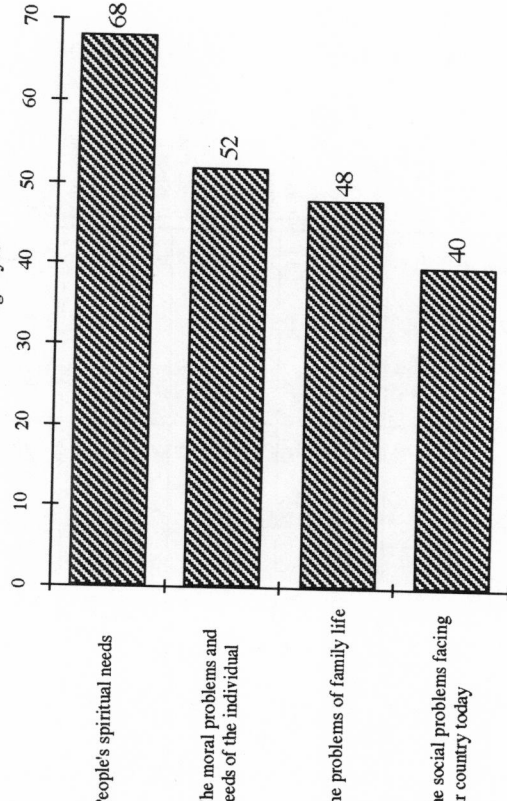

Percentage "yes"

People's spiritual needs — 68

The moral problems and needs of the individual — 52

The problems of family life — 48

The social problems facing our country today — 40

V151. Independently of whether you go to church or not, would you say you are...

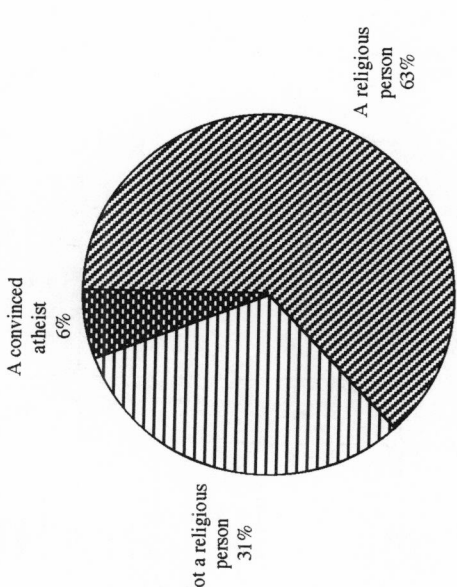

A convinced atheist 6%

A religious person 63%

Not a religious person 31%

V151 IS RESPONDENT RELIGIOUS

Independently of whether you go to church or not, would you say you are a religious person, not a religious person, or a convinced atheist? (% "religious person")

	Total	Gender		Age			Education			Income			Political Affinity			Values		
		Male	Female	16-29	30-49	50+	Lower	Medium	Upper	Lower	Middle	Upper	Left	Center	Right	Mat	Mixed	Postmat
India	84	82	85	82	83	87	85	85	81	86	81	84	82	83	81	86	81	79
Nigeria	93	91	96	92	93	98	96	94	90	94	91	92	95	89	96	96	91	88
China	05	04	06	06	04	06	06	05	03	04	04	07	na	na	na	06	03	10
Romania	75	68	81	63	70	86	87	71	63	75	78	70	71	74	72	80	73	56
Turkey	75	69	80	68	76	83	85	65	45	81	78	63	49	77	87	85	75	62
Poland	95	93	97	95	96	95	98	98	75	96	98	92	89	96	94	97	95	94
Bulgaria	36	29	43	29	28	49	53	31	26	40	35	27	19	36	43	39	34	38
Chile	77	70	83	70	77	87	81	76	73	80	75	74	65	79	80	79	77	72
Czechoslovakia	46	40	51	34	36	66	61	39	39	51	43	44	32	46	53	51	45	36
South Africa	83	77	89	79	84	90	82	83	87	82	82	87	83	82	83	85	82	84
Lithuania	55	45	64	39	47	73	80	49	37	65	50	38	na	na	na	69	52	42
Hungary	57	52	62	33	46	76	71	45	38	70	48	43	29	55	66	61	55	40
Argentina	73	64	82	66	71	82	77	72	68	80	74	68	44	72	81	79	76	57
Brazil	88	86	89	83	89	94	93	87	82	92	89	82	82	88	91	90	87	84
Mexico	75	71	79	72	73	86	75	80	70	71	80	74	64	74	80	80	74	70
Belarus	41	34	48	36	38	53	61	42	34	48	41	34	40	36	53	43	41	26
Russia	56	40	68	54	50	64	67	57	48	62	55	50	45	54	60	59	54	56
Moscow	40	27	51	44	33	48	52	42	36	42	41	33	41	38	36	47	35	45
Latvia	54	37	66	56	49	61	81	57	41	58	56	50	na	na	na	55	56	38
Estonia	21	14	27	20	17	29	29	21	15	24	19	19	na	na	na	23	19	20
Portugal	69	59	78	52	74	82	79	48	49	81	63	54	59	67	77	79	63	51
South Korea	na	na	na	na	na	na	na	na	na	na	na	na	na	na	na	na	na	na
Ireland	72	67	78	61	72	80	76	72	54	83	70	67	51	71	78	75	73	68
North Ireland	72	64	78	60	69	83	73	66	76	69	69	69	54	72	75	72	72	59
Slovenia	73	68	79	66	71	79	87	69	51	86	69	53	54	71	72	82	71	59
Spain	70	59	79	54	66	85	74	65	53	80	69	59	52	75	86	78	68	53
East Germany	38	31	44	23	34	50	40	40	28	48	37	29	18	45	53	48	36	39
Britain	56	47	65	30	56	71	57	56	52	62	54	47	47	55	64	61	57	51
Italy	86	81	91	80	83	92	87	80	73	90	83	70	72	93	90	94	87	76
Netherlands	61	56	63	46	67	69	69	60	53	57	64	58	45	64	76	70	62	57
Belgium	68	60	75	51	67	79	73	66	61	67	66	70	45	73	79	72	70	58
Austria	81	74	85	72	81	85	84	79	80	84	81	79	70	79	84	89	82	75
France	51	47	54	40	45	64	54	49	45	50	49	50	35	58	68	58	51	44
Canada	71	65	77	63	68	82	77	70	68	73	72	66	58	73	74	80	72	64
United States	84	82	87	79	82	89	84	86	82	88	83	82	65	86	90	89	84	81
Iceland	75	66	84	67	73	86	86	80	63	na	na	na	68	75	78	81	75	56
West Germany	65	57	72	47	61	78	69	58	63	67	65	64	51	69	76	71	70	53
Denmark	73	63	82	58	71	85	80	68	71	76	75	61	60	77	60	74	76	56
Finland	59	53	66	40	58	76	66	59	55	65	57	57	46	64	53	83	58	56
Norway	48	39	56	36	43	60	60	40	49	53	41	48	40	48	na	48	49	37
Sweden	31	25	39	26	28	40	32	28	37	32	34	28	27	32	34	30	34	26
Japan	26	20	32	20	25	32	30	27	20	32	23	28	24	23	33	29	24	26
Switzerland	74	67	80	65	71	80	76	74	65	78	72	64	62	73	79	81	75	66
Total	**63**	**56**	**69**	**54**	**60**	**72**	**70**	**60**	**55**	**66**	**61**	**57**	**54**	**66**	**71**	**68**	**62**	**55**

Ranking:

Poland	95
Nigeria	93
Brazil	88
Italy	86
India	84
United States	84
South Africa	83
Austria	81
Chile	77
Romania	75
Turkey	75
Mexico	75
Iceland	75
Switzerland	74
Argentina	73
Slovenia	73
Denmark	73
Ireland	72
North Ireland	72
Canada	71
Spain	70
Portugal	69
Belgium	68
West Germany	65
Netherlands	61
Finland	59
Hungary	57
Russia	56
Britain	56
Lithuania	55
Latvia	54
France	51
Norway	48
Czechoslovakia	46
Belarus	41
Moscow	40
East Germany	38
Bulgaria	36
Sweden	31
Japan	26
Estonia	21
China	05

Note: Countries in the left column are ranked according to GNP per capita. / The percentages in the bottom row give each country an equal weight. / na=not ascertained.

V152 ANSWERS: MORAL PROBLEMS

Generally speaking, do you think that your church is giving, in your country, adequate answers to the moral problems and needs of the individual? (% "yes")

	Total	Gender		Age			Education			Income			Political Affinity			Values		
		Male	Female	16-29	30-49	50+	Lower	Medium	Upper	Lower	Middle	Upper	Left	Center	Right	Mat	Mixed	Postmat
India	38	37	39	36	40	39	46	37	36	42	38	34	37	38	40	35	40	39
Nigeria	86	83	91	85	88	85	95	87	82	84	88	84	86	84	87	89	86	79
China	na	na	na	na	na	na	na	na	na	na	na	na	na	na	na	na	na	na
Romania	62	60	64	51	55	76	76	na	55	60	64	60	58	60	60	68	60	38
Turkey	50	47	54	49	46	59	60	39	27	59	51	40	36	49	62	56	53	37
Poland	na	na	na	na	na	na	na	na	na	na	na	na	na	na	na	na	na	na
Bulgaria	49	44	54	41	43	60	62	46	43	54	48	41	39	47	58	50	48	58
Chile	77	78	77	69	80	84	83	73	76	81	76	75	79	79	70	76	77	80
Czechoslovakia	na	na	na	na	na	na	na	na	na	na	na	na	na	na	na	na	na	na
South Africa	na	na	na	na	na	na	na	na	na	na	na	na	na	na	na	na	na	na
Lithuania	na	na	na	na	na	na	na	na	na	na	na	na	na	na	na	na	na	na
Hungary	79	75	81	59	72	86	82	74	77	81	77	69	72	79	77	80	77	69
Argentina	42	39	45	35	39	52	52	39	27	53	39	32	27	43	45	51	43	29
Brazil	44	40	47	37	43	58	64	39	20	58	43	29	36	36	51	53	39	25
Mexico	65	62	68	63	65	70	66	68	59	68	65	57	44	67	72	73	62	57
Belarus	83	84	83	76	83	89	84	82	84	86	80	84	84	80	81	82	84	86
Russia	88	90	87	81	85	94	91	85	88	87	90	85	87	86	85	89	87	87
Moscow	87	87	87	83	85	92	85	89	86	87	90	80	89	84	79	88	87	84
Latvia	88	90	87	78	93	90	86	88	88	83	89	92	na	na	na	85	89	87
Estonia	na	na	na	na	na	na	na	na	na	na	na	na	na	na	na	na	na	na
Portugal	57	53	61	44	53	73	65	36	43	69	50	45	46	55	66	68	54	34
South Korea	na	na	na	na	na	na	na	na	na	na	na	na	na	na	na	54	na	34
Ireland	42	42	43	31	38	53	48	37	30	54	45	30	18	38	56	52	43	27
North Ireland	55	51	58	44	49	69	57	56	42	58	59	50	32	59	54	71	51	48
Slovenia	64	67	61	52	61	74	69	60	60	71	61	53	53	65	72	66	64	56
Spain	40	33	47	24	34	60	46	28	27	56	39	30	23	43	62	53	38	20
East Germany	58	56	60	46	61	64	57	61	63	60	56	59	51	58	69	59	55	65
Britain	34	29	39	31	28	42	37	29	26	46	27	25	32	35	32	35	34	34
Italy	55	49	60	44	48	67	56	47	40	63	52	33	35	68	55	65	56	42
Netherlands	36	38	36	38	32	40	40	36	32	30	35	31	22	34	50	47	42	24
Belgium	42	39	45	30	37	53	44	42	39	44	39	38	30	42	49	50	41	35
Austria	47	45	48	37	42	56	53	43	46	52	45	43	41	43	56	58	48	38
France	38	38	38	29	29	55	42	33	37	39	33	38	26	43	59	48	42	23
Canada	55	53	57	52	49	65	63	57	47	60	56	50	47	55	57	71	57	43
United States	68	64	72	62	64	73	69	70	63	69	71	63	55	67	73	72	69	62
Iceland	37	35	39	35	36	40	44	40	29	46	37	na	28	39	42	45	36	24
West Germany	41	36	45	25	31	57	44	33	41	24	19	39	28	40	56	58	43	27
Denmark	20	17	23	11	15	33	32	15	18	24	20	13	14	20	25	31	19	15
Finland	25	25	25	11	21	46	29	24	24	34	21	22	12	31	30	39	24	24
Norway	41	42	40	28	36	54	54	24	24	45	36	39	32	47	43	47	40	33
Sweden	19	22	16	19	13	24	22	17	38	17	20	39	14	19	24	30	19	12
Japan	28	25	31	23	27	32	19	17	23	37	21	28	24	25	34	31	27	16
Switzerland	na	na	na	na	na	na	na	na	na	na	na	na	na	na	na	na	na	na
Total	**53**	**51**	**55**	**45**	**49**	**62**	**58**	**49**	**47**	**58**	**52**	**47**	**42**	**52**	**57**	**59**	**52**	**44**

Ranking:

Russia	88
Latvia	88
Moscow	87
Nigeria	86
Belarus	83
Hungary	79
Chile	77
United States	68
Mexico	65
Slovenia	64
Romania	62
East Germany	58
Portugal	57
North Ireland	55
Italy	55
Canada	55
Turkey	50
Bulgaria	49
Austria	47
Brazil	44
Argentina	42
Ireland	42
Belgium	42
West Germany	41
Norway	41
Spain	40
India	38
France	38
Iceland	37
Netherlands	36
Britain	34
Japan	28
Finland	25
Denmark	20
Sweden	19

Note: Countries in the left column are ranked according to GNP per capita. / The percentages in the bottom row give each country an equal weight. / na=not ascertained.

V153 ANSWERS: FAMILY LIFE

Generally speaking, do you think that your church is giving, in your country, adequate answers to the problems of family life? (% "yes")

	Total	Gender		Age			Education			Income			Political Affinity			Values		
		Male	Female	16-29	30-49	50+	Lower	Medium	Upper	Lower	Middle	Upper	Left	Center	Right	Mat	Mixed	Postmat
India	28	26	31	26	30	31	39	27	25	34	26	25	29	25	25	27	28	23
Nigeria	86	84	89	84	88	91	93	87	82	85	87	89	86	86	86	90	84	80
China	na	na	na	na	na	na	na	na	na	na	na	na	na	na	na	na	na	na
Romania	53	50	56	44	46	65	66	48	44	52	54	53	55	49	50	62	48	32
Turkey	34	32	35	32	32	39	44	22	11	41	35	24	20	33	42	38	37	20
Poland	na	na	na	na	na	na	na	na	na	na	na	na	na	na	na	na	na	na
Bulgaria	38	32	43	31	28	51	55	31	31	44	35	29	25	35	46	38	37	44
Chile	83	83	83	80	83	86	87	82	78	86	82	79	83	84	79	81	83	84
Czechoslovakia	na	na	na	na	na	na	na	na	na	na	na	na	na	na	na	na	na	na
South Africa	na	na	na	na	na	na	na	na	na	na	na	na	na	na	na	na	na	na
Lithuania	na	na	na	na	na	na	na	na	na	na	na	na	na	na	na	na	na	na
Hungary	70	67	72	53	60	80	74	63	74	72	66	71	60	70	73	69	71	54
Argentina	49	45	53	43	46	58	58	45	38	60	50	35	29	51	47	60	50	32
Brazil	51	47	56	45	52	61	67	49	27	65	49	37	44	45	60	59	48	33
Mexico	64	60	69	61	64	73	66	65	58	65	65	59	47	63	70	73	62	58
Belarus	83	84	83	76	83	89	84	82	84	86	80	84	84	80	81	82	84	86
Russia	74	73	74	62	67	87	82	73	69	76	76	68	75	68	76	76	72	76
Moscow	87	87	87	83	85	92	85	89	86	87	90	80	89	84	79	88	87	84
Latvia	63	56	67	48	67	74	77	63	58	57	65	65	na	na	na	59	66	63
Estonia	34	31	35	39	29	37	37	30	35	28	38	47	40	58	65	50	39	na
Portugal	56	52	61	48	49	72	63	36	46	65	51	47	40	58	65	66	53	42
South Korea	na	na	na	na	na	na	na	na	na	na	na	na	na	na	na	na	na	na
Ireland	36	37	35	25	32	47	43	29	24	46	37	26	17	31	47	43	37	24
North Ireland	59	57	61	49	55	70	60	56	64	59	59	55	43	62	58	72	55	51
Slovenia	54	56	52	47	51	62	60	51	49	61	50	47	49	56	65	59	52	50
Spain	42	36	47	25	39	59	48	29	27	57	39	30	26	47	64	52	40	21
East Germany	43	40	46	34	44	49	41	45	51	48	41	41	36	43	56	48	41	47
Britain	36	33	40	31	30	45	39	32	30	46	34	26	35	36	37	37	35	40
Italy	47	43	51	37	38	61	48	42	44	57	42	28	28	61	48	54	48	38
Netherlands	34	31	35	39	29	37	37	30	35	28	38	28	20	33	46	50	39	21
Belgium	37	35	38	26	30	48	40	38	28	41	39	36	23	37	43	45	36	29
Austria	34	29	37	23	29	42	39	30	33	37	32	33	32	31	39	44	34	28
France	28	30	27	19	22	42	33	21	28	31	26	29	16	32	48	37	29	20
Canada	56	54	57	52	50	65	62	57	49	59	57	50	48	56	58	72	56	47
United States	69	66	73	62	66	75	73	70	66	69	72	66	54	71	75	74	71	63
Iceland	40	34	46	36	40	44	46	41	34	na	34	29	33	43	40	42	40	30
West Germany	35	32	38	23	24	50	37	29	33	41	34	34	25	35	47	48	36	24
Denmark	13	11	16	07	09	22	21	09	11	16	12	08	10	11	18	19	12	11
Finland	27	26	28	18	22	45	26	26	22	37	26	18	16	30	30	50	27	23
Norway	29	30	28	17	23	44	47	24	25	34	25	28	21	33	31	34	28	21
Sweden	14	15	13	13	08	23	19	11	11	16	13	14	09	15	17	22	14	08
Japan	22	19	25	14	21	29	28	22	17	30	18	21	15	22	24	24	22	10
Switzerland	na	na	na	na	na	na	na	na	na	na	na	na	na	na	na	na	na	na
Total	**48**	**45**	**50**	**40**	**44**	**57**	**54**	**44**	**43**	**53**	**47**	**43**	**39**	**48**	**52**	**54**	**47**	**40**

Ranking:

Moscow	87
Nigeria	86
Chile	83
Belarus	83
Russia	74
Hungary	70
United States	69
Mexico	64
Latvia	63
North Ireland	59
Portugal	56
Canada	56
Slovenia	54
Romania	53
Brazil	51
Argentina	49
Italy	47
East Germany	43
Spain	42
Iceland	40
Bulgaria	38
Belgium	37
Ireland	36
Britain	36
West Germany	35
Turkey	34
Netherlands	34
Austria	34
Norway	29
India	28
France	28
Finland	27
Japan	22
Sweden	14
Denmark	13

Note: Countries in the left column are ranked according to GNP per capita. / The percentages in the bottom row give each country an equal weight. / na=not ascertained.

V154 ANSWERS: SPIRITUAL NEEDS

Generally speaking, do you think that your church is giving, in your country, adequate answers to people's spiritual needs?
(% "yes")

	Total	Gender		Age			Education			Income			Political Affinity			Values		
		Male	Female	16-29	30-49	50+	Lower	Medium	Upper	Lower	Middle	Upper	Left	Center	Right	Mat	Mixed	Postmat
India	59	57	61	57	59	63	63	56	60	60	56	59	57	63	60	53	62	66
Nigeria	89	86	93	89	90	85	91	90	87	88	90	91	90	89	90	92	89	78
China	na	na	na	na	na	na	na	na	na	na	na	na	na	na	na	na	na	na
Romania	78	74	81	73	72	86	85	74	74	75	80	77	74	78	75	83	76	55
Turkey	59	59	59	56	56	67	64	54	45	64	59	52	45	62	65	66	58	52
Poland	na	na	na	na	na	na	na	na	na	na	na	na	na	na	na	na	na	na
Bulgaria	56	51	61	62	48	62	63	54	54	60	58	52	44	55	64	54	59	55
Chile	86	86	86	81	87	90	93	82	83	90	85	83	87	86	83	86	85	88
Czechoslovakia	na	na	na	na	na	na	na	na	na	na	na	na	na	na	na	na	na	na
South Africa	na	na	na	na	na	na	na	na	na	na	na	na	na	na	na	na	na	na
Lithuania	na	na	na	na	na	na	na	na	na	na	na	na	na	na	na	na	na	na
Hungary	90	86	94	82	87	94	92	90	79	91	90	88	86	90	92	91	91	80
Argentina	59	56	61	55	53	67	67	57	48	67	59	52	42	59	66	68	59	45
Brazil	57	53	60	54	54	68	73	54	33	68	55	47	48	52	65	64	54	41
Mexico	80	76	86	79	78	87	81	78	78	82	80	77	67	82	81	85	79	75
Belarus	83	84	83	76	83	89	84	82	84	86	80	84	67	80	81	82	84	86
Russia	92	91	92	87	92	94	92	93	90	92	92	90	84	92	94	92	91	94
Moscow	87	87	92	83	85	92	85	89	86	87	90	80	89	84	79	88	91	84
Latvia	87	89	86	85	87	91	91	89	83	85	85	90	89	84	77	86	88	85
Estonia	na	na	na	na	na	na	na	na	na	na	na	na	na	na	na	na	na	na
Portugal	62	59	65	55	57	73	68	50	48	71	57	55	44	63	71	71	59	46
South Korea	na	na	na	na	na	na	na	na	na	na	na	na	na	na	na	na	na	na
Ireland	71	68	73	62	69	78	74	69	56	78	71	63	47	72	76	73	73	60
North Ireland	80	80	80	74	77	87	80	84	69	76	85	75	64	85	75	90	76	78
Slovenia	77	76	78	77	72	81	81	75	70	83	72	72	64	75	72	85	75	80
Spain	54	46	61	43	48	69	59	44	40	63	52	46	39	58	75	64	52	37
East Germany	64	61	66	60	62	67	64	66	62	64	64	63	54	67	71	64	62	68
Britain	63	59	66	63	62	64	64	62	55	66	62	63	57	65	65	64	63	61
Italy	72	66	76	62	67	82	73	63	54	78	68	63	59	78	77	77	74	60
Netherlands	55	52	57	62	52	53	54	58	53	48	53	64	45	53	68	68	59	47
Belgium	58	55	60	49	52	67	60	57	55	59	56	58	46	58	65	61	60	49
Austria	68	66	70	68	66	71	70	67	72	69	65	70	64	65	75	69	68	68
France	59	57	61	52	55	69	58	57	66	55	58	66	51	65	78	60	61	55
Canada	75	75	76	72	72	83	79	78	69	78	78	70	69	75	80	85	76	69
United States	84	82	86	81	83	85	83	83	85	84	86	83	73	85	88	84	84	83
Iceland	58	57	58	51	60	62	67	61	48	na	67	67	51	59	58	59	58	49
West Germany	68	63	72	57	64	76	70	63	65	70	67	67	58	72	72	75	70	59
Denmark	49	45	52	41	44	60	61	43	45	48	50	44	38	48	56	54	52	32
Finland	51	48	54	53	45	65	54	52	48	61	51	41	45	55	52	61	52	46
Norway	55	50	60	43	52	66	71	52	50	58	50	55	46	60	57	57	55	46
Sweden	51	48	53	53	47	54	57	52	39	50	54	49	48	51	53	56	54	42
Japan	42	37	47	39	37	49	49	39	41	46	35	44	31	38	46	51	41	23
Switzerland	na	na	na	na	na	na	na	na	na	na	na	na	na	na	na	na	na	na
Total	68	65	70	64	65	74	72	66	62	71	67	66	59	68	72	72	68	61

Ranking:

Russia	92
Hungary	90
Nigeria	89
Moscow	87
Latvia	87
Chile	86
United States	84
Belarus	83
Mexico	80
North Ireland	80
Romania	78
Slovenia	77
Canada	75
Italy	72
Ireland	71
Austria	68
West Germany	68
East Germany	64
Britain	63
Portugal	62
India	59
Turkey	59
Argentina	59
France	59
Belgium	58
Iceland	58
Brazil	57
Bulgaria	56
Netherlands	55
Norway	55
Spain	54
Finland	51
Sweden	51
Denmark	49
Japan	42

Note: Countries in the left column are ranked according to GNP per capita. / The percentages in the bottom row give each country an equal weight. / na=not ascertained.

V155 ANSWERS: SOCIAL PROBLEMS

Generally speaking, do you think that your church is giving, in your country, adequate answers to the social problems facing our country today? (% "yes")

	Total	Gender		Age			Education			Income			Political Affinity			Values		
		Male	Female	16-29	30-49	50+	Lower	Medium	Upper	Lower	Middle	Upper	Left	Center	Right	Mat	Mixed	Postmat
India	24	24	24	23	23	28	29	23	23	26	24	22	25	26	23	20	27	24
Nigeria	83	81	86	82	82	89	91	85	77	84	80	86	83	81	82	88	80	77
China	na	na	na	na	na	na	na	na	na	na	na	na	na	na	na	na	na	na
Romania	32	30	35	22	27	45	43	30	23	33	33	31	31	31	32	39	29	21
Turkey	29	27	31	30	26	33	38	18	12	39	28	21	16	29	40	28	34	20
Poland	na	na	na	na	na	na	na	na	na	na	na	na	na	na	na	na	na	na
Bulgaria	23	21	24	20	18	29	33	19	18	21	24	20	13	22	28	22	23	16
Chile	76	77	74	69	78	81	79	74	73	80	74	74	77	77	74	71	77	78
Czechoslovakia	na	na	na	na	na	na	na	na	na	na	na	na	na	na	na	na	na	na
South Africa	na	na	na	na	na	na	na	na	na	na	na	na	na	na	na	na	na	na
Lithuania	na	na	na	na	na	na	na	na	na	na	na	na	na	na	na	na	na	na
Hungary	55	51	59	24	44	69	63	44	53	64	48	39	50	54	61	54	57	39
Argentina	37	33	41	30	33	47	47	33	25	49	34	26	18	37	38	43	39	26
Brazil	42	39	45	33	42	58	60	36	27	54	40	31	36	35	50	50	38	28
Mexico	47	44	51	46	45	55	49	51	37	50	47	40	30	48	52	53	42	40
Belarus	83	84	83	76	83	89	84	82	84	86	80	84	84	80	81	82	84	86
Russia	60	55	62	47	55	71	66	62	52	61	62	56	48	55	64	65	56	53
Moscow	87	87	87	83	85	92	85	89	86	87	90	80	89	84	79	88	87	84
Latvia	42	33	46	29	41	59	54	49	27	39	52	35	na	na	na	45	45	35
Estonia	na	na	na	na	na	na	na	na	na	na	na	na	na	na	na	na	na	na
Portugal	44	38	49	36	39	56	52	30	25	54	39	34	34	44	51	53	39	34
South Korea	33	32	34	26	28	44	37	30	24	43	30	26	17	29	44	36	34	29
Ireland	33	48	55	39	50	64	56	48	42	51	57	45	43	56	46	63	48	50
North Ireland	52	48	49	39	47	57	53	42	52	55	43	49	39	53	50	48	50	41
Slovenia	49	49	49	39	47	57	53	42	52	55	43	49	39	53	50	48	50	41
Spain	33	26	39	19	30	50	39	57	58	47	58	60	22	34	52	43	31	16
East Germany	58	56	60	51	58	63	59	57	58	57	58	60	47	63	65	53	58	61
Britain	29	27	31	25	24	37	32	23	25	38	23	24	28	30	27	30	28	34
Italy	43	40	46	37	37	53	44	41	32	51	40	35	27	54	40	51	43	35
Netherlands	33	30	34	31	31	37	34	33	31	25	36	33	29	32	37	47	36	25
Belgium	29	26	32	17	25	39	32	28	25	32	31	26	18	31	34	33	30	20
Austria	39	37	41	26	36	48	42	38	37	38	40	38	39	34	48	49	39	35
France	24	23	24	16	19	35	27	18	25	25	23	23	17	26	39	32	25	15
Canada	44	41	46	38	37	56	54	43	37	53	42	37	35	56	44	53	44	36
United States	57	54	60	47	52	65	62	60	50	58	61	51	43	57	63	60	58	51
Iceland	24	23	25	26	21	28	31	24	19	31	29	26	14	30	26	26	33	18
West Germany	33	28	37	20	25	48	36	25	38	39	29	31	27	33	41	44	33	28
Denmark	08	07	10	07	06	12	13	05	08	07	07	09	05	07	15	10	08	09
Finland	12	13	11	09	09	23	15	12	11	18	11	08	05	13	20	30	13	08
Norway	19	18	19	14	15	27	28	17	15	22	15	19	17	19	12	20	18	13
Sweden	12	14	10	16	08	14	13	13	08	12	12	12	09	10	15	14	14	05
Japan	07	06	08	04	07	10	10	07	04	12	04	07	04	06	07	06	08	02
Switzerland	na	na	na	na	na	na	na	na	na	na	na	na	na	na	na	na	na	na
Total	**40**	**38**	**42**	**33**	**37**	**49**	**45**	**37**	**34**	**44**	**40**	**36**	**33**	**40**	**44**	**44**	**40**	**34**

Ranking:

Moscow	87
Nigeria	83
Belarus	83
Chile	76
Russia	60
East Germany	58
United States	57
Hungary	55
North Ireland	52
Slovenia	49
Mexico	47
Portugal	44
Canada	44
Italy	43
Brazil	42
Latvia	42
Austria	39
Argentina	37
Ireland	33
Spain	33
Netherlands	33
West Germany	33
Romania	32
Turkey	29
Britain	29
Belgium	29
India	24
France	24
Iceland	24
Bulgaria	23
Norway	19
Finland	12
Sweden	12
Denmark	08
Japan	07

Note: Countries in the left column are ranked according to GNP per capita. / The percentages in the bottom row give each country an equal weight. / na=not ascertained.

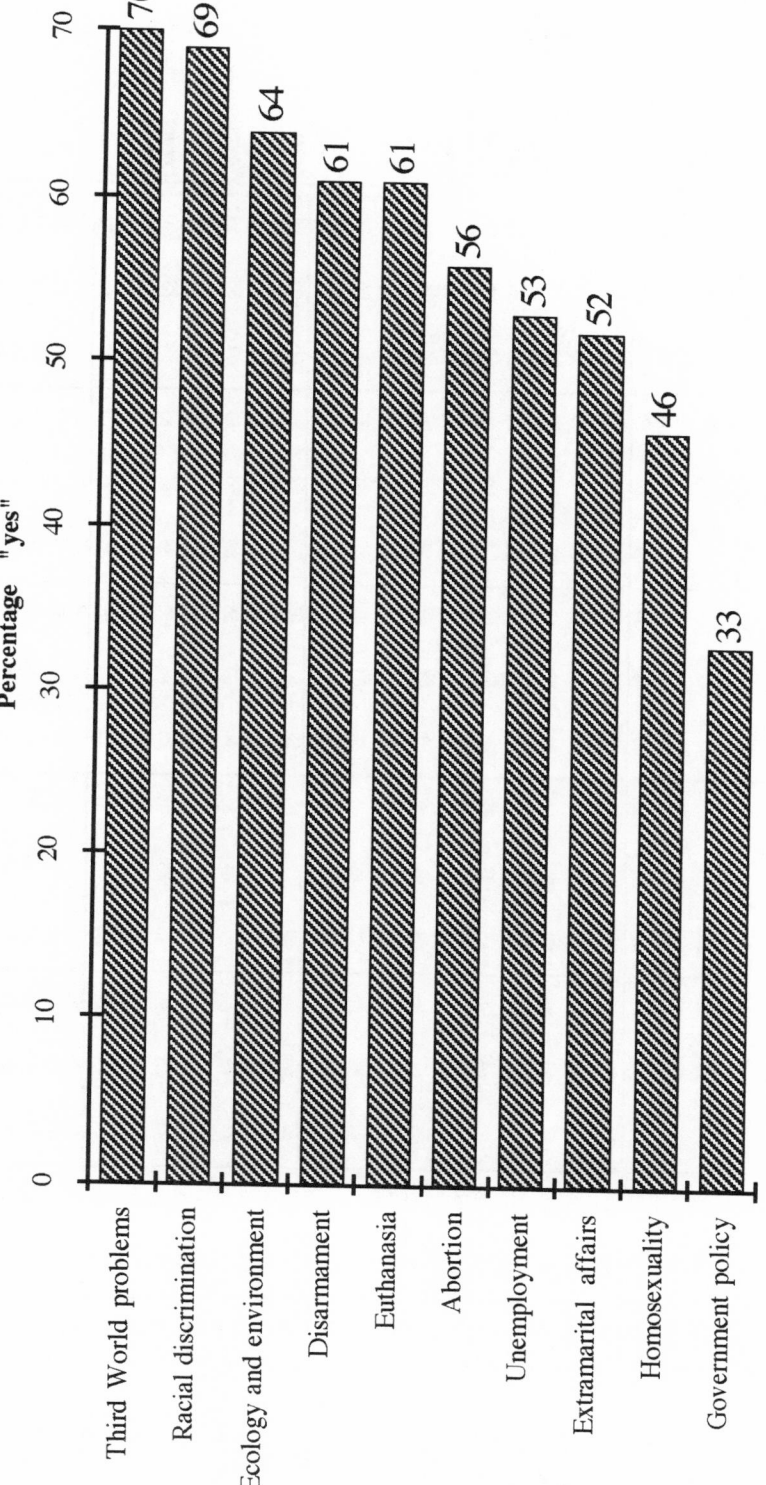

V156-V165. Do you think it is proper for churches to speak out on:

V156 SPEAK OUT: DISARMAMENT

Do you think it is proper for churches to speak out on: Disarmament (% "yes")

	Total	Gender		Age			Education			Income			Political Affinity			Values		
		Male	Female	16-29	30-49	50+	Lower	Medium	Upper	Lower	Middle	Upper	Left	Center	Right	Mat	Mixed	Postmat
India	32	35	29	32	32	32	26	29	38	31	31	34	36	35	34	32	35	31
Nigeria	77	78	76	75	79	85	75	75	80	77	79	75	72	83	79	77	76	88
China	na	na	na	na	na	na	na	na	na	na	na	na	na	na	na	na	na	na
Romania	65	65	66	61	59	74	69	65	62	70	65	62	67	65	64	70	62	61
Turkey	38	42	34	35	39	42	42	34	29	40	41	33	30	36	50	42	39	32
Poland	na	na	na	na	na	na	na	na	na	na	na	na	na	na	na	na	na	na
Bulgaria	57	61	54	57	55	61	55	53	67	63	57	53	49	63	57	54	57	72
Chile	66	74	58	63	72	61	59	63	78	59	66	73	77	62	69	53	67	81
Czechoslovakia	na	na	na	na	na	na	na	na	na	na	na	na	na	na	na	na	na	na
South Africa	na	na	na	na	na	na	na	na	na	na	na	na	na	na	na	na	na	na
Lithuania	na	na	na	na	na	na	na	na	na	na	na	na	na	na	na	na	na	na
Hungary	65	68	62	57	64	70	68	59	75	66	64	68	64	66	71	64	66	68
Argentina	63	65	61	63	64	63	61	63	67	60	65	65	68	64	59	58	64	69
Brazil	72	70	73	71	72	73	75	71	69	75	71	68	75	70	73	72	71	76
Mexico	65	65	64	64	67	64	64	61	69	63	66	67	64	63	69	66	64	66
Belarus	na	na	na	na	na	na	na	na	na	na	na	na	na	na	na	na	na	na
Russia	89	88	89	90	88	88	90	87	90	88	88	90	89	89	77	86	91	89
Moscow	86	87	85	83	86	86	82	88	85	88	83	86	87	84	77	84	86	88
Latvia	na	na	na	na	na	na	na	na	na	na	na	na	na	na	na	na	na	na
Estonia	na	na	na	na	na	na	na	na	na	na	na	na	na	na	na	na	na	na
Portugal	64	63	65	62	64	66	63	67	65	66	61	63	73	62	61	60	65	74
South Korea	na	na	na	na	na	na	na	na	na	na	na	na	na	na	na	na	na	na
Ireland	67	67	68	68	65	69	64	70	76	66	66	68	62	68	69	64	67	72
North Ireland	66	63	68	62	68	66	67	66	61	71	69	58	68	63	63	67	65	69
Slovenia	48	51	45	47	51	45	47	49	49	51	45	48	55	50	49	44	48	59
Spain	56	55	58	60	57	54	54	56	67	59	55	59	56	59	55	56	55	63
East Germany	88	87	89	84	88	90	88	85	91	88	86	90	86	89	89	84	88	90
Britain	58	60	56	60	62	54	56	57	73	56	61	63	70	61	48	51	58	70
Italy	70	71	70	69	69	71	70	76	62	75	71	73	68	79	66	66	70	75
Netherlands	66	64	67	65	69	61	60	67	71	64	63	77	72	66	62	55	63	75
Belgium	48	48	48	46	46	51	44	48	55	47	47	53	47	49	56	42	47	55
Austria	44	43	44	49	44	41	43	44	49	38	41	53	44	43	47	41	41	52
France	51	56	47	53	47	55	50	48	60	49	51	57	54	57	47	40	50	64
Canada	59	57	60	56	61	57	52	57	67	57	58	63	73	57	54	48	57	67
United States	54	54	54	47	60	50	48	52	60	50	55	57	65	53	54	47	51	66
Iceland	74	72	75	69	74	78	76	68	75	55	57	57	85	72	66	71	72	86
West Germany	56	54	58	55	54	60	55	57	63	56	57	53	61	57	53	49	53	66
Denmark	45	50	40	51	50	35	29	44	56	42	45	57	64	43	37	31	43	72
Finland	77	75	78	82	77	70	72	75	81	72	77	81	89	77	70	79	75	80
Norway	59	57	61	68	56	55	51	54	67	65	56	62	73	53	55	50	60	77
Sweden	62	64	61	64	67	57	51	64	77	57	63	66	72	58	61	62	58	78
Japan	53	52	54	56	50	54	51	52	56	64	44	54	64	48	47	62	50	60
Switzerland	43	44	43	52	42	41	41	44	52	48	45	44	62	44	37	36	40	55
Total	61	62	61	61	62	61	59	60	66	61	60	63	67	61	60	58	60	69

Ranking:

Russia	89
East Germany	88
Moscow	86
Nigeria	77
Finland	77
Iceland	74
Brazil	72
Italy	70
Ireland	67
Chile	66
North Ireland	66
Netherlands	66
Romania	65
Hungary	65
Mexico	65
Portugal	64
Argentina	63
Sweden	62
Canada	59
Norway	59
Britain	58
Bulgaria	57
Spain	56
West Germany	56
United States	54
Japan	53
France	51
Slovenia	48
Belgium	48
Denmark	45
Austria	44
Switzerland	43
Turkey	38
India	32

V157 SPEAK OUT: ABORTION

Do you think it is proper for churches to speak out on: Abortion (% "yes")

		Gender		Age			Education			Income			Political Affinity			Values		
	Total	Male	Female	16-29	30-49	50+	Lower	Medium	Upper	Lower	Middle	Upper	Left	Center	Right	Mat	Mixed	Postmat
India	16	18	15	15	17	17	11	16	19	15	13	21	20	19	15	13	20	17
Nigeria	86	86	87	86	87	89	86	85	88	86	91	86	90	92	80	92	84	82
China	na	na	na	na	na	na	na	na	na	na	na	na	na	na	na	na	na	na
Romania	51	49	53	41	47	61	57	49	46	53	54	45	49	50	49	na	na	na
Turkey	42	41	42	38	42	46	44	39	36	41	46	36	30	43	46	58	47	38
Poland	na	na	na	na	na	na	na	na	na	na	na	na	na	na	na	na	na	na
Bulgaria	39	41	36	41	37	39	29	38	49	41	40	34	39	43	47	51	41	32
Chile	80	81	79	81	84	71	72	82	87	71	81	88	82	79	81	75	80	86
Czechoslovakia	na	na	na	na	na	na	na	na	na	na	na	na	na	na	na	na	na	na
South Africa	na	na	na	na	na	na	na	na	na	na	na	na	na	na	na	na	na	na
Lithuania	na	na	na	na	na	na	na	na	na	na	na	na	na	na	na	na	na	na
Hungary	50	52	48	45	46	56	58	41	50	56	46	43	45	49	61	52	48	49
Argentina	70	69	71	68	71	70	68	70	74	70	67	75	69	71	71	70	70	68
Brazil	64	62	67	67	63	61	60	67	65	62	69	63	67	64	61	65	63	67
Mexico	73	70	76	74	72	71	70	76	79	70	74	74	64	73	79	75	72	74
Belarus	na	na	na	na	na	na	na	na	na	na	na	na	na	na	na	na	na	na
Russia	67	66	67	63	63	74	69	70	63	68	67	65	68	64	65	67	67	62
Moscow	66	63	68	57	64	74	70	64	66	68	65	65	66	64	62	67	65	69
Latvia	na	na	na	na	na	na	na	na	na	na	na	na	na	na	na	na	na	na
Estonia	na	na	na	na	na	na	na	na	na	na	na	na	na	na	na	na	na	na
Portugal	65	62	68	66	64	65	63	65	72	65	66	64	65	62	72	65	66	68
South Korea	na	na	na	na	na	na	na	na	na	na	na	na	na	na	na	na	na	na
Ireland	82	82	82	76	80	88	81	84	82	81	85	82	71	82	86	84	82	81
North Ireland	74	73	74	63	72	82	76	71	62	69	78	67	82	69	75	81	72	69
Slovenia	24	27	22	25	22	27	25	22	27	26	23	26	23	24	37	24	24	29
Spain	57	53	61	56	56	60	58	54	60	63	57	54	52	60	66	60	59	53
East Germany	57	54	60	49	58	61	56	60	58	62	55	56	46	62	64	62	57	57
Britain	56	59	54	53	56	58	53	54	78	54	56	58	60	54	58	54	55	61
Italy	60	56	63	57	57	64	60	60	59	65	55	57	42	75	63	63	60	55
Netherlands	47	55	44	45	43	54	45	41	56	47	49	52	45	42	55	41	48	47
Belgium	43	42	43	34	37	54	42	41	46	44	41	45	33	44	54	44	44	39
Austria	49	50	48	46	48	50	53	45	49	46	47	52	44	41	59	48	49	49
France	38	39	36	32	35	46	38	36	40	35	36	40	32	37	55	41	37	37
Canada	56	58	55	53	55	61	58	54	59	55	58	56	57	55	63	62	56	55
United States	67	69	66	64	70	65	64	66	70	66	68	69	61	67	71	64	68	68
Iceland	44	43	45	45	48	50	50	41	42	na	na	na	48	47	39	46	42	54
West Germany	53	52	55	41	48	65	55	48	56	53	53	54	42	54	67	67	55	43
Denmark	39	42	37	45	41	32	30	36	45	36	38	45	49	36	38	29	40	51
Finland	74	72	78	79	75	69	72	70	81	65	73	85	77	75	72	71	73	79
Norway	59	63	55	65	57	59	53	52	70	63	57	64	63	58	62	53	59	74
Sweden	47	51	43	45	51	44	34	47	65	47	43	50	54	42	48	46	44	56
Japan	41	45	37	43	40	40	40	39	46	43	32	51	42	45	40	50	37	49
Switzerland	41	42	41	37	41	43	39	41	52	47	42	36	49	43	42	44	39	47
Total	55	55	55	53	54	58	54	54	59	56	55	56	54	55	59	56	55	56

Ranking:

Nigeria	86
Ireland	82
Chile	80
North Ireland	74
Finland	74
Mexico	73
Argentina	70
Russia	67
United States	67
Moscow	66
Portugal	65
Brazil	64
Italy	60
Norway	59
Spain	57
East Germany	57
Britain	56
Canada	56
West Germany	53
Romania	51
Hungary	50
Austria	49
Netherlands	47
Sweden	47
Iceland	44
Belgium	43
Turkey	42
Japan	41
Switzerland	41
Bulgaria	39
Denmark	39
France	38
Slovenia	24
India	16

Note: Countries in the left column are ranked according to GNP per capita. / The percentages in the bottom row give each country an equal weight. / na=not ascertained.

V158 SPEAK OUT: THIRD WORLD

Do you think it is proper for churches to speak out on: Third World problems (% "yes")

	Total	Gender		Age			Education			Income			Political Affinity			Values		
		Male	Female	16-29	30-49	50+	Lower	Medium	Upper	Lower	Middle	Upper	Left	Center	Right	Mat	Mixed	Postmat
India	25	26	23	24	26	25	20	24	28	24	24	26	26	29	25	22	28	21
Nigeria	87	86	88	86	88	80	87	84	88	85	89	87	89	90	85	92	83	86
China	na	na	na	na	na	na	na	na	na	na	na	na	na	na	na	na	na	na
Romania	60	58	61	60	54	65	63	60	55	63	62	54	50	62	59	63	57	61
Turkey	39	41	37	36	42	41	44	36	25	41	41	35	29	40	47	44	40	33
Poland	na	na	na	na	na	na	na	na	na	na	na	na	na	na	na	na	na	na
Bulgaria	42	43	40	41	42	40	33	42	48	42	44	40	34	46	46	40	40	54
Chile	73	76	69	70	77	69	70	70	79	68	71	79	80	71	72	68	71	83
Czechoslovakia	na	na	na	na	na	na	na	na	na	na	na	na	na	na	na	na	na	na
South Africa	na	na	na	na	na	na	na	na	na	na	na	na	na	na	na	na	na	na
Lithuania	na	na	na	na	na	na	na	na	na	na	na	na	na	na	na	na	na	na
Hungary	70	73	68	71	71	69	69	67	89	66	73	75	72	71	74	69	71	74
Argentina	60	59	60	58	63	58	56	57	67	57	57	67	67	58	62	52	62	64
Brazil	63	60	67	61	65	63	63	63	64	62	63	64	68	63	61	60	64	74
Mexico	66	65	66	63	68	66	66	62	68	64	68	67	68	65	68	65	65	70
Belarus	na	na	na	na	na	na	na	na	na	na	na	na	na	na	na	na	na	na
Russia	70	69	71	68	71	70	67	68	73	68	70	73	70	69	55	66	73	71
Moscow	57	57	57	49	58	62	67	58	55	57	58	58	56	58	67	60	56	59
Latvia	na	na	na	na	na	na	na	na	na	na	na	na	na	na	na	na	na	na
Estonia	na	na	na	na	na	na	na	na	na	na	na	na	na	na	na	na	na	na
Portugal	81	74	87	82	77	82	79	82	85	82	78	80	85	82	77	76	81	88
South Korea	na	na	na	82	82	80	79	83	92	75	83	93	79	80	86	82	80	87
Ireland	93	92	95	95	91	94	93	95	92	92	95	93	91	93	95	93	93	96
North Ireland	90	86	93	84	91	94	90	90	90	90	94	86	96	92	84	89	90	93
Slovenia	46	46	45	52	45	41	44	43	52	47	42	50	47	49	54	40	47	57
Spain	80	77	83	83	81	78	80	80	83	81	80	81	78	82	84	83	79	83
East Germany	95	95	95	93	96	95	94	96	96	95	95	95	95	96	93	89	95	96
Britain	78	77	78	80	80	75	75	81	89	76	74	83	85	78	75	78	77	83
Italy	87	85	89	88	84	89	87	90	90	89	88	88	80	93	91	87	87	88
Netherlands	82	78	84	83	83	80	82	81	83	80	82	87	83	83	81	75	85	81
Belgium	69	67	71	67	67	72	67	69	71	68	61	71	61	74	75	63	71	69
Austria	82	81	82	86	82	80	79	83	87	75	83	86	79	80	86	82	80	87
France	74	76	72	71	74	76	72	74	79	71	75	79	71	78	79	68	75	78
Canada	74	74	75	75	75	72	70	72	81	73	76	76	83	74	73	74	73	77
United States	60	61	59	59	63	57	50	58	69	56	59	66	66	61	63	56	58	69
Iceland	81	77	84	80	81	80	80	79	82	83	82	84	83	85	75	76	82	85
West Germany	83	81	85	80	81	87	83	82	84	82	82	84	81	86	84	80	82	85
Denmark	64	66	61	72	67	54	46	66	72	60	64	71	73	62	61	44	65	82
Finland	84	83	86	85	85	84	82	82	88	82	81	90	89	83	83	90	89	89
Norway	78	78	78	86	77	74	74	76	82	81	76	78	83	77	77	71	80	91
Sweden	77	76	79	78	79	75	70	78	87	73	77	80	82	74	80	69	76	86
Japan	44	44	43	53	36	50	48	45	39	57	36	44	47	44	38	55	42	53
Switzerland	49	48	51	51	45	53	50	50	46	55	52	40	64	51	45	47	46	58
Total	**70**	**69**	**70**	**70**	**70**	**69**	**68**	**69**	**72**	**69**	**69**	**71**	**71**	**71**	**70**	**67**	**69**	**74**

Ranking:

East Germany	95
Ireland	93
North Ireland	90
Nigeria	87
Italy	87
Finland	84
West Germany	83
Netherlands	82
Austria	82
Portugal	81
Iceland	81
Spain	80
Britain	78
Norway	78
Sweden	77
France	74
Canada	74
Chile	73
Hungary	70
Russia	70
Belgium	69
Mexico	66
Denmark	64
Brazil	63
Romania	60
Argentina	60
United States	60
Moscow	57
Switzerland	49
Slovenia	46
Japan	44
Bulgaria	42
Turkey	39
India	25

Note: Countries in the left column are ranked according to GNP per capita. / The percentages in the bottom row give each country an equal weight. / na=not ascertained.

V159 SPEAK OUT: AFFAIRS

Do you think it is proper for churches to speak out on: Extramarital affairs   (% "yes")

	Total	Gender Male	Gender Female	Age 16-29	Age 30-49	Age 50+	Education Lower	Education Medium	Education Upper	Income Lower	Income Middle	Income Upper	Pol. Aff. Left	Pol. Aff. Center	Pol. Aff. Right	Values Mat	Values Mixed	Values Postmat
India	19	20	18	20	19	19	15	17	24	19	17	22	22	22	17	16	22	23
Nigeria	89	89	90	89	90	89	86	89	91	87	95	87	95	92	88	94	87	89
China	na	na	na	47	54	73	67	54	58	66	62	52	60	61	54	na	55	51
Romania	59	55	64	47	54	63	65	67	65	66	66	64	59	69	70	66	55	61
Turkey	66	68	64	66	63	70	65	67	70	67	66	64	59	69	74	70	68	71
Poland	na	na	na	na	na	na	na	na	na	na	na	na	na	na	na	na	na	na
Bulgaria	48	46	50	46	48	50	41	48	54	50	46	46	46	53	53	44	48	58
Chile	79	78	81	76	83	77	76	79	83	77	78	84	82	78	77	75	79	85
Czechoslovakia	na	na	na	na	na	na	na	na	na	na	na	na	na	na	na	na	na	na
South Africa	na	na	na	na	na	na	na	na	na	na	na	na	na	na	na	na	na	na
Lithuania	na	na	na	na	na	na	na	na	na	na	na	na	na	na	na	na	na	na
Hungary	41	40	42	28	34	53	48	31	49	49	32	43	29	39	51	41	41	32
Argentina	64	63	65	60	68	62	63	63	67	69	61	66	59	64	60	67	64	60
Brazil	64	60	69	60	66	67	63	63	59	70	62	61	61	62	69	68	62	54
Mexico	68	65	71	67	69	69	66	72	70	63	71	72	59	70	74	70	68	71
Belarus	na	na	na	na	na	na	78	69	66	72	71	69	68	70	66	74	68	64
Russia	70	67	72	59	67	81	72	62	66	71	71	69	65	64	68	64	65	61
Moscow	65	60	68	55	65	71	57	62	67	66	61	69	65	64	68	64	65	61
Latvia	na	na	na	na	na	na	na	na	na	na	na	na	na	na	na	na	na	na
Estonia	na	na	na	na	na	na	na	na	na	na	na	na	na	na	na	na	na	na
Portugal	55	46	63	54	51	58	54	50	59	54	57	52	51	54	59	58	52	55
South Korea	na	na	na	na	na	na	na	na	na	na	na	na	na	na	na	na	na	na
Ireland	72	71	73	65	70	78	72	72	69	76	71	69	61	71	76	79	71	65
North Ireland	71	67	74	59	69	82	74	64	72	71	68	66	74	71	67	75	71	64
Slovenia	23	22	23	18	21	28	27	19	22	26	20	22	17	24	28	21	23	24
Spain	53	49	57	46	54	58	55	45	49	62	51	47	46	56	57	58	53	46
East Germany	36	36	37	24	36	44	36	32	39	38	36	35	27	39	41	45	35	35
Britain	52	53	52	45	51	57	49	50	72	53	45	54	53	50	58	55	51	54
Italy	43	41	45	38	38	50	43	45	26	47	39	35	28	56	43	45	44	39
Netherlands	35	42	32	35	32	39	31	32	42	36	35	35	33	33	40	32	36	34
Belgium	33	32	34	26	29	41	32	30	40	32	31	36	25	33	43	31	30	33
Austria	31	28	32	26	29	34	37	27	20	30	31	31	24	26	38	35	30	30
France	36	37	36	31	34	44	37	33	42	34	32	42	28	41	50	46	36	32
Canada	50	52	49	45	47	59	52	49	51	49	49	52	48	50	53	52	52	45
United States	74	75	73	73	75	73	70	71	81	73	74	74	65	76	80	77	75	72
Iceland	46	46	47	39	48	52	45	43	49	45	44	44	44	47	49	49	45	48
West Germany	31	29	33	20	22	44	33	24	33	35	29	29	25	30	41	48	29	23
Denmark	50	53	47	58	49	45	45	50	53	50	48	52	57	44	53	39	52	57
Finland	76	74	79	82	76	72	75	72	82	72	74	83	78	78	74	76	73	83
Norway	49	51	47	47	48	52	47	42	56	53	47	52	51	46	52	44	48	66
Sweden	35	40	31	40	37	30	24	37	50	34	34	37	37	31	40	33	33	45
Japan	27	30	23	25	28	28	25	27	28	29	22	32	21	28	30	34	23	41
Switzerland	34	34	34	30	32	37	32	34	39	41	34	30	38	35	35	37	32	37
Total	**51**	**51**	**52**	**47**	**50**	**55**	**51**	**49**	**54**	**53**	**50**	**52**	**48**	**52**	**55**	**53**	**51**	**51**

Ranking:

Nigeria	89
Chile	79
Finland	76
United States	74
Ireland	72
North Ireland	71
Russia	70
Mexico	68
Turkey	66
Moscow	65
Argentina	64
Brazil	64
Romania	59
Portugal	55
Spain	53
Britain	52
Canada	50
Denmark	50
Norway	49
Bulgaria	48
Iceland	46
Italy	43
Hungary	41
East Germany	36
France	36
Netherlands	35
Sweden	35
Switzerland	34
Belgium	33
Austria	31
West Germany	31
Japan	27
Slovenia	23
India	19

Note: Countries in the left column are ranked according to GNP per capita. / The percentages in the bottom row give each country an equal weight. / na=not ascertained.

V160 SPEAK OUT: UNEMPLOYMENT

Do you think it is proper for churches to speak out on: Unemployment (% "yes")

	Total	Gender		Age			Education			Income			Political Affinity			Values			Ranking	
		Male	Female	16-29	30-49	50+	Lower	Middle	Upper	Lower	Middle	Upper	Left	Center	Right	Mat	Mixed	Postmat		
India	27	28	25	26	28	24	23	25	30	28	25	27	28	32	25	24	29	29	Nigeria	90
Nigeria	90	88	92	89	89	94	92	89	90	89	91	88	88	91	89	92	88	89	Russia	78
China	na	na	na	na	na	na	44	29	28	38	35	29	28	38	25	41	29	24	Ireland	78
Romania	34	32	35	23	33	41	44	29	28	38	35	33	28	38	50	41	29	24	Chile	75
Turkey	39	38	41	36	40	44	46	32	23	39	45	33	29	38	50	43	42	29	Finland	75
Poland	na	na	na	na	na	na	na	na	na	na	na	na	na	na	na	na	na	na	Brazil	69
Bulgaria	47	49	44	45	44	50	40	43	57	52	47	40	40	52	56	44	45	66	Moscow	69
Chile	75	76	74	71	79	74	75	73	78	76	72	76	82	73	71	70	75	85	East Germany	69
Czechoslovakia	na	na	na	na	na	na	na	na	na	na	na	na	na	na	na	na	na	na	Portugal	67
South Africa	na	na	na	na	na	na	na	na	na	na	na	na	na	na	na	na	na	na	North Ireland	66
Lithuania	na	na	na	na	na	na	na	na	na	na	na	na	na	na	na	na	na	na	Argentina	64
Hungary	61	61	61	58	61	62	60	58	75	63	59	60	60	62	69	60	63	58	Mexico	63
Argentina	64	60	67	53	68	67	66	63	63	68	65	62	61	65	58	62	64	66	Hungary	61
Brazil	69	66	72	66	70	74	74	68	65	72	71	64	71	65	72	72	67	72	Italy	61
Mexico	63	61	66	62	65	61	62	61	66	62	63	67	55	63	69	64	62	64	Spain	59
Belarus	na	na	na	na	na	na	na	na	na	81	77	77	77	78	69	76	80	78	United States	51
Russia	78	76	80	77	78	80	78	79	78	81	77	77	77	78	69	76	80	78	Britain	48
Moscow	69	68	69	64	70	69	70	68	68	67	68	72	70	66	60	73	67	67	Bulgaria	47
Latvia	na	na	na	na	na	na	na	na	na	na	na	na	na	na	na	na	na	na	Norway	47
Estonia	45	41	48	44	46	45	42	46	48	52	37	49	47	45	52	43	44	57	Slovenia	45
Portugal	67	62	71	63	67	71	66	70	69	68	68	66	69	68	65	67	65	78	Netherlands	43
South Korea	59	na	na	na	na	na	na	na	na	60	56	61	55	61	63	62	58	59	West Germany	42
Ireland	78	78	77	70	77	83	78	78	78	81	75	79	73	77	80	76	79	76	Turkey	39
North Ireland	66	65	67	51	67	75	67	64	66	68	65	60	60	66	62	70	65	64	France	39
Slovenia	45	41	48	44	46	45	42	46	48	52	37	49	47	45	52	43	44	57	Canada	39
Spain	59	55	62	53	60	63	60	56	59	60	56	61	55	61	63	62	58	59	Austria	38
East Germany	69	71	67	65	71	70	68	69	73	68	67	71	70	70	67	61	68	76	Sweden	38
Britain	48	47	48	43	48	50	46	44	60	50	43	47	60	49	37	38	48	57	Iceland	35
Italy	61	59	63	52	57	70	61	64	64	67	60	56	57	68	56	60	63	59	Romania	34
Netherlands	43	43	43	40	45	44	42	39	49	43	43	49	45	43	42	41	40	50	Denmark	34
Belgium	26	26	26	20	25	32	25	23	35	28	27	28	26	27	33	25	26	29	Switzerland	34
Austria	38	37	39	34	38	40	36	38	43	32	38	43	42	38	40	34	36	45	Japan	31
France	39	39	38	24	39	50	38	33	51	37	36	44	39	40	41	34	39	43	India	27
Canada	39	37	40	34	37	44	34	35	47	39	37	42	45	39	39	30	38	45	Belgium	26
United States	51	51	52	51	54	48	47	48	58	48	51	53	57	50	52	46	50	59		
Iceland	35	32	37	24	37	43	36	31	36	na	na	na	44	32	29	32	34	47		
West Germany	42	41	42	38	38	47	40	41	54	43	41	41	46	41	41	35	39	51		
Denmark	34	35	34	33	39	29	25	33	40	33	31	42	51	30	31	22	32	59		
Finland	75	73	77	80	76	68	71	71	81	72	71	82	74	80	69	71	73	80		
Norway	47	46	48	50	45	47	42	43	52	54	43	47	55	46	43	40	46	69		
Sweden	38	39	36	39	42	30	27	37	57	33	38	40	47	31	39	29	34	53		
Japan	31	36	26	37	27	34	33	30	33	43	28	29	42	32	25	34	30	41		
Switzerland	34	33	35	35	32	35	34	32	41	41	33	31	43	38	30	29	33	40		
Total	52	51	53	49	53	55	51	50	56	54	52	53	55	53	51	50	52	58		

Note: Countries in the left column are ranked according to GNP per capita. / The percentages in the bottom row give each country an equal weight. / na=not ascertained.

V161 SPEAK OUT: RACIAL DISCRIMINATION

Do you think it is proper for churches to speak out on: Racial discrimination (% "yes")

	Total	Gender		Age			Education			Income			Political Affinity			Values		
		Male	Female	16-29	30-49	50+	Lower	Medium	Upper	Lower	Middle	Upper	Left	Center	Right	Mat	Mixed	Postmat
India	27	28	24	27	27	23	19	25	32	25	25	29	30	29	28	24	29	30
Nigeria	85	84	87	85	86	77	83	83	89	84	88	83	82	91	84	89	83	81
China	na	na	na	na	na	na	na	na	na	na	na	na	na	na	na	na	na	na
Romania	60	60	60	54	58	65	62	57	61	63	59	59	52	63	57	61	58	67
Turkey	49	49	48	49	46	51	49	50	43	47	51	47	42	48	56	52	49	43
Poland	na	na	na	na	na	na	na	na	na	na	na	na	na	na	na	na	na	na
Bulgaria	56	58	54	58	58	52	45	56	65	60	56	53	50	62	65	49	56	80
Chile	79	81	76	79	81	74	72	78	87	73	79	86	84	79	79	68	80	89
Czechoslovakia	na	na	na	na	na	na	na	na	na	na	na	na	na	na	na	na	na	na
South Africa	na	na	na	na	na	na	na	na	na	na	na	na	na	na	na	na	na	na
Lithuania	na	na	na	na	na	na	na	na	na	na	na	na	na	na	na	na	na	na
Hungary	66	67	65	67	68	65	64	65	82	66	65	70	69	66	73	67	67	55
Argentina	70	69	70	74	70	66	64	71	80	70	66	77	75	69	74	66	70	74
Brazil	72	71	73	76	72	65	66	74	79	72	72	75	79	72	67	71	73	76
Mexico	76	75	77	76	76	73	74	75	82	73	77	81	74	76	78	74	76	82
Belarus	na	na	na	na	na	na	na	na	na	na	na	na	na	na	na	na	na	na
Russia	82	81	83	78	85	82	78	80	86	81	81	83	84	82	71	78	84	88
Moscow	80	80	80	78	79	81	77	78	81	81	77	82	81	78	72	76	81	83
Latvia	na	na	na	na	na	na	na	na	na	na	na	na	na	na	na	na	na	na
Estonia	na	na	na	na	na	na	na	na	na	na	na	na	na	na	na	na	na	na
Portugal	78	75	80	81	76	76	72	88	89	73	80	82	82	78	76	70	80	91
South Korea	na	na	na	na	na	na	na	na	na	na	na	na	na	na	na	na	na	na
Ireland	83	82	85	86	82	83	78	89	93	77	83	89	80	83	86	82	82	89
North Ireland	75	77	73	72	74	78	74	74	83	70	76	72	82	74	67	66	73	78
Slovenia	44	47	41	54	45	36	39	43	54	41	42	54	51	47	53	38	44	65
Spain	75	72	78	78	76	72	73	78	79	78	74	76	74	78	75	75	75	77
East Germany	87	88	86	87	89	85	78	88	92	84	88	89	89	87	84	83	86	91
Britain	69	71	67	70	69	68	65	73	85	64	69	73	77	68	67	67	66	78
Italy	81	80	82	85	81	79	80	86	83	82	79	87	78	87	78	75	81	87
Netherlands	72	72	72	76	71	70	65	72	81	73	68	81	76	71	73	63	71	77
Belgium	57	56	58	61	56	55	52	56	69	52	54	62	54	59	65	47	58	64
Austria	68	69	67	72	68	65	66	68	77	61	67	75	65	67	73	57	66	76
France	59	62	57	56	58	63	56	58	68	55	56	66	59	66	59	53	59	67
Canada	69	70	68	69	71	66	59	67	79	63	69	74	77	69	69	60	70	72
United States	72	72	71	70	78	67	64	68	83	63	74	78	76	73	74	70	71	77
Iceland	83	81	86	83	84	83	82	81	86	na	74	78	91	80	79	82	83	90
West Germany	75	75	75	73	74	76	73	76	83	73	74	78	76	76	73	68	74	81
Denmark	50	57	43	60	56	36	29	53	60	45	50	63	67	45	48	33	50	69
Finland	85	82	88	90	85	79	81	83	89	81	84	89	89	85	81	79	84	88
Norway	73	73	72	76	73	70	63	67	83	74	74	76	80	73	70	64	74	88
Sweden	68	68	67	72	71	64	56	69	84	63	69	70	73	64	72	57	65	82
Japan	62	62	62	72	59	59	60	62	64	64	61	62	66	61	53	75	55	74
Switzerland	58	57	58	66	55	56	54	59	65	64	60	57	71	61	55	47	56	68
Total	69	69	69	71	69	66	64	69	76	66	68	72	72	70	69	65	69	76

Ranking:

East Germany	87
Nigeria	85
Finland	85
Ireland	83
Iceland	83
Russia	82
Italy	81
Moscow	80
Chile	79
Portugal	78
Mexico	76
North Ireland	75
Spain	75
West Germany	75
Norway	73
Brazil	72
Netherlands	72
United States	72
Argentina	70
Britain	69
Canada	69
Austria	68
Sweden	68
Hungary	66
Japan	62
Romania	60
France	59
Switzerland	58
Belgium	57
Bulgaria	56
Denmark	50
Turkey	49
Slovenia	44
India	27

Note: Countries in the left column are ranked according to GNP per capita. / The percentages in the bottom row give each country an equal weight. / na=not ascertained.

V162 SPEAK OUT: EUTHANASIA

Do you think it is proper for churches to speak out on: Euthanasia   (% "yes")

	Total	Gender Male	Gender Female	Age 16-29	Age 30-49	Age 50+	Educ. Lower	Educ. Medium	Educ. Upper	Income Lower	Income Middle	Income Upper	Pol. Left	Pol. Center	Pol. Right	Values Mat	Values Mixed	Values Postmat	Ranking	%
India	23	24	21	23	23	19	16	22	26	22	22	24	27	25	21	19	25	33	Finland	82
Nigeria	76	76	77	77	76	67	73	75	79	76	79	76	70	83	78	79	76	69	Ireland	79
China	na	na	na	na	na	na	na	na	na	na	na	na	na	na	na	na	na	na	East Germany	79
Romania	52	52	53	44	52	59	63	46	49	53	55	49	51	50	53	56	49	53	Nigeria	76
Turkey	na	na	na	na	na	na	na	na	na	na	na	na	na	na	na	na	na	na	Chile	74
Poland	na	na	na	na	na	na	na	na	na	na	na	na	na	na	na	na	na	na	West Germany	71
Bulgaria	51	49	53	58	53	44	44	53	54	56	53	46	52	54	54	45	51	68	Iceland	70
Chile	74	76	71	70	78	72	65	74	83	67	72	83	79	73	72	62	75	84	Mexico	67
Czechoslovakia	na	na	na	na	na	na	na	na	na	na	na	na	na	na	na	na	na	na	North Ireland	67
South Africa	na	na	na	na	na	na	na	na	na	na	na	na	na	na	na	na	na	na	Norway	67
Lithuania	na	na	na	na	na	na	na	na	na	na	na	na	na	na	na	na	na	na	Argentina	66
Hungary	60	60	60	57	55	66	63	55	67	66	55	59	58	58	68	60	61	51	Austria	66
Argentina	66	64	69	63	69	66	62	65	74	69	61	71	62	68	73	66	67	65	Russia	65
Brazil	60	56	63	58	60	62	59	58	65	60	58	60	63	60	55	63	58	56	Moscow	65
Mexico	67	64	70	66	67	69	64	68	73	63	68	73	58	67	73	71	65	66	Italy	65
Belarus	na	na	na	na	na	na	na	na	na	na	na	na	na	na	na	na	na	na	United States	64
Russia	65	64	66	65	65	65	64	68	63	65	63	66	66	65	56	65	65	67	Britain	62
Moscow	65	60	69	65	65	65	62	67	65	66	63	68	65	66	73	65	64	67	Hungary	60
Latvia	na	na	na	na	na	na	na	na	na	na	na	na	na	na	na	na	na	na	Brazil	60
Estonia	na	na	na	na	na	na	na	na	na	na	na	na	na	na	na	na	na	na	Portugal	60
Portugal	60	56	63	59	58	61	57	61	68	58	59	61	61	54	67	59	60	64	Canada	60
South Korea	na	na	na	na	na	na	na	na	na	na	na	na	na	na	na	na	na	na	Spain	59
Ireland	79	76	82	76	76	84	77	82	79	78	81	80	69	79	83	80	79	79	Sweden	59
North Ireland	67	63	69	59	73	65	65	69	69	65	73	65	64	68	64	75	65	61	Denmark	58
Slovenia	32	33	32	36	31	32	34	29	35	33	30	35	34	32	41	27	33	46	Japan	55
Spain	59	54	64	58	60	60	60	57	61	65	58	60	54	63	68	63	60	58	Romania	52
East Germany	79	78	79	77	81	77	76	82	86	76	79	81	79	79	75	75	77	85	Netherlands	52
Britain	62	64	60	56	65	63	58	66	80	60	60	66	66	59	67	61	61	66	Bulgaria	51
Italy	65	61	68	63	64	67	64	71	67	71	62	63	55	76	63	66	65	64	France	51
Netherlands	52	57	49	51	49	57	45	45	61	48	52	60	48	51	59	45	52	53	Switzerland	50
Belgium	45	43	47	41	41	51	42	45	49	46	42	50	40	46	54	43	46	46	Belgium	45
Austria	66	66	65	66	66	65	67	65	65	63	63	72	59	65	70	58	65	70	Slovenia	32
France	51	52	50	46	48	57	50	48	57	47	46	60	44	55	62	50	51	51	India	23
Canada	60	60	60	58	60	61	55	59	65	58	64	60	66	59	62	64	60	59		
United States	64	64	64	64	69	59	60	59	73	56	68	68	64	64	70	59	64	70		
Iceland	70	69	71	71	69	70	74	68	68	na	na	na	73	76	64	74	68	71		
West Germany	71	71	72	66	70	76	71	71	77	70	71	74	66	73	76	73	71	71		
Denmark	58	61	56	66	62	46	45	59	64	53	60	65	70	54	56	46	58	69		
Finland	82	81	83	89	82	74	77	78	89	73	80	92	80	81	83	68	81	86		
Norway	67	69	65	73	66	65	59	59	79	71	67	69	73	66	70	61	68	79		
Sweden	59	59	57	60	62	54	44	54	76	55	59	59	64	55	63	55	56	67		
Japan	55	56	53	54	54	55	53	54	57	55	47	62	49	56	56	63	52	57		
Switzerland	50	50	49	49	48	52	48	50	56	55	51	48	59	54	49	49	47	57		
Total	61	60	62	60	61	61	58	60	66	60	60	63	60	62	64	60	60	64		

Note: Countries in the left column are ranked according to GNP per capita. / The percentages in the bottom row give each country an equal weight. / na=not ascertained.

V163 SPEAK OUT: HOMOSEXUALITY

Do you think it is proper for churches to speak out on: Homosexuality (% "yes")

	Total	Gender		Age			Education			Income			Political Affinity			Values		
		Male	Female	16-29	30-49	50+	Lower	Medium	Upper	Lower	Middle	Upper	Left	Center	Right	Mat	Mixed	Postmat
India	12	13	11	12	12	15	12	11	15	13	10	15	14	16	11	09	16	09
Nigeria	85	85	85	83	87	83	84	81	90	83	89	86	84	90	84	88	84	79
China	na	na	na	na	na	na	na	na	na	na	na	na	na	na	na	na	na	na
Romania	52	52	52	43	54	57	58	48	52	55	54	48	54	51	49	55	50	48
Turkey	54	57	52	51	55	59	56	56	46	52	55	55	47	56	61	55	56	50
Poland	na	na	na	na	na	na	na	na	na	na	na	na	na	na	na	na	na	na
Bulgaria	33	35	31	39	33	29	21	32	43	35	31	31	32	38	42	30	32	42
Chile	74	75	73	74	76	70	68	75	80	69	72	80	79	73	72	66	75	81
Czechoslovakia	na	na	na	na	na	na	na	na	na	na	na	na	na	na	na	na	na	na
South Africa	na	na	na	na	na	na	na	na	na	na	na	na	na	na	na	na	na	na
Lithuania	na	na	na	na	na	na	na	na	na	na	na	na	na	na	na	na	na	na
Hungary	44	44	44	34	42	51	49	37	50	51	37	47	39	46	54	45	43	44
Argentina	60	57	64	56	63	60	57	61	64	62	57	58	56	62	60	58	62	59
Brazil	52	50	53	48	54	54	53	51	53	54	49	50	51	50	51	52	52	47
Mexico	60	56	64	62	60	54	56	64	68	56	62	67	53	61	67	60	61	64
Belarus	na	na	na	na	na	na	na	na	na	na	na	na	na	na	na	na	na	na
Russia	67	66	68	62	68	70	66	66	69	67	71	66	69	67	54	66	68	68
Moscow	63	63	62	55	65	65	56	62	64	66	57	66	63	62	67	61	64	63
Latvia	na	na	na	na	na	na	na	na	na	na	na	na	na	na	na	na	na	na
Estonia	na	na	na	na	na	na	na	na	na	na	na	na	na	na	na	na	na	na
Portugal	44	41	46	44	45	43	41	47	50	40	47	45	53	39	45	44	43	47
South Korea	na	na	na	na	na	na	na	na	na	na	na	na	na	na	na	na	na	na
Ireland	61	60	63	50	58	71	63	60	57	59	70	64	54	58	67	69	61	51
North Ireland	66	65	66	54	67	73	63	72	69	65	62	57	64	68	62	71	65	62
Slovenia	22	23	21	25	21	22	19	20	29	23	20	26	26	20	30	20	23	27
Spain	44	40	48	39	46	46	45	39	46	50	44	42	39	48	44	45	45	42
East Germany	46	48	43	41	48	46	44	47	51	46	45	46	43	45	46	48	44	50
Britain	47	50	45	39	48	51	44	45	66	47	43	49	50	45	51	49	45	53
Italy	40	40	40	36	34	48	40	41	29	47	34	32	30	50	37	41	40	37
Netherlands	34	43	30	31	30	42	32	27	42	33	37	36	31	32	38	35	32	36
Belgium	30	28	26	22	24	34	25	26	32	27	27	28	24	26	32	28	28	25
Austria	28	30	27	26	31	32	34	28	27	29	31	31	30	26	36	28	30	31
France	28	30	27	20	27	37	30	25	31	31	24	29	22	32	39	31	29	26
Canada	47	49	45	44	45	53	45	47	50	48	49	44	43	47	52	50	48	44
United States	61	64	57	54	64	60	56	57	68	55	64	63	56	61	68	57	62	61
Iceland	29	28	30	28	26	35	36	22	32	34	26	28	31	31	25	34	25	39
West Germany	29	29	29	22	23	39	30	26	32	22	26	28	23	29	36	25	27	32
Denmark	34	34	34	33	40	28	24	34	38	32	33	40	45	29	32	22	32	51
Finland	71	67	75	77	72	60	69	65	78	65	66	81	72	73	67	65	68	77
Norway	45	48	43	46	44	46	40	40	53	48	45	49	46	44	49	41	44	61
Sweden	38	40	34	39	42	32	26	38	58	36	37	41	43	33	42	36	35	47
Japan	27	30	25	25	31	23	25	27	29	27	22	36	22	29	27	32	26	35
Switzerland	31	32	30	28	31	32	29	27	40	36	30	29	37	34	31	32	28	37
Total	**46**	**46**	**45**	**42**	**46**	**48**	**44**	**44**	**50**	**47**	**45**	**47**	**45**	**46**	**48**	**46**	**45**	**48**

Ranking:

Country	%
Nigeria	85
Chile	74
Finland	71
Russia	67
North Ireland	66
Moscow	63
Ireland	61
United States	61
Argentina	60
Mexico	60
Turkey	54
Romania	52
Brazil	52
Britain	47
Canada	47
East Germany	46
Norway	45
Hungary	44
Portugal	44
Spain	44
Italy	40
Sweden	38
Netherlands	34
Denmark	34
Bulgaria	33
Switzerland	31
Austria	30
Iceland	29
West Germany	29
France	28
Belgium	27
Japan	27
Slovenia	22
India	12

Note: Countries in the left column are ranked according to GNP per capita. / The percentages in the bottom row give each country an equal weight. / na=not ascertained.

V164 SPEAK OUT: ECOLOGY

Do you think it is proper for churches to speak out on: Ecology and environmental issues (% "yes")

Country	Total	Gender		Age			Education			Income			Political Affinity			Values		
		Male	Female	16-29	30-49	50+	Lower	Medium	Upper	Lower	Middle	Upper	Left	Center	Right	Mat	Mixed	Postmat
India	32	35	29	32	33	29	25	30	38	29	31	36	33	37	36	29	37	28
Nigeria	82	82	81	81	82	84	80	83	81	85	81	78	78	87	83	87	77	89
China	na	na	na	na	na	na	na	na	na	na	na	na	na	na	na	na	na	na
Romania	58	58	59	46	55	69	60	56	59	64	59	54	48	61	57	63	55	57
Turkey	56	59	53	53	59	56	59	57	43	56	57	55	46	56	66	58	57	51
Poland	na	na	na	na	na	na	na	na	na	na	na	na	na	na	na	na	na	na
Bulgaria	73	73	73	71	73	74	73	70	77	74	73	71	67	76	80	67	73	87
Chile	79	81	77	77	82	77	76	79	81	77	79	80	84	78	79	71	79	88
Czechoslovakia	na	na	na	na	na	na	na	na	na	na	na	na	na	na	na	na	na	na
South Africa	na	na	na	na	na	na	na	na	na	na	na	na	na	na	na	na	na	na
Lithuania	na	na	na	na	na	na	na	na	na	na	na	na	na	na	na	na	na	na
Hungary	77	79	75	76	76	79	76	77	84	76	75	86	76	80	80	75	79	76
Argentina	67	66	69	62	71	68	65	67	72	68	68	71	69	67	71	63	69	69
Brazil	77	77	78	78	77	76	78	78	74	77	79	76	82	76	78	78	78	76
Mexico	69	69	70	68	70	72	69	69	72	66	73	73	68	68	74	69	68	73
Belarus	na	na	na	na	na	na	na	na	na	na	na	na	na	na	na	na	na	na
Russia	94	91	95	93	94	93	93	93	94	94	94	93	92	94	91	93	94	93
Moscow	94	92	95	90	95	95	90	94	95	94	93	94	95	92	88	96	93	94
Latvia	na	na	na	na	na	na	na	na	na	na	na	na	na	na	na	na	na	na
Estonia	na	na	na	na	na	na	na	na	na	na	na	na	na	na	na	na	na	na
Portugal	71	68	73	71	68	73	70	73	73	70	72	70	74	69	70	69	70	83
South Korea	60	60	60	61	62	57	57	62	66	58	54	64	59	57	64	55	59	66
Ireland	65	64	67	52	70	69	64	71	62	67	70	55	81	65	62	67	64	68
North Ireland	58	59	58	57	60	58	54	58	66	61	54	62	63	60	67	53	60	68
Slovenia	59	56	61	61	58	59	58	58	62	61	54	62	63	60	67	53	60	68
Spain	59	56	61	61	58	59	58	58	62	58	58	60	58	61	55	58	60	62
East Germany	88	88	88	84	89	90	87	87	92	88	87	90	87	90	85	86	88	91
Britain	64	65	63	66	68	60	61	66	77	64	66	70	73	64	60	56	66	68
Italy	61	60	63	57	57	68	61	64	62	66	60	67	59	69	56	56	62	64
Netherlands	58	55	59	62	56	58	52	59	65	59	61	60	66	56	55	54	56	64
Belgium	36	37	34	32	35	38	34	33	44	38	33	36	37	37	40	30	36	40
Austria	55	54	56	49	53	60	57	54	58	54	54	57	58	57	55	52	54	59
France	41	42	40	38	41	43	39	38	49	42	39	42	43	43	39	32	40	50
Canada	53	52	53	49	53	55	45	48	64	51	54	56	64	51	55	43	52	59
United States	61	61	61	58	64	59	55	59	68	56	62	65	70	61	63	52	62	67
Iceland	57	53	62	51	56	68	61	50	58	60	53	58	68	56	49	53	57	66
West Germany	57	55	59	54	55	61	56	56	65	53	53	58	61	58	53	51	54	65
Denmark	41	42	39	45	46	30	27	42	47	36	40	50	60	35	34	26	37	67
Finland	85	83	88	92	86	78	81	83	90	79	86	91	85	89	81	90	83	88
Norway	62	62	61	66	58	64	60	57	68	70	61	61	70	61	58	56	61	81
Sweden	61	59	62	58	63	61	55	61	73	56	64	63	67	59	61	52	59	74
Japan	52	53	52	55	51	53	44	54	54	57	47	55	56	51	50	57	52	65
Switzerland	na	na	na	na	na	na	na	na	na	na	na	na	na	na	na	na	na	na
Total	**64**	**63**	**64**	**62**	**64**	**65**	**61**	**63**	**68**	**64**	**64**	**66**	**67**	**64**	**63**	**61**	**63**	**70**

Ranking:

Russia	94
Moscow	94
East Germany	88
Finland	85
Nigeria	82
Chile	79
Hungary	77
Brazil	77
Bulgaria	73
Portugal	71
Mexico	69
Argentina	67
North Ireland	65
Britain	64
Norway	62
Italy	61
United States	61
Sweden	61
Ireland	60
Spain	59
Romania	58
Slovenia	58
Netherlands	58
Iceland	57
West Germany	57
Turkey	56
Austria	55
Canada	53
Japan	52
France	41
Denmark	41
Belgium	36
India	32

Note: Countries in the left column are ranked according to GNP per capita. / The percentages in the bottom row give each country an equal weight. / na=not ascertained.

V165 SPEAK OUT: GOVERNMENT
Do you think it is proper for churches to speak out on: Government policy (% "yes")

	Total	Gender		Age			Education			Income			Political Affinity			Values			Ranking:	
		Male	Female	16-29	30-49	50+	Lower	Medium	Upper	Lower	Middle	Upper	Left	Center	Right	Mat	Mixed	Postmat		
India	22	23	20	22	21	23	19	22	23	22	24	21	22	27	23	19	25	25	Nigeria	76
Nigeria	76	76	77	75	78	74	78	74	78	72	79	81	78	81	80	83	73	74	Russia	71
China	na	na	na	na	na	na	na	na	na	na	na	na	na	na	na	na	na	na	Moscow	71
Romania	20	20	21	11	19	28	27	16	20	27	21	15	16	21	20	25	16	20	East Germany	52
Turkey	22	20	23	23	21	21	27	15	12	24	22	18	13	18	32	17	26	15	Hungary	45
Poland	na	na	na	na	na	na	na	na	na	na	na	na	na	na	na	na	na	na	North Ireland	43
Bulgaria	40	40	41	41	37	43	39	38	44	41	42	39	33	42	42	35	41	48	Chile	42
Chile	42	47	37	39	43	43	41	40	44	39	40	47	60	37	36	30	42	60	Bulgaria	40
Czechoslovakia	na	na	na	na	na	na	na	na	na	na	na	na	na	na	na	na	na	na	United States	40
South Africa	na	na	na	na	na	na	na	na	na	na	na	na	na	na	na	na	na	na	Finland	37
Lithuania	na	na	na	na	na	na	na	na	na	na	na	na	na	na	na	na	na	na	Britain	36
Hungary	45	44	46	43	44	47	49	42	42	50	40	43	40	46	52	41	48	50	Ireland	35
Argentina	30	26	33	25	32	31	31	29	29	29	30	32	38	26	26	23	31	34	Mexico	34
Brazil	33	32	35	30	35	38	38	30	39	36	29	34	34	31	38	32	33	33	Brazil	33
Mexico	34	32	36	32	35	34	33	33	34	33	36	32	29	34	38	36	31	41	Netherlands	31
Belarus	na	na	na	na	na	na	na	na	na	na	na	na	na	na	na	na	na	na	Norway	31
Russia	71	65	76	67	71	74	74	72	67	75	70	67	66	71	65	71	70	73	Argentina	30
Moscow	71	67	74	68	71	72	70	69	72	68	72	72	72	65	68	68	72	72	Canada	30
Latvia	na	na	na	na	na	na	na	na	na	na	na	na	na	na	na	na	na	na	Sweden	29
Estonia	na	na	na	na	na	na	na	na	na	na	na	na	na	na	na	na	na	na	Spain	27
Portugal	15	14	15	12	18	14	14	14	19	13	14	16	21	14	13	13	15	19	Japan	26
South Korea	na	na	na	na	na	na	na	na	na	na	na	na	na	na	na	na	na	na	Italy	23
Ireland	35	35	36	29	35	39	32	39	42	37	31	38	31	31	43	37	35	33	India	22
North Ireland	43	40	46	26	45	53	46	43	28	52	46	30	33	43	45	49	42	37	Turkey	22
Slovenia	18	20	16	21	16	16	19	18	18	21	16	18	13	19	28	18	19	13	Romania	20
Spain	27	25	30	28	26	28	27	23	32	29	26	27	28	27	26	27	27	30	Denmark	20
East Germany	52	48	56	47	51	56	55	50	44	54	49	52	43	60	51	49	53	52	Iceland	19
Britain	36	38	35	37	41	32	34	34	54	35	36	38	52	37	25	23	36	51	Slovenia	18
Italy	23	20	25	25	18	26	23	26	16	26	20	17	16	31	21	23	25	19	West Germany	18
Netherlands	31	31	30	33	30	29	25	30	38	33	36	29	34	30	30	36	31	41	Austria	17
Belgium	16	15	17	14	14	19	16	15	20	17	16	16	16	15	21	16	17	15	Belgium	16
Austria	17	12	19	16	16	17	17	16	17	17	16	16	18	15	19	13	15	21	France	16
France	16	16	16	10	18	19	16	13	21	18	11	18	17	19	15	14	16	18	Portugal	15
Canada	30	29	31	29	29	32	26	26	29	30	30	32	40	29	32	23	29	34		
United States	40	42	37	40	44	36	35	37	47	39	39	44	44	37	47	35	38	47		
Iceland	19	19	19	18	19	21	19	16	21	na	na	na	24	18	16	18	19	24		
West Germany	18	16	20	17	16	21	17	19	23	24	16	16	17	20	17	16	17	21		
Denmark	20	20	19	21	25	13	12	18	26	19	19	24	34	16	15	11	18	37		
Finland	37	35	39	42	39	28	33	31	46	38	30	46	34	39	34	45	34	41		
Norway	31	31	32	37	30	29	26	29	36	35	29	33	36	33	28	28	30	49		
Sweden	29	29	28	34	32	24	20	30	44	25	33	30	33	25	31	20	26	44		
Japan	26	26	26	33	22	29	29	28	19	44	16	23	37	21	18	25	27	34		
Switzerland	na	na	na	na	na	na	na	na	na	na	na	na	na	na	na	na	na	na		
Total	33	32	34	32	33	34	32	31	35	35	32	33	34	33	33	31	33	37		

Note: Countries in the left column are ranked according to GNP per capita. / The percentages in the bottom row give each country an equal weight. / na=not ascertained.

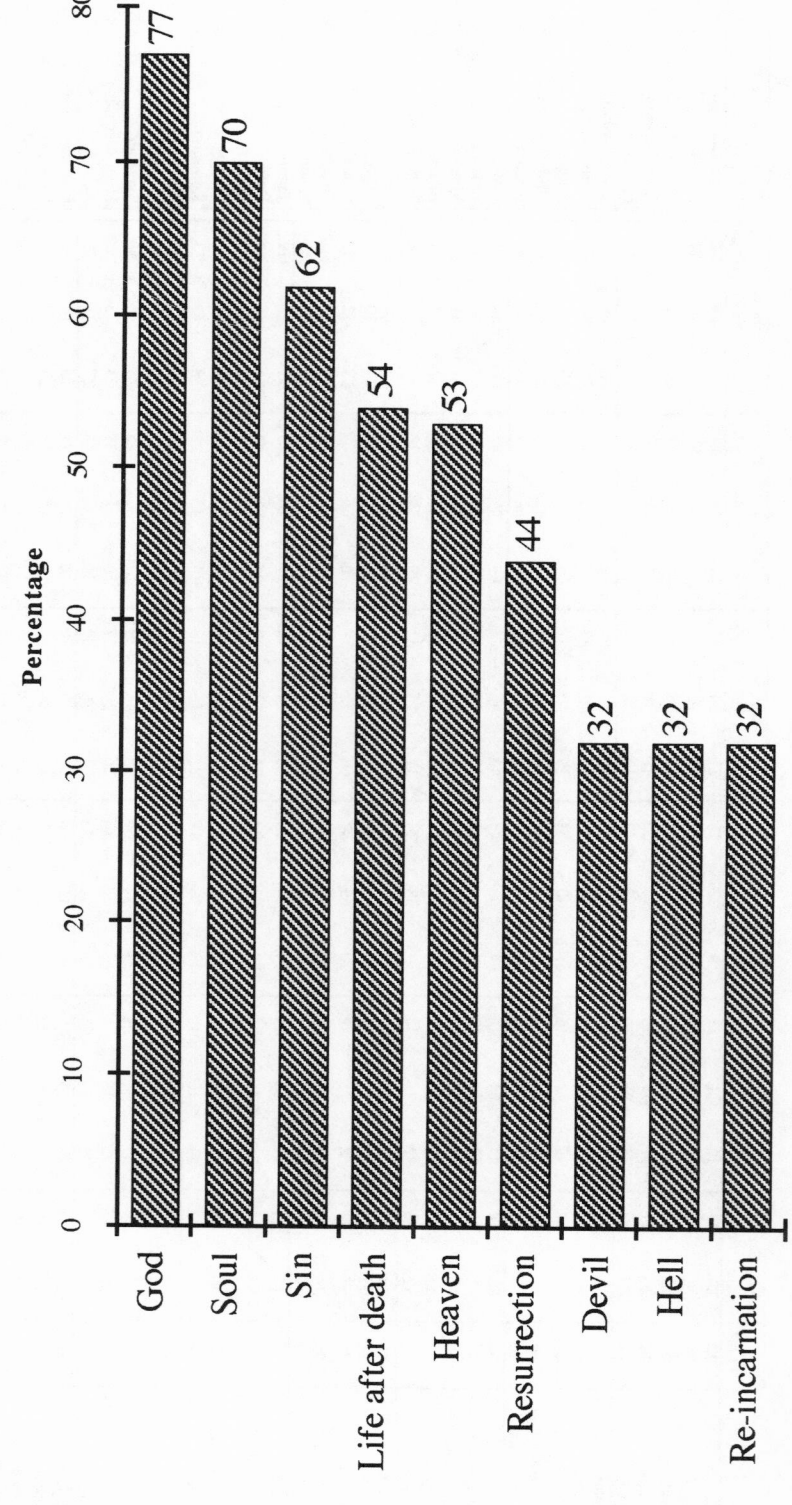

V166-V174. Which, if any, of the following do you believe in?

Percentage

V166 BELIEF IN GOD
Which, if any, of the following do you believe in? God (% "yes")

	Total	Gender		Age			Education			Income			Political Affinity			Values			Ranking:	
		Male	Female	16-29	30-49	50+	Lower	Medium	Upper	Lower	Middle	Upper	Left	Center	Right	Mat	Mixed	Postmat		
India	94	92	96	91	95	94	97	95	91	95	95	91	89	95	94	95	93	89	Nigeria	100
Nigeria	100	100	100	100	100	100	100	100	100	100	100	100	100	100	100	100	100	100	Brazil	99
China	na	na	na	na	na	na	na	na	na	na	na	na	na	na	na	na	na	na	South Africa	98
Romania	94	91	97	90	94	96	98	92	90	94	94	93	94	93	92	96	92	93	Ireland	98
Turkey	na	na	na	na	na	na	na	na	na	na	na	na	na	na	na	na	na	na	Poland	97
Poland	97	95	98	97	97	96	99	98	82	97	98	95	92	97	95	99	95	99	North Ireland	97
Bulgaria	40	31	49	37	31	53	62	33	30	46	38	32	26	38	42	41	38	48	United States	96
Chile	95	93	97	94	96	96	97	94	93	96	96	92	90	96	98	96	96	91	Chile	95
Czechoslovakia	na	na	na	na	na	na	na	na	na	na	na	na	na	na	na	na	na	na	India	94
South Africa	98	96	99	97	98	99	97	98	97	97	98	98	97	98	97	98	98	96	Romania	94
Lithuania	na	na	na	na	na	na	na	na	na	na	na	na	na	na	na	na	na	na	Mexico	93
Hungary	65	57	74	42	52	85	81	52	42	76	58	51	38	65	71	68	65	44	Argentina	92
Argentina	92	89	95	88	92	96	96	90	88	94	95	88	71	93	94	96	93	83	Italy	91
Brazil	99	98	99	99	98	100	99	99	97	100	99	97	98	98	99	99	99	96	Canada	89
Mexico	93	91	96	92	93	95	94	95	91	93	93	92	82	94	96	96	93	90	Austria	87
Belarus	43	32	52	38	40	52	57	46	34	51	41	36	41	39	57	46	42	31	Portugal	86
Russia	44	27	57	38	36	56	60	41	36	53	41	34	30	41	43	50	39	48	Spain	86
Moscow	41	28	52	49	34	46	57	42	36	40	42	41	42	36	38	47	37	40	Iceland	85
Latvia	58	45	64	60	53	66	90	60	43	57	57	60	na	61	na	56	61	46	Britain	85
Estonia	na	na	na	na	na	na	na	na	na	na	na	na	na	na	na	na	na	na	West Germany	78
Portugal	86	79	92	75	88	94	92	72	71	92	84	74	79	86	89	93	83	72	Finland	76
South Korea	na	na	na	na	na	na	na	na	na	na	na	na	na	na	na	na	na	na	Belgium	69
Ireland	98	96	99	95	98	99	99	97	96	97	98	97	86	99	99	98	98	96	Hungary	65
North Ireland	97	93	99	96	95	99	97	95	96	99	96	94	96	97	96	98	96	95	Norway	65
Slovenia	63	58	67	58	57	71	81	55	38	76	59	40	42	60	65	72	61	44	Japan	65
Spain	86	79	91	78	82	94	90	79	74	92	86	78	72	92	93	93	85	71	Netherlands	64
East Germany	36	29	43	24	32	49	38	39	29	49	36	26	16	42	54	45	34	39	Denmark	64
Britain	78	69	86	63	76	89	81	77	67	84	77	69	70	80	82	80	80	70	Slovenia	63
Italy	91	86	94	89	88	94	91	88	86	94	90	82	80	95	95	96	91	84	France	62
Netherlands	64	64	64	52	66	75	70	66	55	58	67	65	46	67	81	78	66	58	Latvia	58
Belgium	69	63	75	51	68	81	74	68	61	68	63	71	47	75	79	75	71	58	Sweden	45
Austria	87	82	90	78	88	89	89	86	83	88	86	87	73	85	90	92	87	82	Russia	44
France	62	58	65	51	55	77	65	60	57	61	58	62	47	69	77	70	63	53	Belarus	43
Canada	89	85	93	85	87	94	91	91	85	75	89	85	81	90	91	96	89	83	Moscow	41
United States	96	95	97	95	94	98	97	97	85	97	97	94	87	97	98	98	96	93	Bulgaria	40
Iceland	85	78	92	78	84	95	93	87	78	na	na	na	81	87	86	90	85	73	East Germany	36
West Germany	78	71	84	62	75	89	82	71	70	80	76	77	64	80	88	85	82	68		
Denmark	64	56	73	50	58	82	74	61	61	69	64	52	46	68	71	69	68	41		
Finland	76	67	86	57	76	89	78	74	61	75	74	79	63	77	83	89	78	69		
Norway	65	56	74	53	60	78	81	59	62	70	60	63	57	67	69	65	66	56		
Sweden	45	38	53	34	40	62	48	41	48	47	46	41	36	49	51	50	47	39		
Japan	65	55	73	69	60	68	68	67	55	68	61	63	39	62	68	70	63	45		
Switzerland	na	na	na	na	na	na	na	na	na	na	na	na	na	na	na	na	na	na		
Total	76	70	81	70	73	83	82	74	69	78	75	71	66	77	81	80	76	69		

Note: Countries in the left column are ranked according to GNP per capita. / The percentages in the bottom row give each country an equal weight. / na=not ascertained.

V167 LIFE AFTER DEATH

Which, if any, of the following do you believe in? Life after death (% "yes")

	Total	Gender		Age			Education			Income			Political Affinity			Values		
		Male	Female	16-29	30-49	50+	Lower	Medium	Upper	Lower	Middle	Upper	Left	Center	Right	Mat	Mixed	Postmat
India	41	41	40	36	42	50	52	38	39	48	39	38	35	39	45	43	37	47
Nigeria	82	84	81	83	82	84	78	83	84	81	82	85	88	78	83	83	82	84
China	na	na	na	na	na	na	na	na	na	na	na	na	na	na	na	na	na	na
Romania	58	51	65	52	49	69	75	49	47	62	60	52	56	54	56	62	53	62
Turkey	80	79	81	79	78	87	82	80	71	80	84	77	60	85	89	89	81	69
Poland	78	72	84	77	76	82	83	79	62	81	80	74	69	74	79	82	76	81
Bulgaria	18	12	23	18	15	21	25	15	16	22	17	13	11	15	21	18	16	25
Chile	70	65	74	68	69	72	67	68	77	70	66	73	68	68	75	70	70	67
Czechoslovakia	na	na	na	na	na	na	na	na	na	na	na	na	na	na	na	na	na	na
South Africa	78	73	83	71	80	87	80	76	85	75	79	86	76	78	76	81	77	74
Lithuania	26	na	na	21	na	37	30	21	28	35	21	18	13	25	42	27	25	26
Hungary	26	22	31	21	17	37	30	21	28	35	21	18	13	25	42	27	25	26
Argentina	65	59	69	68	61	67	56	67	73	63	67	65	54	66	69	60	67	64
Brazil	74	72	75	74	72	75	71	74	80	73	72	74	74	76	72	71	75	82
Mexico	61	56	68	58	62	69	63	58	58	63	59	60	55	59	67	66	62	53
Belarus	18	13	22	16	15	25	32	17	13	26	16	14	18	14	23	17	18	20
Russia	21	14	27	19	16	29	32	21	15	26	18	19	13	19	25	24	20	20
Moscow	23	13	31	32	16	27	28	25	20	19	27	22	24	18	24	26	19	29
Latvia	30	28	32	38	25	29	47	29	26	27	30	33	24	na	na	19	34	26
Estonia	na	na	na	na	na	na	na	na	na	na	na	na	na	na	na	na	na	na
Portugal	39	28	49	28	36	52	43	28	33	47	34	32	32	36	50	40	38	31
South Korea	na	na	na	na	na	na	na	na	na	na	na	na	na	na	na	na	na	na
Ireland	83	81	85	75	82	90	82	84	87	85	83	83	67	84	89	85	84	82
North Ireland	78	71	84	66	78	88	78	83	69	80	80	75	65	76	82	84	75	81
Slovenia	28	25	32	30	23	33	40	22	17	36	25	20	24	24	39	31	27	25
Spain	52	42	60	46	45	62	53	52	47	55	50	48	35	57	71	58	49	42
East Germany	21	18	23	16	21	24	20	29	18	26	20	17	9	24	33	19	20	23
Britain	52	41	62	45	50	58	52	57	45	54	49	48	45	54	54	56	52	48
Italy	68	59	76	69	64	71	69	67	59	72	67	63	52	79	70	72	69	63
Netherlands	47	45	48	48	46	47	41	49	52	46	49	46	40	46	58	39	46	49
Belgium	44	39	49	39	39	53	41	45	48	43	37	48	34	45	57	43	45	44
Austria	56	48	62	60	56	55	56	57	55	56	56	57	49	51	64	60	57	54
France	44	37	50	46	38	50	39	47	52	38	46	48	38	46	61	47	42	46
Canada	69	63	74	68	69	70	69	67	71	72	70	66	65	70	71	75	69	66
United States	74	76	80	73	79	80	74	79	80	79	77	77	63	79	83	82	80	70
Iceland	81	73	89	80	78	87	87	80	77	na	na	na	75	85	81	86	80	71
West Germany	50	41	58	42	45	59	52	48	47	53	46	52	43	51	56	57	51	45
Denmark	34	25	43	33	31	37	40	30	33	40	31	24	31	31	37	32	34	31
Finland	60	50	72	58	58	64	64	56	64	60	61	59	53	58	65	67	58	65
Norway	45	34	56	46	37	53	58	39	44	56	35	41	41	43	47	42	47	38
Sweden	38	28	50	47	39	33	33	40	43	40	42	34	34	39	41	34	41	34
Japan	54	42	65	73	48	49	53	57	50	59	49	53	34	57	45	51	56	47
Switzerland	64	54	73	65	64	64	64	64	65	68	61	55	63	61	63	65	64	64
Total	**53**	**47**	**59**	**52**	**50**	**58**	**56**	**52**	**51**	**54**	**51**	**50**	**46**	**53**	**58**	**54**	**53**	**51**

Ranking:

Country	
Ireland	83
Nigeria	82
Iceland	81
Turkey	80
Poland	78
South Africa	78
North Ireland	78
United States	74
Brazil	74
Chile	70
Canada	69
Italy	68
Argentina	65
Switzerland	64
Mexico	61
Finland	60
Romania	58
Austria	56
Latvia	54
Japan	52
Spain	52
Britain	52
West Germany	50
Netherlands	47
Norway	45
Belgium	44
France	44
India	41
Portugal	39
Sweden	38
Denmark	34
Latvia	30
Slovenia	28
Hungary	26
Moscow	23
Russia	21
East Germany	21
Bulgaria	18
Belarus	18

Note: Countries in the left column are ranked according to GNP per capita. / The percentages in the bottom row give each country an equal weight. / na=not ascertained.

V168 BELIEF IN SOUL

Which, if any, of the following do you believe in? A soul (% "yes")

	Total	Gender		Age			Education			Income			Political Affinity			Values		
		Male	Female	16-29	30-49	50+	Lower	Medium	Upper	Lower	Middle	Upper	Left	Center	Right	Mat	Mixed	Postmat
India	75	73	78	71	77	82	81	75	73	78	75	72	76	72	74	79	72	73
Nigeria	92	92	93	91	92	100	91	92	92	93	93	93	95	92	91	92	92	97
China	na	na	na	na	na	na	na	na	na	na	na	na	na	na	na	na	na	na
Romania	76	70	82	70	70	85	89	70	68	80	78	71	76	73	78	80	72	83
Turkey	87	86	88	84	85	94	89	86	75	88	89	82	68	90	96	95	87	76
Poland	86	81	91	89	84	86	90	86	69	88	89	81	75	85	88	90	83	89
Bulgaria	38	31	44	42	34	41	42	34	41	37	36	41	27	37	51	34	37	53
Chile	81	78	84	78	80	87	82	77	86	79	81	83	78	81	86	80	82	80
Czechoslovakia	na	na	na	na	na	na	na	na	na	na	na	na	na	na	na	na	na	na
South Africa	91	89	94	90	92	94	93	91	93	92	91	94	90	88	91	92	91	91
Lithuania	na	na	na	na	na	na	na	na	na	na	na	na	na	na	na	na	na	na
Hungary	14	15	14	09	11	19	16	11	16	15	15	14	08	16	24	14	15	17
Argentina	81	75	87	82	79	84	80	79	83	83	86	75	70	82	84	81	82	79
Brazil	84	82	87	86	82	85	84	83	87	84	84	83	83	85	84	82	85	86
Mexico	72	68	76	71	70	78	73	69	71	73	67	72	64	71	73	76	71	64
Belarus	45	36	53	47	44	45	49	55	44	58	52	46	46	39	51	41	47	54
Russia	54	45	61	58	52	54	56	55	52	56	52	48	48	53	53	54	53	67
Moscow	59	46	68	65	55	59	54	55	61	56	62	59	62	54	52	58	56	71
Latvia	78	67	84	80	78	76	74	74	86	75	78	81	na	na	na	74	80	71
Estonia	na	na	na	na	na	na	na	na	na	na	na	na	na	na	na	na	na	na
Portugal	66	55	76	57	62	78	72	51	55	75	65	54	53	63	77	71	63	78
South Korea	na	na	na	na	na	na	na	na	na	na	na	na	na	na	na	na	na	na
Ireland	88	87	na	80	87	95	90	87	81	94	89	82	67	89	92	92	88	85
North Ireland	92	86	90	88	88	100	93	90	90	99	93	84	89	91	94	95	92	85
Slovenia	46	43	49	49	42	49	57	41	33	54	43	35	35	42	55	46	46	47
Spain	65	54	75	58	61	74	67	60	63	73	62	62	51	71	81	71	63	54
East Germany	37	33	41	29	35	45	36	43	38	44	37	32	23	42	50	41	35	41
Britain	70	59	80	65	71	73	68	75	71	69	70	70	66	69	73	69	72	65
Italy	78	67	87	71	72	81	78	75	73	80	77	70	61	85	82	80	79	72
Netherlands	75	67	77	79	77	75	73	77	75	76	76	73	68	76	83	80	74	78
Belgium	60	56	64	51	58	68	58	61	63	58	58	64	44	65	74	57	61	41
Austria	73	64	78	73	72	72	70	73	75	72	72	73	72	69	76	71	72	56
France	55	50	60	56	48	62	52	56	61	52	52	59	47	63	69	57	56	75
Canada	85	79	90	81	84	88	87	83	85	87	85	80	77	84	89	88	85	55
United States	93	90	95	93	92	93	93	93	92	91	93	92	83	89	94	96	92	81
Iceland	88	82	94	85	87	94	91	88	85	na	na	na	87	89	87	89	88	86
West Germany	75	66	82	72	70	81	77	70	74	77	72	75	70	75	79	82	74	73
Denmark	47	39	56	47	42	53	45	41	53	53	43	43	51	45	48	35	49	51
Finland	73	64	82	71	73	74	75	69	76	72	71	76	67	71	77	76	69	80
Norway	54	44	66	52	73	63	63	49	55	63	47	51	50	54	58	50	57	80
Sweden	58	47	70	60	61	54	49	59	73	57	60	56	54	59	63	53	58	63
Japan	75	68	82	85	73	72	76	77	77	79	73	73	63	76	72	81	76	56
Switzerland	81	74	86	80	80	82	79	82	84	82	81	76	81	80	78	76	80	85
Total	70	63	75	68	68	74	71	68	69	71	69	67	63	69	74	70	69	70

Ranking:

Country	
United States	93
Nigeria	92
North Ireland	92
South Africa	91
Ireland	88
Iceland	88
Turkey	87
Poland	86
Canada	85
Brazil	84
Chile	81
Argentina	81
Switzerland	81
Latvia	78
Italy	78
Romania	76
India	75
Netherlands	75
West Germany	75
Japan	75
Austria	73
Finland	73
Mexico	72
Britain	70
Portugal	66
Spain	65
Belgium	60
Moscow	59
Sweden	58
France	55
Russia	54
Norway	54
Denmark	47
Slovenia	46
Belarus	45
Bulgaria	38
East Germany	37
Hungary	14

Note: Countries in the left column are ranked according to GNP per capita. / The percentages in the bottom row give each country an equal weight. / na=not ascertained.

V169 BELIEF IN DEVIL

Which, if any, of the following do you believe in? The Devil (% "yes")

	Total	Gender Male	Gender Female	Age 16-29	Age 30-49	Age 50+	Education Lower	Education Medium	Education Upper	Income Lower	Income Middle	Income Upper	Political Affinity Left	Political Affinity Center	Political Affinity Right	Values Mat	Values Mixed	Values Postmat
India	27	27	28	23	28	32	37	27	22	32	26	23	26	27	24	27	26	23
Nigeria	45	44	48	43	45	66	44	46	45	61	39	30	43	44	45	38	47	67
China	na	na	na	na	na	na	na	na	na	na	na	na	na	na	na	na	na	na
Romania	42	37	48	32	39	52	52	39	34	49	40	41	41	39	39	47	38	46
Turkey	69	69	69	68	68	74	72	71	56	70	72	65	48	74	77	78	68	60
Poland	51	47	55	53	46	55	55	51	33	52	56	43	44	51	51	53	49	51
Bulgaria	10	08	11	10	07	13	15	07	09	13	07	08	04	09	13	12	08	15
Chile	50	49	51	47	49	56	53	45	53	50	52	47	46	51	49	54	50	43
Czechoslovakia	na	na	na	na	na	na	na	na	na	na	na	na	na	na	na	na	na	na
South Africa	51	47	56	48	52	55	46	52	67	46	50	63	53	53	47	52	51	53
Lithuania	na	na	na	na	na	na	na	na	na	na	na	na	na	na	na	na	na	na
Hungary	19	17	21	12	15	26	24	14	19	24	17	14	16	18	23	20	19	14
Argentina	47	44	50	49	45	48	42	48	52	50	51	40	40	46	55	48	48	43
Brazil	44	41	47	43	44	45	47	45	34	47	44	39	42	42	43	43	45	40
Mexico	44	40	50	44	41	54	46	41	41	46	40	44	32	42	41	52	42	33
Belarus	10	08	13	13	11	08	11	11	10	12	09	10	11	06	21	08	11	18
Russia	15	11	18	18	11	18	22	14	12	17	12	14	13	12	17	16	14	19
Moscow	20	16	24	24	18	19	21	23	18	19	20	23	21	18	20	21	18	26
Latvia	09	08	10	15	06	08	14	10	06	08	10	09	na	na	na	05	12	00
Estonia	na	na	na	na	na	na	na	na	na	na	na	na	na	na	na	na	na	na
Portugal	28	22	33	18	24	40	33	12	20	34	22	22	21	27	32	31	24	13
South Korea	na	na	na	na	na	na	na	na	na	na	na	na	na	na	na	na	na	na
Ireland	55	52	58	42	54	65	55	54	58	58	52	52	39	56	60	63	54	50
North Ireland	76	71	79	75	71	81	74	79	81	79	76	73	70	72	80	73	74	88
Slovenia	17	15	18	12	12	24	25	15	10	22	15	09	10	13	26	18	17	09
Spain	32	24	39	22	29	44	35	29	22	43	29	24	19	35	45	41	29	21
East Germany	10	09	10	07	10	11	09	15	07	13	10	07	04	10	21	08	09	13
Britain	33	29	36	30	32	35	33	34	31	35	33	33	32	32	33	28	35	33
Italy	42	35	48	37	37	48	43	35	32	48	35	24	25	52	45	48	44	29
Netherlands	16	19	15	11	17	21	19	15	16	14	17	17	07	13	29	23	16	13
Belgium	19	16	22	10	16	28	22	18	15	21	16	19	10	17	25	19	22	13
Austria	23	19	25	20	22	26	24	22	25	27	21	20	19	18	29	29	25	16
France	20	18	23	18	17	26	22	20	18	22	20	19	15	25	30	27	20	18
Canada	43	42	45	44	40	47	48	43	41	48	43	38	30	45	48	45	44	38
United States	70	69	71	73	70	69	71	71	67	69	72	65	45	71	78	78	72	55
Iceland	19	22	16	17	15	28	21	19	18	na	na	na	14	20	20	20	19	19
West Germany	18	13	23	12	13	25	20	16	11	22	16	15	11	19	23	29	18	13
Denmark	10	08	13	07	09	15	14	07	11	16	07	06	10	10	12	07	11	08
Finland	31	28	34	37	28	41	38	32	26	36	30	27	10	31	34	38	31	30
Norway	24	22	26	20	21	31	33	21	23	30	20	23	17	25	29	21	26	16
Sweden	12	12	12	13	11	14	11	12	14	12	14	11	09	13	14	18	12	09
Japan	19	14	24	28	16	16	21	19	17	22	20	14	17	14	17	22	19	10
Switzerland	28	24	31	26	26	31	29	27	29	36	27	18	22	28	33	28	30	22
Total	32	29	34	29	29	37	34	30	29	35	31	28	26	32	36	34	32	29

Ranking:

North Ireland	76
United States	70
Turkey	69
Ireland	55
Poland	51
South Africa	51
Chile	50
Argentina	47
Nigeria	45
Brazil	44
Mexico	44
Canada	43
Romania	42
Italy	42
Britain	33
Spain	32
Finland	31
Portugal	28
Switzerland	28
India	27
Norway	24
Austria	23
Moscow	20
France	20
Hungary	19
Belgium	19
Iceland	19
Japan	19
West Germany	18
Slovenia	17
Netherlands	16
Russia	15
Sweden	12
Bulgaria	10
Belarus	10
East Germany	10
Denmark	10
Latvia	09

Note: Countries in the left column are ranked according to GNP per capita. / The percentages in the bottom row give each country an equal weight. / na=not ascertained.

V170 BELIEF IN HELL
Which, if any, of the following do you believe in? Hell (% "yes")

	Total	Gender		Age			Education			Income			Political Affinity			Values			Ranking:	
		Male	Female	16-29	30-49	50+	Lower	Medium	Upper	Lower	Middle	Upper	Left	Center	Right	Mat	Mixed	Postmat		
India	39	37	43	34	40	49	54	41	30	48	na	na	33	38	42	43	36	33	Turkey	85
Nigeria	51	49	54	49	51	65	48	54	50	65	44	39	45	51	51	45	53	70	North Ireland	73
China	na	na	na	na	na	na	na	na	na	na	na	na	na	na	na	na	na	na	United States	71
Romania	43	36	49	35	36	53	56	38	31	46	43	39	37	38	39	48	37	46	Poland	54
Turkey	85	85	85	84	84	91	90	80	71	86	89	80	65	89	94	94	86	73	Ireland	53
Poland	54	49	58	59	49	56	58	55	30	56	58	46	48	55	54	57	52	54	South Africa	52
Bulgaria	11	08	14	10	08	15	17	10	08	14	10	09	04	08	15	12	09	17	Nigeria	51
Chile	45	43	47	41	42	55	50	39	46	48	45	41	41	46	43	51	46	31	Mexico	48
Czechoslovakia	na	na	na	na	na	na	na	na	na	na	na	na	na	na	na	na	na	na	Chile	45
South Africa	52	47	56	47	54	56	46	53	64	46	50	65	52	53	48	53	51	51	Romania	43
Lithuania	na	na	na	na	na	na	na	na	na	na	na	na	na	na	na	na	na	na	Italy	42
Hungary	16	14	18	10	11	24	20	13	13	23	11	13	07	15	23	16	16	11	Canada	42
Argentina	41	38	44	43	40	42	37	45	45	46	41	38	32	41	52	43	43	36	Argentina	41
Brazil	39	34	44	39	37	43	44	39	28	44	39	33	35	38	41	38	41	34	India	39
Mexico	48	43	55	48	46	56	51	45	42	51	45	46	35	46	48	56	47	31	Brazil	39
Belarus	09	07	11	10	08	11	16	09	07	10	08	10	08	06	23	10	08	12	Japan	32
Russia	16	10	22	18	12	21	25	16	12	20	13	12	10	14	18	19	14	20	Spain	30
Moscow	14	08	19	13	12	16	20	15	12	12	14	16	14	11	16	18	10	20	Britain	28
Latvia	07	07	07	10	04	10	21	06	04	05	10	07	na	na	na	02	10	03	Finland	27
Estonia	na	na	na	na	na	na	na	na	na	na	na	na	na	na	na	na	na	na	Portugal	25
Portugal	25	20	30	16	20	38	31	11	15	32	20	21	17	22	32	31	21	11	Switzerland	24
South Korea	na	na	na	na	na	na	na	na	na	na	na	na	na	na	na	na	na	na	Austria	20
Ireland	53	51	54	39	51	63	54	51	48	57	49	48	37	53	55	60	52	46	Norway	19
North Ireland	73	68	76	66	67	82	73	75	64	75	73	66	54	68	80	72	72	78	Slovenia	17
Slovenia	17	15	19	16	13	23	27	11	10	24	14	10	10	14	24	20	17	10	Belgium	17
Spain	30	22	37	17	26	44	33	25	20	43	26	22	16	34	45	41	26	16	France	17
East Germany	09	08	10	06	10	11	09	14	07	13	08	08	04	10	19	07	09	12	Hungary	16
Britain	28	26	29	28	28	28	28	30	22	31	24	26	28	28	26	23	30	27	Russia	16
Italy	42	33	51	35	37	51	44	31	31	48	37	23	23	54	44	51	43	31	West Germany	15
Netherlands	13	16	11	10	12	17	17	08	12	12	12	12	03	09	27	18	13	10	Moscow	14
Belgium	17	15	19	08	14	26	19	16	13	18	12	16	09	15	22	18	18	11	Netherlands	13
Austria	20	18	22	15	19	24	22	19	19	23	20	16	15	16	26	26	21	15	Iceland	12
France	17	15	20	14	13	24	20	15	14	18	17	16	11	21	30	28	16	12	Bulgaria	11
Canada	42	39	44	43	39	44	43	42	39	46	41	34	29	43	46	46	43	34	Belarus	09
United States	71	71	70	74	70	71	74	74	64	74	72	65	44	73	77	79	73	57	East Germany	09
Iceland	12	14	10	10	10	18	11	14	12	na	na	na	07	14	14	12	12	11	Denmark	08
West Germany	15	11	18	09	11	21	17	13	08	20	14	11	08	17	18	28	14	10	Sweden	08
Denmark	08	07	10	06	06	13	11	05	08	13	07	03	07	08	10	08	09	05	Latvia	07
Finland	27	24	31	28	23	37	33	27	25	34	25	25	16	29	31	45	26	27		
Norway	19	18	21	17	17	24	27	16	19	24	16	17	12	21	23	17	21	13		
Sweden	08	09	06	08	08	09	08	08	07	07	09	08	05	08	09	12	08	06		
Japan	32	20	43	44	27	30	35	33	26	35	29	29	26	29	25	32	32	25		
Switzerland	24	21	27	18	23	29	25	24	20	32	24	11	16	24	31	29	26	17		
Total	31	28	34	28	28	37	35	29	26	35	30	27	23	31	36	34	31	27		

Note: Countries in the left column are ranked according to GNP per capita. / The percentages in the bottom row give each country an equal weight. / na=not ascertained.

V171 BELIEF IN HEAVEN

Which, if any, of the following do you believe in? Heaven (% "yes")

	Total	Gender		Age			Education			Income			Political Affinity			Values		
		Male	Female	16-29	30-49	50+	Lower	Medium	Upper	Lower	Middle	Upper	Left	Center	Right	Mat	Mixed	Postmat
India	43	41	46	39	43	53	58	45	33	52	42	36	39	42	45	47	41	34
Nigeria	96	94	97	95	96	98	97	97	93	96	96	94	97	94	97	98	94	93
China	na	na	na	na	na	na	na	na	na	na	na	na	na	na	na	na	na	na
Romania	58	50	65	46	50	71	79	50	39	60	61	53	53	52	57	65	52	53
Turkey	87	87	88	84	86	93	93	80	73	89	90	81	68	90	97	95	88	74
Poland	80	75	85	83	76	83	87	81	51	83	81	76	73	79	79	86	75	87
Bulgaria	16	11	20	14	11	22	26	13	11	18	14	12	07	13	20	18	14	19
Chile	77	72	82	76	75	82	86	72	73	83	79	67	70	78	78	85	77	67
Czechoslovakia	na	na	na	na	na	na	na	na	na	na	na	na	na	na	na	na	na	na
South Africa	91	88	94	90	91	94	93	91	86	91	92	91	87	92	90	93	90	86
Lithuania	na	na	na	na	na	na	na	na	na	na	na	na	na	na	na	na	na	na
Hungary	27	23	30	16	17	41	36	19	15	38	19	16	09	23	37	27	27	19
Argentina	69	63	75	67	69	72	76	66	62	77	73	59	48	68	77	79	70	54
Brazil	76	72	80	76	73	82	87	76	55	87	79	63	68	73	83	82	75	54
Mexico	70	64	77	69	67	81	71	72	66	73	66	67	57	66	75	78	71	50
Belarus	12	08	16	10	11	16	23	12	08	14	11	11	11	10	25	13	11	16
Russia	18	11	24	18	13	25	28	18	13	22	16	14	10	17	20	21	17	18
Moscow	17	09	23	17	14	22	25	19	14	15	17	19	17	13	21	25	12	22
Latvia	12	11	12	13	06	19	35	10	06	11	15	09	na	na	na	06	15	03
Estonia	na	na	na	na	na	na	na	na	na	na	na	na	na	na	na	na	na	na
Portugal	56	47	64	41	50	75	69	30	28	70	53	38	48	50	65	69	48	33
South Korea	na	na	na	na	na	na	na	na	na	na	na	na	na	na	na	na	na	na
Ireland	90	86	93	83	88	95	92	88	81	95	88	86	68	90	94	92	90	85
North Ireland	90	83	95	83	89	95	94	84	81	95	93	82	88	89	90	92	90	86
Slovenia	30	27	34	26	24	40	46	23	14	39	27	19	22	24	33	36	29	19
Spain	52	39	63	39	45	68	57	45	35	66	49	39	32	58	72	65	48	32
East Germany	25	21	29	16	20	36	27	27	16	36	25	17	10	27	43	35	23	24
Britain	59	48	69	48	55	68	63	52	45	69	54	47	55	60	57	64	60	51
Italy	54	44	63	50	46	63	56	42	32	59	51	34	33	67	58	64	55	42
Netherlands	37	35	37	31	36	44	42	39	29	32	37	32	22	33	55	55	40	27
Belgium	34	28	39	24	29	45	37	34	27	36	26	33	18	34	43	37	36	25
Austria	47	38	53	42	45	52	50	47	38	52	46	42	41	42	52	57	50	36
France	32	25	39	28	28	41	37	29	27	34	32	32	21	38	47	45	33	23
Canada	72	66	77	72	66	79	81	72	66	78	71	65	53	73	76	84	74	61
United States	87	85	89	89	85	88	91	90	80	91	87	81	63	88	92	90	89	78
Iceland	57	51	63	45	57	74	72	58	46	na	na	na	43	65	57	72	56	34
West Germany	38	29	46	26	29	51	43	31	23	44	35	33	23	41	48	59	39	24
Denmark	19	14	25	16	14	29	31	14	17	28	17	08	14	17	25	23	20	12
Finland	55	47	63	46	52	69	61	52	55	57	55	52	38	54	64	60	55	53
Norway	44	35	54	36	38	56	61	40	39	53	38	38	35	46	48	45	46	26
Sweden	31	25	38	28	28	36	35	29	28	29	33	29	25	32	34	40	33	21
Japan	43	29	56	62	39	37	41	46	39	48	38	40	25	41	38	42	44	36
Switzerland	44	37	50	33	41	52	46	45	34	54	39	28	24	41	52	53	47	33
Total	51	45	57	47	47		59	48	42	56	50	44	41	52	58	58	51	42

Ranking:

Country	
Nigeria	96
South Africa	91
Ireland	90
North Ireland	90
Turkey	87
United States	87
Poland	80
Chile	77
Brazil	76
Canada	72
Mexico	70
Argentina	69
Britain	59
Romania	58
Iceland	57
Portugal	56
Finland	55
Italy	54
Spain	52
Austria	47
Norway	44
Switzerland	44
India	43
Japan	43
West Germany	38
Netherlands	37
Belgium	34
France	32
Sweden	31
Slovenia	30
Hungary	27
East Germany	25
Denmark	19
Russia	18
Moscow	17
Bulgaria	16
Belarus	12
Latvia	12

Note: Countries in the left column are ranked according to GNP per capita. / The percentages in the bottom row give each country an equal weight. / na=not ascertained.

V172 BELIEF IN SIN

Which, if any, of the following do you believe in? Sin (% "yes")

	Total	Gender Male	Gender Female	Age 16-29	Age 30-49	Age 50+	Educ. Lower	Educ. Medium	Educ. Upper	Income Lower	Income Middle	Income Upper	Pol. Left	Pol. Center	Pol. Right	Values Mat	Values Mixed	Values Postmat
India	67	65	70	64	68	71	70	67	66	68	66	68	65	66	67	73	64	54
Nigeria	62	61	63	58	63	82	58	62	63	74	56	52	55	65	58	55	63	83
China	na	na	na	na	na	na	na	na	na	na	na	na	na	na	na	na	na	na
Romania	77	72	81	67	75	84	86	73	70	78	78	75	77	74	76	83	71	80
Turkey	91	91	91	88	91	96	96	87	75	93	93	86	74	95	96	96	93	80
Poland	91	87	95	91	91	90	93	92	79	94	91	88	83	91	92	94	88	95
Bulgaria	30	25	35	25	26	38	37	28	27	31	28	29	19	30	34	31	29	32
Chile	88	85	91	87	87	93	92	87	86	91	89	84	82	90	89	93	89	81
Czechoslovakia	na	na	na	na	na	na	na	na	na	na	na	na	na	na	na	na	na	na
South Africa	69	65	73	64	73	73	64	71	83	62	68	83	71	70	68	70	69	73
Lithuania	na	na	na	na	na	na	na	na	na	na	na	na	na	na	na	na	na	na
Hungary	39	35	43	25	33	50	46	33	35	44	36	34	29	39	47	39	40	29
Argentina	72	68	75	66	71	77	77	68	68	78	74	63	50	70	80	78	75	54
Brazil	82	81	83	83	79	86	89	83	63	89	85	72	50	81	86	87	80	66
Mexico	74	68	80	72	71	83	75	78	67	74	73	70	75	75	78	80	74	57
Belarus	48	39	55	39	47	56	58	46	45	54	44	45	54	42	56	48	46	50
Russia	47	37	55	45	44	53	54	44	47	49	47	43	48	44	50	47	47	56
Moscow	48	37	56	47	43	54	51	47	47	48	50	41	41	43	49	49	44	54
Latvia	51	49	52	48	45	63	62	50	47	50	48	53	50	na	na	51	52	52
Estonia	na	na	na	na	na	na	na	na	na	na	na	na	na	na	na	na	na	na
Portugal	68	59	77	55	68	81	77	51	48	75	69	56	60	67	72	75	65	50
South Korea	na	na	na	na	na	na	na	na	na	na	na	na	na	na	na	na	na	na
Ireland	87	84	89	81	89	88	89	84	83	88	86	85	67	90	92	90	88	81
North Ireland	91	89	93	89	89	95	92	90	93	91	91	92	89	84	78	91	92	88
Slovenia	47	44	42	42	42	54	58	39	36	56	45	31	29	46	53	51	46	35
Spain	56	45	66	44	50	71	61	47	42	71	52	47	40	42	71	69	53	37
East Germany	37	33	40	25	34	46	37	39	31	45	36	29	24	64	50	41	34	41
Britain	72	69	74	60	76	75	71	74	72	74	69	75	70	39	74	73	72	70
Italy	73	67	80	68	68	81	75	65	65	79	73	57	53	71	78	80	75	64
Netherlands	43	46	42	32	44	53	47	38	43	40	44	43	26	46	59	55	45	38
Belgium	45	41	49	33	40	57	45	45	44	47	41	49	32	46	55	48	45	40
Austria	66	59	71	61	67	68	68	65	62	71	65	63	62	60	74	69	69	59
France	43	40	46	38	36	55	46	41	41	42	39	45	30	51	64	55	42	37
Canada	74	73	76	73	71	78	75	77	70	73	75	72	61	77	76	81	76	66
United States	89	89	89	92	87	91	89	90	87	89	89	88	77	91	91	94	89	84
Iceland	70	67	73	62	67	85	77	73	64	na	na	na	71	65	73	72	72	54
West Germany	63	56	69	50	57	74	68	55	56	64	62	60	46	66	76	76	65	51
Denmark	24	18	30	18	16	38	35	17	22	35	19	14	18	24	27	26	25	17
Finland	66	61	72	58	62	82	65	65	66	68	65	65	56	67	70	83	65	64
Norway	44	42	47	32	36	45	67	37	39	54	38	39	36	47	47	na	na	na
Sweden	31	31	31	23	25	45	37	26	31	30	35	29	25	31	36	38	31	32
Japan	28	24	32	36	26	26	29	29	24	28	28	24	21	26	22	32	27	22
Switzerland	64	60	67	61	56	72	66	64	54	72	61	53	49	64	70	62	68	53
Total	**61**	**57**	**65**	**55**	**58**	**69**	**65**	**59**	**56**	**64**	**60**	**57**	**52**	**62**	**66**	**65**	**61**	**55**

Ranking:

Turkey	91
Poland	91
North Ireland	91
United States	89
Chile	88
Ireland	87
Brazil	82
Romania	77
Mexico	74
Canada	74
Italy	73
Argentina	72
Britain	72
Iceland	70
South Africa	69
Portugal	68
India	67
Austria	66
Finland	66
Switzerland	64
West Germany	63
Nigeria	62
Spain	56
Latvia	51
Belarus	48
Moscow	48
Russia	47
Slovenia	47
Belgium	45
Norway	44
Netherlands	43
France	43
Hungary	39
East Germany	37
Sweden	31
Bulgaria	30
Japan	28
Denmark	24

Note: Countries in the left column are ranked according to GNP per capita. / The percentages in the bottom row give...

V173 RESURRECTION

Which, if any, of the following do you believe in? Resurrection of the dead (% "yes")

	Total	Gender		Age			Education			Income			Political Affinity			Values		
		Male	Female	16-29	30-49	50+	Lower	Medium	Upper	Lower	Middle	Upper	Left	Center	Right	Mat	Mixed	Postmat
India	09	11	08	07	10	12	14	08	08	14	08	07	09	08	09	09	09	07
Nigeria	89	87	91	90	86	91	90	89	88	85	89	92	89	85	92	92	87	84
China	na	na	na	na	na	na	na	na	na	na	na	na	na	na	na	na	na	na
Romania	50	43	56	41	45	60	71	39	37	52	54	42	48	46	45	56	44	45
Turkey	83	81	85	79	83	89	87	79	69	83	86	79	61	86	93	91	84	70
Poland	83	78	87	83	80	85	88	83	61	86	84	77	72	82	83	88	80	83
Bulgaria	16	11	21	17	14	18	20	14	17	20	12	14	10	15	24	14	15	29
Chile	69	62	75	66	70	72	74	64	69	73	68	67	63	69	73	75	68	64
Czechoslovakia	na	na	na	na	na	na	na	na	na	na	na	na	na	na	na	na	na	na
South Africa	76	71	82	72	77	85	80	75	73	76	77	79	70	78	78	77	77	70
Lithuania	na	na	na	na	na	na	na	na	na	na	na	na	na	na	na	na	na	na
Hungary	27	24	31	16	18	42	36	20	16	38	19	21	10	26	39	29	26	21
Argentina	50	44	57	48	53	49	49	52	51	49	53	47	33	53	57	55	51	43
Brazil	67	62	71	60	68	76	78	63	55	72	67	59	61	64	72	67	67	46
Mexico	58	52	65	57	55	65	58	60	55	60	53	58	42	55	62	64	57	46
Belarus	10	08	11	09	09	11	14	10	08	11	08	14	10	08	18	10	09	15
Russia	08	08	09	08	08	10	11	08	07	10	08	08	05	08	11	13	11	12
Moscow	13	10	16	17	12	13	17	12	13	13	14	16	14	10	11	07	19	18
Latvia	16	10	19	19	08	26	45	17	06	15	16	17	na	na	na	na	na	03
Estonia	na	na	na	na	na	na	na	na	na	na	na	na	na	na	na	na	na	na
Portugal	38	29	46	24	36	54	45	26	23	51	31	25	27	35	48	44	35	19
South Korea	na	75	78	na	na	na	na	73	70	na	79	69	na	na	na	80	76	74
Ireland	77	75	81	60	77	87	81	73	70	84	79	69	55	78	83	80	76	74
North Ireland	77	73	81	63	74	89	80	73	68	85	71	68	74	76	77	80	75	76
Slovenia	22	20	25	17	19	29	32	17	12	31	19	32	15	17	35	20	18	27
Spain	39	29	47	29	33	51	40	39	32	46	34	32	23	45	61	46	37	27
East Germany	20	17	22	15	19	23	19	27	17	25	19	16	07	23	33	20	18	23
Britain	37	30	44	26	36	44	37	37	36	41	33	33	31	35	42	44	53	28
Italy	53	43	63	47	47	62	54	53	45	60	51	35	35	66	60	57	55	26
Netherlands	30	30	30	22	33	36	32	29	29	27	33	29	20	28	46	35	32	28
Belgium	32	28	35	28	28	42	31	31	35	33	23	33	45	43	60	56	53	44
Austria	51	42	57	51	49	53	53	51	42	56	47	51	20	34	47	35	30	28
France	30	27	33	27	25	38	28	29	36	28	29	51	38	60	58	66	57	50
Canada	56	50	63	50	55	63	62	56	52	61	55	51	45	75	80	66	57	59
United States	73	67	78	65	72	76	72	75	69	76	71	71	40	54	55	80	75	39
Iceland	51	46	56	46	32	61	57	50	47	45	35	38	28	41	55	53	53	30
West Germany	40	31	47	28	20	52	44	32	24	28	21	14	19	21	50	53	41	20
Denmark	23	17	29	18	19	30	29	17	24	28	21	14	31	50	26	21	23	51
Finland	49	44	56	47	46	59	52	46	52	52	46	51	26	34	57	56	48	25
Norway	32	28	37	29	26	42	48	27	30	38	26	30	16	23	35	33	33	15
Sweden	21	19	25	18	19	27	20	20	25	24	23	19	10	10	26	25	12	10
Japan	11	09	13	20	10	07	09	13	10	09	12	10	10	10	08	09	12	42
Switzerland	48	40	55	41	47	52	48	47	47	56	47	32	38	48	50	47	50	38
Total	**43**	**38**	**47**	**38**	**41**	**50**	**48**	**41**	**41**	**46**	**41**	**39**	**34**	**44**	**50**	**46**	**43**	**38**

Ranking:

Nigeria	89
Turkey	83
Poland	83
Ireland	77
North Ireland	76
South Africa	73
United States	69
Chile	67
Brazil	58
Mexico	56
Canada	53
Italy	51
Austria	51
Iceland	51
Romania	50
Argentina	50
Finland	49
Switzerland	48
West Germany	40
Spain	39
Portugal	38
Britain	37
Belgium	32
Norway	32
Netherlands	30
France	30
Hungary	27
Denmark	23
Slovenia	22
Sweden	21
East Germany	20
Bulgaria	16
Latvia	16
Moscow	13
Japan	11
Belarus	09
India	09
Russia	08

Note: Countries in the left column are ranked according to GNP per capita. / The percentages in the bottom row give each country an equal weight. / na=not ascertained.

V174 RE-INCARNATION
Which, if any, of the following do you believe in? Re-incarnation (% "yes")

	Total	Gender Male	Female	Age 16-29	30-49	50+	Education Lower	Medium	Upper	Income Lower	Middle	Upper	Political Affinity Left	Center	Right	Values Mat	Mixed	Postmat	Ranking:	
India	91	90	93	93	91	88	87	92	92	87	92	93	92	92	91	92	91	93	India	91
Nigeria	39	37	42	40	37	51	41	41	37	40	39	35	35	38	38	35	40	49	Brazil	57
China	na	na	na	na	na	na	na	na	na	na	na	na	na	na	na	na	na	na	Turkey	54
Romania	24	21	27	32	21	22	21	25	26	30	22	23	24	24	26	19	25	46	Japan	50
Turkey	54	51	56	48	55	60	61	45	37	55	57	47	40	55	61	57	54	49	Chile	49
Poland	26	24	28	37	22	24	26	26	26	24	24	29	19	29	28	28	24	35	Latvia	45
Bulgaria	25	19	32	33	24	22	24	24	31	29	22	24	20	26	33	22	24	45	South Africa	43
Chile	49	47	50	42	51	55	56	43	48	52	47	46	46	48	49	59	45	46	Mexico	43
Czechoslovakia	na	na	na	na	na	na	na	na	na	na	na	na	na	na	na	na	na	na	Iceland	40
South Africa	43	41	45	47	39	43	53	42	18	52	47	23	45	36	45	38	45	48	Nigeria	39
Lithuania	na	na	na	na	na	na	na	na	na	na	na	na	na	na	na	na	na	na	Argentina	39
Hungary	23	21	26	21	14	33	30	18	14	30	20	13	13	22	35	25	22	18	Switzerland	36
Argentina	39	36	42	40	41	36	43	40	31	34	45	37	30	37	44	36	42	37	Finland	34
Brazil	57	55	59	55	57	60	61	55	54	57	60	54	58	58	60	52	59	64	Moscow	33
Mexico	43	40	47	42	42	48	46	43	34	47	39	40	33	41	42	47	43	31	North Ireland	33
Belarus	24	19	29	29	26	16	20	25	25	25	24	24	27	17	33	19	25	44	Canada	31
Russia	22	18	24	26	21	20	21	23	21	18	22	22	18	22	19	19	23	29	Portugal	29
Moscow	33	24	40	43	32	25	19	31	35	31	34	33	37	27	26	31	29	51	Britain	29
Latvia	45	45	44	57	45	28	36	44	47	43	44	48	na	na	na	35	46	50	Austria	29
Estonia	na	na	na	na	na	na	na	na	na	na	na	na	na	na	na	na	na	na	Spain	28
Portugal	29	23	34	23	28	36	33	22	19	37	24	20	22	26	35	30	27	23	France	28
South Korea	na	na	na	na	na	na	na	na	na	na	na	na	na	na	na	na	na	na	Italy	27
Ireland	20	23	18	18	20	23	23	17	23	29	16	16	19	19	21	17	22	18	Poland	26
North Ireland	33	35	31	24	38	33	35	33	16	44	32	25	35	30	36	32	32	33	United States	26
Slovenia	17	19	16	26	14	16	19	16	17	19	15	18	19	20	20	11	20	20	West Germany	26
Spain	28	22	34	28	25	32	30	34	17	31	27	24	21	31	36	31	28	23	Bulgaria	25
East Germany	13	10	15	10	11	16	13	14	09	17	11	09	06	15	18	19	12	12	Romania	24
Britain	29	22	35	30	30	27	29	31	22	29	30	26	23	29	34	35	29	24	Belarus	24
Italy	27	23	31	28	22	30	28	16	20	32	20	16	21	24	28	29	28	22	Hungary	23
Netherlands	22	15	24	23	26	13	16	29	21	22	23	17	26	23	16	17	20	25	Russia	22
Belgium	16	12	20	20	18	12	16	17	15	18	15	15	15	17	16	17	17	14	Netherlands	22
Austria	29	24	33	36	30	26	28	30	28	31	27	30	28	27	32	33	28	31	Ireland	20
France	28	24	31	32	29	24	24	33	29	26	28	30	24	30	34	30	28	28	Sweden	20
Canada	31	27	36	33	37	23	31	32	30	35	34	27	28	33	27	30	31	31	Slovenia	17
United States	26	22	29	16	25	29	29	27	21	28	27	22	27	24	26	27	24	23	Denmark	17
Iceland	40	35	44	48	36	35	41	42	37	41	42	na	33	42	42	38	41	36	Belgium	16
West Germany	26	23	28	26	24	26	25	30	20	26	23	27	25	13	29	25	25	25	Norway	15
Denmark	17	12	21	21	18	11	10	18	19	17	17	17	24	29	15	11	17	22	East Germany	13
Finland	34	32	36	31	36	30	40	35	28	36	33	34	28	38	34	33	34	33		
Norway	15	12	19	22	15	11	14	16	15	19	11	15	14	14	17	10	17	20		
Sweden	20	13	29	27	19	15	16	24	19	19	26	15	18	18	24	19	17	19		
Japan	50	40	60	74	47	35	42	54	49	50	47	49	42	53	39	48	53	45		
Switzerland	36	30	41	36	38	32	37	34	39	38	37	27	40	33	31	32	36	36		
Total	**32**	**29**	**36**	**35**	**32**	**31**	**32**	**32**	**29**	**34**	**31**	**29**	**29**	**31**	**34**	**31**	**32**	**34**		

Note: Countries in the left column are ranked according to GNP per capita. / The percentages in the bottom row give each country an equal weight. / na=not ascertained.

V175. Which of these statements comes closest to your beliefs?

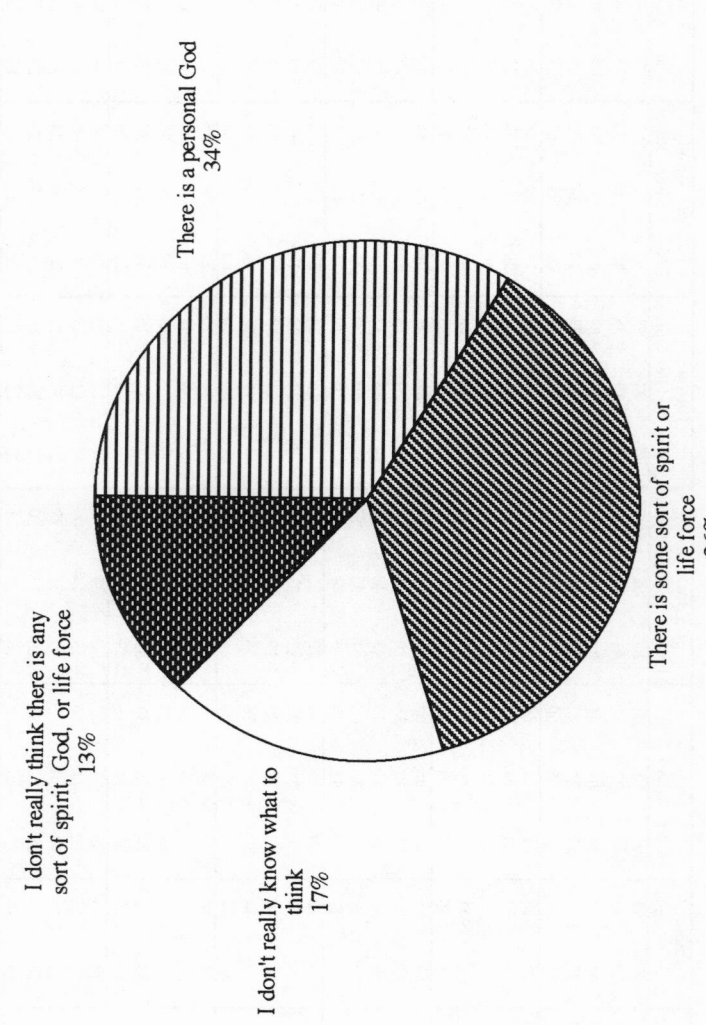

There is a personal God
34%

There is some sort of spirit or
life force
36%

I don't really think there is any
sort of spirit, God, or life force
13%

I don't really know what to
think
17%

V175 WHAT IS GOD

Which of these statements* comes closest to your beliefs? % "There is a personal God."

Country	Total	Gender		Age			Education			Income			Political Affinity			Values		
		Male	Female	16-29	30-49	50+	Lower	Medium	Upper	Lower	Middle	Upper	Left	Center	Right	Mat	Mixed	Postmat
India	30	28	34	26	30	39	46	30	23	37	30	26	21	34	36	31	29	25
Nigeria	68	68	69	67	68	82	77	68	64	69	66	71	65	70	69	69	69	53
China	03	03	04	04	03	03	03	04	02	03	03	04	na	na	na	03	03	07
Romania	36	35	38	26	30	49	58	27	22	36	41	32	40	33	32	43	33	15
Turkey	na	na	na	na	na	na	na	na	na	na	na	na	na	na	na	na	na	na
Poland	na	na	na	na	na	na	na	na	na	na	na	na	na	na	na	na	na	na
Bulgaria	10	09	11	09	08	14	16	09	07	11	07	10	05	10	15	12	10	11
Chile	52	51	54	45	54	61	60	47	50	55	54	47	43	55	52	59	52	42
Czechoslovakia	na	na	na	na	na	na	na	na	na	na	na	na	na	na	na	na	na	na
South Africa	na	na	na	na	na	na	na	na	na	na	na	na	na	na	na	na	na	na
Lithuania	21	17	24	12	14	36	40	17	08	29	15	11	na	na	na	24	21	20
Hungary	40	33	46	23	26	58	53	28	22	50	33	25	18	36	52	44	37	21
Argentina	58	54	62	52	55	67	62	54	57	66	58	52	39	59	65	68	59	44
Brazil	56	55	58	50	54	71	71	53	38	68	54	47	47	54	62	63	53	44
Mexico	56	51	62	54	54	67	71	59	49	60	55	50	42	55	62	65	53	50
Belarus	06	04	07	05	04	10	10	06	04	07	06	04	04	06	08	07	05	08
Russia	08	05	10	03	05	14	15	07	05	12	06	06	04	06	13	10	07	05
Moscow	07	05	08	06	06	08	11	08	05	07	06	09	04	06	09	06	07	03
Latvia	10	08	12	08	09	16	20	10	09	12	11	09	07	06	09	12	10	07
Estonia	07	05	08	05	07	09	09	07	05	09	06	09	na	na	na	07	06	03
Portugal	62	52	70	48	60	76	70	48	38	71	57	46	52	56	72	71	57	39
South Korea	na	na	na	na	na	na	na	na	na	na	na	na	na	na	na	na	na	na
Ireland	67	62	72	60	60	79	70	65	63	73	68	63	na	na	na	69	68	62
North Ireland	66	56	74	54	65	76	70	61	55	68	62	67	49	64	79	66	69	56
Slovenia	22	21	24	16	20	29	32	16	14	29	20	15	50	70	66	25	21	19
Spain	49	42	55	34	45	63	52	46	36	58	47	42	14	18	31	59	47	33
East Germany	17	14	20	12	18	20	17	22	14	21	17	14	36	52	57	17	16	21
Britain	33	26	40	21	31	42	33	34	34	37	26	28	05	19	30	39	32	28
Italy	67	61	73	62	61	75	68	58	60	74	64	46	28	33	36	77	67	57
Netherlands	27	32	25	15	26	42	33	26	20	22	26	27	50	77	69	34	29	20
Belgium	32	28	35	16	26	47	36	31	24	36	26	33	13	22	47	41	30	26
Austria	29	22	34	24	26	34	34	27	19	35	28	25	20	32	41	39	30	23
France	22	20	23	18	17	34	23	20	23	23	20	24	21	25	35	26	21	20
Canada	44	39	49	39	39	56	54	42	39	49	43	37	16	21	37	53	45	36
United States	69	67	71	68	66	73	74	68	66	71	70	66	30	47	46	81	71	57
Iceland	51	44	59	39	51	66	64	55	39	na	na	na	44	69	82	62	49	38
West Germany	25	18	31	14	18	37	29	20	17	30	23	22	41	51	58	41	25	17
Denmark	20	17	24	12	19	28	28	17	18	25	19	12	17	24	35	22	21	14
Finland	29	25	32	24	25	43	28	17	27	31	31	24	14	20	24	49	28	26
Norway	30	24	36	26	25	38	45	25	27	39	23	27	20	30	32	30	30	21
Sweden	16	14	17	13	14	20	16	13	20	16	15	16	13	16	17	20	16	13
Japan	05	03	06	06	03	06	04	05	04	04	06	03	01	04	05	07	04	03
Switzerland	23	19	26	15	21	28	22	23	24	28	19	15	15	20	31	32	24	15
Total	34	30	37	27	31	42	40	31	28	37	31	29	27	36	42	39	33	26

Ranking:

Country	
United States	69
Nigeria	68
Ireland	67
Italy	67
North Ireland	66
Portugal	62
Argentina	58
Brazil	56
Mexico	56
Chile	52
Iceland	51
Spain	49
Canada	44
Hungary	40
Romania	36
Britain	33
Belgium	32
India	30
Norway	30
Austria	29
Finland	29
Netherlands	27
West Germany	25
Switzerland	23
Slovenia	22
France	22
Lithuania	21
Denmark	20
East Germany	17
Sweden	16
Bulgaria	10
Latvia	10
Russia	08
Moscow	07
Estonia	07
Belarus	06
Japan	05
China	03

Note: Countries in the left column are ranked according to GNP per capita. / The percentages in the bottom row give each country an equal weight. / na=not ascertained.

* The other statements offered were: "There is some sort of spirit or life force;" "I don't really know what to think;" "I don't really think there is any sort of spirit, God, or life force."

V176. And how important is God in your life? 10 means "very important" and 1 "not at all important."

Bar chart showing Percentage on the vertical axis (0 to 30) against a scale from [1] Not at all to [10] Very:

- [1] Not at all: 17
- [2]: 6
- [3]: 6
- [4]: 4
- [5]: 10
- [6]: 7
- [7]: 7
- [8]: 9
- [9]: 6
- [10] Very: 29

V176 IMPORTANCE OF GOD

And how important is God in your life? Please use this card to indicate- 10 means very important and 1 means not at all important. (% "very important"—codes 7 to 10)

	Total	Gender		Age			Education			Income			Political Affinity			Values		
		Male	Female	16-29	30-49	50+	Lower	Medium	Upper	Lower	Middle	Upper	Left	Center	Right	Mat	Mixed	Postmat
India	68	62	74	60	71	77	76	69	63	67	70	66	58	62	77	70	65	65
Nigeria	98	98	98	98	98	97	99	99	97	98	97	100	98	98	99	98	98	97
China	03	03	04	04	04	02	02	04	03	04	02	03	na	na	na	04	03	04
Romania	67	61	74	59	63	77	81	60	61	68	68	67	63	67	65	72	64	63
Turkey	86	84	89	81	86	95	92	83	66	88	90	81	63	91	96	95	87	74
Poland	87	81	93	83	83	93	94	86	66	89	88	83	76	87	88	89	86	88
Bulgaria	20	17	23	15	18	26	31	17	15	21	17	18	10	17	25	21	19	24
Chile	84	77	90	80	85	89	89	83	79	88	84	79	72	86	89	88	84	78
Czechoslovakia	na	na	na	na	na	na	na	na	na	na	na	na	na	na	na	na	na	na
South Africa	88	85	92	87	88	92	89	88	88	88	89	88	83	88	89	89	88	87
Lithuania	na	na	na	na	na	na	na	na	na	na	na	na	na	na	na	na	na	na
Hungary	40	32	48	22	24	62	56	25	29	55	30	23	15	37	53	44	37	26
Argentina	74	70	78	65	74	81	79	75	67	81	78	66	51	75	77	83	73	65
Brazil	94	92	96	93	94	96	96	94	87	96	96	89	91	93	96	96	93	89
Mexico	82	77	87	80	82	86	83	85	75	81	83	79	64	83	90	87	81	70
Belarus	22	16	27	16	19	34	36	21	17	26	21	18	22	17	30	26	20	15
Russia	21	12	29	15	17	30	34	20	16	26	21	14	14	19	21	25	19	21
Moscow	23	16	28	20	19	32	35	21	21	24	23	21	23	19	23	29	19	20
Latvia	26	18	31	30	19	34	46	28	17	24	24	30	na	na	na	26	27	23
Estonia	na	na	na	na	na	na	na	na	na	na	na	na	na	na	na	na	na	na
Portugal	57	45	67	40	58	73	68	35	34	70	49	42	49	53	66	67	53	33
South Korea	na	na	na	na	na	na	na	na	na	na	na	na	na	na	na	na	na	na
Ireland	74	69	78	56	70	88	80	69	55	84	73	65	49	70	86	76	75	68
North Ireland	73	61	82	49	71	92	77	70	55	77	73	61	61	70	80	77	74	60
Slovenia	30	26	33	25	25	38	41	25	15	38	25	22	22	22	47	36	28	22
Spain	48	36	59	33	44	64	53	42	34	58	46	39	32	49	67	55	48	32
East Germany	36	22	30	15	24	35	27	27	20	34	28	19	12	29	42	33	24	28
Britain	36	27	44	16	29	54	37	35	30	43	29	25	32	34	40	43	34	34
Italy	65	55	73	58	58	75	66	55	59	72	61	46	44	77	72	77	62	58
Netherlands	33	37	32	20	34	47	39	31	29	32	32	33	17	31	52	49	37	22
Belgium	39	33	44	24	33	54	41	39	33	43	35	36	24	39	53	41	39	35
Austria	41	41	40	42	42	40	41	41	39	36	41	44	32	39	47	41	40	43
France	27	23	31	15	20	43	31	23	25	28	25	25	16	31	42	36	25	23
Canada	62	53	70	51	58	76	72	60	57	70	62	53	50	64	64	78	60	59
United States	77	74	79	68	73	84	79	79	71	80	75	73	54	77	85	84	77	70
Iceland	47	37	57	29	46	71	63	44	37	na	na	na	37	50	49	51	48	33
West Germany	39	31	46	25	31	53	42	32	35	43	35	37	25	39	52	50	41	28
Denmark	18	11	25	08	14	30	25	12	19	24	18	09	13	18	22	19	19	13
Finland	42	34	49	25	40	59	46	42	39	49	37	41	38	39	47	53	39	45
Norway	27	23	32	16	21	43	47	20	25	35	22	23	20	28	32	28	28	15
Sweden	19	16	22	13	15	30	20	15	23	20	22	16	13	19	22	23	21	11
Japan	20	16	23	12	17	28	27	19	15	22	17	20	12	20	24	24	19	14
Switzerland	56	48	63	47	49	68	56	57	56	64	52	42	46	55	61	66	59	42
Total	**50**	**44**	**55**	**41**	**47**	**60**	**56**	**47**	**43**	**54**	**48**	**45**	**41**	**51**	**59**	**55**	**49**	**44**

Ranking:

Nigeria	98
Brazil	94
South Africa	88
Poland	87
Turkey	86
Chile	84
Mexico	82
United States	77
Argentina	74
Ireland	74
North Ireland	73
India	68
Romania	67
Italy	65
Canada	62
Portugal	57
Switzerland	56
Spain	48
Iceland	47
Finland	42
Austria	41
Hungary	40
Belgium	39
West Germany	39
Britain	36
Netherlands	33
Slovenia	30
France	27
Norway	27
Latvia	26
East Germany	26
Moscow	23
Belarus	22
Russia	21
Bulgaria	20
Japan	20
Sweden	19
Denmark	18
China	03

Note: Countries in the left column are ranked according to GNP per capita. / The percentages in the bottom row give each country an equal weight. / na=not ascertained.

V177. Do you find that you get comfort and strength from religion?

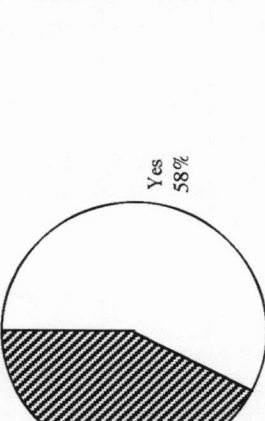

Yes
58%

No
42%

V178. Do you take some moments of prayer, meditation, or contemplation, or something like that?

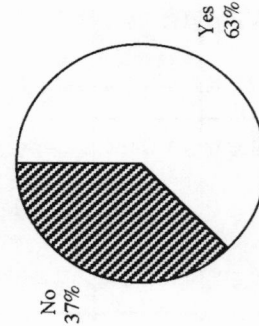

Yes
63%

No
37%

V179. How often do you pray to God outside of religious services?

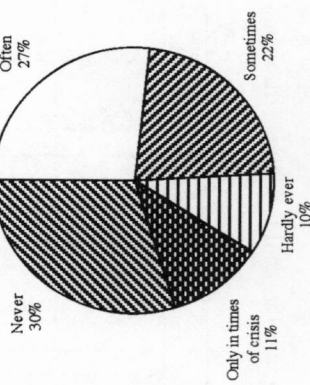

Often
27%

Sometimes
22%

Hardly ever
10%

Only in times
of crisis
11%

Never
30%

V177 COMFORT IN RELIGION

Do you find that you get comfort and strength from religion? (% "yes")

	Total	Gender		Age			Education			Income			Political Affinity			Values		
		Male	Female	16-29	30-49	50+	Lower	Medium	Upper	Lower	Middle	Upper	Left	Center	Right	Mat	Mixed	Postmat
India	81	79	83	76	82	88	90	82	75	83	81	78	76	82	84	82	80	75
Nigeria	96	95	98	95	97	100	99	96	95	97	97	96	98	95	97	99	94	97
China	04	04	04	05	03	04	03	05	03	04	02	05	na	na	na	05	02	08
Romania	76	70	82	65	72	86	89	70	67	80	75	74	75	73	73	81	72	65
Turkey	88	85	90	83	87	97	94	83	67	93	91	79	66	91	99	95	90	75
Poland	90	86	93	86	89	93	95	90	66	90	91	88	81	90	88	93	88	90
Bulgaria	33	24	41	27	26	44	49	28	26	35	31	27	17	33	36	33	32	33
Chile	83	77	89	75	85	91	91	80	77	88	83	77	73	85	88	89	82	74
Czechoslovakia	na	na	na	na	na	na	na	na	na	na	na	na	na	na	na	na	na	na
South Africa	89	84	94	87	90	91	89	89	87	87	91	89	83	89	89	91	89	86
Lithuania	na	na	na	na	na	na	na	na	na	na	na	na	na	na	na	na	na	na
Hungary	49	39	59	24	36	71	65	35	34	62	41	33	21	48	57	53	48	26
Argentina	66	57	73	53	65	76	70	61	62	75	66	55	45	65	74	72	67	55
Brazil	86	82	90	82	87	93	94	85	78	90	88	81	81	85	91	92	84	75
Mexico	77	70	85	74	77	86	77	82	73	75	78	77	58	77	83	84	76	69
Belarus	31	24	38	26	28	43	46	35	22	34	30	29	30	27	44	38	27	37
Russia	35	21	45	24	29	48	49	33	28	39	34	31	24	32	41	39	32	38
Moscow	32	22	39	27	27	42	47	30	29	33	32	28	32	29	28	35	30	30
Latvia	37	24	44	38	26	56	69	30	20	34	36	38	32	29	28	39	37	30
Estonia	na	na	na	na	na	na	na	na	na	na	na	na	na	na	na	na	na	na
Portugal	67	57	77	54	69	78	74	49	56	76	63	56	51	67	75	77	61	57
South Korea	na	na	na	na	na	na	na	na	na	na	na	na	na	na	na	na	na	na
Ireland	83	79	87	67	85	93	87	82	69	89	84	78	61	83	91	90	83	77
North Ireland	77	62	88	63	72	91	81	71	64	85	78	63	74	74	76	84	76	63
Slovenia	51	44	58	40	47	63	66	45	35	67	46	33	40	44	63	59	50	36
Spain	56	39	69	35	51	76	61	48	39	69	54	44	37	63	75	67	53	35
East Germany	31	25	37	20	28	43	33	32	25	42	30	24	13	37	48	41	29	32
Britain	45	33	55	25	41	60	44	48	42	49	41	37	41	42	52	51	44	42
Italy	71	60	82	60	65	84	73	63	56	79	68	46	50	83	79	82	72	59
Netherlands	45	44	46	35	45	57	48	42	45	43	48	44	31	44	65	54	48	37
Belgium	47	39	54	25	40	66	52	44	40	50	42	44	26	50	59	53	48	37
Austria	61	50	68	50	54	71	68	55	57	69	57	58	52	53	68	72	64	47
France	36	31	40	26	28	52	38	34	33	35	34	39	22	41	55	47	36	27
Canada	62	53	71	50	57	79	75	60	55	70	61	54	47	65	65	76	63	52
United States	80	78	83	72	77	87	84	83	75	83	81	76	60	81	89	86	81	74
Iceland	75	64	86	62	75	89	86	76	66	na	na	na	74	74	77	81	76	54
West Germany	45	32	55	26	35	63	49	35	39	52	41	40	29	47	59	61	45	34
Denmark	27	18	37	14	22	44	37	19	27	35	24	18	19	28	32	29	29	18
Finland	49	43	56	30	47	73	56	48	47	57	43	49	40	50	54	72	48	48
Norway	36	28	43	21	28	54	55	27	33	44	30	29	29	39	36	39	35	26
Sweden	27	22	33	23	22	38	25	25	34	28	29	24	20	29	31	32	28	21
Japan	42	32	50	21	38	61	54	41	32	52	40	41	35	37	51	49	37	42
Switzerland	na	na	na	na	na	na	na	na	na	na	na	na	na	na	na	na	na	na
Total	**57**	**49**	**64**	**46**	**53**	**69**	**65**	**54**	**49**	**61**	**55**	**51**	**48**	**59**	**66**	**64**	**56**	**50**

Ranking:

Nigeria	96
Poland	90
South Africa	89
Turkey	88
Brazil	86
Chile	83
Ireland	83
India	81
United States	80
Mexico	77
North Ireland	77
Romania	76
Iceland	75
Italy	71
Portugal	67
Argentina	66
Canada	62
Austria	61
Spain	56
Slovenia	51
Hungary	49
Finland	49
Belgium	47
Britain	45
Netherlands	45
West Germany	45
Japan	42
Latvia	37
France	36
Norway	36
Russia	35
Bulgaria	33
Moscow	32
Belarus	31
East Germany	31
Denmark	27
Sweden	27
China	04

Note: Countries in the left column are ranked according to GNP per capita. / The percentages in the bottom row give each country an equal weight. / na=not ascertained.

V178 PRAYER/MEDITATION

Do you take some moments of prayer, meditation, or contemplation, or something like that? (% "yes")

	Total	Gender		Age			Education			Income			Political Affinity			Values			Ranking:	
		Male	Female	16-29	30-49	50+	Lower	Medium	Upper	Lower	Middle	Upper	Left	Center	Right	Mat	Mixed	Postmat		
India	85	83	88	82	87	87	87	85	84	85	85	86	83	88	83	87	84	87	Nigeria	99
Nigeria	99	98	99	98	99	100	100	98	98	98	99	98	99	99	98	99	98	100	Turkey	90
China	20	16	26	28	16	16	19	20	21	22	19	17	na	na	na	18	21	28	Poland	89
Romania	86	80	93	83	83	92	93	85	80	89	87	84	84	85	84	90	84	83	Brazil	89
Turkey	90	88	92	86	89	96	95	87	71	95	93	82	74	93	96	94	92	78	Romania	86
Poland	89	84	94	84	89	92	94	88	78	91	91	84	81	89	89	91	88	92	South Africa	86
Bulgaria	36	27	43	36	30	41	43	31	35	36	35	31	23	35	41	34	34	47	India	85
Chile	85	80	90	79	87	93	87	83	86	86	85	83	79	86	88	88	84	84	Chile	85
Czechoslovakia	na	na	na	na	na	na	na	na	na	na	na	na	na	na	na	na	na	na	Ireland	84
South Africa	86	82	89	81	88	91	83	86	92	81	86	91	84	85	87	85	86	85	United States	84
Lithuania	na	na	na	na	na	na	na	na	na	na	na	na	na	na	na	na	na	na	Mexico	82
Hungary	58	46	69	44	47	74	68	49	43	68	52	45	36	56	68	61	56	35	North Ireland	76
Argentina	75	67	82	67	75	82	77	74	73	84	76	69	62	74	81	78	78	63	Italy	76
Brazil	89	87	92	86	90	94	94	88	83	91	91	85	87	88	91	89	88	93	Argentina	75
Mexico	82	77	87	80	82	87	83	87	77	83	82	79	70	82	87	84	82	75	Canada	74
Belarus	40	29	50	38	39	46	49	39	38	41	38	42	42	34	45	40	40	45	Austria	72
Russia	37	22	48	33	31	46	44	35	34	41	36	33	30	36	37	40	34	45	West Germany	70
Moscow	49	35	60	51	46	52	52	44	51	45	52	49	50	47	39	53	48	45	Netherlands	68
Latvia	66	56	71	65	67	66	58	67	67	70	69	58	na	na	na	66	65	80	Latvia	66
Estonia	na	na	na	na	na	na	na	na	na	na	na	na	na	na	na	na	na	na	Norway	64
Portugal	61	46	75	48	61	75	69	45	48	70	56	50	48	60	69	65	59	47	Spain	62
South Korea	na	na	na	na	na	na	na	na	na	na	na	na	na	na	na	na	na	na	Portugal	61
Ireland	84	80	88	71	87	90	88	81	72	89	84	79	69	85	87	86	84	83	Hungary	58
North Ireland	76	69	81	65	74	86	77	79	62	77	71	72	82	73	73	77	77	67	Belgium	55
Slovenia	45	37	52	40	39	55	59	38	30	58	39	30	38	36	54	53	42	35	Britain	54
Spain	62	46	76	48	60	75	66	54	52	71	61	55	49	68	78	70	58	52	East Germany	53
East Germany	53	47	57	43	51	60	52	52	55	58	51	49	41	55	65	61	49	57	Moscow	49
Britain	54	44	62	35	55	64	52	58	60	55	53	48	50	53	60	53	55	53	France	46
Italy	76	65	85	71	72	82	76	75	72	77	76	66	64	82	82	80	76	72	Iceland	46
Netherlands	68	66	69	63	72	69	65	65	75	69	69	70	63	68	77	63	70	67	Slovenia	45
Belgium	55	48	62	42	51	68	55	55	56	56	53	59	42	58	66	56	54	57	Denmark	43
Austria	72	62	78	62	70	77	77	68	70	75	71	70	65	68	76	75	71	72	Japan	41
France	46	40	51	43	39	55	45	42	55	40	47	52	38	49	64	46	45	49	Belarus	40
Canada	74	66	80	65	72	83	80	70	74	79	73	69	68	75	76	83	72	74	Russia	37
United States	84	82	87	76	83	88	84	85	83	87	83	80	73	84	89	88	84	80	Bulgaria	36
Iceland	46	35	57	34	49	56	54	42	43	na	69	68	41	47	47	46	46	43	Sweden	34
West Germany	70	62	76	55	66	80	70	67	72	73	69	68	66	69	78	76	69	68	Finland	22
Denmark	43	31	55	34	40	54	49	38	44	49	39	36	36	42	48	42	44	40	China	20
Finland	22	20	24	15	15	47	37	20	17	35	18	15	21	25	18	42	21	20		
Norway	64	59	70	59	63	70	62	54	76	66	62	67	68	63	68	58	66	71		
Sweden	34	28	40	28	31	41	28	33	44	33	36	33	30	35	35	34	34	33		
Japan	41	36	46	27	39	55	51	41	34	46	41	41	41	39	45	48	39	43		
Switzerland	na	na	na	na	na	na	na	na	na	na	na	na	na	na	na	na	na	na		
Total	63	56	70	56	61	71	66	61	61	67	63	60	58	64	69	66	63	62		

Note: Countries in the left column are ranked according to GNP per capita. / The percentages in the bottom row give each country an equal weight. / na=not ascertained.

V179 HOW OFTEN PRAY

How often do you pray to God outside of religious services? Would you say often, sometimes, hardly ever, only in times of crisis, or never? (% "often" or "sometimes")

	Total	Gender		Age			Education			Income			Political Affinity			Values			Ranking:
		Male	Female	16-29	30-49	50+	Lower	Medium	Upper	Lower	Middle	Upper	Left	Center	Right	Mat	Mixed	Postmat	
India	73	68	78	66	77	78	76	73	72	72	73	74	68	75	73	76	72	63	Nigeria 97
Nigeria	97	97	98	97	97	100	99	97	97	97	96	97	99	97	98	99	96	99	Brazil 87
China	06	04	10	08	05	06	05	07	06	na	na	na	na	na	na	na	na	na	Ireland 81
Romania	72	62	81	63	66	82	83	65	67	75	72	68	66	71	69	79	67	60	United States 78
Turkey	na	na	na	na	na	na	na	na	na	na	na	na	na	na	na	na	na	na	Chile 76
Poland	na	na	na	na	na	na	na	na	na	na	na	na	na	na	na	na	na	na	North Ireland 75
Bulgaria	21	14	26	16	17	28	29	16	19	25	15	17	10	21	28	22	19	27	India 73
Chile	76	66	85	68	76	87	83	74	69	80	75	72	63	78	79	83	75	68	Romania 72
Czechoslovakia	na	na	na	na	na	na	na	na	na	na	na	na	na	na	na	na	na	na	Mexico 71
South Africa	na	na	na	na	na	na	na	na	na	na	na	na	na	na	na	na	na	na	Italy 67
Lithuania	na	na	na	na	na	na	na	na	na	na	na	na	na	na	na	na	na	na	Argentina 66
Hungary	38	26	49	22	24	58	50	28	29	51	30	23	15	36	48	44	34	21	Canada 62
Argentina	66	56	75	57	66	74	68	65	63	79	65	55	44	65	72	72	68	53	Portugal 58
Brazil	87	82	92	84	87	92	91	86	81	89	89	84	82	89	89	88	87	86	Austria 57
Mexico	71	64	80	70	70	76	71	76	68	69	72	71	55	72	77	75	70	58	Spain 56
Belarus	16	10	21	10	13	28	33	14	13	21	16	12	14	14	26	20	14	12	Finland 53
Russia	17	08	25	09	12	30	28	15	13	21	17	12	10	15	18	22	14	17	Iceland 51
Moscow	16	07	23	15	14	21	24	15	15	18	16	15	16	14	13	22	15	12	Netherlands 46
Latvia	28	16	34	29	22	35	39	30	19	27	25	29	na	na	na	28	30	11	West Germany 46
Estonia	na	na	na	na	na	na	na	na	na	na	na	na	na	na	na	na	na	na	Britain 43
Portugal	58	41	73	40	57	75	64	42	45	66	51	47	43	56	67	66	53	41	Belgium 41
South Korea	na	na	na	na	na	na	na	na	na	na	na	na	na	na	na	na	na	na	Hungary 38
Ireland	81	75	86	65	81	91	88	76	62	90	83	72	58	81	88	84	81	78	Slovenia 38
North Ireland	75	60	85	56	73	89	77	72	66	83	76	62	71	75	71	75	76	64	Japan 38
Slovenia	38	30	45	30	33	48	53	31	20	50	35	19	29	30	44	48	35	20	Norway 36
Spain	56	39	70	39	52	73	61	49	41	66	54	47	37	63	77	66	53	40	France 34
East Germany	28	21	34	17	24	38	29	28	24	38	26	21	10	34	39	36	27	27	Latvia 28
Britain	43	29	55	24	38	58	44	44	37	46	39	32	38	42	45	46	43	42	East Germany 28
Italy	67	53	80	58	63	77	68	61	55	73	65	48	51	77	73	76	68	58	Denmark 25
Netherlands	46	45	47	33	50	56	52	44	43	44	48	45	30	48	63	58	48	39	Sweden 25
Belgium	41	32	49	23	35	58	44	40	37	45	38	39	23	44	52	45	41	35	Bulgaria 21
Austria	57	44	64	44	51	67	63	53	49	64	55	52	48	50	63	69	58	46	Russia 17
France	34	26	42	26	27	49	38	32	29	35	32	35	21	40	54	43	35	27	Belarus 16
Canada	62	53	72	50	60	76	74	59	58	67	64	54	50	65	63	74	62	57	Moscow 16
United States	78	74	83	70	76	84	82	79	74	80	79	74	54	79	87	85	80	68	China 06
Iceland	51	38	64	37	51	69	60	54	42	na	na	na	43	53	52	56	50	44	
West Germany	46	35	56	26	39	63	50	37	41	52	42	43	30	50	57	60	47	35	
Denmark	25	15	35	14	19	40	35	20	23	33	21	16	14	26	32	25	26	17	
Finland	53	45	62	38	50	72	60	52	51	60	51	49	42	53	59	71	52	52	
Norway	36	26	46	28	29	50	52	27	36	45	28	31	30	36	41	39	36	24	
Sweden	25	17	33	20	21	35	25	22	29	25	30	22	22	24	28	28	26	22	
Japan	38	30	45	27	35	51	46	39	30	44	35	40	38	35	44	40	38	40	
Switzerland	na	na	na	na	na	na	na	na	na	na	na	na	na	na	na	na	na	na	
Total	**49**	**40**	**57**	**39**	**46**	**60**	**56**	**46**	**44**	**54**	**48**	**44**	**40**	**52**	**57**	**55**	**49**	**42**	

Note: Countries in the left column are ranked according to GNP per capita. / The percentages in the bottom row give each country an equal weight. / na=not ascertained.

V180 HOME SATISFACTION

Overall, how satisfied or dissatisfied are you with your home life?

(% "satisfied"—codes 7 to 10 from a ten point scale where 1=Dissatisfied and 10= Satisfied)

	Total	Gender		Age			Education			Income			Political Affinity			Values			Ranking:	
		Male	Female	16-29	30-49	50+	Lower	Medium	Upper	Lower	Middle	Upper	Left	Center	Right	Mat	Mixed	Postmat		
India	65	64	67	63	67	63	50	66	72	49	68	76	58	61	73	65	68	67	North Ireland	91
Nigeria	71	66	78	71	71	75	70	68	74	61	71	86	72	66	73	73	69	71	Netherlands	91
China	77	75	81	68	81	80	77	77	77	73	80	78	na	na	na	78	76	70	Denmark	91
Romania	62	63	61	61	66	59	57	63	66	41	61	77	61	64	63	61	63	62	Ireland	89
Turkey	54	54	55	52	59	51	52	54	64	42	54	69	52	53	59	50	56	57	Canada	89
Poland	86	88	85	84	87	86	85	87	88	83	84	92	84	84	92	85	86	92	Sweden	89
Bulgaria	46	50	42	47	47	45	40	47	48	33	44	64	45	43	50	46	46	42	Switzerland	89
Chile	83	83	83	79	84	85	81	85	81	78	85	85	77	83	87	84	82	83	Iceland	88
Czechoslovakia	70	73	66	69	70	70	64	71	77	61	76	71	72	67	73	67	70	71	United States	87
South Africa	60	59	61	57	61	66	46	64	92	36	62	90	56	70	78	63	59	63	Poland	86
Lithuania	50	56	45	52	50	49	50	50	50	46	52	54	na	na	na	47	51	50	Britain	85
Hungary	73	75	72	74	74	71	71	75	75	67	77	81	74	76	75	73	73	73	Belgium	85
Argentina	79	80	79	77	82	79	82	77	80	73	83	83	74	81	84	81	78	80	Chile	83
Brazil	81	84	78	78	82	84	81	81	82	78	81	86	78	81	84	81	81	80	Norway	83
Mexico	76	75	77	74	79	73	72	82	81	70	77	85	69	77	85	76	77	74	Brazil	81
Belarus	55	65	47	48	57	58	54	53	58	55	58	52	55	57	59	56	55	52	Italy	81
Russia	58	64	53	56	59	58	56	56	61	56	60	60	60	57	63	57	59	55	Portugal	80
Moscow	61	70	54	63	61	60	63	58	63	59	63	62	62	58	68	63	62	57	Finland	80
Latvia	44	46	42	46	40	49	40	43	45	42	43	45	na	na	na	43	42	51	Argentina	79
Estonia	47	51	44	51	47	44	44	48	49	45	52	47	na	na	na	46	49	48	Spain	78
Portugal	80	79	81	76	84	82	82	81	74	81	84	80	81	79	84	82	81	74	China	77
South Korea	66	61	71	64	69	63	54	64	75	56	67	81	53	62	73	67	68	55	Mexico	76
Ireland	89	88	89	85	89	91	88	90	91	83	91	92	84	88	94	91	88	89	West Germany	76
North Ireland	91	88	92	84	91	95	88	96	90	80	95	95	75	93	93	97	89	89	Hungary	73
Slovenia	68	68	69	69	72	64	63	69	78	59	71	82	69	70	66	67	68	75	East Germany	73
Spain	78	81	75	75	83	75	77	81	78	68	82	82	76	78	82	77	80	77	France	72
East Germany	73	76	71	65	77	74	72	75	78	67	73	79	75	72	73	67	74	73	Nigeria	71
Britain	85	87	83	78	87	87	85	86	85	82	84	91	82	84	90	87	85	83	Czechoslovakia	70
Italy	81	82	79	79	87	82	81	81	69	80	81	71	78	83	79	82	81	77	Slovenia	68
Netherlands	91	94	90	92	91	89	90	88	95	85	96	96	91	91	92	87	93	90	South Korea	66
Belgium	85	87	83	84	87	84	81	89	86	83	87	90	83	86	88	83	87	86	India	65
Austria	59	60	59	70	62	51	56	61	61	56	59	62	56	59	63	58	57	66	Romania	62
France	72	74	70	71	71	75	70	76	72	66	73	79	70	74	78	72	73	73	Japan	62
Canada	89	89	90	87	88	92	88	90	90	84	90	94	87	90	92	95	88	90	Moscow	61
United States	87	88	86	84	86	89	84	88	88	78	90	94	83	88	90	87	86	91	South Africa	60
Iceland	88	88	88	84	93	87	89	88	89	na	na	na	90	85	89	86	89	89	Austria	59
West Germany	76	77	76	72	79	76	75	76	79	69	76	82	72	78	82	71	77	78	Russia	58
Denmark	91	92	91	90	92	91	90	91	91	86	93	94	86	93	95	87	93	86	Belarus	55
Finland	80	81	80	83	80	78	77	81	81	79	80	81	79	75	84	85	80	80	Turkey	54
Norway	83	83	84	87	87	76	75	85	86	72	90	88	77	86	87	81	85	84	Lithuania	50
Sweden	89	88	90	86	89	91	87	88	89	92	81	95	87	90	91	94	89	88	Estonia	47
Japan	62	60	65	62	64	60	53	63	69	53	61	72	71	57	71	64	62	63	Bulgaria	46
Switzerland	89	89	90	88	90	89	91	88	90	88	92	93	87	89	92	93	90	86	Latvia	44
Total	73	74	73	72	75	73	70	74	76	66	74	79	73	75	79	73	74	73		

Note: Countries in the left column are ranked according to GNP per capita. / The percentages in the bottom row give each country an equal weight. / na=not ascertained.

V181. Marital status

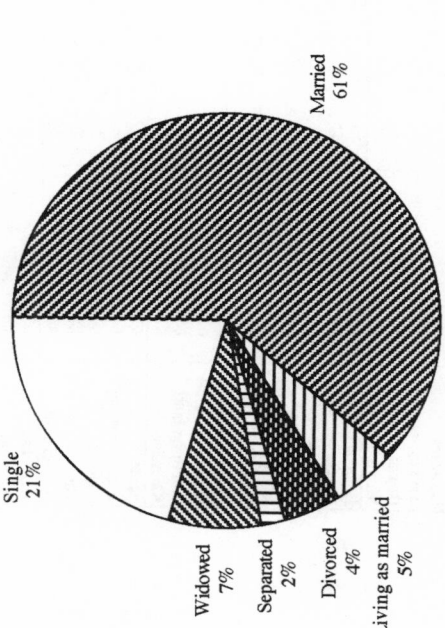

Married
61%

Single
21%

Widowed
7%

Separated
2%

Divorced
4%

Living as married
5%

V182. Have you been married before

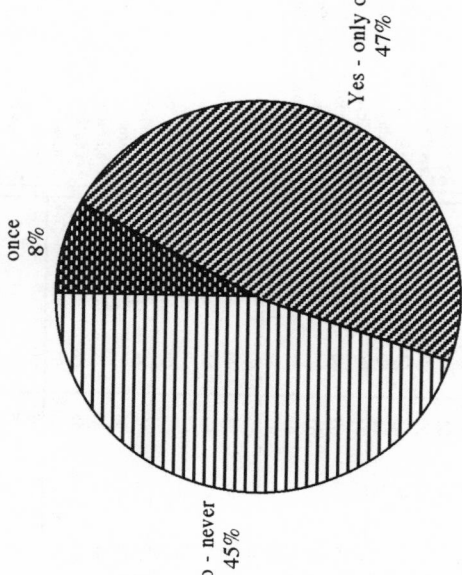

Yes - only once
47%

Yes - more than
once
8%

No - never
45%

V181 MARITAL STATUS
Are you currently... (% "married")

	Total	Gender		Age			Education			Income			Political Affinity			Values		
		Male	Female	16-29	30-49	50+	Lower	Medium	Upper	Lower	Middle	Upper	Left	Center	Right	Mat	Mixed	Postmat
India	69	65	73	37	90	82	77	65	68	67	70	69	64	67	71	70	67	69
Nigeria	51	45	61	26	81	77	72	43	51	52	52	53	50	52	47	59	45	52
China	77	78	75	41	95	89	80	73	80	77	79	77	na	na	na	82	74	72
Romania	67	70	64	35	82	73	74	62	65	61	71	66	69	66	65	74	63	51
Turkey	72	71	72	42	94	78	80	66	43	71	76	67	69	69	78	78	73	59
Poland	73	76	71	39	88	76	69	73	84	72	75	73	79	74	75	69	76	67
Bulgaria	75	77	73	50	86	77	77	76	72	71	78	78	81	75	69	76	75	67
Chile	54	57	52	31	70	63	62	53	47	48	59	56	52	57	56	55	55	52
Czechoslovakia	67	70	63	47	81	63	59	67	81	45	81	71	72	67	63	65	68	65
South Africa	51	49	53	18	77	65	56	46	71	41	50	71	48	55	59	58	49	38
Lithuania	61	69	54	32	79	67	58	60	70	54	71	61	na	na	na	60	61	58
Hungary	70	76	63	50	81	67	68	71	68	61	75	78	76	74	62	69	71	68
Argentina	59	58	60	27	76	67	64	56	54	53	62	63	56	61	56	63	59	56
Brazil	50	51	50	30	62	64	61	46	44	49	51	52	44	50	51	53	48	47
Mexico	46	49	42	21	67	63	52	43	31	46	47	47	44	44	51	50	47	37
Belarus	72	82	64	56	80	72	69	72	74	77	74	65	70	79	71	71	72	75
Russia	68	77	62	51	81	65	67	67	71	70	71	68	72	69	69	69	69	65
Moscow	70	78	63	61	76	65	62	67	72	72	70	65	71	65	83	69	71	64
Latvia	67	77	61	49	77	69	62	66	71	67	67	68	na	na	na	71	66	69
Estonia	57	66	50	38	71	58	44	59	67	57	61	54	58	na	na	59	58	49
Portugal	57	59	54	23	79	69	69	39	38	61	62	45	58	57	55	67	53	38
South Korea	65	60	68	14	89	88	83	62	59	49	74	84	46	58	73	74	62	35
Ireland	62	61	62	20	85	65	68	56	48	56	69	65	53	64	63	65	63	55
North Ireland	65	60	68	40	81	65	70	61	38	50	76	69	68	67	61	63	66	60
Slovenia	67	66	68	32	81	74	61	68	77	63	72	64	71	65	60	72	66	52
Spain	62	62	62	25	84	69	68	58	38	54	67	63	60	64	61	72	63	49
East Germany	64	72	57	47	79	59	61	67	72	33	79	79	64	64	66	53	65	66
Britain	60	64	56	31	77	61	60	58	58	47	68	68	51	64	65	56	62	58
Italy	61	65	58	20	78	71	64	40	38	63	64	59	61	58	55	68	63	58
Netherlands	56	58	55	30	71	64	69	58	40	34	70	73	47	58	65	61	62	47
Belgium	60	59	60	29	75	66	62	63	48	46	67	63	51	64	63	60	62	54
Austria	63	69	59	25	80	65	64	62	63	45	73	67	63	62	65	60	64	61
France	57	54	59	24	71	67	56	62	49	46	61	69	54	60	59	56	59	49
Canada	58	61	56	28	73	68	57	61	56	37	64	71	50	61	63	64	58	59
United States	64	68	59	42	71	66	58	66	66	49	65	79	58	67	66	64	64	64
Iceland	54	51	57	19	70	68	60	54	50	na	62	65	59	52	55	56	55	45
West Germany	54	58	51	19	72	61	61	43	47	40	62	65	48	54	62	59	58	47
Denmark	51	50	53	14	64	65	56	47	52	36	56	72	43	57	72	53	52	70
Finland	70	72	68	41	81	65	51	71	78	47	76	83	72	69	66	65	70	53
Norway	63	64	61	22	74	76	72	60	60	40	71	79	54	68	50	69	62	46
Sweden	53	51	54	18	63	70	59	44	58	62	27	77	54	55	50	56	55	46
Japan	76	77	74	23	92	87	83	76	67	72	82	74	68	75	66	79	73	75
Switzerland	61	63	59	27	73	65	62	63	51	40	74	67	56	66	60	66	62	56
Total	**62**	**64**	**61**	**32**	**78**	**69**	**65**	**60**	**59**	**54**	**67**	**68**	**60**	**63**	**63**	**65**	**62**	**56**

Ranking:

China	77
Japan	76
Bulgaria	75
Poland	73
Turkey	72
Belarus	72
Hungary	70
Moscow	70
Finland	70
India	69
Russia	68
Romania	67
Czechoslovakia	67
Latvia	67
Slovenia	67
South Korea	65
North Ireland	65
East Germany	64
United States	64
Austria	63
Norway	63
Ireland	62
Spain	62
Lithuania	61
Italy	61
Switzerland	61
Britain	60
Belgium	60
Argentina	59
Canada	58
Estonia	57
Portugal	57
France	57
Netherlands	56
Chile	54
Iceland	54
West Germany	54
Sweden	53
Nigeria	51
South Africa	51
Denmark	51
Brazil	50
Mexico	46

Note: Countries in the left column are ranked according to GNP per capita. / The percentages in the bottom row give each country an equal weight. / na=not ascertained.

V182 MARRIED BEFORE

Have you been married before? (% No–Never)

	Total	Gender		Age			Education			Income			Political Affinity			Values		
		Male	Female	16-29	30-49	50+	Lower	Medium	Upper	Lower	Middle	Upper	Left	Center	Right	Mat	Mixed	Postmat
India	94	94	94	95	95	91	90	95	95	94	93	95	97	93	95	95	94	94
Nigeria	44	51	32	70	12	07	22	51	44	44	42	41	46	41	49	37	48	45
China	21	20	21	61	04	01	16	26	23	19	19	22	na	na	na	15	27	26
Romania	80	83	77	97	82	68	74	86	80	72	82	84	80	78	82	78	82	79
Turkey	85	86	84	96	86	69	81	89	97	79	87	89	86	83	87	80	86	90
Poland	na	na	na	na	na	na	na	na	na	na	na	na	na	na	na	na	na	na
Bulgaria	13	14	12	47	05	02	03	15	20	12	13	14	09	12	21	08	13	28
Chile	80	84	76	93	79	63	72	86	82	74	83	83	84	80	81	76	81	82
Czechoslovakia	75	81	70	94	78	60	67	79	78	59	80	86	77	74	75	72	76	80
South Africa	na	na	na	na	na	na	na	na	na	na	na	na	na	na	na	na	na	na
Lithuania	na	na	na	na	na	na	na	na	na	na	na	na	na	na	na	na	na	na
Hungary	76	83	70	88	81	69	70	82	82	69	80	82	79	77	78	76	77	78
Argentina	65	67	63	67	67	62	66	66	61	63	70	63	63	66	73	71	64	58
Brazil	02	02	02	04	01	01	02	02	00	02	03	00	01	03	01	02	02	02
Mexico	77	76	78	91	71	54	73	77	87	74	78	79	76	77	77	74	78	83
Belarus	na	na	na	na	na	na	na	na	na	na	na	na	na	na	na	na	na	na
Russia	19	21	18	45	14	08	12	23	20	74	16	23	18	20	19	15	22	22
Moscow	71	78	64	87	69	61	65	73	71	67	73	71	72	69	71	67	72	69
Latvia	na	na	na	na	na	na	na	na	na	na	na	na	na	na	na	na	na	na
Estonia	na	na	na	na	na	na	na	na	na	na	na	na	na	na	na	na	na	na
Portugal	31	33	29	75	10	06	17	50	68	21	30	47	30	32	31	20	33	57
South Korea	na	na	na	na	na	na	na	na	na	na	na	na	na	na	na	na	na	na
Ireland	30	34	27	79	12	15	19	41	50	27	25	31	41	30	26	22	30	40
North Ireland	23	30	18	58	16	10	18	31	33	13	28	27	32	22	22	16	21	30
Slovenia	88	92	84	99	90	79	85	90	89	85	89	91	94	89	93	85	90	85
Spain	72	75	68	91	72	57	67	79	85	65	77	65	76	70	59	68	70	85
East Germany	18	20	15	47	11	06	17	24	15	24	13	15	23	14	17	09	17	23
Britain	22	25	19	63	10	08	18	31	33	18	21	28	28	22	17	21	22	21
Italy	27	31	24	79	17	04	25	48	50	22	28	37	30	26	30	16	26	28
Netherlands	29	27	29	68	15	15	11	31	48	40	19	20	36	27	22	13	25	39
Belgium	24	30	18	69	11	06	14	24	41	25	23	21	32	21	23	14	23	36
Austria	09	08	09	38	09	03	07	10	09	03	10	12	10	08	09	05	08	13
France	29	32	26	72	17	07	24	29	40	31	26	25	31	29	22	21	27	41
Canada	66	71	61	89	63	49	53	70	70	58	67	69	65	65	67	53	68	68
United States	60	60	60	81	59	52	54	61	63	55	58	67	58	60	64	56	62	59
Iceland	95	97	92	98	86	94	100	91	94	91	94	98	94	94	98	97	94	100
West Germany	26	29	23	78	17	04	16	44	42	24	26	26	37	25	14	11	22	41
Denmark	16	20	13	66	14	00	05	20	20	08	24	19	24	14	14	14	15	22
Finland	71	72	70	91	72	49	65	71	74	57	74	79	68	70	70	59	70	75
Norway	na	na	na	na	na	na	na	na	na	na	na	na	na	na	na	na	na	na
Sweden	74	82	66	99	66	44	64	83	71	70	72	72	68	75	76	73	72	81
Japan	20	21	19	78	07	02	08	21	32	19	15	20	25	22	11	15	24	22
Switzerland	na	na	na	na	na	na	na	na	na	na	na	na	na	na	na	na	na	na
Total	48	51	45	75	42	33	41	53	56	44	46	49	51	48	48	43	48	54

Ranking:

Iceland	95
India	94
Slovenia	88
Turkey	85
Romania	80
Chile	80
Mexico	77
Hungary	76
Czechoslovakia	75
Sweden	74
Spain	72
Moscow	71
Finland	71
Canada	66
Argentina	65
United States	60
Nigeria	44
Portugal	31
Ireland	30
Netherlands	29
France	29
Italy	27
West Germany	26
Belgium	24
North Ireland	23
Britain	22
China	21
Japan	20
Russia	19
East Germany	18
Denmark	16
Bulgaria	13
Austria	09
Brazil	02

Note: Countries in the left column are ranked according to GNP per capita. / The percentages in the bottom row give each country an equal weight. / na=not ascertained.

V183-V189. Do (did) you and your partner share any of the following?

Percentage

	Percentage
Moral attitudes	61
Social attitudes	56
Sexual attitudes	54
Attitudes towards religion	50
Political attitudes	40
None of these	4
Don't know	4

V183 PARTNER: RELIGION
Do (did) you and your partner share any of the following?   Attitudes towards religion   (% "yes")

	Total	Gender		Age			Education			Income			Political Affinity			Values			Ranking:	
		Male	Female	16-29	30-49	50+	Lower	Medium	Upper	Lower	Middle	Upper	Left	Center	Right	Mat	Mixed	Postmat		
India	62	55	69	31	80	80	80	59	55	64	63	58	53	58	68	64	58	60	Turkey	71
Nigeria	54	46	65	28	83	95	78	46	52	55	55	54	52	56	47	62	49	49	India	62
China	37	35	41	18	47	44	42	34	37	40	40	32	na	na	na	40	35	35	United States	62
Romania	59	59	60	27	66	74	73	51	53	64	60	56	62	58	58	68	56	36	Slovenia	60
Turkey	71	69	73	39	89	89	82	62	36	74	75	63	61	71	76	80	73	54	Switzerland	60
Poland	na	na	na	na	na	na	na	na	na	na	na	na	na	na	na	na	na	na	Romania	59
Bulgaria	54	53	55	31	57	66	70	47	52	59	54	54	58	61	44	58	55	44	Norway	59
Chile	53	53	53	25	65	74	64	48	45	54	55	49	47	56	56	60	51	48	North Ireland	58
Czechoslovakia	na	na	na	na	na	na	na	na	na	na	na	na	na	na	na	na	na	na	Hungary	56
South Africa	na	na	na	na	na	na	na	na	na	na	na	na	na	na	na	na	na	na	Ireland	56
Lithuania	43	45	42	16	54	56	53	38	54	41	47	43	na	na	na	48	42	39	Spain	56
Hungary	56	55	57	29	54	68	62	49	54	61	50	55	55	57	53	58	55	48	Iceland	56
Argentina	48	46	50	21	57	60	55	43	42	54	49	45	36	48	51	53	49	41	Sweden	56
Brazil	49	49	49	27	60	72	55	43	35	54	49	45	33	37	46	45	38	24	Canada	55
Mexico	44	46	42	18	61	79	66	46	40	46	46	45	41	56	62	61	58	46	Nigeria	54
Belarus	39	43	35	26	61	73	64	51	30	45	45	43	39	58	63	68	57	51	Bulgaria	54
Russia	42	42	42	29	39	50	46	35	40	48	36	36	67	57	59	39	39	42	Chile	53
Moscow	42	45	40	33	43	49	43	38	45	42	45	42	47	58	66	44	40	47	Denmark	53
Latvia	34	39	31	28	36	47	27	34	47	32	33	37	na	na	na	28	38	38	Italy	52
Estonia	47	55	41	26	55	57	42	45	59	49	45	46	na	na	na	53	49	39	Netherlands	51
Portugal	39	35	43	11	47	59	48	23	22	49	45	46	na	na	na	53	49	34	Brazil	49
South Korea	na	na	na	na	na	na	na	na	na	na	na	na	na	na	na	na	na	na	Britain	49
Ireland	56	54	58	na	na	72	na	na	40	na	62	54	40	47	58	45	38	46	Argentina	48
North Ireland	58	57	59	15	59	79	66	46	40	61	61	54	41	56	52	61	58	45	Estonia	47
Slovenia	60	58	62	26	65	73	64	51	38	70	61	47	39	58	63	68	57	51	Austria	47
Spain	56	50	61	32	64	74	62	42	54	64	59	55	53	57	49	68	53	39	France	46
East Germany	38	38	38	20	41	44	37	31	46	66	56	49	50	64	66	39	53	39	Mexico	44
Britain	49	44	53	22	48	63	48	49	49	33	39	42	52	55	39	39	37	40	Belgium	44
Italy	52	50	54	25	57	72	54	37	49	51	48	46	30	40	44	59	48	44	Lithuania	43
Netherlands	51	54	50	15	54	68	57	54	41	58	53	41	45	58	45	63	52	45	Russia	42
Belgium	44	42	46	32	50	53	46	42	41	40	55	66	40	56	58	56	46	41	Moscow	42
Austria	47	44	49	22	48	58	56	42	41	41	47	51	47	43	52	47	46	40	Belarus	39
France	46	45	47	20	52	52	45	51	39	49	48	45	44	49	48	57	47	41	Portugal	39
Canada	55	55	56	29	52	72	59	56	52	43	49	50	53	57	56	50	47	40	West Germany	39
United States	62	63	61	34	61	73	60	63	63	49	59	60	50	64	68	58	55	55	East Germany	38
Iceland	56	55	56	39	62	65	56	60	68	58	63	68	52	55	61	68	62	57	Finland	38
West Germany	39	37	41	10	39	55	44	29	54	na	na	na	30	40	53	54	55	55	China	37
Denmark	53	53	53	26	62	64	60	50	34	40	38	42	45	58	55	54	41	29	Latvia	34
Finland	38	39	38	30	40	41	30	39	41	44	62	58	31	42	41	35	55	43	Japan	34
Norway	59	57	61	40	66	67	63	59	41	65	66	69	55	63	60	64	59	44		
Sweden	56	54	57	35	60	71	61	52	56	42	42	39	56	62	51	59	57	50		
Japan	34	32	35	08	39	43	39	33	30	32	34	39	34	35	43	44	33	35		
Switzerland	60	57	62	28	61	72	61	64	38	56	63	58	50	62	64	70	61	51		
Total	**50**	**49**	**51**	**25**	**56**	**64**	**55**	**46**	**45**	**51**	**51**	**49**	**46**	**52**	**54**	**55**	**49**	**44**		

Note: Countries in the left column are ranked according to GNP per capita. / The percentages in the bottom row give each country an equal weight. / na=not ascertained.

V184 PARTNER: MORAL

Do (did) you and your partner share any of the following? Moral attitudes (% "yes")

	Total	Gender		Age			Education			Income			Political Affinity			Values		
		Male	Female	16-29	30-49	50+	Lower	Medium	Upper	Lower	Middle	Upper	Left	Center	Right	Mat	Mixed	Postmat
India	63	58	67	33	81	81	73	59	61	59	65	63	55	55	68	66	48	60
Nigeria	54	46	65	28	82	93	77	46	52	54	54	56	53	55	47	62	48	49
China	70	69	72	34	87	85	73	66	72	72	72	68	na	na	na	77	65	61
Romania	63	65	60	28	70	77	72	53	64	64	62	62	64	62	64	69	59	47
Turkey	73	71	75	41	92	90	83	66	42	74	76	69	67	73	78	82	75	57
Poland	na	na	na	na	na	na	na	na	na	na	na	na	na	na	na	na	na	na
Bulgaria	68	68	68	39	70	83	79	63	65	71	70	67	75	73	63	70	69	55
Chile	60	60	61	31	73	82	72	56	52	58	64	61	58	63	59	66	59	58
Czechoslovakia	na	na	na	na	na	na	na	na	na	na	na	na	na	na	na	na	na	na
South Africa	na	na	na	na	na	na	na	na	na	na	na	na	na	na	na	na	na	na
Lithuania	48	53	44	19	57	64	54	43	66	45	52	48	na	na	na	52	47	45
Hungary	75	74	76	43	79	85	78	73	71	74	75	77	75	79	77	78	74	65
Argentina	67	62	70	28	80	81	75	61	58	67	68	71	62	66	66	70	67	61
Brazil	59	58	60	34	71	81	73	53	51	63	58	57	47	60	65	64	56	51
Mexico	47	48	45	20	64	76	51	45	34	48	47	47	47	44	51	52	47	40
Belarus	56	62	51	39	62	63	54	49	64	60	56	53	54	62	56	60	54	63
Russia	56	59	55	35	61	65	58	52	60	64	58	55	60	62	53	62	53	56
Moscow	67	69	65	53	68	74	64	59	72	67	66	68	69	62	79	67	68	66
Latvia	46	52	42	35	51	50	35	43	55	47	49	44	na	na	na	42	49	49
Estonia	50	57	45	29	59	60	47	50	56	51	48	52	na	na	na	57	51	36
Portugal	48	45	50	17	60	66	57	35	23	55	48	36	47	47	49	53	48	32
South Korea	na	na	na	na	na	na	na	na	na	na	na	na	na	na	na	na	na	na
Ireland	62	59	65	20	77	75	71	54	49	63	68	62	55	62	67	66	63	56
North Ireland	68	64	72	38	75	82	75	63	41	67	78	67	64	68	71	71	69	62
Slovenia	64	64	65	34	71	77	62	64	70	64	68	57	64	64	63	73	61	59
Spain	67	62	71	27	81	84	74	58	44	73	69	62	63	68	71	82	65	51
East Germany	54	55	53	33	61	59	51	53	66	46	59	57	55	54	49	62	54	50
Britain	69	67	70	39	76	80	70	69	46	68	70	72	63	69	77	74	69	65
Italy	64	61	67	18	72	86	66	47	53	69	65	53	60	68	65	75	65	54
Netherlands	62	64	61	39	68	78	71	60	60	46	69	79	56	64	68	67	66	55
Belgium	54	51	57	30	63	62	54	55	50	48	57	63	53	58	60	57	56	50
Austria	55	55	56	24	59	66	60	51	60	49	59	55	53	53	60	52	56	56
France	59	59	59	34	73	63	55	65	57	50	64	70	60	62	59	60	59	58
Canada	68	68	69	39	79	82	69	70	66	58	72	77	66	70	70	68	68	70
United States	72	73	71	45	75	82	68	72	75	63	72	83	68	74	75	76	72	71
Iceland	71	66	75	49	82	76	70	75	69	na	na	na	71	72	71	71	70	72
West Germany	50	50	50	17	54	65	54	40	48	49	48	55	43	51	62	61	52	42
Denmark	63	62	65	30	73	78	69	59	63	51	70	79	59	68	66	61	64	57
Finland	55	57	54	37	61	57	46	55	60	40	63	59	60	53	60	47	53	63
Norway	70	69	71	40	78	79	75	66	71	52	77	83	64	74	74	74	70	66
Sweden	66	64	67	39	70	82	69	59	73	76	51	76	68	67	65	66	66	65
Japan	44	45	43	11	54	51	42	46	40	38	46	50	44	42	59	54	45	48
Switzerland	70	68	71	37	75	79	70	73	57	61	77	73	65	73	71	80	69	67
Total	61	60	62	32	70	74	65	57	57	59	63	63	60	63	64	65	61	56

Ranking:

Hungary	75
Turkey	73
United States	72
Iceland	71
China	70
Norway	70
Switzerland	70
Britain	69
Bulgaria	68
North Ireland	68
Canada	68
Argentina	67
Moscow	67
Spain	67
Sweden	66
Slovenia	64
Italy	64
India	63
Romania	63
Denmark	63
Ireland	62
Netherlands	62
Chile	60
Brazil	59
France	59
Belarus	56
Russia	56
Austria	55
Finland	55
Nigeria	54
East Germany	54
Belgium	54
Estonia	50
West Germany	50
Lithuania	48
Portugal	48
Mexico	47
Latvia	46
Japan	44

Note: Countries in the left column are ranked according to GNP per capita. / The percentages in the bottom row give each country an equal weight. / na=not ascertained.

V185 PARTNER: SOCIAL

Do (did) you and your partner share any of the following? Social attitudes (% "yes")

Country	Total	Gender Male	Gender Female	Age 16-29	Age 30-49	Age 50+	Education Lower	Education Medium	Education Upper	Income Lower	Income Middle	Income Upper	Political Left	Political Center	Political Right	Values Mat	Values Mixed	Values Postmat
India	60	56	64	31	78	77	67	58	59	56	62	61	56	58	65	64	58	56
Nigeria	52	44	64	27	79	91	74	45	51	51	52	56	51	53	46	60	47	44
China	54	52	57	24	68	67	56	52	54	53	54	57	na	na	na	58	52	48
Romania	57	60	55	28	66	68	65	51	57	55	59	57	57	59	56	62	55	46
Turkey	71	68	74	40	89	88	82	61	42	75	75	64	63	71	77	80	74	53
Poland	na	na	na	na	na	na	na	na	na	na	na	na	na	na	na	na	na	na
Bulgaria	59	59	59	34	63	70	63	57	59	na	59	61	68	62	56	64	58	57
Chile	52	54	51	26	65	69	59	51	46	49	56	51	51	53	52	56	52	50
Czechoslovakia	na	na	na	na	na	na	na	na	na	na	na	na	na	na	na	na	na	na
South Africa	na	na	na	na	na	na	na	na	na	na	na	na	na	na	na	na	na	na
Lithuania	43	47	40	19	54	53	45	39	62	40	47	44	na	na	na	43	44	39
Hungary	61	61	62	39	65	67	62	59	64	59	61	68	68	64	58	62	62	48
Argentina	65	61	69	31	79	77	71	63	56	68	67	66	63	65	65	70	65	59
Brazil	56	56	57	30	69	79	70	50	49	61	52	55	45	57	64	60	54	49
Mexico	41	43	40	19	58	61	46	37	31	41	43	44	43	39	46	46	42	35
Belarus	60	63	56	42	67	63	56	54	66	61	61	57	60	63	56	60	59	64
Russia	53	54	52	36	58	58	51	47	59	58	57	54	56	58	50	55	51	60
Moscow	68	70	67	55	72	70	64	59	74	68	68	67	71	62	71	65	70	67
Latvia	46	52	43	34	52	48	29	43	58	46	48	46	na	na	na	43	48	49
Estonia	50	56	45	33	57	58	43	50	58	52	47	50	na	na	na	52	52	51
Portugal	40	40	41	15	54	53	46	33	25	42	45	50	43	42	39	44	41	30
South Korea	na	na	na	na	na	na	na	na	na	na	na	na	na	na	na	na	na	na
Ireland	60	57	62	20	73	72	68	51	43	61	65	59	51	60	58	51	61	60
North Ireland	61	56	65	30	68	76	65	60	56	66	65	62	43	63	65	63	62	59
Slovenia	62	62	62	31	70	73	56	63	71	64	64	53	65	64	67	69	60	49
Spain	66	63	68	27	79	82	72	58	42	70	67	62	63	65	71	80	64	58
East Germany	50	50	49	24	53	58	55	48	58	43	56	47	51	50	46	55	54	46
Britain	67	67	68	35	56	77	50	48	53	48	53	44	51	50	55	58	48	51
Italy	56	54	58	36	77	77	69	63	64	68	66	70	61	66	76	71	68	64
Netherlands	58	63	56	14	64	76	58	43	32	62	55	44	53	61	55	66	57	50
Belgium	52	51	53	35	61	79	52	55	45	43	67	70	52	59	65	64	62	50
Austria	50	50	49	27	60	61	55	46	46	47	53	62	53	52	55	55	54	46
France	53	56	50	24	53	58	50	55	53	48	56	71	45	51	51	51	48	51
Canada	63	60	65	31	64	59	64	58	60	55	66	52	54	55	52	52	54	64
United States	69	71	67	38	71	75	63	63	73	61	70	70	60	65	63	58	62	68
Iceland	66	63	69	47	73	77	65	63	46	na	na	62	67	70	74	73	65	68
West Germany	48	47	50	46	75	73	52	49	61	47	48	52	43	49	56	67	50	62
Denmark	60	61	60	19	53	61	64	55	54	49	69	72	57	64	62	61	61	41
Finland	47	44	50	32	67	74	37	45	61	37	51	52	55	42	52	54	46	62
Norway	60	60	61	30	50	54	70	55	52	65	76	68	60	61	62	47	59	49
Sweden	58	59	58	38	59	77	64	52	61	60	50	67	61	59	58	65	59	59
Japan	38	38	38	09	47	44	37	39	38	31	39	46	33	40	56	61	41	42
Switzerland	69	69	68	37	72	79	70	71	52	62	76	68	64	73	68	45	68	64
Total	**56**	**57**	**57**	**31**	**65**	**68**	**59**	**53**	**53**	**55**	**58**	**58**	**56**	**58**	**60**	**60**	**57**	**52**

Ranking:

Turkey	71
United States	69
Switzerland	69
Moscow	68
Britain	67
Spain	66
Iceland	66
Argentina	65
Canada	63
Slovenia	62
Hungary	61
North Ireland	61
India	60
Belarus	60
Ireland	60
Denmark	60
Norway	60
Bulgaria	59
Netherlands	58
Sweden	58
Romania	57
Brazil	56
Italy	56
China	54
Russia	53
France	53
Nigeria	52
Chile	52
Belgium	52
Estonia	50
East Germany	50
Austria	50
West Germany	48
Finland	47
Latvia	46
Lithuania	43
Mexico	41
Portugal	40
Japan	38

Note: Countries in the left column are ranked according to GNP per capita. / The percentages in the bottom row give each country an equal weight. / na=not ascertained.

V186 PARTNER: POLITICS
Do (did) you and your partner share any of the following? Political attitudes (% "yes")

	Total	Gender		Age			Education			Income			Political Affinity			Values		
		Male	Female	16-29	30-49	50+	Lower	Medium	Upper	Lower	Middle	Upper	Left	Center	Right	Mat	Mixed	Postmat
India	29	25	35	17	38	35	28	31	25	23	31	34	28	31	31	28	31	37
Nigeria	23	20	27	11	36	39	34	17	25	24	24	24	17	25	28	27	21	14
China	44	42	46	16	56	55	44	40	48	43	47	41	na	na	na	46	43	33
Romania	38	41	34	18	44	44	39	37	38	41	39	34	43	36	39	40	35	41
Turkey	59	57	61	32	74	76	67	51	36	64	59	55	53	60	65	69	61	41
Poland	na	na	na	na	na	na	na	na	na	na	na	na	na	na	na	na	na	na
Bulgaria	51	49	52	27	54	60	57	47	51	54	50	54	55	52	51	54	51	48
Chile	32	33	31	15	44	38	31	31	35	24	33	42	41	31	34	28	32	40
Czechoslovakia	na	na	na	na	na	na	na	na	na	na	na	na	na	na	na	na	na	na
South Africa	na	na	na	na	na	na	na	na	na	na	na	na	na	na	na	na	na	na
Lithuania	38	43	34	15	48	48	39	34	58	35	44	37	na	na	na	38	39	35
Hungary	43	41	44	25	47	46	40	43	54	39	42	55	51	46	40	44	43	28
Argentina	45	41	49	21	56	51	46	45	41	44	43	50	43	48	50	42	45	49
Brazil	34	32	37	16	41	54	46	28	31	39	31	33	25	32	44	39	32	27
Mexico	21	23	19	10	30	29	22	20	21	18	25	26	30	18	27	21	24	19
Belarus	36	38	34	24	39	40	29	30	45	39	33	36	39	32	34	37	36	41
Russia	38	40	37	25	42	42	32	35	45	41	42	41	44	41	44	39	37	46
Moscow	51	52	50	42	54	53	44	43	58	52	50	51	55	47	58	48	54	53
Latvia	41	43	39	31	45	44	30	37	53	43	41	39	na	na	na	40	42	51
Estonia	42	47	38	28	50	45	34	40	58	43	40	43	na	na	na	44	44	42
Portugal	26	26	26	09	29	39	29	22	15	28	26	22	33	23	24	25	26	23
South Korea	na	na	na	na	na	na	na	na	na	na	na	na	na	na	na	na	na	na
Ireland	37	34	40	10	43	49	44	30	30	42	39	35	30	38	39	40	39	28
North Ireland	44	45	44	21	47	57	46	45	31	47	47	43	29	42	54	51	45	33
Slovenia	43	43	43	22	45	55	40	42	50	44	46	38	48	43	42	51	40	41
Spain	46	43	49	18	54	59	51	38	32	54	47	43	46	45	51	59	44	33
East Germany	42	42	41	30	47	44	39	39	53	32	43	49	49	39	38	33	42	43
Britain	47	45	48	26	51	55	46	47	48	49	50	50	45	44	56	54	46	44
Italy	36	36	37	10	40	50	38	29	24	40	37	33	36	41	39	39	37	34
Netherlands	45	53	42	31	46	60	53	45	36	33	51	57	37	47	53	51	50	36
Belgium	32	28	36	16	36	39	34	31	30	28	34	39	28	33	38	31	34	30
Austria	33	33	33	12	32	43	37	29	42	29	35	34	41	32	36	36	32	33
France	41	41	41	23	49	46	39	46	39	35	44	50	47	42	38	39	42	39
Canada	43	42	44	20	48	57	44	43	43	37	42	52	47	42	49	38	42	46
United States	48	51	46	27	48	58	47	48	50	43	49	56	50	47	55	51	48	48
Iceland	43	43	42	25	50	51	43	46	40	na	34	na	43	38	50	42	42	47
West Germany	33	32	33	13	36	42	34	30	35	28	34	36	36	31	40	39	32	32
Denmark	44	43	45	20	46	59	53	45	38	40	49	49	44	44	49	44	45	37
Finland	28	25	30	15	26	42	22	26	32	23	30	28	30	24	34	41	27	26
Norway	52	53	51	26	56	64	61	49	51	43	55	61	51	53	53	56	51	52
Sweden	51	51	51	25	53	71	55	48	51	56	38	62	55	53	51	59	52	44
Japan	20	20	21	03	23	27	21	21	18	17	17	29	28	21	27	21	22	24
Switzerland	44	45	44	25	43	54	44	46	37	37	49	48	43	48	46	51	43	44
Total	40	40	40	21	45	49	41	37	40	38	40	42	41	39	43	42	40	37

Ranking:

Turkey	59
Norway	52
Bulgaria	51
Moscow	51
Sweden	51
United States	48
Britain	47
Spain	46
Argentina	45
Netherlands	45
China	44
North Ireland	44
Denmark	44
Switzerland	44
Hungary	43
Slovenia	43
Canada	43
Iceland	43
Estonia	42
East Germany	42
Latvia	41
France	41
Romania	38
Lithuania	38
Russia	38
Ireland	37
Belarus	36
Italy	36
Brazil	34
Austria	33
West Germany	33
Chile	32
Belgium	32
India	29
Finland	28
Portugal	26
Nigeria	23
Mexico	21
Japan	20

Note: Countries in the left column are ranked according to GNP per capita. / The percentages in the bottom row give each country an equal weight. / na=not ascertained.

V187 PARTNER: SEX

Do (did) you and your partner share any of the following?   Sexual attitudes   (% "yes")

		Gender		Age			Education			Income			Political Affinity			Values		
	Total	Male	Female	16-29	30-49	50+	Lower	Medium	Upper	Lower	Middle	Upper	Left	Center	Right	Mat	Mixed	Postmat
India	55	52	58	31	73	62	61	53	55	49	58	57	52	58	54	54	56	57
Nigeria	48	43	56	24	75	83	65	41	48	49	49	48	44	49	41	56	42	52
China	43	43	42	19	54	51	42	42	43	44	44	40	na	na	na	46	39	46
Romania	55	57	53	31	67	58	57	50	58	54	54	56	51	57	57	57	53	49
Turkey	67	64	71	39	85	79	75	62	41	67	70	65	65	67	71	74	68	55
Poland	na	na	na	na	na	na	na	na	na	na	na	na	na	na	na	na	na	na
Bulgaria	59	58	60	42	63	64	63	60	55	60	61	61	66	61	60	60	60	50
Chile	53	55	52	31	68	61	59	50	52	47	57	56	55	54	53	54	54	55
Czechoslovakia	na	na	na	na	na	na	na	na	na	na	na	na	na	na	na	na	na	na
South Africa	na	na	na	na	na	na	na	na	na	na	na	na	na	na	na	na	na	na
Lithuania	38	42	34	21	53	37	31	37	55	35	42	36	na	na	na	36	37	44
Hungary	64	64	65	48	74	62	63	66	68	57	68	74	69	67	70	63	66	63
Argentina	63	59	66	33	79	68	67	60	57	64	64	66	64	64	62	63	62	62
Brazil	57	54	60	34	70	74	69	52	50	61	55	56	47	58	63	63	54	47
Mexico	40	43	36	19	57	52	42	39	33	39	41	44	44	38	45	45	40	34
Belarus	40	44	37	35	45	37	28	39	46	43	41	37	41	44	30	39	41	50
Russia	40	43	38	35	50	32	31	39	48	44	43	42	44	46	41	36	42	47
Moscow	57	56	58	54	61	53	50	51	62	57	58	58	61	54	61	56	58	62
Latvia	39	43	36	43	42	28	20	39	46	41	38	39	na	na	na	35	40	47
Estonia	45	50	41	38	54	40	30	49	51	49	41	43	na	na	na	48	47	37
Portugal	39	38	39	18	53	46	45	28	24	39	43	32	45	38	37	39	39	33
South Korea	na	na	na	na	na	na	na	na	na	na	na	na	na	na	na	na	na	na
Ireland	59	55	62	20	74	70	66	51	49	60	61	62	52	60	63	62	61	51
North Ireland	63	59	65	37	70	73	68	59	41	57	73	63	46	65	66	66	63	58
Slovenia	62	61	63	34	73	69	56	65	70	62	65	58	66	63	61	71	59	56
Spain	64	60	67	30	79	75	70	57	42	68	66	61	65	64	62	77	63	52
East Germany	43	45	41	39	54	35	38	51	57	27	49	52	51	38	42	32	43	50
Britain	62	59	64	38	70	68	61	62	63	60	64	70	57	61	69	65	62	59
Italy	51	48	53	17	62	62	53	38	29	54	53	46	48	57	48	56	52	46
Netherlands	64	65	64	41	72	79	75	65	50	47	75	76	58	66	68	71	68	57
Belgium	50	46	53	30	61	53	49	53	45	44	55	61	47	55	51	51	53	45
Austria	45	45	45	29	53	46	43	46	53	35	53	43	46	44	50	38	45	49
France	55	54	56	38	69	55	50	62	56	46	62	70	58	60	51	54	56	56
Canada	62	60	65	38	73	72	63	64	60	53	65	72	59	64	64	58	63	64
United States	68	68	68	46	72	75	63	70	70	62	71	75	71	69	70	73	67	70
Iceland	71	67	76	52	84	72	70	74	71	na	na	na	73	74	70	71	72	66
West Germany	42	44	41	21	52	46	45	36	41	35	44	51	38	44	48	46	43	41
Denmark	66	64	68	40	75	75	72	61	66	50	77	82	60	69	68	66	66	65
Finland	43	43	44	37	47	38	31	44	48	33	47	48	39	42	50	38	43	45
Norway	70	69	72	44	80	75	72	70	69	55	75	85	67	73	71	74	70	68
Sweden	68	66	69	43	75	81	72	62	73	80	52	81	70	71	66	72	69	63
Japan	21	20	21	06	23	27	20	21	21	19	17	28	20	20	32	29	22	23
Switzerland	67	66	67	42	74	70	70	67	53	57	76	74	63	71	66	71	66	67
Total	54	53	55	34	64	59	54	52	52	50	56	57	54	57	57	56	54	52

Ranking:

Iceland	71
Norway	70
United States	68
Sweden	68
Turkey	67
Switzerland	67
Denmark	66
Hungary	64
Spain	64
Netherlands	64
Argentina	63
North Ireland	63
Slovenia	62
Britain	62
Canada	62
Bulgaria	59
Ireland	59
Brazil	57
Moscow	57
India	55
Romania	55
France	55
Chile	53
Italy	51
Belgium	50
Nigeria	48
Estonia	45
Austria	45
China	43
East Germany	43
Finland	43
West Germany	42
Mexico	40
Belarus	40
Russia	40
Latvia	39
Portugal	39
Lithuania	38
Japan	21

Note: Countries in the left column are ranked according to GNP per capita. / The percentages in the bottom row give each country an equal weight. / na=not ascertained.

V190-V196. Do (did) you and your parents share any of the following?

Percentage

Moral attitudes	68
Social attitudes	61
Attitudes towards religion	60
Political attitudes	39
Sexual attitudes	24
None of these	8
Don't know	8

V190 PARENTS: RELIGION

Do (did) you and your parents share any of the following? Attitudes towards religion (% "yes")

		Gender		Age			Education			Income			Political Affinity			Values		
	Total	Male	Female	16-29	30-49	50+	Lower	Medium	Upper	Lower	Middle	Upper	Left	Center	Right	Mat	Mixed	Postmat
India	81	80	81	80	83	77	79	83	79	79	81	81	78	82	85	83	80	83
Nigeria	88	86	92	88	88	90	93	88	86	88	89	89	92	88	91	91	88	80
China	31	30	32	30	36	23	33	31	30	32	35	26	na	na	na	31	31	32
Romania	76	72	81	63	73	88	87	72	68	76	80	73	80	76	69	84	72	62
Turkey	85	82	87	86	85	82	88	83	73	86	87	81	75	88	91	88	87	76
Poland	na	na	na	na	na	na	na	na	na	na	na	na	na	na	na	na	na	na
Bulgaria	54	52	56	48	52	60	63	51	52	53	52	59	54	56	50	54	56	46
Chile	72	71	74	71	72	75	71	75	71	69	72	77	68	73	78	73	73	71
Czechoslovakia	na	na	na	na	na	na	na	na	na	na	na	na	na	na	na	na	na	na
South Africa	na	na	na	na	na	na	na	na	na	na	na	na	na	na	na	na	na	na
Lithuania	50	45	55	38	50	61	60	47	48	54	48	44	na	na	na	60	47	44
Hungary	63	57	68	50	57	72	68	56	60	69	57	57	56	65	69	65	61	50
Argentina	61	58	63	49	64	65	60	58	62	64	56	57	46	65	64	67	61	52
Brazil	69	67	70	67	67	76	70	69	67	74	67	65	64	69	72	71	68	65
Mexico	78	77	79	77	78	81	78	80	77	79	78	80	76	76	83	82	78	76
Belarus	43	40	46	43	42	46	47	43	43	47	41	43	46	37	47	44	43	52
Russia	49	43	54	47	49	52	46	48	52	54	50	49	47	54	55	53	46	55
Moscow	46	42	48	50	44	46	42	43	48	43	44	52	46	47	39	44	47	45
Latvia	34	30	38	33	37	32	30	35	35	35	39	32	na	na	na	34	36	29
Estonia	46	43	48	45	47	46	43	45	52	50	41	45	45	na	na	47	49	44
Portugal	55	49	61	51	54	61	56	55	53	60	53	51	45	54	65	54	55	53
South Korea	na	na	na	na	na	na	na	na	na	na	na	na	na	na	na	na	na	na
Ireland	76	73	79	63	73	87	82	72	58	90	75	66	na	na	na	78	64	67
North Ireland	80	73	84	71	75	90	82	76	76	82	73	78	47	77	83	80	78	78
Slovenia	68	64	71	64	63	76	77	65	56	73	67	60	64	79	84	78	79	59
Spain	64	57	71	51	61	78	68	61	50	73	67	54	64	67	70	74	65	59
East Germany	43	40	46	39	44	45	43	45	43	46	43	41	52	71	78	41	64	51
Britain	58	51	64	51	54	67	57	60	62	59	60	57	40	43	50	67	43	46
Italy	65	57	73	53	58	79	66	56	66	71	60	46	50	58	67	74	58	51
Netherlands	56	57	56	49	55	67	57	59	52	57	58	55	54	74	76	67	65	56
Belgium	50	47	53	39	45	62	52	49	48	54	48	51	49	56	66	52	50	49
Austria	49	46	51	42	49	53	56	45	41	52	49	45	37	54	60	58	51	50
France	56	53	58	46	53	65	57	57	51	57	54	57	46	44	57	65	58	40
Canada	65	60	69	62	60	72	67	64	63	67	66	65	48	60	72	73	65	44
United States	72	68	75	64	68	78	73	70	71	73	71	71	55	66	67	75	72	62
Iceland	71	67	75	62	72	78	73	70	71	na	na	na	68	74	79	69	73	68
West Germany	41	36	44	36	33	51	43	35	41	44	37	42	34	43	76	51	42	62
Denmark	66	64	69	67	61	72	71	70	61	68	70	60	54	68	51	68	68	34
Finland	43	44	43	37	40	58	44	43	44	42	45	43	36	45	73	56	42	54
Norway	67	62	72	66	63	71	74	65	64	66	67	65	62	70	50	71	68	45
Sweden	60	58	63	61	59	62	62	58	61	66	56	62	54	65	67	66	61	51
Japan	35	32	38	30	33	42	36	36	34	35	35	41	38	39	63	46	36	28
Switzerland	74	71	76	68	70	79	75	73	69	78	73	71	62	75	46	81	76	64
Total	**60**	57	63	55	58	66	62	59	57	62	59	58	56	64	68	64	60	55

Ranking:

Nigeria	88
Turkey	85
India	81
North Ireland	80
Mexico	78
Romania	76
Ireland	76
Switzerland	74
Chile	72
United States	72
Iceland	71
Brazil	69
Slovenia	68
Norway	67
Denmark	66
Italy	65
Canada	65
Spain	64
Hungary	63
Argentina	61
Sweden	60
Britain	58
Netherlands	56
France	56
Portugal	55
Bulgaria	54
Lithuania	50
Belgium	50
Russia	49
Austria	49
Moscow	46
Estonia	46
Belarus	43
East Germany	43
Finland	43
West Germany	41
Japan	35
Latvia	34
China	31

Note: Countries in the left column are ranked according to GNP per capita. / The percentages in the bottom row give each country an equal weight / na=not ascertained.

V191 PARENTS: MORAL

Do (did) you and your parents share any of the following? Moral attitudes (% "yes")

	Total	Gender		Age			Education			Income			Political Affinity			Values		
		Male	Female	16-29	30-49	50+	Lower	Medium	Upper	Lower	Middle	Upper	Left	Center	Right	Mat	Mixed	Postmat
India	82	83	80	83	83	76	74	83	85	77	83	85	79	85	86	83	82	87
Nigeria	92	92	92	93	91	93	94	91	93	90	93	95	94	90	95	93	92	89
China	72	70	76	69	81	61	69	77	72	77	72	67	na	na	na	76	69	67
Romania	74	75	72	55	72	87	82	66	74	76	74	71	76	74	71	78	70	73
Turkey	88	87	89	90	89	84	90	88	81	90	88	87	83	91	89	87	89	87
Poland	na	na	na	na	na	na	na	na	na	na	na	na	na	na	na	na	na	na
Bulgaria	64	66	62	46	64	74	69	59	70	66	64	65	73	70	62	65	60	59
Chile	79	79	80	80	80	79	74	82	84	71	80	88	81	80	81	76	81	85
Czechoslovakia	na	na	na	na	na	na	na	na	na	na	na	na	na	na	na	na	na	na
South Africa	na	na	na	na	na	na	na	na	na	na	na	na	na	na	na	na	na	na
Lithuania	56	54	58	45	58	65	58	54	66	58	57	53	na	na	na	59	55	60
Hungary	74	72	76	71	70	78	72	73	86	72	75	77	76	76	84	73	74	75
Argentina	84	84	85	80	84	87	81	85	87	83	84	84	82	87	86	85	83	85
Brazil	75	76	74	72	76	79	72	77	75	75	74	78	70	78	78	77	75	69
Mexico	78	77	79	76	79	81	76	83	82	76	78	84	78	77	81	81	78	77
Belarus	60	59	61	56	65	55	56	54	68	62	57	63	61	63	52	62	60	70
Russia	63	61	64	55	65	64	59	59	69	66	64	66	67	69	63	66	60	64
Moscow	68	64	71	63	70	68	59	63	73	65	69	70	68	73	68	68	69	64
Latvia	47	42	51	40	52	46	31	44	59	48	50	45	na	na	na	45	49	49
Estonia	52	52	53	40	56	61	44	51	65	52	51	54	na	na	na	54	53	63
Portugal	64	62	65	61	63	66	61	68	68	62	65	66	58	63	71	62	63	72
South Korea	na	na	na	na	na	na	na	na	na	na	na	na	na	na	na	na	na	na
Ireland	72	71	73	61	69	81	75	68	70	81	72	65	49	71	79	70	75	63
North Ireland	78	80	77	74	75	85	79	79	69	74	78	78	68	77	83	74	80	76
Slovenia	65	64	66	59	62	73	67	64	65	64	69	62	64	67	73	72	63	59
Spain	72	68	75	61	71	81	74	70	64	74	73	70	68	76	80	79	73	63
East Germany	54	53	56	48	56	58	52	56	65	56	56	52	56	52	58	59	55	52
Britain	69	68	70	66	67	73	65	78	77	70	70	72	67	67	79	75	68	68
Italy	77	74	80	67	74	85	77	74	75	79	77	75	72	83	83	82	77	73
Netherlands	68	74	67	64	65	78	65	71	69	66	70	77	63	70	77	65	72	66
Belgium	59	59	59	54	56	65	57	59	62	60	57	63	58	61	64	56	60	63
Austria	47	45	49	43	45	51	48	44	57	44	46	52	49	45	51	48	47	48
France	69	67	71	59	66	80	69	68	72	68	69	71	67	75	78	72	72	64
Canada	78	74	81	73	75	85	74	78	80	77	78	82	75	78	82	83	77	77
United States	79	77	81	72	80	82	72	81	84	75	82	83	74	82	86	78	80	81
Iceland	78	73	83	72	80	83	74	80	81	na	na	na	75	77	85	69	81	84
West Germany	42	39	44	32	37	50	42	39	44	45	39	42	32	46	49	48	44	34
Denmark	69	67	71	59	66	79	71	71	66	70	65	72	62	68	76	64	70	66
Finland	51	49	53	45	48	63	52	51	51	47	54	51	46	54	55	65	50	51
Norway	75	75	75	70	72	81	76	70	78	71	78	77	71	76	81	74	76	72
Sweden	69	69	69	66	65	77	67	70	75	65	69	73	69	69	73	69	69	71
Japan	50	48	52	38	57	47	41	51	59	38	54	60	58	59	61	59	52	56
Switzerland	76	74	77	66	73	83	77	75	77	77	76	80	66	79	80	83	78	67
Total	68	67	70	62	68	73	67	68	72	68	69	70	67	72	74	70	69	68

Ranking:

Nigeria	92
Turkey	88
Argentina	84
India	82
Chile	79
United States	79
Mexico	78
North Ireland	78
Canada	78
Iceland	78
Italy	77
Switzerland	76
Brazil	75
Norway	75
Romania	74
Hungary	74
China	72
Ireland	72
Spain	72
Britain	69
France	69
Denmark	69
Sweden	69
Moscow	68
Netherlands	68
Slovenia	65
Bulgaria	64
Portugal	64
Russia	63
Belarus	60
Belgium	59
Lithuania	56
East Germany	54
Estonia	52
Finland	51
Japan	50
Latvia	47
Austria	47
West Germany	42

Note: Countries in the left column are ranked according to GNP per capita. / The percentages in the bottom row give each country an equal weight. / na=not ascertained.

V192 PARENTS: SOCIAL

Do (did) you and your parents share any of the following?   Social attitudes   (% "yes")

	Total	Gender		Age			Education			Income			Political Affinity			Values			Ranking:	
		Male	Female	16-29	30-49	50+	Lower	Medium	Upper	Lower	Middle	Upper	Left	Center	Right	Mat	Mixed	Postmat		
India	78	80	76	78	80	71	70	79	80	70	79	79	76	81	83	81	79	76	Turkey	80
Nigeria	78	76	82	76	80	84	82	81	73	74	77	83	83	74	83	79	78	78	Argentina	80
China	47	44	53	41	55	41	47	50	44	50	46	46	na	67	na	50	46	39	India	78
Romania	64	63	65	50	62	75	73	59	59	63	64	64	66	67	59	69	61	51	Nigeria	78
Turkey	80	78	82	78	81	80	85	71	71	83	81	77	74	80	85	81	81	75	Switzerland	76
Poland	na	na	na	na	na	na	na	na	na	na	na	na	na	na	na	na	na	na	United States	72
Bulgaria	58	60	57	48	60	63	56	59	63	60	57	64	62	66	58	60	57	66	North Ireland	70
Chile	69	71	68	72	68	67	62	73	74	60	71	78	72	67	75	64	71	75	Chile	69
Czechoslovakia	na	na	na	na	na	na	na	na	na	na	na	na	na	na	na	na	na	na	Brazil	69
South Africa	na	na	na	na	na	na	na	na	na	na	na	na	na	na	na	na	na	na	Spain	69
Lithuania	52	52	52	44	53	58	50	51	61	53	52	49	na	64	61	54	52	46	Iceland	69
Hungary	60	59	61	67	58	59	53	64	75	57	62	62	69	64	61	58	61	65	Norway	69
Argentina	80	82	78	83	77	80	75	82	83	81	78	79	79	83	83	78	80	81	Canada	68
Brazil	69	70	69	65	71	74	67	70	71	69	67	72	65	72	73	71	69	63	Ireland	67
Mexico	63	62	64	64	64	56	60	63	71	58	63	76	65	61	69	64	64	64	Slovenia	67
Belarus	56	55	57	58	63	42	38	58	62	56	55	57	61	57	42	53	58	56	Netherlands	67
Russia	51	50	51	50	53	48	44	49	57	53	51	54	53	57	52	50	51	55	Denmark	66
Moscow	60	58	61	68	63	48	41	60	64	55	62	61	63	63	49	56	60	66	Romania	64
Latvia	41	40	42	40	46	33	33	38	50	45	42	38	na	63	na	38	44	44	Britain	64
Estonia	49	48	49	50	49	47	42	49	55	50	45	50	41	46	52	47	51	58	Mexico	63
Portugal	46	47	45	51	44	43	42	61	50	43	48	50	41	46	52	39	48	57	Italy	63
South Korea	na	na	na	na	na	na	na	na	na	na	na	na	na	na	na	na	na	na	France	63
Ireland	67	65	69	62	66	72	68	65	68	72	69	63	55	66	73	64	70	62	Sweden	61
North Ireland	70	74	67	65	66	77	70	66	79	67	66	73	50	67	79	68	69	73	Hungary	60
Slovenia	67	67	67	62	66	70	64	68	69	66	68	66	67	70	74	71	65	62	Moscow	60
Spain	69	67	71	66	67	74	70	71	65	71	70	68	68	72	76	76	69	67	Bulgaria	58
East Germany	56	56	56	57	57	54	54	58	64	55	54	59	62	55	49	57	54	61	Belarus	56
Britain	64	67	62	62	64	66	62	68	74	64	65	67	63	62	74	71	64	64	East Germany	56
Italy	63	62	64	55	62	69	63	60	65	67	64	58	60	69	70	67	63	63	Belgium	56
Netherlands	67	72	66	62	65	77	66	69	67	59	73	72	61	67	76	70	70	63	Lithuania	52
Belgium	56	54	58	56	52	61	56	56	57	59	52	58	56	56	61	57	56	59	Russia	51
Austria	45	44	45	55	43	42	41	47	45	38	45	50	47	43	49	37	45	47	Estonia	49
France	63	61	64	61	57	69	65	64	54	66	62	60	63	64	69	67	62	61	China	47
Canada	68	66	71	63	67	75	65	70	69	64	69	76	62	70	72	74	69	66	West Germany	47
United States	72	70	75	72	70	75	69	73	74	73	74	70	64	74	81	70	73	73	Portugal	46
Iceland	69	67	70	71	65	72	66	69	70	na	na	na	67	69	70	66	69	70	Austria	45
West Germany	47	45	50	46	46	50	46	48	53	48	44	51	47	50	48	47	48	50	Finland	42
Denmark	66	67	65	58	64	74	68	65	65	64	70	63	58	69	69	67	66	66	Latvia	41
Finland	42	44	39	40	38	54	35	39	48	40	42	43	38	37	51	47	39	47	Japan	37
Norway	69	71	67	66	65	76	76	64	71	70	70	70	67	71	70	67	70	70		
Sweden	61	65	57	57	58	66	60	61	61	62	64	62	62	58	67	59	62	58		
Japan	37	36	38	25	42	36	30	38	41	31	39	44	37	42	48	43	39	39		
Switzerland	76	74	78	72	74	81	77	76	75	78	79	77	67	80	82	80	79	68		
Total	61	61	62	59	61	63	59	62	64	60	62	63	61	64	67	62	62	62		

Note: Countries in the left column are ranked according to GNP per capita. / The percentages in the bottom row give each country an equal weight. / na=not ascertained.

V193 PARENTS: POLITICS

Do (did) you and your parents share any of the following? Political attitudes (% "yes")

	Total	Gender Male	Gender Female	Age 16-29	Age 30-49	Age 50+	Education Lower	Education Medium	Education Upper	Income Lower	Income Middle	Income Upper	Political Affinity Left	Political Affinity Center	Political Affinity Right	Values Mat	Values Mixed	Values Postmat	Ranking
India	31	33	30	34	31	27	23	33	33	27	28	39	33	36	39	30	34	41	Turkey 62
Nigeria	33	34	32	33	33	35	31	33	35	32	35	32	27	34	47	34	35	26	North Ireland 54
China	36	34	38	28	45	28	34	38	35	37	40	29	na	na	na	37	35	33	Norway 53
Romania	38	40	37	30	37	45	40	36	40	36	39	39	41	42	38	41	35	41	Ireland 49
Turkey	62	61	64	61	61	67	68	52	54	67	61	60	58	61	72	64	66	52	Sweden 49
Poland	na	na	na	na	na	na	na	na	na	na	na	na	na	na	na	na	na	na	United States 48
Bulgaria	47	49	44	38	48	50	49	45	51	46	46	52	53	46	49	50	46	50	Bulgaria 47
Chile	39	41	37	46	41	25	24	42	54	27	36	57	49	37	43	27	41	51	Switzerland 47
Czechoslovakia	na	na	na	na	na	na	na	na	na	na	na	na	na	na	na	na	na	na	Argentina 46
South Africa	na	na	na	na	na	na	na	na	na	na	na	na	na	na	na	na	na	na	Britain 45
Lithuania	34	33	35	36	31	35	30	33	43	34	34	34	45	na	na	32	33	43	Netherlands 45
Hungary	38	39	37	37	37	39	34	37	57	35	39	39	45	42	44	38	38	35	Canada 45
Argentina	46	51	41	54	43	42	35	51	56	40	43	50	46	55	54	35	47	55	Moscow 44
Brazil	41	39	43	38	41	45	41	40	45	42	39	42	37	40	52	41	41	40	Slovenia 44
Mexico	34	36	33	39	32	29	32	35	41	29	36	43	37	35	41	31	36	41	Iceland 43
Belarus	34	35	33	42	37	21	23	33	40	31	33	37	38	31	33	31	36	45	Denmark 42
Russia	33	33	32	35	33	30	25	30	40	34	32	36	38	36	29	30	33	45	Brazil 41
Moscow	44	44	43	48	45	37	29	41	48	43	44	43	46	43	49	42	44	47	Spain 41
Latvia	22	21	23	28	23	14	18	22	25	27	26	17	na	na	na	19	23	29	France 41
Estonia	30	31	29	33	30	25	26	29	35	29	28	31	na	na	na	30	31	41	Chile 39
Portugal	25	28	22	32	19	23	20	33	38	22	26	28	21	24	32	19	26	35	Romania 38
South Korea	na	na	na	na	na	na	na	na	na	na	na	na	na	na	na	na	na	na	Hungary 38
Ireland	49	52	47	43	44	58	52	46	47	55	48	47	37	51	52	47	52	45	Italy 37
North Ireland	54	52	56	46	53	61	52	58	59	56	53	49	36	54	62	63	51	53	China 36
Slovenia	44	45	44	41	41	50	45	43	44	45	45	43	41	44	62	47	43	46	Lithuania 34
Spain	41	39	42	35	38	47	42	36	38	45	39	37	39	42	49	43	43	34	Mexico 34
East Germany	34	38	30	41	36	27	32	37	38	30	33	37	40	31	34	23	35	35	Belarus 34
Britain	45	46	44	47	44	44	43	49	52	45	51	50	50	41	55	53	44	45	East Germany 34
Italy	37	35	38	34	34	40	37	38	26	38	36	44	34	44	48	38	36	38	Finland 34
Netherlands	45	51	42	41	40	55	49	43	41	40	43	48	39	40	60	47	49	38	Nigeria 33
Belgium	29	29	30	25	25	37	31	28	28	30	29	33	22	29	42	29	31	26	Russia 33
Austria	26	29	24	26	25	27	26	25	31	21	26	30	31	24	30	22	25	32	India 31
France	41	41	42	41	37	46	43	40	39	46	40	42	42	42	54	47	43	36	Estonia 30
Canada	45	45	44	45	41	50	44	45	45	43	44	49	47	45	51	46	44	48	Belgium 29
United States	48	48	47	46	45	52	48	48	48	48	49	49	43	49	58	43	48	52	Austria 26
Iceland	43	42	43	40	39	53	44	43	41	na	na	na	40	40	52	40	44	39	Portugal 25
West Germany	25	29	22	29	24	24	23	31	26	22	24	30	27	23	33	23	26	26	West Germany 25
Denmark	42	42	42	32	38	56	45	45	39	41	45	40	40	39	51	42	42	38	Latvia 22
Finland	34	31	37	30	29	49	35	28	40	32	35	34	30	26	46	47	31	37	Japan 18
Norway	53	53	54	39	50	66	64	50	51	56	54	52	49	57	55	55	54	47	
Sweden	49	51	48	44	47	56	49	51	50	51	52	50	56	47	52	51	50	49	
Japan	18	16	20	12	18	21	14	17	22	16	15	25	23	16	27	20	19	23	
Switzerland	47	48	47	44	46	49	45	49	51	46	49	58	43	50	53	51	48	43	
Total	**39**	**40**	**38**	**38**	**37**	**41**	**37**	**39**	**42**	**38**	**39**	**41**	**39**	**40**	**47**	**39**	**39**	**41**	

Note: Countries in the left column are ranked according to GNP per capita. / The percentages in the bottom row give each country an equal weight. / na=not ascertained.

V194 PARENTS: SEX

Do (did) you and your parents share any of the following? Sexual attitudes (% "yes")

	Total	Gender		Age			Education			Income			Political Affinity			Values			Ranking:	
		Male	Female	16-29	30-49	50+	Lower	Medium	Upper	Lower	Middle	Upper	Left	Center	Right	Mat	Mixed	Postmat		
India	08	08	09	08	09	08	08	08	09	08	08	09	10	11	05	07	10	08	Turkey	48
Nigeria	20	18	24	18	22	32	20	21	19	23	19	22	16	24	22	23	20	16	United States	43
China	17	16	18	11	21	16	15	17	18	20	18	12	na	na	na	20	15	15	North Ireland	39
Romania	30	28	31	18	30	37	34	26	30	33	30	27	30	34	26	32	28	30	Canada	37
Turkey	48	49	48	44	49	54	53	40	41	52	47	46	40	50	54	50	49	44	Netherlands	36
Poland	na	na	na	na	na	na	na	na	na	na	na	na	na	na	na	na	na	na	Switzerland	36
Bulgaria	27	25	28	21	23	35	32	25	26	27	28	30	30	27	26	31	27	20	Brazil	33
Chile	29	31	28	35	29	23	20	33	36	24	26	40	30	30	33	27	30	33	Slovenia	33
Czechoslovakia	na	na	na	na	na	na	na	na	na	na	na	na	na	na	na	na	na	na	Ireland	31
South Africa	na	na	na	na	na	na	na	na	na	na	na	na	na	na	na	na	na	na	Denmark	31
Lithuania	11	09	13	07	09	17	14	10	12	13	11	08	na	na	na	10	12	10	Romania	30
Hungary	26	26	26	24	24	28	23	27	36	23	28	24	26	27	30	26	24	35	Britain	30
Argentina	25	25	25	34	25	18	20	30	30	21	22	27	24	29	29	22	26	28	Norway	30
Brazil	33	34	32	30	30	41	35	30	39	31	31	36	31	34	38	33	32	35	Sweden	30
Mexico	24	25	23	29	21	18	21	27	30	21	23	30	24	23	31	19	25	28	Chile	29
Belarus	11	11	11	12	12	08	07	10	13	11	09	13	13	10	07	08	13	14	Spain	29
Russia	14	13	14	13	13	15	12	10	18	13	16	14	15	14	14	12	15	13	Bulgaria	27
Moscow	18	15	20	22	14	20	13	17	19	19	17	18	15	24	21	19	18	13	Iceland	27
Latvia	07	07	07	10	07	05	10	07	06	07	07	07	na	na	na	04	07	09	Hungary	26
Estonia	16	16	16	15	17	16	14	17	16	16	15	17	na	na	na	16	17	19	Argentina	25
Portugal	12	10	13	08	08	10	10	15	16	10	13	14	08	13	12	09	10	21	Italy	25
South Korea	na	na	na	na	na	na	na	na	na	na	na	na	na	na	na	na	na	na	Mexico	24
Ireland	31	31	32	27	26	40	35	28	23	38	31	25	18	34	32	32	34	26	France	23
North Ireland	39	41	38	36	36	45	41	31	52	30	34	44	29	38	46	48	38	31	Belgium	22
Slovenia	33	35	32	32	36	38	36	31	32	32	36	29	31	34	44	36	32	35	Nigeria	20
Spain	29	27	30	23	25	37	31	21	24	36	29	22	23	32	32	31	31	22	Moscow	18
East Germany	10	09	10	12	11	08	09	11	12	09	11	10	13	07	13	08	09	14	China	17
Britain	30	28	31	31	29	30	27	35	39	29	35	34	28	29	35	30	30	33	Finland	17
Italy	25	24	27	25	20	31	26	24	18	27	26	14	20	30	35	27	25	27	Estonia	16
Netherlands	36	36	36	36	27	32	28	39	41	37	38	38	33	37	39	36	38	33	Russia	14
Belgium	22	21	23	23	18	25	23	21	22	24	21	23	15	23	29	21	22	24	Portugal	12
Austria	11	12	11	18	09	10	10	12	13	09	10	14	19	10	13	08	11	12	Japan	12
France	23	24	24	26	20	24	26	21	20	27	22	24	25	27	24	26	23	22	Lithuania	11
Canada	37	33	40	41	34	37	33	38	38	35	36	42	33	38	39	33	37	38	Belarus	11
United States	43	39	46	42	41	45	41	41	46	43	45	43	41	41	54	39	43	46	Austria	11
Iceland	27	25	30	32	26	23	26	24	31	na	na	na	22	28	32	24	29	22	East Germany	10
West Germany	08	08	08	09	11	09	08	08	08	10	06	08	06	07	12	10	08	06	India	08
Denmark	31	29	33	37	29	30	28	36	26	28	35	26	30	29	32	27	33	26	West Germany	08
Finland	17	15	18	20	11	28	16	15	20	16	17	18	07	13	24	21	17	15	Latvia	07
Norway	30	29	31	36	29	28	27	28	33	29	33	31	29	33	31	26	31	35		
Sweden	30	31	30	43	29	22	28	32	30	28	32	30	24	28	39	31	31	28		
Japan	12	09	14	08	11	15	11	12	11	09	11	16	16	11	18	15	12	13		
Switzerland	36	36	37	43	36	33	34	38	37	35	39	41	31	40	37	45	36	32		
Total	24	23	25	25	22	25	23	23	25	24	24	24	23	26	29	24	24	24		

Note: Countries in the left column are ranked according to GNP per capita. / The percentages in the bottom row give each country an equal weight. / na=not ascertained.

V197. If someone said that individuals should have the chance to enjoy complete sexual freedom without being restricted, would you tend to agree or disagree?

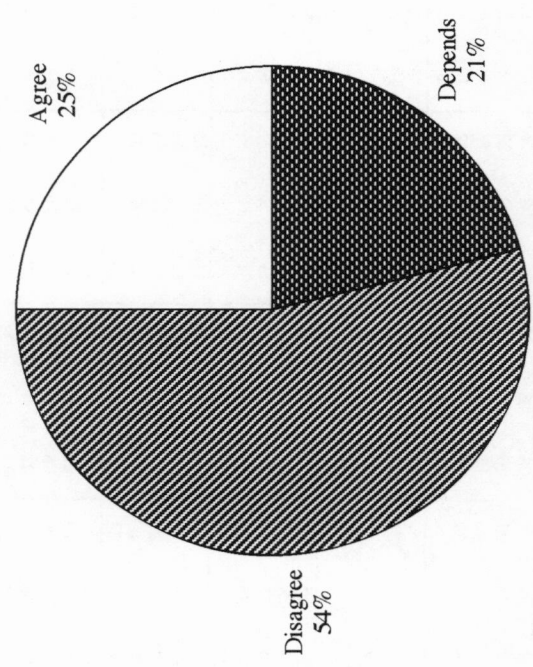

Agree
25%

Disagree
54%

Depends
21%

V197 SEXUAL FREEDOM

If someone said that individuals should have the chance to enjoy complete sexual freedom without being restricted, would you tend to agree or disagree? (% "tend to agree")

	Total	Gender		Age			Education			Income			Political Affinity			Values		
		Male	Female	16-29	30-49	50+	Lower	Medium	Upper	Lower	Middle	Upper	Left	Center	Right	Mat	Mixed	Postmat
India	07	09	04	10	06	04	05	08	07	09	06	07	07	07	08	06	08	08
Nigeria	22	22	21	23	23	09	26	19	23	18	23	23	26	21	24	18	25	22
China	05	07	03	08	05	02	04	06	05	04	06	06	na	na	na	03	06	13
Romania	17	21	14	27	19	09	09	22	21	18	16	18	17	15	24	10	23	22
Turkey	24	24	24	34	19	17	18	29	41	18	21	33	34	21	19	12	26	34
Poland	22	28	17	27	25	17	22	24	15	20	22	24	18	22	23	24	22	21
Bulgaria	30	36	24	50	30	17	22	31	34	26	28	38	28	31	34	20	32	49
Chile	18	24	13	22	18	15	15	19	21	16	18	23	25	17	16	15	17	26
Czechoslovakia	10	15	06	16	10	06	08	12	09	10	09	12	09	09	12	10	10	12
South Africa	24	31	18	33	23	09	24	26	14	28	26	13	31	20	25	20	26	28
Lithuania	27	35	19	36	26	20	24	28	23	22	30	31	31	na	na	19	29	36
Hungary	18	24	13	32	21	09	16	21	14	15	19	22	24	20	18	14	20	30
Argentina	39	45	34	51	43	26	33	46	43	33	36	51	61	38	42	31	38	53
Brazil	29	35	23	35	31	17	24	32	30	28	28	32	34	29	29	27	30	36
Mexico	31	35	27	36	30	21	31	30	32	32	31	32	46	30	27	27	32	40
Belarus	18	21	15	31	13	13	13	22	15	15	17	21	20	17	13	12	21	19
Russia	16	22	12	27	16	08	11	18	17	15	14	19	20	15	23	11	20	21
Moscow	23	24	21	31	22	17	14	23	24	20	24	26	24	20	20	21	21	36
Latvia	17	23	13	24	16	12	20	18	13	17	20	14	na	na	na	11	18	19
Estonia	25	34	18	37	26	10	24	26	24	24	24	29	na	na	na	23	25	37
Portugal	na	28	20	37	22	14	20	34	33	19	28	29	28	25	22	19	25	40
South Korea	na	na	16	na	16	07	na	na	na	na	na	na	na	na	na	na	18	27
Ireland	17	19	16	na	16	07	14	21	18	15	15	20	25	20	08	09	18	27
North Ireland	22	29	18	35	16	14	14	21	31	16	16	26	41	32	21	23	31	33
Slovenia	45	52	38	55	41	42	45	49	38	43	47	44	54	30	34	46	45	38
Spain	55	62	49	75	61	40	50	68	66	50	60	63	66	52	43	39	58	76
East Germany	49	54	44	60	51	40	48	53	48	42	47	55	53	49	45	38	48	55
Britain	31	35	27	56	30	16	31	30	31	30	33	32	41	32	21	23	31	38
Italy	39	45	33	45	30	25	37	30	57	34	43	47	54	30	34	24	39	55
Netherlands	33	31	33	44	32	20	28	33	38	37	33	38	40	34	23	28	28	41
Belgium	28	32	25	38	32	18	25	30	30	32	31	24	35	29	22	27	27	31
Austria	39	39	39	52	40	31	35	43	34	38	39	39	48	40	36	36	37	45
France	32	34	31	43	36	19	30	36	30	32	34	32	41	28	27	24	30	40
Canada	24	29	18	36	25	11	19	24	26	20	25	25	36	20	22	16	24	29
United States	25	28	22	36	28	18	27	27	23	24	28	23	37	24	21	22	25	29
Iceland	24	25	22	32	24	11	22	18	29	na	38	37	18	29	23	26	21	31
West Germany	36	41	32	53	39	24	34	45	31	33	38	37	40	37	31	24	36	42
Denmark	11	13	10	20	11	04	06	15	11	09	13	12	15	09	10	06	11	15
Finland	12	18	06	19	12	06	13	12	12	13	12	11	11	11	12	12	12	12
Norway	10	13	08	21	08	06	05	12	12	13	11	08	12	08	12	08	10	16
Sweden	22	27	18	35	22	13	21	25	18	22	27	18	21	25	18	22	21	27
Japan	13	19	08	21	10	12	15	11	17	16	12	12	26	10	18	12	15	19
Switzerland	44	45	44	29	41	55	46	44	39	50	47	46	38	48	48	51	45	37
Total	**25**	**29**	**21**	**35**	**25**	**17**	**23**	**28**	**26**	**24**	**26**	**27**	**31**	**25**	**24**	**21**	**26**	**32**

Ranking:

Spain	55
East Germany	49
Slovenia	45
Switzerland	44
Argentina	39
Italy	39
Austria	39
West Germany	36
Netherlands	33
France	32
Mexico	31
Britain	31
Bulgaria	31
Brazil	30
Belgium	28
Lithuania	27
Estonia	25
United States	25
Turkey	24
South Africa	24
Portugal	24
Canada	24
Iceland	24
Moscow	23
Nigeria	22
Poland	22
North Ireland	22
Sweden	22
Chile	18
Hungary	18
Belarus	18
Romania	17
Latvia	17
Ireland	17
Russia	16
Japan	13
Finland	12
Denmark	11
Czechoslovakia	10
Norway	10
India	07
China	05

Note: Countries in the left column are ranked according to GNP per capita. / The percentages in the bottom row give each country an equal weight. / na=not ascertained.

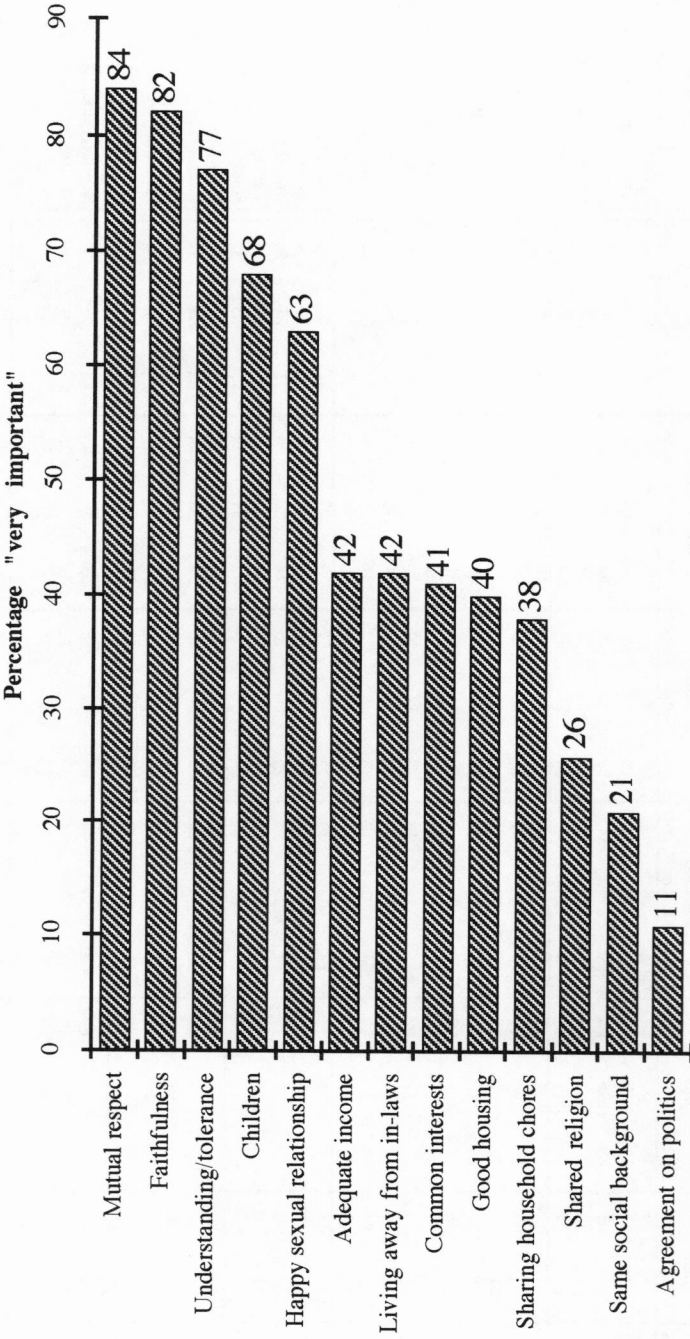

V198-V210. Things that make a marriage successful.

Percentage "very important"

V198 FAITHFULNESS

Here is a list of things which some people think make for a successful marriage. Please tell me, for each one, whether you think it is very important, rather important, or not very important for a successful marriage: Faithfulness (% "very important")

	Total	Gender		Age			Education			Income			Political Affinity			Values		
		Male	Female	16-29	30-49	50+	Lower	Medium	Upper	Lower	Middle	Upper	Left	Center	Right	Mat	Mixed	Postmat
India	94	93	94	94	94	91	91	94	94	92	95	94	94	94	99	95	94	89
Nigeria	99	98	99	99	98	100	99	99	98	99	99	97	99	98	99	99	99	93
China	90	88	95	86	92	93	92	90	90	90	92	90	na	na	na	92	89	83
Romania	77	74	79	73	74	82	82	76	71	81	78	71	76	80	70	82	74	63
Turkey	87	86	89	87	86	89	89	90	75	90	89	83	85	87	89	90	88	81
Poland	na	na	na	na	na	na	na	na	na	na	na	na	na	na	na	na	na	na
Bulgaria	63	62	64	57	56	76	75	62	55	64	64	58	66	64	56	70	63	44
Chile	92	92	92	92	92	91	93	90	93	89	93	92	89	93	92	93	92	90
Czechoslovakia	na	na	na	na	na	na	na	na	na	na	na	na	na	na	na	na	na	na
South Africa	na	na	na	na	na	na	na	na	na	na	na	na	na	na	na	na	na	na
Lithuania	70	66	73	68	68	74	76	67	75	73	69	66	na	na	na	72	71	62
Hungary	84	82	87	78	82	89	89	81	75	86	85	75	82	83	85	86	83	83
Argentina	85	85	86	80	84	90	88	84	81	86	87	81	71	86	86	93	83	83
Brazil	76	73	80	73	77	80	80	75	74	78	75	74	72	73	80	82	73	68
Mexico	81	77	85	81	81	80	79	84	83	77	81	87	69	83	88	82	82	73
Belarus	79	78	80	69	78	91	89	80	74	82	80	75	80	78	75	85	77	70
Russia	77	75	79	73	75	83	85	77	73	80	78	71	70	77	72	80	77	63
Moscow	66	64	69	60	64	74	87	70	59	70	66	60	64	65	78	74	66	51
Latvia	74	73	75	71	76	76	86	75	69	78	76	71	na	na	na	81	75	64
Estonia	61	57	64	57	60	64	66	61	55	63	58	59	na	na	na	67	57	56
Portugal	77	73	82	75	73	84	82	69	67	82	76	72	72	77	81	83	76	66
South Korea	90	91	88	92	88	89	82	89	95	90	87	93	88	87	85	88	91	93
Ireland	93	91	96	90	92	97	94	92	92	94	93	94	88	93	93	94	93	94
North Ireland	94	91	96	87	95	98	96	93	86	96	95	90	89	96	95	99	94	89
Slovenia	80	76	84	81	76	85	83	81	75	82	80	77	73	82	79	85	79	72
Spain	79	74	83	69	77	87	83	71	67	85	79	74	73	78	87	85	79	67
East Germany	78	73	83	73	75	84	80	80	68	85	79	72	69	83	79	90	81	67
Britain	90	89	92	89	88	93	92	86	83	92	89	87	88	90	91	90	91	87
Italy	85	80	89	85	78	90	86	76	58	87	89	82	75	89	85	90	86	87
Netherlands	88	86	89	91	83	92	91	90	83	86	92	84	82	89	85	91	92	81
Belgium	85	82	88	81	83	91	88	85	81	87	85	83	74	87	89	85	86	79
Austria	83	79	86	80	76	91	87	81	83	87	83	80	75	81	87	89	85	75
France	74	72	76	71	70	82	79	73	67	76	76	68	69	78	76	87	75	66
Canada	91	90	91	89	88	90	93	91	90	91	91	87	88	92	91	87	92	88
United States	94	93	95	93	94	96	96	95	93	95	94	89	87	95	96	96	95	92
Iceland	90	86	94	90	89	91	91	93	87	na	na	95	88	91	91	92	90	88
West Germany	78	73	82	69	75	85	83	71	63	81	78	74	66	82	83	86	82	66
Denmark	81	79	84	83	74	88	88	87	74	85	80	74	69	83	93	87	85	63
Finland	75	73	77	71	72	88	86	73	72	74	78	72	76	73	95	85	74	76
Norway	91	89	92	95	87	92	93	90	91	91	91	89	89	92	94	92	91	85
Sweden	89	88	91	92	89	89	92	89	83	92	89	88	89	86	90	95	90	87
Japan	73	71	74	65	73	77	76	73	70	71	73	77	69	70	81	79	73	66
Switzerland	81	78	83	79	76	86	85	80	67	84	79	71	67	81	85	94	83	67
Total	82	80	85	80	80	87	86	82	77	84	82	79	78	84	85	87	83	75

Ranking:

Nigeria	99
India	94
North Ireland	94
United States	94
Ireland	93
Chile	92
Canada	91
Norway	91
China	90
South Korea	90
Britain	90
Iceland	90
Sweden	89
Netherlands	88
Turkey	87
Argentina	85
Italy	85
Belgium	85
Hungary	84
Austria	83
Mexico	81
Denmark	81
Switzerland	81
Slovenia	80
Belarus	79
Spain	79
East Germany	78
West Germany	78
Romania	77
Russia	77
Portugal	77
Brazil	76
Finland	75
Latvia	74
France	74
Japan	73
Lithuania	70
Moscow	66
Bulgaria	63
Estonia	61

Note: Countries in the left column are ranked according to GNP per capita. / The percentages in the bottom row give each country an equal weight. / na=not ascertained.

V199 ADEQUATE INCOME

Here is a list of things which some people think make for a successful marriage. Please tell me, for each one, whether you think it is very important, rather important, or not very important for a successful marriage: An adequate income (% "very important")

	Total	Gender Male	Gender Female	Age 16-29	Age 30-49	Age 50+	Education Lower	Education Medium	Education Upper	Income Lower	Income Middle	Income Upper	Political Affinity Left	Political Affinity Center	Political Affinity Right	Values Mat	Values Mixed	Values Postmat
India	59	59	59	59	61	54	57	62	57	57	64	56	61	53	63	58	60	55
Nigeria	75	74	77	73	77	74	78	77	72	74	71	77	67	75	76	75	75	81
China	31	31	31	27	35	29	38	29	24	31	34	28	na	na	na	34	28	19
Romania	45	46	44	40	47	47	50	46	38	46	46	43	47	47	45	47	45	36
Turkey	58	58	58	53	58	66	63	53	43	62	59	53	59	59	57	66	57	51
Poland	na	na	na	na	na	na	na	na	na	na	na	na	na	na	na	na	na	na
Bulgaria	45	43	48	43	49	43	46	46	43	48	46	38	42	44	49	51	43	44
Chile	67	67	67	60	69	75	76	62	63	76	66	59	64	66	66	74	66	60
Czechoslovakia	na	na	na	na	na	na	na	na	na	na	na	na	na	na	na	na	na	na
South Africa	na	na	na	na	na	na	na	na	na	na	na	na	na	na	na	na	na	na
Lithuania	36	35	36	33	39	35	38	36	31	33	36	40	49	54	43	37	38	31
Hungary	52	51	52	44	52	54	59	48	32	56	51	40	49	54	43	52	52	48
Argentina	44	47	42	42	41	49	49	47	31	41	48	39	44	43	50	50	43	39
Brazil	55	56	55	54	53	61	57	57	45	60	55	49	57	48	60	58	54	49
Mexico	55	56	54	54	55	60	56	57	51	54	53	61	54	54	56	61	53	51
Belarus	66	67	65	64	64	72	78	66	61	67	62	70	68	63	68	69	66	60
Russia	54	52	55	59	56	47	54	60	48	58	54	49	47	52	56	58	52	40
Moscow	52	51	52	46	54	51	65	61	42	54	50	49	49	54	52	56	52	39
Latvia	35	33	36	34	37	31	46	37	27	38	33	33	na	na	na	44	32	25
Estonia	30	31	30	32	30	28	32	32	25	29	30	34	na	na	na	36	28	22
Portugal	49	51	47	45	49	52	53	41	38	49	46	47	54	48	47	57	46	33
South Korea	34	39	31	31	34	40	43	33	32	34	32	38	35	34	35	37	33	26
Ireland	52	54	50	41	53	58	60	45	34	57	54	47	49	50	56	56	55	38
North Ireland	40	46	36	34	32	53	44	35	28	47	34	34	32	37	45	46	40	36
Slovenia	40	37	44	31	39	48	49	38	29	47	42	24	33	40	39	42	41	27
Spain	46	44	48	36	44	56	52	36	30	56	48	39	44	42	48	57	43	36
East Germany	28	29	27	22	23	37	32	23	14	33	30	22	25	29	30	43	27	22
Britain	35	35	34	25	33	42	40	26	17	43	29	27	32	35	34	40	37	20
Italy	32	32	32	23	30	39	33	22	28	35	28	19	30	35	31	38	32	25
Netherlands	24	33	21	15	18	44	36	24	13	25	25	14	15	22	30	48	28	12
Belgium	45	44	46	35	45	52	53	45	31	45	45	41	39	47	43	56	48	30
Austria	30	31	30	18	28	38	33	28	29	32	30	29	38	28	29	36	33	22
France	40	38	38	33	38	42	45	33	28	43	38	32	33	41	40	48	39	28
Canada	40	40	39	35	35	49	53	39	30	48	40	30	33	39	40	47	41	34
United States	46	44	46	41	41	50	53	48	37	49	44	42	39	44	47	52	47	36
Iceland	40	41	38	32	35	57	45	42	34	45	45	41	38	40	43	51	37	25
West Germany	26	28	24	19	27	29	28	22	23	26	27	24	22	24	32	34	27	17
Denmark	11	13	08	09	09	13	15	10	08	13	10	07	06	12	12	19	09	09
Finland	32	32	32	27	28	48	46	31	27	43	27	29	32	35	31	59	33	27
Norway	21	24	17	14	17	30	38	21	12	27	18	16	20	20	20	29	18	09
Sweden	23	24	21	15	21	31	33	17	18	25	24	19	20	24	21	29	24	12
Japan	55	54	55	50	58	54	56	55	53	56	51	59	49	49	60	62	53	46
Switzerland	35	35	35	21	31	45	37	36	19	38	33	24	22	35	40	54	37	18
Total	42	43	42	37	41	47	48	41	34	45	41	38	40	42	44	49	42	33

Ranking:

Nigeria	75
Chile	67
Belarus	66
India	59
Turkey	58
Mexico	55
Japan	55
Brazil	55
Russia	54
Moscow	52
Ireland	52
Hungary	52
Portugal	49
United States	46
Spain	46
Romania	45
Bulgaria	45
Belgium	45
Argentina	44
Slovenia	40
North Ireland	40
Iceland	40
Canada	40
France	38
Lithuania	36
Switzerland	35
Latvia	35
Britain	35
South Korea	34
Italy	32
Finland	32
China	31
Estonia	30
Austria	30
East Germany	28
West Germany	26
Netherlands	24
Sweden	23
Norway	21
Denmark	11

Note: Countries in the left column are ranked according to GNP per capita. / The percentages in the bottom row give each country an equal weight. / na=not ascertained.

V200 SAME BACKGROUND

Here is a list of things which some people think make for a successful marriage. Please tell me, for each one, whether you think it is very important, rather important, or not very important for a successful marriage: Being of the same social background (% "very important")

	Total	Gender		Age			Education			Income			Political Affinity			Values			Ranking:	
		Male	Female	16-29	30-49	50+	Lower	Medium	Upper	Lower	Middle	Upper	Left	Center	Right	Mat	Mixed	Postmat		
India	47	46	48	44	50	47	47	49	45	49	47	43	47	44	49	47	46	52	Nigeria	49
Nigeria	49	49	48	45	54	40	50	50	46	49	46	52	52	46	47	50	47	52	India	47
China	13	13	14	13	14	13	19	10	15	13	15	12	na	na	na	16	11	19	Turkey	47
Romania	25	26	24	18	25	29	24	23	28	23	26	25	30	27	22	25	24	26	Chile	34
Turkey	47	44	51	44	47	52	50	47	37	47	49	45	44	47	49	51	49	38	Mexico	30
Poland	na	na	na	na	na	na	na	na	na	na	na	na	na	na	na	na	na	na	United States	29
Bulgaria	18	16	20	13	20	19	17	21	14	15	20	17	18	19	19	22	17	15	Brazil	28
Chile	34	31	36	19	35	52	48	27	25	42	33	24	25	34	45	44	34	20	Argentina	26
Czechoslovakia	na	na	na	na	na	na	na	na	na	na	na	na	na	na	na	na	na	na	Portugal	26
South Africa	na	na	na	na	na	na	na	na	na	na	na	na	na	na	na	na	na	na	Romania	25
Lithuania	08	07	08	04	07	12	11	07	06	09	06	08	na	na	na	08	09	08	Ireland	25
Hungary	16	15	17	08	11	24	20	12	10	21	13	08	13	17	15	17	15	18	Spain	25
Argentina	26	26	25	16	23	35	30	21	20	25	25	25	25	22	32	30	26	20	Slovenia	24
Brazil	28	29	27	17	29	46	40	24	19	38	24	22	25	20	37	32	27	17	Japan	23
Mexico	30	30	31	26	29	43	31	31	28	30	27	38	22	28	36	33	29	27	South Korea	22
Belarus	16	17	15	09	15	26	29	15	13	14	15	20	16	14	21	22	12	13	Belgium	22
Russia	09	08	09	07	09	10	10	10	08	08	09	10	08	06	13	09	08	18	North Ireland	21
Moscow	12	10	13	07	11	16	26	09	10	12	12	11	10	11	18	15	11	07	Britain	21
Latvia	12	10	13	10	11	15	18	12	10	12	14	11	na	na	na	12	12	11	Netherlands	21
Estonia	08	07	08	07	08	07	07	07	08	08	08	06	na	na	na	08	08	11	France	21
Portugal	26	25	26	14	25	37	32	10	12	33	22	16	28	20	31	32	23	15	Canada	20
South Korea	22	24	19	20	22	23	25	22	19	20	19	14	20	21	31	24	19	15	Bulgaria	18
Ireland	22	24	19	20	22	23	29	22	19	16	15	10	14	23	21	29	27	17	Italy	17
North Ireland	21	17	18	10	14	25	23	16	10	24	17	13	11	na	18	29	27	07	Hungary	16
Slovenia	24	23	25	11	24	32	30	19	08	26	19	18	18	20	24	20	23	18	Belarus	16
Spain	25	24	26	15	25	32	29	14	15	34	25	19	21	22	30	32	24	15	Switzerland	16
East Germany	07	05	08	04	04	11	08	05	03	na	06	05	04	07	09	14	06	03	Austria	15
Britain	21	18	23	10	17	30	23	16	14	16	15	14	19	19	22	26	21	15	Iceland	14
Italy	17	17	18	10	14	25	18	16	10	24	17	22	17	23	22	26	27	12	Norway	14
Netherlands	21	17	22	11	17	39	28	20	07	26	20	13	16	15	24	20	23	11	China	13
Belgium	22	21	24	10	24	29	26	21	18	23	19	18	14	21	27	27	24	15	Moscow	12
Austria	15	14	15	08	12	20	19	11	13	16	15	12	15	23	28	31	21	16	Latvia	12
France	21	23	19	07	20	28	12	10	19	24	17	19	14	14	16	21	16	08	West Germany	12
Canada	20	18	22	14	16	31	30	18	16	26	20	13	18	21	23	29	20	16	Denmark	12
United States	29	26	32	21	22	39	41	27	22	34	26	16	19	30	30	40	21	17	Sweden	12
Iceland	14	12	16	08	11	29	19	13	11	na	09	11	11	17	16	16	14	20	Russia	09
West Germany	12	12	12	07	10	16	12	10	12	14	15	11	09	11	18	18	13	08	Lithuania	08
Denmark	12	10	12	04	09	21	10	09	09	15	10	07	05	14	13	14	11	16	Estonia	08
Finland	08	08	08	07	05	18	16	06	06	13	06	06	05	08	09	14	11	10	Finland	08
Norway	14	15	13	06	10	28	32	09	10	20	12	11	12	16	13	25	08	05	East Germany	07
Sweden	12	14	14	06	10	21	18	10	10	15	14	11	11	16	13	16	13	12		
Japan	23	19	27	23	20	28	25	22	23	22	21	27	19	25	27	24	25	13		
Switzerland	16	14	19	07	14	23	17	18	10	17	16	15	13	13	22	24	17	12		
Total	21	20	21	14	19	28	26	18	16	23	20	18	19	21	25	25	20	16		

Note: Countries in the left column are ranked according to GNP per capita. / The percentages in the bottom row give each country an equal weight. / na=not ascertained

V201 MUTUAL RESPECT

Here is a list of things which some people think make for a successful marriage. Please tell me, for each one, whether you think it is very important, rather important, or not very important for a successful marriage. Mutual respect and appreciation (% "very important")

	Total	Gender Male	Gender Female	Age 16-29	Age 30-49	Age 50+	Education Lower	Education Medium	Education Upper	Income Lower	Income Middle	Income Upper	Pol. Affinity Left	Pol. Affinity Center	Pol. Affinity Right	Values Mat	Values Mixed	Values Postmat
India	80	80	79	80	81	77	70	80	85	71	81	86	81	76	80	78	81	84
Nigeria	97	97	97	96	98	98	99	96	97	97	96	97	98	97	96	97	97	99
China	82	80	85	79	84	82	85	82	83	84	83	80	80	na	na	84	80	81
Romania	82	80	85	85	81	82	78	85	83	82	83	81	80	82	85	79	84	89
Turkey	89	88	90	91	88	89	88	92	90	89	88	91	92	89	88	83	91	90
Poland	na	na	na	na	na	na	na	na	na	na	na	na	na	na	na	na	na	na
Bulgaria	68	68	69	65	69	76	63	69	74	71	66	69	63	71	72	69	69	64
Chile	96	95	96	95	96	96	95	95	97	93	96	97	94	96	95	95	95	96
Czechoslovakia	na	na	na	na	na	na	na	na	na	na	na	na	na	na	na	na	na	na
South Africa	na	na	na	na	na	na	na	na	na	na	na	na	na	na	na	na	na	na
Lithuania	65	62	68	71	66	60	55	67	71	61	67	69	na	na	na	59	67	70
Hungary	90	87	92	85	89	92	90	89	94	90	90	90	85	90	90	91	88	90
Argentina	90	92	89	86	91	93	89	91	90	91	89	90	90	91	91	94	88	91
Brazil	73	72	74	69	75	76	73	72	77	72	71	75	74	70	73	74	72	78
Mexico	88	86	89	87	88	88	85	89	93	87	86	91	87	87	90	87	88	84
Belarus	85	80	89	82	86	88	82	86	84	87	85	84	87	85	74	86	86	83
Russia	78	75	80	80	78	76	75	77	80	75	79	79	75	77	70	75	80	81
Moscow	82	77	86	80	81	87	84	82	82	83	83	79	84	80	71	83	80	88
Latvia	74	68	77	79	71	73	68	74	75	70	72	76	na	na	na	67	77	69
Estonia	74	70	77	74	76	71	69	74	78	75	71	74	na	na	na	74	74	78
Portugal	83	80	86	83	80	86	83	80	84	84	83	83	83	82	84	80	85	85
South Korea	68	69	66	70	65	69	61	65	74	69	63	71	67	67	68	65	69	73
Ireland	83	79	88	81	84	85	81	86	90	81	86	85	82	81	88	81	85	83
North Ireland	83	84	82	84	77	88	80	86	93	85	81	83	89	81	87	80	83	91
Slovenia	87	85	89	90	86	88	86	88	88	86	86	91	87	89	90	88	87	88
Spain	78	75	80	77	77	80	78	78	80	77	77	80	79	80	80	80	77	81
East Germany	78	73	82	77	79	78	77	79	80	78	77	78	79	78	71	75	78	80
Britain	84	83	86	77	83	89	82	83	87	85	80	86	83	84	87	85	85	82
Italy	90	89	91	90	90	89	90	90	92	89	91	97	93	89	91	92	88	93
Netherlands	93	92	94	92	95	91	91	93	95	93	94	95	95	94	93	93	93	95
Belgium	87	84	89	87	88	85	85	87	90	85	86	90	85	90	86	85	86	92
Austria	82	79	85	80	80	86	84	80	90	82	80	85	80	83	81	84	82	83
France	84	81	87	81	87	84	82	87	86	81	86	85	85	83	82	82	85	89
Canada	92	92	93	93	94	90	94	90	96	91	93	94	95	92	93	90	92	94
United States	92	91	93	89	93	92	89	90	96	92	92	93	91	92	95	91	91	95
Iceland	96	94	98	95	97	96	95	96	97	na	na	na	96	96	97	96	96	95
West Germany	79	76	81	77	80	79	78	80	85	78	80	80	80	82	76	75	79	82
Denmark	83	78	88	82	84	84	79	83	86	80	83	86	87	82	83	74	84	91
Finland	83	80	86	86	82	83	88	80	86	86	82	83	91	82	81	79	82	87
Norway	93	91	96	95	93	93	92	92	96	94	93	94	94	93	93	94	93	95
Sweden	91	89	93	90	94	90	87	92	95	90	90	94	90	91	92	86	92	93
Japan	74	70	77	74	75	72	70	74	76	65	74	83	77	76	77	75	75	76
Switzerland	90	88	92	92	90	90	88	91	94	89	89	90	93	88	90	90	90	92
Total	**84**	**81**	**86**	**83**	**84**	**84**	**82**	**84**	**87**	**83**	**83**	**85**	**85**	**85**	**84**	**82**	**84**	**86**

Ranking:

Nigeria	97
Chile	96
Iceland	96
Netherlands	93
Norway	93
Canada	92
United States	92
Sweden	91
Hungary	90
Argentina	90
Italy	90
Switzerland	90
Turkey	89
Mexico	88
Slovenia	87
Belgium	87
Belarus	85
Britain	84
France	84
Portugal	83
Ireland	83
North Ireland	83
Denmark	83
Finland	83
China	82
Romania	82
Moscow	82
Austria	82
India	80
West Germany	79
Russia	78
Spain	78
East Germany	78
Latvia	74
Estonia	74
Japan	74
Brazil	73
Bulgaria	68
South Korea	68
Lithuania	65

Note: Countries in the left column are ranked according to GNP per capita. / The percentages in the bottom row give each country an equal weight. / na=not ascertained.

V202 SHARED RELIGION

Here is a list of things which some people think make for a successful marriage. Please tell me, for each one, whether you think it is very important, rather important, or not very important for a successful marriage. Shared religious beliefs (% "very important")

Country	Total	Gender		Age			Education			Income			Political Affinity			Values		
		Male	Female	16-29	30-49	50+	Lower	Medium	Upper	Lower	Middle	Upper	Left	Center	Right	Mat	Mixed	Postmat
India	40	38	43	34	43	47	48	41	34	48	37	37	40	40	40	41	38	31
Nigeria	83	78	89	81	84	90	88	85	79	85	80	85	84	80	86	87	80	82
China	06	06	05	04	07	05	05	05	05	05	07	05	na	na	na	07	04	06
Romania	31	28	34	17	26	44	42	25	23	33	35	24	35	28	30	38	26	19
Turkey	68	64	72	66	64	77	78	61	33	75	73	54	47	70	80	73	71	52
Poland	na	na	na	na	na	na	na	na	na	na	na	na	na	na	na	na	na	na
Bulgaria	14	12	16	08	12	20	21	13	10	16	11	12	08	14	16	17	14	08
Chile	52	46	58	40	52	70	69	47	37	66	52	35	39	54	53	67	50	36
Czechoslovakia	na	na	na	na	na	na	na	na	na	na	na	na	na	na	na	na	na	na
South Africa	na	na	na	na	na	na	na	na	na	na	na	na	na	na	na	na	na	na
Lithuania	14	12	16	07	08	26	29	09	12	19	10	09	14	21	22	17	13	09
Hungary	22	18	26	09	14	35	31	13	18	31	16	10	11	23	37	23	22	18
Argentina	28	25	31	18	27	36	34	24	22	34	26	22	28	24	37	32	29	19
Brazil	35	33	38	24	38	50	51	31	19	47	32	26	33	24	48	45	30	23
Mexico	50	46	56	46	49	64	51	57	42	53	47	50	33	50	57	60	47	39
Belarus	14	15	14	09	12	26	27	13	11	14	12	16	14	13	19	19	12	11
Russia	11	08	13	08	07	17	17	09	08	12	09	10	08	08	11	12	10	12
Moscow	11	11	12	08	10	15	18	10	10	11	12	11	11	13	09	13	10	12
Latvia	09	06	11	06	08	14	15	09	07	09	07	10	na	na	na	07	08	16
Estonia	08	08	07	05	08	09	09	07	07	08	04	11	na	na	na	07	08	02
Portugal	34	30	38	21	29	51	43	17	16	46	27	21	29	30	40	40	31	18
South Korea	21	27	16	15	22	27	30	20	18	22	19	22	17	21	22	22	21	19
Ireland	33	30	35	15	27	50	41	25	18	48	35	19	16	30	38	40	33	25
North Ireland	37	34	39	18	28	60	44	31	10	50	33	17	11	37	45	48	37	22
Slovenia	34	31	36	18	34	44	43	29	24	43	30	23	23	32	38	40	33	18
Spain	29	22	34	15	24	43	34	17	14	41	28	19	17	28	42	43	25	15
East Germany	16	13	18	08	13	22	17	14	13	20	15	12	10	16	21	22	14	14
Britain	19	15	23	06	11	34	21	16	11	29	14	09	19	16	21	20	21	12
Italy	26	22	30	18	19	38	28	16	09	32	22	09	18	30	30	36	26	18
Netherlands	16	19	15	09	11	31	26	12	09	20	14	09	08	12	28	25	20	06
Belgium	22	20	24	09	21	32	27	22	13	24	21	19	10	24	30	29	23	14
Austria	23	20	24	11	17	32	30	17	14	32	21	15	27	16	28	32	25	12
France	17	16	17	08	12	27	22	11	13	19	11	15	13	14	22	26	15	12
Canada	28	26	30	16	22	46	44	25	21	34	31	17	16	29	31	37	29	22
United States	44	42	46	33	38	54	55	44	36	52	42	37	29	43	52	52	45	33
Iceland	18	17	19	10	13	37	29	15	12	na	na	na	13	17	22	24	15	20
West Germany	14	11	16	05	09	22	16	09	10	19	13	10	07	13	23	25	14	06
Denmark	16	11	21	12	12	23	26	15	11	21	13	07	09	18	18	18	16	11
Finland	13	12	14	11	08	26	21	14	08	21	08	12	09	15	13	36	11	12
Norway	24	22	26	16	17	37	43	18	20	30	22	18	21	27	22	28	24	12
Sweden	18	16	20	14	15	24	23	15	14	20	21	14	14	20	18	26	19	12
Japan	18	17	20	13	15	28	24	18	13	22	15	21	19	17	22	23	19	09
Switzerland	21	15	26	08	16	32	25	19	13	30	16	12	13	17	30	31	23	10
Total	**26**	**24**	**28**	**17**	**23**	**37**	**34**	**22**	**18**	**32**	**24**	**20**	**21**	**27**	**32**	**32**	**25**	**19**

Note: Countries in the left column are ranked according to GNP per capita. / The percentages in the bottom row give each country an equal weight. / na=not ascertained.

Ranking:

Nigeria	83
Turkey	68
Chile	52
Mexico	50
United States	44
India	40
North Ireland	37
Brazil	35
Portugal	34
Slovenia	34
Ireland	33
Romania	31
Spain	29
Argentina	28
Canada	28
Italy	26
Norway	24
Austria	23
Hungary	22
Belgium	22
South Korea	21
Switzerland	21
Britain	19
Iceland	18
Sweden	18
Japan	18
France	17
East Germany	16
Netherlands	16
Denmark	16
Bulgaria	14
Lithuania	14
Belarus	14
West Germany	14
Finland	13
Russia	11
Moscow	11
Latvia	09
Estonia	08
China	06

V203 GOOD HOUSING

Here is a list of things which some people think make for a successful marriage. Please tell me, for each one, whether you think it is very important, rather important, or not very important for a successful marriage: Good housing   (% "very important")

	Total	Gender		Age			Education			Income			Political Affinity			Values		
		Male	Female	16-29	30-49	50+	Lower	Medium	Upper	Lower	Middle	Upper	Left	Center	Right	Mat	Mixed	Postmat
India	41	39	42	39	43	37	41	40	41	39	41	40	35	42	50	37	43	44
Nigeria	74	73	74	74	72	79	75	77	69	76	70	68	72	73	72	69	76	80
China	25	27	23	24	27	23	34	25	17	26	26	23	na	na	na	28	23	17
Romania	51	49	52	45	51	54	55	51	45	49	53	49	54	50	49	55	49	32
Turkey	50	47	52	46	50	54	58	40	27	53	50	45	43	51	48	52	54	36
Poland	na	na	na	na	na	na	na	na	na	na	na	na	na	na	na	na	na	na
Bulgaria	43	43	42	36	42	47	44	43	38	43	45	41	37	42	42	46	41	37
Chile	61	59	62	53	61	71	74	58	47	73	60	47	61	56	64	69	59	50
Czechoslovakia	na	na	na	na	na	na	na	na	na	na	na	na	na	na	na	na	na	na
South Africa	na	na	na	na	na	na	na	na	na	na	na	na	na	na	na	na	na	na
Lithuania	33	31	35	31	38	30	37	33	27	32	33	36	na	na	na	35	34	23
Hungary	51	51	52	40	53	54	58	46	43	56	51	43	48	57	45	53	49	58
Argentina	40	42	38	30	39	48	48	39	27	40	39	35	31	39	44	47	39	33
Brazil	47	49	46	42	47	57	58	46	26	58	48	37	44	41	55	53	45	32
Mexico	44	44	43	42	42	51	44	47	39	45	39	48	37	44	46	48	42	40
Belarus	61	61	61	60	61	63	72	65	53	64	59	61	62	60	57	65	62	39
Russia	51	47	54	56	53	46	52	55	47	54	52	47	42	52	55	53	51	40
Moscow	52	48	54	51	53	50	70	57	44	55	50	49	51	49	64	55	53	41
Latvia	45	41	47	39	47	49	56	46	39	45	40	48	na	na	na	54	45	34
Estonia	35	32	38	39	34	33	38	36	30	35	29	41	37	44	46	38	32	32
Portugal	52	53	51	45	53	58	58	44	34	58	48	43	59	48	55	61	51	27
South Korea	07	08	06	06	08	08	15	06	05	09	07	04	11	06	07	08	07	05
Ireland	46	43	49	28	50	54	55	38	30	57	51	37	39	44	51	52	49	32
North Ireland	36	43	31	24	32	50	45	28	03	42	40	20	43	34	37	39	36	33
Slovenia	39	36	42	30	41	43	44	35	36	44	38	35	35	39	37	42	40	22
Spain	40	37	43	31	39	48	44	32	29	50	40	36	37	39	43	49	37	33
East Germany	41	39	42	38	37	46	45	37	27	41	44	38	40	42	40	51	41	37
Britain	37	36	38	25	31	50	44	25	18	51	31	22	36	36	37	40	39	27
Italy	25	24	26	18	22	31	25	23	15	28	19	19	25	23	31	30	27	16
Netherlands	33	36	32	27	27	48	46	30	21	37	33	20	28	31	35	48	37	22
Belgium	39	38	41	30	41	44	46	40	27	41	38	35	29	41	40	45	43	26
Austria	40	40	41	25	38	49	43	38	37	41	42	39	47	39	41	47	43	30
France	37	36	37	30	37	42	41	34	31	42	33	35	35	34	39	43	37	32
Canada	33	34	32	27	30	41	45	33	24	39	33	26	26	33	33	32	34	30
United States	40	39	40	37	31	49	52	43	26	49	38	31	27	40	43	48	40	31
Iceland	33	35	31	28	25	52	44	31	26	na	na	na	28	35	38	45	31	15
West Germany	26	26	25	20	24	30	28	20	22	27	25	26	21	25	33	33	28	17
Denmark	30	30	30	23	26	35	38	30	24	33	28	25	29	31	27	31	30	23
Finland	22	22	22	15	19	31	31	21	19	25	18	23	22	23	21	59	20	18
Norway	23	22	23	07	15	42	46	20	14	29	22	24	19	23	24	32	20	11
Sweden	39	39	38	30	33	51	51	35	26	46	39	35	34	40	38	48	40	28
Japan	35	34	36	25	33	45	42	34	30	39	30	40	30	30	40	43	32	27
Switzerland	34	33	35	18	31	45	37	36	16	37	32	22	30	32	41	48	36	24
Total	**40**	**39**	**40**	**33**	**38**	**44**	**47**	**38**	**30**	**44**	**39**	**35**	**37**	**40**	**42**	**46**	**40**	**31**

Ranking:

Nigeria	74
Chile	61
Belarus	61
Moscow	52
Portugal	52
Romania	51
Hungary	51
Russia	51
Turkey	50
Brazil	47
Ireland	46
Latvia	45
Mexico	44
Bulgaria	43
India	41
East Germany	41
Argentina	40
Spain	40
Austria	40
United States	40
Slovenia	39
Belgium	39
Sweden	39
Britain	37
France	37
North Ireland	36
Estonia	35
Japan	35
Switzerland	34
Lithuania	33
Netherlands	33
Canada	33
Iceland	33
Denmark	30
West Germany	26
China	25
Italy	25
Norway	23
Finland	22
South Korea	07

Note: Countries in the left column are ranked according to GNP per capita. / The percentages in the bottom row give each country an equal weight. / na=not ascertained.

V204 POLITICS

Here is a list of things which some people think make for a successful marriage. Please tell me, for each one, whether you think it is very important, rather important, or not very important for a successful marriage: Agreement on politics (% "very important")

		Gender		Age			Education			Income			Political Affinity			Values			Ranking:	
	Total	Male	Female	16-29	30-49	50+	Lower	Medium	Upper	Lower	Middle	Upper	Left	Center	Right	Mat	Mixed	Postmat		
India	12	11	13	11	11	13	13	12	10	14	10	11	14	13	11	08	14	14	Turkey	35
Nigeria	20	20	19	21	17	23	20	21	18	21	19	16	21	18	25	23	19	12	China	24
China	24	21	28	15	26	32	21	23	29	22	30	21	na	na	na	25	24	17	Nigeria	20
Romania	07	09	06	05	06	10	08	07	08	06	06	09	14	06	10	07	08	09	Chile	18
Turkey	35	32	38	30	35	40	39	30	25	41	30	33	40	32	36	32	37	32	Mexico	18
Poland	na	na	na	na	na	na	na	na	na	na	na	na	na	na	na	na	na	na	Bulgaria	15
Bulgaria	15	14	15	11	14	18	12	16	16	11	17	17	16	14	21	15	13	24	Portugal	15
Chile	18	18	18	12	20	24	24	16	14	20	17	16	23	15	23	19	17	22	Spain	15
Czechoslovakia	na	na	na	na	na	na	na	na	na	na	na	na	na	na	na	na	na	na	Slovenia	14
South Africa	na	na	na	na	na	na	na	na	na	na	na	na	na	na	na	na	na	na	Brazil	13
Lithuania	08	09	07	05	05	13	07	07	09	07	09	05	na	na	na	08	07	10	Latvia	13
Hungary	11	10	11	04	08	16	13	08	11	14	08	08	11	11	11	12	10	05	India	12
Argentina	08	09	07	05	06	12	08	09	07	08	10	06	07	08	14	07	08	09	East Germany	12
Brazil	13	13	14	09	13	21	21	10	08	20	12	08	10	07	21	16	12	07	United States	12
Mexico	18	19	17	16	19	21	18	21	15	17	18	19	16	18	19	20	16	20	Hungary	11
Belarus	09	10	08	06	07	17	13	08	09	08	07	12	10	07	13	11	08	10	Moscow	10
Russia	08	08	08	07	08	10	07	08	09	05	10	09	12	07	09	09	07	12	South Korea	10
Moscow	10	09	10	07	09	13	13	09	09	11	07	12	08	10	21	15	08	08	North Ireland	10
Latvia	13	12	14	09	13	18	18	11	15	10	13	14	na	na	na	11	14	12	Italy	10
Estonia	06	05	06	02	05	11	05	04	09	05	05	07	na	na	na	04	06	09	Sweden	10
Portugal	15	15	16	11	13	21	17	11	12	19	12	12	20	11	19	19	12	15	Belarus	09
South Korea	10	12	08	10	11	07	16	10	07	10	12	05	17	10	07	09	10	12	Belgium	09
Ireland	04	04	04	00	05	06	06	02	00	08	03	03	03	04	06	04	05	03	Switzerland	09
North Ireland	10	09	10	07	05	17	12	08	00	14	05	03	04	06	18	12	10	04	Lithuania	08
Slovenia	14	14	13	07	13	18	15	13	11	15	13	12	09	13	21	16	13	07	Argentina	08
Spain	15	14	16	08	14	21	18	07	08	23	15	09	12	12	21	23	13	08	Russia	08
East Germany	12	09	15	08	12	15	10	15	19	13	11	12	19	08	09	12	12	13	Austria	08
Britain	07	07	07	04	05	11	07	06	08	08	07	04	08	06	08	07	07	06	France	08
Italy	10	08	11	07	08	14	11	06	03	13	07	09	11	09	11	12	09	10	Japan	08
Netherlands	07	12	06	05	04	14	11	07	04	10	07	01	05	05	12	20	08	03	Romania	07
Belgium	09	10	08	06	08	12	10	10	05	08	09	09	06	09	15	10	09	07	Britain	07
Austria	08	07	08	04	05	12	11	06	04	09	09	05	12	06	09	10	09	04	Netherlands	07
France	08	08	07	04	05	13	09	05	07	07	05	08	09	05	11	09	07	08	West Germany	07
Canada	06	06	05	03	04	10	11	04	04	06	05	04	05	03	08	06	05	07	Norway	07
United States	12	12	11	10	07	16	22	10	06	15	10	08	08	10	15	14	12	07	Estonia	06
Iceland	05	06	03	03	04	09	09	03	03	na	na	na	03	04	08	06	05	03	Canada	06
West Germany	07	07	06	05	05	09	06	06	10	08	06	07	08	05	10	08	07	06	Iceland	05
Denmark	04	03	05	00	05	07	06	04	03	06	02	04	05	03	04	05	03	04	Finland	05
Finland	05	05	05	05	01	14	16	02	02	11	03	01	03	05	05	22	04	03	Ireland	04
Norway	07	07	06	06	03	14	16	05	04	12	04	04	07	05	07	08	06	04	Denmark	04
Sweden	10	08	12	06	07	18	15	06	08	11	13	07	09	10	13	18	09	07		
Japan	08	07	09	04	06	13	10	08	06	10	04	11	09	08	08	07	07	15		
Switzerland	09	08	09	06	06	13	09	10	04	10	07	03	08	05	12	10	10	05		
Total	**11**	**11**	**11**	**08**	**09**	**15**	**13**	**10**	**09**	**12**	**10**	**11**	**11**	**09**	**14**	**13**	**11**	**10**		

Note: Countries in the left column are ranked according to GNP per capita. / The percentages in the bottom row give each country an equal weight. / na=not ascertained.

V205   UNDERSTANDING

Here is a list of things which some people think make for a successful marriage. Please tell me, for each one, whether you think it is very important, rather important, or not very important for a successful marriage: Understanding and tolerance   (% "very important")

	Total	Gender		Age			Education			Income			Political Affinity			Values		
		Male	Female	16-29	30-49	50+	Lower	Medium	Upper	Lower	Middle	Upper	Left	Center	Right	Mat	Mixed	Postmat
India	81	81	82	82	82	79	71	82	86	74	81	99	84	78	99	82	82	84
Nigeria	99	98	100	98	99	100	99	98	99	99	99	99	97	99	99	98	99	99
China	70	67	75	72	71	67	69	71	75	70	72	68	na	na	na	70	72	76
Romania	72	68	77	73	69	76	74	72	70	75	72	70	73	71	73	75	70	77
Turkey	80	76	84	79	80	81	80	82	76	80	81	80	81	81	77	80	80	81
Poland	na	na	na	na	na	na	na	na	na	na	na	na	na	na	na	na	na	na
Bulgaria	63	62	65	65	63	61	57	65	69	62	63	69	58	69	63	63	63	65
Chile	90	90	90	87	91	92	90	90	90	87	90	94	90	91	89	91	89	92
Czechoslovakia	na	na	na	na	na	na	na	na	na	na	na	na	na	na	na	na	na	na
South Africa	na	na	na	na	na	na	na	na	na	na	na	na	na	na	na	na	na	na
Lithuania	33	32	34	34	35	31	31	32	44	33	31	36	na	na	na	32	32	33
Hungary	76	74	79	76	75	77	72	78	89	75	78	79	79	79	76	79	74	80
Argentina	89	89	88	83	90	92	90	88	88	87	88	88	90	89	91	92	87	89
Brazil	70	68	73	67	72	73	67	70	78	70	70	70	69	67	73	72	69	73
Mexico	82	79	84	82	81	80	79	86	85	81	79	85	83	80	84	83	81	81
Belarus	69	66	72	65	69	74	67	66	73	69	71	67	72	66	63	64	74	59
Russia	67	62	71	71	66	66	64	66	70	65	70	69	65	68	53	64	69	67
Moscow	74	67	80	73	73	77	67	74	75	75	71	77	74	75	67	75	72	79
Latvia	62	57	65	63	61	62	55	60	67	61	65	61	na	na	na	53	64	67
Estonia	57	51	62	58	55	59	55	57	58	58	52	59	na	na	na	54	59	55
Portugal	76	73	78	75	76	76	76	80	72	76	76	73	75	75	77	78	75	69
South Korea	73	72	74	82	68	69	66	68	82	75	69	75	69	73	75	70	72	84
Ireland	81	76	86	76	82	85	79	83	88	81	80	83	71	80	89	81	83	77
North Ireland	81	78	82	72	78	89	82	80	72	81	77	77	64	80	86	82	83	73
Slovenia	78	76	80	76	79	78	76	77	84	78	75	84	83	82	74	79	78	78
Spain	73	71	75	75	71	74	73	74	74	72	74	78	76	76	76	75	71	78
East Germany	74	72	76	73	75	74	72	78	79	76	73	73	79	73	70	68	73	79
Britain	86	85	87	80	85	90	85	87	90	87	87	85	85	86	85	85	87	85
Italy	80	77	82	75	80	82	80	81	79	79	82	88	82	83	78	80	78	84
Netherlands	87	85	88	89	86	88	87	87	89	87	87	86	85	89	88	92	88	86
Belgium	78	77	79	76	80	76	75	78	82	74	78	80	74	80	76	74	78	82
Austria	83	79	84	81	82	84	84	82	88	81	83	83	78	82	85	79	82	85
France	74	72	77	71	76	75	73	74	79	72	74	75	75	73	73	69	74	80
Canada	84	81	87	84	83	84	81	83	88	83	82	87	83	84	85	81	83	88
United States	83	81	85	82	85	82	81	82	86	81	81	88	85	84	84	78	83	86
Iceland	86	81	92	85	88	83	82	87	89	na	na	na	90	84	85	87	86	84
West Germany	77	74	80	80	79	75	74	82	86	77	77	79	81	78	73	69	77	83
Denmark	80	77	84	80	80	81	77	83	80	79	75	87	82	81	79	73	81	82
Finland	70	70	69	78	68	68	70	64	76	70	68	72	65	65	69	79	67	74
Norway	84	82	86	85	84	84	79	81	90	82	84	89	84	84	85	81	85	89
Sweden	89	85	93	91	88	89	84	89	94	85	88	91	86	88	92	81	89	94
Japan	77	73	80	85	78	71	69	77	83	74	78	79	82	79	78	80	78	75
Switzerland	86	83	89	87	84	88	84	88	89	87	85	85	91	84	85	83	86	90
Total	77	74	79	77	77	77	74	77	80	76	76	80	79	79	79	76	77	79

Ranking:

Nigeria	99
Chile	90
Argentina	89
Sweden	89
Netherlands	87
Britain	86
Iceland	86
Switzerland	86
Canada	84
Norway	84
Austria	83
United States	83
Mexico	82
India	81
Ireland	81
North Ireland	81
Turkey	80
Italy	80
Denmark	80
Slovenia	78
Belgium	78
West Germany	77
Japan	77
Hungary	76
Portugal	76
Moscow	74
East Germany	74
France	74
South Korea	73
Spain	73
Romania	72
China	70
Brazil	70
Finland	70
Belarus	69
Russia	67
Bulgaria	63
Latvia	62
Estonia	57
Lithuania	33

Note: Countries in the left column are ranked according to GNP per capita. / The percentages in the bottom row give each country an equal weight. / na=not ascertained.

V206 AWAY FROM IN-LAWS

Here is a list of things which some people think make for a successful marriage. Please tell me, for each one, whether you think it is very important, rather important, or not very important for a successful marriage: Living apart from your in-laws (% "very important")

	Total	Gender Male	Gender Female	Age 16-29	Age 30-49	Age 50+	Education Lower	Education Medium	Education Upper	Income Lower	Income Middle	Income Upper	Political Affinity Left	Political Affinity Center	Political Affinity Right	Values Mat	Values Mixed	Values Postmat	Ranking:	
India	20	21	18	18	20	22	22	21	17	24	18	17	21	20	19	18	21	18	France	64
Nigeria	57	58	57	55	60	56	53	62	54	61	55	53	57	54	56	62	54	62	Netherlands	59
China	08	06	11	06	11	06	06	09	09	07	12	07	na	na	na	08	09	09	Switzerland	59
Romania	40	36	44	44	46	31	32	44	44	41	41	38	44	38	46	35	42	53	Nigeria	57
Turkey	42	44	40	43	41	41	40	44	46	40	40	45	46	44	35	40	43	43	Belgium	57
Poland	na	na	na	na	na	na	na	na	na	na	na	na	na	na	na	na	na	na	Portugal	54
Bulgaria	43	37	49	55	46	33	26	50	48	43	45	42	40	44	48	44	40	60	North Ireland	54
Chile	53	52	54	52	54	52	55	50	55	55	54	49	51	51	63	56	53	51	Britain	54
Czechoslovakia	na	na	na	na	na	na	na	na	na	na	na	na	na	na	na	na	na	na	Denmark	54
South Africa	na	na	na	na	na	na	na	na	na	na	na	na	na	na	na	na	na	na	Sweden	54
Lithuania	35	31	38	41	40	25	25	36	49	34	36	36	na	na	na	36	36	29	Chile	53
Hungary	48	47	48	42	53	45	48	46	52	46	50	44	47	49	52	47	49	45	Canada	51
Argentina	41	42	40	44	42	37	39	45	44	40	43	43	50	45	44	42	37	52	Belarus	50
Brazil	48	45	51	48	49	47	49	47	51	47	49	46	52	43	47	48	48	46	Moscow	49
Mexico	40	39	42	40	40	41	40	39	40	37	39	49	42	42	40	37	41	48	Hungary	48
Belarus	50	51	49	51	51	45	41	52	51	47	49	53	52	49	44	51	51	43	Brazil	48
Russia	36	33	38	44	40	25	29	39	36	35	36	36	35	34	37	32	37	51	United States	47
Moscow	49	41	56	45	53	46	48	50	48	51	47	48	49	46	47	51	49	49	Ireland	46
Latvia	42	38	46	35	46	43	43	43	41	39	45	43	na	na	na	44	42	37	Italy	46
Estonia	42	39	44	46	46	31	34	44	43	41	42	43	na	na	na	37	42	45	East Germany	44
Portugal	54	52	55	57	50	53	55	58	51	55	51	51	58	51	54	59	52	45	Bulgaria	43
South Korea	05	06	04	03	06	05	12	05	02	06	05	05	06	05	04	06	04	03	Iceland	43
Ireland	46	45	47	49	51	40	47	47	38	44	45	49	42	44	52	42	48	49	Turkey	42
North Ireland	54	61	49	45	60	55	57	54	38	57	61	47	50	56	57	60	53	56	Latvia	42
Slovenia	31	29	34	28	36	28	28	30	40	30	32	33	32	33	40	31	32	25	Estonia	42
Spain	36	33	38	39	36	34	36	34	40	39	36	37	39	33	35	38	33	41	Norway	42
East Germany	44	44	43	47	46	40	44	45	44	40	44	47	48	44	40	38	44	47	Argentina	41
Britain	54	56	53	53	55	54	54	58	48	57	62	50	54	54	54	50	57	50	Romania	40
Italy	46	44	47	52	52	37	44	55	60	41	55	56	52	44	46	40	46	51	Mexico	40
Netherlands	59	60	59	54	61	61	61	59	56	58	61	57	61	58	59	61	58	60	West Germany	37
Belgium	57	55	58	59	61	51	55	58	59	54	52	57	58	54	55	55	58	58	Russia	36
Austria	36	35	37	36	37	36	35	36	46	30	38	40	49	37	35	34	36	40	Spain	36
France	64	61	67	63	69	59	62	65	65	61	67	65	66	59	60	64	63	67	Austria	36
Canada	51	47	54	51	50	52	53	53	47	56	51	56	52	50	53	53	52	51	Lithuania	35
United States	47	46	47	49	48	45	47	49	44	49	47	43	48	48	45	44	47	47	Slovenia	31
Iceland	43	41	45	35	49	43	42	44	43	na	na	na	40	44	47	46	42	43	Finland	24
West Germany	37	39	36	44	40	31	37	38	42	37	39	37	41	38	33	32	38	39	India	20
Denmark	54	52	56	52	55	54	55	56	52	53	54	57	52	54	57	53	53	52	China	08
Finland	24	23	24	20	24	25	25	18	29	24	17	31	21	20	26	36	25	18	Japan	07
Norway	42	39	44	41	40	44	48	42	38	44	41	42	45	39	41	43	40	45	South Korea	05
Sweden	54	51	58	47	56	56	56	54	47	54	53	53	52	55	53	56	56	45		
Japan	07	06	08	08	06	08	10	07	06	09	05	08	06	08	06	08	06	08		
Switzerland	59	55	63	56	60	59	60	60	55	62	54	58	61	56	57	67	59	55		
Total	**42**	**41**	**44**	**42**	**45**	**40**	**41**	**44**	**43**	**42**	**42**	**42**	**45**	**43**	**44**	**43**	**42**	**43**		

Note: Countries in the left column are ranked according to GNP per capita. / The percentages in the bottom row give each country an equal weight. / na=not ascertained.

V207 HAPPY SEXUAL LIFE

Here is a list of things which some people think make for a successful marriage. Please tell me, for each one, whether you think it is very important, rather important, or not very important for a successful marriage: Happy sexual relationship (% "very important")

	Total	Gender		Age			Education			Income			Political Affinity			Values		
		Male	Female	16-29	30-49	50+	Lower	Medium	Upper	Lower	Middle	Upper	Left	Center	Right	Mat	Mixed	Postmat
India	78	79	76	78	79	74	72	79	79	74	79	92	78	78	81	77	79	78
Nigeria	91	92	91	91	93	86	95	91	91	92	91	92	90	92	90	94	90	92
China	37	38	36	39	39	32	43	34	40	36	43	35	60	na	na	35	39	49
Romania	59	59	59	70	60	52	45	65	68	59	58	61	60	58	65	51	63	76
Turkey	73	72	74	77	74	65	69	79	78	71	70	80	77	72	72	64	74	82
Poland	na	na	na	na	na	na	na	na	na	na	na	na	na	na	na	na	na	na
Bulgaria	48	49	47	64	52	34	33	51	57	44	46	57	51	47	52	42	49	64
Chile	74	77	71	73	79	68	73	74	76	71	73	79	77	74	74	77	72	80
Czechoslovakia	na	na	na	na	na	na	na	na	na	na	na	na	na	na	na	na	na	na
South Africa	na	na	na	na	na	na	na	na	na	na	na	na	na	na	na	na	na	na
Lithuania	37	38	36	46	42	23	25	39	48	34	35	45	na	na	na	32	38	42
Hungary	69	73	66	77	76	60	62	76	75	60	76	77	75	72	68	67	70	78
Argentina	81	82	80	78	83	81	80	84	81	79	80	83	84	83	81	78	82	84
Brazil	72	71	73	72	74	68	66	75	74	71	74	70	74	69	75	73	71	72
Mexico	77	76	77	80	78	66	74	81	82	74	77	82	81	79	77	69	80	76
Belarus	58	60	56	66	58	50	51	58	60	57	57	60	62	51	60	52	61	61
Russia	46	50	44	65	52	27	34	52	48	43	47	47	52	47	48	42	48	57
Moscow	62	62	63	66	67	51	51	64	63	58	64	63	64	62	57	61	63	66
Latvia	59	59	59	71	60	44	53	60	60	59	61	59	na	na	na	49	64	60
Estonia	53	55	51	65	54	37	47	55	53	51	50	58	na	na	na	51	53	53
Portugal	69	71	67	75	71	61	68	73	70	62	76	71	76	68	70	70	71	64
South Korea	na	na	na	na	na	na	na	na	na	na	na	na	na	na	na	na	na	na
Ireland	68	69	67	70	70	64	68	69	63	68	66	68	65	65	74	63	70	68
North Ireland	69	67	71	55	75	73	73	65	52	74	70	62	57	68	73	69	69	71
Slovenia	61	58	63	62	66	55	60	61	63	61	60	63	59	65	62	60	61	59
Spain	63	66	60	71	66	53	59	71	71	57	65	60	69	63	62	60	64	73
East Germany	54	60	49	66	56	45	51	64	57	49	58	56	60	53	50	40	54	60
Britain	66	69	65	70	63	70	69	61	59	70	68	60	67	65	68	69	67	64
Italy	67	71	64	70	72	61	66	72	77	66	73	74	73	66	65	65	67	71
Netherlands	62	67	60	58	61	68	66	61	58	61	61	63	59	59	67	67	66	53
Belgium	65	65	65	67	69	59	60	68	68	61	68	68	63	67	67	60	67	64
Austria	57	56	57	67	58	51	51	60	60	51	56	63	59	57	56	45	58	60
France	68	68	67	69	76	59	66	71	67	68	67	72	70	67	63	68	67	70
Canada	72	74	71	71	73	73	76	73	69	75	73	72	72	73	71	67	74	72
United States	71	71	71	71	70	71	76	71	67	75	69	67	67	71	72	71	72	71
Iceland	73	71	75	74	71	75	80	75	67	na	55	53	73	70	77	81	70	69
West Germany	51	55	47	62	59	38	49	54	53	45	55	53	53	52	49	41	52	53
Denmark	65	65	65	68	66	62	60	71	64	61	65	69	63	63	68	57	67	62
Finland	61	64	58	66	66	60	61	62	61	65	60	61	68	64	58	61	62	60
Norway	62	64	60	64	60	63	63	65	59	60	62	68	59	63	64	64	61	61
Sweden	67	68	65	69	66	67	69	67	63	70	65	67	65	66	67	68	67	68
Japan	28	29	28	32	28	25	21	28	36	26	24	35	25	30	34	32	27	39
Switzerland	68	70	66	68	69	66	69	67	67	68	68	69	70	67	67	69	68	67
Total	**63**	**64**	**62**	**67**	**65**	**57**	**60**	**65**	**64**	**61**	**63**	**65**	**66**	**65**	**66**	**61**	**64**	**66**

Ranking:

Nigeria	91
Argentina	81
India	78
Mexico	77
Chile	74
Turkey	73
Iceland	73
Brazil	72
Canada	72
United States	71
Hungary	69
Portugal	69
North Ireland	69
Ireland	68
France	68
Switzerland	68
Italy	67
Sweden	67
Britain	66
Belgium	65
Denmark	65
Spain	63
Moscow	62
Netherlands	62
Norway	62
Slovenia	61
Finland	61
Romania	59
Latvia	59
Belarus	58
Austria	57
East Germany	54
Estonia	53
West Germany	51
Bulgaria	48
Russia	46
China	37
Lithuania	37
Japan	28

Note: Countries in the left column are ranked according to GNP per capita. / The percentages in the bottom row give each country an equal weight. / na=not ascertained.

V208 SHARE HOUSEHOLD CHORES

Here is a list of things which some people think make for a successful marriage. Please tell me, for each one, whether you think it is very important, rather important, or not very important for a successful marriage: Sharing household chores   (% "very important")

	Total	Gender		Age			Education			Income			Political Affinity			Values		
		Male	Female	16-29	30-49	50+	Lower	Medium	Upper	Lower	Middle	Upper	Left	Center	Right	Mat	Mixed	Postmat
India	58	57	60	60	59	53	53	61	58	57	55	60	65	58	56	54	61	69
Nigeria	67	68	66	67	68	61	68	73	60	78	59	64	69	62	69	64	70	64
China	35	34	38	33	35	39	41	35	29	36	34	36	na	na	na	38	33	32
Romania	42	38	47	34	40	50	45	43	38	48	45	34	42	42	42	47	40	32
Turkey	31	27	36	32	30	33	32	30	34	34	30	31	33	30	32	29	32	33
Poland	na	na	na	na	na	na	na	na	na	na	na	na	na	na	na	na	na	na
Bulgaria	42	36	47	38	40	45	42	45	34	42	45	37	39	44	34	44	41	37
Chile	62	60	63	54	64	70	71	58	54	72	59	53	55	61	63	66	61	60
Czechoslovakia	na	na	na	na	na	na	na	na	na	na	na	na	na	na	na	na	na	na
South Africa	na	na	na	na	na	na	na	na	na	na	na	na	na	na	na	na	na	na
Lithuania	25	20	29	22	23	29	27	24	25	26	26	20	na	na	na	26	24	28
Hungary	40	36	43	36	37	44	47	34	35	44	38	37	38	40	37	40	40	56
Argentina	53	50	56	47	53	58	58	58	47	55	53	49	48	47	56	53	53	52
Brazil	37	35	39	34	37	42	44	35	31	44	35	31	36	28	44	40	35	32
Mexico	47	45	50	51	44	45	44	52	55	48	45	50	46	48	51	43	48	49
Belarus	29	26	32	26	28	35	38	29	26	31	25	31	29	27	32	29	29	30
Russia	38	31	43	36	38	40	43	41	32	41	41	33	29	39	35	42	35	34
Moscow	30	29	32	29	27	37	45	32	26	33	27	32	28	30	36	35	29	26
Latvia	31	23	37	29	31	34	38	31	29	32	34	29	36	na	na	34	31	26
Estonia	19	15	22	20	16	21	15	21	17	21	18	16	na	na	na	22	17	17
Portugal	50	45	53	54	49	45	50	48	47	49	52	45	51	51	49	51	49	45
South Korea	na	na	na	na	na	na	na	na	na	na	na	na	na	na	na	na	na	na
Ireland	38	36	41	42	40	34	39	38	34	39	38	38	41	36	41	32	41	37
North Ireland	45	51	41	42	43	49	47	48	21	49	43	41	36	44	50	45	44	47
Slovenia	35	32	38	33	36	35	38	31	35	36	36	31	33	36	39	35	36	24
Spain	40	38	41	47	37	36	40	38	41	46	40	37	42	40	34	40	38	44
East Germany	30	26	33	32	29	30	31	33	23	32	32	26	35	28	24	32	30	30
Britain	44	45	43	48	40	45	45	45	39	50	40	43	43	46	41	37	46	46
Italy	30	29	31	37	31	28	30	31	30	32	30	23	36	29	26	25	31	33
Netherlands	34	35	34	39	32	32	31	36	35	39	32	33	45	30	29	34	32	38
Belgium	38	39	38	41	38	36	38	37	40	43	44	34	38	42	36	41	37	39
Austria	29	29	29	32	26	30	29	29	31	29	31	26	35	30	29	32	28	29
France	35	36	35	34	38	34	35	33	39	35	36	34	38	32	27	33	32	44
Canada	53	53	53	60	52	47	57	51	52	55	54	52	58	51	48	51	53	54
United States	47	48	46	53	46	46	53	46	45	49	48	45	42	47	51	44	47	49
Iceland	42	44	41	46	42	40	45	43	40	na	na	na	52	38	41	44	40	53
West Germany	21	20	23	28	21	17	19	23	27	22	22	21	25	22	18	14	20	28
Denmark	48	46	51	53	50	42	44	53	47	44	50	54	49	46	48	45	49	45
Finland	25	22	28	36	21	24	35	22	24	32	19	25	33	22	20	52	25	19
Norway	34	30	37	46	31	28	30	33	35	36	31	36	39	33	29	29	34	43
Sweden	48	45	51	56	47	42	48	50	43	49	49	44	49	50	41	44	48	51
Japan	10	10	10	12	09	10	08	09	15	13	09	12	08	08	13	10	11	17
Switzerland	33	35	31	41	30	32	34	31	35	35	30	30	39	29	31	37	32	33
Total	38	37	40	40	37	38	40	39	36	41	38	36	41	38	39	39	38	39

Ranking:

Nigeria	67
Chile	62
India	58
Canada	53
Argentina	53
Portugal	50
Sweden	48
Denmark	48
United States	47
Mexico	47
North Ireland	45
Britain	44
Romania	42
Iceland	42
Bulgaria	42
Spain	40
Hungary	40
Russia	38
Ireland	38
Belgium	38
Brazil	37
Slovenia	35
France	35
China	35
Norway	34
Netherlands	34
Switzerland	33
Turkey	31
Latvia	31
Moscow	30
Italy	30
East Germany	30
Belarus	29
Austria	29
Lithuania	25
Finland	25
West Germany	21
Estonia	19
Japan	10

Note: Countries in the left column are ranked according to GNP per capita. / The percentages in the bottom row give each country an equal weight. / na=not ascertained.

V209 CHILDREN

Here is a list of things which some people think make for a successful marriage. Please tell me, for each one, whether you think it is very important, rather important, or not very important for a successful marriage: Children (% "very important")

	Total	Gender		Age			Education			Income			Political Affinity			Values		
		Male	Female	16-29	30-49	50+	Lower	Medium	Upper	Lower	Middle	Upper	Left	Center	Right	Mat	Mixed	Postmat
India	79	77	82	77	82	78	80	81	na	75	81	na	80	77	83	82	78	77
Nigeria	94	94	94	95	91	98	96	95	92	95	92	94	92	93	95	94	94	90
China	55	51	60	45	63	50	64	53	48	58	58	48	75	na	na	60	50	50
Romania	68	71	66	53	69	78	74	65	64	74	69	67	75	68	61	75	66	42
Turkey	69	66	73	63	72	76	77	63	46	74	67	67	61	73	72	72	72	59
Poland	na	na	na	na	na	na	na	na	na	na	na	na	na	na	na	na	na	na
Bulgaria	84	83	84	82	85	82	81	86	81	82	83	87	86	82	80	86	83	79
Chile	92	92	93	93	92	92	94	93	90	93	93	90	91	93	93	93	93	90
Czechoslovakia	na	na	na	na	na	na	na	na	na	na	na	na	na	na	na	na	na	na
South Africa	na	na	na	na	na	na	na	na	na	na	na	na	na	na	na	na	na	na
Lithuania	66	60	71	60	69	67	65	66	64	62	72	63	na	na	na	71	65	62
Hungary	85	84	86	82	85	87	86	85	83	85	85	85	88	84	82	85	84	95
Argentina	88	88	88	81	91	89	89	89	88	86	87	89	85	87	93	89	88	85
Brazil	60	60	60	53	63	66	65	60	50	64	59	56	53	57	67	65	57	49
Mexico	75	74	76	75	74	75	74	83	73	75	73	79	71	73	81	74	76	65
Belarus	81	80	83	73	84	85	84	81	81	85	82	78	83	79	81	84	81	77
Russia	80	76	83	77	81	80	83	80	78	83	80	76	78	79	79	83	79	74
Moscow	74	71	77	68	76	76	84	78	69	77	75	67	73	76	75	78	73	70
Latvia	78	74	81	75	79	79	84	75	81	82	81	72	73	na	na	81	79	72
Estonia	74	67	79	68	76	77	70	75	73	79	69	70	71	73	81	73	75	75
Portugal	65	64	66	56	68	70	71	62	44	72	63	55	65	63	66	68	65	49
South Korea	na	na	na	na	na	na	na	na	na	na	na	na	na	na	na	na	na	na
Ireland	62	59	65	53	66	64	66	60	49	66	64	59	59	62	61	63	62	63
North Ireland	69	70	68	61	68	76	75	65	38	74	73	58	46	68	75	72	67	73
Slovenia	73	69	76	67	75	74	72	72	75	73	73	72	73	74	73	75	71	71
Spain	68	66	70	63	69	72	70	67	59	71	69	67	67	72	74	71	66	69
East Germany	65	59	70	59	66	67	65	64	65	64	67	64	65	66	60	63	64	68
Britain	58	56	60	48	55	67	63	50	43	68	55	49	52	62	56	61	59	55
Italy	65	64	65	54	61	74	67	49	39	70	59	54	59	68	67	76	65	52
Netherlands	56	57	56	45	56	70	71	57	39	50	64	52	46	58	61	72	61	44
Belgium	55	52	58	50	54	59	58	54	49	54	55	51	45	58	56	63	56	44
Austria	63	60	66	54	66	65	66	63	57	61	68	61	64	61	65	67	65	58
France	65	61	69	60	66	68	67	65	59	66	65	63	63	63	68	72	65	59
Canada	66	62	69	62	66	73	73	68	57	68	66	64	57	66	66	66	67	63
United States	65	63	67	58	62	71	67	69	59	68	65	62	49	68	68	73	68	56
Iceland	66	64	67	51	68	79	69	69	62	na	na	na	65	68	66	75	65	50
West Germany	44	40	48	32	45	50	48	37	39	45	45	43	38	47	46	48	46	38
Denmark	42	37	47	24	42	57	56	40	36	49	42	35	36	44	45	54	42	30
Finland	60	59	62	53	58	72	61	56	58	61	59	62	64	63	56	79	62	53
Norway	61	61	61	51	57	71	72	60	56	57	61	62	53	63	63	68	59	53
Sweden	61	62	61	54	63	66	69	60	53	66	54	66	61	64	60	63	63	55
Japan	52	52	52	44	53	55	54	53	45	52	53	51	52	48	54	55	52	46
Switzerland	54	51	56	47	49	62	55	56	39	54	49	43	39	51	61	72	54	41
Total	68	66	70	61	68	72	71	67	60	69	68	65	64	68	69	72	68	62

Ranking:

Nigeria	94
Chile	92
Argentina	88
Hungary	85
Bulgaria	84
Belarus	81
Russia	80
India	79
Latvia	78
Mexico	75
Moscow	74
Estonia	74
Slovenia	73
Turkey	69
North Ireland	69
Romania	68
Spain	68
Lithuania	66
Canada	66
Iceland	66
Portugal	65
East Germany	65
Italy	65
France	65
United States	65
Austria	63
Ireland	62
Norway	61
Sweden	61
Brazil	60
Finland	60
Britain	58
Netherlands	56
China	55
Belgium	55
Switzerland	54
Japan	52
West Germany	44
Denmark	42

Note: Countries in the left column are ranked according to GNP per capita. / The percentages in the bottom row give each country an equal weight. / na=not ascertained.

V210 COMMON INTERESTS

Here is a list of things which some people think make for a successful marriage. Please tell me, for each one, whether you think it is very important, rather important, or not very important for a successful marriage: Tastes and interests in common   (% "very important")

	Total	Gender Male	Gender Female	Age 16-29	Age 30-49	Age 50+	Education Lower	Education Medium	Education Upper	Income Lower	Income Middle	Income Upper	Pol. Aff. Left	Pol. Aff. Center	Pol. Aff. Right	Values Mat	Values Mixed	Values Postmat
India	48	47	50	47	50	47	45	50	47	46	49	49	54	43	47	45	50	50
Nigeria	78	75	81	78	79	68	81	80	74	79	74	78	79	72	80	77	79	71
China	34	33	34	40	32	29	33	33	37	33	37	31	48	43	na	31	35	50
Romania	43	40	46	44	43	43	39	46	45	46	43	41	48	43	42	44	42	48
Turkey	61	59	63	59	62	62	64	62	47	64	55	65	62	59	67	57	65	57
Poland	na	na	na	na	na	na	na	na	na	na	na	na	na	na	na	na	na	na
Bulgaria	38	36	40	32	38	41	35	39	38	34	40	41	34	41	39	42	36	37
Chile	63	60	66	57	64	71	68	62	59	70	61	58	60	62	64	66	62	63
Czechoslovakia	na	na	na	na	na	na	na	na	na	na	na	na	na	na	na	na	na	na
South Africa	na	na	na	na	na	na	na	na	na	na	na	na	na	na	na	na	na	na
Lithuania	21	21	22	24	21	19	22	21	22	24	19	19	na	na	na	25	20	17
Hungary	44	41	46	31	43	50	45	43	41	47	43	36	42	46	44	44	43	54
Argentina	61	60	63	50	63	68	63	63	60	61	57	63	57	60	64	62	62	59
Brazil	43	42	45	36	46	51	50	42	36	49	41	39	40	36	52	49	39	39
Mexico	60	56	65	63	57	61	58	68	60	60	59	62	53	64	63	56	62	59
Belarus	46	44	47	44	43	53	44	48	44	45	44	48	48	43	41	45	45	50
Russia	37	35	39	35	35	41	37	39	35	35	41	37	32	39	32	35	38	42
Moscow	45	42	48	40	44	52	60	47	41	47	45	42	44	47	47	52	43	43
Latvia	30	24	35	33	29	30	32	30	30	27	27	34	na	na	na	26	34	25
Estonia	29	26	31	34	25	29	28	30	26	30	25	29	na	na	na	29	28	33
Portugal	51	51	52	49	51	55	54	53	41	57	51	40	52	52	50	54	50	42
South Korea	20	26	14	22	19	17	19	19	21	20	20	18	19	22	18	20	18	25
Ireland	40	36	44	39	39	42	42	38	41	45	40	38	34	40	43	39	41	41
North Ireland	40	38	41	28	36	52	44	38	14	49	38	31	18	40	44	45	36	49
Slovenia	35	31	39	29	36	38	41	33	26	40	34	28	26	34	36	41	34	21
Spain	46	46	46	42	44	51	49	40	39	55	47	40	46	44	49	53	50	47
East Germany	43	40	45	44	38	47	45	38	38	46	43	40	39	46	38	42	41	49
Britain	50	48	51	43	46	57	53	43	41	60	43	43	47	49	54	53	50	46
Italy	50	47	53	49	47	53	51	46	45	51	47	47	48	49	52	52	51	47
Netherlands	27	34	25	24	24	36	33	26	23	26	26	24	26	27	30	37	30	21
Belgium	39	38	40	36	38	43	42	38	36	43	40	36	33	42	38	46	40	32
Austria	66	63	68	69	64	66	68	66	58	65	66	67	65	67	66	59	68	65
France	38	37	39	32	37	44	44	36	27	40	35	35	35	36	40	44	38	34
Canada	50	51	50	51	45	56	58	48	48	52	47	49	45	49	52	50	52	47
United States	49	50	50	46	45	54	57	47	46	54	47	46	48	47	52	54	50	43
Iceland	27	26	28	21	27	36	33	28	23	na	na	na	20	31	30	32	26	20
West Germany	48	46	50	49	50	46	46	49	53	47	46	50	49	50	45	41	50	48
Denmark	21	21	21	18	16	27	28	17	19	24	18	16	19	20	20	23	21	15
Finland	10	11	10	10	07	19	17	09	09	15	10	07	08	11	12	27	09	10
Norway	23	23	22	17	18	31	35	18	21	26	23	19	23	23	22	29	21	17
Sweden	30	28	32	27	25	41	35	25	32	31	33	28	25	29	32	37	32	22
Japan	27	25	30	40	24	24	22	29	30	24	24	33	24	31	24	27	28	24
Switzerland	31	30	33	27	28	37	34	30	25	32	25	28	26	28	32	44	31	25
Total	**41**	**40**	**43**	**39**	**39**	**45**	**44**	**40**	**37**	**44**	**40**	**39**	**40**	**42**	**43**	**43**	**41**	**40**

Ranking:

Nigeria	78
Austria	66
Chile	63
Turkey	61
Argentina	61
Mexico	60
Portugal	51
Britain	50
Italy	50
Canada	50
United States	49
India	48
West Germany	48
Belarus	46
Spain	46
Moscow	45
Hungary	44
Romania	43
Brazil	43
East Germany	43
Ireland	40
North Ireland	40
Belgium	39
Bulgaria	38
France	38
Russia	37
Slovenia	35
China	34
Switzerland	31
Latvia	30
Sweden	30
Estonia	29
Netherlands	27
Iceland	27
Japan	27
Norway	23
Lithuania	21
Denmark	21
South Korea	20
Finland	10

Note: Countries in the left column are ranked according to GNP per capita. / The percentages in the bottom row give each country an equal weight. / na=not ascertained.

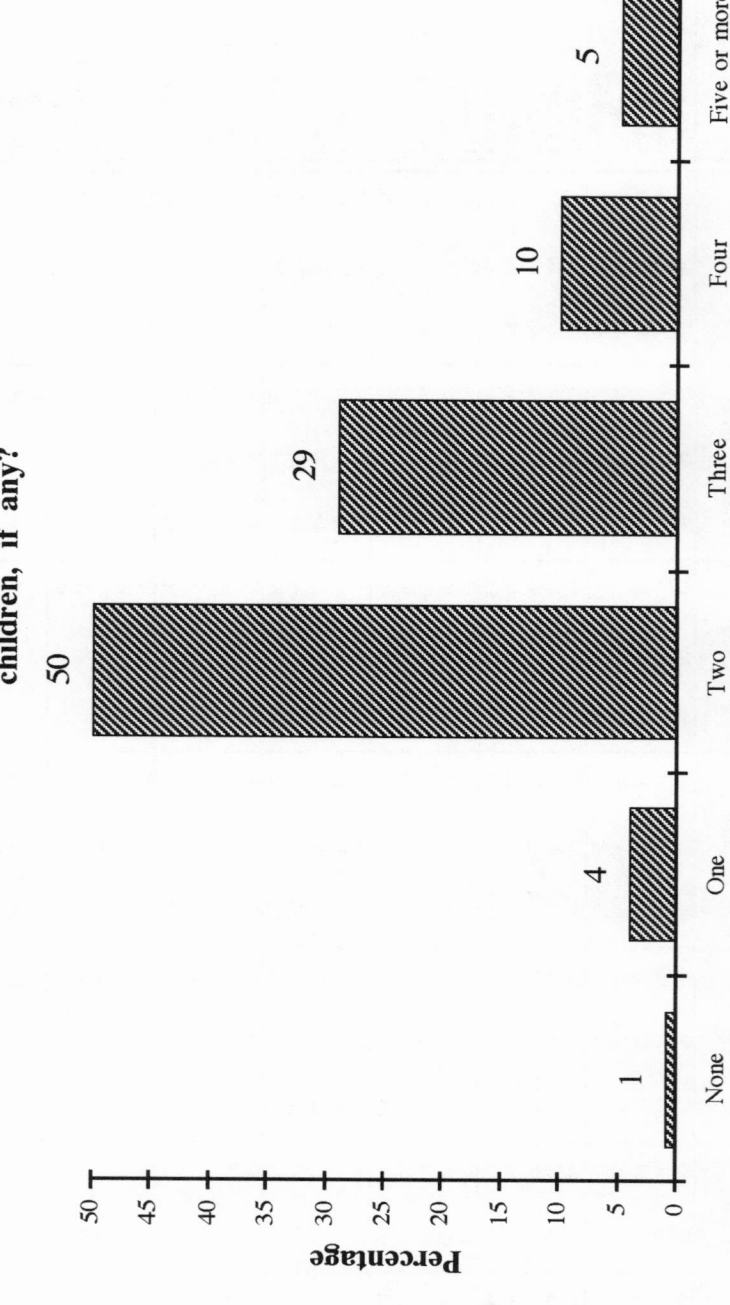

V213. What do you think is the ideal size of the family - how many children, if any?

V213 IDEAL NUMBER OF CHILDREN

What do you think is the ideal size of the family - how many children, if any?
(% two or fewer—codes 0 to 2)

	Total	Gender		Age			Education			Income			Political Affinity			Values			Ranking:	
		Male	Female	16-29	30-49	50+	Lower	Medium	Upper	Lower	Middle	Upper	Left	Center	Right	Mat	Mixed	Postmat		
India	72	71	73	83	83	55	52	74	80	62	72	81	76	72	75	74	74	74	China	93
Nigeria	06	06	05	05	06	11	04	05	07	05	07	05	03	06	06	05	05	13	East Germany	83
China	93	93	94	97	94	88	93	94	97	92	96	94	na	na	na	91	96	94	South Korea	78
Romania	70	69	70	85	73	56	56	77	77	66	69	74	68	73	67	65	72	79	West Germany	74
Turkey	71	69	73	79	69	63	63	82	86	67	71	77	82	76	56	66	69	82	India	72
Poland	58	58	58	66	64	49	47	64	76	54	64	59	59	61	56	52	61	63	Turkey	71
Bulgaria	68	64	71	77	73	56	54	78	63	66	64	74	71	64	70	70	67	66	Moscow	71
Chile	36	38	35	48	33	24	34	40	35	38	41	34	37	39	29	34	36	39	Romania	70
Czechoslovakia	70	68	71	78	72	61	63	74	69	69	71	70	70	70	69	70	70	66	Czechoslovakia	70
South Africa	35	35	35	39	36	26	23	40	48	28	30	54	40	40	36	37	35	31	Bulgaria	68
Lithuania	36	35	36	46	39	24	26	39	41	38	37	45	na	na	na	33	36	42	Portugal	68
Hungary	67	68	66	77	71	60	64	72	62	66	70	66	68	68	62	64	70	68	Hungary	67
Argentina	44	48	41	47	41	45	46	48	37	45	44	44	47	42	44	49	41	47	Austria	66
Brazil	54	53	54	64	51	41	44	56	64	50	56	57	62	56	49	50	56	60	Slovenia	65
Mexico	50	49	51	58	47	34	49	52	52	49	55	48	55	53	46	44	53	55	Spain	65
Belarus	56	53	58	69	57	40	43	58	58	53	56	60	58	53	51	52	58	49	Britain	64
Russia	49	46	52	57	54	40	40	55	50	47	52	54	46	52	45	50	49	51	Italy	61
Moscow	71	69	73	74	70	70	71	76	68	69	71	77	71	70	70	69	73	69	Belgium	61
Latvia	40	37	43	40	42	37	41	41	38	39	41	50	na	na	na	38	42	33	Poland	58
Estonia	43	43	44	54	41	35	44	45	39	38	47	53	na	na	na	46	41	39	Sweden	58
Portugal	68	73	63	75	72	58	66	79	68	65	75	71	71	70	63	69	67	77	Denmark	57
South Korea	78	81	76	86	81	58	67	83	78	77	82	74	83	81	75	76	80	81	Belarus	56
Ireland	24	22	25	30	28	15	22	26	23	22	23	29	34	23	21	24	24	21	Netherlands	55
North Ireland	42	47	39	50	50	29	40	49	39	39	41	56	29	42	45	38	43	43	United States	55
Slovenia	65	65	64	67	69	59	62	67	65	64	65	67	61	67	49	64	66	57	Norway	55
Spain	65	71	61	75	68	55	63	76	69	63	68	66	71	64	58	63	64	75	Switzerland	55
East Germany	83	85	81	91	83	78	84	81	79	79	86	85	86	83	80	82	85	78	Brazil	54
Britain	64	67	61	70	70	55	65	65	54	61	66	65	66	64	64	69	64	58	Mexico	50
Italy	61	67	56	64	67	55	61	60	61	59	64	72	69	54	58	60	59	67	Finland	50
Netherlands	55	58	54	57	57	50	59	49	58	60	55	53	59	55	47	51	56	57	Russia	49
Belgium	61	63	59	60	64	59	64	63	51	58	62	57	61	59	56	68	61	55	France	49
Austria	66	69	64	70	68	61	62	69	68	62	67	69	71	69	61	60	66	68	Canada	49
France	49	50	47	55	50	42	51	49	40	50	48	42	49	46	46	41	52	44	Argentina	44
Canada	49	51	48	54	54	39	43	52	50	48	50	52	54	48	46	46	51	46	Estonia	43
United States	55	55	54	56	61	48	45	55	62	47	58	62	61	57	52	48	55	59	North Ireland	42
Iceland	24	29	19	33	25	11	17	30	27	na	na	na	23	26	24	25	23	32	Latvia	40
West Germany	74	75	72	75	80	68	74	74	70	70	76	75	75	76	69	71	75	72	Japan	38
Denmark	57	61	54	64	62	46	47	66	57	50	62	64	58	54	59	54	58	62	Chile	36
Finland	50	54	46	50	51	48	52	53	46	52	52	48	53	44	54	50	49	52	Lithuania	36
Norway	55	59	51	59	60	46	47	57	57	49	58	56	54	52	56	56	53	56	South Africa	35
Sweden	58	61	56	57	58	58	56	63	51	60	58	58	56	53	66	65	58	54	Ireland	24
Japan	38	38	39	57	35	31	28	39	46	39	36	38	36	39	32	42	39	37	Iceland	24
Switzerland	55	60	50	55	59	50	56	56	46	56	68	72	53	60	57	50	56	53	Nigeria	06
Total	55	57	54	62	58	47	51	59	56	54	58	60	58	56	53	54	56	56		

Note: Countries in the left column are ranked according to GNP per capita. / The percentages in the bottom row give each country an equal weight. / na=not ascertained.

V214. If someone says a child needs a home with both a father and a mother to grow up happily, would you tend to agree or disagree?

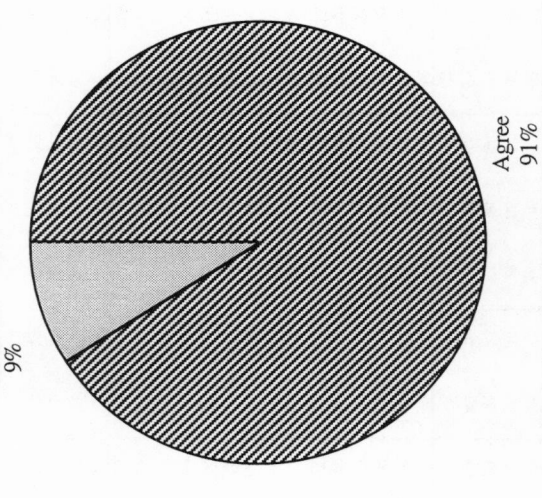

V215. Do you think that a woman has to have children in order to be fulfilled or is this not necessary?

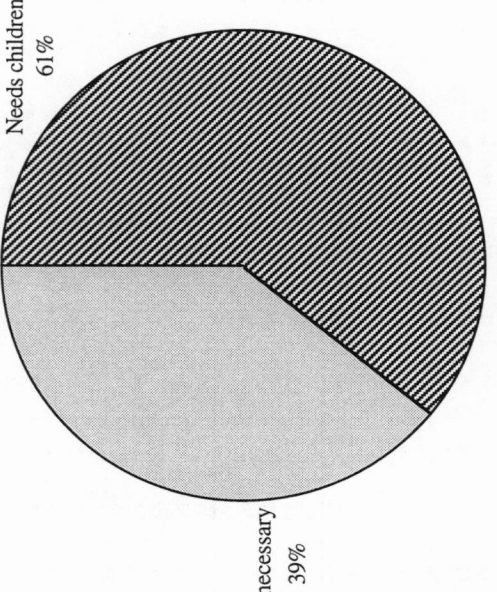

V214 CHILD NEED PARENTS

If someone says a child needs a home with both a father and a mother to grow up happily, would you tend to agree or disagree? (% "tend to agree")

	Total	Gender		Age			Education			Income			Political Affinity			Values			Ranking:
		Male	Female	16-29	30-49	50+	Lower	Medium	Upper	Lower	Middle	Upper	Left	Center	Right	Mat	Mixed	Postmat	
India	97	97	97	97	97	97	98	97	97	96	98	97	96	98	96	97	97	96	Czechoslovakia 99
Nigeria	98	98	99	96	98	93	97	96	98	96	98	97	94	97	97	98	96	95	Hungary 99
China	98	98	99	97	99	99	98	98	98	98	98	99	na	na	na	99	98	96	Latvia 99
Romania	97	97	96	97	99	98	98	95	97	97	97	96	96	97	na	97	96	95	Estonia 99
Turkey	96	97	95	94	96	95	98	93	92	97	96	94	93	96	97	98	96	94	China 98
Poland	98	99	98	96	96	99	98	99	98	99	98	94	98	99	99	98	98	100	Poland 98
Bulgaria	95	95	96	96	96	94	94	97	94	95	96	95	96	95	94	96	95	93	India 97
Chile	93	95	91	91	92	96	94	91	93	92	92	94	93	93	93	93	93	92	Nigeria 97
Czechoslovakia	99	100	99	99	99	100	100	99	100	99	99	100	100	99	99	100	99	99	Romania 97
South Africa	92	95	90	92	91	95	94	92	90	93	92	91	89	91	92	94	92	87	Russia 97
Lithuania	94	94	94	93	96	93	92	95	94	93	92	91	89	91	92	92	95	93	East Germany 97
Hungary	99	99	98	98	99	99	99	99	98	99	99	99	98	99	na	99	98	98	Italy 97
Argentina	95	94	96	93	95	97	96	95	93	97	95	95	94	97	92	99	98	93	Turkey 96
Brazil	88	92	84	86	86	95	94	87	81	89	89	87	89	84	91	90	89	76	Moscow 96
Mexico	88	89	86	87	88	89	88	87	86	88	87	89	76	89	89	91	89	73	Bulgaria 95
Belarus	na	na	na	na	na	na	na	na	na	na	na	na	na	na	na	91	na	na	Argentina 95
Russia	97	98	97	97	98	97	97	97	97	97	98	97	98	98	96	98	97	97	Japan 95
Moscow	96	97	96	95	97	97	96	95	98	97	96	96	97	97	93	96	96	97	Lithuania 94
Latvia	99	99	99	99	99	100	99	99	98	98	100	96	99	99	na	100	99	99	Slovenia 94
Estonia	99	99	98	98	99	98	99	99	98	98	98	100	na	na	na	99	98	100	Austria 94
Portugal	93	94	92	90	89	99	97	88	84	96	94	87	92	94	90	99	98	100	France 94
South Korea	na	na	na	na	na	na	na	na	na	na	na	na	na	na	na	95	92	86	West Germany 94
Ireland	83	86	80	74	78	93	86	80	73	85	85	81	76	82	87	na	na	na	Chile 93
North Ireland	81	84	78	73	77	90	83	77	72	84	72	82	54	84	83	85	84	75	Portugal 93
Slovenia	94	95	93	93	93	95	94	94	94	92	96	92	92	95	93	81	83	71	South Africa 92
Spain	91	92	90	84	90	97	93	88	83	96	90	88	87	90	91	93	90	85	Belgium 92
East Germany	97	98	96	96	97	98	97	95	100	98	97	97	96	97	99	99	97	86	Spain 91
Britain	74	80	69	58	71	87	75	73	72	78	72	71	74	70	83	78	75	69	Brazil 88
Italy	97	97	97	96	95	98	97	95	90	97	97	93	95	97	99	99	98	93	Mexico 88
Netherlands	74	88	69	69	69	88	80	74	68	68	74	79	62	78	83	83	78	67	Finland 86
Belgium	92	94	90	88	91	96	94	92	88	89	93	92	86	93	93	93	93	86	Norway 86
Austria	94	96	92	87	92	97	96	93	87	93	94	93	94	92	96	97	94	91	Sweden 85
France	94	95	92	90	94	96	94	94	92	94	93	94	91	97	95	96	94	93	Ireland 83
Canada	78	83	73	69	78	85	84	77	75	73	79	80	73	79	80	87	77	75	North Ireland 81
United States	73	80	66	64	68	82	76	74	70	76	73	72	66	72	80	73	75	68	Iceland 79
Iceland	79	86	73	78	76	84	85	79	73	na	na	na	73	83	78	85	77	70	Canada 78
West Germany	94	96	93	90	93	97	96	91	94	95	94	93	91	95	98	97	95	91	Britain 74
Denmark	73	78	67	70	66	83	74	74	67	74	70	71	63	74	80	81	74	57	Netherlands 74
Finland	86	90	81	82	85	91	86	89	83	84	87	86	84	87	86	88	86	85	United States 73
Norway	86	92	79	80	82	94	92	86	82	85	88	85	82	85	88	88	86	75	Denmark 73
Sweden	85	90	80	83	83	91	90	84	79	85	82	88	82	86	87	91	86	79	
Japan	95	96	95	94	94	98	96	95	96	96	94	97	92	93	97	97	96	88	
Switzerland	na	na	na	na	na	na	na	na	na	na	na	na	na	na	na	na	na	na	
Total	91	93	89	88	90	94	93	90	88	91	91	91	86	90	91	93	91	87	

Note: Countries in the left column are ranked according to GNP per capita. / The percentages in the bottom row give each country an equal weight. / na=not ascertained.

V215 WOMAN NEEDS CHILD

Do you think that a woman has to have children in order to be fulfilled or is this not necessary? (% "needs children")

Country	Total	Gender Male	Gender Female	Age 16-29	Age 30-49	Age 50+	Education Lower	Education Medium	Education Upper	Income Lower	Income Middle	Income Upper	Political Left	Political Center	Political Right	Values Mat	Values Mixed	Values Postmat	Ranking
India	89	88	89	86	90	91	93	89	86	90	87	89	87	90	87	88	89	82	Belarus 97
Nigeria	87	86	89	87	86	91	95	89	82	88	86	85	86	85	87	91	86	78	Hungary 96
China	46	46	46	39	47	51	52	41	44	44	41	52	na	na	na	51	41	37	Latvia 96
Romania	85	85	84	75	85	90	92	81	82	81	87	86	88	85	83	90	84	64	Bulgaria 92
Turkey	72	69	75	63	74	82	84	56	47	78	74	62	62	73	77	79	74	58	Russia 92
Poland	79	78	79	68	75	88	86	74	75	81	78	77	82	72	84	82	77	76	Estonia 91
Bulgaria	92	91	92	87	89	97	97	91	87	94	91	88	94	89	89	94	92	82	India 89
Chile	64	62	65	55	64	74	72	59	61	70	63	59	59	65	67	68	65	55	Lithuania 89
Czechoslovakia	87	88	86	84	88	88	89	87	86	86	88	87	90	87	86	87	88	82	Nigeria 87
South Africa	70	71	70	66	71	77	82	66	50	84	69	54	65	66	66	71	71	63	Czechoslovakia 87
Lithuania	89	88	89	79	94	90	87	89	92	86	92	88	na	na	na	88	89	84	Romania 85
Hungary	96	98	95	93	97	97	97	95	94	97	95	98	95	97	96	95	98	95	Moscow 85
Argentina	60	63	58	61	55	65	64	58	54	61	57	62	56	61	62	65	60	54	Denmark 82
Brazil	56	59	54	46	60	68	70	51	48	62	54	51	55	51	59	63	53	38	Poland 79
Mexico	52	52	52	44	56	64	55	55	41	60	48	42	39	52	52	56	53	24	South Korea 76
Belarus	97	98	97	96	97	99	99	96	99	96	98	98	98	97	97	98	97	97	Japan 76
Russia	92	93	92	90	92	94	93	92	91	93	92	91	92	92	93	94	91	89	France 75
Moscow	85	86	83	80	86	86	86	86	83	86	84	84	84	84	83	83	86	83	Turkey 72
Latvia	96	96	96	95	96	97	98	95	98	98	96	95	na	na	na	97	97	94	South Africa 70
Estonia	91	89	92	88	93	90	90	91	92	92	91	89	na	na	na	92	90	94	Italy 67
Portugal	61	56	66	46	60	76	67	53	46	69	55	54	56	60	65	69	58	44	East Germany 66
South Korea	76	72	80	66	79	86	86	75	73	75	77	78	64	75	81	81	73	67	Chile 64
Ireland	26	27	25	18	24	33	32	22	10	36	23	21	23	23	31	28	26	24	Portugal 61
North Ireland	32	39	27	16	30	46	40	20	11	36	45	20	22	29	39	38	29	30	Argentina 60
Slovenia	58	53	62	40	60	67	64	54	53	62	59	49	52	57	67	62	58	41	Slovenia 58
Spain	46	44	47	33	41	59	52	35	26	55	45	38	38	46	52	55	44	32	Brazil 56
East Germany	66	63	68	53	66	74	69	56	63	68	68	64	64	66	68	75	67	59	Mexico 52
Britain	21	25	18	12	16	31	23	20	15	28	20	18	21	19	21	22	23	17	Austria 51
Italy	67	67	68	55	60	81	69	57	43	73	60	61	63	69	67	78	68	54	China 46
Netherlands	09	12	08	03	08	19	16	07	03	08	08	04	06	03	18	25	09	04	Spain 46
Belgium	46	47	45	36	42	56	52	43	38	52	42	39	45	47	49	53	48	31	Belgium 46
Austria	51	51	51	32	43	66	59	45	44	61	51	39	51	46	56	69	53	36	West Germany 45
France	75	77	72	67	71	84	76	77	67	76	76	70	70	79	76	86	75	65	Iceland 42
Canada	24	27	20	17	23	30	30	22	22	24	26	21	13	24	28	37	22	21	North Ireland 32
United States	20	22	17	22	14	22	24	21	15	22	21	16	14	19	22	24	20	16	Switzerland 31
Iceland	42	45	39	31	36	68	56	38	35	na	na	na	34	46	56	51	41	25	Ireland 26
West Germany	45	45	45	28	37	59	53	31	31	50	45	40	30	47	57	71	46	26	Canada 24
Denmark	82	86	79	77	82	85	84	79	84	82	81	83	78	82	85	79	83	81	Norway 23
Finland	20	23	16	14	18	30	24	22	16	27	19	15	14	21	23	33	24	09	Britain 21
Norway	23	29	18	16	18	34	35	22	18	28	24	19	19	25	23	33	21	21	Sweden 21
Sweden	21	26	16	16	19	27	28	18	15	20	23	19	22	20	19	29	23	11	United States 20
Japan	76	76	77	71	71	83	81	78	66	75	78	76	73	75	76	78	78	63	Finland 20
Switzerland	31	34	29	22	26	41	33	31	25	36	28	24	19	27	42	41	33	20	Netherlands 09
Total	61	61	60	53	59	68	66	57	54	64	61	57	54	58	61	66	61	52	

Note: Countries in the left column are ranked according to GNP per capita. / The percentages in the bottom row give each country an equal weight. / na=not ascertained.

V217. If a woman wants to have a child as a single parent but she doesn't want to have a stable relationship with a man, do you approve or disapprove?

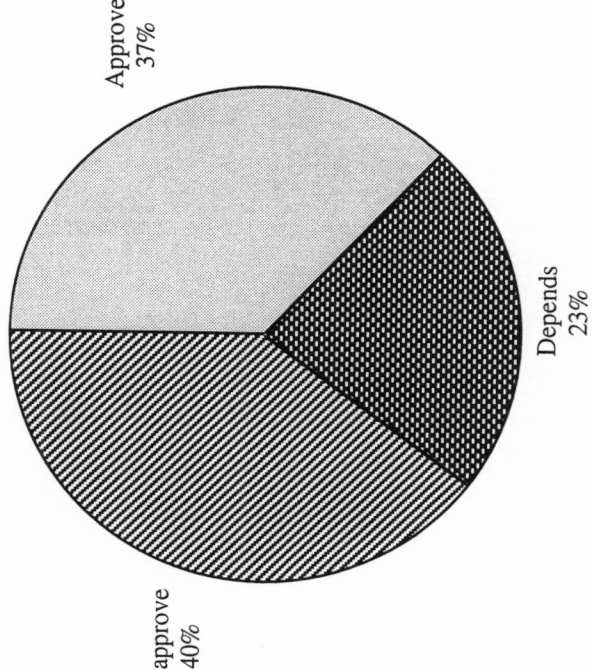

Approve
37%

Depends
23%

Disapprove
40%

V216. Marriage is an out-dated institution

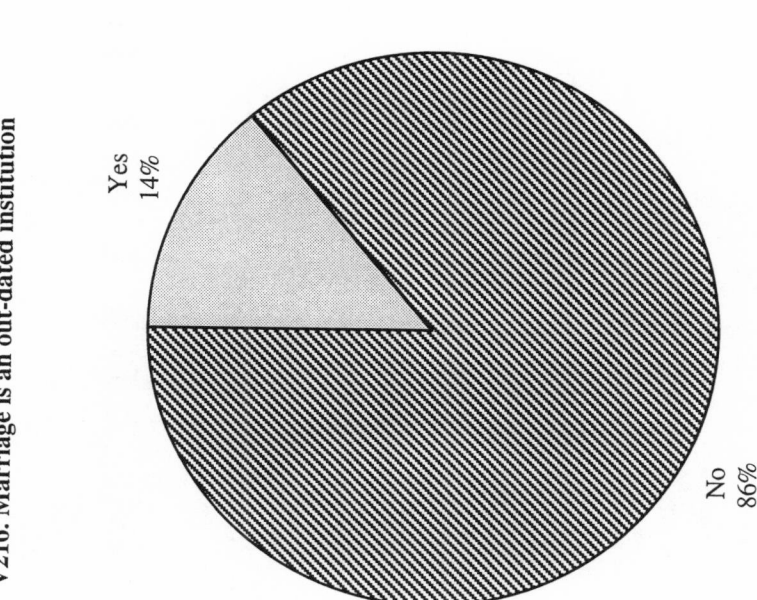

Yes
14%

No
86%

V216 MARRIAGE OUTDATED

Do you agree or disagree with the following statement? "Marriage is an out-dated institution" (% "agree")

	Total	Gender		Age			Education			Income			Political Affinity			Values		
		Male	Female	16-29	30-49	50+	Lower	Medium	Upper	Lower	Middle	Upper	Left	Center	Right	Mat	Mixed	Postmat
India	05	06	03	06	04	03	02	10	11	04	04	16	05	05	05	06	03	07
Nigeria	13	13	13	15	10	16	10	16	11	14	10	16	15	10	15	11	14	19
China	15	15	15	19	15	12	20	15	11	17	16	13	na	na	na	14	17	11
Romania	09	10	07	12	09	06	07	10	09	10	09	08	14	06	12	06	10	15
Turkey	11	11	11	10	11	13	12	10	10	15	08	11	11	10	14	10	13	10
Poland	08	09	07	09	08	07	07	12	09	08	06	09	05	08	09	06	09	05
Bulgaria	11	11	11	17	12	05	07	12	12	10	13	10	10	09	11	08	10	19
Chile	15	15	15	18	16	10	16	16	14	18	16	10	17	14	15	15	15	18
Czechoslovakia	10	10	10	14	09	08	11	11	06	12	09	10	10	09	11	09	09	18
South Africa	13	15	12	17	13	08	16	14	04	17	14	05	15	09	15	09	15	18
Lithuania	09	12	07	17	07	06	10	10	03	10	07	12	na	na	na	10	09	13
Hungary	11	14	09	13	12	10	12	12	05	11	12	11	11	09	22	11	11	18
Argentina	09	10	09	14	11	05	11	09	08	09	08	10	21	09	05	06	10	12
Brazil	27	27	28	31	28	20	24	30	25	30	27	25	30	28	26	26	28	35
Mexico	17	18	16	17	18	14	17	19	15	16	17	19	27	17	14	13	17	25
Belarus	16	16	16	20	14	18	26	16	13	19	16	13	16	17	14	13	18	20
Russia	15	16	14	25	13	09	14	16	14	12	13	18	15	12	16	12	14	18
Moscow	14	15	13	15	14	12	15	15	13	11	17	14	16	13	11	13	16	17
Latvia	09	10	08	15	07	05	10	10	06	06	09	10	na	na	na	04	09	09
Estonia	11	12	10	16	08	09	10	12	09	10	09	14	na	na	na	11	10	18
Portugal	23	28	19	28	23	19	24	27	17	23	28	20	27	23	20	22	24	28
South Korea	na	na	na	na	na	na	na	na	na	na	na	na	na	na	na	na	na	na
Ireland	10	12	08	15	09	08	11	09	10	12	07	09	25	10	14	07	10	12
North Ireland	14	13	16	22	15	08	16	13	07	21	14	11	21	13	11	11	14	22
Slovenia	18	20	15	18	20	15	17	19	17	18	17	18	23	17	14	17	19	10
Spain	17	20	14	27	20	08	14	23	28	09	17	24	27	14	08	09	17	36
East Germany	14	17	12	21	15	10	14	14	14	16	13	13	16	14	14	09	14	16
Britain	18	19	16	24	20	12	19	14	12	19	20	13	24	18	09	16	18	20
Italy	14	16	11	12	17	12	14	14	21	13	13	15	20	10	11	10	13	18
Netherlands	20	20	20	23	22	12	18	15	27	25	17	17	32	17	12	13	16	27
Belgium	22	24	21	29	24	16	22	21	26	25	25	19	34	22	13	23	20	27
Austria	12	11	12	19	13	08	10	13	13	14	12	11	17	11	12	10	11	16
France	29	31	27	30	35	23	26	32	31	34	27	28	35	26	19	21	28	37
Canada	13	15	10	16	14	09	13	13	11	16	11	12	17	13	08	07	12	17
United States	08	08	08	10	07	08	10	09	05	10	06	06	09	08	07	09	07	08
Iceland	06	08	05	08	07	03	07	05	07	na	na	na	06	08	04	05	07	08
West Germany	15	16	14	28	18	06	11	20	25	14	15	15	30	11	06	07	11	27
Denmark	18	20	16	24	20	11	17	21	17	18	20	18	26	18	13	24	16	25
Finland	13	14	13	19	13	07	12	14	11	12	15	13	18	11	09	03	13	13
Norway	10	12	08	14	10	08	09	10	11	11	11	10	12	09	10	11	09	17
Sweden	14	17	11	14	16	13	14	16	10	15	19	12	19	14	11	12	13	16
Japan	07	07	07	03	07	10	11	07	05	08	07	06	09	06	05	05	06	07
Switzerland	13	15	11	20	14	10	13	13	17	16	11	18	23	13	07	09	12	17
Total	**14**	**15**	**13**	**18**	**14**	**10**	**14**	**14**	**13**	**15**	**14**	**13**	**19**	**13**	**12**	**11**	**14**	**18**

Ranking:

29	France
27	Brazil
23	Portugal
22	Belgium
20	Netherlands
18	Slovenia
18	Britain
18	Denmark
17	Mexico
17	Spain
16	Belarus
15	China
15	Chile
15	Russia
15	West Germany
14	Moscow
14	North Ireland
14	East Germany
14	Italy
14	Sweden
13	Nigeria
13	South Africa
13	Canada
13	Finland
13	Switzerland
12	Austria
11	Turkey
11	Bulgaria
11	Hungary
11	Estonia
10	Czechoslovakia
10	Ireland
10	Norway
09	Romania
09	Lithuania
09	Argentina
09	Latvia
08	Poland
08	United States
07	Japan
06	Iceland
05	India

Note: Countries in the left column are ranked according to GNP per capita. / The percentages in the bottom row give each country an equal weight. / na=not ascertained.

V217 WOMAN SINGLE PARENT

If a woman wants to have a child as a single parent but she doesn't want to have a stable relationship with a man, do you approve or disapprove? (% "approve")

	Total	Gender Male	Gender Female	Age 16-29	Age 30-49	Age 50+	Education Lower	Education Medium	Education Upper	Income Lower	Income Middle	Income Upper	Pol. Affinity Left	Pol. Affinity Center	Pol. Affinity Right	Values Mat	Values Mixed	Values Postmat
India	03	04	02	03	02	02	05	03	10	03	02	03	05	03	02	03	02	04
Nigeria	09	10	08	09	08	07	06	09	06	06	10	08	12	09	08	08	09	11
China	06	07	04	09	05	04	06	06	06	05	05	06	na	na	na	05	06	17
Romania	38	37	39	49	39	29	27	42	45	36	37	40	35	37	41	31	42	47
Turkey	07	07	06	08	07	04	03	08	19	04	05	11	10	06	05	04	06	11
Poland	18	15	20	13	21	16	14	19	21	20	15	17	23	16	17	20	16	16
Bulgaria	47	44	50	58	55	31	24	52	60	48	42	52	44	52	58	40	46	68
Chile	60	58	61	58	64	54	58	61	59	57	63	58	61	61	59	65	58	63
Czechoslovakia	23	24	21	25	27	16	19	25	24	19	25	24	18	23	26	20	24	25
South Africa	19	20	18	23	18	13	22	18	13	21	21	12	25	18	21	17	20	21
Lithuania	55	50	58	59	56	50	49	57	55	54	56	55	na	na	na	50	54	66
Hungary	39	41	36	44	43	32	36	40	45	35	41	43	49	38	42	34	41	53
Argentina	58	56	59	61	63	49	56	59	59	54	59	61	73	57	60	51	58	65
Brazil	51	47	55	61	53	30	34	57	62	54	59	58	56	54	46	44	55	62
Mexico	43	42	44	49	43	26	41	44	49	43	51	46	56	45	39	33	47	50
Belarus	47	42	50	49	46	45	49	46	46	47	46	46	50	44	41	46	46	48
Russia	42	36	46	44	43	39	36	45	42	45	41	44	47	41	42	43	40	44
Moscow	48	42	53	45	50	47	40	44	53	45	49	53	51	44	49	45	49	52
Latvia	26	25	26	22	26	28	19	26	26	23	25	28	na	na	na	21	29	25
Estonia	32	30	34	33	34	29	29	33	34	32	31	35	na	na	na	33	34	32
Portugal	40	39	40	51	43	26	35	49	51	33	47	44	40	43	38	30	47	46
South Korea	na	na	na	na	na	na	na	na	na	na	na	na	na	na	na	na	na	na
Ireland	23	23	23	47	22	09	17	29	30	15	24	27	44	24	14	17	24	28
North Ireland	25	27	22	40	28	10	24	28	18	26	23	30	44	25	23	25	22	38
Slovenia	60	55	64	50	64	62	53	63	66	58	61	61	56	61	63	62	59	58
Spain	65	66	64	83	72	45	60	76	79	48	70	72	78	63	52	54	69	80
East Germany	34	33	35	36	36	30	31	40	42	26	39	37	45	30	27	21	35	38
Britain	36	39	32	56	41	18	37	30	34	31	43	38	41	38	28	31	34	44
Italy	39	41	37	45	45	33	38	39	48	37	42	43	50	35	35	31	38	50
Netherlands	44	36	47	52	48	29	37	47	48	44	42	46	59	41	28	37	38	55
Belgium	32	33	31	35	36	26	28	33	37	33	32	39	37	34	28	28	38	39
Austria	39	40	39	45	40	35	38	40	45	37	39	42	41	43	28	28	31	47
France	39	40	37	38	43	35	39	40	36	40	42	37	43	37	37	37	38	41
Canada	38	37	38	48	42	24	31	38	42	36	38	43	52	35	34	30	38	43
United States	38	36	40	52	45	26	38	38	40	38	35	41	56	36	32	31	37	46
Iceland	84	82	85	77	88	84	82	85	84	na	na	na	87	87	80	85	85	73
West Germany	23	23	24	33	26	15	19	30	32	22	24	25	32	22	16	11	20	36
Denmark	67	67	66	69	75	56	54	70	72	59	69	79	72	64	66	56	66	83
Finland	56	56	56	61	59	43	49	55	60	49	59	59	70	55	52	49	56	61
Norway	27	24	31	30	29	24	25	26	30	32	28	26	37	25	25	30	28	38
Sweden	25	21	29	19	24	33	25	23	30	27	25	24	30	24	24	23	23	38
Japan	15	13	17	25	17	05	07	15	24	14	16	14	31	16	10	11	17	30
Switzerland	38	39	36	44	43	28	37	38	36	34	40	41	52	37	29	33	34	50
Total	**37**	**36**	**38**	**42**	**40**	**30**	**33**	**39**	**41**	**34**	**37**	**38**	**45**	**37**	**35**	**32**	**37**	**44**

Ranking:

Iceland	84
Denmark	67
Spain	65
Chile	60
Slovenia	60
Argentina	58
Finland	56
Lithuania	55
Brazil	51
Moscow	48
Bulgaria	47
Belarus	47
Netherlands	44
Mexico	43
Russia	42
Portugal	40
Hungary	39
Italy	39
Austria	39
France	39
Romania	38
Canada	38
United States	38
Switzerland	38
Britain	36
East Germany	34
Estonia	32
Belgium	32
Norway	27
Latvia	26
North Ireland	25
Sweden	25
Czechoslovakia	23
Ireland	23
West Germany	23
South Africa	19
Poland	18
Japan	15
Nigeria	09
Turkey	07
China	06
India	03

Note: Countries in the left column are ranked according to GNP per capita. / The percentages in the bottom row give each country an equal weight. / na=not ascertained.

V218-V223. The changing roles of men and women

Percentage "strongly agree" or "agree"

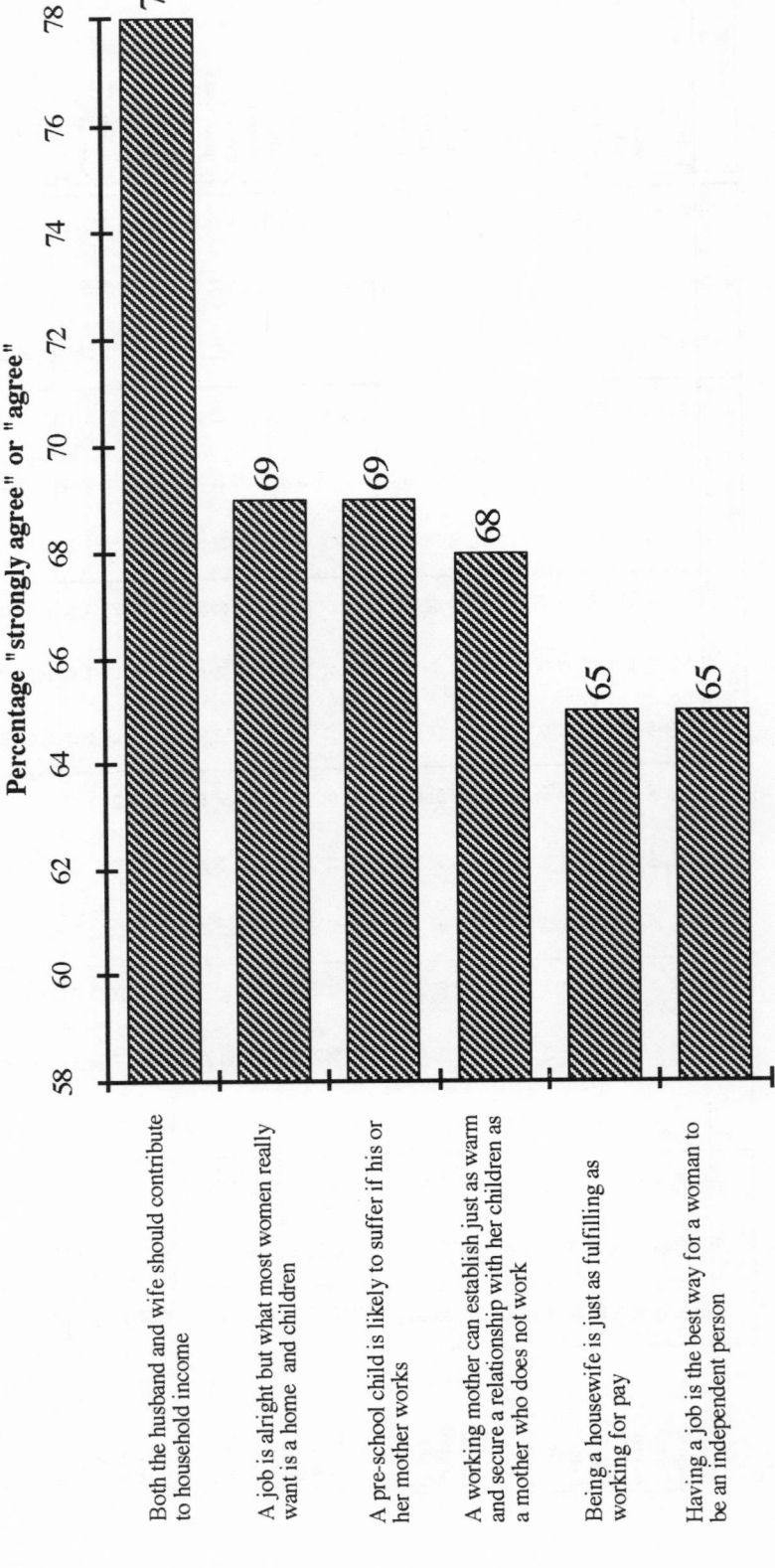

V218 WORKING MOTHER

People talk about the changing roles of men and women today. For each of the following statements, can you tell me how much you agree with each. "A working mother can establish just as warm and secure a relationship with her children as a mother who does not work" (% "strongly agree" or "agree")

	Total	Gender		Age			Education			Income			Political Affinity			Values		
		Male	Female	16-29	30-49	50+	Lower	Medium	Upper	Lower	Middle	Upper	Left	Center	Right	Mat	Mixed	Postmat
India	58	55	60	59	58	54	55	56	61	57	55	61	64	63	50	52	61	75
Nigeria	65	63	68	68	63	55	56	68	66	63	68	66	66	67	63	67	65	60
China	91	90	92	91	91	90	91	91	90	90	91	91	na	na	na	92	90	87
Romania	84	83	85	90	84	81	83	85	84	82	84	87	84	86	81	84	84	88
Turkey	57	55	58	65	56	45	52	59	73	51	55	65	65	56	48	50	56	66
Poland	na	na	na	na	na	na	na	na	na	na	na	na	na	na	na	na	na	na
Bulgaria	61	60	61	64	60	60	64	60	58	51	64	67	64	55	50	58	63	48
Chile	72	69	74	73	72	70	68	73	74	70	70	76	70	73	70	73	70	78
Czechoslovakia	59	53	64	61	59	58	58	57	68	57	60	60	65	59	53	56	59	64
South Africa	na	na	na	na	na	na	na	na	na	na	na	na	na	na	na	na	na	na
Lithuania	42	44	41	48	37	43	40	43	43	40	45	45	na	na	na	44	43	36
Hungary	70	67	72	79	70	66	67	73	68	71	67	75	71	71	66	69	69	78
Argentina	74	69	78	75	76	70	70	73	81	69	73	81	80	73	73	67	76	78
Brazil	64	61	68	68	64	57	55	65	79	60	62	71	68	67	63	60	66	75
Mexico	64	61	68	69	64	51	59	70	76	61	64	71	75	64	67	58	66	79
Belarus	65	65	66	67	66	64	69	67	62	63	68	65	64	67	66	65	64	64
Russia	64	62	65	62	63	66	66	66	60	63	64	64	57	65	62	64	65	52
Moscow	61	61	60	58	62	62	63	62	59	59	61	64	57	66	68	66	59	58
Latvia	47	42	50	47	46	50	48	48	45	43	50	48	na	na	na	51	45	53
Estonia	82	80	83	83	80	82	88	81	77	84	81	80	na	na	na	81	83	78
Portugal	76	72	80	86	78	66	71	84	89	75	75	85	75	78	78	73	79	78
South Korea	43	50	36	49	42	33	39	41	47	47	40	38	51	40	43	41	43	52
Ireland	63	59	66	77	67	50	52	73	82	52	59	74	75	63	58	55	64	71
North Ireland	71	66	74	80	69	66	69	70	83	68	60	80	79	70	67	67	70	80
Slovenia	74	71	77	83	74	68	71	77	75	71	74	81	71	77	71	70	75	77
Spain	67	63	70	76	70	56	63	76	76	59	69	70	71	68	63	59	69	75
East Germany	57	52	60	63	58	52	54	59	64	53	52	63	65	56	47	48	58	58
Britain	70	67	73	77	76	61	67	77	76	67	71	75	75	71	65	68	67	79
Italy	63	62	64	76	65	54	62	74	76	58	69	77	68	61	62	60	60	74
Netherlands	75	62	79	76	83	62	64	78	85	74	78	84	83	74	70	63	71	83
Belgium	74	71	76	80	77	66	68	74	84	71	74	82	75	74	74	63	74	84
Austria	53	46	57	55	54	50	53	52	56	46	53	59	56	57	50	47	51	58
France	73	73	73	75	77	68	69	76	80	72	72	80	78	73	70	66	74	79
Canada	70	64	75	73	73	58	62	70	76	67	66	75	81	70	64	67	69	74
United States	72	64	81	81	76	65	70	71	75	65	72	77	81	72	65	67	71	78
Iceland	82	77	86	82	87	72	76	80	87	na	na	na	84	81	82	75	82	96
West Germany	41	37	45	47	47	33	37	47	56	37	42	47	49	43	31	25	38	56
Denmark	83	81	84	82	87	79	81	82	85	79	83	89	87	82	82	75	83	90
Finland	94	92	96	96	94	92	92	94	95	94	93	94	94	95	94	94	94	95
Norway	69	62	77	70	74	63	57	67	78	62	68	78	74	68	69	65	70	80
Sweden	73	65	82	70	75	72	67	73	82	72	67	75	79	73	71	62	71	83
Japan	89	85	93	89	92	84	86	90	90	88	89	89	87	87	88	87	88	90
Switzerland	na	na	na	na	na	na	na	na	na	na	na	na	na	na	na	na	na	na
Total	**68**	**65**	**70**	**72**	**69**	**62**	**65**	**70**	**73**	**64**	**67**	**72**	**72**	**68**	**65**	**64**	**68**	**73**

Ranking:

Finland	94
China	91
Japan	89
Romania	84
Denmark	83
Estonia	82
Iceland	82
Portugal	76
Netherlands	75
Argentina	74
Slovenia	74
Belgium	74
France	73
Sweden	73
Chile	72
United States	72
North Ireland	71
Hungary	70
Britain	70
Canada	70
Norway	69
Spain	67
Nigeria	65
Belarus	65
Brazil	64
Mexico	64
Russia	64
Ireland	63
Italy	63
Bulgaria	61
Moscow	61
Czechoslovakia	59
India	58
Turkey	57
East Germany	57
Austria	53
Latvia	47
South Korea	43
Lithuania	42
West Germany	41

Note: Countries in the left column are ranked according to GNP per capita. / The percentages in the bottom row give each country an equal weight. / na=not ascertained.

V219 CHILD WILL SUFFER

People talk about the changing roles of men and women today. For each of the following statements, can you tell me how much you agree with each. "A pre-school child is likely to suffer if his or her mother works" (% "strongly agree" or "agree")

	Total	Gender Male	Gender Female	Age 16-29	Age 30-49	Age 50+	Education Lower	Education Medium	Education Upper	Income Lower	Income Middle	Income Upper	Political Affinity Left	Political Affinity Center	Political Affinity Right	Values Mat	Values Mixed	Values Postmat
India	92	92	na	90	94	91	95	92	92	91	94	90	93	92	89	92	91	94
Nigeria	54	57	50	51	58	55	58	52	55	53	55	56	54	57	53	58	53	47
China	61	61	61	56	65	60	65	57	64	61	60	62	na	na	na	61	61	72
Romania	58	57	59	49	60	63	61	58	56	57	60	57	53	57	62	57	58	63
Turkey	85	88	82	84	85	85	88	85	73	86	87	81	81	85	89	85	86	81
Poland	na	na	na	na	na	na	na	na	na	na	na	na	na	na	na	na	na	na
Bulgaria	76	73	79	73	75	80	81	73	78	82	74	71	74	75	87	78	75	82
Chile	82	82	82	81	82	84	86	81	79	85	83	79	84	82	79	84	82	83
Czechoslovakia	78	80	76	64	80	84	81	76	78	80	77	77	75	77	82	81	78	73
South Africa	na	na	na	na	na	na	na	na	na	na	na	na	na	na	na	na	na	na
Lithuania	90	87	92	85	94	90	88	89	97	88	92	91	na	na	na	89	90	92
Hungary	70	71	70	54	68	79	78	63	60	75	68	63	62	71	73	72	69	76
Argentina	78	79	77	74	76	83	82	76	72	82	79	72	67	78	80	80	78	71
Brazil	75	76	75	72	75	81	86	74	59	84	76	66	73	71	79	79	73	70
Mexico	78	79	76	76	77	82	80	76	73	79	79	74	72	78	78	82	78	68
Belarus	81	81	82	76	81	89	91	78	81	80	81	83	83	82	75	83	81	76
Russia	70	69	71	64	71	73	68	66	75	69	74	70	81	66	65	69	69	84
Moscow	84	83	85	79	83	89	85	80	87	83	83	87	86	83	83	85	84	85
Latvia	92	90	93	89	94	93	93	91	95	94	93	90	na	na	na	90	94	89
Estonia	91	89	91	85	94	91	89	90	92	91	93	88	na	na	na	90	92	85
Portugal	84	85	83	78	82	93	89	77	72	90	80	81	87	85	80	90	82	76
South Korea	72	72	71	71	72	71	75	70	73	71	72	74	65	72	74	72	71	73
Ireland	53	60	46	38	51	65	65	42	31	64	56	42	43	52	59	61	52	46
North Ireland	44	50	39	35	43	51	48	41	24	46	52	36	36	42	52	45	44	40
Slovenia	67	70	64	50	63	81	74	64	59	71	67	58	62	66	70	71	66	60
Spain	56	53	58	42	51	71	61	46	42	67	55	46	49	60	56	64	54	45
East Germany	79	80	77	74	78	82	80	79	74	83	78	74	72	80	86	89	77	76
Britain	55	57	52	38	52	67	57	48	53	60	49	49	49	52	63	56	57	43
Italy	78	78	78	71	74	85	79	72	59	81	74	68	72	83	77	81	78	73
Netherlands	56	73	50	50	49	74	67	51	49	57	55	47	41	57	69	73	60	45
Belgium	61	65	57	51	57	71	70	60	45	64	59	55	57	59	62	71	61	50
Austria	83	84	82	81	84	83	83	83	80	84	82	83	75	84	83	82	83	84
France	65	68	63	60	61	73	73	61	55	70	61	61	63	65	71	74	65	60
Canada	53	58	48	42	53	62	62	51	48	55	57	46	44	53	60	61	53	49
United States	52	57	46	42	45	60	56	54	45	55	52	47	44	51	56	53	54	46
Iceland	52	58	45	45	47	70	63	53	43	na	na	na	41	57	54	61	51	32
West Germany	84	87	82	79	81	90	87	82	77	89	82	82	79	85	90	93	86	77
Denmark	32	36	28	22	21	52	45	27	28	40	28	21	20	32	40	42	33	16
Finland	52	60	44	36	51	72	54	59	44	59	53	47	51	54	54	71	55	43
Norway	46	54	36	36	42	56	61	44	40	50	44	40	36	47	48	53	44	30
Sweden	74	81	66	71	67	83	86	73	55	77	67	69	68	75	76	84	76	60
Japan	70	70	69	71	64	79	70	71	65	72	67	71	60	68	77	76	69	67
Switzerland	na	na	na	na	na	na	na	na	na	na	na	na	na	na	na	na	na	na
Total	69	71	67	62	68	76	74	67	63	72	69	65	63	68	70	73	69	65

Ranking:

India	92
Latvia	92
Estonia	91
Lithuania	90
Turkey	85
Moscow	84
Portugal	84
West Germany	84
Austria	83
Chile	82
Belarus	81
East Germany	79
Czechoslovakia	78
Argentina	78
Mexico	78
Italy	78
Bulgaria	76
Brazil	75
Sweden	74
South Korea	72
Hungary	70
Russia	70
Japan	70
Slovenia	67
France	65
China	61
Belgium	61
Romania	58
Spain	56
Netherlands	56
Britain	55
Nigeria	54
Ireland	53
Canada	53
United States	52
Iceland	52
Finland	52
Norway	46
North Ireland	44
Denmark	32

Note: Countries in the left column are ranked according to GNP per capita. / The percentages in the bottom row give each country an equal weight. / na=not ascertained.

V220 WOMEN WANT HOME/CHILD

People talk about the changing roles of men and women today. For each of the following statements, can you tell me how much you agree with each. "A job is alright but what most women really want is a home and children" (% "strongly agree" or "agree")

	Total	Gender Male	Gender Female	Age 16-29	Age 30-49	Age 50+	Education Lower	Education Medium	Education Upper	Income Lower	Income Middle	Income Upper	Pol. Aff. Left	Pol. Aff. Center	Pol. Aff. Right	Values Mat	Values Mixed	Values Postmat
India	91	91	91	91	91	92	95	92	88	91	92	90	90	89	91	92	90	91
Nigeria	87	88	86	84	89	91	91	87	84	88	88	86	88	84	87	87	87	84
China	78	81	72	78	79	75	81	78	72	80	76	77	na	na	na	80	74	44
Romania	82	84	80	73	81	88	90	79	74	82	83	80	83	83	78	86	80	68
Turkey	88	89	87	86	88	90	95	84	60	93	90	79	79	87	93	91	89	78
Poland	na	na	na	na	na	na	na	na	na	na	na	na	na	na	na	na	na	na
Bulgaria	90	92	88	89	88	92	92	91	87	91	90	88	89	89	92	89	90	90
Chile	77	78	76	71	76	88	87	77	65	86	77	68	73	77	79	84	78	64
Czechoslovakia	93	93	93	93	92	94	93	93	93	92	95	91	92	94	92	93	94	90
South Africa	na	na	na	na	na	na	na	na	na	na	na	na	na	na	na	na	na	na
Lithuania	97	96	97	98	96	96	94	98	94	97	97	95	na	na	na	96	97	96
Hungary	76	81	72	67	72	84	85	67	71	81	73	69	75	76	73	78	74	82
Argentina	73	79	69	65	70	83	88	66	56	81	73	62	55	72	74	81	75	57
Brazil	72	76	69	67	71	82	88	70	47	81	72	64	67	70	79	79	70	55
Mexico	61	64	57	55	63	73	65	64	45	67	56	56	48	59	63	70	57	49
Belarus	81	83	78	79	80	83	84	81	79	83	80	78	81	80	75	78	83	80
Russia	91	92	90	92	92	89	91	91	91	92	91	90	92	90	84	90	92	91
Moscow	81	85	79	79	81	83	90	83	78	83	79	83	81	82	77	86	80	75
Latvia	90	93	89	91	89	93	92	92	86	91	91	89	na	na	na	92	90	83
Estonia	85	87	84	86	84	86	87	85	84	86	83	86	na	na	na	88	86	77
Portugal	62	60	63	44	61	80	74	48	28	77	60	38	57	58	65	76	55	38
South Korea	70	66	73	60	72	81	81	73	61	72	66	73	56	67	75	77	69	47
Ireland	59	62	55	42	55	72	71	47	35	73	66	39	48	55	65	69	59	44
North Ireland	53	56	51	38	45	72	59	46	31	64	50	43	39	53	57	60	53	40
Slovenia	77	80	73	69	72	86	85	76	62	85	75	63	66	71	83	83	76	60
Spain	57	57	57	37	50	78	66	43	30	76	57	40	46	53	61	70	54	36
East Germany	50	50	49	35	44	64	58	37	28	62	48	40	33	53	65	75	48	42
Britain	45	48	43	31	34	63	52	32	27	61	42	24	40	43	48	49	46	35
Italy	72	72	71	55	69	84	74	57	40	79	66	53	60	77	79	83	72	59
Netherlands	37	43	36	28	30	61	54	35	22	37	35	27	26	37	47	76	42	21
Belgium	61	62	60	47	57	74	72	60	43	71	59	50	57	61	58	73	63	45
Austria	62	64	60	48	57	72	67	59	51	69	62	55	61	59	63	80	64	45
France	68	70	67	60	63	80	75	67	53	75	64	58	60	75	74	83	70	53
Canada	43	45	42	29	37	64	63	43	29	56	43	31	26	47	43	55	46	34
United States	56	58	54	48	48	65	69	60	41	65	55	47	36	56	64	66	58	43
Iceland	71	75	67	62	65	93	84	74	60	na	na	na	62	75	71	79	73	43
West Germany	51	53	49	33	39	70	60	37	31	60	52	42	39	52	65	78	55	29
Denmark	25	25	25	22	20	34	38	26	17	31	27	13	16	29	27	37	25	10
Finland	42	53	32	26	36	74	52	50	28	52	42	34	34	46	45	67	44	34
Norway	51	53	48	33	43	72	79	56	32	60	50	40	44	54	49	65	48	28
Sweden	na	na	na	na	na	na	na	na	na	na	na	na	na	na	na	na	na	na
Japan	81	84	78	78	79	86	85	84	68	88	84	74	73	76	87	88	80	60
Switzerland	na	na	na	na	na	na	na	na	na	na	na	na	na	na	na	na	na	na
Total	**69**	**71**	**67**	**61**	**66**	**79**	**77**	**66**	**56**	**75**	**68**	**61**	**59**	**67**	**69**	**78**	**69**	**58**

Ranking:

Lithuania	97
Czechoslovakia	93
India	91
Russia	91
Bulgaria	90
Latvia	90
Turkey	88
Nigeria	87
Estonia	85
Romania	82
Belarus	81
Moscow	81
Japan	81
China	78
Chile	77
Slovenia	77
Hungary	76
Argentina	73
Brazil	72
Italy	72
Iceland	71
South Korea	70
France	68
Portugal	62
Austria	62
Mexico	61
Belgium	61
Ireland	59
Spain	57
United States	56
North Ireland	53
West Germany	51
Norway	51
East Germany	50
Britain	45
Canada	43
Finland	42
Netherlands	37
Denmark	25

Note: Countries in the left column are ranked according to GNP per capita. / The percentages in the bottom row give each country an equal weight. / na=not ascertained.

V221 HOUSEWIFE FULFILLED

People talk about the changing roles of men and women today. For each of the following statements, can you tell me how much you agree with each. "Being a housewife is just as fulfilling as working for pay" (% "strongly agree" or "agree")

	Total	Gender Male	Gender Female	Age 16-29	Age 30-49	Age 50+	Education Lower	Education Medium	Education Upper	Income Lower	Income Middle	Income Upper	Political Affinity Left	Political Affinity Center	Political Affinity Right	Values Mat	Values Mixed	Values Postmat	Ranking:
India	46	45	48	46	46	47	49	47	44	53	44	43	41	52	50	44	49	47	China 88
Nigeria	49	48	50	48	49	51	53	50	46	47	51	47	51	49	46	49	47	56	Bulgaria 87
China	88	90	87	83	91	91	90	90	85	90	84	91	na	na	na	92	85	87	Russia 86
Romania	48	52	45	38	48	56	64	42	38	50	47	48	46	46	48	52	49	29	Lithuania 85
Turkey	79	78	80	76	78	84	83	76	63	84	82	70	71	76	86	81	80	72	Moscow 84
Poland	na	na	na	na	na	na	na	na	na	na	na	na	na	na	na	na	na	na	Japan 83
Bulgaria	87	86	88	89	85	88	89	86	87	86	88	86	87	87	85	89	87	83	Belarus 81
Chile	74	75	72	65	74	86	86	71	62	81	73	65	68	74	75	80	75	62	Turkey 79
Czechoslovakia	39	42	37	30	34	52	47	36	32	43	37	39	36	39	42	42	40	29	Hungary 76
South Africa	na	na	na	na	na	na	na	na	na	na	na	na	na	na	na	na	na	na	United States 76
Lithuania	85	87	83	85	83	87	91	86	72	85	84	85	na	na	na	87	85	84	Chile 74
Hungary	76	79	73	70	70	84	83	68	72	81	72	70	67	77	78	76	76	76	Ireland 72
Argentina	62	67	58	55	58	71	72	54	51	66	62	52	44	63	61	65	63	52	Estonia 71
Brazil	61	63	58	52	63	72	78	56	41	72	60	51	56	57	66	64	59	53	Canada 71
Mexico	68	70	66	66	69	75	72	69	57	73	65	65	56	68	73	78	68	56	Iceland 71
Belarus	81	86	77	83	80	81	83	84	78	82	80	81	83	80	73	79	82	84	North Ireland 70
Russia	86	91	83	87	85	87	87	87	85	87	87	83	88	87	85	85	87	87	Mexico 68
Moscow	84	89	80	84	83	87	89	83	84	83	85	85	85	84	78	86	83	89	South Korea 67
Latvia	66	71	62	70	63	66	71	70	57	68	64	64	na	na	na	70	62	70	Belgium 67
Estonia	71	75	67	70	69	74	75	71	65	72	69	70	na	na	na	70	72	76	Latvia 66
Portugal	49	52	45	36	45	64	60	23	28	59	46	35	45	47	48	57	45	33	Slovenia 63
South Korea	67	70	64	61	69	72	68	66	68	62	68	74	63	66	69	68	66	65	Austria 63
Ireland	72	73	71	56	68	86	81	59	68	83	75	62	62	69	76	82	71	62	Argentina 62
North Ireland	70	69	71	55	67	86	75	68	45	78	76	60	61	67	75	69	73	58	Sweden 62
Slovenia	63	69	57	59	58	70	75	58	48	75	60	49	53	59	59	67	62	47	Brazil 61
Spain	61	63	60	47	56	77	68	44	44	75	60	48	50	63	66	71	58	47	Spain 61
East Germany	34	36	33	23	27	48	39	25	22	45	31	26	19	37	48	55	32	27	Britain 60
Britain	60	57	63	46	51	77	66	45	51	71	56	42	60	60	59	63	60	57	France 60
Italy	57	62	52	48	51	66	58	45	28	61	54	42	47	62	65	65	56	50	Italy 57
Netherlands	53	56	52	49	47	66	63	50	44	52	57	48	42	53	62	75	57	39	Denmark 55
Belgium	67	71	64	59	64	74	74	64	58	70	64	61	62	66	69	75	66	59	West Germany 54
Austria	63	66	62	52	55	75	69	61	47	74	64	53	64	61	63	79	64	52	Finland 54
France	60	63	57	51	54	73	66	59	47	62	58	54	57	58	60	68	61	50	Netherlands 53
Canada	71	70	72	63	68	80	79	70	66	77	72	64	67	72	70	73	72	70	Norway 53
United States	76	75	76	65	74	81	79	76	73	79	75	72	65	76	79	76	77	72	Nigeria 49
Iceland	71	74	69	69	66	84	81	67	67	na	na	na	66	75	72	76	73	50	Portugal 49
West Germany	54	56	53	38	44	71	62	40	46	63	56	46	44	55	65	73	57	39	Romania 48
Denmark	55	54	57	44	53	67	63	52	53	59	53	50	50	60	56	52	58	46	India 46
Finland	54	56	51	51	46	76	61	56	47	64	54	44	48	56	52	70	55	48	Czechoslovakia 39
Norway	53	54	53	42	50	65	67	51	49	63	50	54	49	55	53	57	52	48	East Germany 34
Sweden	62	63	63	59	59	67	73	58	55	66	65	58	60	63	63	74	63	52	
Japan	83	86	80	77	79	93	87	82	81	85	82	84	82	80	89	87	84	71	
Switzerland	na	na	na	na	na	na	na	na	na	na	na	na	na	na	na	na	na	na	
Total	65	67	63	59	62	74	72	61	56	70	64	60	58	64	66	71	65	58	

Note: Countries in the left column are ranked according to GNP per capita. / The percentages in the bottom row give each country an equal weight. / na=not ascertained.

V222 WAY TO INDEPENDENCE

People talk about the changing roles of men and women today. For each of the following statements, can you tell me how much you agree with each. "Having a job is the best way for a woman to be an independent person" (% "strongly agree" or "agree")

	Total	Gender		Age			Education			Income			Political Affinity			Values			Ranking:	
		Male	Female	16-29	30-49	50+	Lower	Medium	Upper	Lower	Middle	Upper	Left	Center	Right	Mat	Mixed	Postmat		
India	58	56	62	60	57	60	59	59	58	66	54	56	59	63	51	60	57	51	Denmark	81
Nigeria	62	60	64	65	58	57	56	65	60	57	65	59	58	62	61	62	61	64	Portugal	80
China	75	71	81	77	74	76	72	65	79	71	75	81	na	na	na	76	76	67	Spain	79
Romania	68	61	75	74	68	64	66	76	68	69	67	69	71	67	73	65	69	77	France	79
Turkey	45	34	57	47	42	47	45	36	61	51	41	44	49	47	37	43	44	52	Japan	78
Poland	na	na	na	na	na	na	na	na	na	na	na	na	na	na	na	na	na	na	Finland	77
Bulgaria	63	53	72	65	62	64	65	63	61	61	66	61	61	63	59	69	61	52	China	75
Chile	72	70	74	76	69	71	73	71	73	77	70	71	68	73	74	74	72	71	East Germany	75
Czechoslovakia	55	50	59	46	53	63	59	52	54	61	54	49	57	53	56	58	54	55	West Germany	75
South Africa	na	na	na	na	na	na	na	na	na	na	na	na	na	na	na	na	na	na	Norway	75
Lithuania	41	36	45	31	38	52	50	36	51	48	34	36	na	45	na	42	42	32	Brazil	74
Hungary	48	49	46	41	46	52	49	45	53	51	45	46	45	48	52	49	46	47	Italy	74
Argentina	63	63	63	66	63	60	64	64	56	64	61	66	67	65	60	63	63	62	Austria	74
Brazil	74	68	81	75	75	73	76	75	70	79	74	69	75	74	73	74	75	74	Sweden	74
Mexico	62	58	66	64	59	62	61	63	64	61	63	63	66	60	63	61	63	64	Slovenia	73
Belarus	62	56	67	56	61	70	74	60	60	63	60	65	61	62	76	69	58	51	Chile	72
Russia	58	51	63	48	58	64	64	55	57	57	63	57	53	58	56	60	58	47	North Ireland	70
Moscow	58	52	62	43	60	65	70	54	57	60	58	53	56	60	63	64	55	60	Belgium	70
Latvia	62	51	68	53	64	65	58	60	67	60	67	59	na	na	na	69	63	53	Romania	68
Estonia	56	51	60	49	58	61	54	53	68	57	53	58	66	60	63	60	53	68	Britain	68
Portugal	80	75	85	82	78	81	78	85	84	79	80	81	82	79	80	78	81	51	Bulgaria	63
South Korea	34	42	28	36	34	33	39	34	32	37	35	29	47	33	32	32	34	39	Argentina	63
Ireland	61	62	60	70	58	57	59	62	67	61	58	60	60	60	64	54	63	62	Nigeria	62
North Ireland	70	68	71	75	68	67	71	67	69	68	68	68	61	72	70	74	69	61	Mexico	62
Slovenia	73	69	77	64	72	81	78	67	78	73	72	75	77	69	70	76	73	73	Belarus	62
Spain	79	75	83	80	81	77	79	82	76	78	83	77	83	79	78	78	81	81	Latvia	62
East Germany	75	74	75	78	75	73	74	73	80	73	74	76	82	74	64	67	75	77	Ireland	61
Britain	68	65	70	67	70	66	69	61	67	64	67	70	70	69	64	66	68	72	United States	60
Italy	74	70	78	77	77	70	74	79	84	72	76	78	78	74	72	73	74	78	India	58
Netherlands	56	52	57	63	53	52	53	57	58	63	51	56	65	51	51	46	52	64	Russia	58
Belgium	70	68	72	72	69	70	74	65	72	72	67	71	73	71	67	70	70	70	Moscow	58
Austria	74	71	76	77	74	72	74	74	76	75	71	77	75	74	73	74	74	73	Estonia	56
France	79	77	81	80	77	79	76	79	84	78	76	82	79	79	80	73	80	81	Netherlands	56
Canada	55	56	54	57	55	57	53	56	54	55	56	54	63	54	54	61	56	53	Czechoslovakia	55
United States	60	60	60	62	59	59	61	60	57	62	58	60	57	57	57	58	59	61	Canada	55
Iceland	43	42	43	39	47	40	45	38	44	na	na	na	50	40	39	42	41	54	Hungary	48
West Germany	75	73	77	81	77	71	74	77	80	75	73	77	82	76	68	64	75	82	Turkey	45
Denmark	81	79	82	81	83	84	81	82	80	80	81	81	84	80	80	83	80	81	Iceland	43
Finland	77	75	79	72	75	82	84	76	80	80	81	79	75	80	76	87	78	73	Lithuania	41
Norway	75	77	74	77	74	79	80	69	79	79	76	73	77	75	71	77	73	79	South Korea	34
Sweden	74	76	72	71	71	80	73	73	75	80	72	72	77	74	74	71	75	75		
Japan	78	76	81	76	78	80	80	80	78	80	77	80	77	78	82	82	78	73		
Switzerland	na	na	na	na	na	na	na	na	na	na	na	na	na	na	na	na	na	na		
Total	65	62	68	64	64	66	66	64	67	67	64	65	68	65	64	65	64	65		

Note: Countries in the left column are ranked according to GNP per capita. / The percentages in the bottom row give each country an equal weight. / na=not ascertained.

V223 HUSBAND AND WIFE CONTRIBUTE TO HOUSEHOLD INCOME

People talk about the changing roles of men and women today. For each of the following statements, can you tell me how much you agree with each. "Both the husband and wife should contribute to household income" (% "strongly agree" or "agree")

	Total	Gender		Age			Education			Income			Political Affinity			Values		
		Male	Female	16-29	30-49	50+	Lower	Medium	Upper	Lower	Middle	Upper	Left	Center	Right	Mat	Mixed	Postmat
India	82	78	85	83	80	81	79	83	81	86	81	78	80	83	86	85	80	84
Nigeria	94	94	94	94	93	93	90	95	94	96	92	94	95	93	94	93	94	97
China	95	94	98	94	96	95	97	95	93	97	94	94	na	na	na	97	95	87
Romania	91	90	93	93	90	92	92	91	91	88	94	91	92	92	92	93	91	85
Turkey	85	78	92	83	88	85	84	85	90	88	84	85	88	87	79	85	86	85
Poland	na	na	na	na	na	na	na	na	na	na	na	na	na	na	na	na	na	na
Bulgaria	83	80	86	79	83	85	90	84	77	80	85	83	85	83	72	89	82	66
Chile	88	83	92	87	87	88	89	86	89	91	87	85	87	86	92	88	82	88
Czechoslovakia	88	85	90	86	87	90	89	87	87	88	89	86	92	88	82	90	87	86
South Africa	na	na	na	na	na	na	na	na	na	na	na	na	na	na	na	na	na	na
Lithuania	75	73	77	74	72	80	78	75	71	76	77	70	na	na	na	77	78	66
Hungary	83	81	84	83	80	86	87	80	72	86	82	75	79	85	85	84	82	83
Argentina	77	71	84	85	73	77	75	81	79	80	80	71	81	76	75	72	79	82
Brazil	93	91	96	93	93	94	95	92	94	94	93	92	93	92	93	94	93	92
Mexico	82	79	85	87	80	72	79	86	88	79	84	83	89	82	80	79	84	92
Belarus	83	82	84	80	81	89	87	84	80	86	82	82	80	87	89	87	81	73
Russia	80	77	82	74	78	86	87	81	74	81	82	75	69	81	76	83	79	66
Moscow	69	64	73	63	64	81	87	71	64	73	68	63	64	74	75	79	67	62
Latvia	77	74	80	71	78	82	86	78	72	79	79	75	na	na	na	86	76	70
Estonia	81	79	82	76	80	86	85	79	79	81	81	80	89	na	na	81	80	88
Portugal	98	98	98	99	97	97	97	100	98	97	98	98	98	97	98	97	98	97
South Korea	59	62	57	61	56	63	70	59	54	62	60	52	60	57	60	59	59	58
Ireland	70	68	73	76	70	67	67	75	71	73	66	68	71	72	64	62	72	76
North Ireland	83	82	83	84	78	86	84	82	75	88	81	81	64	85	83	87	81	80
Slovenia	93	92	95	91	93	96	95	93	90	94	93	94	91	92	96	95	93	88
Spain	85	83	86	87	85	83	85	83	86	87	86	82	87	83	79	83	86	86
East Germany	88	85	90	91	86	87	89	84	87	88	88	87	92	87	80	88	89	84
Britain	70	67	72	71	65	74	74	65	51	75	69	58	73	71	63	71	69	71
Italy	80	77	83	82	80	79	79	84	96	80	83	76	84	79	76	79	80	83
Netherlands	32	26	34	37	32	24	26	29	40	40	31	27	45	28	20	25	26	42
Belgium	67	66	68	71	67	64	68	66	68	71	64	64	72	67	56	68	67	68
Austria	73	70	76	78	72	72	74	72	78	73	75	70	76	77	70	73	73	74
France	80	80	80	81	76	83	83	77	80	83	76	79	77	81	76	81	80	80
Canada	69	68	69	77	66	64	70	68	68	73	67	66	73	67	65	72	70	66
United States	67	65	71	78	63	66	72	68	63	73	68	60	69	67	63	67	68	65
Iceland	68	68	69	67	69	70	71	64	69	na	na	na	72	66	68	70	67	75
West Germany	64	60	68	74	64	58	62	68	64	61	65	65	69	63	57	55	61	75
Denmark	71	68	74	75	64	76	80	72	66	76	71	63	67	73	68	78	69	71
Finland	78	79	76	81	75	80	81	79	74	79	76	77	86	76	76	75	78	78
Norway	74	73	76	76	71	77	74	74	75	78	70	75	83	72	69	73	74	83
Sweden	87	87	87	87	85	90	90	87	84	89	88	87	85	91	85	89	88	86
Japan	46	39	52	49	44	47	47	47	43	48	42	49	39	50	38	43	45	56
Switzerland	na	na	na	na	na	na	na	na	na	na	na	na	na	na	na	na	na	na
Total	78	75	80	79	76	79	80	78	76	80	78	75	78	78	74	78	77	77

Ranking:

Portugal	98
China	95
Nigeria	94
Brazil	93
Slovenia	93
Romania	91
Chile	88
Czechoslovakia	88
East Germany	88
Sweden	87
Turkey	85
Spain	85
Bulgaria	83
Hungary	83
Belarus	83
North Ireland	83
India	82
Mexico	82
Estonia	81
Russia	80
Italy	80
France	80
Finland	78
Argentina	77
Latvia	77
Lithuania	75
Norway	74
Austria	73
Denmark	71
Ireland	70
Britain	70
Moscow	69
Canada	69
Iceland	68
Belgium	67
United States	67
West Germany	64
South Korea	59
Japan	46
Netherlands	32

Note: Countries in the left column are ranked according to GNP per capita. / The percentages in the bottom row give each country an equal weight. / na=not ascertained.

V224. Love and respect for one's parents

One does not have to respect and love parents who have not earned it by their behaviour and attitudes.
26%

Regardless of the qualities and faults of one's parents, one must always love and respect them.
74%

V225. Parents' responsibilities to their children

Parents have a life of their own and should not be asked to sacrifice their own well-being for the sake of their children
21%

Neither
13%

Parents' duty is to do their best for their children even at the expense of their own well-being
66%

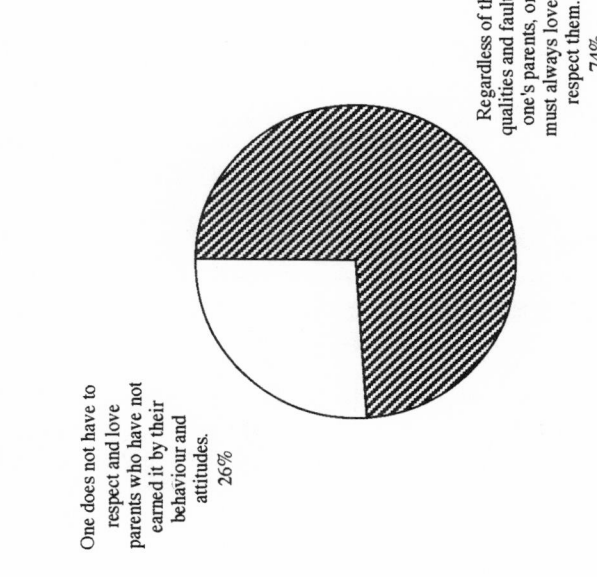

V224 RESPECT PARENTS

With which of these two statements do you tend to agree? A. Regardless of what the qualities and faults of one's parents are, one must always love and respect them. B. One does not have the duty to respect and love parents who have not earned it by their behaviour and attitudes.
(% "tend to agree with statement A")

	Total	Gender		Age			Education			Income			Political Affinity			Values			Ranking	
		Male	Female	16-29	30-49	50+	Lower	Medium	Upper	Lower	Middle	Upper	Left	Center	Right	Mat	Mixed	Postmat		
India	84	83	86	82	86	86	90	85	81	86	85	82	81	85	83	87	82	81	South Korea	94
Nigeria	87	85	89	87	86	86	89	86	87	88	87	82	88	85	85	85	88	78	Brazil	90
China	75	74	77	73	77	76	85	76	61	76	76	74	na	na	na	82	69	64	Chile	88
Romania	83	82	83	70	84	91	88	82	78	81	84	83	88	84	78	88	82	64	Nigeria	87
Turkey	83	82	83	76	84	90	88	76	69	86	84	77	71	83	88	88	85	70	South Africa	87
Poland	84	82	87	85	83	85	86	85	77	84	84	85	83	82	86	83	85	85	India	84
Bulgaria	83	84	83	84	80	88	88	81	82	80	83	85	84	83	82	90	82	77	Poland	84
Chile	88	88	88	84	89	93	91	88	86	90	90	85	85	89	87	92	88	81	Italy	84
Czechoslovakia	67	65	69	63	64	73	72	65	62	70	66	66	66	70	60	72	65	65	Romania	83
South Africa	87	88	86	87	87	88	93	86	73	90	89	78	80	83	85	88	88	78	Turkey	83
Lithuania	80	80	81	78	88	80	83	79	82	82	80	79	na	na	na	79	82	78	Bulgaria	83
Hungary	81	81	81	79	79	84	84	80	73	86	79	74	75	80	89	80	82	90	Belarus	83
Argentina	75	74	75	68	76	79	78	72	69	80	77	70	54	74	83	83	76	60	Slovenia	82
Brazil	90	90	90	89	90	91	91	92	82	92	92	87	83	91	93	92	89	83	Hungary	81
Mexico	78	76	80	73	80	86	79	80	73	80	77	71	55	81	85	80	77	69	Lithuania	80
Belarus	83	83	83	77	84	86	85	83	71	86	82	82	80	86	88	89	81	71	Moscow	80
Russia	76	73	78	75	75	77	78	78	72	78	75	71	67	77	77	80	72	79	North Ireland	80
Moscow	80	80	79	75	81	80	84	79	79	82	78	80	79	80	83	81	80	74	Spain	80
Latvia	72	75	70	68	72	77	73	75	65	68	71	74	na	na	na	75	70	69	Japan	79
Estonia	62	64	60	59	62	63	66	60	62	63	59	61	na	na	na	65	60	49	Mexico	78
Portugal	77	78	76	74	77	76	83	71	58	83	74	69	74	75	79	83	76	58	Ireland	78
South Korea	94	94	93	94	94	92	93	93	94	92	94	94	90	95	94	94	94	91	Portugal	77
Ireland	78	76	79	69	79	83	82	75	61	84	81	68	67	75	82	82	78	71	Belgium	77
North Ireland	80	83	78	71	79	87	81	80	69	77	80	73	71	80	79	86	78	76	France	77
Slovenia	82	80	84	76	82	86	86	82	76	86	82	75	71	81	79	87	82	66	Russia	76
Spain	80	76	82	72	76	88	82	77	71	87	78	73	71	80	88	85	78	69	East Germany	76
East Germany	76	70	82	66	73	86	80	73	64	82	76	71	65	81	82	84	77	72	China	75
Britain	68	69	67	68	61	73	71	67	51	74	65	63	67	69	63	71	69	60	Argentina	75
Italy	84	81	87	78	83	88	85	73	80	88	80	72	77	88	86	89	84	77	Austria	75
Netherlands	38	45	36	32	31	54	46	39	27	36	44	24	24	40	45	59	42	24	United States	75
Belgium	77	76	78	65	72	88	85	73	65	85	74	69	66	78	80	87	77	66	Latvia	72
Austria	75	72	76	67	67	84	80	73	60	82	73	71	69	72	74	89	76	61	Switzerland	70
France	77	76	78	71	76	83	81	78	64	78	75	74	68	79	82	85	78	71	Canada	69
Canada	69	70	69	70	65	74	82	71	57	77	68	62	58	71	67	85	71	57	Britain	68
United States	75	76	72	75	71	78	80	79	65	79	77	67	63	75	77	79	76	69	Czechoslovakia	67
Iceland	61	67	55	58	61	65	72	63	51	na	na	na	47	63	67	72	59	48	West Germany	63
West Germany	63	60	64	45	56	77	69	53	49	66	60	61	40	67	75	84	68	40	Estonia	62
Denmark	47	44	50	39	44	57	63	40	42	53	46	31	32	49	50	58	48	28	Iceland	61
Finland	40	38	42	36	35	55	51	45	29	53	42	27	30	45	39	70	42	30	Sweden	51
Norway	45	47	43	39	42	53	56	47	38	50	44	38	40	46	47	52	44	32	Denmark	47
Sweden	51	54	47	48	48	57	60	49	39	55	56	45	47	56	46	64	53	37	Norway	45
Japan	79	77	81	68	81	81	77	82	72	77	80	80	77	75	83	81	75	75	Finland	40
Switzerland	70	69	71	62	66	77	70	73	56	70	68	65	51	71	75	85	71	58	Netherlands	38
Total	74	74	74	69	73	79	79	73	66	77	74	69	66	75	76	81	74	65		

Note: Countries in the left column are ranked according to GNP per capita. / The percentages in the bottom row give each country an equal weight. / na=not ascertained.

V225 PARENTS' DUTY

Which of the following statements* best describes your views about parents' responsibilities to their children?

% "Parents' duty is to do their best for their children even at the expense of their own well-being"

	Total	Gender		Age			Education			Income			Political Affinity			Values		
		Male	Female	16-29	30-49	50+	Lower	Middle	Upper	Lower	Middle	Upper	Left	Center	Right	Mat	Mixed	Postmat
India	78	76	80	72	80	84	85	74	78	79	78	77	74	77	77	79	76	66
Nigeria	89	89	89	88	90	91	86	90	89	89	89	90	90	88	89	89	90	80
China	61	59	64	47	65	70	68	60	48	67	60	55	na	na	89	67	56	45
Romania	85	85	85	77	84	91	92	82	80	86	88	81	86	86	na	88	85	69
Turkey	67	64	69	60	70	70	70	63	57	70	67	63	64	66	79	75	67	55
Poland	63	67	60	58	61	68	68	63	52	62	65	63	66	60	66	63	64	61
Bulgaria	58	58	58	55	54	66	70	59	47	56	60	59	57	56	68	71	54	43
Chile	80	82	79	73	83	88	87	78	76	86	79	75	77	82	78	86	80	75
Czechoslovakia	41	44	39	37	38	48	49	37	39	41	44	38	41	42	40	47	40	35
South Africa	88	88	87	88	87	89	89	88	81	88	88	85	81	88	86	90	88	81
Lithuania	38	39	36	34	28	49	51	34	32	40	38	31	na	na	na	37	39	35
Hungary	62	65	59	47	56	73	68	58	43	68	59	50	67	61	64	64	61	45
Argentina	79	80	78	69	79	86	87	72	73	85	81	74	64	78	81	88	80	65
Brazil	81	84	78	72	85	82	88	81	69	85	81	78	76	80	84	86	79	70
Mexico	74	74	74	68	77	80	74	78	69	74	75	68	63	71	78	80	74	57
Belarus	46	50	43	39	45	55	61	43	44	49	46	43	44	47	50	50	45	34
Russia	51	50	52	44	46	62	60	51	46	55	54	44	47	52	55	56	49	41
Moscow	44	45	44	32	43	56	57	44	42	44	43	45	42	45	43	54	41	44
Latvia	51	53	50	47	50	59	66	52	45	49	54	50	na	na	na	59	51	48
Estonia	55	54	56	54	52	61	67	54	45	60	55	49	na	na	na	60	55	48
Portugal	84	86	82	76	84	91	87	84	72	87	83	80	83	84	82	85	84	74
South Korea	38	36	41	23	43	52	53	38	32	39	37	42	31	33	44	44	35	25
Ireland	73	73	74	60	74	82	80	67	64	81	76	66	62	73	76	75	74	68
North Ireland	82	82	81	68	81	91	84	75	83	86	82	76	68	81	84	89	78	82
Slovenia	72	74	70	65	71	78	78	67	70	74	74	65	63	73	76	76	71	64
Spain	75	72	78	63	73	86	80	71	58	87	73	68	68	74	84	83	73	64
East Germany	72	70	73	62	69	80	73	68	67	75	70	70	65	73	75	80	73	62
Britain	74	75	73	63	71	83	76	67	72	81	69	71	74	73	76	76	74	72
Italy	79	80	79	66	71	89	81	70	67	82	79	77	74	83	79	85	80	74
Netherlands	62	77	57	53	58	79	68	59	59	63	62	62	53	61	71	71	65	56
Belgium	64	67	62	56	59	74	70	63	54	70	67	58	57	64	70	69	65	57
Austria	61	61	62	45	62	68	70	56	53	64	63	57	59	60	64	70	65	48
France	81	82	79	75	79	86	81	82	77	79	81	82	79	81	79	80	82	79
Canada	67	70	64	64	66	71	72	67	63	70	69	63	68	66	65	77	65	68
United States	75	78	72	76	71	78	77	77	72	80	76	70	71	74	78	78	76	73
Iceland	50	57	43	36	51	65	56	46	47	na	na	na	44	57	51	50	52	38
West Germany	54	53	55	44	44	67	59	46	43	59	55	48	41	55	63	72	57	38
Denmark	52	50	54	40	49	64	61	46	51	58	49	45	44	55	55	53	53	42
Finland	49	55	42	46	45	61	57	52	41	56	46	46	49	49	52	65	48	47
Norway	73	78	67	57	73	82	84	73	66	72	77	67	65	76	73	80	71	59
Sweden	63	65	61	57	59	75	69	63	57	64	62	65	60	63	65	72	64	57
Japan	40	41	38	29	40	46	44	40	35	41	41	39	37	36	45	43	40	32
Switzerland	69	70	68	59	65	78	74	69	54	70	71	63	56	71	74	83	69	61
Total	**65**	**66**	**64**	**57**	**64**	**74**	**72**	**63**	**58**	**68**	**66**	**62**	**62**	**67**	**69**	**71**	**65**	**57**

Ranking:

Nigeria	89
South Africa	88
Romania	85
Portugal	84
North Ireland	82
Brazil	81
France	81
Chile	80
Argentina	79
Italy	79
India	78
Spain	75
United States	75
Mexico	74
Britain	74
Ireland	73
Norway	73
Slovenia	72
East Germany	72
Switzerland	69
Turkey	67
Canada	67
Belgium	64
Poland	63
Sweden	63
Hungary	62
Netherlands	62
China	61
Austria	61
Bulgaria	58
Estonia	55
West Germany	54
Denmark	52
Russia	51
Latvia	51
Iceland	50
Finland	49
Belarus	46
Moscow	44
Czechoslovakia	41
Japan	40
Lithuania	38
South Korea	38

Note: Countries in the left column are ranked according to GNP per capita. / The percentages in the bottom row give each country an equal weight. / na=not ascertained.

* The other statement offered was: "Parents have a life of their own and should not be asked to sacrifice their own well-being for the sake of their children."

V226-V236. Here is a list of qualities which children can be encouraged to learn at home. Which, if any, do you consider to be especially important? Please choose up to five.

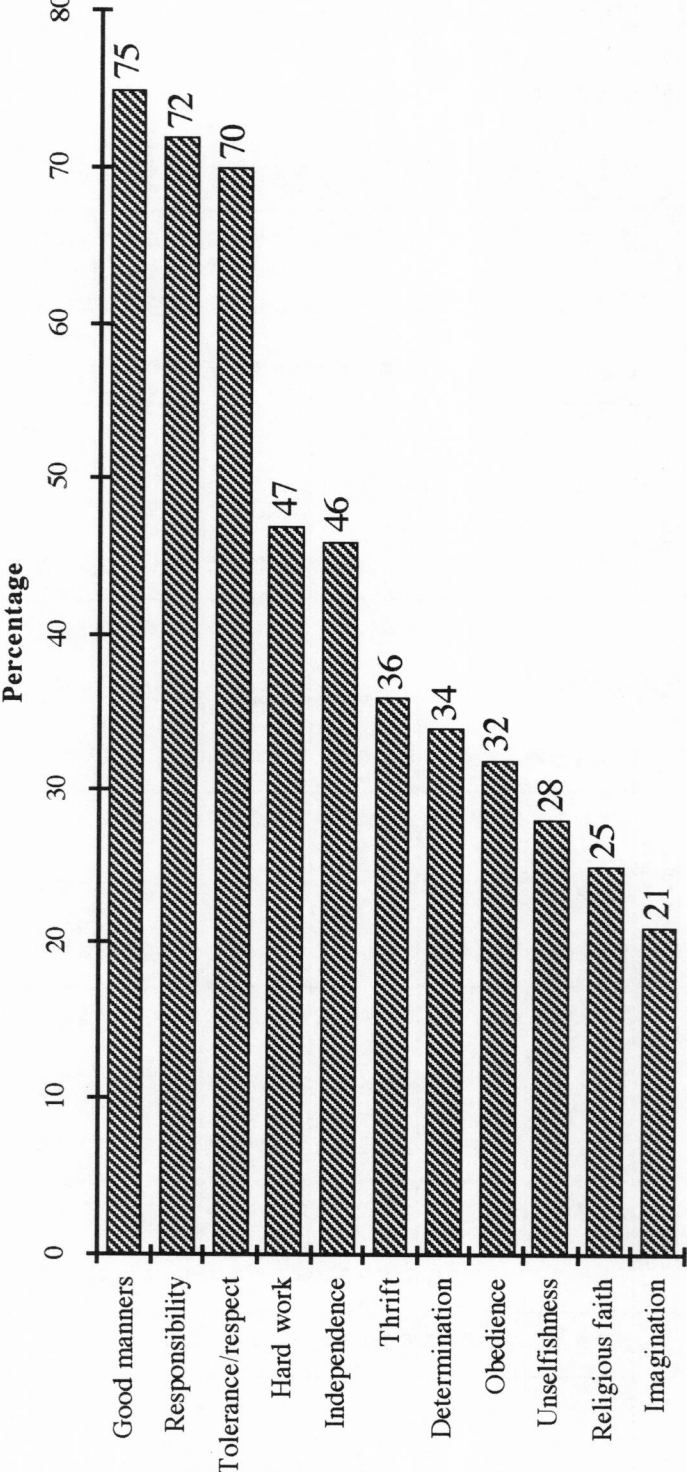

Percentage

Good manners	75
Responsibility	72
Tolerance/respect	70
Hard work	47
Independence	46
Thrift	36
Determination	34
Obedience	32
Unselfishness	28
Religious faith	25
Imagination	21

V226 GOOD MANNERS

Here is a list of qualities which children can be encouraged to learn at home. Which, if any, do you consider to be especially important?

Good manners (% "mentioned")

	Total	Gender		Age			Education			Income			Political Affinity			Values		
		Male	Female	16-29	30-49	50+	Lower	Medium	Upper	Lower	Middle	Upper	Left	Center	Right	Mat	Mixed	Postmat
India	94	94	94	95	94	94	94	94	95	95	94	94	96	93	93	95	93	93
Nigeria	97	97	98	98	96	100	97	98	97	97	98	96	96	97	97	97	97	99
China	53	52	53	58	56	41	55	56	50	51	55	52	na	na	na	54	51	63
Romania	92	91	94	90	93	94	95	94	87	92	94	91	96	93	na	95	92	79
Turkey	92	92	92	89	93	94	96	89	76	97	92	87	84	93	96	97	93	81
Poland	na	na	na	na	na	na	na	na	na	na	na	na	na	na	na	na	na	na
Bulgaria	72	70	74	71	72	73	68	77	69	na	71	74	76	72	74	77	71	71
Chile	90	91	90	89	90	92	94	92	83	93	93	83	88	91	88	94	89	87
Czechoslovakia	86	85	88	82	83	93	90	87	77	89	87	82	85	88	84	90	86	75
South Africa	81	82	80	84	78	79	89	81	50	88	84	63	76	76	77	81	81	78
Lithuania	35	33	37	50	33	25	28	37	39	32	35	43	na	na	na	29	36	44
Hungary	77	76	78	77	74	80	78	77	71	86	77	74	76	na	74	79	75	68
Argentina	78	76	80	77	76	82	85	78	68	80	80	70	62	79	81	90	78	64
Brazil	77	78	76	82	74	72	74	81	64	79	76	74	72	77	83	79	77	66
Mexico	73	74	72	73	74	74	75	71	71	72	74	76	64	75	77	81	74	56
Belarus	71	69	73	77	72	65	71	71	70	75	71	67	72	72	68	72	72	59
Russia	57	50	63	63	59	52	52	61	57	59	54	57	56	58	57	58	57	58
Moscow	57	52	61	62	58	51	58	60	54	56	56	59	54	63	58	58	57	52
Latvia	53	49	56	61	51	49	49	55	52	52	55	53	na	na	na	52	56	48
Estonia	74	72	76	71	74	78	76	75	72	75	71	77	na	na	na	77	74	68
Portugal	82	83	81	78	79	88	86	76	71	85	81	78	79	81	84	88	79	74
South Korea	93	93	93	92	93	95	95	93	93	93	92	95	89	93	94	94	93	91
Ireland	75	71	78	71	74	77	81	68	63	81	80	65	65	74	75	79	76	64
North Ireland	95	95	95	93	94	96	95	95	90	99	96	89	93	97	94	99	94	93
Slovenia	89	88	90	87	89	91	91	89	85	92	96	83	81	89	91	93	89	78
Spain	80	78	82	72	78	89	85	77	63	89	82	72	72	83	83	91	80	78
East Germany	67	65	68	58	64	74	71	61	56	70	66	64	59	72	67	77	69	55
Britain	89	88	90	87	89	90	92	87	73	89	90	88	83	91	90	92	91	81
Italy	79	78	81	76	77	83	81	71	57	80	77	72	71	78	88	86	81	67
Netherlands	80	80	80	78	78	86	85	87	66	80	81	72	69	83	88	88	87	67
Belgium	72	71	72	64	70	78	79	72	59	75	71	71	59	74	74	80	74	59
Austria	78	79	78	71	77	83	82	77	68	80	81	74	75	80	76	88	82	65
France	53	51	55	46	52	52	61	52	33	57	51	42	41	49	64	70	56	33
Canada	75	76	74	77	74	78	81	79	65	73	73	68	64	77	75	79	78	64
United States	76	77	76	78	71	81	85	79	66	84	73	71	63	78	73	82	77	70
Iceland	90	90	90	88	90	92	91	90	88	na	na	na	87	91	92	93	89	78
West Germany	67	64	69	58	62	74	71	62	50	69	68	61	53	70	73	77	71	52
Denmark	66	66	66	66	61	72	76	70	57	71	68	55	50	68	72	82	70	34
Finland	82	80	84	78	81	87	83	82	81	84	80	82	76	80	90	97	83	77
Norway	77	76	78	74	74	82	84	83	68	76	78	73	64	76	86	87	77	53
Sweden	78	78	78	74	74	84	88	78	61	79	78	77	77	79	78	89	83	58
Japan	83	82	83	80	82	86	87	84	75	86	83	82	71	79	86	87	80	72
Switzerland	59	59	60	53	55	66	64	59	45	60	60	62	44	65	66	71	61	49
Total	**76**	**75**	**77**	**75**	**75**	**78**	**79**	**76**	**68**	**78**	**76**	**72**	**72**	**79**	**80**	**82**	**77**	**67**

Ranking:

Nigeria	97
North Ireland	95
India	94
South Korea	93
Romania	92
Turkey	92
Chile	90
Iceland	90
Slovenia	89
Britain	89
Czechoslovakia	86
Japan	83
Portugal	82
Finland	82
South Africa	81
Spain	80
Netherlands	80
Italy	79
Argentina	78
Austria	78
Sweden	78
Hungary	77
Brazil	77
Norway	77
United States	76
Ireland	75
Canada	75
Estonia	74
Mexico	73
Bulgaria	72
Belgium	72
Belarus	71
East Germany	67
West Germany	67
Denmark	66
Switzerland	59
Russia	57
Moscow	57
China	53
Latvia	53
France	53
Lithuania	35

Note: Countries in the left column are ranked according to GNP per capita. / The percentages in the bottom row give each country an equal weight. / na=not ascertained.

V227 INDEPENDENCE

Here is a list of qualities which children can be encouraged to learn at home. Which, if any, do you consider to be especially important? Independence (% "mentioned")

	Total	Gender		Age			Education			Income			Political Affinity			Values			Ranking:	
		Male	Female	16-29	30-49	50+	Lower	Medium	Upper	Lower	Middle	Upper	Left	Center	Right	Mat	Mixed	Postmat		
India	30	30	29	32	29	27	30	29	31	31	28	29	30	33	28	24	34	30	Iceland	89
Nigeria	16	17	16	18	15	14	12	18	17	16	16	18	18	16	20	15	17	23	Norway	86
China	84	83	86	90	83	79	83	84	88	83	85	85	na	na	na	82	85	89	China	84
Romania	24	27	20	37	23	16	13	28	32	18	20	33	23	23	32	15	28	43	Lithuania	81
Turkey	19	22	17	25	18	12	13	20	47	14	16	29	35	17	14	13	16	36	Denmark	81
Poland	na	na	na	na	na	na	na	na	na	na	na	na	na	na	na	na	na	na	Latvia	73
Bulgaria	62	65	60	69	65	55	48	64	75	64	61	64	69	62	74	56	62	85	West Germany	73
Chile	31	30	31	34	31	25	23	30	40	27	32	34	36	29	30	20	33	38	Hungary	70
Czechoslovakia	21	24	17	25	22	16	16	23	21	20	20	21	22	20	23	16	21	32	East Germany	67
South Africa	16	14	18	16	17	15	11	17	33	08	16	28	19	20	19	15	16	23	Japan	65
Lithuania	81	83	79	85	83	75	72	83	86	78	81	88	na	na	na	79	82	82	Austria	63
Hungary	70	70	70	74	76	63	63	76	79	64	74	76	77	73	66	69	71	68	Bulgaria	62
Argentina	43	41	46	54	49	28	30	51	59	29	41	55	71	44	44	31	42	62	Finland	57
Brazil	27	25	28	32	24	22	17	28	42	17	27	35	32	28	24	21	28	44	South Korea	54
Mexico	47	46	49	48	47	48	46	46	53	41	47	62	59	48	46	40	49	58	United States	52
Belarus	31	35	28	37	33	24	25	32	33	24	34	36	32	33	26	26	34	36	Netherlands	51
Russia	29	35	25	36	31	23	21	31	32	25	26	38	40	26	27	25	31	39	Mexico	47
Moscow	43	48	39	46	47	34	31	40	47	39	47	43	45	42	39	38	41	61	Canada	44
Latvia	73	78	69	73	73	71	69	72	75	74	69	74	na	na	na	72	72	75	Argentina	43
Estonia	43	47	39	48	44	35	36	43	49	39	43	47	na	na	na	43	40	42	Moscow	43
Portugal	24	23	24	33	25	14	16	38	43	13	28	36	29	25	19	13	27	45	Estonia	43
South Korea	54	55	54	57	56	45	43	58	56	52	57	53	57	54	54	52	56	59	Ireland	43
Ireland	43	43	43	51	47	34	36	51	52	30	43	52	57	47	36	34	42	59	Britain	43
North Ireland	37	34	39	41	39	33	37	35	45	42	33	44	39	32	41	40	33	49	Switzerland	42
Slovenia	33	37	29	37	33	29	26	36	40	26	34	42	39	34	32	25	34	54	North Ireland	37
Spain	37	38	36	49	43	22	31	47	57	23	37	50	49	35	32	27	41	49	Spain	37
East Germany	67	65	68	79	70	55	64	71	74	59	69	71	73	67	61	53	67	72	Belgium	36
Britain	43	37	49	48	45	38	42	43	50	40	42	43	47	45	36	43	41	52	Sweden	36
Italy	31	31	31	43	33	21	29	37	36	26	34	47	38	27	27	24	29	42	Slovenia	33
Netherlands	51	47	52	54	55	40	40	54	58	53	48	60	63	50	43	35	48	61	Chile	31
Belgium	36	36	35	44	42	24	30	36	47	28	37	41	44	37	32	24	34	50	Belarus	31
Austria	63	63	64	76	72	50	55	67	82	52	66	68	66	64	62	49	61	76	Italy	31
France	27	26	28	34	31	17	20	31	36	24	31	31	35	25	18	15	23	47	India	30
Canada	44	41	47	50	48	33	31	44	53	40	41	51	53	43	43	29	44	51	Russia	29
United States	52	46	60	59	56	45	51	48	59	53	48	56	63	51	49	55	50	59	Brazil	27
Iceland	89	84	93	92	91	82	85	91	91	na	na	na	90	87	91	89	88	96	France	27
West Germany	73	74	72	86	79	61	69	81	81	68	72	79	80	74	63	52	72	86	Romania	24
Denmark	81	79	83	84	86	72	73	83	83	76	84	87	88	80	78	76	81	90	Portugal	24
Finland	57	52	61	64	61	40	53	51	65	52	54	64	57	58	56	50	54	63	Czechoslovakia	21
Norway	86	83	89	90	89	81	74	87	91	80	88	92	86	87	87	82	87	97	Turkey	19
Sweden	36	34	39	39	39	32	25	39	48	32	35	40	38	33	40	20	36	49	Nigeria	16
Japan	65	68	61	62	68	62	60	65	68	61	65	67	71	69	62	63	66	76	South Africa	16
Switzerland	42	44	41	56	48	31	39	43	53	38	47	56	67	41	36	33	38	60		
Total	47	47	47	53	49	39	40	49	55	41	46	52	51	44	42	40	47	57		

Note: Countries in the left column are ranked according to GNP per capita. / The percentages in the bottom row give each country an equal weight. / na=not ascertained.

V228 HARD WORK

Here is a list of qualities which children can be encouraged to learn at home. Which, if any, do you consider to be especially important? Hard work (% "mentioned")

	Total	Gender Male	Gender Female	Age 16-29	Age 30-49	Age 50+	Education Lower	Education Medium	Education Upper	Income Lower	Income Middle	Income Upper	Political Left	Political Center	Political Right	Values Mat	Values Mixed	Values Postmat	Ranking
India	67	71	63	68	66	67	66	68	66	71	64	66	66	69	68	69	66	62	Russia 93
Nigeria	82	83	79	81	83	84	79	80	84	85	80	80	86	84	77	82	82	80	Lithuania 92
China	65	66	62	51	65	80	71	60	58	67	62	65	na	70	na	70	59	57	Estonia 92
Romania	71	70	72	58	68	83	83	67	63	72	74	67	75	70	65	81	66	49	Bulgaria 91
Turkey	73	73	72	67	73	79	77	68	63	79	74	64	67	73	76	78	73	64	Latvia 91
Poland	na	na	na	na	na	na	na	na	na	na	na	na	na	na	na	na	na	na	Czechoslovakia 85
Bulgaria	91	90	92	85	91	95	95	92	86	91	93	90	90	92	90	93	92	79	Nigeria 82
Chile	12	14	11	10	13	15	16	09	13	15	11	10	14	12	10	14	12	09	Belarus 80
Czechoslovakia	85	85	85	78	83	92	88	82	88	89	86	80	88	83	85	89	84	82	Iceland 78
South Africa	30	32	28	32	27	32	36	28	20	38	28	21	26	26	28	32	28	34	Moscow 75
Lithuania	92	92	92	88	91	96	94	91	96	92	93	92	na	na	na	93	92	92	Turkey 73
Hungary	70	70	70	62	69	75	80	63	50	77	68	56	57	72	57	70	70	70	Romania 71
Argentina	53	53	53	46	49	63	58	51	44	64	53	44	45	53	50	54	55	46	Hungary 70
Brazil	52	51	52	47	49	63	70	47	31	61	53	41	49	44	57	61	47	33	India 67
Mexico	23	27	19	18	24	35	28	14	16	28	22	17	22	20	23	29	22	17	Portugal 67
Belarus	80	81	79	72	82	85	82	79	80	81	79	81	80	80	81	85	78	75	China 65
Russia	93	92	93	89	93	95	95	93	91	94	92	92	92	92	90	93	93	84	South Korea 64
Moscow	75	75	75	66	75	82	83	75	73	78	74	71	74	77	71	80	75	70	Argentina 53
Latvia	91	88	93	88	93	93	89	92	90	92	92	90	na	na	na	96	91	84	France 53
Estonia	92	92	92	88	93	96	91	92	92	93	91	92	na	na	na	93	93	92	Brazil 52
Portugal	67	70	65	54	67	80	76	53	44	73	67	59	70	70	63	76	66	43	United States 49
South Korea	64	56	71	58	64	77	64	60	69	58	64	73	63	61	66	65	65	58	Spain 48
Ireland	28	33	23	22	25	35	30	23	32	34	26	24	32	28	28	32	28	22	Belgium 36
North Ireland	29	38	23	29	27	32	31	25	31	30	32	30	21	27	36	40	26	29	Switzerland 36
Slovenia	32	37	28	27	30	38	39	26	28	35	32	27	29	30	27	36	31	25	Canada 35
Spain	48	46	49	36	48	57	52	40	35	59	48	36	45	45	44	59	46	32	Slovenia 32
East Germany	16	19	13	11	11	24	18	08	13	17	16	15	14	15	20	33	15	10	Japan 31
Britain	29	35	23	30	26	30	30	27	27	28	30	31	27	27	32	32	29	24	South Africa 30
Italy	27	30	23	18	24	34	28	17	15	30	22	18	25	25	27	31	29	18	North Ireland 29
Netherlands	13	20	11	11	07	25	17	12	10	13	15	07	07	13	19	21	17	05	Britain 29
Belgium	36	39	34	29	33	44	42	36	26	41	35	25	36	33	34	49	38	22	Ireland 28
Austria	14	16	13	12	11	18	16	14	11	18	15	10	09	11	19	14	16	11	Italy 27
France	53	55	51	47	48	62	59	51	39	56	48	50	47	50	67	64	55	38	Mexico 23
Canada	35	40	30	34	33	38	39	35	33	35	34	37	30	35	43	42	34	33	East Germany 16
United States	49	55	41	46	47	51	57	48	43	49	45	50	48	48	52	55	50	41	West Germany 15
Iceland	78	79	77	76	78	81	78	83	75	na	na	na	73	80	78	82	78	75	Austria 14
West Germany	15	17	12	08	12	21	18	09	09	15	15	13	09	14	23	29	14	08	Netherlands 13
Denmark	02	04	01	05	02	02	03	01	03	01	01	02	08	03	02	03	03	01	Chile 12
Finland	06	05	06	08	06	03	05	06	06	05	03	10	08	06	07	06	06	07	Norway 07
Norway	07	08	06	03	05	10	09	06	06	08	04	09	05	06	09	08	06	04	Finland 06
Sweden	05	08	02	06	04	06	07	05	04	06	06	03	05	05	07	08	05	04	Sweden 05
Japan	31	32	29	14	29	44	39	27	32	34	29	33	33	28	39	32	29	29	Denmark 02
Switzerland	36	37	35	25	29	47	38	35	28	39	32	34	25	37	41	51	39	20	
Total	48	50	46	43	47	54	52	45	43	50	47	44	42	43	45	53	48	41	

Note: Countries in the left column are ranked according to GNP per capita. / The percentages in the bottom row give each country an equal weight. / na=not ascertained.

V229 RESPONSIBILITY

Here is a list of qualities which children can be encouraged to learn at home. Which, if any, do you consider to be especially important?
Feeling of responsibility (% "mentioned")

	Total	Gender Male	Gender Female	Age 16-29	Age 30-49	Age 50+	Education Lower	Education Medium	Education Upper	Income Lower	Income Middle	Income Upper	Pol. Aff. Left	Pol. Aff. Center	Pol. Aff. Right	Values Mat	Values Mixed	Values Postmat	Ranking
India	60	61	59	58	62	60	58	58	64	58	57	64	62	63	58	59	61	60	Iceland 94
Nigeria	36	39	31	37	37	21	27	35	41	34	39	36	31	42	34	31	40	38	South Korea 91
China	67	68	65	67	66	69	63	67	72	63	68	71	na	na	na	67	68	65	Norway 90
Romania	56	55	57	64	58	50	45	61	65	56	56	56	53	60	51	53	57	67	Sweden 89
Turkey	66	67	65	69	67	60	56	80	87	59	64	77	68	68	65	56	66	76	Chile 88
Poland	na	na	na	na	na	na	na	na	na	na	na	na	na	na	na	na	na	na	Denmark 86
Bulgaria	68	66	70	71	70	63	56	71	74	66	71	71	71	68	72	68	69	69	Netherlands 85
Chile	88	88	88	89	89	88	86	89	91	84	90	91	90	88	89	86	89	91	Austria 85
Czechoslovakia	65	61	69	58	71	63	61	64	77	64	65	66	69	67	60	66	64	72	West Germany 85
South Africa	45	45	44	42	47	45	39	46	60	37	45	54	48	47	47	44	45	41	East Germany 84
Lithuania	72	74	71	73	78	67	62	74	84	70	72	79	na	na	na	69	74	77	Japan 84
Hungary	66	69	63	62	69	64	60	70	75	62	66	77	66	70	65	67	64	70	Finland 83
Argentina	80	81	80	81	83	77	78	83	83	80	81	83	78	83	83	81	80	80	Belarus 82
Brazil	72	69	74	74	71	69	61	75	85	63	74	80	75	77	67	69	72	82	Italy 82
Mexico	77	76	77	77	79	72	74	76	85	73	78	81	79	77	75	76	77	82	Moscow 81
Belarus	82	80	83	80	82	81	73	80	86	81	82	81	83	80	78	78	83	84	Argentina 80
Russia	70	69	70	69	72	67	62	70	73	65	72	74	71	74	61	67	72	64	Mexico 77
Moscow	81	82	81	83	82	79	68	84	82	82	81	81	81	82	86	84	82	76	Portugal 77
Latvia	75	75	76	69	77	79	71	74	79	79	76	73	na	na	na	76	76	80	Switzerland 77
Estonia	76	76	76	73	81	72	71	76	82	75	76	78	na	na	na	70	80	78	Estonia 76
Portugal	77	76	77	79	79	72	73	86	85	72	77	85	78	78	77	71	79	88	Latvia 75
South Korea	91	92	90	89	92	91	90	93	89	88	92	92	88	91	92	91	91	89	Spain 75
Ireland	61	60	62	62	63	59	59	62	64	56	59	67	60	61	62	62	60	65	Canada 75
North Ireland	38	45	34	33	45	35	38	38	35	37	33	47	54	31	46	25	41	47	Lithuania 72
Slovenia	71	74	69	77	75	64	58	79	84	66	72	83	80	73	78	68	71	87	Brazil 72
Spain	75	77	73	79	76	70	72	82	82	65	75	83	78	80	77	72	77	82	Belgium 72
East Germany	84	82	85	84	88	80	82	85	92	80	84	87	89	84	80	73	84	90	France 72
Britain	48	47	49	45	46	51	46	51	55	46	47	49	48	47	49	45	47	52	United States 72
Italy	82	82	82	86	85	77	81	87	87	80	84	88	83	77	79	76	83	88	Slovenia 71
Netherlands	85	87	85	82	89	84	83	84	89	83	85	95	88	86	87	71	88	88	Russia 70
Belgium	72	72	72	74	75	68	66	72	85	66	70	78	74	77	73	58	73	85	Bulgaria 68
Austria	85	83	86	88	85	83	82	86	90	78	85	90	86	85	83	81	84	88	China 67
France	72	72	72	72	72	70	67	77	73	67	73	75	74	74	71	66	72	76	Turkey 66
Canada	75	72	78	74	75	76	74	76	75	76	73	76	73	77	72	73	77	74	Hungary 66
United States	72	69	75	64	72	75	75	69	73	72	70	73	78	71	67	72	72	72	Czechoslovakia 65
Iceland	94	92	96	95	94	93	93	94	95	na	na	na	94	94	93	96	93	93	Ireland 61
West Germany	85	83	86	86	86	83	83	86	91	83	86	86	86	86	82	77	85	90	India 60
Denmark	86	87	85	86	87	84	76	87	90	83	87	91	92	85	85	76	88	91	Romania 56
Finland	83	80	86	86	83	80	79	81	86	79	84	84	90	80	83	77	81	87	Britain 48
Norway	90	88	92	91	92	87	82	90	93	85	92	92	90	91	91	87	91	95	South Africa 45
Sweden	89	88	91	87	90	90	86	88	93	85	90	91	91	85	92	89	88	92	North Ireland 38
Japan	84	85	83	85	83	86	77	86	79	86	82	85	74	85	87	81	85	82	Nigeria 36
Switzerland	77	77	78	79	79	75	77	77	81	78	78	84	81	80	77	67	77	86	
Total	**73**	**73**	**73**	**73**	**75**	**71**	**69**	**75**	**79**	**70**	**73**	**77**	**75**	**74**	**73**	**70**	**74**	**77**	

Note: Countries in the left column are ranked according to GNP per capita. / The percentages in the bottom row give each country an equal weight. / na=not ascertained.

V230 IMAGINATION

Here is a list of qualities which children can be encouraged to learn at home. Which, if any, do you consider to be especially important? Imagination (% "mentioned")

	Total	Gender Male	Gender Female	Age 16-29	Age 30-49	Age 50+	Education Lower	Education Medium	Education Upper	Income Lower	Income Middle	Income Upper	Political Affinity Left	Political Affinity Center	Political Affinity Right	Values Mat	Values Mixed	Values Postmat
India	22	25	20	23	24	18	21	24	22	22	23	22	26	24	22	19	25	33
Nigeria	06	07	05	07	06	05	02	06	07	05	08	07	06	09	04	07	06	11
China	27	26	27	36	26	17	25	29	32	24	30	27	na	na	na	22	30	43
Romania	17	22	12	28	18	10	09	22	21	17	18	16	19	17	20	12	20	33
Turkey	23	26	21	25	25	18	15	34	42	20	22	29	37	22	16	17	21	38
Poland	na	na	na	na	na	na	na	na	na	na	na	na	na	na	na	na	na	na
Bulgaria	16	19	14	21	19	11	11	15	24	18	15	18	16	19	18	10	17	30
Chile	32	36	28	37	30	29	26	34	37	29	34	34	34	33	33	28	32	42
Czechoslovakia	07	08	06	08	07	07	07	07	07	08	07	07	06	07	09	05	08	10
South Africa	08	08	07	09	08	06	05	09	15	07	08	10	12	09	09	06	09	09
Lithuania	06	07	06	08	08	04	04	07	09	07	04	09	na	na	na	05	06	11
Hungary	09	12	07	09	11	09	07	10	13	09	11	06	12	10	11	08	11	10
Argentina	31	34	29	44	33	19	20	37	45	25	31	45	48	34	29	19	30	50
Brazil	12	15	10	15	13	08	08	13	18	08	17	14	17	12	10	10	14	14
Mexico	31	32	29	34	30	25	30	30	34	31	33	31	35	33	32	24	33	39
Belarus	07	07	07	09	08	03	05	04	11	07	06	08	08	06	06	06	07	20
Russia	11	13	10	15	12	08	08	10	15	11	10	14	16	10	14	08	13	16
Moscow	30	31	29	33	30	28	26	25	34	30	30	30	31	29	30	24	31	45
Latvia	11	15	09	14	11	09	11	10	15	10	07	16	15	na	na	05	12	20
Estonia	13	14	12	19	13	06	09	13	16	14	13	11	na	na	na	07	14	15
Portugal	20	23	18	29	20	12	14	27	39	14	21	27	24	20	19	14	23	33
South Korea	06	05	07	10	05	03	05	05	08	06	07	05	09	08	05	04	07	12
Ireland	14	16	13	25	16	06	08	19	32	04	12	24	32	15	09	11	12	25
North Ireland	14	15	13	22	13	08	09	15	41	12	16	22	25	14	12	09	12	29
Slovenia	10	13	07	10	14	06	09	10	12	09	11	11	13	10	16	09	10	13
Spain	34	38	31	45	39	21	29	45	49	20	36	47	42	33	29	25	38	45
East Germany	28	30	27	40	33	17	23	39	42	23	28	34	39	24	25	14	24	47
Britain	18	20	17	21	24	12	16	22	27	13	19	25	26	18	14	13	17	29
Italy	15	17	13	23	16	08	13	27	28	13	19	20	22	13	10	07	14	26
Netherlands	24	18	27	27	30	12	14	19	41	29	19	34	43	18	15	10	17	38
Belgium	18	21	16	27	22	09	10	20	30	13	18	22	27	17	16	11	16	31
Austria	24	25	23	35	30	14	20	25	39	19	23	30	27	24	27	09	21	40
France	23	27	19	30	26	14	21	18	36	21	23	23	31	18	18	15	21	34
Canada	23	25	21	27	27	14	14	21	32	19	26	24	37	21	23	15	19	33
United States	27	26	27	33	31	20	25	23	32	24	26	27	37	25	21	26	25	33
Iceland	49	48	51	51	52	43	40	53	55	na	na	na	56	47	48	44	48	73
West Germany	32	33	31	48	39	17	24	44	53	28	31	38	45	30	22	14	27	53
Denmark	37	40	34	44	46	22	20	37	46	34	35	50	53	35	32	20	34	66
Finland	26	30	23	38	25	18	23	24	30	26	27	26	29	25	24	21	22	36
Norway	31	27	36	46	36	16	11	31	42	31	31	37	39	27	32	22	32	53
Sweden	40	37	44	43	46	32	31	45	46	43	39	41	43	42	38	27	39	54
Japan	24	25	23	33	25	16	17	24	31	23	24	26	32	24	20	19	24	41
Switzerland	30	33	29	41	36	20	26	30	52	30	32	38	55	31	23	18	27	47
Total	21	23	20	27	23	14	16	23	30	18	21	24	29	21	20	15	21	33

Ranking:

Iceland	49
Sweden	40
Denmark	37
Spain	34
Chile	32
West Germany	32
Argentina	31
Mexico	31
Norway	31
Moscow	30
Switzerland	30
East Germany	28
China	27
United States	27
Finland	26
Netherlands	24
Austria	24
Japan	24
Turkey	23
France	23
Canada	23
India	22
Portugal	20
Britain	18
Belgium	18
Romania	17
Bulgaria	16
Ireland	15
Italy	14
North Ireland	14
Estonia	13
Brazil	12
Russia	11
Latvia	11
Slovenia	10
Hungary	09
South Africa	08
Czechoslovakia	07
Belarus	07
Nigeria	06
Lithuania	06
South Korea	06

Note: Countries in the left column are ranked according to GNP per capita. / The percentages in the bottom row give each country an equal weight. / na=not ascertained.

V231 TOLERANCE/RESPECT

Here is a list of qualities which children can be encouraged to learn at home. Which, if any, do you consider to be especially important?
Tolerance and respect for other people (% "mentioned")

	Total	Gender		Age			Education			Income			Political Affinity			Values			Ranking:	
		Male	Female	16-29	30-49	50+	Lower	Medium	Upper	Lower	Middle	Upper	Left	Center	Right	Mat	Mixed	Postmat		
India	59	58	61	61	57	62	55	60	61	57	57	63	58	57	63	65	55	61	Iceland	93
Nigeria	75	75	75	74	77	70	76	74	76	74	74	77	75	74	72	78	75	64	Sweden	91
China	62	60	65	58	63	63	66	60	62	62	63	59	na	na	na	64	59	52	Netherlands	87
Romania	56	53	60	50	55	61	61	55	52	57	55	57	54	54	63	57	55	59	Denmark	81
Turkey	69	69	69	67	72	67	68	70	71	70	66	73	72	72	64	66	69	74	Belarus	80
Poland	na	na	na	na	na	na	na	na	na	na	na	na	na	na	na	na	na	na	North Ireland	80
Bulgaria	52	52	51	54	50	52	47	52	54	48	58	51	53	56	47	47	54	53	Canada	80
Chile	79	77	81	77	80	80	80	79	80	76	79	81	78	79	75	79	79	82	Chile	79
Czechoslovakia	64	63	65	70	64	60	57	67	68	60	65	67	68	61	68	59	64	76	Britain	79
South Africa	61	59	63	63	60	62	64	60	56	68	59	54	62	62	52	57	63	65	Finland	79
Lithuania	57	57	57	58	60	53	49	58	63	53	59	61	na	na	na	52	59	62	Argentina	78
Hungary	62	58	65	71	62	58	52	71	67	55	63	81	64	64	71	62	62	53	France	78
Argentina	78	76	79	71	79	81	78	79	77	76	80	80	77	79	75	79	78	74	West Germany	77
Brazil	66	67	64	62	69	65	63	66	71	61	70	66	67	67	65	65	65	68	Switzerland	77
Mexico	64	62	68	65	65	62	64	67	65	64	67	64	71	64	63	60	65	71	Ireland	76
Belarus	80	77	82	77	81	80	78	79	82	81	78	80	81	78	79	80	81	81	Nigeria	75
Russia	70	66	74	66	71	72	70	70	71	73	72	67	67	71	63	70	70	76	Slovenia	75
Moscow	72	68	76	69	74	73	73	72	73	73	73	71	74	71	74	74	70	77	East Germany	74
Latvia	70	65	73	70	69	70	63	69	72	71	71	69	na	na	na	67	71	64	Moscow	72
Estonia	70	66	75	66	75	72	69	71	71	70	73	70	na	na	na	68	72	81	Spain	71
Portugal	69	66	71	75	68	64	65	79	74	63	74	72	69	70	73	64	72	80	United States	71
South Korea	55	58	54	69	49	49	36	54	66	56	52	61	60	54	56	51	57	69	Russia	70
Ireland	76	73	79	76	79	74	74	80	77	74	75	80	69	76	80	75	77	80	Latvia	70
North Ireland	80	77	82	79	81	78	78	83	86	78	85	79	81	80	78	80	82	73	Estonia	70
Slovenia	75	74	75	74	75	75	74	76	74	73	76	77	68	77	75	72	75	78	Turkey	69
Spain	71	72	71	76	70	68	69	71	78	66	71	76	69	70	73	68	72	81	Portugal	69
East Germany	74	71	78	77	80	67	70	81	86	71	73	79	84	71	64	64	73	81	Belgium	69
Britain	79	77	81	81	78	79	77	83	85	78	85	79	81	80	78	77	74	81	Brazil	66
Italy	66	65	67	66	72	61	65	72	78	62	74	77	72	65	67	56	80	82	Italy	66
Netherlands	87	83	89	85	93	83	84	88	90	86	89	93	92	90	83	77	66	78	Austria	66
Belgium	69	68	70	70	70	68	67	67	78	64	72	74	75	73	68	60	70	79	Czechoslovakia	64
Austria	66	62	68	68	73	58	60	69	73	59	65	74	78	67	63	48	66	74	Mexico	64
France	78	77	79	81	78	76	74	80	84	76	81	81	82	80	69	72	77	86	Norway	64
Canada	80	80	80	78	82	81	76	81	82	79	80	83	87	79	78	72	79	85	China	62
United States	71	70	73	62	73	74	71	68	76	64	74	77	75	73	67	66	71	79	Hungary	62
Iceland	93	91	95	92	94	93	90	94	95	na	90	na	94	94	92	94	92	96	South Africa	61
West Germany	77	74	78	74	79	74	73	81	88	75	78	79	81	77	72	61	76	88	Japan	60
Denmark	81	79	83	78	85	77	71	82	85	77	84	86	84	83	77	69	82	89	India	59
Finland	79	75	83	77	79	82	72	79	82	75	80	81	82	79	78	74	78	82	Lithuania	57
Norway	64	59	69	62	69	59	50	57	77	59	66	71	69	62	65	57	65	80	Romania	56
Sweden	91	90	92	88	94	90	88	90	96	89	90	94	90	92	89	87	90	95	South Korea	55
Japan	60	58	61	67	60	53	45	63	66	52	63	64	61	64	60	60	62	70	Bulgaria	52
Switzerland	77	76	78	79	81	72	76	76	77	76	79	79	86	78	74	67	75	89		
Total	71	69	73	71	73	69	68	72	75	68	72	73	74	72	70	67	71	76		

Note: Countries in the left column are ranked according to GNP per capita. / The percentages in the bottom row give each country an equal weight. / na=not ascertained.

V232 THRIFT

Here is a list of qualities which children can be encouraged to learn at home. Which, if any, do you consider to be especially important?
Thrift, saving money and things (% "mentioned")

	Total	Gender Male	Gender Female	Age 16-29	Age 30-49	Age 50+	Educ Lower	Educ Medium	Educ Upper	Income Lower	Income Middle	Income Upper	Pol Left	Pol Center	Pol Right	Values Mat	Values Mixed	Values Postmat	Ranking	
India	24	24	na	24	25	26	30	26	08	26	28	20	26	25	22	24	22	30	Iceland	69
Nigeria	08	09	08	07	08	16	08	10	08	09	08	08	05	09	10	08	07	16	Russia	61
China	56	57	53	44	56	68	61	56	42	62	49	54	na	na	na	60	52	43	Slovenia	58
Romania	37	35	38	22	35	48	51	30	27	43	35	34	40	38	31	47	31	16	East Germany	58
Turkey	36	33	39	36	35	39	43	29	20	40	40	27	33	35	39	45	37	25	China	56
Poland	na	na	na	na	na	na	na	na	na	na	na	na	na	na	na	na	na	na	Austria	55
Bulgaria	39	37	42	27	34	52	61	36	24	42	43	33	38	40	24	53	35	14	Belarus	53
Chile	29	31	27	22	30	36	36	26	21	34	29	22	23	30	30	33	29	21	South Korea	53
Czechoslovakia	48	48	48	44	44	56	56	47	38	49	52	42	49	47	49	54	48	36	Hungary	49
South Africa	17	19	16	16	20	15	18	17	12	19	18	15	18	16	22	19	17	12	Czechoslovakia	48
Lithuania	37	34	39	22	37	49	49	34	26	41	40	22	na	na	na	48	36	15	Sweden	48
Hungary	49	47	51	41	48	54	56	45	33	57	45	39	43	51	48	54	46	45	Latvia	46
Argentina	15	15	14	10	13	19	19	12	11	19	14	12	09	14	16	20	13	12	West Germany	46
Brazil	29	30	28	24	30	36	36	26	25	33	27	26	28	25	35	32	28	21	Switzerland	42
Mexico	33	34	32	35	31	35	36	26	29	35	33	30	25	32	36	38	33	26	Japan	40
Belarus	53	50	56	45	52	63	63	52	50	59	52	49	47	59	66	60	50	39	Bulgaria	39
Russia	61	57	64	52	61	66	70	61	55	67	62	54	54	63	68	68	57	45	Moscow	39
Moscow	39	38	41	37	37	44	56	44	33	44	38	34	38	38	44	41	41	28	Finland	38
Latvia	46	46	46	39	51	45	50	49	40	51	47	43	na	na	na	55	44	40	Romania	37
Estonia	35	33	37	30	29	50	47	32	30	36	36	33	na	na	na	44	32	25	Lithuania	37
Portugal	31	31	32	21	34	39	39	11	19	41	27	23	32	30	32	44	28	08	Turkey	36
South Korea	53	53	54	43	58	59	70	54	45	56	53	51	46	51	56	60	51	35	Belgium	36
Ireland	22	23	21	17	20	26	26	18	17	26	24	17	15	23	22	26	22	17	France	36
North Ireland	25	23	26	18	19	36	27	28	07	36	32	15	18	27	26	22	28	18	Estonia	35
Slovenia	58	57	58	47	61	61	66	56	45	60	59	51	43	54	57	69	55	40	Mexico	33
Spain	18	17	19	13	17	23	20	14	12	24	18	16	16	18	21	22	18	11	Portugal	31
East Germany	58	57	59	45	52	72	65	50	38	65	60	51	51	60	63	78	61	42	Chile	29
Britain	26	25	28	20	21	35	31	19	14	37	22	18	27	27	24	32	29	15	Brazil	29
Italy	29	30	28	17	27	38	30	20	18	32	24	19	27	28	29	36	30	20	Italy	29
Netherlands	28	27	28	23	24	39	36	30	15	28	32	14	20	28	33	48	32	17	United States	29
Belgium	36	34	37	30	29	45	44	35	21	42	34	31	31	33	33	47	37	20	Netherlands	28
Austria	55	56	55	39	50	67	62	53	36	63	59	43	51	53	56	74	56	42	Britain	26
France	36	33	38	29	33	44	44	33	20	40	36	27	28	35	44	49	38	20	North Ireland	25
Canada	21	22	21	17	18	29	30	20	16	27	21	17	13	22	21	29	21	18	India	24
United States	29	29	29	27	26	32	39	27	23	32	29	22	22	26	32	35	29	22	Ireland	22
Iceland	69	70	67	62	65	84	74	71	64	na	na	na	66	72	68	76	68	57	Norway	22
West Germany	46	42	48	28	38	61	55	30	26	52	45	39	33	48	54	71	49	26	Canada	21
Denmark	19	19	18	12	12	31	35	15	12	26	16	10	13	18	21	29	18	08	Denmark	19
Finland	38	40	36	30	36	50	44	41	31	43	37	35	44	39	36	56	38	34	Spain	18
Norway	22	23	21	10	17	35	35	23	13	29	18	16	20	26	19	33	19	10	South Africa	17
Sweden	48	48	49	40	46	55	60	45	34	50	54	43	45	52	47	64	52	30	Argentina	15
Japan	40	37	44	39	39	44	51	37	38	43	39	41	40	34	38	41	39	32	Nigeria	08
Switzerland	42	43	42	32	36	52	48	42	21	43	44	37	26	45	48	55	45	28		
Total	**37**	**37**	**37**	**29**	**35**	**45**	**45**	**34**	**27**	**41**	**36**	**30**	**32**	**36**	**37**	**45**	**36**	**26**		

Note: Countries in the left column are ranked according to GNP per capita. / The percentages in the bottom row give each country an equal weight. / na=not ascertained.

V233 DETERMINATION

Here is a list of qualities which children can be encouraged to learn at home. Which, if any, do you consider to be especially important? Determination, perseverance (% "mentioned")

	Total	Gender		Age			Education			Income			Political Affinity			Values			Ranking:	
		Male	Female	16-29	30-49	50+	Lower	Medium	Upper	Lower	Middle	Upper	Left	Center	Right	Mat	Mixed	Postmat		
India	28	28	27	30	27	24	19	27	33	24	27	32	32	27	24	28	29	20	Iceland	75
Nigeria	21	24	18	21	23	19	20	18	25	19	24	22	22	23	19	17	22	32	Japan	59
China	45	46	43	61	45	25	39	47	60	44	46	45	na	na	na	38	51	63	East Germany	54
Romania	40	43	38	55	42	30	28	42	55	38	40	43	39	42	44	33	44	58	Estonia	51
Turkey	20	24	17	22	20	19	15	27	31	17	21	24	18	24	19	21	19	23	West Germany	49
Poland	na	na	na	na	na	na	na	na	na	na	na	na	na	na	na	na	na	na	China	45
Bulgaria	41	43	39	50	45	30	28	40	55	41	40	43	44	41	52	29	44	55	Moscow	44
Chile	31	34	28	33	32	27	22	32	42	21	31	43	38	30	29	21	33	37	Czechoslovakia	42
Czechoslovakia	42	45	39	41	49	34	33	44	53	39	42	47	47	40	44	35	44	51	Slovenia	42
South Africa	28	28	28	28	29	26	23	29	44	24	24	40	35	30	30	26	28	35	Bulgaria	41
Lithuania	34	46	24	39	36	28	26	37	36	29	35	44	na	na	na	30	34	39	Romania	40
Hungary	12	14	11	16	15	09	07	17	16	09	16	12	21	13	14	11	14	05	Belarus	40
Argentina	29	31	27	34	31	23	22	31	40	24	27	38	46	33	25	22	28	41	Russia	40
Brazil	26	30	22	27	29	20	15	26	53	14	25	39	27	31	24	18	29	48	Latvia	40
Mexico	37	37	38	39	38	28	34	40	44	32	42	40	45	36	42	28	40	48	Belgium	39
Belarus	40	48	32	47	38	36	31	41	41	35	40	45	42	37	35	35	42	48	Austria	39
Russia	40	46	35	47	42	32	34	39	45	36	38	49	46	42	51	37	41	44	France	39
Moscow	44	48	41	49	46	38	33	46	45	45	43	46	47	42	39	39	43	52	Canada	38
Latvia	40	46	36	43	39	39	42	37	46	36	39	44	na	na	na	39	38	53	Finland	38
Estonia	51	57	46	58	55	37	41	53	55	47	53	54	45	46	na	46	54	53	Mexico	37
Portugal	23	23	24	33	24	13	15	36	46	13	28	35	25	23	28	14	27	44	United States	36
South Korea	31	29	33	32	33	25	34	36	25	35	30	27	35	34	28	32	31	29	Lithuania	34
Ireland	26	33	19	35	26	19	19	31	44	14	24	38	32	27	26	20	24	36	Norway	33
North Ireland	18	21	16	29	15	14	15	21	31	10	19	23	18	21	12	15	17	27	Sweden	33
Slovenia	42	43	41	51	44	33	32	45	57	35	43	54	53	46	44	37	42	62	Chile	31
Spain	22	24	21	24	25	19	20	27	31	17	22	27	26	25	15	23	24	26	South Korea	31
East Germany	54	56	52	58	58	48	51	58	63	46	57	58	61	52	49	45	56	52	Britain	31
Britain	31	33	29	37	33	26	26	38	47	24	33	37	31	32	33	28	29	38	Netherlands	30
Italy	27	29	25	35	30	18	25	39	36	20	35	40	30	25	30	19	26	37	Denmark	30
Netherlands	30	36	28	22	36	30	29	27	34	26	34	39	34	30	29	15	29	37	Argentina	29
Belgium	39	41	37	40	44	33	33	39	51	30	45	49	43	41	40	29	39	49	India	28
Austria	39	42	37	43	42	34	37	40	43	31	40	45	36	40	41	30	36	50	South Africa	28
France	39	43	35	38	40	38	32	41	53	31	39	51	40	42	44	27	40	49	Italy	27
Canada	38	38	37	43	41	30	27	36	48	29	38	51	47	38	39	32	35	46	Brazil	26
United States	36	35	36	39	41	30	35	32	42	29	37	41	39	36	33	35	34	42	Ireland	26
Iceland	75	76	74	74	74	78	74	78	75	na	75	na	72	77	75	73	75	80	Portugal	23
West Germany	49	51	47	50	53	47	49	48	58	45	50	54	50	50	51	45	49	52	Spain	22
Denmark	30	33	28	34	33	25	26	30	33	26	33	34	33	28	33	26	30	38	Nigeria	21
Finland	38	40	37	44	43	22	35	36	44	35	34	47	36	42	39	29	37	43	Turkey	20
Norway	33	35	30	35	34	30	26	33	36	28	34	39	33	31	37	25	35	44	North Ireland	18
Sweden	33	34	31	31	32	36	31	31	42	33	28	37	33	29	40	25	32	41	Hungary	12
Japan	59	58	60	65	57	57	63	60	51	58	61	53	62	58	59	56	59	62		
Switzerland	na	na	na	na	na	na	na	na	na	na	na	na	na	na	na	na	na	na		
Total	**36**	**38**	**33**	**40**	**38**	**30**	**30**	**37**	**44**	**30**	**35**	**41**	**38**	**36**	**36**	**30**	**36**	**44**		

Note: Countries in the left column are ranked according to GNP per capita. / The percentages in the bottom row give each country an equal weight. / na=not ascertained.

V234 RELIGIOUS FAITH

Here is a list of qualities which children can be encouraged to learn at home. Which, if any, do you consider to be especially important? Religious faith (% "mentioned")

	Total	Gender Male	Gender Female	Age 16-29	Age 30-49	Age 50+	Educ Lower	Educ Medium	Educ Upper	Income Lower	Income Middle	Income Upper	Pol Left	Pol Center	Pol Right	Values Mat	Values Mixed	Values Postmat	Ranking	
India	29	26	32	24	31	35	40	28	24	28	31	27	22	27	31	29	28	22	Nigeria	74
Nigeria	74	68	82	74	73	79	83	76	68	74	72	77	79	71	74	78	71	75	Ireland	57
China	01	02	01	01	01	02	01	01	01	01	02	01	na	na	na	01	01	02	United States	55
Romania	43	39	48	31	37	57	61	35	33	46	48	36	45	42	39	52	39	26	Chile	54
Turkey	44	41	48	42	43	49	55	33	15	53	47	32	28	43	60	51	47	28	South Africa	50
Poland	na	na	na	na	na	na	na	na	na	na	na	na	na	na	na	na	na	na	Iceland	50
Bulgaria	11	09	12	12	07	14	17	09	07	12	08	09	04	08	15	10	11	13	Brazil	46
Chile	54	48	60	49	59	54	61	52	48	60	54	47	44	56	55	61	55	44	Turkey	44
Czechoslovakia	15	16	15	10	10	26	26	11	09	19	14	14	10	16	18	21	13	14	North Ireland	44
South Africa	50	44	55	47	51	51	50	49	52	48	51	52	42	51	49	52	49	42	Romania	43
Lithuania	21	16	26	10	15	37	40	16	12	28	19	09	na	21	na	27	19	15	Mexico	40
Hungary	24	21	26	14	16	34	32	16	19	32	18	14	10	21	35	25	22	18	Italy	37
Argentina	28	26	31	22	27	34	31	26	25	34	30	22	14	26	39	34	28	20	Canada	31
Brazil	46	40	53	42	46	55	51	46	38	53	47	39	38	46	50	53	44	33	India	29
Mexico	40	37	44	37	41	47	41	41	37	43	39	38	27	40	44	50	38	31	Argentina	28
Belarus	06	05	07	04	05	10	15	06	03	06	05	08	06	04	12	07	05	06	Portugal	25
Russia	08	06	10	05	05	14	13	07	06	08	08	07	07	06	07	09	07	12	Hungary	24
Moscow	12	11	12	13	12	12	13	12	12	11	13	10	13	10	16	11	12	13	Switzerland	24
Latvia	09	08	10	06	09	14	18	09	07	10	10	08	na	na	na	09	10	11	Spain	23
Estonia	03	02	04	03	03	04	05	03	03	06	02	01	na	na	na	03	03	05	Austria	23
Portugal	25	21	30	18	21	36	31	10	16	35	19	17	16	21	33	31	21	11	Lithuania	21
South Korea	19	23	16	17	21	16	21	18	19	19	18	21	15	21	19	20	18	22	Slovenia	21
Ireland	57	55	59	41	56	69	63	52	42	72	53	47	38	54	68	64	58	46	West Germany	20
North Ireland	44	41	47	40	37	56	46	45	35	50	43	32	36	48	42	55	43	33	South Korea	19
Slovenia	21	20	22	16	17	29	31	14	14	26	19	15	15	16	38	27	20	12	Britain	19
Spain	23	17	28	13	19	34	25	18	16	30	20	19	12	28	37	30	21	14	East Germany	16
East Germany	16	14	18	09	16	21	17	18	13	20	17	13	06	18	27	22	15	16	Belgium	16
Britain	19	17	21	07	15	29	19	19	17	24	14	13	17	15	27	26	18	15	Czechoslovakia	15
Italy	37	31	43	29	32	46	37	38	29	43	32	25	19	49	39	47	37	25	Norway	14
Netherlands	13	16	12	08	12	20	16	11	12	09	15	12	04	09	26	17	14	09	Netherlands	13
Belgium	16	14	17	07	12	24	18	16	12	19	15	15	09	14	25	19	15	12	France	13
Austria	23	19	26	15	19	30	28	20	16	30	22	17	21	18	28	24	26	16	Finland	13
France	13	10	15	08	09	20	14	10	13	15	10	11	08	13	25	16	14	09	Moscow	12
Canada	31	28	33	21	28	41	41	28	25	38	34	20	24	31	31	38	32	23	Bulgaria	11
United States	55	53	57	48	52	60	59	59	48	57	57	49	38	54	63	62	58	43	Latvia	09
Iceland	50	46	54	38	46	71	60	50	42	na	na	na	41	51	53	55	49	39	Denmark	09
West Germany	20	15	24	08	13	32	23	13	17	25	18	16	09	21	29	31	22	10	Russia	08
Denmark	09	07	11	03	06	17	18	05	07	14	07	03	02	09	13	13	09	04	Japan	07
Finland	13	12	14	10	10	22	19	12	12	17	11	13	09	13	13	21	13	12	Belarus	06
Norway	14	12	17	11	12	18	20	12	13	19	12	11	08	16	15	14	14	08	Sweden	06
Sweden	06	07	05	06	06	07	08	08	08	08	05	07	05	06	08	10	07	03	Estonia	03
Japan	07	06	08	08	05	10	07	07	05	12	06	07	07	06	08	09	05	06	China	01
Switzerland	24	19	29	17	23	28	24	24	27	32	21	14	12	24	32	27	27	15		
Total	**26**	23	28	20	23	32	31	23	21	29	24	21	20	27	33	30	25	20		

Note: Countries in the left column are ranked according to GNP per capita. / The percentages in the bottom row give each country an equal weight. / na=not ascertained.

V235 UNSELFISHNESS

Here is a list of qualities which children can be encouraged to learn at home. Which, if any, do you consider to be especially important?
Unselfishness (% "mentioned")

	Total	Gender		Age			Education			Income			Political Affinity			Values		
		Male	Female	16-29	30-49	50+	Lower	Medium	Upper	Lower	Middle	Upper	Left	Center	Right	Mat	Mixed	Postmat
India	32	30	34	33	31	31	30	33	31	29	35	na	32	30	31	33	32	31
Nigeria	17	17	18	16	18	23	23	17	16	20	17	15	13	16	20	17	17	12
China	31	30	32	28	29	37	27	32	31	31	30	32	na	na	na	28	36	22
Romania	20	19	21	23	23	15	14	24	22	17	18	24	15	23	20	17	21	27
Turkey	28	25	31	32	28	21	23	31	42	24	29	32	31	30	23	21	28	35
Poland	na	na	na	na	na	na	na	na	na	na	na	na	na	na	na	na	na	na
Bulgaria	22	23	22	24	23	21	17	23	26	25	18	21	21	21	26	25	21	23
Chile	08	09	07	09	08	07	05	10	10	06	08	09	09	08	07	08	07	11
Czechoslovakia	38	37	39	41	39	35	35	39	40	39	39	35	34	38	42	33	39	45
South Africa	20	20	20	20	20	20	17	21	25	20	17	23	24	20	19	16	22	22
Lithuania	33	33	33	36	33	32	25	35	40	31	35	35	na	na	na	29	34	42
Hungary	26	29	23	25	28	24	21	30	31	24	27	29	29	27	27	26	26	23
Argentina	05	06	03	02	06	06	05	05	04	04	05	06	08	04	04	05	04	06
Brazil	28	27	30	33	28	21	19	32	35	23	28	35	32	32	23	22	31	44
Mexico	11	11	11	12	12	06	10	09	14	09	11	15	14	11	12	07	11	17
Belarus	27	26	28	29	27	24	21	27	29	27	28	26	27	26	29	25	28	30
Russia	24	25	23	22	22	27	22	24	25	22	24	25	22	26	17	24	24	22
Moscow	32	29	34	30	31	35	26	28	36	30	31	38	32	29	29	30	33	29
Latvia	16	15	16	19	14	15	11	15	19	12	20	16	na	na	na	11	17	20
Estonia	25	23	26	21	29	22	21	26	26	23	28	25	na	na	na	24	25	31
Portugal	28	26	30	33	27	25	25	39	32	25	34	27	34	28	27	23	31	37
South Korea	11	10	11	13	10	07	04	10	15	10	11	10	17	11	09	08	11	15
Ireland	53	50	55	60	50	50	52	55	49	51	56	53	53	53	52	51	54	50
North Ireland	49	43	53	49	60	37	47	50	59	49	42	56	46	52	48	42	51	51
Slovenia	33	30	36	38	33	30	27	37	37	31	31	43	47	33	39	25	35	49
Spain	12	14	09	11	10	13	12	10	13	14	10	10	10	13	14	13	10	12
East Germany	09	08	09	06	09	10	07	12	10	09	09	07	08	09	08	13	07	10
Britain	57	58	57	65	63	48	55	64	60	52	67	61	60	58	56	54	56	67
Italy	39	36	41	43	45	31	38	46	48	39	41	42	48	38	35	31	39	48
Netherlands	22	25	21	28	18	21	21	24	21	25	41	42	26	24	16	17	19	28
Belgium	27	25	30	29	27	27	27	26	32	27	24	28	31	29	26	28	25	34
Austria	07	07	07	07	07	08	06	08	07	07	08	06	14	05	08	09	07	07
France	40	35	45	39	41	39	40	38	43	44	40	41	44	43	30	39	40	42
Canada	42	44	41	43	43	41	42	42	42	40	44	43	42	44	41	41	43	42
United States	37	34	40	37	39	35	35	37	38	35	36	39	43	37	32	43	34	41
Iceland	75	73	78	73	77	75	71	80	76	na	na	na	77	74	76	70	76	80
West Germany	08	08	07	06	08	08	08	08	07	08	09	07	08	07	08	10	07	07
Denmark	50	46	55	56	52	45	46	54	50	50	53	50	58	47	47	45	51	60
Finland	21	23	18	27	22	13	13	20	26	17	23	22	26	17	22	24	19	25
Norway	10	12	07	12	09	08	05	06	16	09	10	11	12	09	09	06	10	16
Sweden	29	31	28	38	28	24	23	32	33	29	26	31	35	27	29	22	27	41
Japan	44	47	41	50	45	40	37	43	54	35	48	48	42	49	41	46	46	43
Switzerland	37	36	38	43	39	33	35	36	52	35	38	41	49	33	33	31	34	48
Total	28	28	29	30	29	26	25	29	31	26	28	29	31	28	27	26	28	32

Ranking:

Iceland	75
Britain	57
Ireland	53
Denmark	50
North Ireland	49
Japan	44
Canada	42
France	40
Italy	39
Czechoslovakia	38
United States	37
Switzerland	37
Lithuania	33
Slovenia	33
India	32
Moscow	32
China	31
Sweden	29
Turkey	28
Brazil	28
Portugal	28
Belarus	27
Belgium	27
Hungary	26
Estonia	25
Russia	24
Bulgaria	22
Netherlands	22
Finland	21
Romania	20
South Africa	20
Nigeria	17
Latvia	16
Spain	12
Mexico	11
South Korea	11
Norway	10
East Germany	09
Chile	08
West Germany	08
Austria	07
Argentina	05

Note: Countries in the left column are ranked according to GNP per capita. / The percentages in the bottom row give each country an equal weight. / na=not ascertained.

V236 OBEDIENCE

Here is a list of qualities which children can be encouraged to learn at home. Which, if any, do you consider to be especially important?
Obedience (% "mentioned")

	Total	Gender Male	Gender Female	Age 16-29	Age 30-49	Age 50+	Education Lower	Education Medium	Education Upper	Income Lower	Income Middle	Income Upper	Pol. Aff. Left	Pol. Aff. Center	Pol. Aff. Right	Values Mat	Values Mixed	Values Postmat	Ranking	
India	56	55	56	55	56	59	58	57	54	60	54	54	53	53	61	56	56	50	Nigeria	71
Nigeria	71	70	73	73	69	67	80	74	63	74	67	71	73	64	78	75	70	56	Iceland	68
China	09	08	09	05	07	15	06	10	02	10	07	08	na	na	na	11	06	02	India	56
Romania	20	20	19	28	19	15	11	25	24	19	18	22	21	22	21	14	23	28	North Ireland	56
Turkey	31	31	32	27	32	37	39	23	11	37	33	24	32	29	32	38	31	26	France	53
Poland	na	na	na	na	na	na	na	na	na	na	na	na	na	na	na	na	na	na	Chile	52
Bulgaria	19	16	21	16	15	25	33	17	08	19	15	17	12	18	12	24	18	04	Hungary	45
Chile	52	51	54	51	53	52	57	55	41	60	53	44	47	54	49	64	51	39	Mexico	45
Czechoslovakia	28	27	29	27	22	36	36	27	15	32	27	25	27	30	24	34	27	18	Portugal	45
South Africa	42	46	38	42	41	42	48	41	25	44	46	33	35	38	45	49	38	40	South Africa	42
Lithuania	25	23	26	22	21	30	37	23	09	30	23	16	na	na	na	33	24	10	Spain	42
Hungary	45	42	47	53	41	45	49	41	33	48	44	34	49	44	36	42	47	45	Brazil	41
Argentina	32	30	34	32	29	35	39	28	21	38	33	24	17	28	32	28	32	19	Slovenia	40
Brazil	41	40	43	44	40	39	47	42	27	49	39	36	37	39	40	43	40	27	Britain	39
Mexico	45	44	47	45	46	45	45	48	43	50	42	39	29	47	46	53	43	30	United States	39
Belarus	23	24	21	18	23	26	35	25	15	26	22	20	23	21	24	28	19	20	Belgium	37
Russia	26	25	27	23	22	32	42	26	16	32	25	18	16	26	28	31	23	15	Ireland	35
Moscow	17	17	16	14	14	22	34	18	13	19	16	15	16	14	16	22	17	06	Italy	34
Latvia	15	13	17	16	16	13	25	18	07	18	15	15	na	na	na	19	15	08	Netherlands	33
Estonia	19	19	19	23	11	27	37	16	08	23	17	14	na	na	na	26	16	12	Argentina	32
Portugal	45	47	43	41	45	49	53	35	23	54	41	35	37	43	50	54	40	31	Turkey	31
South Korea	18	19	17	15	17	28	31	17	13	22	17	15	13	19	18	21	16	14	Norway	31
Ireland	35	31	39	34	34	38	39	35	17	44	38	25	30	34	33	35	39	25	Czechoslovakia	28
North Ireland	56	51	60	49	57	60	61	53	31	61	56	44	68	52	57	65	57	42	Canada	28
Slovenia	40	39	40	39	38	43	48	39	26	61	40	29	31	36	40	47	39	19	Russia	26
Spain	42	41	43	36	38	51	47	35	26	53	41	31	37	36	49	54	39	31	Lithuania	25
East Germany	24	23	25	19	16	36	29	18	11	36	20	17	14	26	36	41	24	17	Austria	25
Britain	39	38	40	39	36	43	43	35	27	48	35	33	33	41	40	45	41	29	Finland	25
Italy	34	33	35	28	30	41	36	21	12	38	27	23	26	38	34	44	34	21	Sweden	25
Netherlands	33	32	33	41	26	33	37	35	25	33	30	22	21	33	35	53	34	23	East Germany	24
Belgium	37	37	38	39	38	36	41	41	23	42	40	30	29	34	36	49	38	26	Belarus	23
Austria	25	27	24	24	20	30	29	24	16	33	25	18	27	23	25	34	27	17	West Germany	22
France	53	52	54	46	57	54	51	53	56	51	55	56	53	57	50	50	53	55	Romania	20
Canada	28	26	31	28	27	32	35	23	15	36	27	22	22	28	27	39	29	20	Denmark	20
United States	39	39	39	32	35	43	47	41	31	48	38	32	33	37	43	45	41	32	Switzerland	20
Iceland	68	69	67	71	68	51	75	71	61	42	40	31	60	70	69	77	68	47	Bulgaria	19
West Germany	22	21	24	15	16	32	29	13	09	na	22	16	13	23	30	45	23	09	Estonia	19
Denmark	20	22	19	22	15	25	26	23	15	28	20	12	11	25	19	33	20	09	South Korea	18
Finland	25	24	26	28	22	31	36	28	16	24	27	18	18	28	25	38	27	19	Moscow	17
Norway	31	33	30	32	25	31	45	38	18	30	29	21	24	35	30	39	31	20	Latvia	15
Sweden	25	26	23	25	20	31	39	22	07	36	29	18	26	24	21	39	28	11	Japan	10
Japan	10	10	10	14	08	11	12	09	11	10	08	12	02	07	13	13	08	08	China	09
Switzerland	20	20	21	19	19	23	26	18	11	22	21	18	11	20	21	32	23	08		
Total	**33**	**32**	**34**	**32**	**31**	**37**	**40**	**32**	**22**	**37**	**31**	**26**	**30**	**34**	**35**	**41**	**33**	**23**		

Note: Countries in the left column are ranked according to GNP per capita. / The percentages in the bottom row give each country an equal weight. / na=not ascertained.

V237-V240. Do you approve or disapprove of abortion under the following circumstances?

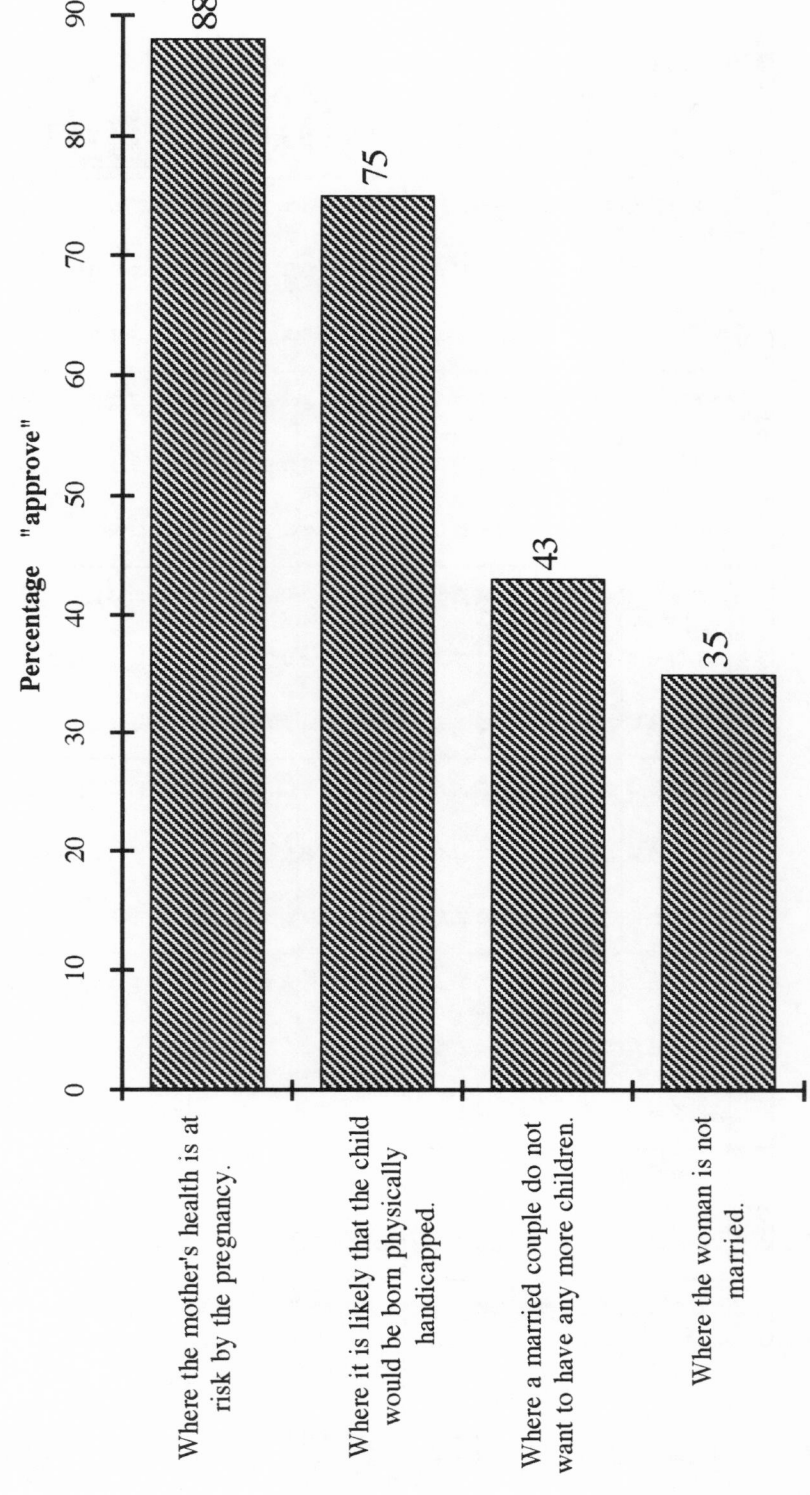

V237 ABORTION: MOTHER'S HEALTH

Do you approve or disapprove of abortion under the following circumstances? Where the mother's health is at risk by the pregnancy. (% "approve")

	Total	Gender		Age			Education			Income			Political Affinity			Values		
		Male	Female	16-29	30-49	50+	Lower	Medium	Upper	Lower	Middle	Upper	Left	Center	Right	Mat	Mixed	Postmat
India	91	90	91	91	92	87	89	91	91	91	91	89	90	92	92	90	92	92
Nigeria	69	70	66	66	72	65	59	63	78	65	75	70	65	72	69	65	72	67
China	91	92	90	89	93	91	86	93	91	91	90	92	na	na	na	91	92	91
Romania	88	90	87	89	91	86	85	90	91	85	91	88	91	88	93	85	90	94
Turkey	84	83	84	85	85	79	81	87	90	81	84	87	86	83	84	84	84	82
Poland	89	89	90	92	91	85	84	91	96	89	89	89	86	92	86	86	92	83
Bulgaria	92	92	92	96	93	89	87	93	76	89	92	95	94	92	91	94	90	88
Chile	75	75	76	76	78	71	72	78	76	69	78	78	76	79	73	76	74	99
Czechoslovakia	na	na	na	na	na	na	na	na	na	na	na	na	na	na	na	na	na	83
South Africa	73	71	76	72	76	70	62	76	95	65	70	91	75	79	79	73	73	75
Lithuania	89	88	90	91	92	85	83	90	93	86	92	91	na	na	na	91	88	91
Hungary	92	92	92	89	93	93	91	94	90	91	93	94	89	94	93	93	91	95
Argentina	77	77	77	77	81	73	72	82	78	69	79	83	80	80	79	73	78	80
Brazil	86	86	87	88	89	81	80	89	89	83	90	89	87	89	85	86	86	91
Mexico	82	83	79	83	83	75	80	80	87	77	86	86	90	83	78	82	82	87
Belarus	89	89	89	89	90	87	83	90	90	91	89	88	89	89	86	88	89	92
Russia	71	74	69	73	71	71	67	70	75	68	71	77	76	75	69	69	72	78
Moscow	84	83	84	82	85	84	71	83	87	79	84	91	86	84	79	84	83	86
Latvia	93	93	93	91	95	91	87	93	94	92	93	94	na	na	na	93	92	97
Estonia	94	94	93	90	95	94	91	93	97	95	94	91	na	na	na	93	94	96
Portugal	90	92	88	94	92	83	87	98	94	85	92	96	92	91	88	93	90	94
South Korea	na	na	na	na	na	na	na	na	na	na	na	na	na	na	na	na	na	na
Ireland	65	67	63	79	72	48	60	69	73	52	67	74	80	65	62	63	65	69
North Ireland	78	78	79	74	85	75	78	79	83	75	82	85	67	79	88	80	78	80
Slovenia	92	91	93	92	93	92	87	95	97	90	92	96	95	95	88	92	92	91
Spain	86	89	83	94	91	75	84	89	90	75	90	88	95	88	72	83	89	94
East Germany	96	97	96	98	97	94	96	97	97	95	97	97	99	96	95	98	96	97
Britain	93	91	95	95	95	90	92	95	95	89	94	96	92	94	93	89	93	94
Italy	91	91	92	91	94	90	92	90	95	91	94	91	92	89	92	89	93	91
Netherlands	94	93	94	92	96	93	92	97	93	95	93	97	97	93	93	90	94	97
Belgium	92	93	92	96	96	87	91	92	96	89	93	94	96	92	92	92	92	93
Austria	93	95	92	96	95	91	94	93	94	90	94	95	96	95	90	92	92	97
France	94	92	94	91	96	93	91	94	94	91	95	97	95	92	97	92	92	97
Canada	92	92	92	92	94	90	90	92	94	89	92	95	96	93	89	90	95	95
United States	86	85	86	85	88	84	78	87	90	84	86	90	94	86	83	83	92	94
Iceland	97	96	97	94	99	98	95	99	97	na	na	na	98	96	97	97	85	90
West Germany	96	97	95	99	98	94	95	98	98	95	97	96	98	97	93	97	97	99
Denmark	98	97	98	98	98	93	97	97	96	96	99	98	99	97	97	92	96	98
Finland	93	91	94	93	94	90	89	91	96	89	95	93	98	91	92	96	94	91
Norway	98	97	98	96	98	99	98	97	98	96	98	98	97	98	98	98	98	98
Sweden	97	98	97	96	98	98	98	98	99	98	97	98	98	97	98	94	98	99
Japan	95	94	96	92	97	98	90	97	95	92	97	98	94	96	96	98	97	91
Switzerland	na	na	na	na	na	na	na	na	na	na	na	na	na	na	na	na	na	na
Total	**88**	**88**	**88**	**89**	**90**	**85**	**85**	**89**	**91**	**85**	**89**	**91**	**90**	**89**	**87**	**87**	**88**	**90**

Ranking:

Denmark	98
Norway	98
Iceland	97
Sweden	97
East Germany	96
West Germany	96
Japan	95
Estonia	94
Netherlands	94
France	94
Latvia	93
Britain	93
Austria	93
Finland	93
Bulgaria	92
Hungary	92
Slovenia	92
Belgium	92
Canada	92
India	91
China	91
Italy	91
Portugal	90
Poland	89
Lithuania	89
Belarus	89
Romania	88
Brazil	86
Spain	86
United States	86
Turkey	84
Moscow	84
Mexico	82
North Ireland	78
Argentina	77
Chile	75
South Africa	73
Russia	71
Nigeria	69
Ireland	65

Note: Countries in the left column are ranked according to GNP per capita. / The percentages in the bottom row give each country an equal weight. / na=not ascertained.

V238 ABORTION: HANDICAPPED

Do you approve or disapprove of abortion under the following circumstances? Where it is likely that the child would be born physically handicapped. (% "approve")

	Total	Gender Male	Gender Female	Age 16-29	Age 30-49	Age 50+	Education Lower	Education Medium	Education Upper	Income Lower	Income Middle	Income Upper	Political Affinity Left	Political Affinity Center	Political Affinity Right	Values Mat	Values Mixed	Values Postmat
India	68	67	70	67	72	63	62	69	71	67	69	69	68	70	69	69	69	65
Nigeria	44	43	45	42	47	42	37	45	46	42	47	46	42	45	49	43	44	56
China	94	94	94	96	95	92	90	96	97	93	95	94	na	na	na	94	94	98
Romania	81	79	82	84	85	74	75	83	83	78	81	82	76	84	85	77	82	91
Turkey	77	70	83	79	79	67	73	80	84	70	77	84	84	79	66	73	78	78
Poland	74	72	75	67	80	71	65	77	88	72	77	74	73	77	71	76	73	67
Bulgaria	91	91	91	93	94	86	86	92	95	89	91	93	92	92	93	92	90	97
Chile	41	36	45	33	44	47	44	41	37	40	43	40	40	43	41	47	40	37
Czechoslovakia	95	95	95	94	97	94	94	96	96	94	96	96	97	96	93	96	95	93
South Africa	45	43	48	43	50	40	30	50	77	35	43	73	56	48	52	43	47	46
Lithuania	89	86	92	89	94	84	81	91	94	85	92	93	na	na	na	88	88	92
Hungary	92	91	92	88	94	91	90	94	91	89	94	90	90	94	89	92	91	93
Argentina	59	56	61	52	63	59	58	63	55	51	58	63	66	62	57	56	60	58
Brazil	53	49	57	50	55	55	49	53	63	51	51	57	55	54	54	53	53	52
Mexico	58	57	59	62	59	44	57	55	61	53	62	62	73	58	50	51	60	63
Belarus	91	89	93	93	92	87	87	92	92	92	93	88	91	92	89	92	91	89
Russia	84	85	83	85	84	84	79	84	87	79	84	86	87	85	82	84	84	89
Moscow	80	77	83	78	81	82	70	80	83	74	83	86	82	80	74	83	79	82
Latvia	95	95	95	94	97	93	85	96	97	97	95	94	na	na	na	95	95	95
Estonia	95	94	96	92	96	96	94	95	96	95	94	95	na	na	na	95	96	93
Portugal	77	77	78	78	82	72	74	87	81	71	80	84	80	80	74	75	79	81
South Korea	na	na	na	na	na	na	na	na	na	na	na	na	na	na	na	na	na	na
Ireland	32	35	29	32	38	26	36	27	32	28	35	34	45	34	25	37	32	28
North Ireland	50	53	48	41	50	57	50	51	52	47	59	54	46	47	65	54	50	47
Slovenia	90	88	91	87	93	88	84	93	94	88	89	94	89	92	80	90	89	90
Spain	76	77	74	83	82	64	75	77	78	65	80	79	86	75	59	75	79	82
East Germany	84	84	83	86	83	83	84	81	86	83	84	84	88	83	84	85	86	78
Britain	80	77	82	77	81	80	79	83	77	76	80	87	77	80	84	78	80	77
Italy	77	76	78	72	84	74	77	76	77	75	78	82	86	71	77	74	79	77
Netherlands	65	63	65	55	71	67	67	61	67	65	65	72	71	64	59	62	65	67
Belgium	77	76	78	76	83	73	77	77	76	78	76	78	84	77	72	84	79	69
Austria	81	82	80	74	81	81	82	81	77	80	82	79	87	83	76	85	80	79
France	91	89	92	87	94	91	88	94	90	89	92	92	90	92	90	88	91	92
Canada	63	63	64	57	67	64	61	65	63	60	61	67	73	61	62	62	63	67
United States	55	54	54	54	54	55	50	54	59	54	55	57	73	53	51	49	55	60
Iceland	90	91	90	85	91	95	88	95	89	na	na	na	90	88	93	93	89	90
West Germany	80	82	79	82	85	76	79	85	85	79	83	81	85	81	77	74	80	83
Denmark	84	84	83	80	87	83	81	85	84	82	87	84	87	82	85	88	82	84
Finland	90	89	92	88	92	89	84	89	94	90	90	91	97	89	90	96	91	87
Norway	70	74	67	60	72	76	75	71	67	67	70	73	68	71	71	76	68	63
Sweden	80	82	78	74	78	86	83	78	76	74	79	82	75	81	82	85	79	78
Japan	77	78	77	78	80	73	66	81	81	72	78	80	77	75	86	79	79	65
Switzerland	na	na	na	na	na	na	na	na	na	na	na	na	na	na	na	na	na	na
Total	75	74	76	73	78	73	72	76	78	72	76	77	76	73	72	75	75	75

Ranking:

Czechoslovakia	95
Latvia	95
Estonia	95
China	94
Hungary	92
Bulgaria	91
Belarus	91
France	91
Slovenia	90
Iceland	90
Finland	90
Lithuania	89
Russia	84
East Germany	84
Denmark	84
Romania	81
Austria	81
Moscow	80
Britain	80
West Germany	80
Sweden	80
Turkey	77
Portugal	77
Italy	77
Belgium	77
Japan	77
Spain	76
Poland	74
Norway	70
India	68
Netherlands	65
Canada	63
Argentina	59
Mexico	58
United States	55
Brazil	53
North Ireland	50
South Africa	45
Nigeria	44
Chile	41
Ireland	32

Note: Countries in the left column are ranked according to GNP per capita. / The percentages in the bottom row give each country an equal weight. / na=not ascertained.

V239 ABORTION: MOTHER UNMARRIED

Do you approve or disapprove of abortion under the following circumstances? Where the woman is not married. (% "approve")

	Total	Gender Male	Gender Female	Age 16-29	Age 30-49	Age 50+	Education Lower	Education Medium	Education Upper	Income Lower	Income Middle	Income Upper	Political Affinity Left	Political Affinity Center	Political Affinity Right	Values Mat	Values Mixed	Values Postmat
India	71	70	73	70	73	70	72	73	69	76	73	66	70	75	65	73	71	68
Nigeria	16	17	14	20	12	04	09	17	17	18	14	19	21	17	14	14	17	21
China	76	72	81	73	77	76	80	77	71	73	75	80	na	na	na	83	68	70
Romania	51	49	53	58	55	42	48	54	50	50	50	53	44	56	50	46	55	52
Turkey	64	55	73	65	65	62	68	63	53	61	66	65	66	66	63	65	66	58
Poland	13	14	13	10	15	13	13	12	17	13	12	15	12	15	13	14	13	14
Bulgaria	64	60	66	62	68	59	64	63	67	62	62	64	66	63	64	68	61	66
Chile	07	08	06	06	08	06	08	06	05	08	06	05	09	05	06	08	06	07
Czechoslovakia	93	92	94	89	96	92	91	94	95	91	94	93	94	93	93	94	93	89
South Africa	11	11	11	12	11	09	07	12	19	08	10	17	17	11	14	08	12	18
Lithuania	29	25	31	34	31	21	22	29	36	27	32	28	na	na	na	25	28	33
Hungary	43	40	45	36	44	44	43	42	43	39	45	44	41	47	37	47	40	33
Argentina	19	20	17	21	20	15	19	20	19	18	17	21	30	18	19	12	19	25
Brazil	13	15	11	14	13	12	14	12	18	13	11	15	16	12	13	12	13	21
Mexico	17	17	17	19	17	11	16	18	18	18	18	14	32	15	12	12	17	29
Belarus	39	38	40	45	39	32	35	37	42	33	38	47	41	36	32	39	37	54
Russia	42	42	42	42	44	40	41	42	43	43	45	45	46	41	41	43	42	45
Moscow	48	47	49	44	51	46	43	53	46	49	43	56	49	49	41	50	46	56
Latvia	46	44	47	44	48	44	46	43	51	45	45	46	na	na	na	41	44	56
Estonia	25	24	25	22	26	26	25	25	25	21	26	29	23	21	18	22	24	26
Portugal	21	21	20	20	21	20	21	18	23	21	23	19	23	21	18	21	20	21
South Korea	na	na	na	na	na	na	na	na	na	na	na	na	na	na	na	na	na	na
Ireland	08	09	07	12	07	05	07	07	16	07	06	10	13	09	04	09	07	09
North Ireland	16	18	14	16	16	15	12	21	24	13	13	27	22	13	20	14	15	24
Slovenia	44	46	42	43	47	41	39	45	52	39	46	50	48	46	34	42	44	55
Spain	29	33	25	41	33	15	24	36	45	18	34	35	42	27	15	18	30	45
East Germany	17	20	16	23	17	14	17	17	20	15	17	20	25	14	15	15	17	20
Britain	35	33	37	35	36	35	32	42	44	33	35	41	39	33	38	32	34	41
Italy	23	25	21	26	27	19	23	27	24	21	22	29	36	16	22	20	22	29
Netherlands	32	31	33	32	37	26	27	32	38	35	29	39	46	26	28	28	30	39
Belgium	27	27	26	25	31	23	24	27	31	28	26	27	35	27	24	26	26	29
Austria	17	18	16	16	18	15	16	16	20	15	16	19	22	19	13	13	15	22
France	30	31	28	27	32	29	25	30	40	30	30	30	40	26	23	26	28	34
Canada	32	32	33	35	34	28	25	29	42	27	30	42	49	30	31	25	31	40
United States	30	28	32	31	32	28	23	25	42	23	31	36	55	27	24	19	30	40
Iceland	22	23	21	24	27	13	15	25	26	na	na	na	32	17	21	18	21	37
West Germany	22	23	20	32	28	11	19	26	30	21	23	22	31	20	13	13	19	31
Denmark	57	61	54	62	63	47	40	60	65	49	58	67	70	52	56	47	58	70
Finland	67	68	66	74	72	48	54	65	75	62	63	77	71	70	63	61	65	73
Norway	45	45	45	51	51	34	30	46	52	38	45	54	46	41	49	46	43	52
Sweden	41	44	38	47	44	31	31	43	50	34	38	47	40	39	43	40	39	45
Japan	58	58	57	58	61	52	47	57	69	47	59	62	59	57	69	59	61	53
Switzerland	na	na	na	na	na	na	na	na	na	na	na	na	na	na	na	na	na	na
Total	**36**	**35**	**36**	**37**	**38**	**31**	**32**	**36**	**40**	**34**	**36**	**39**	**40**	**34**	**32**	**33**	**35**	**40**

Ranking:

Czechoslovakia	93
China	76
India	71
Finland	67
Turkey	64
Bulgaria	64
Japan	58
Denmark	57
Romania	51
Moscow	48
Latvia	46
Norway	45
Slovenia	44
Hungary	43
Russia	42
Sweden	41
Belarus	39
Britain	35
Netherlands	32
Canada	32
France	30
United States	30
Lithuania	29
Spain	29
Belgium	27
Estonia	25
Italy	23
Iceland	22
West Germany	22
Portugal	21
Argentina	19
Mexico	17
East Germany	17
Austria	17
Nigeria	16
North Ireland	16
Poland	13
Brazil	13
South Africa	11
Ireland	08
Chile	07

Note: Countries in the left column are ranked according to GNP per capita. / The percentages in the bottom row give each country an equal weight. / na=not ascertained.

V240 ABORTION: NOT WANT CHILD

Do you approve or disapprove of abortion under the following circumstances? Where a married couple do not want to have any more children. (% "approve")

	Total	Gender		Age			Education			Income			Political Affinity			Values			Ranking:	
		Male	Female	16-29	30-49	50+	Lower	Medium	Upper	Lower	Middle	Upper	Left	Center	Right	Mat	Mixed	Postmat		
India	61	61	60	63	63	52	54	62	63	64	60	59	63	61	58	62	61	59	China	93
Nigeria	28	31	24	31	26	11	17	30	31	32	27	24	31	29	30	26	30	31	Bulgaria	77
China	93	92	94	91	94	94	91	95	92	94	93	92	na	na	na	94	93	89	Moscow	75
Romania	67	65	69	76	75	54	59	73	69	67	67	68	60	72	71	60	71	81	Estonia	73
Turkey	62	57	68	64	68	51	57	72	69	55	59	75	76	64	50	62	62	63	Slovenia	70
Poland	26	28	25	19	31	25	22	27	40	24	27	29	32	29	25	27	26	26	Hungary	69
Bulgaria	77	75	78	82	82	67	66	76	87	72	79	80	80	77	78	76	75	88	Romania	67
Chile	14	15	13	12	16	13	15	13	14	15	14	12	18	12	17	15	14	15	Russia	67
Czechoslovakia	34	36	33	32	39	31	30	35	40	30	34	38	39	32	34	37	33	35	Latvia	67
South Africa	13	13	12	15	12	11	09	14	17	10	12	16	19	12	16	08	14	23	Belarus	66
Lithuania	45	45	45	51	53	32	32	48	56	41	48	50	na	na	na	45	44	52	Denmark	63
Hungary	69	68	70	70	74	64	65	74	62	64	72	74	68	75	63	66	72	75	Turkey	62
Argentina	25	25	25	27	26	22	25	25	27	25	24	28	44	26	19	19	24	35	India	61
Brazil	15	18	12	15	16	15	15	14	22	14	14	17	18	14	17	14	15	23	Finland	61
Mexico	19	21	18	20	22	12	19	18	21	19	20	22	36	18	14	14	21	27	Sweden	52
Belarus	66	67	66	71	68	57	57	66	70	62	67	70	70	63	55	63	68	70	Japan	50
Russia	67	66	67	71	71	58	60	70	68	67	66	71	74	66	62	64	68	71	East Germany	48
Moscow	75	72	77	75	79	67	63	77	76	73	76	76	77	75	58	76	74	81	France	48
Latvia	67	66	67	63	71	63	52	67	71	67	67	67	na	na	na	68	67	64	Norway	46
Estonia	73	68	77	70	77	71	69	74	74	73	69	76	na	na	na	73	72	75	Lithuania	45
Portugal	37	36	37	39	42	29	31	48	49	31	39	41	49	36	28	33	39	42	Britain	41
South Korea	na	na	na	na	na	na	na	na	na	na	na	na	na	na	na	na	na	na	Portugal	37
Ireland	08	09	08	12	09	06	09	06	15	10	06	08	15	08	06	09	07	11	Czechoslovakia	34
North Ireland	17	19	15	15	17	17	15	21	17	19	10	27	21	16	19	13	17	22	West Germany	31
Slovenia	70	69	72	72	75	64	60	76	81	65	71	81	75	75	56	64	73	72	Spain	30
Spain	30	34	28	42	36	17	25	40	49	21	36	38	46	31	16	18	32	51	Canada	30
East Germany	48	52	45	55	51	42	46	51	56	40	50	55	62	45	36	37	50	50	Netherlands	29
Britain	41	42	39	40	41	41	39	46	42	39	41	46	47	39	41	36	40	47	Austria	29
Italy	26	29	23	27	32	20	26	28	28	22	29	36	40	18	25	20	25	35	Nigeria	28
Netherlands	29	29	30	33	32	21	22	28	39	30	30	37	45	26	21	18	23	43	Iceland	27
Belgium	24	25	22	24	29	18	21	23	30	27	23	24	32	24	20	22	21	31	Poland	26
Austria	29	31	27	24	32	28	29	29	27	28	28	31	37	34	23	23	28	35	Italy	26
France	48	47	48	43	54	45	43	49	57	48	48	53	52	51	42	42	47	53	United States	26
Canada	30	31	29	30	35	24	21	28	40	27	28	39	49	26	30	20	28	41	Argentina	25
United States	26	26	26	24	30	24	24	20	36	20	26	33	50	25	19	14	25	39	Belgium	24
Iceland	27	31	23	28	30	20	21	26	32	na	na	na	36	20	27	23	27	36	Mexico	19
West Germany	31	32	29	40	36	21	28	34	37	30	30	31	44	27	22	19	28	41	North Ireland	17
Denmark	63	66	60	65	71	54	48	69	68	54	62	75	75	60	60	54	62	83	Brazil	15
Finland	61	62	60	68	63	51	53	57	70	60	58	67	66	64	58	50	60	65	Chile	14
Norway	46	47	45	44	52	40	34	49	49	39	49	50	48	41	50	47	45	51	South Africa	13
Sweden	52	55	49	50	53	54	47	54	57	46	48	58	56	47	54	49	50	58	Ireland	08
Japan	50	52	48	48	56	42	41	49	61	42	50	53	48	54	52	51	51	47		
Switzerland	na	na	na	na	na	na	na	na	na	na	na	na	na	na	na	na	na	na		
Total	**44**	**44**	**43**	**45**	**47**	**38**	**38**	**45**	**49**	**42**	**44**	**48**	**49**	**40**	**37**	**40**	**43**	**50**		

Note: Countries in the left column are ranked according to GNP per capita. / The percentages in the bottom row give each country an equal weight. / na=not ascertained.

V241. How interested would you say you are in politics?

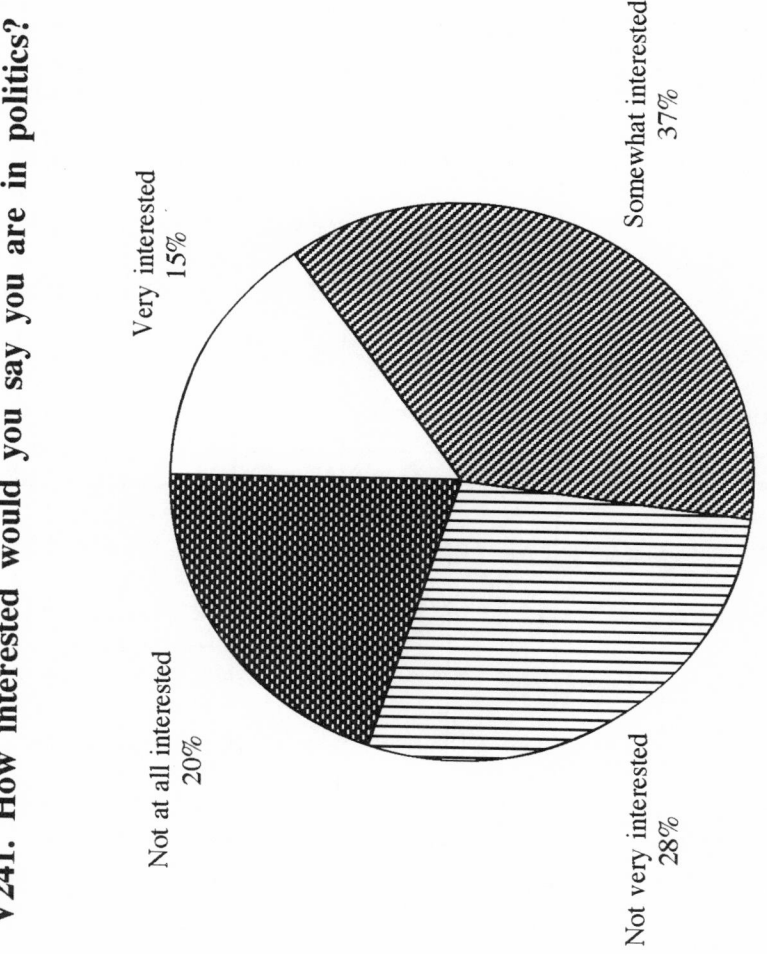

Very interested
15%

Somewhat interested
37%

Not at all interested
20%

Not very interested
28%

V241 INTERESTED IN POLITICS

How interested would you say you are in politics? (% "very interested" or "somewhat interested")

	Total	Gender Male	Gender Female	Age 16-29	Age 30-49	Age 50+	Education Lower	Education Medium	Education Upper	Income Lower	Income Middle	Income Upper	Political Affinity Left	Political Affinity Center	Political Affinity Right	Values Mat	Values Mixed	Values Postmat
India	47	56	36	50	46	42	28	30	53	41	36	50	58	46	53	45	50	59
Nigeria	35	40	27	34	35	46	41	30	38	35	36	33	23	39	55	32	37	33
China	67	71	62	64	70	66	61	73	72	67	68	67	na	na	na	62	73	75
Romania	18	24	12	14	20	18	11	17	30	17	16	20	19	17	28	13	18	43
Turkey	48	57	39	49	48	46	40	55	71	41	44	62	68	42	57	37	47	63
Poland	49	60	38	38	51	52	37	53	71	46	50	51	69	49	61	42	52	49
Bulgaria	73	79	68	78	80	61	49	77	88	67	76	79	79	77	85	69	73	87
Chile	37	44	30	41	39	28	25	37	52	26	38	48	63	30	37	21	37	60
Czechoslovakia	na	na	49	na	na	na	na	na	na	na	na	na	na	na	na	na	na	na
South Africa	57	65	49	60	56	50	37	63	82	47	54	74	76	60	73	49	59	69
Lithuania	74	82	67	62	83	75	61	75	92	71	77	75	na	na	na	67	77	81
Hungary	52	60	44	50	58	47	41	60	70	41	56	73	68	60	67	53	51	53
Argentina	30	34	27	29	30	31	20	31	44	24	30	37	55	34	39	18	31	45
Brazil	46	52	40	50	47	37	29	49	71	37	43	57	51	49	55	38	50	67
Mexico	38	45	30	39	39	33	34	35	53	33	40	46	65	32	44	33	38	58
Belarus	na	na	na	na	na	na	na	na	na	na	na	na	na	na	na	na	na	na
Russia	53	63	45	42	58	54	38	48	67	48	55	62	77	56	56	46	56	67
Moscow	72	78	66	65	72	75	56	66	79	69	72	77	79	68	73	66	73	83
Latvia	79	84	76	68	81	88	70	76	89	77	82	79	na	na	na	74	82	85
Estonia	60	68	54	47	67	64	43	61	77	56	62	65	na	na	na	54	64	76
Portugal	31	36	26	36	28	28	22	38	60	21	29	49	45	28	33	22	34	53
South Korea	73	68	77	73	73	73	69	72	76	68	76	76	82	72	71	67	75	86
Ireland	37	45	30	31	40	38	31	41	57	25	36	47	45	32	52	31	37	44
North Ireland	34	37	32	33	33	36	29	38	55	34	34	46	39	27	51	31	32	49
Slovenia	58	64	52	55	62	54	42	63	78	50	57	74	73	70	78	53	58	69
Spain	25	32	19	28	32	17	20	30	45	12	23	39	42	25	30	16	27	43
East Germany	85	89	81	85	90	79	82	87	95	78	84	91	93	86	81	62	88	89
Britain	49	56	43	43	52	50	42	62	72	44	53	62	53	43	68	45	48	57
Italy	29	40	18	30	32	25	26	47	53	27	35	51	41	29	33	17	27	45
Netherlands	58	72	54	50	62	63	47	56	74	53	64	75	69	57	65	39	58	67
Belgium	30	36	24	31	33	26	18	30	51	22	34	40	37	33	42	15	28	47
Austria	54	64	47	48	60	51	52	54	63	43	56	61	66	54	59	37	53	66
France	38	45	31	31	38	42	32	36	57	26	41	53	54	28	50	22	38	52
Canada	58	62	54	49	58	67	50	56	68	51	60	66	65	57	76	49	56	69
United States	61	65	57	54	64	62	53	57	72	52	60	72	70	61	70	50	60	73
Iceland	47	52	41	44	54	38	33	46	58	na	43	50	55	40	54	36	49	61
West Germany	69	81	59	62	76	68	64	75	90	63	70	76	80	67	81	50	70	81
Denmark	54	65	44	50	59	52	39	52	65	51	54	66	68	51	59	33	56	70
Finland	48	56	39	42	47	54	49	46	49	48	47	49	61	42	53	38	45	56
Norway	72	78	65	70	75	69	66	66	81	70	75	77	79	68	80	62	74	90
Sweden	47	53	40	39	46	54	37	46	66	49	43	50	59	37	56	40	43	63
Japan	62	74	51	47	64	70	63	59	70	59	59	71	87	65	76	59	68	75
Switzerland	66	69	63	49	66	73	66	67	63	61	71	71	68	73	72	57	66	70
Total	**52**	**59**	**45**	**48**	**54**	**51**	**43**	**53**	**66**	**46**	**53**	**60**	**62**	**49**	**59**	**43**	**53**	**64**

Ranking:

East Germany	85
Latvia	79
Lithuania	74
Bulgaria	73
South Korea	73
Moscow	72
Norway	72
West Germany	69
China	67
Switzerland	66
Japan	62
United States	61
Estonia	60
Slovenia	58
Netherlands	58
Canada	58
South Africa	57
Austria	54
Denmark	54
Russia	53
Hungary	52
Poland	49
Britain	49
Turkey	48
Finland	48
India	47
Iceland	47
Sweden	47
Brazil	46
Mexico	38
France	38
Chile	37
Ireland	37
Nigeria	35
North Ireland	34
Portugal	31
Argentina	30
Belgium	30
Italy	29
Spain	25
Romania	18
Romania	18

Note: Countries in the left column are ranked according to GNP per capita. / The percentages in the bottom row give each country an equal weight. / na=not ascertained.
The Swiss survey asked about interest in international politics, national politics, regional politics, and community politics. Responses to the question about community politics (which showed the highest levels of interest) were used here.

V242-V246. Political action

V242-V246. Political action

Percentage "might do"

Action	Percentage
Signing a petition	34
Joining in boycotts	37
Attending lawful demonstrations	40
Joining unofficial strikes	23
Occupying buildings or factories	14

Percentage "have done"

Action	Percentage
Signing a petition	43
Joining in boycotts	9
Attending lawful demonstrations	21
Joining unofficial strikes	6
Occupying buildings or factories	2

V242 SIGN PETITION

I'm going to read out some different forms of political action that people can take, and I'd like you to tell me whether you have actually done any of these things, whether you might do it, or would never, under any circumstances, do it. Signing a petition (% "might do")

	Total	Gender		Age			Education			Income			Political Affinity			Values		
		Male	Female	16-29	30-49	50+	Lower	Medium	Upper	Lower	Middle	Upper	Left	Center	Right	Mat	Mixed	Postmat
India	45	44	47	53	43	32	35	48	46	44	na	32	42	48	52	44	47	47
Nigeria	32	37	26	34	31	23	26	29	39	30	37	32	24	37	37	30	34	35
China	na	na	na	na	na	na	na	na	na	na	na	na	na	na	na	na	na	na
Romania	41	43	38	44	43	31	36	55	37	40	42	42	47	43	36	30	42	52
Turkey	52	55	49	54	54	47	43	55	64	52	52	51	56	62	50	46	55	51
Poland	39	42	37	47	39	36	31	44	38	39	41	38	45	41	42	37	41	37
Bulgaria	34	38	29	41	34	23	23	39	38	27	34	39	36	36	34	24	36	40
Chile	na	na	na	na	na	na	na	na	na	na	na	na	na	na	na	na	na	na
Czechoslovakia	47	51	44	56	45	36	46	50	36	54	48	40	54	49	48	42	50	53
South Africa	29	29	28	27	28	31	33	29	19	29	28	28	na	na	na	30	29	19
Lithuania	30	29	28	27	34	23	25	37	26	24	36	34	29	34	34	31	29	36
Hungary	33	32	33	39	34	26	25	37	35	25	36	39	29	41	43	27	35	34
Argentina	30	27	34	31	30	30	32	31	22	35	31	25	28	30	32	31	31	22
Brazil	44	44	45	48	46	31	40	53	52	45	44	43	37	45	47	43	45	46
Mexico	52	52	51	49	54	49	49	52	53	52	53	49	50	59	44	52	52	55
Belarus	44	46	43	45	46	42	37	45	48	44	49	45	49	49	45	41	46	52
Russia	47	51	44	47	48	46	36	51	47	48	46	48	47	51	na	50	45	54
Moscow	23	23	24	25	22	24	29	26	18	18	26	25	na	na	na	23	25	16
Latvia	39	37	40	41	36	39	37	40	35	37	41	38	na	na	na	42	38	30
Estonia	46	47	44	49	46	42	48	48	35	48	50	38	41	47	45	46	47	45
Portugal	42	42	42	36	45	43	45	43	39	42	44	42	41	42	43	47	41	29
South Korea	40	40	39	39	41	39	42	40	30	43	44	32	32	41	43	47	41	29
Ireland	27	25	29	31	21	31	30	27	07	35	23	22	29	27	26	27	28	20
North Ireland	15	15	14	17	11	18	21	14	13	21	12	13	10	16	35	33	34	31
Slovenia	34	39	29	34	38	25	31	38	31	32	38	28	41	37	35	33	34	40
Spain	36	40	33	49	38	25	35	39	41	24	37	44	41	46	31	39	41	17
East Germany	25	22	28	20	22	33	29	22	14	32	21	22	17	28	26	27	26	11
Britain	17	19	15	15	13	21	18	15	18	21	13	14	14	14	23	15	15	30
Italy	35	33	36	31	31	35	36	34	27	34	31	30	26	40	40	37	34	28
Netherlands	33	31	34	41	30	28	37	34	27	36	31	30	25	29	42	26	30	45
Belgium	27	24	30	26	27	28	28	35	23	22	28	32	18	31	29	35	30	23
Austria	30	34	28	36	30	28	26	35	21	29	30	24	22	31	31	31	31	21
France	29	29	29	37	11	18	34	27	11	21	12	13	20	16	13	23	16	09
Canada	15	15	14	17	16	18	21	14	13	26	19	14	17	18	18	23	21	14
United States	20	19	21	31	27	18	25	22	13	19	19	14	17	18	29	33	39	29
Iceland	37	39	34	38	36	35	37	39	35	31	34	30	34	38	39	43	34	20
West Germany	32	30	33	32	27	35	35	29	16	31	34	22	21	32	27	30	27	14
Denmark	25	28	23	35	22	22	25	27	25	24	31	46	16	29	49	36	46	47
Finland	46	45	47	49	47	38	46	49	42	34	53	46	45	46	49	30	28	22
Norway	28	29	26	32	22	28	24	34	24	28	31	30	16	29	27	30	25	19
Sweden	24	27	21	22	19	29	31	24	13	22	30	23	15	27	23	26	26	20
Japan	25	25	25	37	22	24	24	26	25	32	23	21	18	21	23	21	19	10
Switzerland	17	14	19	21	16	15	17	18	11	17	16	18	08	21	16	14	19	10
Total	**34**	**34**	**33**	**37**	**33**	**31**	**33**	**36**	**30**	**34**	**35**	**32**	**31**	**37**	**35**	**34**	**35**	**31**

Ranking:

Poland	52
Belarus	52
South Africa	47
Moscow	47
Portugal	46
Finland	46
India	45
Mexico	44
Russia	44
South Korea	42
Turkey	41
Ireland	40
Bulgaria	39
Estonia	37
Iceland	36
Spain	35
Italy	34
Chile	34
Slovenia	33
Argentina	33
Netherlands	32
Nigeria	32
West Germany	32
Hungary	30
Brazil	30
Austria	30
Lithuania	29
France	29
Norway	28
North Ireland	27
Belgium	27
East Germany	25
Denmark	25
Japan	25
Sweden	24
Latvia	23
United States	20
Britain	17
Switzerland	17
Canada	15

Note: Countries in the left column are ranked according to GNP per capita. / The percentages in the bottom row give each country an equal weight. / na=not ascertained.

V243 JOIN BOYCOTT

I'm going to read out some different forms of political action that people can take, and I'd like you to tell me whether you have actually done any of these things, whether you might do it, or would never, under any circumstances, do it. Joining in boycotts (% "might do")

	Total	Gender Male	Gender Female	Age 16-29	Age 30-49	Age 50+	Education Lower	Education Medium	Education Upper	Income Lower	Income Middle	Income Upper	Political Affinity Left	Political Affinity Center	Political Affinity Right	Values Mat	Values Mixed	Values Postmat
India	45	45	43	52	43	32	33	45	48	46	44	44	44	49	45	44	45	47
Nigeria	25	29	18	27	24	15	19	23	30	26	29	21	19	30	30	21	26	31
China	na	na	na	na	na	na	na	na	na	na	na	na	na	na	na	na	na	na
Romania	na	na	na	na	na	na	na	na	na	na	na	na	na	na	na	na	na	na
Turkey	23	27	19	28	24	12	16	34	33	18	21	30	42	19	18	12	23	35
Poland	35	39	30	42	41	24	21	41	51	33	36	34	36	41	39	24	39	44
Bulgaria	33	34	31	45	41	16	15	36	44	32	31	35	32	37	47	23	33	53
Chile	11	15	08	17	11	05	06	12	18	09	12	14	24	08	08	04	13	18
Czechoslovakia	na	na	na	na	na	na	na	na	na	na	na	na	na	na	na	na	na	na
South Africa	36	37	36	42	36	26	33	38	42	41	35	36	45	34	39	30	40	40
Lithuania	60	66	55	67	63	51	48	62	70	56	62	67	na	na	na	55	60	71
Hungary	14	18	11	22	18	08	06	20	34	08	17	26	22	15	19	13	15	19
Argentina	09	10	08	14	08	06	04	12	14	04	10	13	29	10	09	03	08	21
Brazil	36	35	38	42	38	24	25	40	45	30	40	41	42	38	32	30	40	47
Mexico	35	39	31	40	34	25	33	35	41	35	35	30	49	34	30	29	35	43
Belarus	38	40	36	50	41	19	18	41	41	36	38	38	44	34	23	25	43	62
Russia	36	45	30	45	41	24	27	37	41	31	37	37	46	39	37	30	39	48
Moscow	41	48	35	46	44	31	20	41	45	44	44	42	49	34	32	36	41	54
Latvia	37	48	30	40	40	27	30	34	45	30	39	40	na	na	na	30	38	46
Estonia	40	47	35	49	45	25	28	43	46	39	40	42	na	na	na	34	44	53
Portugal	31	36	27	39	32	22	24	35	52	29	27	41	35	33	29	23	36	39
South Korea	50	46	53	53	53	37	39	48	57	47	50	53	51	52	48	45	52	61
Ireland	33	38	29	50	34	21	26	39	53	19	32	44	47	34	32	27	33	42
North Ireland	30	32	28	39	34	18	27	27	56	19	29	45	32	31	30	25	29	40
Slovenia	46	51	42	53	49	38	36	49	58	40	51	49	61	52	52	41	47	57
Spain	26	32	21	41	28	13	21	31	41	12	27	38	36	30	19	15	29	39
East Germany	32	40	24	44	39	17	26	32	51	21	32	40	44	26	29	09	31	43
Britain	34	38	31	44	41	23	32	36	47	29	35	46	39	39	27	30	34	44
Italy	46	47	44	58	51	33	44	60	50	41	51	55	53	42	53	35	47	53
Netherlands	36	35	36	48	34	26	27	37	46	37	36	47	49	36	28	20	33	47
Belgium	28	33	23	44	29	17	20	29	41	26	28	34	30	32	27	12	27	45
Austria	25	29	23	31	30	19	19	27	40	15	27	32	23	28	27	10	24	37
France	40	46	35	52	42	30	33	45	51	31	47	46	46	42	35	20	42	52
Canada	43	44	43	56	42	34	31	46	48	41	43	46	33	47	44	42	43	46
United States	45	49	41	57	45	39	39	46	48	38	48	50	39	51	43	42	46	46
Iceland	53	58	47	57	50	52	47	56	56	na	na	na	47	59	53	46	56	49
West Germany	37	42	32	48	41	27	31	47	43	31	38	42	47	38	27	17	35	50
Denmark	32	33	31	40	39	17	20	29	40	25	31	42	42	30	27	24	32	42
Finland	69	70	67	73	73	54	55	71	73	60	72	72	63	71	70	63	68	72
Norway	52	56	47	60	59	38	34	54	58	47	54	61	53	54	52	44	54	59
Sweden	62	63	60	69	61	55	60	64	61	60	60	65	63	62	65	61	61	65
Japan	53	57	48	36	60	53	45	52	62	46	59	57	67	66	51	54	57	60
Switzerland	na	na	na	na	na	na	na	na	na	na	na	na	na	na	na	na	na	na
Total	**37**	**41**	**34**	**45**	**40**	**27**	**29**	**40**	**47**	**32**	**38**	**42**	**42**	**38**	**35**	**29**	**38**	**47**

Ranking:

Finland	69
Sweden	62
Lithuania	60
Iceland	53
Japan	53
Norway	52
South Korea	50
Slovenia	46
Italy	46
India	45
United States	45
Canada	43
Moscow	41
Estonia	40
France	40
Belarus	38
Latvia	37
West Germany	37
South Africa	36
Brazil	36
Russia	36
Netherlands	36
Poland	35
Mexico	35
Britain	34
Bulgaria	33
Ireland	33
East Germany	32
Denmark	32
Portugal	31
North Ireland	30
Belgium	28
Spain	26
Nigeria	25
Austria	25
Turkey	23
Hungary	14
Chile	11
Argentina	09

Note: Countries in the left column are ranked according to GNP per capita. / The percentages in the bottom row give each country an equal weight. / na=not ascertained.

V244 LAWFUL DEMONSTRATION

I'm going to read out some different forms of political action that people can take, and I'd like you to tell me whether you have actually done any of these things, whether you might do it, or would never, under any circumstances, do it. Attending lawful demonstrations (% "might do")

	Total	Gender		Age			Education			Income			Political Affinity			Values			Ranking:	
		Male	Female	16-29	30-49	50+	Lower	Medium	Upper	Lower	Middle	Upper	Left	Center	Right	Mat	Mixed	Postmat		
India	43	46	39	52	40	31	32	45	45	na	na	na	43	45	45	43	44	47	Sweden	59
Nigeria	30	35	23	33	29	17	21	31	33	na	na	na	31	33	31	25	31	42	Czechoslovakia	56
China	na	na	na	na	na	na	na	na	na	na	na	na	na	na	na	na	na	na	Norway	56
Romania	na	na	na	na	na	na	na	na	na	na	na	na	na	na	na	na	na	na	Belarus	55
Turkey	32	42	21	38	31	22	21	44	55	26	30	39	49	26	34	16	32	49	Iceland	53
Poland	51	53	48	55	56	42	44	54	57	53	50	48	49	59	51	41	55	54	Finland	53
Bulgaria	48	49	48	63	53	34	25	56	56	48	49	51	47	55	46	42	50	61	Moscow	52
Chile	24	26	22	30	22	16	16	27	29	19	25	28	26	25	28	20	26	24	Poland	51
Czechoslovakia	56	52	59	59	56	54	57	57	50	54	57	56	53	58	56	54	56	57	Lithuania	51
South Africa	41	44	39	46	41	33	37	43	46	45	40	41	53	42	45	35	45	42	Slovenia	50
Lithuania	51	50	51	55	51	47	49	53	44	49	51	56	na	na	na	46	54	55	Portugal	49
Hungary	27	33	22	46	32	15	17	36	36	18	33	38	44	30	33	22	31	40	Bulgaria	48
Argentina	21	25	18	27	24	14	14	23	29	15	21	31	43	23	25	11	21	34	United States	44
Brazil	40	40	41	52	38	22	28	46	42	37	41	43	42	45	39	35	44	37	India	43
Mexico	43	47	38	50	41	32	41	48	47	41	42	48	43	43	45	43	44	40	Mexico	43
Belarus	55	55	55	57	57	46	46	56	57	52	60	50	60	53	37	48	59	58	Canada	43
Russia	42	46	39	47	47	34	30	43	48	38	43	47	57	43	43	37	44	60	Russia	42
Moscow	52	56	48	54	57	41	44	54	52	51	52	54	60	45	40	49	52	62	Latvia	42
Latvia	42	44	41	39	44	42	44	45	37	42	44	41	na	na	na	43	45	27	Estonia	42
Estonia	42	44	41	47	46	31	35	44	46	41	47	40	na	na	na	43	41	43	Ireland	42
Portugal	49	52	46	58	48	40	47	49	55	50	46	52	46	52	48	44	53	46	West Germany	42
South Korea	33	29	37	35	35	24	27	33	36	32	35	33	32	36	32	29	38	33	South Africa	41
Ireland	42	41	42	55	40	35	35	49	48	32	40	48	41	43	43	39	41	47	Netherlands	41
North Ireland	31	31	31	41	31	24	29	31	48	31	25	39	33	28	40	26	31	43	Brazil	40
Slovenia	50	54	47	60	54	39	41	57	57	46	52	55	64	54	57	45	51	64	Italy	37
Spain	34	37	31	44	36	25	34	37	33	24	36	38	36	44	33	30	39	35	Britain	35
East Germany	34	31	38	35	36	34	37	32	27	35	37	32	37	35	27	35	36	29	Spain	34
Britain	35	38	31	48	42	21	31	44	41	27	36	48	34	38	32	27	36	40	East Germany	34
Italy	37	36	38	43	38	33	38	35	37	38	39	32	31	42	42	34	41	33	South Korea	33
Netherlands	41	41	41	52	41	29	33	47	44	35	47	45	37	47	39	28	43	42	Austria	33
Belgium	29	30	29	41	29	22	25	32	33	28	29	33	24	33	34	24	32	30	Turkey	32
Austria	33	37	31	49	39	21	25	37	41	22	35	41	26	38	33	14	33	43	France	32
France	32	34	31	45	33	22	29	36	36	32	35	29	28	40	30	27	35	32	Denmark	32
Canada	43	43	43	55	45	30	30	47	47	38	47	43	38	45	46	36	43	45	North Ireland	31
United States	44	45	42	62	43	36	34	46	48	38	45	48	34	50	41	36	45	46	Nigeria	30
Iceland	53	54	51	61	53	42	49	56	53	na	na	na	50	57	53	50	55	46	Belgium	29
West Germany	42	47	37	49	49	32	40	49	39	33	47	46	40	44	42	27	44	45	Hungary	27
Denmark	32	35	29	41	32	24	23	38	32	26	35	37	28	33	35	30	33	29	Japan	25
Finland	53	58	49	68	58	28	37	58	57	42	56	61	52	57	50	40	53	58	Chile	24
Norway	56	58	53	69	58	43	41	66	53	51	59	53	54	59	55	53	58	53	Argentina	21
Sweden	59	62	56	67	59	51	58	65	48	60	55	62	54	61	61	51	62	58	Switzerland	21
Japan	25	29	22	21	31	19	16	25	35	22	23	32	31	35	23	22	31	27		
Switzerland	21	23	19	32	26	10	19	19	32	18	22	26	30	21	16	12	18	31		
Total	40	42	38	48	42	31	34	44	44	37	41	43	42	43	40	34	42	44		

Note: Countries in the left column are ranked according to GNP per capita. / The percentages in the bottom row give each country an equal weight. / na=not ascertained.

V245   UNOFFICIAL STRIKES

I'm going to read out some different forms of political action that people can take, and I'd like you to tell me whether you have actually done any of these things, whether you might do it, or would never, under any circumstances, do it. Joining unofficial strikes (% "might do")

		Gender		Age			Education			Income			Political Affinity			Values		
	Total	Male	Female	16-29	30-49	50+	Lower	Medium	Upper	Lower	Middle	Upper	Left	Center	Right	Mat	Mixed	Postmat
India	16	19	13	22	15	08	13	16	18	17	16	15	22	17	15	14	18	25
Nigeria	14	15	13	16	13	04	10	15	15	13	16	15	18	13	15	13	16	09
China	na	na	na	na	na	na	na	na	na	na	na	na	na	na	na	na	na	na
Romania	na	na	na	na	na	na	na	na	na	na	na	na	na	na	na	na	na	na
Turkey	06	07	06	11	05	01	04	07	18	06	03	10	18	04	02	01	06	15
Poland	24	30	18	35	27	16	15	30	26	22	28	22	23	30	26	16	27	31
Bulgaria	25	27	23	42	27	13	13	27	33	25	24	27	21	28	38	19	26	41
Chile	16	22	11	21	17	10	09	16	26	10	16	24	29	14	11	08	17	27
Czechoslovakia	na	na	na	na	na	na	na	na	na	na	na	na	na	na	na	na	na	na
South Africa	24	29	18	33	21	11	24	25	15	30	24	13	36	18	21	17	26	35
Lithuania	50	60	41	63	55	34	36	54	56	42	52	65	na	na	na	40	51	64
Hungary	27	36	19	43	35	14	16	36	46	17	33	41	41	29	29	25	29	39
Argentina	11	13	09	19	11	05	07	11	18	07	08	17	34	11	10	05	08	26
Brazil	19	19	19	28	17	07	11	20	34	13	22	23	26	21	15	14	21	33
Mexico	36	42	28	40	36	25	35	33	42	37	35	38	55	32	30	30	36	46
Belarus	29	32	26	45	30	11	15	31	32	26	30	31	36	23	13	16	34	52
Russia	30	38	24	48	33	15	17	32	35	27	32	33	44	31	27	19	35	52
Moscow	32	40	25	40	35	20	16	33	34	28	34	35	40	24	20	19	32	58
Latvia	30	40	23	37	32	17	19	28	37	27	29	33	40	24	20	19	32	57
Estonia	19	22	16	26	22	07	14	19	24	19	19	18	24	19	18	12	19	42
Portugal	19	21	17	27	19	11	15	17	36	17	19	24	24	19	18	13	22	25
South Korea	na	na	na	na	na	na	na	na	na	na	na	na	na	na	na	na	na	na
Ireland	23	27	21	45	22	11	18	27	38	16	24	27	45	25	18	13	23	37
North Ireland	17	19	17	34	17	07	18	08	38	11	18	21	36	16	14	07	19	27
Slovenia	08	10	06	12	09	04	06	08	11	06	09	11	13	09	12	06	08	16
Spain	21	26	17	40	22	07	16	28	42	08	22	31	33	21	13	10	24	37
East Germany	15	18	13	30	17	05	13	20	20	11	17	17	33	11	11	07	15	23
Britain	19	19	19	33	21	09	17	21	28	16	22	23	24	17	10	14	18	27
Italy	18	20	15	30	22	06	17	26	25	15	21	17	34	12	13	09	17	28
Netherlands	22	21	22	30	24	09	11	22	34	25	17	27	40	19	10	11	17	33
Belgium	18	20	16	22	22	07	13	17	29	13	21	21	30	17	13	07	17	29
Austria	08	10	06	17	10	02	05	08	14	05	07	12	15	08	06	03	06	15
France	25	26	24	35	31	12	18	28	36	22	29	28	39	21	12	14	26	32
Canada	28	30	26	43	30	14	18	28	37	21	29	36	46	25	24	17	27	36
United States	30	34	26	52	32	19	23	26	40	25	30	37	43	30	26	21	29	38
Iceland	20	23	18	26	23	09	13	18	28	13	15	15	31	14	20	12	21	40
West Germany	14	16	11	25	18	05	09	19	26	13	15	27	30	10	04	04	10	28
Denmark	23	23	24	40	26	08	16	25	26	20	24	23	36	22	17	15	22	41
Finland	35	38	31	48	38	16	26	29	46	32	38	33	40	41	29	19	33	42
Norway	58	57	59	73	58	49	46	63	59	54	60	57	57	62	55	54	59	65
Sweden	41	44	37	62	47	17	32	48	42	40	40	41	53	42	33	26	38	59
Japan	13	17	09	14	16	09	10	11	22	11	14	16	29	15	09	10	17	17
Switzerland	22	26	18	33	27	12	20	20	37	19	27	29	53	20	10	08	18	41
Total	**23**	**27**	**20**	**35**	**25**	**12**	**17**	**24**	**31**	**20**	**24**	**27**	**34**	**21**	**18**	**15**	**24**	**36**

Ranking:

Norway	58
Lithuania	50
Sweden	41
Mexico	36
Finland	35
Moscow	32
Russia	30
Latvia	30
United States	30
Belarus	29
Canada	28
Hungary	27
Bulgaria	25
France	25
Poland	24
South Africa	24
Ireland	23
Denmark	23
Netherlands	22
Switzerland	22
Spain	21
Iceland	20
Brazil	19
Estonia	19
Portugal	19
Britain	19
Italy	18
Belgium	18
North Ireland	17
India	16
Chile	16
East Germany	15
Nigeria	14
West Germany	14
Japan	13
Argentina	11
Slovenia	08
Austria	08
Turkey	06

Note: Countries in the left column are ranked according to GNP per capita. / The percentages in the bottom row give each country an equal weight. / na=not ascertained.

V246 OCCUPY BUILDING

I'm going to read out some different forms of political action that people can take, and I'd like you to tell me whether you have actually done any of these things, whether you might do it, or would never, under any circumstances, do it. Occupying buildings or factories (% "might do")

	Total	Gender Male	Gender Female	Age 16-29	Age 30-49	Age 50+	Education Lower	Education Medium	Education Upper	Income Lower	Income Middle	Income Upper	Pol. Aff. Left	Pol. Aff. Center	Pol. Aff. Right	Values Mat	Values Mixed	Values Postmat
India	06	07	04	07	05	04	03	06	06	05	06	06	09	05	05	05	06	10
Nigeria	11	13	08	14	na	na	09	10	12	10	15	07	09	10	14	na	na	na
China	na	na	na	na	na	na	na	na	na	na	na	na	na	na	na	na	na	na
Romania	na	03	02	04	03	01	02	03	06	02	02	05	06	01	03	00	03	06
Turkey	03	03	02	04	03	01	02	03	06	02	02	05	06	01	03	00	03	06
Poland	19	26	13	26	24	11	13	25	17	21	20	17	19	22	23	12	22	25
Bulgaria	14	16	13	22	18	05	05	17	17	15	14	12	09	16	27	07	15	29
Chile	11	14	08	16	11	03	08	11	14	07	13	13	20	09	07	05	11	22
Czechoslovakia	na	na	na	na	na	na	na	na	na	na	na	na	na	na	na	na	na	na
South Africa	24	32	17	33	24	09	22	27	15	27	28	16	40	20	25	18	27	38
Lithuania	21	30	13	32	17	15	14	23	20	19	22	24	na	na	na	19	20	35
Hungary	04	06	02	09	04	02	03	04	04	03	06	02	05	03	08	03	05	00
Argentina	08	10	06	16	08	03	04	10	14	06	09	12	33	06	07	02	06	22
Brazil	12	13	12	17	11	06	09	12	21	12	11	14	19	11	11	07	15	21
Mexico	29	35	22	34	28	17	27	26	37	30	27	28	48	26	22	21	29	40
Belarus	12	15	09	20	12	04	07	14	11	10	13	13	14	11	09	06	13	20
Russia	12	19	07	24	13	05	08	13	14	12	11	14	17	11	19	07	15	21
Moscow	14	19	11	19	15	08	04	14	16	12	15	17	19	07	07	09	15	20
Latvia	05	08	04	06	07	02	07	05	05	03	05	07	na	na	na	06	05	08
Estonia	07	12	03	08	09	03	05	08	06	06	07	09	na	na	na	02	09	14
Portugal	11	12	10	13	12	09	09	11	20	10	10	13	16	09	11	10	11	15
South Korea	37	31	42	44	38	21	27	35	44	35	39	35	46	40	32	29	43	46
Ireland	19	24	15	31	20	10	18	19	30	14	21	21	39	19	16	10	20	28
North Ireland	08	11	06	13	10	03	08	04	21	05	08	10	21	07	07	05	08	12
Slovenia	12	15	09	14	15	08	10	12	16	11	13	13	17	13	13	12	12	15
Spain	23	28	18	41	24	07	17	29	43	09	25	34	38	22	15	10	24	44
East Germany	14	18	11	23	17	06	11	21	20	09	15	18	23	10	12	04	13	22
Britain	10	11	09	17	12	04	09	10	15	07	10	12	20	10	03	04	09	19
Italy	20	21	18	32	21	10	19	21	18	19	22	17	33	15	15	12	19	28
Netherlands	22	26	21	29	23	14	13	21	36	23	21	30	41	21	09	11	16	37
Belgium	21	24	18	31	27	09	15	21	31	19	24	24	36	20	15	10	18	36
Austria	06	06	06	14	07	02	04	07	11	05	06	08	13	06	05	01	05	12
France	25	26	24	36	31	11	21	27	32	22	29	28	40	21	10	13	26	32
Canada	21	24	17	34	21	09	16	19	27	20	20	24	35	18	19	14	19	29
United States	17	19	15	31	19	10	12	16	24	15	18	20	29	16	15	10	16	26
Iceland	09	13	05	14	11	02	06	07	14	na	na	na	17	07	06	06	08	25
West Germany	10	11	08	19	11	04	07	14	19	09	10	10	25	06	03	01	06	22
Denmark	07	07	06	08	10	02	04	06	09	06	06	10	22	02	02	05	03	23
Finland	20	21	19	40	19	04	21	15	25	23	18	19	30	24	11	09	18	26
Norway	10	12	08	15	14	03	03	10	14	10	10	12	22	08	05	06	08	30
Sweden	19	19	20	36	21	05	11	23	25	18	21	18	28	19	14	10	14	41
Japan	07	10	04	07	09	04	04	07	08	04	08	09	20	08	03	03	08	13
Switzerland	na	na	na	na	na	na	na	na	na	na	na	na	na	na	na	na	na	na
Total	**14**	**17**	**12**	**22**	**16**	**07**	**11**	**15**	**19**	**13**	**15**	**16**	**24**	**13**	**12**	**09**	**14**	**24**

Ranking:

South Korea	37
Mexico	29
France	25
South Africa	24
Spain	23
Netherlands	22
Lithuania	21
Belgium	21
Canada	21
Italy	20
Finland	20
Poland	19
Ireland	19
Sweden	19
United States	17
Bulgaria	14
Moscow	14
East Germany	14
Brazil	12
Belarus	12
Russia	12
Slovenia	12
Nigeria	11
Chile	11
Portugal	11
Britain	10
West Germany	10
Norway	10
Iceland	09
Argentina	08
North Ireland	08
Estonia	07
Denmark	07
Japan	07
India	06
Austria	06
Latvia	05
Hungary	04
Turkey	03

Note: Countries in the left column are ranked according to GNP per capita. / The percentages in the ranked column in the bottom row give each country an equal weight. / na=not ascertained.

V247. What is more important, freedom or equality?

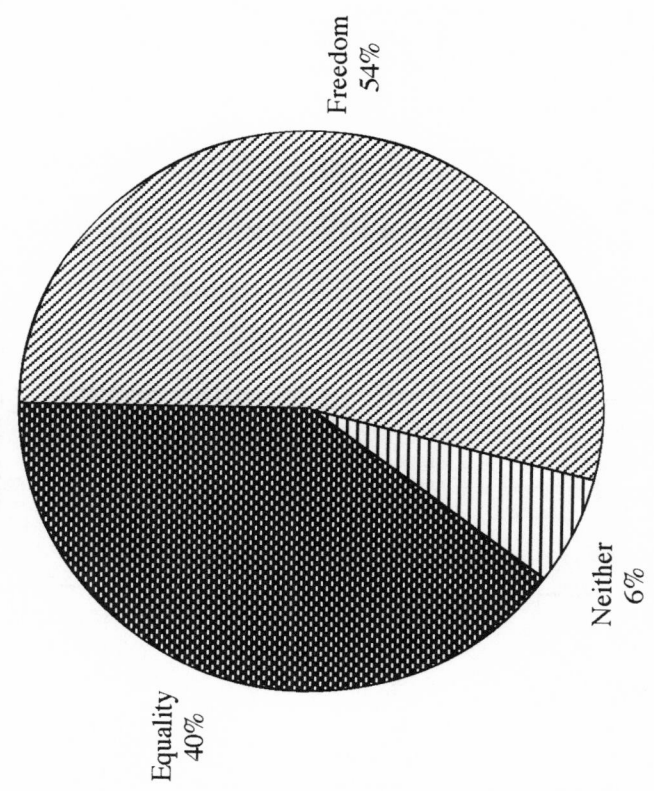

Freedom
54%

Neither
6%

Equality
40%

V247 FREEDOM & EQUALITY

"I find that both freedom and equality are important. But if I were to choose one or the other, I would consider personal freedom more important, that is, everyone can live in freedom and develop without hinderance." (% "agree" with this statement)

	Total	Gender		Age			Education			Income			Political Affinity			Values		
		Male	Female	16-29	30-49	50+	Lower	Medium	Upper	Lower	Middle	Upper	Left	Center	Right	Mat	Mixed	Postmat
India	45	48	41	43	46	44	42	45	45	47	40	48	43	50	47	43	47	44
Nigeria	62	63	61	63	60	64	68	61	61	62	61	62	71	59	60	58	64	63
China	21	22	19	32	17	13	22	19	24	19	19	25	na	na	na	15	24	51
Romania	54	57	52	62	55	48	47	56	61	57	51	56	37	55	65	42	62	75
Turkey	58	66	50	57	57	61	54	64	63	63	53	57	61	57	60	54	58	61
Poland	55	56	54	59	53	57	54	52	73	55	54	57	58	53	61	52	57	55
Bulgaria	48	50	46	56	53	37	34	47	58	47	43	53	46	47	58	38	49	69
Chile	53	55	51	51	54	54	55	49	56	53	52	54	48	53	63	53	55	49
Czechoslovakia	42	47	38	42	43	42	36	44	50	43	41	43	33	41	52	35	44	49
South Africa	48	50	47	44	51	50	40	48	75	41	45	67	49	53	58	55	46	39
Lithuania	73	78	68	82	72	65	66	74	81	67	74	82	na	na	na	67	74	81
Hungary	51	51	51	52	54	48	46	53	65	46	52	62	44	54	58	51	52	47
Argentina	58	61	54	55	58	60	56	56	60	58	53	62	42	60	68	59	59	55
Brazil	41	44	38	39	40	46	47	38	41	45	35	41	36	42	46	43	40	41
Mexico	61	63	58	61	61	60	60	59	65	52	63	74	50	63	70	65	61	59
Belarus	41	45	37	48	40	35	32	39	46	36	43	44	43	39	42	38	41	54
Russia	45	48	43	58	46	36	40	46	47	43	43	49	56	44	43	36	51	60
Moscow	53	55	52	65	55	41	39	49	59	48	57	58	59	48	49	49	50	78
Latvia	58	63	54	64	56	55	47	55	66	52	65	57	na	na	na	53	57	69
Estonia	71	75	67	72	74	64	69	69	78	67	73	74	na	na	na	66	72	79
Portugal	42	47	38	49	40	36	37	52	52	37	39	51	38	42	44	41	42	49
South Korea	51	51	50	49	52	50	40	55	51	45	52	59	46	47	54	51	53	43
Ireland	45	47	44	46	46	44	46	51	51	43	45	45	45	42	51	48	44	45
North Ireland	64	63	65	59	59	75	59	74	69	69	53	72	64	62	73	72	64	51
Slovenia	42	41	43	51	41	37	41	40	46	35	42	55	39	43	49	39	40	65
Spain	43	44	41	49	39	41	40	48	50	42	41	43	40	46	53	41	44	42
East Germany	50	57	45	52	53	46	50	47	55	48	51	52	43	52	65	43	50	55
Britain	65	67	63	63	64	68	65	68	63	62	67	67	54	66	76	68	66	57
Italy	46	47	44	45	46	46	46	45	49	47	42	44	39	47	56	40	49	44
Netherlands	56	59	55	58	57	53	51	59	59	57	59	63	51	58	63	47	60	55
Belgium	52	56	48	53	55	48	49	51	58	49	54	58	44	52	60	48	51	56
Austria	64	67	62	63	62	66	61	65	70	60	66	65	64	62	68	53	64	69
France	53	58	49	58	54	53	51	52	63	47	51	61	46	51	72	48	54	55
Canada	61	60	61	61	59	63	60	61	62	54	65	62	51	62	67	60	64	56
United States	71	73	69	68	71	74	67	72	73	70	72	69	65	72	78	71	72	69
Iceland	45	48	41	52	40	43	43	44	45	na	na	na	29	45	59	42	46	43
West Germany	66	70	62	69	67	63	64	69	70	59	66	72	58	69	74	59	69	66
Denmark	62	64	59	64	62	60	56	68	61	60	57	70	46	60	79	53	67	49
Finland	74	72	77	73	77	70	75	71	78	66	77	78	64	77	80	75	76	70
Norway	67	68	66	72	65	66	60	66	71	62	66	74	55	67	76	63	70	55
Sweden	67	69	64	66	69	64	60	68	75	60	61	74	50	67	82	58	69	66
Japan	46	50	42	41	48	46	40	48	55	43	45	49	44	55	49	49	46	51
Switzerland	58	58	57	52	59	58	58	57	56	54	55	57	47	60	63	54	58	59
Total	54	57	52	56	54	52	51	54	59	52	53	59	49	54	61	51	55	57

Ranking:

Finland	74
Lithuania	73
Estonia	71
United States	71
Norway	67
Sweden	67
West Germany	66
Britain	65
North Ireland	64
Austria	64
Nigeria	62
Denmark	62
Mexico	61
Canada	61
Turkey	58
Argentina	58
Latvia	58
Switzerland	58
Netherlands	56
Poland	55
Romania	54
Chile	53
Moscow	53
France	53
Belgium	52
Hungary	51
South Korea	51
East Germany	50
Bulgaria	48
South Africa	48
Italy	46
Japan	46
India	45
Russia	45
Ireland	45
Iceland	45
Spain	43
Czechoslovakia	42
Portugal	42
Slovenia	42
Brazil	41
Belarus	41
China	21

Note: Countries in the left column are ranked according to GNP per capita. / The percentages in the bottom row give each country an equal weight. / na=not ascertained.
The other statement offered in this question was: "Certainly both freedom and equality are important. But if I were to choose one or the other, I would consider equality more important, that is, that nobody is underprivileged and that social class differences are not so strong."

V248. In political matters, people talk of "the left" and "the right." How would you place your views on this scale, generally speaking?

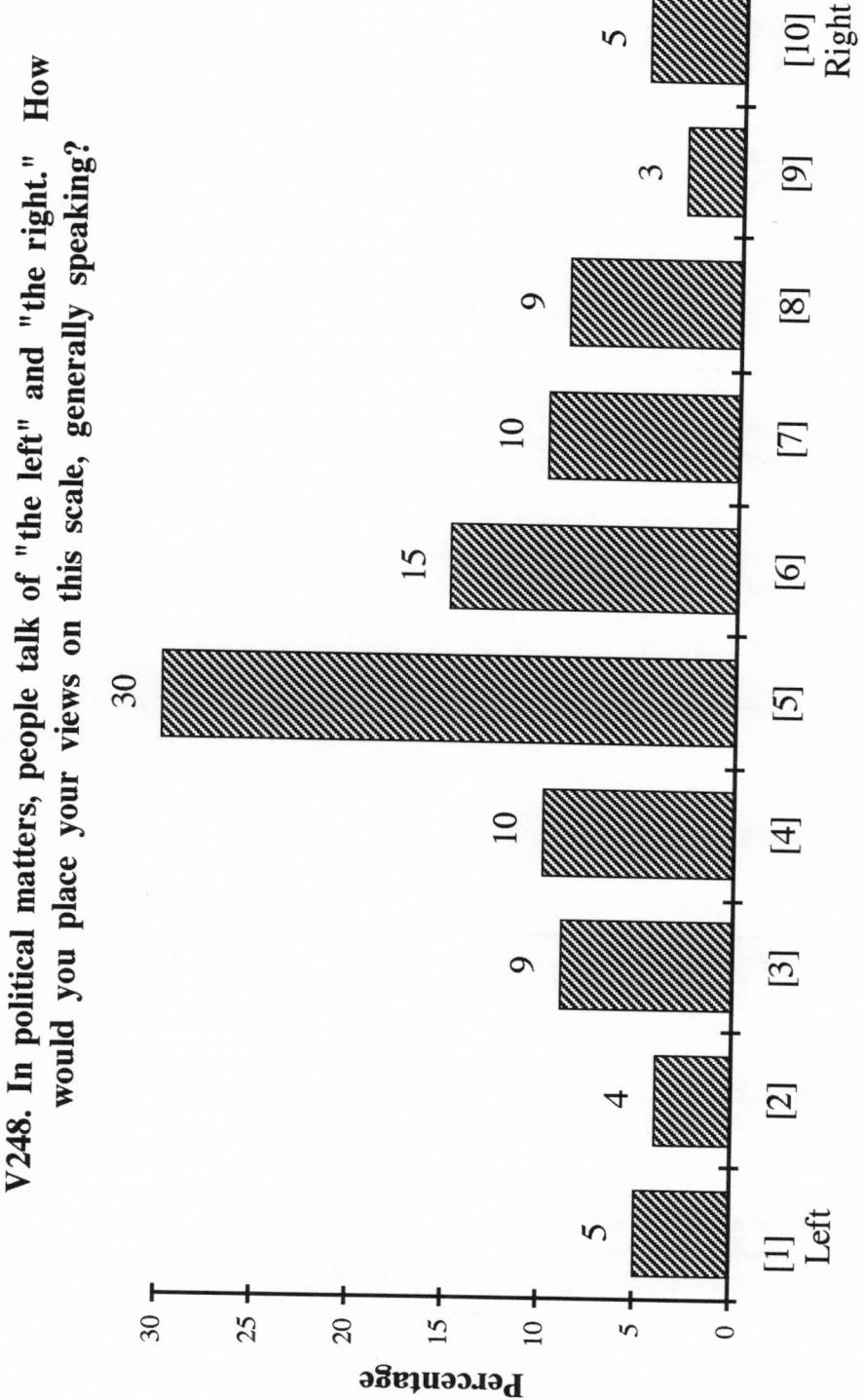

V248 LEFT-RIGHT SELF PLACEMENT: % LEFT

In political matters, people talk of "the left" and "the right." How would you place your views on this scale, generally speaking?
(% "Left"—points 1 to 4 from the scale)

	Total	Gender		Age			Education			Income			Political Affinity			Values			Ranking:	
		Male	Female	16-29	30-49	50+	Lower	Medium	Upper	Lower	Middle	Upper	Left	Center	Right	Mat	Mixed	Postmat		
India	30	33	26	32	29	26	19	32	31	28	31	29	100	00	00	30	30	36	Moscow	64
Nigeria	22	23	20	22	24	13	19	21	24	20	23	21	100	00	00	22	22	25	Belarus	60
China	na	na	na	na	na	na	na	na	na	na	na	na	na	na	na	na	na	na	Spain	50
Romania	19	20	17	18	14	23	21	18	16	21	17	18	100	00	00	25	16	05	France	42
Turkey	25	25	24	28	27	15	19	31	38	25	20	29	100	00	00	13	23	43	Italy	41
Poland	20	22	17	12	19	26	22	18	22	21	17	21	100	00	00	21	20	14	South Africa	39
Bulgaria	31	34	28	22	34	31	36	31	28	29	30	32	100	00	00	37	31	11	East Germany	36
Chile	30	36	25	32	30	27	30	29	33	31	29	31	100	00	00	19	30	43	Russia	33
Czechoslovakia	22	24	20	18	24	22	21	20	29	22	21	23	100	00	00	26	22	13	Netherlands	33
South Africa	39	39	38	43	40	26	38	39	41	42	42	31	100	00	00	27	43	57	Bulgaria	31
Lithuania	na	na	na	na	na	na	na	na	na	na	na	na	na	na	na	na	na	na	India	30
Hungary	18	21	15	22	18	16	16	18	26	13	19	24	100	00	00	16	20	13	Chile	30
Argentina	18	18	17	24	17	12	16	15	20	17	18	19	100	00	00	10	15	31	Brazil	30
Brazil	30	32	29	39	30	13	23	32	38	28	32	31	100	00	00	24	33	45	Iceland	30
Mexico	21	23	17	21	21	21	22	17	20	21	22	20	100	00	00	14	21	34	West Germany	29
Belarus	60	64	57	58	65	52	54	59	63	56	62	62	100	00	00	46	65	84	Sweden	28
Russia	33	37	29	30	36	31	22	28	41	27	33	39	100	00	00	24	35	58	Belgium	27
Moscow	64	65	64	65	66	61	49	62	68	61	67	66	100	00	00	50	67	80	Norway	27
Latvia	na	na	na	na	na	na	na	na	na	na	na	na	na	na	na	na	na	na	Turkey	25
Estonia	na	na	na	na	na	na	na	na	na	na	na	na	na	na	na	na	na	na	Britain	24
Portugal	23	27	20	21	26	23	24	24	21	25	25	18	100	00	00	20	25	29	Denmark	24
South Korea	14	14	13	20	13	04	10	12	17	12	15	11	100	00	00	08	14	34	Portugal	23
Ireland	12	14	10	21	12	07	11	12	21	09	10	16	100	00	00	07	11	22	Slovenia	23
North Ireland	10	09	11	15	14	03	12	04	10	09	11	08	100	00	00	02	11	19	Switzerland	23
Slovenia	23	22	25	19	26	24	23	21	27	19	24	27	100	00	00	15	25	33	Nigeria	22
Spain	50	55	45	56	55	38	48	49	58	46	53	52	100	00	00	39	49	68	Czechoslovakia	22
East Germany	36	37	35	42	39	28	30	40	52	29	34	42	100	00	00	23	35	43	Mexico	21
Britain	24	25	23	29	25	20	24	18	30	26	25	19	100	00	00	16	22	38	Finland	21
Italy	41	43	38	42	47	34	40	45	59	42	38	44	100	00	00	32	38	54	Poland	20
Netherlands	33	28	35	33	40	23	26	33	40	44	28	32	100	00	00	10	25	51	Romania	19
Belgium	27	30	25	34	30	20	26	27	30	34	27	23	100	00	00	26	24	35	Hungary	18
Austria	11	11	12	12	11	12	12	11	10	13	11	11	100	00	00	13	10	13	Argentina	18
France	42	44	40	42	48	35	38	42	48	39	45	45	100	00	00	27	39	57	United States	17
Canada	16	17	15	17	20	10	12	14	21	17	17	19	100	00	00	06	14	25	Canada	16
United States	17	17	17	17	19	14	13	13	22	15	16	18	100	00	00	08	13	30	Japan	16
Iceland	30	26	34	25	32	30	25	26	35	na	31	24	100	00	00	27	28	44	South Korea	14
West Germany	29	31	27	38	33	15	25	33	41	29	31	27	100	00	00	17	21	50	Ireland	12
Denmark	24	24	25	26	31	20	18	24	28	23	27	27	100	00	00	18	19	51	Austria	11
Finland	21	18	24	14	20	27	21	23	18	23	24	15	100	00	00	13	22	20	North Ireland	10
Norway	27	28	27	33	29	21	30	25	29	34	30	20	100	00	00	19	25	55		
Sweden	28	30	24	22	33	25	31	28	23	31	31	24	100	00	00	25	24	40		
Japan	16	17	15	23	14	15	18	15	15	18	15	16	100	00	00	13	17	26		
Switzerland	23	25	22	36	25	16	21	22	37	24	29	20	100	00	00	10	17	43		
Total	27	28	26	29	29	23	25	26	32	27	28	27	100	00	00	20	26	38		

Note: Countries in the left column are ranked according to GNP per capita. / The percentages in the bottom row give each country an equal weight. / na=not ascertained.

V248 LEFT-RIGHT SELF PLACEMENT: % CENTER

In political matters, people talk of "the left" and "the right." How would you place your views on this scale, generally speaking?
(% "Center"—points 5 to 6 from the scale)

	Total	Gender		Age			Education			Income			Political Affinity			Values		
		Male	Female	16-29	30-49	50+	Lower	Medium	Upper	Lower	Middle	Upper	Left	Center	Right	Mat	Mixed	Postmat
India	41	39	44	41	41	41	51	39	41	44	39	42	00	100	00	40	42	41
Nigeria	44	40	50	41	47	49	43	44	44	44	45	46	00	100	00	46	42	51
China	na	na	na	na	na	na	na	na	na	na	na	na	na	na	na	na	na	na
Romania	53	51	54	51	56	51	53	53	51	52	54	52	00	100	00	58	50	43
Turkey	51	47	55	49	49	55	52	48	48	47	55	50	00	100	00	59	51	41
Poland	50	47	53	66	50	42	46	55	45	45	57	50	00	100	00	48	52	50
Bulgaria	47	44	51	48	44	51	49	45	49	49	50	45	00	100	00	46	49	43
Chile	52	49	54	52	48	56	52	54	49	49	55	49	00	100	00	59	52	44
Czechoslovakia	49	45	53	52	49	46	51	49	42	51	48	47	00	100	00	52	47	49
South Africa	32	29	36	30	34	34	30	33	31	28	32	39	00	100	00	37	31	25
Lithuania	na	na	na	na	na	na	na	na	na	na	na	na	na	na	na	na	na	na
Hungary	65	60	71	62	65	66	64	66	60	67	62	64	00	100	00	67	62	70
Argentina	61	61	61	55	64	64	63	65	57	64	63	57	00	100	00	65	63	55
Brazil	39	39	39	38	41	38	30	42	44	35	40	43	00	100	00	37	40	42
Mexico	48	45	51	48	49	44	48	48	47	48	47	46	00	100	00	49	47	44
Belarus	30	28	31	32	27	34	29	32	28	32	30	28	00	100	00	37	28	13
Russia	56	53	60	59	54	57	65	61	50	60	59	51	00	100	00	62	55	39
Moscow	27	27	27	27	29	25	30	28	26	29	27	25	00	100	00	37	25	16
Latvia	na	na	na	na	na	na	na	na	na	na	na	na	na	na	na	na	na	na
Estonia	na	na	na	na	na	na	na	na	na	na	na	na	na	na	na	na	na	na
Portugal	46	47	45	49	46	43	46	45	48	45	48	46	00	100	00	48	45	44
South Korea	36	39	34	43	37	24	39	39	32	42	37	27	00	100	00	33	40	40
Ireland	55	53	56	55	58	52	55	56	45	57	56	51	00	100	00	53	54	60
North Ireland	57	53	60	54	62	53	58	55	52	56	58	53	00	100	00	57	58	50
Slovenia	63	63	63	68	60	63	62	63	64	65	65	59	00	100	00	68	63	51
Spain	33	30	36	32	31	37	34	35	27	35	32	30	00	100	00	37	35	25
East Germany	46	42	49	42	44	51	50	42	36	50	48	41	00	100	00	55	47	39
Britain	50	45	55	54	50	47	52	47	40	50	49	48	00	100	00	46	52	47
Italy	42	40	44	40	39	46	43	36	30	40	45	40	00	100	00	49	43	34
Netherlands	37	37	37	42	35	35	39	39	33	36	41	34	00	100	00	46	39	32
Belgium	42	40	43	39	42	43	46	40	38	38	41	42	00	100	00	39	42	43
Austria	48	45	49	54	49	44	47	49	43	44	50	48	00	100	00	44	46	54
France	38	39	37	43	34	39	38	40	36	45	42	34	00	100	00	46	39	31
Canada	58	57	59	60	56	59	63	62	49	60	59	59	00	100	00	69	58	54
United States	54	51	58	50	57	55	58	60	46	55	54	54	00	100	00	61	55	50
Iceland	34	34	35	41	34	33	43	32	30	43	39	35	00	100	00	38	35	23
West Germany	48	43	53	50	46	48	51	46	34	49	48	46	00	100	00	46	52	54
Denmark	41	40	42	37	38	47	49	39	38	45	42	34	00	100	00	45	41	31
Finland	36	35	37	45	34	35	45	40	28	50	33	28	00	100	00	53	35	36
Norway	39	35	42	34	39	42	45	44	31	37	39	35	00	100	00	45	39	26
Sweden	37	34	40	41	35	36	43	37	27	43	39	33	00	100	00	45	39	30
Japan	54	50	58	59	56	47	50	54	56	53	60	48	00	100	00	51	54	64
Switzerland	47	45	50	41	46	52	51	47	36	45	46	49	00	100	00	51	50	39
Total	**46**	**44**	**48**	**47**	**46**	**46**	**48**	**46**	**41**	**47**	**47**	**44**	**00**	**100**	**00**	**49**	**46**	**41**

Ranking:

Hungary	65
Slovenia	63
Argentina	61
Canada	58
North Ireland	57
Russia	56
Ireland	55
United States	54
Japan	54
Romania	53
Chile	52
Turkey	51
Poland	50
Britain	50
Czechoslovakia	49
Mexico	48
Austria	48
West Germany	48
Bulgaria	47
Switzerland	47
Portugal	46
East Germany	46
Nigeria	44
Italy	42
Belgium	42
India	41
Denmark	41
Brazil	39
Norway	39
France	38
Netherlands	37
Sweden	37
South Korea	36
Finland	36
Iceland	34
Spain	33
South Africa	32
Belarus	30
Moscow	27

Note: Countries in the left column are ranked according to GNP per capita. / The percentages in the bottom row give each country an equal weight. / na=not ascertained.

V248 LEFT-RIGHT SELF PLACEMENT: % RIGHT

In political matters, people talk of "the left" and "the right." How would you place your views on this scale, generally speaking?
(% "Right"—points 7 to 10 from the scale)

	Total	Gender		Age			Education			Income			Political Affinity			Values			Ranking:	
		Male	Female	16-29	30-49	50+	Lower	Medium	Upper	Lower	Middle	Upper	Left	Center	Right	Mat	Mixed	Postmat		
India	29	29	29	27	30	33	30	29	29	28	29	30	00	00	100	30	28	23	South Korea	50
Nigeria	34	37	30	37	30	38	39	35	32	36	32	33	00	00	100	32	37	25	Finland	43
China	na	na	na	na	na	na	na	na	na	na	na	na	na	na	na	na	na	na	Austria	41
Romania	29	29	28	31	30	26	26	29	33	28	29	30	00	00	100	na	na	na	Iceland	36
Turkey	25	28	21	23	23	30	29	21	15	28	25	21	00	00	100	28	26	17	Denmark	35
Poland	30	31	30	22	32	33	33	27	34	35	26	29	00	00	100	32	28	36	Sweden	35
Bulgaria	22	23	21	30	22	18	15	24	23	22	20	23	00	00	100	17	20	46	Nigeria	34
Chile	18	15	22	16	21	17	19	18	19	20	15	20	00	00	100	22	18	14	Norway	34
Czechoslovakia	30	32	28	31	27	33	28	31	29	28	31	31	00	00	100	22	31	39	Ireland	33
South Africa	29	32	26	27	26	40	32	28	28	30	27	30	00	00	100	37	27	18	North Ireland	33
Lithuania	na	na	na	na	na	na	na	na	na	na	na	na	na	na	na	na	na	na	Mexico	32
Hungary	18	20	15	16	18	18	20	16	14	20	18	12	00	00	100	17	19	17	Brazil	31
Argentina	21	21	21	21	20	23	21	20	23	19	20	24	00	00	100	26	23	14	Portugal	31
Brazil	31	29	33	23	29	49	47	27	19	37	29	26	00	00	100	40	27	13	Belgium	31
Mexico	32	32	32	31	31	35	30	34	33	31	31	34	00	00	100	38	32	23	Japan	31
Belarus	10	08	12	10	08	14	17	08	09	12	08	11	00	00	100	16	08	03	Poland	30
Russia	11	11	12	11	10	12	14	12	10	13	09	10	00	00	100	15	10	03	Czechoslovakia	30
Moscow	09	09	09	08	05	15	21	10	05	10	06	10	00	00	100	13	08	04	Netherlands	30
Latvia	na	na	na	na	na	na	na	na	na	na	na	na	na	na	na	na	na	na	Switzerland	30
Estonia	na	na	na	na	na	na	na	na	na	na	na	na	na	na	na	na	na	na	India	29
Portugal	31	26	35	30	28	34	30	31	31	30	27	36	00	00	100	32	30	27	Romania	29
South Korea	50	48	52	37	51	71	51	49	52	46	47	62	00	00	100	59	47	27	South Africa	29
Ireland	33	32	34	24	30	41	34	32	34	34	34	33	00	00	100	40	35	18	United States	29
North Ireland	33	39	29	31	25	45	29	41	38	35	31	39	00	00	100	42	31	31	Britain	27
Slovenia	14	15	13	13	15	14	15	16	09	17	11	14	00	00	100	18	12	16	Canada	26
Spain	17	15	19	12	13	25	18	15	14	20	14	18	00	00	100	25	16	07	Turkey	25
East Germany	18	21	16	16	18	21	20	18	12	21	18	17	00	00	100	23	18	18	West Germany	23
Britain	27	31	22	17	25	34	23	36	30	24	26	33	00	00	100	38	26	16	Bulgaria	22
Italy	18	18	17	18	14	20	17	19	11	18	18	16	00	00	100	19	19	12	Argentina	21
Netherlands	30	36	28	25	25	42	35	28	27	20	31	34	00	00	100	44	37	17	France	20
Belgium	31	30	32	27	28	37	28	33	32	27	32	36	00	00	100	36	34	22	Chile	18
Austria	41	44	39	34	40	45	42	40	47	43	39	42	00	00	100	44	44	33	Hungary	18
France	20	18	22	15	18	26	24	18	15	16	18	23	00	00	100	27	22	12	East Germany	18
Canada	26	26	26	23	24	30	25	23	30	23	25	30	00	00	100	25	28	21	Italy	18
United States	29	32	25	33	24	32	29	27	32	29	30	28	00	00	100	31	32	20	Spain	17
Iceland	36	40	32	38	34	37	34	42	34	34	na	na	00	00	100	36	37	33	Slovenia	14
West Germany	23	26	21	12	21	32	24	22	24	22	21	26	00	00	100	37	27	09	Russia	11
Denmark	35	37	33	37	32	38	33	37	35	32	31	39	00	00	100	37	40	14	Belarus	10
Finland	43	47	38	41	45	38	35	37	54	27	43	57	00	00	100	33	43	45	Moscow	09
Norway	34	37	31	33	32	37	25	32	40	28	32	45	00	00	100	36	36	18		
Sweden	35	36	35	37	32	38	26	35	51	26	31	43	00	00	100	30	37	31		
Japan	31	33	28	18	30	38	32	31	29	32	25	37	00	00	100	36	29	11		
Switzerland	30	31	29	23	30	32	29	32	26	31	25	32	00	00	100	39	33	18		
Total	27	28	26	25	26	32	28	27	27	26	25	29	00	00	100	31	28	21		

Note: Countries in the left column are ranked according to GNP per capita. / The percentages in the bottom row give each country an equal weight / na=not ascertained.

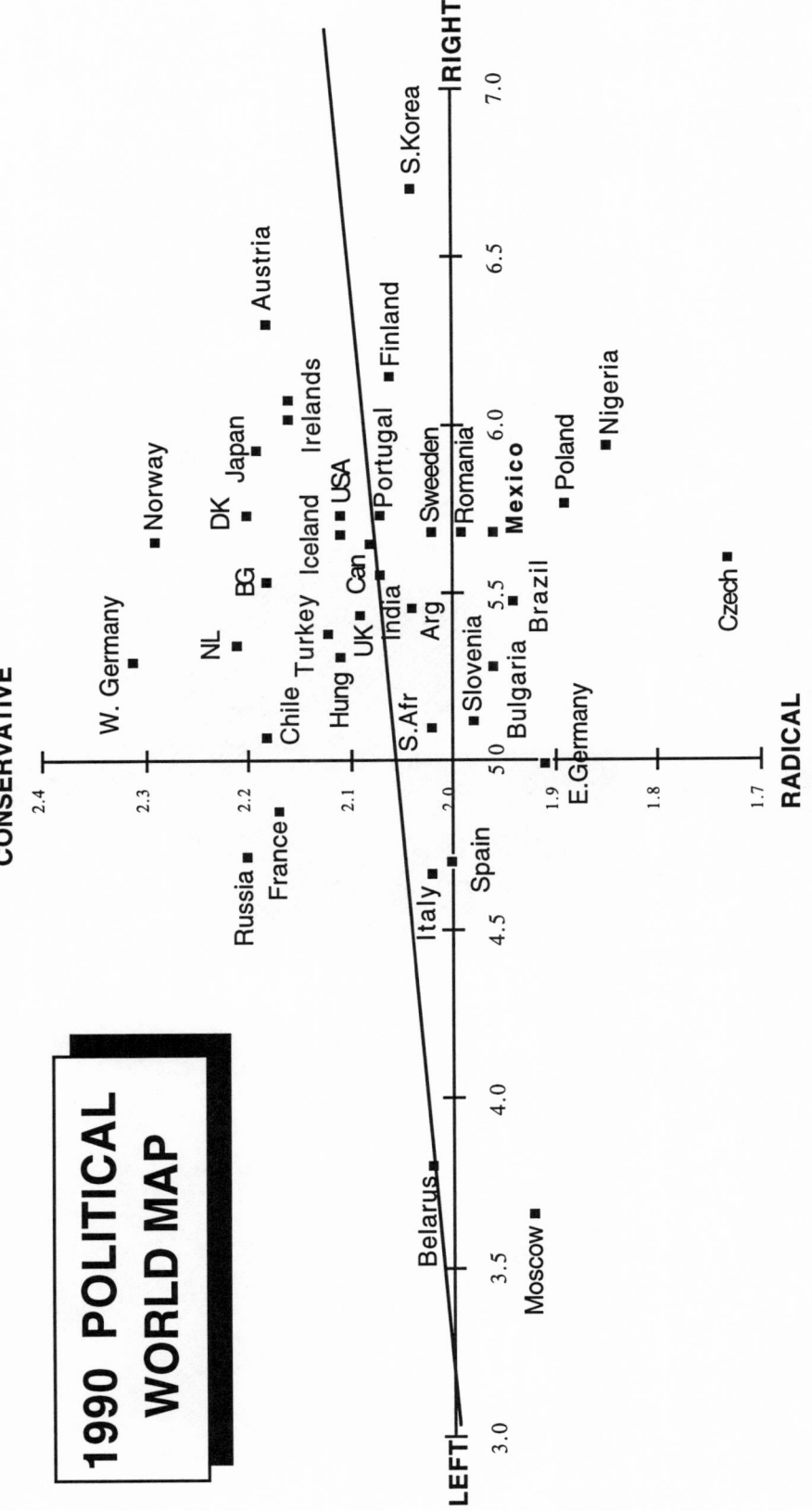

1990 POLITICAL WORLD MAP

CONSERVATIVE

LEFT

RIGHT

RADICAL

M. Basáñez, R. Inglehart and A. Moreno, *Human Values and Beleifs: Cross Cultural Sourcebook*

V249. Attitudes toward society

Our present society must be
valiantly defended against all
subversive forces
17%

The entire way our society is
organised must be radically
changed by revolutionary action
12%

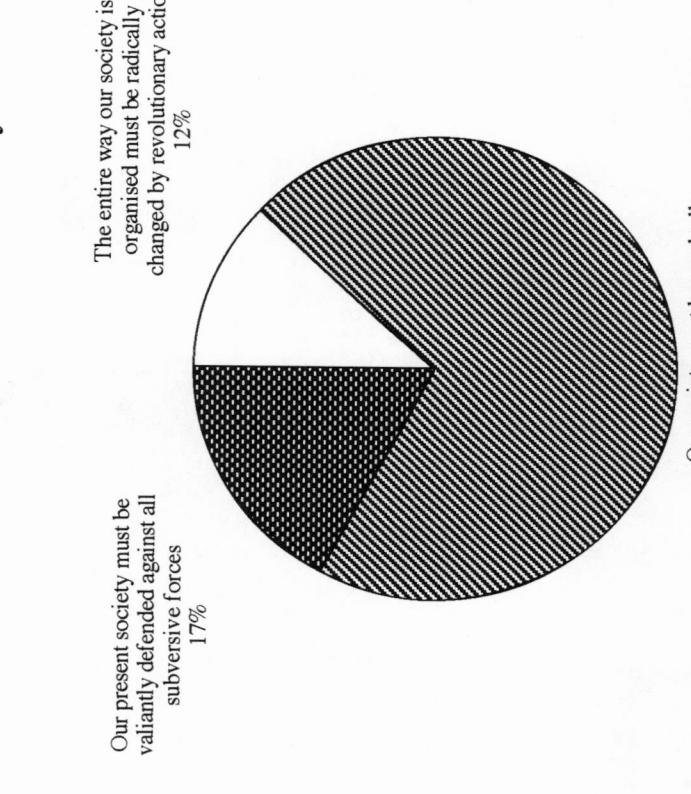

Our society must be gradually
improved by reforms
71%

V249 SOCIETAL CHANGE: % RADICAL

On this card are three basic kinds of attitudes concerning the society we live in. Please choose the one which best describes your own opinion. (% "The entire way our society is organised must be radically changed by revolutionary action")

	Total	Gender		Age			Education			Income			Political Affinity			Values			Ranking:	
		Male	Female	16-29	30-49	50+	Lower	Medium	Upper	Lower	Middle	Upper	Left	Center	Right	Mat	Mixed	Postmat		
India	14	16	12	16	13	12	10	14	16	15	14	13	22	17	07	13	15	12	Czechoslovakia	42
Nigeria	28	31	24	31	26	19	21	28	31	29	26	27	33	22	32	27	28	31	Moscow	33
China	05	07	03	08	05	02	06	05	06	04	05	06	na	na	na	03	06	21	Lithuania	32
Romania	na	na	na	na	na	na	na	na	na	na	na	na	na	na	na	na	na	na	Latvia	31
Turkey	14	15	12	17	12	11	11	16	22	17	11	14	30	10	06	07	13	24	Nigeria	28
Poland	23	26	19	25	21	24	23	23	22	26	23	20	25	23	23	19	25	21	Belarus	26
Bulgaria	22	24	21	27	21	20	18	20	29	24	17	23	19	22	34	13	23	45	Poland	23
Chile	05	05	06	08	04	03	07	05	04	08	05	03	10	03	06	04	05	09	Bulgaria	22
Czechoslovakia	42	47	38	42	43	42	36	44	50	43	41	43	33	41	52	35	44	49	Estonia	22
South Africa	19	20	18	20	19	17	19	20	14	18	20	16	23	17	13	16	19	32	South Africa	19
Lithuania	32	37	27	39	35	22	25	32	38	28	33	38	na	na	na	26	33	37	Mexico	17
Hungary	06	08	04	07	09	03	05	07	09	05	08	04	09	05	02	07	06	03	Russia	17
Argentina	08	09	06	10	06	07	06	08	10	07	07	09	31	05	10	04	07	15	Brazil	16
Brazil	16	18	15	23	14	08	10	18	22	15	15	18	26	16	10	12	18	34	India	14
Mexico	17	19	13	15	17	18	20	13	10	17	18	16	31	14	09	15	17	12	Turkey	14
Belarus	26	30	23	33	25	23	17	26	30	25	26	28	33	17	10	18	28	53	Slovenia	14
Russia	17	23	13	27	19	09	10	18	21	14	18	19	29	16	17	08	22	32	East Germany	13
Moscow	33	41	28	39	34	29	26	31	37	28	35	38	43	20	12	21	35	52	Argentina	08
Latvia	31	35	28	40	27	29	26	29	37	31	33	30	na	na	na	26	30	43	South Korea	07
Estonia	22	27	16	27	23	13	16	21	27	21	21	23	12	11	na	12	24	40	Italy	07
Portugal	04	04	03	05	02	04	05	03	03	04	04	05	04	01	04	04	05	01	United States	07
South Korea	07	08	07	11	06	06	10	05	09	11	03	06	20	06	04	05	09	13	Hungary	06
Ireland	04	06	02	05	04	03	04	03	05	03	04	03	14	03	01	04	04	03	Sweden	06
North Ireland	05	05	05	13	02	03	06	00	10	06	05	01	11	04	04	03	05	07	China	05
Slovenia	14	12	17	11	16	14	15	17	11	20	12	10	12	11	na	12	14	19	Chile	05
Spain	04	05	03	05	05	01	03	04	07	02	04	05	08	01	02	01	02	10	North Ireland	05
East Germany	13	16	10	17	12	10	12	16	13	13	09	14	10	14	17	09	13	13	Britain	05
Britain	05	05	05	07	06	04	06	04	03	05	07	01	11	04	01	05	05	07	Canada	05
Italy	07	08	06	10	06	06	07	09	09	08	05	06	11	01	09	07	06	10	Portugal	04
Netherlands	02	02	02	03	03	02	02	02	02	02	02	02	02	01	02	03	02	02	Ireland	04
Belgium	03	04	03	04	04	02	03	04	02	02	04	02	06	03	02	03	03	05	Spain	04
Austria	02	02	02	05	02	01	03	03	01	02	02	03	04	01	03	04	02	01	France	04
France	04	06	03	06	05	02	05	04	03	04	07	03	06	04	03	06	03	04	Belgium	03
Canada	05	04	06	08	06	02	08	04	04	08	05	03	05	05	03	03	05	05	Iceland	03
United States	07	07	06	09	07	06	09	08	05	06	09	04	07	06	07	09	06	08	Finland	03
Iceland	03	04	02	05	02	03	05	03	02	na	04	02	03	05	03	05	03	03	Netherlands	02
West Germany	02	02	02	02	02	02	02	02	03	02	02	03	03	01	01	01	02	02	Austria	02
Denmark	02	01	02	01	01	03	02	03	04	04	03	00	04	04	03	03	02	06	West Germany	02
Finland	03	03	03	04	03	03	01	02	02	05	03	02	04	04	01	03	05	06	Denmark	02
Norway	02	01	04	04	03	01	03	03	02	02	03	02	03	02	02	04	02	04	Norway	02
Sweden	06	05	07	09	07	03	07	08	02	05	10	04	08	06	05	10	06	05	Japan	02
Japan	02	01	03	03	02	02	03	02	02	03	02	02	02	02	00	01	02	02		
Switzerland	na	na	na	na	na	na	na	na	na	na	na	na	na	na	na	na	na	na		
Total	**12**	**13**	**10**	**15**	**12**	**10**	**11**	**12**	**13**	**12**	**12**	**12**	**15**	**09**	**09**	**10**	**12**	**17**		

Note: Countries in the left column are ranked according to GNP per capita. / The percentages in the bottom row give each country an equal weight. / na=not ascertained.

V249 SOCIETAL CHANGE: % GRADUAL REFORM (MODERATE)

On this card are three basic kinds of attitudes concerning the society we live in. Please choose the one which best describes your own opinion. (% "Our society must be gradually improved by reforms")

	Total	Gender		Age			Education			Income			Political Affinity			Values			Ranking:	
		Male	Female	16-29	30-49	50+	Lower	Medium	Upper	Lower	Middle	Upper	Left	Center	Right	Mat	Mixed	Postmat		
India	69	66	73	64	72	71	72	68	68	68	66	66	58	70	77	72	68	62	Spain	91
Nigeria	59	58	60	53	64	70	69	58	56	61	60	58	54	62	56	58	60	59	Finland	88
China	70	70	71	73	70	67	65	69	84	66	70	76	na	na	na	67	74	72	Sweden	86
Romania	na	na	na	na	na	na	na	na	na	na	na	na	na	na	na	na	na	na	Portugal	85
Turkey	61	63	58	59	63	60	55	68	72	56	63	63	59	62	61	61	59	63	East Germany	84
Poland	65	65	66	69	66	63	60	67	74	61	68	68	66	69	63	62	66	70	Italy	83
Bulgaria	59	61	58	58	61	58	55	64	57	58	61	62	61	62	53	60	61	49	Canada	82
Chile	72	75	68	67	75	73	64	72	80	64	71	80	71	77	60	63	74	75	Iceland	82
Czechoslovakia	42	38	46	38	41	47	50	41	33	42	44	40	52	42	37	46	43	31	Argentina	81
South Africa	60	61	60	61	60	58	60	59	68	58	60	65	59	66	54	62	59	57	South Korea	81
Lithuania	59	55	61	54	56	65	60	58	59	60	58	57	na	na	na	65	57	49	Britain	81
Hungary	77	78	75	78	79	73	67	83	86	68	81	88	84	77	70	77	76	82	Austria	78
Argentina	81	80	82	78	84	81	81	81	82	80	80	81	63	85	76	82	82	78	Hungary	77
Brazil	74	73	74	68	77	78	72	74	76	70	73	78	65	76	77	77	73	64	Denmark	77
Mexico	71	68	75	74	69	65	68	72	78	70	70	72	61	72	76	72	69	80	Japan	77
Belarus	46	47	45	41	49	44	42	46	46	44	48	43	44	51	45	47	45	33	Ireland	76
Russia	49	51	47	46	49	51	47	45	53	48	47	56	51	54	45	49	48	51	North Ireland	75
Moscow	41	39	43	40	45	36	30	42	43	41	42	42	39	50	38	44	42	32	Netherlands	75
Latvia	59	56	60	52	62	59	52	60	57	59	57	60	78	na	na	63	60	47	Belgium	75
Estonia	61	59	63	55	64	63	57	62	64	64	60	58	na	na	na	68	60	50	France	75
Portugal	85	88	83	82	86	88	83	93	88	85	85	85	88	88	80	83	86	89	United States	75
South Korea	81	78	85	81	83	79	69	82	87	75	87	85	76	82	83	80	83	83	Brazil	74
Ireland	76	75	77	87	73	72	72	80	88	69	77	82	78	79	73	76	74	85	Slovenia	73
North Ireland	75	75	74	74	75	75	73	77	79	70	73	85	71	76	73	77	73	79	Chile	72
Slovenia	73	75	72	79	73	71	69	71	83	64	76	83	82	76	73	70	74	80	Mexico	71
Spain	91	90	92	91	91	91	91	91	90	90	90	90	89	94	89	91	93	87	China	70
East Germany	84	81	86	80	85	86	84	83	84	82	90	82	88	83	76	86	83	85	India	69
Britain	81	80	81	85	84	75	77	86	93	71	80	91	76	83	81	80	80	83	West Germany	66
Italy	83	83	84	82	87	81	83	87	73	81	86	91	82	86	79	80	84	85	Norway	66
Netherlands	75	68	78	76	82	64	69	74	83	75	71	82	83	76	69	50	73	84	Poland	65
Belgium	75	75	75	81	74	73	75	71	84	72	75	80	78	74	74	66	75	85	Turkey	61
Austria	78	79	77	80	82	73	73	80	85	77	76	81	79	80	75	66	76	87	Estonia	61
France	75	77	72	70	74	79	70	77	81	72	74	76	80	74	71	71	74	78	South Africa	60
Canada	82	83	81	82	84	79	82	82	88	74	85	87	85	82	80	81	82	84	Nigeria	59
United States	75	74	77	80	79	69	67	73	84	71	75	83	83	77	70	76	74	80	Bulgaria	59
Iceland	82	82	83	86	86	71	74	82	89	na	na	na	84	84	80	80	81	95	Lithuania	59
West Germany	66	66	66	75	73	55	62	72	75	65	66	69	79	67	50	47	61	85	Latvia	59
Denmark	77	79	74	80	80	66	67	77	82	74	77	83	88	75	69	68	75	89	Russia	49
Finland	88	87	90	90	89	84	88	86	90	86	89	89	92	86	85	80	90	85	Belarus	46
Norway	66	71	60	74	73	53	49	63	78	58	71	77	76	61	67	60	65	90	Czechoslovakia	42
Sweden	86	88	84	87	88	83	79	86	94	85	79	92	87	86	86	81	84	92	Moscow	41
Japan	77	77	77	80	77	76	71	77	81	71	81	77	90	80	65	71	77	91		
Switzerland	na	na	na	na	na	na	na	na	na	na	na	na	na	na	na	na	na	na		
Total	71	71	71	71	73	69	67	72	75	68	71	74	73	74	69	69	71	73		

Note: Countries in the left column are ranked according to GNP per capita. / The percentages in the bottom row give each country an equal weight. / na=not ascertained.

V249 SOCIETAL CHANGE: % DEFEND SOCIETY (CONSERVATIVE)

On this card are three basic kinds of attitudes concerning the society we live in. Please choose the one which best describes your own opinion.
(% "Our present society must be valiantly defended against all subversive forces")

	Total	Gender		Age			Education			Income			Political Affinity			Values			Ranking:	
		Male	Female	16-29	30-49	50+	Lower	Medium	Upper	Lower	Middle	Upper	Left	Center	Right	Mat	Mixed	Postmat		
India	17	19	15	20	15	17	17	18	17	17	20	15	20	14	16	15	17	27	Russia	34
Nigeria	13	11	16	16	10	11	11	15	12	10	15	15	13	16	12	15	12	10	West Germany	32
China	25	24	26	18	26	31	29	26	10	30	24	18	na	na	na	30	20	08	Norway	31
Romania	na	na	na	na	na	na	na	na	na	na	na	na	na	na	na	na	na	na	Belarus	28
Turkey	26	22	30	24	26	29	35	17	06	28	26	23	11	28	33	32	28	13	Turkey	26
Poland	12	09	15	07	13	14	17	10	04	13	09	13	10	09	14	19	10	08	China	25
Bulgaria	19	16	21	14	18	22	27	17	14	17	22	15	20	17	14	27	16	06	Moscow	25
Chile	23	20	27	26	21	24	29	23	16	28	24	18	19	21	34	33	21	17	Chile	23
Czechoslovakia	15	15	16	20	16	12	14	16	17	14	15	18	16	17	11	20	13	20	Netherlands	23
South Africa	21	20	22	19	21	24	21	22	19	24	20	20	18	17	34	23	22	12	Denmark	22
Lithuania	10	08	12	07	09	13	14	10	03	13	10	05	na	na	na	09	10	14	South Africa	21
Hungary	17	14	21	14	12	24	28	10	05	28	11	09	07	18	21	17	18	15	North Ireland	21
Argentina	11	11	12	12	10	12	13	10	08	13	13	10	06	10	23	15	11	08	Belgium	21
Brazil	10	09	11	09	10	14	18	08	02	16	12	04	09	09	13	12	10	03	France	21
Mexico	13	14	12	11	14	17	12	16	12	13	12	12	08	14	15	14	13	08	Japan	21
Belarus	28	24	32	27	27	33	41	28	24	32	25	29	23	33	45	35	26	13	Ireland	20
Russia	34	27	40	28	32	41	43	37	26	37	35	26	21	31	38	43	30	17	Austria	20
Moscow	25	20	30	22	21	35	45	27	20	31	23	21	19	30	51	35	23	17	Bulgaria	19
Latvia	11	08	12	08	11	12	23	11	06	11	10	11	na	na	na	12	10	10	United States	18
Estonia	17	13	21	18	13	24	28	17	09	16	18	18	na	na	na	20	17	10	India	17
Portugal	11	08	13	13	12	08	13	05	09	11	11	11	08	08	16	13	09	10	Hungary	17
South Korea	15	15	09	08	12	15	21	14	04	14	10	09	04	12	13	15	09	04	Estonia	17
Ireland	20	19	21	07	23	25	24	17	08	28	18	15	07	19	26	21	22	12	Czechoslovakia	15
North Ireland	21	20	21	14	23	22	21	23	10	24	22	14	18	20	23	20	22	14	Iceland	15
Slovenia	12	13	12	10	11	16	17	12	07	16	12	08	06	13	08	16	12	02	Britain	14
Spain	06	06	05	05	04	08	06	05	03	08	06	04	03	05	09	08	05	04	Nigeria	13
East Germany	04	03	04	03	04	04	04	01	03	05	06	04	02	03	07	05	04	02	Mexico	13
Britain	14	15	14	08	11	21	17	10	04	24	13	08	13	13	18	15	15	10	Canada	13
Italy	10	09	10	08	07	12	10	04	18	11	09	04	06	10	12	13	10	05	Poland	12
Netherlands	23	30	20	21	17	34	29	23	16	24	27	16	15	23	30	47	25	14	Slovenia	12
Belgium	21	21	22	15	22	24	22	25	14	26	22	18	17	23	24	32	23	10	Argentina	11
Austria	20	19	21	15	16	26	25	18	15	21	22	17	18	19	22	30	22	12	Latvia	11
France	21	17	25	24	21	19	25	19	17	24	20	21	15	22	27	23	23	17	Portugal	11
Canada	13	13	13	10	12	17	19	14	08	19	11	10	08	13	17	16	13	11	South Korea	11
United States	18	18	17	11	14	25	24	20	12	23	17	14	10	17	24	15	20	12	Lithuania	10
Iceland	15	14	15	09	12	26	21	15	09	na	na	na	13	12	17	15	16	03	Brazil	10
West Germany	32	32	32	24	25	43	37	26	22	33	32	30	18	32	49	53	38	13	Italy	10
Denmark	22	20	24	14	19	31	30	22	17	25	21	17	11	23	29	29	23	10	Finland	09
Finland	09	11	07	06	08	14	11	11	06	09	09	10	05	08	14	17	08	10	Sweden	08
Norway	31	27	36	23	24	45	49	34	21	39	27	22	21	36	32	37	34	06	Spain	06
Sweden	08	07	10	04	05	15	14	06	03	10	11	04	05	08	09	09	10	03	East Germany	04
Japan	21	22	20	17	21	23	25	22	17	27	17	21	08	18	35	28	21	08		
Switzerland	na	na	na	na	na	na	na	na	na	na	na	na	na	na	na	na	na	na		
Total	**17**	**16**	**19**	**14**	**16**	**22**	**23**	**17**	**12**	**20**	**17**	**14**	**12**	**17**	**23**	**22**	**17**	**10**		

Note: Countries in the left column are ranked according to GNP per capita. / The percenages in the bottom row give each country an equal weight. / na=not ascertained.

V250. Income equality

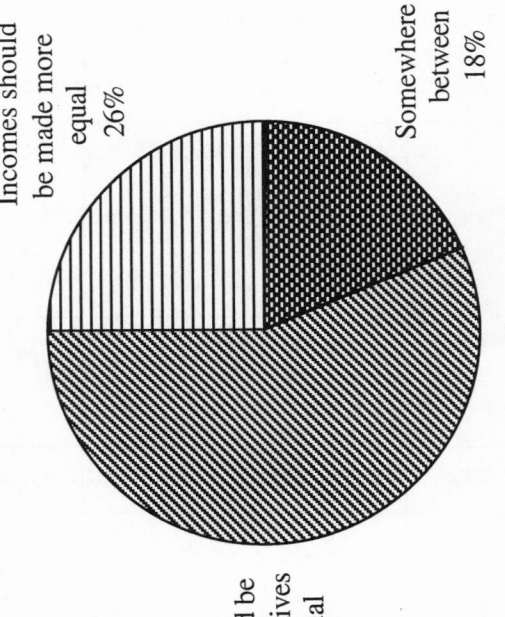

Incomes should be made more equal
26%

Somewhere in between
18%

There should be greater incentives for individual effort
56%

V251. Ownership of business and industry

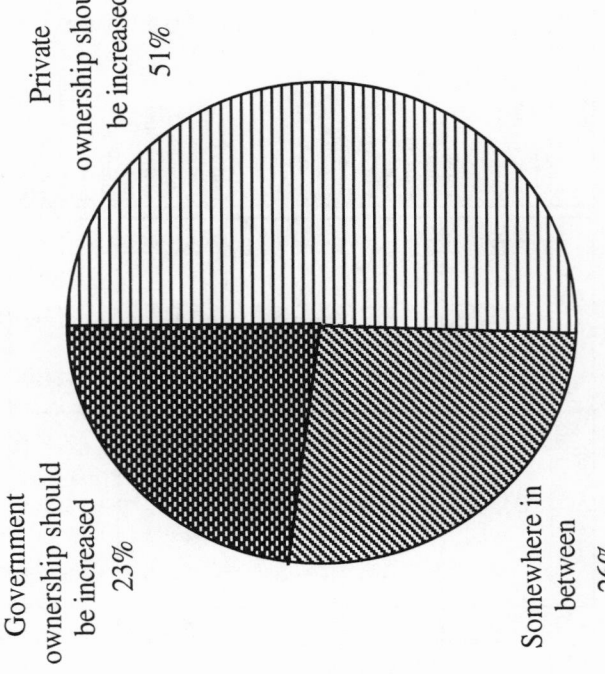

Private ownership should be increased
51%

Government ownership should be increased
23%

Somewhere in between
26%

V250 INCOME EQUALITY

"There should be greater incentives for individual effort" (% "agree"—codes 7 to 10 from a ten-point scale)

	Total	Gender		Age			Education			Income			Political Affinity			Values		
		Male	Female	16-29	30-49	50+	Lower	Medium	Upper	Lower	Middle	Upper	Left	Center	Right	Mat	Mixed	Postmat
India	47	49	44	47	47	47	34	46	54	38	46	55	42	44	58	49	47	44
Nigeria	74	74	72	73	74	70	72	71	77	73	75	73	72	73	77	75	74	74
China	80	81	79	85	80	76	77	79	89	81	81	80	na	na	na	74	86	93
Romania	55	59	51	62	58	47	39	58	72	46	51	67	36	55	77	43	62	80
Turkey	31	33	30	35	29	29	30	31	36	26	32	36	19	33	42	25	34	30
Poland	79	81	78	77	80	80	75	80	94	77	77	85	80	80	84	76	81	83
Bulgaria	61	65	58	71	67	48	43	58	83	60	60	67	57	59	76	49	65	80
Chile	47	48	46	48	45	47	42	47	52	41	45	55	40	48	55	43	46	53
Czechoslovakia	78	80	76	80	80	74	69	81	85	74	80	80	76	77	82	69	81	82
South Africa	37	34	39	28	41	45	22	38	80	21	31	72	36	46	45	42	34	35
Lithuania	73	77	69	75	75	69	65	74	85	67	74	84	na	na	na	63	74	80
Hungary	49	57	41	51	56	41	34	59	75	34	54	78	50	53	59	44	52	65
Argentina	65	67	63	62	67	65	57	65	76	56	64	72	53	70	74	61	67	65
Brazil	48	46	50	46	51	47	41	49	61	42	48	53	44	51	50	45	50	48
Mexico	50	50	50	52	51	43	47	48	61	39	54	67	42	49	61	44	53	49
Belarus	71	74	68	67	73	70	66	67	77	69	70	75	75	64	74	69	71	87
Russia	63	68	58	64	70	52	54	61	68	58	64	68	70	61	66	52	68	80
Moscow	78	82	75	81	79	75	62	76	82	72	82	83	83	74	68	66	81	87
Latvia	68	76	63	70	69	65	49	65	80	63	68	72	na	74	na	58	70	83
Estonia	77	82	73	78	80	72	73	76	87	74	81	78	na	na	na	58	79	90
Portugal	25	26	24	34	22	19	18	35	43	17	23	39	16	27	33	73	21	32
South Korea	39	40	38	32	39	52	35	38	39	34	38	51	25	35	46	42	38	34
Ireland	58	59	58	58	63	54	44	67	69	44	58	69	47	60	65	55	57	68
North Ireland	67	69	66	49	67	68	50	72	76	71	71	75	54	63	80	62	69	67
Slovenia	48	51	45	45	50	42	34	51	68	33	52	68	57	53	63	42	48	69
Spain	32	33	31	38	32	27	29	38	38	23	31	39	25	40	46	30	32	34
East Germany	74	79	69	77	78	68	70	78	84	66	74	81	75	74	83	60	75	77
Britain	58	65	52	58	59	58	55	68	64	47	66	69	41	59	78	63	59	51
Italy	47	52	43	49	51	43	46	62	56	40	53	70	40	51	59	46	46	54
Netherlands	48	57	45	45	48	54	50	47	48	38	50	61	28	50	71	41	56	40
Belgium	50	52	48	54	51	46	41	54	61	43	46	59	34	55	64	41	53	51
Austria	42	47	39	43	44	39	40	42	57	30	44	50	47	42	41	36	42	45
France	40	43	37	42	37	39	36	40	48	29	37	52	23	49	64	35	40	44
Canada	63	64	62	61	64	64	56	65	67	56	61	72	55	61	77	58	65	59
United States	62	66	58	57	65	63	51	64	68	56	67	65	50	61	74	58	62	68
Iceland	47	55	39	52	47	41	41	55	46	na	na	na	27	48	64	47	48	41
West Germany	52	55	48	53	54	49	50	52	56	44	52	58	44	52	63	51	55	46
Denmark	57	60	53	59	52	61	52	60	56	53	53	62	26	55	80	51	61	38
Finland	61	65	57	60	61	48	50	58	70	49	56	77	35	52	83	61	61	62
Norway	47	52	41	49	45	48	36	45	54	38	46	61	26	44	72	66	60	62
Sweden	58	63	53	56	58	62	51	57	73	53	48	68	32	56	82	56	50	35
Japan	34	43	26	30	36	35	31	34	39	26	34	44	33	31	53	33	39	26
Switzerland	na	na	na	na	na	na	49	na	na	50	na	na	38	na	na	na	na	na
Total	56	59	53	57	57	53	49	57	66	49	56	66	45	54	66	52	58	59

Ranking:

China	80
Poland	79
Czechoslovakia	78
Moscow	78
Estonia	77
Nigeria	74
East Germany	74
Lithuania	73
Belarus	71
Latvia	68
North Ireland	67
Argentina	65
Russia	63
Canada	63
United States	62
Bulgaria	61
Finland	61
Ireland	58
Britain	58
Sweden	58
Denmark	57
Romania	55
West Germany	52
Mexico	50
Belgium	49
Hungary	48
Brazil	48
Slovenia	48
Netherlands	47
India	47
Chile	47
Italy	47
Iceland	47
Norway	47
Austria	42
France	40
South Korea	39
South Africa	37
Japan	34
Spain	32
Turkey	31
Portugal	25

Note: Countries in the left column are ranked according to GNP per capita. / The percentages in the bottom row give each country an equal weight. / na=not ascertained.

V251 OWNERSHIP OF BUSINESS

"Government ownership of business and industry should be increased" (% "agree"—codes 7 to 10 from a ten-point scale)

	Total	Gender Male	Gender Female	Age 16-29	Age 30-49	Age 50+	Education Lower	Education Medium	Education Upper	Income Lower	Income Middle	Income Upper	Political Affinity Left	Political Affinity Center	Political Affinity Right	Values Mat	Values Mixed	Values Postmat
India	31	29	32	30	33	28	31	29	33	29	31	31	37	24	33	29	32	26
Nigeria	50	49	51	51	49	39	54	49	48	49	52	46	48	48	52	53	48	44
China	61	58	65	48	62	74	70	59	47	69	59	53	na	na	na	70	57	15
Romania	31	26	37	26	30	36	45	29	17	38	34	24	49	29	23	41	26	07
Turkey	42	36	48	43	40	43	49	34	25	51	43	30	51	37	41	39	45	37
Poland	24	22	26	17	22	29	31	22	11	27	24	19	31	23	18	27	23	19
Bulgaria	20	20	21	14	19	25	33	19	12	19	20	20	24	17	16	24	21	05
Chile	41	39	43	45	40	38	46	40	37	48	42	33	48	36	42	41	40	47
Czechoslovakia	19	17	21	12	17	28	27	17	14	24	20	15	30	18	12	25	18	11
South Africa	25	25	24	27	23	22	32	24	08	36	25	10	27	17	16	20	26	32
Lithuania	28	22	33	18	29	36	34	28	16	34	26	19	na	na	na	36	27	20
Hungary	17	16	19	18	17	17	20	15	08	20	17	13	21	17	17	17	17	23
Argentina	18	14	21	24	14	17	21	17	15	22	16	13	31	15	15	20	16	20
Brazil	37	30	44	39	35	35	44	37	21	46	36	26	37	28	44	40	35	30
Mexico	24	23	27	25	26	18	23	30	24	25	25	21	32	17	26	24	23	24
Belarus	42	37	47	33	42	54	55	41	40	47	40	42	38	42	72	54	38	18
Russia	40	32	46	27	38	51	53	37	35	44	40	34	24	36	51	52	34	10
Moscow	31	26	36	23	27	44	55	36	24	38	28	26	24	34	57	42	31	14
Latvia	22	17	25	15	22	28	28	24	15	19	22	22	na	na	na	30	20	16
Estonia	19	15	23	18	18	22	22	20	15	19	19	19	25	14	17	26	17	07
Portugal	18	16	19	17	20	16	17	23	17	18	20	15	25	14	17	19	16	23
South Korea	29	37	21	27	29	29	45	31	18	35	27	21	33	24	30	31	27	23
Ireland	15	14	16	12	16	16	16	15	11	16	14	15	23	12	16	11	15	18
North Ireland	21	21	20	21	22	18	21	22	14	32	17	14	25	16	28	18	21	23
Slovenia	17	13	20	08	17	24	23	14	12	23	16	08	16	14	13	23	15	08
Spain	36	38	35	37	39	32	35	37	39	36	42	33	46	33	24	39	35	37
East Germany	09	08	09	08	08	10	09	07	09	10	06	10	13	07	07	14	09	03
Britain	22	24	20	19	23	23	24	17	18	26	23	16	36	18	16	22	20	31
Italy	18	17	19	18	18	19	18	19	15	22	15	09	24	12	15	16	18	21
Netherlands	10	10	10	09	10	11	10	09	12	16	07	08	14	10	06	09	08	14
Belgium	14	13	14	13	14	14	15	14	10	19	15	09	22	13	11	10	15	13
Austria	08	08	08	07	05	11	10	05	08	12	06	07	14	08	06	11	08	05
France	18	19	18	17	22	15	19	19	14	19	23	16	26	14	12	26	16	19
Canada	10	10	10	13	08	09	09	10	10	14	08	08	14	09	09	06	10	12
United States	07	08	07	10	07	07	07	08	07	09	08	05	09	06	10	08	08	08
Iceland	11	09	12	11	10	11	12	11	09	na	na	na	19	09	05	08	10	16
West Germany	09	08	09	11	10	07	08	09	14	10	10	07	19	06	03	09	07	12
Denmark	11	10	11	12	11	09	09	11	11	10	10	11	24	09	04	07	10	17
Finland	06	06	05	01	06	08	08	07	03	08	06	03	19	03	02	16	05	06
Norway	14	12	16	12	14	15	15	14	13	17	15	11	23	13	08	11	14	17
Sweden	14	12	18	13	12	16	14	14	12	16	20	10	28	11	06	19	12	17
Japan	17	16	19	18	18	15	17	19	14	20	16	17	31	11	15	14	15	29
Switzerland	na	na	na	na	na	na	na	na	na	na	na	na	na	na	na	na	na	na
Total	23	21	24	21	22	24	27	22	18	27	23	19	28	19	21	25	22	19

Ranking:

61	China
50	Nigeria
42	Turkey
42	Belarus
41	Chile
40	Russia
37	Brazil
36	Spain
31	India
31	Romania
31	Moscow
29	South Korea
28	Lithuania
25	South Africa
24	Poland
24	Mexico
22	Latvia
22	Britain
21	North Ireland
20	Bulgaria
19	Czechoslovakia
19	Estonia
18	Argentina
18	Portugal
18	Italy
18	France
17	Hungary
17	Slovenia
17	Japan
15	Ireland
14	Belgium
14	Norway
14	Sweden
11	Iceland
11	Denmark
10	Netherlands
10	Canada
09	East Germany
09	West Germany
08	Austria
07	United States
06	Finland

Note: Countries in the left column are ranked according to GNP per capita. / The percentages in the bottom row give each country an equal weight. / na=not ascertained.

V252. Responsibility to provide

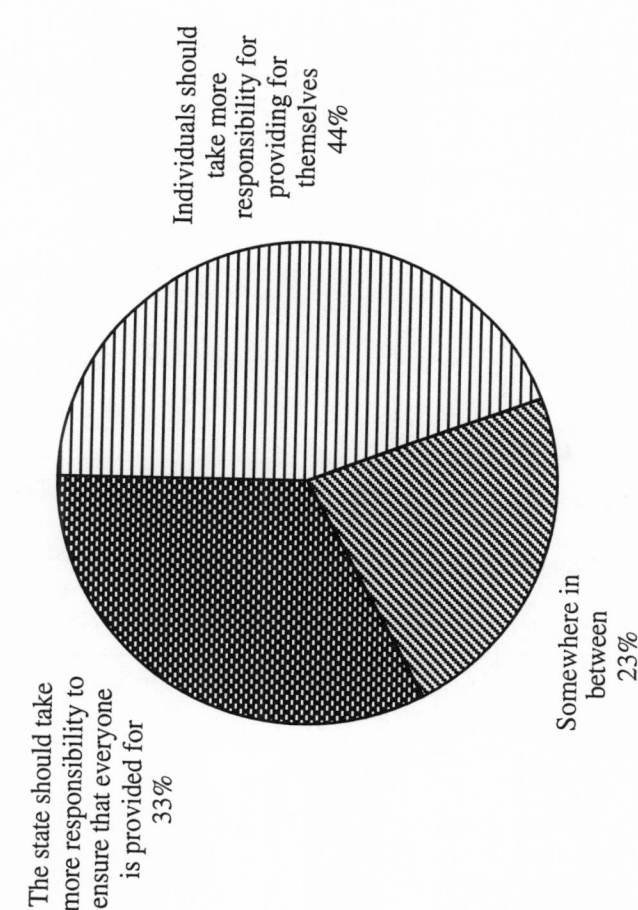

Individuals should take more responsibility for providing for themselves
44%

Somewhere in between
23%

The state should take more responsibility to ensure that everyone is provided for
33%

V252 RESPONSIBILITY

"The state should take more responsibility to ensure that everyone is provided for"   (% "agree"—codes 7 to 10 from a ten-point scale)

	Total	Gender		Age			Education			Income			Political Affinity			Values		
		Male	Female	16-29	30-49	50+	Lower	Medium	Upper	Lower	Middle	Upper	Left	Center	Right	Mat	Mixed	Postmat
India	20	18	23	19	21	22	24	19	21	21	17	23	24	18	21	19	20	19
Nigeria	54	56	50	54	54	46	52	51	57	50	58	53	51	56	55	49	56	60
China	33	33	33	31	32	37	34	34	28	28	32	41	na	na	na	37	30	26
Romania	37	32	41	33	39	37	42	38	27	43	37	31	46	40	29	43	34	14
Turkey	50	48	53	52	51	47	53	48	41	57	50	43	62	48	43	43	54	51
Poland	37	38	36	37	34	39	48	33	17	36	36	38	32	35	35	37	38	31
Bulgaria	35	31	39	33	34	38	42	36	27	37	36	29	32	32	32	43	34	18
Chile	55	54	56	59	52	53	58	54	53	58	58	48	60	55	45	57	56	52
Czechoslovakia	40	38	41	40	38	42	47	39	29	42	43	34	44	41	34	49	38	26
South Africa	39	42	36	44	36	36	50	37	12	51	41	17	38	31	36	32	42	49
Lithuania	44	39	48	45	42	44	47	42	44	44	47	37	na	na	na	44	45	42
Hungary	50	49	51	49	49	51	55	47	42	58	46	41	50	49	49	51	50	29
Argentina	33	32	35	39	32	31	36	32	30	40	35	23	47	31	37	39	32	29
Brazil	41	36	46	44	39	40	45	43	27	46	44	33	44	36	45	42	41	43
Mexico	35	36	33	34	36	34	35	37	32	38	31	34	36	34	30	32	36	30
Belarus	43	40	45	41	43	46	46	44	42	46	41	43	45	39	50	40	46	41
Russia	32	29	35	32	31	34	35	35	28	35	30	27	25	30	39	38	29	19
Moscow	35	29	40	36	33	38	31	42	31	42	33	29	33	40	38	38	35	31
Latvia	55	45	62	55	56	55	49	59	50	58	57	52	na	na	na	59	57	38
Estonia	35	32	37	32	36	37	36	36	28	35	38	31	36	34	30	42	32	19
Portugal	28	25	31	33	26	24	28	30	25	29	33	21	36	28	24	30	28	26
South Korea	25	28	23	31	22	21	24	25	25	30	23	19	35	24	22	21	25	42
Ireland	30	26	33	38	30	25	31	30	20	37	28	26	41	29	23	24	30	36
North Ireland	36	37	35	44	40	26	37	35	28	46	29	33	46	37	30	24	36	49
Slovenia	44	40	48	47	45	41	48	46	34	53	44	28	46	39	36	45	45	28
Spain	44	44	45	43	47	42	44	40	48	43	47	45	50	47	41	43	44	49
East Germany	23	21	24	18	19	29	25	14	20	30	20	17	26	19	18	37	22	16
Britain	33	33	32	36	30	33	36	23	30	39	32	28	44	32	21	32	32	39
Italy	39	37	41	45	39	37	41	25	42	44	35	29	44	33	36	38	38	44
Netherlands	23	18	26	21	26	22	28	24	18	27	22	17	29	21	17	29	24	20
Belgium	29	29	30	29	30	29	31	29	25	35	33	28	33	24	26	29	29	31
Austria	14	10	17	13	12	17	16	13	15	17	14	12	22	13	11	24	13	12
France	19	15	22	20	18	18	22	18	12	24	20	13	20	17	14	23	18	17
Canada	19	18	21	25	19	14	24	18	18	28	18	14	24	18	18	18	20	18
United States	14	15	12	18	13	11	12	15	12	15	14	12	21	11	13	12	13	15
Iceland	26	22	30	24	28	24	29	19	28	na	na	na	39	26	17	24	25	38
West Germany	22	18	26	26	21	21	23	21	18	27	23	18	32	19	16	24	21	24
Denmark	16	15	17	22	17	11	17	17	15	20	17	12	27	15	11	14	15	23
Finland	20	19	21	07	22	26	26	25	10	23	22	15	33	17	15	22	22	15
Norway	21	20	22	27	22	16	22	21	20	23	21	18	32	18	15	20	20	36
Sweden	11	11	11	15	09	08	13	10	08	11	13	08	15	11	05	13	09	12
Japan	55	51	60	53	55	57	60	56	48	59	55	51	68	47	48	51	57	62
Switzerland	na	na	na	na	na	na	na	na	na	na	na	na	na	na	na	na	na	na
Total	33	31	35	34	33	32	36	32	28	37	33	29	38	31	29	34	33	32

Ranking:

Chile	55
Latvia	55
Japan	55
Nigeria	54
Turkey	50
Hungary	50
Lithuania	44
Slovenia	44
Spain	44
Belarus	43
Brazil	41
Czechoslovakia	40
South Africa	39
Italy	39
Romania	37
Poland	37
North Ireland	36
Bulgaria	35
Mexico	35
Moscow	35
Estonia	35
China	33
Argentina	33
Britain	33
Russia	32
Ireland	30
Belgium	29
Portugal	28
Iceland	26
South Korea	25
East Germany	23
Netherlands	23
West Germany	22
Norway	21
India	20
Finland	20
France	19
Canada	19
Denmark	16
Austria	14
United States	14
Sweden	11

Note: Countries in the left column are ranked according to GNP per capita. / The percentages in the bottom row give each country an equal weight. / na=not ascertained.

V253. People who are unemployed...

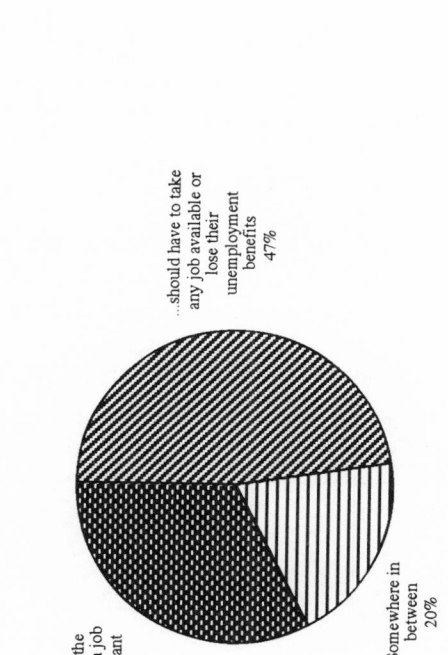

...should have to take any job available or lose their unemployment benefits
47%

Somewhere in between
20%

...should have the right to refuse a job they do not want
33%

V254. Competition

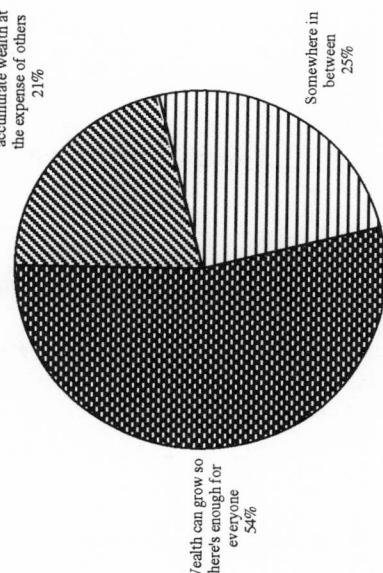

Competition is good. It stimulates people to work hard and develop new ideas
71%

Competition is harmful. It brings out the worst in people
12%

Somewhere in between
17%

V255. Hard work

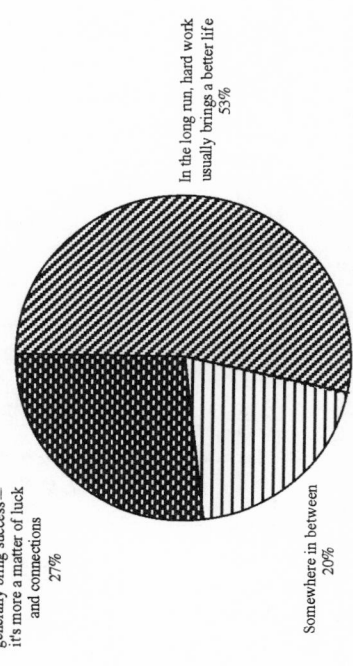

In the long run, hard work usually brings a better life
53%

Hard work doesn't generally bring success — it's more a matter of luck and connections
27%

Somewhere in between
20%

V256. Wealth

People can only accumulate wealth at the expense of others
21%

Somewhere in between
25%

Wealth can grow so there's enough for everyone
54%

V253 UNEMPLOYED

"People who are unemployed should have the right to refuse a job they do not want" (% "agree"—codes 7 to 10 from a ten-point scale)

	Total	Gender		Age			Education			Income			Political Affinity			Values		
		Male	Female	16-29	30-49	50+	Lower	Medium	Upper	Lower	Middle	Upper	Left	Center	Right	Mat	Mixed	Postmat
India	20	21	na	21	20	18	12	20	24	14	20	26	21	19	26	19	21	21
Nigeria	29	30	26	28	31	31	23	26	34	32	32	21	24	26	36	26	28	43
China	36	36	38	47	36	25	35	37	42	32	40	38	na	na	na	32	40	44
Romania	42	41	43	57	45	30	33	48	46	37	42	47	38	44	50	37	46	49
Turkey	na	na	na	na	na	na	na	na	na	na	na	na	na	na	na	na	na	na
Poland	39	40	38	50	45	27	30	46	39	41	37	40	38	41	37	29	43	53
Bulgaria	59	59	60	66	65	48	42	63	68	58	60	61	53	52	76	53	60	73
Chile	26	28	23	29	26	21	23	26	28	27	24	26	30	25	21	25	24	31
Czechoslovakia	41	40	41	47	47	29	33	44	47	37	42	44	47	41	35	40	39	53
South Africa	28	29	27	32	26	22	22	32	21	30	29	22	35	22	27	19	31	38
Lithuania	45	46	44	52	49	35	34	46	60	42	45	52	na	na	na	40	45	54
Hungary	39	44	35	43	43	34	38	39	48	38	38	45	45	36	40	36	41	60
Argentina	23	24	23	27	23	20	18	26	30	21	25	45	36	21	24	21	23	28
Brazil	38	39	38	44	37	29	30	41	43	35	42	39	47	36	36	34	41	44
Mexico	31	31	29	31	33	23	29	30	35	27	31	36	39	27	30	26	32	40
Belarus	39	38	40	45	39	34	30	38	44	37	36	44	43	35	27	28	43	58
Russia	41	43	39	52	44	29	32	45	41	38	38	43	45	35	42	35	43	56
Moscow	51	52	50	61	50	45	38	50	54	47	53	56	54	48	39	42	53	61
Latvia	68	70	67	71	72	57	51	69	72	68	67	70	na	na	na	65	70	78
Estonia	57	60	54	56	63	49	51	57	63	57	54	59	na	na	na	50	59	69
Portugal	27	28	27	35	29	18	26	29	33	26	29	29	27	28	26	22	29	40
South Korea	33	34	32	44	31	19	20	36	35	34	33	28	39	35	30	31	32	45
Ireland	37	35	39	38	40	34	37	37	39	41	36	36	51	33	38	34	38	38
North Ireland	39	47	32	47	35	37	38	39	38	47	35	40	46	37	39	30	43	36
Slovenia	11	12	11	16	13	07	10	12	13	12	11	14	15	09	11	09	12	18
Spain	30	34	27	41	33	19	26	38	43	23	33	36	40	32	20	19	32	45
East Germany	40	39	42	45	47	31	38	45	47	34	41	45	51	38	30	28	40	49
Britain	37	39	35	43	35	35	37	34	39	39	40	33	48	36	26	30	36	44
Italy	16	16	17	21	16	13	15	24	33	18	15	14	23	15	12	13	14	25
Netherlands	28	25	30	27	37	18	24	28	35	37	22	22	47	23	15	21	23	38
Belgium	29	30	29	35	33	23	27	30	34	29	32	28	41	27	23	19	29	41
Austria	16	15	17	21	18	12	13	17	28	13	15	21	26	15	15	11	14	22
France	25	22	28	30	31	16	20	27	37	23	31	26	38	22	13	17	22	38
Canada	30	30	29	32	33	23	32	29	28	35	30	22	36	28	26	31	28	31
United States	26	27	26	29	27	23	24	30	22	28	30	20	34	23	26	23	26	30
Iceland	22	21	24	25	18	27	20	24	24	na	na	na	31	21	19	18	21	38
West Germany	25	24	25	36	27	16	21	29	37	26	25	24	42	21	13	14	20	39
Denmark	26	24	28	28	31	19	26	23	27	25	30	23	48	23	13	21	24	40
Finland	12	12	12	13	14	07	14	14	09	17	09	11	26	09	06	12	10	17
Norway	12	13	12	13	14	10	13	13	12	14	11	13	17	10	10	11	12	19
Sweden	19	19	19	27	17	14	19	19	20	18	24	15	26	21	13	18	18	24
Japan	24	23	26	22	24	27	23	26	23	29	23	21	38	24	27	14	30	32
Switzerland	na	na	na	na	na	na	na	na	na	na	na	na	na	na	na	na	na	na
Total	32	33	32	37	34	26	27	34	36	32	33	33	37	28	27	27	33	42

Ranking:

Latvia	68
Bulgaria	59
Estonia	57
Moscow	51
Lithuania	45
Romania	42
Czechoslovakia	41
Russia	41
East Germany	40
Poland	39
Hungary	39
Belarus	39
North Ireland	39
Brazil	38
Ireland	37
Britain	37
China	36
South Korea	33
Mexico	31
Spain	30
Canada	30
Nigeria	29
Belgium	29
South Africa	28
Netherlands	28
Portugal	27
Chile	26
United States	26
Denmark	26
France	25
West Germany	25
Japan	24
Argentina	23
Iceland	22
India	20
Sweden	19
Italy	16
Austria	16
Finland	12
Norway	12
Slovenia	11

Note: Countries in the left column are ranked according to GNP per capita. / The percentages in the bottom row give each country an equal weight. / na=not ascertained.

V254 COMPETITION

"Competition is harmful. It brings out the worst in people" (% "agree"—codes 7 to 10 from a ten-point scale)

		Gender		Age			Education			Income			Political Affinity			Values			Ranking:	
	Total	Male	Female	16-29	30-49	50+	Lower	Medium	Upper	Lower	Middle	Upper	Left	Center	Right	Mat	Mixed	Postmat			
India	07	07	07	07	07	07	12	07	06	14	20	26	06	08	08	06	08	05	Turkey	23
Nigeria	07	06	09	08	07	04	09	08	06	32	32	21	07	09	08	05	08	11	Spain	22
China	05	03	08	05	04	07	09	03	03	32	40	38	na	na	na	08	03	00	Chile	21
Romania	06	04	08	06	05	06	08	06	03	37	42	47	11	04	05	09	04	01	Portugal	19
Turkey	23	20	27	21	21	30	30	14	09	na	na	na	19	21	27	20	27	17	Brazil	18
Poland	12	13	11	12	13	12	17	10	07	41	37	40	15	10	13	14	11	12	Italy	18
Bulgaria	07	05	08	07	07	06	09	06	03	58	60	61	05	07	03	10	05	03	Mexico	16
Chile	21	20	22	22	20	21	25	19	19	27	24	26	21	20	21	22	20	20	North Ireland	16
Czechoslovakia	05	04	06	05	05	06	08	04	04	37	42	44	06	06	03	09	04	04	Belgium	16
South Africa	14	14	15	14	14	15	19	13	05	30	29	22	15	11	14	14	14	18	France	16
Lithuania	10	10	10	07	10	13	14	10	05	42	45	52	na	na	na	14	10	04	Britain	15
Hungary	13	13	14	16	10	15	16	10	10	38	38	45	14	12	20	12	14	15	South Africa	14
Argentina	11	09	14	14	13	08	16	10	07	21	25	25	18	08	11	09	11	16	Netherlands	14
Brazil	18	17	20	20	19	14	23	17	13	35	42	39	18	18	20	19	18	15	Hungary	13
Mexico	16	15	17	18	15	13	16	16	14	27	31	36	19	13	16	15	15	15	Belarus	13
Belarus	13	11	15	15	11	16	21	13	10	37	36	44	10	13	28	18	11	08	Ireland	13
Russia	12	10	14	09	11	17	18	12	09	38	38	43	07	14	24	18	09	05	Denmark	13
Moscow	09	08	10	05	09	12	15	09	07	47	53	56	06	12	19	12	08	09	Japan	13
Latvia	08	06	09	06	09	09	14	09	04	68	67	70	na	na	na	11	07	07	Poland	12
Estonia	08	07	08	06	06	12	12	08	04	57	54	59	na	na	na	10	07	03	Russia	12
Portugal	19	19	20	18	21	19	21	16	16	26	29	29	25	18	16	21	17	25	Argentina	11
South Korea	09	11	07	05	08	15	22	07	04	34	33	28	09	07	09	10	07	08	Lithuania	10
Ireland	13	12	15	14	14	12	14	12	11	41	36	36	17	13	10	13	12	16	Canada	10
North Ireland	16	16	17	20	22	08	19	14	07	47	35	40	21	17	14	11	18	20	United States	10
Slovenia	09	08	09	09	08	09	09	10	07	12	11	14	11	06	09	10	08	09	Moscow	09
Spain	22	22	22	28	23	17	22	21	26	23	33	36	29	23	15	20	22	27	South Korea	09
East Germany	08	06	10	06	07	10	10	06	04	34	41	45	06	08	12	13	08	07	Slovenia	09
Britain	15	15	14	13	16	16	16	14	11	39	40	33	21	13	11	17	14	17	Latvia	08
Italy	18	16	20	21	18	17	19	16	22	18	15	14	22	14	15	17	19	19	Estonia	08
Netherlands	14	12	14	10	15	14	15	12	14	37	22	22	17	13	10	14	13	15	East Germany	08
Belgium	16	15	18	18	18	13	17	17	14	29	32	28	21	15	12	16	16	18	West Germany	08
Austria	07	05	08	06	07	07	06	07	14	13	15	21	09	05	07	10	06	06	Finland	08
France	16	17	16	17	16	16	19	14	14	23	31	26	17	15	14	21	15	11	India	07
Canada	10	10	10	11	11	07	10	11	08	35	30	22	10	09	08	09	10	11	Nigeria	07
United States	10	12	08	09	09	10	12	11	07	28	30	20	12	10	11	12	10	09	Bulgaria	07
Iceland	05	06	04	07	03	05	07	03	04	na	na	na	07	05	03	08	03	07	Austria	07
West Germany	08	07	09	09	08	07	07	09	09	26	25	24	12	06	04	11	06	09	Norway	07
Denmark	13	10	17	13	16	11	17	14	11	25	30	23	20	13	09	14	13	16	Sweden	07
Finland	08	08	08	04	08	10	14	08	05	17	09	11	16	08	04	19	09	04	Romania	06
Norway	07	06	08	05	08	06	10	07	05	14	11	13	12	06	04	07	07	06	China	05
Sweden	07	05	10	09	06	06	09	07	06	18	24	15	09	08	03	08	07	08	Czechoslovakia	05
Japan	13	10	17	13	13	14	16	14	10	29	23	21	16	11	10	12	13	11	Iceland	05
Switzerland	na	na	na	na	na	na	na	na	na	na	na	na	na	na	na	na	na	na		
Total	**12**	**11**	**13**	**12**	**12**	**12**	**15**	**11**	**09**	**32**	**33**	**33**	**14**	**11**	**12**	**13**	**11**	**11**		

Note: Countries in the left column are ranked according to GNP per capita. / The percentages in the bottom row give each country an equal weight. / na=not ascertained.

V255 HARD WORK

"Hard work doesn't generally bring success—it's more a matter of luck and connections" (% "agree"—codes 7 to 10 from a ten-point scale)

	Total	Gender		Age			Education			Income			Political Affinity			Values		
		Male	Female	16-29	30-49	50+	Lower	Medium	Upper	Lower	Middle	Upper	Left	Center	Right	Mat	Mixed	Postmat
India	11	10	13	10	12	10	11	11	11	08	12	13	14	10	12	10	12	10
Nigeria	19	19	19	21	18	05	19	18	20	17	23	17	15	20	19	16	18	36
China	35	35	35	41	36	26	31	36	41	29	37	41	na	na	na	32	36	56
Romania	19	14	24	27	20	14	19	22	15	23	18	17	19	17	19	20	19	12
Turkey	28	25	31	30	30	21	29	28	22	31	28	25	36	28	23	24	28	32
Poland	44	44	45	42	48	42	41	47	44	43	45	45	45	45	44	43	45	41
Bulgaria	17	14	20	24	20	09	14	19	17	19	18	13	13	14	20	15	18	17
Chile	30	28	31	35	27	25	34	28	27	32	31	25	31	31	24	33	28	29
Czechoslovakia	22	20	25	24	21	23	26	22	17	22	22	23	26	22	19	30	20	18
South Africa	13	15	12	13	13	14	14	13	10	14	13	11	13	12	17	14	13	11
Lithuania	43	36	49	43	43	43	48	43	34	48	39	39	na	na	na	46	46	27
Hungary	28	29	26	22	31	27	28	27	25	28	28	26	32	29	28	27	28	36
Argentina	31	29	33	35	30	28	27	35	33	31	29	33	45	31	28	31	31	30
Brazil	61	60	62	63	64	54	58	63	59	60	65	59	62	64	59	58	63	66
Mexico	25	25	25	26	26	23	23	32	27	25	22	30	31	21	27	25	26	27
Belarus	25	19	30	29	25	21	18	28	24	26	22	27	25	23	28	22	26	28
Russia	22	19	25	21	27	18	19	23	24	19	23	19	19	20	27	23	22	20
Moscow	29	24	32	34	30	23	18	33	28	32	30	22	30	25	27	30	27	32
Latvia	38	29	44	42	37	33	37	40	34	41	31	40	na	na	na	47	36	30
Estonia	25	25	24	31	26	16	23	26	24	25	22	26	na	na	na	28	22	24
Portugal	43	43	42	46	44	37	42	40	48	43	44	39	49	42	40	40	43	49
South Korea	15	16	13	16	15	12	15	15	14	17	14	13	20	15	12	15	14	15
Ireland	29	28	29	31	32	24	30	28	26	33	31	25	37	29	24	24	31	28
North Ireland	19	19	20	25	25	10	20	23	17	16	20	19	29	19	18	14	20	24
Slovenia	21	21	22	21	23	20	23	23	22	25	21	14	15	22	19	21	21	19
Spain	40	43	37	43	42	35	40	38	41	33	44	42	44	41	31	35	41	44
East Germany	11	10	12	13	09	11	11	12	11	12	11	10	11	09	11	13	11	09
Britain	29	28	30	30	31	28	32	25	21	31	34	25	36	29	22	30	29	33
Italy	32	31	33	30	37	30	33	26	36	35	30	25	36	27	31	34	31	35
Netherlands	31	31	31	31	31	29	32	32	28	39	26	22	39	25	24	45	26	33
Belgium	29	26	31	30	30	26	31	28	25	30	32	25	31	27	23	28	30	26
Austria	16	14	17	17	16	16	18	16	10	19	15	16	22	16	15	16	15	18
France	21	19	22	21	22	19	22	20	18	24	23	16	22	20	14	24	21	17
Canada	18	17	19	19	18	16	20	17	18	21	17	13	20	18	16	16	19	16
United States	13	13	14	14	14	11	15	15	10	16	13	10	12	13	13	11	13	15
Iceland	16	16	16	20	14	15	14	17	17	na	na	na	21	16	13	16	16	16
West Germany	21	20	22	29	23	15	20	20	26	24	22	18	34	17	11	18	19	25
Denmark	46	43	49	48	49	41	45	49	44	48	45	47	60	46	38	40	46	50
Finland	15	15	15	16	14	16	16	17	12	21	14	11	21	15	09	16	15	14
Norway	25	22	29	24	28	23	28	26	23	27	27	21	34	23	20	25	24	28
Sweden	28	26	31	24	31	28	33	26	26	30	33	24	37	27	19	24	27	35
Japan	15	14	16	13	17	14	19	14	14	16	16	13	19	15	09	15	15	12
Switzerland	na	na	na	na	na	na	na	na	na	na	na	na	na	na	na	na	na	na
Total	26	25	28	28	27	23	26	27	25	28	27	24	29	24	22	26	26	27

Ranking:

Brazil	61
Denmark	46
Poland	44
Lithuania	43
Portugal	43
Spain	40
Latvia	38
China	35
Italy	32
Argentina	31
Netherlands	31
Chile	30
Moscow	29
Ireland	29
Britain	29
Belgium	29
Turkey	28
Hungary	28
Sweden	28
Mexico	25
Belarus	25
Estonia	25
Norway	25
Czechoslovakia	22
Russia	22
Slovenia	21
France	21
West Germany	21
Nigeria	19
Romania	19
North Ireland	19
Canada	18
Bulgaria	17
Austria	16
Iceland	16
South Korea	15
Finland	15
Japan	15
South Africa	13
United States	13
India	11
East Germany	11

Note: Countries in the left column are ranked according to GNP per capita. / The percentages in the bottom row give each country an equal weight. / na=not ascertained.

V256 WEALTH ACCUMULATION

"Wealth can grow so there's enough for everyone" (% "agree"—codes 7 to 10 from a ten point scale)

	Total	Gender		Age			Education			Income			Political Affinity			Values		
		Male	Female	16-29	30-49	50+	Lower	Medium	Upper	Lower	Middle	Upper	Left	Center	Right	Mat	Mixed	Postmat
India	50	50	49	49	50	51	47	51	49	49	44	55	55	49	51	51	49	49
Nigeria	47	47	46	47	48	38	39	46	51	47	47	47	39	45	54	51	43	54
China	72	72	73	64	76	77	74	72	70	76	69	71	na	na	na	75	72	55
Romania	48	50	47	49	50	46	43	49	55	41	48	54	43	50	55	46	49	56
Turkey	46	47	45	44	50	43	49	41	42	48	42	49	36	48	54	42	48	46
Poland	72	71	73	69	73	73	69	73	77	71	71	74	72	67	79	71	71	82
Bulgaria	54	52	55	53	57	51	53	54	56	52	49	62	48	51	65	54	55	53
Chile	68	65	70	64	69	70	69	67	67	70	64	69	65	66	73	68	66	72
Czechoslovakia	44	45	44	42	45	46	45	44	43	43	43	47	38	41	55	40	46	50
South Africa	72	74	71	70	73	74	76	70	71	75	72	69	67	72	75	74	71	71
Lithuania	63	63	63	57	63	70	65	61	74	65	64	60	na	na	na	59	65	68
Hungary	60	62	58	61	57	63	60	58	67	62	58	61	54	62	67	57	62	74
Argentina	63	60	66	59	61	67	63	66	61	64	62	62	59	60	72	61	63	64
Brazil	63	62	63	56	64	75	69	62	55	65	62	61	57	61	71	67	60	60
Mexico	50	49	51	51	50	44	48	51	53	47	53	50	53	47	55	48	50	62
Belarus	61	62	60	50	62	69	69	56	64	63	63	57	64	55	63	63	61	57
Russia	51	54	48	51	51	51	52	49	52	50	50	54	55	49	50	50	51	52
Moscow	53	56	50	46	53	59	55	53	52	53	52	55	56	50	47	50	54	57
Latvia	47	52	44	38	46	61	39	46	52	52	46	45	na	na	na	51	45	51
Estonia	55	54	56	51	57	57	58	53	59	56	58	51	na	47	na	49	58	72
Portugal	34	33	35	29	35	38	35	32	32	35	33	34	29	30	42	36	30	45
South Korea	54	52	56	48	57	57	49	55	56	50	53	62	36	52	61	58	52	45
Ireland	50	46	53	41	48	57	50	50	51	50	50	52	45	50	54	47	49	55
North Ireland	47	42	51	34	47	56	54	39	28	60	49	40	36	44	55	47	48	42
Slovenia	39	39	39	41	40	37	37	39	42	34	41	46	42	38	42	34	40	48
Spain	41	38	44	45	42	37	39	48	45	40	39	45	41	45	48	38	41	47
East Germany	74	73	75	65	75	78	75	72	69	74	75	73	71	76	74	71	76	71
Britain	46	46	46	41	46	48	47	41	39	46	39	50	40	45	52	50	44	45
Italy	64	61	67	60	64	67	64	66	47	63	67	67	59	66	73	62	65	64
Netherlands	64	68	62	56	66	68	65	63	63	66	64	62	70	55	67	61	66	62
Belgium	52	51	54	47	53	55	51	52	55	51	54	56	48	55	60	47	55	53
Austria	64	65	63	60	64	65	62	66	61	61	64	66	67	65	62	62	63	66
France	42	42	42	37	39	48	41	43	39	43	40	45	36	41	48	47	40	41
Canada	62	59	65	62	60	63	64	60	62	60	62	61	50	61	69	64	60	65
United States	46	45	47	47	44	47	44	45	49	46	48	44	41	45	51	45	45	48
Iceland	61	57	65	58	59	69	62	64	58	na	na	na	58	62	64	58	63	55
West Germany	55	53	57	48	53	62	56	55	53	55	51	59	47	57	62	55	58	51
Denmark	47	42	53	41	50	47	46	50	47	46	49	46	55	42	50	39	48	49
Finland	49	51	47	40	49	58	53	49	47	49	47	51	54	40	53	70	47	50
Norway	48	45	51	42	45	54	56	46	45	49	45	47	44	49	48	55	45	46
Sweden	43	40	48	35	45	48	44	38	54	40	44	44	42	40	46	40	42	50
Japan	38	38	38	36	38	39	40	40	31	35	39	36	40	31	41	39	37	40
Switzerland	na	na	na	na	na	na	na	na	na	na	na	na	na	na	na	na	na	na
Total	54	53	55	50	54	57	54	53	54	54	53	55	50	52	58	54	54	56

Ranking:

East Germany	74
China	72
Poland	72
South Africa	72
Chile	68
Italy	64
Netherlands	64
Austria	64
Lithuania	63
Argentina	63
Brazil	63
Canada	62
Belarus	61
Iceland	61
Hungary	60
Estonia	55
West Germany	55
Bulgaria	54
South Korea	54
Moscow	53
Belgium	52
Russia	51
India	50
Mexico	50
Ireland	50
Finland	49
Romania	48
Norway	48
Nigeria	47
Latvia	47
North Ireland	47
Denmark	47
Turkey	46
Britain	46
United States	46
Czechoslovakia	44
Sweden	43
France	42
Spain	41
Slovenia	39
Japan	38
Portugal	34

Note: Countries in the left column are ranked according to GNP per capita. / The percentages in the bottom row give each country an equal weight. / na=not ascertained.

V257. There is a lot of talk these days about what the aims of this country should be for the next ten years. Would you please say which one of these you, yourself, consider the most important?

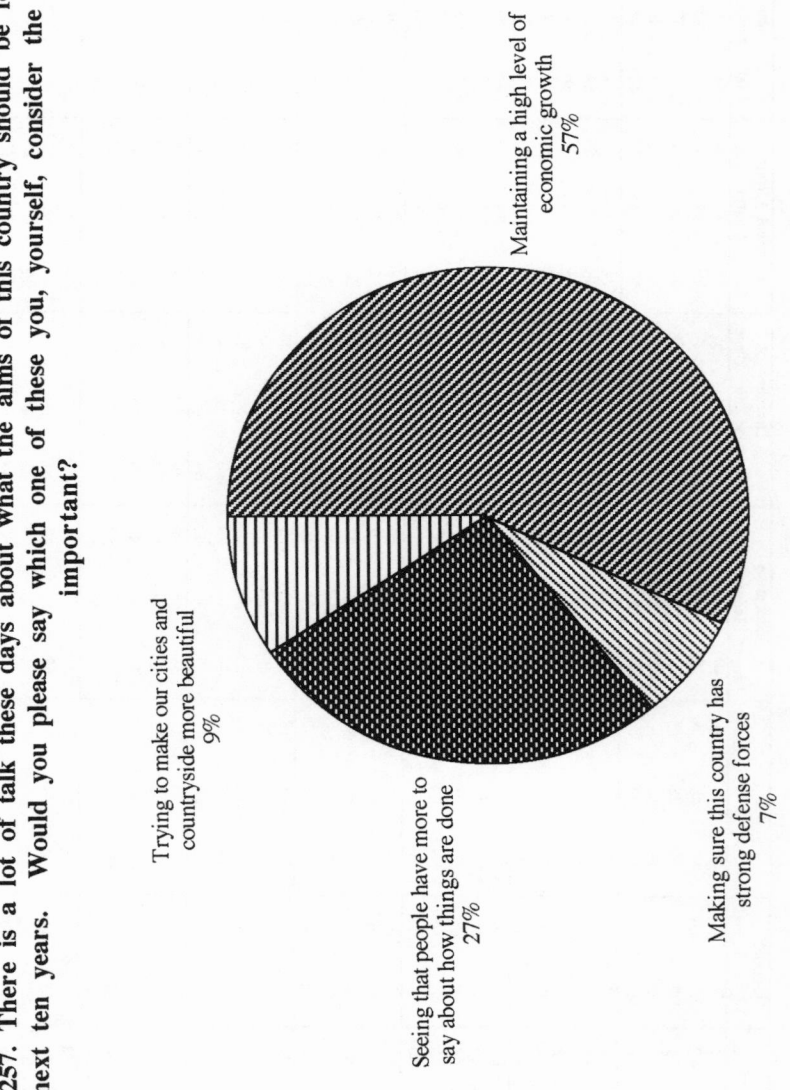

Trying to make our cities and
countryside more beautiful
9%

Seeing that people have more to
say about how things are done
27%

Maintaining a high level of
economic growth
57%

Making sure this country has
strong defense forces
7%

V257 COUNTRY'S GOALS: ECONOMIC GROWTH

There is a lot of talk these days about what the aims of this country should be for the next ten years. On this card are listed some of the goals which different people would give top priority. Would you please say which one of these you, yourself, consider the most important?
(% "Maintaining a high level of economic growth")

	Total	Gender		Age			Education			Income			Political Affinity			Values		
		Male	Female	16-29	30-49	50+	Lower	Medium	Upper	Lower	Middle	Upper	Left	Center	Right	Mat	Mixed	Postmat
India	54	56	52	54	54	56	41	51	62	52	49	62	54	60	53	59	53	49
Nigeria	67	71	61	65	69	67	62	63	72	67	66	67	63	68	66	73	64	58
China	66	67	66	70	68	59	61	68	79	63	66	66	na	na	na	63	70	76
Romania	na	na	na	na	na	na	na	na	na	na	na	na	na	na	na	na	na	na
Turkey	59	63	55	62	61	52	54	68	69	55	61	62	60	59	61	62	58	60
Poland	74	76	73	73	74	75	67	78	85	72	74	78	76	77	74	78	73	66
Bulgaria	76	80	72	82	76	71	67	73	88	76	72	79	78	76	82	73	76	86
Chile	66	69	63	61	72	64	64	66	67	60	68	71	62	67	73	69	68	58
Czechoslovakia	66	70	63	68	71	59	52	72	78	66	68	72	63	67	69	66	66	58
South Africa	54	57	51	50	56	58	44	56	80	43	51	76	61	62	58	55	55	43
Lithuania	76	80	73	79	83	67	60	79	91	71	78	86	na	na	na	74	76	82
Hungary	63	66	60	61	66	61	52	70	87	54	67	78	63	65	66	66	60	55
Argentina	66	69	64	61	65	73	65	68	67	64	66	69	58	72	69	74	68	52
Brazil	51	55	47	50	54	50	42	54	58	48	50	56	47	55	54	52	53	32
Mexico	62	65	59	64	61	56	60	60	76	58	62	69	59	65	66	64	62	52
Belarus	73	73	73	74	74	69	65	69	80	67	75	76	74	77	59	73	73	73
Russia	72	74	70	74	73	70	63	71	79	68	72	75	78	75	69	73	71	74
Moscow	77	77	76	79	78	72	56	72	84	70	80	76	81	77	57	74	75	82
Latvia	83	82	83	80	84	84	74	82	86	78	80	80	na	na	na	84	82	79
Estonia	80	80	79	79	81	78	71	81	85	78	79	87	na	na	na	81	82	71
Portugal	71	74	69	73	77	63	69	72	80	61	74	81	67	70	77	72	79	63
South Korea	52	48	55	43	54	63	59	56	43	52	51	56	37	48	58	59	74	30
Ireland	55	57	53	50	52	63	51	58	57	46	57	61	41	56	59	65	51	45
North Ireland	53	52	54	53	50	60	49	55	55	45	53	58	29	52	64	70	54	47
Slovenia	64	66	62	66	63	63	50	67	81	57	68	70	69	69	57	68	49	67
Spain	46	48	43	41	46	49	45	49	43	53	44	41	41	50	49	59	45	29
East Germany	73	77	69	70	78	69	72	71	77	66	73	78	70	72	84	68	75	68
Britain	43	49	38	41	45	42	40	48	53	34	43	59	28	40	66	55	42	32
Italy	43	47	39	44	45	40	42	52	35	39	45	54	35	47	46	51	44	30
Netherlands	41	49	39	41	41	43	38	44	41	31	44	52	26	45	58	42	50	30
Belgium	42	46	37	39	41	44	39	44	42	38	37	51	35	44	55	42	44	36
Austria	52	58	48	43	50	58	53	52	52	51	53	53	51	54	51	60	56	39
France	52	55	49	50	48	58	46	59	57	45	52	62	51	56	64	51	55	46
Canada	56	57	55	49	58	60	52	59	55	51	57	60	36	58	65	66	59	44
United States	54	52	55	46	53	57	51	55	54	46	54	60	46	57	53	66	56	41
Iceland	53	58	47	52	54	52	48	60	51	na	51	na	41	51	65	55	54	37
West Germany	49	53	45	39	52	52	47	45	41	43	51	53	33	55	63	58	56	31
Denmark	47	55	40	50	44	49	47	51	45	46	45	52	24	50	62	58	50	27
Finland	34	37	31	31	37	30	32	36	34	32	29	43	24	28	46	43	36	29
Norway	48	51	45	54	46	47	43	45	54	40	46	57	36	47	60	53	49	24
Sweden	51	56	46	43	53	55	51	50	54	48	46	56	36	50	67	63	54	37
Japan	43	46	39	43	43	49	44	43	40	35	45	47	31	44	53	49	42	29
Switzerland	28	34	23	27	28	29	28	29	29	19	27	36	11	32	40	34	30	21
Total	58	61	55	56	59	58	53	60	64	53	58	64	49	58	62	62	59	50

Ranking:

Latvia	83
Estonia	80
Moscow	77
Bulgaria	76
Lithuania	76
Poland	74
Belarus	73
East Germany	73
Russia	72
Portugal	71
Nigeria	67
China	66
Chile	66
Czechoslovakia	66
Argentina	66
Slovenia	64
Hungary	63
Mexico	62
Turkey	59
Canada	56
Ireland	55
India	54
South Africa	54
United States	54
North Ireland	53
Iceland	53
South Korea	52
Austria	52
France	52
Brazil	51
Sweden	51
West Germany	49
Norway	48
Denmark	47
Spain	46
Britain	43
Italy	43
Japan	43
Belgium	42
Netherlands	41
Finland	34
Switzerland	28

Note: Countries in the left column are ranked according to GNP per capita. / The percentages in the bottom row give each country an equal weight. / na=not ascertained.

V257 COUNTRY'S GOALS: GIVING PEOPLE MORE SAY AT THEIR JOBS

There is a lot of talk these days about what the aims of this country should be for the next ten years. On this card are listed some of the goals which different people would give top priority. Would you please say which one of these you, yourself, consider the most important?
(% "Seeing that people have more to say about how things are done at their jobs and in their communities")

	Total	Gender		Age			Education			Income			Political Affinity			Values		
		Male	Female	16-29	30-49	50+	Lower	Medium	Upper	Lower	Middle	Upper	Left	Center	Right	Mat	Mixed	Postmat
India	09	08	10	09	08	08	07	08	16	09	09	08	11	07	08	07	09	11
Nigeria	17	16	18	16	17	20	19	17	16	18	17	15	17	14	20	11	19	25
China	02	03	02	03	03	02	02	03	03	02	01	04	na	na	na	02	03	07
Romania	na	na	na	na	na	na	na	na	na	na	na	na	na	na	na	na	na	na
Turkey	12	12	13	14	11	14	10	14	19	12	13	13	23	11	08	07	11	24
Poland	17	16	17	19	19	14	20	15	12	18	17	14	15	17	13	11	18	28
Bulgaria	16	13	19	12	16	18	19	19	09	17	19	13	13	17	14	16	18	09
Chile	25	24	26	30	21	24	24	25	28	26	23	25	32	25	14	17	25	36
Czechoslovakia	25	22	28	24	22	28	33	22	18	26	26	21	30	24	22	21	27	21
South Africa	26	25	27	28	26	21	28	27	14	28	31	15	25	23	20	19	28	39
Lithuania	13	11	15	13	13	12	13	14	07	14	15	07	na	na	na	11	14	14
Hungary	22	22	21	26	25	17	25	21	10	23	22	15	22	22	19	17	25	35
Argentina	25	24	25	31	28	17	23	25	26	24	25	25	40	24	16	12	24	45
Brazil	26	26	26	28	27	20	21	26	37	22	27	29	33	28	17	18	28	59
Mexico	25	24	25	22	26	29	26	25	22	26	26	20	33	23	18	20	25	36
Belarus	17	18	17	18	17	18	18	21	14	19	18	15	17	16	23	15	18	21
Russia	15	16	15	18	17	12	15	17	14	15	17	14	16	14	17	11	17	24
Moscow	14	15	12	13	15	13	24	16	11	17	11	15	12	15	17	10	16	14
Latvia	08	09	07	09	09	04	11	08	06	09	09	07	na	na	na	03	10	11
Estonia	12	11	12	11	13	11	14	11	11	12	14	10	na	na	na	09	12	24
Portugal	15	15	15	14	13	18	17	21	15	18	16	11	22	15	11	11	15	27
South Korea	25	25	25	34	23	15	17	21	34	36	26	23	41	27	19	17	28	45
Ireland	35	32	38	41	39	27	36	35	31	36	34	33	51	36	29	22	35	50
North Ireland	31	30	32	34	39	20	36	28	17	33	32	32	57	34	17	16	33	42
Slovenia	29	28	31	34	32	30	40	27	16	36	25	24	22	25	37	24	32	30
Spain	39	38	40	47	41	31	37	38	49	30	43	42	48	37	31	23	40	60
East Germany	19	17	20	23	17	18	19	21	17	20	19	17	24	18	09	10	17	26
Britain	40	36	44	45	42	36	40	41	36	45	41	31	59	42	20	25	40	56
Italy	38	36	40	41	39	35	38	36	52	41	37	30	49	32	31	22	37	60
Netherlands	52	43	55	54	52	48	53	52	50	62	48	40	68	49	36	48	43	65
Belgium	38	35	41	42	42	34	41	35	39	41	43	31	47	39	30	34	37	47
Austria	29	28	30	35	34	22	27	30	31	26	30	32	29	30	28	17	25	45
France	36	33	39	38	41	29	39	33	32	40	39	28	41	32	22	31	34	45
Canada	34	32	36	40	35	28	31	33	38	37	33	34	54	33	26	18	32	47
United States	26	25	28	31	29	21	25	24	30	31	23	25	40	24	20	14	24	41
Iceland	39	33	45	36	43	37	40	30	44	na	na	na	52	41	26	36	37	60
West Germany	34	32	35	44	35	27	31	37	42	36	35	31	53	30	18	14	29	54
Denmark	40	33	48	36	48	35	35	37	46	39	45	39	63	37	27	28	39	66
Finland	54	49	61	55	52	59	54	54	56	54	61	47	68	58	42	39	53	61
Norway	43	41	44	39	47	39	41	47	39	47	45	45	54	43	32	36	42	68
Sweden	33	28	38	38	35	28	33	34	34	39	39	28	51	35	17	20	30	51
Japan	31	28	34	42	30	24	26	31	34	34	28	30	45	29	18	21	36	43
Switzerland	42	38	46	47	49	33	42	41	46	45	46	41	63	40	31	32	38	58
Total	27	25	29	29	28	24	27	27	27	28	28	24	38	28	22	19	27	39

Ranking:

Finland	54
Netherlands	52
Norway	43
Switzerland	42
Britain	40
Denmark	40
Spain	39
Iceland	39
Italy	38
Belgium	38
France	36
Ireland	35
Canada	34
West Germany	34
Sweden	33
North Ireland	31
Japan	31
Slovenia	29
Austria	29
South Africa	26
Brazil	26
United States	26
Chile	25
Czechoslovakia	25
Argentina	25
Mexico	25
South Korea	25
Hungary	22
East Germany	19
Nigeria	17
Poland	17
Belarus	17
Bulgaria	16
Russia	15
Portugal	15
Moscow	14
Lithuania	13
Turkey	12
Estonia	12
India	09
Latvia	08
China	02

Note: Countries in the left column are ranked according to GNP per capita. / The percentages in the bottom row give each country an equal weight. / na=not ascertained.

V259. If you had to choose, which one of the things on this card would you say is most important?

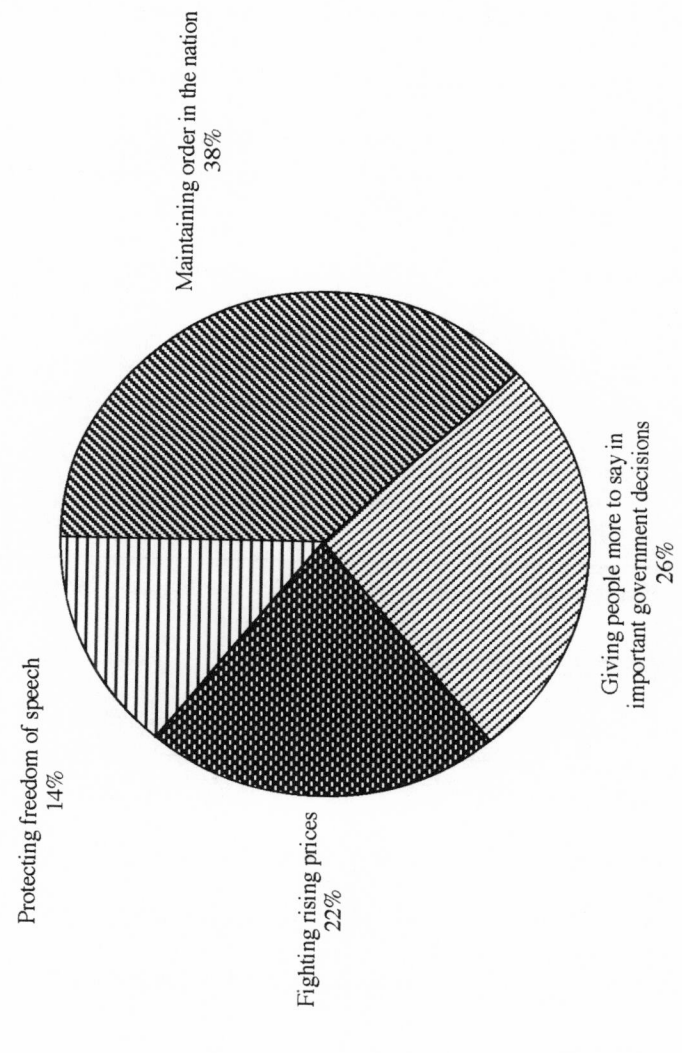

Maintaining order in the nation
38%

Giving people more to say in
important government decisions
26%

Fighting rising prices
22%

Protecting freedom of speech
14%

V259 COUNTRY'S GOALS: MAINTAIN ORDER

If you had to choose, which one of the things on this card would you say is most important?

(% "Maintaining order in the nation")

	Total	Gender		Age			Education			Income			Political Affinity			Values		
		Male	Female	16-29	30-49	50+	Lower	Medium	Upper	Lower	Middle	Upper	Left	Center	Right	Mat	Mixed	Postmat
India	43	46	40	43	44	45	34	43	49	38	42	51	45	46	51	65	36	70
Nigeria	43	42	43	44	41	42	42	44	42	40	44	42	44	40	49	60	38	60
China	67	65	69	63	65	74	67	70	60	73	65	61	na	na	na	80	61	78
Romania	60	61	60	53	57	67	60	62	57	55	62	62	67	63	54	70	61	57
Turkey	20	22	19	15	20	30	24	15	16	24	18	19	09	25	20	40	19	49
Poland	26	26	27	26	22	31	28	25	25	27	26	24	28	22	27	47	20	79
Bulgaria	51	50	52	43	51	56	56	53	44	46	53	54	63	50	40	73	49	87
Chile	39	37	42	34	40	47	45	38	34	44	37	37	24	43	47	73	39	82
Czechoslovakia	44	45	43	35	43	51	46	41	49	43	49	39	44	44	44	56	46	66
South Africa	38	41	36	37	37	43	35	39	48	34	35	50	32	42	48	60	30	77
Lithuania	29	30	29	27	30	30	34	28	29	29	31	26	na	na	na	56	23	70
Hungary	37	39	35	30	32	44	36	37	40	35	38	37	36	40	39	52	25	65
Argentina	35	35	36	30	36	39	40	32	32	34	35	30	23	33	44	71	31	81
Brazil	31	32	30	24	31	41	42	29	13	37	27	26	25	26	37	52	18	70
Mexico	28	31	26	29	28	28	30	24	28	25	28	35	17	27	37	51	25	62
Belarus	44	46	43	35	46	51	46	42	46	44	43	47	38	51	57	69	35	98
Russia	59	57	60	51	55	69	67	57	56	59	59	58	48	59	71	75	53	86
Moscow	41	41	41	35	41	45	40	41	42	37	46	38	36	50	49	71	35	87
Latvia	54	51	57	46	54	64	57	57	49	53	55	55	na	na	na	82	51	64
Estonia	59	58	59	55	59	61	57	61	56	59	60	58	na	na	na	72	58	71
Portugal	34	33	35	28	35	40	38	23	28	36	33	32	28	32	40	58	28	65
South Korea	43	41	45	35	45	54	48	46	37	43	40	48	32	40	49	59	37	59
Ireland	24	27	21	17	22	30	25	23	20	27	24	22	11	22	32	48	22	70
North Ireland	36	31	39	32	30	43	34	39	35	30	36	36	07	31	49	65	34	60
Slovenia	27	27	26	19	26	33	27	25	29	24	29	27	21	27	33	52	18	66
Spain	33	32	34	19	30	47	38	25	17	47	34	22	23	33	45	67	27	70
East Germany	37	40	35	26	37	44	39	32	33	37	36	37	29	40	44	59	46	66
Britain	25	26	24	19	22	31	24	33	21	25	24	27	09	25	43	51	24	60
Italy	29	28	29	19	26	37	29	24	21	29	28	28	16	36	36	58	27	65
Netherlands	27	33	24	16	23	43	38	25	16	23	29	24	12	27	41	61	38	31
Belgium	21	20	22	17	18	28	25	21	14	24	17	21	13	19	27	47	20	40
Austria	41	44	39	31	31	54	48	37	33	48	41	35	37	36	45	73	51	53
France	28	25	30	27	20	35	34	25	15	33	26	16	17	33	41	63	27	54
Canada	21	18	24	20	18	25	23	21	19	20	18	23	11	21	26	61	21	69
United States	28	26	29	30	24	31	32	27	26	27	29	25	15	27	34	60	29	52
Iceland	49	51	48	46	43	64	60	58	36	na	na	na	36	52	58	74	47	68
West Germany	37	38	37	24	31	50	43	28	28	41	37	34	18	40	56	75	46	54
Denmark	59	59	60	52	55	69	74	58	51	63	62	48	39	61	69	82	67	59
Finland	11	13	09	04	07	26	18	11	07	17	08	09	08	10	14	56	12	77
Norway	64	64	65	53	61	75	78	65	56	66	62	63	48	69	70	78	68	46
Sweden	38	40	37	27	32	56	54	35	21	40	40	37	30	40	43	69	45	55
Japan	35	37	32	26	35	39	37	33	37	32	33	41	20	31	53	63	29	60
Switzerland	32	31	32	20	26	43	34	33	17	36	29	17	10	33	41	72	35	46
Total	**38**	**38**	**38**	**32**	**36**	**45**	**42**	**37**	**33**	**38**	**37**	**36**	**27**	**37**	**44**	**63**	**36**	**65**

Ranking:

China	67
Norway	64
Romania	60
Russia	59
Estonia	59
Denmark	59
Latvia	54
Bulgaria	51
Iceland	49
Czechoslovakia	44
Belarus	44
India	43
Nigeria	43
South Korea	43
Moscow	41
Austria	41
Chile	39
South Africa	38
Sweden	38
Hungary	37
East Germany	37
West Germany	37
North Ireland	36
Argentina	35
Japan	35
Portugal	34
Spain	33
Switzerland	32
Brazil	31
Lithuania	29
Italy	29
Mexico	28
France	28
United States	28
Slovenia	27
Netherlands	27
Poland	26
Britain	25
Ireland	24
Belgium	21
Canada	21
Turkey	20
Finland	11

Note: Countries in the left column are ranked according to GNP per capita. / The percentages in the bottom row give each country an equal weight. / na=not ascertained.

V259 COUNTRY'S GOALS: GIVING PEOPLE MORE SAY IN GOVERNMENT DECISIONS

If you had to choose, which one of the things on this card would you say is most important?
(% "Giving people more to say in important government decisions")

	Total	Gender		Age			Education			Income			Political Affinity			Values			Ranking:	
		Male	Female	16-29	30-49	50+	Lower	Medium	Upper	Lower	Middle	Upper	Left	Center	Right	Mat	Mixed	Postmat		
India	18	19	16	19	18	14	12	19	19	16	19	17	21	17	18	35	27	30	Finland	59
Nigeria	20	22	17	20	22	13	21	19	21	18	18	25	15	21	20	40	27	40	Canada	43
China	14	16	12	20	14	08	07	15	23	12	15	16	na	na	na	21	22	22	Moscow	39
Romania	12	14	10	18	14	06	07	12	18	11	13	12	10	11	18	30	15	43	Belarus	35
Turkey	23	22	24	27	25	13	22	27	22	20	24	26	31	20	22	60	24	51	East Germany	35
Poland	27	32	23	26	34	21	21	30	35	24	27	32	33	32	27	53	33	21	Lithuania	32
Bulgaria	29	30	27	38	30	22	16	28	41	29	29	32	21	31	42	27	34	13	Argentina	32
Chile	31	37	27	38	32	21	19	33	45	22	32	42	47	29	29	27	29	19	Ireland	32
Czechoslovakia	27	27	27	37	27	21	25	31	20	26	26	30	25	28	27	44	32	34	Chile	31
South Africa	27	27	28	31	28	20	23	30	28	27	30	24	41	25	21	40	37	23	United States	31
Lithuania	32	36	28	40	34	23	13	37	36	27	37	34	na	na	na	45	39	30	Bulgaria	29
Hungary	18	20	17	24	24	10	15	22	17	14	21	26	25	16	23	48	32	35	Spain	29
Argentina	32	38	28	41	32	26	22	37	45	23	36	42	52	36	24	29	30	19	Britain	29
Brazil	22	25	20	26	25	11	12	24	39	16	23	30	31	26	15	48	33	30	Italy	29
Mexico	23	23	23	26	21	19	22	19	30	22	25	22	37	23	21	49	25	39	Japan	29
Belarus	35	37	33	43	35	26	23	37	36	31	36	36	43	28	17	31	48	02	Slovenia	28
Russia	24	29	21	32	28	14	14	24	30	22	24	29	38	23	17	25	35	14	Sweden	28
Moscow	39	43	36	46	40	33	26	35	44	36	39	45	47	27	28	29	47	13	Poland	27
Latvia	26	28	24	35	25	18	15	26	29	28	23	25	na	na	na	18	32	36	Czechoslovakia	27
Estonia	21	23	20	26	22	16	15	21	29	20	21	23	na	na	na	28	28	29	South Africa	27
Portugal	22	25	19	31	18	16	16	42	27	23	23	30	25	23	20	42	27	35	North Ireland	27
South Korea	15	15	14	24	11	08	10	11	21	15	16	10	23	13	14	41	19	41	Latvia	26
Ireland	32	30	35	44	33	24	27	38	38	24	32	38	40	36	26	52	33	30	Austria	26
North Ireland	27	28	26	29	30	22	27	24	35	26	31	34	43	26	25	35	29	40	Iceland	26
Slovenia	28	30	26	39	28	22	22	30	35	27	27	34	34	30	30	48	37	34	West Germany	26
Spain	29	32	26	38	32	17	23	37	44	16	30	36	38	24	22	33	29	31	Russia	24
East Germany	35	34	36	43	39	26	30	43	45	29	34	41	48	29	27	41	30	34	Turkey	23
Britain	29	29	30	37	33	21	29	29	30	25	32	31	41	30	19	49	29	40	Mexico	23
Italy	29	32	26	33	34	21	28	37	28	28	32	30	37	26	23	42	27	35	Brazil	22
Netherlands	16	15	16	15	18	15	14	14	21	18	16	14	21	13	15	39	09	69	Portugal	22
Belgium	18	19	17	16	21	16	15	17	25	16	19	20	20	21	18	53	16	61	Estonia	21
Austria	26	26	26	29	31	21	22	29	25	19	28	30	29	28	24	27	21	48	France	21
France	21	24	18	23	24	17	16	24	30	16	22	31	26	20	16	37	15	47	Nigeria	20
Canada	43	44	41	45	45	39	41	40	47	47	44	41	55	41	42	40	40	31	India	18
United States	31	31	31	30	34	29	27	31	35	31	33	29	37	33	26	40	32	48	Hungary	18
Iceland	26	23	28	24	34	13	15	23	35	na	na	na	37	22	23	26	29	32	Belgium	18
West Germany	26	28	24	32	31	19	24	29	33	22	30	26	41	23	16	25	19	46	Switzerland	18
Denmark	16	16	17	21	18	12	08	19	20	14	15	23	32	15	09	19	11	41	Netherlands	16
Finland	59	59	59	66	63	44	48	59	64	46	64	65	68	55	57	44	56	23	Denmark	16
Norway	14	13	14	20	15	08	06	13	18	13	14	15	24	13	08	23	15	54	South Korea	15
Sweden	28	25	32	31	35	17	24	29	34	26	27	32	40	26	23	32	25	45	China	14
Japan	29	31	28	41	25	28	29	32	24	33	28	28	37	32	16	37	39	41	Norway	14
Switzerland	18	21	17	24	19	16	16	18	28	16	20	20	35	16	14	28	12	54	Romania	12
Total	26	27	25	31	28	19	20	28	31	23	27	29	35	25	23	37	29	35		

Note: Countries in the left column are ranked according to GNP per capita. / The percentages in the bottom row give each country an equal weight. / na=not ascertained.

V261. Here is another list. In your opinion, which one of these is most important?

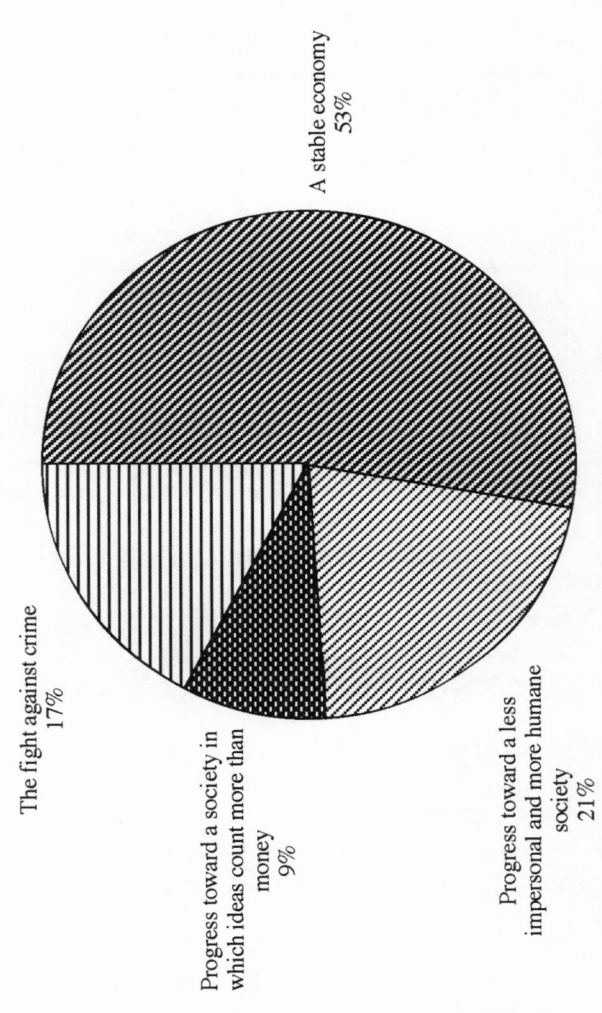

The fight against crime
17%

Progress toward a society in
which ideas count more than
money
9%

A stable economy
53%

Progress toward a less
impersonal and more humane
society
21%

V261 COUNTRY'S GOALS: A STABLE ECONOMY

Here is another list. In your opinion, which one of these is most important?
(% "A stable economy")

	Total	Gender		Age			Education			Income			Political Affinity			Values			Ranking:	
		Male	Female	16-29	30-49	50+	Lower	Medium	Upper	Lower	Middle	Upper	Left	Center	Right	Mat	Mixed	Postmat		
India	44	47	41	41	47	46	34	42	52	40	42	52	39	52	49	49	44	36	China	83
Nigeria	61	66	53	58	63	71	64	57	64	59	63	62	56	62	67	63	61	52	Bulgaria	83
China	83	82	85	80	82	88	81	84	84	81	79	89	na	na	na	86	82	63	Slovenia	81
Romania	67	70	65	63	68	70	72	64	67	67	65	71	67	69	68	72	67	41	Latvia	77
Turkey	36	42	28	32	40	34	31	44	39	32	35	40	31	36	44	44	35	27	Poland	73
Poland	73	75	71	65	79	70	70	72	84	74	70	75	79	76	76	72	73	66	East Germany	73
Bulgaria	83	83	82	83	84	81	77	83	86	79	84	87	85	84	82	82	84	79	Belarus	70
Chile	56	60	53	54	57	58	56	57	56	55	56	60	52	60	62	62	60	42	Romania	67
Czechoslovakia	63	69	58	57	72	57	50	69	71	57	67	65	67	61	66	62	65	60	Hungary	67
South Africa	46	46	45	42	47	51	34	48	73	35	43	71	49	54	55	60	43	42	Moscow	67
Lithuania	61	67	55	62	70	49	44	65	70	56	62	70	na	na	na	55	64	59	Russia	65
Hungary	67	72	63	64	72	64	59	74	73	61	70	74	72	69	64	68	67	56	Argentina	64
Argentina	64	65	62	60	66	65	67	66	57	62	64	63	53	61	71	71	70	37	Czechoslovakia	63
Brazil	30	33	26	27	34	29	26	28	44	23	27	38	27	36	27	28	32	22	Nigeria	61
Mexico	53	55	51	52	55	51	55	48	52	52	53	57	47	54	59	59	54	36	Lithuania	61
Belarus	70	73	68	70	76	59	63	68	75	66	74	71	72	72	69	69	72	53	Estonia	60
Russia	65	69	63	64	71	59	53	65	74	60	67	71	73	68	60	66	65	61	Iceland	58
Moscow	67	70	65	63	71	65	50	66	72	62	70	70	69	71	46	67	69	61	Chile	56
Latvia	77	74	80	72	80	78	70	80	75	80	76	76	na	na	na	81	78	64	Canada	54
Estonia	60	65	55	53	65	60	54	61	62	57	61	64	na	na	na	64	60	41	Mexico	53
Portugal	47	55	41	50	49	43	46	55	48	45	48	52	40	52	50	51	47	45	South Korea	53
South Korea	53	55	51	40	57	63	65	59	39	53	54	56	40	50	58	63	49	26	North Ireland	51
Ireland	49	54	43	46	51	48	46	52	53	44	54	51	41	49	52	57	49	37	Austria	51
North Ireland	51	50	52	36	55	57	51	51	52	37	60	51	43	52	53	71	46	44	United States	50
Slovenia	81	83	79	78	81	82	79	81	85	78	85	80	76	83	78	85	80	72	Denmark	50
Spain	36	37	36	34	37	38	38	36	31	37	39	30	35	38	39	45	37	25	Ireland	49
East Germany	73	75	70	68	72	75	74	66	73	70	70	76	67	75	80	68	77	64	West Germany	49
Britain	40	45	35	38	41	41	39	42	44	34	40	48	27	40	54	52	41	26	Portugal	47
Italy	30	34	26	19	30	36	30	26	13	30	31	27	25	32	30	41	30	18	South Africa	46
Netherlands	32	46	27	25	32	41	35	31	30	25	36	40	24	34	43	31	35	29	Norway	46
Belgium	32	36	28	31	33	32	30	34	33	30	30	38	29	36	40	29	37	25	India	44
Austria	51	61	44	41	50	56	53	50	46	47	51	55	51	53	49	51	55	41	Japan	44
France	26	30	23	22	26	29	24	27	30	20	27	29	27	26	33	30	28	18	Britain	40
Canada	54	54	54	48	54	59	54	59	48	49	54	56	37	56	59	70	57	40	Finland	40
United States	50	51	49	45	49	53	51	52	46	51	49	47	30	52	55	60	53	36	Sweden	39
Iceland	58	66	49	55	57	62	58	65	52	na	na	na	44	60	71	63	59	38	Turkey	36
West Germany	49	55	44	41	50	53	54	43	37	45	50	52	36	54	61	58	55	33	Spain	36
Denmark	50	56	44	50	46	55	57	50	47	49	49	49	30	48	63	65	52	24	Netherlands	32
Finland	40	45	36	36	37	52	44	48	30	49	39	34	35	44	41	55	43	33	Belgium	32
Norway	46	54	38	36	45	54	54	48	41	44	46	50	37	47	54	52	46	28	Brazil	30
Sweden	39	43	35	29	39	45	43	36	36	36	37	42	32	38	47	45	41	28	Italy	30
Japan	44	45	42	32	42	55	54	42	38	49	39	45	32	40	55	54	43	27	France	26
Switzerland	26	30	23	17	26	30	25	27	23	19	26	31	12	30	29	39	29	12	Switzerland	26
Total	53	57	50	48	55	55	51	54	54	50	53	56	46	53	55	58	54	41		

Note: Countries in the left column are ranked according to GNP per capita. / The percentages in the bottom row give each country an equal weight. / na=not ascertained.

V261 COUNTRY'S GOALS: HUMANE SOCIETY

Here is another list. In your opinion, which one of these is most important?

(% "Progress toward a less impersonal and more humane society")

	Total	Gender		Age			Education			Income			Political Affinity			Values			Ranking:	
		Male	Female	16-29	30-49	50+	Lower	Medium	Upper	Lower	Middle	Upper	Left	Center	Right	Mat	Mixed	Postmat		
India	20	19	22	24	18	19	18	21	21	18	21	07	26	18	05	18	22	30	Finland	48
Nigeria	07	07	08	07	08	00	06	06	10	07	08	07	07	09	05	04	08	13	Japan	44
China	06	07	05	09	05	04	03	06	09	07	06	05	na	na	na	03	06	26	Switzerland	37
Romania	10	10	11	13	12	08	06	13	12	10	11	10	08	11	12	08	11	25	South Korea	36
Turkey	27	23	32	25	26	32	28	28	20	28	27	25	30	26	23	23	27	31	France	33
Poland	09	09	09	13	05	10	10	08	04	09	09	07	07	07	09	10	08	11	Sweden	31
Bulgaria	09	08	09	10	08	10	11	08	08	13	09	04	08	10	08	07	09	14	Netherlands	30
Chile	22	23	20	22	24	17	16	22	27	17	23	25	29	21	15	12	19	40	West Germany	30
Czechoslovakia	09	07	10	10	06	11	09	07	13	08	08	10	10	09	08	06	08	17	Mexico	28
South Africa	17	17	18	20	16	14	18	18	13	19	17	13	20	17	15	12	20	23	Italy	27
Lithuania	13	12	14	14	15	11	10	14	17	13	14	12	na	na	na	12	11	21	Turkey	27
Hungary	08	07	09	15	08	06	07	09	13	06	10	11	09	10	10	05	10	23	Brazil	27
Argentina	18	20	16	22	19	15	12	21	27	14	20	21	30	22	08	07	16	38	Spain	27
Brazil	27	28	27	27	30	23	21	29	34	25	29	29	31	27	25	23	29	38	Norway	27
Mexico	28	28	28	30	28	26	25	35	33	29	29	26	37	28	24	21	28	43	Belgium	26
Belarus	11	09	12	12	10	12	09	11	12	11	11	11	13	08	15	06	11	34	Iceland	25
Russia	09	10	08	11	07	09	07	08	11	08	09	10	12	10	07	04	11	21	Estonia	24
Moscow	12	09	13	17	10	10	09	08	14	11	10	16	15	07	12	05	13	22	Portugal	24
Latvia	13	15	11	19	12	08	04	13	15	11	12	14	na	na	na	08	12	28	Chile	22
Estonia	24	22	25	30	24	17	18	24	29	22	25	25	na	na	na	18	24	51	Canada	22
Portugal	24	22	27	26	24	23	22	27	31	20	26	28	30	25	20	18	27	33	Britain	21
South Korea	36	32	40	54	30	21	17	29	54	35	36	34	50	41	30	23	41	72	Denmark	21
Ireland	19	17	21	24	21	14	14	24	29	12	15	27	33	19	17	11	18	33	India	20
North Ireland	19	22	17	28	22	10	18	20	21	20	12	28	21	22	15	06	21	31	Austria	20
Slovenia	09	09	10	11	09	08	09	08	11	10	07	11	12	10	08	04	10	19	Ireland	19
Spain	27	28	25	33	28	19	22	33	41	20	26	34	31	24	22	14	26	47	North Ireland	19
East Germany	17	15	19	18	19	14	15	23	18	18	17	15	22	14	12	14	13	29	Argentina	18
Britain	21	19	24	25	23	18	18	30	29	20	24	23	35	20	14	10	20	38	South Africa	17
Italy	28	29	28	32	30	18	27	38	61	27	28	34	32	25	26	15	27	43	East Germany	17
Netherlands	30	24	33	29	36	23	21	31	40	27	31	38	45	26	20	12	25	42	United States	16
Belgium	26	24	28	26	29	24	23	26	34	22	28	26	30	27	23	19	24	36	Lithuania	13
Austria	20	16	22	24	23	16	16	22	25	17	22	19	13	21	26	13	17	31	Latvia	13
France	33	33	34	35	36	29	31	34	38	29	37	36	39	30	26	23	32	47	Moscow	12
Canada	22	23	21	24	24	16	16	18	30	23	21	26	37	21	17	09	18	36	Belarus	11
United States	16	15	17	17	21	10	15	11	23	10	15	23	36	15	09	08	13	27	Romania	10
Iceland	25	19	31	28	29	15	18	21	34	na	na	na	34	25	17	14	26	50	Poland	09
West Germany	30	26	33	34	32	25	25	34	42	30	31	30	40	27	20	19	24	46	Bulgaria	09
Denmark	21	20	23	19	26	17	15	20	26	21	20	26	39	21	12	08	18	46	Czechoslovakia	09
Finland	48	47	50	52	52	34	38	42	61	39	48	56	50	46	49	27	45	60	Russia	09
Norway	27	24	30	35	29	19	14	21	38	26	30	30	40	25	20	13	29	55	Slovenia	09
Sweden	31	27	35	32	35	26	23	31	45	31	33	32	38	27	30	17	28	46	Hungary	08
Japan	44	45	43	50	46	37	37	42	54	38	49	43	58	47	35	34	46	66	Nigeria	07
Switzerland	37	38	37	43	41	32	33	38	51	37	40	40	53	36	35	15	33	61	China	06
Total	21	20	22	24	22	17	17	22	27	19	22	23	28	21	18	13	21	36		

Note: Countries in the left column are ranked according to GNP per capita. / The percentages in the bottom row give each country an equal weight. / na=not ascertained.

V263. Of course, we all hope that there will not be another war, but if it were to come to that, would you be willing to fight for your country?

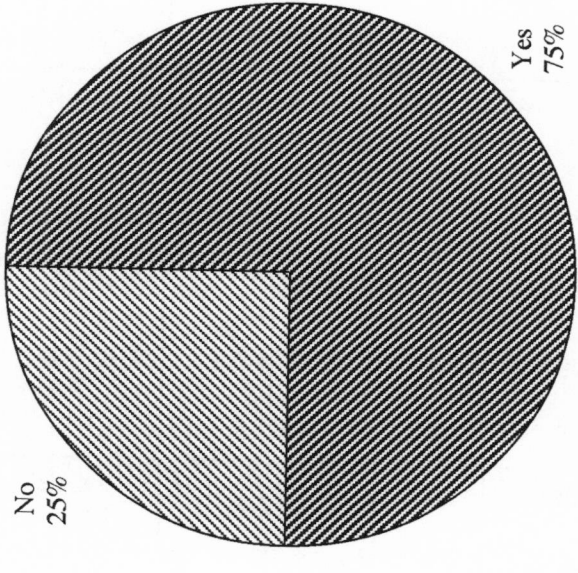

Yes
75%

No
25%

V263 WILLING TO FIGHT FOR COUNTRY

Of course, we all hope that there will not be another war, but if it were to come to that, would you be willing to fight for your country? (% "yes")

	Total	Gender Male	Gender Female	Age 16-29	Age 30-49	Age 50+	Education Lower	Education Medium	Education Upper	Income Lower	Income Middle	Income Upper	Political Affinity Left	Political Affinity Center	Political Affinity Right	Values Mat	Values Mixed	Values Postmat	Ranking:	
India	92	94	89	94	93	86	88	92	94	92	91	93	93	94	91	93	93	92	China	97
Nigeria	80	86	71	82	76	82	80	84	76	82	81	77	85	79	84	80	82	67	Latvia	97
China	97	98	97	97	97	98	97	98	98	99	98	96	na	na	na	97	98	94	Slovenia	95
Romania	92	94	89	91	95	90	91	94	90	88	94	93	94	93	89	93	92	87	Turkey	93
Turkey	93	94	91	91	93	94	94	94	86	92	95	91	85	95	95	95	92	91	India	92
Poland	92	94	91	97	96	86	88	97	90	91	94	94	93	96	90	91	93	95	Romania	92
Bulgaria	91	93	90	94	93	88	86	94	92	88	94	93	96	94	89	92	93	84	Poland	92
Chile	83	85	81	85	82	82	86	83	79	86	83	79	81	83	90	86	83	82	Belarus	92
Czechoslovakia	66	71	62	67	65	67	67	67	63	64	67	68	67	65	70	64	67	73	Estonia	92
South Africa	70	77	63	75	72	55	56	77	78	63	68	85	67	81	86	69	72	62	Bulgaria	91
Lithuania	84	95	73	89	93	70	71	87	88	80	87	87	na	na	na	73	87	91	Norway	91
Hungary	77	84	70	88	89	61	71	82	86	66	83	87	87	78	77	72	80	84	Denmark	89
Argentina	63	68	58	57	67	64	65	55	69	60	72	57	54	65	73	63	65	57	Sweden	89
Brazil	36	30	42	40	36	29	28	37	50	30	40	40	40	36	27	32	38	42	Finland	88
Mexico	74	81	65	78	75	62	73	70	80	75	72	72	75	71	81	77	75	78	South Korea	87
Belarus	92	96	89	90	94	91	89	93	92	89	94	92	93	89	92	93	92	91	Lithuania	84
Russia	84	87	81	85	86	80	79	83	87	84	84	83	85	83	83	81	86	79	Russia	84
Moscow	75	86	66	66	77	77	76	77	74	73	76	76	75	79	72	79	75	73	Chile	83
Latvia	97	98	97	96	98	98	97	98	96	98	99	96	na	na	na	99	97	95	Nigeria	80
Estonia	92	94	90	92	94	89	92	93	92	91	92	95	95	97	na	90	94	96	United States	80
Portugal	68	80	56	69	74	62	69	68	67	67	71	69	66	70	71	74	68	65	Switzerland	78
South Korea	87	80	94	87	87	87	82	89	87	86	89	86	79	86	90	86	88	84	Hungary	77
Ireland	61	72	50	64	65	55	62	60	57	60	65	60	57	63	62	53	62	67	Iceland	77
North Ireland	61	66	57	55	65	60	60	64	58	59	70	62	58	55	71	64	59	67	Moscow	75
Slovenia	95	97	94	99	96	92	94	97	97	95	95	98	95	97	95	95	95	97	Britain	75
Spain	62	64	60	58	64	63	66	61	42	62	65	54	52	70	76	71	61	48	Mexico	74
East Germany	53	58	49	63	60	41	54	54	49	42	59	59	56	50	56	35	58	49	Netherlands	71
Britain	75	81	69	75	79	72	74	80	71	73	76	84	71	77	82	76	76	71	South Africa	70
Italy	31	40	24	30	37	28	31	34	29	35	31	39	25	36	41	30	32	32	Portugal	68
Netherlands	71	66	73	78	71	63	68	73	72	65	74	69	62	72	78	69	75	66	Canada	68
Belgium	41	44	38	41	41	38	37	45	43	44	41	41	31	48	45	42	42	39	Czechoslovakia	66
Austria	66	73	62	69	74	57	63	70	64	58	70	69	64	67	69	60	69	63	Austria	66
France	66	67	65	59	71	67	69	64	62	63	69	67	59	70	77	72	69	57	France	66
Canada	68	73	63	69	67	69	65	68	70	66	69	71	53	72	78	59	71	68	Argentina	63
United States	80	86	72	82	78	80	76	81	80	77	81	81	68	82	86	76	81	79	Spain	62
Iceland	77	79	76	72	82	76	80	82	72	na	na	na	68	78	85	81	78	62	Ireland	61
West Germany	42	51	33	40	44	42	46	37	33	40	44	42	25	44	63	51	49	25	North Ireland	61
Denmark	89	90	89	86	92	89	88	90	89	86	93	92	87	88	94	89	92	84	East Germany	53
Finland	88	89	87	81	88	94	85	89	89	85	88	91	79	89	93	82	90	86	West Germany	42
Norway	91	94	89	91	91	91	88	93	92	89	94	92	85	92	95	91	92	87	Belgium	41
Sweden	89	92	85	82	88	93	93	87	86	93	85	89	88	87	92	89	90	85	Brazil	36
Japan	20	26	14	08	18	33	27	17	21	27	19	21	19	19	41	29	20	06	Italy	31
Switzerland	78	78	77	67	77	83	77	79	74	75	82	80	60	83	83	83	78	73	Japan	20
Total	**74**	**78**	**70**	**74**	**76**	**72**	**73**	**75**	**74**	**72**	**76**	**75**	**69**	**74**	**77**	**74**	**76**	**71**		

Note: Countries in the left column are ranked according to GNP per capita. / The percentages in the bottom row give each country an equal weight. / na=not ascertained.

V264-V270. Here is a list of various changes in our way of life that might take place in the near future. Please tell me for each one, if it were to happen whether you think it would be a good thing, a bad thing, or don't you mind?

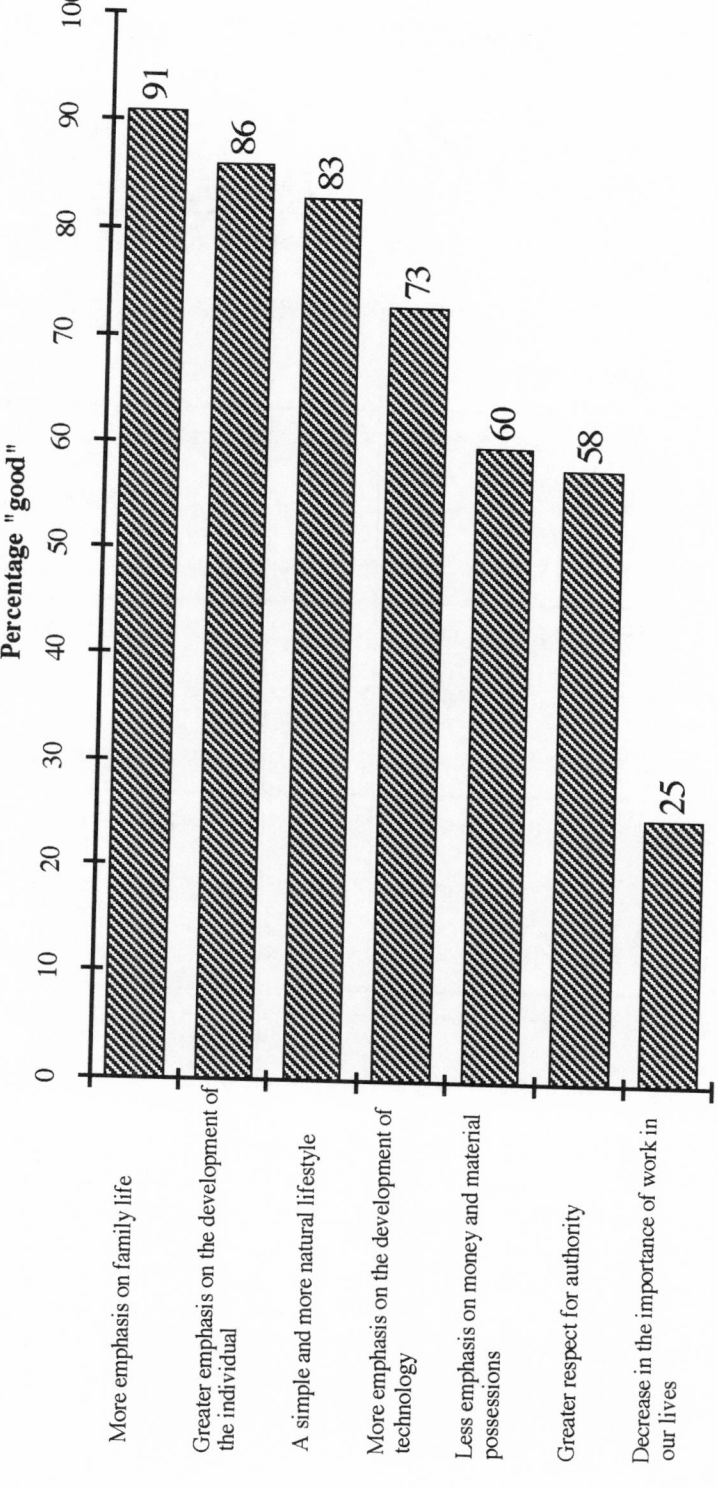

Percentage "good"

More emphasis on family life — 91

Greater emphasis on the development of the individual — 86

A simple and more natural lifestyle — 83

More emphasis on the development of technology — 73

Less emphasis on money and material possessions — 60

Greater respect for authority — 58

Decrease in the importance of work in our lives — 25

V264 LESS EMPHASIS ON MONEY

Here is a list of various changes in our way of life that might take place in the near future. Please tell me for each one, if it were to happen whether you think it would be a good thing, a bad thing, or don't you mind? "Less emphasis on money and material possessions" (% "good")

	Total	Gender Male	Gender Female	Age 16-29	Age 30-49	Age 50+	Education Lower	Education Medium	Education Upper	Income Lower	Income Middle	Income Upper	Political Affinity Left	Political Affinity Center	Political Affinity Right	Values Mat	Values Mixed	Values Postmat	Ranking	
India	43	46	40	43	43	46	36	44	47	45	42	45	47	49	36	48	44	38	Switzerland	82
Nigeria	64	64	64	64	64	58	62	60	69	65	64	61	64	66	61	68	62	59	Spain	81
China	67	65	69	62	68	70	67	66	73	67	69	66	na	na	na	66	70	55	Denmark	78
Romania	na	na	na	na	na	na	na	na	na	na	na	na	na	na	na	na	na	na	Ireland	73
Turkey	56	58	53	59	54	54	51	61	66	57	53	59	66	55	51	59	50	68	Italy	72
Poland	59	57	61	59	60	59	53	64	62	57	57	64	60	61	66	60	57	67	Argentina	71
Bulgaria	61	59	62	68	61	57	55	63	63	64	64	56	62	63	65	64	59	59	France	71
Chile	60	58	62	58	63	57	57	60	64	57	59	65	63	59	58	59	60	63	United States	71
Czechoslovakia	52	49	55	52	50	54	51	52	55	54	51	51	58	52	49	53	52	51	Finland	71
South Africa	45	42	47	42	46	49	38	45	67	34	43	63	42	50	52	47	42	51	Mexico	68
Lithuania	33	31	36	38	34	29	23	37	36	31	35	36	na	na	na	27	36	37	China	67
Hungary	44	41	47	48	44	42	41	45	57	42	45	49	44	45	47	45	44	35	Sweden	66
Argentina	71	70	73	65	75	73	71	69	74	68	74	70	77	75	61	68	70	79	Belgium	65
Brazil	62	59	65	65	59	62	61	62	64	60	64	62	61	62	61	62	62	64	Nigeria	64
Mexico	68	67	69	67	68	68	67	71	69	68	70	68	74	68	67	67	71	67	Britain	64
Belarus	60	60	61	59	62	58	65	59	60	60	69	51	61	60	62	61	61	57	Netherlands	64
Russia	42	40	43	40	40	45	38	42	43	45	41	41	42	42	43	45	39	35	Portugal	63
Moscow	61	58	63	55	63	63	60	60	63	63	63	55	63	63	56	64	63	56	South Korea	63
Latvia	na	na	na	na	na	na	na	na	na	na	na	na	na	na	na	na	na	na	Brazil	62
Estonia	na	na	na	na	na	na	na	na	na	na	na	na	na	na	na	na	na	na	Canada	62
Portugal	63	60	67	67	60	63	61	70	69	60	69	65	65	62	64	57	68	67	Bulgaria	61
South Korea	63	63	63	68	60	62	63	60	67	63	61	65	67	60	64	61	64	66	Moscow	61
Ireland	73	70	76	73	71	76	71	74	84	71	72	79	74	73	76	74	74	71	Chile	60
North Ireland	60	50	67	50	63	64	57	58	83	55	56	69	57	61	58	66	59	56	Belarus	60
Slovenia	50	47	52	52	46	52	46	51	53	47	52	51	53	48	60	49	50	47	North Ireland	60
Spain	81	79	82	79	82	80	80	81	84	81	82	81	84	82	76	81	82	83	Norway	60
East Germany	49	44	53	51	50	47	46	52	58	50	51	47	58	47	39	46	46	56	Poland	59
Britain	64	59	68	55	68	66	61	72	69	64	65	60	72	63	61	60	62	73	Iceland	59
Italy	72	70	74	73	71	71	72	75	76	72	73	72	80	71	61	68	71	79	Turkey	56
Netherlands	64	62	64	59	67	64	61	68	75	70	60	65	77	64	54	53	59	75	Austria	55
Belgium	65	62	67	62	65	66	61	65	71	67	63	67	68	66	64	62	63	73	Czechoslovakia	52
Austria	55	48	60	55	56	55	54	55	60	57	54	57	56	54	54	50	55	59	West Germany	51
France	71	70	72	71	71	70	69	74	70	69	71	60	76	70	61	66	71	75	Slovenia	50
Canada	62	57	66	58	63	63	57	61	66	66	63	62	71	60	62	55	61	67	East Germany	49
United States	71	68	74	65	75	69	71	68	75	69	69	75	77	70	71	69	70	78	South Africa	45
Iceland	59	54	65	56	61	61	61	56	66	na	na	na	70	64	49	51	62	65	Hungary	44
West Germany	51	45	55	52	48	51	48	52	63	52	51	48	60	49	42	47	46	62	India	43
Denmark	78	72	83	68	83	80	80	76	78	81	76	77	83	79	75	77	76	86	Russia	42
Finland	71	68	74	74	74	60	61	68	80	63	70	80	84	70	66	57	69	79	Japan	41
Norway	60	55	64	59	63	56	52	54	69	61	59	60	65	61	56	50	63	70	Lithuania	33
Sweden	66	59	73	63	69	63	63	63	75	66	66	66	76	65	58	57	63	77		
Japan	41	42	40	43	41	41	35	39	53	39	42	45	60	44	42	41	44	62		
Switzerland	82	80	84	80	84	83	81	83	90	83	82	81	90	81	79	78	81	89		
Total	**60**	**58**	**63**	**59**	**61**	**60**	**58**	**61**	**67**	**60**	**61**	**62**	**66**	**61**	**59**	**58**	**60**	**64**		

Note: Countries in the left column are ranked according to GNP per capita. / The percentages in the bottom row give each country an equal weight. / na=not ascertained.

V265 DECREASE WORK IMPORTANCE

Here is a list of various changes in our way of life that might take place in the near future. Please tell me for each one, if it were to happen whether you think it would be a good thing, a bad thing, or don't you mind? "Decrease in the importance of work in our lives" (% "good")

	Total	Gender		Age			Education			Income			Political Affinity			Values		
		Male	Female	16-29	30-49	50+	Lower	Medium	Upper	Lower	Middle	Upper	Left	Center	Right	Mat	Mixed	Postmat
India	07	08	06	06	07	08	09	07	06	09	06	05	08	08	06	05	08	09
Nigeria	15	14	15	16	12	14	12	15	15	12	14	20	19	18	11	16	14	14
China	08	09	08	08	09	08	08	06	12	07	09	08	na	na	na	06	10	17
Romania	na	na	na	na	na	na	na	na	na	na	na	na	na	na	na	na	na	na
Turkey	16	15	17	18	15	16	19	13	11	20	14	15	20	14	15	18	15	16
Poland	30	30	29	24	33	30	31	32	16	29	30	31	29	30	30	28	29	33
Bulgaria	41	40	42	44	40	41	44	43	39	44	43	38	40	39	47	40	42	43
Chile	18	17	20	17	19	18	23	17	15	22	18	14	17	17	21	21	17	16
Czechoslovakia	08	08	08	09	10	05	09	08	05	06	10	07	06	08	08	08	08	09
South Africa	14	14	14	15	13	14	11	15	20	10	15	18	17	16	14	13	13	22
Lithuania	12	13	12	16	12	09	07	15	08	11	13	14	na	na	na	08	13	16
Hungary	25	26	25	30	23	25	28	22	22	29	23	19	27	23	29	27	24	21
Argentina	20	23	17	23	20	16	17	21	19	18	17	25	27	23	19	18	17	28
Brazil	19	19	18	20	17	20	28	16	11	21	17	16	21	15	25	21	17	16
Mexico	28	27	29	27	30	28	30	26	23	32	29	24	27	27	28	33	28	19
Belarus	28	28	28	26	29	28	30	31	24	30	31	22	31	23	24	27	28	28
Russia	26	25	27	30	24	24	25	29	23	28	25	26	21	29	37	30	23	22
Moscow	33	29	36	30	35	32	33	35	32	33	31	37	33	38	34	38	32	30
Latvia	na	na	na	na	na	na	na	na	na	na	na	na	na	na	na	na	na	na
Estonia	na	na	na	na	na	na	na	na	na	na	na	na	na	na	na	na	na	na
Portugal	38	39	37	40	41	33	37	37	42	34	40	44	41	36	37	38	40	36
South Korea	16	17	16	14	17	20	27	18	09	21	16	11	16	17	16	18	17	09
Ireland	22	21	24	26	25	18	23	22	19	20	23	23	32	22	19	18	23	26
North Ireland	22	23	22	21	24	22	23	21	21	24	23	23	21	23	24	20	25	18
Slovenia	12	12	12	14	10	13	15	12	06	13	13	08	13	11	14	11	13	07
Spain	50	52	49	55	51	46	48	57	55	47	54	56	54	55	43	46	53	58
East Germany	15	15	14	18	14	13	15	12	13	17	14	13	14	15	15	15	14	16
Britain	33	36	30	32	38	28	33	29	36	31	36	34	44	31	26	28	31	45
Italy	25	26	24	25	28	22	25	23	23	24	26	30	30	23	25	20	25	30
Netherlands	36	34	36	38	38	29	33	31	44	42	32	37	45	31	33	28	30	46
Belgium	42	42	42	47	44	37	41	42	44	43	45	39	51	41	38	42	42	46
Austria	23	22	23	26	28	17	20	25	23	17	24	29	31	23	22	22	21	29
France	35	35	36	36	38	32	36	37	31	39	35	32	41	32	30	31	37	37
Canada	31	31	31	32	34	27	30	28	36	30	32	32	39	31	26	29	29	38
United States	23	22	24	25	26	19	24	25	20	22	21	26	23	22	25	25	23	24
Iceland	33	30	36	34	35	27	24	31	41	na	na	na	44	30	27	25	34	43
West Germany	35	36	33	42	39	27	32	41	37	33	38	35	49	31	24	19	33	45
Denmark	27	27	27	29	32	19	24	24	31	28	25	31	43	24	20	22	25	45
Finland	24	27	20	36	25	10	21	24	25	21	22	28	27	22	24	25	22	27
Norway	17	15	18	21	21	09	07	16	22	15	18	19	21	15	15	14	16	26
Sweden	27	27	28	37	28	17	22	29	30	26	28	25	31	25	27	22	24	37
Japan	06	08	03	10	05	04	04	05	08	05	07	06	11	07	03	05	06	13
Switzerland	46	44	47	46	53	38	44	48	47	43	47	48	56	45	36	39	44	53
Total	25	25	25	27	26	22	24	25	24	24	25	25	29	25	24	23	24	28

Ranking:

Spain	50
Switzerland	46
Belgium	42
Bulgaria	41
Portugal	38
Netherlands	36
France	35
West Germany	35
Moscow	33
Britain	33
Iceland	33
Canada	31
Poland	30
Mexico	28
Belarus	28
Denmark	27
Sweden	27
Russia	26
Hungary	25
Italy	25
Finland	24
Austria	23
United States	23
Ireland	22
North Ireland	22
Argentina	20
Brazil	19
Chile	18
Norway	17
Turkey	16
South Korea	16
Nigeria	15
East Germany	15
South Africa	14
Lithuania	12
Slovenia	12
China	08
Czechoslovakia	08
India	07
Japan	06

Note: Countries in the left column are ranked according to GNP per capita. / The percentages in the bottom row give each country an equal weight. / na=not ascertained.

V266 TECHNOLOGICAL DEVELOPMENT

Here is a list of various changes in our way of life that might take place in the near future. Please tell me for each one, if it were to happen whether you think it would be a good thing, a bad thing, or don't you mind? "More emphasis on the development of technology" (% "good")

	Total	Gender		Age			Education			Income			Political Affinity			Values		
		Male	Female	16-29	30-49	50+	Lower	Medium	Upper	Lower	Middle	Upper	Left	Center	Right	Mat	Mixed	Postmat
India	85	88	81	88	84	78	70	86	91	79	85	89	89	87	89	86	86	89
Nigeria	96	97	93	96	95	93	93	97	96	96	94	97	94	95	99	98	96	96
China	95	95	95	93	96	96	95	97	97	96	96	94	na	na	na	95	96	96
Romania	na	na	na	na	na	na	na	na	na	na	na	na	na	na	na	na	na	na
Turkey	90	93	87	91	90	89	89	91	95	89	89	93	93	90	91	88	90	92
Poland	89	91	88	88	91	89	87	91	93	89	88	92	92	90	91	85	91	96
Bulgaria	81	84	79	84	85	75	67	85	90	78	85	88	84	88	87	81	82	87
Chile	73	80	67	72	76	70	69	74	78	64	77	80	73	75	77	68	76	78
Czechoslovakia	85	90	80	85	88	81	78	87	92	80	88	86	86	84	88	78	87	88
South Africa	82	81	83	82	83	83	78	84	86	76	85	88	80	85	82	84	81	84
Lithuania	88	91	86	86	91	88	86	89	92	85	91	92	na	na	na	89	88	90
Hungary	75	82	70	76	78	72	68	82	81	71	77	83	83	78	74	75	77	67
Argentina	78	84	73	78	78	78	75	80	81	75	79	80	72	81	83	74	78	82
Brazil	78	84	72	80	77	77	72	79	87	74	79	82	79	78	82	77	79	81
Mexico	78	80	77	80	79	73	76	83	81	74	83	83	78	78	82	81	81	81
Belarus	84	86	82	82	86	84	79	81	89	84	86	83	87	82	85	84	84	89
Russia	84	88	81	88	86	80	78	83	89	83	86	87	90	89	86	82	86	86
Moscow	85	89	81	82	88	81	76	83	88	80	88	86	87	87	79	84	86	89
Latvia	81	89	75	79	82	81	70	81	83	81	76	84	na	na	na	75	83	91
Estonia	84	88	81	84	86	80	73	85	93	80	84	89	na	na	na	80	88	88
Portugal	74	82	68	80	78	66	70	79	88	67	75	84	76	77	77	72	78	85
South Korea	90	89	92	89	90	95	89	88	93	88	92	95	82	92	92	92	91	83
Ireland	61	66	57	56	63	62	59	65	56	55	59	67	52	63	64	54	65	60
North Ireland	60	70	53	55	64	59	57	63	69	62	58	73	54	57	70	63	59	64
Slovenia	87	89	84	85	90	84	77	92	96	83	88	93	90	91	93	84	87	88
Spain	66	70	63	68	68	63	66	73	60	61	69	69	66	69	65	66	71	64
East Germany	83	88	78	87	86	77	82	82	86	73	86	89	84	83	85	75	85	83
Britain	64	71	58	65	65	63	64	65	65	63	67	71	58	63	77	68	64	62
Italy	60	64	57	60	58	62	60	62	75	59	62	65	58	67	60	60	61	58
Netherlands	47	59	42	50	41	50	50	51	38	43	51	48	33	53	55	60	52	36
Belgium	55	59	51	53	56	56	54	57	54	56	58	59	50	59	61	56	58	52
Austria	42	52	35	45	45	37	38	45	43	34	43	48	44	44	42	38	43	41
France	76	80	73	75	78	76	74	79	77	74	77	81	80	73	81	73	77	77
Canada	63	70	57	62	64	64	61	64	64	62	62	68	60	65	68	58	66	62
United States	70	77	64	70	72	69	68	68	76	66	74	72	64	71	80	66	73	69
Iceland	69	79	59	70	67	74	69	71	68	na	na	na	63	69	75	66	73	56
West Germany	52	62	43	55	54	50	52	52	54	43	57	57	44	55	63	49	57	46
Denmark	59	65	52	63	61	54	54	66	57	54	64	62	52	58	67	57	60	57
Finland	68	76	57	68	66	71	60	72	66	70	68	66	60	67	71	65	67	70
Norway	47	58	36	53	47	44	42	49	48	40	51	55	43	43	57	49	48	42
Sweden	35	41	29	34	33	40	39	36	30	38	35	35	33	33	41	39	39	24
Japan	65	69	61	61	68	63	63	65	67	63	66	70	61	70	77	74	69	54
Switzerland	57	64	50	53	54	60	55	58	55	52	58	57	48	62	58	54	58	53
Total	72	78	68	73	74	71	69	74	75	69	74	77	69	72	75	71	74	72

Ranking:

Nigeria	96
China	95
Turkey	90
South Korea	90
Poland	89
Lithuania	88
Slovenia	87
India	85
Czechoslovakia	85
Moscow	85
Belarus	84
Russia	84
Estonia	84
East Germany	83
South Africa	82
Bulgaria	81
Latvia	81
Argentina	78
Brazil	78
Mexico	78
France	76
Hungary	75
Portugal	74
Chile	73
United States	70
Iceland	69
Finland	68
Spain	66
Japan	65
Britain	64
Canada	63
Ireland	61
North Ireland	60
Italy	60
Denmark	59
Switzerland	57
Belgium	55
West Germany	52
Netherlands	47
Norway	47
Austria	42
Sweden	35

Note: Countries in the left column are ranked according to GNP per capita. / The percentages in the bottom row give each country an equal weight. / na=not ascertained.

V267 INDIVIDUAL DEVELOPMENT

Here is a list of various changes in our way of life that might take place in the near future. Please tell me for each one, if it were to happen whether you think it would be a good thing, a bad thing, or don't you mind? "Greater emphasis on the development of the individual"
(% "good")

	Total	Gender		Age			Education			Income			Political Affinity			Values			Ranking:	
		Male	Female	16-29	30-49	50+	Lower	Medium	Upper	Lower	Middle	Upper	Left	Center	Right	Mat	Mixed	Postmat		
India	71	73	69	72	72	67	61	72	75	68	72	73	75	70	76	72	72	75	Belarus	96
Nigeria	93	92	93	91	93	97	90	94	92	92	94	95	90	91	96	95	93	81	Argentina	95
China	40	42	37	51	37	32	34	38	55	36	42	44	na	na	na	29	49	76	Moscow	95
Romania	na	na	na	na	na	na	na	na	na	na	na	na	na	na	na	na	na	na	Poland	94
Turkey	93	93	92	94	93	91	90	96	96	91	93	93	93	93	92	87	94	96	Czechoslovakia	94
Poland	94	93	94	88	95	95	92	94	94	92	94	95	97	93	93	90	96	94	Iceland	94
Bulgaria	87	88	87	92	89	82	79	88	96	88	90	89	90	91	88	85	88	92	Nigeria	93
Chile	90	93	88	90	91	91	85	92	95	84	92	96	92	92	87	87	91	96	Turkey	93
Czechoslovakia	94	94	95	94	95	94	93	95	96	94	94	96	95	94	95	91	95	97	Italy	93
South Africa	90	88	91	89	90	90	89	89	94	88	88	95	87	92	90	92	89	88	Denmark	93
Lithuania	91	92	91	92	92	90	87	92	96	90	91	94	na	na	na	91	91	95	Finland	93
Hungary	72	75	69	73	74	69	65	76	84	67	75	79	76	75	71	70	73	67	Brazil	92
Argentina	95	95	95	93	96	96	94	97	98	93	95	96	96	96	94	94	96	96	Lithuania	91
Brazil	92	92	92	90	92	93	87	93	97	87	94	96	90	94	92	90	92	98	Spain	91
Mexico	88	87	89	88	88	87	85	92	93	85	88	93	89	90	86	89	89	90	Switzerland	91
Belarus	96	96	95	93	97	94	93	94	98	93	97	96	98	93	94	95	96	97	Chile	90
Russia	89	89	89	90	92	86	82	90	94	88	90	92	95	90	87	86	91	91	South Africa	90
Moscow	95	96	94	95	96	93	90	95	96	94	96	94	97	93	99	97	96	95	Ireland	90
Latvia	86	88	85	85	86	89	80	83	94	82	88	88	na	na	na	77	90	89	Russia	89
Estonia	85	87	84	87	86	82	79	86	90	86	86	84	na	na	na	84	87	92	Mexico	88
Portugal	76	76	76	76	80	72	72	84	82	68	81	80	74	77	81	74	79	82	East Germany	88
South Korea	84	84	84	84	83	84	77	84	87	81	83	88	76	85	85	84	84	81	France	88
Ireland	90	87	92	90	91	88	88	93	88	87	89	91	86	93	87	88	89	93	Norway	88
North Ireland	81	84	78	83	82	77	79	81	90	84	72	94	82	79	84	77	83	84	Sweden	88
Slovenia	81	82	80	84	81	78	72	85	89	76	81	88	81	85	90	78	81	87	Bulgaria	87
Spain	91	92	90	91	93	88	90	94	95	88	93	94	93	92	91	93	94	92	United States	87
East Germany	88	91	86	92	92	83	85	95	95	83	90	92	92	89	85	77	90	90	Latvia	86
Britain	78	78	77	74	81	76	75	82	84	76	79	81	79	79	80	77	77	83	Estonia	85
Italy	93	92	94	94	94	92	92	96	95	92	95	98	94	95	92	91	93	95	Canada	85
Netherlands	84	86	84	84	86	83	79	85	89	83	83	90	88	86	84	81	82	91	West Germany	85
Belgium	81	80	82	83	83	79	77	82	87	80	84	84	83	84	83	76	83	87	South Korea	84
Austria	76	77	75	79	79	72	71	77	89	66	77	82	77	76	78	62	76	83	Netherlands	84
France	88	87	89	86	90	87	85	91	92	87	90	89	92	87	82	81	88	94	North Ireland	81
Canada	85	85	84	83	88	83	81	85	87	83	85	88	89	85	87	81	85	90	Slovenia	81
United States	87	87	86	85	88	86	81	85	93	85	85	90	86	89	86	83	87	91	Belgium	81
Iceland	94	93	96	94	95	95	93	89	99	na	86	na	99	92	94	94	94	100	Britain	78
West Germany	85	85	84	90	86	81	82	89	93	82	86	87	85	87	82	72	85	91	Portugal	76
Denmark	93	93	94	89	96	93	89	93	96	92	92	96	98	93	91	89	94	97	Austria	76
Finland	93	91	96	96	94	89	86	94	97	88	97	94	92	93	94	85	93	96	Hungary	72
Norway	88	90	87	89	90	86	79	88	94	84	92	92	89	87	92	84	90	94	India	71
Sweden	88	88	88	86	89	89	85	89	91	91	85	90	89	86	92	87	87	92	Japan	70
Japan	70	73	68	75	70	67	65	69	80	65	69	78	76	75	81	75	75	66	China	40
Switzerland	91	90	92	90	92	91	90	93	90	91	94	89	93	92	88	91	90	95		
Total	86	86	86	86	87	84	82	87	91	83	86	89	88	88	88	83	87	90		

Note: Countries in the left column are ranked according to GNP per capita. / The percentages in the bottom row give each country an equal weight. / na=not ascertained.

V268 RESPECT AUTHORITY

Here is a list of various changes in our way of life that might take place in the near future. Please tell me for each one, if it were to happen whether you think it would be a good thing, a bad thing, or don't you mind? "Greater respect for authority" (% "good")

	Total	Gender Male	Gender Female	Age 16-29	Age 30-49	Age 50+	Education Lower	Education Medium	Education Upper	Income Lower	Income Middle	Income Upper	Pol. Affinity Left	Pol. Affinity Center	Pol. Affinity Right	Values Mat	Values Mixed	Values Postmat
India	54	56	52	54	55	54	50	55	56	51	58	55	57	50	60	56	56	57
Nigeria	91	91	91	91	90	91	88	94	89	92	89	94	90	89	94	97	90	77
China	24	26	22	20	25	30	23	25	25	23	25	27	na	na	na	24	26	19
Romania	na	na	na	na	na	na	na	na	na	na	na	na	na	na	na	na	na	na
Turkey	65	64	66	59	63	77	74	56	38	74	67	52	46	67	73	68	70	46
Poland	73	69	76	67	70	79	73	73	73	72	70	77	75	72	79	73	72	79
Bulgaria	78	79	77	72	78	82	79	78	78	77	84	79	82	82	74	84	78	60
Chile	80	79	81	72	83	86	89	77	72	85	80	75	73	82	84	86	80	74
Czechoslovakia	65	65	65	54	62	75	71	61	66	66	67	61	62	64	70	56	69	62
South Africa	88	88	89	85	89	93	91	88	82	88	89	86	80	91	88	92	87	83
Lithuania	53	54	51	41	51	65	63	51	42	53	53	51	na	na	na	59	53	40
Hungary	61	62	60	53	60	65	63	58	67	62	60	61	59	64	63	59	62	64
Argentina	69	69	69	55	69	80	79	64	57	76	69	58	45	66	73	79	71	50
Brazil	81	79	82	75	80	92	91	80	63	89	81	72	74	78	90	90	77	58
Mexico	65	63	68	59	70	71	65	68	64	64	66	67	49	67	73	73	65	52
Belarus	71	73	69	63	73	76	77	64	76	66	75	72	70	73	77	76	70	65
Russia	68	70	67	59	64	79	71	64	71	71	70	70	70	73	68	71	67	63
Moscow	69	70	68	63	68	76	71	65	71	66	73	71	72	67	67	74	70	63
Latvia	na	70	na	na	na	na	na	na	na	na	na	na	na	na	na	na	na	na
Estonia	na	na	na	na	na	na	na	na	na	na	na	na	na	na	na	na	na	na
Portugal	74	71	76	62	74	84	79	67	58	80	69	68	65	76	78	84	73	52
South Korea	14	15	13	12	14	16	23	15	08	16	13	10	13	13	14	13	16	07
Ireland	83	80	85	68	84	91	87	79	69	89	87	75	58	83	91	92	82	73
North Ireland	82	81	82	65	81	94	85	79	66	79	86	80	82	80	86	95	81	67
Slovenia	66	66	66	59	68	69	64	72	59	67	65	69	55	66	73	68	66	63
Spain	69	69	69	53	66	84	76	62	46	83	69	61	58	69	80	86	71	43
East Germany	57	56	59	46	52	70	62	48	48	63	56	53	49	60	65	75	60	42
Britain	72	70	73	55	73	81	76	71	51	77	75	64	59	72	83	86	72	59
Italy	49	49	49	39	44	59	51	36	36	54	44	42	38	56	51	59	52	31
Netherlands	51	56	49	42	47	67	60	50	41	45	53	50	31	52	69	80	60	32
Belgium	50	46	53	35	43	66	58	50	32	62	45	41	37	52	52	68	52	30
Austria	47	47	48	33	39	61	53	44	40	54	49	39	45	47	49	63	51	30
France	59	57	61	51	51	73	70	53	42	66	59	47	45	59	78	78	62	37
Canada	64	62	66	56	60	77	78	67	51	69	64	58	42	66	69	74	68	54
United States	78	79	77	73	75	84	81	80	73	83	78	72	55	81	85	82	80	70
Iceland	42	44	41	34	41	55	51	34	41	na	na	na	33	46	47	41	45	29
West Germany	30	28	33	16	20	47	37	20	15	37	28	25	14	31	48	55	33	12
Denmark	35	34	36	34	26	46	50	36	26	39	36	22	19	39	41	44	40	10
Finland	26	25	27	23	26	30	34	28	21	30	25	23	17	26	32	38	26	24
Norway	32	32	32	24	28	42	43	30	28	35	30	27	20	35	39	40	32	11
Sweden	22	24	19	22	18	27	33	19	10	27	24	18	18	20	23	32	24	10
Japan	06	05	06	07	05	05	05	06	05	07	05	05	03	05	06	06	05	09
Switzerland	46	44	48	34	38	59	52	45	27	55	42	32	25	48	52	68	49	24
Total	**58**	**57**	**58**	**50**	**56**	**66**	**63**	**55**	**50**	**61**	**58**	**54**	**50**	**60**	**64**	**66**	**59**	**46**

Ranking:

Nigeria	91
South Africa	88
Ireland	83
North Ireland	82
Brazil	81
Chile	80
Bulgaria	78
United States	78
Portugal	74
Poland	73
Britain	72
Belarus	71
Argentina	69
Moscow	69
Spain	69
Russia	68
Slovenia	66
Turkey	65
Czechoslovakia	65
Mexico	65
Canada	64
Hungary	61
France	59
East Germany	57
India	54
Lithuania	53
Netherlands	51
Belgium	50
Italy	49
Austria	47
Switzerland	46
Iceland	42
Denmark	35
Norway	32
West Germany	30
Finland	26
China	24
Sweden	22
South Korea	14
Japan	06

Note: Countries in the left column are ranked according to GNP per capita. / The percentages in the bottom row give each country an equal weight / na=not ascertained.

V269 EMPHASIS FAMILY LIFE

Here is a list of various changes in our way of life that might take place in the near future. Please tell me for each one, if it were to happen whether you think it would be a good thing, a bad thing, or don't you mind? "More emphasis on family life" (% "good")

	Total	Gender Male	Gender Female	Age 16-29	Age 30-49	Age 50+	Education Lower	Education Medium	Education Upper	Income Lower	Income Middle	Income Upper	Political Affinity Left	Political Affinity Center	Political Affinity Right	Values Mat	Values Mixed	Values Postmat
India	75	74	75	73	75	77	72	76	74	70	78	75	72	75	83	77	74	73
Nigeria	92	92	93	91	92	98	95	92	91	89	93	95	90	92	95	95	91	92
China	74	70	80	72	77	70	79	71	71	75	75	71	na	na	na	76	70	85
Romania	na	na	na	na	na	na	na	na	na	na	na	na	na	na	na	na	na	na
Turkey	95	95	94	92	96	97	97	93	90	95	97	92	92	95	98	94	96	94
Poland	97	96	98	93	98	97	95	97	99	96	95	99	98	97	98	95	98	97
Bulgaria	90	88	92	88	90	92	90	92	87	91	91	90	91	91	93	92	91	78
Chile	98	97	98	98	97	97	97	97	99	97	97	99	98	98	98	97	97	99
Czechoslovakia	94	90	98	91	93	96	94	93	94	94	95	91	94	93	95	93	93	96
South Africa	94	94	94	93	94	95	95	93	98	92	94	98	92	97	94	95	94	93
Lithuania	96	95	96	95	96	97	97	96	95	94	96	98	na	na	na	97	96	95
Hungary	94	94	94	94	94	94	94	95	92	94	95	92	94	97	94	96	94	88
Argentina	96	97	96	94	97	98	98	95	95	97	97	94	90	96	97	96	96	95
Brazil	98	97	99	98	98	98	98	98	95	98	99	97	97	97	98	99	98	93
Mexico	91	90	92	90	91	93	91	90	93	91	93	91	90	91	92	94	92	86
Belarus	95	95	95	94	95	96	94	94	96	95	96	94	95	95	96	97	95	92
Russia	95	94	96	94	95	95	96	95	94	95	96	94	94	96	96	96	95	94
Moscow	91	91	92	86	94	91	89	91	92	91	92	90	93	91	93	94	92	91
Latvia	85	79	89	82	85	88	80	85	85	89	85	82	na	na	na	86	84	84
Estonia	86	85	87	87	86	85	87	86	86	85	85	88	na	na	na	85	89	85
Portugal	95	94	96	93	97	96	96	96	93	95	97	93	95	96	95	96	95	97
South Korea	89	90	88	90	86	91	86	88	91	89	87	90	83	89	90	88	90	84
Ireland	94	94	95	91	95	97	97	93	86	96	95	92	80	94	98	96	95	91
North Ireland	92	91	93	82	95	96	93	91	86	93	95	92	89	94	93	100	92	87
Slovenia	91	89	93	91	91	91	89	94	92	89	93	93	87	93	96	92	91	85
Spain	89	87	91	82	90	94	92	89	78	94	90	86	83	94	95	96	92	78
East Germany	92	89	94	84	93	96	93	88	91	91	94	91	88	88	92	96	93	86
Britain	88	85	90	78	89	92	89	88	79	89	87	84	83	88	93	91	88	86
Italy	93	90	95	88	92	96	94	87	81	94	92	83	87	96	94	96	94	87
Netherlands	66	66	67	64	61	77	73	72	52	64	70	61	50	73	76	76	74	54
Belgium	85	81	88	77	84	90	88	86	76	86	84	85	77	86	85	89	88	76
Austria	92	91	93	85	93	95	94	91	88	91	94	92	90	93	92	96	93	89
France	90	89	91	84	91	95	92	92	81	91	91	88	84	92	92	98	91	84
Canada	94	93	94	92	94	94	93	95	92	95	94	93	89	94	96	94	94	93
United States	95	94	95	94	95	96	93	95	96	95	94	95	91	96	96	95	95	96
Iceland	96	94	97	95	96	95	95	94	97	na	na	na	95	96	97	94	96	97
West Germany	87	84	90	76	87	94	91	82	78	88	88	88	78	91	91	94	90	79
Denmark	95	92	97	92	96	95	98	96	91	94	96	92	90	96	95	96	96	87
Finland	96	95	96	96	96	96	91	98	95	94	97	96	95	96	98	100	96	95
Norway	95	95	95	94	95	96	96	95	94	95	95	96	94	96	96	97	96	90
Sweden	85	84	87	85	84	87	89	85	80	89	84	85	81	88	87	92	86	80
Japan	85	87	84	88	87	82	78	86	91	79	86	91	91	87	93	91	90	88
Switzerland	91	89	93	85	89	95	94	90	81	92	90	86	82	93	94	96	92	86
Total	91	89	92	88	91	93	91	90	88	91	91	90	88	93	94	93	91	88

Ranking:

Chile	98
Brazil	98
Poland	97
Lithuania	96
Argentina	96
Iceland	96
Finland	96
Turkey	95
Belarus	95
Russia	95
Portugal	95
United States	95
Denmark	95
Norway	95
Czechoslovakia	94
South Africa	94
Hungary	94
Ireland	94
Canada	94
Italy	93
Nigeria	92
North Ireland	92
East Germany	92
Austria	92
Mexico	91
Moscow	91
Slovenia	91
Switzerland	91
Bulgaria	90
France	90
South Korea	89
Spain	89
Britain	88
West Germany	87
Estonia	86
Latvia	85
Belgium	85
Sweden	85
Japan	85
India	75
China	74
Netherlands	66

Note: Countries in the left column are ranked according to GNP per capita. / The percentages in the bottom row give each country an equal weight. / na=not ascertained.

V270 NATURAL LIFESTYLE

Here is a list of various changes in our way of life that might take place in the near future. Please tell me for each one, if it were to happen whether you think it would be a good thing, a bad thing, or don't you mind? "A simple and more natural lifestyle" (% "good")

	Total	Gender		Age			Education			Income			Political Affinity			Values		
		Male	Female	16-29	30-49	50+	Lower	Medium	Upper	Lower	Middle	Upper	Left	Center	Right	Mat	Mixed	Postmat
India	80	81	79	80	81	78	75	80	83	77	81	81	84	81	83	81	82	84
Nigeria	90	90	89	89	90	97	88	88	92	91	91	87	91	87	92	93	88	86
China	51	51	52	57	49	49	54	51	50	44	56	56	na	na	na	49	53	59
Romania	na	na	na	na	na	na	na	na	na	na	na	na	na	na	na	na	na	na
Turkey	53	54	52	52	53	53	56	47	50	54	51	52	53	53	53	53	54	50
Poland	89	85	92	85	92	87	85	91	94	89	89	88	84	92	90	85	91	85
Bulgaria	82	82	82	77	84	82	77	82	86	84	84	81	83	85	89	81	81	87
Chile	93	93	93	91	96	93	94	91	95	94	94	92	92	94	93	95	92	95
Czechoslovakia	86	85	87	85	87	86	87	86	84	88	86	85	85	88	85	89	86	80
South Africa	86	84	88	83	86	91	87	85	86	83	85	89	80	91	86	88	85	80
Lithuania	89	86	93	90	90	88	85	91	90	88	90	93	na	na	na	86	92	91
Hungary	85	84	86	88	85	84	84	86	87	85	86	84	84	87	87	84	86	88
Argentina	92	91	93	89	92	94	95	90	88	94	93	87	86	92	89	92	92	92
Brazil	93	91	94	90	94	94	94	94	86	96	94	91	90	93	93	95	91	91
Mexico	83	82	85	83	84	82	83	83	85	81	86	83	79	87	81	86	84	86
Belarus	90	90	90	90	89	91	91	90	90	87	93	90	90	89	na	91	89	91
Russia	89	88	90	88	90	90	88	90	90	89	89	90	91	89	92	89	90	86
Moscow	87	86	88	88	88	85	85	87	88	89	87	84	90	86	87	89	88	90
Latvia	80	77	83	73	82	87	80	81	80	81	83	78	na	na	na	80	81	78
Estonia	84	81	86	81	84	86	83	84	84	84	83	84	na	na	na	84	85	83
Portugal	92	89	94	81	94	93	96	96	88	88	93	91	93	94	89	91	93	92
South Korea	66	67	65	59	67	75	71	67	61	66	66	66	59	63	69	66	66	64
Ireland	87	85	88	78	89	91	89	87	87	91	88	83	79	86	90	87	89	84
North Ireland	86	87	85	82	87	87	87	88	76	89	85	76	86	92	86	83	89	82
Slovenia	90	89	91	86	91	91	87	91	92	87	93	89	91	92	90	89	90	93
Spain	93	93	93	92	94	93	93	93	90	92	94	94	93	93	93	95	95	91
East Germany	66	60	71	61	62	72	64	68	69	71	64	62	69	65	60	68	65	65
Britain	80	75	83	73	79	84	85	71	63	84	80	73	81	81	75	79	80	82
Italy	93	91	95	91	93	95	94	90	95	94	94	88	95	94	91	94	94	94
Netherlands	78	72	80	68	82	84	85	71	78	82	78	71	83	75	77	81	78	79
Belgium	84	82	85	76	85	87	87	82	81	86	84	81	87	88	78	85	85	84
Austria	85	81	88	80	86	87	87	83	89	86	85	89	86	90	79	88	84	86
France	92	90	93	89	92	93	93	92	89	96	89	81	93	94	87	94	91	90
Canada	84	82	87	80	86	86	89	85	81	89	85	81	83	84	85	86	84	87
United States	85	83	87	81	85	88	83	86	86	87	86	83	85	86	83	83	86	87
Iceland	79	74	84	74	78	87	77	78	81	na	na	na	78	80	80	77	80	78
West Germany	63	58	66	55	59	70	63	59	70	67	60	60	66	64	58	59	61	69
Denmark	85	80	89	75	88	88	89	84	82	87	85	79	85	87	82	85	85	83
Finland	91	87	95	87	92	90	89	92	90	90	90	92	92	95	86	90	91	90
Norway	80	76	84	71	79	87	85	75	82	82	83	75	86	83	75	81	79	89
Sweden	90	88	92	86	93	90	94	88	88	94	92	88	91	93	87	88	90	92
Japan	76	76	76	71	78	76	71	76	80	71	74	83	87	77	86	83	79	84
Switzerland	91	89	92	84	92	92	91	91	87	92	92	86	93	91	86	90	90	93
Total	83	81	85	80	84	85	84	83	82	84	84	82	84	85	83	84	84	84

Ranking:

Chile	93
Brazil	93
Spain	93
Italy	93
Argentina	92
Portugal	92
France	92
Finland	91
Switzerland	91
Nigeria	90
Belarus	90
Slovenia	90
Sweden	90
Poland	89
Lithuania	89
Russia	89
Moscow	87
Ireland	87
Czechoslovakia	86
South Africa	86
North Ireland	86
Hungary	85
Austria	85
United States	85
Denmark	85
Estonia	84
Belgium	84
Canada	84
Mexico	83
Bulgaria	82
India	80
Latvia	80
Britain	80
Norway	80
Iceland	79
Netherlands	78
Japan	76
South Korea	66
East Germany	66
West Germany	63
Turkey	53
China	51

Note: Countries in the left column are ranked according to GNP per capita. / The percentages in the bottom row give each country an equal weight. / na=not ascertained.

V271. In the long run, do you think the scientific advances we are making will help or harm mankind?

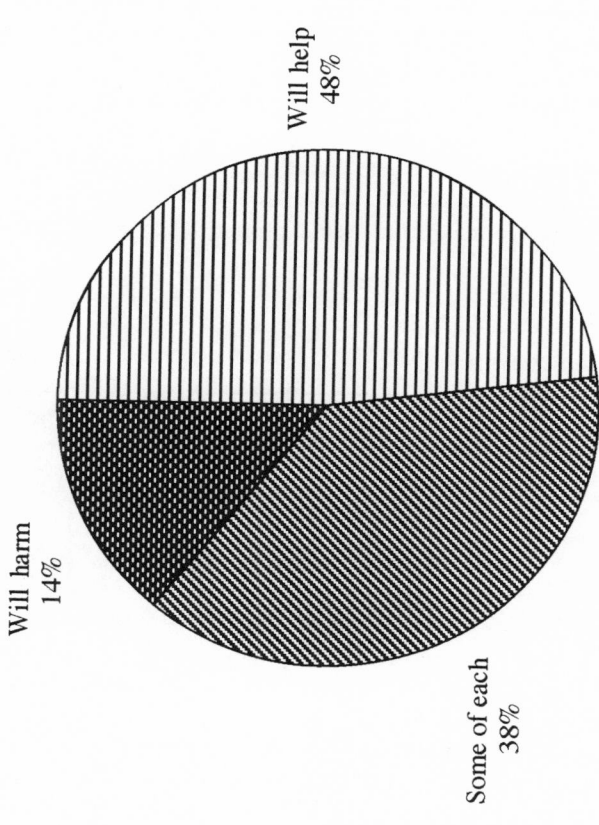

Will help
48%

Will harm
14%

Some of each
38%

V271 SCIENTIFIC ADVANCES WILL HELP MANKIND

In the long run, do you think the scientific advances we are making will help or harm mankind? (% "will help")

	Total	Gender		Age			Education			Income			Political Affinity			Values		
		Male	Female	16-29	30-49	50+	Lower	Medium	Upper	Lower	Middle	Upper	Left	Center	Right	Mat	Mixed	Postmat
India	51	53	48	51	51	50	55	52	47	57	49	47	52	50	50	52	49	44
Nigeria	79	76	84	80	78	80	80	81	77	78	80	80	82	78	80	84	77	74
China	58	58	59	50	59	66	63	58	48	63	54	57	na	na	na	63	56	35
Romania	na	na	na	na	na	na	na	na	na	na	na	na	na	na	na	na	na	na
Turkey	72	76	68	66	75	76	77	64	64	77	73	66	70	72	72	75	74	61
Poland	70	70	69	65	72	70	70	67	79	64	74	73	69	70	77	70	70	67
Bulgaria	62	63	61	61	63	61	57	63	64	57	64	65	66	62	60	66	60	58
Chile	43	47	38	43	41	44	39	42	48	38	40	51	45	43	45	39	44	43
Czechoslovakia	30	36	24	28	30	30	30	29	32	31	29	29	31	29	31	25	32	30
South Africa	57	60	55	58	58	54	59	57	54	60	55	55	55	51	66	58	57	57
Lithuania	61	61	61	55	55	73	74	58	57	62	61	59	na	55	na	60	62	61
Hungary	55	63	47	50	55	57	56	53	58	54	55	57	63	55	63	52	57	68
Argentina	47	51	43	44	48	47	47	46	47	44	42	51	44	46	65	48	49	39
Brazil	64	65	63	62	63	69	69	61	64	64	63	63	60	61	73	66	62	63
Mexico	44	45	44	47	42	44	44	46	45	42	47	42	39	45	49	47	45	37
Belarus	38	40	36	31	38	44	39	35	40	34	37	42	39	36	38	40	36	49
Russia	60	62	58	60	57	62	62	59	59	61	58	66	60	62	64	60	59	59
Moscow	45	45	45	39	43	53	53	42	45	46	46	42	45	43	49	43	46	48
Latvia	34	40	31	26	34	45	42	31	38	31	34	37	na	na	na	40	33	35
Estonia	52	58	48	49	55	53	55	50	56	50	55	53	39	45	na	51	54	61
Portugal	47	49	45	51	46	43	45	52	49	48	41	53	47	47	48	46	48	45
South Korea	40	36	44	37	40	46	44	38	41	39	41	41	33	39	44	42	39	36
Ireland	40	44	36	40	39	41	39	40	41	38	38	43	44	41	40	37	40	42
North Ireland	46	50	42	48	41	49	43	51	52	42	41	57	37	41	60	48	42	55
Slovenia	41	47	36	34	41	47	44	39	41	43	41	40	36	40	53	44	41	33
Spain	46	49	43	51	43	44	43	52	53	45	44	49	46	46	48	45	48	44
East Germany	52	58	47	52	55	50	53	49	54	47	55	55	52	53	55	49	53	54
Britain	48	55	41	55	49	43	43	51	70	41	55	56	50	44	58	55	44	53
Italy	37	44	30	32	40	37	36	45	40	37	39	52	36	42	38	37	38	38
Netherlands	37	42	35	38	39	32	34	36	41	32	34	44	34	37	39	46	37	34
Belgium	34	36	32	34	35	33	29	34	44	30	43	38	30	33	44	31	34	37
Austria	31	34	29	30	35	27	28	31	44	25	30	38	34	31	32	24	32	33
France	42	45	39	40	45	39	38	45	45	40	41	51	45	43	46	37	42	46
Canada	55	59	52	55	55	53	50	55	59	45	55	56	60	52	62	50	57	55
United States	63	68	57	60	63	65	56	63	67	56	65	68	67	62	64	60	63	57
Iceland	54	61	48	53	60	47	50	60	54	na	na	na	47	57	62	52	55	54
West Germany	39	46	34	38	42	38	39	38	45	34	40	45	33	41	52	40	44	33
Denmark	43	51	35	45	45	39	36	43	47	37	48	51	38	45	46	43	45	42
Finland	42	47	36	33	41	50	35	40	47	40	40	44	29	36	56	29	41	44
Norway	36	47	24	43	39	29	21	40	39	27	39	50	34	28	50	34	36	45
Sweden	47	56	37	44	49	48	41	47	57	42	41	54	45	45	54	43	47	52
Japan	26	32	19	23	27	26	25	25	27	29	24	25	29	21	36	30	25	22
Switzerland	na	na	na	na	na	na	na	na	na	na	na	na	na	na	na	na	na	na
Total	48	52	44	46	48	49	47	48	51	46	48	51	47	47	53	48	48	48

Ranking:

Nigeria	79
Turkey	72
Poland	70
Brazil	64
United States	63
Bulgaria	62
Lithuania	61
Russia	60
China	58
South Africa	57
Hungary	55
Canada	55
Iceland	54
Estonia	52
East Germany	52
India	51
Britain	48
Argentina	47
Portugal	47
Sweden	47
North Ireland	46
Spain	46
Moscow	45
Mexico	44
Chile	43
Denmark	43
France	42
Finland	42
Slovenia	41
South Korea	40
Ireland	40
West Germany	39
Belarus	38
Italy	37
Netherlands	37
Norway	36
Latvia	34
Belgium	34
Austria	31
Czechoslovakia	30
Japan	26

Note: Countries in the left column are ranked according to GNP per capita. / The percentages in the bottom row give each country an equal weight. / na=not ascertained.

V272-V285. Please look at this card and tell me, for each item listed, how much confidence you have in them, is it a great deal, quite a lot, not very much, or none at all?

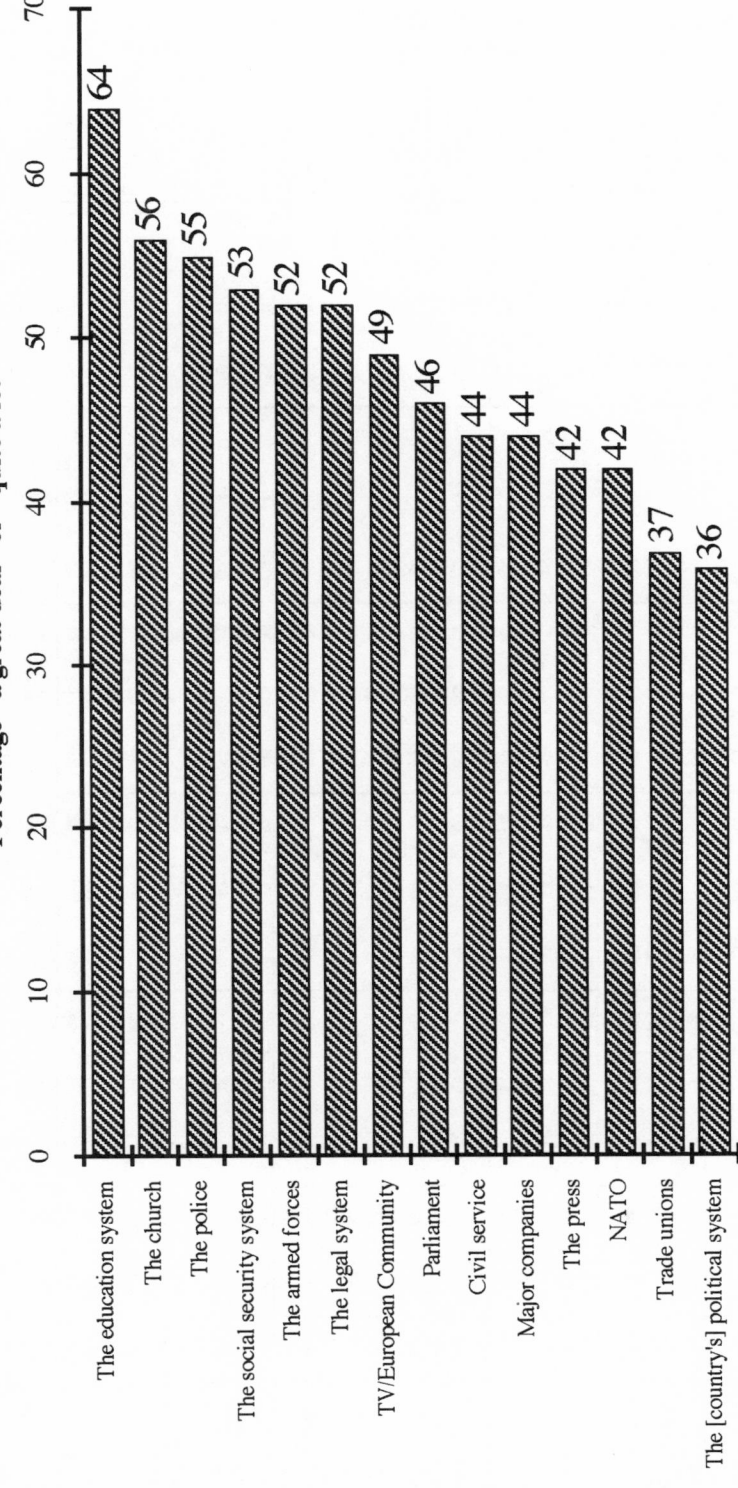

Percentage "a great deal" or "quite a lot"

V272 CONFIDENCE: CHURCH

For each item listed, how much confidence do you have in them, is it a great deal, quite a lot, not very much, or none at all? The church (% "a great deal" or "quite a lot")

	Total	Gender Male	Gender Female	Age 16-29	Age 30-49	Age 50+	Education Lower	Education Medium	Education Upper	Income Lower	Income Middle	Income Upper	Pol. Aff. Left	Pol. Aff. Center	Pol. Aff. Right	Values Mat	Values Mixed	Values Postmat	Ranking	
India	85	82	89	82	87	86	94	88	77	89	88	80	79	85	87	86	84	80	Nigeria	88
Nigeria	88	84	93	88	86	95	93	90	83	86	86	91	88	85	90	92	86	80	India	85
China	05	05	05	07	03	05	03	05	05	04	03	07	na	na	na	05	03	11	Poland	84
Romania	72	67	78	60	67	86	89	65	61	74	74	69	75	72	64	81	69	47	South Africa	83
Turkey	66	62	69	61	63	78	80	51	27	75	71	49	40	67	80	80	69	40	North Ireland	80
Poland	84	82	85	81	81	88	88	84	69	84	84	84	76	83	87	86	83	83	Chile	76
Bulgaria	30	24	36	28	21	41	44	24	25	36	24	24	17	28	37	28	29	35	Mexico	76
Chile	76	75	77	70	79	81	80	74	73	76	77	75	78	77	73	77	76	74	Brazil	75
Czechoslovakia	43	40	46	32	36	59	55	37	40	48	40	43	28	42	55	43	43	43	Lithuania	73
South Africa	83	78	87	83	82	85	86	83	75	83	86	77	78	80	82	82	84	83	Romania	72
Lithuania	73	70	77	62	72	85	85	68	80	75	72	72	na	na	na	75	73	71	Ireland	72
Hungary	56	52	60	33	46	75	67	44	52	65	48	52	34	57	64	58	56	43	United States	68
Argentina	45	40	50	33	44	57	52	43	37	57	46	33	19	45	54	55	47	26	Iceland	68
Brazil	75	69	81	72	72	85	83	74	58	83	76	66	67	72	80	79	74	59	Turkey	66
Mexico	76	73	80	74	76	85	77	83	69	79	74	73	55	78	83	82	75	64	Russia	65
Belarus	53	50	56	48	52	61	65	53	49	57	50	52	52	66	59	55	52	56	Latvia	64
Russia	65	58	70	63	63	69	70	67	60	68	68	62	62	66	64	66	64	75	Canada	64
Moscow	55	52	58	50	53	63	64	53	55	54	57	55	58	54	43	61	53	54	Italy	63
Latvia	64	65	63	62	64	67	66	64	64	69	64	61	na	na	na	60	64	71	South Korea	58
Estonia	54	55	53	49	55	57	59	53	52	56	51	53	na	na	na	50	55	68	Hungary	56
Portugal	56	46	66	42	53	73	66	31	39	70	48	43	37	53	70	69	51	29	Portugal	56
South Korea	58	65	51	54	60	58	54	58	59	59	56	58	51	60	57	56	60	54	Moscow	55
Ireland	72	70	74	56	70	86	79	67	57	83	71	66	44	71	83	79	72	65	Estonia	54
North Ireland	80	71	86	67	74	95	83	73	76	84	78	70	68	79	85	92	76	71	Belarus	53
Slovenia	39	37	41	36	35	46	53	31	25	50	33	29	27	37	51	45	37	29	Belgium	50
Spain	46	35	55	27	37	67	51	37	26	60	44	35	24	51	70	58	41	26	Austria	50
East Germany	43	40	46	30	41	53	44	43	41	49	42	39	25	50	55	48	41	47	France	50
Britain	43	33	52	32	38	53	44	40	39	51	36	32	38	44	44	53	41	37	Denmark	47
Italy	63	54	71	54	55	76	64	56	56	71	59	51	42	76	71	73	63	52	Spain	46
Netherlands	31	34	30	22	28	47	39	30	24	27	35	29	13	30	52	48	36	19	Argentina	45
Belgium	50	44	55	35	43	65	54	48	44	50	44	51	28	52	65	58	52	37	Norway	45
Austria	50	45	53	38	44	60	57	46	37	57	49	43	43	42	60	62	53	37	Czechoslovakia	43
France	50	47	52	37	45	65	53	48	43	51	44	50	35	60	68	59	53	38	East Germany	43
Canada	64	58	69	55	58	78	74	64	55	68	65	54	48	67	63	77	64	57	Britain	43
United States	68	68	68	63	66	72	71	68	65	74	69	62	67	66	73	69	69	66	West Germany	40
Iceland	68	62	74	60	67	79	78	70	59	na	na	na	65	66	72	79	66	50	Slovenia	39
West Germany	40	33	46	21	31	57	44	32	33	46	36	37	22	42	56	57	43	24	Sweden	38
Denmark	47	41	54	34	44	62	55	43	47	51	45	40	34	51	54	52	49	34	Finland	32
Finland	32	28	36	23	28	51	37	33	28	38	34	24	25	36	37	53	32	27	Netherlands	31
Norway	45	42	47	33	39	59	60	38	43	51	40	43	33	51	50	50	44	28	Bulgaria	30
Sweden	38	35	41	29	33	50	39	34	41	37	36	38	36	35	45	51	39	26	Japan	11
Japan	11	12	11	05	09	19	18	10	07	14	11	09	13	11	15	16	10	11	China	05
Switzerland	na	na	na	na	na	na	na	na	na	na	na	na	na	na	na	na	na	na		
Total	56	52	59	47	52	66	62	52	49	60	54	51	45	57	63	62	56	48		

Note: Countries in the left column are ranked according to GNP per capita. / The percentages in the bottom row give each country an equal weight. / na=not ascertained.

V273 CONFIDENCE: ARMED FORCES

For each item listed, how much confidence do you have in them, is it a great deal, quite a lot, not very much, or none at all?
The armed forces (% "a great deal" or "quite a lot")

	Total	Gender Male	Gender Female	Age 16-29	Age 30-49	Age 50+	Education Lower	Education Medium	Education Upper	Income Lower	Income Middle	Income Upper	Political Affinity Left	Political Affinity Center	Political Affinity Right	Values Mat	Values Mixed	Values Postmat	Ranking Country	Ranking
India	93	94	92	94	92	92	90	93	94	91	94	93	94	93	93	91	95	94	India	93
Nigeria	61	61	61	64	57	58	66	66	54	55	63	72	67	61	63	69	59	33	Turkey	91
China	90	90	90	84	92	94	93	89	87	91	91	89	na	na	na	93	89	75	China	90
Romania	82	83	81	73	81	90	90	82	73	81	85	80	86	83	75	89	81	55	Romania	82
Turkey	91	90	92	88	91	96	95	90	75	94	93	87	78	95	95	98	93	77	Britain	81
Poland	65	66	64	49	65	73	77	61	39	64	64	67	73	59	60	73	62	59	South Korea	80
Bulgaria	69	69	69	55	67	79	81	64	64	69	73	66	77	69	58	82	68	39	North Ireland	79
Chile	41	39	42	33	41	50	43	42	36	40	40	43	24	41	63	51	41	24	Bulgaria	69
Czechoslovakia	39	36	42	35	37	45	44	39	27	40	41	35	46	38	36	40	40	28	Russia	69
South Africa	61	59	62	55	61	70	54	61	81	40	57	79	53	66	69	69	57	49	Brazil	67
Lithuania	22	22	21	18	21	25	26	21	15	24	22	14	na	na	na	28	20	09	Poland	65
Hungary	52	51	53	38	51	58	59	46	36	55	48	49	45	54	47	52	52	43	Norway	65
Argentina	28	28	29	27	24	35	33	26	25	36	32	21	13	26	36	35	31	13	Nigeria	61
Brazil	67	68	66	60	66	81	75	65	55	73	66	63	57	66	76	73	64	49	South Africa	61
Mexico	47	49	44	44	49	51	48	45	46	49	46	43	35	48	55	53	48	29	Belarus	61
Belarus	61	61	61	51	60	74	77	60	58	63	64	57	56	67	68	76	56	47	Ireland	61
Russia	69	67	71	57	67	79	81	68	63	72	69	65	51	72	73	79	65	42	Canada	57
Moscow	46	48	43	33	44	59	69	48	39	51	45	37	39	53	59	61	44	22	Finland	57
Latvia	25	24	25	22	24	30	27	25	24	20	26	26	na	na	na	28	25	08	France	56
Estonia	23	23	23	19	21	29	28	22	20	23	25	21	na	na	na	30	20	12	Hungary	52
Portugal	47	46	48	38	48	56	55	60	31	56	43	39	48	45	49	60	41	31	Sweden	49
South Korea	80	80	79	68	83	91	87	86	68	81	79	83	62	75	88	89	77	49	Italy	48
Ireland	61	59	63	45	57	75	67	56	44	71	63	53	40	60	70	61	60	54	United States	48
North Ireland	79	76	81	65	81	86	78	81	72	82	89	79	64	77	90	89	76	76	Mexico	47
Slovenia	45	48	43	45	47	43	48	47	36	47	46	43	37	49	54	50	44	43	Portugal	47
Spain	37	33	41	20	29	57	43	26	22	54	34	28	23	37	59	55	32	18	Moscow	46
East Germany	14	13	16	13	11	18	15	15	12	13	15	14	17	15	06	17	15	09	Denmark	45
Britain	81	80	82	78	79	85	83	82	69	82	82	81	72	82	89	88	84	68	Slovenia	45
Italy	48	43	53	39	44	57	50	36	17	52	47	32	29	56	61	58	50	34	Chile	41
Netherlands	32	35	30	33	27	36	31	36	27	32	32	29	19	35	42	43	37	20	West Germany	40
Belgium	33	30	36	31	27	40	36	32	30	37	30	27	26	37	36	42	36	20	Czechoslovakia	39
Austria	29	27	30	21	24	37	35	24	27	36	28	22	26	25	33	41	31	17	Spain	37
France	56	56	57	46	54	67	60	58	44	53	58	55	44	62	79	64	61	41	Belgium	33
Canada	57	51	63	52	52	68	68	57	48	65	56	47	38	61	56	71	58	48	Netherlands	32
United States	48	51	46	51	44	52	49	51	45	54	46	50	49	45	53	49	49	49	Austria	29
Iceland	24	22	26	29	20	25	27	27	19	na	na	na	10	22	40	27	25	11	Argentina	28
West Germany	40	41	39	28	35	51	44	34	30	41	39	40	21	42	60	55	46	21	Latvia	25
Denmark	46	46	45	48	41	50	47	44	46	45	46	44	27	45	58	46	50	26	Iceland	24
Finland	57	60	53	54	52	74	63	59	51	59	58	55	35	62	64	68	54	61	Japan	24
Norway	65	67	63	60	64	70	66	66	63	63	65	66	47	70	76	68	67	47	Estonia	23
Sweden	49	52	46	46	43	58	56	48	39	51	43	49	43	46	59	53	52	39	Lithuania	22
Japan	24	27	22	16	23	33	31	23	20	21	28	25	18	23	40	32	24	17	East Germany	14
Switzerland	na	na	na	na	na	na	na	na	na	na	na	na	na	na	na	na	na	na		
Total	**52**	**52**	**52**	**46**	**50**	**59**	**57**	**51**	**45**	**55**	**53**	**50**	**44**	**54**	**60**	**60**	**52**	**38**		

Note: Countries in the left column are ranked according to GNP per capita. / The percentages in the bottom row give each country an equal weight. / na=not ascertained.

V274 CONFIDENCE: EDUCATION

For each item listed, how much confidence do you have in them, is it a great deal, quite a lot, not very much, or none at all?
The education system (% "a great deal" or "quite a lot")

	Total	Gender Male	Gender Female	Age 16-29	Age 30-49	Age 50+	Education Lower	Education Medium	Education Upper	Income Lower	Income Middle	Income Upper	Political Affinity Left	Political Affinity Center	Political Affinity Right	Values Mat	Values Mixed	Values Postmat
India	73	69	78	72	74	72	78	74	70	75	75	70	66	72	78	73	72	69
Nigeria	84	80	90	87	79	84	85	89	78	81	83	87	84	84	85	86	84	71
China	93	91	95	90	93	96	95	92	89	93	90	96	86	76	na	96	90	78
Romania	79	81	78	70	79	85	84	81	70	76	82	78	86	76	78	83	78	65
Turkey	65	56	75	60	65	75	79	52	27	75	69	50	48	67	72	74	70	42
Poland	75	75	75	66	76	79	85	72	52	74	76	74	69	72	73	79	73	71
Bulgaria	53	53	53	43	46	67	76	50	36	53	56	52	52	52	42	67	50	28
Chile	73	73	74	71	73	78	79	73	67	81	73	66	73	73	74	79	74	65
Czechoslovakia	61	59	63	63	53	69	70	59	49	63	63	56	64	61	58	63	60	59
South Africa	77	77	78	79	76	77	84	76	58	84	79	63	71	75	77	80	77	70
Lithuania	57	56	58	49	49	71	75	53	42	61	53	51	na	na	na	60	57	51
Hungary	61	63	59	61	57	64	66	58	48	66	59	50	52	62	59	60	61	63
Argentina	38	37	39	37	35	44	49	33	25	52	42	22	29	34	41	49	38	25
Brazil	67	65	69	65	64	75	80	64	49	77	65	57	57	64	73	72	65	49
Mexico	76	75	78	76	76	80	76	80	75	78	76	74	65	79	81	80	78	57
Belarus	43	44	43	38	41	54	57	42	40	42	46	41	40	44	57	55	37	31
Russia	55	52	57	46	50	67	71	55	45	58	55	52	41	54	58	63	51	37
Moscow	26	25	28	21	24	35	60	31	17	31	24	22	21	25	46	37	25	14
Latvia	53	50	54	48	47	69	73	54	45	59	50	51	na	na	na	65	52	46
Estonia	48	46	49	39	45	62	57	46	42	47	48	49	45	na	na	53	47	39
Portugal	51	45	57	41	53	61	59	35	37	62	48	38	45	52	52	64	45	34
South Korea	64	68	61	52	68	77	77	73	48	67	66	63	44	66	68	72	62	41
Ireland	73	72	74	67	70	79	72	74	71	74	77	71	58	72	81	78	72	70
North Ireland	66	61	69	74	60	66	64	69	72	73	68	67	61	65	69	74	65	60
Slovenia	67	71	64	58	67	75	69	66	67	69	66	68	65	69	80	71	66	63
Spain	67	63	69	60	61	77	72	59	47	81	68	58	62	69	69	77	67	50
East Germany	40	37	43	40	36	45	42	39	35	42	40	38	45	42	31	43	42	35
Britain	47	48	47	49	45	49	48	45	45	54	46	44	47	49	44	48	48	46
Italy	48	45	51	40	43	58	51	34	25	51	47	32	38	54	47	58	48	40
Netherlands	67	67	67	70	65	66	66	72	62	64	72	65	69	70	60	62	68	66
Belgium	73	72	73	69	72	76	73	73	72	73	76	73	70	72	78	74	75	71
Austria	65	64	65	66	62	67	70	63	54	65	67	62	66	62	66	73	66	58
France	66	64	68	66	69	63	69	65	61	70	63	58	70	67	50	75	64	63
Canada	73	73	72	77	72	70	73	75	70	70	72	73	71	74	70	78	73	70
United States	55	56	53	57	55	54	51	58	53	54	56	55	60	53	56	52	54	58
Iceland	80	77	83	80	82	78	80	78	82	na	na	na	84	79	82	74	82	87
West Germany	54	51	56	49	52	58	55	51	50	53	55	54	46	55	60	58	58	47
Denmark	81	81	81	78	82	82	83	77	83	79	83	81	84	82	77	81	81	80
Finland	78	80	76	71	78	83	76	83	73	76	80	77	78	78	80	74	80	73
Norway	79	79	78	75	79	81	84	79	76	79	82	76	80	83	75	78	78	81
Sweden	70	70	71	74	69	67	71	71	67	73	67	68	78	70	67	74	71	67
Japan	46	48	44	35	45	56	52	44	44	41	49	51	44	42	62	53	47	38
Switzerland	na	na	na	na	na	na	na	na	na	na	na	na	na	na	na	na	na	na
Total	**64**	**62**	**65**	**60**	**62**	**69**	**70**	**62**	**55**	**66**	**64**	**59**	**60**	**64**	**65**	**68**	**63**	**55**

Ranking:

China	93
Nigeria	84
Denmark	81
Iceland	80
Romania	79
Norway	79
Finland	78
South Africa	77
Mexico	76
Poland	75
India	73
Chile	73
Ireland	73
Belgium	73
Canada	73
Sweden	70
Brazil	67
Slovenia	67
Spain	67
Netherlands	67
North Ireland	66
France	66
Turkey	65
Austria	65
South Korea	64
Czechoslovakia	61
Hungary	61
Lithuania	57
Russia	55
United States	55
West Germany	54
Bulgaria	53
Latvia	53
Portugal	51
Estonia	48
Italy	48
Britain	47
Japan	46
Belarus	43
East Germany	40
Argentina	38
Moscow	26

Note: Countries in the left column are ranked according to GNP per capita. / The percentages in the bottom row give each country an equal weight. / na=not ascertained.

V275 CONFIDENCE: LEGAL SYSTEM

For each item listed, how much confidence do you have in them, is it a great deal, quite a lot, not very much, or none at all?
The legal system (% "a great deal" or "quite a lot")

	Total	Gender		Age			Education			Income			Political Affinity			Values		
		Male	Female	16-29	30-49	50+	Lower	Medium	Upper	Lower	Middle	Upper	Left	Center	Right	Mat	Mixed	Postmat
India	64	61	67	62	64	66	67	64	61	64	65	61	60	63	69	64	64	60
Nigeria	64	63	67	67	60	70	66	69	60	54	69	72	62	66	69	69	64	44
China	76	72	80	70	77	80	82	76	67	81	75	70	na	na	na	81	73	42
Romania	48	49	46	46	45	51	53	48	40	41	52	47	56	46	40	53	45	30
Turkey	64	59	69	61	62	72	71	57	41	67	65	59	48	66	70	77	64	45
Poland	48	45	52	53	42	53	56	48	25	44	51	51	42	49	50	54	46	42
Bulgaria	46	42	48	46	40	52	60	43	38	39	48	51	51	42	37	50	47	23
Chile	45	44	45	41	45	49	48	47	38	48	46	41	39	45	54	54	43	37
Czechoslovakia	43	40	45	51	36	46	46	43	38	45	44	39	41	44	43	41	43	37
South Africa	74	74	74	73	74	75	76	72	78	73	74	77	73	70	74	80	72	62
Lithuania	39	38	39	35	32	48	51	38	21	45	33	33	na	na	na	44	38	34
Hungary	60	60	59	65	53	64	59	61	53	60	59	59	55	59	64	61	59	54
Argentina	23	22	25	24	20	27	28	20	20	33	25	17	23	20	21	26	23	21
Brazil	44	43	46	39	42	58	60	38	36	54	42	36	33	41	54	51	42	27
Mexico	53	53	54	51	54	61	55	54	49	53	55	53	36	54	65	61	53	37
Belarus	26	23	29	22	23	36	41	23	23	24	28	26	22	27	43	38	21	11
Russia	38	36	40	35	33	47	50	37	33	38	38	36	30	39	33	42	38	20
Moscow	18	16	19	17	13	25	31	21	13	21	17	14	14	17	33	27	15	12
Latvia	36	32	39	36	32	47	45	38	30	39	37	33	na	na	na	46	33	34
Estonia	33	33	32	29	29	42	40	32	27	32	32	35	na	na	na	35	33	22
Portugal	41	39	43	36	40	46	44	29	41	46	38	36	41	39	44	35	33	35
South Korea	67	68	66	59	69	73	70	72	59	64	68	70	48	66	72	74	63	48
Ireland	47	46	48	49	45	49	46	47	53	48	51	44	36	47	55	47	48	45
North Ireland	56	48	61	51	52	64	52	65	59	63	56	56	46	56	61	47	48	45
Slovenia	51	54	48	47	51	53	53	50	49	51	49	55	55	52	55	68	54	49
Spain	49	47	50	41	43	60	53	42	33	51	48	39	44	48	57	53	50	55
East Germany	41	37	45	40	39	45	42	42	38	42	41	41	42	45	33	41	44	34
Britain	54	51	56	52	54	54	50	59	66	48	48	63	42	54	65	63	53	37
Italy	32	30	34	32	27	36	32	31	40	33	31	34	26	35	33	34	32	46
Netherlands	64	65	64	67	67	56	55	64	74	62	59	73	73	61	60	63	53	29
Belgium	45	43	46	48	41	46	43	45	48	48	43	44	39	46	52	47	60	75
Austria	58	58	59	60	56	60	60	58	53	57	58	59	57	57	61	50	44	41
France	58	57	59	59	58	56	55	57	66	58	54	59	63	55	59	58	59	58
Canada	54	52	57	51	51	54	53	56	53	51	55	58	51	55	51	65	57	52
United States	58	54	61	56	61	57	59	61	54	60	56	60	55	52	57	58	58	51
Iceland	67	67	66	71	67	68	61	61	69	na	na	na	62	69	70	64	67	57
West Germany	65	65	66	63	70	66	67	67	60	64	na	67	57	67	76	73	68	68
Denmark	79	81	78	79	82	77	76	77	84	74	81	86	77	78	85	75	80	83
Finland	66	64	69	74	63	69	68	63	69	63	68	67	60	63	72	50	69	64
Norway	75	78	73	79	79	70	65	71	85	74	78	79	76	76	77	73	75	83
Sweden	56	57	56	59	57	54	50	55	66	56	54	58	58	54	58	51	56	64
Japan	62	64	61	50	64	70	65	60	65	53	66	71	64	66	77	70	66	55
Switzerland	na	na	na	na	na	na	na	na	na	na	na	na	na	na	na	na	na	na
Total	52	51	53	51	50	56	55	51	49	52	52	52	49	53	57	56	51	45

Ranking:

Denmark	79
China	76
Norway	75
South Africa	74
South Korea	67
Iceland	67
Finland	66
West Germany	65
India	64
Nigeria	64
Turkey	64
Netherlands	64
Japan	62
Hungary	60
Austria	58
France	58
United States	58
North Ireland	56
Sweden	56
Britain	54
Canada	54
Mexico	53
Slovenia	51
Spain	49
Romania	48
Poland	48
Ireland	47
Bulgaria	46
Chile	45
Belgium	45
Brazil	44
Czechoslovakia	43
Portugal	41
East Germany	41
Lithuania	39
Russia	38
Latvia	36
Estonia	33
Italy	32
Belarus	26
Argentina	23
Moscow	18

Note: Countries in the left column are ranked according to GNP per capita. / The percentages in the bottom row give each country an equal weight. / na=not ascertained.

V276 CONFIDENCE: PRESS

For each item listed, how much confidence do you have in them, is it a great deal, quite a lot, not very much, or none at all?
The press (% "a great deal" or "quite a lot")

	Total	Gender Male	Gender Female	Age 16-29	Age 30-49	Age 50+	Education Lower	Education Medium	Education Upper	Income Lower	Income Middle	Income Upper	Pol. Aff. Left	Pol. Aff. Center	Pol. Aff. Right	Values Mat	Values Mixed	Values Postmat
India	66	66	66	67	66	62	62	66	67	63	67	65	64	69	71	62	70	70
Nigeria	71	71	72	75	65	86	79	75	64	66	72	78	74	74	73	73	72	60
China	55	54	56	54	54	58	58	53	54	58	57	49	na	na	na	58	53	39
Romania	28	35	21	31	25	28	26	28	30	23	30	29	26	25	35	23	29	52
Turkey	42	39	45	39	44	43	47	37	29	45	43	39	43	43	36	45	43	36
Poland	47	52	42	51	40	52	52	45	37	44	51	47	44	43	54	52	44	45
Bulgaria	35	36	35	39	32	37	38	33	36	35	31	40	33	31	41	33	37	36
Chile	43	48	38	40	45	43	43	45	40	43	43	44	50	43	40	42	42	49
Czechoslovakia	43	47	40	47	43	41	43	44	39	43	42	45	36	44	47	37	44	51
South Africa	58	63	54	62	56	56	63	59	38	66	64	39	65	50	53	54	61	57
Lithuania	68	70	66	74	62	67	68	68	64	67	66	72	na	na	na	67	67	74
Hungary	40	44	36	51	35	40	40	40	41	42	38	39	45	37	41	38	42	39
Argentina	27	26	28	31	25	28	28	29	27	30	26	30	30	27	30	28	28	24
Brazil	55	56	54	55	55	55	56	54	55	55	56	52	55	53	58	54	56	50
Mexico	49	50	47	46	52	49	51	46	45	48	49	51	44	47	56	54	50	34
Belarus	25	27	24	30	23	26	26	27	24	24	26	25	27	22	22	28	23	30
Russia	44	43	44	45	39	48	46	43	43	44	45	40	45	39	43	43	45	38
Moscow	31	30	32	34	27	34	40	32	28	32	30	31	31	23	39	26	31	42
Latvia	60	61	60	65	60	55	52	61	61	65	61	57	na	na	na	63	59	70
Estonia	64	65	62	69	62	61	67	62	64	63	64	64	na	na	na	63	64	75
Portugal	36	38	34	36	32	39	36	33	36	41	29	62	36	36	33	39	34	29
South Korea	66	66	66	63	66	73	70	70	60	67	69	62	51	66	71	69	67	56
Ireland	36	36	36	31	35	41	36	36	41	40	34	35	33	35	45	34	36	39
North Ireland	16	16	17	15	14	19	18	11	17	14	19	14	21	14	16	17	13	22
Slovenia	50	51	48	50	51	47	50	51	47	49	49	53	53	50	54	51	49	45
Spain	45	48	42	46	42	47	45	46	44	48	45	44	49	43	49	44	49	43
East Germany	21	22	20	21	21	22	22	21	18	24	17	22	20	22	22	27	20	23
Britain	14	13	15	10	12	18	13	12	21	15	10	14	13	13	15	18	14	10
Italy	39	37	41	42	36	40	39	40	47	39	40	48	36	39	48	37	41	40
Netherlands	34	43	31	36	35	30	27	29	48	37	32	39	45	33	28	17	30	44
Belgium	44	47	41	47	42	40	41	43	52	42	44	47	53	42	46	41	44	52
Austria	18	17	18	14	16	21	20	15	19	16	20	17	16	14	21	19	18	16
France	38	38	38	41	40	34	36	37	47	38	40	39	44	39	35	34	37	44
Canada	46	47	46	48	47	44	46	49	43	45	46	39	48	47	46	50	45	48
United States	56	55	58	55	57	56	57	59	53	56	56	56	51	57	54	56	59	49
Iceland	20	21	20	23	18	21	22	26	14	na	na	na	14	22	26	22	20	16
West Germany	34	36	33	34	36	33	35	32	38	34	38	33	38	34	34	40	33	35
Denmark	31	31	31	26	31	35	31	23	37	32	27	33	31	32	30	30	30	35
Finland	38	42	33	44	39	29	31	35	44	31	37	45	31	39	40	30	37	40
Norway	43	44	42	49	44	39	43	42	45	43	na	46	43	45	43	38	46	42
Sweden	33	32	34	34	32	32	27	38	33	34	34	30	29	33	38	32	33	34
Japan	56	56	55	53	52	63	59	55	52	54	56	59	58	57	64	59	58	52
Switzerland	na	na	na	na	na	na	na	na	na	na	na	na	na	na	na	na	na	na
Total	**42**	**43**	**41**	**43**	**41**	**43**	**43**	**42**	**41**	**43**	**43**	**43**	**40**	**39**	**42**	**42**	**42**	**43**

Ranking:

Nigeria	71
Lithuania	68
India	66
South Korea	66
Estonia	64
Latvia	60
South Africa	58
United States	56
Japan	56
China	55
Brazil	55
Slovenia	50
Mexico	49
Poland	47
Canada	46
Spain	45
Russia	44
Belgium	44
Chile	43
Czechoslovakia	43
Norway	43
Turkey	42
Hungary	40
Italy	39
France	38
Finland	38
Portugal	36
Ireland	36
Bulgaria	35
Netherlands	34
West Germany	34
Sweden	33
Moscow	31
Denmark	31
Romania	28
Argentina	27
Belarus	25
East Germany	21
Iceland	20
Austria	18
North Ireland	16
Britain	14

Note: Countries in the left column are ranked according to GNP per capita. / The percentages in the bottom row give each country an equal weight. / na=not ascertained.

V277 CONFIDENCE: UNIONS

For each item listed, how much confidence do you have in them, is it a great deal, quite a lot, not very much, or none at all?
Trade unions (% "a great deal" or "quite a lot")

	Total	Gender		Age			Education			Income			Political Affinity			Values			Ranking:	
		Male	Female	16-29	30-49	50+	Lower	Medium	Upper	Lower	Middle	Upper	Left	Center	Right	Mat	Mixed	Postmat		
India	52	52	52	53	53	47	56	53	49	55	56	46	57	55	54	50	54	56	South Korea	67
Nigeria	66	63	71	69	62	68	72	72	58	60	68	72	67	68	67	68	67	52	Nigeria	66
China	42	41	43	42	43	40	39	44	41	41	45	38	na	na	na	41	42	41	South Africa	61
Romania	30	35	25	24	32	32	35	30	23	27	33	28	31	28	31	32	29	26	Norway	59
Turkey	40	35	47	37	42	42	48	32	25	48	39	34	40	40	42	44	41	36	Netherlands	54
Poland	23	23	24	26	21	24	30	20	14	22	25	22	22	22	25	31	21	14	India	52
Bulgaria	32	32	32	34	29	34	40	31	26	31	36	29	32	29	29	36	32	21	Iceland	51
Chile	47	51	44	44	50	48	47	47	48	44	52	46	61	46	41	45	48	54	Brazil	48
Czechoslovakia	27	26	27	26	24	31	30	28	18	28	27	23	30	26	26	25	27	28	Chile	47
South Africa	61	66	56	69	59	49	75	62	21	79	68	24	70	51	55	51	65	76	Russia	47
Lithuania	27	23	30	26	23	31	36	26	17	28	27	23	na	na	na	30	25	28	Denmark	46
Hungary	30	29	31	31	25	35	36	26	18	36	27	21	36	29	32	31	30	21	Ireland	43
Argentina	08	07	09	09	06	09	09	08	07	11	08	04	09	07	08	10	09	06	China	42
Brazil	48	45	51	48	48	47	53	44	53	50	45	48	50	43	50	45	50	50	Turkey	40
Mexico	38	39	37	37	39	41	41	34	34	41	36	37	36	36	42	44	37	27	Spain	40
Belarus	25	23	27	24	26	24	35	26	20	22	28	23	25	25	29	34	21	19	Sweden	40
Russia	47	42	51	42	43	55	59	47	41	47	49	17	36	46	54	54	45	24	Mexico	38
Moscow	22	20	25	24	19	27	44	26	16	28	20	17	17	24	39	29	21	19	Belgium	37
Latvia	24	20	27	20	24	28	28	26	19	26	25	22	na	na	na	37	21	18	West Germany	36
Estonia	27	22	31	24	24	34	31	27	24	28	27	25	na	na	na	29	26	28	Austria	35
Portugal	29	29	29	27	26	34	30	29	26	36	25	24	43	28	21	32	27	28	Canada	35
South Korea	67	66	67	72	67	56	67	68	65	69	71	56	78	69	62	61	69	78	Italy	34
Ireland	43	43	42	45	41	43	38	47	52	43	41	43	55	42	43	37	45	33	United States	33
North Ireland	24	28	22	21	20	30	27	19	21	29	23	21	32	22	24	23	22	33	Bulgaria	32
Slovenia	27	31	23	29	28	24	28	29	22	28	26	28	30	25	29	25	28	19	France	32
Spain	40	41	38	37	40	40	40	39	39	41	43	37	53	37	33	37	42	42	Finland	32
East Germany	28	29	27	32	25	28	29	26	26	25	28	30	38	25	18	30	28	26	Romania	30
Britain	26	26	25	29	22	28	27	20	29	28	25	23	43	23	15	22	26	32	Hungary	30
Italy	34	32	35	32	31	37	34	32	18	35	33	34	40	32	29	31	35	34	Portugal	29
Netherlands	54	58	53	65	50	49	47	59	57	54	59	50	66	54	41	48	48	67	East Germany	28
Belgium	37	39	36	42	35	37	42	35	33	42	36	33	47	33	33	41	37	37	Czechoslovakia	27
Austria	35	38	33	30	33	39	37	34	35	36	36	33	40	35	33	37	35	33	Lithuania	27
France	32	32	32	36	34	28	31	33	33	34	31	30	46	29	21	25	33	35	Estonia	27
Canada	35	36	34	40	35	30	34	36	34	34	33	36	47	31	35	33	34	38	Slovenia	27
United States	33	33	33	32	32	36	38	35	28	33	36	30	39	34	29	30	36	29	Britain	26
Iceland	51	44	58	52	49	54	61	46	46	na	na	na	60	52	41	56	51	41	Japan	26
West Germany	36	38	34	39	36	34	37	34	36	39	41	31	50	35	25	33	34	42	Belarus	25
Denmark	46	43	50	48	48	43	50	39	51	46	54	39	61	49	31	49	44	54	Latvia	24
Finland	32	29	36	37	30	33	36	32	30	37	31	29	50	34	22	38	32	30	North Ireland	24
Norway	59	56	62	63	59	57	60	58	60	64	61	54	73	62	45	54	61	65	Poland	23
Sweden	40	39	42	41	39	41	46	41	29	44	40	36	56	42	24	40	42	40	Moscow	22
Japan	26	24	28	28	25	25	29	25	25	24	28	26	41	25	23	25	29	30	Argentina	08
Switzerland	na	na	na	na	na	na	na	na	na	na	na	na	na	na	na	na	na	na		
Total	37	36	38	38	36	37	41	36	33	38	38	33	45	37	34	37	37	36		

Note: Countries in the left column are ranked according to GNP per capita. / The percentages in the bottom row give each country an equal weight. / na=not ascertained.

V278 CONFIDENCE: POLICE

For each item listed, how much confidence do you have in them, is it a great deal, quite a lot, not very much, or none at all?
The police (% "a great deal" or "quite a lot")

	Total	Gender Male	Gender Female	Age 16-29	Age 30-49	Age 50+	Education Lower	Education Medium	Education Upper	Income Lower	Income Middle	Income Upper	Pol. Affinity Left	Pol. Affinity Center	Pol. Affinity Right	Values Mat	Values Mixed	Values Postmat	Ranking	
India	39	37	43	39	39	42	45	38	38	42	39	38	39	40	43	41	39	34	Denmark	89
Nigeria	44	43	46	44	42	53	49	51	35	37	47	51	50	43	43	45	45	29	Norway	88
China	68	66	71	62	69	74	73	67	61	70	69	65	na	na	na	76	63	29	Ireland	86
Romania	45	45	45	47	41	48	53	45	35	42	47	45	53	43	39	52	40	39	Iceland	85
Turkey	63	54	71	58	61	74	73	51	35	68	68	51	35	69	72	78	64	41	Canada	84
Poland	30	32	29	29	22	40	39	27	16	33	27	32	34	30	31	39	27	27	North Ireland	80
Bulgaria	46	44	48	40	41	57	63	43	38	48	48	44	50	46	36	54	48	21	Britain	77
Chile	59	59	58	51	61	66	61	59	55	57	59	62	46	64	70	67	59	48	Finland	76
Czechoslovakia	32	31	33	35	27	36	34	32	28	35	32	29	38	31	30	32	33	27	United States	75
South Africa	64	59	68	58	63	77	66	62	69	61	62	74	48	63	74	75	59	51	Sweden	75
Lithuania	29	28	29	25	22	38	41	26	21	33	24	24	na	na	na	34	27	26	Netherlands	73
Hungary	51	51	50	48	48	54	54	48	44	52	49	50	50	50	55	52	50	45	West Germany	70
Argentina	26	26	27	26	19	34	35	22	20	35	29	17	13	27	24	37	25	15	China	68
Brazil	38	39	38	34	35	50	50	35	25	48	33	32	29	35	48	43	37	21	Austria	68
Mexico	32	32	32	31	31	38	33	31	31	33	30	30	20	33	41	36	31	26	Italy	67
Belarus	22	18	24	15	21	30	28	19	22	21	24	20	20	21	31	30	18	16	France	67
Russia	35	32	37	25	31	47	43	33	33	34	39	32	27	36	33	41	33	24	South Africa	64
Moscow	19	18	21	14	16	29	37	18	17	23	18	15	13	24	29	29	17	11	Turkey	63
Latvia	20	18	22	20	17	27	29	21	17	23	21	18	na	na	na	29	19	10	Chile	59
Estonia	19	20	18	17	17	25	23	18	19	21	21	15	na	na	na	24	18	10	Japan	59
Portugal	44	43	46	37	40	56	49	30	37	55	37	36	36	43	49	54	39	34	Spain	58
South Korea	53	57	50	45	53	67	64	58	42	56	53	51	33	50	61	60	52	25	South Korea	53
Ireland	86	83	88	77	86	91	86	87	78	87	87	85	66	87	92	88	87	80	Slovenia	52
North Ireland	80	76	83	68	78	90	78	84	83	83	90	79	64	83	82	86	78	76	Hungary	51
Slovenia	52	54	49	50	52	52	53	50	51	51	51	54	48	50	54	57	50	43	Belgium	51
Spain	58	54	61	46	54	69	63	52	44	65	63	54	49	58	68	70	57	43	Bulgaria	46
East Germany	39	38	40	38	34	44	42	33	32	43	37	36	40	40	34	44	42	28	Romania	45
Britain	77	75	79	73	76	80	77	81	73	78	76	79	64	79	85	88	78	64	Nigeria	44
Italy	67	64	69	62	63	74	68	63	46	69	66	68	58	73	70	75	67	57	Portugal	44
Netherlands	73	70	74	79	72	69	70	75	76	64	75	79	69	75	73	71	76	71	India	39
Belgium	51	49	53	48	46	58	54	51	46	57	50	47	44	50	59	60	53	40	East Germany	39
Austria	68	67	69	60	64	74	70	66	63	70	69	64	63	67	70	75	70	58	Brazil	38
France	67	65	68	64	63	72	68	68	59	68	62	69	61	70	75	71	70	57	Russia	35
Canada	84	81	88	81	86	89	86	86	80	82	83	86	77	86	87	88	85	82	Czechoslovakia	32
United States	75	73	78	72	73	79	75	73	77	72	75	78	65	77	80	79	76	68	Mexico	32
Iceland	85	82	87	82	84	89	81	83	83	na	na	na	82	87	85	84	85	85	Poland	30
West Germany	70	68	71	58	65	80	75	64	57	71	73	67	55	74	80	80	75	57	Lithuania	29
Denmark	89	89	90	89	88	91	91	87	90	86	92	90	82	89	94	92	92	75	Argentina	26
Finland	76	76	76	71	76	81	77	75	77	73	79	77	68	75	79	74	77	74	Belarus	22
Norway	88	87	89	91	87	87	83	88	90	87	89	88	87	89	89	89	89	81	Latvia	20
Sweden	75	73	77	74	73	78	73	75	75	77	71	75	74	71	80	75	76	72	Moscow	19
Japan	59	60	57	46	62	63	62	57	58	51	66	62	52	61	76	67	61	38	Estonia	19
Switzerland	na	na	na	na	na	na	na	na	na	na	na	na	na	na	na	na	na	na		
Total	**55**	**53**	**56**	**51**	**52**	**61**	**59**	**53**	**49**	**55**	**54**	**53**	**50**	**58**	**61**	**61**	**54**	**44**		

Note: Countries in the left column are ranked according to GNP per capita. / The percentages in the bottom row give each country an equal weight. / na=not ascertained.

V279 CONFIDENCE: PARLIAMENT

For each item listed, how much confidence do you have in them, is it a great deal, quite a lot, not very much, or none at all?
Parliament (% "a great deal" or "quite a lot")

	Total	Gender		Age			Education			Income			Political Affinity			Values			Ranking:	
		Male	Female	16-29	30-49	50+	Lower	Medium	Upper	Lower	Middle	Upper	Left	Center	Right	Mat	Mixed	Postmat		
India	67	66	67	66	67	66	63	68	66	66	68	66	68	69	71	69	67	61	China	81
Nigeria	54	52	56	57	49	55	52	59	49	49	58	58	49	60	55	60	52	40	Poland	79
China	81	80	83	75	82	88	85	82	71	89	80	73	na	na	na	88	78	39	Latvia	73
Romania	21	22	19	18	17	27	26	20	15	15	23	23	25	21	16	26	18	15	Estonia	69
Turkey	58	50	66	53	57	67	69	46	27	64	61	48	37	62	64	71	59	39	India	67
Poland	79	78	80	68	80	84	80	79	77	80	77	79	79	77	86	77	79	80	South Africa	66
Bulgaria	49	49	48	47	46	54	55	46	47	51	46	48	50	49	43	50	49	44	Lithuania	66
Chile	63	67	61	61	67	61	60	61	71	59	64	69	73	62	70	56	66	72	Chile	63
Czechoslovakia	44	44	45	46	39	50	46	45	39	47	45	41	38	44	50	37	45	58	Norway	59
South Africa	66	64	68	62	67	72	71	64	61	70	64	64	64	65	57	71	66	51	Turkey	58
Lithuania	66	66	66	70	59	69	71	65	60	64	67	68	na	na	na	64	67	73	Nigeria	54
Hungary	40	38	41	39	38	42	41	37	46	40	37	46	35	40	44	42	38	44	Iceland	54
Argentina	17	17	16	14	15	20	17	15	20	18	16	22	24	15	21	21	16	14	Netherlands	52
Brazil	24	23	25	22	22	32	33	22	15	33	21	17	18	21	31	27	23	16	West Germany	51
Mexico	35	35	34	35	35	35	35	30	38	35	35	33	26	38	42	39	35	27	Ireland	50
Belarus	29	27	31	25	27	39	35	27	30	30	30	27	28	30	34	39	24	28	Bulgaria	49
Russia	47	44	49	38	41	60	58	45	42	51	46	45	34	50	50	55	43	31	France	48
Moscow	27	24	29	23	25	33	44	28	23	31	26	21	23	28	36	37	25	17	Russia	47
Latvia	73	71	74	72	71	76	80	73	69	79	76	66	na	na	na	74	72	82	Sweden	47
Estonia	69	67	70	67	68	72	71	67	72	71	64	70	na	na	na	70	71	75	North Ireland	46
Portugal	34	33	34	31	31	39	35	27	33	37	27	34	30	33	38	35	31	35	Britain	46
South Korea	34	36	32	25	34	50	51	39	21	40	33	29	24	34	37	37	35	18	United States	46
Ireland	50	50	51	40	48	59	52	49	47	58	51	46	30	49	64	59	48	46	Czechoslovakia	44
North Ireland	46	43	49	41	37	59	43	51	52	49	52	49	25	46	56	59	41	49	Belgium	43
Slovenia	36	43	29	29	39	37	35	33	42	34	34	42	39	35	43	36	35	39	Denmark	42
Spain	32	33	31	28	32	35	33	28	32	34	32	33	37	36	31	33	35	26	East Germany	41
East Germany	41	40	42	34	40	46	42	36	40	41	39	42	34	45	47	40	41	31	Austria	41
Britain	46	50	43	36	47	51	42	56	57	43	46	55	36	42	66	52	47	39	Hungary	40
Italy	32	30	34	32	27	36	32	32	28	34	33	29	26	35	32	29	34	31	Canada	38
Netherlands	52	59	49	52	50	55	47	53	56	43	53	60	48	53	58	52	53	51	Slovenia	36
Belgium	43	41	45	42	42	45	40	41	51	43	38	48	42	42	49	45	43	42	Mexico	35
Austria	41	41	41	37	39	45	44	39	43	42	40	41	45	39	45	42	42	39	Portugal	34
France	48	48	48	52	47	47	45	50	54	47	44	48	52	49	49	52	48	47	South Korea	34
Canada	38	35	41	40	32	43	39	36	40	36	37	39	34	38	43	39	39	37	Finland	34
United States	46	45	46	43	39	53	46	44	47	40	49	48	39	46	52	48	46	44	Spain	32
Iceland	54	55	52	52	51	60	56	51	52	na	na	na	59	53	50	56	53	53	Italy	32
West Germany	51	52	49	41	47	59	52	46	50	50	50	53	37	53	67	60	54	40	Belarus	29
Denmark	42	43	41	44	40	43	40	40	46	38	40	45	37	38	51	40	44	35	Japan	29
Finland	34	34	34	29	32	44	32	31	40	34	33	36	34	31	39	29	35	34	Moscow	27
Norway	59	61	57	59	60	58	55	53	67	59	60	64	58	62	61	58	59	61	Brazil	24
Sweden	47	48	46	43	48	49	46	44	56	48	41	50	56	46	46	43	45	58	Romania	21
Japan	29	30	28	18	29	38	39	25	29	28	29	32	22	26	45	39	30	16	Argentina	17
Switzerland	na	na	na	na	na	na	na	na	na	na	na	na	na	na	na	na	na	na		
Total	46	46	46	43	44	51	49	45	46	47	45	47	40	44	48	49	46	43		

Note: Countries in the left column are ranked according to GNP per capita. / The percentages in the bottom row give each country an equal weight. / na=not ascertained. In Russia, substitutions were made for V279-V285. V279=Parliament (USSR); V281=Government (USSR); V282=Parliament (Russia); V283=TV; V284=Government (Russia); V285=Soviet political system.

V280 CONFIDENCE: CIVIL SERVICE

For each item listed, how much confidence do you have in them, is it a great deal, quite a lot, not very much, or none at all? Civil service (% "a great deal" or "quite a lot")

	Total	Gender		Age			Education			Income			Political Affinity			Values			Ranking:	
		Male	Female	16-29	30-49	50+	Lower	Medium	Upper	Lower	Middle	Upper	Left	Center	Right	Mat	Mixed	Postmat		
India	74	74	74	77	74	69	68	74	76	72	77	72	73	76	76	73	76	74	Poland	79
Nigeria	76	75	77	77	72	83	73	78	73	73	76	81	73	80	73	78	76	59	Nigeria	76
China	59	60	59	57	60	62	67	58	50	61	60	59	na	na	na	62	60	27	India	74
Romania	31	33	29	26	26	38	37	31	21	25	34	30	29	30	27	36	27	21	South Korea	61
Turkey	50	41	59	43	52	59	60	38	28	56	50	45	33	49	58	60	53	31	South Africa	60
Poland	79	78	79	68	76	87	82	77	76	78	80	79	77	76	86	76	80	78	China	59
Bulgaria	30	30	31	35	29	29	34	33	22	26	34	33	35	27	24	33	31	21	Ireland	59
Chile	49	53	46	47	51	51	52	48	47	52	50	47	52	50	54	51	50	50	United States	59
Czechoslovakia	32	29	36	32	28	39	39	31	24	32	33	32	39	31	31	34	33	27	North Ireland	58
South Africa	60	62	59	61	58	63	67	60	40	65	64	48	55	56	59	64	60	46	Lithuania	52
Lithuania	52	52	52	50	45	61	59	52	41	57	49	48	na	na	na	58	51	46	Denmark	51
Hungary	50	49	50	52	49	50	52	47	48	51	47	52	48	51	47	51	47	64	Turkey	50
Argentina	07	06	09	06	05	11	09	05	08	09	06	08	07	06	09	12	07	04	Hungary	50
Brazil	49	48	50	49	44	56	54	47	45	54	50	44	45	47	53	50	49	42	Canada	50
Mexico	28	27	29	28	28	30	29	26	27	27	29	27	18	31	33	31	28	23	Chile	49
Belarus	20	18	21	18	17	27	30	19	17	20	21	18	18	17	32	30	15	11	Brazil	49
Russia	48	43	52	40	42	61	62	48	40	53	48	42	37	49	53	57	44	24	France	49
Moscow	14	14	16	12	13	20	35	15	10	19	12	12	11	14	30	23	12	10	Russia	48
Latvia	34	29	37	34	31	39	35	35	32	37	32	34	na	na	na	43	33	31	Netherlands	46
Estonia	39	40	37	40	35	43	40	39	35	40	36	39	na	na	na	41	39	41	Iceland	46
Portugal	32	32	31	26	29	39	35	22	26	40	24	26	27	30	37	39	26	28	Britain	44
South Korea	61	62	60	55	61	71	66	63	56	63	60	60	52	60	64	64	61	50	Norway	44
Ireland	59	56	63	53	58	65	59	61	59	64	58	57	45	58	66	67	58	54	Sweden	44
North Ireland	58	54	60	55	48	69	58	58	55	56	62	56	46	58	59	63	55	60	Belgium	43
Slovenia	40	44	37	38	41	41	41	39	40	38	38	51	43	41	39	42	39	40	Austria	42
Spain	34	32	36	27	29	43	37	24	27	43	35	27	31	34	34	41	35	24	Slovenia	40
East Germany	18	16	20	15	15	23	21	13	10	20	18	17	14	23	15	23	19	14	Estonia	39
Britain	44	41	48	39	40	51	44	47	45	50	43	40	43	45	46	50	44	40	West Germany	39
Italy	27	25	28	25	23	32	28	19	14	27	30	14	20	29	30	31	28	21	Latvia	34
Netherlands	46	49	45	49	42	48	44	50	44	37	54	47	48	45	46	40	46	48	Spain	34
Belgium	43	41	44	38	40	48	45	43	37	48	44	38	41	44	42	54	46	28	Japan	34
Austria	42	42	42	36	36	50	44	40	36	42	40	42	43	38	47	46	44	36	Finland	33
France	49	49	49	43	50	53	49	49	50	47	45	49	51	49	44	59	51	39	Czechoslovakia	32
Canada	50	48	52	54	45	53	58	49	44	53	49	47	45	51	48	59	50	47	Portugal	32
United States	59	59	59	61	51	65	63	59	55	62	59	55	51	59	64	64	60	51	Romania	31
Iceland	46	44	48	42	48	48	55	39	45	na	na	na	47	50	43	45	46	48	Bulgaria	30
West Germany	39	37	40	30	34	47	41	34	35	38	39	40	29	40	53	46	43	26	Mexico	28
Denmark	51	50	53	44	51	57	55	47	53	51	44	60	53	51	51	48	52	53	Italy	27
Finland	33	33	34	26	34	38	32	29	39	28	35	36	28	27	40	41	32	35	Belarus	20
Norway	44	42	46	45	44	43	46	41	46	44	46	40	48	43	41	45	42	47	East Germany	18
Sweden	44	44	45	38	45	48	44	43	46	47	39	46	53	43	42	44	44	45	Moscow	14
Japan	34	35	32	21	34	43	30	30	35	29	33	42	28	33	51	38	36	25	Argentina	07
Switzerland	na	na	na	na	na	na	na	na	na	na	na	na	na	na	na	na	na	na		
Total	44	43	45	41	41	49	47	42	39	45	43	42	40	43	46	48	44	38		

Note: Countries in the left column are ranked according to GNP per capita. / The percentages in the bottom row give each country an equal weight. / na=not ascertained. In Slovenia, V280 "Civil service" was worded as "Local administration," to distinguish it from Yugoslav authority. In Russia, substitutions were made for V279-V285: V279=Parliament (USSR); V281=Government (USSR); V282=Parliament (Russia); V283=TV; V284=Government (Russia); V285=Soviet political system.

V281 CONFIDENCE: COMPANIES

For each item listed, how much confidence do you have in them, is it a great deal, quite a lot, not very much, or none at all?
Major companies (% "a great deal" or "quite a lot")

	Total	Gender		Age			Education			Income			Political Affinity			Values			Ranking:	
		Male	Female	16-29	30-49	50+	Lower	Medium	Upper	Lower	Middle	Upper	Left	Center	Right	Mat	Mixed	Postmat		
India	61	62	61	64	60	58	62	61	62	57	64	62	63	62	68	60	64	57	Nigeria	76
Nigeria	76	76	77	78	72	86	72	81	74	72	79	81	75	80	75	76	77	67	South Africa	76
China	36	36	36	38	33	39	40	33	35	36	36	35	na	na	na	34	38	38	Poland	71
Romania	35	35	35	31	35	38	40	39	23	30	37	36	46	33	30	40	33	18	France	67
Turkey	29	24	34	28	28	32	36	21	14	29	30	29	17	29	37	28	34	17	Italy	62
Poland	71	71	70	66	68	76	76	71	52	69	73	70	64	67	78	67	71	74	India	61
Bulgaria	34	36	32	44	32	31	32	38	30	32	34	37	38	34	28	29	38	28	Brazil	58
Chile	53	55	51	48	55	56	54	52	51	53	53	53	43	55	67	57	55	45	Chile	53
Czechoslovakia	27	26	28	28	24	30	29	27	21	27	27	26	37	26	20	30	27	19	Norway	53
South Africa	76	77	76	77	75	79	79	76	71	76	78	74	76	78	72	80	76	68	Sweden	53
Lithuania	16	20	13	23	15	12	14	18	12	14	16	23	na	na	na	11	17	24	Ireland	52
Hungary	34	33	35	42	31	34	37	32	28	38	32	31	37	35	35	33	35	34	Canada	51
Argentina	25	27	23	23	23	28	29	19	22	26	22	25	17	23	37	31	24	17	United States	51
Brazil	58	60	56	56	57	64	62	55	60	60	55	58	54	58	63	60	57	54	Belgium	50
Mexico	46	46	45	45	47	44	44	42	52	39	49	54	32	46	57	54	46	36	Britain	48
Belarus	37	34	40	35	35	44	49	35	36	37	37	37	36	40	42	43	35	37	Netherlands	48
Russia	46	43	48	35	40	61	57	45	41	51	45	45	29	49	50	55	42	25	North Ireland	47
Moscow	36	35	37	37	33	40	50	40	31	41	34	30	32	38	49	44	34	31	Mexico	46
Latvia	11	13	10	17	08	11	13	12	10	10	11	13	na	na	na	09	12	16	Russia	46
Estonia	15	22	10	21	14	12	14	16	15	14	17	17	na	na	na	12	17	25	East Germany	46
Portugal	45	43	46	46	37	52	46	42	42	50	37	43	36	46	49	52	42	31	Portugal	45
South Korea	35	39	33	32	35	44	43	39	27	37	35	36	25	35	38	41	33	20	Spain	43
Ireland	52	53	52	56	53	50	49	58	50	50	58	54	45	52	57	54	53	48	Austria	42
North Ireland	47	42	51	47	51	50	46	51	45	47	52	48	36	46	50	50	46	52	Finland	41
Slovenia	33	39	27	30	31	37	37	30	28	33	33	32	36	32	32	35	32	28	Iceland	40
Spain	43	42	44	38	40	48	46	40	32	33	43	42	37	49	56	49	45	33	West Germany	38
East Germany	46	52	41	43	48	45	47	45	43	39	48	50	37	50	55	42	46	47	Denmark	38
Britain	48	48	48	48	51	47	46	57	50	46	51	55	36	50	58	55	48	42	Belarus	37
Italy	62	63	62	60	61	66	62	65	62	58	71	70	56	68	69	67	63	56	China	36
Netherlands	48	49	48	59	43	44	43	55	47	41	48	55	36	55	56	49	52	43	Moscow	36
Belgium	50	49	51	54	50	48	46	50	58	47	49	54	42	50	60	53	53	43	Romania	35
Austria	42	46	39	35	39	47	45	40	40	40	40	46	41	41	45	46	42	40	South Korea	35
France	67	66	67	69	62	70	67	64	70	65	66	70	59	72	85	68	68	63	Bulgaria	34
Canada	51	51	52	51	50	54	55	52	48	47	53	55	43	52	58	60	53	45	Hungary	34
United States	51	54	48	51	43	58	51	50	52	52	54	49	36	53	58	57	53	42	Slovenia	33
Iceland	40	42	37	44	40	33	43	40	37	na	na	na	26	38	53	40	40	35	Turkey	29
West Germany	38	42	35	31	37	43	40	37	36	34	40	42	27	40	54	49	42	25	Japan	28
Denmark	38	43	33	41	34	40	40	36	40	35	38	43	25	38	49	40	41	24	Czechoslovakia	27
Finland	41	44	37	45	41	37	37	46	37	33	44	45	22	42	47	35	41	43	Argentina	25
Norway	53	58	47	51	51	50	46	53	56	48	54	59	46	52	61	50	55	44	Lithuania	16
Sweden	53	57	49	51	49	60	47	55	57	50	46	58	40	50	69	50	55	48	Estonia	15
Japan	28	29	27	22	28	31	31	26	29	23	28	33	21	29	39	36	30	20	Latvia	11
Switzerland	na	na	na	na	na	na	na	na	na	na	na	na	na	na	na	na	na	na		
Total	44	45	43	44	42	46	45	44	41	42	44	46	39	47	53	46	44	38		

Note: Countries in the left column are ranked according to GNP per capita. / The percentages in the bottom row give each country an equal weight. / na=not ascertained.
In Russia, substitutions were made for V279-V285: V279=Parliament (USSR); V282=Parliament (Russia); V283=TV; V284=Government (Russia);
V285=Soviet political system.

V282 CONFIDENCE: SOCIAL SECURITY

For each item listed, how much confidence do you have in them, is it a great deal, quite a lot, not very much, or none at all?
The social security system (% "a great deal" or "quite a lot")

	Total	Gender Male	Gender Female	Age 16-29	Age 30-49	Age 50+	Education Lower	Education Medium	Education Upper	Income Lower	Income Middle	Income Upper	Political Affinity Left	Political Affinity Center	Political Affinity Right	Values Mat	Values Mixed	Values Postmat
India	67	69	66	68	68	65	65	70	65	69	67	67	62	72	75	72	67	59
Nigeria	65	64	66	69	59	63	68	69	59	59	66	73	72	63	62	67	65	54
China	81	78	84	77	80	85	85	80	73	83	79	78	na	na	na	86	78	52
Romania	36	38	34	31	31	44	42	39	25	28	41	36	45	36	31	42	34	19
Turkey	75	74	76	71	75	80	81	71	56	77	80	68	60	76	81	81	77	62
Poland	43	42	43	46	36	47	50	42	23	39	49	41	35	42	47	44	42	43
Bulgaria	36	35	36	35	32	39	44	38	25	32	34	41	37	34	24	42	35	19
Chile	54	56	51	48	57	56	58	55	45	57	56	49	49	54	60	57	56	45
Czechoslovakia	42	39	45	40	35	52	47	41	35	47	40	39	42	42	42	40	43	40
South Africa	60	61	59	61	59	60	67	59	40	65	61	52	55	56	59	63	61	46
Lithuania	53	50	55	51	46	61	63	52	34	57	52	42	na	na	na	57	54	48
Hungary	50	47	54	52	44	56	53	49	44	55	48	43	49	51	54	53	49	39
Argentina	20	21	19	20	17	22	24	18	15	23	22	14	17	17	26	24	20	14
Brazil	32	32	32	28	30	42	47	28	16	46	30	18	23	29	38	37	29	24
Mexico	48	49	48	45	52	49	48	49	48	46	49	51	33	50	57	54	49	39
Belarus	32	32	33	22	30	47	49	30	29	31	34	32	31	34	37	48	24	25
Russia	67	67	66	65	64	71	70	66	65	70	68	63	71	64	69	66	66	76
Moscow	24	22	26	17	21	34	46	28	17	25	24	21	21	25	40	33	23	11
Latvia	37	34	39	36	32	51	45	39	31	37	41	36	na	na	na	45	37	28
Estonia	46	42	49	41	42	58	50	45	44	47	46	44	na	na	na	49	46	44
Portugal	47	45	49	42	45	55	52	36	37	56	44	38	43	45	53	57	42	35
South Korea	98	98	98	98	97	99	94	99	99	98	97	99	96	96	98	98	98	99
Ireland	59	59	60	53	61	62	61	58	52	66	60	54	45	57	70	65	61	46
North Ireland	48	48	48	46	36	62	50	46	38	53	49	47	36	44	57	51	48	40
Slovenia	40	43	37	37	37	45	43	38	37	40	40	41	37	40	43	45	38	40
Spain	50	48	52	40	44	62	55	38	36	62	52	40	48	52	51	62	49	35
East Germany	58	59	58	57	54	63	60	51	56	61	55	58	56	60	55	58	60	53
Britain	34	34	33	27	28	42	35	26	39	40	32	31	27	34	37	36	33	30
Italy	38	36	41	35	32	45	39	30	29	41	37	25	31	43	40	45	39	32
Netherlands	68	73	67	70	64	72	67	67	70	59	74	75	63	70	72	66	71	67
Belgium	67	68	67	65	63	72	69	66	67	73	66	69	73	65	68	73	67	64
Austria	68	68	67	57	63	76	73	64	61	71	66	67	68	67	70	76	68	62
France	70	71	69	63	69	76	71	69	69	71	66	73	72	72	63	76	68	68
Canada	61	63	60	58	55	73	68	59	60	66	61	59	63	63	62	72	60	62
United States	53	54	51	46	35	72	60	55	45	61	55	40	49	51	55	57	53	48
Iceland	69	70	68	64	69	76	71	66	70	na	na	na	70	67	71	70	68	73
West Germany	70	69	71	63	67	77	70	71	66	68	72	71	64	71	78	70	74	64
Denmark	69	70	69	67	72	68	67	66	73	69	69	68	70	66	73	72	70	66
Finland	75	75	74	69	74	81	74	72	77	76	73	75	70	75	77	73	75	73
Norway	48	52	45	40	46	57	55	45	49	59	74	44	57	50	42	48	48	53
Sweden	46	47	46	49	45	42	43	48	47	45	44	46	59	47	37	47	45	51
Japan	44	44	43	41	40	51	50	42	41	43	43	46	46	44	53	46	47	40
Switzerland	na	na	na	na	na	na	na	na	na	na	na	na	na	na	na	na	na	na
Total	**54**	**53**	**54**	**50**	**50**	**60**	**58**	**52**	**48**	**55**	**53**	**51**	**51**	**53**	**56**	**58**	**53**	**47**

Ranking:

South Korea	98
China	81
Turkey	75
Finland	75
France	70
West Germany	70
Iceland	69
Denmark	69
Netherlands	68
Austria	68
India	67
Russia	67
Belgium	67
Nigeria	65
Canada	61
South Africa	60
Ireland	59
East Germany	58
Chile	54
Lithuania	53
United States	53
Hungary	50
Spain	50
Mexico	48
North Ireland	48
Norway	48
Portugal	47
Sweden	46
Estonia	46
Japan	44
Poland	43
Czechoslovakia	42
Slovenia	40
Italy	38
Latvia	37
Romania	36
Bulgaria	36
Britain	34
Brazil	32
Belarus	32
Moscow	24
Argentina	20

Note: Countries in the left column are ranked according to GNP per capita. / The percentages in the bottom row give each country an equal weight. / na=not ascertained.
In Russia, substitutions were made for V279-V285. V279=Parliament (USSR); V280=Government (USSR); V281=Government (USSR); V282=Parliament (Russia); V283=TV; V284=Government (Russia); V285=Soviet political system.

V283 CONFIDENCE: T.V./EUROPEAN COMMUNITY

For each item listed, how much confidence do you have in them, is it a great deal, quite a lot, not very much, or none at all?
TV/European Community* (% "a great deal" or "quite a lot")

	Total	Gender		Age			Education			Income			Political Affinity			Values		
		Male	Female	16-29	30-49	50+	Lower	Medium	Upper	Lower	Middle	Upper	Left	Center	Right	Mat	Mixed	Postmat
India	33	33	32	36	31	28	40	29	36	31	33	34	29	36	43	31	34	36
Nigeria	69	69	69	75	62	65	67	73	66	63	74	73	72	71	70	68	70	64
China	30	30	29	40	26	21	19	28	40	23	31	34	na	na	na	23	33	43
Romania	na	na	na	na	na	na	na	na	na	na	na	na	na	na	na	na	na	na
Turkey	37	33	41	37	35	39	41	34	25	37	39	35	33	38	37	42	37	31
Poland	na	na	na	na	na	na	na	na	na	na	na	na	na	na	na	na	na	na
Bulgaria	50	52	48	63	51	42	33	54	60	51	48	55	51	51	62	38	52	74
Chile	32	37	28	24	37	36	29	33	35	26	33	39	37	32	33	30	32	38
Czechoslovakia	66	70	61	70	68	60	57	69	71	62	64	71	54	64	78	55	68	77
South Africa	na	na	na	na	na	na	na	na	na	na	na	na	na	na	na	na	na	na
Lithuania	na	na	na	na	na	na	na	na	na	na	na	na	na	na	na	na	na	na
Hungary	63	68	59	64	65	61	58	67	67	61	64	66	64	65	71	62	63	78
Argentina	na	na	na	na	na	na	na	na	na	na	na	na	na	na	na	na	na	na
Brazil	38	38	37	36	35	45	37	38	40	39	39	37	32	41	43	35	40	32
Mexico	27	28	26	27	29	22	26	27	31	21	31	38	26	28	36	28	28	27
Belarus	na	na	na	na	na	na	na	na	na	na	na	na	na	na	na	na	na	na
Russia	56	55	56	58	51	60	62	58	50	57	59	50	54	54	52	56	56	45
Moscow	23	20	26	23	22	25	42	31	15	30	23	13	21	23	33	31	22	15
Latvia	na	na	na	na	na	na	na	na	na	na	na	na	na	na	na	na	na	na
Estonia	na	na	na	na	na	na	na	na	na	na	na	na	na	na	na	na	na	na
Portugal	57	59	55	61	56	53	54	64	60	52	55	67	46	62	59	57	57	60
South Korea	na	na	na	na	na	na	na	na	na	na	na	na	na	na	na	na	na	na
Ireland	71	72	70	74	67	72	68	74	72	67	70	76	56	71	79	70	71	68
North Ireland	49	47	50	54	45	50	49	45	62	42	57	48	50	46	53	45	48	55
Slovenia	46	48	43	40	49	46	45	45	47	40	47	54	43	47	57	45	46	49
Spain	48	50	46	49	45	50	48	44	51	48	49	48	51	52	50	49	50	48
East Germany	64	72	57	59	66	64	64	62	51	59	62	69	55	69	75	53	65	67
Britain	47	51	44	48	47	47	45	50	57	44	54	47	50	49	44	45	46	55
Italy	74	76	73	78	72	74	74	80	69	70	81	84	67	81	79	73	74	77
Netherlands	58	59	58	60	57	57	59	60	56	47	64	57	52	59	66	54	59	59
Belgium	66	66	67	72	64	64	60	67	76	65	67	68	69	67	71	65	66	71
Austria	na	na	na	na	na	na	na	na	na	na	na	na	na	na	na	na	na	na
France	73	73	72	76	68	75	67	75	82	67	72	79	76	76	69	72	71	77
Canada	50	47	52	48	50	52	54	52	44	46	50	50	38	54	46	56	51	44
United States	45	44	46	44	39	50	48	45	41	48	46	40	44	43	46	54	43	43
Iceland	36	34	39	46	35	24	32	39	38	46	49	50	27	37	45	37	38	28
West Germany	48	47	48	47	45	50	46	50	50	46	49	50	45	49	50	46	49	47
Denmark	39	43	35	44	35	40	35	41	40	36	36	40	22	35	56	36	42	31
Finland	47	49	46	59	45	45	46	44	52	41	50	49	33	39	60	46	47	48
Norway	40	42	39	43	41	38	30	38	48	33	41	53	29	37	54	38	42	36
Sweden	58	58	58	58	53	63	53	59	64	53	52	65	37	52	79	62	58	56
Japan	27	27	26	30	27	24	22	25	36	22	26	33	31	33	34	28	33	29
Switzerland	na	na	na	na	na	na	na	na	na	na	na	na	na	na	na	na	na	na
Total	49	50	48	51	47	48	47	50	51	46	51	52	45	50	56	48	50	50

Ranking:

Italy	74
France	73
Ireland	71
Nigeria	69
Czechoslovakia	66
Belgium	66
East Germany	64
Hungary	63
Netherlands	58
Sweden	58
Portugal	57
Russia	56
Bulgaria	50
Canada	50
North Ireland	49
Spain	48
West Germany	48
Britain	47
Finland	47
Slovenia	46
United States	45
Norway	40
Denmark	39
Brazil	38
Turkey	37
Iceland	36
India	33
Chile	32
China	30
Mexico	27
Japan	27
Moscow	23

Note: Countries in the left column are ranked according to GNP per capita. / The percentages in the bottom row give each country an equal weight. / na=not ascertained.
* In West European countries and China, V283 refers to the European Community; elsewhere, it refers to TV newscasters. In Russia, substitutions were made for V279-V285:
V279=Parliament (USSR); V281=Government (USSR); V282=Parliament (Russia); V283=TV; V284=Government (Russia); V285=Soviet political system.

V284 CONFIDENCE: NATO

For each item listed, how much confidence do you have in them, is it a great deal, quite a lot, not very much, or none at all? NATO (% "a great deal" or "quite a lot")

		Gender		Age			Education			Income			Political Affinity			Values		
	Total	Male	Female	16-29	30-49	50+	Lower	Medium	Upper	Lower	Middle	Upper	Left	Center	Right	Mat	Mixed	Postmat
India	35	34	37	38	35	26	35	32	38	31	37	36	35	34	44	30	39	39
Nigeria	55	55	54	56	51	61	57	57	52	51	57	59	53	56	57	60	52	52
China	22	21	23	30	21	12	12	22	30	18	22	27	na	na	na	17	26	26
Romania	47	51	42	51	45	46	44	50	45	45	47	49	41	44	55	43	48	54
Turkey	47	43	51	47	44	52	54	41	30	51	48	42	35	50	52	55	48	34
Poland	na	na	na	na	na	na	na	na	na	na	na	na	na	na	na	na	na	na
Bulgaria	28	29	26	36	27	23	22	29	30	27	27	30	21	27	43	22	26	50
Chile	29	34	25	25	34	28	24	31	33	23	30	37	35	29	35	27	32	29
Czechoslovakia	35	37	34	33	38	33	33	36	38	36	32	39	24	31	51	24	38	44
South Africa	na	na	na	na	na	na	na	na	na	na	na	na	na	na	na	na	na	na
Lithuania	42	42	42	44	38	44	43	42	31	45	40	35	36	39	56	40	43	42
Hungary	na	na	na	na	na	na	na	na	na	na	na	na	na	na	na	na	na	na
Argentina	na	na	na	na	na	na	na	na	na	na	na	na	na	na	na	na	na	na
Brazil	na	na	na	na	na	na	na	na	na	na	na	na	na	na	na	na	na	na
Mexico	27	27	26	28	28	21	24	28	33	20	30	35	25	26	37	26	27	28
Belarus	na	na	na	na	na	na	na	na	na	na	na	na	na	na	na	na	na	na
Russia	68	68	69	65	66	72	73	67	66	71	71	63	74	68	69	65	69	79
Moscow	20	17	23	21	19	21	38	26	13	28	17	14	16	22	27	29	18	15
Latvia	na	na	na	na	na	na	na	na	na	na	na	na	na	na	na	na	na	na
Estonia	na	na	na	na	na	na	na	na	na	na	na	na	na	na	na	na	na	na
Portugal	35	38	32	40	29	35	33	37	41	35	28	42	26	35	41	37	34	37
South Korea	na	na	na	na	na	na	na	na	na	na	na	na	na	na	na	na	na	na
Ireland	59	59	59	60	60	59	58	60	59	60	61	61	44	62	66	59	61	53
North Ireland	53	60	48	54	51	57	51	58	59	45	68	61	50	64	61	60	50	57
Slovenia	25	27	24	27	26	27	27	26	22	25	26	24	22	25	33	26	26	16
Spain	19	17	20	16	15	25	20	16	14	24	17	13	14	19	22	24	18	10
East Germany	18	19	18	17	16	21	19	18	14	20	17	18	09	24	26	15	19	20
Britain	60	64	55	54	61	61	58	67	56	58	62	61	55	64	65	64	60	54
Italy	54	53	54	51	51	58	54	56	33	52	56	54	40	64	68	58	55	45
Netherlands	50	49	51	55	48	49	49	59	43	39	54	54	33	54	67	54	55	44
Belgium	46	43	49	48	42	49	46	46	49	45	43	45	39	47	54	53	48	36
Austria	na	na	na	na	na	na	na	na	na	na	na	na	na	na	na	na	na	na
France	60	55	65	56	56	64	57	66	55	62	57	56	55	65	68	64	62	53
Canada	50	52	49	47	51	53	48	51	51	44	52	54	39	54	56	43	53	51
United States	52	53	51	52	46	58	49	54	51	48	50	56	47	56	51	58	50	52
Iceland	35	33	38	39	31	38	38	40	31	40	41	44	18	36	50	37	37	24
West Germany	42	43	41	34	39	49	45	36	36	40	41	44	30	43	58	52	47	27
Denmark	52	56	48	51	49	56	50	55	51	48	52	53	32	50	70	45	56	37
Finland	29	29	30	28	29	30	30	32	25	24	32	30	17	21	43	35	29	29
Norway	67	72	61	65	69	65	57	68	71	61	67	77	52	68	82	69	69	49
Sweden	36	36	36	30	33	46	38	35	37	36	32	39	15	33	55	39	39	28
Japan	27	26	27	29	26	26	25	24	33	23	26	31	26	33	34	32	30	28
Switzerland	na	na	na	na	na	na	na	na	na	na	na	na	na	na	na	na	na	na
Total	41	42	41	41	40	43	41	43	40	40	42	43	34	43	51	43	43	39

Ranking:

Russia	68
Norway	67
Britain	60
France	60
Ireland	59
Nigeria	55
Italy	54
North Ireland	53
United States	52
Denmark	52
Netherlands	50
Canada	50
Romania	47
Turkey	47
Belgium	46
Hungary	42
West Germany	42
Sweden	36
India	35
Czechoslovakia	35
Portugal	35
Iceland	35
Chile	29
Finland	29
Bulgaria	28
Mexico	27
Japan	27
Slovenia	25
China	22
Moscow	20
Spain	19
East Germany	18

Note: Countries in the left column are ranked according to GNP per capita. / The percentages in the bottom row give each country an equal weight. / na=not ascertained.
In Russia, substitutions were made for V279-V285. V279=Parliament (USSR); V280=Parliament (Russia); V281=Government (USSR); V282=Parliament (Russia); V283=TV; V284=Government (Russia); V285=Soviet political system.

V285   CONFIDENCE: POLITICAL SYSTEM

For each item listed, how much confidence do you have in them, is it a great deal, quite a lot, not very much, or none at all?
The [country's] political system (% "a great deal" or "quite a lot")

Country	Total	Gender		Age			Education			Income			Political Affinity			Values		
		Male	Female	16-29	30-49	50+	Lower	Medium	Upper	Lower	Middle	Upper	Left	Center	Right	Mat	Mixed	Postmat
India	55	56	54	56	56	51	55	58	52	55	58	52	56	60	60	56	56	63
Nigeria	38	37	40	42	31	46	48	38	34	34	40	41	34	44	46	44	36	21
China	80	78	83	73	81	88	82	81	75	85	79	75	na	na	na	88	77	40
Romania	na	na	na	na	na	na	na	na	na	na	na	na	na	na	na	na	na	na
Turkey	49	44	55	46	46	61	61	37	22	54	56	39	30	52	61	59	51	33
Poland	09	10	09	14	09	07	10	09	07	08	09	11	14	11	07	12	08	10
Bulgaria	29	31	26	25	25	36	41	26	23	28	33	25	34	28	23	32	29	19
Chile	50	57	45	50	54	46	46	50	56	47	49	58	63	50	54	41	51	66
Czechoslovakia	44	45	43	40	44	47	42	44	47	44	42	46	30	41	59	35	45	62
South Africa	58	56	59	56	57	62	55	58	60	53	58	62	57	66	48	63	57	40
Lithuania	13	12	13	08	10	20	12	12	15	16	10	11	na	na	na	17	12	06
Hungary	na	na	na	na	na	na	na	na	na	na	na	na	na	na	na	na	na	na
Argentina	na	na	na	na	na	na	na	na	na	na	na	na	na	na	na	na	na	na
Brazil	na	na	na	na	na	na	na	na	na	na	na	na	na	na	na	na	na	na
Mexico	30	32	28	28	33	29	30	29	33	26	33	35	21	30	42	34	30	30
Belarus	23	24	22	17	22	29	35	18	23	22	23	23	21	21	31	31	18	17
Russia	46	42	48	35	42	58	58	44	40	48	45	43	37	49	48	55	42	22
Moscow	23	24	23	19	19	33	51	24	17	28	20	20	17	26	38	36	19	15
Latvia	18	15	21	17	18	21	25	19	15	17	19	18	na	na	na	19	19	08
Estonia	17	15	19	17	14	22	20	16	16	19	15	15	na	na	na	22	15	12
Portugal	na	na	na	na	na	na	na	na	na	na	na	na	na	na	na	na	na	na
South Korea	na	na	na	na	na	na	na	na	na	na	na	na	na	na	na	na	na	na
Ireland	na	na	na	na	na	na	na	na	na	na	na	na	na	na	na	na	na	na
North Ireland	na	na	na	na	na	na	na	na	na	na	na	na	na	na	na	na	na	na
Slovenia	na	na	na	na	na	na	na	na	na	na	na	na	na	na	na	na	na	na
Spain	23	24	23	18	24	26	25	16	22	24	22	24	28	27	23	22	26	20
East Germany	na	na	na	na	na	na	na	na	na	na	na	na	na	na	na	na	na	na
Britain	na	na	na	na	na	na	na	na	na	na	na	na	na	na	na	na	na	na
Italy	na	na	na	na	na	na	na	na	na	na	na	na	na	na	na	na	na	na
Netherlands	na	na	na	na	na	na	na	na	na	na	na	na	na	na	na	na	na	na
Belgium	na	na	na	na	na	na	na	na	na	na	na	na	na	na	na	na	na	na
Austria	na	na	na	na	na	na	na	na	na	na	na	na	na	na	na	na	na	na
France	na	na	na	na	na	na	na	na	na	na	na	na	na	na	na	na	na	na
Canada	38	37	38	35	37	40	37	34	44	34	38	42	38	39	43	46	37	39
United States	55	58	53	53	49	63	57	51	59	52	59	55	53	57	61	59	55	54
Iceland	na	na	na	na	na	na	na	na	na	na	na	na	na	na	na	na	na	na
West Germany	na	na	na	na	na	na	na	na	na	na	na	na	na	na	na	na	na	na
Denmark	na	na	na	na	na	na	na	na	na	na	na	na	na	na	na	na	na	na
Finland	na	na	na	na	na	na	na	na	na	na	na	na	na	na	na	na	na	na
Norway	na	na	na	na	na	na	na	na	na	na	na	na	na	na	na	na	na	na
Sweden	na	na	na	na	na	na	na	na	na	na	na	na	na	na	na	na	na	na
Japan	na	na	na	na	na	na	na	na	na	na	na	na	na	na	na	na	na	na
Switzerland	na	na	na	na	na	na	na	na	na	na	na	na	na	na	na	na	na	na
Total	37	37	37	34	35	41	42	35	35	37	37	37	36	40	43	41	36	30

Ranking:

China	80
South Africa	58
India	55
United States	55
Chile	50
Turkey	49
Russia	46
Czechoslovakia	44
Nigeria	38
Canada	38
Mexico	30
Bulgaria	29
Belarus	23
Moscow	23
Spain	23
Latvia	18
Estonia	17
Lithuania	13
Poland	09

Note: Countries in the left column are ranked according to GNP per capita. / The percentages in the bottom row give each country an equal weight. / na=not ascertained.
In Russia, substitutions were made for V279-V285: V279=Parliament (Russia); V281=Government (USSR); V282=Parliament (USSR); V283=TV; V284=Government (Russia); V285=Soviet political system.

V286. On this card are listed some things people have said make them proud of their country. Do any of these things make you proud of this country?

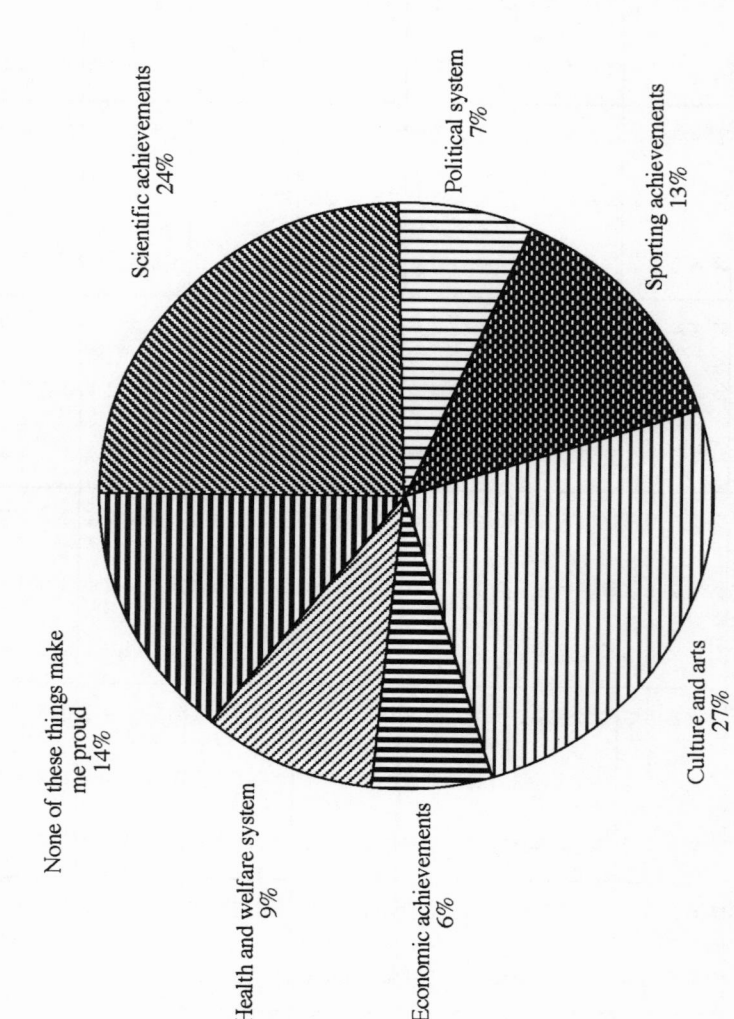

V286 WHAT PROUD OF

On this card are listed some things people have said make them proud of [their country]. Do any of these things make you proud of this country? (% "scientific achievements")

	Total	Gender		Age			Education			Income			Political Affinity			Values			Ranking:	
		Male	Female	16-29	30-49	50+	Lower	Medium	Upper	Lower	Middle	Upper	Left	Center	Right	Mat	Mixed	Postmat		
India	44	46	42	40	48	46	51	45	41	46	47	39	46	43	48	47	41	46	United States	47
Nigeria	10	10	10	11	09	06	07	11	10	08	13	10	07	15	07	08	12	06	India	44
China	30	31	30	32	28	32	34	31	23	30	24	33	na	na	na	30	31	20	Mexico	32
Romania	na	na	na	na	na	na	na	na	na	na	na	na	na	na	na	na	na	na	China	30
Turkey	26	29	23	20	30	29	26	27	26	23	30	26	20	29	30	29	26	23	Turkey	26
Poland	na	na	na	na	na	na	na	na	na	na	na	na	na	na	na	na	na	na	Canada	26
Bulgaria	na	na	na	na	na	na	na	na	na	na	na	na	na	na	na	na	na	na	Spain	18
Chile	17	17	17	15	19	17	17	18	15	16	19	16	15	19	17	19	17	14	Chile	17
Czechoslovakia	na	na	na	na	na	na	na	na	na	na	na	na	na	na	na	na	na	na	Lithuania	17
South Africa	na	na	na	na	na	na	na	na	na	na	na	na	na	na	na	na	na	na	Nigeria	10
Lithuania	17	15	19	12	12	26	25	15	16	18	19	10	na	na	na	17	17	18	Estonia	10
Hungary	na	na	na	na	na	na	na	na	na	na	na	na	na	na	na	na	na	na	Latvia	08
Argentina	na	na	na	na	na	na	na	na	na	na	na	na	na	na	na	na	na	na		
Brazil	na	na	na	na	na	na	na	na	na	na	na	na	na	na	na	na	na	na		
Mexico	32	33	31	32	32	31	30	36	35	29	32	38	29	33	35	34	32	29		
Belarus	na	na	na	na	na	na	na	na	na	na	na	na	na	na	na	na	na	na		
Russia	na	na	na	na	na	na	na	na	na	na	na	na	na	na	na	na	na	na		
Moscow	na	na	na	na	na	na	na	na	na	na	na	na	na	na	na	na	na	na		
Latvia	08	11	07	08	07	10	16	08	07	07	09	08	na	na	na	07	08	08		
Estonia	10	11	10	10	09	13	13	09	11	10	08	13	na	na	na	08	12	09		
Portugal	na	na	na	na	na	na	na	na	na	na	na	na	na	na	na	na	na	na		
South Korea	na	na	na	na	na	na	na	na	na	na	na	na	na	na	na	na	na	na		
Ireland	na	na	na	na	na	na	na	na	na	na	na	na	na	na	na	na	na	na		
North Ireland	na	na	na	na	na	na	na	na	na	na	na	na	na	na	na	na	na	na		
Slovenia	na	na	na	na	na	na	na	na	na	na	na	na	na	na	na	na	na	na		
Spain	18	20	16	15	21	16	19	13	17	11	15	11	16	15	26	20	18	15		
East Germany	na	na	na	na	na	na	na	na	na	na	na	na	na	na	na	na	na	na		
Britain	na	na	na	na	na	na	na	na	na	na	na	na	na	na	na	na	na	na		
Italy	na	na	na	na	na	na	na	na	na	na	na	na	na	na	na	na	na	na		
Netherlands	na	na	na	na	na	na	na	na	na	na	na	na	na	na	na	na	na	na		
Belgium	na	na	na	na	na	na	na	na	na	na	na	na	na	na	na	na	na	na		
Austria	na	na	na	na	na	na	na	na	na	na	na	na	na	na	na	na	na	na		
France	na	na	na	na	na	na	na	na	na	na	na	na	na	na	na	na	na	na		
Canada	26	29	24	25	27	27	20	26	32	23	26	31	22	27	29	24	27	25		
United States	47	45	50	46	45	50	44	50	46	46	50	46	45	48	45	47	48	47		
Iceland	na	na	na	na	na	na	na	na	na	na	na	na	na	na	na	na	na	na		
West Germany	na	na	na	na	na	na	na	na	na	na	na	na	na	na	na	na	na	na		
Denmark	na	na	na	na	na	na	na	na	na	na	na	na	na	na	na	na	na	na		
Finland	na	na	na	na	na	na	na	na	na	na	na	na	na	na	na	na	na	na		
Norway	na	na	na	na	na	na	na	na	na	na	na	na	na	na	na	na	na	na		
Sweden	na	na	na	na	na	na	na	na	na	na	na	na	na	na	na	na	na	na		
Japan	na	na	na	na	na	na	na	na	na	na	na	na	na	na	na	na	na	na		
Switzerland	na	na	na	na	na	na	na	na	na	na	na	na	na	na	na	na	na	na		
Total	24	25	23	22	24	25	25	24	23	22	24	23	25	29	30	24	24	22		

Note: Countries in the left column are ranked according to GNP per capita. / The percentages in the bottom row give each country an equal weight. / na=not ascertained.

V289. How much do you trust the government to do what is right? Do you trust it almost always, most of the time, only some of the time, or almost never?

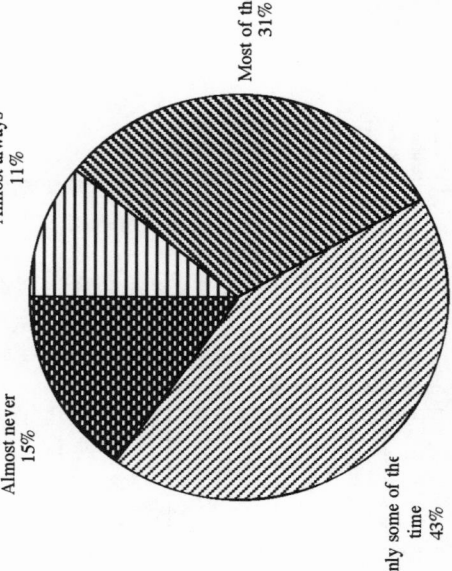

Most of the time
31%

Almost always
11%

Almost never
15%

Only some of the
time
43%

V288. Generally speaking, would you say that this country is run by a few big interests looking out for themselves, or that it is run for the benefit of all the people?

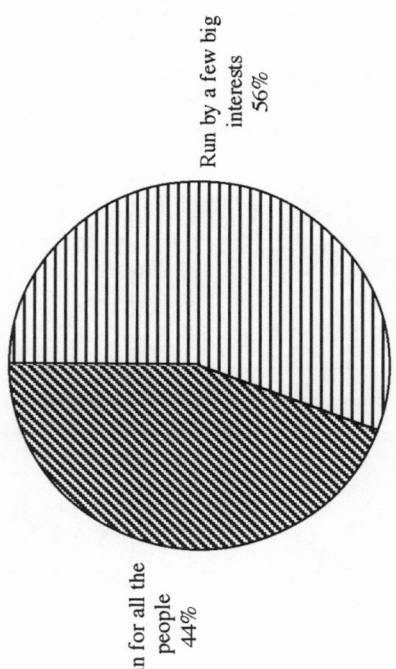

Run by a few big
interests
56%

Run for all the
people
44%

V288 COUNTRY RUN BY

Generally speaking, would you say that this country is run by a few big interests looking out for themselves, or that it is run for the benefit of all the people? (% "run by a few big interests")

	Total	Gender		Age			Education			Income			Political Affinity			Values		
		Male	Female	16-29	30-49	50+	Lower	Medium	Upper	Lower	Middle	Upper	Left	Center	Right	Mat	Mixed	Postmat
India	55	57	54	56	55	56	52	53	60	53	55	57	61	57	46	55	57	48
Nigeria	78	80	76	76	83	70	78	74	82	76	79	83	79	79	77	73	80	81
China	08	09	07	13	06	05	03	08	13	06	06	11	na	na	na	04	08	52
Romania	na	na	na	na	na	na	na	na	na	na	na	na	na	na	na	na	na	na
Turkey	53	59	47	58	55	41	44	63	75	50	49	61	71	51	43	43	52	66
Poland	na	na	na	na	na	na	na	na	na	na	na	na	na	na	na	na	na	na
Bulgaria	na	na	na	na	na	na	na	na	na	na	na	na	na	na	na	na	na	na
Chile	45	48	42	43	48	42	41	46	48	40	44	50	45	47	40	46	43	48
Czechoslovakia	67	69	66	69	70	63	68	67	67	66	69	67	79	68	57	73	67	55
South Africa	na	na	na	na	na	na	na	na	na	na	na	na	na	na	na	na	na	na
Lithuania	50	47	52	46	57	46	40	52	58	47	51	55	na	na	na	52	51	38
Hungary	na	na	na	na	na	na	na	na	na	na	na	na	na	na	na	na	na	na
Argentina	na	na	na	na	na	na	na	na	na	na	na	na	na	na	na	na	na	na
Brazil	na	na	na	na	na	na	na	na	na	na	na	na	na	na	na	na	na	na
Mexico	81	82	80	82	82	78	80	79	88	80	82	86	93	83	71	77	83	89
Belarus	na	na	na	na	na	na	na	na	na	na	na	na	na	na	na	na	na	na
Russia	na	na	na	na	na	na	na	na	na	na	na	na	na	na	na	na	na	na
Moscow	na	na	na	na	na	na	na	na	na	na	na	na	na	na	na	na	na	na
Latvia	35	37	33	33	38	30	22	35	38	31	31	40	na	na	na	40	33	29
Estonia	54	54	54	48	57	54	48	54	59	52	57	53	na	na	na	53	53	56
Portugal	na	na	na	na	na	na	na	na	na	na	na	na	na	na	na	na	na	na
South Korea	na	na	na	na	na	na	na	na	na	na	na	na	na	na	na	na	na	na
Ireland	na	na	na	na	na	na	na	na	na	na	na	na	na	na	na	na	na	na
North Ireland	na	na	na	na	na	na	na	na	na	na	na	na	na	na	na	na	na	na
Slovenia	na	na	na	na	na	na	na	na	na	na	na	na	na	na	na	na	na	na
Spain	51	50	51	57	49	47	47	59	63	45	50	55	48	49	58	42	50	63
East Germany	na	na	na	na	na	na	na	na	na	na	na	na	na	na	na	na	na	na
Britain	na	na	na	na	na	na	na	na	na	na	na	na	na	na	na	na	na	na
Italy	na	na	na	na	na	na	na	na	na	na	na	na	na	na	na	na	na	na
Netherlands	na	na	na	na	na	na	na	na	na	na	na	na	na	na	na	na	na	na
Belgium	na	na	na	na	na	na	na	na	na	na	na	na	na	na	na	na	na	na
Austria	na	na	na	na	na	na	na	na	na	na	na	na	na	na	na	na	na	na
France	na	na	na	na	na	na	na	na	na	na	na	na	na	na	na	na	na	na
Canada	70	71	70	67	71	71	75	71	65	76	70	65	71	73	59	67	70	73
United States	68	68	68	63	70	67	76	64	66	69	68	66	71	66	64	69	66	70
Iceland	na	na	na	na	na	na	na	na	na	na	na	na	na	na	na	na	na	na
West Germany	na	na	na	na	na	na	na	na	na	na	na	na	na	na	na	na	na	na
Denmark	na	na	na	na	na	na	na	na	na	na	na	na	na	na	na	na	na	na
Finland	na	na	na	na	na	na	na	na	na	na	na	na	na	na	na	na	na	na
Norway	na	na	na	na	na	na	na	na	na	na	na	na	na	na	na	na	na	na
Sweden	na	na	na	na	na	na	na	na	na	na	na	na	na	na	na	na	na	na
Japan	na	na	na	na	na	na	na	na	na	na	na	na	na	na	na	na	na	na
Switzerland	na	na	na	na	na	na	na	na	na	na	na	na	na	na	na	na	na	na
Total	55	56	54	55	57	52	52	56	60	53	55	58	69	64	57	53	55	59

Ranking:

Mexico	81
Nigeria	78
Canada	70
United States	68
Czechoslovakia	67
India	55
Estonia	54
Turkey	53
Spain	51
Lithuania	50
Chile	45
Latvia	35
China	08

Note: Countries in the left column are ranked according to GNP per capita. / The percentages in the bottom row give each country an equal weight. / na=not ascertained.

V289 TRUST GOVERNMENT

How much do you trust the government to do what is right? Do you trust it almost always, most of the time, only some of the time, or almost never? (% "almost always" or "most of the time")

		Gender		Age			Education			Income			Political Affinity			Values		
	Total	Male	Female	16-29	30-49	50+	Lower	Medium	Upper	Lower	Middle	Upper	Left	Center	Right	Mat	Mixed	Postmat
India	43	46	41	43	45	41	42	46	41	44	47	40	42	49	50	43	45	46
Nigeria	26	26	26	26	22	47	31	29	21	24	28	27	30	25	27	31	25	15
China	na	na	na	na	na	na	na	na	na	na	na	na	na	na	na	na	na	na
Romania	na	na	na	na	na	na	na	na	na	na	na	na	na	na	na	na	na	na
Turkey	32	30	33	28	29	41	39	23	14	37	34	24	13	35	42	44	32	17
Poland	na	na	na	na	na	na	na	na	na	na	na	na	na	na	na	na	na	na
Bulgaria	na	na	na	na	na	na	na	na	na	na	na	na	na	na	na	na	na	na
Chile	59	64	55	57	61	61	59	58	62	58	59	63	70	61	47	51	61	67
Czechoslovakia	44	45	42	39	44	47	39	45	48	44	46	41	34	40	56	35	45	56
South Africa	na	na	na	na	na	na	na	na	na	na	na	na	na	na	na	na	na	na
Lithuania	59	61	57	59	58	60	56	59	63	56	61	63	na	na	na	52	59	73
Hungary	na	na	na	na	na	na	na	na	na	na	na	na	na	na	na	na	na	na
Argentina	na	na	na	na	na	na	na	na	na	na	na	na	na	na	na	na	na	na
Brazil	na	na	na	na	na	na	na	na	na	na	na	na	na	na	na	na	na	na
Mexico	24	23	26	23	25	27	26	26	20	25	23	23	12	25	34	27	23	17
Belarus	na	na	na	na	na	na	na	na	na	na	na	na	na	na	na	na	na	na
Russia	na	na	na	na	na	na	na	na	na	na	na	na	na	na	na	na	na	na
Moscow	na	na	na	na	na	na	na	na	na	na	na	na	na	na	na	na	na	na
Latvia	58	54	60	54	56	66	65	60	51	57	62	55	na	na	na	58	58	62
Estonia	65	64	65	66	65	63	70	62	68	65	61	67	na	na	na	62	67	71
Portugal	na	na	na	na	na	na	na	na	na	na	na	na	na	na	na	na	na	na
South Korea	na	na	na	na	na	na	na	na	na	na	na	na	na	na	na	na	na	na
Ireland	na	na	na	na	na	na	na	na	na	na	na	na	na	na	na	na	na	na
North Ireland	na	na	na	na	na	na	na	na	na	na	na	na	na	na	na	na	na	na
Slovenia	na	na	na	na	na	na	na	na	na	na	na	na	na	na	na	na	na	na
Spain	28	29	27	22	25	36	31	19	20	36	28	28	33	32	19	31	29	19
East Germany	na	na	na	na	na	na	na	na	na	na	na	na	na	na	na	na	na	na
Britain	na	na	na	na	na	na	na	na	na	na	na	na	na	na	na	na	na	na
Italy	na	na	na	na	na	na	na	na	na	na	na	na	na	na	na	na	na	na
Netherlands	na	na	na	na	na	na	na	na	na	na	na	na	na	na	na	na	na	na
Belgium	na	na	na	na	na	na	na	na	na	na	na	na	na	na	na	na	na	na
Austria	na	na	na	na	na	na	na	na	na	na	na	na	na	na	na	na	na	na
France	na	na	na	na	na	na	na	na	na	na	na	na	na	na	na	na	na	na
Canada	20	19	21	22	17	23	18	19	23	19	19	21	15	20	25	30	19	20
United States	41	39	44	50	35	44	42	41	42	40	43	41	35	42	46	44	43	36
Iceland	na	na	na	na	na	na	na	na	na	na	na	na	na	na	na	na	na	na
West Germany	na	na	na	na	na	na	na	na	na	na	na	na	na	na	na	na	na	na
Denmark	na	na	na	na	na	na	na	na	na	na	na	na	na	na	na	na	na	na
Finland	na	na	na	na	na	na	na	na	na	na	na	na	na	na	na	na	na	na
Norway	na	na	na	na	na	na	na	na	na	na	na	na	na	na	na	na	na	na
Sweden	na	na	na	na	na	na	na	na	na	na	na	na	na	na	na	na	na	na
Japan	na	na	na	na	na	na	na	na	na	na	na	na	na	na	na	na	na	na
Switzerland	na	na	na	na	na	na	na	na	na	na	na	na	na	na	na	na	na	na
Total	**42**	**42**	**41**	**41**	**40**	**46**	**43**	**41**	**39**	**42**	**43**	**41**	**32**	**37**	**38**	**42**	**42**	**42**

Ranking:

Estonia	65
Chile	59
Lithuania	59
Latvia	58
Czechoslovakia	44
India	43
United States	41
Turkey	32
Spain	28
Nigeria	26
Mexico	24
Canada	20

Note: Countries in the left column are ranked according to GNP per capita. / The percentages in the bottom row give each country an equal weight. / na=not ascertained.

V290-V295. There are a number of groups and movements looking for public support. For each of the following movements, which I read out, can you tell me whether you approve or disapprove of this movement?

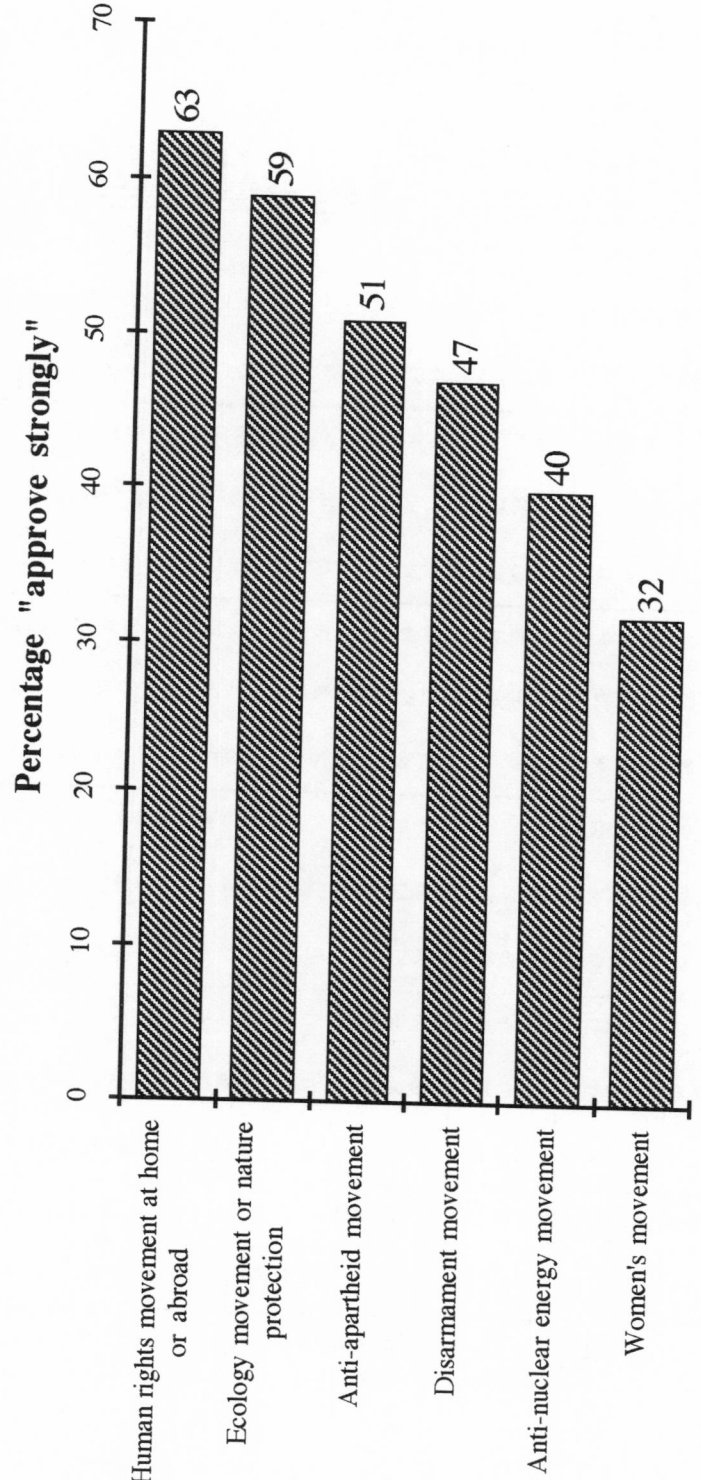

Percentage "approve strongly"

V290 ECOLOGY MOVEMENT

There are a number of groups and movements looking for public support. For each of the following movements, which I read out, can you tell me whether you approve or disapprove of this movement? Ecology movement or nature protection (% "strongly approve")

Country	Total	Gender Male	Gender Female	Age 16-29	Age 30-49	Age 50+	Educ Lower	Educ Medium	Educ Upper	Income Lower	Income Middle	Income Upper	Pol. Left	Pol. Center	Pol. Right	Values Mat	Values Mixed	Values Postmat	Ranking	
India	61	66	55	61	61	61	50	58	67	56	60	64	64	60	63	59	64	55	Moscow	83
Nigeria	61	63	58	62	61	50	55	63	61	63	61	57	na	59	63	63	61	52	Brazil	82
China	56	57	53	60	53	56	49	53	66	57	58	54	na	na	na	48	63	62	Poland	81
Romania	56	56	55	60	49	58	53	57	56	51	60	53	59	52	56	55	57	51	East Germany	79
Turkey	52	53	50	54	49	54	50	52	57	56	48	51	51	52	53	48	53	52	Belarus	78
Poland	81	82	80	77	83	81	80	81	86	79	83	81	77	81	89	78	81	85	Chile	77
Bulgaria	75	75	74	78	74	73	70	75	76	75	71	79	72	74	84	72	75	83	Argentina	77
Chile	77	81	73	75	79	76	71	77	83	71	76	84	79	77	80	70	78	83	Portugal	76
Czechoslovakia	54	51	58	53	53	58	54	56	50	58	52	53	52	55	56	50	57	52	Bulgaria	75
South Africa	69	66	72	69	69	69	66	70	73	65	71	72	66	70	72	71	69	63	South Korea	74
Lithuania	54	54	54	55	53	56	57	53	56	54	58	50	na	na	na	55	54	53	Russia	73
Hungary	70	70	71	75	68	70	67	74	72	66	73	77	68	73	70	71	69	69	Spain	73
Argentina	82	76	78	79	77	76	76	79	78	75	77	78	83	73	74	72	75	84	Austria	73
Brazil	70	82	82	86	79	80	80	84	79	82	86	81	82	82	79	82	82	76	Hungary	70
Mexico	78	68	71	71	71	64	68	69	76	65	72	77	74	66	73	65	70	76	Mexico	70
Belarus	78	81	76	79	77	79	83	75	80	77	80	77	80	77	74	75	80	84	West Germany	70
Russia	73	69	75	75	69	76	76	75	68	77	72	68	68	74	66	73	73	66	South Africa	69
Moscow	83	81	84	81	81	86	87	83	81	86	81	81	83	80	75	83	81	86	India	61
Latvia	48	49	48	48	47	50	56	47	48	60	47	42	na	na	na	46	48	59	Nigeria	61
Estonia	49	47	50	46	50	49	48	51	45	52	45	47	81	74	77	49	48	65	Japan	59
Portugal	76	75	77	76	77	75	75	75	80	75	78	73	81	74	77	71	80	79	China	56
South Korea	74	74	75	76	71	81	73	72	77	76	73	75	65	76	76	74	76	69	Romania	56
Ireland	50	47	54	48	53	49	49	51	61	46	53	52	51	48	56	51	49	56	Czechoslovakia	54
North Ireland	38	36	39	34	38	41	42	27	41	45	38	37	31	40	38	27	40	47	Lithuania	54
Slovenia	54	53	54	47	54	57	55	50	58	57	51	52	54	55	63	55	52	60	Slovenia	54
Spain	73	72	74	79	74	67	72	78	73	68	74	77	78	69	69	63	78	79	Netherlands	54
East Germany	79	77	81	79	75	82	78	80	80	79	78	80	82	79	74	72	79	82	Canada	54
Britain	47	45	50	46	50	46	46	47	54	45	49	47	52	47	44	42	45	58	Switzerland	53
Italy	50	47	53	54	46	51	50	49	67	52	52	41	53	47	52	46	49	59	Turkey	52
Netherlands	54	52	55	57	54	51	48	52	63	54	54	53	71	49	45	39	53	61	Ireland	50
Belgium	49	48	51	54	51	45	48	48	54	50	47	44	56	49	42	45	47	59	Italy	50
Austria	73	67	76	78	72	71	69	74	81	68	75	75	76	76	70	65	73	76	France	50
France	50	49	50	48	54	47	49	51	50	50	52	49	56	46	36	45	50	57	Estonia	49
Canada	54	54	54	55	56	50	47	54	59	53	53	56	61	52	52	45	52	64	Belgium	49
United States	45	45	45	49	51	38	33	45	53	44	45	48	58	44	39	40	44	53	Latvia	48
Iceland	37	31	43	42	32	38	35	38	37	na	na	na	48	38	37	38	34	47	Britain	47
West Germany	70	69	71	73	74	64	64	76	88	67	68	75	79	69	62	50	69	83	Norway	47
Denmark	30	27	32	31	32	26	16	30	37	30	29	30	47	27	22	12	30	44	United States	45
Finland	28	22	34	32	27	25	31	24	31	35	24	26	44	31	19	33	26	31	Sweden	41
Norway	47	43	51	59	50	36	40	44	54	39	46	45	61	48	36	43	47	61	North Ireland	38
Sweden	41	35	47	45	43	34	33	43	48	39	42	39	45	41	37	29	39	53	Iceland	37
Japan	59	57	62	57	58	64	61	58	61	60	58	62	75	59	58	57	64	60	Denmark	30
Switzerland	53	47	58	59	53	50	49	57	52	53	59	48	72	53	43	42	51	66	Finland	28
Total	59	58	61	61	59	58	57	59	63	60	60	60	65	60	58	55	60	65		

Note: Countries in the left column are ranked according to GNP per capita. / The percentages in the bottom row give each country an equal weight. / na=not ascertained.

V291   ANTI-NUCLEAR ENERGY

There are a number of groups and movements looking for public support. For each of the following movements, which I read out, can you tell me whether you approve or disapprove of this movement? Anti-nuclear energy movement (% "strongly approve")

	Total	Gender		Age			Education			Income			Political Affinity			Values		
		Male	Female	16-29	30-49	50+	Lower	Medium	Upper	Lower	Middle	Upper	Left	Center	Right	Mat	Mixed	Postmat
India	38	41	33	38	37	42	34	36	40	35	35	41	34	35	47	38	38	37
Nigeria	54	55	53	56	52	48	51	55	54	52	55	54	58	55	53	56	53	55
China	56	56	57	54	56	61	61	55	54	59	53	57	na	na	na	58	56	39
Romania	34	30	37	32	32	37	33	35	33	31	34	35	38	34	32	37	34	17
Turkey	26	26	26	25	24	32	29	22	23	31	24	23	26	25	31	25	28	24
Poland	66	61	71	58	65	72	68	67	60	73	63	61	65	64	70	71	64	67
Bulgaria	51	42	58	49	49	53	48	50	52	50	47	52	40	50	58	55	49	53
Chile	50	53	48	46	52	52	45	50	56	44	52	54	57	47	50	44	52	53
Czechoslovakia	24	20	28	19	21	31	30	22	19	25	24	25	19	25	28	22	25	40
South Africa	41	38	43	43	41	35	41	42	28	42	43	33	40	37	38	42	39	47
Lithuania	27	28	25	24	24	32	33	24	29	29	26	25	na	na	na	22	27	36
Hungary	43	37	48	40	40	46	46	41	35	44	46	29	38	41	40	46	40	40
Argentina	54	47	60	51	56	52	53	56	54	56	52	48	61	48	50	52	52	59
Brazil	60	58	62	61	60	58	57	61	60	61	61	59	64	61	51	59	60	65
Mexico	44	42	46	40	48	45	45	38	44	40	49	48	56	42	40	43	44	47
Belarus	44	39	48	40	43	49	56	45	38	52	40	41	43	42	52	51	41	42
Russia	41	32	47	37	36	48	48	45	32	47	41	35	30	36	51	47	38	26
Moscow	40	31	47	37	37	47	49	47	34	42	38	38	40	42	36	46	38	40
Latvia	41	39	42	37	37	52	54	40	38	47	41	37	na	na	na	42	40	55
Estonia	28	29	27	24	27	34	31	28	24	31	24	26	na	na	na	21	32	33
Portugal	60	55	64	55	67	57	60	64	54	63	66	49	56	62	59	58	60	60
South Korea	34	37	31	42	32	25	27	30	41	32	33	37	44	38	27	27	33	59
Ireland	52	47	57	52	56	47	50	54	49	47	54	51	51	51	56	49	52	54
North Ireland	22	20	23	24	20	14	29	18	19	22	24	15	31	20	12	17	19	28
Slovenia	40	38	43	40	38	43	42	40	35	41	42	37	35	28	25	45	38	39
Spain	64	62	66	68	67	60	64	64	59	64	66	63	71	57	54	54	69	69
East Germany	41	33	48	42	35	46	44	41	30	44	39	38	39	42	32	42	41	43
Britain	20	20	21	24	20	19	21	18	19	22	24	15	31	20	12	17	19	28
Italy	33	28	37	32	34	32	18	28	35	21	32	22	36	28	25	32	31	37
Netherlands	31	25	37	28	33	30	33	30	31	35	30	25	51	24	16	28	32	36
Belgium	38	36	41	39	40	37	31	38	35	38	38	29	49	35	30	39	38	39
Austria	63	58	67	64	66	61	61	63	73	58	66	66	64	64	61	52	63	71
France	28	23	32	30	31	27	27	28	28	29	27	24	34	25	15	27	28	36
Canada	32	27	37	34	34	27	30	33	33	35	32	30	28	23	17	27	32	29
United States	25	22	28	29	28	21	23	26	25	23	25	29	36	24	17	23	23	19
Iceland	58	51	64	60	56	58	57	62	55	na	na	na	72	56	48	56	57	62
West Germany	37	32	43	41	44	30	33	43	47	37	35	38	56	34	19	25	31	57
Denmark	26	23	30	24	31	22	26	24	28	30	25	22	42	25	16	16	24	19
Finland	23	16	31	23	24	23	32	23	19	26	24	20	28	24	17	41	23	34
Norway	45	40	51	51	45	42	44	44	47	50	45	39	61	44	34	42	45	60
Sweden	20	13	27	19	22	15	18	19	24	18	23	18	27	21	13	17	18	45
Japan	60	60	59	57	62	58	57	58	66	61	61	59	73	62	53	62	60	65
Switzerland	29	28	31	31	31	28	30	27	38	33	32	24	60	27	17	17	26	45
Total	**41**	**37**	**43**	**40**	**41**	**41**	**42**	**40**	**39**	**41**	**40**	**37**	**46**	**40**	**37**	**39**	**40**	**44**

Ranking:

Poland	66
Spain	64
Austria	63
Brazil	60
Portugal	60
Japan	60
Iceland	58
China	56
Nigeria	54
Argentina	54
Ireland	52
Bulgaria	51
Chile	50
Norway	45
Mexico	44
Belarus	44
Hungary	43
South Africa	41
Russia	41
Latvia	41
East Germany	41
Moscow	40
Slovenia	40
India	38
Belgium	38
West Germany	37
Romania	34
South Korea	34
Italy	33
Canada	32
Netherlands	31
Switzerland	29
Estonia	28
France	28
Lithuania	27
Turkey	26
Denmark	26
United States	25
Czechoslovakia	24
Finland	23
North Ireland	22
Britain	20
Sweden	20

Note: Countries in the left column are ranked according to GNP per capita. / The percentages in the bottom row give each country an equal weight. / na=not ascertained.

V292 DISARMAMENT

There are a number of groups and movements looking for public support. For each of the following movements, which I read out, can you tell me whether you approve or disapprove of this movement? Disarmament movement (% "strongly approve")

	Total	Gender		Age			Education			Income			Political Affinity			Values			Ranking:	
		Male	Female	16-29	30-49	50+	Lower	Medium	Upper	Lower	Middle	Upper	Left	Center	Right	Mat	Mixed	Postmat		
India	43	47	38	42	43	48	38	39	49	39	40	48	44	42	48	40	45	44	Poland	76
Nigeria	55	56	52	55	55	53	52	55	55	58	52	55	59	53	58	59	53	54	Brazil	74
China	41	40	43	34	43	48	41	38	46	39	44	42	na	na	na	41	42	37	East Germany	74
Romania	60	58	61	59	55	65	61	59	59	59	63	56	62	62	54	63	58	49	Argentina	73
Turkey	39	40	38	38	40	41	38	39	47	44	37	37	50	37	37	34	40	44	Belarus	71
Poland	76	78	74	73	76	79	73	80	75	77	76	76	69	78	82	74	76	82	Bulgaria	70
Bulgaria	70	67	72	68	70	72	68	71	70	73	68	67	66	69	76	74	69	73	Moscow	70
Chile	61	68	55	57	64	64	55	61	69	53	64	66	67	61	55	51	63	71	Portugal	70
Czechoslovakia	54	55	54	51	51	61	56	52	59	56	54	54	52	54	57	52	55	56	Spain	68
South Africa	33	33	34	36	32	32	34	35	25	35	37	24	31	33	29	33	34	32	Hungary	65
Lithuania	01	02	01	01	01	02	03	01	00	02	01	01	na	na	na	02	01	01	Russia	63
Hungary	65	70	60	56	67	67	60	68	76	61	69	65	65	68	67	63	67	70	Iceland	63
Argentina	73	71	75	68	77	72	72	76	71	72	76	68	80	69	69	72	70	81	Chile	61
Brazil	74	77	72	72	76	77	70	76	77	71	76	78	74	73	72	71	76	81	Romania	60
Mexico	56	58	53	54	60	50	57	49	57	52	61	57	66	54	54	48	57	63	Mexico	56
Belarus	71	71	70	68	70	74	79	68	70	73	71	66	71	73	65	67	72	72	Austria	56
Russia	63	62	65	63	59	69	67	66	59	67	62	59	63	60	69	64	64	52	Nigeria	55
Moscow	70	70	71	67	70	73	81	67	70	74	67	70	72	69	62	68	68	85	Japan	55
Latvia	03	02	04	04	02	05	06	04	01	01	04	04	na	na	na	02	04	01	Czechoslovakia	54
Estonia	02	03	01	02	02	03	05	02	00	02	03	01	na	na	na	02	02	02	Ireland	50
Portugal	70	71	70	66	73	73	71	73	66	71	76	63	74	72	66	65	74	71	Slovenia	50
South Korea	31	26	35	35	28	32	31	26	36	30	31	31	43	33	26	22	34	53	Italy	50
Ireland	50	48	51	53	51	46	47	53	52	48	50	52	49	47	57	45	50	56	West Germany	47
North Ireland	17	21	15	22	19	12	19	15	14	16	13	12	19	19	14	04	22	18	Belgium	44
Slovenia	50	50	49	43	51	52	48	48	54	49	48	53	52	50	49	48	49	61	India	43
Spain	68	67	69	74	70	61	67	70	69	65	69	69	76	62	59	58	72	74	Norway	42
East Germany	74	70	77	74	74	74	73	71	78	73	75	74	83	72	64	64	75	77	China	41
Britain	17	17	16	20	17	14	17	12	20	18	20	15	28	15	09	13	16	22	Canada	40
Italy	50	47	53	54	47	50	50	47	56	51	49	46	54	47	46	49	49	55	Turkey	39
Netherlands	33	31	33	30	34	33	30	33	35	40	31	27	52	29	17	26	30	37	France	36
Belgium	44	44	45	47	46	41	44	45	45	44	46	36	54	41	36	43	42	51	South Africa	33
Austria	56	49	60	62	55	53	54	57	56	53	60	53	59	58	50	53	52	65	Netherlands	33
France	36	38	34	39	39	30	36	37	35	37	35	37	46	30	17	32	32	47	South Korea	31
Canada	40	41	39	47	43	30	32	41	45	41	39	40	53	39	36	26	39	49	Sweden	31
United States	27	27	26	32	28	24	26	26	29	25	29	28	37	27	20	22	25	36	Switzerland	31
Iceland	63	58	68	65	62	65	65	64	61	na	na	na	76	63	54	62	63	70	Finland	30
West Germany	47	42	52	52	52	41	52	52	62	47	48	48	64	46	30	35	43	64	United States	27
Denmark	26	21	32	30	28	21	25	29	26	29	25	24	41	27	15	17	25	41	Denmark	26
Finland	30	27	34	23	31	35	36	28	30	34	28	30	52	28	20	31	30	30	North Ireland	17
Norway	42	40	44	51	41	37	43	40	43	48	41	37	58	38	33	39	41	57	Britain	17
Sweden	31	28	33	37	32	22	28	31	32	28	36	27	40	31	21	20	30	40	Latvia	03
Japan	55	58	51	49	56	57	52	52	64	59	55	53	81	59	49	59	55	62	Estonia	02
Switzerland	31	30	32	39	33	26	31	30	37	34	33	29	58	28	22	19	29	44	Lithuania	01
Total	**46**	**46**	**47**	**47**	**47**	**46**	**46**	**46**	**48**	**46**	**47**	**45**	**57**	**49**	**45**	**43**	**46**	**52**		

Note: Countries in the left column are ranked according to GNP per capita. / The percentages in the bottom row give each country an equal weight. / na=not ascertained.

V293 HUMAN RIGHTS

There are a number of groups and movements looking for public support. For each of the following movements, which I read out, can you tell me whether you approve or disapprove of this movement? Human rights movement at home or abroad   (% "strongly approve")

	Total	Gender		Age			Education			Income			Political Affinity			Values			Ranking:	
		Male	Female	16-29	30-49	50+	Lower	Medium	Upper	Lower	Middle	Upper	Left	Center	Right	Mat	Mixed	Postmat		
India	62	64	59	61	62	61	52	61	66	58	60	66	65	59	64	60	63	67	Nigeria	86
Nigeria	86	88	83	86	86	88	83	87	85	88	83	86	87	83	89	85	86	87	Brazil	84
China	27	24	31	35	24	20	25	27	29	24	29	28	na	na	na	21	28	56	Moscow	82
Romania	73	71	75	78	72	69	67	76	74	71	75	72	69	73	76	69	74	86	Portugal	82
Turkey	61	63	59	58	63	61	59	62	67	64	58	60	71	60	59	52	62	68	Bulgaria	79
Poland	74	75	74	70	75	76	68	79	76	70	79	75	73	77	79	68	77	80	Spain	78
Bulgaria	79	78	80	85	77	79	80	81	76	83	76	79	77	78	80	76	80	85	Belarus	77
Chile	76	81	71	74	76	77	74	76	79	74	76	78	89	75	62	66	78	86	Chile	76
Czechoslovakia	61	61	61	59	59	64	62	58	66	60	61	62	57	60	64	51	63	70	Poland	74
South Africa	72	73	71	77	69	68	76	73	54	80	75	53	76	73	58	66	75	78	Romania	73
Lithuania	41	41	40	45	34	44	44	41	36	41	43	35	na	na	na	37	42	42	South Africa	72
Hungary	65	67	63	68	67	62	59	70	70	60	67	71	66	70	57	64	65	73	South Korea	71
Argentina	69	66	71	71	71	65	68	70	67	69	71	67	84	66	63	58	70	79	Slovenia	71
Brazil	84	82	87	86	85	81	82	86	84	83	87	84	85	87	79	82	85	92	Russia	70
Mexico	65	66	64	66	65	61	63	60	73	59	67	76	78	62	65	59	67	76	Argentina	69
Belarus	77	80	75	77	78	76	77	77	78	80	74	78	83	73	63	71	81	88	Italy	67
Russia	70	69	71	72	68	72	71	71	69	71	71	70	68	69	69	66	72	83	Norway	66
Moscow	82	81	84	80	83	83	82	83	82	81	84	82	85	80	73	79	84	90	Hungary	65
Latvia	48	48	48	46	48	49	50	48	47	48	48	48	na	na	na	48	49	56	Mexico	65
Estonia	27	27	27	27	28	25	31	26	25	29	25	25	na	na	na	23	28	42	East Germany	65
Portugal	82	81	83	82	85	79	80	86	86	81	82	80	84	82	82	77	84	84	Iceland	64
South Korea	71	70	72	78	68	67	61	70	77	72	69	69	75	74	68	66	73	83	Ireland	63
Ireland	63	59	67	67	64	60	60	67	67	58	67	65	68	60	70	58	63	71	India	62
North Ireland	33	37	30	39	36	25	39	25	14	33	30	25	52	33	28	17	37	40	France	62
Slovenia	71	71	72	72	72	70	70	71	75	69	71	74	72	76	78	64	73	84	Turkey	61
Spain	78	78	79	83	81	72	76	85	88	71	80	82	85	74	77	66	83	87	Czechoslovakia	61
East Germany	65	62	67	68	65	62	62	66	73	64	62	68	72	65	56	52	65	72	Netherlands	59
Britain	41	44	39	40	47	37	38	46	54	37	45	49	54	38	40	32	40	53	Sweden	59
Italy	67	66	68	70	68	64	66	73	73	68	69	72	73	66	58	60	65	79	Switzerland	59
Netherlands	59	55	60	63	59	54	51	59	66	62	60	63	76	55	48	60	55	70	Canada	58
Belgium	54	54	54	60	54	50	49	54	62	49	55	55	64	55	45	39	52	65	Austria	56
Austria	56	51	59	60	57	53	52	58	62	50	58	59	61	60	50	46	53	70	Belgium	54
France	62	64	60	66	67	54	57	65	69	59	63	67	75	59	48	44	60	80	West Germany	54
Canada	58	55	62	64	62	49	54	57	63	59	57	59	72	58	55	46	57	69	Finland	53
United States	51	49	52	53	56	45	45	47	59	47	49	58	65	49	47	38	49	64	United States	51
Iceland	64	61	68	66	65	61	64	65	65	na	na	63	72	68	57	61	65	69	Denmark	51
West Germany	54	49	58	61	55	49	48	61	69	52	54	56	68	53	42	30	52	70	Japan	50
Denmark	51	49	54	55	55	42	43	52	55	52	50	52	62	52	45	35	52	66	Latvia	48
Finland	53	46	61	58	52	60	60	53	50	52	55	46	67	55	44	46	52	58	Lithuania	41
Norway	66	64	68	75	68	58	58	62	74	70	64	68	75	62	64	63	65	84	Britain	41
Sweden	59	58	60	70	58	54	51	60	69	50	60	60	67	53	60	43	59	72	North Ireland	33
Japan	50	49	51	49	53	46	47	50	54	50	46	55	64	53	43	46	51	69	China	27
Switzerland	59	57	60	65	61	54	57	59	63	59	66	59	79	60	52	39	56	77	Estonia	27
Total	**62**	**61**	**63**	**65**	**63**	**59**	**60**	**63**	**65**	**61**	**62**	**63**	**72**	**64**	**60**	**54**	**63**	**73**		

Note: Countries in the left column are ranked according to GNP per capita.   / The percentages in the bottom row give each country an equal weight. / na=not ascertained.

V294 WOMEN'S MOVEMENT

There are a number of groups and movements looking for public support. For each of the following movements, which I read out, can you tell me whether you approve or disapprove of this movement? Women's movement (% "strongly approve")

	Total	Gender		Age			Education			Income			Political Affinity			Values			Ranking:	
		Male	Female	16-29	30-49	50+	Lower	Medium	Upper	Lower	Middle	Upper	Left	Center	Right	Mat	Mixed	Postmat		
India	50	41	61	48	51	49	47	51	49	46	50	52	51	46	49	48	50	57	South Africa	56
Nigeria	50	40	65	51	46	57	48	54	47	50	52	49	52	49	48	52	50	40	India	50
China	28	19	42	29	24	32	32	26	29	29	32	22	na	na	na	28	28	24	Nigeria	50
Romania	32	22	42	32	32	32	38	31	27	38	31	29	34	31	31	33	33	25	Belarus	50
Turkey	48	38	58	49	49	44	50	44	47	53	45	45	51	51	39	43	49	50	Moscow	50
Poland	49	43	53	43	52	48	51	50	35	49	50	47	44	51	45	50	47	53	Poland	49
Bulgaria	46	37	53	46	42	51	49	49	37	48	46	43	44	43	42	52	46	38	Russia	49
Chile	31	28	34	31	27	36	33	32	25	33	30	28	35	27	27	32	31	27	Turkey	48
Czechoslovakia	23	20	26	21	22	27	30	21	20	26	24	20	23	26	19	24	23	20	Bulgaria	46
South Africa	56	45	66	56	56	55	58	56	49	58	58	46	54	56	51	52	58	57	Brazil	43
Lithuania	33	28	36	32	26	39	42	30	27	34	34	26	na	na	na	33	33	33	South Korea	42
Hungary	36	35	37	30	37	38	41	33	28	38	37	30	34	38	34	35	35	48	Slovenia	42
Argentina	29	28	30	29	30	29	30	34	24	32	29	25	38	25	32	26	30	30	Latvia	40
Brazil	43	40	47	39	46	45	52	41	30	49	44	35	41	36	47	44	43	38	Ireland	37
Mexico	28	23	34	29	28	24	30	25	25	30	28	21	35	28	21	22	30	25	Canada	37
Belarus	50	48	51	48	46	60	48	48	49	55	45	50	49	51	51	53	49	42	Hungary	36
Russia	49	39	56	47	45	55	53	52	43	52	50	45	39	45	46	49	50	43	Spain	36
Moscow	50	43	55	41	49	57	64	53	45	56	49	40	48	52	49	52	52	34	Austria	34
Latvia	40	31	45	40	38	42	38	41	37	45	40	36	na	na	na	41	39	45	Lithuania	33
Estonia	31	26	34	29	32	30	34	32	26	33	28	29	35	28	21	32	31	28	Romania	32
Portugal	24	22	25	17	27	28	28	19	13	30	27	12	27	24	21	23	26	19	United States	32
South Korea	42	56	29	47	40	37	41	42	42	45	39	38	42	43	40	38	44	50	Chile	31
Ireland	37	28	45	44	39	31	34	42	37	32	38	40	37	35	40	30	38	44	Estonia	31
North Ireland	18	18	18	19	18	17	22	11	10	22	15	09	26	17	16	09	21	18	Argentina	29
Slovenia	42	39	44	37	41	45	44	41	39	43	42	38	44	40	40	42	41	44	East Germany	29
Spain	36	34	38	40	37	30	36	36	35	38	37	36	44	33	24	28	40	38	China	28
East Germany	29	23	33	26	27	32	30	22	27	31	30	25	35	29	14	25	30	27	Mexico	28
Britain	19	17	21	21	17	21	19	18	23	21	19	18	29	18	15	18	19	24	Portugal	24
Italy	13	11	14	16	13	11	12	14	13	13	10	09	14	13	09	12	10	18	Belgium	24
Netherlands	18	19	18	14	18	23	16	15	23	25	17	14	31	13	11	10	14	25	Japan	24
Belgium	24	21	27	24	25	24	26	24	22	26	24	18	28	22	19	23	24	29	Czechoslovakia	23
Austria	34	27	38	33	34	34	32	36	31	38	34	30	43	34	31	29	32	41	France	23
France	23	25	22	24	24	22	25	21	22	25	18	24	28	18	15	24	22	25	Iceland	23
Canada	37	31	42	41	39	30	38	35	39	41	34	37	48	34	31	30	36	44	West Germany	22
United States	32	29	36	41	32	28	29	31	37	32	30	37	48	31	25	26	30	43	Sweden	21
Iceland	23	19	28	20	26	24	23	20	25	na	na	na	36	23	16	22	22	34	Norway	20
West Germany	22	14	28	24	25	18	20	23	27	22	20	21	33	19	14	13	17	34	Switzerland	20
Denmark	12	09	15	11	12	13	13	13	11	15	12	07	20	10	07	10	11	21	Britain	19
Finland	16	11	21	18	14	19	21	14	16	20	16	13	26	15	11	18	14	20	North Ireland	18
Norway	20	17	23	20	19	22	24	19	19	24	19	15	30	18	12	19	19	29	Netherlands	18
Sweden	21	18	24	20	17	26	24	20	17	23	26	14	27	20	15	14	22	22	Finland	16
Japan	24	19	30	25	23	26	25	25	23	25	22	27	36	26	15	18	25	39	Italy	13
Switzerland	20	19	21	17	22	19	19	20	23	20	20	21	39	17	13	14	16	32	Denmark	12
Total	32	28	36	32	32	33	34	32	30	35	32	29	37	31	28	30	32	34		

Note: Countries in the left column are ranked according to GNP per capita. / The percentages in the bottom row give each country an equal weight. / na=not ascertained.

V295 ANTI-APARTHEID

There are a number of groups and movements looking for public support. For each of the following movements, which I read out, can you tell me whether you approve or disapprove of this movement? Anti-apartheid movement (% "strongly approve")

	Total	Gender		Age			Education			Income			Political Affinity			Values		
		Male	Female	16-29	30-49	50+	Lower	Medium	Upper	Lower	Middle	Upper	Left	Center	Right	Mat	Mixed	Postmat
India	53	55	51	53	53	55	42	52	58	47	48	61	50	52	60	53	53	58
Nigeria	83	86	78	82	83	87	81	82	84	84	83	83	75	83	86	84	82	76
China	48	49	46	47	47	58	46	45	55	52	47	44	na	na	na	46	49	44
Romania	50	48	53	55	49	49	50	51	50	51	50	50	49	53	46	52	50	44
Turkey	46	47	45	46	46	46	41	50	59	48	42	48	53	46	42	37	46	56
Poland	52	50	55	51	53	53	50	53	54	53	51	53	54	55	49	49	52	60
Bulgaria	54	53	54	55	52	63	58	51	54	57	50	53	54	54	50	52	55	58
Chile	60	63	57	60	61	57	49	60	71	54	56	71	67	60	54	50	61	68
Czechoslovakia	na	na	na	na	na	na	na	na	na	na	na	na	na	na	na	na	na	na
South Africa	62	64	60	70	59	53	74	61	33	75	70	30	71	54	46	53	66	73
Lithuania	13	14	11	16	07	15	20	12	04	16	10	10	na	na	na	11	13	16
Hungary	48	50	46	52	51	44	40	52	69	42	52	57	58	50	39	48	47	63
Argentina	69	69	70	72	73	63	63	72	76	66	71	70	74	68	67	58	69	83
Brazil	70	71	69	68	71	73	67	69	80	67	71	73	71	68	66	67	71	81
Mexico	59	60	58	60	60	55	57	55	67	53	63	67	69	56	55	52	59	68
Belarus	56	61	52	53	55	62	55	54	59	61	53	57	60	55	48	57	56	62
Russia	56	54	57	51	52	63	57	55	56	55	58	56	55	54	45	54	57	56
Moscow	59	61	57	54	60	61	59	60	58	62	57	56	62	52	45	57	59	63
Latvia	32	32	32	35	32	30	38	30	34	40	31	29	na	na	na	30	33	39
Estonia	14	16	12	19	13	11	17	14	11	16	10	15	na	na	na	10	15	26
Portugal	65	63	67	65	64	67	62	76	66	67	64	64	69	67	60	53	71	69
South Korea	61	61	62	65	59	58	54	60	65	63	59	61	60	63	na	56	63	73
Ireland	57	53	61	61	57	53	52	61	72	51	55	63	58	55	39	54	56	66
North Ireland	34	44	26	62	33	28	33	32	43	32	26	34	48	29	36	25	35	44
Slovenia	52	53	51	55	52	49	47	49	64	49	51	60	59	53	51	46	53	64
Spain	73	73	73	77	76	67	71	79	77	65	75	78	80	70	63	61	77	82
East Germany	49	49	49	50	50	47	47	50	55	47	47	53	63	46	31	33	49	56
Britain	36	38	35	44	39	29	31	43	54	32	40	43	46	35	30	25	34	54
Italy	55	55	55	62	59	47	54	63	69	54	59	55	63	55	45	44	53	70
Netherlands	49	45	50	53	50	41	41	50	56	49	54	48	63	55	45	27	41	66
Belgium	42	42	42	50	43	35	39	40	49	39	45	36	68	46	34	35	41	66
Austria	43	40	45	50	46	37	36	46	56	39	43	47	56	39	32	35	39	54
France	52	52	52	57	57	43	43	58	65	47	53	59	50	46	37	24	38	62
Canada	48	46	50	56	50	37	36	47	56	42	50	49	67	45	30	35	48	74
United States	37	36	39	39	46	27	34	34	43	32	36	45	62	36	43	37	46	56
Iceland	49	43	55	49	49	35	45	48	52	na	na	na	54	36	27	28	35	47
West Germany	49	44	53	58	51	41	42	57	62	45	48	52	59	48	43	43	48	65
Denmark	42	40	43	47	44	34	31	42	47	44	39	44	63	48	32	28	43	68
Finland	43	37	51	47	43	42	43	40	48	46	43	42	56	41	33	22	40	64
Norway	52	50	54	63	54	41	41	46	62	53	50	55	57	38	39	33	42	48
Sweden	55	52	58	65	52	51	49	56	61	49	60	53	66	49	45	39	54	72
Japan	43	41	45	47	44	37	39	39	51	33	44	47	63	51	33	41	53	70
Switzerland	43	42	44	55	47	34	39	45	53	40	50	49	57	44	33	24	42	63
Total	**50**	**50**	**51**	**54**	**51**	**47**	**47**	**51**	**56**	**49**	**50**	**52**	**61**	**51**	**46**	**42**	**50**	**61**

Ranking:

Nigeria	83
Spain	73
Brazil	70
Argentina	69
Portugal	65
South Africa	62
South Korea	61
Chile	60
Mexico	59
Moscow	59
Ireland	57
Belarus	56
Russia	56
Italy	55
Sweden	55
Bulgaria	54
India	53
Poland	52
Slovenia	52
France	52
Norway	52
Romania	50
East Germany	49
West Germany	49
China	48
Hungary	48
Canada	48
Turkey	46
Austria	43
Finland	43
Japan	43
Switzerland	43
Belgium	42
Denmark	42
United States	37
Britain	36
North Ireland	34
Latvia	32
Estonia	14
Lithuania	13

Note: Countries in the left column are ranked according to GNP per capita. / The percentages in the bottom row give each country an equal weight. / na=not ascertained.

V296-V319. Please tell me for each of the following statements whether you think it can always be justified, never be justified, or something in between.

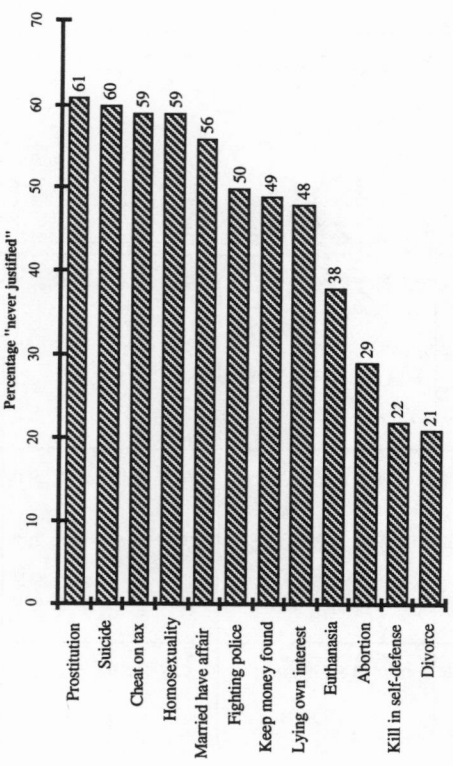

Percentage "never justified"

V296-V319. Please tell me for each of the following statements whether you think it can always be justified, never be justified, or something in between (continued).

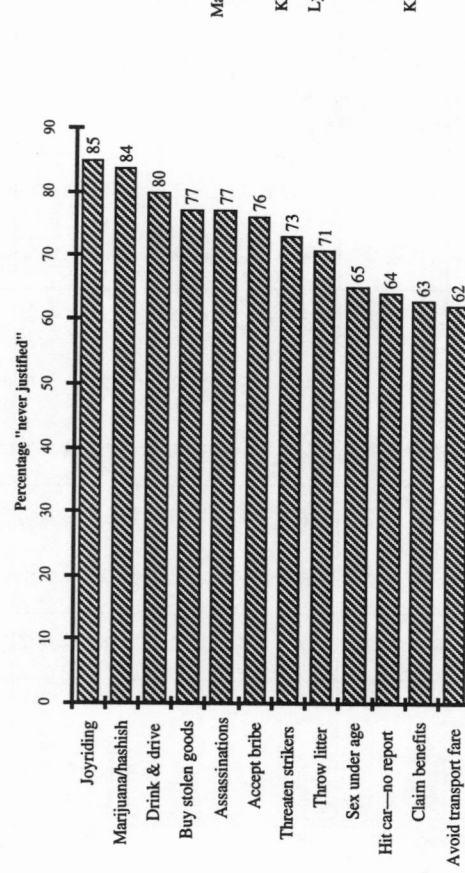

Percentage "never justified"

V296 CLAIM BENEFITS

Please tell me for each of the following statements whether you think it can always be justified, never be justified, or something in between. Claiming government benefits which you are not entitled to (% "never justified"—code 1 from a ten-point scale where 1=never and 10=always)

	Total	Gender Male	Gender Female	Age 16-29	Age 30-49	Age 50+	Education Lower	Education Medium	Education Upper	Income Lower	Income Middle	Income Upper	Political Affinity Left	Political Affinity Center	Political Affinity Right	Values Mat	Values Mixed	Values Postmat	Ranking:	
India	77	76	79	75	79	79	81	75	78	72	80	76	76	77	72	77	78	65	Turkey	84
Nigeria	69	71	66	67	70	84	75	66	70	68	66	65	65	67	69	65	70	68	Denmark	81
China	76	76	77	69	78	82	80	73	75	76	77	73	na	na	na	78	75	65	Norway	80
Romania	71	73	69	60	72	77	74	67	73	75	71	67	70	70	72	70	72	71	Argentina	79
Turkey	84	85	83	78	86	89	83	88	79	85	81	83	87	83	80	90	82	81	South Korea	78
Poland	65	65	65	48	69	71	67	61	79	67	63	61	62	64	71	65	65	63	India	77
Bulgaria	69	67	69	63	69	71	73	69	65	71	68	63	60	67	78	72	66	69	South Africa	77
Chile	51	47	54	38	54	63	55	48	49	40	43	46	48	48	52	49	51	48	North Ireland	77
Czechoslovakia	02	02	03	03	02	02	03	02	01	02	02	00	01	02	03	01	03	01	China	76
South Africa	77	73	80	71	77	87	78	76	79	71	70	78	73	72	75	83	74	69	Latvia	75
Lithuania	61	57	65	48	61	72	66	59	64	63	61	55	na	na	na	65	62	54	Sweden	75
Hungary	67	67	68	49	70	73	69	65	64	61	59	69	68	68	71	69	65	78	Switzerland	75
Argentina	79	78	80	69	80	86	81	82	73	80	73	75	71	77	75	79	80	76	East Germany	74
Brazil	72	72	72	63	76	80	75	69	77	66	64	66	70	71	69	74	70	70	Iceland	73
Mexico	25	24	26	24	26	24	24	27	26	22	23	21	20	24	27	30	24	19	Brazil	72
Belarus	58	62	54	47	62	60	61	54	60	55	56	56	56	57	66	56	58	64	Romania	71
Russia	66	62	68	55	63	75	69	65	65	66	65	65	65	61	63	67	65	66	Netherlands	71
Moscow	53	51	54	42	54	60	56	53	53	47	53	51	51	54	48	55	53	49	Spain	70
Latvia	75	70	78	62	77	85	79	75	73	78	73	69	na	na	na	75	76	70	Britain	70
Estonia	63	64	63	54	65	70	64	62	65	64	59	59	na	na	na	66	61	72	Canada	70
Portugal	58	53	63	47	62	66	61	55	52	51	57	56	52	59	62	64	57	41	Nigeria	69
South Korea	78	74	82	71	78	89	81	79	75	73	79	84	73	74	82	81	77	72	Bulgaria	69
Ireland	69	65	72	53	66	81	70	68	64	70	64	74	46	66	81	70	70	64	Ireland	69
North Ireland	77	76	78	48	79	95	81	73	62	76	80	74	71	72	88	88	78	60	Austria	69
Slovenia	51	49	52	35	52	60	53	48	51	52	47	48	48	47	49	53	50	43	United States	69
Spain	70	69	71	59	71	77	74	68	56	74	68	60	62	64	75	78	67	64	Italy	68
East Germany	74	70	78	63	70	85	75	74	73	78	73	70	73	76	70	82	76	64	Hungary	67
Britain	70	68	72	49	69	82	70	72	66	69	67	71	59	70	78	75	70	65	Japan	67
Italy	68	68	68	58	70	72	67	71	74	67	70	74	71	69	68	64	68	71	Russia	66
Netherlands	71	77	69	55	72	87	82	69	61	63	75	79	64	72	77	79	76	63	Poland	65
Belgium	52	50	55	41	52	60	55	50	51	45	51	53	43	52	58	55	53	49	Estonia	63
Austria	69	66	71	48	67	80	73	67	58	74	67	66	69	69	68	77	70	62	Lithuania	61
France	40	41	39	26	40	49	39	37	46	36	32	46	40	36	45	44	38	39	Belarus	58
Canada	70	67	72	57	68	83	74	72	64	72	69	68	60	71	75	73	69	71	Portugal	58
United States	69	70	68	51	69	77	72	65	72	66	67	71	64	72	77	73	68	70	West Germany	57
Iceland	73	72	74	57	78	85	80	67	72	na	51	na	75	69	75	78	72	63	Moscow	53
West Germany	57	53	61	42	53	69	61	50	53	57	52	58	43	58	68	70	60	44	Belgium	52
Denmark	81	78	84	68	81	91	86	80	79	81	76	86	70	82	87	83	83	69	Chile	51
Finland	13	16	11	04	12	24	14	15	11	13	12	13	16	12	13	21	13	13	Slovenia	51
Norway	80	75	84	63	80	90	90	76	78	79	83	74	74	82	80	83	78	82	France	40
Sweden	75	73	77	58	79	84	79	70	79	74	73	78	72	73	78	78	76	71	Mexico	25
Japan	67	69	66	49	69	77	74	66	63	69	67	69	69	60	76	72	65	61	Finland	13
Switzerland	75	75	76	57	75	83	76	77	65	74	71	74	66	78	78	82	76	71	Czechoslovakia	02
Total	64	63	65	52	65	73	67	63	63	63	62	63	60	63	66	68	64	60		

Note: Countries in the left column are ranked according to GNP per capita. / The percentages in the bottom row give each country an equal weight. / na=not ascertained.

V297 AVOID TRANSPORT FARE

Please tell me for each of the following statements whether you think it can always be justified, never be justified, or something in between.
Avoiding a fare on public transport (% "never justified" — code 1 from a ten-point scale where 1=never and 10=always)

	Total	Gender Male	Gender Female	Age 16-29	Age 30-49	Age 50+	Education Lower	Education Medium	Education Upper	Income Lower	Income Middle	Income Upper	Political Affinity Left	Political Affinity Center	Political Affinity Right	Values Mat	Values Mixed	Values Postmat
India	84	83	85	83	85	85	85	83	85	84	84	84	85	82	79	86	83	69
Nigeria	61	64	57	61	59	79	64	59	62	58	60	58	56	59	63	56	63	66
China	80	79	81	73	81	85	79	81	76	78	83	75	65	na	na	82	78	72
Romania	64	63	66	48	68	71	69	59	67	67	64	58	65	67	56	70	61	52
Turkey	76	77	74	68	79	83	78	73	69	77	71	73	68	76	78	82	77	66
Poland	na	na	na	na	na	na	na	na	na	na	na	na	na	na	na	na	na	na
Bulgaria	65	64	65	49	52	71	70	66	59	64	61	63	58	64	74	74	62	52
Chile	60	57	62	48	65	70	64	58	57	54	53	58	50	61	66	63	59	59
Czechoslovakia	na	na	na	na	na	na	na	na	na	na	na	na	na	na	na	na	na	na
South Africa	na	na	na	na	na	na	na	na	na	na	na	na	na	na	na	na	na	na
Lithuania	56	53	60	31	53	81	72	52	49	64	51	46	na	na	na	64	54	51
Hungary	59	56	61	38	52	73	70	50	41	59	48	47	61	59	53	60	57	61
Argentina	73	72	73	60	77	78	75	70	73	67	72	73	60	68	76	77	72	68
Brazil	67	67	68	61	67	77	72	64	69	61	62	62	63	65	69	70	65	62
Mexico	32	30	35	32	32	35	34	25	34	29	30	30	23	31	37	38	31	32
Belarus	50	52	47	34	50	65	59	43	53	49	46	48	48	51	55	55	48	40
Russia	54	50	57	40	52	66	62	53	50	55	50	52	50	51	54	57	53	41
Moscow	44	42	45	27	43	55	57	46	39	39	42	41	39	50	51	49	43	40
Latvia	61	55	64	38	64	80	69	61	56	62	61	54	na	na	na	67	61	62
Estonia	61	57	63	43	62	76	70	58	58	61	58	57	na	na	na	63	60	59
Portugal	57	57	57	43	63	65	60	55	48	53	55	51	49	58	58	63	56	36
South Korea	69	64	73	52	73	86	75	71	63	64	65	75	54	68	72	75	67	49
Ireland	58	53	62	43	58	67	60	59	43	63	61	54	39	58	63	56	62	48
North Ireland	72	71	73	45	75	88	78	66	48	71	73	69	57	73	77	81	74	51
Slovenia	63	61	65	44	66	73	64	62	65	64	58	64	59	63	58	66	64	49
Spain	68	64	72	50	73	77	73	67	48	76	65	62	58	68	74	78	65	56
East Germany	73	68	78	56	69	89	76	69	68	83	71	67	70	76	69	83	74	66
Britain	60	57	62	40	55	76	60	58	59	64	53	57	52	57	71	63	59	55
Italy	67	69	65	49	70	76	67	68	57	69	68	66	65	70	69	71	65	66
Netherlands	56	62	54	39	55	77	71	52	44	52	62	52	45	58	63	76	60	44
Belgium	59	57	62	43	57	72	66	58	50	56	57	54	44	62	62	68	62	45
Austria	66	61	69	46	63	77	69	66	50	77	63	88	68	65	65	78	67	56
France	55	54	57	41	52	70	56	58	51	54	51	55	52	57	56	57	57	49
Canada	63	59	66	48	55	76	65	65	57	66	61	58	50	64	66	66	62	64
United States	62	63	61	43	62	70	67	61	59	63	61	60	50	62	66	66	61	60
Iceland	56	54	57	40	59	71	66	54	49	na	56	49	50	55	59	62	56	37
West Germany	53	48	57	33	49	67	58	43	47	56	50	49	37	57	59	63	57	40
Denmark	75	70	81	56	75	90	85	73	71	74	72	78	65	77	79	82	77	58
Finland	54	51	58	35	54	71	60	57	48	53	56	51	59	50	56	66	55	51
Norway	76	73	79	55	77	89	91	75	70	75	76	70	67	82	76	78	77	68
Sweden	68	64	72	48	69	81	79	61	64	69	73	64	69	69	64	76	70	59
Japan	79	79	78	58	81	89	87	79	70	78	79	81	77	77	79	82	78	74
Switzerland	79	76	82	58	78	89	82	81	59	77	77	74	63	81	83	88	79	73
Total	**63**	**61**	**65**	**47**	**64**	**75**	**69**	**61**	**57**	**64**	**62**	**60**	**56**	**64**	**65**	**69**	**63**	**55**

Ranking:

India	84
China	80
Japan	79
Switzerland	79
Turkey	76
Norway	76
Denmark	75
Argentina	73
East Germany	73
North Ireland	72
South Korea	69
Spain	68
Sweden	68
Brazil	67
Italy	67
Austria	66
Bulgaria	65
Romania	64
Slovenia	63
Canada	63
United States	62
Nigeria	61
Latvia	61
Estonia	61
Chile	60
Britain	60
Hungary	59
Belgium	59
Ireland	58
Portugal	57
Lithuania	56
Netherlands	56
Iceland	56
France	55
Russia	54
Finland	54
West Germany	53
Belarus	50
Moscow	44
Mexico	32

Note: Countries in the left column are ranked according to GNP per capita. / The percentages in the bottom row give each country an equal weight. / na=not ascertained.

V298 CHEAT ON TAX

Please tell me for each of the following statements whether you think it can always be justified, never be justified, or something in between. Cheating on tax if you have the chance   (% "never justified"—code 1 from a ten-point scale where 1=never and 10=always)

	Total	Gender		Age			Education			Income			Political Affinity			Values			Ranking:	
		Male	Female	16-29	30-49	50+	Lower	Medium	Upper	Lower	Middle	Upper	Left	Center	Right	Mat	Mixed	Postmat		
India	82	80	85	81	83	84	84	82	81	82	83	80	82	81	78	84	81	71	South Korea	91
Nigeria	64	67	60	65	62	77	64	63	66	64	60	60	59	61	64	58	67	68	Turkey	90
China	82	82	83	75	84	87	82	84	80	81	86	78	na	na	na	83	83	64	India	82
Romania	69	69	69	57	69	76	72	63	72	71	67	66	72	70	63	73	66	62	China	82
Turkey	90	91	90	87	92	93	91	91	84	90	92	88	89	90	91	93	89	91	Japan	82
Poland	51	49	53	37	49	61	53	48	60	52	50	45	56	49	50	53	51	41	Argentina	81
Bulgaria	60	58	62	52	63	62	66	60	57	56	59	59	55	59	64	65	59	51	Chile	78
Chile	78	76	80	71	80	83	77	76	80	71	78	79	76	77	75	75	78	77	North Ireland	71
Czechoslovakia	na	na	na	na	na	na	na	na	na	na	na	na	na	na	na	na	na	na	Slovenia	70
South Africa	68	63	72	61	68	80	73	67	55	62	63	60	60	63	63	72	66	62	Romania	69
Lithuania	58	53	62	48	54	71	68	55	53	63	54	47	na	na	na	65	56	56	United States	69
Hungary	62	58	65	46	59	71	69	57	46	63	52	50	58	61	56	64	60	57	South Africa	68
Argentina	81	80	83	72	82	88	82	82	79	82	81	75	69	80	82	83	83	76	Latvia	68
Brazil	65	62	68	59	66	74	73	64	56	66	60	56	62	62	67	68	64	60	East Germany	68
Mexico	41	37	45	41	39	43	40	38	44	38	39	33	27	40	43	45	41	43	Estonia	66
Belarus	47	51	45	30	49	61	59	40	51	42	45	48	45	49	54	51	48	30	Switzerland	66
Russia	56	51	59	39	52	69	62	52	55	52	56	54	53	54	48	59	54	42	Brazil	65
Moscow	41	36	45	27	39	55	47	41	40	38	40	36	36	47	42	43	41	33	Spain	65
Latvia	68	63	72	55	68	83	71	70	63	69	69	59	na	na	na	76	67	69	Nigeria	64
Estonia	66	60	71	54	66	78	72	65	63	67	63	63	na	na	na	68	65	69	Austria	63
Portugal	45	42	47	32	47	55	47	41	40	40	44	35	39	46	46	48	42	42	Hungary	62
South Korea	91	90	92	88	91	96	88	92	91	88	90	92	86	93	91	92	90	89	Canada	61
Ireland	50	44	56	42	47	58	50	51	41	52	51	48	40	46	57	48	52	44	Bulgaria	60
North Ireland	71	64	76	50	69	87	74	69	52	74	67	62	52	72	76	79	72	54	Iceland	59
Slovenia	70	63	75	48	73	80	71	69	67	74	66	62	58	67	70	74	69	55	Denmark	59
Spain	65	62	67	50	67	74	69	63	47	75	61	54	56	62	68	72	63	52	Lithuania	58
East Germany	68	59	75	55	64	80	72	63	55	79	63	60	65	71	61	81	69	58	Sweden	58
Britain	55	51	59	41	51	68	56	55	49	62	44	49	52	54	60	59	55	58	Italy	57
Italy	57	56	59	46	57	65	57	61	56	59	59	53	60	59	55	58	56	50	Russia	56
Netherlands	44	44	43	34	42	56	48	41	42	43	47	40	42	43	44	51	46	37	Britain	55
Belgium	38	35	41	29	36	45	42	36	32	33	39	28	35	34	36	44	39	31	Poland	51
Austria	63	59	66	49	59	73	66	63	48	74	62	54	63	63	59	76	64	54	Ireland	50
France	48	43	53	37	51	55	51	48	40	48	47	40	44	49	41	59	48	41	France	48
Canada	61	57	64	50	58	73	67	62	54	67	57	54	46	63	62	67	61	58	Belarus	47
United States	69	70	69	56	68	76	74	69	66	70	68	64	56	70	71	72	67	72	Portugal	45
Iceland	59	57	61	48	59	71	66	56	55	na	na	na	56	55	60	62	57	60	Norway	45
West Germany	42	36	47	30	36	53	46	36	31	44	39	35	27	45	47	52	45	29	Netherlands	44
Denmark	59	52	66	50	55	71	72	55	55	64	49	53	56	62	55	68	58	51	West Germany	42
Finland	42	35	48	32	39	57	50	44	36	45	40	36	46	40	38	53	42	38	Finland	42
Norway	45	40	51	37	40	56	61	39	43	48	41	31	49	48	37	47	44	47	Mexico	41
Sweden	58	51	66	51	54	66	69	51	55	59	62	50	64	59	48	64	59	52	Moscow	41
Japan	82	82	83	74	82	88	87	83	78	83	80	84	80	82	85	83	82	82	Belgium	38
Switzerland	66	60	71	50	62	76	68	66	54	67	61	52	56	66	66	75	66	59		
Total	61	58	64	51	60	71	66	60	56	62	59	55	56	60	60	66	61	56		

Note: Countries in the left column are ranked according to GNP per capita. / The percentages in the bottom row give each country an equal weight. / na=not ascertained.

V299 BUY STOLEN GOODS

Please tell me for each of the following statements whether you think it can always be justified, never be justified, or something in between. Buying something you knew was stolen (% "never justified"—code 1 from a ten-point scale where 1=never and 10=always)

		Gender		Age			Education			Income			Political Affinity			Values			Ranking:
	Total	Male	Female	16-29	30-49	50+	Lower	Medium	Upper	Lower	Middle	Upper	Left	Center	Right	Mat	Mixed	Postmat	
India	84	82	85	83	84	84	84	83	85	82	85	83	86	82	77	85	83	71	South Korea 92
Nigeria	71	72	68	68	71	89	70	70	72	73	68	67	63	71	72	66	73	75	Argentina 90
China	73	72	75	65	76	77	74	73	72	72	79	66	na	na	na	73	74	61	Denmark 89
Romania	78	75	80	70	77	83	83	75	75	81	78	73	81	82	70	82	75	69	Turkey 87
Turkey	87	86	88	83	89	90	88	88	81	86	89	85	83	87	88	88	86	88	East Germany 87
Poland	86	84	87	75	88	89	87	85	89	86	87	82	87	84	87	87	86	81	Sweden 87
Bulgaria	76	71	80	68	78	78	79	74	77	76	74	75	70	76	81	81	76	67	Switzerland 87
Chile	84	81	86	77	87	89	86	81	85	81	82	88	79	85	84	81	85	83	Poland 86
Czechoslovakia	na	na	na	na	na	na	na	na	na	na	na	na	59	74	74	79	67	55	Brazil 86
South Africa	70	65	75	61	70	85	72	67	81	56	64	79	59	74	74	79	67	55	North Ireland 86
Lithuania	72	67	76	53	74	86	80	69	72	75	70	66	na	na	na	78	70	66	Norway 86
Hungary	81	77	84	69	79	87	82	80	72	73	69	73	80	82	75	85	77	83	Austria 85
Argentina	90	90	90	80	90	97	92	89	87	91	91	87	82	88	90	91	90	88	India 84
Brazil	86	84	88	79	89	94	90	84	84	87	86	83	80	87	87	89	84	85	Chile 84
Mexico	50	46	55	49	49	54	51	45	51	46	52	43	40	48	56	55	50	50	Slovenia 84
Belarus	69	68	69	55	70	79	72	62	74	68	66	65	66	70	72	71	68	62	Iceland 83
Russia	80	75	84	63	80	90	84	78	79	82	80	78	76	78	79	83	79	69	Hungary 81
Moscow	71	64	76	56	71	81	83	65	71	67	67	65	70	71	75	73	71	63	Ireland 81
Latvia	76	74	77	55	80	92	79	76	76	75	74	73	na	na	na	83	76	76	Russia 80
Estonia	78	71	85	64	81	89	80	78	79	79	77	74	na	na	na	83	78	70	Japan 80
Portugal	73	70	76	59	79	81	76	76	60	77	74	63	72	73	71	77	72	60	Romania 78
South Korea	92	91	94	87	95	97	92	93	92	89	94	94	86	93	94	94	92	88	Estonia 78
Ireland	81	77	84	64	83	89	81	82	72	84	81	79	60	80	91	83	81	78	Spain 78
North Ireland	86	84	88	67	87	98	89	86	69	90	90	79	71	88	87	91	87	78	United States 77
Slovenia	84	80	88	69	90	89	83	85	87	84	85	81	81	82	80	85	84	82	Bulgaria 76
Spain	78	75	81	63	83	85	82	76	62	83	75	73	71	74	86	85	76	69	Latvia 76
East Germany	87	82	91	78	84	95	87	87	85	92	84	84	88	88	84	90	87	84	Italy 75
Britain	71	67	75	49	67	88	70	73	76	77	59	71	68	68	66	75	71	66	China 73
Italy	75	73	76	57	74	86	75	70	72	77	74	70	76	75	74	77	75	70	Portugal 73
Netherlands	70	73	68	50	71	89	82	65	61	64	68	73	64	70	75	88	71	63	Canada 73
Belgium	69	65	73	51	68	81	73	68	62	67	66	67	59	70	69	72	71	62	Lithuania 72
Austria	85	80	88	70	87	90	87	85	79	90	83	82	83	85	84	92	85	81	Nigeria 71
France	66	63	68	47	68	78	68	64	63	65	60	66	58	67	71	73	66	59	Moscow 71
Canada	73	68	79	57	73	87	78	73	71	74	71	73	65	76	75	78	72	74	Britain 71
United States	77	77	78	62	78	82	79	76	71	76	75	78	70	78	77	77	75	81	South Africa 70
Iceland	83	77	88	65	91	95	82	83	76	na	na	na	78	85	82	88	81	77	Netherlands 70
West Germany	70	64	75	53	67	81	87	64	64	70	70	66	59	72	73	75	74	60	West Germany 70
Denmark	89	83	95	76	90	97	94	87	87	87	89	87	81	90	92	95	89	77	Finland 70
Finland	70	66	76	51	73	80	70	69	72	69	67	75	73	65	75	67	70	71	Belarus 69
Norway	86	81	91	68	87	96	94	80	87	86	86	85	84	91	82	88	85	82	Belgium 69
Sweden	87	82	93	70	91	95	91	81	91	86	87	87	88	88	85	89	88	83	France 66
Japan	80	80	81	69	81	86	85	81	74	82	78	80	81	79	82	82	78	82	Mexico 50
Switzerland	87	84	89	67	87	95	89	87	76	85	87	85	78	88	87	93	86	86	
Total	**78**	**75**	**81**	**65**	**79**	**87**	**81**	**77**	**76**	**78**	**77**	**76**	**74**	**79**	**80**	**82**	**78**	**73**	

Note: Countries in the left column are ranked according to GNP per capita. / The percentages in the bottom row give each country an equal weight. / na=not ascertained.

Please tell me for each of the following statements whether you think it can always be justified, never be justified, or something in between. Taking and driving away a car belonging to someone else joyriding (% "never justified" – code 1 from a ten-point scale where 1=never and 10=always)

Country	Total	Gender		Age			Education			Income			Political Affinity			Values		
		Male	Female	16-29	30-49	50+	Lower	Medium	Upper	Lower	Middle	Upper	Left	Center	Right	Mat	Mixed	Postmat
India	84	83	86	83	85	87	86	84	84	85	85	82	88	81	77	85	84	73
Nigeria	63	65	60	61	64	77	64	63	62	65	60	57	55	62	63	55	68	64
China	85	83	88	77	88	89	88	86	79	87	89	78	88	na	na	87	83	74
Romania	87	82	92	81	87	91	90	84	87	88	87	83	88	89	85	89	86	82
Turkey	88	88	89	85	91	90	89	89	84	86	92	87	87	87	91	88	88	90
Poland	na	na	na	na	na	na	na	na	na	na	na	na	na	na	na	na	na	na
Bulgaria	86	84	88	84	88	85	87	86	85	85	85	87	83	86	87	91	86	77
Chile	88	86	89	81	91	91	90	86	87	87	87	87	86	87	90	86	87	88
Czechoslovakia	na	na	na	na	na	na	na	na	na	na	na	na	na	na	na	na	na	na
South Africa	na	na	na	na	na	na	na	na	na	na	na	na	na	na	na	na	na	na
Lithuania	94	91	96	87	94	99	97	93	94	96	93	89	na	85	82	97	94	91
Hungary	85	84	86	76	85	89	87	86	72	78	74	81	87	85	82	87	83	91
Argentina	95	95	94	90	95	97	95	97	93	96	94	95	90	93	97	95	95	93
Brazil	90	89	91	85	94	94	93	89	88	90	89	90	86	91	91	92	89	84
Mexico	56	51	62	54	55	62	57	50	58	55	52	51	47	54	59	57	57	57
Belarus	75	78	72	61	77	82	83	69	78	75	68	73	74	72	80	78	75	66
Russia	93	92	94	87	94	96	94	94	74	94	94	93	92	92	91	95	93	87
Moscow	75	73	77	61	75	86	84	73	74	71	72	73	73	76	83	78	74	72
Latvia	92	91	93	84	95	97	93	94	90	92	92	90	na	na	na	95	92	92
Estonia	93	90	94	87	94	96	94	91	94	92	91	88	na	na	na	92	93	92
Portugal	87	87	88	83	89	90	88	84	78	87	88	85	88	87	86	88	87	89
South Korea	83	84	83	75	85	95	91	84	79	82	82	87	75	82	86	86	83	73
Ireland	95	95	95	91	95	98	95	96	93	96	97	95	92	95	99	94	96	95
North Ireland	98	98	99	97	98	100	99	99	97	99	97	99	100	98	100	100	98	96
Slovenia	90	86	93	81	93	92	88	90	94	90	90	89	85	90	88	90	90	87
Spain	84	82	86	75	87	87	85	85	77	88	83	78	79	81	89	87	83	79
East Germany	93	92	95	86	94	97	94	92	93	94	93	93	92	94	91	96	94	89
Britain	89	88	90	82	89	94	89	89	90	90	85	92	86	87	93	91	89	87
Italy	83	81	84	72	83	89	83	81	82	82	82	82	78	83	80	83	84	79
Netherlands	80	78	80	70	83	85	86	79	74	76	80	81	78	81	82	89	82	75
Belgium	83	81	86	72	88	91	86	83	79	80	81	85	79	83	84	88	83	80
Austria	94	91	95	89	96	94	93	94	95	95	93	93	89	95	92	96	94	93
France	84	82	86	77	85	88	83	85	80	83	84	84	77	86	87	87	84	78
Canada	83	80	86	76	84	88	87	84	80	83	82	81	83	83	87	87	84	82
United States	88	88	88	80	89	90	88	86	91	88	87	88	83	89	89	88	87	90
Iceland	72	70	74	60	73	87	84	72	63	na	na	na	63	73	77	80	72	54
West Germany	88	86	90	80	89	92	89	85	89	88	88	88	83	90	90	88	91	84
Denmark	96	94	98	91	97	98	96	96	89	95	95	98	79	96	97	96	96	93
Finland	78	75	81	69	79	84	73	80	77	81	79	74	79	76	80	74	81	73
Norway	89	86	93	79	89	96	95	85	90	89	89	87	88	91	87	91	89	85
Sweden	97	95	99	92	98	98	98	97	96	99	97	96	97	96	97	99	98	93
Japan	91	91	92	88	93	93	92	92	91	90	89	93	93	91	89	91	92	87
Switzerland	85	82	87	67	84	93	87	85	73	86	81	81	73	84	89	91	85	79
Total	**86**	**84**	**87**	**79**	**87**	**91**	**88**	**85**	**84**	**86**	**85**	**85**	**83**	**85**	**87**	**88**	**86**	**82**

Ranking:

North Ireland	98
Sweden	97
Denmark	96
Argentina	95
Ireland	95
Lithuania	94
Austria	94
Russia	93
Estonia	93
East Germany	93
Latvia	92
Japan	91
Brazil	90
Slovenia	90
Britain	89
Norway	89
Turkey	88
Chile	88
United States	88
West Germany	88
Romania	87
Portugal	87
Bulgaria	86
China	85
Hungary	85
Switzerland	85
India	84
Spain	84
France	84
South Korea	83
Italy	83
Belgium	83
Canada	83
Netherlands	80
Finland	78
Belarus	75
Moscow	75
Iceland	72
Nigeria	63
Mexico	56

Note: Countries in the left column are ranked according to GNP per capita. / The percentages in the bottom row give each country an equal weight. / na=not ascertained.

V301   MARIJUANA/HASHISH

Please tell me for each of the following statements whether you think it can always be justified, never be justified, or something in between. Taking the drug marijuana or hashish (% "never justified"—code 1 from a ten-point scale where 1=never and 10=always)

	Total	Gender Male	Gender Female	Age 16-29	Age 30-49	Age 50+	Education Lower	Education Medium	Education Upper	Income Lower	Income Middle	Income Upper	Political Affinity Left	Political Affinity Center	Political Affinity Right	Values Mat	Values Mixed	Values Postmat	Ranking:
India	91	91	92	92	91	91	90	92	92	90	92	91	93	92	86	93	91	82	China 96
Nigeria	71	71	72	71	71	89	70	73	71	70	71	68	68	73	71	68	73	77	Argentina 95
China	96	96	97	95	97	97	97	96	96	97	97	95	na	na	na	97	97	91	East Germany 95
Romania	91	89	94	81	93	95	96	91	86	93	90	90	94	93	85	96	89	80	Lithuania 94
Turkey	93	92	94	91	94	95	95	91	87	93	95	91	93	92	94	96	92	92	Russia 94
Poland	91	89	93	80	95	95	93	92	87	90	91	88	89	91	89	91	92	86	South Korea 94
Bulgaria	88	87	88	85	88	90	91	87	87	88	84	88	89	87	90	93	87	81	Turkey 93
Chile	90	87	93	84	93	95	92	91	87	90	89	90	85	90	93	95	88	89	Sweden 93
Czechoslovakia	77	74	79	66	76	85	79	77	72	79	75	74	81	77	73	80	76	70	Latvia 92
South Africa	84	79	88	78	85	92	83	83	86	71	79	87	72	86	82	89	81	76	Japan 92
Lithuania	94	91	96	86	94	100	99	92	95	95	92	91	na	na	na	97	94	84	India 91
Hungary	90	86	93	86	88	93	93	88	78	80	75	81	91	89	87	92	88	91	Romania 91
Argentina	95	94	95	91	95	97	97	97	91	97	95	93	87	96	94	96	95	93	Poland 91
Brazil	91	90	93	88	92	96	96	91	82	93	92	86	86	91	95	95	90	83	Brazil 91
Mexico	69	63	76	67	67	78	69	71	69	68	64	59	58	65	75	76	69	63	North Ireland 91
Belarus	85	86	83	73	89	88	88	82	86	83	82	78	85	82	84	85	86	78	Norway 91
Russia	94	91	95	86	94	98	97	95	90	95	94	92	91	93	93	97	92	82	Chile 90
Moscow	83	79	86	70	85	91	93	84	80	81	77	79	82	83	87	86	84	75	Hungary 90
Latvia	92	91	93	83	96	95	89	93	92	94	92	90	na	na	na	93	93	87	Estonia 89
Estonia	89	87	91	83	90	94	88	90	87	88	85	85	na	na	na	92	89	86	Bulgaria 88
Portugal	82	78	85	64	88	93	89	69	62	89	78	69	80	83	79	89	80	63	Ireland 88
South Korea	94	94	94	88	96	100	98	94	92	98	93	96	85	94	96	98	92	85	Slovenia 88
Ireland	88	85	91	77	87	96	94	84	67	94	92	80	70	88	92	94	88	81	Austria 86
North Ireland	91	91	91	78	92	99	94	90	69	96	92	83	82	90	96	99	90	80	Belarus 85
Slovenia	88	84	91	73	91	93	89	89	82	89	89	77	76	87	91	92	88	67	Italy 85
Spain	82	78	85	67	84	91	85	80	67	88	79	75	72	82	89	90	81	68	Belgium 85
East Germany	95	94	95	90	94	98	95	93	95	95	95	94	93	95	95	98	96	91	South Africa 84
Britain	77	71	81	63	68	92	82	69	56	86	67	66	70	75	80	86	77	64	Moscow 83
Italy	85	82	88	72	84	95	87	73	73	88	83	65	78	90	88	93	86	77	France 83
Netherlands	66	71	64	51	64	84	84	64	47	61	71	56	51	68	77	87	74	48	West Germany 83
Belgium	85	83	87	76	84	92	90	86	74	84	82	81	74	85	86	91	87	76	Portugal 82
Austria	86	81	90	71	87	92	91	83	82	93	86	80	81	88	83	92	88	78	Spain 82
France	83	82	84	71	82	93	86	82	78	86	83	80	76	87	87	91	86	71	Iceland 80
Canada	65	61	69	53	69	84	79	68	51	77	63	55	39	70	67	77	68	55	Finland 79
United States	74	72	77	67	81	83	80	76	68	78	72	67	55	76	77	80	75	67	Switzerland 79
Iceland	80	79	82	68	82	94	86	84	69	na	82	81	74	80	85	87	81	76	Czechoslovakia 77
West Germany	83	81	84	66	87	92	91	75	67	83	84	78	81	86	83	91	87	78	Britain 77
Denmark	73	65	81	54	69	91	86	72	63	77	71	61	53	80	67	84	74	50	United States 74
Finland	79	75	84	70	81	84	79	82	77	78	83	74	79	78	82	85	80	76	Denmark 73
Norway	91	89	94	82	91	98	97	91	88	88	94	88	87	95	90	96	91	81	Nigeria 71
Sweden	93	92	95	88	92	98	97	92	89	95	93	94	94	93	92	99	94	90	Mexico 69
Japan	92	91	93	88	93	95	92	93	89	91	91	91	90	90	91	94	92	88	Netherlands 66
Switzerland	79	74	83	54	75	92	84	80	54	79	74	69	57	81	84	96	81	62	Canada 65
Total	**85**	**83**	**87**	**76**	**85**	**93**	**89**	**84**	**78**	**86**	**84**	**80**	**78**	**85**	**86**	**91**	**86**	**77**	

Note: Countries in the left column are ranked according to GNP per capita. / The percentages in the bottom row give each country an equal weight. / na=not ascertained.

V302 KEEP MONEY FOUND

Please tell me for each of the following statements whether you think it can always be justified, never be justified, or something in between.
Keeping money that you have found (% "never justified"—code 1 from a ten-point scale where 1=never and 10=always)

	Total	Gender Male	Gender Female	Age 16-29	Age 30-49	Age 50+	Education Lower	Education Medium	Education Upper	Income Lower	Income Middle	Income Upper	Political Affinity Left	Political Affinity Center	Political Affinity Right	Values Mat	Values Mixed	Values Postmat
India	62	58	67	60	62	69	61	61	65	60	61	60	63	63	53	61	63	58
Nigeria	45	47	42	41	46	75	43	41	50	47	36	39	37	46	43	38	48	57
China	66	64	70	54	69	76	63	68	68	65	71	62	na	na	na	69	65	57
Romania	43	42	43	31	42	50	47	42	38	42	37	38	48	44	37	47	41	28
Turkey	70	65	74	65	72	73	73	66	59	69	69	64	56	71	74	68	72	66
Poland	na	na	na	na	na	na	na	na	na	na	na	na	na	na	na	na	na	na
Bulgaria	72	66	77	61	74	76	76	74	65	72	68	71	69	70	72	81	70	57
Chile	43	39	46	35	40	57	48	40	40	39	33	33	39	40	46	46	41	42
Czechoslovakia	34	33	36	19	28	51	43	29	35	40	32	26	34	33	37	34	35	32
South Africa	na	na	na	na	na	na	na	na	na	na	na	na	na	na	na	na	na	na
Lithuania	57	52	61	33	58	75	68	52	60	62	54	46	na	na	na	63	55	54
Hungary	44	42	46	29	36	56	53	34	33	44	35	33	39	44	47	44	42	56
Argentina	45	42	48	29	45	58	55	41	37	44	38	35	34	37	49	53	44	38
Brazil	48	45	51	36	51	63	63	43	37	39	34	32	42	42	52	54	45	40
Mexico	23	22	25	23	21	31	23	30	21	20	17	17	16	21	26	27	22	20
Belarus	54	57	51	36	54	69	64	47	57	54	49	47	50	58	55	59	52	44
Russia	54	45	60	36	50	68	62	52	50	55	51	49	46	51	53	60	51	37
Moscow	44	41	46	24	44	56	60	44	39	41	40	36	39	48	55	53	41	35
Latvia	na	na	na	na	na	na	na	na	na	na	na	na	na	na	na	na	na	na
Estonia	na	na	na	na	na	na	na	na	na	na	na	na	na	na	na	na	na	na
Portugal	39	34	43	27	39	49	42	36	28	41	30	22	29	38	42	41	37	34
South Korea	68	68	68	52	74	82	81	69	62	66	67	74	60	66	71	73	66	56
Ireland	62	56	67	43	64	71	66	61	42	69	63	57	43	61	70	62	65	53
North Ireland	69	59	75	37	73	86	76	64	32	70	73	60	61	70	69	79	70	42
Slovenia	72	66	77	49	78	80	72	73	70	72	71	69	65	70	67	75	73	52
Spain	50	45	54	32	53	60	55	45	33	56	45	38	39	46	61	58	49	33
East Germany	46	42	50	29	43	59	50	41	35	56	41	37	38	51	43	58	46	40
Britain	49	42	55	26	44	66	51	48	40	55	46	37	41	45	58	53	49	43
Italy	42	41	43	25	42	54	44	31	40	45	38	30	39	42	42	47	44	33
Netherlands	47	51	46	24	50	68	58	46	36	41	48	46	39	46	53	56	51	38
Belgium	38	36	40	20	34	53	44	38	25	38	30	34	31	35	43	45	38	32
Austria	70	65	73	51	69	79	74	68	62	74	69	67	70	72	67	78	72	63
France	42	42	43	24	37	60	48	40	33	38	35	36	34	44	46	57	41	32
Canada	36	32	39	25	30	51	46	36	28	41	31	27	22	36	40	33	38	32
United States	36	31	41	26	31	46	47	36	28	42	32	31	23	40	31	43	36	31
Iceland	50	45	55	28	49	78	70	49	36	na	44	32	51	47	50	59	49	34
West Germany	40	35	44	20	35	53	43	33	35	44	34	32	26	41	48	47	42	30
Denmark	67	62	71	41	69	83	81	62	62	67	65	61	58	70	69	79	64	63
Finland	29	29	30	16	26	48	39	32	21	38	30	19	31	30	28	49	30	23
Norway	60	56	64	39	56	77	76	59	53	59	59	56	56	63	58	67	58	50
Sweden	53	48	58	34	52	70	67	46	45	56	57	47	49	58	51	60	55	46
Japan	59	58	61	41	57	76	70	60	48	64	57	57	55	56	61	61	57	50
Switzerland	67	63	70	47	62	79	70	68	50	67	61	63	55	69	70	80	66	61
Total	51	48	54	35	50	65	58	49	44	52	48	44	44	50	52	57	51	43

Ranking:

Bulgaria	72
Slovenia	72
Turkey	70
Austria	70
North Ireland	69
South Korea	68
Denmark	67
Switzerland	67
China	66
India	62
Ireland	62
Norway	60
Japan	59
Lithuania	57
Belarus	54
Russia	54
Sweden	53
Spain	50
Iceland	50
Britain	49
Brazil	48
Netherlands	47
East Germany	46
Nigeria	45
Argentina	45
Hungary	44
Moscow	44
Romania	43
Chile	43
Italy	42
France	42
West Germany	40
Portugal	39
Belgium	38
Canada	36
United States	36
Czechoslovakia	34
Finland	29
Mexico	23

Note: Countries in the left column are ranked according to GNP per capita. / The percentages in the bottom row give each country an equal weight. / na=not ascertained.

V303 LYING OWN INTEREST

Please tell me for each of the following statements whether you think it can always be justified, never be justified, or something in between. Lying in your own interest (% "never justified"—code 1 from a ten-point scale where 1=never and 10=always)

Country	Total	Gender Male	Gender Female	Age 16-29	Age 30-49	Age 50+	Education Lower	Education Medium	Education Upper	Income Lower	Income Middle	Income Upper	Political Affinity Left	Political Affinity Center	Political Affinity Right	Values Mat	Values Mixed	Values Postmat
India	58	56	61	56	58	65	63	58	56	61	56	54	61	57	47	58	57	62
Nigeria	45	47	43	45	43	60	52	44	44	46	38	40	39	46	45	41	47	44
China	34	35	33	36	32	35	35	37	30	30	31	34	na	na	na	37	31	28
Romania	38	39	37	29	32	48	49	31	31	36	38	33	44	36	33	44	34	24
Turkey	67	69	65	61	69	74	71	67	49	69	66	63	59	66	72	68	68	64
Poland	63	61	64	52	57	73	68	61	53	66	62	57	64	60	61	63	62	59
Bulgaria	70	67	73	64	70	75	73	72	65	69	70	69	65	72	76	80	67	63
Chile	64	61	66	54	67	72	67	63	60	63	61	63	62	62	66	65	63	64
Czechoslovakia	29	28	31	21	25	41	41	24	25	35	27	22	27	30	29	29	31	23
South Africa	62	57	67	54	63	75	66	60	63	58	55	63	51	61	62	69	59	53
Lithuania	58	53	63	40	56	76	68	56	54	65	56	46	na	na	na	64	57	59
Hungary	40	38	41	30	35	48	48	31	33	43	32	29	35	37	46	38	40	50
Argentina	65	63	67	53	66	73	73	61	58	70	67	54	55	58	68	70	67	55
Brazil	63	62	63	55	64	73	75	59	49	66	56	53	57	59	64	70	58	57
Mexico	31	29	32	30	28	38	32	28	29	28	31	27	20	29	32	37	30	27
Belarus	47	52	44	34	46	63	57	43	49	50	44	45	45	48	49	51	46	36
Russia	50	44	54	33	44	66	63	47	44	50	49	48	40	47	49	56	46	39
Moscow	42	41	42	27	39	56	54	40	40	40	38	43	37	45	49	47	40	39
Latvia	61	53	67	45	63	75	70	61	58	60	59	59	na	na	na	67	62	61
Estonia	47	46	48	39	46	58	50	47	46	46	46	48	na	na	na	50	46	44
Portugal	38	36	40	26	40	48	44	28	24	43	35	27	31	40	39	44	36	25
South Korea	70	68	72	61	73	78	72	72	66	70	68	71	63	66	74	72	68	69
Ireland	52	48	56	35	52	64	54	53	36	59	54	47	34	49	62	49	55	47
North Ireland	60	53	66	26	63	81	67	54	32	74	65	41	50	62	64	72	59	48
Slovenia	67	63	71	48	70	78	71	63	67	69	68	58	57	63	71	72	66	55
Spain	52	48	55	34	55	60	56	47	36	64	49	41	41	49	55	58	50	39
East Germany	37	31	41	22	31	51	40	31	26	48	30	30	31	41	31	53	35	32
Britain	40	36	44	24	38	48	37	39	34	47	35	35	33	38	47	47	40	35
Italy	50	50	51	35	51	59	56	45	48	52	48	40	33	50	48	54	49	48
Netherlands	25	24	26	17	26	34	31	22	22	27	22	25	22	21	33	33	27	19
Belgium	30	29	31	17	28	41	35	28	24	30	29	23	22	29	33	39	28	23
Austria	39	35	42	29	35	47	40	39	33	49	36	31	49	38	36	55	39	31
France	34	33	35	22	29	48	37	33	27	35	32	27	51	35	33	42	33	28
Canada	46	42	49	31	45	58	56	45	39	55	42	39	29	48	46	51	46	41
United States	56	56	55	44	51	65	63	57	48	61	52	51	41	58	57	56	57	50
Iceland	69	66	73	57	71	83	85	75	55	na	na	na	66	69	71	76	68	61
West Germany	25	20	29	13	20	35	28	19	18	31	22	19	17	24	30	31	27	17
Denmark	59	53	65	43	59	71	69	59	54	60	59	54	51	62	60	66	60	48
Finland	31	31	32	18	30	48	42	31	27	37	31	28	34	29	34	38	31	32
Norway	56	51	62	38	52	72	76	58	43	62	57	44	50	63	51	66	54	39
Sweden	55	48	63	41	58	62	73	46	46	55	59	51	54	58	51	65	57	45
Japan	55	51	58	39	54	66	67	55	42	57	54	51	52	49	53	57	51	45
Switzerland	51	46	55	37	46	62	53	53	36	53	48	37	37	48	59	67	52	39
Total	50	47	52	38	48	61	56	47	42	52	47	43	44	49	51	55	49	43

Ranking:

Bulgaria	70
South Korea	70
Iceland	69
Turkey	67
Slovenia	67
Argentina	65
Chile	64
Poland	63
Brazil	63
South Africa	62
Latvia	61
North Ireland	60
Denmark	59
India	58
Lithuania	58
United States	56
Norway	56
Sweden	55
Japan	55
Ireland	52
Spain	52
Switzerland	51
Russia	50
Italy	50
Belarus	47
Estonia	47
Canada	46
Nigeria	45
Moscow	42
Hungary	40
Britain	40
Austria	39
Romania	38
Portugal	38
East Germany	37
China	34
France	34
Mexico	31
Finland	31
Belgium	30
Czechoslovakia	29
Netherlands	25
West Germany	25

Note: Countries in the left column are ranked according to GNP per capita. / The percentages in the bottom row give each country an equal weight. / na=not ascertained.

V304 MARRIED HAVE AFFAIR

Please tell me for each of the following statements whether you think it can always be justified, never be justified, or something in between. Married men/women having an affair (% "never justified" –code 1 from a ten-point scale where 1=never and 10=always)

	Total	Gender		Age			Education			Income			Political Affinity			Values		
		Male	Female	16-29	30-49	50+	Lower	Medium	Upper	Lower	Middle	Upper	Left	Center	Right	Mat	Mixed	Postmat
India	91	90	93	91	91	93	94	92	89	90	92	89	92	89	91	92	90	93
Nigeria	58	58	58	58	57	72	62	55	61	56	51	55	na	56	58	57	59	62
China	72	68	79	61	74	84	78	73	60	76	71	70	na	na	na	82	67	33
Romania	62	53	71	49	62	71	74	60	51	60	63	59	62	64	57	73	57	30
Turkey	87	85	90	82	90	90	93	82	73	92	89	79	81	86	91	92	89	77
Poland	69	66	71	63	66	75	76	68	46	70	68	64	64	67	69	70	69	62
Bulgaria	49	43	55	32	43	65	72	46	32	47	49	40	44	44	46	62	46	22
Chile	63	53	72	56	63	72	70	61	56	65	60	55	56	62	65	69	62	56
Czechoslovakia	31	26	36	26	23	44	44	26	24	36	30	23	30	32	30	38	30	26
South Africa	73	69	77	69	72	82	77	71	73	65	66	74	64	75	71	78	70	67
Lithuania	61	49	70	48	53	78	75	57	53	67	56	50	na	na	na	69	59	53
Hungary	64	52	75	48	59	74	73	57	46	64	56	49	58	62	58	66	62	68
Argentina	72	60	82	63	73	77	77	72	62	76	72	56	54	71	70	74	73	67
Brazil	68	54	80	61	68	79	78	65	57	69	62	57	58	66	70	73	65	67
Mexico	43	36	50	40	42	49	43	41	42	41	40	35	32	42	44	44	43	40
Belarus	45	46	44	31	44	62	62	41	43	47	40	39	42	46	56	52	43	33
Russia	51	44	56	37	47	64	65	51	43	53	51	43	40	47	52	58	48	34
Moscow	29	26	32	21	24	41	44	32	23	31	24	19	24	33	43	34	27	26
Latvia	48	42	52	35	47	62	56	48	44	48	44	41	na	na	na	53	46	41
Estonia	31	25	35	25	26	44	42	30	21	31	30	27	na	na	na	36	29	24
Portugal	62	46	74	45	66	74	68	43	52	68	52	51	54	60	66	68	59	36
South Korea	72	74	70	58	74	88	84	71	67	69	73	72	56	68	78	75	71	60
Ireland	69	64	75	59	65	81	76	66	47	77	74	60	49	66	78	72	71	61
North Ireland	78	70	84	55	79	93	84	78	41	82	82	68	68	80	79	86	76	71
Slovenia	43	34	50	26	44	53	51	43	28	47	40	31	24	38	41	46	44	22
Spain	59	49	68	35	61	76	67	46	36	68	56	48	45	57	70	71	56	40
East Germany	57	49	64	43	52	71	62	54	42	67	55	44	43	63	62	72	57	49
Britain	53	49	56	41	47	65	58	41	35	63	44	44	49	53	52	56	55	43
Italy	52	43	60	36	45	68	54	35	33	57	43	27	40	58	44	62	52	38
Netherlands	45	48	44	35	44	59	62	41	32	43	54	32	32	46	54	59	50	34
Belgium	52	49	54	41	47	64	59	52	38	52	50	47	36	51	56	63	52	40
Austria	52	42	58	42	47	60	57	49	42	59	52	44	47	52	50	67	53	40
France	35	32	37	27	32	44	42	30	25	36	31	25	24	35	41	48	35	21
Canada	55	49	60	50	48	65	62	57	46	64	52	44	36	58	56	61	52	48
United States	71	68	75	67	67	77	77	72	63	76	69	64	50	73	75	74	71	66
Iceland	72	69	74	71	67	81	82	75	61	na	na	na	64	72	74	78	70	64
West Germany	43	35	50	29	35	57	49	36	25	49	39	36	28	44	52	54	46	29
Denmark	67	61	73	62	62	77	82	70	56	70	64	61	51	73	68	77	69	46
Finland	42	37	47	43	38	51	55	44	34	50	42	33	33	47	42	65	43	35
Norway	62	59	66	52	56	76	84	63	50	63	61	52	50	68	61	69	62	40
Sweden	63	61	65	65	60	64	73	61	50	69	59	60	60	66	58	77	63	51
Japan	47	44	49	31	42	64	63	47	29	55	43	42	35	40	47	48	42	41
Switzerland	56	49	61	46	49	67	62	55	35	60	48	43	31	55	61	73	59	36
Total	**58**	**52**	**63**	**48**	**55**	**69**	**67**	**55**	**46**	**60**	**55**	**49**	**48**	**58**	**60**	**65**	**57**	**46**

Ranking:

India	91
Turkey	87
North Ireland	78
South Africa	73
China	72
Argentina	72
South Korea	72
Iceland	72
United States	71
Poland	69
Ireland	69
Brazil	68
Denmark	67
Hungary	64
Chile	63
Sweden	63
Romania	62
Portugal	62
Norway	62
Lithuania	61
Spain	59
Nigeria	58
East Germany	57
Switzerland	56
Canada	55
Britain	53
Italy	52
Belgium	52
Austria	52
Russia	51
Bulgaria	49
Latvia	48
Japan	47
Belarus	45
Netherlands	45
Mexico	43
Slovenia	43
West Germany	43
Finland	42
France	35
Czechoslovakia	31
Estonia	31
Moscow	29

Note: Countries in the left column are ranked according to GNP per capita. / The percentages in the bottom row give each country an equal weight. / na=not ascertained.

V305 SEX UNDER AGE

Please tell me for each of the following statements whether you think it can always be justified, never be justified, or something in between.
Sex under the legal age of consent (% "never justified"—code 1 from a ten-point scale where 1=never and 10=always)

	Total	Gender		Age			Education			Income			Political Affinity			Values		
		Male	Female	16-29	30-49	50+	Lower	Medium	Upper	Lower	Middle	Upper	Left	Center	Right	Mat	Mixed	Postmat
India	90	88	91	88	90	91	92	90	87	89	90	87	92	88	84	89	90	91
Nigeria	54	56	51	51	55	77	55	54	53	54	44	45	46	50	54	52	54	57
China	76	74	78	66	77	83	79	75	71	78	75	73	na	na	na	79	74	52
Romania	81	77	86	65	83	91	91	77	76	79	81	78	84	82	74	90	77	57
Turkey	88	85	91	80	93	92	92	85	77	90	88	84	85	88	87	94	87	84
Poland	73	69	77	54	71	84	80	72	52	76	71	67	70	69	69	77	73	56
Bulgaria	57	51	62	35	54	72	75	56	41	53	58	46	58	52	53	70	55	25
Chile	77	73	80	66	81	86	84	76	69	80	75	70	73	77	77	79	77	71
Czechoslovakia	56	52	61	40	53	72	64	52	56	62	57	48	60	57	53	60	57	42
South Africa	74	73	76	67	77	83	77	72	77	60	68	77	65	75	76	79	72	67
Lithuania	72	64	79	42	75	93	85	68	72	79	71	54	na	na	na	78	72	59
Hungary	89	87	92	73	94	92	88	91	85	77	77	84	86	91	88	90	89	85
Argentina	73	69	75	56	75	82	82	69	61	81	72	59	45	71	77	76	76	59
Brazil	72	67	76	58	75	88	88	68	51	81	68	54	63	68	74	79	67	62
Mexico	45	39	53	38	47	61	47	46	40	44	40	39	31	42	49	52	43	42
Belarus	81	81	80	63	85	90	86	76	84	78	78	78	80	80	84	85	81	68
Russia	64	57	70	44	60	82	75	61	61	64	65	60	56	62	64	71	62	41
Moscow	77	76	79	52	79	92	88	78	75	74	72	70	74	78	88	85	76	67
Latvia	na	na	na	na	na	na	na	na	na	na	na	na	na	na	na	na	na	na
Estonia	na	na	na	na	na	na	na	na	na	na	na	na	na	na	na	na	na	na
Portugal	57	49	63	36	58	74	65	41	34	63	45	40	49	55	60	69	50	36
South Korea	na	na	na	na	na	na	na	na	na	na	na	na	na	na	na	na	na	na
Ireland	86	82	89	61	66	78	70	71	61	76	71	62	67	85	93	89	87	80
North Ireland	89	84	92	70	91	99	92	91	59	96	91	82	86	88	90	94	89	80
Slovenia	31	27	35	11	29	46	39	28	23	32	27	17	25	27	40	37	30	19
Spain	69	64	73	42	71	85	76	55	46	81	65	55	55	70	77	78	68	48
East Germany	77	73	80	65	73	88	80	74	67	83	74	71	69	78	82	84	79	68
Britain	74	73	75	50	75	87	78	71	58	81	67	68	74	70	78	82	74	68
Italy	50	41	57	30	43	66	52	35	41	56	38	27	40	55	49	62	50	33
Netherlands	17	20	16	09	14	31	22	14	13	15	16	10	08	15	24	34	18	09
Belgium	36	32	39	18	31	51	45	33	23	36	33	28	22	37	40	50	36	20
Austria	70	68	72	61	66	78	70	71	61	76	71	62	65	71	67	79	73	57
France	38	36	39	24	31	54	43	35	29	39	30	30	28	39	42	50	38	25
Canada	52	48	56	36	51	66	63	51	45	58	47	41	38	56	51	48	55	46
United States	65	65	66	49	61	76	73	66	59	70	64	62	50	67	68	73	66	59
Iceland	40	36	44	23	39	64	60	34	29	na	52	46	35	39	40	53	37	27
West Germany	54	53	55	30	50	69	61	43	37	59	52	46	37	57	66	70	56	40
Denmark	99	98	99	98	98	99	100	99	98	99	98	99	96	100	99	100	99	95
Finland	38	34	42	16	35	61	57	37	30	43	35	32	33	36	42	63	40	27
Norway	99	98	99	97	98	100	99	99	98	98	99	98	99	98	98	99	99	97
Sweden	98	97	98	95	99	99	97	97	99	97	98	98	99	97	97	99	98	97
Japan	55	55	55	24	56	75	66	56	41	55	55	55	41	51	60	58	52	47
Switzerland	63	59	66	46	56	76	67	64	38	65	57	45	42	62	66	80	65	47
Total	**66**	**63**	**69**	**51**	**66**	**79**	**73**	**64**	**57**	**69**	**64**	**60**	**59**	**65**	**68**	**73**	**66**	**55**

Ranking:

Denmark	99
Norway	99
Sweden	98
India	90
Hungary	89
North Ireland	89
Turkey	88
Ireland	86
Romania	81
Belarus	81
Chile	77
Moscow	77
East Germany	77
China	76
South Africa	74
Britain	74
Poland	73
Argentina	73
Lithuania	72
Brazil	72
Austria	70
Spain	69
United States	65
Russia	64
Switzerland	63
Bulgaria	57
Portugal	57
Czechoslovakia	56
Japan	55
Nigeria	54
West Germany	54
Canada	52
Italy	50
Mexico	45
Iceland	40
France	38
Finland	38
Belgium	36
Slovenia	31
Netherlands	17

Note: Countries in the left column are ranked according to GNP per capita. / The percentages in the bottom row give each country an equal weight. / na=not ascertained.

V306 ACCEPT BRIBE

Please tell me for each of the following statements whether you think it can always be justified, never be justified, or something in between. Someone accepting a bribe in the course of their duties (% "never justified"—code 1 from a ten-point scale where 1=never and 10=always)

	Total	Gender		Age			Education			Income			Political Affinity			Values			Ranking:
		Male	Female	16-29	30-49	50+	Lower	Medium	Upper	Lower	Middle	Upper	Left	Center	Right	Mat	Mixed	Postmat	
India	86	87	85	85	86	88	86	85	87	84	86	87	88	83	81	88	85	76	Argentina 95
Nigeria	66	67	64	62	68	77	70	65	65	67	64	62	63	64	67	64	66	71	Turkey 92
China	87	86	88	79	88	93	88	87	83	91	86	82	na	na	na	88	87	72	Denmark 91
Romania	68	71	66	57	67	76	74	64	66	67	69	65	68	67	67	70	67	62	Brazil 88
Turkey	92	92	91	89	93	94	93	91	84	92	95	86	90	91	91	93	90	93	China 87
Poland	83	82	84	70	86	88	84	83	84	86	82	78	87	80	83	84	84	81	India 86
Bulgaria	81	77	85	79	80	85	85	81	81	83	81	76	77	81	90	86	79	81	Chile 85
Chile	85	84	85	78	86	92	86	83	86	84	83	86	83	85	83	86	85	82	Russia 85
Czechoslovakia	57	56	59	52	55	63	60	55	59	62	56	53	62	56	58	56	58	55	South Korea 85
South Africa	80	75	85	75	81	88	82	78	83	71	76	81	76	80	80	83	79	75	Ireland 85
Lithuania	60	60	60	42	63	72	66	56	66	61	57	57	na	na	na	62	59	60	North Ireland 85
Hungary	70	68	71	64	66	76	75	64	62	66	61	61	68	72	61	71	67	76	Iceland 84
Argentina	95	93	96	93	96	95	95	96	96	96	94	93	93	93	96	97	94	95	Switzerland 84
Brazil	88	86	90	83	91	93	91	87	87	89	88	86	84	88	88	89	86	93	Poland 83
Mexico	55	50	60	51	57	60	54	53	57	51	54	52	47	53	58	61	54	61	Spain 83
Belarus	75	79	70	64	77	80	83	70	76	72	72	71	73	74	78	74	76	67	Bulgaria 81
Russia	85	83	87	75	86	91	90	84	84	88	87	82	84	84	83	87	85	78	Slovenia 81
Moscow	76	75	78	63	77	85	88	77	74	75	70	74	76	78	65	78	76	76	South Africa 80
Latvia	76	70	81	62	79	88	80	75	71	83	74	71	na	na	na	77	78	74	United States 80
Estonia	70	63	75	56	68	86	72	69	65	71	69	65	na	na	na	71	69	60	Norway 80
Portugal	74	74	74	62	79	81	76	75	63	78	71	68	70	74	73	76	72	69	Italy 77
South Korea	85	86	84	85	83	91	90	87	81	86	84	83	79	86	86	85	85	86	Canada 77
Ireland	85	82	88	75	88	89	86	85	77	87	88	77	70	84	83	85	76	76	Moscow 76
North Ireland	85	81	88	73	87	90	86	89	66	87	84	71	70	85	65	86	85	74	Latvia 76
Slovenia	81	74	86	60	84	90	81	80	80	82	78	75	72	79	80	86	80	63	Belarus 75
Spain	83	81	84	72	86	88	84	84	76	86	82	79	80	79	85	86	80	80	Britain 75
East Germany	64	60	67	52	61	75	66	62	57	74	59	58	62	66	59	71	64	59	Portugal 74
Britain	75	72	78	61	73	84	75	77	68	81	71	69	73	73	79	74	75	74	Finland 74
Italy	77	77	77	66	77	83	76	82	83	80	77	75	78	76	77	78	76	79	Sweden 74
Netherlands	68	65	69	56	69	80	75	63	64	65	68	72	70	67	68	70	69	65	Austria 72
Belgium	61	58	64	43	62	72	65	59	58	61	57	59	55	61	60	62	63	55	Japan 71
Austria	72	66	76	61	69	79	75	70	64	76	72	66	72	72	68	81	73	65	Hungary 70
France	64	62	66	50	62	77	65	63	62	64	66	59	64	62	62	66	65	61	Estonia 70
Canada	77	73	80	66	76	86	83	75	74	79	74	76	71	79	76	75	76	78	Romania 68
United States	80	81	81	73	81	83	81	81	79	83	77	80	75	80	84	82	79	82	Netherlands 68
Iceland	84	80	88	78	84	93	92	85	78	na	na	na	83	86	82	85	84	85	Nigeria 66
West Germany	63	57	67	53	59	71	64	60	59	66	61	59	58	64	64	66	63	60	East Germany 64
Denmark	91	87	95	85	93	94	90	90	89	93	91	90	91	92	89	88	92	90	France 64
Finland	74	72	76	58	79	75	75	74	74	76	74	74	74	75	72	76	74	73	West Germany 63
Norway	80	78	82	67	79	90	89	76	80	80	83	73	83	82	76	81	79	83	Belgium 61
Sweden	74	68	80	72	69	80	81	69	73	71	77	73	74	74	70	77	72	76	Lithuania 60
Japan	71	68	74	61	68	82	77	71	63	76	69	67	69	67	67	72	67	75	Czechoslovakia 57
Switzerland	84	80	88	76	82	90	87	84	76	86	81	83	81	85	85	92	83	84	Mexico 55
Total	76	74	78	67	77	84	80	75	74	78	75	73	74	76	76	78	76	74	

Note: Countries in the left column are ranked according to GNP per capita. / The percentages in the bottom row give each country an equal weight. / na=not ascertained.

V307 HOMOSEXUALITY

Please tell me for each of the following statements whether you think it can always be justified, never be justified, or something in between. Homosexuality (% "never justified"—code 1 from a ten-point scale where 1=never and 10=always)

	Total	Gender		Age			Education			Income			Political Affinity			Values			Ranking:	
		Male	Female	16-29	30-49	50+	Lower	Medium	Upper	Lower	Middle	Upper	Left	Center	Right	Mat	Mixed	Postmat		
India	94	94	94	93	95	92	96	93	94	94	96	93	94	92	93	94	95	86	India	94
Nigeria	73	76	68	72	73	88	78	71	73	74	73	69	67	75	73	69	74	83	China	93
China	93	91	95	89	94	94	96	94	88	94	91	91	na	na	na	96	90	82	South Korea	91
Romania	87	84	90	75	88	94	95	85	80	89	87	84	90	89	81	94	85	65	Lithuania	89
Turkey	85	85	84	78	88	91	89	82	72	87	86	79	83	82	90	89	85	80	Russia	89
Poland	81	82	80	68	78	89	86	80	64	81	80	74	76	78	83	86	81	64	Romania	87
Bulgaria	81	80	82	74	83	83	87	82	76	77	79	82	82	78	79	86	82	63	Turkey	85
Chile	78	78	78	73	77	86	83	78	73	82	78	70	75	77	79	80	78	72	Hungary	85
Czechoslovakia	39	39	39	31	34	48	47	35	32	37	33	28	40	39	36	43	38	27	Belarus	84
South Africa	78	80	77	76	77	85	86	76	64	74	75	69	71	76	78	84	75	76	Latvia	84
Lithuania	89	85	92	79	88	98	96	87	88	91	88	83	na	na	na	92	88	82	Poland	81
Hungary	85	83	86	83	82	88	88	82	80	78	71	66	86	85	81	87	83	78	Bulgaria	81
Argentina	63	65	62	50	61	74	73	56	51	69	58	50	44	62	63	73	64	46	Chile	78
Brazil	73	79	67	69	71	83	84	71	57	78	70	60	67	69	77	80	70	61	South Africa	78
Mexico	58	58	58	55	58	68	60	58	53	58	54	49	42	55	64	65	57	48	Estonia	78
Belarus	84	86	82	75	85	91	92	82	83	83	82	77	84	83	84	86	84	78	Nigeria	73
Russia	89	88	89	82	88	95	96	90	84	90	88	85	80	90	87	93	88	70	Brazil	73
Moscow	72	75	71	57	73	83	86	76	68	72	64	68	68	76	85	82	71	60	Moscow	72
Latvia	84	84	84	73	87	90	93	86	78	87	84	78	na	na	na	87	84	86	Portugal	67
Estonia	78	78	79	71	78	88	84	78	72	78	77	71	na	na	na	86	77	69	Slovenia	66
Portugal	67	71	63	57	64	79	74	54	48	74	61	56	60	67	70	77	64	42	North Ireland	65
South Korea	91	91	91	88	92	94	92	91	90	88	91	93	85	91	93	93	90	85	Argentina	63
Ireland	52	58	47	35	47	69	66	39	28	69	59	29	37	52	59	57	55	38	Japan	61
North Ireland	65	61	69	36	66	85	70	65	33	73	66	50	34	41	46	81	63	48	Mexico	58
Slovenia	66	62	69	50	67	74	73	63	57	70	59	43	48	62	67	78	63	43	United States	57
Spain	46	44	47	23	43	62	51	34	28	56	36	29	33	43	48	53	42	30	Norway	53
East Germany	50	52	48	35	42	66	54	44	36	53	47	35	38	52	59	73	51	34	Ireland	52
Britain	42	46	39	27	35	57	47	34	25	51	28	30	34	41	46	51	43	28	Austria	52
Italy	49	50	48	34	41	64	51	32	26	57	35	20	41	52	49	59	49	34	East Germany	50
Netherlands	20	26	17	12	15	31	30	10	16	10	11	06	12	13	26	31	21	05	Italy	49
Belgium	46	48	44	33	41	58	54	44	33	48	49	33	37	47	48	62	48	25	Switzerland	49
Austria	52	52	51	43	45	60	60	47	36	58	49	40	59	51	48	68	54	34	Spain	46
France	42	48	37	29	36	59	51	37	29	49	32	31	29	45	41	60	42	27	Belgium	46
Canada	40	46	34	33	35	51	54	39	28	48	35	26	27	41	54	57	45	21	Sweden	45
United States	57	60	53	48	49	67	67	60	44	65	55	42	31	56	66	66	59	42	Denmark	44
Iceland	30	36	23	20	25	49	42	27	21	na	33	na	21	32	33	39	29	13	Britain	42
West Germany	38	40	36	21	31	51	43	29	24	40	33	24	25	35	50	60	38	21	France	42
Denmark	44	51	36	30	36	61	64	38	25	46	35	25	31	47	43	57	45	21	Canada	40
Finland	36	43	28	30	28	59	50	37	25	39	32	35	27	33	54	61	36	30	Czechoslovakia	39
Norway	53	59	47	38	46	70	79	55	36	51	45	32	41	58	43	65	50	36	West Germany	38
Sweden	45	50	38	41	40	52	60	39	29	63	58	58	43	47	43	59	47	27	Finland	36
Japan	61	67	55	47	57	76	71	61	51	58	58	58	58	56	61	69	56	43	Iceland	30
Switzerland	49	51	47	33	40	62	54	48	30	49	35	28	31	47	57	65	52	26	Netherlands	20
Total	**63**	**65**	**61**	**53**	**60**	**74**	**71**	**60**	**52**	**66**	**60**	**53**	**52**	**60**	**63**	**72**	**63**	**50**		

Note: Countries in the left column are ranked according to GNP per capita. / The percentages in the bottom row give each country an equal weight. / na=not ascertained.

V308 PROSTITUTION

Please tell me for each of the following statements whether you think it can always be justified, never be justified, or something in between. Prostitution (% "never justified"—code 1 from a ten-point scale where 1=never and 10=always)

	Total	Gender Male	Gender Female	Age 16-29	Age 30-49	Age 50+	Educ Lower	Educ Medium	Educ Upper	Income Lower	Income Middle	Income Upper	Pol. Aff. Left	Pol. Aff. Center	Pol. Aff. Right	Values Mat	Values Mixed	Values Postmat	Ranking Country	Ranking
India	84	81	87	83	84	85	86	84	83	83	82	84	83	79	82	87	81	76	China	92
Nigeria	68	70	64	66	66	95	70	65	69	65	64	67	62	70	69	62	69	79	India	84
China	92	90	96	88	94	94	95	93	90	94	93	89	na	na	na	94	91	83	Turkey	83
Romania	80	73	86	65	80	89	91	76	70	79	79	76	85	82	70	90	76	45	South Africa	81
Turkey	83	80	86	80	82	90	89	80	64	85	85	76	75	83	88	88	84	75	Romania	80
Poland	76	71	80	69	72	83	85	74	49	75	76	72	69	72	73	82	73	64	South Korea	79
Bulgaria	72	66	77	60	68	85	86	73	59	68	70	69	71	70	70	84	70	47	Chile	78
Chile	78	76	79	74	78	83	82	77	73	82	76	70	72	79	79	82	77	72	Lithuania	78
Czechoslovakia	43	33	52	29	37	58	56	38	33	48	42	32	44	45	39	48	42	34	Hungary	78
South Africa	81	78	83	81	79	84	89	79	62	78	79	67	74	79	77	84	79	75	Russia	78
Lithuania	78	66	89	65	73	95	92	75	71	84	75	67	na	na	na	84	78	71	Poland	76
Hungary	78	72	84	69	75	85	85	72	69	74	67	63	80	76	76	82	76	69	Argentina	75
Argentina	75	71	79	64	71	87	82	71	65	80	71	63	53	74	75	82	75	63	Brazil	75
Brazil	75	72	78	70	75	84	85	73	61	80	75	65	69	72	77	80	72	65	Belarus	73
Mexico	52	48	56	48	51	62	53	56	45	50	50	42	43	51	54	60	53	36	Bulgaria	72
Belarus	73	68	78	60	73	88	86	71	71	71	73	65	71	74	81	82	71	59	Japan	71
Russia	78	67	86	63	77	89	89	78	71	81	78	72	65	76	74	87	74	56	Nigeria	68
Moscow	61	53	69	46	57	79	82	65	55	62	54	56	57	65	70	74	60	46	Latvia	68
Latvia	68	53	77	50	70	82	78	69	62	68	66	60	na	na	na	79	67	58	Portugal	68
Estonia	63	55	69	52	61	79	72	63	55	61	66	55	na	na	na	72	60	54	Norway	66
Portugal	68	65	71	60	67	77	73	59	57	74	65	55	62	69	69	75	66	53	Sweden	66
South Korea	79	83	77	68	83	89	88	81	73	79	77	80	64	76	84	85	76	69	North Ireland	65
Ireland	61	59	64	48	55	75	69	56	39	75	64	47	46	59	65	68	60	45	Estonia	63
North Ireland	65	49	77	43	62	84	71	64	31	77	64	46	56	67	65	78	64	48	Slovenia	63
Slovenia	63	51	73	44	61	77	72	61	47	69	61	42	47	58	63	76	59	43	Moscow	61
Spain	50	44	55	34	46	66	56	41	32	62	43	36	37	50	63	58	46	37	Ireland	61
East Germany	53	43	62	36	48	69	58	45	41	63	50	45	45	56	53	74	54	41	United States	61
Britain	43	37	48	33	32	58	46	37	31	53	25	31	39	40	45	52	43	30	Italy	60
Italy	60	53	65	49	53	72	62	45	31	67	49	36	51	66	56	69	60	49	Iceland	54
Netherlands	21	23	20	14	15	34	30	15	16	19	17	14	09	19	32	31	25	09	East Germany	53
Belgium	48	45	51	36	43	61	58	46	34	53	45	39	38	49	49	62	52	28	Mexico	52
Austria	49	41	54	40	44	57	56	46	34	56	46	40	47	46	48	65	51	35	Spain	50
France	48	46	50	34	45	62	55	44	38	52	40	39	37	47	57	62	47	37	Austria	49
Canada	44	37	50	35	39	56	57	46	30	53	40	32	24	47	41	54	46	32	Belgium	48
United States	61	58	65	53	56	69	68	65	50	66	59	51	35	62	66	67	63	50	France	48
Iceland	54	47	61	45	48	76	70	54	42	na	na	na	51	54	50	62	52	46	Denmark	45
West Germany	36	29	41	23	25	50	42	27	20	42	32	23	22	36	44	53	38	19	Switzerland	45
Denmark	45	40	50	37	37	60	60	45	36	50	43	31	35	49	45	59	44	29	Canada	44
Finland	31	25	38	24	25	54	48	29	26	38	28	21	27	32	33	61	31	26	Czechoslovakia	43
Norway	66	61	72	50	61	83	84	65	58	72	59	55	61	62	66	75	63	50	Britain	43
Sweden	66	58	76	64	60	74	75	62	59	65	68	62	66	65	64	73	66	60	West Germany	36
Japan	71	67	76	57	71	82	78	73	61	77	68	67	60	67	69	80	65	64	Finland	31
Switzerland	45	41	49	27	38	59	48	46	28	48	36	28	26	43	52	64	48	25	Netherlands	21
Total	62	57	67	52	59	75	71	60	51	66	60	53	53	61	62	72	62	50		

Note: Countries in the left column are ranked according to GNP per capita. / The percentages in the bottom row give each country an equal weight. / na=not ascertained.

V309 ABORTION

Please tell me for each of the following statements whether you think it can always be justified, never be justified, or something in between.
Abortion (% "never justified" —code 1 from a ten-point scale where 1=never and 10=always)

		Gender		Age			Education			Income			Political Affinity			Values		
	Total	Male	Female	16-29	30-49	50+	Lower	Medium	Upper	Lower	Middle	Upper	Left	Center	Right	Mat	Mixed	Postmat
India	39	39	40	36	38	50	51	38	35	43	37	35	42	39	29	38	38	39
Nigeria	53	53	53	51	53	75	50	57	51	49	48	61	54	50	58	52	54	50
China	16	15	16	15	15	17	19	15	11	14	16	14	na	na	na	16	15	15
Romania	25	24	27	15	22	34	35	18	22	26	21	23	33	21	24	31	23	08
Turkey	40	41	40	34	37	56	48	29	23	48	37	25	25	40	44	44	42	31
Poland	43	44	42	43	37	50	51	42	20	44	42	36	42	38	47	43	44	36
Bulgaria	29	31	28	18	24	40	44	25	16	25	27	21	19	27	30	34	29	14
Chile	76	76	77	73	76	81	79	78	71	81	75	69	74	76	77	80	76	72
Czechoslovakia	09	10	09	11	06	12	12	08	09	09	07	07	06	09	12	10	09	11
South Africa	66	66	65	66	62	72	80	63	36	66	65	43	55	61	59	67	66	58
Lithuania	31	32	29	24	24	43	43	28	22	36	25	22	na	na	na	32	31	29
Hungary	27	28	26	22	25	31	31	23	25	27	23	17	28	24	23	27	27	30
Argentina	48	47	48	44	42	57	52	45	44	51	43	40	31	44	53	56	47	38
Brazil	66	63	69	63	66	73	78	65	45	74	63	54	59	63	71	71	64	51
Mexico	43	40	47	40	40	57	44	44	37	42	36	35	30	39	47	49	41	42
Belarus	28	30	26	24	24	39	44	28	21	25	25	25	27	24	39	31	25	16
Russia	20	20	20	18	17	26	28	21	15	16	21	17	14	20	21	22	20	11
Moscow	14	15	14	13	12	17	28	14	10	15	10	07	12	15	16	13	14	10
Latvia	27	24	30	21	25	39	40	28	22	28	19	22	na	na	na	36	26	08
Estonia	15	16	14	16	13	17	22	14	11	13	17	13	na	na	na	15	14	11
Portugal	28	25	31	20	25	39	34	14	18	33	24	15	20	29	28	32	26	14
South Korea	40	40	40	38	39	45	59	40	31	49	34	28	30	41	41	40	40	36
Ireland	53	51	54	43	46	65	58	49	36	69	49	41	35	50	58	57	54	43
North Ireland	41	33	46	33	39	48	47	34	17	54	43	23	41	43	33	39	42	38
Slovenia	19	18	19	15	18	22	26	15	09	18	14	08	10	16	28	21	18	15
Spain	33	28	38	18	26	49	38	24	21	45	23	21	19	34	52	40	29	20
East Germany	21	18	24	08	17	34	25	14	15	27	19	15	12	26	25	31	22	15
Britain	19	19	20	15	16	25	23	12	08	27	11	10	19	18	18	25	20	12
Italy	26	22	29	23	19	33	25	25	30	30	17	12	16	30	23	27	26	21
Netherlands	13	13	13	12	10	19	19	09	10	12	09	06	07	11	18	20	13	09
Belgium	24	23	25	16	21	32	27	25	15	29	20	18	13	21	31	27	25	16
Austria	34	31	35	25	29	41	40	29	28	39	31	28	36	30	35	47	35	23
France	20	22	18	16	12	30	26	14	14	24	13	10	11	22	24	29	20	10
Canada	23	22	23	21	18	29	32	23	15	29	20	13	14	22	26	26	23	18
United States	35	34	37	36	27	43	48	38	21	43	31	24	17	33	40	47	35	25
Iceland	12	09	15	12	07	20	22	07	07	na	na	na	10	11	13	18	11	04
West Germany	19	16	22	11	12	29	23	12	10	23	17	15	08	19	27	32	21	07
Denmark	na	na	na	na	na	na	na	na	na	na	na	na	na	na	na	na	na	na
Finland	14	15	12	14	08	24	23	15	07	17	09	06	11	13	14	26	13	12
Norway	16	15	16	10	12	23	30	15	09	18	12	09	12	16	16	21	14	09
Sweden	15	12	16	11	13	18	23	10	09	15	16	10	09	17	13	20	17	05
Japan	29	27	30	20	25	41	34	31	18	38	25	22	19	24	30	28	26	22
Switzerland	56	52	59	44	51	67	63	54	35	63	48	36	36	55	65	75	59	36
Total	31	30	32	26	27	40	39	28	22	35	28	23	25	31	34	36	31	24

Ranking:

76	Chile
66	South Africa
66	Brazil
56	Switzerland
53	Nigeria
53	Ireland
48	Argentina
43	Poland
43	Mexico
41	North Ireland
40	Turkey
40	South Korea
39	India
35	United States
34	Austria
33	Spain
31	Lithuania
29	Bulgaria
29	Japan
28	Belarus
28	Portugal
27	Hungary
27	Latvia
26	Italy
25	Romania
24	Belgium
23	Canada
21	East Germany
20	Russia
20	France
19	Slovenia
19	Britain
19	West Germany
16	China
16	Norway
15	Estonia
15	Sweden
14	Moscow
14	Finland
13	Netherlands
12	Iceland
09	Czechoslovakia

Note: Countries in the left column are ranked according to GNP per capita. / The percentages in the bottom row give each country an equal weight. / na=not ascertained.

V310 DIVORCE

Please tell me for each of the following statements whether you think it can always be justified, never be justified, or something in between.

Divorce (% "never justified" — code 1 from a ten-point scale where 1=never and 10=always)

	Total	Gender		Age			Education			Income			Political Affinity			Values		
		Male	Female	16-29	30-49	50+	Lower	Medium	Upper	Lower	Middle	Upper	Left	Center	Right	Mat	Mixed	Postmat
India	52	50	54	48	53	60	64	54	43	58	51	45	53	49	42	53	48	46
Nigeria	44	45	45	43	42	70	45	44	43	38	42	49	46	42	43	43	45	42
China	16	16	15	12	16	21	20	14	11	14	17	15	na	na	na	18	13	14
Romania	25	25	26	17	23	32	36	19	20	21	24	22	33	23	25	30	23	09
Turkey	27	21	34	24	25	37	35	15	10	32	21	20	14	24	31	34	27	19
Poland	33	34	32	26	28	41	41	30	14	31	33	29	32	27	38	36	32	26
Bulgaria	33	32	33	22	27	45	48	30	17	29	31	26	25	32	33	40	31	18
Chile	49	48	51	43	51	57	59	47	40	55	45	38	41	50	51	54	49	42
Czechoslovakia	08	08	08	05	04	13	12	06	06	11	05	05	08	07	09	10	07	07
South Africa	53	51	54	55	48	59	67	50	22	58	53	28	45	47	47	56	52	49
Lithuania	25	24	26	16	19	37	41	20	20	29	22	15	na	na	na	30	24	24
Hungary	26	28	25	19	23	33	31	22	18	25	25	12	34	23	24	27	25	42
Argentina	32	33	31	23	31	39	38	27	26	31	22	17	11	26	32	43	29	23
Brazil	39	37	40	32	37	55	56	35	18	42	29	24	32	33	44	44	36	26
Mexico	29	26	34	27	28	38	31	26	26	29	22	23	23	26	32	32	28	28
Belarus	22	25	19	18	19	31	40	20	17	22	19	19	21	19	33	27	19	13
Russia	18	16	19	13	15	22	23	19	13	15	17	13	10	15	21	19	17	09
Moscow	11	09	12	11	08	16	23	11	08	13	07	05	09	12	17	15	09	12
Latvia	20	17	22	17	18	29	35	21	14	21	12	15	na	na	na	25	20	07
Estonia	12	14	10	12	10	15	14	12	10	10	16	11	na	na	na	10	12	07
Portugal	20	16	24	11	19	30	26	09	08	23	17	09	15	17	24	29	15	09
South Korea	40	37	42	28	41	54	62	42	26	43	37	34	31	37	43	45	39	10
Ireland	31	32	31	21	22	21	39	24	13	46	33	16	19	26	39	37	32	18
North Ireland	28	24	30	18	22	30	32	23	08	30	20	14	19	33	16	27	29	21
Slovenia	20	19	20	15	16	14	26	17	10	18	16	08	19	16	20	23	19	19
Spain	25	20	28	08	18	40	30	13	10	33	15	11	11	24	11	29	21	11
East Germany	14	13	15	07	12	21	16	13	08	17	13	10	05	17	35	21	14	12
Britain	12	12	13	08	08	19	15	09	06	14	06	06	12	11	19	14	13	08
Italy	21	18	24	14	16	23	22	06	17	17	06	17	13	25	15	29	15	10
Netherlands	07	09	07	05	05	14	13	04	04	24	13	07	03	04	11	19	08	15
Belgium	18	18	19	11	14	21	22	18	11	18	16	11	12	18	24	27	18	11
Austria	19	17	20	12	14	25	23	17	07	23	16	13	17	19	17	33	18	10
France	13	15	11	06	09	21	18	09	07	14	07	06	07	12	17	17	13	07
Canada	15	17	13	11	10	23	27	13	09	21	13	07	07	16	16	17	15	12
United States	20	19	20	20	14	24	32	19	11	21	19	13	12	16	23	25	20	13
Iceland	05	07	04	06	03	08	10	04	02	na	na	14	04	06	08	09	04	03
West Germany	10	15	11	04	05	16	13	05	04	12	07	06	05	10	13	15	11	03
Denmark	17	07	19	13	14	23	29	14	12	17	13	07	08	21	16	23	17	11
Finland	07	07	07	07	04	15	17	06	04	08	04	03	02	06	09	11	07	11
Norway	16	17	14	11	14	20	28	16	08	18	13	09	12	16	16	21	13	12
Sweden	09	08	09	07	09	11	14	07	04	08	08	06	08	09	12	14	10	12
Japan	19	22	17	12	15	31	29	18	12	24	16	12	13	14	24	21	18	13
Switzerland	26	27	26	16	20	37	32	24	14	27	20	12	11	24	31	46	27	12
Total	23	22	24	18	20	31	31	20	14	25	20	16	18	22	25	28	22	16

Ranking:

South Africa	53
India	52
Chile	49
Nigeria	44
South Korea	40
Brazil	39
Poland	33
Bulgaria	33
Argentina	32
Ireland	31
Mexico	29
North Ireland	28
Turkey	27
Hungary	26
Switzerland	26
Romania	25
Lithuania	25
Spain	25
Belarus	22
Italy	21
Latvia	20
Portugal	20
Slovenia	20
United States	20
Austria	19
Japan	19
Russia	18
Belgium	18
Denmark	17
China	16
Norway	16
Canada	15
East Germany	14
France	13
Estonia	12
Britain	12
Moscow	11
West Germany	10
Sweden	09
Czechoslovakia	08
Netherlands	07
Finland	07
Iceland	05

Note: Countries in the left column are ranked according to GNP per capita. / The percentages in the bottom row give each country an equal weight. / na=not ascertained.

V311 FIGHTING POLICE

Please tell me for the following statements whether you think it can always be justified, never be justified, or something in between. Fighting with the police (% "never justified" —code 1 from a ten-point scale where 1=never and 10=always)

	Total	Gender Male	Gender Female	Age 16-29	Age 30-49	Age 50+	Education Lower	Education Medium	Education Upper	Income Lower	Income Middle	Income Upper	Political Affinity Left	Political Affinity Center	Political Affinity Right	Values Mat	Values Mixed	Values Postmat	Ranking:	
India	61	56	66	55	63	68	72	60	56	61	63	54	58	61	51	56	62	52	Denmark	83
Nigeria	50	52	47	48	49	70	54	50	47	50	45	45	47	48	53	45	52	55	Brazil	77
China	45	43	46	38	44	52	54	44	34	46	39	46	na	na	na	48	43	26	Romania	76
Romania	76	75	78	66	74	85	82	72	76	77	79	71	82	77	71	81	76	53	Argentina	73
Turkey	45	40	50	39	45	54	56	29	26	53	41	31	31	44	51	58	45	28	Switzerland	71
Poland	50	48	51	40	50	56	51	50	43	46	49	51	50	50	48	55	49	38	North Ireland	68
Bulgaria	54	52	56	44	49	66	65	52	46	53	53	50	49	53	52	67	51	36	Ireland	67
Chile	61	59	63	49	63	75	72	60	48	67	59	48	44	65	63	73	59	46	Norway	66
Czechoslovakia	24	23	24	14	18	37	32	20	20	26	22	18	24	24	25	27	23	19	Hungary	65
South Africa	61	60	62	54	60	76	67	60	46	54	58	57	46	59	68	68	59	49	Britain	63
Lithuania	32	27	36	20	28	46	43	29	27	37	28	22	na	na	na	41	29	23	Sweden	62
Hungary	65	62	67	54	60	74	75	57	48	65	54	52	58	69	55	68	62	71	India	61
Argentina	73	71	75	60	72	83	80	71	63	81	69	61	50	71	73	83	72	62	Chile	61
Brazil	77	75	79	68	79	89	89	75	57	83	76	67	68	74	81	85	73	59	South Africa	61
Mexico	29	28	31	29	26	35	30	27	27	29	26	21	19	30	31	30	30	25	Spain	61
Belarus	31	31	30	20	29	45	48	25	30	29	28	31	26	28	51	39	28	14	Austria	57
Russia	37	31	42	22	31	55	46	36	34	37	38	36	26	35	48	46	33	19	Belgium	56
Moscow	25	24	26	16	22	37	46	26	20	26	22	21	21	28	34	34	24	15	Slovenia	55
Latvia	31	28	33	21	30	44	47	31	26	32	25	28	na	na	na	38	33	14	Bulgaria	54
Estonia	42	39	45	27	41	61	52	39	41	40	42	40	na	na	na	49	39	43	East Germany	52
Portugal	51	50	53	34	55	64	58	46	29	57	51	40	35	51	58	60	49	26	Italy	52
South Korea	35	34	37	21	38	50	60	36	22	37	33	30	20	33	40	40	35	14	Portugal	51
Ireland	67	65	70	49	65	82	74	65	37	78	70	59	42	67	74	73	70	53	France	51
North Ireland	68	62	72	51	59	89	75	65	31	73	73	53	46	68	74	77	67	54	Nigeria	50
Slovenia	55	50	59	36	54	69	62	52	48	57	55	44	40	50	52	65	53	25	Poland	50
Spain	61	57	64	45	56	77	68	50	39	74	58	48	35	57	72	73	58	42	Canada	50
East Germany	52	45	59	36	45	70	58	46	36	65	49	43	42	57	40	74	52	42	United States	50
Britain	63	60	65	44	54	81	68	56	41	73	54	52	47	63	73	77	63	49	Iceland	47
Italy	52	50	54	38	47	64	54	36	34	58	48	32	41	53	59	61	51	42	China	45
Netherlands	50	44	35	22	35	59	52	34	24	31	39	29	27	36	48	58	42	25	Turkey	45
Belgium	56	52	60	39	53	69	64	56	38	55	54	48	43	57	53	71	58	38	West Germany	43
Austria	57	52	59	43	54	66	61	56	49	63	56	53	59	54	51	75	59	43	Estonia	42
France	51	49	54	39	50	62	57	50	39	51	50	45	43	51	57	59	54	37	Japan	42
Canada	50	48	51	36	44	68	66	50	37	57	47	38	37	53	46	61	51	41	Russia	37
United States	50	51	49	39	43	61	59	52	40	58	51	40	37	53	49	55	51	42	Netherlands	37
Iceland	47	49	46	37	40	73	63	49	35	na	na	na	35	49	53	58	46	32	South Korea	35
West Germany	43	37	48	26	36	58	49	36	25	48	40	38	26	44	55	53	47	29	Lithuania	32
Denmark	83	81	85	75	81	92	91	85	77	85	84	77	69	87	87	93	86	62	Belarus	31
Finland	26	25	27	09	23	48	39	28	17	33	26	17	30	26	24	50	27	17	Latvia	31
Norway	66	67	64	44	62	84	85	65	56	68	65	60	53	71	69	75	66	41	Mexico	29
Sweden	62	62	63	48	59	76	74	57	51	64	65	59	59	64	62	76	65	43	Finland	26
Japan	42	45	40	27	38	60	59	40	31	46	42	37	33	35	51	48	37	26	Moscow	25
Switzerland	71	67	75	57	64	85	78	71	47	75	65	62	48	72	75	89	74	54	Czechoslovakia	24
Total	**51**	**49**	**53**	**39**	**49**	**65**	**61**	**49**	**39**	**55**	**50**	**44**	**42**	**53**	**56**	**61**	**51**	**38**		

Note: Countries in the left column are ranked according to GNP per capita. / The percentages in the bottom row give each country an equal weight. / na=not ascertained.

V312 EUTHANASIA

Please tell me for each of the following statements whether you think it can always be justified, never be justified, or something in between. Euthanasia terminating the life of the incurably sick (% "never justified"—code 1 from a ten-point scale where 1=never and 10=always)

	Total	Gender		Age			Education			Income			Political Affinity			Values		
		Male	Female	16-29	30-49	50+	Lower	Medium	Upper	Lower	Middle	Upper	Left	Center	Right	Mat	Mixed	Postmat
India	57	55	59	52	58	63	62	57	54	52	55	50	57	54	51	56	55	57
Nigeria	56	58	54	55	56	74	57	56	57	54	49	50	60	56	54	51	58	71
China	24	24	24	21	25	26	29	23	13	17	16	13	na	na	na	26	21	14
Romania	54	54	54	40	50	65	61	50	48	51	51	44	62	48	47	61	51	30
Turkey	70	69	71	63	72	78	76	62	53	70	68	51	60	69	75	70	71	65
Poland	67	66	68	60	63	75	74	66	48	67	68	61	57	69	68	71	66	60
Bulgaria	52	52	51	41	49	62	63	48	46	44	48	49	45	50	57	58	49	47
Chile	68	67	70	59	70	79	79	67	58	70	64	56	60	69	66	74	67	62
Czechoslovakia	na	na	na	na	na	na	na	na	na	na	na	na	na	na	na	na	na	na
South Africa	61	59	62	61	57	66	75	59	24	66	60	30	54	54	48	62	60	59
Lithuania	45	47	44	35	44	55	56	43	38	46	40	39	na	na	na	54	43	37
Hungary	48	49	47	38	45	57	53	46	37	43	38	34	48	47	48	49	47	57
Argentina	61	58	64	48	60	72	71	57	51	64	56	44	32	58	56	72	61	46
Brazil	71	68	73	64	70	83	86	67	51	77	62	58	63	66	77	81	65	54
Mexico	38	34	43	35	36	50	39	40	34	38	32	31	23	36	43	48	36	33
Belarus	40	46	35	29	41	50	57	35	39	37	35	30	35	42	57	43	40	33
Russia	54	51	56	44	50	64	64	54	47	49	47	51	47	52	54	58	51	44
Moscow	36	36	37	27	34	46	52	39	30	33	29	28	33	37	50	38	36	35
Latvia	48	47	48	36	49	58	56	50	42	38	43	41	na	na	na	49	52	31
Estonia	40	40	40	36	39	47	45	42	30	39	35	34	na	na	na	42	39	38
Portugal	53	52	54	42	55	63	61	47	27	56	45	37	45	55	53	58	51	30
South Korea	na	na	na	na	na	na	na	na	na	na	na	na	na	na	na	na	na	na
Ireland	56	52	60	47	51	69	59	56	43	63	58	49	38	53	68	57	59	49
North Ireland	43	37	46	32	43	49	48	37	21	49	39	25	46	48	32	44	42	36
Slovenia	51	48	55	38	50	63	57	51	44	52	42	35	39	43	55	59	50	29
Spain	45	40	49	26	40	61	51	32	26	52	36	28	31	45	55	55	43	27
East Germany	43	39	45	32	40	52	45	39	38	45	36	36	41	42	42	47	43	36
Britain	23	23	24	19	17	32	27	17	14	30	14	15	22	22	24	26	24	19
Italy	47	40	52	39	39	57	48	32	45	52	37	24	36	54	44	55	47	36
Netherlands	13	18	11	11	08	23	20	09	09	13	10	04	04	10	22	21	15	06
Belgium	23	22	24	13	17	35	29	21	15	24	21	17	14	20	28	29	23	16
Austria	42	37	45	29	39	49	45	38	43	45	37	36	41	42	39	49	42	36
France	24	25	23	20	17	34	31	17	18	23	18	17	17	26	29	31	24	16
Canada	25	23	27	16	20	37	38	23	17	31	22	15	13	26	27	34	25	19
United States	34	34	33	24	28	43	47	34	23	36	33	23	20	33	37	42	33	26
Iceland	22	21	23	13	17	33	37	19	12	na	na	na	18	21	25	27	21	15
West Germany	33	31	35	25	30	39	36	27	30	34	29	30	26	33	37	32	34	32
Denmark	26	22	31	19	23	36	43	21	20	28	19	12	19	30	25	43	24	16
Finland	14	14	14	12	11	24	25	14	10	20	09	07	07	19	13	41	15	08
Norway	32	29	34	19	28	45	53	28	25	37	24	23	28	35	30	39	30	22
Sweden	21	19	22	13	20	27	28	18	15	20	24	14	23	21	15	26	23	12
Japan	21	22	19	13	17	32	31	20	12	24	17	14	19	13	25	19	20	11
Switzerland	32	29	34	23	23	44	34	33	21	31	21	17	12	29	38	46	35	16
Total	**42**	**40**	**43**	**34**	**39**	**52**	**50**	**39**	**32**	**43**	**37**	**32**	**35**	**41**	**44**	**47**	**41**	**34**

Ranking:

Brazil	71	East Germany	43
Turkey	70	Austria	42
Chile	68	Belarus	40
Poland	67	Estonia	40
South Africa	61	Mexico	38
Argentina	61	Moscow	36
India	57	United States	34
Nigeria	56	West Germany	33
Ireland	56	Norway	32
Romania	54	Switzerland	32
Russia	54	Denmark	26
Portugal	53	Canada	25
Bulgaria	52	China	24
Slovenia	51	France	24
Hungary	48	Britain	23
Latvia	48	Belgium	23
Italy	47	Iceland	22
Lithuania	45	Sweden	21
Spain	45	Japan	21
North Ireland	43	Finland	14
		Netherlands	13

Note: Countries in the left column are ranked according to GNP per capita. / The percentages in the bottom row give each country an equal weight. / na=not ascertained.

V313 SUICIDE

Please tell me for each of the following statements whether you think it can always be justified, never be justified, or something in between.
Suicide (% "never justified"—code 1 from a ten-point scale where 1=never and 10=always)

Country	Total	Gender Male	Gender Female	Age 16-29	Age 30-49	Age 50+	Education Lower	Education Medium	Education Upper	Income Lower	Income Middle	Income Upper	Political Affinity Left	Political Affinity Center	Political Affinity Right	Values Mat	Values Mixed	Values Postmat	Ranking Country	Ranking Value
India	82	80	84	80	83	84	85	82	80	82	80	82	85	77	73	84	79	75	Brazil	90
Nigeria	74	78	68	73	72	93	77	74	73	73	74	68	74	74	75	70	75	79	Argentina	83
China	55	53	59	43	58	64	63	53	48	56	55	52	na	na	na	60	52	37	India	82
Romania	77	79	75	65	78	84	81	76	73	75	76	75	84	75	na	83	76	50	Chile	82
Turkey	81	82	81	77	83	86	83	81	72	84	80	77	75	80	86	84	81	79	Turkey	81
Poland	75	74	77	64	74	83	81	74	63	73	75	74	72	74	76	77	76	69	South Africa	78
Bulgaria	68	67	69	66	66	72	70	69	66	62	72	67	59	70	71	74	67	62	Romania	77
Chile	82	80	84	78	83	87	87	80	80	85	79	78	75	85	81	85	81	82	Poland	75
Czechoslovakia	na	na	na	na	na	na	na	na	na	na	na	na	na	na	na	na	na	na	Nigeria	74
South Africa	78	78	78	75	78	83	85	77	62	78	77	67	73	76	72	83	76	72	Hungary	73
Lithuania	70	68	72	58	68	82	83	67	63	72	70	59	na	na	na	75	70	62	Portugal	72
Hungary	73	73	73	67	74	74	75	72	64	68	62	66	71	75	71	70	75	78	Spain	72
Argentina	83	82	85	79	82	88	85	84	82	83	81	79	72	84	85	87	86	72	Lithuania	70
Brazil	90	89	91	85	92	93	93	89	83	90	89	87	88	89	90	91	89	88	Italy	70
Mexico	51	50	53	50	51	57	51	53	52	51	44	45	37	49	57	57	50	45	Bulgaria	68
Belarus	64	67	60	51	65	73	70	61	63	65	60	55	62	62	69	69	61	56	Russia	68
Russia	68	66	69	60	65	75	74	69	62	70	64	63	56	69	75	74	64	58	South Korea	66
Moscow	47	50	45	33	47	57	62	47	44	45	41	45	45	52	49	52	46	40	Belarus	64
Latvia	64	64	64	49	67	76	73	65	61	61	62	59	na	na	na	70	66	54	Latvia	64
Estonia	59	57	61	50	58	71	66	62	46	59	54	53	na	na	na	64	57	55	Ireland	63
Portugal	72	74	69	65	72	78	75	73	57	74	69	66	63	77	70	77	70	62	United States	62
South Korea	66	64	69	51	70	84	76	69	59	63	64	72	53	65	71	71	66	47	Denmark	60
Ireland	63	61	65	51	64	71	70	59	40	71	69	51	42	64	69	62	66	56	Estonia	59
North Ireland	58	59	58	45	53	74	64	55	29	63	65	34	46	61	55	62	60	44	Slovenia	59
Slovenia	59	59	59	45	59	69	62	58	55	58	56	47	51	58	56	65	59	36	North Ireland	58
Spain	72	69	75	56	73	83	77	63	55	78	68	61	61	72	82	81	71	56	Norway	58
East Germany	56	56	56	46	52	65	59	53	43	62	53	50	44	60	63	69	54	52	Japan	58
Britain	40	42	37	29	38	48	44	32	29	46	35	30	36	38	45	42	41	33	Switzerland	58
Italy	70	67	74	65	64	79	72	56	58	77	63	47	65	72	72	76	71	61	Iceland	57
Netherlands	32	40	30	20	31	48	45	29	20	28	30	23	18	30	44	55	37	17	East Germany	56
Belgium	51	52	50	39	47	61	57	51	38	51	48	43	37	50	54	60	54	35	China	55
Austria	50	47	51	39	46	57	52	49	41	55	47	45	50	48	48	61	52	38	Canada	53
France	34	37	32	30	30	42	42	30	22	35	30	27	22	37	39	47	34	22	Mexico	51
Canada	53	55	51	48	48	63	55	55	42	52	52	42	37	56	50	61	54	47	Belgium	51
United States	62	62	62	61	61	64	69	65	53	70	63	49	47	63	65	67	63	55	Austria	50
Iceland	57	59	55	56	52	67	69	59	47	na	na	na	50	56	59	63	57	41	Moscow	47
West Germany	43	41	44	31	38	53	46	39	34	45	38	38	31	43	52	48	46	33	Sweden	47
Denmark	60	57	62	57	54	69	72	58	54	63	59	44	48	61	64	68	62	37	West Germany	43
Finland	33	32	34	23	28	53	38	40	22	43	29	24	36	30	35	46	36	24	Britain	40
Norway	58	60	55	39	59	70	74	59	49	61	60	49	48	63	58	65	58	38	France	34
Sweden	47	48	47	47	44	51	57	48	29	45	47	42	44	49	45	55	51	31	Finland	33
Japan	58	55	61	53	55	67	66	61	46	64	55	50	51	52	53	58	58	44	Netherlands	32
Switzerland	58	56	59	45	52	68	63	57	37	64	47	40	30	57	65	77	60	39		
Total	**62**	**62**	**62**	**53**	**60**	**71**	**68**	**61**	**52**	**64**	**60**	**54**	**54**	**62**	**64**	**68**	**62**	**51**		

Note: Countries in the left column are ranked according to GNP per capita. / The percentages in the bottom row give each country an equal weight. / na=not ascertained.

V314 HIT CAR–NO REPORT

Please tell me for each of the following statements whether you think it can always be justified, never be justified, or something in between. Failing to report damage you've done accidentally to a parked vehicle (% "never justified"—code 1 from a ten-point scale where 1=never and 10=always)

	Total	Gender		Age			Education			Income			Political Affinity			Values		
		Male	Female	16-29	30-49	50+	Lower	Medium	Upper	Lower	Middle	Upper	Left	Center	Right	Mat	Mixed	Postmat
India	75	73	78	72	77	79	78	76	73	76	75	72	78	73	65	76	74	69
Nigeria	54	54	54	52	53	82	59	56	51	55	52	48	49	55	54	49	57	52
China	52	50	54	45	52	59	55	50	47	57	49	46	na	na	na	57	49	33
Romania	73	71	75	60	74	79	79	70	69	77	74	66	74	73	70	77	72	52
Turkey	79	76	81	72	82	85	82	77	68	78	80	75	72	79	81	80	79	77
Poland	na	na	na	na	na	na	na	na	na	na	na	na	na	na	na	na	na	na
Bulgaria	70	64	75	59	69	76	78	69	64	68	70	64	66	67	76	74	69	58
Chile	62	59	65	52	62	77	70	59	57	63	55	58	61	58	64	64	62	57
Czechoslovakia	na	na	na	na	na	na	na	na	na	na	na	na	na	na	na	na	na	na
South Africa	na	na	na	na	na	na	na	na	na	na	na	na	na	na	na	na	na	na
Lithuania	52	47	57	32	53	67	65	47	57	58	48	37	na	na	na	54	51	49
Hungary	67	66	67	52	70	70	68	67	58	60	59	61	64	68	66	69	64	69
Argentina	79	76	81	69	78	86	85	80	66	84	77	67	66	75	79	84	78	73
Brazil	67	63	70	56	69	81	80	63	52	73	60	57	62	60	71	70	65	61
Mexico	33	31	35	30	32	41	35	31	27	31	29	31	22	31	38	37	33	31
Belarus	53	56	50	40	53	64	64	48	53	50	50	52	49	57	55	55	52	41
Russia	60	50	68	46	55	76	69	60	56	62	60	54	50	58	60	70	55	42
Moscow	40	36	45	23	39	56	53	41	37	41	35	39	36	46	44	45	40	34
Latvia	57	54	60	42	56	77	65	59	52	58	54	53	na	na	na	63	58	58
Estonia	58	58	58	44	57	75	65	57	54	56	56	57	na	na	na	58	60	56
Portugal	67	63	70	52	75	75	71	65	55	68	67	54	61	66	69	73	64	57
South Korea	72	73	71	60	74	86	81	72	67	70	70	77	67	67	76	75	71	61
Ireland	65	59	71	47	66	77	68	66	51	71	68	60	48	62	76	63	69	59
North Ireland	69	68	70	43	70	86	72	70	45	66	73	60	64	69	68	73	71	50
Slovenia	70	68	72	48	73	81	72	69	67	73	68	58	61	66	66	76	69	48
Spain	74	71	77	60	75	84	79	71	58	81	73	65	66	69	77	80	73	64
East Germany	69	65	73	53	67	82	72	68	61	76	63	66	67	70	67	78	70	61
Britain	51	46	56	32	50	64	52	54	46	59	46	43	48	49	55	57	51	44
Italy	62	63	61	48	63	69	63	55	55	64	60	54	61	60	60	67	60	59
Netherlands	60	58	61	51	60	70	64	60	56	53	62	64	50	64	65	66	62	55
Belgium	65	62	68	53	66	73	69	66	58	62	63	58	58	66	65	72	67	57
Austria	78	74	81	63	79	83	79	78	71	83	77	74	77	76	77	84	80	69
France	60	59	61	45	61	72	63	58	59	58	57	59	59	58	60	66	59	57
Canada	64	63	65	52	62	76	75	61	58	66	64	60	54	66	65	68	64	62
United States	65	65	66	55	64	70	70	65	60	68	62	62	54	66	66	68	63	66
Iceland	80	77	83	73	79	91	89	83	72	68	na	na	80	76	82	84	80	73
West Germany	64	59	68	48	63	73	68	58	53	61	64	64	53	67	70	64	68	57
Denmark	84	80	88	72	86	91	91	84	80	85	83	83	78	84	86	84	86	77
Finland	62	59	65	56	63	64	59	64	60	60	62	61	62	63	59	73	65	52
Norway	78	75	82	63	75	91	92	75	74	79	79	73	77	82	75	84	77	73
Sweden	69	67	71	59	66	81	79	66	61	72	69	66	68	70	82	79	72	57
Japan	79	76	81	71	77	85	84	79	71	80	78	77	78	75	70	80	76	75
Switzerland	79	75	83	65	77	87	84	79	63	77	77	73	64	80	81	93	81	68
Total	65	63	68	53	66	76	71	64	59	66	63	60	61	66	68	70	65	58

Ranking:

Denmark	84
Iceland	80
Turkey	79
Argentina	79
Japan	79
Switzerland	79
Austria	78
Norway	78
India	75
Spain	74
Romania	73
South Korea	72
Bulgaria	70
Slovenia	70
North Ireland	69
East Germany	69
Sweden	69
Hungary	67
Brazil	67
Portugal	67
Ireland	65
Belgium	65
United States	65
Canada	64
West Germany	64
Chile	62
Italy	62
Finland	62
Russia	60
Netherlands	60
France	60
Estonia	58
Latvia	57
Nigeria	54
Belarus	53
China	52
Lithuania	52
Britain	51
Moscow	40
Mexico	33

Note: Countries in the left column are ranked according to GNP per capita. / The percentages in the bottom row give each country an equal weight.   na=not ascertained.

V315   THREATEN STRIKERS

Please tell me for each of the following statements whether you think it can always be justified, never be justified, or something in between. Threatening workers who refuse to join a strike (% "never justified"—code 1 from a ten-point scale where 1=never and 10=always)

		Gender		Age			Education			Income			Political Affinity			Values		
	Total	Male	Female	16-29	30-49	50+	Lower	Medium	Upper	Lower	Middle	Upper	Left	Center	Right	Mat	Mixed	Postmat
India	80	79	82	79	81	82	82	81	79	78	80	80	81	77	59	83	77	78
Nigeria	54	54	55	52	53	77	57	54	54	56	48	48	45	53	na	50	56	56
China	70	69	72	60	75	74	73	72	65	73	71	66	na	na	76	74	67	59
Romania	77	74	80	72	80	78	79	76	77	81	76	74	78	77	na	79	78	66
Turkey	79	79	80	72	83	85	81	80	70	77	77	79	72	81	79	82	79	76
Poland	64	64	65	57	68	65	63	72	67	61	62	65	67	62	65	69	63	60
Bulgaria	69	69	70	64	71	71	70	70	63	66	67	71	62	67	80	75	69	59
Chile	85	85	85	81	87	89	87	83	85	84	84	85	83	85	84	83	85	85
Czechoslovakia	na	na	na	na	na	na	na	na	na	na	na	na	na	na	na	na	na	na
South Africa	74	71	77	67	77	84	74	73	85	64	66	81	65	76	74	83	70	66
Lithuania	76	73	78	67	77	82	80	75	73	78	74	70	na	na	na	78	75	77
Hungary	80	81	80	79	81	81	80	82	72	70	70	74	81	80	79	80	79	94
Argentina	95	94	95	91	95	96	95	95	94	95	95	90	87	94	95	96	95	93
Brazil	80	80	81	73	83	88	87	79	71	82	79	74	72	80	82	85	78	68
Mexico	58	55	62	54	62	62	57	64	57	55	56	52	55	55	61	55	59	67
Belarus	67	71	63	58	70	70	69	64	70	61	62	65	67	65	65	67	68	70
Russia	76	71	80	68	75	82	77	76	75	77	75	72	72	73	76	78	76	71
Moscow	65	61	68	54	65	73	72	66	63	65	55	63	64	67	64	66	66	61
Latvia	86	83	88	85	86	86	77	86	88	90	82	80	na	na	na	84	87	86
Estonia	81	79	83	74	81	89	82	81	82	79	75	80	na	na	na	80	82	83
Portugal	76	75	76	72	77	78	75	80	75	75	76	71	69	78	76	77	75	72
South Korea	86	85	86	81	87	90	90	85	85	82	83	86	80	84	88	86	86	80
Ireland	77	75	78	63	78	84	78	76	69	80	80	73	57	75	85	78	78	72
North Ireland	81	78	83	65	81	92	83	84	59	78	80	77	82	80	86	86	82	67
Slovenia	72	67	77	56	77	78	72	71	73	72	73	61	66	70	73	76	72	58
Spain	81	78	84	74	81	86	83	82	71	84	78	77	73	81	81	84	80	76
East Germany	72	67	77	62	70	81	75	69	66	76	70	69	71	75	64	78	73	69
Britain	73	72	74	62	70	82	74	70	70	76	69	73	66	72	80	79	72	70
Italy	76	73	79	70	78	80	76	77	80	77	74	73	75	76	73	79	75	76
Netherlands	70	73	69	62	73	75	72	69	69	66	72	74	68	71	72	71	71	69
Belgium	73	68	77	67	74	76	73	73	68	67	67	70	64	72	74	72	75	68
Austria	76	71	79	68	77	79	75	77	79	78	76	74	76	77	72	78	78	71
France	74	74	74	70	77	74	72	76	76	69	75	77	71	75	75	75	73	76
Canada	66	66	67	58	66	74	73	66	62	70	65	61	52	69	68	70	66	67
United States	71	69	74	67	71	73	76	71	67	75	68	68	61	71	75	79	69	69
Iceland	74	73	75	65	74	84	83	73	67	na	na	na	67	75	75	76	73	69
West Germany	67	64	70	60	66	72	68	66	62	65	67	67	61	66	74	66	68	65
Denmark	81	76	86	74	80	89	86	80	80	85	72	85	70	81	88	81	82	77
Finland	29	30	28	22	27	41	36	29	27	37	25	25	16	26	37	48	28	27
Norway	77	74	81	76	76	87	86	74	76	78	75	73	71	79	79	80	78	66
Sweden	79	77	81	73	80	83	80	80	75	76	80	81	76	78	81	83	80	73
Japan	80	76	84	77	83	79	81	81	78	84	76	80	71	78	74	82	79	76
Switzerland	83	78	86	82	78	88	85	84	70	86	80	75	80	80	86	88	83	79
Total	**74**	**72**	**76**	**67**	**75**	**80**	**76**	**74**	**71**	**74**	**72**	**72**	**68**	**73**	**75**	**77**	**74**	**71**

Ranking:

Argentina	95
Latvia	86
South Korea	86
Chile	85
Switzerland	83
Estonia	81
North Ireland	81
Spain	81
Denmark	81
India	80
Hungary	80
Brazil	80
Japan	80
Turkey	79
Sweden	79
Romania	77
Ireland	77
Norway	77
Lithuania	76
Russia	76
Portugal	76
Italy	76
Austria	76
South Africa	74
France	74
Iceland	74
Britain	73
Belgium	73
Slovenia	72
East Germany	72
United States	71
China	70
Netherlands	70
Bulgaria	69
Belarus	67
West Germany	67
Canada	66
Moscow	65
Poland	64
Mexico	58
Nigeria	54
Finland	29

Note: Countries in the left column are ranked according to GNP per capita. / The percentages in the bottom row give each country an equal weight. / na=not ascertained.

V316 KILL IN SELF-DEFENSE

Please tell me for each of the following statements whether you think it can always be justified, never be justified, or something in between.

Killing in self-defense (% "never justified" — code 1 from a ten-point scale where 1=never and 10=always)

	Total	Gender Male	Gender Female	Age 16-29	Age 30-49	Age 50+	Education Lower	Education Medium	Education Upper	Income Lower	Income Middle	Income Upper	Political Affinity Left	Political Affinity Center	Political Affinity Right	Values Mat	Values Mixed	Values Postmat	Ranking	
India	39	35	43	39	38	44	43	41	35	37	32	32	44	35	31	34	39	46	Japan	51
Nigeria	41	36	46	40	39	61	48	41	36	29	28	37	40	40	37	38	41	41	Turkey	46
China	15	16	14	15	14	18	22	13	12	08	13	09	na	na	na	16	14	16	Chile	43
Romania	37	34	39	34	34	41	41	34	33	31	34	28	34	37	33	41	35	14	Nigeria	41
Turkey	46	40	52	42	47	50	53	38	32	36	36	32	38	44	45	47	49	38	Austria	41
Poland	23	21	25	22	24	22	21	25	20	20	16	22	16	21	24	27	22	16	India	39
Bulgaria	29	29	30	25	29	33	38	29	20	22	24	24	22	25	30	35	28	20	South Africa	39
Chile	43	37	48	38	44	50	52	40	35	42	36	28	37	42	45	48	41	38	Spain	38
Czechoslovakia	na	na	na	na	na	na	na	na	na	na	na	na	na	na	na	na	na	na	Romania	37
South Africa	39	38	40	37	37	48	54	34	10	43	35	12	34	32	32	44	37	39	Slovenia	37
Lithuania	22	16	26	17	20	27	25	21	20	23	15	18	na	na	na	25	21	17	Hungary	36
Hungary	36	33	38	33	30	42	41	30	35	33	29	18	37	32	32	35	36	38	East Germany	36
Argentina	31	23	37	21	33	36	36	32	18	27	20	13	14	24	26	36	31	23	Switzerland	36
Brazil	35	28	41	32	32	46	49	33	15	28	24	16	29	29	39	36	31	28	Brazil	35
Mexico	25	21	29	25	22	31	25	31	19	20	19	15	19	23	29	39	33	13	South Korea	33
Belarus	13	11	14	09	11	19	22	13	09	12	08	07	10	09	24	14	26	13	Argentina	31
Russia	15	10	19	11	14	20	23	15	11	11	11	07	08	13	20	17	13	02	Denmark	31
Moscow	12	10	14	09	08	21	19	08	12	07	08	07	09	14	28	14	15	11	Bulgaria	29
Latvia	23	20	26	22	22	30	35	24	19	17	15	06	na	na	na	17	11	13	Sweden	27
Estonia	15	12	17	13	12	21	24	13	10	11	14	14	na	na	na	14	11	23	North Ireland	26
Portugal	24	26	23	18	23	31	28	14	13	23	08	16	na	na	na	27	23	07	Italy	26
South Korea	33	37	29	22	36	43	57	35	18	23	18	10	24	24	23	28	22	19	West Germany	26
Ireland	25	22	28	17	21	34	32	19	14	31	26	13	23	32	36	38	30	21	Mexico	26
North Ireland	26	20	30	18	21	34	28	19	14	31	26	13	17	22	30	22	28	19	Ireland	25
Slovenia	37	30	43	31	35	42	42	35	30	29	34	24	26	26	29	27	26	16	Portugal	24
Spain	38	34	42	26	36	49	43	29	23	41	29	23	26	34	29	42	37	10	Poland	23
East Germany	36	31	40	27	28	48	39	34	26	42	27	23	29	35	36	46	37	22	Latvia	23
Britain	16	13	19	07	14	24	20	08	07	21	14	23	26	39	40	42	36	32	France	23
Italy	26	19	31	19	23	32	26	19	24	21	14	05	16	14	17	19	16	11	Lithuania	22
Netherlands	15	17	15	09	15	23	22	12	11	27	18	09	26	25	20	32	24	19	Belgium	22
Belgium	22	18	27	20	20	28	27	22	14	14	12	11	12	15	20	20	16	12	Iceland	21
Austria	41	37	44	32	39	47	41	42	32	42	33	10	16	22	19	28	23	13	Norway	21
France	23	22	24	18	19	31	29	18	16	21	19	36	39	40	40	57	42	29	United States	18
Canada	14	14	14	13	11	20	25	13	09	21	11	11	22	22	20	28	21	22	Britain	16
United States	18	15	20	16	16	19	28	19	07	16	13	07	11	14	14	16	15	12	China	15
Iceland	21	19	24	13	13	32	34	18	14	17	na	09	18	15	17	24	16	14	Russia	15
West Germany	26	21	30	17	21	31	29	22	18	26	20	18	20	20	22	29	20	10	Estonia	15
Denmark	31	22	39	22	25	31	22	25	24	27	25	17	25	25	26	27	26	21	Netherlands	15
Finland	13	13	13	09	11	20	24	30	32	25	32	08	23	32	32	41	31	19	Canada	14
Norway	21	19	24	11	20	31	39	21	13	17	09	17	12	15	17	31	11	13	Belarus	13
Sweden	27	23	31	13	25	38	40	21	16	23	26	19	23	23	22	29	19	15	Finland	13
Japan	51	48	55	38	48	64	60	53	40	58	48	45	51	46	47	33	30	16	Moscow	12
Switzerland	36	30	42	28	32	44	37	40	19	35	27	18	22	34	34	48	47	44		
Total	28	24	31	22	26	35	35	26	19	26	22	17	24	27	28	32	27	21		

Note: Countries in the left column are ranked according to GNP per capita. / The percentages in the bottom row give each country an equal weight. / na=not ascertained.

V317 ASSASSINATIONS

Please tell me for each of the following statements whether you think it can always be justified, never be justified, or something in between. Political assassinations (% "never justified"—code 1 from a ten-point scale where 1=never and 10=always)

	Total	Gender		Age			Education			Income			Political Affinity			Values		
		Male	Female	16-29	30-49	50+	Lower	Medium	Upper	Lower	Middle	Upper	Left	Center	Right	Mat	Mixed	Postmat
India	82	80	85	80	83	84	86	82	82	81	83	79	84	77	63	84	79	76
Nigeria	64	67	59	61	66	78	65	62	65	65	61	58	63	63	63	58	65	75
China	na	na	na	na	na	na	na	na	na	na	na	na	na	na	na	na	na	na
Romania	82	80	83	70	84	88	88	77	80	87	83	75	83	83	78	86	81	65
Turkey	na	na	na	na	na	na	na	na	na	na	na	na	na	na	na	na	na	na
Poland	72	71	72	62	71	78	71	72	70	68	70	71	72	72	68	77	71	65
Bulgaria	74	74	74	72	72	77	79	74	70	72	71	74	69	73	81	78	73	74
Chile	88	87	90	81	92	94	91	85	90	88	87	88	83	90	89	90	89	85
Czechoslovakia	na	na	na	na	na	na	na	na	na	na	na	na	na	na	na	na	na	na
South Africa	76	74	79	70	78	85	85	73	71	71	71	72	70	74	70	82	75	65
Lithuania	80	78	83	67	84	88	90	77	81	84	79	75	na	na	na	86	79	75
Hungary	86	85	87	76	86	91	88	84	88	77	73	80	88	86	87	87	86	89
Argentina	93	92	93	87	93	97	93	93	91	92	91	92	86	92	93	94	94	87
Brazil	92	91	92	90	92	94	92	91	91	93	92	89	87	92	92	93	91	86
Mexico	54	52	57	54	53	57	51	60	58	50	53	50	45	54	57	58	54	57
Belarus	65	69	61	52	67	73	63	59	71	62	60	63	61	68	69	66	65	63
Russia	78	77	79	66	78	86	84	74	78	77	78	77	77	77	75	81	77	67
Moscow	64	64	63	51	63	76	66	62	64	60	59	63	63	60	65	61	64	65
Latvia	78	78	77	65	81	85	73	78	79	75	75	76	na	na	na	73	80	79
Estonia	75	72	79	65	78	82	76	76	73	75	70	70	na	na	na	78	73	74
Portugal	83	82	84	76	85	89	86	81	75	84	86	77	75	86	85	89	81	73
South Korea	74	72	75	66	75	83	78	75	70	70	73	74	68	69	78	77	71	65
Ireland	73	68	77	66	71	79	75	74	61	72	79	67	51	74	76	69	76	70
North Ireland	78	72	82	63	78	88	80	81	55	75	77	73	71	83	73	80	77	77
Slovenia	76	73	79	65	78	83	75	77	79	75	76	73	76	73	71	80	75	71
Spain	85	83	87	77	86	90	88	84	74	89	85	79	77	86	88	90	84	77
East Germany	91	91	91	85	92	93	91	88	92	92	92	88	88	94	89	94	91	90
Britain	69	68	70	55	67	79	72	68	53	75	67	65	64	67	74	69	71	65
Italy	88	86	90	82	88	91	89	83	81	89	90	84	84	91	89	86	90	85
Netherlands	74	79	72	63	77	82	79	75	73	66	80	72	68	74	80	77	75	70
Belgium	75	72	78	67	73	82	78	75	69	78	71	71	69	76	73	79	77	67
Austria	87	83	90	82	86	90	88	87	84	90	86	86	87	87	84	92	88	82
France	69	70	69	62	69	76	71	68	69	70	62	71	67	69	68	68	71	69
Canada	72	70	75	62	72	81	77	73	68	76	72	69	63	74	73	75	73	70
United States	72	71	75	67	71	76	76	74	67	77	69	68	67	72	71	77	69	76
Iceland	88	89	88	84	88	93	90	93	84	84	85	na	84	87	91	92	87	89
West Germany	79	77	81	74	79	83	81	77	76	82	75	79	73	81	82	83	82	74
Denmark	94	92	95	89	94	97	97	94	92	92	92	94	91	94	94	94	95	88
Finland	57	54	61	53	58	58	57	53	61	60	55	56	67	53	56	52	57	59
Norway	91	90	92	85	91	95	95	92	88	92	92	89	91	93	90	92	91	89
Sweden	88	87	90	84	89	91	91	89	82	89	89	88	91	88	87	90	90	84
Japan	74	70	77	64	73	81	77	75	66	77	74	72	74	70	73	75	71	69
Switzerland	83	81	85	78	78	90	87	84	66	82	82	75	66	87	84	95	85	72
Total	**78**	**77**	**79**	**70**	**78**	**84**	**80**	**77**	**75**	**78**	**76**	**75**	**74**	**78**	**78**	**80**	**78**	**74**

Ranking:

Denmark	94
Argentina	93
Brazil	92
East Germany	91
Norway	91
Chile	88
Italy	88
Iceland	88
Sweden	88
Austria	87
Hungary	86
Spain	85
Portugal	83
Switzerland	83
India	82
Romania	82
Lithuania	80
West Germany	79
Russia	78
Latvia	78
North Ireland	78
South Africa	76
Slovenia	75
Estonia	75
Belgium	75
Bulgaria	74
South Korea	74
Netherlands	74
Japan	74
Ireland	73
Poland	72
Canada	72
United States	72
Britain	69
France	69
Belarus	65
Nigeria	64
Moscow	64
Finland	57
Mexico	54

Note: Countries in the left column are ranked according to GNP per capita. / The percentages in the bottom row give each country an equal weight. / na=not ascertained.

V318 THROW LITTER

Please tell me for each of the following statements whether you think it can always be justified, never be justified, or something in between. Throwing away litter in a public place (% "never justified"—code 1 from a ten-point scale where 1=never and 10=always)

	Total	Gender		Age			Education			Income			Political Affinity			Values		
		Male	Female	16-29	30-49	50+	Lower	Medium	Upper	Lower	Middle	Upper	Left	Center	Right	Mat	Mixed	Postmat
India	85	84	85	85	84	85	83	85	85	84	84	84	89	81	76	87	82	78
Nigeria	66	68	62	65	65	75	68	65	66	66	66	61	57	67	68	59	70	66
China	77	77	78	75	79	77	81	74	83	78	83	71	na	na	na	77	79	78
Romania	84	82	86	80	86	86	86	82	86	84	85	82	86	83	84	85	83	87
Turkey	85	85	84	81	88	86	84	86	85	83	87	83	86	86	82	85	85	83
Poland	na	na	na	na	na	na	na	na	na	na	na	na	na	na	na	na	na	na
Bulgaria	79	74	83	73	81	80	80	79	78	79	78	75	71	80	82	81	79	72
Chile	82	82	82	76	84	88	86	79	80	82	82	82	79	82	84	81	82	83
Czechoslovakia	na	na	na	na	na	na	na	na	na	na	na	na	na	na	na	na	na	na
South Africa	na	na	na	na	na	na	na	na	na	na	na	na	na	na	na	na	na	na
Lithuania	69	64	74	51	74	80	74	67	76	73	67	62	na	na	na	71	69	69
Hungary	67	64	69	54	64	75	73	62	57	67	59	62	65	69	66	67	66	68
Argentina	86	85	87	81	86	90	88	87	84	87	83	84	83	80	92	84	88	85
Brazil	85	83	87	79	88	91	85	85	80	89	84	82	82	84	85	89	84	77
Mexico	57	56	58	56	58	58	56	56	61	54	57	51	51	58	59	60	58	56
Belarus	70	69	71	59	70	83	80	66	72	68	66	70	68	73	69	70	72	61
Russia	70	62	76	56	67	82	74	68	69	71	72	67	65	65	69	77	66	62
Moscow	60	54	66	48	60	71	65	61	59	59	57	55	60	62	56	63	60	58
Latvia	89	84	93	84	90	93	89	89	90	91	88	87	na	na	na	89	90	85
Estonia	78	72	83	71	78	85	75	80	76	80	73	73	na	na	na	78	77	76
Portugal	73	71	75	70	76	73	73	75	74	72	78	70	69	75	73	76	72	72
South Korea	88	86	89	80	90	95	89	89	85	87	85	91	88	84	90	89	86	88
Ireland	70	66	74	54	74	77	70	71	68	74	67	72	59	70	77	70	72	67
North Ireland	61	59	62	32	53	88	62	64	43	64	63	54	46	59	71	71	60	47
Slovenia	75	74	77	64	79	79	74	77	76	77	74	71	68	76	67	80	75	61
Spain	80	76	82	70	83	84	82	79	70	86	78	74	77	73	83	83	77	72
East Germany	65	59	71	52	60	79	68	61	58	74	62	60	63	66	63	76	65	60
Britain	64	60	67	43	62	77	65	65	64	68	56	66	55	64	70	64	63	63
Italy	76	73	79	69	75	82	78	78	80	78	75	74	77	76	78	78	75	76
Netherlands	64	67	63	48	67	79	72	62	57	59	67	63	61	64	68	67	67	59
Belgium	69	64	73	57	70	75	74	68	61	69	67	65	67	70	66	77	67	67
Austria	67	62	70	59	66	72	67	67	56	73	68	62	69	68	63	76	68	60
France	75	75	75	70	79	76	73	73	77	72	74	78	77	73	72	77	75	75
Canada	73	72	74	60	75	82	69	73	71	77	74	71	71	74	73	76	72	76
United States	72	72	72	63	70	79	77	74	66	75	71	69	66	74	73	73	72	74
Iceland	66	63	70	52	67	83	74	66	60	74	na	na	64	68	66	76	65	51
West Germany	62	56	67	52	63	67	63	59	63	62	60	63	55	64	64	63	63	60
Denmark	79	75	84	64	82	88	89	76	79	80	80	79	72	82	81	79	82	68
Finland	42	37	48	27	41	58	48	45	37	46	42	39	49	37	42	47	45	35
Norway	70	65	75	47	65	90	91	65	63	75	70	62	66	72	68	78	69	55
Sweden	52	47	56	38	49	67	63	45	46	55	55	46	51	53	50	59	53	46
Japan	73	72	73	61	73	80	78	73	68	70	69	74	68	70	73	79	69	70
Switzerland	na	na	na	na	na	na	na	na	na	na	na	na	na	na	na	na	na	na
Total	72	69	74	62	72	80	76	71	69	73	71	69	68	71	72	75	72	68

Ranking:

Latvia	89
South Korea	88
Argentina	86
India	85
Turkey	85
Brazil	85
Romania	84
Chile	82
Spain	80
Bulgaria	79
Denmark	79
Estonia	78
China	77
Italy	76
Slovenia	75
France	75
Portugal	73
Canada	73
Japan	73
United States	72
Belarus	70
Russia	70
Ireland	70
Norway	70
Lithuania	69
Belgium	69
Hungary	67
Austria	67
Nigeria	66
Iceland	66
East Germany	65
Britain	64
Netherlands	64
West Germany	62
North Ireland	61
Moscow	60
Mexico	57
Sweden	52
Finland	42

Note: Countries in the left column are ranked according to GNP per capita. / The percentages in the bottom row give each country an equal weight. / na=not ascertained.

V319 DRINK & DRIVE

Please tell me for each of the following statements whether you think it can always be justified, never be justified, or something in between. Driving under the influence of alcohol (% "never justified" – code 1 from a ten-point scale where 1=never and 10=always)

	Total	Gender		Age			Education			Income			Political Affinity			Values			Ranking:	
		Male	Female	16-29	30-49	50+	Lower	Medium	Upper	Lower	Middle	Upper	Left	Center	Right	Mat	Mixed	Postmat		
India	88	86	91	87	87	89	88	88	86	89	88	86	92	86	79	88	87	83	Argentina	93
Nigeria	74	75	74	74	73	88	76	76	72	75	72	72	71	74	75	71	75	84	Brazil	91
China	86	86	87	85	87	86	87	86	86	89	86	83	na	na	na	87	85	85	North Ireland	90
Romania	83	78	88	74	83	88	90	81	76	87	82	79	81	85	na	87	81	70	Denmark	90
Turkey	88	86	89	85	90	87	90	84	82	88	89	84	88	87	86	88	89	83	Sweden	89
Poland	82	77	86	70	80	89	83	81	80	80	83	79	84	78	84	83	82	75	India	88
Bulgaria	86	84	89	83	85	90	92	85	84	85	87	84	79	87	87	88	88	76	Turkey	88
Chile	87	83	90	81	88	93	90	87	82	90	87	83	84	86	85	88	86	84	Norway	88
Czechoslovakia	na	na	na	na	na	na	na	na	na	na	na	na	na	na	na	na	na	na	Chile	87
South Africa	86	85	88	84	87	89	91	85	79	77	82	79	84	85	82	89	86	82	East Germany	87
Lithuania	73	63	82	55	75	87	84	69	76	79	69	66	na	na	na	77	73	64	China	86
Hungary	86	82	90	78	84	91	90	83	81	78	76	75	85	87	83	88	84	86	Bulgaria	86
Argentina	93	90	96	90	94	95	94	95	90	96	92	89	86	92	91	94	94	92	South Africa	86
Brazil	91	88	93	86	92	96	95	89	86	93	90	88	87	90	91	92	90	89	Hungary	86
Mexico	59	54	64	56	60	64	60	59	57	59	58	49	50	59	61	64	59	55	Britain	86
Belarus	75	72	77	67	75	82	79	71	78	74	71	70	74	74	74	74	77	64	South Korea	85
Russia	83	76	89	71	83	93	89	84	80	86	85	79	80	80	79	89	81	71	Italy	85
Moscow	77	72	82	63	77	88	85	77	76	77	71	73	76	79	78	80	78	72	Romania	83
Latvia	77	70	81	66	77	89	82	77	74	80	74	73	na	na	na	84	76	77	Russia	83
Estonia	76	68	83	64	76	82	82	75	75	74	74	77	na	na	na	80	75	68	Canada	83
Portugal	76	70	81	63	81	83	78	73	68	77	78	70	75	78	71	82	73	67	Poland	82
South Korea	85	87	82	82	84	91	91	84	82	86	84	83	84	83	86	86	84	83	United States	82
Ireland	81	74	87	67	82	88	84	79	69	87	79	78	72	80	85	80	82	79	Ireland	81
North Ireland	90	88	92	81	92	96	90	94	86	96	88	89	79	92	93	92	92	82	Spain	81
Slovenia	72	62	80	54	73	82	76	69	66	77	68	63	63	71	64	80	69	61	Netherlands	81
Spain	81	76	85	68	83	89	84	77	71	89	80	74	75	78	85	85	79	75	Iceland	80
East Germany	87	80	92	76	86	94	87	86	85	90	84	85	88	86	83	91	86	85	Finland	79
Britain	86	82	90	83	82	91	88	87	76	90	84	82	87	85	86	90	85	86	Moscow	77
Italy	85	82	88	77	83	91	85	81	89	87	85	75	84	86	85	88	85	82	Latvia	77
Netherlands	81	73	84	78	82	84	86	81	76	77	84	77	82	84	78	91	82	78	Estonia	76
Belgium	67	58	75	54	64	78	74	66	55	68	61	60	54	71	65	72	67	62	Portugal	76
Austria	72	63	78	67	68	78	73	72	69	78	72	68	74	74	69	79	73	67	Belarus	75
France	70	63	76	67	68	75	73	67	69	75	66	66	64	71	72	81	69	64	Japan	75
Canada	83	79	86	77	80	90	87	81	80	85	82	80	82	83	82	86	83	83	Nigeria	74
United States	82	81	84	75	80	88	86	81	80	86	80	79	76	83	82	82	82	83	Lithuania	73
Iceland	80	75	86	71	81	90	92	82	70	na	na	na	80	79	78	86	79	72	Switzerland	73
West Germany	64	54	72	54	60	73	67	59	59	68	61	62	59	66	64	68	66	59	Slovenia	72
Denmark	90	86	95	89	90	92	94	91	88	93	88	90	88	92	89	93	91	86	Austria	72
Finland	79	74	85	75	80	80	77	81	77	77	81	77	79	78	80	79	80	77	France	70
Norway	88	82	94	83	85	95	94	86	86	88	87	83	85	90	87	91	88	80	Belgium	67
Sweden	89	84	94	87	88	91	93	89	81	90	93	86	90	90	86	92	90	84	West Germany	64
Japan	75	72	78	56	75	87	85	76	63	79	71	74	68	72	72	76	73	65	Mexico	59
Switzerland	73	66	79	59	68	83	73	75	58	78	69	57	63	71	74	87	73	64		
Total	81	76	85	73	80	87	84	80	76	82	79	76	78	81	80	84	80	76		

Note: Countries in the left column are ranked according to GNP per capita. / The percentages in the bottom row give each country an equal weight. / na=not ascertained.

V320. Which of these geographical groups would you say you belong to first of all?

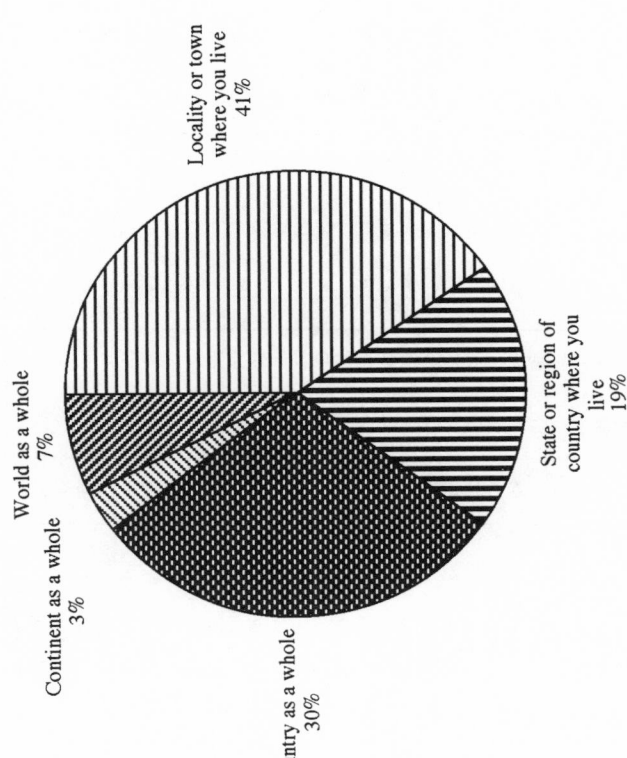

Locality or town where you live
41%

State or region of country where you live
19%

Country as a whole
30%

Continent as a whole
3%

World as a whole
7%

V322. How proud are you to be (nationality)?

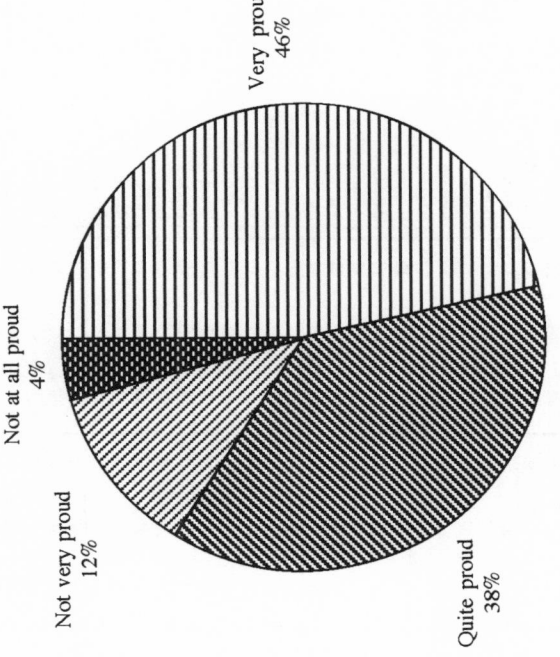

Very proud
46%

Quite proud
38%

Not very proud
12%

Not at all proud
4%

V320 GEOGRAPHICAL GROUPS: TOWN

Which of these geographical groups would you say you belong to first of all?
(% "Locality or town where you live")

	Total	Gender		Age			Education			Income			Political Affinity			Values			Ranking:	
		Male	Female	16-29	30-49	50+	Lower	Medium	Upper	Lower	Middle	Upper	Left	Center	Right	Mat	Mixed	Postmat		
India	37	37	38	33	39	44	50	37	40	47	32	34	35	33	31	40	33	25	Norway	69
Nigeria	40	42	36	37	41	57	46	37	40	39	42	39	46	43	35	35	44	33	Hungary	58
China	42	39	47	35	44	47	52	38	33	45	41	37	na	na	na	46	38	34	Sweden	56
Romania	48	43	53	46	45	52	57	48	37	51	49	45	48	49	46	51	49	27	Belarus	52
Turkey	34	30	37	31	33	39	34	32	34	32	37	32	31	34	32	38	33	31	Denmark	52
Poland	29	30	28	25	27	34	37	25	18	30	30	27	31	29	29	36	27	18	Bulgaria	51
Bulgaria	51	49	52	45	49	56	59	55	36	46	51	56	51	46	42	55	51	37	Moscow	51
Chile	33	31	34	34	31	33	37	33	27	38	32	28	30	35	28	35	34	29	Switzerland	51
Czechoslovakia	32	31	32	34	30	31	37	30	25	31	32	32	30	36	25	36	30	27	Romania	48
South Africa	38	33	42	37	37	41	46	34	31	43	36	31	28	34	37	40	37	30	North Ireland	48
Lithuania	25	21	29	24	25	27	28	26	16	30	24	18	na	na	na	32	25	13	Belgium	47
Hungary	58	58	58	58	51	64	65	52	48	65	55	45	51	56	50	57	59	53	Slovenia	46
Argentina	28	26	30	30	28	28	25	35	26	26	28	33	26	29	37	30	28	27	Spain	46
Brazil	37	34	40	37	37	36	43	35	32	40	34	34	39	35	35	40	36	26	Ireland	44
Mexico	38	37	39	38	35	48	41	36	32	40	38	33	32	38	39	45	38	35	Netherlands	44
Belarus	52	50	54	47	49	65	69	51	47	53	56	47	47	57	61	63	49	31	China	42
Russia	33	30	35	35	30	35	34	37	29	44	37	37	29	33	31	34	33	27	Italy	41
Moscow	51	48	54	48	51	55	59	58	46	53	54	44	50	53	47	57	49	47	France	41
Latvia	34	30	36	37	30	39	30	36	31	33	29	37	na	na	na	40	33	24	Iceland	41
Estonia	31	32	31	30	31	33	31	32	30	31	30	33	32	38	39	29	32	27	Nigeria	40
Portugal	40	38	43	35	39	47	45	30	31	49	36	30	37	40	39	40	41	32	Portugal	40
South Korea	18	18	18	15	18	22	42	18	06	28	15	07	17	21	17	19	19	13	Britain	40
Ireland	44	42	46	37	47	46	46	44	31	45	45	41	43	45	42	48	45	37	South Africa	38
North Ireland	48	44	51	40	48	55	47	50	52	48	56	41	32	50	48	65	48	22	Mexico	38
Slovenia	46	42	49	40	48	47	52	46	34	51	42	44	44	41	47	48	45	42	India	37
Spain	46	43	48	45	44	49	49	40	35	56	46	37	44	46	37	53	43	40	Brazil	37
East Germany	25	20	30	20	22	32	28	22	17	44	34	29	22	27	19	36	26	16	United States	37
Britain	40	34	45	40	36	43	42	35	32	44	33	32	42	42	31	41	42	32	Japan	36
Italy	41	40	43	35	42	45	42	37	24	45	37	33	40	42	36	49	42	32	Austria	35
Netherlands	44	38	47	42	47	44	49	49	34	40	46	42	38	47	44	55	47	37	West Germany	35
Belgium	47	44	49	40	47	51	53	45	37	47	45	44	42	46	49	52	48	38	Turkey	34
Austria	35	32	36	29	30	41	39	33	17	38	36	29	38	32	33	44	35	28	Latvia	34
France	41	38	43	34	42	44	45	41	28	48	40	31	34	45	42	54	43	24	Chile	33
Canada	31	30	32	30	32	30	37	31	26	35	30	26	25	33	24	38	32	25	Russia	33
United States	37	34	41	34	35	41	41	38	34	40	38	33	31	47	38	44	36	35	Finland	33
Iceland	41	44	37	35	38	51	50	43	32	na	na	na	34	40	45	55	37	27	Czechoslovakia	32
West Germany	35	33	37	29	30	43	42	26	20	49	38	31	29	36	41	48	37	25	Estonia	31
Denmark	52	52	53	44	56	55	64	51	47	53	56	43	51	56	47	65	51	42	Canada	31
Finland	33	30	36	35	29	41	34	39	25	35	35	26	33	32	32	34	36	25	Poland	29
Norway	69	68	71	63	68	74	73	72	64	67	69	70	66	72	69	77	67	59	Argentina	28
Sweden	56	55	58	53	55	61	67	54	43	58	59	54	57	58	54	70	58	43	Lithuania	25
Japan	36	35	38	37	33	41	43	35	32	37	37	34	26	33	38	34	35	30	East Germany	25
Switzerland	51	50	52	39	50	57	52	54	34	56	47	50	34	54	58	66	51	42	South Korea	18
Total	40	38	42	37	39	45	46	40	32	44	40	36	38	41	39	46	40	31		

Note: Countries in the left column are ranked according to GNP per capita. ¹ The percentages in the bottom row give each country an equal weight. / na=not ascertained.

V320 GEOGRAPHICAL GROUPS: COUNTRY

Which of these geographical groups would you say you belong to first of all?

(% "The country as a whole")

Country	Total	Gender		Age			Education			Income			Political Affinity			Values		
		Male	Female	16-29	30-49	50+	Lower	Medium	Upper	Lower	Middle	Upper	Left	Center	Right	Mat	Mixed	Postmat
India	39	40	38	42	39	33	29	40	43	30	43	42	42	42	43	40	41	40
Nigeria	30	30	30	31	28	25	33	28	31	31	28	29	23	27	33	36	26	27
China	38	40	36	42	37	36	30	42	43	36	37	42	na	na	na	36	42	36
Romania	32	36	28	33	33	30	26	33	38	30	30	35	35	31	30	31	33	32
Turkey	46	48	43	43	48	45	50	43	30	50	46	40	39	47	50	49	46	39
Poland	52	49	55	48	52	54	48	53	65	54	50	52	46	50	55	47	54	56
Bulgaria	30	30	30	28	31	30	28	27	36	34	29	26	31	34	30	31	30	39
Chile	40	39	40	33	42	45	40	41	38	39	40	39	40	38	44	40	39	39
Czechoslovakia	32	30	33	28	32	35	33	30	34	33	32	30	37	31	30	31	32	29
South Africa	33	35	31	32	35	31	24	37	42	27	32	44	43	36	34	30	35	36
Lithuania	03	04	03	02	03	04	02	03	07	03	03	02	na	na	na	04	03	01
Hungary	27	26	29	24	31	25	23	30	40	21	30	40	33	29	32	28	27	29
Argentina	58	58	58	55	58	60	63	51	57	62	58	53	55	56	49	62	56	56
Brazil	30	33	28	28	33	31	28	32	29	29	35	31	28	33	30	29	31	29
Mexico	28	29	28	26	31	29	26	36	29	28	25	36	27	31	26	27	28	21
Belarus	12	12	12	09	14	12	08	11	15	10	12	15	13	10	12	10	13	23
Russia	10	10	11	08	10	12	12	08	12	10	12	17	09	11	10	13	09	05
Moscow	19	20	17	18	19	18	18	17	19	18	17	21	17	22	20	20	18	19
Latvia	06	08	04	06	07	04	06	05	07	03	09	06	na	na	na	07	07	00
Estonia	08	10	07	07	09	10	09	09	06	09	08	07	na	na	na	10	08	02
Portugal	27	27	26	30	28	23	24	28	36	22	30	34	25	26	29	25	25	38
South Korea	58	60	57	57	58	60	40	53	74	48	59	69	56	54	62	59	56	65
Ireland	37	38	37	42	34	37	34	39	50	35	36	42	39	36	41	37	36	44
North Ireland	22	24	18	24	23	18	21	23	21	16	15	25	18	21	22	09	24	29
Slovenia	42	42	41	46	39	42	37	44	48	36	47	41	39	44	41	39	43	39
Spain	29	29	29	20	30	35	31	24	27	26	28	29	24	28	44	31	31	21
East Germany	09	07	11	07	12	09	09	09	12	12	13	14	20	05	02	08	10	07
Britain	32	35	29	23	31	33	26	28	35	25	28	36	33	30	41	35	30	34
Italy	28	24	31	31	24	31	28	26	18	28	27	29	26	29	35	29	29	25
Netherlands	34	38	33	33	33	37	34	32	37	39	33	33	38	32	36	32	34	36
Belgium	22	21	22	21	18	25	23	23	17	24	22	20	15	22	22	29	23	16
Austria	27	28	27	23	31	26	26	28	35	25	28	28	33	28	27	19	29	28
France	28	30	26	25	25	33	28	28	28	28	25	29	26	27	34	23	29	30
Canada	40	40	40	35	37	46	39	38	42	38	40	43	35	40	47	39	40	38
United States	31	34	27	29	30	33	29	32	31	27	34	32	29	32	31	32	30	32
Iceland	48	46	51	51	50	42	39	43	59	na	na	na	57	48	44	37	52	53
West Germany	14	15	14	14	13	15	14	15	13	14	13	18	12	16	14	15	16	10
Denmark	22	22	22	27	21	19	15	24	24	21	19	29	21	27	25	23	21	29
Finland	41	43	40	35	44	41	34	35	53	40	39	46	40	38	44	47	40	44
Norway	14	15	13	15	15	13	12	12	17	13	13	16	11	14	16	13	16	10
Sweden	25	23	26	26	25	22	17	26	33	22	23	28	21	23	29	15	25	31
Japan	43	45	41	41	42	46	42	43	44	42	42	46	43	44	47	44	45	46
Switzerland	17	17	17	19	15	18	19	16	16	13	18	15	15	17	20	16	17	17
Total	**29**	**30**	**29**	**28**	**30**	**30**	**27**	**29**	**32**	**28**	**29**	**31**	**30**	**31**	**33**	**29**	**30**	**30**

Ranking:

Country	Ranking
Argentina	58
South Korea	58
Poland	52
Iceland	48
Turkey	46
Japan	43
Slovenia	42
Finland	41
Chile	40
Canada	40
India	39
China	38
Ireland	37
Netherlands	34
South Africa	33
Romania	32
Czechoslovakia	32
Britain	32
United States	31
Nigeria	30
Bulgaria	30
Brazil	30
Spain	29
Mexico	28
Italy	28
France	28
Hungary	27
Portugal	27
Austria	27
Sweden	25
North Ireland	22
Belgium	22
Denmark	22
Moscow	19
Switzerland	17
West Germany	14
Norway	14
Belarus	12
Russia	10
East Germany	09
Estonia	08
Latvia	06
Lithuania	03

Note: Countries in the left column are ranked according to GNP per capita. / The percentages in the bottom row give each country an equal weight. / na=not ascertained.

V320 GEOGRAPHICAL GROUPS: COSMOPOLITAN

Which of these geographical groups would you say you belong to first of all?

(% "The world as a whole" or the continent/subcontinent)

	Total	Gender		Age			Education			Income			Political Affinity			Values			Ranking:	
		Male	Female	16-29	30-49	50+	Lower	Medium	Upper	Lower	Middle	Upper	Left	Center	Right	Mat	Mixed	Postmat		
India	09	10	08	11	08	07	06	08	13	07	08	12	10	09	10	08	10	13	Brazil	22
Nigeria	20	20	21	21	22	05	13	21	23	21	18	24	18	19	24	20	20	27	Nigeria	20
China	04	04	04	07	04	01	04	05	06	04	05	04	na	na	na	03	04	13	Italy	20
Romania	05	06	05	07	06	04	03	04	09	04	06	05	04	05	09	02	05	24	United States	19
Turkey	09	11	08	13	08	04	05	14	20	07	06	15	15	09	04	05	09	16	Mexico	18
Poland	07	08	05	12	07	04	04	08	09	04	08	09	08	07	06	05	07	11	Belgium	18
Bulgaria	11	12	11	17	13	05	04	10	20	13	10	10	08	12	20	07	11	24	France	18
Chile	13	17	10	15	13	12	10	12	19	08	15	17	19	11	12	10	13	20	Russia	16
Czechoslovakia	13	15	12	15	15	10	08	15	16	12	13	15	10	13	17	10	13	19	Portugal	14
South Africa	11	13	09	15	11	07	06	14	13	08	15	09	15	11	10	08	12	18	Finland	14
Lithuania	06	07	04	09	06	03	05	06	06	06	03	09	na	na	na	04	06	10	Chile	13
Hungary	09	10	08	11	11	06	06	09	10	07	10	09	09	na	15	09	09	11	Czechoslovakia	13
Argentina	11	14	09	13	12	09	09	13	13	09	11	12	15	11	12	05	13	14	Netherlands	13
Brazil	22	22	22	23	21	21	18	22	28	21	20	24	23	24	21	19	22	35	Canada	13
Mexico	18	19	16	21	18	09	16	18	25	15	21	18	25	17	17	14	17	32	Britain	12
Belarus	06	07	05	07	07	03	05	06	06	06	04	07	06	05	05	03	07	07	West Germany	12
Russia	16	15	16	20	17	12	15	16	16	22	20	12	14	16	15	14	16	23	Switzerland	12
Moscow	11	10	12	15	10	09	10	09	13	11	10	13	12	10	11	07	11	19	Bulgaria	11
Latvia	05	07	04	08	05	03	01	05	07	03	06	06	na	na	na	02	06	10	South Africa	11
Estonia	05	05	04	08	04	03	04	05	03	04	06	04	na	na	na	05	04	12	Argentina	11
Portugal	14	15	13	15	16	11	11	22	18	10	16	17	18	15	10	10	17	12	Moscow	11
South Korea	na	na	na	na	na	na	na	na	na	na	na	na	na	na	na	na	na	na	Spain	10
Ireland	05	07	04	04	06	05	05	05	06	06	04	06	07	06	04	02	06	07	East Germany	10
North Ireland	08	06	09	11	09	04	08	09	03	09	06	11	25	07	04	02	08	18	India	09
Slovenia	04	06	03	04	05	03	03	04	08	04	06	04	06	05	03	03	05	08	Turkey	09
Spain	10	12	08	16	11	04	06	19	18	05	09	15	14	09	06	04	10	21	Hungary	09
East Germany	10	11	08	13	10	08	08	10	16	12	16	13	14	09	08	05	10	13	North Ireland	08
Britain	12	15	10	17	14	07	12	10	18	09	12	17	14	12	10	08	11	18	Poland	07
Italy	20	24	15	26	24	12	17	31	56	16	25	28	24	19	19	13	17	34	Austria	07
Netherlands	13	17	09	14	13	11	08	09	24	15	10	19	16	11	11	06	11	18	Sweden	07
Belgium	18	21	15	24	21	10	12	17	31	16	21	19	30	18	12	09	16	29	Lithuania	06
Austria	07	08	06	10	08	04	05	07	15	04	07	09	10	08	06	02	05	13	Belarus	06
France	18	17	18	25	18	12	15	16	28	13	20	24	24	13	13	11	13	34	Romania	05
Canada	13	14	12	15	14	10	10	14	15	13	13	13	24	11	13	07	12	18	Latvia	05
United States	19	18	21	23	21	15	17	18	21	22	14	21	26	18	17	13	19	23	Estonia	05
Iceland	05	06	05	08	05	02	03	07	06	05	02	06	05	07	04	03	05	11	Ireland	05
West Germany	12	13	11	19	13	07	08	17	22	12	14	13	21	10	05	04	08	23	Iceland	05
Denmark	04	05	03	05	13	04	00	04	05	03	03	04	06	01	04	01	03	10	China	04
Finland	14	15	13	15	17	06	16	12	16	11	14	17	16	14	12	00	13	20	Slovenia	04
Norway	04	05	03	05	04	02	02	04	04	05	02	05	05	03	04	01	03	10	Denmark	04
Sweden	07	07	05	10	05	06	03	07	12	05	08	06	06	06	06	04	05	12	Norway	04
Japan	03	03	03	04	03	01	02	03	04	03	03	03	09	02	02	02	03	08	Japan	03
Switzerland	12	13	11	21	13	07	09	12	23	12	13	10	24	11	06	03	11	19		
Total	11	12	10	14	11	07	08	11	15	10	11	12	15	11	10	07	10	18	Total	18

Note: Countries in the left column are ranked according to GNP per capita. / The percentages in the bottom row give each country an equal weight. / na=not ascertained.

How proud are you to be British [substitute own nationality for 'British']? (% "very proud")

	Total	Gender		Age			Education			Income			Political Affinity			Values			Ranking:	
		Male	Female	16-29	30-49	50+	Lower	Medium	Upper	Lower	Middle	Upper	Left	Center	Right	Mat	Mixed	Postmat		
India	75	78	72	75	78	68	65	77	77	76	74	75	80	73	79	80	72	77	Ireland	77
Nigeria	68	67	70	68	67	79	79	70	61	68	68	66	72	69	67	76	65	58	United States	76
China	43	43	44	35	44	52	47	45	33	50	41	36	na	47	41	48	41	20	India	75
Romania	48	48	48	33	45	61	60	41	44	48	49	48	57	47	41	54	47	26	Poland	69
Turkey	67	67	67	56	70	81	73	64	44	71	70	60	49	72	73	73	69	55	Nigeria	68
Poland	69	66	71	53	68	77	71	68	66	66	68	72	66	67	71	65	72	65	Turkey	67
Bulgaria	39	38	40	27	34	52	53	36	31	35	39	41	43	38	25	52	37	12	South Africa	64
Chile	53	53	54	42	57	63	61	49	49	59	52	49	44	56	54	61	51	49	Brazil	64
Czechoslovakia	25	25	25	19	21	35	35	21	21	30	24	21	28	24	25	25	26	21	Canada	61
South Africa	64	65	64	65	63	66	62	67	57	62	67	61	62	64	68	66	65	53	Slovenia	59
Lithuania	41	41	42	36	34	52	50	36	51	40	41	42	na	na	na	38	42	43	Mexico	56
Hungary	47	49	45	41	41	56	52	43	36	54	43	38	38	50	45	45	48	58	Argentina	55
Argentina	55	53	56	47	51	66	62	47	53	64	57	43	33	53	65	66	52	50	North Ireland	54
Brazil	64	65	63	54	65	81	78	61	46	69	66	59	53	61	74	71	61	48	Britain	54
Mexico	56	57	55	53	57	61	57	61	52	55	53	61	51	58	59	54	56	55	Iceland	54
Belarus	35	39	30	28	32	46	38	33	35	35	36	32	32	37	36	34	33	37	Chile	53
Russia	26	23	29	15	19	43	39	23	23	29	28	22	22	24	34	33	23	11	Austria	53
Moscow	20	21	19	12	16	33	39	21	15	23	19	17	16	23	43	30	17	11	Latvia	49
Latvia	49	44	52	44	47	59	67	48	45	60	49	43	na	na	na	50	52	47	Romania	48
Estonia	30	27	32	24	30	34	29	29	32	30	28	30	na	na	na	27	31	39	Hungary	47
Portugal	42	42	42	37	43	46	44	40	35	46	40	39	37	43	42	46	42	33	South Korea	45
South Korea	45	42	48	40	47	52	59	47	37	50	43	41	44	42	47	44	47	40	Spain	45
Ireland	77	77	77	75	75	80	78	78	66	78	76	78	68	75	81	83	77	70	Norway	45
North Ireland	54	55	52	44	48	66	58	50	35	64	49	40	61	48	61	58	51	56	China	43
Slovenia	59	57	61	57	57	62	59	62	53	61	60	52	39	65	65	66	57	44	Portugal	42
Spain	45	41	49	35	40	58	49	39	35	52	44	38	36	43	59	53	44	32	Denmark	42
East Germany	29	32	26	25	23	37	34	23	13	33	30	26	16	32	42	36	30	25	Lithuania	41
Britain	54	53	55	42	47	67	57	53	37	59	57	47	43	53	66	63	54	43	Italy	41
Italy	41	43	40	34	37	50	43	30	21	49	36	30	31	45	50	49	41	36	Sweden	41
Netherlands	21	20	22	13	21	31	29	23	11	24	22	15	16	22	25	38	24	13	Bulgaria	39
Belgium	29	28	30	22	26	36	36	28	16	40	28	21	21	30	29	39	30	16	Finland	38
Austria	53	54	53	37	51	62	61	48	42	59	53	47	64	53	50	63	56	40	Switzerland	38
France	35	35	35	24	33	45	42	31	23	43	37	24	26	34	45	47	37	21	Belarus	35
Canada	61	58	63	56	56	70	66	62	54	62	60	59	49	62	64	63	65	52	France	35
United States	76	74	79	71	69	85	81	79	69	77	78	74	61	78	80	82	77	71	Estonia	30
Iceland	54	51	57	47	53	66	58	60	47	na	na	na	49	53	59	61	53	42	East Germany	29
West Germany	20	23	17	14	17	25	24	15	10	21	22	17	08	21	34	29	24	07	Belgium	29
Denmark	42	39	46	39	40	48	57	43	33	45	45	33	33	44	46	53	44	25	Japan	29
Finland	38	38	38	34	37	45	42	38	36	40	40	34	28	37	46	41	37	40	Russia	26
Norway	45	43	47	43	41	50	51	49	37	43	41	44	35	46	51	49	47	24	Czechoslovakia	25
Sweden	41	39	42	38	35	48	54	37	24	45	45	36	39	42	39	47	43	31	Netherlands	21
Japan	29	31	27	19	23	44	38	26	27	33	27	30	27	24	43	32	29	23	Moscow	20
Switzerland	38	37	39	24	31	51	42	41	13	42	38	28	18	38	45	56	41	20	West Germany	20
Total	47	46	47	39	44	56	53	45	38	50	46	42	41	47	52	52	47	38		

Note: Countries in the left column are ranked according to GNP per capita. / The percentages in the bottom row give each country an equal weight. / na=not ascertained.

V323. Boldness vs. caution

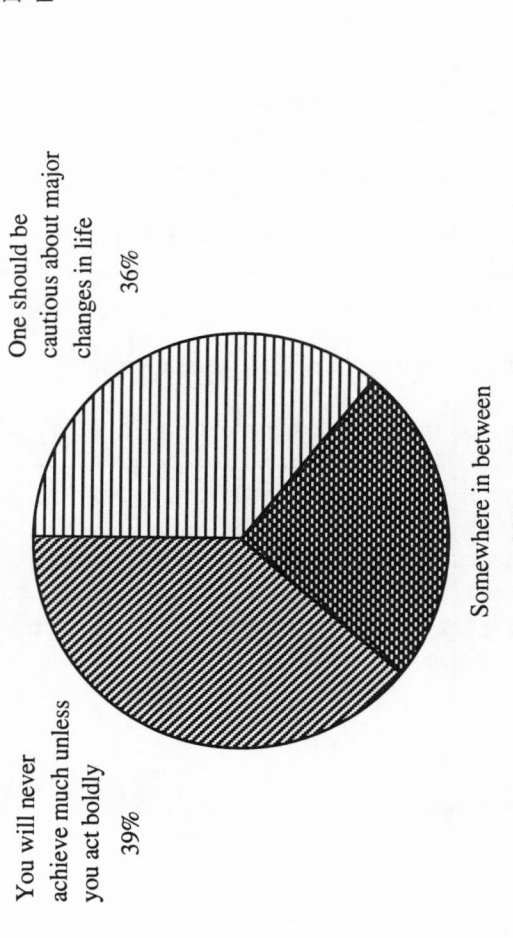

One should be
cautious about major
changes in life
36%

You will never
achieve much unless
you act boldly
39%

Somewhere in between
25%

V324. New ideas vs. old ones

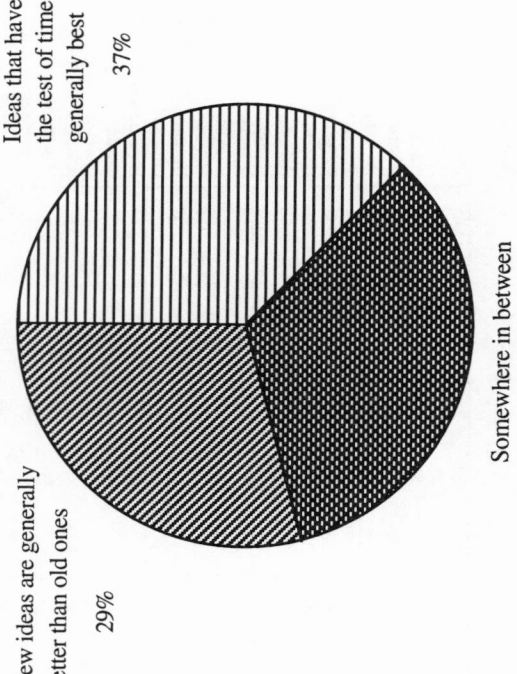

Ideas that have stood
the test of time are
generally best
37%

New ideas are generally
better than old ones
29%

Somewhere in between
34%

V323 BOLDNESS VS. CAUTION
"You will never achieve much unless you act boldly" (% "agree"—codes 7 to 10)

	Total	Gender Male	Gender Female	Age 16-29	Age 30-49	Age 50+	Education Lower	Education Medium	Education Upper	Income Lower	Income Middle	Income Upper	Pol. Affinity Left	Pol. Affinity Center	Pol. Affinity Right	Values Mat	Values Mixed	Values Postmat	Ranking	
India	42	44	41	43	43	39	31	43	46	29	42	53	46	39	49	44	41	48	Finland	81
Nigeria	38	41	34	41	38	25	35	39	39	33	42	42	38	44	37	35	39	52	Sweden	76
China	22	24	19	28	21	16	22	23	23	21	22	23	na	na	na	18	25	37	Poland	66
Romania	30	32	29	40	35	19	21	35	35	29	27	35	27	29	41	25	32	49	Iceland	61
Turkey	40	42	37	46	37	35	37	44	44	39	36	44	43	39	36	32	41	45	Netherlands	60
Poland	66	68	64	75	69	58	58	68	84	64	63	71	67	67	69	58	68	79	East Germany	53
Bulgaria	39	44	34	53	41	28	28	41	44	37	42	41	36	39	44	35	39	55	Italy	51
Chile	23	24	23	28	23	16	21	24	25	24	22	25	25	20	31	22	24	26	West Germany	49
Czechoslovakia	28	33	23	30	31	22	23	28	34	24	27	32	24	25	35	22	28	36	Denmark	48
South Africa	39	40	38	42	37	35	40	38	40	37	41	40	44	34	43	35	40	47	Moscow	44
Lithuania	43	46	41	57	40	34	30	49	39	41	43	49	na	na	na	35	46	59	Estonia	44
Hungary	35	43	28	47	43	23	26	42	42	26	40	48	41	36	47	31	39	35	Lithuania	43
Argentina	30	29	30	39	31	21	24	35	34	21	28	35	34	31	31	23	29	39	Norway	43
Brazil	21	22	19	25	19	16	18	20	31	16	21	25	25	23	18	18	22	32	India	42
Mexico	24	27	20	24	25	22	22	22	30	23	23	28	26	24	24	25	23	30	Belgium	42
Belarus	34	36	32	39	36	23	28	34	34	33	32	37	36	32	26	27	36	48	Britain	41
Russia	32	36	29	43	33	23	25	33	36	29	30	37	39	30	39	26	35	46	Turkey	40
Moscow	44	53	38	47	46	40	43	44	44	44	47	41	44	45	47	36	47	47	Bulgaria	39
Latvia	34	33	35	41	32	31	32	36	31	37	31	36	na	na	na	32	36	34	South Africa	39
Estonia	44	49	40	51	47	31	40	43	49	41	44	48	na	na	na	39	45	63	Austria	39
Portugal	25	26	24	33	25	16	22	32	30	19	25	32	25	26	25	19	28	27	Nigeria	38
South Korea	35	34	36	47	34	19	30	33	40	36	35	34	45	37	31	30	36	52	Hungary	35
Ireland	32	37	27	40	34	25	29	33	47	23	36	37	41	29	36	30	31	37	South Korea	35
North Ireland	29	27	31	32	32	26	28	36	35	31	28	33	29	30	32	16	33	38	France	35
Slovenia	27	29	25	29	30	21	21	29	34	25	27	29	26	26	34	19	29	38	Belarus	34
Spain	29	32	26	39	30	19	26	35	37	20	30	30	34	30	23	24	29	38	Latvia	34
East Germany	53	58	48	64	58	40	49	61	60	43	58	58	56	54	53	31	53	64	Canada	34
Britain	41	46	37	48	41	37	37	49	53	37	41	53	33	38	54	35	42	45	Russia	32
Italy	51	52	50	64	56	38	50	60	61	45	54	67	60	44	50	46	48	63	Ireland	32
Netherlands	60	57	61	70	61	47	52	61	68	63	53	66	66	59	56	50	58	66	United States	32
Belgium	42	47	37	53	48	29	35	43	52	33	46	51	41	44	45	31	40	55	Romania	30
Austria	39	42	36	52	43	29	37	39	46	29	40	46	39	42	37	29	37	50	Argentina	30
France	35	37	32	41	38	26	31	35	44	29	36	43	35	38	35	26	34	44	North Ireland	29
Canada	34	38	31	38	36	30	28	32	43	33	35	38	43	32	39	23	33	44	Spain	29
United States	32	34	30	37	33	28	27	30	37	32	30	35	44	29	34	28	30	39	Czechoslovakia	28
Iceland	61	63	60	62	62	57	58	66	60	na	na	na	56	62	64	59	61	66	Slovenia	27
West Germany	49	54	45	64	55	36	42	61	65	41	49	57	60	47	46	31	47	64	Portugal	25
Denmark	48	52	44	60	51	35	32	47	56	45	46	57	60	42	51	32	49	61	Mexico	24
Finland	81	81	81	88	83	70	77	80	84	78	80	84	87	78	83	61	81	84	Chile	23
Norway	43	43	42	54	52	23	18	41	56	38	43	53	46	36	52	36	44	55	Japan	23
Sweden	76	74	79	79	83	64	65	80	85	73	73	82	78	75	78	67	73	89	China	22
Japan	23	26	20	28	23	19	20	22	27	20	22	27	41	19	26	20	24	33	Brazil	21
Switzerland	na	na	na	na	na	na	na	na	na	na	na	na	na	na	na	na	na	na		
Total	39	42	37	47	41	31	34	42	45	35	39	44	43	39	42	32	40	49		

Note: Countries in the left column are ranked according to GNP per capita. / The percentages in the bottom row give each country an equal weight. / na=not ascertained.
The contrasting statement was: "One should be cautious about making major changes in life."

V324 NEW IDEAS VS. OLD ONES
"New ideas are generally better than old ones" (% "agree"—codes 7 to 10)

	Total	Gender		Age			Education			Income			Political Affinity			Values		
		Male	Female	16-29	30-49	50+	Lower	Medium	Upper	Lower	Middle	Upper	Left	Center	Right	Mat	Mixed	Postmat
India	26	27	26	27	28	23	21	26	29	19	29	30	28	24	33	22	30	31
Nigeria	40	41	39	44	38	25	33	45	39	38	40	46	43	36	46	37	43	36
China	14	16	12	19	12	13	16	13	13	14	13	16	na	na	na	14	14	20
Romania	25	29	21	30	28	19	19	28	29	22	24	29	24	25	33	21	26	36
Turkey	44	46	42	46	46	37	45	44	37	42	45	44	52	41	45	34	49	42
Poland	40	43	37	38	39	42	46	38	29	39	35	46	43	36	45	39	41	37
Bulgaria	40	40	39	46	42	32	35	42	39	37	42	41	35	37	48	37	39	51
Chile	42	42	41	47	40	37	44	41	40	44	43	39	43	39	48	42	42	40
Czechoslovakia	30	35	25	33	29	28	27	31	31	26	32	32	28	29	32	27	30	34
South Africa	46	50	42	52	46	34	45	48	30	46	49	36	55	36	46	40	48	57
Lithuania	29	33	25	36	27	24	34	29	21	30	28	27	na	na	na	28	27	42
Hungary	22	25	20	27	25	17	22	24	17	22	22	23	27	22	22	17	26	40
Argentina	32	34	30	44	33	21	31	34	34	25	34	34	39	34	41	28	33	35
Brazil	38	40	37	42	36	35	39	41	28	42	43	32	37	35	45	41	37	34
Mexico	34	36	33	40	33	22	32	40	38	36	33	34	43	31	36	33	35	36
Belarus	28	30	26	34	26	25	28	30	25	29	26	29	30	25	26	29	25	43
Russia	19	23	16	28	19	13	16	21	19	18	19	19	21	17	28	17	20	24
Moscow	29	34	25	34	28	25	34	26	29	27	31	27	30	22	32	28	29	33
Latvia	26	29	25	27	27	24	23	26	27	27	23	28	na	na	na	25	27	25
Estonia	33	36	31	45	30	27	33	33	35	30	35	37	na	na	na	29	35	41
Portugal	37	38	36	48	39	25	34	51	38	32	43	38	43	37	34	31	43	36
South Korea	23	22	24	28	23	16	25	25	20	24	24	19	27	22	23	21	25	24
Ireland	29	29	28	40	30	20	27	32	27	24	30	31	33	25	31	23	32	28
North Ireland	24	28	21	34	29	13	25	24	17	25	26	25	25	27	23	15	25	36
Slovenia	25	26	23	33	27	19	21	25	29	21	26	28	29	25	28	21	25	35
Spain	37	40	35	49	40	24	35	41	45	27	41	42	40	39	30	26	40	49
East Germany	31	35	27	39	30	27	29	35	34	26	33	32	35	29	33	20	31	37
Britain	23	26	20	28	24	19	25	17	24	25	24	26	21	22	26	22	25	22
Italy	29	33	26	35	33	23	27	32	31	29	30	30	32	25	27	23	29	28
Netherlands	32	30	33	33	34	28	34	30	33	30	29	34	32	33	27	34	31	32
Belgium	26	27	25	27	27	18	23	28	27	31	32	25	29	21	28	25	26	27
Austria	24	28	21	32	28	17	22	24	32	19	23	28	26	27	22	22	22	29
France	21	21	21	25	23	17	23	20	19	25	19	17	24	19	15	18	22	29
Canada	30	32	27	35	29	24	26	28	34	29	29	32	32	26	30	27	30	29
United States	20	20	21	20	22	19	23	20	19	20	23	18	26	20	21	20	30	20
Iceland	21	26	17	19	21	25	24	20	21	na	na	na	17	18	26	23	20	24
West Germany	25	29	22	33	29	18	22	31	30	22	28	28	34	23	21	16	23	35
Denmark	31	37	26	41	31	25	36	30	22	28	30	38	31	29	35	30	33	26
Finland	24	22	25	26	25	17	24	25	22	24	23	23	20	21	25	25	24	23
Norway	33	36	31	40	35	26	26	39	31	31	35	37	32	32	35	34	32	39
Sweden	36	36	36	38	38	35	34	37	37	43	32	35	38	36	37	33	38	34
Japan	05	06	05	05	04	07	06	05	06	08	05	04	05	06	03	04	06	07
Switzerland	na	na	na	na	na	na	na	na	na	na	na	na	na	na	na	na	na	na
Total	29	31	27	35	30	23	28	30	28	28	30	30	32	28	31	26	30	33

Ranking:

South Africa	46
Turkey	44
Chile	42
Nigeria	40
Poland	40
Bulgaria	40
Brazil	38
Portugal	37
Spain	37
Sweden	36
Mexico	34
Estonia	33
Norway	33
Argentina	32
Netherlands	32
East Germany	31
Denmark	31
Czechoslovakia	30
Canada	30
Lithuania	29
Moscow	29
Ireland	29
Italy	29
Belarus	28
India	26
Latvia	26
Belgium	26
Romania	25
Slovenia	25
West Germany	25
North Ireland	24
Austria	24
Finland	24
South Korea	23
Britain	23
Hungary	22
France	21
Iceland	21
United States	20
Russia	19
China	14
Japan	05

Note: Countries in the left column are ranked according to GNP per capita. / The percentages in the bottom row give each country an equal weight. / na=not ascertained.
The contrasting statement was: "Ideas that have stood the test of time are generally best."

V325. Changes in life

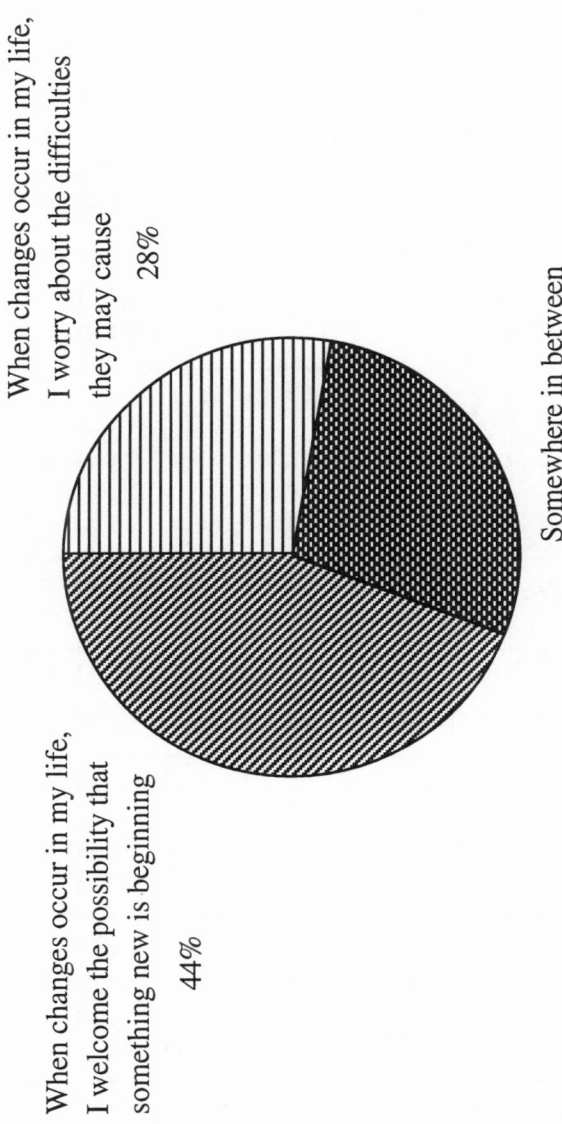

When changes occur in my life,
I worry about the difficulties
they may cause
28%

Somewhere in between
28%

When changes occur in my life,
I welcome the possibility that
something new is beginning

44%

V325 ADAPTING TO CHANGE

"When changes occur in my life, I welcome the possibility that something new is beginning" (% "agree"—codes 7 to 10)

	Total	Gender		Age			Education			Income			Political Affinity			Values			Ranking:	
		Male	Female	16-29	30-49	50+	Lower	Medium	Upper	Lower	Middle	Upper	Left	Center	Right	Mat	Mixed	Postmat		
India	54	55	54	57	54	47	41	54	60	43	56	62	57	55	60	55	55	63	Nigeria	61
Nigeria	61	65	54	59	64	56	57	58	64	59	59	63	54	60	63	55	61	81	Finland	61
China	46	49	40	57	44	36	41	48	52	46	46	44	na	na	na	40	50	67	Argentina	60
Romania	32	38	26	43	32	25	24	36	38	28	30	39	29	29	45	27	35	48	Chile	59
Turkey	57	62	52	63	57	46	53	59	71	52	57	62	65	56	57	44	58	68	Turkey	57
Poland	na	na	na	na	na	na	na	na	na	na	na	na	na	na	na	na	na	na	Netherlands	56
Bulgaria	45	50	41	52	51	33	33	47	52	43	44	51	44	44	53	39	46	57	Brazil	55
Chile	59	58	60	61	59	57	56	60	62	57	60	61	59	57	65	57	59	67	Mexico	55
Czechoslovakia	36	44	29	47	35	31	29	38	45	31	38	39	35	34	42	26	39	46	India	54
South Africa	na	na	na	na	na	na	na	na	na	na	na	na	na	na	na	na	na	na	Canada	54
Lithuania	42	46	38	56	34	36	39	44	36	42	37	47	44	37	45	39	42	51	Iceland	51
Hungary	37	45	30	49	42	28	30	43	45	29	42	45	44	37	45	32	40	51	Denmark	51
Argentina	60	61	60	71	62	50	55	69	60	49	67	61	65	61	67	58	59	64	Sweden	50
Brazil	55	54	56	61	52	50	47	58	61	50	58	59	57	59	54	54	55	64	Norway	49
Mexico	55	55	55	58	57	42	52	60	62	51	57	64	64	55	54	52	58	63	China	46
Belarus	37	41	33	45	35	30	38	38	35	34	36	41	39	33	35	35	36	55	Bulgaria	45
Russia	28	29	27	39	29	18	22	30	29	25	26	31	34	25	39	23	30	41	Italy	44
Moscow	36	38	34	38	38	29	37	33	37	34	37	36	37	31	32	29	35	49	United States	43
Latvia	40	39	40	46	38	34	28	42	38	43	39	38	na	na	na	39	39	42	Lithuania	42
Estonia	33	36	31	48	31	21	29	34	34	29	33	41	na	na	na	29	35	52	Slovenia	42
Portugal	39	42	37	55	37	27	33	56	51	32	41	47	46	39	38	33	45	43	Britain	41
South Korea	40	38	41	48	40	25	34	38	45	37	40	40	45	39	39	33	43	55	Ireland	41
Ireland	41	43	39	54	45	28	35	45	53	36	41	43	54	37	40	31	42	49	Belgium	41
North Ireland	37	41	34	45	40	28	33	41	55	33	35	43	43	38	33	17	42	51	France	41
Slovenia	42	44	41	50	42	37	41	42	46	40	43	47	41	43	49	38	43	58	Latvia	40
Spain	39	41	37	50	40	27	35	47	48	28	40	42	43	38	35	33	39	51	South Korea	40
East Germany	39	42	37	46	41	33	38	40	42	36	40	42	39	40	43	24	39	48	Portugal	39
Britain	42	47	38	51	43	36	40	48	43	40	45	50	40	40	49	38	44	42	Spain	39
Italy	44	48	41	57	50	31	43	54	63	39	48	61	49	41	41	38	42	54	East Germany	39
Netherlands	56	56	56	58	62	46	53	52	65	55	55	60	68	56	45	39	55	64	West Germany	39
Belgium	41	44	39	56	44	29	32	44	55	40	45	47	46	43	43	32	38	58	Hungary	37
Austria	36	39	35	52	41	26	32	39	45	27	38	43	41	38	35	25	34	49	Belarus	37
France	41	41	41	44	46	34	37	42	50	39	41	50	46	39	37	33	41	50	North Ireland	37
Canada	54	54	54	59	55	48	52	54	56	56	54	58	58	54	52	51	54	59	Czechoslovakia	36
United States	43	44	43	46	48	37	37	42	49	48	42	48	51	44	44	38	43	48	Moscow	36
Iceland	51	48	54	56	54	40	44	54	55	na	na	na	48	51	55	46	51	67	Austria	36
West Germany	39	43	36	56	44	27	34	47	55	33	38	45	50	37	34	21	38	54	Estonia	33
Denmark	51	57	45	61	56	36	38	53	57	46	41	50	57	43	55	46	50	63	Romania	32
Finland	61	61	60	73	61	47	47	63	64	57	59	65	62	54	66	27	62	64	Japan	32
Norway	49	54	44	60	53	37	39	51	52	48	50	52	50	47	54	45	49	64	Russia	28
Sweden	50	50	50	58	50	42	38	53	62	44	52	52	51	46	55	43	47	61		
Japan	32	34	29	38	31	29	23	32	38	30	26	41	47	27	37	27	37	43		
Switzerland	na	na	na	na	na	na	na	na	na	na	na	na	na	na	na	na	na	na		
Total	45	47	42	53	46	35	39	47	51	41	45	49	49	44	47	37	45	56		

Note: Countries in the left column are ranked according to GNP per capita. / The percentages in the bottom row give each country an equal weight. / na=not ascertained.
The contrasting statement was: "When changes occur in my life I worry about the difficulties they may cause."

V326-V334. A variety of characteristics are listed here. Could you take a look at them and select those which apply to you?

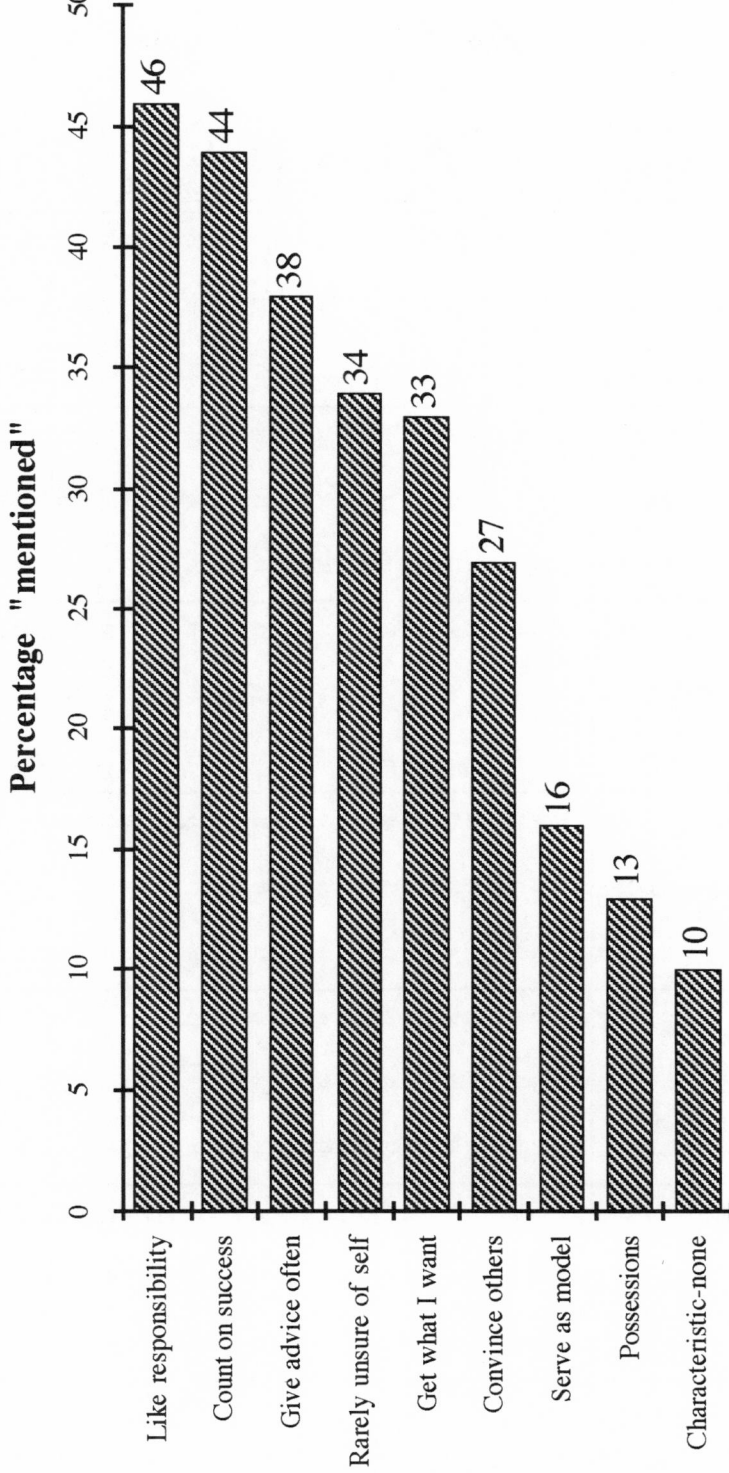

Percentage "mentioned"

V326 COUNT ON SUCCESS

A variety of characteristics are listed here. Could you take a look at them and select those which apply to you?
"I usually count on being successful in everything I do" (% "mentioned")

	Total	Gender		Age			Education			Income			Political Affinity			Values		
		Male	Female	16-29	30-49	50+	Lower	Medium	Upper	Lower	Middle	Upper	Left	Center	Right	Mat	Mixed	Postmat
India	61	64	58	65	63	51	47	62	69	56	60	67	66	63	69	60	68	68
Nigeria	68	67	70	70	67	54	60	69	70	66	69	70	68	67	73	67	68	74
China	79	79	79	75	83	76	79	80	79	81	80	81	na	na	na	79	81	67
Romania	30	33	26	25	31	31	32	29	28	18	32	35	27	29	34	30	30	28
Turkey	62	66	59	57	65	67	68	54	50	70	59	61	59	66	64	63	64	56
Poland	na	na	na	na	na	na	na	na	na	na	na	na	na	na	na	na	na	na
Bulgaria	56	63	50	57	55	55	55	57	55	50	59	64	59	54	56	59	54	58
Chile	70	74	67	70	71	71	67	71	74	68	70	74	72	70	73	69	70	74
Czechoslovakia	36	41	31	32	37	38	33	35	44	32	36	41	34	32	43	33	38	32
South Africa	na	na	na	na	na	na	na	na	na	na	na	na	na	na	na	na	na	na
Lithuania	47	53	41	45	47	48	49	45	50	44	47	53	na	na	na	47	46	49
Hungary	39	46	33	41	42	37	38	39	46	36	41	46	41	42	48	40	39	38
Argentina	66	72	62	70	68	62	64	68	68	59	68	68	61	71	70	68	65	67
Brazil	42	46	37	45	40	38	40	42	44	39	40	44	41	32	30	43	41	37
Mexico	59	60	58	62	61	49	55	65	70	51	66	68	61	71	70	56	64	64
Belarus	46	53	39	45	46	46	43	44	48	39	48	50	48	43	50	45	45	53
Russia	45	54	39	49	46	42	39	48	47	42	46	50	50	48	50	45	45	47
Moscow	44	52	39	46	42	47	48	40	46	39	48	49	45	47	46	48	44	42
Latvia	18	22	15	18	18	18	18	18	19	14	15	22	na	na	na	14	19	15
Estonia	46	54	40	54	46	39	41	48	48	43	47	50	41	57	71	41	49	53
Portugal	71	77	65	76	76	60	68	82	73	66	72	78	67	72	77	71	74	72
South Korea	na	na	na	na	na	na	na	na	na	na	na	na	na	na	na	na	na	na
Ireland	40	42	38	44	43	34	35	44	50	37	41	43	32	41	41	32	42	44
North Ireland	30	40	23	41	28	25	29	29	38	26	24	37	29	32	30	34	28	36
Slovenia	58	64	52	56	58	58	58	60	54	56	61	58	56	59	64	59	58	52
Spain	37	43	31	45	38	29	34	47	41	26	36	43	37	43	38	37	38	43
East Germany	60	71	52	60	60	61	59	62	64	57	62	63	59	61	68	50	63	57
Britain	35	40	31	39	36	32	34	37	36	34	36	38	28	37	38	33	36	37
Italy	18	21	16	19	17	15	18	17	21	19	16	16	16	18	21	20	17	18
Netherlands	37	43	35	39	35	38	35	37	40	39	39	38	35	42	37	30	40	36
Belgium	53	57	49	54	54	49	50	52	61	47	57	63	48	59	59	49	53	60
Austria	60	69	54	64	61	57	59	60	69	57	62	61	60	60	63	55	60	62
France	56	60	53	59	61	50	54	59	57	54	58	62	54	63	57	52	59	56
Canada	63	67	60	64	64	62	65	63	61	60	66	65	58	65	65	63	64	63
United States	59	65	54	66	58	58	52	60	64	53	61	65	52	61	65	60	60	59
Iceland	85	87	82	82	88	82	81	84	89	na	na	na	82	87	89	85	84	89
West Germany	65	72	58	68	69	60	63	64	76	56	68	71	64	69	68	56	67	67
Denmark	09	13	05	10	09	08	08	08	10	06	10	11	07	08	12	07	10	09
Finland	39	43	35	43	40	34	33	35	46	37	40	40	36	36	44	32	37	44
Norway	19	24	13	23	18	18	20	19	19	20	17	23	21	18	19	20	20	16
Sweden	55	59	50	59	53	54	53	55	55	52	52	58	52	53	59	59	56	52
Japan	14	18	10	14	15	13	11	15	17	12	13	20	17	20	15	14	16	20
Switzerland	na	na	na	na	na	na	na	na	na	na	na	na	na	na	na	na	na	na
Total	48	53	44	50	49	45	46	49	51	44	48	51	47	50	52	47	49	49

Ranking:

Iceland	85
China	79
Portugal	71
Chile	70
Nigeria	68
Argentina	66
West Germany	65
Canada	63
Turkey	62
India	61
East Germany	60
Austria	60
Mexico	59
United States	59
Slovenia	58
Bulgaria	56
France	56
Sweden	55
Belgium	53
Lithuania	47
Belarus	46
Estonia	46
Russia	45
Moscow	44
Brazil	42
Ireland	40
Hungary	39
Finland	39
Spain	37
Netherlands	37
Czechoslovakia	36
Britain	35
Romania	30
North Ireland	30
Norway	19
Latvia	18
Italy	18
Japan	14
Denmark	09

Note: Countries in the left column are ranked according to GNP per capita. / The percentages in the bottom row give each country an equal weight. / na=not ascertained.

V327 CONVINCE OTHERS

A variety of characteristics are listed here. Could you take a look at them and select those which apply to you?
"I enjoy convincing others of my opinion" (% "mentioned")

	Total	Gender		Age			Education			Income			Political Affinity			Values		
		Male	Female	16-29	30-49	50+	Lower	Medium	Upper	Lower	Middle	Upper	Left	Center	Right	Mat	Mixed	Postmat
India	30	33	26	32	28	31	23	27	37	28	27	35	31	31	34	30	32	25
Nigeria	57	59	53	58	56	54	57	54	60	53	59	59	57	55	67	53	59	52
China	31	28	35	26	30	39	31	32	25	35	33	25	na	na	na	31	30	43
Romania	45	46	44	40	44	49	46	43	46	46	43	47	46	45	49	42	46	51
Turkey	46	46	47	50	44	46	45	50	47	44	49	47	51	48	46	46	47	45
Poland	na	na	na	na	na	na	na	na	na	na	na	na	na	na	na	na	na	na
Bulgaria	32	36	29	36	32	30	25	31	42	26	36	42	41	31	41	27	33	48
Chile	20	22	17	15	20	26	21	19	19	25	17	17	23	18	18	22	19	18
Czechoslovakia	33	38	27	33	33	31	27	34	40	28	34	36	40	26	38	30	34	31
South Africa	na	na	na	na	na	na	na	na	na	na	na	na	na	na	na	na	na	na
Lithuania	37	39	34	33	35	41	39	34	45	36	38	36	na	na	na	36	36	40
Hungary	50	56	45	59	52	45	42	56	66	41	56	61	65	50	53	51	50	55
Argentina	21	22	20	22	20	21	24	19	18	21	18	22	20	19	26	19	22	21
Brazil	36	37	34	39	34	33	34	37	34	37	36	34	40	33	38	36	34	43
Mexico	33	34	32	31	34	36	32	33	37	32	32	39	40	32	36	30	36	35
Belarus	23	24	22	21	23	25	19	21	27	21	22	26	23	23	28	23	21	38
Russia	19	21	18	18	18	21	17	16	23	19	18	23	24	19	22	19	18	33
Moscow	22	23	22	21	21	25	20	21	24	22	22	26	23	20	30	20	25	21
Latvia	25	27	24	29	22	26	25	23	24	24	23	26	na	na	na	26	26	33
Estonia	20	23	17	20	22	17	16	20	24	15	20	27	na	na	na	20	20	25
Portugal	24	25	23	25	22	25	22	25	30	24	20	28	25	22	29	25	26	20
South Korea	na	na	na	na	na	na	na	na	na	na	na	na	na	na	na	na	na	na
Ireland	20	21	19	25	20	17	16	23	31	16	16	27	25	19	19	16	21	22
North Ireland	16	25	10	20	14	16	12	19	35	13	11	23	21	14	20	14	15	29
Slovenia	26	30	22	24	25	29	24	28	26	26	27	23	31	27	32	28	26	16
Spain	14	17	12	15	13	14	12	20	18	11	14	18	17	14	17	11	15	18
East Germany	36	40	32	35	36	35	34	36	41	33	36	37	40	33	39	30	36	39
Britain	22	26	19	25	19	23	21	21	31	18	23	27	24	20	26	22	20	29
Italy	27	29	24	24	27	28	26	30	29	26	27	33	28	27	32	25	27	29
Netherlands	30	36	27	31	27	32	33	29	27	32	29	27	34	26	32	25	31	29
Belgium	22	27	18	28	23	18	18	22	33	20	23	25	23	23	25	14	24	29
Austria	31	33	30	33	34	28	29	32	36	28	32	34	47	28	32	31	30	34
France	26	30	22	29	26	24	21	28	34	20	28	35	28	29	28	16	28	31
Canada	26	30	21	30	25	24	24	24	31	24	25	31	34	26	30	19	27	29
United States	26	31	21	32	25	25	25	24	30	25	25	29	30	26	27	27	26	25
Iceland	19	23	16	24	18	16	17	20	21	na	na	na	17	17	24	20	19	19
West Germany	38	43	34	46	39	34	35	39	54	34	40	43	48	36	39	30	38	44
Denmark	39	42	36	48	38	32	31	46	38	39	39	42	46	36	41	29	42	40
Finland	55	60	50	70	56	40	45	54	61	54	53	59	50	55	59	47	51	65
Norway	24	25	22	34	20	21	22	23	25	24	26	22	28	21	23	21	24	30
Sweden	33	37	29	36	31	32	30	33	37	32	30	35	35	31	34	29	33	38
Japan	10	12	07	12	10	08	08	08	15	10	08	11	12	11	10	09	12	09
Switzerland	na	na	na	na	na	na	na	na	na	na	na	na	na	na	na	na	na	na
Total	29	32	27	32	29	29	27	30	34	28	29	33	33	28	33	27	30	33

Ranking:

Nigeria	57
Finland	55
Hungary	50
Turkey	46
Romania	45
Denmark	39
West Germany	38
Lithuania	37
Brazil	36
East Germany	36
Czechoslovakia	33
Mexico	33
Sweden	33
Bulgaria	32
China	31
Austria	31
India	30
Netherlands	30
Italy	27
Slovenia	26
France	26
Canada	26
United States	26
Latvia	25
Portugal	24
Norway	24
Belarus	23
Moscow	22
Britain	22
Belgium	22
Argentina	21
Chile	20
Estonia	20
Ireland	20
Russia	19
Iceland	19
North Ireland	16
Spain	14
Japan	10

Note: Countries in the left column are ranked according to GNP per capita. / The percentages in the bottom row give each country an equal weight. / na=not ascertained.

V328 SERVE AS MODEL

A variety of characteristics are listed here. Could you take a look at them and select those which apply to you?

"I often notice that I serve as a model for others" (% "mentioned")

	Total	Gender Male	Gender Female	Age 16-29	Age 30-49	Age 50+	Education Lower	Education Medium	Education Upper	Income Lower	Income Middle	Income Upper	Political Affinity Left	Political Affinity Center	Political Affinity Right	Values Mat	Values Mixed	Values Postmat
India	29	31	26	28	29	30	21	30	32	31	28	28	37	29	27	26	32	36
Nigeria	55	56	54	55	58	47	47	55	59	52	57	57	57	53	62	52	58	53
China	15	15	16	13	16	17	17	14	16	16	19	11	na	na	21	14	17	09
Romania	22	22	22	08	22	31	28	17	22	24	22	19	21	25	21	24	21	17
Turkey	45	47	43	37	47	53	49	40	34	42	46	49	37	47	54	44	47	40
Poland	na	na	na	na	na	na	na	na	na	na	na	na	na	na	na	na	na	na
Bulgaria	10	11	10	09	08	13	14	09	08	09	10	12	12	09	10	08	11	11
Chile	21	23	20	16	22	27	22	20	22	22	22	19	19	21	24	22	21	21
Czechoslovakia	19	19	18	15	14	27	26	16	15	18	20	18	18	18	20	22	17	19
South Africa	na	na	na	na	na	na	na	na	na	na	na	na	na	na	na	na	na	na
Lithuania	13	14	13	07	11	22	23	10	14	15	14	08	na	na	na	14	14	09
Hungary	13	15	11	10	16	12	10	14	23	11	14	14	20	14	15	13	13	08
Argentina	25	26	24	23	26	25	25	26	23	23	25	23	19	25	26	24	23	29
Brazil	19	20	18	18	19	20	17	19	22	16	20	22	19	19	21	16	20	24
Mexico	24	24	24	24	24	25	23	28	24	22	25	27	27	25	26	22	26	26
Belarus	11	11	11	08	10	15	12	10	11	10	11	11	11	13	10	13	10	19
Russia	09	09	09	05	08	13	11	07	09	09	10	09	07	09	14	11	08	08
Moscow	11	10	11	09	10	12	18	11	09	11	11	10	10	09	17	16	10	06
Latvia	09	10	09	10	09	09	07	09	09	05	10	10	na	na	na	10	08	08
Estonia	09	09	08	09	08	10	09	08	09	08	06	11	na	na	na	09	09	07
Portugal	12	14	11	09	11	16	15	07	08	15	11	09	10	16	10	14	12	13
South Korea	na	na	na	na	na	na	na	na	na	na	na	na	na	na	na	na	na	na
Ireland	07	06	08	07	07	08	07	07	09	07	08	08	06	07	09	10	06	07
North Ireland	05	07	03	07	03	06	05	06	03	03	04	06	00	06	04	06	06	00
Slovenia	29	33	25	26	28	32	30	29	28	29	30	27	30	32	33	30	29	31
Spain	05	07	04	05	04	06	05	07	06	06	05	07	06	07	07	05	06	06
East Germany	28	29	27	24	30	28	26	26	37	24	27	32	30	26	32	27	27	29
Britain	09	10	09	08	09	10	08	13	09	10	09	11	07	09	11	08	11	08
Italy	24	25	23	21	29	22	23	33	38	22	28	32	25	26	24	22	24	29
Netherlands	15	19	14	11	17	19	14	16	17	18	11	20	14	17	17	11	17	15
Belgium	11	12	09	10	12	10	10	10	13	11	10	12	09	09	15	08	11	12
Austria	27	33	24	30	30	24	25	27	36	19	30	31	28	29	28	20	28	30
France	05	06	05	05	06	05	06	05	03	05	05	06	06	04	06	05	06	04
Canada	20	19	21	19	22	18	18	19	22	18	18	22	21	20	23	16	20	20
United States	21	22	20	25	23	18	16	22	24	21	22	22	18	24	23	18	21	23
Iceland	15	17	12	13	15	16	11	14	18	na	na	na	13	16	15	16	14	12
West Germany	31	33	28	30	33	30	29	31	39	24	30	38	32	29	35	26	31	32
Denmark	07	09	06	06	08	07	06	08	07	07	06	08	08	07	08	07	07	07
Finland	28	32	24	24	30	27	24	27	31	23	31	29	28	28	30	18	26	35
Norway	05	07	04	03	05	06	08	05	04	06	04	05	04	05	06	06	04	08
Sweden	17	16	19	18	17	18	15	17	22	16	18	18	17	15	18	14	17	18
Japan	11	15	08	08	12	13	10	12	10	10	12	15	15	13	15	10	13	15
Switzerland	na	na	na	na	na	na	na	na	na	na	na	na	na	na	na	na	na	na
Total	18	19	17	16	18	19	18	18	19	17	18	19	18	19	20	17	18	18

Ranking:

Nigeria	55
Turkey	45
West Germany	31
India	29
Slovenia	29
East Germany	28
Finland	28
Austria	27
Argentina	25
Mexico	24
Italy	24
Romania	22
Chile	21
United States	21
Canada	20
Czechoslovakia	19
Brazil	19
Sweden	17
China	15
Netherlands	15
Iceland	15
Lithuania	13
Hungary	13
Portugal	12
Belarus	11
Moscow	11
Belgium	11
Japan	11
Bulgaria	10
Russia	09
Latvia	09
Estonia	09
Britain	09
Ireland	07
Denmark	07
North Ireland	05
Spain	05
France	05
Norway	05

Note: Countries in the left column are ranked according to GNP per capita. / The percentages in the bottom row give each country an equal weight. / na=not ascertained.

V329 GET WHAT I WANT

A variety of characteristics are listed here. Could you take a look at them and select those which apply to you?
"I am good at getting what I want" (% "mentioned")

	Total	Gender		Age			Education			Income			Political Affinity			Values			Ranking:	
		Male	Female	16-29	30-49	50+	Lower	Medium	Upper	Lower	Middle	Upper	Left	Center	Right	Mat	Mixed	Postmat		
India	32	33	30	34	30	31	20	31	39	27	32	36	31	34	34	30	35	35	Portugal	78
Nigeria	53	53	53	55	50	46	46	57	51	53	53	53	57	49	61	49	55	58	Hungary	58
China	26	24	28	31	27	17	30	27	21	29	27	19	na	na	na	24	27	26	Slovenia	56
Romania	52	51	53	53	53	51	49	54	54	43	53	58	54	53	57	52	52	51	Turkey	54
Turkey	54	52	55	52	56	54	54	55	50	52	55	55	58	53	52	54	54	52	Nigeria	53
Poland	na	na	na	na	na	na	na	na	na	na	na	na	na	na	na	na	na	na	Romania	52
Bulgaria	43	45	42	41	47	40	39	46	43	38	43	55	48	44	43	45	43	41	Czechoslovakia	50
Chile	27	28	25	25	27	28	30	26	23	27	28	24	22	27	32	29	26	23	Sweden	49
Czechoslovakia	50	50	50	55	50	47	46	53	50	44	53	53	50	48	54	47	50	56	West Germany	48
South Africa	na	na	na	na	na	na	na	na	na	na	na	na	na	na	na	na	na	na	Netherlands	47
Lithuania	41	45	37	44	39	39	40	41	42	36	41	51	na	na	na	33	42	50	Finland	45
Hungary	58	59	58	58	60	57	58	59	58	56	59	63	51	62	69	60	59	48	Bulgaria	43
Argentina	36	35	38	36	40	32	37	35	34	36	37	30	38	32	41	41	35	35	Brazil	42
Brazil	42	43	41	43	42	39	42	43	38	40	43	43	39	42	43	43	40	46	Lithuania	41
Mexico	23	23	24	24	24	22	23	26	22	20	23	31	21	25	28	23	25	28	Austria	41
Belarus	34	34	34	44	36	21	36	34	34	31	36	35	35	33	40	36	34	34	Iceland	39
Russia	31	34	29	40	33	22	26	32	32	30	32	32	30	34	38	28	33	28	East Germany	38
Moscow	33	34	33	41	32	29	32	34	33	30	36	37	35	30	38	35	32	38	Argentina	36
Latvia	31	32	30	29	33	27	24	31	33	28	34	30	na	na	na	28	31	41	Belarus	34
Estonia	29	32	28	36	30	22	27	28	35	24	31	36	na	na	na	27	31	44	Moscow	33
Portugal	78	78	77	82	83	69	75	86	81	69	83	87	82	77	78	76	82	79	India	32
South Korea	na	na	na	na	na	na	na	na	na	na	na	na	na	na	na	na	na	na	Russia	31
Ireland	27	23	30	30	25	26	23	30	33	20	25	34	28	29	23	22	28	28	Latvia	31
North Ireland	16	17	15	25	14	12	14	13	38	12	10	22	14	17	18	17	17	13	Belgium	30
Slovenia	56	62	50	59	59	50	51	60	58	51	60	58	51	61	63	57	56	49	Estonia	29
Spain	20	23	17	25	21	15	18	26	23	12	21	28	20	24	22	18	21	25	Chile	27
East Germany	38	41	35	42	37	37	37	43	38	37	37	40	41	36	40	32	39	41	Ireland	27
Britain	24	24	25	34	21	22	23	26	29	19	23	31	24	23	26	25	25	22	Canada	27
Italy	21	22	21	32	21	15	21	19	24	21	18	26	22	17	28	22	20	23	China	26
Netherlands	47	49	46	54	44	42	40	45	57	41	48	51	49	51	44	32	51	48	Britain	24
Belgium	30	31	29	34	32	25	28	29	35	26	32	37	29	32	36	27	30	33	France	24
Austria	41	43	40	49	41	39	42	39	51	35	43	46	47	41	40	35	42	45	United States	24
France	24	22	26	31	26	18	23	27	22	23	30	22	24	23	31	26	24	25	Mexico	23
Canada	27	27	27	33	26	23	26	27	28	24	27	30	26	27	29	31	27	28	Denmark	22
United States	24	24	23	31	24	21	24	24	27	19	24	28	24	24	25	25	24	22	Italy	21
Iceland	39	38	41	44	42	28	32	37	46	39	51	46	35	37	47	37	39	45	Spain	20
West Germany	48	54	44	50	53	44	46	51	54	39	51	55	49	49	51	42	50	50	Norway	20
Denmark	22	23	21	33	23	13	13	24	26	20	20	30	25	19	24	20	22	26	North Ireland	16
Finland	45	48	42	56	47	34	39	41	54	43	47	46	40	46	46	29	45	49	Japan	10
Norway	20	22	18	30	18	15	14	20	23	15	22	24	19	19	21	21	19	27		
Sweden	49	46	51	53	48	45	38	51	60	48	39	55	48	48	52	39	51	51		
Japan	10	11	08	11	11	06	07	10	12	06	11	12	09	12	07	08	12	14		
Switzerland	na	na	na	na	na	na	na	na	na	na	na	na	na	na	na	na	na	na		
Total	36	37	35	40	37	31	33	37	39	32	37	40	36	37	39	34	37	38		

Note: Countries in the left column are ranked according to GNP per capita. / The percentages in the bottom row give each country an equal weight. / na=not ascertained

V330 POSSESSIONS

A variety of characteristics are listed here. Could you take a look at them and select those which apply to you?
"I own many things others envy me for" (% "mentioned")

	Total	Gender Male	Gender Female	Age 16-29	Age 30-49	Age 50+	Education Lower	Education Medium	Education Upper	Income Lower	Income Middle	Income Upper	Political Affinity Left	Political Affinity Center	Political Affinity Right	Values Mat	Values Mixed	Values Postmat
India	15	16	14	16	15	14	12	16	16	13	17	16	18	17	14	13	18	13
Nigeria	32	30	35	35	30	21	28	37	29	33	34	34	39	32	35	29	35	34
China	10	09	13	10	12	08	10	10	13	08	13	10	na	na	na	08	12	17
Romania	24	23	24	18	29	22	25	25	20	21	22	27	24	25	24	24	24	15
Turkey	26	25	26	22	25	32	28	22	24	22	25	31	23	27	31	27	25	26
Poland	na	na	na	na	na	na	na	na	na	na	na	na	na	na	na	na	na	na
Bulgaria	17	16	18	18	17	16	15	18	17	14	20	20	15	19	25	15	19	13
Chile	15	16	14	12	13	21	17	14	12	15	14	15	15	15	16	19	14	11
Czechoslovakia	15	14	16	13	15	16	17	15	10	13	16	15	12	15	18	18	15	10
South Africa	na	na	na	na	na	na	na	na	na	na	na	na	na	na	na	na	na	na
Lithuania	15	13	17	14	11	20	24	13	09	16	12	16	na	na	na	15	14	17
Hungary	18	19	17	19	21	14	15	20	23	17	16	26	22	19	27	15	21	13
Argentina	15	14	15	14	16	14	16	15	13	15	15	14	07	14	14	16	14	13
Brazil	20	20	20	19	22	18	20	20	22	19	22	21	21	19	23	21	20	15
Mexico	19	18	20	19	19	20	19	20	19	18	19	22	16	18	26	23	19	14
Belarus	19	16	21	17	18	21	22	15	21	15	20	21	19	19	21	19	18	28
Russia	13	11	14	13	14	11	10	12	15	12	12	17	15	12	16	12	13	17
Moscow	16	15	16	15	15	17	16	17	15	14	17	17	16	14	23	17	15	17
Latvia	08	08	09	08	08	10	11	09	07	07	07	10	10	na	na	10	09	07
Estonia	11	09	13	12	11	10	13	10	12	07	09	16	na	na	na	13	11	05
Portugal	23	21	25	19	27	23	24	18	24	23	21	24	18	26	24	27	24	14
South Korea	na	na	na	na	na	na	na	na	na	na	na	na	na	na	na	na	na	na
Ireland	07	08	06	09	07	06	05	10	03	04	05	08	11	06	06	05	07	08
North Ireland	04	06	03	05	03	06	03	06	10	04	06	05	11	03	07	05	04	04
Slovenia	25	25	25	20	26	26	28	25	21	22	27	26	23	25	28	30	23	19
Spain	06	07	05	05	06	07	05	07	07	07	05	08	05	06	11	06	05	08
East Germany	19	18	20	16	16	23	20	15	19	20	18	19	16	20	20	18	20	15
Britain	09	06	11	07	06	12	09	09	07	10	06	08	09	06	12	13	09	06
Italy	12	12	11	10	14	12	13	10	16	10	14	16	11	15	14	14	12	11
Netherlands	11	13	10	07	13	14	13	11	10	11	11	12	08	12	13	10	12	10
Belgium	09	10	08	09	08	10	07	11	09	08	07	11	06	10	11	09	10	09
Austria	22	21	23	21	25	20	22	22	26	21	22	25	18	22	24	18	22	25
France	06	07	05	05	06	06	05	04	10	05	05	08	05	05	11	05	05	08
Canada	11	12	09	11	10	06	11	11	10	08	13	10	10	10	13	11	11	09
United States	10	12	07	09	08	11	10	11	08	09	10	09	07	10	14	10	11	06
Iceland	10	14	07	11	08	15	10	10	12	na	na	na	08	09	16	13	10	10
West Germany	26	26	25	21	29	26	25	26	29	19	25	33	22	28	29	24	27	24
Denmark	10	10	09	09	07	13	11	08	10	10	07	07	06	09	12	10	11	06
Finland	27	28	27	30	25	31	20	24	35	25	26	32	25	28	29	29	26	31
Norway	06	07	05	06	05	08	08	05	05	07	04	06	05	05	08	07	06	02
Sweden	15	14	16	14	13	17	11	16	19	13	12	17	10	14	20	17	16	13
Japan	03	03	03	06	02	02	03	02	05	03	02	04	05	03	02	03	03	06
Switzerland	na	na	na	na	na	na	na	na	na	na	na	na	na	na	na	na	na	na
Total	**15**	**15**	**15**	**14**	**15**	**15**	**15**	**15**	**15**	**14**	**15**	**17**	**14**	**15**	**18**	**15**	**15**	**14**

Ranking:

Nigeria	32
Finland	27
Turkey	26
West Germany	26
Slovenia	25
Romania	24
Portugal	23
Austria	22
Brazil	20
Mexico	19
Belarus	19
East Germany	19
Hungary	18
Bulgaria	17
Moscow	16
India	15
Chile	15
Czechoslovakia	15
Lithuania	15
Argentina	15
Sweden	15
Russia	13
Italy	12
Estonia	11
Netherlands	11
Canada	11
China	10
United States	10
Iceland	10
Denmark	10
Britain	09
Belgium	09
Latvia	08
Ireland	07
Spain	06
France	06
Norway	06
North Ireland	04
Japan	03

Note: Countries in the left column are ranked according to GNP per capita. / The percentages in the bottom row give each country an equal weight. / na=not ascertained.

V331 LIKE RESPONSIBILITY

A variety of characteristics are listed here. Could you take a look at them and select those which apply to you?
"I like to assume responsibility" (% "mentioned")

	Total	Gender		Age			Education			Income			Political Affinity			Values		
		Male	Female	16-29	30-49	50+	Lower	Medium	Upper	Lower	Middle	Upper	Left	Center	Right	Mat	Mixed	Postmat
India	65	70	59	69	63	61	48	65	73	61	60	73	68	71	67	71	66	61
Nigeria	75	74	77	72	81	70	67	76	79	76	77	73	76	76	79	75	76	75
China	26	30	20	18	27	34	23	25	32	26	27	25	na	na	na	23	28	46
Romania	47	50	44	41	52	46	39	47	57	43	48	49	43	50	53	43	48	62
Turkey	73	77	69	71	77	70	67	80	87	67	72	82	80	74	72	67	71	84
Poland	na	na	na	na	na	na	na	na	na	na	na	na	na	na	na	na	na	na
Bulgaria	40	44	36	40	41	38	26	44	48	38	40	48	49	40	52	36	41	48
Chile	69	72	66	69	69	69	67	69	71	68	70	68	70	70	64	71	69	69
Czechoslovakia	30	31	29	23	27	38	29	26	43	29	30	30	38	27	30	29	30	34
South Africa	na	na	na	na	na	na	na	na	na	na	na	na	na	na	na	na	na	na
Lithuania	32	38	26	25	31	39	28	32	39	29	34	34	na	na	na	30	32	43
Hungary	52	54	51	38	60	50	46	56	66	47	53	67	59	58	57	52	53	58
Argentina	69	69	70	64	71	72	66	72	69	68	73	70	65	72	72	72	69	68
Brazil	63	64	62	58	66	66	62	61	72	61	64	66	61	63	66	72	63	64
Mexico	61	61	62	58	65	60	58	61	70	54	64	72	57	63	69	62	64	65
Belarus	31	33	29	25	31	36	28	27	36	30	29	34	30	34	33	35	29	34
Russia	24	27	23	20	24	28	19	22	31	21	28	28	34	25	26	23	25	28
Moscow	31	35	28	18	32	39	27	27	35	30	31	33	33	31	35	33	34	23
Latvia	18	19	17	15	16	24	11	15	25	15	20	18	na	na	na	14	21	20
Estonia	20	25	16	15	22	22	13	21	26	18	13	30	na	na	na	16	23	29
Portugal	64	66	62	66	71	55	59	74	72	55	68	75	65	67	65	64	66	71
South Korea	na	na	na	na	na	na	na	na	na	na	na	na	na	na	na	na	na	na
Ireland	49	50	48	51	56	47	42	55	62	34	48	61	51	48	54	46	48	57
North Ireland	41	48	36	60	48	37	38	43	62	39	39	53	43	41	46	43	43	42
Slovenia	47	53	41	67	42	45	37	51	57	42	46	60	59	48	62	48	45	52
Spain	33	38	30	56	38	27	30	40	42	27	33	41	37	37	36	30	37	38
East Germany	59	63	55	36	63	57	55	58	72	52	59	64	66	55	59	44	61	60
Britain	44	49	39	53	46	41	39	53	58	38	49	52	41	43	51	42	45	45
Italy	53	56	50	46	56	48	52	60	56	50	60	55	54	51	56	54	51	57
Netherlands	56	65	52	54	53	59	46	58	64	51	57	68	63	59	51	41	56	61
Belgium	43	48	39	48	46	38	35	45	55	41	46	60	43	46	48	31	44	57
Austria	51	55	49	51	56	47	49	52	61	53	62	67	49	54	52	44	51	56
France	57	62	53	60	60	53	51	64	65	48	62	67	61	57	55	51	58	64
Canada	65	65	64	67	65	63	63	62	69	65	65	67	66	66	67	64	65	68
United States	61	61	59	56	67	57	56	59	68	60	59	69	60	64	64	57	61	66
Iceland	68	66	69	71	71	63	63	68	71	na	54	65	68	67	72	68	66	76
West Germany	55	63	48	59	59	53	51	57	71	47	54	77	55	56	59	48	54	61
Denmark	68	70	67	71	71	58	54	70	75	62	72	77	67	68	73	58	73	67
Finland	72	76	68	72	75	66	57	74	78	71	71	76	71	75	74	65	71	77
Norway	61	61	60	63	65	54	51	58	68	59	60	72	61	61	66	57	62	72
Sweden	88	85	90	85	89	88	88	87	89	88	88	90	88	87	89	85	88	89
Japan	12	15	09	10	10	15	13	10	14	14	10	13	18	14	12	12	13	17
Switzerland	na	na	na	na	na	na	na	na	na	na	na	na	na	na	na	na	na	na
Total	**51**	**54**	**48**	**49**	**53**	**49**	**45**	**52**	**59**	**46**	**51**	**56**	**56**	**55**	**57**	**48**	**51**	**55**

Ranking:

Sweden	88
Nigeria	75
Turkey	73
Finland	72
Chile	69
Argentina	69
Iceland	68
Denmark	68
India	65
Canada	65
Portugal	64
Brazil	63
Mexico	61
United States	61
Norway	61
East Germany	59
France	57
Netherlands	56
West Germany	55
Italy	53
Hungary	52
Austria	51
Ireland	49
Romania	47
Slovenia	47
Britain	44
Belgium	43
North Ireland	41
Bulgaria	40
Spain	33
Lithuania	32
Belarus	31
Moscow	31
Czechoslovakia	30
China	26
Russia	24
Estonia	20
Latvia	18
Japan	12

Note: Countries in the left column are ranked according to GNP per capita. / The percentages in the bottom row give each country an equal weight. / na=not ascertained.

V332 RARELY UNSURE OF SELF

A variety of characteristics are listed here. Could you take a look at them and select those which apply to you?
"I am rarely unsure about how I should behave" (% "mentioned")

	Total	Gender Male	Gender Female	Age 16-29	Age 30-49	Age 50+	Education Lower	Education Medium	Education Upper	Income Lower	Income Middle	Income Upper	Political Affinity Left	Political Affinity Center	Political Affinity Right	Values Mat	Values Mixed	Values Postmat
India	40	42	38	na	40	37	29	41	45	31	40	42	39	40	38	42	42	42
Nigeria	34	33	34	39	29	18	27	39	30	33	33	36	na	28	38	34	34	34
China	32	32	32	30	31	37	31	32	34	33	35	28	35	40	37	28	36	39
Romania	37	36	39	42	40	32	33	42	38	35	41	36	35	40	37	34	39	32
Turkey	68	76	61	70	67	69	63	76	76	66	67	74	75	69	67	66	67	73
Poland	na	na	na	na	na	na	na	na	na	na	na	na	na	na	na	na	na	na
Bulgaria	33	34	31	37	30	33	29	34	34	28	37	38	35	33	38	31	33	39
Chile	50	50	49	48	50	52	49	47	54	48	50	51	49	50	49	48	52	48
Czechoslovakia	52	51	52	52	49	55	50	51	56	51	52	51	52	53	50	49	54	45
South Africa	na	na	na	na	na	na	na	na	na	na	na	na	na	na	na	na	na	na
Lithuania	28	28	28	28	27	29	30	28	27	27	32	26	na	na	na	29	28	29
Hungary	46	45	47	44	48	46	41	51	46	42	48	52	48	50	55	47	46	48
Argentina	47	46	48	46	44	51	46	52	45	49	48	44	44	48	49	49	47	45
Brazil	32	32	32	32	33	32	31	31	41	29	32	36	31	33	38	31	33	32
Mexico	45	44	46	46	45	44	43	48	48	43	44	49	44	44	53	45	47	48
Belarus	41	41	40	38	45	36	39	41	41	34	42	47	42	40	48	40	40	50
Russia	35	36	35	38	37	31	31	36	37	36	36	36	38	36	47	35	34	38
Moscow	38	40	37	43	37	36	35	38	39	33	41	44	37	41	44	36	38	42
Latvia	13	16	11	15	13	10	17	13	10	08	13	15	na	na	na	11	13	09
Estonia	33	35	31	34	33	33	32	35	30	31	36	35	35	na	na	31	35	42
Portugal	37	39	36	36	35	40	36	45	34	35	39	39	35	39	39	33	40	47
South Korea	36	na	na	na	na	na	na	na	na	na	na	na	na	na	na	33	na	33
Ireland	32	31	34	35	34	29	27	38	44	27	34	37	29	34	35	30	33	35
North Ireland	33	30	36	33	34	33	30	39	41	37	24	40	32	34	36	29	36	31
Slovenia	41	44	39	31	43	46	39	42	43	41	42	43	47	40	47	42	40	46
Spain	36	40	33	35	35	37	37	34	30	33	36	41	36	43	35	38	39	33
East Germany	39	42	37	40	37	40	39	36	44	36	40	41	41	37	43	35	40	40
Britain	40	40	39	40	42	38	38	47	41	35	41	48	35	37	50	41	40	40
Italy	31	33	29	34	28	31	30	35	33	29	32	40	29	32	40	29	32	32
Netherlands	30	40	27	29	28	35	29	34	27	26	29	35	27	30	33	23	33	29
Belgium	33	35	31	32	33	35	33	32	34	30	33	36	37	34	34	28	35	34
Austria	39	44	36	44	39	37	37	40	45	36	40	43	40	39	40	42	38	41
France	27	30	25	26	28	29	25	30	30	30	25	28	24	33	33	25	29	28
Canada	36	37	36	36	35	39	35	38	35	36	37	38	34	38	39	31	38	37
United States	41	39	43	37	39	44	39	39	45	38	41	44	45	42	39	39	42	41
Iceland	41	39	43	44	40	40	37	41	44	na	na	na	40	35	52	38	42	45
West Germany	45	49	41	45	48	42	44	45	51	37	46	52	45	46	50	43	45	45
Denmark	32	36	27	31	36	28	21	35	36	27	31	43	29	29	40	26	35	30
Finland	46	48	43	46	45	46	43	46	46	45	47	44	38	53	46	41	46	47
Norway	24	27	21	27	23	24	21	22	28	20	29	25	26	23	27	26	24	23
Sweden	57	56	57	55	60	53	50	60	60	57	50	60	54	58	57	52	57	59
Japan	14	17	11	11	14	15	11	15	16	12	15	15	14	19	17	12	17	15
Switzerland	na	na	na	na	na	na	na	na	na	na	na	na	na	na	na	na	na	na
Total	37	39	36	38	37	37	35	39	39	35	38	40	39	39	42	36	38	39

Ranking:

Turkey	68
Sweden	57
Czechoslovakia	52
Chile	50
Argentina	47
Hungary	46
Finland	46
Mexico	45
West Germany	45
Belarus	41
Slovenia	41
United States	41
Iceland	41
India	40
Britain	40
East Germany	39
Austria	39
Moscow	38
Romania	37
Portugal	37
Spain	36
Canada	36
Russia	35
Nigeria	34
Bulgaria	33
Estonia	33
North Ireland	33
Belgium	33
China	32
Brazil	32
Ireland	32
Denmark	32
Italy	31
Netherlands	30
Lithuania	28
France	27
Norway	24
Japan	14
Latvia	13

Note: Countries in the left column are ranked according to GNP per capita. / The percentages in the bottom row give each country an equal weight. / na=not ascertained.

V333 GIVE ADVICE OFTEN

A variety of characteristics are listed here. Could you take a look at them and select those which apply to you?
"I often give others advice" (% "mentioned")

	Total	Gender Male	Gender Female	Age 16-29	Age 30-49	Age 50+	Education Lower	Education Medium	Education Upper	Income Lower	Income Middle	Income Upper	Political Affinity Left	Political Affinity Center	Political Affinity Right	Values Mat	Values Mixed	Values Postmat
India	47	49	45	44	47	51	46	47	47	46	48	45	48	47	44	49	47	47
Nigeria	88	85	92	86	87	98	92	88	86	91	82	92	88	87	89	87	88	84
China	25	27	22	19	23	35	25	24	25	24	29	21	na	na	na	24	25	32
Romania	50	47	53	37	44	64	57	48	45	50	52	48	54	52	50	57	46	42
Turkey	69	65	73	57	73	82	75	64	53	74	71	65	61	72	72	72	69	66
Poland	na	na	na	na	na	na	na	na	na	na	na	na	na	na	na	na	na	na
Bulgaria	24	25	23	18	19	35	30	22	23	24	26	24	28	25	20	27	24	26
Chile	53	53	52	54	48	60	54	50	55	53	52	53	51	52	57	55	52	51
Czechoslovakia	32	32	33	25	30	39	33	30	38	31	33	32	36	29	35	34	32	30
South Africa	na	na	na	na	na	na	na	na	na	na	na	na	na	na	na	na	na	na
Lithuania	43	42	44	33	41	53	54	40	39	44	43	41	na	na	na	41	44	41
Hungary	44	46	42	44	46	42	38	50	46	36	47	57	48	49	48	45	42	50
Argentina	50	51	49	55	45	52	49	53	45	50	50	54	43	50	57	55	48	48
Brazil	50	49	51	44	50	59	58	46	45	54	51	46	47	46	55	54	47	42
Mexico	48	44	53	45	48	55	46	54	48	44	50	53	47	52	44	46	50	41
Belarus	23	20	24	17	22	30	26	20	23	23	19	27	21	22	31	24	21	34
Russia	23	21	24	20	17	30	24	22	22	23	24	24	25	20	32	24	21	25
Moscow	22	20	24	20	21	26	26	24	21	21	23	24	21	22	30	27	22	16
Latvia	18	20	17	18	16	23	19	18	20	14	22	19	na	na	na	22	19	20
Estonia	29	29	29	25	31	30	23	29	34	30	25	30	na	na	na	29	30	32
Portugal	50	48	52	43	49	57	52	51	42	52	53	44	50	49	55	53	49	42
South Korea	na	na	na	na	na	na	na	na	na	na	na	na	na	na	na	na	na	na
Ireland	52	48	55	50	49	56	52	52	54	43	55	57	51	54	49	49	51	59
North Ireland	42	44	40	38	43	43	42	40	45	47	41	44	46	41	43	39	45	40
Slovenia	34	36	31	30	37	32	30	34	41	35	32	34	38	35	44	35	33	37
Spain	26	27	26	27	23	29	25	31	30	27	24	32	24	30	33	28	28	26
East Germany	58	60	57	54	60	59	56	59	64	53	59	62	59	59	58	54	59	60
Britain	50	52	48	51	53	47	49	53	53	42	54	57	48	48	52	56	48	53
Italy	40	42	39	43	37	42	40	45	33	41	41	41	43	39	41	39	42	40
Netherlands	43	56	38	41	39	49	37	44	47	40	45	47	44	41	46	39	42	44
Belgium	31	35	28	30	33	30	27	33	36	30	33	37	35	31	33	22	32	39
Austria	52	51	52	52	53	51	52	52	54	52	50	55	55	54	50	57	50	53
France	23	24	22	25	20	23	25	20	21	23	23	24	22	25	26	23	23	23
Canada	42	44	40	48	39	40	40	42	44	43	41	43	47	44	42	38	44	42
United States	43	45	42	48	43	42	38	45	45	45	43	42	44	43	46	39	44	44
Iceland	50	52	47	55	53	39	38	51	58	na	na	na	48	50	52	50	48	62
West Germany	56	58	54	54	57	56	56	56	58	53	60	58	58	55	61	58	56	58
Denmark	46	47	46	51	50	38	38	49	49	43	48	50	50	44	47	46	46	53
Finland	55	56	54	64	59	37	52	51	61	50	55	59	51	57	55	41	52	64
Norway	33	35	31	37	37	25	26	31	38	31	36	35	34	32	37	29	34	40
Sweden	58	56	60	65	58	52	53	58	65	56	55	60	55	59	59	48	60	63
Japan	27	33	22	30	25	29	23	27	32	18	29	35	37	32	31	28	33	38
Switzerland	na	na	na	na	na	na	na	na	na	na	na	na	na	na	na	na	na	na
Total	42	43	42	41	42	45	42	42	43	41	43	44	44	44	46	42	42	44

Ranking:

Nigeria	88
Turkey	69
East Germany	58
Sweden	58
West Germany	56
Finland	55
Chile	53
Ireland	52
Austria	52
Romania	50
Argentina	50
Brazil	50
Portugal	50
Britain	50
Iceland	50
Mexico	48
India	47
Denmark	46
Hungary	44
Lithuania	43
Netherlands	43
United States	43
North Ireland	42
Canada	42
Italy	40
Slovenia	34
Norway	33
Czechoslovakia	32
Belgium	31
Estonia	29
Japan	27
Spain	26
China	25
Bulgaria	24
Belarus	23
Russia	23
France	23
Moscow	22
Latvia	18

Note: Countries in the left column are ranked according to GNP per capita. / The percentages in the bottom row give each country an equal weight. / na=not ascertained.

V335-V339. I am going to read out some statements about the government and the economy. For each one, could you tell me how much you agree or disagree?

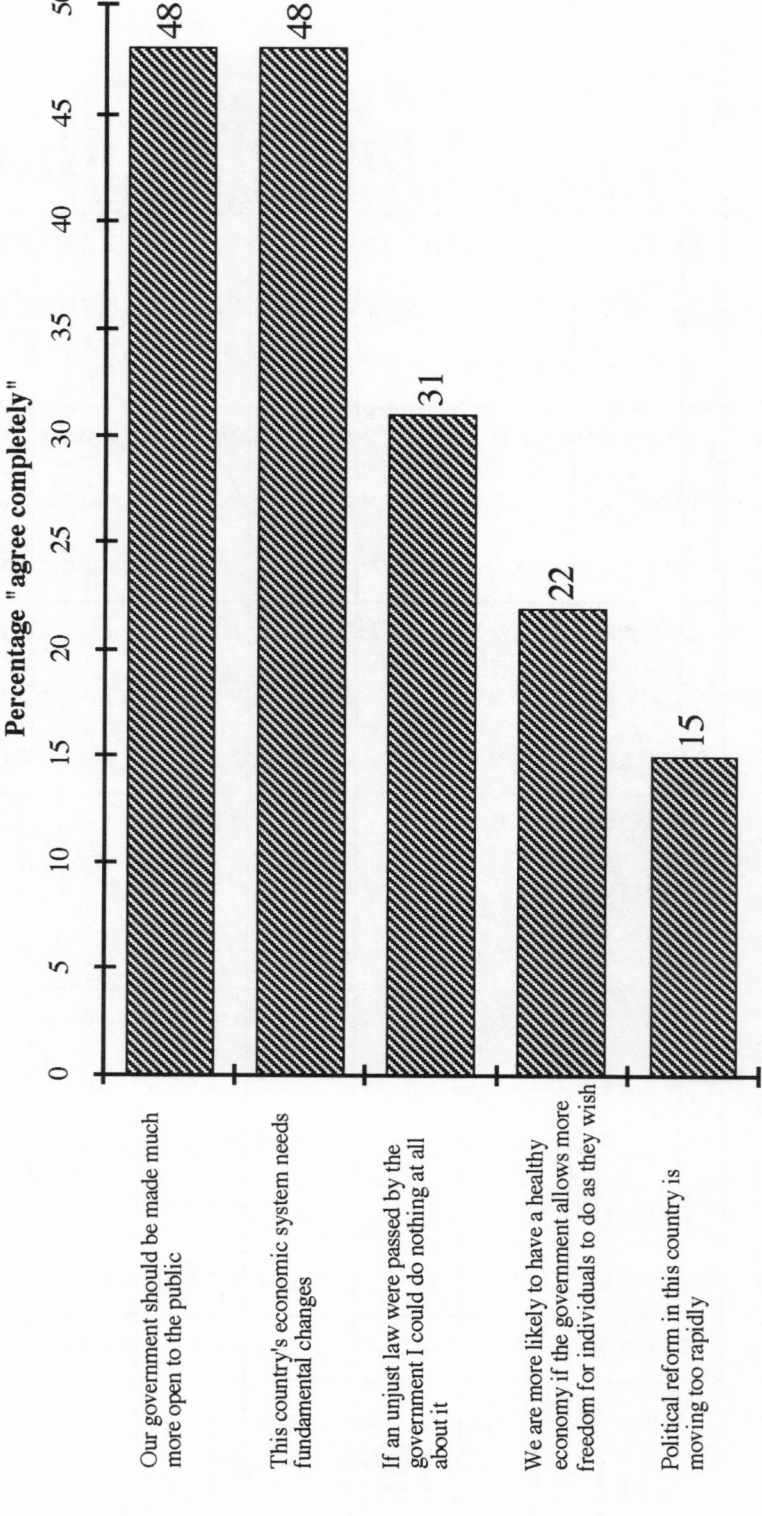

Percentage "agree completely"

V335 ECONOMY NEEDS CHANGES

I am going to read out some statements about the government and the economy. For each one, could you tell me how much you agree or disagree? "This country's economic system needs fundamental changes" (% "strongly agree")

	Total	Gender		Age			Education			Income			Political Affinity			Values		
		Male	Female	16-29	30-49	50+	Lower	Medium	Upper	Lower	Middle	Upper	Left	Center	Right	Mat	Mixed	Postmat
India	53	57	47	52	54	53	39	54	56	54	51	53	59	51	48	52	54	48
Nigeria	86	89	81	86	86	84	83	86	87	82	87	91	87	82	92	83	87	86
China	na	na	na	na	na	na	na	na	na	na	na	na	na	na	na	na	na	na
Romania	50	54	46	49	52	48	42	52	57	49	49	52	44	50	59	46	51	68
Turkey	28	31	24	27	30	26	25	31	36	27	28	29	41	26	24	19	28	40
Poland	71	73	69	69	73	71	65	74	80	76	67	70	71	68	79	67	73	71
Bulgaria	73	75	71	77	75	69	64	71	84	72	73	75	69	74	85	68	73	88
Chile	55	56	53	51	56	57	64	53	46	64	59	40	64	52	48	55	55	56
Czechoslovakia	62	67	57	62	67	56	47	67	74	53	67	65	54	58	73	51	64	76
South Africa	56	58	53	58	56	51	59	56	43	60	58	45	62	49	51	51	59	56
Lithuania	52	58	47	55	56	46	48	51	65	49	55	55	na	na	na	47	53	58
Hungary	69	72	66	72	71	65	64	71	80	64	72	78	71	69	72	69	68	74
Argentina	82	83	80	81	83	80	81	83	86	76	84	85	84	82	83	78	83	82
Brazil	88	87	89	89	88	86	86	89	84	87	89	89	90	87	88	86	89	93
Mexico	54	55	52	53	56	50	51	53	61	51	59	53	71	52	45	45	56	66
Belarus	69	73	65	67	71	68	63	67	73	67	68	72	74	62	66	61	72	81
Russia	77	81	74	82	80	70	69	76	83	73	79	80	86	76	72	71	80	89
Moscow	74	74	74	75	75	73	58	68	81	70	75	80	82	66	54	70	75	84
Latvia	83	82	84	83	84	82	80	83	81	86	81	82	90	na	na	83	83	82
Estonia	74	77	72	71	79	70	66	75	79	72	70	81	71	52	45	72	74	81
Portugal	34	35	34	33	34	36	35	41	24	33	40	29	43	33	30	36	34	33
South Korea	34	33	35	35	35	30	37	32	35	35	34	31	48	34	29	29	34	55
Ireland	38	40	37	35	44	34	44	34	22	43	42	32	47	40	29	34	39	40
North Ireland	33	37	31	29	37	33	32	40	28	35	34	26	43	33	32	24	36	40
Slovenia	51	50	53	42	49	61	53	50	51	55	49	51	43	51	51	24	36	48
Spain	41	43	39	44	43	36	36	49	53	34	40	48	45	36	45	34	41	52
East Germany	87	87	86	87	89	85	85	92	89	85	86	89	81	90	93	78	87	90
Britain	30	31	30	29	28	33	34	24	21	40	31	22	44	31	16	23	32	34
Italy	35	38	33	32	36	37	36	30	22	37	31	24	40	32	33	36	35	34
Netherlands	07	06	07	06	06	10	10	06	05	09	06	03	10	05	04	10	07	06
Belgium	15	14	15	13	16	15	17	15	09	16	13	11	18	14	11	19	15	12
Austria	14	14	15	17	15	13	13	20	17	13	16	13	23	15	09	14	14	15
France	21	23	19	20	21	22	24	20	15	25	23	16	19	19	19	24	21	20
Canada	39	40	38	34	40	42	47	42	30	47	38	34	40	39	37	29	40	43
United States	32	32	33	34	33	32	32	36	29	39	32	29	32	32	31	32	32	34
Iceland	27	27	28	20	29	34	35	25	09	na	05	na	31	27	25	35	29	34
West Germany	06	06	05	06	06	05	05	05	09	08	05	05	11	04	05	04	04	10
Denmark	53	50	56	46	55	57	60	56	47	58	54	51	46	58	53	54	56	44
Finland	20	19	22	18	19	26	34	19	15	28	19	15	20	23	17	29	21	18
Norway	28	24	33	25	29	29	39	31	20	30	27	26	31	25	29	30	29	19
Sweden	46	43	49	40	45	52	51	43	43	45	48	43	33	45	52	49	49	34
Japan	08	08	08	10	07	09	10	09	04	17	04	06	12	06	05	03	10	07
Switzerland	na	na	na	na	na	na	na	na	na	na	na	na	na	na	na	na	na	na
Total	48	49	47	47	49	47	47	48	48	49	49	47	49	45	45	45	49	51

Ranking:

Brazil	88
East Germany	87
Nigeria	86
Latvia	83
Argentina	82
Russia	77
Moscow	74
Estonia	74
Bulgaria	73
Poland	71
Hungary	69
Belarus	69
Czechoslovakia	62
South Africa	56
Chile	55
Mexico	54
India	53
Denmark	53
Lithuania	52
Slovenia	51
Romania	50
Sweden	46
Spain	41
Canada	39
Ireland	38
Italy	35
Portugal	34
South Korea	34
North Ireland	33
United States	32
Britain	30
Turkey	28
Norway	28
Iceland	27
France	21
Finland	20
Belgium	15
Austria	14
Japan	08
Netherlands	07
West Germany	06

Note: Countries in the left column are ranked according to GNP per capita. / The percentages in the bottom row give each country an equal weight. / na=not ascertained.

V336 GOVERNMENT MORE OPEN

I am going to read out some statements about the government and the economy. For each one, could you tell me how much you agree or disagree? "Our government should be made much more open to the public" (% "strongly agree")

	Total	Gender		Age			Education			Income			Political Affinity			Values		
		Male	Female	16-29	30-49	50+	Lower	Medium	Upper	Lower	Middle	Upper	Left	Center	Right	Mat	Mixed	Postmat
India	48	53	42	48	49	45	33	48	54	45	48	80	56	40	na	47	49	52
Nigeria	74	75	72	74	74	79	74	76	72	73	71	80	81	73	77	70	76	83
China	na	na	na	na	na	na	na	na	na	na	na	na	na	na	na	na	na	na
Romania	43	47	39	41	42	45	46	43	39	44	44	40	36	44	44	42	43	41
Turkey	40	45	35	38	41	40	37	44	47	43	39	39	51	37	40	28	41	52
Poland	48	52	45	50	49	46	43	52	52	48	49	48	46	47	48	40	52	49
Bulgaria	74	73	74	75	76	70	68	73	78	74	73	76	67	75	82	68	75	79
Chile	55	59	51	54	54	58	60	54	50	64	53	49	58	54	52	53	56	58
Czechoslovakia	53	56	50	52	53	53	53	53	51	51	55	52	57	54	47	53	53	55
South Africa	46	48	43	48	45	41	51	45	34	51	47	33	52	41	41	40	48	54
Lithuania	26	30	22	25	27	27	27	26	26	26	27	24	na	na	na	28	26	23
Hungary	67	71	63	72	69	63	64	71	68	61	73	69	72	68	67	65	69	80
Argentina	64	65	62	58	66	66	67	65	60	65	66	59	70	60	62	60	64	68
Brazil	86	86	85	86	87	83	91	86	75	88	86	83	90	81	86	83	88	86
Mexico	51	54	48	52	53	46	48	53	59	51	52	51	68	50	42	44	53	62
Belarus	65	71	59	60	65	69	65	65	65	66	64	63	70	61	50	55	69	80
Russia	61	62	60	62	63	57	59	63	59	62	59	60	66	57	54	52	66	74
Moscow	66	65	67	64	69	63	59	70	65	67	67	66	73	57	52	60	67	77
Latvia	61	66	58	60	62	61	65	62	58	62	58	63	na	na	na	54	65	65
Estonia	43	45	42	47	42	41	45	43	42	42	44	46	na	na	na	43	43	48
Portugal	45	47	44	42	47	48	46	53	37	51	46	38	60	42	38	46	46	46
South Korea	35	31	40	39	32	37	40	30	39	34	34	38	51	35	32	27	39	53
Ireland	46	45	47	39	51	46	50	44	37	47	50	43	57	47	41	32	47	62
North Ireland	45	51	40	46	52	36	46	46	35	49	42	37	64	49	32	24	52	47
Slovenia	51	51	50	48	47	58	54	49	50	52	51	49	52	53	40	47	53	50
Spain	46	49	44	51	48	40	42	56	57	38	48	51	51	41	46	38	45	59
East Germany	59	54	63	53	55	65	63	54	46	64	62	51	62	58	47	69	56	59
Britain	40	42	38	42	39	40	43	32	37	45	40	35	57	43	22	25	41	56
Italy	38	39	37	36	40	37	39	33	29	41	35	34	46	32	34	34	36	48
Netherlands	20	21	20	16	19	27	26	19	15	25	17	15	23	15	20	26	19	20
Belgium	33	33	32	28	35	34	38	32	25	31	34	31	38	31	26	37	33	32
Austria	47	48	47	52	48	45	48	47	50	49	48	46	53	52	41	46	45	55
France	33	32	35	28	37	34	38	32	25	36	33	30	33	30	34	34	34	34
Canada	50	51	49	48	50	51	55	53	42	56	52	43	52	51	46	36	50	58
United States	34	35	32	34	37	29	32	36	32	37	33	34	36	34	31	22	33	45
Iceland	25	25	26	24	27	24	30	24	23	45	na	na	30	26	22	25	25	32
West Germany	40	38	41	46	38	38	41	40	37	45	42	33	51	38	24	31	37	51
Denmark	48	46	49	45	54	48	50	51	44	47	53	46	56	51	39	36	48	58
Finland	42	40	44	45	42	38	54	43	33	47	42	35	45	45	36	45	40	46
Norway	37	38	36	35	34	42	48	41	27	43	36	32	44	35	33	38	36	47
Sweden	56	57	55	53	54	60	62	55	48	55	60	52	52	56	56	53	58	52
Japan	30	32	27	30	31	27	28	29	32	38	27	28	46	29	24	20	34	42
Switzerland	na	na	na	na	na	na	na	na	na	na	na	na	na	na	na	na	na	na
Total	48	49	47	47	49	48	49	49	45	50	49	46	55	47	44	43	49	55

Ranking:

Brazil	86
Nigeria	74
Bulgaria	74
Hungary	67
Moscow	66
Belarus	65
Argentina	64
Russia	61
Latvia	61
East Germany	59
Sweden	56
Chile	55
Czechoslovakia	53
Mexico	51
Slovenia	51
Canada	50
India	48
Poland	48
Denmark	48
Austria	47
South Africa	46
Ireland	46
Spain	46
Portugal	45
North Ireland	45
Romania	43
Estonia	43
Finland	42
Turkey	40
Britain	40
West Germany	40
Italy	38
Norway	37
South Korea	35
United States	34
Belgium	33
France	33
Japan	30
Lithuania	26
Iceland	25
Netherlands	20

Note: Countries in the left column are ranked according to GNP per capita. / The percentages in the bottom row give each country an equal weight. / na=not ascertained.

V337 INDIVIDUAL FREEDOM

I am going to read out some statements about the government and the economy. For each one, could you tell me how much you agree or disagree? "We are more likely to have a healthy economy if the government allows more freedom for individuals to do as they wish" (% "strongly agree")

	Total	Gender		Age			Education			Income			Political Affinity			Values		
		Male	Female	16-29	30-49	50+	Lower	Medium	Upper	Lower	Middle	Upper	Left	Center	Right	Mat	Mixed	Postmat
India	23	25	20	22	na	26	16	24	24	22	22	24	25	20	27	24	23	20
Nigeria	25	25	24	24	26	22	28	27	21	25	25	22	39	18	26	23	24	34
China	na	na	na	na	na	na	na	na	na	na	na	na	na	na	na	na	na	na
Romania	32	36	28	32	36	29	25	33	39	28	32	36	25	32	42	21	36	67
Turkey	20	24	16	18	19	24	21	19	20	24	18	17	22	20	22	18	20	23
Poland	na	na	na	na	na	na	na	na	na	na	na	na	na	na	na	na	na	na
Bulgaria	47	51	43	45	48	46	46	42	54	51	42	49	37	48	55	40	47	63
Chile	24	27	21	17	23	35	30	22	18	28	24	19	21	23	28	26	25	19
Czechoslovakia	03	04	02	04	03	03	04	03	03	05	02	03	02	02	05	03	03	05
South Africa	na	na	na	na	na	na	na	na	na	na	na	na	na	na	na	na	na	na
Lithuania	24	28	20	24	24	24	27	22	28	23	24	25	32	32	41	19	25	32
Hungary	33	38	28	26	35	33	35	31	27	33	33	35	28	32	41	28	37	42
Argentina	28	27	28	21	30	30	28	26	30	24	26	27	28	26	32	23	30	27
Brazil	61	61	61	54	64	68	74	58	43	69	57	55	58	56	65	61	60	62
Mexico	13	14	11	11	13	16	15	08	11	14	12	13	14	13	11	11	12	14
Belarus	30	34	27	29	28	36	29	29	32	32	30	31	34	25	28	23	32	46
Russia	32	34	30	35	30	33	32	33	31	32	29	34	41	27	35	26	34	47
Moscow	42	45	40	34	44	44	38	37	45	36	43	48	49	33	27	32	40	66
Latvia	42	49	36	44	37	51	44	41	44	38	40	46	na	na	na	35	45	54
Estonia	25	25	24	29	23	24	23	25	25	21	25	29	19	10	15	22	24	41
Portugal	14	13	15	12	14	16	15	13	10	18	11	10	19	10	15	15	13	13
South Korea	11	11	12	11	12	16	15	10	35	12	11	10	18	12	09	09	12	21
Ireland	15	16	14	09	18	15	18	13	16	16	15	14	17	17	09	12	17	14
North Ireland	10	15	06	12	09	14	10	12	07	16	05	07	11	07	12	05	10	16
Slovenia	18	19	16	18	14	09	21	18	03	18	17	21	17	18	19	16	19	12
Spain	23	23	23	19	25	24	23	23	13	25	22	20	20	20	26	22	24	24
East Germany	45	48	43	41	46	48	47	45	38	44	47	45	37	50	51	47	44	49
Britain	13	14	11	10	12	14	16	06	07	16	12	09	15	11	13	07	14	14
Italy	12	13	10	11	12	12	12	10	04	13	08	07	13	08	16	11	11	13
Netherlands	05	06	05	04	04	08	08	03	04	08	05	03	03	04	08	05	06	03
Belgium	16	17	15	16	15	17	17	16	14	15	18	18	17	15	15	17	16	16
Austria	26	31	23	28	27	24	23	27	35	20	24	33	33	25	25	20	26	29
France	15	17	13	12	17	15	16	13	16	15	14	17	10	14	23	13	16	17
Canada	11	13	09	07	11	14	15	11	07	14	12	07	10	11	11	09	12	09
United States	10	12	08	09	10	14	10	11	07	11	09	10	09	09	14	06	11	11
Iceland	11	15	08	08	12	15	14	10	10	na	08	na	05	10	18	12	10	14
West Germany	08	08	07	07	07	08	09	06	05	08	07	07	07	08	06	08	07	08
Denmark	18	18	19	15	17	22	20	19	17	22	14	19	09	20	23	21	18	15
Finland	25	27	22	26	24	26	36	23	21	29	25	21	16	25	28	37	24	26
Norway	12	15	09	12	11	14	13	11	13	12	10	17	07	10	20	10	14	08
Sweden	27	31	22	25	21	34	30	25	23	27	26	24	16	25	36	21	30	24
Japan	04	04	04	07	03	02	05	03	05	06	02	04	07	03	04	02	04	07
Switzerland	na	na	na	na	na	na	na	na	na	na	na	na	na	na	na	na	na	na
Total	**22**	**24**	**20**	**20**	**22**	**24**	**23**	**21**	**20**	**23**	**21**	**22**	**21**	**20**	**23**	**19**	**22**	**26**

Ranking:

Brazil	61
Bulgaria	47
East Germany	45
Moscow	42
Latvia	42
Hungary	33
Romania	32
Russia	32
Belarus	30
Argentina	28
Sweden	27
Austria	26
Nigeria	25
Estonia	25
Finland	25
Chile	24
Lithuania	24
India	23
Spain	23
Turkey	20
Slovenia	18
Denmark	18
Belgium	16
Ireland	15
France	15
Portugal	14
Mexico	13
Britain	13
Italy	12
Norway	12
South Korea	11
Canada	11
Iceland	11
North Ireland	10
United States	10
West Germany	08
Netherlands	05
Japan	04
Czechoslovakia	03

Note: Countries in the left column are ranked according to GNP per capita. / The percentages in the bottom row give each country an equal weight. / na=not ascertained.

V338 HELPLESS: UNJUST LAW

I am going to read out some statements about the government and the economy. For each one, could you tell me how much you agree or disagree? "If an unjust law were passed by the government I could do nothing at all about it" (% "strongly agree")

	Total	Gender Male	Gender Female	Age 16-29	Age 30-49	Age 50+	Education Lower	Education Medium	Education Upper	Income Lower	Income Middle	Income Upper	Political Affinity Left	Political Affinity Center	Political Affinity Right	Values Mat	Values Mixed	Values Postmat	Ranking	
India	08	08	07	08	07	08	08	07	08	09	07	08	06	na	na	08	na	08	Slovenia	65
Nigeria	41	41	41	40	43	40	44	42	39	46	40	37	48	39	37	51	36	40	Latvia	55
China	na	na	na	na	na	na	na	na	na	na	na	na	na	na	na	na	na	na	Poland	51
Romania	47	47	47	46	48	47	49	45	47	51	43	49	46	49	44	48	48	39	Russia	50
Turkey	18	15	20	15	17	24	21	15	10	21	17	16	15	16	22	16	20	13	Bulgaria	49
Poland	51	47	56	47	50	56	55	50	49	49	54	52	53	46	49	59	50	37	Estonia	49
Bulgaria	49	47	50	42	46	57	55	52	38	56	46	42	43	50	47	54	48	41	Romania	47
Chile	21	20	23	18	22	26	25	22	15	23	22	19	19	21	21	29	21	14	Hungary	46
Czechoslovakia	27	24	29	25	26	26	29	25	25	30	24	26	33	27	20	33	26	16	Belarus	45
South Africa	29	27	31	27	30	32	40	25	18	37	26	23	22	25	31	38	25	20	Moscow	45
Lithuania	43	40	45	39	42	47	47	41	43	44	44	38	na	na	na	47	43	33	Sweden	44
Hungary	46	46	46	37	47	49	48	46	32	50	46	39	43	48	39	48	45	35	Lithuania	43
Argentina	32	29	34	34	30	32	34	31	28	32	29	31	21	29	34	35	34	23	Nigeria	41
Brazil	31	31	31	25	29	46	44	28	18	38	31	24	26	28	32	33	30	23	Denmark	38
Mexico	17	15	20	18	17	17	19	16	13	17	15	20	16	16	13	16	17	13	Austria	36
Belarus	45	47	43	38	44	53	53	42	44	43	43	49	45	44	47	43	46	43	France	33
Russia	50	46	54	45	51	52	52	54	46	55	48	46	48	48	53	54	49	42	Argentina	32
Moscow	45	38	51	41	45	50	46	44	46	45	45	44	43	48	45	48	43	50	Spain	32
Latvia	55	51	58	51	54	64	56	57	52	56	54	55	na	na	na	56	56	52	Brazil	31
Estonia	49	45	53	48	50	50	58	48	43	48	52	47	na	na	na	55	47	39	Portugal	31
Portugal	31	31	31	27	32	35	35	25	22	38	30	22	26	31	34	40	28	13	East Germany	30
South Korea	11	13	09	09	12	11	18	10	09	13	10	10	08	14	09	10	13	10	West Germany	30
Ireland	20	18	21	19	20	19	24	15	14	25	22	15	18	18	19	19	22	13	South Africa	29
North Ireland	16	21	12	18	16	16	16	21	07	14	09	18	07	15	20	16	18	11	Czechoslovakia	27
Slovenia	65	62	67	53	65	73	67	66	59	71	62	58	52	64	58	68	64	52	Finland	27
Spain	32	31	33	28	33	35	33	36	25	35	31	30	28	30	35	36	32	26	Belgium	25
East Germany	30	27	33	25	27	36	32	25	27	32	30	29	33	29	22	42	31	24	Italy	24
Britain	17	17	18	16	16	19	19	12	12	21	19	12	21	17	13	15	18	18	Chile	21
Italy	24	23	25	19	23	27	25	16	11	25	20	18	24	20	28	31	24	18	Ireland	20
Netherlands	11	16	09	06	07	22	17	09	06	14	13	08	08	11	13	26	09	08	Norway	20
Belgium	25	24	26	21	25	29	29	27	15	27	23	26	20	24	25	34	26	18	Japan	20
Austria	36	36	36	28	34	41	40	33	35	36	37	36	41	36	33	35	38	31	Turkey	18
France	33	33	34	29	39	31	37	32	27	37	34	29	28	32	39	39	33	31	Mexico	17
Canada	15	16	15	15	15	16	23	15	11	17	18	11	14	17	13	21	15	13	Britain	17
United States	09	07	11	09	09	08	12	09	05	09	10	06	06	07	09	11	09	05	North Ireland	16
Iceland	12	12	11	10	11	16	15	12	09	na	na	na	13	11	12	12	12	10	Canada	15
West Germany	30	28	33	28	30	32	34	26	22	33	28	27	28	32	26	39	31	24	Iceland	12
Denmark	38	37	40	32	33	49	53	43	27	44	38	26	31	42	37	49	39	25	South Korea	11
Finland	27	27	27	23	24	38	38	32	16	34	25	24	23	29	23	39	27	26	Netherlands	11
Norway	20	20	20	10	17	30	33	20	13	24	19	15	20	17	20	25	20	08	United States	09
Sweden	44	46	42	39	39	54	56	44	27	44	48	41	36	49	45	55	47	31	India	08
Japan	20	20	19	18	19	23	24	19	18	23	22	17	26	19	17	18	22	09		
Switzerland	na	na	na	na	na	na	na	na	na	na	na	na	na	na	na	na	na	na		
Total	31	30	32	27	30	35	36	30	25	34	31	29	27	29	29	35	31	24		

Note: Countries in the left column are ranked according to GNP per capita. / The percentages in the bottom row give each country an equal weight. / na=not ascertained.

V339 POLITICAL REFORM RAPID

I am going to read out some statements about the government and the economy. For each one, could you tell me how much you agree or disagree? "Political reform in this country is moving too rapidly" (% "strongly agree")

	Total	Gender Male	Gender Female	Age 16-29	Age 30-49	Age 50+	Education Lower	Education Medium	Education Upper	Income Lower	Income Middle	Income Upper	Pol. Affinity Left	Pol. Affinity Center	Pol. Affinity Right	Values Mat	Values Mixed	Values Postmat
India	08	09	06	08	07	09	07	07	08	08	07	08	10	08	06	07	07	15
Nigeria	38	36	42	40	37	29	38	43	34	35	41	42	52	37	36	47	35	32
China	na	na	na	na	na	na	na	na	na	na	na	na	na	na	na	na	na	na
Romania	18	18	19	14	21	19	22	18	14	24	20	13	24	19	11	22	17	04
Turkey	10	11	10	11	09	12	13	08	05	12	11	09	09	10	15	12	10	10
Poland	40	42	38	39	42	39	36	43	44	42	38	40	41	37	44	34	43	44
Bulgaria	11	09	13	11	09	15	12	11	09	09	13	11	10	12	09	15	11	03
Chile	21	21	22	20	21	24	29	20	15	28	21	16	18	21	26	26	22	15
Czechoslovakia	11	10	12	08	13	11	13	11	09	11	13	10	17	12	06	12	11	07
South Africa	48	54	43	53	47	41	55	48	28	59	51	28	62	40	46	38	52	63
Lithuania	16	16	16	14	15	19	18	14	22	17	17	12	na	na	na	18	17	09
Hungary	22	20	24	16	23	23	31	17	04	27	22	12	20	21	20	23	21	13
Argentina	16	14	17	16	15	17	19	13	12	23	13	14	06	14	20	21	15	13
Brazil	41	41	40	39	39	46	50	42	16	51	38	32	38	38	44	43	40	29
Mexico	12	11	13	12	11	15	13	12	09	14	11	10	11	11	14	13	11	08
Belarus	09	09	09	08	08	11	14	10	06	07	11	09	07	11	12	11	08	09
Russia	11	09	12	10	09	13	12	12	09	11	10	12	07	11	20	14	09	07
Moscow	10	09	11	08	09	13	17	09	09	11	08	12	06	13	18	16	08	05
Latvia	18	16	19	13	17	24	25	19	14	15	17	19	na	na	na	19	19	07
Estonia	19	17	20	13	18	26	29	18	12	18	18	20	na	na	na	25	17	10
Portugal	09	10	07	07	08	10	11	08	02	10	08	07	09	07	10	11	08	06
South Korea	12	13	11	08	13	15	23	12	06	14	11	09	12	09	13	13	11	07
Ireland	04	03	06	03	04	06	07	02	00	06	05	04	03	05	04	03	05	04
North Ireland	06	07	05	01	06	08	08	01	00	11	03	03	00	06	08	07	06	04
Slovenia	28	25	32	22	25	37	36	27	17	33	31	15	23	26	21	30	29	17
Spain	13	13	14	09	14	16	15	11	09	19	12	09	10	11	12	16	13	10
East Germany	29	26	32	22	27	37	30	28	29	33	28	27	42	25	14	47	28	24
Britain	08	07	08	07	06	09	09	06	03	12	07	03	12	07	05	06	09	06
Italy	07	07	07	05	07	08	07	04	02	09	04	04	06	07	05	09	07	05
Netherlands	03	03	03	03	01	07	04	02	02	05	05	01	02	03	04	05	04	01
Belgium	09	07	11	07	08	11	12	09	04	12	10	06	07	09	09	11	10	05
Austria	08	08	09	09	08	08	09	08	10	09	08	10	10	08	08	11	09	05
France	11	09	13	11	13	09	13	10	07	14	11	09	08	10	13	19	10	06
Canada	08	09	08	08	08	10	16	08	04	12	08	09	08	08	07	10	09	07
United States	06	06	08	06	04	08	12	06	03	09	06	03	04	04	10	07	07	04
Iceland	06	06	06	03	05	12	12	04	03	na	na	na	06	06	07	09	05	06
West Germany	14	13	16	11	14	17	17	11	08	16	13	12	12	16	11	20	15	09
Denmark	21	17	25	12	19	29	32	20	15	29	20	10	17	25	16	30	19	22
Finland	06	06	06	05	04	12	12	06	03	12	04	02	06	08	05	19	07	06
Norway	08	08	09	06	07	12	13	11	03	09	09	07	07	10	07	11	08	03
Sweden	20	17	24	18	21	22	26	19	11	22	28	12	10	23	21	26	22	13
Japan	05	05	05	05	06	06	08	04	04	12	02	05	04	05	06	03	06	03
Switzerland	na	na	na	na	na	na	na	na	na	na	na	na	na	na	na	na	na	na
Total	15	15	16	13	15	17	19	14	10	18	15	12	15	15	15	18	15	12

Ranking:

South Africa	48
Brazil	41
Poland	40
Nigeria	38
East Germany	29
Slovenia	28
Hungary	22
Chile	21
Denmark	21
Sweden	20
Estonia	19
Romania	18
Latvia	18
Lithuania	16
Argentina	16
West Germany	14
Spain	13
Mexico	12
South Korea	12
Bulgaria	11
Czechoslovakia	11
Russia	11
France	11
Turkey	10
Moscow	10
Belarus	09
Portugal	09
Belgium	09
India	08
Britain	08
Austria	08
Canada	08
Norway	08
Italy	07
North Ireland	06
United States	06
Iceland	06
Finland	06
Japan	05
Ireland	04
Netherlands	03

Note: Countries in the left column are ranked according to GNP per capita. / The percentages in the bottom row give each country an equal weight. / na=not ascertained.

V340-V345. I now want to ask you how much you trust various groups of people: Using the responses on this card, could you tell me how much you trust...

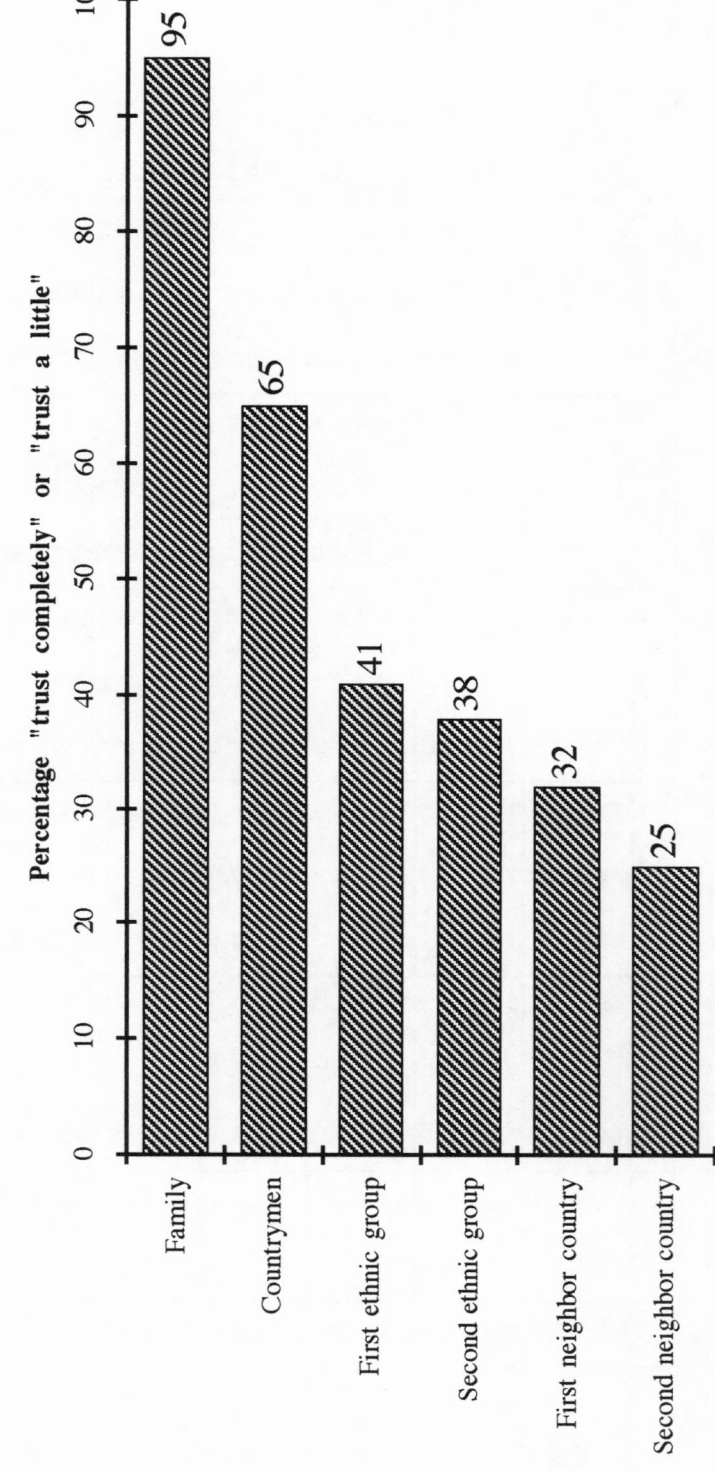

V340 TRUST: FAMILY

I now want to ask you how much you trust various groups of people: Using the responses on this card, could you tell me how much you trust... Your family (% "trust them completely" or "trust them a little")

	Total	Gender Male	Female	Age 16-29	30-49	50+	Education Lower	Medium	Upper	Income Lower	Middle	Upper	Pol. Aff. Left	Center	Right	Values Mat	Mixed	Postmat
India	99	99	99	99	100	98	99	100	99	99	99	96	99	99	100	99	99	99
Nigeria	95	95	94	94	95	98	94	94	96	95	95	97	96	96	97	93	96	95
China	98	98	98	97	98	99	99	98	97	85	99	95	na	na	na	98	98	98
Romania	92	92	91	92	90	93	92	91	93	85	94	95	90	92	89	91	92	93
Turkey	98	99	98	98	98	99	98	98	99	97	99	98	98	98	98	99	98	99
Poland	82	84	80	80	85	79	78	83	91	79	83	84	80	81	88	81	83	81
Bulgaria	95	94	96	95	93	97	95	96	94	95	97	94	96	95	94	97	95	89
Chile	93	94	92	92	94	93	92	96	95	89	94	95	94	92	93	92	93	93
Czechoslovakia	97	96	97	97	97	97	97	96	97	96	94	96	99	96	96	97	97	95
South Africa	84	84	85	85	84	84	82	84	95	83	82	92	82	86	86	87	84	82
Lithuania	96	96	96	96	97	95	94	96	97	95	97	96	na	na	na	95	97	94
Hungary	96	97	96	97	96	96	95	97	98	95	97	98	100	96	97	96	97	95
Argentina	96	97	96	97	95	95	96	96	97	94	96	99	95	96	98	95	96	97
Brazil	95	97	94	94	97	96	93	95	98	94	95	97	93	96	95	95	95	97
Mexico	96	95	96	94	97	97	95	96	97	95	96	97	93	96	97	97	96	95
Belarus	95	95	95	94	95	94	95	94	95	96	96	92	95	94	92	95	96	92
Russia	55	54	55	50	55	58	58	51	56	53	54	58	58	51	53	56	53	64
Moscow	96	97	95	94	97	97	95	95	97	54	97	94	96	95	97	96	96	95
Latvia	97	97	96	96	96	98	95	96	97	96	97	94	na	na	na	95	97	97
Estonia	97	97	97	95	99	95	98	98	96	97	96	96	na	na	na	97	97	100
Portugal	97	98	97	96	98	98	97	98	96	98	100	95	98	96	97	98	97	97
South Korea	97	96	97	96	97	97	95	96	98	97	97	96	95	96	98	97	97	98
Ireland	98	98	98	99	97	98	95	98	98	95	98	99	95	96	97	97	96	97
North Ireland	99	99	98	100	98	100	99	100	100	98	100	100	100	100	99	100	98	97
Slovenia	98	99	97	99	98	98	97	99	99	99	98	99	97	99	95	98	99	100
Spain	97	97	97	97	98	97	97	98	97	97	98	96	96	97	98	98	98	99
East Germany	98	98	98	97	99	98	98	98	99	96	100	99	98	98	99	96	99	95
Britain	98	98	99	98	98	99	98	98	99	99	99	98	98	99	99	98	99	97
Italy	96	97	97	95	98	96	96	97	94	99	97	98	97	98	95	96	96	97
Netherlands	89	87	89	91	88	86	85	91	90	83	91	92	88	86	91	91	88	88
Belgium	92	92	92	91	89	94	92	91	93	91	90	92	90	93	93	94	92	90
Austria	98	98	97	98	98	98	98	98	94	96	99	95	97	98	96	99	97	98
France	94	95	93	95	95	92	92	99	95	91	95	99	94	94	98	94	94	94
Canada	98	97	99	99	97	97	97	98	99	98	98	98	97	98	98	99	98	97
United States	98	98	98	98	98	99	98	97	99	99	99	99	97	98	99	99	98	99
Iceland	98	98	98	98	97	98	98	95	98	na	na	96	97	98	97	97	98	93
West Germany	95	95	95	95	96	94	95	99	97	92	96	98	93	96	99	93	96	93
Denmark	99	99	99	99	99	99	100	96	99	98	100	98	98	99	95	99	99	98
Finland	96	96	96	96	96	98	93	97	96	97	98	98	95	98	98	100	98	93
Norway	97	97	97	99	96	98	95	97	98	95	95	97	96	98	95	99	97	96
Sweden	98	98	98	97	98	99	98	97	97	99	99	97	98	98	98	99	98	97
Japan	98	98	98	97	98	96	97	99	99	96	na	na	99	na	na	99	98	na
Switzerland	na	na	na	na	na	na	na	na	98	na	na	na	na	na	na	na	na	na
Total	**95**	**95**	**95**	**94**	**95**	**95**	**94**	**95**	**96**	**94**	**94**	**95**	**94**	**94**	**95**	**95**	**95**	**94**

Ranking:

India	99
North Ireland	99
Denmark	99
China	99
Turkey	98
Ireland	98
Slovenia	98
East Germany	98
Britain	98
Austria	98
Canada	98
United States	98
Iceland	98
Sweden	98
Japan	98
Czechoslovakia	97
Latvia	97
Estonia	97
Portugal	97
South Korea	97
Spain	97
Norway	97
Lithuania	96
Hungary	96
Argentina	96
Mexico	96
Moscow	96
Italy	96
Finland	96
Nigeria	95
Bulgaria	95
Brazil	95
Belarus	95
West Germany	95
France	94
Chile	93
Romania	92
Belgium	92
Netherlands	89
South Africa	84
Poland	82
Russia	55

Note: Countries in the left column are ranked according to GNP per capita. / The percentages in the bottom row give each country an equal weight. / na=not ascertained.

V341 TRUST: OWN NATIONALITY

I now want to ask you how much you trust various groups of people: Using the responses on this card, could you tell me how much you trust... People of respondent's own nationality (% "trust them completely" or "trust them a little")

	Total	Gender Male	Gender Female	Age 16-29	Age 30-49	Age 50+	Education Lower	Education Medium	Education Upper	Income Lower	Income Middle	Income Upper	Political Affinity Left	Political Affinity Center	Political Affinity Right	Values Mat	Values Mixed	Values Postmat
India	90	90	91	90	91	89	92	92	88	94	88	89	88	90	94	93	89	86
Nigeria	40	42	36	37	41	53	39	38	42	36	43	47	40	45	35	39	42	28
China	65	65	66	54	68	74	69	64	62	65	66	66	na	na	na	70	63	44
Romania	52	57	48	38	49	65	62	46	49	49	54	53	54	52	42	57	50	44
Turkey	81	81	81	75	82	87	85	73	77	85	82	75	75	81	85	86	82	71
Poland	36	40	33	30	34	42	39	35	28	35	33	40	34	32	45	38	35	37
Bulgaria	74	75	73	68	70	84	88	70	68	72	79	69	74	77	67	82	73	59
Chile	64	67	62	58	64	74	67	63	63	68	62	64	69	61	65	64	64	67
Czechoslovakia	48	52	45	40	45	58	54	45	46	51	48	46	48	49	48	50	48	47
South Africa	33	32	34	35	31	34	38	32	27	40	30	27	34	29	33	34	33	31
Lithuania	86	87	86	87	86	87	87	86	87	85	89	87	na	na	na	85	88	86
Hungary	53	55	51	49	49	57	54	52	49	53	51	59	55	54	57	54	51	60
Argentina	58	59	57	47	59	66	66	51	56	64	63	55	55	56	60	60	58	57
Brazil	62	64	61	55	63	72	70	60	56	68	58	58	58	62	64	64	61	62
Mexico	70	72	67	66	72	74	70	69	70	73	68	67	64	70	72	75	70	66
Belarus	64	70	59	61	63	70	72	59	66	61	66	65	63	64	69	70	62	58
Russia	45	46	43	41	43	49	47	42	45	42	47	45	45	45	43	45	43	42
Moscow	50	53	48	44	50	55	56	48	50	50	50	50	50	50	55	53	50	42
Latvia	82	78	84	81	80	87	83	84	77	85	81	81	na	na	na	78	83	88
Estonia	81	82	81	80	82	82	78	83	81	81	79	84	na	na	na	83	82	67
Portugal	77	77	77	73	79	80	76	81	78	79	76	78	79	75	79	78	77	80
South Korea	74	74	74	70	74	81	79	76	69	75	74	74	71	71	76	75	73	71
Ireland	81	82	80	80	79	84	83	78	83	82	81	79	78	80	86	85	80	79
North Ireland	69	78	63	63	63	81	70	71	59	67	73	62	68	70	70	66	70	67
Slovenia	84	88	79	81	85	84	84	84	83	82	86	82	78	88	81	87	82	80
Spain	63	63	63	56	65	67	65	59	63	66	67	55	64	59	64	66	64	61
East Germany	69	72	66	59	72	71	72	65	60	67	71	69	54	76	79	71	69	68
Britain	68	68	68	64	63	74	68	70	63	74	64	67	65	69	70	68	69	66
Italy	39	39	39	32	42	41	40	36	27	39	43	39	37	41	45	41	39	39
Netherlands	57	59	56	53	57	60	60	54	56	50	59	63	52	56	62	58	57	55
Belgium	51	50	52	41	50	59	54	49	49	54	51	54	45	52	56	54	51	52
Austria	70	71	69	59	71	74	72	69	68	70	72	67	69	70	73	74	70	68
France	59	63	55	58	58	69	59	61	56	60	56	62	61	61	57	58	60	58
Canada	80	80	80	74	78	87	84	80	77	80	80	80	70	77	84	84	80	79
United States	75	76	73	72	74	78	73	77	74	75	74	77	72	77	75	72	74	79
Iceland	61	58	64	51	65	64	62	58	61	na	na	na	65	59	62	58	61	66
West Germany	66	67	65	56	63	74	70	60	54	66	67	65	50	72	78	78	71	52
Denmark	81	80	82	71	84	85	85	77	82	81	82	82	80	72	80	78	81	85
Finland	74	77	72	64	77	77	71	73	77	68	77	77	70	72	81	64	73	78
Norway	83	83	83	82	84	83	83	84	83	82	86	84	83	84	84	81	84	89
Sweden	75	76	74	67	78	78	76	72	77	75	71	77	79	73	76	67	76	76
Japan	52	54	50	41	55	57	47	55	50	49	53	54	53	52	65	60	50	53
Switzerland	na	na	na	na	na	na	na	na	na	na	na	na	na	na	na	na	na	na
Total	**65**	**67**	**64**	**59**	**65**	**71**	**68**	**64**	**63**	**66**	**66**	**65**	**62**	**64**	**66**	**67**	**65**	**63**

Ranking:

India	90
Lithuania	86
Slovenia	84
Norway	83
Latvia	82
Turkey	81
Estonia	81
Ireland	81
Denmark	81
Canada	80
Portugal	77
United States	75
Sweden	75
Bulgaria	74
South Korea	74
Finland	74
Mexico	70
Austria	70
North Ireland	69
East Germany	69
Britain	68
West Germany	66
China	65
Chile	64
Belarus	64
Spain	63
Brazil	62
Iceland	61
France	59
Argentina	58
Netherlands	57
Hungary	53
Romania	52
Japan	52
Belgium	51
Moscow	50
Czechoslovakia	48
Russia	45
Nigeria	40
Italy	39
Poland	36
South Africa	33

Note: Countries in the left column are ranked according to GNP per capita. / The percentages in the bottom row give each country an equal weight. / na=not ascertained.

V342 TRUST: FIRST DOMESTIC ETHNIC GROUP

I now want to ask you how much you trust various groups of people: Using the responses on this card, could you tell me how much you trust... First domestic ethnic group (% "trust them completely" or "trust them a little")

		Gender		Age			Education			Income			Political Affinity			Values		
	Total	Male	Female	16-29	30-49	50+	Lower	Medium	Upper	Lower	Middle	Upper	Left	Center	Right	Mat	Mixed	Postmat
India	88	87	88	88	88	87	90	89	85	92	85	86	83	87	93	90	86	84
Nigeria	49	56	39	46	52	60	47	46	54	44	52	59	48	54	46	49	50	46
China	35	39	29	28	36	44	34	34	38	34	34	36	na	na	na	39	33	22
Romania	na	na	na	na	na	na	na	na	na	na	na	na	na	na	na	12	09	na
Turkey	10	10	10	11	09	11	11	08	09	09	10	10	06	09	15	12	09	09
Poland	09	12	07	11	09	09	12	09	02	09	05	14	08	09	09	08	09	08
Bulgaria	24	24	24	30	24	21	30	23	21	21	27	22	19	24	22	26	24	18
Chile	52	57	48	44	56	60	55	52	48	55	54	48	58	49	52	49	52	56
Czechoslovakia	29	31	27	24	28	33	28	29	31	31	26	30	33	30	24	27	30	26
South Africa	22	18	26	19	22	29	22	21	31	22	19	32	20	23	27	28	20	15
Lithuania	74	78	71	79	74	71	67	76	80	72	76	77	na	na	na	71	74	86
Hungary	na	na	na	na	na	na	na	na	na	na	na	na	na	na	na	na	na	na
Argentina	na	na	na	na	na	na	na	na	na	na	na	na	na	na	na	na	na	na
Brazil	62	62	61	60	62	64	63	63	56	63	65	58	61	61	64	60	64	58
Mexico	55	56	53	52	57	58	55	54	56	56	56	52	57	54	58	55	55	54
Belarus	na	na	na	na	na	na	na	na	na	na	na	na	na	na	na	na	na	na
Russia	na	na	na	na	na	na	na	na	na	na	na	na	na	na	na	na	na	na
Moscow	na	na	na	na	na	na	na	na	na	na	na	na	na	na	na	na	na	na
Latvia	68	71	66	65	68	73	57	70	69	70	68	67	na	na	na	63	70	77
Estonia	62	65	59	59	65	60	58	63	61	61	59	66	na	na	na	62	63	47
Portugal	na	na	na	na	na	na	na	na	na	na	na	na	na	na	na	na	na	na
South Korea	19	16	22	17	19	23	17	21	18	19	20	19	21	14	23	22	17	15
Ireland	na	na	na	na	na	na	na	na	na	na	na	na	na	na	na	na	na	na
North Ireland	na	na	na	na	na	na	na	na	na	na	na	na	na	na	na	na	na	na
Slovenia	11	13	10	08	15	10	09	11	16	09	14	12	14	11	05	07	13	17
Spain	21	23	20	24	23	18	21	18	27	16	21	26	25	19	18	17	24	24
East Germany	na	na	na	na	na	na	na	na	na	na	na	na	na	na	na	na	na	na
Britain	na	na	na	na	na	na	na	na	na	na	na	na	na	na	na	na	na	na
Italy	na	na	na	na	na	na	na	na	na	na	na	na	na	na	na	na	na	na
Netherlands	na	na	na	na	na	na	na	na	na	na	na	na	na	na	na	na	na	na
Belgium	na	na	na	na	na	na	na	na	na	na	na	na	na	na	na	na	na	na
Austria	na	na	na	na	na	na	na	na	na	na	na	na	na	na	na	na	na	na
France	na	na	na	na	na	na	na	na	na	na	na	na	na	na	na	na	na	na
Canada	58	58	59	53	57	64	59	57	59	51	62	59	52	58	65	64	58	57
United States	61	61	60	61	62	59	60	60	63	59	59	64	64	63	57	57	60	67
Iceland	na	na	na	na	na	na	na	na	na	na	na	na	na	na	na	na	na	na
West Germany	na	na	na	na	na	na	na	na	na	na	na	na	na	na	na	na	na	na
Denmark	na	na	na	na	na	na	na	na	na	na	na	na	na	na	na	na	na	na
Finland	na	na	na	na	na	na	na	na	na	na	na	na	na	na	na	na	na	na
Norway	na	na	na	na	na	na	na	na	na	na	na	na	na	na	na	na	na	na
Sweden	na	na	na	na	na	na	na	na	na	na	na	na	na	na	na	na	na	na
Japan	12	13	11	12	13	11	12	11	15	13	14	11	25	14	09	17	11	19
Switzerland	na	na	na	na	na	na	na	na	na	na	na	na	na	na	na	na	na	na
Total	41	43	40	40	42	43	40	41	42	40	41	42	37	36	37	41	41	40

Ranking:

India	88
Lithuania	74
Latvia	68
Brazil	62
Estonia	62
United States	61
Canada	58
Mexico	55
Chile	52
Nigeria	49
China	35
Czechoslovakia	29
Bulgaria	24
South Africa	22
Spain	21
South Korea	19
Japan	12
Slovenia	11
Turkey	10
Poland	09

Note: Countries in the left column are ranked according to GNP per capita. / The percentages in the bottom row give each country an equal weight. / na=not ascertained.

V343 TRUST: SECOND DOMESTIC ETHNIC GROUP

I now want to ask you how much you trust various groups of people. Using the responses on this card, could you tell me how much you trust... Second domestic ethnic group (% "trust them completely" or "trust them a little")

	Total	Gender		Age			Education			Income			Political Affinity			Values		
		Male	Female	16-29	30-49	50+	Lower	Medium	Upper	Lower	Middle	Upper	Left	Center	Right	Mat	Mixed	Postmat
India	70	70	69	68	70	71	72	68	71	72	66	71	65	70	73	72	68	66
Nigeria	41	45	34	37	44	53	37	40	43	42	39	47	37	43	40	36	43	42
China	37	39	34	29	38	45	39	36	37	39	34	37	na	na	na	40	36	24
Romania	na	na	na	na	na	na	na	na	na	na	na	na	na	na	na	na	na	na
Turkey	08	10	05	08	07	09	08	08	05	07	08	08	04	07	11	08	08	07
Poland	07	08	07	11	06	06	09	07	03	08	04	10	04	08	07	05	09	05
Bulgaria	12	12	11	14	11	11	16	12	06	12	11	10	06	13	11	12	12	07
Chile	48	52	44	38	52	59	53	48	43	50	50	44	53	45	50	47	48	51
Czechoslovakia	03	04	02	03	03	03	03	02	04	05	02	02	02	03	03	03	03	01
South Africa	36	37	34	41	33	30	42	35	17	47	36	15	39	26	33	32	37	40
Lithuania	75	80	70	79	72	74	68	76	80	71	78	78	na	na	na	71	74	85
Hungary	na	na	na	na	na	na	na	na	na	na	na	na	na	na	na	na	na	na
Argentina	na	na	na	na	na	na	na	na	na	na	na	na	na	na	na	na	na	na
Brazil	46	48	44	42	48	49	44	47	44	43	47	47	42	48	52	44	48	46
Mexico	55	55	55	53	58	53	55	57	54	56	55	53	58	55	54	54	55	59
Belarus	na	na	na	na	na	na	na	na	na	na	na	na	na	na	na	na	na	na
Russia	na	na	na	na	na	na	na	na	na	na	na	na	na	na	na	na	na	na
Moscow	68	69	68	64	68	74	61	70	68	70	67	68	na	na	na	63	70	75
Latvia	68	69	68	64	68	74	61	70	65	70	67	61	na	na	na	64	65	53
Estonia	64	66	62	61	66	64	60	65	67	64	61	68	na	na	na	na	na	na
Portugal	na	na	na	na	na	na	na	na	na	na	na	na	na	na	na	na	na	na
South Korea	27	22	31	23	27	33	23	25	31	23	28	32	26	21	32	30	25	19
Ireland	na	na	na	na	na	na	na	na	na	na	na	na	na	na	na	na	na	na
North Ireland	na	na	na	na	na	na	na	na	na	na	na	na	na	na	na	na	na	na
Slovenia	33	36	31	34	35	31	36	31	32	34	34	32	34	34	33	28	36	37
Spain	23	24	21	28	24	17	21	25	29	15	23	31	28	21	18	15	25	30
East Germany	na	na	na	na	na	na	na	na	na	na	na	na	na	na	na	na	na	na
Britain	na	na	na	na	na	na	na	na	na	na	na	na	na	na	na	na	na	na
Italy	na	na	na	na	na	na	na	na	na	na	na	na	na	na	na	na	na	na
Netherlands	na	na	na	na	na	na	na	na	na	na	na	na	na	na	na	na	na	na
Belgium	na	na	na	na	na	na	na	na	na	na	na	na	na	na	na	na	na	na
Austria	na	na	na	na	na	na	na	na	na	na	na	na	na	na	na	na	na	na
France	na	na	na	na	na	na	na	na	na	na	na	na	na	na	na	na	na	na
Canada	46	45	46	39	47	49	42	44	50	41	48	49	46	48	48	41	44	54
United States	56	56	55	56	58	56	54	58	56	53	57	60	63	56	52	54	55	61
Iceland	na	na	na	na	na	na	na	na	na	na	na	na	na	na	na	na	na	na
West Germany	na	na	na	na	na	na	na	na	na	na	na	na	na	na	na	na	na	na
Denmark	na	na	na	na	na	na	na	na	na	na	na	na	na	na	na	na	na	na
Finland	na	na	na	na	na	na	na	na	na	na	na	na	na	na	na	na	na	na
Norway	na	na	na	na	na	na	na	na	na	na	na	na	na	na	na	na	na	na
Sweden	na	na	na	na	na	na	na	na	na	na	na	na	na	na	na	na	na	na
Japan	11	13	10	11	13	10	09	11	15	11	14	11	26	12	10	15	11	19
Switzerland	na	na	na	na	na	na	na	na	na	na	na	na	na	na	na	na	na	na
Total	**38**	**40**	**37**	**37**	**39**	**40**	**38**	**38**	**38**	**38**	**38**	**39**	**33**	**32**	**33**	**37**	**39**	**39**

Ranking:

Lithuania	75
India	70
Latvia	68
Estonia	64
United States	56
Mexico	55
Chile	48
Brazil	46
Canada	46
Nigeria	41
China	37
South Africa	36
Slovenia	33
South Korea	27
Spain	23
Bulgaria	12
Japan	11
Turkey	08
Poland	07
Czechoslovakia	03

Note: Countries in the left column are ranked according to GNP per capita. / The percentages in the bottom row give each country an equal weight. / na=not ascertained.

V344 TRUST: FIRST NEIGHBOR NATIONALITY

I now want to ask you how much you trust various groups of people: Using the responses on this card, could you tell me how much you trust... First neighbor nationality (% "trust them completely" or "trust them a little")

Country	Total	Gender		Age			Education			Income			Political Affinity			Values		
		Male	Female	16-29	30-49	50+	Lower	Medium	Upper	Lower	Middle	Upper	Left	Center	Right	Mat	Mixed	Postmat
India	14	15	na	14	13	18	14	14	15	16	11	17	13	15	17	14	14	17
Nigeria	39	43	32	37	39	54	33	39	41	40	37	43	36	39	38	33	42	40
China	12	13	11	15	13	07	08	11	20	10	11	15	na	na	na	07	15	27
Romania	na	na	na	na	na	na	na	na	na	na	na	na	na	na	na	na	na	na
Turkey	09	10	08	11	07	10	09	09	10	05	10	14	08	12	06	09	09	10
Poland	36	38	34	25	33	45	42	33	33	37	30	42	32	32	45	35	36	37
Bulgaria	52	54	50	66	53	41	37	54	62	51	51	56	43	59	64	39	54	70
Chile	25	26	24	17	27	33	26	24	24	26	27	22	21	25	29	24	26	22
Czechoslovakia	24	26	22	26	25	22	21	26	26	25	23	25	17	22	33	19	25	31
South Africa	28	29	27	32	25	27	29	29	19	28	30	24	30	29	30	31	26	31
Lithuania	44	47	41	46	41	45	49	44	37	46	43	41	na	na	na	42	44	49
Hungary	na	na	na	na	na	na	na	na	na	na	na	na	na	na	na	na	na	na
Argentina	na	na	na	na	na	na	na	na	na	na	na	na	na	na	na	na	na	na
Brazil	35	36	34	32	33	44	37	35	29	36	35	35	28	35	44	36	35	28
Mexico	28	28	28	27	29	27	27	33	26	29	29	25	35	27	26	23	28	32
Belarus	na	na	na	na	na	na	na	na	na	na	na	na	na	na	na	na	na	na
Russia	na	na	na	na	na	na	na	na	na	na	na	na	na	na	na	na	na	na
Moscow	50	55	47	50	47	58	46	52	48	43	52	55	na	na	na	46	50	60
Latvia	50	55	49	53	55	46	46	52	52	51	50	57	na	na	na	57	51	54
Estonia	52	55	49	53	55	46	52	52	58	51	50	57	na	na	na	57	51	54
Portugal	na	na	na	na	na	na	na	na	na	na	na	na	na	na	na	na	na	na
South Korea	20	18	21	11	20	34	24	22	16	20	18	24	12	14	25	25	17	06
Ireland	na	na	na	na	na	na	na	na	na	na	na	na	na	na	na	na	na	na
North Ireland	na	na	na	na	na	na	na	na	na	na	na	na	na	na	na	na	na	na
Slovenia	26	28	24	26	27	25	32	24	20	30	24	22	na	na	23	25	26	25
Spain	28	31	25	34	30	21	26	30	35	17	31	32	33	26	24	20	30	35
East Germany	na	na	na	na	na	na	na	na	na	na	na	na	na	na	na	na	na	na
Britain	na	na	na	na	na	na	na	na	na	na	na	na	na	na	na	na	na	na
Italy	na	na	na	na	na	na	na	na	na	na	na	na	na	na	na	na	na	na
Netherlands	na	na	na	na	na	na	na	na	na	na	na	na	na	na	na	na	na	na
Belgium	na	na	na	na	na	na	na	na	na	na	na	na	na	na	na	na	na	na
Austria	na	na	na	na	na	na	na	na	na	na	na	na	na	na	na	na	na	na
France	na	na	na	na	na	na	na	na	na	na	na	na	na	na	na	na	na	na
Canada	54	53	55	45	52	64	54	54	54	51	56	54	44	56	61	53	54	65
United States	62	64	59	56	60	66	56	63	63	59	60	66	66	63	60	57	62	65
Iceland	na	na	na	na	na	na	na	na	na	na	na	na	na	na	na	na	na	na
West Germany	na	na	na	na	na	na	na	na	na	na	na	na	na	na	na	na	na	na
Denmark	na	na	na	na	na	na	na	na	na	na	na	na	na	na	na	na	na	na
Finland	na	na	na	na	na	na	na	na	na	na	na	na	na	na	na	na	na	na
Norway	na	na	na	na	na	na	na	na	na	na	na	na	na	na	na	na	na	na
Sweden	na	na	na	na	na	na	na	na	na	na	na	na	na	na	na	na	na	na
Japan	12	12	12	14	12	09	09	12	14	12	13	11	24	13	08	17	10	20
Switzerland	na	na	na	na	na	na	na	na	na	na	na	na	na	na	na	na	na	na
Total	33	34	31	32	32	35	33	33	33	32	32	34	29	31	33	31	33	36

Ranking:

United States	62
Canada	54
Bulgaria	52
Estonia	52
Latvia	50
Lithuania	44
Nigeria	39
Poland	36
Brazil	35
South Africa	28
Mexico	28
Spain	28
Slovenia	26
Chile	25
Czechoslovakia	24
South Korea	20
India	14
China	12
Japan	12
Turkey	09

Note: Countries in the left column are ranked according to GNP per capita. / The percentages in the bottom row give each country an equal weight. / na=not ascertained.

V345 TRUST: SECOND NEIGHBOR NATIONALITY

I now want to ask you how much you trust various groups of people: Using the responses on this card, could you tell me how much you trust... Second neighbor nationality (% "trust them completely" or "trust them a little")

	Total	Gender Male	Gender Female	Age 16-29	Age 30-49	Age 50+	Education Lower	Education Medium	Education Upper	Income Lower	Income Middle	Income Upper	Political Affinity Left	Political Affinity Center	Political Affinity Right	Values Mat	Values Mixed	Values Postmat
India	35	40	30	33	35	41	28	33	41	38	29	39	36	36	38	35	37	33
Nigeria	26	29	21	26	25	36	23	25	28	25	26	32	24	28	25	22	29	23
China	10	11	08	12	10	06	07	10	15	08	08	14	na	na	na	06	12	23
Romania	na	na	na	na	na	na	na	na	na	na	na	na	na	na	na	na	na	na
Turkey	03	na	na	04	03	01	02	03	05	02	02	05	04	03	01	02	02	06
Poland	16	16	15	17	15	17	17	16	12	13	14	21	14	16	19	16	16	16
Bulgaria	25	23	26	33	27	17	15	27	30	21	28	27	23	26	27	22	25	23
Chile	23	23	23	18	23	31	27	21	21	26	22	21	30	21	19	22	23	24
Czechoslovakia	10	10	09	07	09	11	09	09	13	11	09	09	10	09	10	08	09	13
South Africa	13	11	14	12	11	18	15	12	13	11	13	13	13	11	14	14	12	17
Lithuania	43	46	40	41	43	43	42	43	44	43	40	46	na	na	na	39	42	52
Hungary	na	na	na	na	na	na	na	na	na	na	na	na	na	na	na	na	na	na
Argentina	na	na	na	na	na	na	na	na	na	na	na	na	na	na	na	na	na	na
Brazil	26	27	25	21	27	34	28	26	23	26	26	25	20	29	30	26	26	27
Mexico	20	20	19	20	19	21	20	24	17	18	21	20	13	21	24	20	20	18
Belarus	na	na	na	na	na	na	na	na	na	na	na	na	na	na	na	na	na	na
Russia	na	na	na	na	na	na	na	na	na	na	na	na	na	na	na	na	na	na
Moscow	na	na	na	na	na	na	na	na	na	na	na	na	na	na	na	41	48	60
Latvia	47	52	44	40	48	55	42	47	50	47	41	51	na	na	na	46	44	39
Estonia	45	43	47	39	49	44	34	47	48	46	45	42	na	na	na	na	na	na
Portugal	09	na	na	na	na	na	na	na	na	na	na	na	na	na	na	na	na	na
South Korea	na	08	10	07	08	15	10	10	08	10	09	09	06	08	11	11	07	07
Ireland	na	na	na	na	na	na	na	na	na	na	na	na	na	na	na	na	na	na
North Ireland	na	na	na	na	na	na	na	na	na	na	na	na	na	na	na	na	na	na
Slovenia	40	43	37	43	38	37	44	39	34	45	38	37	37	40	44	40	40	45
Spain	21	23	20	26	23	17	20	22	29	16	21	28	26	22	17	15	23	29
East Germany	na	na	na	na	na	na	na	na	na	na	na	na	na	na	na	na	na	na
Britain	na	na	na	na	na	na	na	na	na	na	na	na	na	na	na	na	na	na
Italy	na	na	na	na	na	na	na	na	na	na	na	na	na	na	na	na	na	na
Netherlands	na	na	na	na	na	na	na	na	na	na	na	na	na	na	na	na	na	na
Belgium	na	na	na	na	na	na	na	na	na	na	na	na	na	na	na	na	na	na
Austria	na	na	na	na	na	na	na	na	na	na	na	na	na	na	na	na	na	na
France	na	na	na	na	na	na	na	na	na	na	na	na	na	na	na	na	na	na
Canada	37	38	36	32	38	40	35	36	40	34	39	38	38	37	40	33	36	42
United States	52	53	51	50	54	51	51	54	51	50	51	56	59	53	47	51	50	60
Iceland	na	na	na	na	na	na	na	na	na	na	na	na	na	na	na	na	na	na
West Germany	na	na	na	na	na	na	na	na	na	na	na	na	na	na	na	na	na	na
Denmark	na	na	na	na	na	na	na	na	na	na	na	na	na	na	na	na	na	na
Finland	na	na	na	na	na	na	na	na	na	na	na	na	na	na	na	na	na	na
Norway	na	na	na	na	na	na	na	na	na	na	na	na	na	na	na	na	na	na
Sweden	na	na	na	na	na	na	na	na	na	na	na	na	na	na	na	na	na	na
Japan	13	14	12	14	13	12	10	13	15	15	14	12	26	12	11	18	12	20
Switzerland	na	na	na	na	na	na	na	na	na	na	na	na	na	na	na	na	na	na
Total	26	27	25	25	26	27	24	26	27	25	25	27	24	23	24	24	26	29

Ranking:

United States	52
Latvia	47
Estonia	45
Lithuania	43
Slovenia	40
Canada	37
India	35
Nigeria	26
Brazil	26
Bulgaria	25
Chile	23
Spain	21
Mexico	20
Poland	16
South Africa	13
Japan	13
China	10
Czechoslovakia	10
South Korea	09
Turkey	03

Note: Countries in the left column are ranked according to GNP per capita. / The percentages in the bottom row give each country an equal weight. / na=not ascertained.

V346 TRUST: FIRST SUPERPOWER

I now want to ask you how much you trust various groups of people: Using the responses on this card, could you tell me how much you trust... First superpower (% "trust them completely" or "trust them a little")

	Total	Gender Male	Gender Female	Age 16-29	Age 30-49	Age 50+	Education Lower	Education Medium	Education Upper	Income Lower	Income Middle	Income Upper	Political Affinity Left	Political Affinity Center	Political Affinity Right	Values Mat	Values Mixed	Values Postmat	Ranking	
India	28	30	26	27	28	34	25	26	33	38	29	39	27	31	34	25	32	28	Latvia	53
Nigeria	33	38	26	33	33	39	30	34	33	25	26	32	28	35	32	28	37	32	Bulgaria	50
China	09	09	09	09	10	07	08	09	10	08	08	14	na	na	na	07	10	08	Estonia	47
Romania	na	na	na	na	na	na	na	na	na	na	na	na	na	na	na	na	na	na	United States	43
Turkey	13	16	11	14	14	11	13	14	15	02	02	05	17	15	10	12	13	17	Czechoslovakia	42
Poland	13	14	11	08	11	17	15	11	13	13	14	21	12	12	15	11	13	10	Lithuania	42
Bulgaria	50	48	52	43	47	59	62	47	47	21	28	27	55	51	42	57	50	33	Russia	39
Chile	17	18	16	14	17	21	18	17	14	26	22	21	35	15	14	14	16	21	Canada	38
Czechoslovakia	42	48	37	44	42	42	42	43	42	11	09	09	35	38	56	32	46	49	Nigeria	33
South Africa	14	17	12	17	12	12	13	15	12	11	13	13	16	14	14	12	15	22	Brazil	29
Lithuania	42	49	36	41	44	40	39	44	37	43	40	46	na	na	na	40	42	47	India	28
Hungary	na	na	na	na	na	na	na	na	na	na	na	na	na	na	na	na	na	na	Japan	21
Argentina	na	na	na	na	na	na	na	na	na	na	na	na	na	na	na	na	na	na	Spain	19
Brazil	29	30	28	25	30	34	29	29	28	26	26	25	24	31	34	26	31	31	Chile	17
Mexico	15	16	13	15	15	14	16	17	11	18	21	20	17	14	17	13	14	19	Slovenia	16
Belarus	na	na	na	na	na	na	na	na	na	na	na	na	na	na	na	na	na	na	Mexico	15
Russia	39	38	40	37	35	45	41	37	39	na	na	na	39	39	37	40	37	44	South Africa	14
Moscow	na	na	na	na	na	na	na	na	na	na	na	na	na	na	na	na	na	na	Turkey	13
Latvia	53	56	51	54	52	57	48	57	49	47	41	51	50	55	51	50	55	51	Poland	13
Estonia	47	50	45	45	49	46	42	48	51	46	45	42	51	45	38	51	45	38	China	09
Portugal	na	na	na	na	na	na	na	na	na	na	na	na	na	na	na	na	na	na	South Korea	08
South Korea	08	07	08	08	07	09	10	08	06	10	09	09	07	08	08	09	06	10		
Ireland	na	na	na	na	na	na	na	na	na	na	na	na	na	na	na	na	na	na		
North Ireland	na	na	na	na	na	na	na	na	na	na	na	na	na	na	na	na	na	na		
Slovenia	16	18	14	18	16	15	20	15	13	45	38	37	13	17	09	14	16	22		
Spain	19	19	18	22	20	15	18	19	23	16	21	28	22	18	14	13	20	24		
East Germany	na	na	na	na	na	na	na	na	na	na	na	na	na	na	na	na	na	na		
Britain	na	na	na	na	na	na	na	na	na	na	na	na	na	na	na	na	na	na		
Italy	na	na	na	na	na	na	na	na	na	na	na	na	na	na	na	na	na	na		
Netherlands	na	na	na	na	na	na	na	na	na	na	na	na	na	na	na	na	na	na		
Belgium	na	na	na	na	na	na	na	na	na	na	na	na	na	na	na	na	na	na		
Austria	na	na	na	na	na	na	na	na	na	na	na	na	na	na	na	na	na	na		
France	na	na	na	na	na	na	na	na	na	na	na	na	na	na	na	na	na	na		
Canada	38	40	35	34	39	41	33	38	41	34	39	38	39	39	39	31	37	42		
United States	43	46	38	42	43	43	41	42	45	50	51	56	54	43	37	38	41	50		
Iceland	na	na	na	na	na	na	na	na	na	na	na	na	na	na	na	na	na	na		
West Germany	na	na	na	na	na	na	na	na	na	na	na	na	na	na	na	na	na	na		
Denmark	na	na	na	na	na	na	na	na	na	na	na	na	na	na	na	na	na	na		
Finland	na	na	na	na	na	na	na	na	na	na	na	na	na	na	na	na	na	na		
Norway	na	na	na	na	na	na	na	na	na	na	na	na	na	na	na	na	na	na		
Sweden	na	na	na	na	na	na	na	na	na	na	na	na	na	na	na	na	na	na		
Japan	21	23	18	24	20	19	19	20	23	15	14	12	33	22	24	27	20	26		
Switzerland	na	na	na	na	na	na	na	na	na	na	na	na	na	na	na	na	na	na		
Total	28	30	26	27	28	30	28	28	28	25	25	27	27	26	26	26	28	30		

Note: Countries in the left column are ranked according to GNP per capita. / The percentages in the bottom row give each country an equal weight / na=not ascertained.

V347 TRUST: SECOND SUPERPOWER

I now want to ask you how much you trust various groups of people: Using the responses on this card, could you tell me how much you trust... Second superpower (% "trust them completely" or "trust them a little")

	Total	Gender		Age			Education			Income			Political Affinity			Values		
		Male	Female	16-29	30-49	50+	Lower	Medium	Upper	Lower	Middle	Upper	Left	Center	Right	Mat	Mixed	Postmat
India	49	53	44	52	47	49	39	48	54	44	49	53	52	49	56	45	53	62
Nigeria	06	07	06	06	07	06	07	06	07	07	06	05	na	na	na	na	na	na
China	06	06	06	06	07	06	07	06	07	07	06	05	na	na	na	05	07	06
Romania	na	na	na	na	na	na	na	na	na	na	na	na	na	na	na	na	na	na
Turkey	19	25	13	16	20	22	18	22	15	15	18	24	16	21	19	18	19	19
Poland	09	11	06	11	07	10	11	08	03	09	07	11	05	09	08	10	08	05
Bulgaria	11	11	11	13	08	13	14	11	09	10	12	10	10	10	11	12	10	09
Chile	23	24	22	19	25	27	25	23	21	24	24	22	30	20	22	22	22	26
Czechoslovakia	17	19	14	13	14	22	19	15	18	18	15	16	25	17	11	19	16	13
South Africa	11	11	12	11	10	15	13	11	11	10	10	14	10	11	15	12	11	12
Lithuania	34	38	31	34	34	35	40	34	25	37	32	32	na	na	na	35	33	39
Hungary	na	na	na	na	na	na	na	na	na	na	na	na	na	na	na	na	na	na
Argentina	na	na	na	na	na	na	na	na	na	na	na	na	na	na	na	na	na	na
Brazil	31	32	31	30	32	33	30	34	24	30	35	30	27	34	36	29	33	32
Mexico	16	17	15	17	16	14	17	18	12	16	17	14	15	16	17	16	16	18
Belarus	na	na	na	na	na	na	na	na	na	na	na	na	na	na	na	na	na	na
Russia	na	na	na	na	na	na	na	na	na	na	na	na	na	na	na	na	na	na
Moscow	na	na	na	na	na	na	na	na	na	na	na	na	na	na	na	na	na	na
Latvia	47	na	43	40	46	58	39	48	47	43	46	50	na	na	na	44	47	53
Estonia	44	44	43	41	47	42	42	44	46	47	43	40	na	na	na	48	43	38
Portugal	na	na	na	na	na	na	na	na	na	na	na	na	na	na	na	na	na	na
South Korea	14	12	15	12	13	17	16	14	12	14	14	12	12	14	14	14	14	12
Ireland	na	na	na	na	na	na	na	na	na	na	na	na	na	na	na	na	na	na
North Ireland	na	na	na	na	na	na	na	na	na	na	na	na	na	na	na	na	na	na
Slovenia	33	35	31	33	33	32	39	29	28	37	32	27	31	34	31	31	34	31
Spain	na	na	na	na	na	na	na	na	na	na	na	na	na	na	na	na	na	na
East Germany	na	na	na	na	na	na	na	na	na	na	na	na	na	na	na	na	na	na
Britain	na	na	na	na	na	na	na	na	na	na	na	na	na	na	na	na	na	na
Italy	na	na	na	na	na	na	na	na	na	na	na	na	na	na	na	na	na	na
Netherlands	na	na	na	na	na	na	na	na	na	na	na	na	na	na	na	na	na	na
Belgium	na	na	na	na	na	na	na	na	na	na	na	na	na	na	na	na	na	na
Austria	na	na	na	na	na	na	na	na	na	na	na	na	na	na	na	na	na	na
France	na	na	na	na	na	na	na	na	na	na	na	na	na	na	na	na	na	na
Canada	42	43	42	37	43	47	43	41	44	40	43	45	40	43	47	40	42	45
United States	45	47	42	47	45	44	43	45	46	39	45	51	56	47	36	41	43	52
Iceland	na	na	na	na	na	na	na	na	na	na	na	na	na	na	na	na	na	na
West Germany	na	na	na	na	na	na	na	na	na	na	na	na	na	na	na	na	na	na
Denmark	na	na	na	na	na	na	na	na	na	na	na	na	na	na	na	na	na	na
Finland	na	na	na	na	na	na	na	na	na	na	na	na	na	na	na	na	na	na
Norway	na	na	na	na	na	na	na	na	na	na	na	na	na	na	na	na	na	na
Sweden	na	na	na	na	na	na	na	na	na	na	na	na	na	na	na	na	na	na
Japan	11	11	11	13	12	06	08	11	13	10	12	10	20	12	07	13	10	19
Switzerland	na	na	na	na	na	na	na	na	na	na	na	na	na	na	na	na	na	na
Total	**26**	**27**	**24**	**25**	**26**	**27**	**26**	**26**	**24**	**25**	**26**	**26**	**25**	**24**	**24**	**25**	**26**	**27**

Ranking:

India	49
Latvia	47
United States	45
Estonia	44
Canada	42
Lithuania	34
Slovenia	33
Brazil	31
Chile	23
Turkey	19
Czechoslovakia	17
Mexico	16
South Korea	14
Bulgaria	11
South Africa	11
Japan	11
Poland	09
China	06

Note: Countries in the left column are ranked according to GNP per capita. / The percentages in the bottom row give each country an equal weight. / na = not ascertained.

V405 MATERIALIST-POSTMATERIALIST VALUES
(% "Materialist values")

	Total	Gender		Age			Education			Income			Political Affinity			Values			Ranking:	
		Male	Female	16-29	30-49	50+	Lower	Medium	Upper	Lower	Middle	Upper	Left	Center	Right	Mat	Mixed	Postmat		
India	40	40	41	39	42	42	47	42	36	46	38	42	39	38	41	100	00	00	China	51
Nigeria	36	32	42	34	38	38	48	33	34	36	38	34	36	38	34	100	00	00	South Korea	46
China	51	47	56	41	50	63	59	49	36	53	50	48	na	na	na	100	00	00	Hungary	45
Romania	44	37	50	29	40	56	58	41	28	47	47	38	55	46	26	100	00	00	Romania	44
Turkey	25	25	26	17	24	41	31	17	15	30	26	20	12	28	28	100	00	00	India	40
Poland	31	28	35	29	28	36	38	28	23	35	31	27	29	26	29	100	00	00	Brazil	40
Bulgaria	28	26	30	21	26	35	36	28	20	29	30	22	32	26	21	100	00	00	Russia	39
Chile	25	19	31	21	22	36	36	23	14	32	26	15	15	26	27	100	00	00	Nigeria	36
Czechoslovakia	26	23	30	21	24	32	34	23	21	29	26	24	31	28	19	100	00	00	South Africa	35
South Africa	35	34	36	28	36	45	42	31	35	35	32	42	23	38	42	100	00	00	Belarus	34
Lithuania	27	22	32	19	27	35	40	24	22	34	25	17	na	na	na	100	00	00	Portugal	34
Hungary	45	42	49	35	39	55	48	42	48	48	45	35	41	47	42	100	00	00	Estonia	32
Argentina	25	22	28	21	25	30	36	18	15	33	26	20	11	22	25	100	00	00	Poland	31
Brazil	40	38	42	34	39	54	54	38	20	51	36	32	29	35	48	100	00	00	Spain	30
Mexico	25	27	23	22	27	30	29	20	18	28	22	26	15	23	26	100	00	00	Norway	29
Belarus	34	30	38	28	32	45	49	34	29	38	32	34	26	42	54	100	00	00	Japan	29
Russia	39	32	44	26	35	52	52	38	32	44	39	34	26	39	47	100	00	00	Bulgaria	28
Moscow	27	24	29	20	26	34	42	33	20	31	25	22	20	35	38	100	00	00	Slovenia	28
Latvia	27	23	30	19	29	33	30	30	22	30	26	26	na	na	na	100	00	00	Lithuania	27
Estonia	32	28	35	25	31	41	41	33	21	33	32	30	na	na	na	100	00	00	Moscow	27
Portugal	34	32	36	22	36	46	42	21	16	43	32	24	29	35	35	100	00	00	Latvia	27
South Korea	46	48	44	33	49	60	56	50	36	47	44	50	28	41	53	100	00	00	Czechoslovakia	26
Ireland	24	23	24	12	22	25	30	17	14	29	26	19	13	22	27	100	00	00	Turkey	25
North Ireland	22	19	24	13	19	33	23	23	14	22	26	16	17	23	28	100	00	00	Chile	25
Slovenia	28	23	32	17	27	36	31	28	22	32	29	19	17	28	33	100	00	00	Argentina	25
Spain	30	26	33	13	27	46	36	21	11	48	26	21	20	29	40	100	00	00	Mexico	25
East Germany	12	11	13	03	08	22	16	03	05	21	12	05	07	13	13	100	00	00	Italy	25
Britain	20	18	22	15	18	25	21	20	12	24	19	15	13	18	28	100	00	00	Iceland	25
Italy	25	22	27	14	22	33	26	14	07	26	18	17	17	25	25	100	00	00	Ireland	24
Netherlands	10	10	10	07	08	18	18	08	04	11	08	04	03	11	13	100	00	00	North Ireland	22
Belgium	22	20	24	15	19	30	33	19	07	30	22	16	18	17	21	100	00	00	Belgium	22
Austria	14	11	15	07	08	21	20	10	05	21	13	07	15	12	14	100	00	00	France	21
France	21	17	24	18	18	27	28	19	06	26	22	09	12	23	25	100	00	00	Britain	20
Canada	12	10	14	12	11	13	17	11	09	12	11	10	04	13	11	100	00	00	United States	16
United States	16	14	19	14	17	17	22	16	13	19	16	13	08	17	17	100	00	00	Denmark	16
Iceland	25	23	28	25	23	30	35	25	19	na	na	na	22	27	25	100	00	00	West Germany	15
West Germany	15	12	17	06	10	23	19	08	06	20	12	13	08	13	22	100	00	00	Austria	14
Denmark	16	14	18	17	13	20	31	14	10	20	17	08	11	16	15	100	00	00	Sweden	14
Finland	06	05	07	01	05	13	09	06	04	09	05	04	04	09	05	100	00	00	Switzerland	14
Norway	29	28	30	20	27	38	47	30	19	35	27	23	20	32	29	100	00	00	East Germany	12
Sweden	14	14	15	09	12	19	21	14	03	15	19	11	12	16	12	100	00	00	Canada	12
Japan	29	28	30	22	30	32	34	26	30	32	28	27	20	25	32	100	00	00	Netherlands	10
Switzerland	14	12	15	08	11	19	16	14	04	16	13	07	05	13	15	100	00	00	Finland	06
Total	27	24	29	20	25	35	34	24	18	31	26	22	19	26	28	100	00	00		

Note: Countries in the left column are ranked according to GNP per capita. / The percentages in the bottom row give each country an equal weight. / na=not ascertained.
The percentages in the last three columns were omitted because they refer to a cross-tabulation of the same variable.

V405 MATERIALIST-POSTMATERIALIST VALUES
(% "Postmaterialist values")

		Gender		Age			Education			Income			Political Affinity			Values		
	Total	Male	Female	16-29	30-49	50+	Lower	Medium	Upper	Lower	Middle	Upper	Left	Center	Right	Mat	Mixed	Postmat
India	06	07	05	07	06	05	03	06	07	05	07	06	08	07	06	00	00	100
Nigeria	07	08	06	06	10	09	06	06	09	07	08	05	08	08	05	00	00	100
China	06	07	03	08	06	03	01	04	13	05	06	06	na	na	na	00	00	100
Romania	07	09	06	12	08	04	02	06	17	07	06	09	02	07	15	00	00	100
Turkey	20	25	16	28	20	10	11	31	44	13	21	27	37	17	14	00	00	100
Poland	10	11	09	14	11	07	09	10	10	09	07	14	08	11	13	00	00	100
Bulgaria	09	12	07	14	11	05	03	08	18	09	09	10	04	10	22	00	00	100
Chile	19	22	16	21	22	12	11	20	26	14	19	25	29	17	16	00	00	100
Czechoslovakia	11	11	10	18	11	05	06	12	13	09	11	11	06	11	14	00	00	100
South Africa	08	09	08	11	07	06	06	10	09	09	08	07	15	08	06	00	00	100
Lithuania	13	16	10	20	12	07	07	14	18	10	13	19	na	na	na	00	00	100
Hungary	04	05	03	05	05	02	03	04	07	03	05	06	03	05	04	00	00	100
Argentina	19	24	15	28	18	15	10	23	31	12	21	27	42	21	16	00	00	100
Brazil	07	09	05	08	08	04	04	07	16	03	07	11	12	09	03	00	00	100
Mexico	12	12	12	12	12	04	10	08	18	10	12	15	20	12	09	00	00	100
Belarus	07	08	05	09	06	06	04	06	08	05	07	08	10	03	02	00	00	100
Russia	06	08	04	08	07	03	03	05	09	04	07	08	14	06	02	00	00	100
Moscow	13	14	13	21	11	11	06	13	15	11	14	16	17	08	07	00	00	100
Latvia	09	14	06	10	10	08	05	07	15	10	09	09	na	na	na	00	00	100
Estonia	06	08	05	09	07	03	04	06	10	06	06	08	na	na	na	00	00	100
Portugal	12	13	12	21	10	05	05	25	26	07	13	20	15	12	11	00	00	100
South Korea	11	11	11	20	09	01	04	09	18	11	12	08	29	13	06	00	00	100
Ireland	19	18	20	29	19	13	13	26	27	10	17	26	36	22	11	00	00	100
North Ireland	15	21	11	27	14	08	12	17	31	18	19	20	30	14	14	00	00	100
Slovenia	07	09	04	09	07	04	05	05	12	06	04	13	12	07	10	00	00	100
Spain	21	24	17	36	21	08	15	27	39	09	21	28	31	17	10	00	00	100
East Germany	23	23	24	32	28	13	20	34	27	19	23	27	29	20	24	00	00	100
Britain	20	22	18	26	21	15	16	25	34	15	22	24	32	19	12	00	00	100
Italy	22	26	19	33	29	10	20	36	48	19	27	32	32	20	17	00	00	100
Netherlands	36	33	37	40	41	24	24	33	53	37	35	44	57	33	21	00	00	100
Belgium	24	27	20	31	30	13	13	24	46	19	23	33	34	28	19	00	00	100
Austria	25	26	24	37	31	14	18	28	36	17	25	32	30	30	21	00	00	100
France	25	28	23	32	28	17	16	28	43	19	25	40	37	22	17	00	00	100
Canada	26	30	21	26	26	24	20	23	34	23	27	30	43	25	22	00	00	100
United States	23	24	21	21	27	18	18	20	29	19	25	24	43	22	17	00	00	100
Iceland	11	12	09	11	13	06	05	11	15	na	na	na	16	07	10	00	00	100
West Germany	28	29	28	41	34	16	21	38	50	24	28	33	51	25	12	00	00	100
Denmark	16	17	15	17	19	11	06	14	22	14	13	25	34	14	06	00	00	100
Finland	29	33	25	40	28	21	22	26	35	22	29	36	29	29	31	00	00	100
Norway	10	11	08	11	12	05	10	07	16	10	12	10	21	07	06	00	00	100
Sweden	23	23	22	29	27	14	12	24	39	18	24	25	33	18	20	00	00	100
Japan	10	10	10	12	09	09	10	08	15	09	12	09	16	12	04	00	00	100
Switzerland	24	26	22	31	29	15	19	24	44	18	28	35	50	22	16	00	00	100
Total	**15**	**17**	**14**	**20**	**17**	**10**	**10**	**17**	**24**	**12**	**16**	**20**	**25**	**15**	**13**	**00**	**00**	**100**

Ranking:

Netherlands	36
Finland	29
West Germany	28
Canada	26
Austria	25
France	25
Belgium	24
Switzerland	24
East Germany	23
United States	23
Sweden	23
Italy	22
Spain	21
Turkey	20
Britain	20
Chile	19
Argentina	19
Ireland	19
Denmark	16
North Ireland	15
Lithuania	13
Moscow	13
Mexico	12
Portugal	12
Czechoslovakia	11
South Korea	11
Iceland	11
Poland	10
Norway	10
Japan	10
Bulgaria	09
Latvia	09
South Africa	08
Nigeria	07
Romania	07
Brazil	07
Belarus	07
Slovenia	07
India	06
China	06
Russia	06
Estonia	06
Hungary	04

Note: Countries in the left column are ranked according to GNP per capita. / The percentages in the bottom row give each country an equal weight. / na=not ascertained.

Technical Note

Fieldwork, Sampling, Independent Variables Weighting

The World Values Surveys provide a broader range of variation than has ever before been available for analyzing the values and attitudes of mass publics. The 1990–93 surveys were carried out in 43 societies representing almost 70 percent of the world's population and covering the full range of variation, from societies with per capita incomes as low as $300 per year, to societies with per capita incomes as high as $30,000 per year; and from long-established democracies with market economies, to ex-socialist states and authoritarian states. The 1981–1984 surveys provide time series data for 22 of these societies, enabling us to analyze the changes in values and attitudes that took place during the years between the two sets of surveys.

The World Values Surveys grew out of a study launched by the European Values Systems Study Group (EVSSG) under the leadership of Jan Kerkhofs and Ruud de Moor, with an advisory committee consisting of Gordon Heald, Juan Linz, Elisabeth Noelle-Neumann, Jacques Rabier,and Helene Riffault. In 1981, the EVSSG carried out surveys in ten West European societies; it evoked such widespread interest that it was replicated in 14 additional countries.

Findings from these surveys suggested that predictable cultural changes were taking place: many variables showing large intergenerational differences, and were strongly correlated with Postmaterialist values. To monitor possible changes, a new wave of surveys was designed, building on findings from the first wave, but this time designed to be carried out globally. The second wave of surveys was designed and coordinated by the following steering committee: Ruud de Moor, chair; Karel Dobbelaere, Loek Halman, Stephen Harding, Felix Heunks, Ronald Inglehart, Jan Kerkhofs, Renate Koecher, Jacques Rabier, and Noel Timms. Inglehart organized the surveys in non-European countries and in several East European countries.

Most of the first wave World Values surveys were carried out in Spring, 1981, but fieldwork for the South Korean survey took place in 1982 and fieldwork for the Argentine survey was in 1984. Similarly, most of the second wave surveys were carried out in 1990, but two (the Swiss and Polish surveys) completed their fieldwork in 1989; and two surveys (those in Russia and Turkey) were completed in early 1991, while another (in

Slovenia) was carried out in early 1992 and still another (in Romania) was carried out in Spring, 1993.

Fieldwork and Principal Investigators for the 1990 Surveys

Survey organizations, sample sizes, fieldwork period,and the principal investigators for each country are shown below. If not otherwise noted, the investigator is affiliated with the institution that carried out fieldwork:

ARGENTINA—Instituto Gallup de la Argentina (Buenos Aires) n = 1,001; February–April, 1991. Principal investigator, Marita Carballo de Cilley, Catholic University of Argentina.

AUSTRIA—Fessel + GFK Institut (Vienna) n = 1,460; June–July, 1990. Principal investigators, Paul Zulehner, Christian Friesl, University of Vienna.

BELARUS—Institute of Sociology, Belarus Academy of Sciences (Minsk) n = 1,015; October–November, 1990. Principal investigator, Andrei Vardomatski.

BELGIUM—Dimaraso-Gallup, Belgium (Brussels) n = 2,792; June, 1990. Principal investigators, Jan Kerkhofs and Karel Dobbelaere, University of Leuven; and Jacques-Rene Rabier, formerly of the Commission of the European Communities.

BRAZIL—Instituto Gallup de Opiniao Publica (Sao Paolo) n = 1,782; October, 1991–January, 1992. Principal investigator, Carlos Eduardo Meirelles Matheus.

BRITAIN—Gallup (London) n = 1,484; June–September, 1990. Principal investigators, David Barker, Stephen Harding, Gordon Heald, and Noel Timms, University of Leicester.

BULGARIA—National Public Opinion Center (Sofia) n = 1,034; August, 1990. Principal investigators, Andrei Raichev, Kancho Stoichev.

CANADA—Gallup-Canada (Toronto) n = 1,730; May–June, 1990. Principal investigators Neil Nevitte, University of Calgary and Ronald Inglehart, University of Michigan.

CHILE—Centro de Estudios de la Realidad Contemporanea (Santiago) n = 1,500; May, 1990. Principal investigators, Carlos Huneeus and Marta Lagos, Academia de Humanismo Cristiano.

CHINA—China Statistical Information Center (Beijing) n = 1,000; July–December, 1990. Principal investigators Jiang Xingrong, Xiang Zongde, and Ronald Inglehart.

CZECHOSLOVAKIA—Association for Independent Social Analysis (Prague) n = 1,396; September, 1990. Principal investigators, Vladimir Rak, Marek Boguszak and Ivan Gabal, Association for Independent Social Analysis; and Blanka Filipcova, Institute of Sociology, Czechoslovak Academy of Sciences; and Hans Dieter Klingemann, Berlin Science Center for Social Research.

DENMARK—Socialforskningsinstituttet (Danish National Institute of Social Research), (Copenhagen) n = 1,030; April–May, 1990. Principal investigators, Ole Riis and Peter Gundelach, University of Aarhus.

ESTONIA—Mass Communication Research and Information Center (Tallinn) n = 1,008; June–August, 1990. Principal investigators, Mikk Titma, Andrus Saar, and Hans-Dieter Klingemann.

FINLAND—Suomen Gallup [Gallup-Finland] (Helsinki) n = 588; April, 1990. Principal investigators, Leila Lotti and Juhani Pehkonen.

FRANCE—Faits et Opinions (Paris) n = 1,002; June–July, 1990. Principal investigator, Helene Riffault.

(EAST) GERMANY—Institut fuer Demoskopie (Allensbach) n = 1,336; Fall, 1990. Principal investigators, Renate Koecher and Elisabeth Noelle-Neumann.

(WEST) GERMANY—Institut fuer Demoskopie (Allensbach) n = 2,201; June–July, 1990. Principal investigators, Renate Koecher and Elisabeth Noelle-Neumann.

HUNGARY—Gallup, Hungary (Budapest) n = 999; May–June, 1990. Principal investigators Elemer Hankiss and Robert Manchin, Center for Value Sociology, Hungarian Academy of Sciences.

ICELAND—University of Iceland, Social Science Research Institute, n = 702; April, 1990. Principal investigators, Stefan Olafsson and Fridrik Jonsson.

INDIA—Indian Institute of Public Opinion (New Delhi) n = 2,500; July–December, 1990. Principal investigators, Eric de Costa, V.P. Madhok, and Ronald Inglehart.

IRELAND—Economic and Social Research Institute (Dublin) n = 1,000; July–October, 1990. Principal investigator, Michael Fogarty.

NORTHERN IRELAND—n = 304; July–September, 1990. Principal investigators, David Barker, Stephen Harding, Gordon Heald, and Noel Timms.

ITALY—Centro internazionale di recerche sociali sulle aree montane (Trento) n = 2,010; October–November, 1990. Principal investigator, Renzo Gubert, University of Trento.

JAPAN—Nippon Research Center Ltd. [Gallup-Japan] (Tokyo) n = 1011; September, 1990. Principal investigator, Kenji Iijima, Nippon Research Center and Yuji Fukuda and Seiko Yamazaki, Dentsu Institute for Human Studies.

SOUTH KOREA—Ewha University (Seoul) n = 1,251; June–July, 1990. Principal investigator, Soo Young Auh, Ewha University.

LATVIA—Public Opinion Research Group, Latvian Sociological Association (Riga) n = 903; June–August, 1990. Principal investigators, Brigita Zepa and Hans-Dieter Klingemann.

LITHUANIA—Vilnius State University Sociological Laboratory (Vilnius) n = 1,000; June–August, 1990. Principal investigators, Rasa Alishauskiene and Hans-Dieter Klingemann.

MEXICO—Market and Opinion Research International [MORI de Mexico] (Mexico City) n = 1,531; May, 1990. Principal investigators, Miguel Basáñez, Instituto Tecnologico Autonomo de Mexico and Ronald Inglehart.

MOSCOW—Institute of Sociology, Soviet Academy of Sciences (Moscow) n = 1,012; October–November, 1990. Principal investigator Elena Bashkirova and Vladimir Yadov.

NETHERLANDS—Institut voor Sociaal-Wetenschappelijk Onderzoek (Tilburg) n = 1,017; June–August, 1990. Principal investigators, Ruud de Moor, Felix Heunks and Loek Halman, University of Tilburg.

NIGERIA—Research and Marketing Services, Ltd. [Gallup-Nigeria] (Lagos) n = 939; May–June, 1990. Principal investigators Kareem Tejumola and Ronald Inglehart.

NORWAY—survey division of Norwegian Central Bureau of Statistics (Oslo) n = 1,239; April–June, 1990. Principal investigator, Ola Listhaug, University of Trondheim

POLAND—Osrodek Badania Opinii Publicznej [survey unit of Polish Radio-Television] (Warsaw) n = 938; November–December, 1989. Principal investigator, Renata Siemienska, University of Warsaw.

PORTUGAL—EuroExpansao, S.A. (Lisbon) n = 1,185; May–July, 1990. Principal investigators, Luis de Franca, Jorge Vala, and J.C. Jesumo, Instituto de Estudios para o Desenvolvimento.

RUSSIA—Institute for Social and Political Research, Soviet Academy of Sciences (Moscow) n = 1,961; January, 1991. Principal investigator Vladimir Andreyenkov.

ROMANIA—Institute for Research on Quality of Life, Romanian Academy of Sciences (Bucharest) n = 1,103; Spring, 1993. Principal Investigators, Catalin Zamfir, Nicolae Lotreanu, and Mattei Dogan.

SLOVENIA—Center for Public Opinion Research, University of Ljubljana n = 1,035; February, 1992. Principal investigator, Niko Tos.

SOUTH AFRICA—Markinor (Johannesburg) n = 2,736; October–November, 1990. Principal investigator Christine Woessner.

SPAIN—DATA, Madrid n = 2,637; April–May, 1990. Principal investigators, Francisco Andres Orizo, Javier Elzo, Deusto University.

SPAIN—Analisis Sociologicas, Economicos Y Politicos (ASEP) Madrid n = 1,510; May, 1990. Principal investigator, Juan Diez Nicolas, Complutense University, Madrid.

SWEDEN—Svenska Institutet for Opinionsundersokingar (SIFO)[Gallup-Sweden] (Stockholm) n = 1,047; April–May, 1990. Principal investigator, Thorleif Petterson, University of Uppsala.

SWITZERLAND—ISOPUBLIC, Institut Suisse d'Opinion Publique (Zurich) n = 1,400; November 1988–February, 1989. Principal investigator, Anna Melich, University of Geneva and Commission, European Union.

TURKEY—Bogazici University, Department of Political Science (Istanbul) n = 1,030; November, 1990–January, 1991. Principal investigators, Ustun Erguder, Yilmaz Esmer and Ersin Kalaycioglu.

U.S.A.—The Gallup Organization (Princeton) n = 1,839; May–June, 1990. Principal investigators, George Gallup, Alec Gallup, and Max Larsen, The Gallup Organization and Ronald Inglehart, University of Michigan.

Sampling Procedures

All of these surveys were carried out through face to face interviews, with a sampling universe consisting of all adult citizens, ages 18 and older. Representative national samples were interviewed in all cases except for sub-national surveys in Northern Ireland and the greater Moscow region (which was surveyed in *addition* to the entire Russian republic). The quality of the samples varies from country to country. Surveys in Western countries were carried out by professional survey organizations with a great deal of experience, most of them members of the Gallup chain. In other countries they were carried out by the respective national academies of sciences or university-based institutes, some of which had carried out few previous surveys.

Apart from the regional samples mentioned above, national samples were used except in the following cases: In Chile, the sample covers the central portion of the country, which contains 63 percent of the total population; the income level of this region is about 40 percent higher than the national average. In Argentina, sampling was limited to the urbanized central portion of the country, where about 70 percent of the population is concentrated, and which also has above-average incomes. In India, the sample was stratified to allocate 90 percent of the interviews to urban areas and 10 percent to rural areas; and to have 90 percent of the respondents with literate respondents (who are slightly less than 50 percent of the population); in Nigeria, the fieldwork was limited to urban areas plus a sample of rural areas within 100 kilometers of an urban center; and in

China the sample is 90 percent urban. The samples have been weighted accordingly to make the samples replicate the national population parameters more closely.

Fieldwork was carried out by professional survey research organizations in all countries except South Korea and Turkey, where sampling was designed by faculty and interviewing was executed by students from Ewha University and Bogazici University, respectively. In most countries, stratified multistage random sampling was used, with the samples being selected in two stages. First, a random selection of sampling locations was made ensuring that all types of location were represented in proportion to their population. Next, a random selection of individuals was drawn up. In Great Britain, Northern Ireland, Italy, and the Republic of Ireland, individuals were selected from electoral rolls; in Slovenia they were selected from a central registry of citizens. In Norway, Sweden, and Denmark, stratified random samples were interviewed, with response rates averaging 71 percent. The U.S. and Canada used stratified random samples, with three call backs. The Japanese used a stratified multistage random sample, drawing names from records maintained by local government agencies; completed interviews were obtained with 62 percent of the individuals drawn. In some countries, the final selection was made by quota sampling, with quotas assigned on the basis of sex, age, occupation, and region, using census data as a guide to the distribution of each group in the population.

This project was a confederation of equal partners. It was carried out with very little central funding and hence, with little central control. In most countries, funding for fieldwork and analysis was obtained from local sources. Inevitably, the quality of fieldwork varies cross-nationally; and the problems are not restricted to low-income societies.

The Chinese survey used stratified multistage random sampling, first stratifying the provinces according to three levels of economic development, with several provinces being randomly selected within each of these strata. Within each province, approximately 20 sampling points were selected randomly, with five individuals being interviewed at each point. The population was stratified according to rural-urban residence, sex, age, occupation, and education, and within these sampling points, each stratum was sampled by quota, with a 10 percent subsample of illiterate persons. The Indian survey was stratified to cover 14 states representing different geographic and socioeconomic regions of the country, with 2,500 interviews distributed among these states in proportion to their population. Within these 14 states, about 10 percent of the Parliamentary Constituencies were selected and 50 interviews allocated to each one. The interviews were then stratified according to town size, allocating 90 percent to urban areas, but stratifying according to population within the urban sample. A quota sample was then designed which is representative in terms of age and sex, but not education, since the sample design called for 90 percent of the interviews to be carried out with the literate part of the public. Within this segment, interviews were stratified according to education. Interviews were carried out in the eight most widely spoken languages of India, but the rural 10 percent of the sample was confined to the five Hindi-speaking states in the sample. The Nigerian sample was stratified in a similar fashion, with 90 percent of the interviews being carried out with the urban and literate segments of the population. It was then stratified by age, sex, and education, within 17 provinces representing the major ethnic groups in the country. Most surveys in these countries undersample rural and illiterate respondents, who tend to give large numbers of "don't know" responses. Our samples from all three low-income countries underrepresent the rural and illiterate segments of the population; though the samples have been weighted accordingly, this compensates imperfectly. These samples do provide representative coverage of the various regions, cultural groups, age, and gender groups.

The samples from China, India, and Nigeria undersample the illiterate and rural portions of the public and oversample the more educated and urban portions; the weight variable is designed to correct for this problem by giving greater weight to the less educated. The present dataset is weighted to compensate for these and other features of the samples. The samples from both the U.S. and South Africa were stratified by race; the weight variable corrects for this. The Swiss survey is stratified by language group, producing a sample that overrepresents the French-speaking and Italian-speaking groups; it is weighted to obtain a nationally representative sample. The weight variable also corrects for obvious deviations from national population parameters in age and education in other countries. In most cases, the more highly educated are oversampled, and are accordingly weighted less heavily than the less educated. In the 1990 Italian sample, however, the more educated are substantially undersampled, and are weighted more heavily to compensate for it.

As a rough generalization, the surveys from low income countries, and countries in which survey research is new, tend to be less reliable than than those from richer countries and societies with long experience in carrying out survey research. Though there are some exceptions to this generalization, it reflects some rather intractable problems. Richer societies tend to have more accurate census information and other social records, better communications infrastructure, and a longer-established and better developed survey research infrastructure.

The samples from India, Nigeria, and China by design undersampled the illiterate portion of the public and oversampled the urban areas and the more educated strata. Since the oversampled groups tend to have orientations relatively similar to those found in industrial societies, our data probably *underestimate* the size of cross-national differences involving these countries; nevertheless, these three countries frequently show very distinctive orientations. The present dataset is weighted to correct for these (and other) features of sampling; but it would be unrealistic to view the samples from these three countries as fully comparable to those from advanced industrial societies. We considered these societies extremely important, from both substantive and theoretic perspectives; but obtaining random probability samples from them would have required far more funding than was available for this project. We accorded a high priority to including such societies as China, India, and Nigeria, and were willing to accept imperfect samples rather than omit them from this study.

Although these data have numerous imperfections, our experience in analyzing them suggests that the results from most societies are in the right ballpark, in global perspective. A variety of indications point to this conclusion. Figure 1 in the introduction provides one piece of evidence. It shows how the responses of the publics from these 43 societies compare with each other on the two major dimensions of cross-cultural variation (based on responses to scores of items). If there were a great deal of error in measurement, one might expect to find the various societies scattered more or less randomly across these two key dimensions of cross-cultural variation. But the actual results show a remarkably clear and coherent pattern, as is pointed out in more detail in the introduction to this sourcebook.

There are a number of additional indications that the findings from these surveys are at least in the right ballpark. For the most part, when we can check our results against findings from other sources, they are reasonably consistent. Moreover, the pattern of internal correlations shows an excellent fit with theoretical expectations. For example, Postmaterialist values are more prevalent among the young than among the old in nearly all societies; but the strength of this relationship varies a good deal cross-culturally, being strong in those societies that have experienced rapid economic growth during the past several decades, and weak or nonexistent in those that have experienced little or no growth. This is true more broadly: the findings show remarkably coherent patterns in cross-level analyses. With a wide variety of variables, the values and attitudes of the respective publics show strong relationships with logically related macrosocietal characteristics, from economic development level to political institutions. And, as the tables in this book demonstrate, these beliefs and values are consistently related to the GNP per capita of the given societies in a pattern that is consistent with the implications of modernization theory. The overall pattern of cross-national differences is remarkably coherent.

The reader may wonder, To what extent does the set of 43 societies included in this study represent the world's population? While it clearly is *not* a random sample of the world's societies, it does cover about 70 percent of the world's population: having limited resources available, we made a major effort to include the world's most populous societies, and accordingly have undersampled the mini-states. Thus, while the societies that were omitted probably do differ to some extent from those included here, the distribution of beliefs and values in the world as a whole could not differ very radically from those found here, since most of the world's population is *included* here. One of the most striking and important findings that emerges from this study is the fact that there are sizeable and systematic differences between the values and beliefs of the peoples of rich, as compared with poor, societies. This gives us some indication of what we might expect to find in given societies that were not included.

Copies of the original questionnaires used in the various societies can be obtained from the ICPSR survey data archive at the Institute for Social Research, University of Michigan.

Independent and Weighting Variables

The independent variables used for cross tabulation in this sourcebook were gender, age, education, income, political affinity, and materialist-postmaterialist values. With the exception of the variable **gender**, with which the original codes 1="male" and 2="female" were used (the marginals being 49 percent and 51 percent respectively), all other variables were recoded and collapsed into three categories.

The variable **age** was constructed from variable V355 ("age in years"). Collapsing V355 into three categories was a straightforward process shown by the category labels themselves. Thus code 1="16-29" includes categories 16 through 29 from V355; code 2="30-49" includes categories 30 through 49 from V355; and code 3="50+" includes categories 50 through 99 from V355. Any other original codes were treated as missing data. Marginals for the constructed variable age are:

16-29 = 28% / 30-49 = 41% /   50+ = 31%

The variable **education** was constructed from V356 or V375 depending upon the country. A single variable education was constructed for most countries from variable

V356 ("school leaving age") by collapsing the categories as follows: 1="lower" from categories 0 through 5; 2="medium" from categories 6 though 9; and 3="upper" from category 10. Any other original codes were treated as missing data. In 14 countries the variable education was constructed using V375 ("educational system") with the codes collapsed as follows:

Brazil	1=0-2	2=3	3=4
Estonia	1=0-2	2=3-5	3=6
Finland	1=0-3	2=4-5	3=6-7
India	1=0-2	2=3-4	3=5
Latvia	1=0-2	2=3-5	3=6
Lithuania	1=0-2	2=3-5	3=6
Nigeria	1=0-2,9	2=3-4	3=5
Norway	1=0-1	2=2-5	3=6-8
Poland	1=0-2	2=3-5	3=6-7
Turkey	1=0-3,99	2=4-7	3=8-10
South Africa	1=0-3	2=4-6	3=7-9
South Korea	1=0-2	2=3-4	3=5-6
Sweden	1=0-1	2=2-5	3=6
Switzerland	1=0-4	2=5-8	3=9-10

Any other values were treated as missing data.
The marginals for the constructed variable **education** are:

1 "Lower"	33%
2 "Medium"	41%
3 "Upper"	26%

The variable **income** was created from variable V363 ("scale of household income"), which is a ten point scale with 1=lower income level and 10=upper income level. This scale was recoded for each nation into three categories: 1=Lower, 2=Middle; and 3=Upper. The criterion used for recoding was that each category would include a third of the sample as much as possible. Thus, by grouping the lower third, the middle third, and the upper third for each nation we would make our variable more cross-nationally comparable. The following are the codes that fall in each category for each nation:

Codes grouped in each category

	Lower	Middle	Upper
India	1-2	3-4	5-10
Nigeria	1-4	5-7	8-10
China	1-2	3	4-10
Romania	1-3	4-5	6-10
Turkey	1-3	4	5-10
Poland	1-4	5	6-10

Bulgaria	1-4	5	6-10
Chile	1-3	4-6	7-10
Czechoslovakia	1-4	5-6	7-10
South Africa	1-2	3-5	6-8
Lithuania	1-6	7	8-10
Hungary	1-4	5-6	7-10
Argentina	1-2	3-4	5-10
Brazil	1	2	3-10
Mexico	1-3	4-5	6-10
Belarus	1-3	4-5	6-10
Russia	1-3	4-5	6-10
Moscow	1-4	5-6	7-10
Latvia	1-2	3	4-10
Estonia	1-3	4	5-10
Portugal	1-3	4-5	6-10
South Korea	1	4	7, 10
Ireland	1-4	5-7	8-10
North Ireland	1-4	5-7	8-10
Slovenia	1-3	4-5	6-10
Spain	1-2	3-4	5-10
East Germany	1-2	3-5	6-10
Britain	1-5	6-8	9-10
Italy	1-3	4-5	6-10
Netherlands	1-4	5-7	8-10
Belgium	1-4	5-7	8-10
Austria	1-3	4-6	7-10
France	1-3	4-6	7-10
Canada	1-4	5-7	8-10
USA	1-3	4-5	6-10
West Germany	1-2	3-4	5-10
Denmark	1-4	5-7	8-10
Finland	1-7	8-9	10
Norway	1-3	4-7	8-10
Sweden	1	2-8	9
Japan	1-3	4-6	7-10
Switzerland	1, 2, 4	5-6	7, 9, 10

Note that not all nations used the full ten-point scale. In some cases the scale was shortened, or some codes were missing data.

The variable **political affinity** was constructed from V248 (Left-Right self placement). Code 1="Left" included categories 1 through 4; code 2="Center" included categories 5 and 6; and code 3="Right" included categories 7 through 10. The marginals for this variable are:

Left	27%
Center	46%
Right	27%

The variable **values** draws from an index previously developed by Ronald Inglehart. This index is based on the respondent's first and second choices in the original four item Materialist/Postmaterialist values battery (variables V259 and V260). If both Materialist items are given high priority, the score is "1"; if both Postmaterialist items are given high priority, the score is "3" if one Materialist item and one Postmaterialist item are given high priority, the score is "2." If the respondent makes only one or no choices, the result is missing data. In other words, the index is created with a constant value "2" and two conditionals:

Compute Values=2
If ((V259=1 and V260=3) or (V259=3 and V260=1)) Values=1
If ((V259=2 and V260=4) or (V259=4 and V260=2)) Values=3
The marginals for this variable are:

1 "Materialist"   28%
2 "Mixed"   58%
3 "Postmaterialist" 14%

Some of the samples in the 1990–1993 World Values Survey are self-weighting, while others employ a weighting variable that corrects for deviations from national population parameters. We have constructed a new weight variable that incorporates these national weight variables into a still broader weighting system that also gives each country the same weight. This offsets the fact that some countries, such as India and Spain the n's are 2,500 and 4,147 respectively, while in others such as North Ireland and Finland the n's are 304 and 508, respectively.

To do so we created a **weight variable** that gave each country a very nearly equal weight. This weight variable was simply the product of the original weight variable—that created by each country's principal investigator—multiplied by a value that would give each country a weighted sample of 1,000. For example, India's weighted sample of 2,500 was multiplied by 0.4; the product of 2,500 multiplied by 0.4 is 1,000. In other words, the weight variable is the product of the original weight variable multiplied by the specific value that each country needs in order to have a weighted sample of 1,000. Because of rounding, some weighted samples are not exactly 1,000.

Publications based on the 1990 World Values Surveys

Abbruzzese, S. 1992. L'Italia dei valori. *Micromega* 4: 123–32.

Abela, Anthony M. 1992. *Transmitting Values in European Malta. A Study in the Contemporary Values of Modern Society.* Valletta and Rome: Jesuit Publications/ Editrice Pontificia Universita Gregoriana.

Abela, Anthony M. 1992. European values study in Malta. *Melita Theologica*, University of Malta, XLIII: 33–38.

Abela, Anthony M. 1993. Post-secularisation: The social significance of religious values in four Catholic European countries. *Melita Theolgica* XLIV: 39–58.

Abela, Anthony M. 1993. Valori per il futuro di Malta. *La Civilta Cattolica Quaderno* 3429, Roma: 260–69.

Abela, Anthony M. 1994. Values for Malta's future. Social change, values and social policy. In R.G. Sultana and G. Baldacchino (eds.), *Maltese Society. A Sociological Inquiry.* Malta: Mireva Publications.

Abela, Anthony M. 1995. Youth and Religion in Malta. *Social Compass* 42: 59–67.

Abramson, Paul R., and Ronald Inglehart. 1994. Education, security, and postmaterialism. *American Journal of Political Science* 38: 3.

Abramson, Paul R., and Ronald Inglehart. 1994. Generational change: Cohort effects and period effects. In Henk Becker and Piet Hermkens (eds.) *Solidarity of Generations: Demographics, Economic and Social Change and its Consequences.* Amsterdam: Thesis, 1994, pp. 71–109.

Abramson, Paul R., and Ronald Inglehart. 1995. *Value Change in Global Perspective.* Ann Arbor: University of Michigan Press.

Aish-Van Vaerenbergh, Ann-Marie, and Jacques-Rene Rabier. 1994. Algunas reflexiones metodologicas sobre la investigacion estadistica intercultural sobre los valores. In Juan Diez-Nicolas and Ronald Inglehart (eds.), *Cambios en los Valores Sociales y Politicos.* Madrid: Complutense University Press.

Akker, Piet van den, and Sheena Ashford. 1995. Individualism in contemporary Europe. The case of Eastern Europe. In Ruud de Moor (ed.), *Values in Western Society*. Tilburg: Tilburg University Press.

Akker, Piet van den, Loek Halman, and Ruud de Moor. 1993. Primary relations in Western societies. In Peter Ester, Loek Halman, and Ruud de Moor (eds.), *The Individualizing Society: Value Change in Europe and North America*. Tilburg, The Netherlands: Tilburg University Press.

Alishauskene, Rasa. 1994. El humor politica en la poblacion lituana. In Juan Diez Nicolas and Ronald Inglehart (eds.), *Cambios en los Valores Sociales y Politicos*. Madrid: Complutense University Press.

Ashford, A., and Loek Halman. 1994. Changing attitudes in the European community. In C. Rootes and H. Davies (eds.), *Social Change and Political Transformation*, pp. 72–85. London: UCL Press.

Ashford, Sheena, and Noel Timms. 1992. *What Europe Thinks: A Study of Western European Values*. Aldershot: Dartmouth Publishing Co.

Auh, Soo Young. 1991. The impact of value change on democratization in South Korea. *Korean Political Science Review* 25, 2. [In Korean]

Auh, Soo Young. 1994. Cambio de valores y democratizacion en Corea del Sur. In Juan Diez-Nicolas and Ronald Inglehart (eds.), *Cambios en los Valores Sociales y Politicos*. Madrid: Complutense University Press.

Barker, David. 1992. Changing social values in Europe. *Business Ethics. A European Review* 1: 91–103.

Barker, David. 1993. Values and volunteering. In Justin Davis-Smith, *Volunteering in Europe*. Berkhamsted: The Volunteer Centre.

Barker, D., L. Halman, and A. Vloet. 1992. *The European Values Study 1981–1990*. Summary Report. London: The Gordon Cook Foundation.

Basáñez, Miguel. 1993. Is Mexico Headed Toward its Fifth Crisis? In Riordan Roett (ed.), *Political and Economic Liberalization in Mexico*. Boulder: Lynne Rienner.

Basáñez, Miguel. 1993. "Protestant and Catholic Ethics: An Empirical Comparison." Paper presented at conference on *Changing Social and Political Values: A Global Perspective*, Complutense University, Madrid, September 27–October 1.

Basáñez, Miguel. 1994. Winners and Losers of NAFTA in Mexico. In Brenda M. McPhail (ed.), *NAFTA Now! The Changing Political Economy of North America*. Latham, MD: University Press of America.

Basáñez, Miguel, and Alejandro Moreno. 1994. Mexico en la Encuesta Mundial de Valores 1981–1990. In Juan Diez-Nicolas and Ronald Inglehart (eds.), *Cambios en los Valores Sociales y Politicos*. Madrid: Complutense University Press.

Bashkirova, Elena. 1994. Cambio de actitudes politicas y los valores en la URSS y Russia. In Juan Diez-Nicolas and Ronald Inglehart (eds.), *Cambios en los Valores Sociales y Politicos*. Madrid: Complutense University Press.

Becker, Henk. 1995. Generations and Value Change. In Ruud de Moor (ed.), *Values in Western Societies*. Tilburg: Tilburg University Press.

Brechon, Pierre. 1995. Les Europeens et la politique. *Futuribles*, 200 (July–August): 63–84.

Brechon, Pierre. (forthcoming). Religions et politique en Europe. Paris.

Breen, G., and C.T. Whelan. 1993. Social class, class origins and political partisanship in the Republic of Ireland. *European Journal of Political Research 25*.

Broek, Andries van den, and Ruud de Moor. 1993. Eastern Europe after 1989. In Peter Ester, Loek Halman, and Ruud de Moor (eds.), *The Individualizing Society: Value Change in Europe and North America*. Tilburg, The Netherlands: Tilburg University Press.

Broek, Andries van den, and Felix Heunks. 1993. Political culture. Patterns of political orientations and behavior. In Peter Ester, Loek Halman, and Ruud de Moor (eds.), *The Individualizing Society: Value Change in Europe and North America*. Tilburg, The Netherlands: Tilburg University Press.

Capraro, G. 1992. I valori degli Italiani nel contesto Europeo. *Presbyteri* XXVI 9: 679 702.

Capraro, G. 1992. I valori degli Italiani negli anni Ottanta secondo un'indagine Europea. Pp. 197–207 in CET, *Le regioni del Nord-Est, Societa, economia e ambiente*. Padova: Messaggero.

Capraro, G. 1993. Valori Europei e loro trasmissione in un-Europa aperta. In AA.VV. *Anziani e Cultura Europea. Atti del Convegno Naziale della Federuni Trento*. Vicenza: Rezzara.

Capraro, G. 1993. *Sociologia e religione: teoria e ricerca empirica*. Brescia: Morcelliana.

Capraro, G., and R. Gubert. 1993. *I valori degli Europei*. Trento: Regione Autonoma Trentino-Alta Adige.

Carballo de Cilley, Marita, and Carlos Matheus. 1994. Actitudes y valores politicos y laborales: comparacion entre Brasil y Argentina. In Juan Diez-Nicolas and Ronald Inglehart (eds.), *Cambios en los Valores Sociales y Politicos*. Madrid: Complutense University Press.

Chauvel, Louis. 1993. Les valeurs dans la Communaute Europeenne: l'erosion des extremismes. *Observations et Diagnostics Economiques, Revue de l'OPCE*.

Chauvel, Louis. 1995. Valeurs regionales et nationales en Europe. *Futuribles*, 200 (July–August): 167–200.

Chiu, Hei Yuan. 1994. Valores de la educacion en la sociedad Taiwanesa. In Juan Diez Nicolas and Ronald Inglehart (eds.), *Cambios en los Valores Sociales y Politicos*. Madrid: Complutense University Press.

Conci, A. 1993. I valori degli Europei fra evoluzione e nostalgia. *Rivista di Teologia Morale* XXV 1: 55–72.

Dalton, Russell J. 1993. *Politics in Germany*, 2nd edition. New York: Harper Collins.

Dalton, Russell J. 1994. *The Green Rainbow: Environmental Groups in Western Europe*. New Haven: Yale University Press.

Davie, G. 1992. God and Caesar: Religion in a Rapidly Changing Europe. In J. Bailey (ed.), *Social Europe*. London and New York: Longman.

Dentsu Institute for Human Studies. Human Studies No. 7 "Fairness," semi-annual report by Dentsu Institute for Human Studies (in Japanese and English).

Dentsu Institute for Human Studies. Human Studies No. 9 "Sense of Values," semi annual report by Dentsu Institute for Human Studies (in Japanese and English).

Dentsu Institute for Human Studies. Human Studies No. 11 "A New Course for the U.S.; A New Direction for Japan," semi-annual report by Dentsu Institute for Human Studies (in Japanese and English).

Dentsu Institute for Human Studies. *Nihon No Chouryuu (Japanese Trends)—Quality of Society* (in Japanese). PHP-Kennkyuusho Publishing Company.

Dentsu Institute for Human Studies. Forthcoming. *Ibunnka Tositeno Nihon to Amerika.* Tokyo: Nannundou Publishing Company.

Dentsu Institute for Human Studies. Forthcoming. *Ibunnka Likai to Ibunnka Masatsu.* Tokyo: Nihon Keizai Shinnbunnsha.

Dentsu Institute for Human Studies and The Leisure Development Center of Japan. 1994. Japon en una perspectiva comparativa. In Juan Diez-Nicolas and Ronald Inglehart (eds.), *Cambios en los Valores Sociales y Politicos.* Madrid: Complutense University Press.

Diez Medrano, Juan. 1994. El significado de los concepios de izquierda y de derecha: una perspectiva comparada. In Juan Diez-Nicolas and Ronald Inglehart (eds.), *Cambios en los Valores Sociales y Politicos.* Madrid: Complutense University Press.

Diez Nicolas, Juan. 1994. Postmaterialismo y desarollo economico. In *Cambios en los Valores Sociales y Politicos: Una Perspectiva Global.* Juan Diez-Nicolas and Ronald Inglehart (eds), Madrid: Complutense University Press.

Dobbelaere, Karel. 1993. Church involvement and secularization: Making sense of the European case. In E. Barker, J.A. Beckford, and K Dobbelaere (eds.), *Secularization, Rationalism and Sectarism.* Oxford: Clarendon Press.

Dobbelaere, Karel, and Wolfgang Jagodzinski. 1995. Religious cognitions and beliefs. In Jan W. van Deth and Elinor Scarbrough (eds.), *The Impact of Values.* Oxford and New York: Oxford University Press.

Dobbelaere, Karel. 1995. Religion in Europe and North America. In Ruud de Moor (ed.), *Values in Western Societies.* Tilburg: Tilburg University Press.

Dogan, Mattei. 1994. The decline of nationalism within Western Europe. *Comparative Politics*, April: 281–305.

Dogan, Mattei. 1994. The erosion of Nationalism in the European Community. In M. Haller and R. Richter (eds.), *Towards a European Nation?* New York: Sharpe: 31–54.

Dogan, Mattei. 1995. The decline of Class Voting and of Religious Vote in Western Europe. *International Social Science Journal*, 146: 525–38.

Dogan, Mattei. 1995. Le Declin des Croyances Relgieuses en Europe Occidentale. *Revue Internationale des Sciences Sociales*, 3: 461–76.

Dogan, Mattei. 1995. Testing the Concepts of Legitimacy and Trust. In H.E. Chehabi and Alfred Stepan (eds.), *Politics, Society and Democracy: Essays in Honor of Juan Linz.* Boulder: Westview Press.

Doring, H. 1992. Higher education and confidence in institutions: A secondary analysis of the 'European Values Survey', 1981–83. *West European Politics* 15: 126–46.

Duch, Raymond M., and Michael A. Taylor. 1994. A reply to 'Education, security, and postmaterialism.' *American Journal of Political Science* 38:xxx-xxx.

Elzo, Javier. 1994. Nacionalismo, nacionalidad y religion en Euskalerria. In Juan Diez Nicolas and Ronald Inglehart (eds.), *Cambios en los Valores Sociales y Politicos*. Madrid: Complutense University Press.

Elzo, Javier, F. A. Orizo, M. A. Barreda, F. Garmendia, P. G. Blasco, and J. F. Santacoloma. 1992. *Euskalerria ante la Encuesta Europea de Valores. Son Los Vascos Diferentas?* Bilbao: Universidad De Deusto Deiker.

Elzo, Javier, et al. 1991. *Construir Europa: Euskadi*. Editorial Areces.

Elzo, Javier, et al. 1992. *Drogas y Escuela IV*. Escuela Universitaria de Trabajo Social. San Sebastian.

Elzo, Javier, et al. 1992. *Euskadi ante las Drogas 92*. Informe sobre la evolucion del consumo de tasbaco, alcohol y demas drogas en los ultimos diez anos. Servicio Central de Publicaciones del Gobierno Vasco.

Elzo, Javier, et al. 1993. Giovani e religione in Spagna. In Luigi Tomasi (ed.), *Persistenze Valiorioli e Nuovi Orientananti*. Trento: Reverdito Edizioni.

Elzo, Javier, et al. 1994. *Jovenes espanoles*. Editorial S.M. Madrid.

Ester, Peter, and Loek Halman. Forthcoming. Empirical trends in religious and moral beliefs in Western Europe. A cross-sectional longitudinal analysis: 1981–1990. In M. Haller and R. Richter (eds.), *Towards a European Nation? Political Trends in Europe*. New York: Sharpe.

Ester, Peter, Loek Halman, and Ruud de Moor. 1993. Value shift in western societies. In Peter Ester, Loek Halman, and Ruud de Moor (eds.), *The Individualizing Society: Value Change in Europe and North America*. Tilburg, The Netherlands: Tilburg University Press.

Ester, Peter, Loek Halman, and Brigitte Seuren. 1993. Environmental concern in Europe and North America. In Peter Ester, Loek Halman, and Ruud de Moor (eds.), *The Individualizing Society: Value Change in Europe and North America*. Tilburg, The Netherlands: Tilburg University Press.

Ester, Peter, Loek Halman, and H. Vinken. 1992. Zur diffusion und kristallisation von wertorientierungen in der Niederlandischen Bevolkerung. *H.H. Medien, Medienwissenschaftliche Beitrage der Heinrich-Heine-Universitat Dusseldorf*, Heft 2/3 December: 36–59.

Franca, Luis de. 1993. Portugal, valores Europeus, identidade cultural. Lisbon: Instituto de Estudos para o Desenvolvimento.

Fuchs, Dieter, and Hans-Dieter Klingemann. 1995 (forthcoming). Citizens and the state: A changing relationship? In Hans-Dieter Klingemann and Dieter Fuchs (eds.), *Citizens and the State*. Oxford and New York: Oxford University Press.

Gabriel, Oscar W. 1995. "Political Efficacy and Trust." In Jan Van Deth and Elinor Scarbrough (eds.), *The Impact of Values*. Oxford: Oxford University Press.

Galland, Olivier, and Yannick Lemel. 1995. "La Permanence des differences: une comparison des systemes de valeurs entre pays europeens." *Futuribles*, 200 (July–August): 113–30.

Gibbins, John, and Bo Reimer. 1995. "Postmodernism," in Jan Van Deth and Elinor Scarbrough (eds.) *The Impact of Values*. Oxford: Oxford University Press.

Gold, H., and A. Webster. 1990. *New Zealand Values Today*. Palmerston North: Alpha.

Granato, Jim, Ronald Inglehart, and David Leblang. 1996a. "The Effect of Culture on Economic Development: Theory, Hypotheses and Some Empirical Tests." *American Journal of Political Science* (August, forthcoming).

Granato, Jim, Ronald Inglehart, and David Leblang. 1996b. "Cultural Values, Stable Democracy and Economic Development: A Reply." *American Journal of Political Science* (August, forthcoming).

Gubert, Renzo (ed.). 1992. *Persitenze e mutamenti dei Valori degli Italinan nel Contesto Europea*. Trento: Reverdito Edizioni.

Gubert, Renzo. 1995. Analysis of Regional Differences in the Values of European. In Ruud de Moor (ed.), *Values in Western Societies*. Tilburg: Tilburg University Press.

Gundelach, Peter, and Ole Riis. 1993. *Danskernes Voerdier*. Kobenhavn K.: Forlaget Sociologi.

Gundelach, Peter, and Ole Riis. 1994. El retorno al familismo? In Juan Diez-Nicolas and Ronald Inglehart (eds.), *Cambios en los Valores Sociales y Politicos*. Madrid: Complutense University Press.

Gundelach, Peter. 1994. "National Value Differences" Modernization or Institutionalization? *International Journal of Comparative Studies* 35: 37–58.

Halman, Loek. 1992. Culturele identiteit: Waardevol of waardeloos? *Rawoo Lunchlezing* 28, April.

Halman, Loek. 1994. Westerse waarden. Wat weten wij van onze cultuur?   In M. Veldhuis, *Cultuur en Ontwikkeling. Rawoo Lezingenserie 1992*. Den Haag: Rawoo.

Halman, Loek. 1995. La comparazione dei valori nell'European Value Study. La misurazione dei valori e il problema della comparabilita. In R. Gubert and G. Capraro (eds.), *I Valori degli Eurpei negli anni Novanta*. Trento: University of Trento.

Halman, Loek. 1994. Scandinavian values. How special are they? In Thorleif Pettersson and Ole Riis (eds.), *Religious and Moral Values in Scandinavian Countries*. Stockholm: Almqvist Wiksell International.

Halman, Loek. Variations in Tolerance levels in Europe. *European Journal of Criminal Policy and Research*. 2: 15–38.

Halman, Loek, K. Dobbelaere, R. de Moor, and L. Voye. 1992. Godsdienst en kerk in Belgie en Nederland. *Sociologische Gids* 92/5-6: 285–99.

Halman, Loek, and Ruud de Moor. 1993. Comparative research on values. In Peter Ester, Loek Halman, and Ruud de Moor (eds.), *The Individualizing Society: Value Change in Europe and North America*. Tilburg, The Netherlands: Tilburg University Press.

Halman, Loek, and Ruud de Moor. 1993. Religion, churches and moral values. In Peter Ester, Loek Halman, and Ruud de Moor (eds.), *The Individualizing Society: Value*

Change in Europe and North America. Tilburg, The Netherlands: Tilburg University Press.

Halman, Loek, and Ruud de Moor. 1993. Value patterns and modernity. In Peter Ester, Loek Halman, and Ruud de Moor (eds.), *The Individualizing Society: Value Change in Europe and North America.* Tilburg, The Netherlands: Tilburg University Press.

Halman, Loek, and Ruud de Moor. 1994. Individualizacion y cambio de valores en Europa y Norteamerica. In Juan Diez-Nicolas and Ronald Inglehart (eds.), *Cambios en los Valores Sociales y Politicos.* Madrid: Complutense University Press.

Halman, Loek. 1995. Is there a Moral Decline? A cross-national Inquiry into Morality in Contemporary Society. *International Social Science Journal* 145: 419–40.

Halman, Loek, and Thorleif Petterson. 1995. Individualization and Value Fragmentation. In Ruud de Moor (ed.), *Values in Western Societies.* Tilburg: Tilburg University Press.

Hardiman, N., and C.T. Whelan. 1992. *Politics and Values in the Republic of Ireland. Evidence from the European Values Survey.*

Harding, Stephen D., and Frans J. Hikspoors. 1995. New Work Values: In Theory and in Practice. *International Social Science Journal* 145: 441–56.

Honne, Sissel. 1994. Rekkefolgeeffekt—et seigt og magert tema? Om formeffekter I den norske verdiundersokelsen [On Form Effects in the Norwegian Values Survey]. Thesis, Department of Sociology and Political Science, University of Trondheim, 1994.

Hornsby-Smith, M.P., and C.T. Whelan. 1992. *Religious and Moral Values in Ireland. An Analysis of the European Values Survey.*

Hornsby-Smith, M.P., and M. Procter. 1995. Catholic Identity, Religious Context and Environmental Values in Western Europe. *Social Compass* 42: 27–34.

Huenks, Felix, and Frans Hikspoors. 1995. Political Culture, 1960–1990. In Ruud de Moor (ed.) *Values in Western Societies.* Tilburg: Tilburg University Press.

Huseby, Beate, and Ola Listhaug. 1995. Identifications of Norwegians with Europe: The Impact of Values and Center-Periphery Factors. In Ruud de Moor (ed.), *Values in Western Societies.* Tilburg: Tilburg University Press.

Inglehart, Ronald. 1992. Changing values in industrial societies: The case of North America, 1981–1990. *Politics and the Individual* 2, 2:1–31.

Inglehart, Ronald. 1992. Vergleichende wertewandelforschung (revised 2nd edition). In Ferdinand Müeller-Rommel and Dirk Berg-Schlosser (eds.), *Vergleichende Politikwissenschaft* (Leverkusen: Leske Verlag) 125–44.

Inglehart, Ronald. 1993. Democratizacao em perspectiva global. *Opinao Publica* (July August): 9–42.

Inglehart, Ronald. 1993. Modernizacion y post-modernizacion: la cambiante relacion entre el desarrollo economico, cambio cultural y politico. In Juan Diez Nicolas and Ronald Inglehart (eds.), *Cambios en los Valores Sociales y Politicos: Una Perspectiva Global.* Madrid: Complutense University Press.

Inglehart, Ronald. 1994. Les valeurs des europeens: Existe-il un systeme des valeurs europeen? *Futuribles*, November.

Inglehart, Ronald. 1995. Public support for environmental problems: Objective problems and subjective values. *PS Political Science and Politics*.

Inglehart, Ronald. 1995. Changing Values, Economic Development and Political Change. *International Social Science Journal* 145: 379–404.

Inglehart, Ronald, and Paul R. Abramson. 1994. Economic security and value change, 1970–1993. *American Political Science Review*, June: 336–54.

Inglehart, Ronald, and Rudy Andeweg. 1993. Change in Dutch political culture: A silent or a silenced revolution? *West European Politics*, July: 345–61.

Inglehart, Ronald, and Terry N. Clark. 1991. *Nowa Kultura Polityczna* (*The New Political Culture*) (Warsaw). Reprinted in Hungarian as "Az uj politikai kultura," in Gabor Peteri (ed.), *Helyi Demokracia es Ujitasok* (*Reforming Local Democracy*) (Budapest: Alapitvany kiadvanya, 1992) 22–96.

Inglehart, Ronald, Miguel Basáñez, and Neil Nevitte. 1994. *Convergencia en Norteamerica: Comercio, Politica y Cultura*. Mexico: Siglo Veintiuno Editores.

Inglehart, Ronald, Susan Ellis, Jim Granato, and David Leblang. 1996. "Economic Development, Political Culture and Democracy: Bringing the People Back In." Paper presented at annual meeting of Midwest Political Science Association, Chicago.

Jagodzinski, Wolfgang, and Karel Dobbelaere. 1993. Die amtskirchen im prozess der modernisierung. *Kolner Zeitschrift fur Soziologie und Sozialpsychologie* 33: 68–91.

Jagodzinski, Wolfgang, and Karel Dobbelaere. 1995. Religious and ethical pluralism. In Jan W. van Deth and Elinor Scarbrough (eds.), *The Impact of Values*. Oxford and New York: Oxford University Press.

Jagodzinski, Wolfgang, and Karel Dobbelaere. 1995. Secularization and church religiosity. In Jan W. van Deth and Elinor Scarbrough (eds.), *The Impact of Values*. Oxford and New York: Oxford University Press.

Kaase, Max, and Kenneth Newton. 1995. Beliefs in Government. Oxford: Oxford University Press.

Kalaycioglu, Ersin. 1994. Elections and Party Preferences in Turkey. *Comparative Political Studies* 27,3: 402–424.

Kerkhofs, Jan 1990. Europa. Waardenontwikkeling of -ontworteling? *Ondernemen* VKW Brussel, 46: 525–31.

Kerkhofs, Jan. 1992. L'Europe a une nouvelle croisee des chemins; vers une autre echelle de valuers. *Lumen Vitae* 47: 15–24.

Kerkhofs, Jan. 1992. Europa heute -aus der sicht der kirchen. *Communio* 21: 295–304.

Kerkhofs, Jan. 1992. A quel point l'Europe est-elle religieuse? *Concilium* 1992, nr. 240: 97–107.

Kerkhofs, Jan. 1992. Waarden-evolutie van jongeren in een postmoderne cultuur. *Ethische Perspectieven* 2: 3–7.

Kerkhofs, Jan. 1992. Mutations des valeurs en Europe. *L'Entreprise et l'homme* 64:215–20.

Kerkhofs, Jan. 1992. Waardenverschuivingen in Europa en Belgie. *Cultuur in Beweging* 19, 4: 21–24.

Kerkhofs, Jan. 1992. La problematique familiale selon des recentes etudes sur les valeurs. *Cahiers Ceppes*, nr. 3: 137–42.

Kerkhofs, Jan. 1992. L'Europe: Une autre echelle de valeurs. *Christus*, nr. 156, okt.: 499–508.

Kerkhofs, J. 1992. Jongeren en waarden in een postmoderne cultuur. *Korrel Cahier*, Altiora, Averbode: 5–11.

Kerkhofs, Jan., Karel Dobbelaere, Lilianne Voye, and Bernadette Bawin-Legros (eds.). 1992. *De Versnelde Ommekeer*. Tielt: Lannoo.

Klingemann, Hans-Dieter. 1995. The Convergence of Party Positions and Voter Orientations. In Hans-Dieter Klingemann and Dieter Fuchs (eds.), *Citizens and the State*. Oxford and New York: Oxford University Press. 183–205.

Klingemann, Hans-Dieter, and Dieter Fuchs (eds.) 1995. *Citizens and the State*. Oxford: Oxford University Press.

Klingemann, Hans-Dieter, Gurgling Lass, and Katrin Mattusch. 1994.

Nationalitatenkonflikt und mechanismen politischer integration im Baltikum. In Dieter Segert (Hrsg.), *Konfliktregulierung durch Parteien und Politische Stabilitat in Ostmitteleuropa*. Frankfurt/M.: Peter Lang.

Klingemann, Hans-Dieter, Gurgling Lass, and Katrin Mattusch. 1994. La orientacion de valores y la participacion politica en los Estados Balticos. In Juan Diez-Nicolas and Ronald Inglehart (eds.), *Cambios en los Valores Sociales y Politicos*. Madrid: Complutense University Press.

Knutsen, Oddbjorn. 1995. "Left-Right Materialist Orientations." In Jan Van Deth and Elinor Scarbrough (eds.), *The Impact of Values*. Oxford: Oxford University Press.

Knutsen, Oddbjorn, and Elinor Scarbrough. 1995. "Cleavage Politics." In Jan Van Deth and Elinor Scarbrough (eds.), *The Impact of Values*. Oxford: Oxford University Press.

Lambert, Yves. 1993. Effet d'age, de generation et de periode dans l'evolution religieuse. *Revue Francaise de Sociologie*.

Lambert, Yves. 1993. Les jeunes et le christianisme: Le grand defi. In Gallimard (ed.), *Le Debat*.

Lambert, Yves. 1993. Ages, generations et christianisme en France et en Europe. *Revue Francaise de Sociologie*, XXXIV.

Lambert, Yves. 1994. Les regimes confessionels et l'etat du sentiment religieux. In Jean Bauberot, *Religion et Laicite dans l'Europe des Douze*. Paris: Syros.

Lambert, Yves, and Guy Michelat. 1992. *Crepuscule des religions chez les jeunes?* Paris: L'Harmettan.

Lambert, Yves. 1995. Vers une ere post-chretienne? *Futuribles*, 200 (July–August): 85–112.

Larsen, Max D. 1994. Satisfaccion del consumidor con los servicios gubernamentales. In Juan Diez-Nicolas and Ronald Inglehart (eds.), *Cambios en los Valores Sociales y Politicos*. Madrid: Complutense University Press.

Laumenskaite, E. 1991. Does Lithuania return to Christian faith. *Kataliku Pasaulis* 1 [in Lithuanian].

Laumenskaite, E. 1992. The face of religion and its role in the reconstruction of the society in Lithuania. *Religion Today*, Summer 1992, Vol. 7, No. 3.

Laumenskaite, E. 1993. Religion and the church in Lithuania: The present and the perspectives. *Naujasis Zidinys*, No. 7–8.

Laumenskaite, E. Forthcoming. Attitudes to family and religion in Lithuania. In *Religion, Family and Social Changes*. Los Angeles.

Lee, Aie-Rie. 1993. Culture shift and popular protest in South Korea. *Comparative Political Studies* 26, 1:63–80.

Leschinsky, Achim. 1996. *Vorleben oder Nachdenken? Bericht der wissenschaftlischen Begleitung ueber den Modellversuch zum Lernbereich 'Lebensgestaltung-Ethik Religion'* Frankfurt: Verlag Moritz Diesterweg.

Lesthaeghe, Ron, Guy Moors, and Loek Halman. 1992. Living arrangements and values among young adults in the Netherlands, Belgium, France and Germany, 1990. *IPD Working Paper* 1992–3, Brussel: Centrum Sociologie, Vrije Universiteit.

Lesthaeghe, Ron, and Guy Moore. 1995. Living Arrangements and Parenthood: Do Values Matter? In Ruud de Moor (ed.), *Values in Western Societies*. Tilburg: Tilburg University Press.

Lindseth, Odd Helge. 1993. Samme himmel, samme samfunn? Religion som norm-regulator blant protestanter og katolikker i Nord-Amerika og Vest-Europa [One Heaven, One Society? Religion as a Regulator of Norms among Protestants and Catholics in North America and Western Europe]. Thesis, Department of Sociology and Political Science, University of Trondheim.

Lindseth, Odd Helge, and Ola Listhaug. 1994. Religion y valores del trabajo en los noventa: un estudio comparativo de Europa Occidental y Estados Unidos. In Juan Diez-Nicolas and Ronald Inglehart (eds.), *Cambios en los Valores Sociales y Politicos*. Madrid: Complutense University Press.

Lindseth, Odd Helge, and Ola Listhaug. 1994. Religion and work values in the 1990s: A comparative study of Western Europe and North America. In Thorleif Pettersson and Ole Riis (eds.), *Religious and Moral Values in the Scandinavian Countries*. Stockholm: Almquist and Wiksell.

Listhaug, Ola. 1991. Norske verdier 1982–1990: Stabilitet og endring [Norwegian Values 1982–1990: Stability and Change]. *ISS -rapport nr. 30*: University of Trondheim.

Listhaug, Ola. 1995 . The impact of modernization and value change on confidence in institutions. In Ruud de Moor (ed.), *Values in Western Societies*. Tilburg: Tilburg University Press.

Listhaug, Ola, and Beate Huseby. 1990. Values in Norway 1990: Study description and codebook. *ISS -rapport nr. 29*: University of Trondheim.

Listhaug, Ola, and Matti Wiberg. 1995 Confidence in political and private institutions. In Hans-Dieter Klingemann and Dieter Fuchs (eds.), *Citizens and the State: Changing Public Attitudes toward Government in Western Europe*. Oxford and New York: Oxford University Press. 298–322.

Liubsiene, E. 1993. Lithuanian survey of the families raising disabled children. Report for a Regional Seminar for the Baltic States: "The Future of Children with Disabilities in the Baltic States." Vilnius.

Lu, Hai-Qi. 1994. Aproximacion a la posicion de la mujer china en actividades economicas, sociales y politicas. In Juan Diez-Nicolas and Ronald Inglehart (eds.), *Cambios en los Valores Sociales y Politicos*. Madrid: Complutense University Press.

Marques, Guilhermina. 1991. Les valeurs des jeunes Suisses entre 15 et 19 ans. Geneva: Johann Jacobs Foundation.

Mattusch, Katrin. 1994. Demokratisierung und politische kultur im Baltikum. Dissertation: Freie Universitaet Berlin.

Melich, Anna (ed.). 1991. *Les Valeurs des Suisses*. Berne: Lange Verlag. [German version: *Die Werte der Schweizer*. Berne: Lang.]

Melich, Anna. 1994. Insatisfacion nacional y desconfianza europea: el caso de Suiza. In Juan Diez-Nicolas and Ronald Inglehart (eds.), *Cambios en los Valores Sociales y Politicos*. Madrid: Complutense University Press.

Melich, Anna. 1995. National dissatisfaction and distrust in Europe: the case of Switzerland. In Ruud de Moor (ed.), *Values in Western Societies*. Tilburg: Tilburg University Press.

Montero, Jose Ramon, and Mariano Torcal. 1994. Cambio cultural, reemplazo generacional y politica en Espana. In Juan Diez-Nicolas and Ronald Inglehart (eds.), *Cambios en los Valores Sociales y Politicos*. Madrid: Complutense University Press.

de Moor, Ruud. 1995. Religion and Moral Values: The Case of Euthanasia. In Ruud de Moor (ed.), *Values in Western Societies*. Tilburg: Tilburg University Press.

Myers, D.G. 1992. *The Pursuit of Happiness*. New York: William Morrow and Company.

Nas, Masja. 1995. "Green, Greener, Greenest". In Jan W. van Deth and Elinor Scarbrough (eds.), *The Impact of Values*. Oxford and New York: Oxford University Press.

Nevitte, Neil. 1991. New politics, the charter and political participation. In Herman Bakvis (ed.), *Representation, Integration and Political Parties in Canada*. Toronto: Dundurn Press. Vol. 14. Report of the Royal Commission on Electoral Change and Party Financing, 1991: 355–417.

Nevitte, Neil. 1994. Se ha vuelto la gente mas tolerante? Evidencias de la Encuesta Mundial de Valores 1981–1990. In Juan Diez-Nicolas and Ronald Inglehart (eds.), *Cambios en los Valores Sociales y Politicos*. Madrid: Complutense University Press.

Nevitte, Neil. 1996. *The Decline of Deference*. Toronto: Broadview Press.

Nevitte, Neil. Forthcoming. Bringing values "back in": Value change and North American integration. In D. Barry (ed.), *Toward a North American Community? Canada, United States and Mexico*. Boulder, CO: Westview Press.

Nevitte, Neil. Forthcoming. NAFTA: Why not before now? In B. McPhail (ed.), *NAFTA Now! The Changing Political Economy of North America*. University Press of America.

Nevitte, Neil, and Herman Bakvis. 1992. The greening of the Canadian electorate: Environmentalism, ideology and partisanship. In Robert Boardman (ed.), *Canadian Environmental Policy: Ecosystems, Politics and Process*. Don Mills, Ontario: Oxford University Press.

Nevitte, Neil, W. Brandon, and L. Davis. 1993. The American abortion controversy: Lessons from cross-national evidence. *Politics and the Life Sciences* 12 (1), February: 19–30.

Nevitte, Neil, and Ian Brodie. 1993. Evaluating the citizen's constitution theory. *Canadian Journal of Political Science* XXVI, June 2: 235–59.

Nevitte, Neil, and Ian Brodie. 1993. Clarifying differences: A rejoinder to Alan Cairn's defence of the citizen's constitution theory. *Canadian Journal of Political Science* XXVI, June 2: 269–72.

Nevitte, Neil, and Ronald Inglehart. 1992. Directions of value change in North America. In Steven Randall (ed.), *North America Without Borders*. Calgary: University of Calgary Press. 245–59.

Nevitte, Neil, and Ronald Inglehart. 1995. North American value change and integration: Lessons from Western Europe? In Ruud de Moor (ed.), *Values in Western Societies*. Tilburg: Tilburg University Press.

Nevitte, Neil, and Mebs Kanji. 1995. "Explaining Environmental Concern and Action in Canada." *Applied Behavoral Science Review*, 3:1: 85–102.

Nevitte, Neil, and M. Wohlfeld. 1990. Postindustrial value change and support for native issues. *Canadian Ethnic Studies* 22, 3: 56–88.

Orizo, Francisco Andres. 1991. *El Sistema de Valors dels Catalans*. Barcelona: Institut Catala d'Etudes Mediterranis.

Orizo, Francisco Andres. 1991. *Los Nuevos Valores de los Espanoles*. Madrid: Fundacion Santa Maria.

Orizo, Francisco Andres. 1994. Los valores de libertad en Espana. In Juan Diez-Nicolas and Ronald Inglehart (eds.), *Cambios en los Valores Sociales y Politicos*. Madrid: Complutense University Press.

Orizo, Francisco Andres, and Alejandro Sanchez Fernandez. 1993. *El Sistema de Valors dels Catalans*. Barcelona: Institut Catala d'Estudis Mediterranis.

Ortiz, Angel I. Rivera, and Jorge Beritez Nazario. 1994. Cambio en valores e identidad nacional: el caso de Puerto Rico desde una perspectiva comparada. In Juan Diez-Nicolas and Ronald Inglehart (eds.), *Cambios en los Valores Sociales y Politicos*. Madrid: Complutense University Press.

Osti, G. 1993. Dimensioni dell 'insediamento e associazionismo. *Annali di Sociologia-Sociologisches Jahrbuch* 9: 18.

Pettersson, Thorleif. 1994. Individualizacion, secularizacion y cambio de valor moral en la Escandinavia contemporanea. In Juan Diez-Nicolas and Ronald Inglehart (eds.), *Cambios en los Valores Sociales y Politicos*. Madrid: Complutense University Press.

Purvaneckiene, G. 1993. Individo psichologine busena ir seima. *Acta Paedagogica Vilnensia* 2: 128.

Purvaneckiene, G. 1993. Lietuvos motery vertybines orientacijos keiciantis politinei bei ekonominei padeciai. *Visuomene: Politikos, Visuomenes ir Kulturos Zurnalas* 1 (22).

Purvaneckiene, G. 1993. Women in changing Lithuania. In Marina Thoberg (ed.), *Women Around the Baltic Sea. Part I: Estonia, Latvia, and Lithuania.* Sweden: Lund University.

Rehak, J. 1992. Are the Czechs and the Slovaks different? *Czechoslovak Sociological Review* 28: 129–32.

Riffault, Helene. 1993. L'evolution des valeurs en Europe. *Futuribles*, December.

Riffault, Helene. 1994. Resultados de la Encuesta de Valores en Francia. In Juan Diez-Nicolas and Ronald Inglehart (eds.), *Cambios en los Valores Sociales y Politicos.* Madrid: Complutense University Press.

Riffault, Helene. 1994. Le systeme de valeurs des Francais: ce qui a bouge depuis 10 ans. *Les Techniques Psychologiques d'Evaluation des Personnes.* Paris: Actes du Congres International Inetop.

Riffault, Helene (ed.). 1994. *Les Valeurs des Francais.* Paris: Presses Universitaires de France.

Riffault, Helene. Les Europeens et la valeur travail. *Futuribles*, 200 (July–August): 25–46.

Romero, Catalina. 1994. Valores y cambio social en el Peru: algunas diferencias para comparar. In Juan Diez-Nicolas and Ronald Inglehart (eds.), *Cambios en los Valores Sociales y Politicos.* Madrid: Complutense University Press.

Rosa, G. de. 1993. I valori degli italiani nel contesto Europeo. *La Civilta Cattolica* 144, 1.

Roussel, Louis. 1995. Vers une Europe des familles? *Futuribles*, 200 (July–August): 47–62.

Scarbrough, Elinor. 1995. "Materialist-Postmaterialist Value Orientations." In Jan Van Deth and Elinor Scarbrough (eds.), *The Impact of Values.* Oxford: Oxford University Press.

Schuur, Wijbrandt H. van (in cooperation with M. Kruijtbosch). 1992. De affectbalans van vijftigplussers in Europa. In D. Hak and R. Wielers, *Lang Zal Hij Leven! Opstellen van Frans Wasseur ter Gelegenheid van Zijn Vijftigste Verjaardag.* Groningen: Vakgroep Sociologie.

Schuur, Wijbrandt H. van, and Martine Kruijbosch. 1994. El bienestar subjetivo: despliegue de la Escala de Equilibrio Emotivo de Bradburn. In Juan Diez-Nicolas and Ronald Inglehart (eds.), *Cambios en los Valores Sociales y Politicos.* Madrid: Complutense University Press.

Schwqeisguth, Etienne. 1995. La Montee des valeurs individualistes. *Futuribles*, 200 (July–August): 131–66.

Scida, G. 1993. Associazionismo e attivita non-profit in Italia e in Europa. *Aggiornamenti Sociali* XLIV 2: 153–68.

Siemienska, Renata. 1994. (ed.) *Szkoly niepanstwowe w polskim systemie edukacyjnym* (Nonpublic Schools in the Polish Educational System), Kwartalnik Pedagogiczny 1–2 (151–152) (special volume)

Siemienska, Renata. 1996. *Kobiety: nowe wyzwania. Starcie przeszlocsi z terazniejszoscia* (Women and New Challenges. The Clash of the Past and the Present). Warsaw University Press.

Siemienska, Renata. 1990. (with Ronald Inglehart) O procesach demokratyzacyjnych. Globalna i zachodnio-europejska perspektywa. (Democratization in Poland and West Europe) *Panstwo i Kultura Polityczna,* 1990.

Siemienska, Renata. 1992. Zaufanie Polakow do roznych narodow w okresie przemian politycznych i ekonomicznych (Poles' Trust toward Other Nations in the Period of Political and Economic Changes). In Aleksandra Jasinska-Kania (ed.), *Bliscy i dalecy*. Warsaw: Warsaw University Press: 201–7.

Siemienska, Renata. 1993. Gender as a Factor Differentiating Social Positions in Transition to a Market Economy. In Mary Nash (ed.), *From Dictatorship to Democracy: Women in Mediterranean, Central and Eastern Europe*. Barcelona: University of Barcelona Press: 120–68.

Siemienska, Renata. 1994. Polish Women as the Object and Subject of Political Activity in the Communist and Postcommunist Periods, in: B. Nelson and N. Chowdhury (eds.) *Women and Politics Worldwide*, New Haven: Yale University Press. 608–624.

Siemienska, Renata. 1994. Women in the Period of Systemic Changes in Poland, *Journal of Women's History*, vol.5, no.3. 70–90.

Siemienska, Renata. 1994. Some Determinants of Polish Attitudes Toward Other Nations During a Period of Transition. In Russell F. Farnen (ed), *Nationalism, Ethnicity and Identity.Cross-National and Comparative Perspectives*. New Brunswick, NJ and London (U.K.), Transaction Publishers. 327–44.

Siemienska, Renata. 1994. Viejos y nuevos elementos de los valores democraticos en Polonia, desde una perspectiva international. In Juan Diez Nicolas and Ronald Inglehart (eds.), *Tendencias mundiales de cambio en los valores sociales y politicos*. Madrid, Fundesco. 375–404.

Siemienska, Renata. 1994. "Szkola panstwowa i niepanstwowa a wartosci demokratyczne" (Public and Non-public Schools and Democratic Values). In R. Siemienska (ed.), Szkoly niepanstwowe w systemie edukacji w Polsce (Nonpublic Schools in the Polish Educational System). *Kwartalnik Pedagogiczny* 1–2 (151–52): 55–78.

Siemienska, Renata. 1995. "Tradycja i rzeczywistosc: miejsce kobiet w spoleczenstwie" (Tradition and Reality—Women's Status in Society). *Kobieta i Biznes* (Akademicko-gospodarcze Forum). 2–3. 2–6. (published in Polish and English)

Siemienska, Renata. 1995. "Dylematy transformacji w Europie Srodkowej i Wschodniej: Analiza systemu w perspektywie porownawczej" (Dilemmas of Transformation in Central and Eastern Europe. Analysis of the System in Comparative Perspective). In: E. Tarkowska (ed.), *Powroty i kontynuacje* . Wyd. IFiS PAN. 117–35.

Simons, John. 1995. Fertility and Values in 15 Western Countries during the 1980s. In Ruud de Moor (ed.), *Values in Western Societies*. Tilburg: Tilburg University Press.

Stoychev, Kancho. 1994. El espacio politico y las estructuras de valores. In Juan Diez-Nicolas and Ronald Inglehart (eds.), *Cambios en los Valores Sociales y Politicos*. Madrid: Complutense University Press.

Tejumola, Kareem A., Alabas Simpson, and H.O. Akimmagtoe. 1994. Cambio de valores en el ambito del matrimonio y de la familia. In Juan Diez-Nicolas and Ronald Inglehart (eds.), *Cambios en los Valores Sociales y Politicos*. Madrid: Complutense University Press.

Timms, Noel. 1992. *Family and Citizenship. Values in Contemporary Britain*. Aldershot: Dartmouth.

Tomasi, L. 1994. *La Religione dei Giovani Europei*. Milano: Angeli.

Torregrosa Peris, Jose R. 1994. Orientaciones internacionales de los espanoles: entre Europa e Iberoamerica. In Juan Diez-Nicolas and Ronald Inglehart (eds.), *Cambios en los Valores Sociales y Politicos*. Madrid: Complutense University Press.

Tos, Niko. 1994. La (no) religiosidad en Eslovenia. In Juan Diez-Nicolas and Ronald Inglehart (eds.), *Cambios en los Valores Sociales y Politicos*. Madrid: Complutense University Press.

Turner, Frederick C., and Carlos A. Elordi. 1995. Economic Values and the Role of Government in Latin America. *International Social Science Journal* 145: 473–88.

Vala, Jorge. 1994. La emergencia de los valores post-materialistas en Portugal. In Juan Diez-Nicolas and Ronald Inglehart (eds.), *Cambios en los Valores Sociales y Politicos*. Madrid: Complutense University Press.

Van Deth, Jan, and Elinor Scarbrough (eds.), *The Impact of Values*. Oxford: Oxford University Press.

Van Deth, Jan. and Elinor Scarbrough. 1995. "Perspectives on Value Change." In Jan Van Deth and Elinor Scarbrough (eds.), *The Impact of Values*. Oxford: Oxford University Press.

Veenhoven, R. 1993. *Happiness in Nations*. Rotterdam: Risbo.

Villalain, J.L., A. Basterra, and J.M. del Valle. 1992. *La Sociedad Espanola de los 90*. Madrid: Fundacion Santa Maria, Ediciones SM.

Vinken, Henk, Peter Ester, and Henk-Jan Dirven. 1993. Individualization of the life course and cultural divergence between age groups. In Peter Ester, Loek Halman, and Ruud de Moor (eds.), *The Individualizing Society: Value Change in Europe and North America*. Tilburg, The Netherlands: Tilburg University Press.

Voye, Liliane, Bernadette Bawin-Legros, Jan Kerkhofs, and Karel Dobbelaere. 1992. *Belges, Hereux et Satisfaits. Les Valeurs des Belges dans les Annees 90*. Brussels: De Boeck-Wesmael.

Webster, Alan C., Edward E. Drawmeek, and Paul E. Perry. 1994. Multiples culturas de valores en una sociedad pequena: sistemas de valores en la Encuesta de Valores de Nueva Zelanda. In Juan Diez-Nicolas and Ronald Inglehart (eds.), *Cambios en los Valores Sociales y Politicos*. Madrid: Complutense University Press.

Webster, Alan C., and Paul E. Perry. 199X. *The Religious Factor in New Zealand Society*. Palmerston North: Alpha.

Webster, Alan C., and Paul E. Perry. 1992. *What Difference Does It Make?* Values and Faith in a Shifting Culture. Palmerston North: Alpha.

Whelan, C.T. 1992. *Stability and Change in Values and Attitudes Relevant to Women's Participation in the Labour Force and Wider Role in Society: An Analysis of the European Values Survey.*

Whelan, C.T. (ed.) 1994. *Values and Social Change in Ireland.* Dublin: Gill and Macmillan.

Wilson, B., and K. Dobbelaere. 1994. *A Time to Chant.* Oxford: Clarendon Press.

Woessner, Christine. 1994. Sudafrica en la encrucijada. In Juan Diez-Nicolas and Ronald Inglehart (eds.), *Cambios en los Valores Sociales y Politicos.* Madrid: Complutense University Press.

Worcester, Robert M. 1994. Valores y actitudes sociales ante las dimensiones humanas del cambio medioambiental global. In Juan Diez-Nicolas and Ronald Inglehart (eds.), *Cambios en los Valores Sociales y Politicos.* Madrid: Complutense University Press.

World Commission on Culture and Development. 1995. *Our Creative Diversity.* Paris: UNESCO.

Xingrong, Jiang. 1992. An international comparison of morality (in Chinese). State Statistical Bureau, Beijing, China.

Xingrong, Jiang. 1991. More and more people pay attention to the environment (in Chinese). State Statistical Bureau, Beijing, China.

Xingrong, Jiang. 1992. The political, economical, educational and social status of Chinese ladies (in Chinese). State Statistical Bureau, Beijing, China.

Xingrong, Jiang. 1992. Public viewpoint of market economy (in Chinese). State Statistical Bureau, Beijing, China.

Zanders, Harry, and Stephen Harding. Changing World Values in Europe and North America. In Ruud de Moor (ed.), *Values in Western Societies.* Tilburg: Tilburg University Press.

Zanders, Harry. 1993. Changing work values. In Peter Ester, Loek Halman, and Ruud de Moor (eds.), *The Individualizing Society: Value Change in Europe and North America.* Tilburg, The Netherlands: Tilburg University Press.

Zulehner, Paul. 1991. *Vom Untertan zum Freiheitskunstler. Eine Kulturdiagnose anhand der Untersuchungen "Religion im Leben der Osterreicher 1970–1990".* Wien: Herder.

Zulehner, Paul, and Herman Denz. 1993. *Wie Europa Lebt und Glaubt.* Duesseldorf: Patmos.

WORLD VALUES SURVEY
1990 QUESTIONNAIRE

SHOW CARD A

Please say, for each of the following, how important it is in your life.

	Very Important	Quite Important	Not Very Important	Not at all Important	DK
V 4 A) Work	1	2	3	4	9
V 5 B) Family	1	2	3	4	9
V 6 C) Friends, acquaintances	1	2	3	4	9
V 7 D) Leisure time	1	2	3	4	9
V 8 E) Politics	1	2	3	4	9
V 9 F) Religion	1	2	3	4	9

NOTE: Throughout these surveys, "0" is used as a Not Ascertained (N.A.) code. With single-digit variables, "9" is also occasionally used as a N.A. code.

V 10 When you get together with your friends, would you say you discuss political matters frequently, occasionally or never?

* *[INDICATES ITEMS ASKED IN BOTH 1981 and 1990 SURVEYS]*

> 1 Frequently
> 2 Occasionally
> 3 Never
> 9 Don't know

V 11 When you yourself, hold a strong opinion, do you ever find yourself persuading your friends, relatives or fellow workers to share your views? IF SO, does it happen often, from time to time, or rarely?

1 Often
2 From time to time
3 Rarely
4 Never
9 Don't know

<u>SHOW CARD B</u>
I am now going to read out some statements about the environment. For each one I read out, can you tell me whether you agree strongly, agree, disagree or strongly disagree?
(READ OUT EACH STATEMENT AND CODE AN ANSWER FOR EACH)

	Strongly Agree	Agree	Disagree	Strongly Disagree	DK
V 12 A) I would give part of my income if I were certain that the money would be used to prevent environmental pollution	1	2	3	4	9
V 13 B) I would agree to an increase in taxes if the extra money is used to prevent environmental pollution	1	2	3	4	9
V 14 C) The Government has to reduce environmental pollution but it should not cost me any money	1	2	3	4	9
V 15 D) All the talk about pollution makes people too anxious	1	2	3	4	9
V 16 E) If we want to combat unemployment in this country, we shall just have to accept environmental problems	1	2	3	4	9
V 17 F) Protecting the environment and fighting pollution is less urgent than often suggested	1	2	3	4	9

V 18 Taking all things together, would you say you are...(READ OUT, REVERSING ORDER FOR ALTERNATE CONTACTS)
*

    1 Very happy
    2 Quite happy
    3 Not very happy
    4 Not at all happy
    9 Don't know

SHOW CARD C
Please look carefully at the following list of voluntary organisations and activities and say...
    a) which, if any, do you belong to?
    (CODE ALL 'YES' ANSWERS UNDER (a))
    b) which, if any, are you currently doing
    unpaid voluntary work for?
    (CODE ALL 'YES' ANSWERS UNDER (b))
*

	(a) Belong to	(b) Do unpaid work for	
V 19 A) Social welfare services for elderly, handicapped or deprived people	1	V 37	1
V 20 B) Religious or church organisations	1	V 38	1
V 21 C) Education, arts, music or cultural activities	1	V 39	1
V 22 D) Trade unions	1	V 40	1
V 23 E) Political parties or groups	1	V 41	1
V 24 F) Local community action on issues like poverty, employment, housing, racial equality	1	V 42	1
V 25 G) Third world development or human rights	1	V 43	1
V 26 H) Conservation, the environment, ecology	1	V 44	1
V 27 I) Professional associations	1	V 45	1

V 28 J) Youth work (e.g. scouts, guides, youth clubs, etc.)	1	V 46	1
V 29 K) Sports or recreation	1	V 47	1
V 30 L) Women's groups	1	V 48	1
V 31 M) Peace movement	1	V 49	1
V 32 N) Animal rights	1	V 50	1
V 33 O) Voluntary organisations concerned with health	1	V 51	1
V 34 P) Other groups	1	V 52	1
V 35 None	1	V 53	-
V 36 Don't know	9	V 54	-

For V19 to V54, "1" indicates "mentioned, "2" indicates "not mentioned."
The Chinese questionnaire translated "Trade Unions" (V22 and V40) as "Trading Associations," which was chosen by very few people. "Professional Associations" was translated as "occupational organizations," which evokes the (government-sponsored) labor unions; thus, for China, V27 is functionally equivalent to V22.
The Swiss survey used the phrase, "charitable organization," for "social welfare services" in V19 and V37.

SHOW CARD D
Thinking about your reasons for doing voluntary work, please use the following five-point scale to indicate how important each of the reasons below have been in your own case.
(WHERE 1 IS UNIMPORTANT AND 5 IS VERY IMPORTANT)

		Unimportant				Very Important	DK
V 55 A)	A sense of solidarity with the poor and disadvantaged	1	2	3	4	5	9
V 56 B)	Compassion for those in need	1	2	3	4	5	9
V 57 C)	An opportunity to repay something, give something back	1	2	3	4	5	9
V 58 D)	A sense of duty, moral obligation	1	2	3	4	5	9

V 59 E)	Identifying with people who were suffering	1	2	3	4	5	9
V 60 F)	Time on my hands, wanted something worthwhile to do	1	2	3	4	5	9
V 61 G)	Purely for personal satisfaction	1	2	3	4	5	9
V 62 H)	Religious beliefs	1	2	3	4	5	9
V 63 I)	To help give disadvantaged people hope and dignity	1	2	3	4	5	9
V 64 J)	To make a contribution to my local community	1	2	3	4	5	9
V 65 K)	To bring about social or political change	1	2	3	4	5	9
V 66 L)	For social reasons, to meet people	1	2	3	4	5	9
V 67 M)	To gain new skills and useful experience	1	2	3	4	5	9
V 68 N)	I did not want to, but could not refuse	1	2	3	4	5	9

SHOW CARD E
On this list are various groups of people. Could you please sort out any that you would not like to have as neighbours? (CODE AN ANSWER FOR EACH)
*

	Mentioned	Not Mentioned
V 69 A) People with a criminal record	1	2
V 70 B) People of a different race	1	2
V 71 C) Left wing extremists	1	2
V 72 D) Heavy drinkers	1	2
V 73 E) Right wing extremists	1	2
V 74 F) People with large families	1	2

V 75 G) Emotionally unstable people		1	2
V 76 H) Muslims		1	2
V 77 I) Immigrants/foreign workers		1	2
V 78 J) People who have AIDS		1	2
V 79 K) Drug addicts		1	2
V 80 L) Homosexuals		1	2
V 81 M) Jews		1	2
V 82 N) Hindus		1	2

The Slovenian survey and the Lithuanian, Latvian and Estonian surveys asked about "Gypsies," rather than "Hindus," in V82.
The surveys in the Baltic countries asked about "extremists" (not "Left-wing extremists") in V71, and about "people of other nationalities" in V73.

V 83 All in all, how would you describe your state of health these days? Would you say it is... (READ OUT REVERSING ORDER FOR ALTERNATE CONTACTS)
*

    1 Very good
    2 Good
    3 Fair
    4 Poor
    5 Very poor
    9 Don't know

We are interested in the way people are feeling these days. During the past few weeks, did you ever feel...(READ OUT AND MARK ONE CODE FOR EACH STATEMENT)
*

		YES	NO
V 84 A)	Particularly excited or interested in something	1	2
V 85 B)	So restless you couldn't sit long in a chair	1	2
V 86 C)	Proud because someone had complimented you on something you had done	1	2

V 87 D)	Very lonely or remote from other people	1	2
V 88 E)	Pleased about having accomplished something	1	2
V 89 F)	Bored	1	2
V 90 G)	On top of the world/feeling that life is wonderful	1	2
V 91 H)	Depressed or very unhappy	1	2
V 92 I)	That things were going your way	1	2
V 93 J)	Upset because somebody criticized you	1	2

V 94 Generally speaking, would you say that most people can be trusted or that you can't be too careful in dealing with people?
*
    1 Most people can be trusted
    2 Can't be too careful
    9 Don't know

SHOW CARD F
V 95 Some people feel they have completely free choice and control over their lives, and other people feel that what they do has no real effect on what happens to them. Please use the scale to indicate how much freedom of choice and control you feel you have over the way your life turns out.
*

    1   2   3   4   5   6   7   8   9   10
    None at all   A great deal
                              DK = 99

SHOW CARD G
V 96 All things considered, how satisfied are you with your life as a whole these days? Please use this card to help with your answer.
*
    1 2 3 4 5 6 7 8 9 10
Dissatisfied   Satisfied
                      DK = 99

SHOW CARD H
V 97 Why are there people in this country who live in need? Here are four possible reasons. Which one reason do you consider to be most important? (CODE ONE UNDER

(a) BELOW) And which reason do you consider to be the second most important?
(CODE ONE UNDER (b) BELOW)

	V 97 (a) Most important	V 98 (b) Second most important
Because they are unlucky	1	1
Because of laziness and lack of will power	2	2
Because there is injustice in our society	3	3
It's an inevitable part of modern progress	4	4
None of these	5	5
Don't know	9	9

India only: additional codes 6 and 8 refer to ascetic and religious motivations.

SHOW CARD I
Here are some aspects of a job that people say are important. Please look at them and tell me which ones you personally think are important in a job? (CODE ALL MENTIONED)

			Mentioned	Not Mentioned
V 99	A)	Good pay	1	2
V 100	B)	Pleasant people to work with	1	2
V 101	C)	Not too much pressure	1	2
V 102	D)	Good job security	1	2
V 103	E)	Good chances for promotion	1	2
V 104	F)	A job respected by people in general	1	2
V 105	G)	Good hours	1	2
V 106	H)	An opportunity to use initiative	1	2
V 107	I)	A useful job for society	1	2
V 108	J)	Generous holidays	1	2
V 109	K)	Meeting people	1	2
V 110	L)	A job in which you feel you can achieve something	1	2
V 111	M)	A responsible job	1	2
V 112	N)	A job that is interesting	1	2
V 113	O)	A job that meets one's abilities	1	2
V 114		None of these	1	2

ASK ALL WORKING OTHERS SKIP TO V 118
How much pride, if any, do you take in the work that you do? READ OUT
*

V 115   1 A great deal
          2 Some
          3 Little
          4 None
          9 Don't know

Overall, how satisfied or dissatisfied are you with your job?
*

V 116	1	2	3	4	5	6	7	8	9	10
	Dissatisfied								Satisfied	

DK = 99

How free are you to make decisions in your job? Please use this card to indicate how much decision-making freedom you feel you have.
*

V 117	1	2	3	4	5	6	7	8	9	10
	None at all								A great deal	

DK = 99

ASK ALL
Here are some statements about why people work. Irrespective of whether you have a job, or not, which of them comes closest to what you think?

	Mentioned	Not Mentioned	
V 118	1	2	Work is like a business transaction. The more I get paid, the more I do; the less I get paid, the less I do
V 119	1	2	I will always do the best I can, regardless of pay
V 120	1	2	Working for a living is a necessity; I wouldn't work if I didn't have to
V 121	1	2	I enjoy working but I don't let it interfere with the rest of my life
V 122	1	2	I enjoy my work; it's the most important thing in my life
V 123	1	2	I never had a paid job
V 124	1	2	Don't know

Imagine two secretaries, of the same age, doing practically the same job. One finds out that the other earns $50 a week more than she does. The better paid secretary, however, is quicker, more efficient and more reliable at her job. In your opinion, is it fair or not fair that one secretary is paid more than the other?
* **COUNTRIES OTHER THAN U.K.: Please use own currency!**

V 125	1	Fair
	2	Unfair
	9	Don't know

There is a lot of discussion about how business and industry should be managed. Which of these four statements comes closest to your opinion? (CODE ONE ONLY)
*

V 126   1   The owners should run their business or appoint the managers
          2   The owners and the employees should participate in the selection
              of managers
          3   The government should be the owner and appoint the managers
          4   The employees should own the business and should elect the managers
          9   Don't know

People have different ideas about following instructions at work. Some say that one should follow instructions of one's superiors even when one does not fully agree with them. Others say that one should follow one's superior's instructions only when one is convinced that they are right. With which of these two opinions do you agree?
      *

V 127   1   Should follow instructions
                 2   Depends
                 3   Must be convinced first
                 9   Don't know

Do you agree or disagree with the following statements?

		Agree	Neither	Disagree	DK
V 128	A) When jobs are scarce, men have more right to a job than women	1	2	3	9
V 129	B) When jobs are scarce, people should be forced to retire early	1	2	3	9
V 130	C) When jobs are scarce, employers should give priority to British countries other than U.K.: please substitute your nationality people over immigrants	1	2	3	9
V 131	D) It is unfair to give work to handicapped people when able-bodied people can't find jobs	1	2	3	9

How satisfied are you with the financial situation of your household?
*

V 132   1   2   3   4   5   6   7   8   9   10

Dissatisfied   Satisfied
                                                DK = 99

How often, if at all, do you think about the meaning and purpose of life? (READ OUT IN
REVERSE ORDER FOR ALTERNATE CONTACTS)
*
V 133   1 Often
         2 Sometimes
         3 Rarely
         4 Never
         9 Don't know

Do you ever think about death? Would you say ...

V 134   1 Often
         2 Sometimes
         3 Rarely
         4 Never
         9 Don't know

I am going to read out a list of statements about the meaning of life. Please indicate
whether you agree or disagree with each of them. (READ OUT IN REVERSE ORDER
FOR ALTERNATE CONTACTS)

			Agree	Disagree	Neither	DK
V 135	A)	Life is meaningful only because God exists	1	2	3	9
V 136	B)	The meaning of life is that you try to get the best out of it	1	2	3	9
V 137	C)	Death is inevitable, it is pointless to worry about it	1	2	3	9
V 138	D)	Death has a meaning only if you believe in God	1	2	3	9
V 139	E)	If you have lived your life, death is a natural resting point	1	2	3 ·	9
V 140	F)	In my opinion, sorrow and suffering only have meaning				

if you believe in God	1	2	3	9
V 141 G) Life has no meaning	1	2	3	9

SHOW CARD P

Here are two statements which people sometimes make when discussing good and evil. Which one comes closest to your own point of view?

V 142   *

A. There are absolutely clear guidelines about what is good and evil. These always apply to everyone, whatever the circumstances.

B. There can never be absolutely clear guidelines about what is good and evil. What is good and evil depends entirely upon the circumstances at the time.

1 Agree with statement A
2 Disagree with both
3 Agree with statement B
9 Don't know

V 143   a)   Do you belong to a religious denomination?
*

1 Yes - GO TO b)
2 No - GO TO c)

b) (IF YES) Which one? (CODE UNDER (b) BELOW)

c) (IF NO) Were you ever a member of a religious denomination? Which one? (CODE UNDER (c) BELOW)

	V 144 (b) Religious Denomination	V 145 (c) Before
Roman Catholic	1	1
Mainline Protestant	2	2
Fundamentalist Protestant	3	3
Jew	4	4
Muslim	5	5
Hindu	6	6
Buddhist	7	7
Other	8	8
Never	-	0
No answer	9	9

NOTE: Japan, South Korea and many East European countries used different codes from these. For these and other deviations from the above, see V144 and V145 in section on NATION-SPECIFIC CODES.

<u>ASK ALL</u>
V 146 Were you brought up religiously at home?

    1   Yes
    2   No

<u>SHOW CARD Q</u>
V 147 Apart from weddings, funerals and christenings, about how often do you attend religious services these days?
*

    1   More than once a week
    2   Once a week
    3   Once a month
    4   Christmas/Easter day
    5   Other specific holy days
    6   Once a year
    7   Less often
    8   Never, practically never

Do you personally think it is important to hold a religious service for any of the following events?

		Yes	No	DK
V 148	A) Birth'	1	2	9
V 149	B) Marriage	1	2	9
V 150	C) Death	1	2	9

Independently of whether you go to church or not, would you say you are...(READ OUT REVERSING ORDER)
    *
V 151   1   A religious person
         2   Not a religious person
         3   A convinced atheist
         9   Don't know

Generally speaking, do you think that your church is giving, in your country, adequate answers to ... (READ OUT AND CODE ONE ANSWER FOR EACH)
    *

			YES	NO	DK
V 152	A)	The moral problems and needs of the individual	1	2	9

			YES	NO	DK
V 153	B)	The problems of family life	1	2	9
V 154	C)	People's spiritual needs	1	2	9
V 155	D)	The social problems facing our country today	1	2	9

Do you think it is proper for churches to speak out on:

			YES	NO	DK
V 156	A)	Disarmament	1	2	9
V 157	B)	Abortion	1	2	9
V 158	C)	Third World problems	1	2	9
V 159	D)	Extramarital affairs	1	2	9
V 160	E)	Unemployment	1	2	9
V 161	F)	Racial discrimination	1	2	9
V 162	G)	Euthanasia	1	2	9
V 163	H)	Homosexuality	1	2	9
V 164	I)	Ecology and environmental issues	1	2	9
V 165	J) Government policy		1	2	9

Which, if any, of the following do you believe in? (READ OUT AND CODE ONE ANSWER FOR EACH)
*

			YES	NO	DK
V 166	A)	God	1	2	9
V 167	B)	Life after death	1	2	9
V 168	C)	A soul	1	2	9
V 169	D)	The Devil	1	2	9
V 170	E)	Hell	1	2	9
V 171	F)	Heaven	1	2	9
V 172	G)	Sin	1	2	9
V 173	H)	Resurrection of the dead	1	2	9
V 174	I)	Re-incarnation	1	2	9

SHOW CARD R
Which of these statements comes closest to your beliefs?
  (CODE ONE ANSWER ONLY)
*

V 175
  1 There is a personal God
  2 There is some sort of spirit or life force
  3 I don't really know what to think
  4 I don't really think there is any sort of spirit, God, or life force
  9 Not answered

And how important is God in your life? Please use this card to indicate - 10 means very important and 1 means not at all important.
*

V 176   1   2   3   4   5   6   7   8   9   10
                Not at all   Very
                                              DK = 99

Do you find that you get comfort and strength from religion?
*

V 177   1   Yes
           2   No
           9   Don't know

Do you take some moments of prayer, meditation or contemplation or something like that?
*

V 178   1   Yes
           2   No
           9   Don't know

How often do you pray to God outside of religious services? Would you say...

V 179   1   Often
           2   Sometimes
           3   Hardly ever
           4   Only in times of crisis
           5   Never
           9   Don't know

Overall, how satisfied or dissatisfied are you with your home life?
*

V 180   1   2   3   4   5   6   7   8   9   10
                Dissatisfied   Satisfied
                                            DK = 99

Are you currently ....(READ OUT AND CODE ONE ONLY)
*

V 181   1   Married
           2   Living as married
           3   Divorced
           4   Separated
           5   Widowed
           6   Single

Have you been married before?

V 182	1	Yes - more than once
	2	Yes - only once
	3	No - never

NOTE: In the 1990 Dutch survey, V 182 was worded as: "How often have you been married?" 1= once, 2=more than once, 3=more than twice. This question gave rise to confusion in many countries; it was not clear whether being married before meant "have you ever been married?" or "have you ever been married before your <u>present</u> marriage?"

ASK ALL EXCEPT SINGLES
Do (did) you and your partner share any of the following?
  (READ OUT AND CODE ALL MENTIONED)
*

V 183	1	Attitudes towards religion
V 184	1	Moral attitudes
V 185	1	Social attitudes
V 186	1	Political attitudes
V 187	1	Sexual attitudes
V 188	1	None of these
V 189	1	Don't know

For V183-V196, code "2" indicates "not mentioned."

ASK ALL
And how about your parents? Do (did) you and your parents share any of the following?
(READ OUT AND CODE ALL MENTIONED)
*

V 190	1	Attitudes towards religion
V 191	1	Moral attitudes
V 192	1	Social attitudes
V 193	1	Political attitudes
V 194	1	Sexual attitudes
V 195	1	None of these
V 196	1	Don't know

If someone said that individuals should have the chance to enjoy complete sexual freedom without being restricted, would you tend to agree or disagree?
*

V 197	1	Tend to agree
	2	Neither/it depends
	3	Tend to disagree
	9	Don't know

SHOW CARD U

Here is a list of things which some people think make for a successful marriage. Please tell me, for each one, whether you think it is very important, rather important or not very important for a successful marriage:
*

	Very Important	Rather Important	Not very Important
V 198 A) Faithfulness	1	2	3
V 199 B) An adequate income	1	2	3
V 200 C) Being of the same social background	1	2	3
V 201 D) Mutual respect and appreciation	1	2	3
V 202 E) Shared religious beliefs	1	2	3
V 203 F) Good housing	1	2	3
V 204 G) Agreement on politics	1	2	3
V 205 H) Understanding and tolerance	1	2	3
V 206 I) Living apart from your in-laws	1	2	3
V 207 J) Happy sexual relationship	1	2	3
V 208 K) Sharing household chores	1	2	3
V 209 L) Children	1	2	3
V 210 M) Tastes and interests in common	1	2	3

Have you had any children? IF YES, how many?
*

V 211

0	No child - skip to V 213
1	1 child
2	2 children
3	3 children
4	4 children
5	5 children
6	6 children or more
9	No answer

How many of them are still living at home?

V 212

0	No child
1	1 child
2	2 children
3	3 children
4	4 children
5	5 children
6	6 children or more
9	No answer

<u>ASK ALL</u>
What do you think is the ideal size of the family - how many children, if any?

*
V 213

0	None
1	1 child
2	2 children
3	3 children
4	4 children
5	5 children
6	6 children
7	7 children
8	8 children
9	9 children
10	10 or more
99	Don't know

If someone says a child needs a home with both a father and a mother to grow up happily, would you tend to agree or disagree?
*

V 214	1	Tend to agree
	2	Tend to disagree
	9	Don't know

(South Korean 1981 survey contains one undocumented code "4")

Do you think that a woman has to have children in order to be fulfilled or is this not necessary?

	1	Needs children
V 215	2	Not necessary
	3	Don't know (in some countries)
	9	Don't know (in other countries)

Do you agree or disagree with the following statement? (READ OUT)
*

		YES	NO	DK
V 216	Marriage is an out-dated institution	1	2	9

If a woman wants to have a child as a single parent but she doesn't want to have a stable relationship with a man, do you approve or disapprove?
*

V 217	1	Approve
	2	Depends
	3	Disapprove
	9	Don't know

SHOW CARD V
People talk about the changing roles of men and women today. For each of the following statements I read out, can you tell me how much you agree with each. Please use the responses on this card.

		Strongly Agree	Agree	Disagree	Strongly Disagree	DK
V 218	A) A working mother can establish just as warm and secure a relationship with her children as a mother who does not work	1	2	3	4	9
V 219	B) A pre-school child is likely to suffer if his or her mother works	1	2	3	4	9
V 220	C) A job is alright but what most women really want is a home and children	1	2	3	4	9
V 221	D) Being a housewife is just as fulfilling as working for pay	1	2	3	4	9
V 222	E) Having a job is the best way for a woman to be an independent person	1	2	3	4	9
V 223	F) Both the husband and wife should contribute to household income	1	2	3	4	9

SHOW CARD W
With which of these two statements do you tend to agree? (CODE ONE
ANSWER ONLY)
*
V 224

A. Regardless of what the qualities and faults of one's parents are, one must
always love and respect them
B. One does not have the duty to respect and love parents who have not earned
it by their behaviour and attitudes

1   Tend to agree with statement A
2   Tend to agree with statement B
9   Don't know

SHOW CARD X
Which of the following statements best describes your views about
parents' responsibilities to their children? (CODE ONE ONLY)
*
V 225

1 Parents' duty is to do their best for their children even at the expense of their
own well-being

2 Neither
3 Parents have a life of their own and should not be asked to sacrifice their own well-being for the sake of their children
9 Don't know

SHOW CARD Y
Here is a list of qualities which children can be encouraged to learn at home. Which, if any, do you consider to be especially important? Please choose up to five. (CODE FIVE ONLY)
*

	IMPORTANT
V 226 A) Good manners	1
V 227 B) Independence	1
V 228 C) Hard work	1
V 229 D) Feeling of responsibility	1
V 230 E) Imagination	1
V 231 F) Tolerance and respect for other people	1
V 232 G) Thrift, saving money and things	1
V 233 H) Determination, perseverance	1
V 234 I) Religious faith	1
V 235 J) Unselfishness	1
V 236 K) Obedience	1

(V226-V236: code "2" indicates items that were not chosen)

SHOW CARD Z
Do you approve or disapprove of abortion under the following circumstances?
*

		Approve	Disapprove
V 237 A)	Where the mother's health is at risk by the pregnancy	1	2
V 238 B)	Where it is likely that the child would be born physically handicapped	1	2
V 239 C)	Where the woman is not married	1	2
V 240 D)	Where a married couple do not want to have any more children	1	2

How interested would you say you are in politics?

V 241	1	Very interested
	2	Somewhat interested
	3	Not very interested
	4	Not at all interested

9   Don't know

The Swiss survey asked about interest in international politics, national politics, regional politics and community politics. Responses to the question about community politics (which showed the highest levels of interest) were used here.

SHOW CARD AA
Now I'd like you to look at this card. I'm going to read out some different forms of political action that people can take, and I'd like you to tell me, for each one, whether you have actually *done* any of these things, whether you might do it or would never, under any circumstances, do it.
*

		Have Done	Might Do	Would Never Do	DK
V 242	A) Signing a petition	1	2	3	9
V 243	B) Joining in boycotts	1	2	3	9
V 244	C) Attending lawful demonstrations	1	2	3	9
V 245	D) Joining unofficial strikes	1	2	3	9
V 246	E) Occupying buildings or factories	1	2	3	9

(For V242, the normal N.A. code is "0" but "8" was used in some countries)

SHOW CARD BB
V 247 Which of these two statements comes closest to your own opinion?
*

A. I find that both freedom and equality are important. But if I were to choose one or the other, I would consider personal freedom more important, that is, everyone can live in freedom and develop without hinderance.

B. Certainly both freedom and equality are important. But if I were to choose one or the other, I would consider equality more important, that is, that nobody is underprivileged and that social class differences are not so strong.

1   Agree with statement A
2   Agree with Neither/depends
3   Agree with statement B
9   Don't know

SHOW CARD CC
V 248 In political matters, people talk of "the left" and "the right." How would you place your views on this scale, generally speaking?
*

1   2   3   4   5   6   7   8   9   10

Left   Right
                                              DK = 99
                                        Not answered = 98

<u>SHOW CARD DD</u>
V 249 On this card are three basic kinds of attitudes concerning the society we live in.
Please choose the *one* which best describes your own opinion. CODE ONE ONLY
*
    1 The entire way our society is organised must be radically changed by
    revolutionary action
    2 Our society must be gradually improved by reforms
    3 Our present society must be valiantly defended against all subversive forces
    9 Don't know

<u>SHOW CARD EE</u>
Now I'd like you to tell me your views on various issues. How would you place your
views on this scale? 1 means you agree completely with the statement on the left, 10
means you agree completely with the statement on the right, or you can choose any
number in between.
V 250

    1   2   3   4   5   6   7   8   9   10
                                                  DK = 99

A) Incomes should be   There should be greater
made more equal   incentives for individual effort

V 251

    1   2   3   4   5   6   7   8   9   10
                                                  DK = 99

B) Private ownership of   Government ownership of
business and industry   business and industry
should be increased   should be increased

V 252

    1   2   3   4   5   6   7   8   9   10
                                                  DK = 99

C) Individuals should take   The state should take more
more responsibility for   responsibility to ensure that
providing for themselves   everyone is provided for

V 253

    1   2   3   4   5   6   7   8   9   10
                                                  DK = 99

D) People who are unemployed   People who are unemployed
should have to take any job   should have the right to
available or lose their   refuse a job they do not want
unemployment benefits

V 254

1	2	3	4	5	6	7	8	9	10

DK = 99

E) Competition is good. It stimulates people to work hard and develop new ideas | Competition is harmful. It brings out the worst in people

---

V 255

1	2	3	4	5	6	7	8	9	10

DK = 99

F) In the long run, hard work usually brings a better life | Hard work doesn't generally bring success -- it's more a matter of luck and connections

---

V 256

1	2	3	4	5	6	7	8	9	10

DK = 99

G) People can only accumulate wealth at the expense of others | Wealth can grow so there's enough for everyone

---

SHOW CARD FF

There is a lot of talk these days about what the aims of this country should be for the next ten years. On this card are listed some of the goals which different people would give top priority. Would you please say which one of these you, yourself, consider the most important? CODE ONE ANSWER ONLY UNDER a BELOW

And which would be the next most important? CODE ONE ANSWER ONLY UNDER b BELOW

	V 257 (a) First Choice	V 258 (b) Second Choice
Maintaining a high level of economic growth	1	1
Making sure this country has strong defense forces	2	2
Seeing that people have more to say about how things are done at their jobs and in their communities	3	3
Trying to make our cities and countryside more beautiful	4	4
Don't know	9	9

SHOW CARD GG

a) If you had to choose, which one of the things on this card would you say is most important? CODE ONE ANSWER ONLY
*

b) And which would be the next most important? CODE ONE ANSWER ONLY
*

	V 259 (a) First Choice	V 260 (b) Second Choice
Maintaining order in the nation	1	1
Giving people more to say in important government decisions	2	2
Fighting rising prices	3	3
Protecting freedom of speech	4	4
Don't know	9	9

SHOW CARD HH

a) Here is another list. In your opinion, which one of these is most important? CODE ONE ANSWER ONLY

b) And what would be the next most important? CODE ONE ANSWER ONLY

	V 261 (a) First Choice	V 262 (b) Second Choice
A stable economy	1	1
Progress toward a less impersonal and more humane society	2	2
Progress toward a society in which ideas count more than money	3	3
The fight against crime	4	4
Don't know	9	9

V 263 Of course, we all hope that there will not be another war, but if it were to come to that, would you be willing to fight for your country?
*

    1   Yes
    2   No
    9   Don't know

SHOW CARD II
Here is a list of various changes in our way of life that might take place in the near future. Please tell me for each one, if it were to happen whether you think it would be a good thing, a bad thing, or don't you mind?
*

			Good	Don't mind	Bad
V 264	A)	Less emphasis on money and material possessions	1	2	3
V 265	B)	Decrease in the importance of work in our lives	1	2	3
V 266	C)	More emphasis on the development of technology	1	2	3
V 267	D)	Greater emphasis on the development of the individual	1	2	3
V 268	E)	Greater respect for authority	1	2	3
V 269	F)	More emphasis on family life	1	2	3
V 270	G)	A simple and more natural lifestyle	1	2	3

V 271 In the long run, do you think the scientific advances we are making will help or harm mankind?
   *

   1 Will help
   2 Some of each
   3 Will harm
   9 Don't know

SHOW CARD JJ
Please look at this card and tell me, for each item listed, how much confidence you have in them, is it a great deal, quite a lot, not very much or none at all? CODE ONE ANSWER FOR EACH ITEM - READ OUT REVERSING ORDER FOR ALTERNATE CONTACTS

*			A Great Deal	Quite A Lot	Not Very Much	None At All
V 272	A)	The church	1	2	3	4
V 273	B)	The armed forces	1	2	3	4
V 274	C)	The education system	1	2	3	4
V 275	D)	The legal system	1	2	3	4
V 276	E)	The press	1	2	3	4

V 277	F)	Trade unions	1	2	3	4
V 278	G)	The police	1	2	3	4
V 279	H)	Parliament	1	2	3	4
V 280	I)	Civil service	1	2	3	4
V 281	J)	Major companies	1	2	3	4
V 282	K)	The social security system	1	2	3	4
V 283	L)	TV/European Community	1	2	3	4
V 284	M)	NATO	1	2	3	4
V 285	N)	The [American]* political system	1	2	3	4

In West European countries and China, V283 refers to the European Community; elsewhere, it refers to TV newscasters.
The item concerning NATO (V284) was not asked in some countries.
In Slovenia, V280 "Civil service" was worded as "Local administration," to distinguish it from Yugoslav authority.
In Lithuania, Latvia and Estonia, the following changes were made: V276= this republic's (Lithuanian, etc.) mass media; V279=this republic's parliament; V281=cooperatives; V283 the People's Front [Baltic independence movement]; V284=this republic's government; V285=government of the USSR.
In Russia, substitutions were made for V279-V285: V279=Parliament (USSR); V281=Government (USSR); V282=Parliament (Russia); V283=TV; V284=Government (Russia); V285=Soviet political system.

On this card are listed some things people have said make them proud of the [U.S.]* Do any of these things make you proud of this country?
...Is there anything else?
...And is there anything else? [CODE UP TO TWO MENTIONS]

	V 286 First Choice	V 287 Second Choice
[American]* scientific achievements	1	1
The American political system	2	2
American sporting achievements	3	3
American culture and arts	4	4
American economic achievements	5	5
American health and welfare system	6	6
None of these things make me proud	7	7
DK	9	9

*substitute your nation for "U.S." or "American" or "Washington"

In Spain (ASEP survey) only, the codes for V286-V287 were: 0=scientific achievements, 1=the political system, 2=sporting achievements, 3=culture and arts, 4=economic

achievements, 5=health and welfare system, 6=Spain's history, 7=the language, 8=none, 9=D.K.
In China, the above codes were used, with the addition of code 8= "the long, long Chinese history."

V 288 Generally speaking, would you say that this country is run by a few big interests looking out for themselves, or that it is run for the benefit of all the people?

        1 Run by a few big interests
        2 Run for all the people
        9 Don't know

V 289 How much do you trust the government in [Washington]* to do what is right? Do you trust it almost always, most of the time, only some of the time, or almost never?

        1 Almost always
        2 Most of the time
        3 Only some of the time
        4 Almost never

SHOW CARD KK
There are a number of groups and movements looking for public support. For each of the following movements, which I read out, can you tell me whether you approve or disapprove of this movement? READ OUT AND CODE ONE ANSWER FOR EACH. Please use the responses on this card!

		Approve		Disapprove		
		Strongly	Somewhat	Strongly	Somewhat	DK
V 290	A) Ecology movement or nature protection	1	2	3	4	9
V 291	B) Anti-nuclear energy movement	1	2	3	4	9
V 292	C) Disarmament movement	1	2	3	4	9
V 293	D) Human rights movement at home or abroad	1	2	3	4	9
V 294	E) Women's movement	1	2	3	4	9
V 295	F) Anti-apartheid movement	1	2	3	4	9

SHOW CARD LL
Please tell me for each of the following statements whether you think it can always be justified, never be justified, or something in between, using this card. READ OUT STATEMENTS REVERSING ORDER FOR ALTERNATE CONTACTS. CODE

ONE ANSWER FOR EACH STATEMENT

*

V 296	A)	Claiming government benefits which you are not entitled to	1 / 2 / 3 / 4 / 5 / 6 / 7 / 8 / 9 / 10
			Never Always
			DK = 99

| V 297 | B) | Avoiding a fare on public transport | 1 / 2 / 3 / 4 / 5 / 6 / 7 /8 / 9 / 10 |
| | | | DK = 99 |

| V 298 | C) | Cheating on tax if you have the chance | 1 / 2 / 3 / 4 / 5 / 6 / 7 /8 / 9 / 10 |
| | | | DK = 99 |

| V 299 | D) | Buying something you knew was stolen | 1 / 2 / 3 / 4 / 5 / 6 / 7 /8 / 9 / 10 |
| | | | DK = 99 |

| V 300 | E) | Taking and driving away a car belonging to someone else joyriding | 1 / 2 / 3 / 4 / 5 / 6 / 7 / 8 / 9 / 10 |
| | | | DK = 99 |

| V 301 | F) | Taking the drug marijuana or hashish | 1 / 2 / 3 / 4 / 5 / 6 / 7 / 8 / 9 / 10 |
| | | | DK = 99 |

| V 302 | G) | Keeping money that you have found | 1 / 2 / 3 / 4 / 5 / 6 / 7 / 8 / 9 / 10 |
| | | | DK = 99 |

| V 303 | H) | Lying in your own interest | 1 / 2 / 3 / 4 / 5 / 6 / 7 / 8 / 9 / 10 |
| | | | DK = 99 |

| V 304 | I) | Married men/women having an affair | 1 / 2 / 3 / 4 / 5 / 6 / 7 / 8 / 9 / 10 |
| | | | DK = 99 |

| V 305 | J) | Sex under the legal age of consent | 1 / 2 / 3 / 4 / 5 / 6 / 7 / 8 / 9 / 10 |
| | | | DK = 99 |

V 306	K)	Someone accepting a bribe in the course of their duties	1 / 2 / 3 / 4 / 5 / 6 / 7 / 8 / 9 / 10
			Never Always
			DK = 99

| V 307 | L) | Homosexuality | 1 / 2 / 3 / 4 / 5 / 6 / 7 / 8 / 9 / 10 |
| | | | DK = 99 |

| V 308 | M) | Prostitution | 1 / 2 / 3 / 4 / 5 / 6 / 7 / 8 / 9 / 10 |
| | | | DK = 99 |

| V 309 | N) | Abortion | 1 / 2 / 3 / 4 / 5 / 6 / 7 / 8 / 9 / 10 |
| | | | DK = 99 |

| V 310 | O) | Divorce | 1 / 2 / 3 / 4 / 5 / 6 / 7 / 8 / 9 / 10 |
| | | | DK = 99 |

| V 311 | P) | Fighting with the police | 1 / 2 / 3 / 4 / 5 / 6 / 7 / 8 / 9 / 10 |
| | | | DK = 99 |

| V 312 | Q) | Euthanasia terminating the life of the incurably sick | 1 / 2 / 3 / 4 / 5 / 6 / 7 / 8 / 9 / 10 |
| | | | DK = 99 |

| V 313 | R) | Suicide | 1 / 2 / 3 / 4 / 5 / 6 / 7 / 8 / 9 / 10 |
| | | | DK = 99 |

V 314	S)	Failing to report damage you've done accidentally to a parked vehicle	1 / 2 / 3 / 4 / 5 / 6 / 7 / 8 / 9 / 10 DK = 99
V 315	T)	Threatening workers who refuse to join a strike	1 / 2 / 3 / 4 / 5 / 6 / 7 / 8 / 9 / 10 DK = 99
V 316	U)	Killing in self-defence	1 / 2 / 3 / 4 / 5 / 6 / 7 / 8 / 9 / 10 DK = 99
V 317	V)	Political assassinations	1 / 2 / 3 / 4 / 5 / 6 / 7 / 8 / 9 / 10 DK = 99
V 318	W)	Throwing away litter in a public place	1 / 2 / 3 / 4 / 5 / 6 / 7 / 8 / 9 / 10 DK = 99
V 319	X)	Driving under the influence of alcohol	1 / 2 / 3 / 4 / 5 / 6 / 7 / 8 / 9 / 10 DK = 99

SHOW CARD MM

a) Which of these geographical groups would you say you belong to first of all?

b) And the next?

	V 320 (a) First	V 321 (b) Next
Locality or town where you live	1	1
State or region of country where you live	2	2
The U.S. as a whole	3	3
North America	4	4
The world as a whole	5	5
(see nation-specific codes)	6	6
Don't know	9	9

V 322 How proud are you to be British?
[substitute your own nationality for 'British']
*

1 Very proud
2 Quite proud
3 Not very proud
4 Not at all proud
9 Don't know

SHOW CARD NN

Now I want to ask you some questions about your outlook on life. Each card I show you has two contrasting statements on it. Using the scale listed, could you tell me where you would place your own view? 1 means you agree completely with the statement on the left, 10 means you agree completely with the statement on the right, or you can choose any number in between.

V 323   1 2 3 4 5 6 7 8 9 10   DK = 99

A)   One should be cautious about   You will never achieve much
      making major changes in life   unless you act boldly

V 324   1 2 3 4 5 6 7 8 9 10   DK = 99

B)   Ideas that have stood the test   New ideas are generally
      of time are generally best   better than old ones

V 325   1 2 3 4 5 6 7 8 9 10   DK = 99

C)   When changes occur in my life,   When changes occur in my life,
      I worry about the difficulties   I welcome the possibility that
      they may cause   something new is beginning

<u>SHOW CARD OO</u>
A variety of characteristics are listed here. Could you take a look at them and select those which apply to you?

V 326   A) I usually count on being successful in everything I do   1
V 327   B) I enjoy convincing others of my opinion   1
V 328   C) I often notice that I serve as a model for others   1
V 329   D) I am good at getting what I want   1
V 330   E) I own many things others envy me for   1
V 331   F) I like to assume responsibility   1
V 332   G) I am rarely unsure about how I should behave   1
V 333   H) I often give others advice   1
V 334   None of the above   1

(For V327-V334, code "2" indicates "not mentioned")

<u>SHOW CARD PP</u>
I am going to read out some statements about the government and the economy. For each one, could you tell me how much you agree or disagree? Please use the responses on this card.

	Agree com-pletely	Agree somewhat	Neither agree nor disagree	Disagree somewhat	Disagree com-pletey	Don't Know
V 335						
A) This country's economic system needs fundamental changes	1	2	3	4	5	6
V 336						
B) Our government should be made much more open to the public changes	1	2	3	4	5	6
V 337						
C) We are more likely to have a healthy economy if the government allows more freedom for individuals to do as they wish changes	1	2	3	4	5	6
V 338						
D) If an injust law were passed by the government I could do nothing at all about it changes changes	1	2	3	4	5	6
V 339						
E) Political reform in this country is moving too rapidly changes	1	2	3	4	5	6

SHOW CARD QQ

I now want to ask you how much you trust various groups of people: Using the responses on this card, could you tell me how much you trust... READ OUT EACH AND CODE AN ANSWER FOR EACH

		Trust them completely	Trust them a little	Neither trust nor distrust them	Do not trust them very much	Do not trust them at all	Don't Know
V 340 a)	Your family	1	2	3	4	5	6
V 341 b)	The British (*substitute your nationality for 'British'*) in general	1	2	3	4	5	6
V 342 c)	Black Americans	1	2	3	4	5	6
V 343 d)	Hispanic Americans	1	2	3	4	5	6
V 344 e)	Canadians	1	2	3	4	5	6
V 345 f)	Mexicans	1	2	3	4	5	6

V 346 g)	Russians	1	2	3	4	5	6
V 347 h)	Chinese	1	2	3	4	5	6

Here, as elsewhere, "0" indicates N.A.

Items c through h were asked in 15 of the 43 countries surveyed in 1990. The nationalities referred to in these items vary from country to country: items c and d indicate some important ethnic group within the given country; e and f indicate some neighboring nationality; g and h refer to the Americans, the Chinese or the Russians. See Nation-Specific Variables section in ICPSR codebook for details.

V 348 Were you born in the United States [this country]?

    1   Yes

        No (If no): Where were you born?

    2   Latin America
    3   North America
    4   Asia
    5   Europe
    6   Africa
    7   Other

V 349 (If no) In what year did you come to the United States [to this country]?

    1   Within past 2 years
    2   Within past 3-5 years
    3   6-10 years ago
    4   11-15 years ago
    5   More than 15 years ago

V 350 To which of the following groups do you belong above all? Just call out one of the letters on this card. SHOW CARD

    1 [A] Above all, I am an Hispanic American
    2 [B] Above all, I am a Black American
    3 [C] Above all, I am a white American
    4 [D] Above all, I am an Asian American
    5 [E] I am an American first and a member of some ethnic group second
[the groups coded in V350 vary from country to country; see the section on NATION-SPECIFIC CODES in ICPSR codebook for codes used in countries other than the U.S.]

V 351 If there were a general election tomorrow, which party would you vote for? If DON'T KNOW: Which party appeals to you most?
[see NATION-SPECIFIC CODES in ICPSR codebook for codes used in given countries]

V 352 And which party would be your second choice?
[see NATION-SPECIFIC CODES in ICPSR codebook for codes used in given countries]

DEMOGRAPHICS

V 353 Sex of respondent:
*

   1 Male
   2 Female

V 354 a) Can you tell me your date of birth, please ....
*
V 355 b) This means you are .... years old.

NOTE: The surveys carried out in Sweden, South Africa and the Baltic countries did not ascertain the respondent's exact age, but did provide a collapsed six-category age variable: see V404 below.

V 356 At what age did you or will you complete your full time education, either at school or at an institution of higher education? Please exclude apprenticeships. (WRITE IN AGE)
*
Except as noted, the following categories were used in all surveys (see NATION-SPECIFIC CODES below for exceptions):

0. N.A.
1. Completed formal education at 12 years of age or earlier
2. Completed education at 13 years of age
3. Completed education at 14
4. Completed education at 15
5. Completed education at 16
6. Completed education at 17
7. Completed education at 18
8. Completed education at 19
9. Completed education at 20
10. Completed education at 21 years of age or older
99. N.A., D.K.

V 357 Do you live with your parents?
.*

   1 Yes
   2 No

Are you yourself employed now or not?
IF YES: *
About how many hours a week? If more than one job: only for the main job

Has paid employment		V 358
30 hours a week or more	1	
Less than 30 hours a week	2	
Self employed	3	

If no paid employment	
Retired/pensioned	4
Housewife not otherwise employed	5
Student	6
Unemployed	7
Other PLEASE SPECIFY	8

....

b) In which profession/industry do you or did you work? If more than one job, the main job WRITE IN
*

....
....

What is/was your job there? WRITE IN AND CODE BELOW
*
The following codes were used in most countries (see NATION-SPECIFIC CODES below for exceptions):

V 359

1	Employer/manager of establishment with 10 or more employees
2	Employer/manager of establishment with less than 10 employees
3	Professional worker lawyer, accountant, teacher, etc.
4	Middle level non-manual - office worker, etc.
5	Junior level non-manual - office worker, etc.
6	Foreman and supervisor
7	Skilled manual worker
8	Semi-skilled manual worker
9	Unskilled manual worker
10	Farmer: employer, manager on own account
11	Agricultural worker
12	Member of armed forces
13	Never had a job

V 360 Are you the chief wage earner?
*

1	Yes - GO TO V 363
2	No - GO TO V 361
3	Equal wage earner (treated as "Yes") - GO TO V363

V 361

a) Is the chief wage earner employed now or not?

   1 Yes
   2 No

b) In which profession/industry does/did he she work? WRITE IN

    ....
V 362 b) What is/was his/her job? WRITE IN AND CODE BELOW

Most countries used the following codes (see NATION-SPECIFIC CODES below for exceptions):

1	Employer/manager of establishment with 10 or more employees
2	Employer/manager of establishment with less than 10 employees
3	Professional worker lawyer, accountant, teacher, etc.
4	Middle level non-manual - office worker, etc.
5	Junior level non-manual - office worker, etc.
6	Foreman and supervisor
7	Skilled manual worker
8	Semi-skilled manual worker
9	Unskilled manual worker
10	Farmer: employer, manager on own account
11	Agricultural worker
12	Member of armed forces
13	Never had a job

ASK ALL
SHOW INCOME CARD
V 363 Here is a scale of incomes and we would like to know in what group your household is, counting all wages, salaries, pensions and other incomes that come in. Just give the letter of the group your household falls into, before taxes and other deductions.
(see NATION-SPECIFIC CODES below for categories):

1	2	3	4	5	6	7	8	9	10
C	D	E	F	G	H	I	J	K	L

No answer = 98

V 364 INTERVIEWER CODE BY YOURSELF
*   Socio-economic status of respondent
Most countries used the following codes (see NATION-SPECIFIC CODES below for exceptions):

1 AB Upper, upper-middle class
2 C1 Middle, non-manual workers
3 C2 Manual workers - skilled, semi-skilled
4 DE Manual workers - unskilled, unemployed

V 365 a) Time at the end of the interview: ....

V 366 b) Total length of interview   Hours   Minutes

V 367 During the interview the respondent was ....

1 Very interested
2 Somewhat interested
3 Not very interested

a) Town where interview was conducted: _____

[code below]:
V 368 b) Size of town:
Most countries used the following codes (see NATION-SPECIFIC CODES below for exceptions):

1	Under 2,000
2	2,000 - 5,000
3	5 - 10,000
4	10 - 20,000
5	20 - 50,000
6	50 - 100,000
7	100 - 500,000
8	500,000 and more

V 369 Ethnic group [code by observation]:
Unless otherwise noted, all countries used the following coding scheme:

1	Caucasian/white
2	Negro Black
3	South Asian Indian, Pakistani, etc.
4	East Asian Chinese, Japanese, etc.
5	Arabic
6	Other
9	N.A.

V 370 Region where the interview was conducted:
See nation-specific codes in section below. The following is the U.S. example:

1	New England
2	Middle Atlantic states
3	South Atlantic
4	East South Central
5	West South Central
6	East North Central
7	West North Central
8	Rocky Mountain states
9	Northwest
10	California

INDEX